A Half Century of the
Society for Historical Archaeology

Compiled with an introduction by
Benjamin C. Pykles and Ryan W. Saltzgiver

SOCIETY *for*
HISTORICAL
ARCHAEOLOGY

A Society for Historical Archaeology Publication

A Half Century of the Society for Historical Archaeology

© 2016 Society for Historical Archaeology
13017 Wisteria Drive #395
Germantown, MD 20874, U.S.A.

Compiled with an introduction by Benjamin C. Pykles and Ryan W. Saltzgiver

Library of Congress Control Number: 2016957475

Cover Photo: *John Cotter (far left) addressing the International Conference on Historic Archeology on January 6, 1967, shortly after being elected as the first president of the newly formed Society for Historical Archaeology. Photo courtesy of Edward B. Jelks.*

Cover Design by Jennifer Fultz.

www.sha.org

Contents

Part III: Harrington Awards

Part IV: Ruppé Awards

Appendices

Introduction

Benjamin C. Pykles and Ryan W. Saltzgiver

The afternoon of January 5, 1967 was unseasonably warm in Dallas, Texas.[1] Fourteen scholars met in a small room on the campus of Southern Methodist University. On the agenda was a discussion of the prospects for a new professional society devoted to the promotion and advancement of archaeological inquiry into the recent past. The debate was "lively" (Jelks 1993:11) as the discussion ranged from the increasing need for better publication venues to the feasibility of obtaining funding for another annual archaeological meeting. The group even discussed whether a new society was even necessary (Pilling 1967; see also Jelks 1993).

At the time, archaeology at historic-period sites, primarily publicly-toured historic places, was seen as a non-academic "redundant or heuristic" (Schuyler 1993:35) activity by most archaeologists. Scholars working at historic-period sites found it difficult to find avenues for funding, presentations, publications, and networking with other like-minded professionals working in similar contexts. The idea of a new society, devoted exclusively to the promotion and support of historic-period archaeology had been discussed for more than a decade. While a few regional organizations existed to help meet this objective, no national or international organization had been formed. Panels, symposia, and other venues had been successful in starting the conversation, but these efforts were fractious and intermittent. During the annual meeting of the Central States Anthropological Society in April 1966, a panel discussion became an open-forum debate on the feasibility and need for a new society (Jelks 2017). After the meeting, the panelists determined it was time to create an exploratory committee to examine the possibility for a new society. With that goal in mind, the committee organized a conference on historic sites archaeology, held at Southern Methodist University in January 1967.

When they met that warm January afternoon, the fourteen-member committee faced several issues still open for debate. The prospects of creating and operating a new professional society were daunting. The committee members recognized that the field of historical

. . . .

[1] *The day-time high was 65 degrees, which was 19 degrees above the average for that day. The following day was even warmer, with a day-time high of 72 degrees (Farmers' Almanac, 5 January 1967).*

archaeology was laboring against significant external bias and that any new society devoted to its promotion would likely find it difficult to establish its legitimacy under then current conditions. Many of the participants were concerned about the ability of the society to be self-sustaining. Others worried that the annual meeting would become just one more conference for which they would have to drum-up additional funding to attend. While all recognized that new avenues for publication and data sharing were necessary and essential, some were concerned that a national or international society would not provide the appropriate forum.

Despite their concerns, as their discussions continued it became clear to the participants that the society was needed for at least four reasons. First, a real need existed for networking amongst historical archaeologists. Annual conferences would provide an opportunity for interested scholars to interact in ways not then available. Second, the new society, by creating and editing its own journal, would provide new publishing opportunities for archaeologists working at historic sites. Third, the new society could advocate, both through public relations campaigns and through political outreach, for causes of specific interest to archaeologists working at historic places. Finally, the society could foster multi-disciplinary studies of the historic past on a global scale.

Given these primary considerations, the committee determined to formally recommend the creation of a new society dedicated to the promotion of scholarly research in historical archaeology. The following day (January 6, 1967) the committee presented its recommendation to those who had assembled for the conference and the motion was unanimously accepted. At the same time, the group decided on the name of the society, elected their first officers, and established the location of the society's first annual conference to be held the following year. Thus began the Society for Historical Archaeology (SHA).

An examination of what the society and its members have accomplished since that noteworthy day in January 1967 reveals major themes and trends in the development of the discipline of historical archaeology and the SHA over the last half-century. The articles reproduced in this volume document the lives and careers of some of the most prominent and influential figures in this development. It includes articles celebrating the recipients of the society's J. C. Harrington Medal in Historical Archaeology as well as those who have been awarded the society's Carol V. Ruppé Distinguished Service Award. It also includes oral history interviews and memorials for some of the key figures in the history of the society and discipline at large. Compiled in celebration of the society's 50th anniversary, all of the material reprinted here has been previously published in the journal Historical Archaeology since its first issue in 1967.

Although the individuals featured in this volume do not constitute an exhaustive list of "who's who" in historical archaeology's past, they are some of those most prominent figures who significantly helped develop both the field and the society throughout the last fifty years (or earlier). For example, nine of the fourteen members of the committee that formed the SHA in January 1967 are featured in one or more of the pieces reproduced in this volume. Others who served as some of the society's earliest officers are also represented, as are many others who have made (and, in some cases, continue to make) significant contributions since the society's founding. Some of these men and women are better known than others; unfortunately, other important figures are not represented at all. Nevertheless, the lives and careers of those who are featured reveal much about the development of historical archaeology and the rise and growth of the SHA over the last fifty years.

Among other things that are demonstrated in these pieces are clear examples of how the SHA and its members have endeavored to meet the four primary needs of networking, publishing, advocacy, and global research and outreach established by the fourteen-member committee that formed the society in January 1967. For example, the article honoring Patrick H. Garrow, the 2015 recipient of the Carol V. Ruppé Distinguished Service Award, highlights his "most substantial and lasting contribution" as chair of the SHA Conference Committee (Scott-Ireton and Corbin 2015:10). In this capacity, in which he served for many years, Garrow helped expand of one of the primary networking venues for society members and others interested in historical archaeology. As the authors of the article affirm, he "oversaw the growth of the SHA annual meeting from a rather small gathering of a few hundred people to a major annual conference of international proportions attended by over a thousand archaeologists" (Scott-Ireton and Corbin 2015:10).

Other pieces reprinted in this volume highlight the growth and development of the society's publications program. The oral history interview with Ronald L.

Michael (Roberts 2012), editor of the SHA for twenty-seven years, and the article written for his Ruppé Distinguished Service Award (Rodeffer 1998), reveal a great deal about the history of the society's journal, Historical Archaeology, and other publications efforts, as well as highlight the many individuals who assisted Michael in his editorial duties. Similarly, the article for the 2001 Ruppé Distinguished Service Award honoring Norman F. Barka (Brown 2001), and the memorial published after his death in 2008 (Veit 2009), each highlight his role as the society's newsletter editor for twenty years and explain a great deal about the history of the SHA Newsletter, which remains "one of the most recognized newsletters in [the] world" (Brown 2001:6).

The efforts of the society and its members to publicly advocate for the protection and management of the world's archaeological resources are also documented in the pieces reprinted in this volume. An extraordinary example is found in the article honoring María del Pilar Luna Erreguerena as the recipient of the 2011 J. C. Harrington Medal in Historical Archaeology, which documents her life-long efforts to protect Mexico's underwater cultural heritage "against numerous all-out efforts by foreign treasure-hunting companies to search for and salvage shipwreck sites in Mexican waters" (Leshikar-Denton and Carrell 2011:2). This article also documents Erreguerena's efforts to advocate for the protection and preservation of underwater cultural heritage in international forums such as the International Council on Monuments and Sites (ICOMOS), the United Nations Educational, Scientific and Cultural Organization (UNESCO), and the World Archaeological Congress (WAC). Erreguerena's achievements demonstrate that the concerns for advocacy and global outreach first established by the committee that formed the SHA in January 1967 remain important concerns of the society and its members today.

Finally, the pieces reprinted in this volume demonstrate an on-going commitment by the society and its members to foster multi-disciplinary studies of the historic past on a global scale. Take for example the article celebrating Kathleen A. Deagan as the 2004 recipient of the J. C. Harrington Medal in Historical Archaeology highlights "her interdisciplinary approach to research and her lifelong interest in the processes underlying the development of the Hispanic-American cultural tradition" (McKewan 2004:5–6). A similar emphasis is seen in the career of Roberta S. Greenwood, awarded the Harrington Medal in Historical Archaeology in 2001, who "always emphasized the multi-disciplinary aspect

Introduction

of archaeology" (Foster 2001:2), especially in her work on Chinese-American sites. Although, like Deagan and Greenwood, most of the individuals featured in this volume worked primarily at sites in the New World, they understood that the peoples reflected in the sites and material culture they worked with were part of a global cultural system. This understanding that the scope of historical archaeology research is global in scale has been with the society from its beginnings.

A final example of the society's global scope comes from the fascinating oral history interview of Stanley A. South, one of the original fourteen members of the committee that formed the SHA in 1967. Although his research centered mainly on sites in North America, he actively encouraged the practice of historical archaeology elsewhere throughout the world, especially in Latin America. The oral history interview reproduced here documents his response to Latin American colleagues who had "a great need to get their historic site archaeology papers published" (Joseph 2010:140). Using his own funds, South began publishing the series Historical Archaeology in Latin America, which featured papers published in Portuguese, Spanish, and English. He shipped copies of the sixteen resulting volumes "to a representative for each [Latin American] country to be handed out free to their colleagues" (Joseph 2010:140). This emphasis on the global nature of historical archaeology research continues today with members of the SHA practicing historical archaeology on nearly every continent.

As the SHA celebrates its fiftieth anniversary in 2017, it seems appropriate to remember and reflect on those individuals who have made significant contributions to the discipline at large and to the society in particular. The lives and careers of these key figures, as captured in the pieces reproduced in this volume, reveal a great deal about the history of historical archaeology and the SHA over the last fifty years. Indeed, the developments of the last half-century shed light on the trajectory of the discipline and society since the fourteen-member committee gathered in Dallas in January 1967. Since that time, the society they created has grown to become the primary venue, clearinghouse, and advocate for the research, protection, and preservation of historic-period archaeological resources worldwide. An understanding of what the society and its members have accomplished in its first fifty years will provide insight and inspiration as we look ahead to the next half-century.

References

BROWN, MARLEY R., III
2001   Carol V. Ruppé Distinguished Service Award: Norma F. Barka. Historical Archaeology 35(4):4–7.

FARMERS' ALMANAC
1967   Weather History Results for Dallas, Texas (75208), January 5 & 6, 1967, electronic resource accessed October 31, 2016, http://farmersalmanac.com/weather-history/75208/1967/01/06/

FOSTER, JOHN M.
2001   J.C. Harrington Medal in Historical Archaeology: Roberta S. Greenwood. Historical Archaeology 35(4):1–3.

JELKS, EDWARD B.
1993   The Founding Meeting of the Society for Historical Archaeology, 6 January 1967. Historical Archaeology 27(3):10–11.

2017   The Birth of the SHA. Paper Presented at the 50th Annual Conference on Historical and Underwater Archaeology, Society for Historical Archaeology, Fort Worth, Texas, January 4–8, 2017.

JOSEPH, J.W.
2010   An Interview with Stanley South. Historical Archaeology 44(2):132–144.

LESHIKAR-DENTON, MARGARET E., AND TONI L. CARRELL
2011   J.C. Harrington Medal in Historical Archaeology: Maria del Pilar Luna Erreguerena. Historical Archaeology 45(2):1–6.

McKEWAN, BONNIE
2004   J.C. Harrington Medal in Historical Archaeology: Kathleen Deagan. Historical Archaeology 38(4):5–7.

PILLING, ARNOLD
1967   Beginnings. Historical Archaeology 1:1–22.

ROBERTS, DANIEL G.
2012   A Conversation with Ronald L. Michael. Historical Archaeology 46(4):162–182.

RODEFFER, STEPHANIE H.
1998   Carol V. Ruppé Distinguished Service Award: Ronald L. Michael. Historical Archaeology 32(2):2–6.

SCHUYLER, ROBERT L.
1993   The Society for Historical Archaeology, 1967–1992: A Quarter Century of a National Archaeological Society. Historical Archaeology 27(1):35–41.

SCOTT-IRETON, DELLA A., AND ANNALIES CORBIN
2015   Carol V. Ruppé Distinguished Service Award: Patrick H. Garrow. Historical Archaeology 49(2):10–11.

Veit, Richard
2009   Norman F. Barka, 1938–2008. Historical
        Archaeology 43(2):1–8.

· · · · · · · · · · · · · · · ·

Benjamin C. Pykles
Church History Department
The Church of Jesus Christ of the Latter-day Saints
15 East North Temple Street
Salt Lake City, Utah 84150

Ryan W. Saltzgiver
Church History Department
The Church of Jesus Christ of the Latter-day Saints
15 East North Temple Street
Salt Lake City, Utah 84150

Part I:
Oral History Interviews

MELBURN D. THURMAN

Conversations with Lewis R. Binford on Historical Archaeology

Introduction

Had Lewis R. Binford—renowned as an archaeological theorist since the early 1960s—never been specifically concerned with historical archaeology, his contribution to this field, through the field's association with anthropological and archaeological methods and theory, would, nevertheless, still be immense. But Binford has also excavated historic sites, thought deeply about the interrelationships of historical and archaeological data, and made a number of methodological and theoretical contributions of primary interest to historical archaeologists. Indeed, even when Binford's work specific to the field of historical archaeology is considered by itself, he must be ranked as a major figure in this field (Figure 1).

Binford, then, is in a unique position for assessing the current strengths and weaknesses of historical archaeology as a part of archaeological, historical, and anthropological scholarship. So his views on these matters, expressed here, will certainly be of interest to all the toilers in the vineyard of historical archaeology. And in elucidating the logic of his own intellectual development, in which historical archaeology played a substantial role, Binford's retrospective view of his involvement with historical archaeology must provide food for thought for all those who are concerned with the ultimate aims of archaeology in general.

This interview was conducted 7 March 1997, at the Binford home in Dallas, Texas, where he lives with his wife, Nancy Stone, an academically trained archaeologist and talented chef. The home is about a 10-minute drive from the Southern Methodist University campus, where he teaches. The conversations with Binford stretched out from early morning through late evening. About three hours of talks—those specifically concerned with Binford's career in historical archaeology, the field's method and theory, and its place in scholarship—were recorded in a morning session and one in the afternoon.

Binford is now at work on his *magnum opus*, which will generalize about hunting and gathering cultures on a worldwide basis. He works on this at his home, with its mixture of comfortable furniture, striking antique pieces, and mementos of an extraordinary scholarly career, which has taken him to the far corners of the world—the Arctic, Tierra del Fuego, Australia, Europe, Africa, Southeast Asia, and beyond.

A glassed-in, tiled, sunken patio, off the Binford kitchen, is dominated by a mural-sized oil of him in an Eskimo village. This painting, by an admiring British artist, was used on the paperback edition of one of his books. The patio looks out over the garden, where Binford likes to putter around with plants.

But the scholarly heart of the house—what had been the master bedroom—is the two-level study where he writes. The main floor is lined with books on one wall. On the other side of the room is a table with a desktop computer. Behind Binford, when sitting at his computer, is a long bank of file cabinets. The files contain, as Binford says in the interview, "nothing but material on hunters and ethnographic material on hunters and gatherers."

Although most archaeologists are now familiar with the Binford charisma through his public presentations, the massive goodwill he exudes in informal situations can only be suggested by the brackets, such as "[laughs]," in this published interview. He speaks with, what the interviewer's wife used to refer to as, "a really charming accent"—a trace of the South modified by long residence in the Midwest, California, and the Southwest.

In large measure, while Binford's portion of the conversations was spontaneous, the interviewer relied heavily on prepared questions. An edited transcript, with minor changes from the verbatim transcript, was sent to Binford for approval. He asked for only cosmetic modifications, or as he joked in one telephone conversation, "I'm putting verbs in some sentences that don't have them."

The interviewer was an undergraduate student of Binford's at the University of Chicago, and worked under his direction during the Carlyle Reservoir excavations. Later, he took graduate courses with Binford at UCLA.

The interview was undertaken with one over-riding thought in mind: "What would most historical archaeologists ask Binford if they had an opportunity to quiz him about their field?" In fact, the questions of some colleagues, who shall remain anonymous, were solicited before the interview was conducted.

The Interview

[Question:] *Historical archaeology, more than most disciplines, has been very aware of its*

roots. Had Marlon Brando not given the word another meaning, it might be said that some scholars are regarded as the "Godfathers" of the field. Through your career, have you had any contact with, or were you influenced by, the "Godfathers." First, J. C. "Pinky" Harrington?

I first saw Pinky Harrington when I was in junior high school at Norfolk and he was working at Jamestown. I had a field trip arranged through the school I went to. Harrington gave us children a talk on Jamestown and walked us around. This was the first time I had ever seen him. Later I just decided I was interested and went to Jamestown and volunteered at the excavations.

[Q:] *Was that your first excavation?*
Yes.

So I worked as a volunteer. I basically carried things and dug holes where people told me. But

FIGURE 1. Lewis R. Binford at work. (Photo by Nancy M. Stone.)

that was when I met him. I got to know him a bit. And then I didn't see him for years and years.

When I started the pipe stem work, I had, by that time, read a lot of historic sites archaeology because I was working on the ethnohistory of groups in Virginia. And, of course, any time I'd see Harrington's name, I read the paper because I knew him. So I knew his writings and knew his work—early work—on pipe stems. Later, I began to try to apply his early work to material I had collected.

[Q:] *When was that?*
That would have been 1953–1954.

[Q:] *And at what stage were you in your career?*
I had just entered the University of North Carolina. I had just come back from the military. I had been to VPI (Virginia Polytechnic Institute) before. But I had to take all these undergraduate degree courses. I had transferred a bunch of courses. All the science courses were acceptable, but none of the social science courses. I had to take them all again, so I just entered their degree program.

Harrington had given me some—I forget now what it was—piece of information some years before. I couldn't find the note, and he couldn't find it either. We joked that we were losing data [laughs]. So I worked with the pipe stems and a knowledge of Harrington's work. I frequently had questions, and would call him on the phone and we would have long talks. I think I talked about this in one of Stan South's Conference publications. Anyway, I continued to talk to Pinky on the telephone, but when I was at Michigan, I stopped working on pipe stems, and I didn't see him again.

[Q:] *What about Noël Hume?*
I was unaware of Noël Hume until Stanley South started being critical of him. South had made a decision to go into historic sites archaeology, and we talked. He sort of kept me edu-

cated. Up at Michigan, Stanley would keep me informed about what was going on. And we'd write or talk on the phone. Stanley was not happy with the ideas of Noël Hume—particularly about ceramic typology, but also various other things. I think I met him one time when I attended one of Stanley's conferences.

[Q:] *John Cotter?*
That's a different story. You might not have known it, but you were illegally working on John Cotter's money at Carlyle.

[Q:] *Wait a minute, Lew. Are we beyond the statute of limitations?*
Oh, I think so. [MDT laughs.]
At that time there weren't any laws really yet on salvage archaeology. The Corps of Engineers didn't have any legal responsibility to do archaeology at all. But they had decided that they had a kind of moral obligation. So they were looking for people who could finance work in the Carlyle[, Illinois,] Reservoir. But they didn't have any money.

I found some money from Chicago—a little bit. "Mike" [Melvin] Fowler got some from SIU [Southern Illinois University, Carbondale]. But the person who financed that work was Johnny Cotter. I had known Cotter before, and Mike Fowler had also. We called around various government agencies before, looking for somebody who might be sympathetic to what was going on. And John Cotter dumped Park Service money into the Corps of Engineers project at Carlyle and supported us.

He always supported me. Right from the beginning he liked what I was doing. He had been at Jamestown, and he knew about historical work. He always supported me. Right. Every time I needed it, I got John Cotter's support.

[Q:] *Charles Fairbanks?*
Now I knew Chuck, but I didn't ever work with him. I just knew him as an important person and read his work.

[Q:] *"Bunny" Fontana?*

Same thing. Perhaps I interacted with him a little more because of his early ethnohistory on the ceramics of Pima/Papago, which I was interested in getting documented, and he was the only person doing it. But it was more of colleagues talking to one another. And it wasn't . . . "historic" [laughs].

[Q:] *George Quimby was saved for last of the "Godfathers," for Quimby stories have been known to fall from your lips. How did you meet him? Wasn't he then generally known as an eastern U.S. prehistorian?*

Well certainly, when I first met him he was known as an eastern prehistorian. But I actually can't recall when I first met George Quimby. I think, I *think*, that the first time I met him was on an archaeological site up in Wisconsin. I was visiting the site, and Ritzenthaler was excavating.

Subsequently, George used to come to Ann Arbor frequently to look at collections. He was a very diligent comparison person. So, if he had some material, he would travel to wherever there were comparable materials he wanted to look at.

He was a frequent visitor to Ann Arbor when I was a student and would come with some beads or something to compare to the collections. Then there would always be a cocktail party at somebody's house and George and all these people who had gone to Chicago earlier would talk over old times. And this was the context in which I got to know George. Then when I went to Chicago, I got to know him on a much more friendly basis. And I stayed at his house lots of times and we were just good friends.

[Q:] *How did you get together with Quimby for the joint work in the* Fieldiana *series?*

George would go almost every summer and do some fieldwork. Usually it was mainly making surface collections. And he would come back and try to compare the stuff he found.

One year he had some kind of deal with a wealthy person with a yacht, which took them around the shore of Lake Michigan and part of

Lake Superior. They would put the dinghy over and George would go on shore and make surface collections, then get back on the yacht and go to another place.

He found several sites up in the Great Lakes with what he called "strange lithics," and he brought them to me and said, "What are these things?" I looked at them and told him, "Well, I'm not sure, but let's see more." So he made huge collections.

I analyzed these lithic collections and came to the conclusion, basically, that they were not wedges, but cores. At that time, all we knew about the sites George had visited was that they were relatively recent. He thought this was very interesting, and got all excited. So we published a joint paper in *Fieldiana*.

[Q:] *Were you new at Chicago when you wrote that?*

I think I started writing it at Ann Arbor. Maybe I was at Chicago. Anyway, we didn't publish it right away. It was certainly published while I was at Chicago, but I think I started analyzing stones before I left Ann Arbor.

[Q:] *By the time of your Master's thesis, you were concerned with ethnohistorically known tribes. How did you come to select this topic? Was the topic selected before or after your involvement with Joffre Coe's program of excavations? Was the topic considered to be part of the elucidations of this program?*

Many of the sites that I used in that were sites that I'd discovered before I was ever in the university, when I was in the Boy Scouts and when I was just an interested young person. I would go out and find artifacts, as many people have, but pretty quickly stopped collecting them. I didn't save them very much. I put the information on a map. At that time I didn't even know there was a prehistoric past. I just knew there was a history. So, I immediately tried as a high school kid to relate all these sites to the tribes that were known at the time of colonization. I had these little maps of where the various historic tribes were, and the maps of where I'd found sites.

Some of the sites were Archaic and some of them were Woodland, but they were all organized that way. Then later, even before I went into the university, I began to realize that some sites had early colonial items on them, like pipe stems, and others didn't. So I began, in my own little world, a segregation. Later all that stuff was just stored in Norfolk after going into the service.

When I went back to the university, Joffre Coe was into tracing the Siouan tribes, and his whole thing was identifying the archaeology of the Siouan-speakers. It seemed to me that he was doing what I had tried to do as a high school student. So, he said, "Well, if you want to do a Master's thesis, you'll have to do researching; you'll have to do this, and do that." And I said, "Well, look, I have all this stuff," and I showed him the collections that I had and the maps that I had. This stuff was from an area that he had never worked in. It was just to the north of where he had stopped his kind of research.

[Q:] *So you had never worked for him in the field before that?*

No, I hadn't.

Then Joffre said, "Well, why don't you do the ethnohistory and go back and do a survey on top of it?— because you already know some of the land owners, and you already know your way around. Do a modern survey in this area and use that."

I said, "fine." Then I started driving every weekend from Chapel Hill up to the Virginia–North Carolina border, contacting land owners and surveying for sites. And as I read the ethnohistory I became convinced that Joffre Coe was wrong about the trading path from the Virginia Colony. I said it.

In my opinion, I couldn't defend the argument that all those traders were going out from the Virginia Colony to Okenechee Island, up near Clarksville. What everything said was that the trading path was down the edge of the Piedmont, to what would be Roanoke Rapids, North Caro-

lina, not Clarksville, Virginia. So I began to bring in data talking about this. He was not happy. So our first big argument, our first conflict, was over where the first Indian traders out of Virginia Colony were going. And that was a big part of my thesis. It just seemed that what I'd been doing led directly into difficulties with what Joffre was presenting to me as archaeological method.

[Q:] *Did you ever develop the idea that there was a basic difference between historic and prehistoric archaeological data in terms of how the data should be conceptualized?*

No. Joffre was the big believer in the direct historical method. But my view was, look, if you're going to look at the past, you have to take advantage of your knowledge capital—where you have the most knowledge. If you have the most knowledge about the past for Native Americans during the colonization period, and if you want to learn anything about the archaeological record, then the chances for having some control information are going to be greater for the historic period.

I never thought particularly about this, although I was certainly aware of the argument; but it seemed to me, very quickly, that the direct historic approach argument failed—that is, because so much of the historic period was already modified by Europeans. It was very tenuous to take that back into the Pre-Columbian Era and identify a group of people. I never was very comfortable with that, but I was very comfortable in using the knowledge from history and the historical record to give me some idea of what things might look like in the archaeological record of that period.

[Q:] *Yet through the early part of your career you continued to have a good deal of contact with scholars who were involved one way or another with the direct historical approach. Besides Joffre Coe, who also worked on the Cherokees, there was James B. Griffin, who less directly tried to tie the Shawnees to the Fort An-*

cient Aspect, and Albert C. Spaulding, whose most extensive monograph was on Arzberger, a protohistoric Arikara site. Other than Coe, did any other scholars directly or indirectly influence your views on the value, or lack of it, of the direct historical approach?

It always seemed to me that if we had ethnohistorical material we could say "Ok, the Arzberger site is perhaps a proto-Arikara site. Certainly in the case of the Carolina Hill country, many of the sites were historic Cherokee with historical colonial materials. So we have pretty good reason to believe that this stuff is Cherokee.

But what made the direct historical archeological approach to ancient materials possible were all these assumptions about the nature of culture history—that similar squiggles on the pot meant you're in the same tribe.

I always thought that the archaeological record was probably more interesting than that; that ethnicity itself was something that was caused. It just didn't come from God. Ethnicity is something that represents a reorganization of people under new or varying conditions.

Sometimes you have great big ethnic groups and other times you have groups like the Mattole in California, where there are only 200 people in the whole ethnic group and they're an independent language. What is causing that variability is something archaeologists can address—and the historians and ethnographers can never address.

To take these little assumptions of "similarity equals influence" means there was a mindless passing on of customs. Clearly this was probably not the best way of looking at the archaeological record. The past was probably much more interesting than that.

[Q:] *In one of your books, recalling preparation of a paper for a SHA meeting, you say something about "that word historical" in the term "historical archaeology." This seems to imply that you see historical archaeology and archaeology which does not use historical documentation as being, somehow, basically different.*

Is this really the case? And if it is the case, about when, do you think, you developed this perception?

I think your allusion is to a conference I attended after I'd finished the first season of fieldwork with the Nunamiut Eskimo. My comments about the word "historical" were all about one issue. When I worked with the informants up there, they're sitting there trying to remember what they did when they were 20 years old.

Much of what they were doing was the same thing I, as an archaeologist, would do. They were making inferences; they didn't remember. They were bringing in ancillary information, and saying, "well, it must have been; I must have been doing this because of some other circumstantial evidence." It wasn't really historical information. It was just that they had more knowledge with which to make an inference than I did.

Do you see what I'm saying? It was so striking when I worked with the Eskimos—most of what the informants told me was not fact in the sense of an accurate recollection of an event. It was inference, but based upon much more information than I had. It was in this context that I was commenting on history.

But your question goes a little bit beyond that. I never thought there was anything different about historical archaeology. It just, maybe, has a richer body of information to bring to specific archaeological experience. But still the general archaeological experience is no different.

[Q:] *In your publications, you have eloquently developed this position that ethnographic observations are no more "direct" observations than the kind of observations made by archaeologists dealing with the archaeological record. How, then, can one incorporate ethnographic and archaeological observations into a single framework and still be methodologically sound—since there are different sets of presuppositions underlying the two kinds of data?*

In the book I'm writing over here right now [pointing toward his computer], this is the only subject that the book has. That's because there have been so many silly arguments in archaeology about the use of ethnographic observations. And my answer is that the only reliable way to use them is to be able to explain them.

If archaeologists are going to use ethnographic material, they have to treat the ethnographic data just the way they treat the archaeological data. They have to analyze the ethnographic data to come up with explanatory arguments as to why the world was patterned the way it seems to have been patterned when documented by ethnographers.

You have to develop a theory—let's say a theory of group size. In ethnography you get people telling you how big the groups are; in archaeology they're not telling you that. We have to infer it. The archaeological record is not giving us estimates here. We have to use all kinds of circumstantial evidence. But in ethnography people give you estimates, "There were 23 people. There were 17 people." I can't use this until I find out what's causing the variability in group size.

Now, if I find that groups are large in the Tropics, but they are smaller at 35° latitude, and that they're big again in the near-Arctic, but they become very small in the Arctic, then I have a pattern—just like an archaeologist might have a pattern in something he studies.

Then I have to explain why the world was the way it was when documented ethnographically. And if I can explain why group size varies with environment, then I have a theory that should apply to the archaeological record up to some point.

[Q:] *Are you saying that it does not make any difference what method you use, because if you use a method and perceive the pattern, the pattern is there regardless of the method you used in the recognition of the pattern?*

No, I'm not exactly saying that. I'm saying that we know that people lived in groups and ethnographers may give me estimates of the numbers of people. In the archaeological record, we have no direct estimates that we can dig up.

What we have is all kinds of other archaeological evidence, perhaps—maybe even evidence that we don't know how to recognize—which can tell us about group size.

But if I can take ethnographic data and study the pattern in the ethnographic terms—what a group is, how big it is—and show that it varies in regular ways with the environment, the demography, whatever—then I can build a theory of group size. Then I can reason from this theory to the archaeological record and see what correlates with these ethnographic estimates, and perhaps then develop a method for monitoring group size with archaeological observations.

That's basically the procedures I think we have to use. Use ethnographic information as prior knowledge for developing a method to use with the archaeological stuff. But the ethnographic information is not used to *interpret* archaeological material. It only becomes really useful when one has a theory—an explanation—for the variability in the ethnographically documented properties.

[Q:] *So an explanation which will explain all diversities of data can be obtained from any particular class of data?*

Exactly, exactly, exactly. It's just a matter of how you use your resources. If I've got better knowledge here, I develop the argument here. Take it over here and see when it fails, because when it begins to fail I've got a chance to learn something.

[Q:] *But can ethnographic observations really be "tested" with archaeological observations, or vice versa?*

I can develop a theory, an explanation, with ethnographic material. Then I can take that explanation to archaeological properties, and I can find where the properties are consistent with what I expect, and where they differ. And when they differ, perhaps I've reached the limits of the range of variability that was documented ethnographically, and I'm now looking at some variability for which there was no ethnographic documentation. So the first thing the ethnographically derived explanation allows me to do is diagnose that threshold. The second thing it allows me to do is say: "Okay, the most likely situation is that in the ethnographic material I only have this much variability, while in the past I've got this much—What, then, is the likelihood that the same variables are causing the variability where only the ranges of their values differ in the past from the ranges known ethnographically?"

So I've already got a good way of thinking about what it is I may not know. I'm not lost intellectually if I've already done the work on the ethnography.

[Q:] *Your thinking on the interrelationship of ethnographic and archaeological data can be easily analogized to the historical documentation used by historical archaeologists. We have traced the development of this thinking from your first scholarly essays on this at North Carolina. Let's go back to that time for a while.*

Someone told me that there were five graduate students in anthropology at North Carolina when you were there. These were, it was said, you, Stanley South, Aubrey Williams, Ruben Reina, and someone else. Was this the case?

I was a graduate student with Stanley South, Aubrey Williams, Hester Davis (E. Mott Davis's sister), and a Belgian woman whose name now escapes me. But I can see her. She was Belgian, and her training was in Acheulian. And there was a Margaret Mead student by the name of John Grant. And that was essentially it. If Ruben Reina was there, it was for a very short period of time. So it was six of us.

Stanley and I, of course, were learning archaeology with Joffre Coe—but it was all North Carolina. Hester was pretty much the same way, only she had a brother who dug lots of things outside. John Grant was trained by Margaret Mead and had decided to go into archaeology. I don't know why. He knew nothing about archaeology and all he wanted to talk about was the swaddling hypothesis for the Great Russians, or something like that [laughs]. So the Belgian

woman was important to us, because she had archaeological interests outside North Carolina. God, Mel, I wish I could remember the Belgian woman's name.

[Q:] *If the department had only six students, was your contact nevertheless much closer with some than with others? How did you first meet Stanley South? Did you do any significant amount of fieldwork together?*

There were several reasons that South and I were much closer. We were both older. We'd both been in the military. He'd been in the navy. So we were both veterans. Both of us had had a different career earlier. South had been a school teacher; I had been in wildlife biology. We were married. We had families. We shared all those things that we didn't share with all the other students. Hester was unmarried, and so was the Belgian woman. John Grant was married, but they were like teenagers—I mean they were very young. The Belgian woman—I never knew what she was doing in North Carolina—was somewhat older.

Stanley and I met there at the University of North Carolina. We became fast friends the first week we met.

I don't know why, but every time Joffre Coe wanted something done, he would call Stanley and me and say, "I want you to go this weekend and put a test pit on the such-and-such site and bring me the pottery." He was forever sending us off to do things, and we did lots of those things together.

Then we were looking for thesis material. I already had material for my Master's thesis; Stanley had to get his. So Joffre got money from the Virginia Electric and Power Company to do some salvage archaeology at the dam that they were building on the Roanoke River. It was just assumed that I was going to help Stanley dig, and the Roanoke Rapids project paid enough money that we could buy peanut butter and bread, I think. We lived in tents and camped way out in the middle of the reservoir and did the archaeology. And that was one of the big sections of Joffre Coe's doctoral thesis as well.

So Stanley and I did fieldwork together at North Carolina. Hester sometimes came down to see what we were doing, but she didn't do fieldwork with us much. Aubrey didn't. John Grant didn't. I don't know why Joffre didn't get them to do fieldwork.

[Q:] *Can you recollect if South then thought of the possibility of specializing in historical archaeology?*

No, Stanley had no interest in historical archaeology when he started. And part of the reason that Stanley went into historical archaeology in the long run was because it was the only way he could stay in the region and not be told what to do by Joffre Coe. It was the same reason I went to Virginia for my thesis fieldwork, and the same reason I went to Michigan [laughs].

Joffre viewed us as just people in his footsteps. And he also only wanted people who thought just like he did. And if you didn't think like he did, you were a traitor. So Joffre viewed both Stanley and me as traitors, or at least we felt he did. He gave Stan some hard times when he was working in historical research in Carolina. Joffre was never supportive of me after I went to Michigan. Never. No support whatsoever.

[Q:] *You seem to imply in one of your books that your decision to go to the University of Michigan was connected with Joffre Coe having gone there. Was your decision to go a function of Coe's academic lineage, his concern with Leslie White's work, or something else?*

Joffre recommended that I go to Michigan. Although I had problems with him, I thought that was good advice. So I went. And I did want to study with Leslie White.

[Q:] *At Michigan, there were several teachers who seem to have influenced you positively in one way or another. You have several times mentioned the influence of Leslie White's theory, and Albert Spaulding's archaeological outlook. At your famous 1965 American Anthropological Association symposium in Denver, David F. Aberle*

was one of the commentators on the papers. Was the influence of these teachers primarily from the point of theory or method, or both? Do you recall what courses you took at Michigan?

Michigan at that time had a really impressive staff. It was a high-quality department. David Aberle was teaching social organization; Marshall Sahlins was teaching courses in state formation; Elman Service was teaching on hunters and gatherers; Richard Beardsley was teaching Asia and archaeological methods. There was a wealth of really superb teachers.

I had become pretty close to David Aberle because I had taken his courses and found them fascinating. He hired me once to do background research. So I was reading reports of the Indian agencies to the government. These were detailed reports by various Indian agents on what was happening on the reservations in the last part of the last century and the early part of this century. I was just accumulating information, some of which Aberle later used in his peyote book. I got fascinated by social organization really through him. So it was my suggestion that we have Aberle come to the Denver session.

I don't know anywhere today—we never really achieved it at Chicago in the 1960s—where you had really fundamental strong education in all fields of anthropology. At Michigan we had James Sphuler in physical. We had Fred Thieme. We were really strong in physical anthropology. You were really educated in anthropology per se, and that was primary. Then what you did for your thesis was secondary. So it was a superb education in a broad view of anthropology.

This opened up to me areas of relevance that I hadn't even imagined. I learned that it was important to know the ethnography all the way around the world—to know the range of variability.

[Q:] *Do you feel that this is the kind of training that is still absolutely necessary regardless of anthropological specialization, and—specifically for an archaeologist—regardless of the kind of archaeology?*

I do. I think the broader the base of one's knowledge, particularly of the variability in human organized ways of living, the better archaeologist one is going to be.

[Q:] *And should historical archaeologists also have this kind of background?*

Yes. Absolutely—because historical archaeologists usually see their historical materials in a narrow event sequence way, rather than in a systems comparative fashion. I think depth of knowledge is critical to being a good anthropologist, a good archaeologist, and a good historical archaeologist.

[Q:] *I seem to remember that once at Chicago you mentioned that you used to sometimes attend Plains Conferences. I assume that you more often attended Southeast Conferences. In both areas there was then a notable development in the direct historical approach, if more so on the Plains. The Plains, however, in the work of Spaulding, Donald J. Lehmer, and a few others, had a notable quantitative archaeology component. On the other hand, Stanley South's Conference on Historic Sites Archaeology got started in connection with the Southeast Conference.*

Were these factors in your attendance? How would you characterize your involvement with these meetings? At the Southeast Conference, if you gave papers, were they more often directed at prehistorians, those using the direct historical approach, or in South's sessions?

Yes, I certainly attended Plains Conferences, and I read almost all of Waldo Wedel's work and the direct historical approach on the Plains. But my interest in the Plains Conferences was with the early Archaic material that was coming out of the River Basin Surveys on the upper Missouri—not down where the Mandan and Hidatsas were, but upriver.

[Q:] *Let me ask for a clarification here. Was this before or after Willey and Phillips's book came out? One of the problems with their formulation was that they had not been able to iden-*

tify Archaic on the Plains. Was your work connected with that problem?

Yes it was. Willey and Phillips came out when I was a student at North Carolina, but in two installments in *American Anthropologist*. It was not a book, at first. I don't remember when I had the first look at Willey and Phillips, but the issue of the Archaic was a huge one when I became a student. This was because you then didn't have C-14. You had this alleged big temporal gap. And you had the estimates that most people were using. The peopling of the New World was imagined in two waves: the Paleo-Indians, and then another about A.D. 1 That was the magic date. So in the chronology that we were talking about, essentially, all the archaeological record fit between A.D. 1 and Columbus. And then you had Paleo-Indian way down here, and you had this huge gap between.

Once you had the beginnings of C-14, almost everybody was working on this Archaic problem. There was great excitement, and once you began to expand the chronology backward, you began to see an Archaic in places other than New York. Ritchie had defined the Archaic, in 1941, based on New York material. And other people would say, "We don't have any. We just have a lot of projectile points mixed up with pottery."

To get good segregation of the archaeological material, you have to have stratified sites. That's why Joffre Coe's stratigraphic archaeology really impressed Stanley and me. He was way ahead of his time in learning how to find stratified sites. When Stanley and I were students, the only stratified sites in existence in the Southeast were Joffre Coe sites. There was some super-positioning from WPA, but they didn't have any really stratified sites.

[Q:] *Is that primarily in Coe's American Philosophical Society publication?*

That's right. But that was published very late. Joffre had most of those sites before the war [WWII].

[MDT:] *You were talking about the Plains Archaic, and Plains and Southeastern Conferences.*

At that time there were several "capitals" for archaeology. Lincoln, Nebraska, was one of them. Joe Brew was there. All of the offices for the River Basin Surveys people were there. Preston Holder was there, at the university. And Wedel and his people were in and out of there all the time. So it was one of the great field capitals of archaeology.

Atlanta was another one, with A. R. Kelly and all of his people in and out all the time. So you went to Lincoln or Atlanta to find out what was happening in that area of the world. And I started doing that fairly early. I was not in Lincoln paying much attention to the direct historical work. I was there on the problem of the Archaic gap and the excitement of finding and getting chronology on these projectile points—because at Ann Arbor I was working on projectile points.

As far as the Southeast goes, I also attended Southeast Conferences. Stanley South and I participated in the first one that I remember attending. I think we were both at North Carolina then. Both of us were arguing about prehistoric archaeology—with Steve Williams and the Harvard gang—on Duck River materials and the Tennessee Valley stuff. It was not until later that Stanley actually went into historic sites work, when he went to Brunswicktown. About the same time, I had the opportunity to work at Fort Michilimackinac.

This was a time when Stanley and I were both working on historic material. He would send me slides of his ceramics, and I would send him slides of mine, and we would trade a lot of information. That was in 1959 and then again in 1961, because I ran crews those years. Moreau Maxwell ran the crew at Michilimackinac in 1960.

[Q:] *Were you doing pipe stem work then?*

When I went to Fort Michilimackinac, I'd already done a lot of work on the pipe stems from Virginia, even though Joffre had thought it was silly to try to develop a new dating technique for them. He told me I was wasting my time. When I went to Michilimackinac, I just continued the use of what was already done.

[Q:] *Under what circumstances did you first come across W. W. Taylor's book?*

That was in a course with Joffre Coe. And the course was called "theory." We had the two articles in the *American Anthropologist* which later became the Willey and Phillips book. We had Taylor, and we had Duncan Strong's article on the direct historical method. And that was all the readings there were in the methods and theory course. [Laughs.] Well, there were a few others, but there was really nothing to read then. So we all read all those articles many times.

[Q:] *What was Spaulding's reading list like when you got to Michigan?*

The first course I had with Spaulding was in African prehistory. It was a very up-to-date reading list on the literature of the Paleolithic of Africa. This was before there were the potassium-argon dates from Olduvai. We read the prewar stuff of Leakey, and all of Dart's stuff, and Broom, and all those people. But it was before dating. The first dates came in 1959.

[Q:] *Did you have a theory course with Spaulding?*

I did; it was more about method than theory. It was basically on the use of statistics.

[Q:] *What kind of reading list did he have?*

He had a lot of readings on statistical literature.

[Q:] *Do you mean like Brainerd and Robinson and that kind of thing? Or do you mean mathematical statistics?*

Mathematical statistics. We had to learn how to do all these things, and then of course we only had slide rules to work with, or do it all by long hand. Then it was an application. You know, we had to read Brainerd and Robinson and all the seriation strategies in archaeology that required counting things. So we had to read Kroeber's article on Zuni potsherds and we had to read Ford—all the Ford literature. We had to read examples of quantification which, at that time, were only from the lower Mississippi Valley survey by Griffin, Ford, and Willey. We would take data out of that to use as examples for statistics.

[Q:] *I audited your methods and theory course at Chicago—the graduate course. You had a massive reading list. When did you compile that? What were the circumstances?*

Over time. They're just horrible now. When I would take courses, I would not just do what the course required. I used the reading list to get an *entrée* into the literature. Then I'd go and get what was cited in the readings, and read these. I began to accumulate these files, and I still work that way.

These files—[turning]—they're all full, and there's nothing but material on hunters and gatherers. There's no place on Earth that has this much information [laughs] on hunters and gatherers. And that's the way I've always worked. You may have seen the big bibliography on technology I gave out in California.

"Oh, yeah we done that" [mocking himself, laughing, and rifling through the files]. But these are every case. Every file folder is a different known case of hunters and gatherers. And then you pull them out, and there's 35 articles or something in a file [laughs].

When I was a student there was nothing to read. When we took archaeology of Eastern North America, it was going through Griffin's book, *Archaeology of Eastern United States*, focus by focus. That was what it was.

[Q:] *W. W. Taylor once thought of using the term "functional archaeology" for what he finally called the "conjunctive approach" to archaeology. As I recall the development of your work, the basic character of Processual Archaeology*

had been developed by you before you became intrigued by General Systems Theory. Some have criticized General Systems Theory (GST) as being "functionalist" in nature. Was your turn to GST stimulated be Taylor's approach, or were you trying to move beyond functionalism? Indeed, in your opinion, is it possible for any archaeology to move beyond functionalism?

I don't think my views of functionalism have changed very much since I was a student. If you take Radcliffe-Brown, the father of functionalism, as the example, functionalism was psychological anthropology. He was trying to explain things in terms of sentiments and emotional feelings of people, and so the explanation was not that things go together in a system the way I think about it. He thought that things are related in people's minds in terms of overarching concepts, sentiments, and emotions. These are all reductions to motivational kinds of explanations as far as I can see. Radcliffe-Brown was saying, "This happens because people think this way." Functionalism—in the anthropological sense—to me is just another idealistic thing.

Yet, particularly in the world of physics, function has another, very important, meaning. And it means the dynamic role elements or material phenomena play in a system. What is the function of a carburetor? Well it does this, *vis à vis* the maintenance and flow of energy through the system. So my notion of function is this second conceptualization of function. I never paid much attention to functionalism as it developed in anthropology.

When it comes to looking at a system—anything for that matter—there are two things you have to do. You have to ask, "What is the world like?" Because, if I assume that the world is flat, I can waste a hell of a lot of time trying to explain why. So [laughing] you want to know what the world is like. Then you have to define how the world is organized into systems, and how energy flows are integrated.

You can't look at the history of World War II and not understand what a system is. It has various kinds of differentiated roles. There was all kinds of hierarchical state differentiation. There was differential wealth. The United States was essentially financing most of the hardware of the war. And so there were all these integrations of flow of material matter, energy cost, energy sinks. The battlefield is a giant energy sink. So you have to be able to describe the world in ways that are germane. You many not know yet what is really germane. But you have to be able to describe the world in ways that may be germane to the way it works, not what one "feels" about it, or what motivated the participants.

My view is that what people thought about World War II is not of much help in understanding the system involved. (They claim you have to understand how people are used, how people are manipulated, how people are made to be motivated to kill themselves.) You have to be able to look at a system in a more materialist way than this—as a system of energy flows and cycles of nutrients and such things.

So that has been my view of function and structure. Given that view, structure is a statement of the limitations of function; a simple thing. If the piston is going up and down in the engine, then structure is the upper and lower limits of movement for the piston. It—structure—is the constraints on dynamics in a system. So systems have structure, and if dynamics get out of hand, a system blows up, it goes to a new level of organization, or it goes extinct. It just doesn't stay the way it is. That has been my idea of structure and function. When I talked about function, I was not talking about the kinds of things Radcliffe-Brown was talking about.

There is a third usage of "function." This is the archaeologist's view, as when one asks: "What is this used for?" "Is this a skin scraper?" "Is this a lance?" "Is this a projectile point?" I never really thought I could give an answer to such questions until I did analysis and saw what role the artifact played within systems of the sort already mentioned. So I ask about the artifact: "Does it co-vary with bone? Is it more common as an isolated find and less common as a complete item in a village?" Until I can see the patterning, I can't give you much of an opinion.

This is why I argue with Schiffer and others, who want to interpret everything. They make up little stories of the Boy Scout sitting around the fire. They want to see the event. I never thought the event was that important. I want to know how things were constrained by structure and pushed by dynamics, repetitively over time.

That was my idea of structure and function.

[Q:] *You raise a question in my mind. You gave the example of World War II. If someone said, "Lew Binford, we will do the archaeology of World War II," how would one go about doing the archaeology in terms of defining the system operating for carrying out World War II?*

You would have to have a lot of money. [Both laugh.] Almost as much money as there was in the war. But the point is well taken.

[MDT:] *With inflation, maybe a lot more.*

That's right. [Both laugh.] You would have to begin to understand how the events that were taking place in the U.S. were related to the transport of material to the Old World—and related to Nazi submarine warfare. Why did the first big push come in North Africa? Isn't that interesting?

Well the Germans, obviously, were in North Africa with their crack troops. You basically didn't have to go through the North Atlantic in order to get logistics into North Africa. You didn't have to go through England. You didn't have to go anywhere the Luftwaffe could get at you. And if you could get inside the Mediterranean—the mouth of the Mediterranean—that was the easiest place to defend from the air, or against submarines. So don't send all the tanks to England, and then on to Germany. Send them right to the battlefield. And there was only one place on Earth where there could be such a battlefield.

So you didn't want to take the chance of trying to get the material into England, because the submarines had England blocked. Then they were subject to being destroyed by the Luftwaffe. You want to avoid all that. It was a risk reduction strategy that worked like a dream. And basically, once you had North Africa, then you could go through Italy, which was the softest part of the Axis military support. And the Germans weren't anxious to really put their goodies in there. And also they made a stupid mistake with respect to Russia. So, if we could go in through Italy, knock out the Italian support, let the Russians take the brunt of the Panzer divisions, then we could stage England for Europe. It was a whole series of very, very systemic, energetically based decisions that stood behind these victories, and failures sometimes.

[Q:] *But would we be doing the archaeology in North Africa or would we be doing it in the United States?*

Given what we know about the production of the logistics components, we would have to do that out of the United States. Where is the entropy sink? Where is it you're going to spend that production? You don't want to spend it, you want to use it. So you don't want to lose it; you don't want to lose the tanks; you don't want to lose the airplanes. The relation between production highs and expenditure sinks are clues to systems organization.

You would be sampling, given what we know. You wouldn't be digging the battlefields, you wouldn't be doing those kinds of things.

[Q:] *Now you've been talking about the study of the archaeology of World War II. One might interpret what you're saying by analogy with the situation of historical archaeologists who are concerned with the study of the spread of the modern world. By analogy, it might be argued by some that you are suggesting that to do historical archaeology (because the primary logistics systems centered in Europe during that spread), one should be working in Europe to a larger degree than in the New World. Is that what you're saying?*

To some extent. Let me see if I can make an example. They're digging down here in south Texas right now, the *La Belle*, which was one of LaSalle's last ships for a potential French colony at the mouth of the Mississippi. Now why do we

have a colony which is not at the mouth of the Mississippi? They couldn't find the river. And even the ship captain had been there before. The ship is lost out here in a Texas harbor, and there were only four survivors of this entire enterprise, and they ended up walking from south Texas to the French settlements in the Great Lakes. They eventually got home. Now why is this endeavor such an enormous failure as opposed to some other colonial endeavors?

Now that seems to be a reasonable kind of processual question to ask. Why are the French putting all this in here. They have boats, they're loading them up; they're sending people and it fails miserably, whereas some others don't.

If you would compare this failure to the Roanoke colony in Virginia, it has an awful lot of the same characteristics. That is, there wasn't continued logistics. They got in trouble, so they have to send a boat back to England to tell them, because there wasn't a pre-arrangement for support regardless of news. And on and on. There are a whole series of parallels between the failure of LaSalle's expedition and the failure at the Roanoke colony.

Why did the Virginia colony from the time of the Jamestown settlement succeed? It had the same problems. A small group of people arrived among indigenous people. That wasn't necessarily a bad scene to start with. But the first winter they starved; they lost about half or more of the total population when the streams were full of sturgeon. They didn't know about the environment, the local place. But in this case the Virginia colony made it, because the British sponsors sent support without waiting to receive news. The assumption of logistics was made directly—that you need to supply these people regardless of whether it's a Garden of Eden or not, until they get established. Even if they lost about 152 out of 280 original settlers, they made it.

[A malfunction occurred here during recording. Binford then summarized his points which had been made at greater length during the recording failure.]

My only point was this: What questions are historical archeologists trying to answer? Are they doing comparisons? Or are they interpreting their sites? If they are *interpreting* their sites, they are behaving like historians according to my philosophical outlook. They are using prior knowledge to give meaning to their sites. On the other hand, if they're taking their sites and comparing them one to another, trying to control variables, and asking, "What variables were different in this settlement and at that one," then they're putting themselves in the posture of learning about processual phenomena. But if they're just trying to interpret their little site, then they're using ethnographic analogy—historical analogy—and they're arguing with one another about the adequacy of the historical records. If they are doing that, then they're doing nonproductive things. One wants to use prior knowledge to guide analysis so that "new properties of the world" are exposed—rather than simply accomodating new observations to old knowledge and beliefs.

[Q:] *How do you go from site to systemic view when you're dealing with historical sites?*

The same way you do it in other archaeology. It's no different. It's no different at all.

[Q:] *And what is that? How does that go?*

Some of the model is in Stanley South's work, where he basically said, "Okay, within the little world that I've worked, here is the Carolina Pattern. Where does the Carolina Pattern change?" He was saying to historic sites archaeologists, "Here is something to which you can compare your data." We can begin to learn when the world looks different than we would have expected. Then we have a question, "Why is your pattern different than the Carolina Pattern?" That provides a basis from which to begin generalizing—as when South started saying things like, "Look, on the frontier we're getting much higher use of iron in construction than we are in plantation settings. Why?"

[Q:] *Is there a basic difference between looking at sites on the periphery of the system and looking at the core of the system?*

Well, generally.

[Q:] *I mean, can you define the nature of the system from one class, or do you have to have sites from both core and periphery areas?*

Look at it this way. When I dug Fort Michilimackinac, if I had only known what I saw in the site, I would have inferred that this is where porcelain was invented; or I would have had to infer that I was in China. In the classic model I'd been taught in school, the dominant pottery is made locally [laughing]. There was more Chinese porcelain per square inch at Michilimackinac probably than any other place I've ever been, except Southeast Asia—not China, but Southeast Asia.

Why are there no local ceramics at Fort Michilimackinac? There are some, but not many Native American pieces—but not inside the fort. It's outside the fort. This is a funny kind of settlement, yet the entire French period is represented there and there are local crafts. They made their own pipes, they made lots of their own stuff. Yet at the same time, I'm getting penknives with Arabic script saying, "Praise to Allah." Now where is this all coming from? All this is telling me about a system vastly broader than Fort Michilimackinac.

[Q:] *I can't go and excavate in China, at the porcelain factories, can I, and learn about the structure of this system? But aren't the porcelain factories part of the major system of the logistics of this network?*

That's true—because we don't know. But we may not have to know about the porcelain factories in order to compare Fort Michilimackinac with some other frontier fort.

It's my impression that the sources of the late Ming material that the Spanish were transporting across Panama weren't the same sources that the British were trading to. They were trading in north China. I wouldn't necessarily have to know these things to treat the fort in systemic terms.

I wouldn't have to have British King's Eighth Regiment buttons in the excavation to know that this assemblage was British. And what we want to understand is the nature of the system.

Look at it this way. Why is there so much Canton ware at Fort Michilimackinac? When I was a teenager, there was a movie called *Northwest Passage*, and it was about Major Robert Rogers, of the Rangers. The movie depicted Fort Michilimackinac, and Rogers's cabin. Things were so bad he almost committed cannabalism—he almost ate the head of a Native American in his Swedish log cabin [laughs].

Now here I am digging with Maxwell, who was excavating Robert Rogers's house, and it's got molded plaster ceilings, ivory billiard balls, more Venetian glass than you want to imagine.

Now why is all this stuff here? The British are paying the cost of getting this stuff from China, taking it somewhere, and sending it out to Fort Michilimackinac. Now what's this all about? It is paying people to go where they would otherwise never go. It is the perks of being a military officer. It's paying; it's the same thing the Romans did. It's much like Rome. The Romans were successful and so were the British. If you look at the *castella* across the Netherlands, there's more Roman glass in the Barbarian settlements than there is in the Roman forts.

[Q:] *But can the effect of logistics networks only be understood in terms of penetrations such as this on the periphery, or is there a better way to understand them than in studying on the periphery—perhaps through excavations throughout western Europe?*

I think you have to do both. It was not until actual excavations were done in Holland, at the pipe manufacturing centers that anyone realized how different the Dutch methods of manufacturing pipes were as opposed to the British. The pipe-stem technique doesn't work for Dutch pipes. It works for British. If you have mixed samples it still works fairly well. But it's going

to give you an earlier date if you have any Dutch pipes in there. Pipe manufacturing sequences were crucial for learning something about pipes.

You have to do both, but basically, what I'm saying about historical sites in Quebec—and I'm only making one point—is that you don't "interpret" your site. Your site is a datum point with certain potential controls and variables. Its value is realized when it is compared with other sites. And the pattering for which an explanation is sought results, not from the identifications ("this is such-and-such pipe; this is such-and-such house; this is the house of Robert Rogers"). As long as you're staying at that level, rather than saying, "Let's compare houses," or "Let's compare the kilns, or whatever," you're doing what historians do. You're going for the unique, you're going for the particular, you're going for isolating more and more detailed characteristics of events rather than seeing the commonalities and the contrast of events as they're played out in different settings and under different conditions.

[Q:] *Would this be a proper interpretation of what you're saying—that archaeologists work with the sites they have excavated and have at hand, and they should define the system on the basis of what they have at hand?*

Mmm-hmm [agreeing].

But then you use that.

[MDT:] . . . *to define the structure?*

That's the first step. That is telling me that the world's not flat—is telling me something about the world relative to my prior ideas.

[Q:] *How did you come to work with Moreau Maxwell at Mackinac?*

Moreau Maxwell had, as I recall, just recently taken the job at Michigan State. Griffin had been contacted by the Mackinac Island State Park commission about finding somebody to excavate Fort Michilimackinac. So Griffin proposed Moreau Maxwell as an archaeologist they might consider. Moreau then asked Griffin if he had any students who could help, because he hadn't done field archaeology for many years. He had been in the military, and here and there. Griffin said yes—he had me, and he would send me up. So I was sent up there to begin the excavations in 1959 with Moreau Maxwell.

We worked together, but we sort of decided that he would do his thing, and I would do mine. In other words, Moreau Maxwell was hesitant to tell me what to do, and I certainly wasn't going to tell him what to do. He excavated one area in the French quarter, and I excavated the big British barracks that first year. But it was like having two digs.

We were using prisoners out of Marquette Prison for crew. They were all murderers. But we had as many crew as we could handle, so we didn't have a lack of labor.

In '59 we worked together in parallel that way, but decided that afterwards we'd alternate. In '60 Moreau Maxwell excavated; in '61 I excavated. Then I moved to the University of Chicago and said I wasn't going to do it anymore.

So Moreau Maxwell and I had this strange kind of relationship, and I never knew what he was going to say—good, bad, or indifferent.

[Q:] *When I was at Chicago, I remember illustrations, and so on, that were in the laboratory. Were you still working on the report at that time?*

Yes. And that was an unhappy situation, because I did all these drawings and stuff. Maxwell was in charge of the official reports. None of that stuff was ever used. Well, the historians up there used my drawings in popular versions of tour guides. I was really angry because I had put in a huge amount of labor into all that, and written my report, and it was never published or acknowledged.

[Q:] *You mean that report at Chicago was never pubished? That wasn't the published report of Maxwell and Binford?*

The unpublished report was on the season that I was in charge of all the excavations—1961.

That thing that was published with Maxwell was on the 1959 excavations. He never published the material from 1960. And I wrote all that stuff for 1961. And there was money to make the publications.

I still have the manuscripts and all that artifact stuff—huge amounts of typological work and distribution studies and so on.

[Q:] *How did you become acquainted with James Deetz? Did his approach to historical archaeology influence you in any way? If not, why not?*

I don't remember when I first met Deetz. Maybe I heard a paper at a national meeting, or maybe I simply read one, I don't remember. But I became aware of Deetz. And when we were organizing things that were new, at some point, I judged his work to be different, and asked him to be involved in some of the meetings where we did things. And he did get involved. I guess he gave a paper in the '64 meetings and things like that. Basically, I sought him out because I saw a different way of looking at ceramic variability which I thought was interesting.

I didn't really get to know Deetz. I was responsible for him being invited to the "Man the Hunter" conference at Chicago. He had no credentials to be there, but I told Sol Tax they ought to invite him because I wanted to know something more about what he was doing. So they invited him. I guess I spent more time with him at that conference that I'd ever spent before.

Then when I was fired at Chicago, Jim Deetz suggested to [Charles] Erasmus [, chairman of the University of California at Santa Barbara anthropology department,] that I be offered the job they had. I was very grateful for this, because there weren't many jobs then.

When I first got to Santa Barbara, Jim Deetz was on leave, and I never saw him. Then he came back from being on sabbatical and the three of us—Jim Deetz, me, and Loring Brace—taught courses that started at 9 o'clock in the morning and went till noon, back-to-back. Loring

Brace was teaching Paleolithic, so he taught from 9 to 10. I was teaching Middle Paleolithic and methods, and I taught from 10 to 11. And Jim Deetz was teaching historical archaeology and he taught from 11 until 12. [Laughs]. We had these huge classes—I mean they were giant classes of 900 to 1,300 undergraduate students.

In that period I became very disillusioned with Jim Deetz, because of his treatment of students. Then I had a difficult time with him in the firing situation at Santa Barbara in 1966.

[MDT:] *You turned to Paleolithic archaeology while still at Chicago, before going to Santa Barbara.*

The reason I got interested in the Paleolithic was not so much that it was fascinating. There were two reasons. One was a practical reason. I realized early that all students of anthropology, at that time anyway, had to take a basic course in human origins. So the Paleolithic was the only place that an archaeologist had a chance to say something to the entire field of anthropology, in an educational sense. If you're doing something with Paleolithic, you get to talk to all the students. So that was a pragmatic reason.

But the more interesting reason was that I thought it was a field where an argument against idealism could be developed. This was because you couldn't make the assumption that Australopithecus was like us. You had to make the assumption that they were probably different. So you couldn't do these little thought games— "It would be rational for the Australopithecine to do this"—because you had no idea what was rational for an Australopithecine.

This meant you had to develop arguments about circumstantial evidence. You had to demonstrate necessary relationships between material things—not arguments about motive. That was why I was so successful in knocking down positions and in arguments within Paleolithic archaeology. They were all doing the reverse. I mean Glynn Isaac was making Australopithecines just like us, only they needed a "Head Start" program [laughs]. They were just interpreting what they saw in terms of what they knew about us.

Those are the reasons I went into Paleolithic studies. The reason I have gone into ethnography so much is because of its wealth of information that archaeologists need to know in order to reasonably think about variability in archaeological material.

[Q:] *Since you began in the archaeological fields, do you feel there has been really significant advance?*

It's hard to say, because I certainly know I've learned a lot. I have learned a huge amount by virtue of making decisions that forced me to learn more and more. I have certainly published a lot. I've tried to share that with archaeology. People have responded, people have argued about it. People have misused it.

If somebody else tells me they've got a hunting camp, I'm going to vomit—or that they have discovered a residential base camp. That's not the point. Identification is not the point. The point is what is conditioning the variability.

But, yes, archaeology is a much different field today than it was when I was a beginning student.

[Q:] *Was there ever a point in your career where you thought of doing much more with historical materials in archaeology? I remember, in California, you once said how intriguing it would be if an archaeologist controlled the languages and archaeologically investigated "the fall of Rome." It was never clear to me if this was one of your numerous good ideas which you never had any intention of pursuing. Or if it was something to which you had given a great deal of thought.*

I thought about it, but it was never something I thought of pursuing. You know, that's a classic example of what all archaeologists have been talking about—collapse, allegedly. I don't know that it really happened, but [laughs], as far as I know, nobody ever looked at it, to see what it looks like. Is there an archaeological record of the "collapse" of Rome? I doubt it. I don't think you're going to find a layer with pillaging and raping and barbarian pottery. I don't believe it. I'd be very curious, but I don't know. [Both laugh]

[Q:] *Eventually, as you went on to more inclusive development of your theoretical work, you lost contact with some of your early associates. When you went on to Michigan, Chicago, California, and New Mexico, did you maintain contact with Stanley South?*

Oh yes, still do. Of course I maintained contact with various people I got to know at Michigan and that I got to know in California. But Stanley South . . . Stanley South and I have been very, very close all of our careers. Now this doesn't mean that we write every day; we don't. But, any time that something comes up, when I want to know something about historic stuff, I call Stanley and ask him. If he wants to know something about opportunities for students, he calls me. When things happen in our personal lives, we immediately tell each other and try to help. We've just been very close for a long time.

As far as people from Ann Arbor, Charles McNutt has been an old friend, and we are still close friends. He's down at Memphis State. He's had a stroke now. Newman, who's down in Louisiana, I met on the upper Missouri. We've maintained a relationship, not as close, but we always could count on one another. When he wanted to go to China, I wrote recommendations. So it's been a lot of people like that, all over the place.

[Q:] *Since the 1980s, historical archaeologists have been influenced by "meta-historians," such as Braudel, and by similar work from the anthropologist Eric Wolf. Wolf left Chicago just before you joined the anthropology department. Did you ever have any contact with Wolf or meta-historians, and did they influence you in any way?*

I knew Wolf because, when he left Chicago, he went to Ann Arbor and was on the staff there. He was hired at Ann Arbor to teach peas-

ant communities—that general area. On several occasions I went to cocktail parties at Elman Service's home—and subsequent to my leaving Ann Arbor—where I met Wolf and talked to him at some length. He had not become a meta-historian then. He was still into peasant studies and comparative village studies and things like that.

My only contact with Eric as a meta-historian was to write him a note when he was the distinguished lecturer at the American Anthropological Association, and he gave a fairly old-timey, Marxist presentation. I liked it, and told him so.

Braudel I've never read, so I don't know anything about his work. I don't necessarily condemn him because of what people have done with this. Richard Gould is forever citing him and various people, and I think it's silly. But I haven't read his work, so I don't know what it's like.

[Q:] *Most historical archaeologists now see their field as being concerned with the archaeological explanation of the modern world. Do you believe that the basic difficulty for such an archaeology lies, as it does in prehistoric archaeology, in the development of middle range theory?*

The idea that historic archaeology is the explanation of the modern world insures that historic archaeology will never be a science. Science is dedicated to saying, "I'm going to explain the variability in my subject matter." That variability is what I look at in the empirical world. So, physics says, "I'm going to explain variability in physical phenomena, measured in terms of mass, velocity—these kinds of properties." And that's the subject matter of physics. So its problem is generated from the study of its subject matter. That problem comes from patterning in the subject matter, and it is this patterning which is in need of explanation.

My feeling has always been that archaeology as a science is the science of the archaeological record, and that problems arise from comparative study of the archaeological record, and in the recognition of the patterning there.

Any time you run around and say, "I want to use"—let's say abuse—"the archaeological record to answer some problem that I've decided ought to be solved," like gender issues ("what is the role of gender in the past?"), then you're not studying the archaeological record and its patterning; you're using the archaeological record as a vehicle for knowledge of claims about something else.

I'm dedicated to the study of the archaeological record. I think it's the study of the archaeological record—if we're going to make any claims at all—that we have to be concerned with. And that it's historical, or it's Paleo-Indian, or it's Paleolithic makes no difference. We should be dedicated to the study of our subject matter. We should not be sitting around saying, "I'm just studying the archaeolgical record because I might be able to mine some information for totally different purposes—I'm not interested in the archaeological record, as such." That ensures that we're not going to be a science—we're going to be rapists of the archaeological record.

[Q:] *As evolution occurs, systems become more complex. What if we defined historical archaeology in terms of being concerned with a single world system, which is a last systemic development of things in the earlier archaeological record? Would this be acceptable, or would you say it would still be divorcing the subject matter from archaeology in general?*

I think you would still be divorcing it. You have got to demonstrate to me from patterning in the archaeological record that you have a world system. You can't make the assumption and then accommodate the archaeological record to it. You have got to demonstrate to me that, really, what is going on in Paris is of great importance to the mortuary practices of the Celebes Islands. And if you can't, then Paris is irrelevant to that patterning on the Celebes Islands, and all those claims for world systems are bulls**t. Now if you can demonstrate patterning that links all this stuff, great. But that's coming out of the study of the archaeological record, not the romance of somebody's head. [There was here a slight difficulty with the recorder.]

[MDT:] *You were discussing your objections to taking the definition of historical archaeology as the archaeology of the modern world.*

I take a rather strict view of science, and in science one chooses an empirical domain as that which one studies and then the problems which one seeks to solve arise as a result of the study of that domain. So I've always thought that archaeology was the study of the archaeological record and that problems arose from the analytical research that we do, comparatively and otherwise, on the archaeological record.

My experience has been that if that's not the case, then the archaeological record gets abused in the following sense: when archaeologists thought that the major problem was chronology, they dug sites with deep stratigraphic cuts and little narrow trenches to look at things vertically. The result was that they didn't record the data that might be useful to someone who might want to look at the horizontal distributions.

Any time one has a narrow problem, even if a big problem, like the world, the modern world, they have a bias as to what is germane to that. And properties of the archaeological record that aren't in that "search image" get lost and destroyed.

I think, as in physics, any science has to say, "What I do is study a domain"—whether it is a natural one or an artificial one is irrelevant—"Here is the domain of the empirical world that I study. My study leads to the recognition of properties in this domain which we don't understand—and these are our problems." Otherwise you are always accommodating what the archaeological record has to say to some other interest. And the archaeological record never gets really studied.

Any time you decide beforehand what your problem is and then say "all right, I'm going to exploit this for solving my problem," you're in the position of generating accommodating arguments. You are accommodating what you see in the archaeological record—to what you believe about your problem.

[Q:] *Are there people actually doing that?*
All the time.

Let me put it this way. You mentioned earlier the notion of core/periphery. Well, that's been a big idea. And so, students are told, "well, you are working in the periphery," or "you're working in the core—and somehow or another you have to do this in order to do that."

I had a student like this last week, who had been told she was working in the periphery. She was working in central Asia, and she was working on sites that are pretty much 25 miles apart, or a little more. They're tiny little settlements and they're clearly related to the early use of Bactrian camels in transport. They were like Pony Express stations.

Carleton Coon wrote a book which I think is fascinating. I read it maybe once every three years. It's called *Caravan*. He argued that the development of complex systems in the Near East could only be understood in terms of what he called "the Land of Insolence." Now "the Land of Insolence" for Carleton Coon was what constrained state expansion, what caused states to fail, and what basically supported states in the Near East.

The whole notion of process is based on certain assumptions. If at that time a state had to mount an army, and if the army had to live off the land, and if the land is not productive, then you can't have an army there. You can't have an army in the Sahara. You can't have an army in the Libyan Desert. You can't have an army in the Sinai. You can't have an army in Saudi Arabia. You can't have an army in Jordan. [Both laugh.] You can't have an army in the Iranian Plateau. There's nothing for them to eat.

So these are areas where specialists develop. The whole trading characteristics of the Tuareg are related to being able to operate where they are beyond the control of states. But the states couldn't live without them, and they have enormous power relative to their size. If they decide to change their policies, they impact the states in ways that hundred, thousands, of other people making a change would not.

Coon's ideas about the organization of the system in "the Land of Insolence" were very different than this notion that "here's the core, where everything happens," and the parallel in an old diffusionist idea, "Here's where everything was invented," and then just dribbles out to the periphery—making the periphery somehow or other dependent upon the core. I'm not denying synergy, just skeptical of researchers' bias in how it might work.

I don't know that that is the way the world works. That is certainly not the way my parents felt during the depression in Virginia [laughs]. They didn't feel that they were somehow or another dependent upon what happened in Atlanta or Washington. They were dependent upon what they did and how they did it.

I have never been happy with these global notions of power, and centers of diffusion, and great invention, and all that nonsense. Complexity is the differentiation of things. What are the processes that bring into being differentiation ethnic, rural, economic, and all these kinds of groups, as well as states? You can't handle these with what is basically a diffusionist model.

There are so many arguments in archaeology right now. You have George Cowgill sitting in Mesoamerica saying, "I don't think demography has anything to do with complex society." And then you have somebody like Nathan Cohen saying, "I think demography is the cause." None of these things are accurate; none of them. Demography is not the cause; demography happens. On the other hand, changes in the number of people changes the demand for food. It changes the demand for goods. It changes the demand for labor. So there's no way that demography is not important in changing the system. So Cowgill can't be right either.

Most of these kinds of simple-minded positions on what's important cannot be correct, when you think about it. Yet, if you go and design your research in those terms ("I'm going to prove demography doesn't have anything to do with the origins of Tenochtitlán," or something like that), you're going to look at things in a biased way.

But if I say, "the only way I'm going to learn something new is if I can see something I haven't seen before in the relationship between things in the archaeological record," I'm continuously looking for new patterns, new relationships between things. And if I ask, "How do things interact in the statistics, and in the spatial distribution of things in the archaeological record?" Then there's no way I'm not going to learn something. But I'm not going to learn it by claiming that I know the answer before I look.

So I don't think most of those great overarching ideas do anything but make people feel warm and gooey. They certainly don't inspire you to do good archaeology.

[Q:] *Will the documentary record, to your mind, provide the major source for the development of middle range theory in historical archaeology? Or will middle range theory in the field develop primarily from more strictly archaeological work—or from a combination of the two?*

I think documentary knowledge is an absolutely crucial and essential body of prior knowledge for an archaeologist to have if he's going to work in a historic period. I don't think there is any question about that. Here's the information he can think with, and he'd better use it. But whether or not documentary knowledge is going to provide the answers to the archaeological record is another issue. I think you have to study the archaeological record and the problems are going to arise from that subject, and that subject matter used archaeologically.

I may bring my knowledge to bear from documents, but I'm never going to be able to understand the archaeological record by direct analogy to historical documents. The knowledge of history is useful—to help you think with when you are trying to solve archeological problems. But archaeological problems have to be solved within their own domain. I don't think they can be solved in someone else's patch.

The middle range work that is needed in historical archaeology is basically implicated in the question, "How do I diagnose the past from observations on the archaeological record in any accurate sense?" The middle range work has to be done in terms of a problem (or frustration) in trying to deal with the archaeological record. Then documentary work as well as experimental work in comparative study, ethnography, or whatever, may be a major aid in coming up with ways of learning from the archaeological record.

So my view is, the more prior knowledge I have, the better I'm able to think. That's because I then have more intellectual options. That is fundamental. But the problem, once again, comes down to the archaeological record.

Let me just take Fort Michilimackinac. Historians didn't want archaeologists to do anything at Fort Michilimackinac but to prove that this map that they had was accurate. They had a map made in 1742, I think, the so-called Magra map (now dated by historians to 1766). They wanted to reconstruct the fort on the basis of that map, and wanted to make sure we were in the right place. That was what historians wanted done.

Maxwell started digging in one place, and I started digging in another. My initial thoughts were: "Well, if we are in the right place, and if the Magra map is correct—as I had been told—then I want to dig a hole in the middle of the parade ground where I know there have been no structures. There I can see what the natural soil is like inside the fort. Then I will have a basis for understanding what it looks like when it's all disturbed and houses have been built."

I put my first hole down in the middle of the parade field, where there was not supposed to be anything, and came down on the biggest pair of back-to-back dolomite foundations for fireplaces you ever saw. And not only that, as we followed the foundations, we found this was a big structure. I got paired fireplaces.

Well, there's not supposed to be anything here, and the historians are all upset. This is in the middle of the parade ground, and here's this enormous structure. It's obviously of the British period, and there are King's Eighth Regiment buttons everywhere—just incredible stuff.

What the historians didn't know was that the British, during the Revolution, had gotten upset about the Americans, and brought in the King's Eighth Regiment, and secretly built a giant barracks in the only place in the fort that there was any place to build such a building—which was in the middle of the parade ground. The British had all these nice little guys waiting for the Americans when they were going to come north. But the historians didn't know this.

Now what is interesting is that once we found the barracks, they found it in the literature. But they didn't know it before. The literature hadn't changed. So why didn't they know from their giant, wonderful research that there was going to be a barracks? The answer was that they didn't know whether it was propaganda or not. This barracks was referred to in all the documents, but had been dismissed by historians as simply propaganda mounted to scare the Americans. It turned out to be real [laughs].

The historians were totally upset, because, God, here's this magnificent structure—a wonderful story—and we can't move it. It's too big. I mean these are dolomitic foundations for huge fireplaces; can't move it. This is in the middle of the parade ground. What are we going to do?

Their response was to bury it all back up and construct the fort as of 1742, or whatever their target date was. But that was not quite possible, because since 1742 there had been at least four building facies in the fort, and there was very little left, archaeologically, of 1742. We had the French period at the time of Pontiac's rebellion pretty well, but we didn't have much before that. [Laughs.]

Working with the historians was a totally frustrating event. And we were finding stuff that, as archaeologists, we had to deal with. We, of course, got French material in certain sections of the site. If we're doing the archaeology of the modern world, do I throw all of that away? What do I throw away in order to argue about the archaeology of the modern world, rather than to deal with variability in the archaeological record?

[MDT Note: If Binford's use of the "archaeology of the modern world" seems, on this specific point, to be incongruous with common usage of historical archaeologists, they should remember that earlier Binford explicitly denied the value of the simple diffusionist model—which he equated with historical archaeologists' usage of a modern world-system type model. As Binford sees all cultural contact as involving complex interchanges, his main criticism at this point is that the modern world-system type model requires, essentially, a simplistic "acculturative" interpretation, which is not even adequate to explain the found archaeological variability of the locally made French items at the fort.]

[Q:] Once you said that historical archaeology might come to hold the foremost position in archaeological theory building. Did you have middle range theory specifically in mind then?

Yes, I did. Because in a historic context you have lots of different variables that we know—from documents and so on—lots of conditions that you can design experiments with. If I know these conditions are all constant over here and are different over there, then I can compare similar things in different contexts and begin to see the consequences of contextual differences, in orgnization, and so forth. So the more knowledge I have, the more ability I have to design comparative experiments to learn things.

[Q:] Could you exemplify this?

Okay, let me take a very broad example. This is not necesarily all archaeology—some of it is history—but it is an example I know well. If you look at Europe, after the appearance of domesticated plants and animals, you had societies that had both. They had a heavy investment in domesticated animals and agriculture. This is true in Africa. It is true all the way across Europe. It is true in Asia. It's true of South America. But it is not true of America north of Panama. Here there was a major investment in domesticated plants, and there were no effective domesticated animals in pre-Columbian times.

So now—if I want to determine the answer to this question, "What is the effect of having domesticated animals and plants, versus only having plants?"—I can design experiments. I try to hold the demographic scales constant in North America, where they didn't have domesticated animals, to compare it to places in Peru and Europe where they had both domesticated plants and animals.

When you first start playing this game, the first thing you see is what we get from history—and no North Americanist has ever talked about this, for they don't do comparisons. What we get from history is that warfare in North America was never for inhabited land; it was always for uninhabited land. It was warfare over hunting territory. In Europe, warfare was over agricultural lands, it was over inhabited villages. It was over infrastructure. It was never over uninhabited land. Now isn't that interesting?

The entire organization of warfare among Native Americans in North America was in terms of males going off into the hunting territories, taking captives, getting ransoms, doing all these various things. It was a phenomenon of the fall season. It was all about theft. But it was rarely, if ever, about stealing people's agricultural land or their infrastructure.

North of Panama there were effectively no domesticated animals, only domesticated plants. Knowing this, we can ask, "How does such a system compete with other such systems? As soon as you ask about competition, you realize that competition was for totally different things here than it was in Europe. Now that has to have an effect on the way cultural systems develop and change. So you've got an experiment you can do. But you've got to be able to get beyond your little history, to see the difference between archaeology in North America versus archaeology elsewhere. Similarly, trade played different roles. It's really interesting, but we are only providing an example of experimentation.

Another kind of experiment: I suspect that everybody is correct, that Native Americans came into the New World across the Bering Strait.

Well that is a disease filter. Most tropical organisms would not make it across. The people, then, are coming into the New World with a very minimal disease load. They're radiating, for the first time in human history, from north to south, from polar to equatorial settings. All other previous radiations had been from equatorial to polar settings. So we have a reverse process.

Now is a radiation in reverse direction, from the standpoint of ecosystem, different from one that's going the other way? Point number one. Point number two: What is the effect of bringing groups of people into highly productive equatorial settings in which there had been no co-evolution of disease species in the past? The answer is that you're watching the archaeology of a Charlie Chaplin movie. It is speeded up. I've already had students do this in two different theses. The average length of time from the appearance of the first domesticates to the appearance of the first public structures, that aren't palaces or such, in Europe is 6,000 years; in North America it's 1,300 years. Interesting. [Laughs].

We are now getting close to variables. And that is what we want to know about. A difference between having domesticated animals, versus not having them, makes you have differential competition. Having a disease load or not makes for differential rates of cultural evolution. There are fascinating things like these which we want to learn about. And it's a matter of trying to find out where you can hold variables constant, and where you can let them vary, to see the different effects of different variables. Historical approaches generally make it possible to do this, but their focus is wrong.

What is the difference between a colony that is essentially an aristocracy and has an aristocratic core, versus a colony that doesn't? What is the relationship to the initial governing bodies? I think it has to be totally different. We know that in Australia. [Laughs]. And you can compare the setlements that were founded by, in a sense, aristocratic Europeans who were exiled versus prisoners. Oh my God, the contrast in the society in Australia in the early days was staggering.

These are the kind of things we want to get the handle on to begin to see how the world really works and what the important variables are. History gives you a good knowledge background for historical archaeology, and gives you some control over which variables you can say, with confidence, were or were not relevant in a particular place. That is crucial to doing good science. Why don't historians do it?

[Q:] *Since the 1980s, "Post-Processual Archaeology" has appeared, and Mark Leone has been its major figure in historical archaeology. What do you believe are the major contributions, or difficulties, or both, of this approach?*

Post-processual archaeology, in my opinion, is not archaeology. It is anti-science. You can't get much more negative than that. [Laughs.]

Post-processual arguments basically say that we cannot know, we cannot evaluate our own ideas, we cannot learn, we can only reflect the biases of our received knowledge. It says we're all biased, we're all cultural beings, and when we say we have a method by which we may learn something, we are, then, essentially intellectual imperialists. That's their position. The bottom line is that everybody's ideas are equally good, no matter how stupid they are. That's the message of post-processualism.

The position of post-processualism has this nihilistic argument that basically we can't learn because we're prisoners of our own culture, and we don't even know our own biases. It concludes that there is no way of judging who is right or even if there was an actual past that one can correctly know.

Science, of course, makes all the opposite assumptions. It basically makes the assumption that we can learn and that there are methods whereby we can use our prior knowledge to allow us to recognize our ignorance, and in turn that there are ways in which we can manipulate our prior knowledge so that experience can be a teacher of new things. Post-processualists deny this.

Now that Mark Leone is a "good" post-processualist, I would not argue with him when he says some aspects of science are useful. But

then he adopts a posture which is associated with post-processualism, that the explanation for everything in the archaeological record is a reflection of mind. In that sense he is in the post-processualist philosophical domain, but, ironically, he sort of denies the other side of their argument—that you can't learn. He accepts the scientific position that you can learn.

[Nancy Stone enters.]

[Nancy Stone:] *Can I interrupt? But leave it [the recorder] on. Remember—Lew will remember this. Remember when we were in Australia, at Armidale, and people asked, generally, how you know the past? Mark Leone stood up and he said, "Well, in the 19th century we received, or it was presented to us, a theory about why things are the way they are: this was Marxism." And he said, "This explains it." Remember?*

[LRB:] Yes; yes.

[NS:] *Talk about that. He got right up and he said, "We already know why things are the way they are!"*

[LRB:] Yes, I agree. But that's not post-processualism.

[NS:] *No, it's not, and he straddles both domains.*

[LRB:] That's right. [NS exits.]

I agree with what she is saying. But that has been his way. He's not really a post-processualist. He accepts some of the propositions, the mentalism, that the explanation is in the minds of people. But he accepts some of the propositions of science. Then on top of all this, he is a committed Marxist, in a funny sense. But he is a post-World War II Marxist, and they're all idealists. They're not materialists. They have accepted the mind business as well. Mark is not a very pure post-processualist, so he's not a very good one. He's an anachronistic scientist and he's a born-again Marxist. So it's really difficult to talk about him [laughing].

[Q:] *Do you have any other comments on post-processualism?*

I think if you adopt post-processualism there is nothing for you to do but to argue with other people's opinions, because the archaeological record is dismissed as having no inherent structure or patterning independent of our ideas about it. So all you do is argue with other people over their interpretation of it. This is just a non-event. You can't learn anything this way.

[Q:] *Besides your general theoretical work which has had an impact on historical archaeology, you have made contributions specifically to the field, as in your pipe-stem dating formula. Over, say, the last 10 or 15 years, have you tried to keep abreast, at least in a general way, with developments in historical archaeology? If so, how would you evaluate the general direction the field has taken? If not, why not? Is this from dissatisfaction with the course of the field, or in the press of work have you limited yourself to things more directly concerned with your overall theoretical ambitions?*

I really haven't made any effort for a long time to keep up with the literature of historic archaeology. The exception has been that I keep up with the work of Stanley South because we know each other and we talk about what he's doing. So I track what he's doing. And of course he expresses opinions. [Laughs.] So I know something about his opinions regarding the field. But it's just through him; it's not through any independent work of my own. That's the only way I've kept up with it—through Stanley South.

It's not because I wasn't interested; it's just that you can't do everything. [Laughs.] And I have sort of committed myself to demonstrating to archaeology how you actually use ethnographic or historical knowledge. I chose in this case to use ethnographic and historical records of hunting and gathering people.

Periodically, I get students that are interested in historic sites archaeology. I probably have a biased sample, but what most students here at SMU who have come in to me want to know is how to identify things.

[Q:] *You mean objects?*
Objects. So they're really into objectology. I've tried to make them read other stuff, and then they come back and say, "Well, I don't have the

time. There's not enough time in life to learn all the kinds of nails and all the kinds of bullets and all the kinds of this-and-that. I need to really invest my time in being able to identify these things that we find in Civil War sites (or whatever their site happens to be)."

That has been a common kind of experience with students recently. They seem to be overwelmed with the notion of what they have to learn at the practical level to actually do historic sites archaeology. And I can understand that. That is daunting.

I think there is this notion that you have to know everything—what everything that you find is—or you're not qualified. When we started—I'm thinking of Stanley and I—we didn't know what anything was. You know, we were in the process of learning. For instance, none of the ceramic chronology that you have today—not even the work of the British ceramicists, was known in a chronological sense then. The late British sequence from the 1700s was not well documented.

We just had all the stuff, and we basically dealt with it as classes of things that we could see. We could see the difference between, you know, blue-glazed tinwares versus something else, and we dealt with things in those terms. And we began to learn the difference between British and French gun flints, and this kind of stuff, because we could see differences.

I almost feel that being able to look at things and see differences is more important than knowing what the things are; that just developing skills of recognizing things might be the important thing to learn.

[Q:] *You're saying, essentially, that you were operating at the level of a pre-historical archaeologist . . . .*
Right.

. . . going into an area which was not known . . .
Right.

. . . and making the visual differentiation . . .

Sure.

. . . *of artifacts which you could recognize?*
Right.

[Q:] *That's right?*
Yes.

[Q:] *I'm not misinterpreting you?*
That's right. That's right.

At least, for instance, on historic sites in Texas, most of which are Civil War, the students come in and say, "We are CRM people and we have got the contract to do this or that site. How do I learn what it is I'm looking at?" And I say, "I don't know." [Both laugh.] I don't know any books on the Civil War or whatever.

That's really their concern. They're not concerned with, "How do I dig?" or "How do I document an archaeological site?" They seem to be more concerned with passing their little test of competency by being able to identify things. But I don't know that that's really true of all historic sites archaeology. But it seems to be true of some of the CRM stuff.

[Q:] *How long, would you say, has it been since you really made an effort apart from Stanley South, to keep abreast of what has been going on in historical archaeology?*
Oh, I think I tried to keep up with things until maybe the middle 1980s. About 1985—something like that—because I had, by that time, large numbers of students in Albuquerque. I had field projects going on everywhere. We had a larger number of faculty, so I didn't have to teach as great a breadth of subject matter as I used to do. I began to cut back at that point. Mainly because I had so many students and I just couldn't keep up with everything.

[Q:] *Mercifully, we are at the last question, Lew.* [He laughs.] *Are there any points which you feel are relevant which have not been covered, or are there elaborations you would like to make concerning anything already touched on?*
[Very long pause.]

All I can say is that a lot of the thoughts that I had while we were talking came back to one sort of fundamental thing. In terms of goals, in terms of approaches, I don't think there is any difference between historical archaeology and any other kind of archaeology. The subject matter for study is the archaeological record and the patterning in the archaeological record should define our problems.

If we impose on the archaeological record what comes from somewhere else, what comes from history, what comes from the political interests of the time—feminist movements, whatever—I don't think that serves archaeology well. I'm not saying such things aren't important. But unless I can justify from the archaeological record some patterning that implicates those things, then I am trying to find it because I think I'd like to know it. That is the wrong way to go. That generally results in forced accommodations between observations and ideas.

The archaeological record is hard enough to understand if we take it at face value: "Here's what is there; how do we understand it?" Let's work out the methods for being able to relate what we see to past conditions in an accurate way, because we don't do this very well now. Yet half the time archaeologists are walking around talking about "the limitations of the archaeological record."

The archaeological record is only limited because the archaeologist doesn't see any self-evident way of talking about what he wanted to talk about for the past. That is not a measure of limitation, because there are no self-evident facts. The only way we are going to get to the past from the archaeological record is by hard work in the sense of figuring out what are the conditions which unambiguously implicate certain kinds of patterning in the archaeological record. And I think that is true in the historic period as well in the other periods.

I'm perfectly aware that the historic period is better informed— there's more knowledge to bring to bear in doing its archaeology—but I don't think that makes the doing any different. It's like when I was with the Eskimos.

I would go out on sites that these Eskimos had lived on, where they had in fact created the archaeological record I was looking at. We'd clean the site up and look at it. Here's a house, and the guy that lived in the house is standing right inside it.

And I'd ask him, "Why are all the metapodials over here?"

And he'd say, "I don't know why they're over there."

So I'd say,"Well, you did it. You lived here."

"Yeah," he'd say, "but I didn't pay any attention to metapodials; they're just old bones to me."

Yet then we'd walk around the site, and every one of the houses had metapodials in the same place. So I'd say, "look at this."

He'd say: [scoffing] "Crazy Eskimos. I don't know why."

So then we'd leave the site. Maybe three weeks later I'd see the man again. He comes running across the field "I know why. I know. I know why."

I'd say to him, "Hey, what are you talking about?"

"The metapodials," he'd say,"the metapodials! I figured it out."

So half the stuff that we were seeing as archaeologists, the people who produced it didn't understand. That's because they don't live their life in terms of where they throw things away [laughing] or how they push things out of the way, or what their wife does when they're not looking. They don't live their life in those terms. So there is tons of stuff in the archaeological record that informs us about things that even the participants didn't know about.

This is a tremendously interesting asset, with a wonderful potential. We have to basically look at what the patterning is in the archaeological record and use that to define our problems. Because if we want the archaeological record to be what it isn't, we're never going to learn and we're never going to be satisfied. We are always going to say, "It's limited, it doesn't tell me what I want to know." Because we want it to be something it isn't.

[Nancy Stone reenters:] *Now I'm about to serve. Is that a good stopping point?*

[LRB:] Yes, it is.

[NS:] *Do you want the archaeological record to be something it isn't?* [NS begins to leave.]

[LRB:] A lot of people do, and they don't even understand what it is.

You want to have some supper?

ACKNOWLEDGMENTS

The greatest debt is to Lewis R. Binford, for agreeing to this interview. But the debt is compounded, for Lew and Nancy Stone also provided bed and board in Dallas. In addition, Nancy also made great—and successful—efforts to get an extra, last-minute, ticket, so I might accompany them to the ballet. And this treat, to one who is culturally deprived, will long be remembered. Attorney, classics scholar, and nephew, Martin T. Sigillito, and my daughter, Tanya E. Thurman, French graduate student, verified my transcriptions of some words. My son, John A. P. Thurman, Kenyon College '98, made the superlatively accurate verbatim transcript. My heartfelt thanks to all.

MELBURN D. THURMAN
PO BOX 391
STE. GENEVIEVE, MO 63670

DANIEL G. ROBERTS

A Conversation with John L. Cotter

Introduction

I first met John L. Cotter in the winter of 1971, although I doubt if he remembers the circumstances. I was a 24-year old field archaeologist working at Franklin Court, one of the National Park Service's properties at Independence National Historical Park in Philadelphia, and John was Regional Archeologist for the Park Service who was then nearly 60 years of age. The project I was working on was headed by Barbara Liggett, who was under contract to the Park Service to excavate in the basements of a series of five 18th century properties adjacent to the subsurface foundations of Benjamin Franklin's house. The contract was administered, of course, by John Cotter. As I remember it, one day John visited the site, and I happened to be trowelling out artifacts from the bottom of a privy, about 15 feet below grade in a brick-lined shaft no larger than about 3+ feet in circumference (OSHA-compliance was not an archaeological consideration in those days). All of a sudden my attention was directed to the opening above by Barbara Liggett, who wanted to introduce me to a newly-arrived visitor. All I could see was the outline of the head and shoulders of a dapper man with a light gray mustache and goatee wearing a checked fedora peering over the side of the privy. Words to the effect of "How are you, young man?" and "Fine, thank you, nice to meet you" were exchanged, and that was that. I never saw him again or spoke with him for another dozen years, during which time I relocated to the western United States for awhile and John finished his 37-year stint with the National Park Service, his 19-year association with the Department of American Civilization at the University of Pennsylvania, and retired. As most historical archaeologists are probably aware, however, John

didn't really retire, he simply enabled himself to devote more time to writing, research, and mentoring after his official "retirement" in 1979.

I was not one of John's students at Penn, but I did have the good fortune to work closely with him (and Michael Parrington) for nearly 10 years in the preparation of a book on Philadelphia's archaeology, which John talks a bit about in the following interview. The genesis of the book took place in discussions I had with John at the 1983 annual meeting of the Society for American Archaeology in Pittsburgh which, as far as I can remember, was the next time I spoke with him after our "privy meeting" in 1971. I had in mind doing an annotated bibliography on the archaeology of Philadelphia, and I knew John had an enormous stockpile of unpublished reports, notes, etc. in his library. Within about five minutes of approaching him with the annotated bibliography idea, John said "Hell, Dan, let's do a book!" and that, too, was that—the book was officially underway.

During the time we worked closely together I found John to be an incredible source of historical and archaeological knowledge, with a broad-based vision of what archaeology embraces that few can equal. He is truly a generalist, and has an enormous wealth of facts and ideas stored up in his head. The anecdotes he can recall and relate from his exceptionally varied career are a joy to listen to, as I hope the following interview conveys. Although at all times he is a consummate gentleman, he also has a mischievous, even risqué, side to him. During the preparation of the Philadelphia book, for example, one of his principal regrets was that we had only two pornographic pipe tampers to illustrate and represent what he was sure was a robust body of Philadelphia pornographic artifacts destroyed before the archaeologist could lay hands on them or still lying undiscovered beneath the city.

John is probably mostly associated with historical archaeology and, indeed, he was the first recipient of SHA's prestigious Harrington Award in 1983 and the subject of a volume of historic archaeological papers compiled in his honor and published in 1984. But his interests and influences have been remarkably broad over a more than 60 year career, and include, among many other things, involvement in the early man discoveries at Clovis and Lindenmeier; WPA employment in the Kentucky river bottoms; numerous assignments during his National Park Service career, including posts at Tuzigoot, Natchez Trace, and Jamestown; and his involvement in the historical archaeology of the Philadelphia region. When asked in the following interview if he considered himself to be first and foremost an historical archaeologist, he replied "No, I'm just an archaeologist."

The interview took place on two successive weekends in the spring of 1995 at the office that John still maintains at the University of Pennsylvania. Here he puts in about 20 hours a week on research and writing, surrounded by a large and eclectic library of archaeological and historical literature. He has recently been practicing with computer technology with an eye toward imminent emancipation from his old IBM Selectric typewriter, and with the aid of Rick Sprague and Ronn Michael, he finally has concluded his years of labor on a bibliography of historical archaeology which he began in 1964. It is now available on line at The Society for Historical Archaeology's web site.

After the interview was completed, approximately five hours of audio tape were transcribed by Margy Schoettle (a thankless job which she cheerfully and expertly accomplished, claiming all the while that she enjoyed it immensely, and for which I am grateful) and then edited several times by both John and me to correct spellings of proper names and otherwise re-format the interview for the published page. On several occasions during this process John modestly expressed amazement that anyone would take the time to commit his reminiscences to print, but I have steadfastly maintained this is important stuff that needs to be preserved in the SHA archives. I am grateful to John for being such a candid and entertaining interview subject. Most importantly, I am honored to be John's friend and to

call him friend, and I am pleased to have been the one to conduct the following interview.

The Interview

[Q:] *Let's begin by talking about your early life in Denver.*

My life began in Denver 6 December 1911 at Mercy Hospital. A brother predeceased my arrival, and so I grew up an only child. My father was a gentle and lovable man who lacked only one virtue—ambition—if that is a virtue. Although he was a pioneer with the Bell Telephone Company—he started in 1904—he somehow never had a job that he could depend on. He did a lot of traveling, installing PBX's (private branch exchanges) all over the Rocky Mountain West, so we moved around. I grew up vicariously in Butte and Helena, Montana, and then back to Denver; after completing the 4th grade in Denver, I went to La Mesa, California, which is now part of San Diego, and attended a school that had three grades in one room where I had an opportunity to listen to advanced grades and learned the secret of learning without compulsion. Learning by listening to others learn, you learn a lot more and a lot faster, and with discrimination. After that I found myself in Spokane, Washington going to school and then Butte, and Livingston, Montana, then finally to Longmont, Colorado, and back to Denver for my junior high and high school years.

I never thought I would be going to college because my family simply didn't have the means, and college was not in my family's background. My father was born in Dubuque, Iowa, into a big Irish family of which I am the only grandchild of eight children. The Cotters ended up in Denver, Colorado and there he met my mother. My mother came from a large German family and her father, Joseph Henry Becker, was a businessman in Denver and quite a successful one. He had a wholesale liquor and tobacco business supplying the miners in the mountain mining area. He had a man go with a wagon loaded with the things that comfort the miners in the mountains. His name was Julius Kessler—a young, aggressive, and very enterprising salesman who ended up one of the big whiskey makers in the United States. Kessler's Choice was his product, and later on after prohibition, he really went to town. However, aside from that, Henry Becker's business was not a continuing success. He sold out, moved out of Denver and lost his money. My mother went part of the way through East Denver High School, but didn't like math and simply dropped out. But she was an accomplished musician with some very good musical training. She had a beautiful contralto voice and did quite a bit of singing in churches and became well-known in Denver. She married my father, much against the will of his family and hers. He was about 10 years older than she was when she began the various adventures and misadventures of the Cotter family.

By the time I progressed from Morey Junior High School to East Denver High School, I was wondering what I would do afterward, hoping of course that I would get to college. I was the editor of our school paper in East Denver High School and as I graduated the principal, Roscoe C. Hill, called me to his office and he said, "Jack" (I was Jack Cotter in those days), "Jack, I have a job for you this summer, at the Associated Press." I almost dropped. I just couldn't believe this magic had descended upon me. I went down to the Associated Press in Denver, which was located in the *Rocky Mountain News* at the time, and found that the job was 6 o'clock in the evening till 3 o'clock in the morning and my work was taking care of the automatic typewriter which was activated in Kansas City and printed in Denver. I made up 10 carbons, put them in the typewriter and when the typewriter was finished took the carbon copies to the various places where they were to go in the organization. That was my job, and by the time the summer was over, journalism wasn't exactly my idea of a career.

Luckily, I had a scholarship for one-half tuition for one year at the University of Denver and my mother and father had just a tiny nest egg that

they invaded; it made up the other half and I went to the University of Denver and there I got a job with the National Youth Administration. A little later on, when I understood what geology was, I tutored geology. I also washed dishes at a restaurant and managed to help myself along, still expecting I would go into journalism. I got on the school paper and I went ahead with my plans while taking some courses in anthropology.

The University of Denver had a one-man anthropology department which was run by Etienne Bernardo Renaud. Renaud was a quintessential Frenchman who had gotten his doctorate at the University of Denver right after World War I when the University needed people with Ph.D.'s. They accepted his thesis on Edmund Rostand and gave him his doctorate. He meanwhile became interested in anthropology and took some work with an American school abroad, met Aleš Hrdlička and other anthropologists, and toured France. Since he spoke French as a native, he was quite useful. He became acquainted with anthropology and took pains to understand the texts. Pretty soon he was teaching anthropology at the University of Denver. His technique was to have an open book before him as he conducted his class (he simply followed the book), but he was also a very inspirational teacher because he could convey a sense of what a subject was and get you interested in it and enthusiastic about going on with it. He also had a field school in the summer; he had a little car that he would drive out in the field and would always insist that the people in his class who had cars use their own. He would sometimes buy gas for them and sometimes a few groceries and that was it. But it turned out that he usually had a grant from a wealthy party in Denver and he always had a new car at the end of the season.

He had a field class in Santa Fe for a couple of years which I managed to attend. At that time I had gotten to be 20 years old and still didn't know how to drive. We never had a car in the family. I had an uncle in Longmont,

Colorado who was a Ford dealer who told my mother one day that a boy with whom I had gone to school there before I came to Denver had died of scarlet fever. His name was Kernan Gardner, and he had graduated from high school and gone to Colorado University at Fort Collins. His family had given him a Ford roadster with a Stromberg downdraft carburetor and a police head, sexy as hell, black and with mandarin red trimmings, and side-mounted tires with red trimming, luggage rack in back, and a canvas top. They wanted to get rid of it and offered it to my mother for $250. She took $250 of a tiny legacy from a deceased uncle and bought me the car. Since I did not know how to drive, I read up on automobiles, turned on the ignition at 5 o'clock one morning, got it out of the garage when there wasn't anything on the city roads, and practiced. In a month I knew how to drive. That started me on archaeology because then I could join the field parties and feel that I could carry my weight with driving.

[Q:] *Had you been taking anthropology or archaeology courses at this time?*

At that time I had been taking quite a few anthropology courses as well as courses in English, to go into journalism. I found that I had more credits in anthropology than anything else, so I went to the Dean of Men, and said, "I find that I have actually come to a major in anthropology and I don't know whether I can make a living at it. What would you say I'd better do?" And he told me something that I've never forgotten. "If you're interested in something enough you'll make a living in it." So I took him at his word and went ahead.

[Q:] *What was E. B. Renaud like?*

He was the only one in the Anthropology Department and frankly he was a fraud. He wasn't an anthropologist at all. He was a fast-moving, smooth-talking Frenchman with a horrible accent that everybody loved; however, he was quite interesting, certainly to his students.

[Q:] *Didn't Renaud conduct some early research on teshoas and other types of cobble choppers?*

Yes, he did. In Wyoming he would pick up ovate choppers, which we assumed might be just blanks. He would look at one of them and say, "This is a *coup de poing*." For all we knew it was an Aurignacian *coup de poing*, and what the hell it was doing in Wyoming we weren't sure. But there it was in your hand, and the French go by typology.

At that time he didn't know any more about anthropology than to think that typology was the whole game, so he simply said that this was what it was and let you decide how it got there, and when. However, these were not necessarily blanks and I have always wondered just what these peculiar flaked objects really were and why they were there in the valleys of Wyoming.

[Q:] *By this point had you received your Bachelor's degree in anthropology?*

I got my Bachelor's degree and decided I would go on for a M.A., since I had a thesis topic that I was very much interested in, and that was the fluted Folsom point, and I wanted to make a survey to see just what the distribution of it was. I wrote as many letters as I could to people who had said they had found them in other states and I reached as far east as Pennsylvania and even corresponded with people like Edgar B. Howard at the University of Pennsylvania. Finally I realized that, sure enough, we were finding these things all the way from the east coast to the Rocky Mountain West, and down into the Southwest. There was a tremendous spread, but the focus seemed to be in Colorado, which wasn't odd because that's where everybody had been hunting Folsom points. For an M.A. thesis I got up a study based on the first 1,000 Folsom and Yuma points, but when I had just about finished it, Renaud came out with a mimeographed report on "The First 1,000 Folsom and Yuma Points," using my data to extend his 1931-1932 work. It happened that I had shown my work to Jesse D. Figgins, then

Director of the Colorado (now Denver) Museum of Natural History, for whom I had worked at the Weld County Oligocene fossil beds, as well as at the Lindenmeier Folsom site and in the lab preparing specimens. Figgins was outraged and said that I had been hijacked. He had intended to publish my thesis in the Museum Series, and that resulted in his having a falling out with Renaud. I just kept my cool, measured a couple hundred more points, and completed my thesis, with maps and illustrations, including comparable Solutrean and Yuma forms, which Renaud had previously observed. He knew his Old World analogs in form.

[Q:] *How did you feel about Renaud after this?*

Well, I felt a little queasy about him. After all, I was getting my degree from Renaud and I had to go along with him. There was nothing else I could do, so I didn't make any objections and I didn't get indignant about it. I simply took my examination. Renaud had a couple of other faculty members in on the exam who didn't know much about anthropology, so I made out well enough to pass and he helped me make out an application to the University of Pennsylvania for a Harrison Scholarship. To my enormous amazement, and I don't doubt Renaud's also, I got it. So in September of 1935 I sold the Ford roadster, bought a bus ticket, and came to the University of Pennsylvania to begin a serious attack on the problem of getting a Ph.D. in anthropology.

[Q:] *Before we get into that for just a moment—did you have to switch your M.A. topic, since Renaud apparently swiped some of your ideas on your original thesis topic?*

Oh no, my thesis was accepted at the University of Denver and I still have a copy of it and there's one in the Library of the University of Denver. It remains the first documented survey accounting for the North American presence of fluted and Archaic ripple-flaked artifacts.

[Q:] *Before that you had several experiences at early man sites with the Colorado Museum of Natural History. Could you go into that a little more?*

That's right. Jesse D. Figgins had been the one who had recognized the disclosure by Carl Schwascheim and others of the original Folsom site in northeastern New Mexico. The site had been found by a cowboy named George McJunkin in 1908. He had found *Bison oxidentalis* bones in a gully near Folsom after a cloudburst that took out part of the little town. Figgins immediately notified the American Museum of Natural History (AMNH) and the Smithsonian Institution, and they sent parties to verify the find. By 1934 both the AMNH and the Smithsonian were interested in the Lindenmeier site 40 miles north of Fort Collins, Colorado. After I had finished a season at the Weld County Trigonius-Oligocene rhinoceros-fossil quarry, Figgins and Frank Roberts agreed that I could go to an area just above the Smithsonian dig and excavate. So I was chosen as head of a party of three. There was Harvey Goettsche, who was a kid from West Texas, and there was Bob Landberg, who was the assistant to Philip Rhineheimer, who ran the fossil laboratory at the Colorado Museum of Natural History. Bob was Swedish, rather wild, and older than we—I suppose as much as 10 years older than I, and the other kid was a little younger than I. I cased the locality until we found a place to dig. The Lindenmeier site was a spring with a long slope above it which ended in an abrupt eroded scarp of brule clay, and it had eroded continuously ever since the site was occupied some 11,000 years ago. Much of the site was probably lost to erosion but what was left was between the top of the slope and the spring, and in that slope we found quite a few stratified artifact deposits and some bison bones—no mammoth, however. We opened up a 20 x 20 foot area and found a pretty good place above the spring and beyond Frank Roberts' trenches. It had stratigraphy down to the level where Frank was finding things and we found, beside fluted blade debris, half of a lignite bead and half of a bone disc with graved edges. We also found some spalls from the fluted blades that had been chipped so that very sharp little points remained for some purpose—possibly tattooing or at least puncturing. Of course a bone needle would have been just as useful for tattooing. I wrote up our observations, and so we finished that season.

[Q:] *Which season was that?*

This was 1935. I got to meet several people at the Smithsonian, including Carl Miller and Loren Eiseley. Eiseley was held in considerable awe by the rest of us because he had had a poem published in the *American Mercury*, which was heavy stuff at the time. And he also had published in the *Prairie Schooner*, which was one of the very good literary magazines in the Midwest. He had also been continuing his graduate studies at the University of Nebraska. He told us about his travels, and his bumming around the country on the freight trains—a very interesting person. We had Bill Beatty, who was later an anthropologist at the University of Washington, I believe—a very interesting guy and a very fine anthropologist later on. Charles Theodore Rutledge Bohannon, a western galoot from Bethesda, Maryland, was there, and Davey MacAlister, an ethnomusiocologist, was another. We also had at that time Frank Roberts and his wife Linda, who was a very beautiful young woman and a much-admired addition to the camp for all the guys. We would sing at night and we would recall the usual jingles and outrageous stuff that kids in college love, especially in the East, and it was pretty risqué. We got up a saga of Folsom man which we put into music and words. More than 40 years later Davy MacAlister, at a meeting at the University (of Pennsylvania) Museum, told me that a friend of his had gone to the Library of Congress and found among the western lore a legubrious western ditty he and Charles Scoggin had composed, plus this saga of Folsom man. It seems that somebody had put them there on the assumption

that they were part of western lore, which I guess they became. He was quite amused and so was I. I still have a copy of each.

Lindenmeier was the beginning of archaeology for me, followed by the formative years at the University of Pennsylvania, where I was the unpaid graduate assistant for Frank Speck. I could bang a typewriter pretty fast, so I took dictation on the typewriter and made myself useful to Frank, as he was finishing his Nascapi volume and a couple of other projects and articles.

[Q:] *So you started at the University of Pennsylvania in the fall of 1935?*

Yes, in the fall of 1935; by the summer of 1936 I became acquainted with Edgar B. Howard, who had just gotten his doctorate in geology. He was interested in Pleistocene geology and, in particular, the possibility of man's association with the megafauna of the late Pleistocene in North America. That led him to New Mexico and he got acquainted with various collectors there, especially in the Guadeloupe Mountain area around Carlsbad, and near Clovis as well, because there had been some finds of great interest there. At Clovis were mammoth bones and these particular artifacts which were Folsom-like, with fluted surfaces. Around Carlsbad the evidence was in caves and rock shelters. There was an old character by the name of Bill Burnett who was the chief guide there. Burnett Cave was named after him, where the first documented Clovis fluted point was found in the bottom stratum. Bill had a tin shop where he had a sign which said, "We work iron and steel for a living." He liked the double meaning. He was probably the most profane, scatological, and blasphemous individual I had ever met, and yet he was extremely funny.

[Q:] *Was he an archaeologist?*

He was an avocational archaeologist, a forerunner who scouted around and found things in caves and had gotten acquainted with Edgar B. Howard. Now Howard was a gentleman who came from New Orleans originally, a southerner, before he settled on the Philadelphia Main Line. He was a man of considerable means who had married a lady named Elizabeth Newhall and raised a large family—five boys. Howard decided that he would mount a field party to Clovis, New Mexico and the Guadeloupe Mountains and asked me to join him, which I did. The rest of the party was made up of young college undergraduates who had money in the family and whose parents would pay $500 for the season. Multiply that by about 12 or 15 and you get what then was pretty good money. So that gave us the means to mount the field project and then Howard probably put in some himself. I drove out to Carlsbad in the summer of 1936 with C. T. R. Bohannon in his 1928 Model A Ford roadster, which I helped him put together at his parents' home in Bethesda, Maryland. He had disassembled it completely some time before for his own reasons. That's the way he was.

The first season we went out to Clovis after we had been to Carlsbad, and I got acquainted with the Clovis site as well as the old caves in the Carlsbad area. We didn't find anything really spectacular in the caves. At Clovis a gravel pit recently had been excavated and there was a deposit on one side that was clearly interesting. At the juncture of a blue clay and a sandy stratum beneath there were mammoth bones, and above that in the blue clay there were bison bones. The gravel for which the roadbuilders had opened the pit lay below the sandy layer. We decided that since artifacts were being found by collectors below the pit side, the objects had evidently eroded from the banks of the pit. So, that's where we wanted to dig.

The first season we uncovered quite a bit of ground by stripping the blow sand and brown soil above the blue clay and sand. This we managed with a plain slip bucket and later a fresno operated by a guy with a horse to get the topsoil moved in an area so we could uncover the strata that we were interested in. It wasn't a very good way of doing archaeology, but then we knew what we wanted. We wanted to get down where the mammoth was. So that's what we did and we were there for two seasons—the summers of 1936 and 1937. When Howard was off scouting other sites, I was the chief of party. It fell to me to make all the notes, and I triangulated everything in so that I could make a map of everything we found and place artifacts and bones in their relation to each other. Then I made a sketch of the bones in position. We had an "official photographer"— his name was Alexander Biddle Brock. His family had the means to equip him handsomely and he came out in a handsome Oldsmobile roadster and he had a very expensive camera with him—a 35 mm—so what photographs we have, were done by Brock supplemented by the sketches that I made.

I had enough notes to make up a report and I turned them over to Howard. He did exactly the opposite of what Renaud did. He said "Why don't you write it up yourself, Jack." I was again amazed to find that my reports for the two seasons were published by the Academy of Natural Sciences of Philadelphia as part of the *Proceedings* of the Academy. That gave me my first publication in archaeology.

[Q:] *So meanwhile, during the winters, you were taking coursework at Penn?*
Yes, I was taking coursework at Penn. In 1937 I came up for my oral examination, and I worked as hard as I could for it. I also had been working very hard in preparation for the International Symposium on Early Man at the Academy. This symposium was gotten up for the fall of 1937 by Edgar B. Howard after we had come back from the field. His secretary, Virginia Wilkins Tomlin, was the hard-working facilitator, and she was later to become my wife. I had become acquainted with Miss Tomlin during the time I made a museum replica of the 20 x 20 foot section of the gravel pit where we found the greatest concentration of mammoth bones lying in speckled sand below the blue clay. I got some Delaware River sand, put it in the enclosure, then took the top half of each

plaster and burlap cast of the bones and nested the bottom of the casts in the sand with the bones exposed. Then we placed the actual artifacts exactly where they had been. Today I marvel at our faith in the viewers—not an artifact was stolen! The mammoth pit became the main exhibit for the symposium and I was very happy about it. I remember Barnum Brown came from the American Museum of Natural History one day and looked at it. He had been to the original Folsom site and acknowledged that it was authentic, but he hadn't been to the Clovis site. I stood near him wondering whether he'd say anything. Well, he did. He said "Totally fortuitous." Fortuitous! I didn't speak to him. I could have kicked him in the shins at least, but I didn't. I simply melted away into the crowd and said nothing. So I could see that you didn't necessarily get away with your hopes, and that they were sometimes dashed by doubters.

[Q:] *Shortly after this you wound up in Kentucky?*

Yes, I took my prelims and busted them flat, because the preparation that I had gotten at the University of Denver was not up to the standards of the University of Pennsylvania and besides that, I had been putting in long hours with the symposium and its preparations. I had also been working for Frank Speck and I probably had not been doing as much concentrated study as I might have, in retrospect, but at least I had taken courses and I had tried to think in terms of the requirements. I simply didn't think far enough or deep enough, and I didn't make it. D. S. Davidson, Irving L. Hallowell, and Frank Speck were on the committee. I remember I was simply told, "You just have to try this again."

So I thought I would stay at Penn and see if I could make it. By that time I had parlayed the Harrison Scholarship into a Fellowship which gave me a little more money and made it possible for me to stay, but at the same time, my father, who always lied about his age, making

himself 10 years younger than he was, had finally come into his 70s and to the point he faced retirement. Money was therefore once again scarce.

That December I miraculously got word from Jesse Figgins, who had moved to Lexington, Kentucky. He ended his career at the Colorado Museum of Natural History, retired, and moved to Lexington. He had become associated with a man named Burnheim who was going to fund a large museum at Louisville, which was to be a natural history museum. It was also to have a section on the Indians, and Figgins was employed there to get up a complete representation of the Indians of the Southwest. To do this, he wanted full scale figures, and he had gone to Taos Pueblo and got permission to make living casts of the people there. This he did, using Harvey Goettsche, who had worked with me at the Lindenmeier site, as his assistant.

Well, by that time he had met W. S. Webb, who was the head of the Physics Department at the University of Kentucky, and who was a great avocational archaeologist and very serious about conserving the things that were being found by the Tennessee Valley Authority. He had been a major at the artillery school run by the army at Fort Sill, Oklahoma, during World War I. He had gotten acquainted with the Indians there, and was tremendously interested in their lifeways, and then became interested in archaeology. He became aware of the conservation of sites in Kentucky, and by that time, he and Dean W. Funkhauser of the University of Kentucky had written *The Archaeological Survey of Kentucky*, which was the first of the Kentucky series on archaeology. When the Works Progress Administration (WPA) began to operate, he applied for a large grant, and got it. He opened up a number of field projects and the museum project, and he wanted somebody who was an experienced archaeologist to run each project. So Figgins got in touch with me and said he could get me a job in the field at the University of Kentucky WPA project, if I would come immediately. This was in December of 1937. So I picked up my socks and whatever else I had, and was in Lexington, Kentucky in time for Christmas.

[Q:] *Were you now officially employed by the Works Progress Administration?*

No, I was officially working for the University of Kentucky, which administered the WPA-funded Archaeological Survey and we were paid by WPA—we being the crew and the supervising archaeologists. We had several field projects and one museum project, which was located in the Museum of the University of Kentucky, at Lexington. I was sent out to the Green River country of western Kentucky near the village of Island. By that time it was early January and we were to work all winter because the men needed the pay. This was a coal mining area, with small mines that had all failed during the Depression; but the coal miners had hung around because they didn't have any other place to go, and their only livelihood was the WPA. The virtue of the archaeological projects was that all you needed were some shovels, trowels, and a conveyance, and you were in business. The rest was up to the man who was in charge. It was usually a graduate student, usually in archaeology or anthropology, and he would have all these laborers on his hands, to excavate a mound or whatever.

There was a small aboriginal mound near Island only about a foot or a foot-and-a-half high at the apex that was our objective. We had about 40 men on the crew and if you have 40 men and one not-too-large mound that's mostly plowed down, you have something of a challenge to figure out what you're going to do with all these people and how you're going to do it. So, of course I had to lay out a grid which I did at considerable trouble and as fast as I possibly could, and then instructed the guys how to flat-shovel and take just a little earth at a time and save anything that they found. Little by little I got them to understand the difference between coal mining and archaeology.

But I also found this was a practicum in observing human relationships under great stress during the depth of the Depression, in a very poor part of the United States. I lived in a house which was maintained by a widow and her rather homely 25 or 26-year old daughter. I had a room upstairs which was heated by a coal grate, and I was introduced to the science of maintaining a coal fire and how to bank it with slack—slack being slate—so it wouldn't go out altogether. Then in the morning you poked the slate aside, got the coals going, put some fresh coal on it, and got the room warm. By the time it was almost habitable, it was time for you to go. The lady would pack a little lunch for me and I would drive the gang out in a flatbed truck with sides.

I also got an idea of how people lived there during the Depression and what it was like to be an out-of-work coal miner in the poorest part of Kentucky, and how these people were mistreated by those who sold and bought up the mines that had failed. The owners simply got the last of the coal out of the ground, sold the mine, and then failed to meet their last payroll. These guys would show up on Monday morning for the job and I put them in the truck and drove them out with tools, set them to work, and helped teach them something about archaeology. I quickly realized that they had intelligence and human dignity and that they were damned fine people. But they were completely ignorant of what archaeology was, and it was a real challenge to teach them. And I, too, learned a lot.

So that's how we operated, and after about two months or so, I got word that Major Webb had been told by WPA that they had to have a state supervisor of the Archaeological Survey of Kentucky, and usually that was a non-archaeologist. He wanted an archaeologist, and so he made the choice, and he chose me. So I came in and moved to Lexington. Someone took my place and finished up at the Island site, and then went on to other shell mounds, and that became their objective. One of the people who carried on there was Albert Spaulding, incidentally, and another was David Stout, and they became notable professionals later on. Spaulding was there with his wife and four-year old son Ronnie. I would shuffle between the various projects and take the crews various things that they would need and came back with things that they wanted to take back to the laboratory—artifacts and bones, things like that. But I remember at one time, after I had gotten myself a 1938 model Plymouth sedan, I packed as many as 21 burials in boxes, which taught me the science of logistics in packing a car. That's what my job was mainly, facilitating and answering questions, doing things in the laboratory. Also, I helped Bill Haag who was the right bower of Major Webb. He was the man who really kept the project going. He did graduate work at the University of Mississippi, under Jimmy Griffin. He was particularly good at what he did, and he had a good crew there at the museum, which included Ivar Skarland and H. T. E. Hertzberg, physical anthropologists, and also several other people who became pretty notable anthropologists later on.

[Q:] *Roughly how many sites were being excavated at any given time?*

As many as a dozen sites were excavated simultaneously. In western Kentucky shell mound sites were associated with the drainage of the Green River, and in Middle Kentucky, north of Lexington, Adena burial mounds extended up to Cincinnati. These Adena earth mounds had burials in them, and they also extended to eastern Kentucky and Paintsville, in the valleys of the mountains of eastern Kentucky, so we really covered the state pretty well. The only thing we didn't do was carry on archaeological investigations within Mammoth Cave, which always impressed me, but that was in the National Park System, and not part of our objective.

[Q:] *This was all between 1938-1940. Were you continuously employed year-round?*

Yes, it was year-round employment. And every year the project had to be renewed, so that meant we made an application to the Washington office of WPA, and the paper work would go through, and we would or would not get a renewal. The Major wanted to be damned sure that it went through. So I said, "Why don't I go and I'll see it through by hand-processing it." Well, it so happened that the man in charge of WPA archaeology in the Washington office, under Harry Hopkins, who was the head of the whole shebang, was Vincenzo Petrillo. Petrillo was a student of Frank Speck's who had ventured into ethnology and had mounted quite an expedition to Brazil. Petrillo was a rather dashing guy, so he was often photographed. I remember when Petrillo came back from his Brazil expedition, I happened to be at the office with Frank Speck. Petrillo came in and said that he had some tough luck on his expedition, that he had his books and things and equipment in a canoe, and it had overturned and he had lost them. So he salvaged what he could. He had some notes, and he showed them to Frank. Frank went over them cursorily, then took them and dropped them in a wastebasket, and that was my introduction to Vincenzo Petrillo. But he later did some serious teaching, as I understand it. I never really caught up with his later career, but during the WPA years, he was the head of WPA archaeology in the Washington office and so I had at least a Penn connection, since I knew who he was. So I hand-processed the paperwork by going from office to office, from in box to out box, in Washington. It didn't stay in somebody's in box very long. That was my job.

[Q:] *So Major Webb deployed you to Washington to do that?*

That's right. I got the thing hustled through, and he got his money without delay and the project kept on going, which was the big thing.

[Q:] *Do you recall roughly how much money was involved per year?*

We got around $300,000.00 a year. I know in the years that I was there, from 1937-1940, we spent at least a million dollars—which was a hell of a lot of money in those Depression days.

But we had these big projects and they really created a lot of work for many people. We had as many as 200 or 250 people working at one time. WPA archaeology came into existence in 1933 and it really got going in 1934. It started in the Southeast for a good reason. You could work all year round in the Southeast, you see, although there were other projects farther north. Donald Cadzow had one in Pennsylvania, for instance, at Tinicum Island looking for the Printzhof, as well as at Pennsbury, William Penn's country estate, and at various frontier forts. He had some pretty good people working for him, too. Regrettably, Cadzow never published a single report. Major W. S. Webb published a report on everything that he did—everything—and they were almost always under his name.

[Q:] *Did he actually write most of them himself?*

Yes, he did, but there was one man, John Elliott, who worked a large Adena mound just south of Cincinnati. It was called the Wright Mound, and when it came to writing up the report, John was a guy who had a mind of his own, and a pretty good will, and he was very capable. He said to Webb, "This is my project, I would like to write the report. And when it's published I would like to have my name associated with it." And by God, the Major agreed, so the report is authored by Webb and Elliott. But the Major always gave credit to the people who did the field work and to Bill Haag and to anybody who worked on the project.

For instance, when I was stationed at Lexington at the University of Kentucky, where we had the big project centered at the Museum, I worked at the Major's office very often because he had a darkroom for photography. Bill Haag was a good photographer and he taught me procedure in the darkroom so I could do some printing and developing. A fellow named John Buckner was one of the Major's field supervisors and he was

from Paris, Kentucky. His father had been a Japanese diplomat and his mother was a local socialite, a southern belle, and there was a great hoopla when the Japanese diplomat and the very lovely southern girl married. Their son John was the product of this mixed marriage, a gentle, rather gaunt looking patrician with a slightly Oriental cast to his face. He was distinctly a southern gentleman and he had great character, but like many southern gentlemen he just couldn't apply himself to get something done. So here was this big Adena mound project, for which Buckner got his notes so far, but he just couldn't finish them and get the damned thing done so the Major could write up his report. So the Major collared me and said "Cotter, (he always called me Cotter), Cotter, you've got to get these things finished. I want you to do what you can; take those notes that Buckner has written—they won't do the way they are—and finish them up." So I spent night after night getting Buckner's notes to mean something, and redoing his drawings so they could be reproduced, and so on, and that finally went into the published report and Webb gave me credit for it.

[Q:] *With hindsight of over 50 years, how do you feel about what the WPA accomplished—was it a good thing?*

The WPA was the foundation of modern archaeology in the United States and I'll tell you how it happened. You see, Gordon Willey, Stu Neitzel, Jim Ford, Art Kelly, and others in Louisiana and Georgia were the ones who were the students from Harvard, the University of Michigan, and the University of Chicago. Remember, the University of Chicago, under Faye Cooper-Cole, had the big Kincaid site in Illinois, and they were going gangbusters on archaeology there. And at Harvard there were people interested in Southwestern archaeology, such as Alfred Kidder. But Willey worked for Kelly and he met Jim Ford in the Southeast. Jim Ford taught him all about ceramics and seriation, and the serious side of archaeological investigations. That big project at Macon (Okmulgee) embodied the beginnings of American archaeology that later on flowered into modern archaeology, and it was the groundwork of the "New Archaeology," if you can call it that.

[Q:] *Did the Willey and Phillips' volume on method and theory in archaeology spring from these early collaborations?*

Well, in many ways it did. The Willey and Phillips volume is a seminal volume, but when you go back to their personal history, here is Gordon Willey learning about ceramics from Jim Ford, a kid from Mississippi who had worked at the White Apple site and the Fatherland site at Natchez when he was in high school with Moreau B. C. Chambers, who was another Mississippi product. These two had been there on the scene all this time since the 1920s, and when WPA came in needing somebody to put large numbers of people to work, all these bright young fellows managed the first large archaeological projects. They employed dozens and dozens of WPA laborers, including, and this is interesting, an all woman field crew.

[Q:] *At which site was that?*

It was a mound site north of Macon, I think, that was related to the Macon Plateau Mississippian sites in that region. Gordon Willey mentions it in his book *Archaeological Researches in Retrospect.*

[Q:] *Weren't some of the WPA laborers convicts?*

Yes, there were convict laborers, for instance, at Fort Mackina in the 1950s and 1960s. There is no reason why you can't go to a minimum security prison, where you have a lot of young people, and get them interested in doing a careful piece of field work—it's great for rehabilitation. We shouldn't forget that the Civilian Conservation Corps (CCC) also did archaeology at this time, for example, at Jamestown under Pinky Harrington, from 1934 to 1942. The WPA lasted from 1933 to 1942, and as soon as World War II began to loom everybody went into the muni-

tions industries and there were no more work projects needed; that was the end of WPA and CCC.

[Q:] *It must have been daunting to be in charge of dozens if not hundreds of laborers, virtually none of whom was trained.*

Not necessarily. When you're under pressure and you know what you're doing, and you know what you have to do, and you don't have much time to do it, you will do as good a job as if you had time to worry about it and get your interests scattered and things come in to interfere with your objective, and you have to come back to it several times and get it started again.

I can give you an example, for instance. Let's take the Angel site, near Evanston, Indiana in which you had the WPA and later fieldwork going on for years and years. Glenn Black was a devoted scientist and he knew what he was doing, and he took years and years to do that work. That was probably the optimum of using WPA labor, over a long period of time until it was exhausted, and then taking other labor, and so on. Eli Lilly, the head of Lilly pharmaceutical, who was very much interested in archaeology, bankrolled Black's work and published a magnificent account of the Angel site. Sometimes you have all of this possibility and you don't take advantage of it, like Donald Cadzow, who did all this damned field work in Pennsylvania and then didn't write a report. Cadzow had lots of people helping him, but he never followed through. But my point is these young fellows who were in the South, particularly in the Southeast, and in the Southwest too, like Caywood and Spicer at Tuzigoot and other people who took on WPA labor, knew what they were doing. They did their job with large numbers of people under great pressure and in a hurry, but they also produced reports, learned a lot, and got a lot accomplished.

[Q:] *Well, I know many contemporary compliance archaeologists who would agree with you because time constraints are endemic to most compliance archaeology projects today.*

Right you are. It depends on how good you are and whether you follow through with proper reports and get the thing done right; you can louse it up quickly or you can louse it up slowly, but it's still the same lousy job if you don't do it right.

One final note before leaving the projects in Kentucky. I've mentioned C. T. R. Bohannon earlier. Bohannon was a long rifle and I first met him at the Lindemeier site in 1935. I knew that he was in archaeology, and when we had a chance to hire him in Kentucky we did so. I knew he was pretty good. So he went to work at a Greenup County mound that was to be excavated completely. The Major said to Bohannon, "I want you to save everything, rocks, pebbles, everything." Bohannon said "Yes sir, I will do that," and he did. He saved every rock, every pebble, every this, every that, and I came up there, and saw all these cloth bank bags filled with hundreds of pounds of pebbles and sundry detritus. "These are just rocks, Boh," I remonstrated. "Well," he said, "the Major wanted everything saved and this is it." This is the same Bohannon who always did things the tough way, so cantankerous and so contrary, he'd scratch his head when his foot itched.

One day I bounded up the stairs to where he was staying in an upstairs room above a store. I had heard that Bohannon was squiring a lady who had a beard. Everyone was talking about Bohannon and the bearded lady, and I was about to say, "Hey Boh, how about you and the bearded lady?" as I banged on the door. On hearing "Come in," I opened the door, and by God, Bohannon was there and next to him sat the bearded lady, too. He just said, "Meet m'wife Dorothy," and I said, "Certainly happy to meet you." Mrs. Bohannon, I saw, had a very pronounced mustache; she was a southern girl who had been a school teacher in Washington, DC. And so I caught my breath and thought, "My God, I might be dead by now if I had burst in on them and said how about you and the

bearded lady?" But anyway, Dorothy was a very able draftsperson and she would draft up plans and profiles and the two of them made a marvelous report of this site in Greenup County, Kentucky. Bohannon was no slouch as an archaeologist. He was also, as I said, a long rifle, and when World War II broke out he volunteered immediately. But he had one trouble and that was his eyesight wasn't worth a damn and he had glasses with very thick lenses. Whenever he would wrestle (we'd all wrestle and tussle around) he would never take off his glasses. We'd say "Bohannon, take off your glasses, you're gonna smash them." "No, I'm keeping them on." He couldn't see anything without glasses. He memorized the eye chart and passed the eye examination and got into the army.

Bohannon ended up a full colonel. He stayed with the American troops that were marooned in the Philippines and organized guerrilla warfare there. He became an expert in guerrilla warfare and he wrote a book with another army colonel named Valentine on the subject—the most perceptive, analytical book on how to do it right that has ever been written. The crux of it is you've got to be sure that the people who are going to conduct guerrilla warfare in their own country know that the training is for them, not for you. That was overlooked in Vietnam.

[Q:] *Well, that brings us to 1940, when you assumed a position with the National Park Service.*

In April 1940 I had been advised by Civil Service that the examination I had taken at Tucumcari, New Mexico, in 1936 had finally come through. I must have been at the bottom of the barrel by that time, but anyway, I had been selected as the first custodian—the superintendents were then called custodians—at the new National Monument named Tuzigoot, in central Arizona, at a salary of $2,000 a year. I had been getting something like $1,800, so it seemed to me that this Civil Service job was a desideratum because it was a livelihood in the depths of the Depression. I also had my mother and father to think of because my father was very close to retirement. So I decided to take it.

By that time, Virginia Tomlin at the Academy of Natural Sciences here in Philadelphia and I had agreed to marry, but not while I was working on a temporary federal relief project. I think Virginia would have been satisfied to take the chance on it, but I was basically very conservative, if not a fearful individual, when it came to taking chances with my family responsibilities. So I went to Arizona alone and we agreed then that we would wait until I was established in the job.

I arrived on April 30, 1940 in my car packed to the gunnels with everything I possessed and was met by one Ted Smiley, who was the Park Service man who had opened the place up as a temporary assignment the month before. Later on he became quite a light in dendrochronology and was head of the Dendrochronology Lab at Tucson for some years. Ted had taken over the museum that had been erected in 1936 after the archaeological dig by Caywood and Spicer, which started in 1933, got going in 1934 and continued to 1936. They excavated 110 rooms of an old Sinaqua pueblo, dating to about AD 1000 to 1300, and then they built a museum with WPA labor which was 2200 square feet and had 22 glass-topped cases and was a very decent little museum. It was in the pueblo Southwestern style, and the ceiling had rough pole *vegas* with rafters of tule reeds. It was very picturesque, if a little impractical. I found the powder post beetles loved tule reeds and they were infesting it very heavily. In the morning I would find a shower of dust on the 22 glass-topped tables which I would have to clean off. So I had the job of keeping the place up as a lone post monument.

There was an oil furnace put in which by that time was in pretty uncertain condition, having sooted up a great deal. I got somebody from Clarkdale to come up and look at it who was supposed to know something about oil furnaces. I had been there for about two months, when he was working on it. When he got it finished and

turned it on, it promptly blew up, throwing approximately one-half of an inch of soot at the point nearest to the furnace and it graded down toward the end of the room to about one-eighth to one-quarter of an inch of soot covering everything.

That was my introduction to the world of crisis management in taking care of a National Monument. Well, little by little, and without the aid of a vacuum cleaner, I got it cleaned. And then I stopped to consider, here I was a graduate student on my way to a doctorate in anthropology. I was stationed at Tuzigoot National Monument which sometimes had days in which nobody appeared at all. It had a maximum of 8,000 to 10,000 visitors a year, most of whom came in the summer months, and I'd take them all up on the ruins. I wanted to be with them at all times. I'd have to lock up the museum when I went up on the ruins with them. So I debated with myself whether I really wanted to do this or not, and when the furnace blew up I thought about it very carefully, and decided that I would stay.

We had to write up monthly reports—all the Southwestern National Monuments required monthly reports—and these became rather famous in a sense. There were a number of visitors who asked the Park Service to supply them with copies of these monthly reports because these were lone posts for the most part and the superintendents had idiosyncratic ways of describing their lone post adventures; sometimes they were rather unique and humorous.

Less than a year after I opened Tuzigoot in 1940, Virginia and I were married and set up housekeeping in the little apartment that was attached to the museum, and in 1943, March 18th, our daughter, Jean, was born. That March 18 happened to be the very day that Edgar B. Howard died. He was a man who had a congenital heart condition. It ran in his family and I remember when he announced at the Academy of Natural Sciences, "I am turning 50," just as though that was a seal of doom placed on him. In a way it was because in a couple of years he was gone from a heart attack. He had been in World War I as captain, and he had, I think, been in either the infantry or the artillery, I can't remember which. But he volunteered in World War II, was turned down, went out to the munitions industry in La Jolla, California, settled there (which was his wife's Newhall family home), and there he died.

At the Monument, I got some National Youth Administration boys who were available to help stabilize the ruins and put up a retaining wall that had fallen down. They were wonderful kids, ranging from about 16 to 19 years of age, and were mostly from the Clarkdale/Cottonwood area that was near the National Monument in the Verde Valley. The Park Service decided the restoration that had been done in a reconstructed ten-room unit at the foot of the hill on which most of the excavated rooms were was an ill-advised reconstruction and should come down and be restored to its original look. So they asked me to undertake the job. I got these kids organized, took sledge hammers, and we attacked the concrete decking that was on top of each one of the rooms, which proved to be resilient enough not to cave in easily. It was solid, so we just had to literally batter it down, stage by stage. We finally got the walls back down where they had been approximately when the place was restored, hauled away the debris, and made up mixtures of tar, water, cement and earth to simulate the "adobe" without changing the color too much.

In stabilizing the ruins, we found several burials which I left in place as exhibits. I got some glass, put it in front of the burials, left it open and then placed a masking of stones in front which I could lift away quickly to show visitors and replace them so you couldn't see the exhibits.

I was rather proud of that, and years later when I came back for a visit there were something like five people there instead of one, and the ruins were open to the public, but nobody accompanied them there. The museum was open and I asked the person in charge "How is it that nobody accompanies anybody up on the ruins? I used to take everybody up there." And the answer was, "Well, we don't have enough people— short handed." I went up on the ruins and found that I couldn't discover the *in situ* exhibits. I asked about them, and was told, "On no, it was too much trouble, and besides, we couldn't keep them up, so we just covered them over and sealed them in the walls and forgot about them." So that was progress in interpretation and conservation.

[Q:] *This was your first employment as a National Park Service employee?*

Yes, my first employment as a Park Service employee, which lasted 37 years. In 1943, I was taken into the armed forces. I had volunteered for Navy officer training, but as I was about to leave before my first interview, my draft number came up. I was ordered to the Phoenix induction station, and I was asked to take a group of people who were coming down from northern Arizona in a bus. I was given their papers and told, "You are in charge, see that these people get there." So I took the papers and they got aboard and I found that they were all Navajo Indians. They had had a lot to drink and they were contentious. They had various fights all the way down, and I was trying to quell those fights and keep peace, and keep the bus going all at the same time. When we got to Phoenix we all landed in one piece, miraculously, and I went through the physical only to be told, "You're 4F."

"WHAT!" I said, "What's the matter?" "High blood pressure." "I don't have high blood pressure, I've never had high blood pressure." They said, "You've got it now. Any particular stress you've been under?" and I said, "Well, frankly, yes." "Well, if you feel that way, take a bromide, get a hotel room, and come back tomorrow."

I was just stupid enough to do that, and I got in. And instead of going into the Navy as I could have, I chose the Army and went straight into infantry training at Camp Roberts, California.

So I left my wife and by that time my six months old baby girl in the home of my mother and father in Boulder, Colorado. Later they went to the east coast and lived with her mother and father for awhile.

[Q:] *I understand you served in the Normandy invasion.*

Yes, I was supposed to go to the Pacific with our infantry battalion after our 17-week training increment. But, this being the army, they changed their mind at the last minute, and sent us to the European theater. We stayed in the moors in Devon, England, where it was all heather and weather in our staging area.

Finally on D+6, six days after the initial invasion date, we were the first replacements in the 357th Infantry Regiment of the 90th Division. We went in on Utah Beach and were quickly deployed. Our company had lost 80% of its personnel in the six days before, so we were fresh in it. The people who were leading us didn't know too much about what they were doing, and we didn't know anything about what we were doing. So we ended up—just to make it brief—in a hedgerow in a very pleasant wheat field with lots of red poppies. It turned out we were in the way of an armored regiment of Germans breaking out of Cherbourg and coming down the peninsula, getting back before being trapped. All hell broke loose. They knew what they were doing. And they just went right through the fields like the stuff through a tin horn. They spotted the guys in the hedgerow where they never should have been because a tree burst can get everybody. So they just took a mortar and aimed it in our direction.

It came right down on our squad, deployed along the hedgerow, and it got every man in that squad. I could feel the metal going into my left thigh and I didn't know whether I could get up and go or not, but as I was looking around, I saw a 2nd louie there who was covered with blood, and he looked terrible; I thought, "God, he's had it." Then, all of a sudden he got up on his feet and ran like a rabbit, just zoom, he was

gone. I thought, hell, if he can do that, maybe I can do it too. So I found I could walk and I looked for my BAR—I had been given a Browning Automatic Rifle—and the damned mortar shell had exploded and completely covered it with earth, so I couldn't find the thing.

I started to find my way through the wheat field and back toward what I hoped was a first aid station. I picked up somebody's dropped rifle because I was told that you must never give up your rifle, always have your rifle by your side. So I grabbed a rifle that somebody had dropped, adopted it, and kept on going and crossed the road where the Panzer division, the German mobile unit, was still coming up. I crossed the road with a bunch of wounded guys who were trying to get to the aid station. When I was about 300 or 400 feet from the road there was an explosion, something hit me, and it was just as though someone had taken a bucket of water and thrown it full force against me. I looked down and saw a hand, just like an old furnace glove, and I realized that the guy who was in back of me had been hit by a 37 mm tank cannon shell, and he just simply exploded.

So I realized that as far as being in action is concerned, it's just a matter of luck whether you make it or don't. I did make it to the MASH unit, was separated from my mortar fragments, and in due time flown to Churchill Hospital in London, from which I went through rehabilitation, and to the unit which would go back in action. I was sent back to France, and this time landed in Etamps, near Paris, where an old Nazi Luftwaffe unit was. I got word there that I was to come to Paris and not go up to the front with my unit as I was originally supposed to do. Right after that came the Battle of the Bulge. So in Paris I was placed in the Armed Forces Institute and given some fast training, instructing instructors to instruct, and then transferred back to England and stationed in London for one full year. I joined the staff of a mail order college, an Armed Forces correspondence school.

I came back in December 1945 when the American army was suddenly dissolved and sent home. I came back on the aircraft carrier Saratoga with 5,000 other guys in an Atlantic storm, and then resumed my career at Tuzigoot and was there until 1947 as Superintendent. There we had our second child, Lawrence Tomlin Cotter, May 2, 1947 and when he was six weeks old I was transferred to Natchez State Parkway at Tupelo, Mississippi.

The Natchez State Parkway had been the creation of a congressman named John Rankin, also known as Barefoot John, or Honest John, Rankin. Rankin had some property near Tupelo, where he allowed that it would be nice if the Park Service were to buy the property in part, at least, and keep cutting the lawn and weeds on his part, and they could make a memorial road of the old Natchez Trace which ran from Natchez, Mississippi to Nashville, Tennessee through Tupelo.

The Trace had a lot of archaeological sites along it, and I was assigned there to carry on the archaeological survey that had been started by Jesse Jennings three or four years before. Jennings had done a very good job. He had concentrated on the late historic and late prehistoric sites near Tupelo. So I then went to the Bynum site, which was just south of Tupelo a few miles, and later on, down to the Emerald Mound near Natchez. Emerald Mound was 400 feet long and 200 feet wide, 35 feet high, a great truncated platform with secondary mounds at the east and west ends. We excavated tests in the primary mound, got a profile across it, and demonstrated the relationship of this late prehistoric site to others in the southern Mississippi area.

We also excavated the Bynum site. I worked for a time with John Corbett. This was his first job in the Park Service. He was right out of Columbia University, where he had just gotten his Ph.D. He had been at the Trace for about a year or so when the opportunity arose to take charge of the Missouri River Basin archaeology in Lincoln, Nebraska. The Park Service had its Regional Archaeologist in Omaha, and the Smithsonian was to have a supervisor at the University at Lincoln. This was the opening,

and word came from the Washington office that I had a crack at it if I wanted it. And, I suppose stupidly, I said that I wanted to finish the Trace. And so I did, and Corbett took the Omaha job and inside of two years he was the Chief Archaeologist of the National Park Service.

Before he left, Corbett and I produced *The Archaeology of the Bynum Mounds*, which was the first of the archaeological research series in the National Park Service. That appeared in 1951. Then I continued and finished the work at Emerald Mound and also worked at the Gordon site and several other sites along the Parkway, which by that time had had quite a bit of land purchased for it. Some of the road was built, but outside of the fact that the right-of-way was designated, most of it was theoretical still. Where it was built was rather interesting because it was laid out by landscape architects whose main objective was to use a French curve. If you know what a French curve is, you just lay a flexible strip on the drafting table and you make a fancy curve with it. They loved to use those French curves so the Natchez State Parkway was composed mostly of gently curving roadways that curved both to the left and to the right. I could never drive on those roads more than five miles without falling asleep. It's very hazardous driving, actually.

There was one place that was rather low which they filled with ballast, then trucked in more ballast over the new part of the road. But they made one little mistake—the ballast wasn't enough—and as they hauled more and more ballast, they beat up the road so it wasn't passable. Finally they couldn't get the ballast to the end of the road, so they decided to move the Trace to another spot on high ground. Incidentally, the Natchez Trace Parkway is not quite finished yet, even though it was started in 1932, I believe. I don't know how much money the road has cost—it would be interesting to know. But it certainly had some archaeological work done along it, and that was fine while it lasted. From the Trace I went to Washington, DC and took

Corbett's place while he did some Army service which he was called on to do as a reserve officer.

[Q:] *What were your main duties at that time as Acting Chief Archaeologist in Washington?*

It was taking Corbett's place or working with him. And I got acquainted with the operation of the Washington office and got so that I could dictate letters directly to the secretary and correct them quickly and get them out, which is an art unto itself.

[Q:] *Was this position the top archaeological position in the National Park Service?*

That's right, at that time. The way the Park Service was set up, it had field offices in a few parks like Mesa Verde or Casa Grande, where the superintendent would be an archaeologist and he would have other archaeologists working for him. But most of the other National Park Service areas, although they might have been archaeological sites, did not have archaeologists on their staffs, and they would be served by the regional archaeologists who might or might not have a staff. Then next would be the Washington staff and archaeologists.

[Q:] *Were you involved in policy-making at that time?*

I furnished advice when it was sought in the Washington office. While I was there I would sit in on meetings of the Committee for the Recovery of Archaeological Remains (CRAR), and this had included W. S. Webb and Frank H. H. Roberts, Jr., and was headed by John Otis Brew, from the Peabody Museum at Harvard. There was also Walter Leland from the American Council of Learned Societies, so it was a pretty high-powered committee. These people would recommend policy for the Park Service, and usually the Park Service would go along with whatever they recommended. The Park Service regional archaeologists and the Washington archaeologists would meet with them, and that's how I got to know all of these people.

[Q:] *Do you have any notion of how many archaeologists were employed in the Park Service at this time, the early 1950s?*

No, I wouldn't know the exact number, but in the Southwest there was a nucleus of archaeologically trained people whose headquarters was Casa Grande National Monument. Dale King was an archaeologist there, and another was Charlie Steen, both University of Denver graduates in anthropology. There were also archaeologists in the field who had charge of lone post monuments like Tuzigoot (my former post), Navaho National Monument, and Grand Quirira. Once a year they would gather everybody for a meeting at Casa Grande and everybody would have drinks and get tight and their wives would meet each other and then they would go back to their lone post monuments.

[Q:] *And then, after about three years in Washington, you transferred to Jamestown?*

That's right. Jamestown was coming up on its 350th anniversary in 1957, so in 1953 they began to make preparations for the final archaeological push, and they got some money for it. In 1954, I was sent there to take charge. I lived at Williamsburg in a little development and bought the first house we owned in our lives.

Our field project personnel at Jamestown consisted of Ed Jelks and B. Bruce Powell, both trained archaeologists without prior Colonial site experience. They were joined by Joel Shiner who came to help out with some work around the Confederate fort and took some clam bucket tests in the James River, and Louis Caywood, who had excavated at Tuzigoot in 1933-1936 with Ned [Edward H.] Spicer, another University of Arizona graduate student. Caywood did have experience excavating Hudson's Bay Company posts in the Northwest. He came to work at the site of the Ludwell House Group on the first rise just west of the church point. It turned out that that was where the burials of 1609-1610 apparently were, because there were a lot of burials under the ruins of a long rowhouse. The owner of that property, the Association for the Preservation of Virginia Antiquities (APVA), had toyed with the idea of restoring the Ludwell Row, and the man who had hoped to have the restoration in his hands was an architect named Henry Chandlee Forman. He had been the architect who started at Jamestown in 1933 and had insisted that he was in charge of all the archaeological work as well as the architectural work. However, there was an archaeologist named John Winter who really was in charge, and another archaeologist named H. Summerfield Day, and briefly, Alonzo Pond. Forman had assumed the prerogative of not having the archaeologists excavate within five or six feet of the foundation area of any buildings because that was the architect's business, not the archaeologist's. Forman had quarreled bitterly with the archaeologists, and all the time that I was at Jamestown, from 1954 to 1957, he never showed up and he never got in touch with me. I think he wanted to do the Ludwell Row and was disappointed when Caywood found burials in the foundation area under the building and the APVA decided that they would not reconstruct the house. So they simply marked the site and put up a large cross with an inscription from Revelations "These are they which are come out of great tribulation." That was the memorial which marked the end of the project. Caywood went on to excavate Greenspring for the 350th Anniversary Commission and Shiner found the rest of the burials at Ludwell Row.

That's how we began at Jamestown and we found a number of important sites there which had not been disclosed to Pinky Harrington and his first group, which had worked after Chandlee Forman left. Day and Winter were the two archaeologists who had fought so bitterly with Forman. They had departed and Pinky Harrington came aboard in 1936 and continued the project until 1942 with CCC labor. There was a big camp located near Williamsburg and they trucked the CCC boys in.

They did a very good job, so in order to finish that up, our project was organized to continue where Harrington left off. Since the grounds were to be developed and a new museum was to be built, we had to go wherever the landscapers told us we could go. The landscaping people wanted to save trees first. So we had to make our seven miles of exploratory trenches in and out of the trees, which is a horrible thing, of course. We would never do that again but that was our only alternative. It was either that or put down individual potholes the way Forman had.

[Q:] *Seven miles is a lot of trenching.*

It is. We didn't have ground penetrating radar and soil resistivity equipment, so we had to dodge around trees and do the best we could. The result was that we finished our work pretty well, and then guess what happened? They decided that they would cut down all the trees since we found some houses in among them, and how they removed the trees is very interesting. They dynamited the stumps, and the first thing I said was, "For God's sake, don't use any dynamite there, let's go and do a proper job," but no, they dynamited them anyway. The Colonial National Historical Park administration, which consisted of architects, regarded the archaeologists as a necessary nuisance. They furthermore did not appreciate our criticism of their bulldozing down a Confederate earthwork for a parking lot or our criticism of the location of the Visitor Center in the midst of the historic area--and on low ground.

[Q:] *Was your work at Jamestown a fortuitous event in your career?*

It was fortuitous and it was accidental and totally unpremeditated. It was something I hadn't even thought of, just as it had been for Pinky Harrington. The only historical archaeology I had done prior to Jamestown was on the Natchez Trace Parkway near the Bynum site, where I found a burial of an early 1800s Chickasaw chief or factotum who had a musket, a silver crown, and a tin cup at his side buried with him. I had also worked a bit for John D. Rockefeller, Jr., at the Van Cortland Manor House on the

Hudson, excavating to see if I could find something interesting.

[Q:] *What year was that?*

That was in 1951, when I took annual leave and worked for Rockefeller.

[Q:] *How did you get involved in that?*

It was through Colonial Williamsburg. An architect at Colonial Williamsburg, a very nice gentleman named Mario Campiolli, and the archaeologist who preceded Ivor Noël Hume, Moreau Chambers, were aware that archaeological work was to be done at Van Corlandt. Anyway, I was recommended for the Van Cortland job, and that's how I happened to go there. We excavated, among other things, a remarkable privy and found that there was a succession in the late 1800s of bottles of good scotch. Then prohibition came and Anne Van Cortland, who had died there in her 90s, and was the last resident owner of the Van Cortland manor house, had gone to Lydia Pinckam, and there was a stratum of Lydia Pinckam bottles. When prohibition was repealed in 1932, they changed back to scotch, and I could tell then that there was a certain cultural value to what you could observe in a privy if you knew the story, and if you didn't know the story you could estimate it. So it introduced me to the value of historical archaeology.

My point is I was scarcely trained as an historical archaeologist when I went to Jamestown for good and sufficient reason. That is, there wasn't any historical archaeology. The only trained historical archaeologist in the United States that I knew of at that time was Pinky Harrington, who was the Regional Archaeologist for the Southeastern Region of the Park Service. Pinky had a principle of "hands off" for whoever worked at Jamestown. The job was my baby and I was to take care of it in my way, which was a very generous thing for him to do. I shudder at the thought that I knew so little about it. By that time, Pinky knew a lot about historical archaeology and his wife Virginia was an

accomplished historical researcher, so the two of them were the ideal combination to do historical archaeology from the research and the field angles, and I didn't know how little I knew when I arrived at Jamestown.

[Q:] *So how did your on-the-job-training go at Jamestown?*

We simply went on the premise that you get every bit of information you possibly can and then you relate it to whatever the story indicates, and the story was up to the historians, as far as I was concerned. The historian of the National Park Service at Colonial National Historical Park was Charles Hatch, a conventional historian who had been trained at the College of William and Mary where he had gained a Phi Beta Kappa key. Hatch was a smart guy, and he had an infinity of notes on 5x7 cards which nobody could read but himself, and he had accomplished a lot of research, had published about Jamestown, and he had certain fixed ideas. He knew where the first statehouse was because it was where the people who had excavated there originally said it was, and he agreed with them. This was before the Park Service came aboard. He assumed that was that, and he wrote a little brochure stating that this was the site of the first state house, and he lived and died by it.

At one time Hatch met Ed Jelks and me in the laboratory and said, "Frankly, I don't think that archaeology has anything to contribute to Jamestown and it never will." So there was a certain lack of understanding between us and unfortunately, I never got the kind of historical research that was directed to answer archaeological questions, and we didn't know enough about the history of Jamestown to try and ask the right questions. But we did the best we could, and by the time we came to the end of our campaign in 1957, Paul Hudson had come on board as the curator of the Museum. Hudson was a good researcher who knew artifacts, and he helped to clue us in to what the ceramics were and what the glass objects were, and what their relative ages and origins were. He was very good at relating field evidence to documentation.

Thanks to Pinky Harrington's pioneering research, we knew that pipe stems and their variations in diameter indicated relative age, as did the shapes of the bowls, so we took what we had and went as far as we could with it. In retrospect what we did was to tell what we had found and related as much as we could to what we knew or understood about Jamestown, which wasn't too much. We produced a report in 1958, *Archaeological Excavations at Jamestown, Virginia*, which I wrote up with a section by Ed Jelks on ceramics and another section on a burial by Georg Neumann, and a section on the ecology by Johnny Hack. Its main virtue was that it was state of the art at the time. With the exception of the appendices of the book, I wrote all of the text, so it came out under my name. And in its recent re-publication by the Archaeological Society of Virginia, I added 37 typewritten pages of new material to bring the story of Jamestown and its digs up to date with some relation to other 17th century sites of Tidewater Virginia and Maryland. I reviewed the earthfast houses which have gotten so much attention since then, which we found originally at Jamestown, but didn't make a lot of at the time. We have now cast a little more light on the archaeology and history of Jamestown, which I didn't do in the first edition.

[Q:] *What ultimately brought you back to Philadelphia?*

I was assigned to come to Philadelphia as the Regional Archeologist for what was then the Northeast Region of the National Park Service. This was in July of 1957. After I moved to the Philadelphia region with my family, I immediately went down to the University of Pennsylvania, sized it up, and got acquainted with Loren Eiseley, who was the head of the Department of Anthropology at the time. I saw him at a cocktail party shortly after I arrived, and he said "Jack, if there's anything I can do for you just let me know," and I said "I'll be up to your office tomorrow morning if you don't mind." So

I told him I wanted to finish my degree, and he said it was a little late for that, but he would see what could be done.

[Q:] *How many years had it been since you left Penn?*

Twenty.

[Q:] *Had you completed your coursework?*

I had completed my coursework but a lot of it was out of date. I had passed the German and French exams, so I had that out of the way, but I did have a lot of coursework to make up because of the lapse from 1937 to 1957. So I went back and took a course in the history of anthropology from A. I. Hallowell, whose courses I had also taken in 1935-1937. Pete was back at Penn. He had gone to Northwestern and come back to Penn to teach his last years there. Davidson was dead by that time and so was Heinz Wieschoft. He had been killed in a plane wreck in Africa that also took the life of the head of the United Nations, Dag Hammersjold. Frank Speck was also gone by that time. So I went back, took courses for two years and finally got my degree in 1959. At the commencement I sat beside Jane Goodale of Bryn Mawr. She had her thesis on the Kiwi and I had my thesis on Jamestown, which I reworked from the book.

[Q:] *Meanwhile, you were still Regional Archeologist at the Park Service?*

Yes, I was Regional Archeologist and I kept on with that until 1977, another 20 years, and then retired from the Park Service.

[Q:] *But in 1960 you also took a position as Adjunct Associate Professor at Penn.*

Yes, as soon as I got my degree, Tony Garvan said to me, "Why don't you teach a course in historical archaeology since you have this Jamestown book?" He was very much taken with the Jamestown publication and I had had the remarkable foresight to quote Garvan and his *Town Planning in Connecticut*, which had been his thesis. I think it kind of pleased him. And there was a definite relation between the first fort in Jamestown and the English bawn built in Northern Ireland when the British opposed the natives there, very much as they did the natives of Virginia a few years later. The bawn was essentially a defensive house fortification, sometimes enlarged to be a community fortification. So I went ahead and started the first course in historical archaeology in 1960 and kept that up until 1979.

[Q:] *The first course in American historical archaeology?*

Yes, that was the first course in American historical archaeology and about six months later, Steve Williams at Harvard taught a seminar in historical archaeology and that was the next one, to my knowledge. Both of us were very much interested in historical archaeology, Steve in 18th century Louisiana and I in 17th century Virginia.

[Q:] *How were you able to work full-time for the Park Service, which must have been demanding, and yet still find time to squeeze in teaching a course?*

Well, it worked this way—I did teaching on my own time. I took annual leave to do it and if there were a field course, that was on the weekend, so I put in my full time with the Park Service as required, and took my annual leave and free time to devote to the class.

[Q:] *And that was usually in the summertime?*

No, it was year-round, both semesters and also in the summer. Every summer I had a summer field class. So I was working pretty much the whole year. Some years I didn't have a fall or spring class and it varied, but I'd have at least one class during each year.

The thing that I tried to do in the Park Service was everything that was expected of me. I had charge of all of the River Basin work, plus all of the work that was the responsibility of the Northeastern Region of the Park Service. At that time this area included Virginia to Maine, over to Isle Royale, and down to St. Louis. A huge area,

and it included, of course, the Boston area with all of its historic sites, and Philadelphia. Being located in Philadelphia, of course, I was sitting right on top of Independence Park, which is where we had our headquarters, and so I had oversight over all the work that was going on there.

[Q:] *Was it during this time that you had your encounter with Eleanor Roosevelt?*

Yes, I had an idea very early, as soon as I came to Philadelphia, that the best artifact that we had was actually the spoken or written word. The written word is the phoneme and the artifact is the morpheme, so both of them are symbols. The speech is a much more intricate symbol than the artifact, which is seen and not heard, but the symbol of speech includes a lot of complicated business within the brain. Anyway, aside from that I decided that speech as an artifact had to be maintained, and so I wondered why archaeologists shouldn't be involved in the tape-recording of as many important events and people as they possibly could. I got absolutely nowhere with that idea except in the case of getting somebody who was central to an area of historic importance to recall something about it. Eleanor Roosevelt was a natural at Hyde Park, also within the Park Service system. Hyde Park was a national historic site which included FDR's library and the house and grounds.

I wrote to the superintendent and asked him if he could set up a meeting with Mrs. Roosevelt so that I could tape-record a walk through the house with her. We had just gotten a portable tape recorder, when these were brand new. It was a foot long and about six inches wide and very heavy. It came in a holster which you put on your shoulder and wore. It had a lapel mike and a little cassette and it worked pretty well, but if you wanted to play it, you had to transfer it to a reel-to-reel with a patch tape and get it on another system. Anyway, Mrs. Roosevelt said yes, to my great surprise and delight, and Superintendent Atkinson wrote back or called back and said to come up at a certain time.

Mrs. Roosevelt then got in touch with me and said "Why don't you come up the night before and we'll have dinner at my house and we can meet, and the next day I'll take you through the house with the tape recorder?"

So Atkinson, the superintendent, and I went that evening and we had dinner at a long table, with at least 20 guests, including family and friends, in attendance. Mrs. Roosevelt had a lady to help her in the kitchen and she would serve things to Mrs. Roosevelt. I remember the soup came in a tureen and Mrs. Roosevelt ladled out the soup herself and it was passed down to the individuals at the table, all the time keeping up a fascinating conversation. She was a magnificent conversationalist, and what she said was unaffected, made sense, and it was intellectual. It wasn't just chit chat, and so I got to know a little about Mrs. Roosevelt at that time, and next morning at 8 o'clock she was there for our appointment.

It was in October, I think, a cold morning, and she wore an old gray sweater as she drove up in her car. She drove herself, and as she got out of the car, I noticed that the glasses she was wearing were very dirty, almost gray. I wondered how she could see through them, but she never had time to do anything for herself. She was the last person she thought of, and she didn't have time to clean her glasses, so she didn't pay any attention to them.

Mrs. Roosevelt simply said—she had a lovely modulated voice— "Well, Mr. Cotter, I think we're ready now," so I put the tape recorder in the holster and put it on her and adjusted the microphone, and we started over toward the house. As we passed a tall tree, she said that, of course, Hyde Park is where Franklin Roosevelt had grown up. She said "That's where my husband played when he was a boy— it was his ship's mast—that was the cockpit up there, the lookout, and he would climb up there and travel all over the world." And she went on and described this scene as she remembered her husband mentioning it to her—the tree that he had climbed and seen the world from, the mast of a ship sailing away.

Then we went into the house from room to room, and she would stop and mention something that she remembered in connection with each room except for one. At the second floor she went over to a room that had been hers and she walked by it, saying only "This was my room." And I couldn't get her to say anything more about her room.

[Q:] *What year did you interview Mrs. Roosevelt?*

This must have been about 1959, when she was probably in her early 70s. She was a magnificent person to meet, and the trip she made through the house brought back very personal recollections. Sometime later, the tape was made into the guide that takes visitors through the house today.

I also tried to do the same with Mrs. Eisenhower but she wouldn't have it. She was a much different kind of person. She was completely surrounded by the Secret Service, factotums to guard her at Eisenhower's Gettysburg farm, where she was very much aloof and unapproachable. I remember doing some work at Gettysburg National Battlefield Park one time at a little house which was in the Park Service near the Eisenhower estate, and I needed some labor for it. I had arranged for the park to get a couple of maintenance people there for a day or so to work, and in the midst of it one of the factotum's wives said "What are these people doing here, they are supposed to be working for me and doing this, get 'em out of there." So the situation was quite different.

[Q:] *How would you characterize the 37 years you were in the National Park Service?*

There was a lot to do and I worked out a system of getting it done. I usually had a pretty good secretary and I simply kept an orderly routine of everything. I had to budget everything. I had to find the money and then see that it was spent so as to get archaeological jobs done and reports finished. I contracted with what were then called salvage archaeologists, CRM now. I would write out the contracts and the payoff was always when the final report was in and accepted. I would pay in increments but the last increment was withheld until the report was in and satisfactory. This worked pretty well. Jake Gruber, Fred Kinsey, Herb Kraft, and Vince Foley all worked for me, and a good many others. Fred Kinsey and Herb Kraft did a lot of excellent work in the Tocks Island area of northeastern Pennsylvania.

I also had a group at Isle Royale from the University of Michigan on contract, and they looked for the old native copper mining pits dug by the Archaic Indians two to three thousand years ago. They found a 1200 hundred pound mass of copper in the bottom of one of these "glory holes." It had been shored up from the bottom with some kind of wood framing that was still visible at the time it was found, and the Indians had tried to work on that copper mass. They had bashed at it and bashed at it—it was awfully hard to get anything off of a mass of copper with stone tools. Anyway, this copper mass was found, transported and exhibited at the Bicentennial here in Philadelphia and then turned over to the Philadelphia mint and melted for pennies, and that was the end of it. We were hoping to find another copper mass in place again and then make a nice exhibit of it, but we never did. We wanted to get the archaeologists to try making one of these pits with native tools, that is, with sharp elongated rocks and scoops of wood. Tyler Bastian, a graduate student under Jimmy Griffin at the University of Michigan, was one of them, but I could never get them to do it; the work was too difficult.

[Q:] *At a time when most of your colleagues were employed either in museums or academia, did you find your employment in the Park Service rewarding?*

Not altogether. The question should be, was this rewarding for the Park Service? This is the only thing that was really important. I think I did a credibly decent job, especially in getting out reports of work at Jamestown and the Natchez Trace Parkway. It wasn't brilliant but as I've said facetiously many times before, you're never paid for thinking on government time. And in a sense that's true because the group of people that I characteristically worked for and with in the Park Service expected me to merely stand by in case there was something found accidentally. I could go in then, do an archaeological job to find something of interest to report, and display it to the public. This was about it. Nobody was going to read my reports, which would be filed away and probably thrown away in time, as some of those reports were. So actually this was a rather disheartening aspect of working for the government at that time.

[Q:] *So, archaeologists in a sense played "second fiddle" to some of the other professionals, for example, historians, architectural historians, and architects.*

In a sense. The archaeologists in the National Park Service were always under the architects or historians or both. In the Washington office, the chief historian was over the chief archaeologist administratively, and the architects were always the kingpins of the National Park Service because during the Depression, during the CCC days and WPA days, they were out of jobs and were taken in and given CCC or WPA money to work for the Park Service. After the Depression some became the Park Service landscape architects and architects, but many became the administrators, and once they were in that position they were in the catbird seat, you see. That's the story of Arthur Demeray and Conrad Worth, for example. They were landscape architects, but architects first. So their attitude toward archaeology was rather distant and their appreciation of what archaeology was trying to do was equivocal. The historians were inclined to think that archaeology was okay, but it was really an adjunct to history and not too important. And most of it was prehistory anyway, and that was something else again.

[Q:] *I assume there was some kind of burning desire throughout your career to teach, and that's why you took your position at Penn.*

I wanted to teach to teach myself, because the only way you can really learn is by trying to teach others. And so I was beginning to get on to archaeology by trying to teach it and getting my mind together on it, which helped. I was not a terribly good teacher. The only thing I could do well, I think, was to show students, especially graduate students, how they could broaden their horizons and think of new angles on the things they were interested in, and then give them the opportunity to do it, and all the encouragement they needed. And that was very often enough. I found that if you have given really motivated persons the opportunity to do something, the best thing to do is to stand out of the way and watch them do it.

So anyway, about the Park Service. I don't want to scoff at the Park Service for what it was and is. It's a bureaucracy and I am no good at being a bureaucrat. I don't like bureaucracy and the kind of administration that bureaucrats have to be good at, but if you want to see what can be done, just go to the Northeast Region of the Park Service centered in Boston where they have managed to establish a large office with all kinds of people getting something worthwhile done. They have a unit and a museum at Boott Mills that includes archaeologists, supervisors, field personnel, administrators, museum people, and conservators. They get out a whole series of reports on what they're doing, which is just great. Now that's the kind of bureaucratic organization that works, but unfortunately, when I was working that kind of thing wasn't done. It was premature if it were there at all. And there wasn't any part of the Park Service that was organized to be a big office except at the South-

western monuments, where all the obvious archaeological work was. There you had archaeologists, administrators, and all of the support integrated and working as a unit. That was great. Now they have units in each of the Park Service areas plus a big one in Denver. I was one guy in Philadelphia working for the Mid-Atlantic Region, which it finally became and what it was when I left. I was there with one secretary, but now there are many people there doing essentially the same thing, but doing more, and better work, I grant you. There is, besides that, the Denver Service Center which at one time took over my job and made me in charge of the whole eastern United States for a couple of years. But I didn't have a staff. They had a staff in Denver, you see, and I was doing the leg work out in the field. Now they have many people doing the legwork out in the field beside the support group in Denver, and yet the Park Service hasn't grown that much, you know. They don't have that many more archaeological sites in the Park Service—they just do more with what there is. Bureaucracy feeds on itself and it grows accordingly, and the more it feeds on itself, the more it opposes the natural forces of nature by growing larger instead of smaller.

[Q:] *Tell us about the field schools in historical archaeology that you developed at the University of Pennsylvania.*

It wasn't my idea to begin with. I initially tried to teach a course by just simply talking about historical archaeology, telling the history of it, relating what it was, and letting it go at that. Tony Garvan, among others in the Department of American Civilization at Penn, urged me to teach a field course because I wasn't getting enough students. I, too, could sense that I wasn't teaching a very interesting course, and it would be more interesting if the students could do a practicum in the field. So I started teaching historical archaeology field schools in the greater Philadelphia area about 1963 or 1964. I took the class out on field trips and showed them places where archaeology was. At first, digging was

Daniel G. Roberts

something I hesitated to do because I didn't want to impose a group of people who didn't know archaeology and who were in the process of training on a dig which should be done correctly with experienced labor. So I devised the strategy of making a feasibility study by going to the various places and finding out if it were possible to make a real archaeological investigation there. This required doing the necessary background documentation work and field tests to see if there were enough information and enough evidence to make an archaeological job. And that became our objective and it worked pretty well. The field schools really did a limited amount of work in the field, only enough to train people in the techniques of archaeology without destroying too much evidence.

[Q:] *How did you identify sites to take your classes on and what kind of sites were they?*

Wherever they were available. For instance, at the Grange, which is an historic site on the edge of Philadelphia, at Grumblethorpe which is an estate in the Germantown section of Philadelphia, and at Wyck, an historic house also in Germantown. These were places that had archaeological potential.

[Q:] *Were these sites administered by local historical societies?*

That's right. They were usually in the charge of foundations or associations that ran them like Wyck, Grumblethorpe, and Stenton. Stenton was run by the Society of Colonial Dames. I also went to Valley Forge—it was still a state park, not a national park, at the time. I got permission to take a group of students there about 1964 or 1965. Garry Stone was one of the students, and we excavated a couple of hut sites in the Pennsylvania Encampment and wrote it up. Then we went over to the Virginia Encampment and tested there in the early 1970s. By that time, the state of Pennsylvania had transferred Valley Forge to the Park Service and the Park Service had quite a few ambitions for interpretation. I was always hoping that they would clear

enough of Valley Forge to make it possible to delineate the extent of the encampments so that you could look at the landscape and see where they were, but trees being sacred—the park is full of dogwood—archaeology was mostly limited to open space. The same old story.

[Q:] *How was the American Civilization Department at Penn structured?*

The Department of American Civilization sprang mainly from the English Department and was the brainchild of Tony Garvan, Murray Murphy, and one or two others. In the 1960s, there was a collegial attitude among the faculty at the University of Pennsylvania and the historians, anthropologists, economists, and folklorists got together and knew each other and respected each other's work, and we would often refer students back and forth to take courses that related to their particular disciplines.

Today it's a matter of a series of closed compartments, and each compartment appears to be vying for the bucks. The ones who can't get the money fade away and those who can, get the whole bit. The collegial atmosphere has largely dissipated, and instead of having meetings in which, say, the Department of History invites people from Anthropology, American Civilization, Economics, and Sociology to come in and rap with them over lunch—that sort of thing doesn't happen anymore.

But that was the strength in the beginning of the Department of American Civilization. Tony Garvan and Murray Murphy decided that there was a civilization which we find here in this country which is distinct and is worth studying in its own right. Naturally this study has a relation to the subject of history, it relates to sociology, it certainly relates to cultural anthropology, and furthermore, it has something to do with material culture. This is where Murray Murphy was so perceptive and, I think, brilliant. He wrote a little book on historiography, which I think is really splendid, entitled *Our Knowledge of the Historical Past,* which was published in 1973. In it he utilizes his views of historiography and he goes into historical interpretation and historical theory, but he also goes into the use of material culture. Murphy was an authority on pragmatist theory—he wrote his thesis on it. So he had a very interesting background for the study and philosophy of history. He was one man who understood what archaeology was trying to do and that was very helpful, certainly to me. And so did Tony Garvan, because Garvan, of course, was thinking in terms of objects. The Garvan Collection at Yale is famous. His mother was a great collector, so he was thinking in terms of the material objects and what they mean in cultural history. With that beginning, the Department of American Civilization at Penn attracted the attention of those who were interested in material culture, and that's where archaeology came in.

[Q:] *Weren't there three or four emphases that a student could focus on in the Department of American Civilization, with material culture being only one of them?*

Yes, coursework wasn't constrained or exclusively related only to material cultural. There were other aspects of it, including music, art, graphic art, museum work, and other things, as long it was part of American Civilization.

[Q:] *And since you are an historical archaeologist, those students interested in material culture rather than art or music would have been drawn to you.*

That's true. And yet, of course, as I always told each class, there is an archaeology of everything. Computers have an archaeology beginning, of course, with your 10 fingers, which comprised the original computer, and then going on to the abacus, the mechanical computer, and finally the electronic. That's the archaeology of computers. If you want to go into archaeology of, say, cosmetology, you have to go back to the reasons that people put dark around their eyes, especially in hot climates like Egypt. That dark shade under your eyes and around your eyes makes your eyes look bigger, all right, but it also

reduces the glare. You also have these little Paleolithic Venus figurines with the tightly curled hair; that's a coiffeur, and you can be sure they spent a lot of time at it, too. So the permanent wave probably goes back to the Upper Paleolithic, at least. My point is that anything, anything that you mention, has an archaeology and that is what I tried to convey to every student so that whatever they were interested in would have relevance to archaeology.

[Q:] *Since you've had such a varied professional career, perhaps you could give us an idea of what your main interests are in archaeology. How have your interests evolved over the years?*

Well, to begin with, my interest in anthropology and archaeology is simply to do something about my own colossal ignorance because the one thing that impressed me as a kid growing up, especially when I came to high school and college, was how profoundly ignorant I was, and that is no understatement. I really knew very little about anything and, in particular, I didn't know anything about myself. I also didn't know much about the society in which I lived, and didn't know anything about religion or human-kind. So naturally, anthropology, being the study of human-kind itself, was a thing that was a starting place. Ever since then my interests have simply been to try to understand something of the lifeways of a given people at a given site, at a given time in the past. If there's anything that will impress me as long as I live, it is the quotation from Leonardo DaVinci's notebooks "Time and the River." If you have a river going by the place where you are, everything that comes from upstream is the future, and when it arrives you place your hand in it and it is gone in a flash, and everything downstream is the past. In this metaphor there is no present. The past is your only reference because you don't know what is coming from upstream except that it's water. But you do know what's in it once it passes downstream, and that is all you're ever going to know—the past.

My point is simply this—if you're going to know anything about yourself, your times, your activities and be able to guess the future, you have to know something about the past. You have to investigate it scientifically as well as you can, given the fact that you can never go back to the past and live in it. That's impossible because we still don't have a time machine that can put us there. It's a matter of synthesizing a kind of historical fiction. If the archaeologist is worth a damn he or she will try to evoke enough of that past to make it a semblance of life. It's like virtual reality. Nothing is really there that you can put your hands on, but you can simulate it by getting your facts together just as a computer—which is an idiot, of course—has a program that puts all of the plusses and minuses together, and finally comes up with a picture called virtual reality. It isn't reality, but it looks like reality. It's the documentary and archaeological field data that we put into it that really produces an archaeological image.

[Q:] *It sounds like you're the type of archaeologist who can get interested in almost any kind of archaeology.*

Anything, because it's all the same thing, such as at the beginnings of human consciousness— the identifiable humanity—in the hominids that began to walk upright and make primitive tools or use objects. You begin to wonder just what it was like for them to have a child, for instance, and to mate and to have the man and the woman forming a unit together as they undoubtedly did, because that seems to be the basic nature of human-kind. You wonder how the hell a hominid—with all of the hazards of living and of climate and the lack of proper shelter and the hazards of getting food—could manage to birth a baby and care for it to maturity. This was a terrific accomplishment, so you begin to realize how enormously varied and enormously complicated "barbaric life" really was.

[Q:] *Being such a generalist, how do you keep up with the literature?*

I read as long as my eyes will stand it. They're getting worse and worse and pretty soon I may not be able to read, but that's the way it goes. I read as much as I can. And I listen as much as I can to decent programs on TV— sometimes they're rather good. And I see how much I can still absorb, because once you can't absorb anything, I'm not sure just how you'd get along.

[Q:] *I think it's fair to say that most archaeologists would categorize you as an historical archaeologist. Is that the way you view yourself?*

Well, no, I'm just an archaeologist. An archaeologist should be able to place himself in the context of remote prehistory, beginning with the hominids. You must be able to place yourself in the context of the beginnings of human-kind, the beginnings of human occupations wherever and whenever they occurred, both in the New World and the Old, and then go on from there.

[Q:] *Could you tell us about your efforts in public archaeology and public education?*

Briefly, archaeology has a couple of uses. One is to try and present some kind of understanding of the past, but I think its great use is really for education to galvanize the interest of young people in discovery. Because if education is not discovery, then it's not worth a damn. And unless it means the thrill of discovery to the individual who is in the process of education, it becomes a bore. Unfortunately, I have seen many people turned off by boring courses in history, sociology, anthropology, and even archaeology, for that matter. These were courses that were routine, lacking in imagination, and not particularly connected with the interests of the people who took the courses. The people who took the courses didn't see the relevance to themselves and their lives. But all of a sudden, if you experience discovery literally, and what a thrill it is—something you didn't know before, which is interesting, and means something to you—that changes your life a little.

I think archaeology has a definite relevance to early education. I've tried it out with young people in the early grades and found that they're most definitely interested in archaeology. Kids can relate to archaeology, for instance, by projecting themselves into the situation of an Upper Paleolithic kid of nine years old. The old man was out hunting megafauna and the mother was at home trying to fashion some things from leather to make leggings or footsoles and the sister was trying to help her and the kid was trying to learn how to throw a spear. Well, all that is part of the experience of a nine-year-old child at that period, we think, on fairly good evidence. What was it like to be a child at, say, the time of the American Revolution? What were the pastimes and games? Can a nine year old boy of today relate to a nine-year-old boy of 200 years ago as he tries to pitch a coin or a disk up against a wall and see how close he can make it fall against that wall? All this is part of the rhythm of childhood, and if a kid understands that and sees it in the past, and realizes that today nothing is that different, and he or she can begin to associate his or her childhood with the childhoods of the past, then archaeology means something.

[Q:] *Unfortunately, most children in this country are not introduced to archaeology, since there are very few school curricula in archaeology.*

Well, in the Philadelphia area, Lower Merion High School has a teacher named Steven McCarter, who was a student of mine at one time. He teaches historical archaeology and teaches it very well. He has taken his students on field schools at Valley Forge and Gettysburg. Then there was a teacher named Emmanuel Kramer at Cheltenham High School in Cheltenham Township, outside of Philadelphia, and for many years he taught high school historical archaeology, volunteering his students at Independence National Historical Park, Franklin Court, and other places. So, once in a while you'll find a few high school teachers who know archaeology and can convey it, but unfortunately they're damned few.

[Q:] *Why is archaeology so uncommon in secondary schools?*

Because it's uncommon in the primary schools. Nobody regards archaeology as something children can understand. They think it's an arcane subject that is beyond the comprehension of children—which is nonsense. Take, for instance, the University Museum here at Penn. We have thousands of school children going through here year after year after year. They go through in class groups and listen to the docents, who are very nice people and are very good at what they do, tell them, for example, about life in ancient Egypt. But I never heard any of them say this is how it was for the children. What I want to do is have a kids corner in every gallery, and I've proposed this to Jeremy Sabloff, the Director of the Museum, and he's listening. Every gallery should have a kids corner which relates in a hands-on way how it was for children in the subject time period and culture area. It should relate how kids begin to learn to do things, and begin to participate as an adult with the family in a living and learning situation. It could really be gangbusters if you can relate, for example, how a cuneiform tablet was a kid's daily lesson book 2,300 years ago. But the museum exhibitors don't make the connection between the children of the past, their lives, and what they were thinking, and today's children and their lives.

[Q:] *True, but why aren't the school teachers doing this?*

They aren't prepared. They don't know anything about archaeology, and the history that they do know is routine history, events, people, occasions, dates. It sounds as though we've made progress, but have we? If you take a look at our modern junior high school history books, see how much you can understand. But kids really are interested in archaeology, such as the CCC kids who went to Jamestown in the 1930s and worked there. They didn't all become archaeologists. There was not one laborer that I employed who became an archaeologist. But I knew of a great many laborers of all ages who were influenced by what they did at Jamestown because they learned to observe. They learned to do something carefully. They learned to do something with skill and it was appreciated. If you don't do anything else with an individual, you can get him to do something that is carefully done and that he's proud of, gets praise for. If you can do this, you've gone a long way in helping that individual, and archaeology is a terrific vehicle for doing this.

[Q:] *What can you tell us about your current archaeological interests?*

Right now I'm living in a lifecare community in Philadelphia (Logan Square East) in which my wife and I were the first residents in 1984. One of my current interests is in gerontology, and I am very much interested in the American Anthropological Association's section devoted to senior anthropologists. One of the things that challenges a senior anthropologist is what the hell do you do after you've retired without going completely crazy? You get to the point where you recognize the seven stages of humanity when you are an old man sans teeth, sans sight, sans hearing, sans nearly everything. Before that you get to the point where you're just an old man functioning, hopefully, in the sixth stage, not quite in the seventh. But after you retire, you always have the challenge of how to keep on going. And the only way to keep on going is to keep on doing what you've always done in some way because you know how to do it. In other words, if you have a business, go back to the business and volunteer. If you can't get paid for what you do, at least be an advisor.

Here at the Museum, even though I'm not paid, I do have an office, and my wife and I— thrifty souls that we are—saved enough so we can contribute a little to the Museum each year. So they let me have an office, you see, which is a nice thing to do. Anyway, the point is in having this office, I can have my library here, can meet people here, and I can advise students, consult with them, rap with them, and every now and then they'll ask for a person to consult on archaeology, and I can refer them.

I can also be of use to the people at Logan Square East because I can understand some of their problems. What I'm doing there is studying the community as it evolves. Now there are several nice things about a community of geriatrics, and that is if you are one of them yourself, you are a mole, working inside the organization. Furthermore, you speak the language and you know the customs of the people. You don't have to learn a foreign language and you don't have to go to the South Pacific to meet them and live there. You live where you and they are, you are one of them, and you can understand them pretty well. And another thing of course, is that you have an opportunity to participate in everything they do, and you write things down as you go and try to analyze what's happening. If you do that you can keep up your interest in anthropology and you can study this phenomenon of old age.

The thing that impresses me as I look at these old age communities is that they're comprised mostly of women, and as I view them in their living habits, I notice that a great emphasis is placed on food. They always have the best food they can possibly get and as much of it as they can possibly eat. This would kill them in most circumstances except for one thing—their genes. Practically all of them are genetically programmed to live a long time. And so they eat foolishly. They do foolish things and yet they live a long time. Oddly enough, there are many women, but what has happened to the men? And what do the women do for them? They cook for them faithfully and generously all their lives, and the men departed them betimes. They're gone. So the women are left. I think there's some kind of cause and effect here and I don't doubt that their diet had much to do with it.

[Q:] *How are you applying this first-hand knowledge?*

I've got a dossier on Logan Square East. It's very hard to keep up, and it's very hard to gear it into some kind of anthropological framework. There is a group at [nearby] Einstein Hospital which is composed of five anthropologists and they all live on grants and study gerontology—it's sort of a center for geriatrics. We also have a center here at Penn for the study of aging, and I've been interested in both centers. But it's very hard to develop something which will be useful from the standpoint of anthropology, and I haven't quite cracked that yet.

There are some very good books on gerontology. The best of them study old age on a worldwide basis, what the problem is, and how it's handled. Then they discuss the problem of old age in the United States. Of course there are too many old people still living who ordinarily should have been dead a generation or two ago. In the early 1900s they would have had a life expectancy of perhaps 50 or 60 years, and now it tops 80. A woman can expect to live to be 88 or so. A man can expect to live to his early 80s, all because of the availability of modern medicines and decent diets. The population explosion phenomenon is overwhelming in the world, so gerontology becomes tremendously important. And that's why as an anthropologist I'm head over heels interested in gerontology.

[Q:] *Maybe you should try to put together an article on your observations and experiences.*

Well, I've turned over the first part of my notes to the unit at Einstein and they've accepted them graciously and gratefully, but I don't know whether they've used them or not. The notes are not nearly as good as I would like them to be. I would like them carefully structured so that I address intelligent questions to my material, but I can't think of the intelligent questions to ask.

[Q:] *Have you approached it from a participant-observer view? Have you conducted formal interviews?*

I'm with them all the time. I've gotten up a questionnaire, but I haven't disseminated it yet. I'm still working on the questionnaire, and I'm trying to key in certain questions that give me an idea of how these people are thinking. On the other hand, I know that I am kidding myself.

These are all individuals and they all have life stories, and when you try and nail down patterns in these life stories, it's not so easy.

[Q:] *What else is keeping you busy these days?*

I write little essays about topics that intrigue me and I offer them as Forum articles. These are articles in the back of *Archaeology Magazine*, put out by the American Institute of Archaeology. I have fun writing these. For instance, I've written on the triumph of fossil man in existing at all against great odds. I find that a delightful subject. And I've written about Sigmund Freud and artifacts that had been on tour recently and what he thought about archaeology. He was very much interested in classical archaeology, and I relate some of that to Freud and his work. His analysis of the individual was very much like the archaeologist's analysis of the past. He's digging into the mind, we're digging into the earth. Without saying so or even realizing it, Freud seemed to bridge both because he was truly interested in archaeology as he saw it, and was always delving into it, psyching the minds of individuals, which is what we're trying to do with the past.

On the BBC several years ago there was a program on the peopling of the New World, and they asked me to go back to the type site at Clovis at their expense. They wanted me to stand there and make a few comments, which I did. But I found I didn't recognize one damned thing! The gravel pit completely changed and New Mexico State University in Portales—when I was last there it was not much more than a dormitory, a classroom, and a tennis court—suddenly had grown into a large university with over 30,000 students. They had taken great interest in the Clovis type site and had an *in situ* exhibit, and separate from that, a very interesting museum. So I was a living fossil, going back to the place where the real fossils were, trying to identify, or re-identify, the locale which was entirely different from my recollections. This was intriguing to me because in the short space of 60 years, I had suddenly come to a scene which had not only completely changed, but so had my interpretation. Thanks to my having matured and gotten a few ideas in my time, it occurred to me that possibly the ancient people who were at Clovis were trapping animals that were busy seeking water in an increasingly parched landscape in a waterhole, which formed in a drainage course. The hunters might have been trying to trap them there. If you trap an elephant in a waterhole how do you keep the elephant from escaping? Because he can get out of the waterhole faster than he got in, can't he? They must have had something such as cordage to trip him, so it occurred to me for the first time in 50 or 60 years that they may have had some device for bringing the mammoth down so that they could attack and kill it. If that's progress, it shows how long it takes your mind to get together in thinking about things.

[Q:] *You were in on the ground floor when the Society for American Archaeology was formed in the early 1930s. I wonder if you could give us your insights into the SAA's founding, and what national archaeology was like at the time.*

Archaeology at that time was concentrated in the Southwest, Southeast and Midwest. Early participants were Arthur C. Parker, Jimmy Griffin, Douglas Byers, M. R. Harrington, Carl Guthe, W. C. McKern, Henry Collins, E. W. Gifford, Emil Haury, Duncan Strong, Thorne Deuel, W. A. Ritchie, W. S. Webb, Waldo Wedel, Wendell Bennett, and Frank Roberts, Jr. That's the basic roster of the people who were prominent and active in American archaeology at that time.

[Q:] *Were you at the first SAA meeting?*

I don't think I was, I'm trying to remember. I was a student at the University of Denver at the time, and I'm not sure where the first meeting was held. I doubt if I were there, but I went to as many meetings as I possibly could, and if they were held somewhere nearby that was just great.

[Q:] *I assume there were only a hundred or so members of SAA at that time, or fewer.*

Oh yes, less than that. It was a very small beginning, and as I recall, it cost about five bucks a year to be a member. I remember deciding it might be a good investment, although five bucks was a lot of money in those days.

[Q:] *In the mid 1960s you helped form the Society for Historical Archaeology. What can you tell us about that?*

It started with a little panel group that I organized at a meeting of the American Anthropological Association in St. Louis—I think it was in 1965. J. O. Brew, J. Hubert Smith, John Griffin, and Ivor Noël Hume were all on the panel. The purpose of the panel was to discuss historical archaeology. You see, at that time the Society for American Archaeology included some people interested in historical sites. Of course, ever since Pinky Harrington worked at Jamestown, there had been this entity called "historic sites archaeology," so it was there in the background. But some of us were interested in working at historic sites and wanted to be represented at the meetings.

Ed Jelks, John Griffin, and several others were of the opinion that maybe we should form our own organization, but at the time when we met, I had gotten this panel group together with the idea of trying to focus on historical archaeology by defining its purpose and its prospects. I have a copy of that symposium. I referred to it in Volume 1, Number 1 of *Historical Archaeology* and in the retrospective on historical archaeology that we had at the Jamaica meeting in 1992. In 1967 we really got going at a meeting held in Dallas. Ed Jelks was very active in the early years, as was Stan South, Pinky Harrington, Edward Larrabee, and a number of other people.

[Q:] *You were the first editor of the journal, is that correct?*

No, I was the first President, and technically the second editor.

[Q:] *You were both simultaneously?*

Yes, Glenn Little was the first editor, and then he became ill and sent me everything that he had in a shoebox through the mail. I opened up the shoebox and found in the bottom of it a couple of manuscripts, which was all that he had up to then. By that time I had something like three months to get it out, so I immediately got on the phone and got everybody who was supposed to have something to get it in quickly. I then went to a printer in Philadelphia and negotiated the printing of it. We actually managed to get the thing printed up in time for the first meeting, which was in Williamsburg in 1968. I remember taking it in the backseat of our Volkswagen and driving in a sleet storm to Williamsburg. I unloaded the journal copies and made them available to everybody, and that was the beginning of the Society for Historical Archaeology.

[Q:] *Do you remember how many members there were that first year or two?*

I really don't, but I suppose there were no more than a couple hundred or so.

[Q:] *Aside from their different scholarly foci, how would you compare the SHA and the SAA?*

Both organizations have been, let us say, "co-opted" by the intense desire to emphasize theory rather than field work. Neither organization likes to publish reports on fieldwork, although the SHA does publish a lot of articles on material culture studies, mostly rather discursive articles, with attention to the philosophy of the subject rather than straight reporting of accomplishments. If you take a look at the recent issues of *American Antiquity*—here's the issue for April of 1994, for example—you'll see articles like *The Thermal Response of the Clay Cooking Pot*. That's a pretty fancy name for whatever they're talking about, the thermal response—if a cooking pot can make such structural changes. *American Antiquity* is somewhat given to complex analyses and impressive data, and the more involved it is, the more impressive it is.

I think simplification is an art that does not often come easily to modern archaeologists. Of

course it does, oddly enough, to those who try to talk to the lay public. If you take somebody like Jeremy Sabloff, Director of the University Museum here at Penn, he has a book on The Great Cities of Mexico, which is a perfectly clear, succinct, exposition and it doesn't really talk down to the layperson, it lays it out without any jargon. Brian Fagan has books on the Aztecs and on the people of North America, which are perfectly acceptable science reporting, even though they're done without jargon, and they're perfectly clear to the intelligent layperson. So it can be done.

I think that the value of the journal *Historical Archaeology,* when compared to *American Antiquity,* really is its lucidity, its clear and accurate reporting, and its lack of, shall we say, pretense. I see a lot of pretense in much of the complexity of exposition, and a lot of it seems to me to be a matter of archaeologists talking to each other about what they are doing and thinking rather than reporting in a straightforward manner on what they have found and what it means.

[Q:] *Do you find both* Historical Archaeology *and* American Antiquity *of value at this stage in your career?*

Oh yes, I certainly do. I may not read everything from cover to cover, simply because that's physically impossible; but on the other hand, I am aware of what's there and if there's something that is germane to my particular interest I read it. I try to keep up with what's going on in *American Anthropologist* and *Current Anthropology* too, as well as several other journals.

[Q:] *I know you've been honored by the profession on several occasions, particularly later in your career. Could you give us an idea of your thoughts on receiving those awards.*

Well, I'll tell you the award I appreciate really as much as any of them is the one that you and Mike Parrington share with me, and that is the Antoinette Forester Downing Award of the Society for Architectural Historians for our book *The Buried Past: An Archaeological History of Philadelphia.* I always thought that was a very nice thing for an architectural group, rather than an archaeological one, to give to three archaeologists for "excellence as a published architectural survey." Another award I've enjoyed is the David E. Finley award, bestowed by the National Trust for Historic Preservation. This award is given to people who are into historic sites conservation and have made a contribution to that. I've valued that—it was a nice thing to do.

Back in the Bicentennial I also got a certificate of appreciation signed by John Warner at the time he was married to Liz Taylor. She didn't sign it, unfortunately. But anyway, that was for the little booklet *Above Ground Archaeology* that was put out at that time. There was also the J. Alden Mason Award from the Society for Pennsylvania Archaeology—I always was very happy about that. It was very nice of them to remember me and so was the Society for Virginia Archaeology, which gave me their "Archaeologist of the Year" award one time, which I took very kindly to.

[Q:] *Tell us about receiving the J. C. Harrington award from the SHA.*

I do value that award very much because, of course, the Harrington Award is the one real award that the people who are in historical archaeology have for recognition. It was a very nice thing, and I was very happy to get it, believe me.

[Q:] *What do you consider to be your major contributions to the profession?*

The fact of it is I was a rotten teacher as far as classwork was concerned. Getting up and spieling in the classroom, I never considered that I was very good at it. I like to talk, but to get up a formal lecture, no. The thing that always impressed me was that the students were never taking notes. And that's a tip-off, you see. If they don't take notes, you're really not giving them anything they're going to remember, and that always impressed me profoundly—it told me teaching was not my long suit. Therefore, I made it a point to go one-on-one with every stu-

dent in my class. I wanted to get on their particular wave length, know what their interests and intentions were in their careers, know what their background was, and know where they wanted to go. And then I would try and open up an additional perspective in their minds to possibilities they hadn't thought of and would encourage them to do whatever they were doing and possibly show them something about it they hadn't thought of.

[Q:] *So you apparently believe that the bulk of knowledge is made up of ideas rather than facts?*

Oh yes, the facts anybody can acquire, and I learned it's best to assume that people can get the facts themselves if they are sufficiently interested. What you should do is to try to help them organize their own concept of the data, and what they are going to do with their own lives and careers, and to open up new avenues of thought. That is the only real contribution I ever made to teaching, but my students seemed to pick up on that.

[Q:] *I think many of your students, even those who never went on in anthropology or archaeology, received very good training in the historical archaeology of the Philadelphia area.*

Well, Philadelphia was a natural. Of course, since I was with the Park Service and was in the midst of our campaign at Independence National Historical Park, I was able to take the students on various projects there, as well as to sites mentioned earlier, such as Grumblethorpe, Wyck, and Stenton, all in Germantown.

[Q:] *What do you consider to be your lasting contributions to the field?*

One certainly is *Archaeological Excavations at Jamestown, Virginia.* That was published by the GPO in 1958, and I benefited from the work of Pinky Harrington, Ed Jelks, Joel Shiner, B. Bruce Powell, and J. Paul Hudson, among others. We all collaborated in getting the artifacts prepared and analyzed and reported, and then I had the winter of 1956 and the spring of 1957 for getting the material together in published form. I spent weekends and nights working on it, and I did all the typing myself, so the whole thing was done under intense pressure. My wife Virginia helped me proof everything and get it ready, and then Pinky Harrington helped me get it to press, and his help was crucial.

I also consider *The Buried Past: An Archaeological History of Philadelphia* to be another major contribution, co-authored with you and Michael Parrington. As you know, it took nine and a half years to finish that book. One of the reasons that it is a pretty good effort is because it is remarkably free of mistakes, which is one of your contributions. You insisted on, if not perfection, as close as we could possibly come to it, and that was good because there are many instances in which I'm sloppy, particularly with references, and you very justifiably and very correctly told me to go back and get references that should have been cited. I am very happy that you did that. Another reason is that we had the services of Sarah Evans, who is an excellent editor, for the conceptualization of the text. She really made it a seamless whole.

[Q:] *Don't sell your own contributions short. One of the things that I think really comes through in the book is your witty style of writing, which neither Mike Parrington nor I have. You have a way of turning a phrase which Sarah Evans left largely intact, and I'm thankful for that.*

Well, it's interesting that you bring that up because I've always been a witness more than a creator in anthropology. I have never tried to figure out a new way of explaining why humankind operates as it does. I have never been a theoretician, but I have been a witness. I have always been fascinated with observing, first, how people in prehistory and history who are the subject of an archaeological investigation lived their various lifeways, and second, how anthropologists and archaeologists have responded to this interpretive challenge. They talk to each other and they get very elaborate constructs of theory and so on. What they are really doing is trying to figure out what they're doing, and why they're

doing it, and how else they could do what they're doing, and if they do something else, whether it's more important than what they've already done. When you put all that together, you go back to the fundamentals, and it's really to find out what other people did at a different time, you see. And in order to do that you have to go back and try and understand them in their time and in their context of culture. If you can do that, it's a neat trick, but all the theory that you have in the world probably can only encourage you to perceive what you are looking for in the first place and make it perhaps a little better job.

So as far as my own contributions are concerned, it's pretty bald stuff. I've simply tried to say what is there, but in doing so, I couldn't help observe and comment just a little bit, and if that involves a certain amount of wit, I'm happy about it because I see things as being awfully funny very often. The stories of William Penn and Benjamin Franklin, for example, have their humorous aspects, and when you go into the story of Philadelphia, you really understand how this city grew. I think that, little by little, as you add historical data to the archaeological data, and you begin to piece things together, there's a lot that you can laugh at, but there's also a lot that is tragic. But at the same time, it makes the story of the city. Now in *The Buried Past* we didn't relate all that, but we did allude to it and we spoke of the people without history.

[Q:] *One of your publications that I always thought was pretty pioneering for its time (1968) is the* Handbook for Historical Archaeology. *For whatever reason, perhaps because it was privately published, it hasn't gotten a whole lot of play. What are your thoughts on that?*

That was a class project to begin with. The idea was to get together the artifacts most commonly encountered in historical archaeology, classify them, and make them useful to whoever had the handbook. I was going to call it a chapbook at first, which was perhaps more appropriate because a chapbook is really just a little handbook. What was published was Volume 1. There is a

Volume 2, incidentally, which is incomplete. I hoped that I could find somebody to go in with me to expand the first volume and go on to Volume 2 and make this a real handbook, but I didn't find anybody to do it. Dave Orr was going to at first, but it never happened. Ivor Noël Hume thought it was a disgustingly inadequate thing and a shame that students should be so ill-trained that they would do such a wretched job. Well, nobody else did such a handbook. When Noël Hume wrote his book *Historical Archaeology* it was, of course, not really on historical archaeology in general, but on the archaeology of Virginia, and more specifically, on the archaeology of Colonial Williamsburg, and even more specifically, on the archaeology of the 18th century at Colonial Williamsburg. So he had perhaps something less of a framework than I had in mine. I wanted to make it comprehensive. It was a rotten job, true enough, but it was the only one there was at the time, and if I had had a good partner to go in on it, somebody who would stamp around and be very active and carry it on, I think it could have been made into something.

[Q:] *I wonder if you could give us your thoughts on how archaeology has evolved in the 60-plus years that you've been active in it.*

Well, I'm fortunate that I have been able to view archaeology with a certain perspective in as much as I came back to the University of Pennsylvania after being away for 20 years. As I noted earlier, I initially sat in on classes from 1935 to 1937, and then again in the late 1950s, and finally got my degree in 1959. I realized in this interval that things had changed a great deal. I understood what those changes were, but the students who came there in the 1950s did not have this perspective, and I had the experience and a perspective of almost a quarter of a century by that time.

I knew that what I had learned previously was not the true and lively word because in the 1930s we were talking about culture circles, *Kulturekreislehrer*. Everything was in terms of the German concept of the spread of culture

circles throughout the world—a little different from the evolutionary concept. Anyway, we were talking and thinking in those terms at that time, and then when I came back, no word about that at all— completely forgotten. We were talking about psychology and psychoanalysis. Pete Hallowell was talking in terms of the Rohrshach test, which was given to the Saulteaux Indians, and what that meant, and how these people were thinking. So psychology and anthropology were coming together in that respect, and I got a new view of it. Hallowell had been a student at Columbia and had known Franz Boas, and I also knew about Franz Boas through Frank Speck. This was lively stuff because you were in the presence of Franz Boas, and you knew how he taught, and you knew how he wanted to maintain the culture history of the people who were disappearing in the Northwest Coast by learning their languages and transmitting them to students. Boas insisted on speaking the language. I remember Hallowell saying how he watched Boas trying to explain to someone glottal stops, and something in his mouth hit this other guy "splat" in the face. And Boas went right on, and so did the other guy, with neither paying any attention to it because they were intent in what they were doing. They were just splattering saliva all over the place. This was the real thing!

Anyway, this was the kind of experience that I really came to appreciate because I was beginning to get a perspective spanning 20 years. Then I realized that 20 years after that, God knows, there would be other things thought of and talked about, and sure enough, 20 years after that there was something else, so within a decade or two things change rather dramatically in anthropology and archaeology.

[Q:] *During your 20-year "hiatus" from Penn, do you remember having discussions about an overall theoretical framework within which archaeology was being done?*

Well, this is the point. The people who were involved in WPA archaeology during this period—including Al Spaulding, Marion Baugh,

Dave Stout, Ivar Skarland, H. T. C. Hertzberg, John Elliott, Gordon Willey, A. R. Kelly, Jim Ford, among others—were all graduate students trained in archaeology or related subjects, and who all had pretty good academic foundations at that time, the state of the art. And they were damned good, incidentally, Al Spaulding in particular. I think he was a superb field man, and so was Dave Stout.

Well, because we all had so much collected material to study, we went to as many meetings as we could, and rapped with Jimmy Griffin and others. I think we thought we all were on the cutting edge for the time. Webb, however, was less moved by new archaeological thinking then the rest of us.

So we all began to see that Webb was publishing field reports that were descriptive, and the analytical part perhaps was not altogether there. There was more to do, in other words. As they finished their graduate studies and went on, they began to think of this enormous quantity of work. So you had all these young guys who were all beginning to think in terms of what you are going to do with this stuff and what cultural constructs you can get out of it. Ford was beginning to develop the concept of seriation diagrams, and how you could see what styles were beginning and in what quantity, and how those styles became attenuated as they matured through time. Ford also taught ceramics to Gordon Willey, and Willey then took that knowledge to Peru and undertook seriation studies at Ancon. When this all began to come together, it was really the beginning of the "New Archaeology." If it hadn't been for WPA archaeology, I don't think we would have had the "New Archaeology" developing as it has. So then the next step was to refine the "New Archaeology," and we have been doing that ever since.

[Q:] *After WPA, what observations can you make about North American archaeology?*

A lot of the thinking in archaeology in the 1940s and 1950s was in the head of Jimmy Griffin—that remarkable head. I've often wondered if there is anybody still living who remembers Jimmy when he had a head of hair. He was bald when I first met him. He was also quite an athlete, a great swimmer. Jimmy must have taken care of himself because he lived a very long and productive life.

Then people like Gordon Willey began to think in terms of theory, and Walter Taylor wrote his *Study of Archaeology*, which was his thesis at Harvard. All of this took place in the 1940s and 1950s. Joe Caldwell was one of those who also got things going, and then Lew Binford took over from there, and so you have the so-called "New Archaeology." I was just noticing this very excellent book by Bruce Trigger, *A History of Archaeological Thought*, and he mentions that Joe Caldwell in 1959 published an article in *Science* entitled "The New American Archaeology," and so that kind of got us all started.

At the same time the Midwestern Taxonomic System was going great guns, which was W. S. McKern's idea of figuring out how to order the data. And Major Webb was always getting up trait lists. Trait lists were big things at the time. We thought that if you got all the traits you could identify a certain group of people and then match them with the trait lists of another group of people. When so many traits correlated statistically, you would have probable associations. Of course we didn't have computers at that time.

[Q:] *How did you view the "New Archaeology?"*

Well, Lew Binford viewed cultures as humanity's extra-somatic means of adaptation. I like that—extra-somatic—what is body and what is spirit is an interesting thing. When does the spirit jump out of the body and become culture, and is culture manipulable? Is it something that you can analyze and treat as though it were a quantity outside of the body and outside of people? Culture is regarded by many anthropologists as something so concrete that it can be analyzed almost as a species or something that belongs on the biogenetic tree of life. That's a little dicey, I think. By doing this, people get pushed into the background and individuals become amorphous and are lost sight of. The fact of it is, culture is in every individual, and when you're excavating a site, you're not looking at a culture, as much as you are looking at individuals who lived at that site and you're looking at a sample of the things that the individuals did. And when you get it all together, yes, you can quantify it. You can get together all the artifacts which are comparable, and then you can compare them with artifacts from another site, and you can work up your data. Then you begin to hypothesize, and then you get your theories together, and then finally when you get your theories all together, somehow, in some mysterious way, the individuals have been forgotten. This is something that is a trick in archaeology that I don't think we've solved yet.

[Q:] *The two major tenets of the "New Archaeology" back in the late 1960s were 1) an emphasis on a deductive approach to collecting and interpreting data, and 2) an emphasis on trying to devise covering laws of human behavior. How do you feel about those two tenets?*

Well, laws are made to be broken, of course, and unfortunately there is no law that could be imagined by an anthropologist for human-kind that wouldn't have a great many exceptions. Then you question whether it is a law or not, or is it just a pattern of sorts, and what is a pattern? You then try to construct a theory about patterns so that you end up with laws. When you get to the laws, that's when it becomes really dicey, because you can never be sure that you got your definition clear enough that you really have a law that means anything. Kent Flannery and others have pointed out such things as, for instance, the law of the number of houses in a given community will be an indication of how many people lived there. There is a correlation there, but there's also a correlation between the size of a boy's shoe and the height of his body.

[Q:] *What about the old "inductive vs. deductive" debate?*

Well, you simply have to have both of them. You use both approaches as much as you can whenever they are relevant. And if anyone can tell me exactly when they are not relevant, I'd be very willing to listen. When do you have a case in which the deductive approach is totally irrelevant, even dangerous? When is the inductive approach irrelevant? They are two concepts that, when you get right down to it, have only one purpose, and that is, figuring out what people did at a given time, at a given place, and in the context of their times. And so if you find that it's possible to deduce something from a certain piece of evidence, fine. If you can generalize and say something is probable and then test your results, that's great. Why separate them? They go together, as far as I can see.

[Q:] *In 1977, Stanley South published, I believe, the first "covering law" emanating from his focus on pattern recognition which was entitled "The Law of Behavioral By-Product Regularity" which is stated as follows: "The by-product of a specified activity has a consistent frequency relationship to that of all activities in direct proportion to their organized integration." Any comments?*

Sure, you can put it in those words, which make it sufficiently complex to be terribly impressive, but the fact of it is, what South was talking about really is that you have certain things that are done by people, and these are sometimes repetitive. For example, if a woman is doing a lot of laundering, she uses a certain type of soap and a certain type of clothesline on a certain type of a day and, according to the wind, she decides to put it up with a certain type of clothespin or another. Now all of these have a relationship to each other, but they are all only related to one thing, and that is doing the laundry. Now you can make a whole construct out of that and you can deduce various things, and you can show the interrelationship of one to the other. But when you get to the theory of it, according to the temperature of the day, the humidity and whether it's raining or not, and whether the sun is shining or not, you do or you don't use a certain type of clothespin, or you only use a certain segment of the line. As an archaeologist, you have to figure out what's really important. Is it really important that you analyze it to that extent? What does it contribute to our knowledge of doing the laundry in, say, the 19th century in South Philadelphia among people who made an average income of $400 a year and who lived in a father, son, and holy ghost house, and had a little rack up on the roof where they put their laundry out?

With regard to pattern recognition, South should have come to Philadelphia where you can put a wrecked car right outside your door, or somebody will do it for you, and it'll stay there until the cops haul it away. That, of course may be surrounded by bottle caps, pop tops, clothes, and other litter; but on the other hand, if you analyze it, you will probably be confused because you may find that there is also a large bundle of trash which somebody has deposited on your doorstep which has nothing to do with your particular house, but they have favored you by dumping their trash on your property. The city then fails to pick up the trash for a period of two months, until it is well-scattered by the rats and the children and the wind. So we can't always be sure of the way trash was deposited in the past. We assume that people took trash out of their houses and deposited it in a most convenient place. Well, that's dandy, but we weren't there, were we?

[Q:] *Well, certainly we have many instances in the archaeological record of large quantities of trash being deposited under the floor boards of kitchens and outside the back door.*

This is true and, of course, in the case of the Paleolithic caves, they probably weren't as neat as the sow mother is in keeping her nest of piglets clean, which she does very competently. A sow mother will be remarkably tidy about keeping the litter area of her piglets clean. Certainly this is true when compared with some of the evidence from the Southwest where we find human feces scattered around house locations.

[Q:] *One of the things that I find interesting about the fluorescence of the "New Archaeology" in the late 1960s is that coincidentally at about the same time (1966) the National Historic Preservation Act was passed. The passage of that act ushered in a whole new era of compliance archaeology that is conducted under legislative mandates and policies. So we now have new generations of archaeologists coming up who don't view archaeology so much as an academic discipline, but more as an applied profession. I wonder if you could comment on that.*

Yes, I could, because it is now an industry that spends a lot of money, probably well over 200 million a year. It therefore speaks with a voice that can be heard. Back when we were doing archaeology in the WPA days, of course, we were spending a lot of money relative to what money there was to spend, and therefore it gathered a little importance of sorts. But very few of the people who were doing archaeology were keeping good records, and those who were keeping good records did the publishing. As I noted earlier, those like Donald Cadzow here in Pennsylvania, who kept few records at all and left little, simply wasted the opportunity, and that was too bad. Major Webb published everything that he did and that was great. Now, when it comes to the business of compliance archaeology, this is something that has multiplied the quantum of material that we are actually getting to analyze and conserve so that we are severely challenged to do something with it. It's a truism that if an archaeologist excavates and does not make a report, he has destroyed the site for nothing. Everybody who has done compliance archaeology has generated data. Some of it is good, some of it is not so good, some of it is complete, and some of it is very incomplete. Some people have gone into it with competence and others have gone into it with less competence, and some of it has been done by those who have damned little competence at all. And so you have a mix, but the point is that a great quantity has been gotten out of the ground and some of it has been widely published, but most of it has not.

However, contractual obligations, including a written report, must be met in order to be paid. So reports generally exist, and at least one copy should be in each State Historic Preservation Office. Other copies should also be distributed to organizations or individuals who are interested, but the whole thing depends on the proper archiving of this material. There are a lot of CRM outfits that no longer exist. What has happened to their notes, for instance, to say nothing of the artifacts, is a good question. If those notes have been put at risk and now do not exist, then the whole damned thing is a waste, just as though the site had been invaded and destroyed with bulldozers. Those who have made reports that have not been formally published, but which have been archived, have a resource that can be accessed, but there's another catch. Unless material which is gotten out of the ground and reported on is known generally, the tendency is for this to be not only neglected, but very often misconstrued. If you are going into theory, you better have all kinds of data, and unless these data are made public and available, they won't be used. My point is that the CRM archaeologists and SHPOs, whoever is sitting on this mound of reports, has the job of putting them on-line electronically, so that all of this material will be available to everybody. Looking ahead to the 21st century, reports on paper will be old hat—everything will be on-line or on whatever is the medium at that time.

[Q:] *Do you feel that compliance archaeology has made and will continue to make significant contributions, or that it has fallen short of expectations?*

Compliance archaeology has not made the contributions it should. The potential is there but it hasn't been met. Ideally, there should be a journal of CRM archaeology, and there should be a CRM newsletter. They should be gotten out just as often as possible, and they shouldn't be elaborate or expensive. They should all be on-line, with simple indices. There also should be a national organization devoted to CRM archaeology. It should have a national office and there should be a branch in every state.

[Q:] *What do you think of "politically correct archaeology?"*

Well, archaeology that is politically correct probably has extra baggage that isn't worth a damn. There shouldn't be any politics in archaeology, but of course there is and always was, and there always will be.

[Q:] *Can you comment on archaeology the National Park Service way?*

Well, archaeology in the National Park Service was always tied very firmly to development, and development always meant construction of one type or another. Because of the Antiquities Act, the National Historic Preservation Act, and other legislation, the Park Service always had to think of what might happen to the site, and this was supposed to be protected. Many times a superintendent would not know what the archaeologists were talking about or give a damn, and very often his staff didn't know what the archaeologists were talking about either.

Let me give you an example from Morristown, New Jersey. In the 1930s under WPA, Thor Borison, who was a very good military archaeologist, did some work at Fort Nonsense, which was on a hill overlooking Morristown. During the Revolutionary War when the encampment was there, George Washington lived in the nearby Ford Mansion, and this hill was strategically located so that it could command a view of the town. So they built a little fort called Fort Nonsense. The guy who had charge of Morristown for the Park Service was Dr. Francis Ronald. He was a good historian, but he didn't think much about archaeology. When Thor

Borison went to work on top of the hill he located the remains of the fort and reconstructed it. At the same time, the rangers (who were all foresters) let the whole area grow up in trees so that there was no view from the fort. If you are going to interpret it as a fort, for God's sake, you don't let trees grow up around it. But Fran Ronald wasn't thinking that way, and the rangers, one after another, weren't thinking that way either. To finally top it off one ranger in the 1960s finally said, "We've got to make a good turnaround for people when they drive up to the top of Fort Nonsense. Let's take a bulldozer and just smooth it out for them." So they took a bulldozer and completely obliterated the good reconstruction that Thor Borison had made in the 1930s. Then I found out about it and raised hell. It resulted in Ed Rutsch's going back there, making a careful excavation in the 1970s, as I recall, and re-establishing the location of Fort Nonsense. I haven't been back there since, so I don't know whether the Park Service has restored Fort Nonsense or not. But I will bet you one thing, and that is that the damned trees are still growing up around there, so that you can't see anything from the location of the fort.

My point is simply this—the Park Service has always had a concept of doing archaeology because it is required to fulfill the obligations of the Antiquities Act and the National Historic Preservation Act, but it was usually done incidentally to other work. The archaeologists usually had to work with that as a given. Whenever development was taking place in the park system, the archaeologists would try to get there and do some archaeological observation if the place weren't to be completely obliterated. If it were, then we would try to get there first and salvage what was left. It was sort of a touch and go thing. The archaeology was never really ideal, except at Franklin Court in Philadelphia's Independence National Historical Park, where we did have the time and the resources to do a decent job. I think the interpretation there was done right too. When I showed architect Robert Venturi the concept of putting up a frame "shadow house," the idea of which came from a reconstructed picture of a house at Jim Deetz's excavation of Wellfleet on Cape Cod, I said, "Look, you can do that in white ink. How about doing it in structural steel at the site," and he said, "Interesting idea." And that's how that concept got there.

Unhappily, when the Park Service got to doing the Franklin Court museum underground, they conceptualized the entire museum without once mentioning Ben Franklin's house—not once! There's no model of the house, which there could be because we know enough about it. We know what the exterior looked like, since Bill Campball, the architect, came up with two excellent pictures of it. The result is that you go in to the museum and you see a very boring little diorama showing Franklin at Versailles and Franklin in Philadelphia. There should also be a phased interpretation of the building of the house, but there isn't.

So the Park Service, by and large, has never really used archaeology as an interpretive medium as well as it could, although it's tried to in some cases. At Jamestown, it put up a museum, and it put in a very *avant garde* exhibit in the 1970s, and what it was all about was themes as things to be presented. It would say something like "Times were very hard during this period and many people died of starvation. So they made bread, and they didn't make enough of it. Did they make bread first? No, it took them a long while to get the bake oven set up for baking after they got something to bake. So they all starved at first." The story is really very simple—there is a bake oven, they baked bread, but they starved nevertheless. Another theme at Jamestown revolves around a pike and suit of armor. But the colonists didn't use the armor, they got rid of it when they got rid of the Indians. Well, the story is very interesting, but what does it mean? They had equipment which they got from the Tower of London, which is true, but they never used it at Jamestown! You also see Pocahantas's earrings in the museum, but there's a whole story about them that is not told.

The earrings are actually little fish bladders that were mocked up in true pearls, and that's what was given to Pocahantas at the court of England. A nice little present from the Crown! In short, I think the Park Service completely muffed the best interpretations of the story of Jamestown in this nice artistic display of artifacts by not accurately interpreting the artifacts.

[Q:] *Is this sort of thing the "archaeological legacy" of the National Park Service, in your opinion?*

Yes, it goes back to the beginnings of the Park Service. You see, the Park Service started with a group of people who were intent on preserving the western parks, which they did. Yosemite and Yellowstone were the big things, and in the Southwest there were ruins like Montezuma Castle and Casa Grande, which were obviously to be saved, and so they were. But when you came east historical archaeology became connected with the Park Service, and that was by means of historical sites like Jamestown and Independence Park. The Park Service was always dependent on money and circumstance. Where they got their first money was during the Civilian Conservation Corps days when the CCC employed a lot of out-of-work architects, including landscape architects who didn't have a job. So these architects became the architects of the National Park Service, like Conrad L. Worth and Chandlee Forman, the latter previously noted as the architect at Jamestown. They were the old veterans of the CCC days when that was the only game around, and so they came in. The architects ruled the Park Service early on. The next people who came in who had moxie were the historians. There was a man named Herbert Kahler who was in Morristown, New Jersey, and he was a fast-moving gentlemen. He talked to Fran Ronald who was in the Washington office, and he said, "Fran, wouldn't you like to be in Morristown? A nice rural place to be, instead of Washington," and Fran traded places with him for what he thought would be a short while. It turned out to be for a lifetime, and Herb Kahler

stayed in Washington, too. He was a very astute politician and he got a little empire going for himself and his historians, and they were the ones who were in power along with the architects. So archaeology was always in the office of the historians and subservient to them, and they were all doing the bidding of the architects. When you have that combination, with the archaeologists at the bottom of the totem pole, it's easy to see why the archaeologists did not have the power.

[Q:] *Has the Park Service changed in that regard?*

Oh yes, I'm sure it has. A bureaucracy changes all the time, and yet it becomes more of the same. In other words, the more it changes the more it remains the same—it never really changes, it just changes form, it changes its shape. When it wants to reduce its numbers, it simply takes the people out of the main or regional office and puts them in the field. And then when things settle down, they get a few more job openings, they put them back. If one person can do the job, two or four or six people can do it much better. And the more the job costs, the better the job is, the more important it is, and of course the importance of the job is always dependent on the number of bodies one has under him or her. So that's a bureaucracy. It's always a matter of the expansion of power, and the more it expands, the more it impinges on efficiency. That is a law that anthropologists and archaeologists could take seriously. They should study bureaucracies and determine just how a progression of enlargement, aggrandizement, and maximization of power results in the self-preservation of the bureaucracy and a reduction in efficiency. And at a great increase in cost.

[Q:] *But is Park Service archaeology still being done pretty much the same way that it was in the 1950s and 1960s, in your opinion?*

Archaeology is always just archaeology. It's either good or inadequate or bad, and I think that most of the archaeology done in the Park Service is pretty good. You have one very good thing about archaeology in the Park Service, and that is that they have taken seriously the concept of conservation of the data and the artifacts. The Northeastern Region in Boston has done an exemplary job, for instance, of getting out reports on what has been done in the past, and getting these out in good shape. I wish I could say the same for the rest of the regions. The Middle Atlantic Region has a very much smaller staff, and Dave Orr and others have concentrated on archaeological work at various Park Service properties, and very effectively. I'm hoping that all of this will result in published reports.

[Q:] *Earlier you mentioned getting compliance reports on-line. Where do you think the field is moving in the next couple of decades or so?*

It's being moved, as James Joyce would say, as part of the ineluctable modality of the universe. When you can't define something in any better words, but you know it's there, you just attribute it to that and nobody can gainsay you. The fact of it is that archaeology is certainly going to continue and reports will continue to be written, and I hope archived along with the artifacts. Of course, the big problem is what in the hell to do with the artifacts.

[Q:] *What about the curation crisis?*

The curation crisis is on us, it's crucial, and I don't have any idea of how it really can be taken care of, because you have to have expensive facilities. You have to have curators who also cost money, and again, you're going to run up against the same thing we've always run up against. If you've got so many examples of "x" artifacts, if you have so many potsherds, just save a sample of them because they're all the same. Well, that shouldn't happen, because every artifact pertains to a context, and within that context it is very important to keep it.

So what do you do with all of these artifacts? Well, you try to maintain them. The inclination

then is to say that we don't have room for them; therefore, we must warehouse and provide the collection with storage that's inaccessible but still there. In other words, bury it, put it in a vault underground and forget about it. We've had that syndrome before in the Park Service, too. In fact, we've even had people say "just take all this stuff out, bury it, and mark the spot, you can go back to it some day if you need to." Well, that's obviously not the answer, and yet it's better than destroying it and throwing it out in the dump, forgetting it forever, and losing the context.

[Q:] *Do you think ultimately that the Park Service and other agencies will fully embrace selective culling as a matter of fact or policy?*

Selective culling will surely be urged on them by bureaucracy. As soon as it costs too much money, you have to reduce what amounts to the overhead of archaeology, which would be considered to be the conservation of the artifacts, and that's unfortunate. The artifacts are the manifest of what you've done and therefore they must be conserved. The same thing with the reports. Fortunately, the reports can be conserved, and there's no problem with archiving them, I hope. The Park Service has a central archival repository of sorts at Harper's Ferry, West Virginia. I've never visited it, so I don't know how effective it is, or how comprehensive it may be, but some of the past record has been pretty awful. Again, I go back to Morristown where superintendents there urged their staff to get rid of old files that they didn't need, or they just left it up to the secretaries or whoever was there to cull the files. Well, they didn't know the difference between an archaeological report and a report on something that is trivial, irrelevant, and passé, such as the condition of the sinks in the restrooms in 1934. To compare that with the archaeological data on the campsites of Morristown that were excavated in 1934 or so, I'd say the latter is damned important. But when you go to find those reports, you find that some of them have disappeared. People who know archives should be put in charge of culling files pertaining to history, archaeology, geology, and the other sciences, but they frequently aren't.

[Q:] *What else do you see happening in archaeology as we enter the 21st century?*

Archaeology will always remain essentially what it always has been and that is retrieving the evidence and interpreting it. The refinements that have gone into data retrieval are fascinating and will go on, and become even more fascinating in the future. Take, for instance, phytoliths. Whoever thought there were phytoliths 50-100 years ago? How about interpreting diseases from the contents of privies, to cite another example. There are now ways of determining what artifacts were used for, by analyzing traces of blood on them, and the DNA in the blood. This is tremendously important, so as time goes on, we will have more and more sophisticated ways of interpreting data, which I think will be very exciting. But it all comes back to the excavation and recordation of the site with more sophisticated, complete, and accurate means, and then conserving the data so that they can be analyzed again and again. And that means keeping everything, dirt, artifacts, everything, and that's what has not always been done in the past.

[Q:] *Do you have any other closing thoughts you might wish to share?*

Well, yes. You have to keep in mind that the generation of students today is in many respects mentally better equipped and therefore culturally more sophisticated than was the generation when I started at Penn in September of 1935. There is no comparison. Everything then, of course, was gotten from books and discussions, and teaching was simply a matter of conveying information and then discussing it. Today, of course, we have an incredible extension of knowledge. The communication revolution has really changed the picture in such a way that our data are infinite. But the problem is what the hell to do with it. Now we have the job of getting the data in useable form and doing something worth-

while with it. And that, I think, will be the big challenge of the 21st century.

[Q:] *How is that any different from the challenge that you and others had 60 years ago?*

It's just that we now have the means to do a much more comprehensive and detailed job, and it's incremental. That is, you cannot compare the data retrieval capability we had then and the data retrieval capability we have now. And the data storage capability we have now is practically infinite. Library index cards will soon be obsolete.

What we need is a Jules Verne to come back today. Verne had all kinds of concepts in the 19th century, including TV, the electric chair, and the automobile. What we need is somebody who can think that far ahead on the basis of the possibilities, if not the probabilities, that exist at present. There are very few people who can do that effectively. If there are any students in the universities now who can conceptually project forward in time and think with enough depth to see what the possibilities may be in the 21st century and beyond, we'll be tremendously indebted to them given, of course, the enormous problems and dangers that we will have in the 21st century.

I think that most of our future problems can be attributed to a very simple human trait—greed. I think that you can probably trace this through time—I'd love to write a history of human greed from the Lower or Middle Paleolithic. I'm sure it was there before humans were humans. Someone should try to trace greed through the ages. I think he or she would find that most wars are attributable to the unreasoning greed of some particular individual or group of individuals—that's certainly true for World Wars I and II.

I've had some reservations about several things, certainly about the ability of mankind to get rid of greed, and I also wonder if it's possible to do without constructive laws. Take a look at us. We employ more lawyers than any other nation in the history of mankind and we are more litigious than any other nation. So we think in terms of laws just as though they were our lifeline, which they aren't. And so we have predilections, we have inclinations, we have preferences, we have ways of doing things, and we have all kinds of patterns, but when it comes to laws watch out, because man is the most inconsistent animal on the face of the earth. Cockroaches have laws of conduct programmed into them, humans do not. If you want to go into the laws of cockroach behavior, I'm sure you could get a very firm set of immutable laws and be confident that they will maintain for cockroaches, but not for human beings. Humans make laws to live by—and break. Nothing quite holds for what people may do in all times and places.

[Q:] *That sounds like a final indictment of the "New Archaeology."*

Hardly, the "New Archaeology" indicted itself years ago in the court of scholarly opinion.

Daniel G. Roberts
John Milner Associates, Inc.
535 North Church Street
West Chester, PA 19380

Robert L. Schuyler

A Conversation with Edward B. Jelks

Introduction

Edward B. Jelks, a pioneer in Americanist historical archaeology, is one of the founders of The Society for Historical Archaeology. His early career centered on the state of Texas where he directed the River Basin Surveys (1951 to 1965), excavating on both prehistoric and historic sites, established and directed the Texas Archeological Research Laboratory at the University of Texas (1958–1965), and taught at Southern Methodist University (1965–1968). In 1954 he was John L. Cotter's assistant in the second major project at Jamestown, Virginia (1954–1956). Along with his prehistoric research, he worked over almost half a century at a wide variety of historic sites: contact Native American, Spanish colonial, French colonial, and Euroamerican sites in Texas, Illinois, and New York. He also worked at a British military post in Newfoundland and at a copra plantation in Micronesia. In the 1950s he started a life-long study of historic artifacts, especially ceramics and glass trade beads.

In 1968 Jelks left Texas for Illinois State University where he organized an anthropology curriculum and taught undergraduate and graduate courses in archaeology, including a seminar in historical archaeology until his retirement in 1983.

One of Ed Jelks' fundamental contributions to the field was his pivotal role in calling together and organizing a special meeting in January 1967 at Southern Methodist University in Dallas, Texas. Out of this meeting, and a concurrent paper conference, emerged The Society for Historical Archaeology, with Jelks serving as the second SHA President in 1968. If any one individual can be credited with the founding of the SHA it is Edward B. Jelks. He was equally active as a founder and builder of the Society of Professional Archeologists (1976), of which he was the first president. In 1988 The Society for Historical Archaeology honored Jelks with its highest award, the J. C. Harrington Medal.

The interview recorded here took place on Wednesday 5 January 2000 at 7:00 PM at The Society for Historical Archaeology annual meeting in Quebec, Canada and was conducted in the hotel room of Ed and Judy Jelks at the Quebec Hilton.

The Interview

[Q:] First for some background information. When and where were you born and raised?

I was born in Macon, Georgia in 1922. I spent several years in Hollywood, Florida, moving there as an infant, but when I was seven years old, which would be about 1930, we moved to Texas where I was raised in the town of Valley Mills, a community of 1,000 population or so in central Texas not far from Waco.

[Q:] So, most of your childhood then was spent in Texas?

Yes, I was raised in Texas. I graduated from high school at Valley Mills and went on to the University of Texas at Austin for my higher education.

[Q:] Was there anything in either your parents' background, your family background or in your childhood that led you toward archaeology?
No.

[Q:] No, not at all? Well, what was Texas like in the 1930s? This would be central Texas.
Yes, central Texas. Of course that was in the middle of the Great Depression and the economy there was primarily based on cattle and cotton, and it was just a typical small town. It was a hardscrabble existence for many people, and I guess the Protestant Ethic was in vogue.

[Q:] What did your father, or parents, do for a living?

Beginning in the early 19th century, several generations of Jelkses ran the local general store in Hawkinsville, Georgia. About 1890 my grandfather started brick plants in Hawkinsville and Macon, making paving bricks that were sold all over the South. As young men my father and two of his brothers were in the brick business with their father, selling bricks. My grandfather's family had started to go to Florida, to Pompano, when there was nothing down there but a beach, about 1904 or 1905 shortly after a railroad had been built to Miami. They went there to spend the winter. So when the big Florida land boom started in the 1920s they owned a lot of property there, which started to go way up in value. The family sold out the brick business and they all moved down to Florida. When the Florida boom collapsed in 1929 my father and mother moved to Valley Mills, Texas, where my mother's family lived. There my father became a sales agent for a Mexican importing firm. During World War II, while my father, my brother, and I all were in the military service and there was a serious shortage of schoolteachers, my mother taught school in an Austin suburb. She had gotten her teacher's certificate about 1914 and had taught school for several years before her marriage in 1919.

[Q:] Was that Hollywood, Florida?

Well I lived in Hollywood for a time and also in Pompano but mainly in Hollywood. My mother had been born and raised in Valley Mills. Her father was a medical doctor who moved out there from Georgia as a young man, following his brother who was also a doctor.

[Q:] When you were a child in Texas did you ever collect arrowheads?

Yes. Almost all the boys did. I was very active in the Boy Scouts, and that was one of the things we all did. Also, I was inspired by a character named Jesse James Howard, several years older than I, whom I knew growing up in Valley Mills. Jesse was obsessed with Indian lore, Western gunslingers and such, and he went around dressed like Doc Holiday with long hair down to his shoulders, 40 years before the first hippy appeared. He had assembled quite

FIGURE 1. Edward B. Jelks at his home in Normal, Illinois, 2000. (Courtesy of *The Pantagraph*, Bloomington-Normal, Illinois.)

a collection of Indian artifacts. There were a lot of rockshelters in the limestone cliffs, and he dug in them. I used to go and look at his collections and that was one thing that stimulated my interest in what we then called Indian lore.

[Q:] Did you know that arrowhead collecting was related to archaeology?

Well yes, I knew of the field of archaeology but tended to think of it as Classical Archaeology and Old World prehistory. Our school textbooks had pictures of cavemen, Neanderthals and such, and I always thought that was fascinating. But at that time I thought of archaeology as exotic and not something that went on in Texas or the United States. But, of course, I figured out after not too long that there was such a thing locally.

[Q:] Were you the first person in your family to go to college?

No. My father went to Mercer University in Macon and my mother to Bessy Tift College in Forsyth, Georgia and did graduate work at the University of Texas before becoming a schoolteacher in Texas. All four of my grandparents were college graduates.

[Q:] When you finished high school you went to the University of Texas in Austin and you were going to major in premed?

Yes, and it was premed.

[Q:] How did you make that decision?

Well, medicine was sort of a family tradition. My mother's father was a doctor, and one of my father's brothers was a doctor, and other members of the family were doctors, and I was interested in medicine. Primarily I always was interested in science. In my younger days in school they taught in the curriculum a lot about people like Louis Pasteur and other physicians who made discoveries in the field of medicine. I have always been interested in research of various kinds. I did not realize when going through high school that it would be possible to make a career out of American archaeology, and it never entered my mind to think about going into Old World archaeology as a career. Anyway, I started out in pre-medicine.

[Q:] You entered the University of Texas at Austin in 1939?

Yes, 1939 in the Fall.

[Q:] You stopped because of the war?

Right. When the Japanese made their infamous attack on Pearl Harbor in December, like a lot of other young men at the time, in a fit of patriotic zeal, I wanted to join the military. I was in the middle of the fall semester of my junior year at the time, and the easiest way to get a commission was to go into the Army Air Corps . They were recruiting heavily, and my brother did go into that branch. I applied to the Air Corps but was turned down because I did not have 20-20 vision. So I looked around for the second best deal I could find, and I talked with a Navy recruiter, and he said "Well, since you have this major (I was a zoology major, by the way, under premed) we will not start you out at rock bottom in the Navy but rather in the Hospital Corp as Hospital Apprentice First Class," which was the equivalent of a corporal, or something like that, in the Army. So, that is how I entered the Navy.

[Q:] You ended up in the Pacific at Guadalcanal?

Right. I went to boot camp in San Diego and went through three weeks of what would normally be a three or four month program; but they needed bodies quickly. They were taking these kids off the streets and farms, and after quick boot-camp indoctrination, some of them one month later were on ships getting into the thick of the war.

But after I finished boot camp I went up to Mare Island Hospital at Vallejo, California near San Francisco and stayed there for several months getting some further training, including training as an operating room technician, scrub up type, which is what I ultimately ended up doing. Then I was shipped out with a unit to establish a field hospital on Guadalcanal a month or so after the Americans invaded the island to take care of the casualties and also malaria cases and all that kind of stuff.

[Q:] Was fighting still going on when you arrived?

Yes.

[Q:] Did your hospital unit come under fire, were you that close to the front?

Yes, we had bombing raids every night, off and on all night long, which made it difficult to get much sleep. I got a small shrapnel wound in the shoulder during one of the air raids. The closest we came to direct contact with the enemy was in December 1942 when we had been there about two months. The Japanese made one last-ditch effort to repel the Americans, and one afternoon we got word that this assault was under way and Japanese troops were getting closer and closer. They got within about a half a mile of us, and we were ordered to evacuate.

I was in charge of the operating room—four or five other corpsmen and myself—and so we packed up whatever we could put on our backs. The only thing we could do if the Japanese came into the hospital area, which consisted of just tents, would be to head for the hills. The natives on Guadalcanal were very anti-Japanese and we felt they would give us support if we could get away. Several corpsmen would have been left to surrender the patients on the wards. But fortunately the U.S. marines stopped the assault about a half a mile away, and we did not have to go. Incidentally, Bill Sears was a marine on Guadalcanal and involved in a lot of the fighting.

[Q:] Did you know Bill Sears at that time?

No. We became acquainted after the war, and I knew he was in the marines and we talked about it briefly. And it is quite possible that he was there holding the Japanese off from our hospital while we was getting ready to evacuate.

[Q:] When did you leave the service and were you still in the Medical Corp unit?

OK. I came down with a bad case of malaria and they sent me to Auckland, New Zealand to a Navy hospital there, and I fought malaria for several months. On the way our ship was torpedoed, but we were rescued and eventually got to Auckland, stopping on the way at Noumea, New Caledonia. After I recovered from malaria they gave me some soft duty, putting me in charge of a bar at the Navy hospital that opened every night and served beer. So I got to run the bar and I never did get back into the operating room. But while I was in Auckland (for the better part of a year) one of the officers said "Well, you have had college, why don't you apply for Officers Training." So I sent in an application.

They sent us back home to San Diego in July 1944, and after waiting around there for awhile, they gave me a thirty day leave, and I went home to Austin, where Judy and I got married. When I went back to the base in San Diego my orders came through to go to Officers School, and they sent me to Colgate University in Hamilton, New York for a four-month college refresher course. Then I went to Officers School at Notre Dame. When I got through with that and was commissioned as a line-officer ensign, I looked at the different things you could apply for and saw a Japanese language school; so I said, "That's for me."

Very few people at that time in the United States could speak Japanese, and most of those were locked up in detention camps. The government needed to train military people for the impending invasion of Japan, to be able to go there and converse with the Japanese. They sent me to what was then Oklahoma A & M, and is now Oklahoma State, at Stillwater. Our instructors were female schoolteachers they had brought in from Okinawa. The school was supposed to last over a year, but after a couple of months the war ended and I went back to the University of Texas to continue my education under the GI bill.

[Q:] Many years later you went back and dug in the Pacific, you did a copra plantation I think, did that have anything to do with your earlier experiences during the war?

In a way, but my going back was strictly fortuitous. One day in 1978 I got a letter from Tom King, who was then with the National Trust, I guess, and he said they were looking for someone to go down and do what, according to him, would be the first historical archaeology in Micronesia. He did not know much about historical archaeology, and he knew that I had some experience in that area, and he asked me if I would be interested.

Going back to the war, when we were leaving Guadalcanal and heading for Noumea before we got torpedoed, we went through the Marshall Islands—nice coral atolls—and we went close enough so we could see the grass houses, palm trees, and all these people running around the beaches and I said, "Gosh, that is just the classic south seas island paradise." And I always thought I would like to go back and visit one of those islands some day. So when I got the letter from Tom I asked Judy first, "Do you want to go to the Marshall Islands?" and she said "Sure, why not." So the Trust Territory of the Pacific Islands contracted with Judy and me to do the work and away we went.

[Q:] What year was the trip to Micronesia? That was 1978.

[Q:] How long was the project, was it just one season?

Yes, we were supposed to be there about six weeks. It was not actually a dig as it turned out. A Portuguese seaman jumped ship down there in the 1870s, married a daughter of one of the chiefs, and got possession of Likiep Atoll in the Marshall Islands, where he planted all these coconut trees and began producing copra. His son, Joachim de Brum who was quite a character, built this house and had all this furniture brought in from Japan and China and one place and another, along with all these expensive dishes, glassware, and other things. He established a shipyard where he built and repaired wooden ships, training the local Marshallese as woodworkers. He died shortly before World War II, and his children did not want to stay there, so they just locked up the house and it sat there until we went in there in 1978. The roof was leaking, so they sent in a ship with metal roofing, and we had these local people who had been trained as carpenters put a new roof on the house.

We made a complete inventory of everything in the house, and I made scale drawings of the house and grounds. Judy supervised some of the men who rubbed down the furniture with coconut oil and cleaned up the entire house. The men didn't want to work for a woman at first, but Judy charmed them into submission and they were proud of their work at the end.

We knew that Joachim was a photographer and that he had taken photographs of a lot of the Marshallese people, not only on Likiep, but on other islands too. We had hoped that some of his photos were somewhere on the premises. About a week or two before we were to leave I found this big trunk, opened it up, and there were hundreds of big glass negatives taken between 1890 and the1920s of the local people doing ceremonies and other things. A fascinating bunch of stuff. These negatives are now at the museum in Majuro, capital of the Marshalls. Anyway, that was what we did in the Marshalls; it was above-ground archaeology.

I'll tell an anecdote. The usual way to get to Likiep was by boat but, we flew in a chartered amphibian plane, just a small one engine plane, which landed in the lagoon. The pilot had a business hauling people around that part of the Pacific. As we were flying over there he told me a story, which I assumed was apocryphal, about a friend of his who also had a plane who flew people around, and a few years before he had taken an anthropologist to some remote island, left him there, and was supposed to come back in a month or so to pick him up. In a bar one night he was talking to our pilot, who asked him what happened to the anthropologist,

and the second pilot said, "Oh, my God, I forgot him." He went back and picked him up three or four months late, and the anthropologist had lost thirty pounds.

When our six weeks was up on Likiep, guess what happened? Our pilot didn't show up. There was a generator-operated radio on the island, but it was broken and there were no parts for it, so we had no way to contact the outside. We waited and waited for two weeks and didn't know what we were going to do, until one day a little boat came in—it was maybe 30 ft. long run by a man who went around from island to island, just hauling stuff back and forth for people—and he had a couple of helpers with him. They stopped to take on fresh water at a cistern on Likiep, and he had a radio. So I got on the radio and called the governor's office on Majuro and asked "Where is the guy with the plane who was supposed to pick us up." They told me that he and a Peace Corps woman had gone off to San Francisco for the weekend three weeks before and they had not come back yet. So we went out on that small boat which, after a rough trip, got us back safely to Majuro.

[Q:] So, to return to the sequence of events, at the end of the war you returned to Texas and that was when you married Juliet Christian. What was her background and how did you meet her?

When my mother went to the University of Texas in 1913 or 1914 her roommate was Judy's aunt. After graduating with teacher's certificates, they taught school together in a little town in Texas. They kept in touch over the years, were in each other's weddings, and corresponded. So this woman's brother, Judy's father, lived in Austin. He was a lawyer and a state judge there. My family moved to Austin at the time I entered the University of Texas in 1939, and they looked up Judy's father, whom they knew, and that is how I met Judy.

[Q:] And Judy has been not only a wife but also your archaeological partner, is that correct?

Yes. Judy was a city girl, and when I took her out on a dig or two early on she hated it. But after a while she began to like it. When I started out in late 1949 as a full time professional as Robert Stephenson's assistant in the Texas River Basin Surveys program, we would go out to the field in the Spring, March or April, and stay out there until December. Judy and I had one child, a son, Chris, who also got his Ph.D. at the University of Texas and is now an electrical engineer living in Denver. For the first few years, Judy stayed in Austin for the most part, where she worked as a consultant compiling petroleum production statistics for oil producers, taking care of Chris during the extended periods that I was in the field. But in the summer of 1953 she and Chris, then seven years old, spent two months in the field with me at Texarkana Reservoir. We lived in a tent, and both Judy and Chris got a good taste of archaeological fieldwork. They spent many days working the screens, keeping records of artifact bags and the like. We had a guy doing the cooking who gave everybody food poisoning, so Judy kicked him out and took over as cook. That was the first time she went into the field for an extended period of time, but when Chris got older, especially after he was in college, she went out more frequently and before long was attending meetings of the Texas Archeological Society where she met, and became friends with, many of my colleagues. Then she started going regularly to SAA, and later to SHA meetings.

After I started teaching, first at SMU, then at ISU, she became a full partner, helping implement logistics for numerous field projects, maintaining field records, screening and sometimes digging a little, critiquing all my manuscripts before publication (she is an expert copy editor), and becoming a surrogate mother for hundreds of students over the years.

[Q:] So, in 1945 or 1946 you are back from the war, married to Judy, and have returned to the University of Texas in Austin. How did you get into anthropology and archaeology?

I returned to UT on the GI Bill, and as I had a wife and child, I wanted to get some type of college degree and begin making a living without delay. I had decided, after my experiences in the Navy Hospital Corps, not to go into medicine, although I did consider becoming an MD in research. I had always been interested in research but not so much the practice of medicine. I looked into the catalogue of the University of Texas to see the easiest and fastest way to get some kind of degree, and it would have had to be either zoology (my pre-war major) or English (my pre-war minor); so I decided to go for an English degree and become an English professor, or maybe teach high school, or just get a liberal arts degree and go out and get a job. So I got a degree in English literature, taking some anthropology and archaeology courses on the way.

I still had some of my GI Bill left and they were hardly knocking on my door with jobs at that time. So I decided to go for an MA degree and switched over to anthropology as a major and English as a minor. I completed everything for the MA except for the thesis by 1950 and had almost completed the thesis when Robert Stephenson got some money and hired me as his assistant in the River Basin Surveys program.

[Q:] Was G. C. Engerrand one of your instructors and did he influence you to major in anthropology?

Yes, although my major interest was in archaeology and George Engerrand was primarily a cultural anthropologist. Actually he had done some archaeological research years before in Europe and in Mexico. He was a Basque who came to Mexico in the early 20th century, then came to the University of Texas about 1914, and, yes, he did have a strong influence on me.

[Q:] He was primarily a cultural anthropologist?

Yes, a cultural anthropologist who was a Mexican specialist and an Old World specialist who had been trained in Paris, France.

[Q:] Why do you think you moved more toward archaeology rather than cultural anthropology?

Well, I just liked it better I guess. The same reason you chose archaeology perhaps. When I went to the University of Texas I found out you could take courses in Texas archaeology, and that was why I took some archaeology classes. I was also interested in anthropology in general, including ethnography because of my experiences in the Pacific. So that was how I sort of drifted into it without originally intending to become an anthropologist.

[Q:] So from the start you decided to become a North American prehistorian?

The two archaeologists at the University of Texas who taught me were Tom Campbell and Charles Kelley. They taught me North American archaeology and Texas archaeology and, of course, no one was teaching historical archaeology anywhere in those days. I was trained as a prehistorian with a particular interest in the Texas area, including the Caddoan area in eastern Texas and adjacent parts of Louisiana, Arkansas, and Oklahoma; and also the extensions of the Southwestern area into west Texas. And I was strongly influenced by Alex Krieger after I had gotten my Master's Degree.

[Q:] Who supervised your MA thesis and what was the subject of the thesis?

Tom Campbell was my chairman and Engerrand was the second member of my committee. Back in the 1930s the government had built some dams on the Colorado River, which runs right through Austin in the central part of the state, and the University of Texas did salvage archaeology at the reservoir projects with WPA labor, at the same time the TVA salvage archaeology was going on over in the Southeast.

Gilbert McAllister, chairman of the anthropology department at UT administered the program. They had hired people without very much training because there were not any professional archaeologists available then, only people with some experience in digging sites. The man in charge initially had been James Pearce, who had started the anthropology department at UT, one of the very first by the way in the United States, before World War I. Pearce died in 1938, after which Gilbert McAllister took over the program. Dozens of sites were dug under this program, and many of them had not been fully reported. The artifacts and field notes from these excavations were stored in the archaeology lab, so I used the material from several of the sites for my thesis topic, which was to plot the horizontal distribution of projectile types in burned rock middens having no visible stratification. Different distribution patterns for different point types indicated temporal or functional differences in the deposition of the points. I have maintained a strong interest in statistical methods of field analysis ever since.

[Q:] You received your MA Degree in 1950?

No it was 1952, I believe, because I had started to work for Stephenson late in 1949 and didn't finish my thesis until later.

[Q:] It was at this time that you started to work for the River Basin Surveys?

I started fieldwork with Stephenson in the Spring of 1950. In 1951 Stephenson went to the University of Michigan to work on his Ph.D.—he had a Master's degree from Oregon, had been Luther Cressman's student up there—and so when he left I inherited his job as the director of the RBS program in Texas. Over the next few years we began to get more and more money and began to hire more archaeologists. We worked all over the state.

[Q:] About 1950 or 1951 had you heard anything about historical archaeology; did the field have any visibility as a field?

I do not recall anybody mentioning historical archaeology as a special field of study at that time. The first I heard of such was about 1953 when I read Pinky Harrington's article on historic sites archaeology in Jimmie Griffin's monumental *Archaeology of Eastern United States*.

The first place we did RBS fieldwork in 1950 was at Lake Whitney on the Brazos River above Waco, and the very first site we worked on was an historic (18th and 19th century) Indian village, the Stansbury site. Stephenson had done a survey of the reservoir area about 1947, but in those days there was nothing like complete coverage. He had only 2 or 3 weeks to cover an area of 70 to 80 mi.[2], and so he just went in hit or miss asking land owners where they had found arrowheads and collectors where their sites were. He recorded perhaps 50 or 60 sites and there were hundreds in the area that went under the lake. He had to decide by instinct which sites we were going to dig as we would be there only three or four months

We ended up digging at four prehistoric sites (three rockshelters and one open site) and two historic sites (Stansbury and Fort Graham, an army military post built around 1850 at the western edge of the frontier, where we did a little testing). Fort Graham was active for a few years until the beginning of the Civil War when it was abandoned. There were some stone ruins of the fort and I went out a day or two recording those remains because it seemed like it should be done.

At the historic Indian village, the Stansbury Site, we found a lot of European trade goods and didn't know what they were. We were aware that Carlyle Smith and Art Woodward had done some work on trade goods, although I was not aware at the time of George Quimby's work further north. Stephenson knew Carlyle, so we sent some of the materials to him and some to Art Woodward to see if they could identify them. They made some identifications but not many. These were classic trade goods but nobody had much knowledge of them at that time.

Years later, working with RBS archaeologist Lathel Duffield and King Harris, a local amateur, and still later with amateur Ted Hamilton, I got involved in working out what the 18th century French trade guns looked like, with their decorated buttplates, sideplates, and trigger guards. Also, Duffield and I devised a simple typology for basic glass bead forms. It was a lot of fun.

Back to the Stansbury Site, Bob Stephenson turned over tracing down the history of the site to me. I did a lot of library research and tried to get information on the material culture

FIGURE 2. The Stansbury site, location of 18th and 19th century Native American villages on the Brazos River, Whitney Reservoir, Texas, 1950. Standing, left to right: Frank H. H. Roberts, Jr. of the Smithsonian, Director of the River Basin Surveys; Jelks; John Corbett, Chief Archeologist, National Park Service. Local rancher George Benson is crouching in test square. (Courtesy of the Smithsonian Institution.)

of both the Indian materials and the French trade goods. I was able to demonstrate with reasonable certainty that the site was occupied in the late 18th century by a village of Tawakoni (a southern Wichita tribe), and in the middle of the 19th century by a village of Caddo peoples who moved west from east Texas.

[Q:] The Stansbury Site started a theme in your research of looking for documented historic sites and trying to locate them in the field. Was there any influence of William Duncan Strong and other people using the "Direct Historic Approach?"

Yes, I was familiar with the concept and had met Strong at an SAA meeting a time or two and had talked with him about it. There were, and still are, a lot of "lost" historic sites in Texas. The Spanish came in and made a number of settlements, including both missions and presidios, temporarily establishing outposts in central and eastern Texas, but the Indian pressure got so bad that eventually they withdrew back to San Antonio and established a stronghold there. So a lot of the other sites were abandoned. Also there were several explorers such as Cabeza de Vaca, and later others who came up from Mexico into west Texas. And, of course the DeSoto expedition came through the Plains in northern Texas. There was a lot of interest locally by historians in tracing the routes of the explorers. Incidentally, later for my Ph.D., I minored in history largely because of my interest in where the old Spanish sites were located and where the various early expeditions had traveled. I took several courses from H. Bailey Carroll, a well-know historian who taught at UT. He also was very interested in tracing the routes of such explorers. Earlier Herbert E. Bolton had been at the University of Texas before he moved to California, and he had tried to identify some of the mission sites, and also the site of LaSalle's Fort St. Louis of the 1680s. So I read a lot of Bolton's work, and just the idea of trying to find some of these sites I found very fascinating.

[Q:] Was your primary focus on contact native sites or on European sites?

Both. The Spanish and Indian sites went together. The Spaniards would come through on an expedition and record where they went, would stop at an Indian village, and go on to another village. I also got interested in some quantitative issues trying to calculate the distances involved. An explorer usually estimated the number of leagues traveled each day and recorded this along with descriptions of the terrain etc. in a journal. LeRoy Johnson, Jr., Lathel Duffield, and I used these journals to try to trace travel routes on the ground, and we published several papers on our studies. One interesting discovery we made was that when people were going between the same two points in the winter, when it was cold and snowing, their distance estimates were greater than if they were traveling the same route in the summer. Also different people would give different estimates for the same trips.

[Q:] You mention in Stanley South's book, *Pioneers in Historical Archaeology* (1994), that you dug on a Spanish colonial site in west Texas under J. Charles Kelley in 1949, your first experience on an historic site. Did people at that time think that such a site was odd?

I do not think people thought anything about it one way or the other. Kelley was a nationally known scholar who had done a lot of work out in the Big Bend area of Texas on the Jornado Branch of the Mogollon. He had worked out a whole regional chronology, a sequence, with main phases, and he had a couple of historic phases for Indians who were in contact with Spaniards. Kelley was interested in locating early historic sites of both Indians and Spaniards as part of his regional synthesis. There had been some archaeological work done previously at Spanish colonial sites in Texas, notably the Rosario Mission site near Goliad.

[Q:] What about your involvement with historical archaeology in relationship to the Texas Archaeological Society?

In 1962 the idea came to me that there were all these people in Texas interested in archaeology who like to get out in the field and help the professionals, so why not organize the excavation of a significant site using such free labor. King Harris had just discovered a site on the Upper Sabine River which was one of the Indian villages that I had been interested in identifying. It turned out later to be an 18th century village of the Southern Wichita. By that time we knew enough about gun parts and other trade goods

FIGURE 3. Jelks beside gunport at ruins of 18th century Spanish colonial ranch house, Falcon Reservoir on the Rio Grande, Texas, 1953. (Courtesy of the Texas Archeological Research Laboratory, The University of Texas at Austin.

that we could identify the site generally, and later by going back to the documents were able to tell which village it was. So we decided to have a TAS [Texas Archaeological Society] summer dig which I directed. It ran for about three weeks as I recall, and other professionals came out to help. It was very successful. That was the Gilbert Site and the amateurs who worked on the site all participated in writing the final report, which was published by the TAS. I assigned different chapters to different people. As a result of that dig Jay Blaine got interested in gun parts and became a nationally recognized expert on the subject.

I first met Kathleen Gilmore at Gilbert. She heard about the dig, came to visit out of curiosity, got hooked, went back to college, and eventually got her Ph.D. at SMU and became a president of the SHA. The Gilbert Site dig evolved into an annual field school held every summer since 1962 by the TAS. This last year 400 people attended, not all at once of course, but spread out over several weeks. Gilbert was one of many historic Indian sites I have worked at in Texas and Illinois.

[Q:] Between 1954 and 1956 you went off to Jamestown. A question I have always been curious about is why when the NPS decided to do a second major project at Jamestown in 1953, and considering that John Cotter was basically a prehistorian, why did not J. C. Harrington direct the second Jamestown project?

I can answer that easily: I do not know! I can only guess that Pinky, who by that time was stationed in Richmond as director of all the research in the Southeastern Region of the NPS, could have taken on the project if he had chosen to, or possibly the NPS would not let him leave his administrative position to take on a single long-term project. I really do not know.

[Q:] Did you know John Cotter before the Jamestown Project?

Yes, I had known him from SAA conferences. In those days there were only a few archaeologists. The first SAA conference I went to, at Norman, Oklahoma in 1951, may have had 100 people attending, and the meeting was held jointly with the Central States Anthropological Society. I think I met Cotter at that meeting. A bunch of us would get together and sit around in a hotel room and drink whiskey and talk archaeology. I believe I talked to him about the Blackwater Draw (original Clovis) site there.

[Q:] Did you know Louie Caywood or the other Jamestown staff before the project?

No. Cotter was the only one I knew. Joel Shiner, another of the archaeologists at Jamestown, and I got reacquainted later when we both were teaching at Southern Methodist University. Bruce Powell worked on the project, but I did not maintain contact with him after Jamestown.

[Q:] Before you went to Jamestown did you know who J. C. Harrington was and about his relationship to historical archaeology?

As mentioned earlier, the first time I ever heard of historical archaeology, or historic sites archaeology, was in Harrington's article in the Griffin-edited volume, a big thick green book, on archaeology in the Eastern United States. Come to think about it, that may well have had some effect on my recording of buildings and historic sites in the River Basin projects.

[Q:] Did you meet Harrington during the Jamestown Project (1954–1956)?

Yes, Pinky would come down to Jamestown periodically to confer with us about how things were coming along, as he was responsible for the project administratively. John Corbett, the head NPS archaeologist in Washington, also came down a couple of times to check us out. The major consultant was Malcolm Watkins, a ceramics specialist from the Smithsonian, who visited Jamestown frequently for several days at a time to look at the ceramics we were finding and help identify it. Paul Hudson was in charge of accessioning and curating the materials as they came out of the ground.

[Q:] What was your position at Jamestown?

I was Cotter's assistant. There were no formal titles for the archaeological staff, but if there had been I guess I would have been called the assistant director.

[Q:] Did you oversee a certain part of the project, or the whole project?

The way it worked was that the site was divided arbitrarily into several areas and each was assigned an archaeological project number, for example Project 100, 102, and so on. I believe that this was a continuation of a system that Harrington had started years earlier. Shiner was put in charge of the projects on that part of Jamestown owned by the Association for the Preservation of Virginia Antiquities, in the area where the original fort and the old church were located. Shiner went exploring over there for the first fort.

The NPS part of Jamestown was divided into two main areas and I had a crew in one area and Cotter had a crew in the other area. We conferred back and forth all the time. Cotter spent a fair amount of time in Yorktown, Richmond, and Washington D.C. and I was in charge when he was not on the site.

[Q:] What sites at Jamestown did you excavate?

The main section I worked on was the northern part up against the pitch and tar swamp. I also did some work on the south side of the site. Some of the larger features that I dug were an icehouse [Structure 128], a presumed brewhouse [Structure 110], a large brick building [Structure 112], a rowhouse [Structure 115], a small timber-framed house [Structure 116], two large brick houses [Structures 117 and 125], and a well [Well 19]. [The structure numbers and the well number were added after the interview by reference to Cotter's report on Jamestown.]

[Q:] Did you excavate burials?

We found one burial that I remember, Bob, a flexed burial that I am sure was an Indian, but there was nothing buried with it. In fact, as I remember, I had had some experience with paleontologists back in Texas collecting fossils in plaster jackets. The bones were in bad condition, so I surrounded it with a plaster jacket and hauled it away to the lab at Jamestown and have not seen it since! I guess somebody did something with it.

[Q:] How many seasons did you dig at Jamestown?

We dug from November of 1954 all through the winter and the spring and early summer of 1955. There is a little article that Jack and I wrote in *American Antiquity* titled something like "Winter Archaeology at Jamestown" which has pictures of all the snow. We had great big steel drums that we filled up with firewood and kept fires going in them for warmth. We had to come out and warm our hands all the time or we could not dig. Sometimes the ground and the trenches would be frozen; God it was cold!

In the summer of 1955 Cotter sent me over to explore several places at Yorktown Battlefield. One was Redoubt No. 10 in the British line, the location of which was uncertain. I found the two-thirds of the redoubt that survived, the

rest having eroded into the York River. That continued my interest in looking for lost sites.

I did some other work at Yorktown looking for remains of the British earthworks. As you may know, in Yorktown and at Jamestown, the Confederates built big earthworks, massive structures during the Civil War. The question was, were there remains of the British works surviving under these later fortifications? If such remains had survived, they would have to be under the Confederate sites because all the Revolutionary War period earthworks were leveled after the Battle of Yorktown. We did find remnants of some British works under some of these Confederate fortifications. They were little, tiny things. The whole parapet would only be as high as your head with a big ditch behind it, but the Confederate embankments were massive, great big old things, 20 times as massive as the British features. Of course, the difference was because of the improvement in ordinance between the 1780s and the 1860s.

After completing the work at Yorktown that summer I went back to Jamestown and completed some odds and ends of fieldwork there. I spent the fall, winter, and spring (of 1956) working on reports of my work at Yorktown and at Jamestown.

[Q:] When you left Jamestown in 1956 was Cotter still on the site?

Yes, they had a big celebration in 1957 for the 350th anniversary of the founding of Jamestown which I missed, having moved back to the RBS program in Texas in the summer of 1956. Jack stayed on for the celebration and finished writing his report on the archaeology. Everyone called Cotter "Jack" at Jamestown and at SAA meetings previously, but when he moved to Philadelphia everyone started calling him "John."

[Q:] What did you think of the approach at Jamestown that used trenching to explore the site?

It was a very effective technique, better than digging great big holes or dinky little squares. The purpose was to explore a very large area in a limited time, looking primarily for structural remains and other major features. And for that purpose it worked very well. That was Pinky's

FIGURE 4. Field Photo of Ed Jelks recording Structure 117 at Jamestown, Virginia in 1955. (Courtesy of Colonial National Historic Park.)

[J. C. Harrington] design, I am sure. Pinky had set up a coordinate-reference system for Jamestown and we got a transit and set up on his grid. The trenches just followed the grid, north, south, east, and west on 50-foot intervals, and there were miles of trenches before we got through. We removed the plow zone in the trenches until we hit brick foundations, subsurface disturbances, or other anomalies. Although effective for finding large features, it left big areas in the middle of the 50-foot squares that were not explored.

[Q:] Did Harrington in the 1930s open a much bigger area than the excavations your team did in the 1950s?

No, I do not think so. I think it would have been much less. Actually I am not sure, but I think Cotter discusses all the previous digs at Jamestown in his report, including early work by architects on the site.

[Q:] When the artifacts came out of the excavations did your team analyze them or did they go into a lab; what happened to them?

We had all we could do to handle the digging on the project. Paul Hudson ran the lab, so we would bag the artifacts, label them, and send them to him in the lab. He had a crew of people helping him in the lab who would process the materials. There were a couple of chemists from William and Mary who came out for awhile and tried to figure out a way to conserve the iron artifacts but without too much success. They would bake the objects in an oven and try to neutralize the acid. Hudson catalogued everything and put it on storage shelves where it sat for quite some time.

When it came time for working on the report I got interested in the history of the ceramics at Jamestown and I wrote a section of the report on ceramics. Neither I nor Cotter was familiar with the materials when we arrived at Jamestown, Hudson knew a little bit about it, and Malcolm Watkins knew quite a bit about the ceramics from the perspective of a ceramics historian. We were finding all kinds of objects that had never been studied or seen before. Hudson told us fairly soon what Delftware, Stoneware, Cream-ware, and Pearlware were. We had Creamware and Pearlware from an 18th century plantation occupation of the townsite.

One of the interesting things we found is now called "Colonoware" and I was particularly interested in it. Cotter and I and others talked about it, and as it obviously was neither local Indian pottery nor English, and since we knew they had slaves at Jamestown, I suggested maybe it was African. I looked at some reports on African ceramics and I found some types that looked kind of like it. We did not pursue the idea, however. I understand that now they have figured out that, in part at least, it was made by slaves.

[Q:] Was your experience at Jamestown just another historic site or was it a turning point in your interest in the field?

It was a turning point. I invested over two years of my time there, counting the time at Yorktown, and got my apprenticeship in studying European ceramics and other subjects which I had not done before Jamestown. And not only that but it was at this time that I got to know Pinky, Malcolm Watkins, Paul Hudson, and others with some background in historical archaeology and historic artifacts. It then seemed that historical archaeology, or historic sites archaeology, might be a coming field with great potential. It was something I was very interested in, and it looked like an opportunity for me to make a mark in a new area. The door was wide open and there were not many specialists there at the time.

[Q:] At that time did you see both contact sites, like the Gilbert Site, and European sites, like Jamestown, as being equally historic sites?

Yes. It depends on how you define "historical archaeology," but to me in contrast to prehistoric archaeology, if you have some historical documentation related to your field studies, then you have another approach or source of data to base inferences on, rather than just empirical field data. That is what I think of as historical archaeology. That is not "historic sites archaeology" in Harrington's definition, because I think his concept covered only Euroamerican sites.

[Q:] So, you would see historical archaeology as being a unified field on the methodological level?

Yes, in terms of methodology in conducting research you have access to both written documentation and the archaeological data. You combine the two sources of information, so methodologically it is a unified field. Of course in terms of cultural context, historic and prehistoric sites are different.

[Q:] In 1965 you moved into a new phase of your career, the academic world. Was your Ph.D. the first one in archaeology under anthropology at the University of Texas?

It was the first in anthropology at the University of Texas in Austin. At that time it was just THE University of Texas. Later state university systems all over the United States were retooled, taking what had been teachers' colleges, like Illinois State University where I am now, and turning them into multipurpose universities. So now there is a University of Texas at San Antonio, one at Dallas, one at El Paso, and so forth.

[Q:] How did you end up teaching in the Department of Anthropology at Southern Methodist University in Dallas?

As I remember it, I just got a phone call one day in 1965 from Fred Wendorf, who had started the program at SMU the year before. He told me he was interested in developing a curriculum in local Texas archaeology. Wendorf had worked some in that area himself, but had worked mainly in the southwestern U.S. and also had gotten heavily involved in fieldwork at the Aswan Dam project in Egypt. He brought Tony Marx and Joel Shiner, who had worked with him at Aswan to SMU, and Ron Wetherington, who had worked with him in New Mexico, and they were the beginning of the department. Wendorf persuaded the administration at SMU that they should expand the anthropology program by adding someone in Texas archaeology. He was aware that I had just gotten my Ph.D., and so he asked me to come up and join the department. Judy and I went up to Dallas, looked around, and talked with Wendorf. He made me one of those offers that you cannot turn down. So, as I had spent years doing fieldwork, much of it away from home from 1950 to 1965, the thought of a stay-at-home job on a university faculty was enticing as a change of pace.

[Q:] You were hired at SMU as an assistant professor?

An associate professor.

[Q:] Was it a combined sociology-anthropology department?

Yes, it was at that time. A couple of years later Fred got a separate anthropology department started not long before I left Dallas.

[Q:] Was it at SMU that you taught your first class in historical archaeology?

Right. But I had come to SMU to primarily teach Texas prehistory which I did; however, I also wanted to teach historical archaeology. I had never taught before and I was not sure if I would like it or not, but thought I would give it a try.

[Q:] Was the class on historical archaeology a graduate or undergraduate course?

It was a graduate seminar.

[Q:] How frequently was it offered?

Once a year. I was at SMU for three years [1965–1968] and I must have taught it three times.

[Q:] Do you recall any of the topics or the readings that you assigned to the students?

Well, I am trying to remember. I know I assigned Pinky's article on "historic sites archaeology" but it was so long ago it is hard to remember.

[Q:] Was it a hands-on course; did you look at artifacts in class?

Yes, and also fieldwork. We went out and started to look for some of these lost historic sites. In fact, Kathleen Gilmore found one of the Spanish missions on one of the seminar field trips, and she used that for her Master's thesis at SMU.

[Q:] Was Kathleen Gilmore already at SMU when you arrived?

Yes, as soon as Wendorf had started the department, the year before I arrived there, three women, Kathleen, Dessamae Lorraine, and

Norma Hoffrichter, who were buddies and ran around together, matriculated (I guess would be the right word) and signed up for all the archaeology courses.

Dessamae eventually went to the University of Texas at Austin and got her Master's degree there, but then she sort of dropped out of archaeology and I am not sure what happened to her. Norma got her Master's degree at SMU and went to the University of Arkansas where she worked in the anthropology department and the Arkansas Archaeological Survey for years. She retired last year.

[Q:] Were they going to be specialists in prehistoric archaeology originally?

Yes, they started in prehistoric archaeology as that was all that was being offered at SMU before my arrival. We made field trips all the time. I remember taking them to visit a prehistoric site when we came upon the ruins of an old farmstead where you could see some foundations but the house was long gone. You could find the site by the plants growing around it and I was showing them some pottery sherds but they did not seem interested at the time. But once they took my seminar in historical archaeology, we went out to look for lost historic sites and I think that was what got them hooked, especially Kathleen.

[Q:] So, you brought Kathleen Gilmore into historical archaeology?

Yes. I was always interested in research and so many times, Bob, I saw people who would misidentify a site because they did not have a rigorous methodology. I had worked out this method, and taught it to my students, that when you are looking for a lost historic site there are certain procedures you should follow, certain criteria you should employ so when everything fits together with the physical field evidence, you can be fairly certain you have the right place. I have seen so many misidentified sites, working in Texas—but I guess it happens everywhere—where the local lore builds up about a place that leads to popular misidentification.

For example, there is a town called Spanish Fort up on the Red River in Texas. When the first settlers moved into the area in the mid 19th century they saw a bunch of earthworks, and they knew the Spanish had been messing around in that area hundreds of years before; so they said "these are the ruins of an old Spanish fort." What it was actually, was the remains of a fortified Wichita village for which there was good historic documentation. Local residents found gun parts and other items there, but they were French and English trade goods, not Spanish. Anyhow I taught students, including Kathleen Gilmore, to follow a rigorous method for identifying sites to avoid making such mistakes.

[Q:] Was that site Kathleen's Master's thesis?
No. Her thesis was on a Spanish mission in central Texas.

[Q:] Did she also get the Ph.D. under you?
She eventually got her Ph.D. but I was gone from SMU by that time. If I remember correctly she did a dissertation on social organization among the Caddo or something like that.

[Q:] How large were your seminars in historical archaeology?
I averaged maybe ten or twelve students in a class.

[Q:] And most of these students wanted to be primarily prehistorians?
All kinds of people. And those who stayed on in anthropology and archaeology included Kathleen, of course Norma, and Dessamae; Ned Woodall who got his Ph.D. at SMU—he was my assistant up at a 18th and 19th century British military site at Signal Hill in Newfoundland in 1965 and 1966—is now at Wake Forest University where he has been doing primarily prehistoric research, although he did some historical archaeology. Also Jon Gibson who is now at the University of Southwest Louisiana University, and two or three others. I had some success at SMU in getting people pointed in the direction and they stayed in the field.

One other thing before I forget it. I left the University of Texas in early summer of June 1965 and my position at SMU began in September. A few months before I left Austin I saw on the bulletin board an advertisement from Parks Canada saying they were looking for archaeologists. They did not have many trained archaeologists in Canada in 1965, and so they were advertising in American universities. I saw the ad and said "Well that looks kind of interesting" and I sent off my resume and they sent me back a contract to work at Signal Hill, Newfoundland that summer. The contract was with "Her Majesty Elizabeth II Rex" as the party of the first part, and me as the party of the second part etc. So Judy and I went up there, along with Ned and JulieWoodall, and spent the summer of 1965 working at Signal Hill. When I came back to SMU I brought the artifacts from Signal Hill to use in writing a report, and I showed those materials to my class: British artifacts mainly of the early to the mid-19th century. We went back to Signal Hill with the Woodalls the next year in 1966, so we spent two summers there, right in the middle of when I was teaching the historical archaeology seminar at SMU.

[Q:] Did you visit the project at the Fortress of Louisbourg when you were in Canada?

Yes. We stopped there in 1965 and also in 1966. Our son Chris worked at the Louisbourg in 1966.

[Q:] Was Ed Larrabee at Louisbourg?

Yes, Ed Larrabee was there in 1965. Bruce Frye had replaced him in 1966.

[Q:] So you returned to SMU and between 1966 and 1967 you were instrumental in the founding of The Society for Historical Archaeology. What had changed between 1960 and say 1966, had historical archaeology become much more visible?

Yes, I think so. I was pretty far removed from it in Texas because a lot was taking place on the East coast. I think Noël Hume came to Williamsburg shortly after I left Virginia in 1956, and I did not meet him until later. He started to get a great deal of publicity and published *Here Lies Virginia*. That came out early enough that I had my students reading it at SMU as I remember.

[Q:] There was a symposium in Washington D.C. where they discussed historical archaeology at this time and were you there?

I was in the audience. Jack Cotter, Malcolm Watkins, Ed Larrabee, and somebody else, I forget who, were in a panel discussion, and they were talking about historical archaeology. That was in 1965 or 1966. Then in 1966 there was a meeting of the Central States Anthropological Society in St. Louis. I went to that meeting where I heard these same people in a panel giving the same stuff about historic sites archaeology. I was sitting in the audience with Judy and Kathleen Gilmore, and I said to them, "This is the second time I have heard this panel wonder whether there are enough people interested in historical archaeology to form some sort of an organization, and we should get an answer. If I stand up and invite everyone to come to SMU to talk about organizing a society will you ladies help, and they said, Sure."

[Q:] Was this the same panel group?

Pretty much the same. Larrabee, Cotter, Malcolm Watkins, and Arnold Pilling were there and maybe somebody else. So I got up and said I would extend an invitation if people were interested in having a get-together at SMU in Dallas, and I would try to get some financial support if they were interested in coming. Their answer was yes, so we all got together in a hotel that night and made plans.

[Q:] Whose hotel room?

The Jelks. Judy served as recording secretary while the rest of us batted the idea around.

[Q:] Do you remember who was at the meeting in the hotel room?

Cotter, Malcolm Watkins, Arnold Pilling and Ed Larrabee I know were there. There may have been another one or two. We decided to invite to Dallas the leading practitioners in historical archaeology, whoever they might be.

[Q:] Is this the famous "Committee of Fifteen?"

Yes, the "Committee of Fifteen." So we started to write down names. Of course, Pinky Harrington was at the top of the list and we thought of Carlyle Smith and Carl Chapman and G. Hubert Smith, all of whom had worked on historic Indian sites, and Art Woodward and Kenneth Kidd and Charles Fairbanks and Ivor Noël Hume. So we put together a list of fifteen, including at least five of us at that hotel meeting, maybe six.

[Q:] You people drew the list up?

Yes, we drew the list up. Then I went back and talked with the President and the Provost at SMU and asked them to host the meeting and to pay the travel expenses of the fourteen people to come to SMU. And SMU sprang for the money.

[Q:] So you covered all their expenses?

Yes, SMU paid for the plane fares and for the hotel. They all received VIP treatment, including being flown from the airport to the hotel by helicopter. So SMU is owed a vote of gratitude for having financed the meeting. Someone suggested—and I do not remember who—that if we were going to get all these people together why not put on a great big international meeting of historical archaeologists who would be invited to come and give papers. So we decided to do that, and Arnold Pilling was put in charge of organizing the paper conference, while I was in charge of local arrangements in Dallas. We got it all set up and we were really surprised because we had over 100 people show up at that "First International Meeting on Historical Archaeology" or whatever we called it.

[Q:] Regular attendees paid all their own expenses?

Yes. And people gave papers. I cannot remember everyone who was there but Chuck Cleland gave a paper and that was the first time I met him. The conference came off very well and the fifteen people met privately, two or three times, I guess; Kathleen Gilmore and her husband Bob threw a great party for them. Bob belonged to one of these J. R. Ewing type cattleman clubs. It was really swanky, on top of a high-rise building in downtown in Dallas, wonderful dinner, and she and Bob paid for it all. The famous "Committee of Fifteen" came to that dinner—we did not invite the entire one hundred. In addition, Judy and I had two or three cocktail parties at our house for the committee.

The Committee of Fifteen met and started discussions, the first question being: Did we think there were enough people out there interested in historical archaeology to organize a viable society? The opinions were divided and in the beginning Pinky—and this is sort of interesting—said no he did not think there was enough interest. He said that he had been doing this stuff for years and nobody seemed to pay any attention to it. Then someone said look we just sent out this blanket invitation and we got 100 people showing up. So we decided that we did not have a hell of a lot to lose, so let's try it. If it doesn't work we will forget it.

Then we said that if we were going to do that we needed some type of organization, so we arranged for election of officers, which took place next day at the International Conference meeting, where there were a 100 people or more, who voted to form the SHA and elected the first slate of officers. Incidentally, Malcolm Watkins was going to chair that meeting, but he could not come at the last minute and sent Wilcomb Washburn, a historian, to represent the Smithsonian in his place. Wilcomb did not want to chair the organizational meeting, so I ended up chairing it.

[Q:] Wilcomb Washburn is a historian as is Carlos Margain. Where did Margain come from, was he invited by someone?

Yes, Carlos Margain was from Mexico. I did not know him previously and do not know who invited him. He was elected to the first board of directors. We were thinking of historical archaeology as including some people with an historical background as well as an archaeological background. So we had invited historians who were not archaeologists at all. Washburn was a historian and, as I recall, so was Merrill Mattes, another of the participants.

[Q:] The historians tended to drop away from the organization later?

Well, I do not know how many historians we currently have in the society but I assume we have some.

[Q:] Was anyone invited from outside of North America, say, from Europe?

Margain was from Mexico and there were several from Canada, but I don't believe there was anyone from outside North America.

[Q:] What was the issue about a category of "Fellows?" One person, who is slightly younger, who was at the founding meeting told me that some of the older generation in historical archaeology were concerned with losing control of not necessarily the discipline but of a new organization. Is that what the suggested "Fellows" category was all about?

I am trying to remember. We sat down and drafted a preliminary set of categories for membership, and we set a dues structure which was minimal at the time, and we did in the initial draft have a category of "Fellows." It is hard for me to remember the arguments for and against having fellows, but I think the idea was to distinguish between professionals and nonprofessionals, an idea which found fruition eventually in the SOPA-ROPA concept. I do not remember the details. I do know that we talked about it and had it in a draft, but somewhere down the line it was decided to drop the idea of "Fellows." It may have been decided at the meeting in Dallas in the general discussions. I do not recall.

[Q:] Were you surprised by the number of people who showed up for the meeting in Dallas?

I guess I was somewhat surprised. I really thought from one indication and another, going to SAA meetings and regional archaeology meetings, that there was a lot of interest. Another point, Stanley South was one of the other people involved. He had that Historic Site Archaeology Conference going in the Southeast, and he was a bit upset, I think, that the SHA was formed, because he had started to hold regular meetings as an adjunct to the Southeastern Archaeological Conference several years before the Dallas meeting. I do not remember what year. But having gone to some of South's meetings I was aware that there were a number of people out there who were interested in historic sites archaeology as a subdiscipline of the field. I was a little surprised at the number who showed up in Dallas because we had just sent out blanket invitations to be posted on bulletin boards at universities—at departments of anthropology and maybe some history departments. I certainly would have expected 30 or 40 or 50 in retrospect and was a little surprised that we had a little over 100–105 or something like that number.

[Q:] Was Stanley South one of the original members of the Committee of Fifteen?

Yes.

[Q:] Did he suggest that you use his Conference on Historic Site Archaeology rather than forming a new organization?

No. Bob, did you ever go to one of his Conferences? [RLS. "Two or three."] Well he ran it as an adjunct to the Southeastern Conference (SEAC), I guess, all the way through. He put out the publication, papers, and all of that. I attended several of those and there were a number of people there, he got a pretty good attendance; but these were people who primarily had come to the Southeastern Archaeological Conference, the prehistoric conference, some of whom stayed over to go to Stan's conference. But it was certainly my impression that he was somewhat disappointed that what he had started as a regional meeting had not been expanded.

[Q:] Was Stanley South on that earlier panel in Washington, D.C.?

I don't think so but am not certain.

[Q:] When you were setting up the SHA and the Committee of Fifteen did you already know the people on the committee? Let me mention some of the important individuals and ask if you knew them from an earlier period and, if so, when did you meet them?

Carl Chapman: Yes, I had met him at SAA meetings.

Charles Fairbanks: I do not think I had ever met Fairbanks before Dallas, but other people present knew him.

J. C. Harrington you already knew and you knew Ed Larrabee from Louisbourg?

Yes, and also I knew Larrabee from this other panel he was on [in Washington] and we did visit him at Louisbourg.

Ivor Noël Hume: I had never met him before the Dallas meeting, but of course I knew who he was and Cotter knew him very well.

Arnold Pilling: I had never met Arnold until the panel discussion in Washington. [And he was actually the organizer of the paper sessions in Dallas, is that correct?] Yes, he took care of organizing the papers and chaired the paper sessions.

Carlyle Smith: Yes, I had met him at SAA meetings and I had corresponded with him about artifacts, artifacts from the Stansbury and other sites. And Art Woodward I had never met before Dallas, but I had also sent him materials for identification earlier.

G. Hubert Smith: I met him first at the River Basin Surveys office in Lincoln, Nebraska in 1951 and had seen him several other times at Plains Conferences and at other meetings.

James Deetz: I had never met Deetz.

Kenneth Kidd: Also, I had never met Kidd, but other people involved knew him.

Malcolm Watkins: Yes, knew him well by that time from our association at Jamestown and at several subsequent meetings.

Bunny Fontana: No.

Stanley South: Yes, I had met Stanley at his conferences in the Southeast.

[Q:] Had you gone to any of the CHSA meetings before 1966.

Yes, I am sure I did.

[Q:] In 1967 there were 22 "Fellows," most of whom we just discussed. There are five others, however, and I would like to ask the same questions about them. Did you know these individuals before the Dallas meeting and, if so, when and how did you first meet them?

James C. Gifford: I don't recall ever meeting him.

Charles H. Hayes III: I didn't know Hayes before the Dallas meeting.

Merrill J. Mattes: I met Mattes for the first time at the Dallas meeting.

H. Geiger Omwake: I don't remember ever meeting Omwake.

Stephen Williams: I have known Steve since meeting him at a SEAC meeting about 1960.

[Q:] Also by the 1967 Dallas meeting there were other significant, visible researchers in historical archaeology in North America. Several of these scholars did attend the founding meeting and spoke during the open Business Meeting at the Conference. Did you know the following individuals, most of whom were in Dallas, although a few of them were primarily prehistorians, before the 1967 meeting and, if so, when and where did you meet them?

Raymond S. Baby: I knew Ray slightly, having met him at a SAA meeting in the 1950s.

Tyler Bastian: I met Tyler in 1965 when we worked together on the archaeology of the Wichitas. Bob Bell at the University of Oklahoma, Marvin Tong at the Museum of the Great Plains, Bill Newcomb at the Texas Memorial Museum, and I got a grant from the National Science Foundation for a pilot study on the archaeology of the Wichita tribes, which went on for two years. Tong hired Bastian to test several sites in Oklahoma while Ned Woodall and I tested several sites in Texas; then we put out a joint report on the whole project.

Robert T. Bray: I didn't meet Bob until several years after the Dallas meeting.

Col. J. Duncan Campbell: I cannot remember exactly when I met Campbell. I corresponded with him about military buttons for a while.

E. Mott Davis: Mott was hired at the University of Texas in 1956 to replace Alex Krieger, who had moved to California. Mott worked on several RBS sites in East Texas in the late 1950s. We became close friends while we were both in Austin.

Hester Davis: I met Mott's sister, Hester, shortly after she moved to the University of Arkansas, probably in the early 1960s.

James F. Fitting: I first knew Jim while he was in Michigan, before he moved to California. I believe this was after I moved to Illinois in 1968, but I don't remember for sure.

Leif Landberg: I don't remember ever meeting Landberg.

Father John Lee: Ditto for Father John.

William Mayer-Oakes: I first met Mayer-Oakes about 1960 at an SAA meeting. We came to know each other in succeeding years, sharing an interest in the American Society for Conservation Archaeology and other things.

Lee N. Nelson: Don't know him.

Eugene T. Peterson: Ditto.

B. Bruce Powell: I became acquainted with Bruce when he worked with us at Jamestown for a while in the 1950s, but have seen him briefly only once or twice since then.

George I. Quimby: I didn't know Quimby before 1967, but we became good friends later.

Bert Salwen: Ditto.

Albert Schroeder: Schroeder was a NPS archaeologist in the regional office in Santa Fe while I was doing RBS work in Texas. I saw him several times in Santa Fe in the 1950s, and he visited some of my prehistoric digs in Texas. A prehistorian, he did some ethnohistorical research in connection with Indian land claims in the Southwest.

Paul J. F. Schumacher: I got to know Paul and his wife Marietta well through socializing with them for years at SHA meetings. However, I did not know him before 1967.

Hale G. Smith: I met Hale somewhere but do not know him well. I don't think I had met him before 1967.

Roderick Sprague: I didn't know Rick in 1967, but we became good friends later.

Lyle M. Stone: I don't remember the first time I met Lyle, but sometime before the Dallas meeting I wrote a foreword to his publication on artifacts from Fort Michilimackinac, co-authored with J. Jefferson Miller.

Jervis D. Swannack: While I was working at Signal Hill in Newfoundland in 1966, Jervis, then with Parks Canada, visited my dig. I saw him a few time later in Ottawa and at early SHA meetings, but he dropped out of sight some years ago.

James L. Swauger: I don't know Swauger.

Ian C. Walker: Ditto.

[Q:] You were the Second President of The Society for Historical Archaeology (1968). What was your term in that office like? Was it a functioning organization by then or was it still being set up?

Well, it was functioning but certainly not hitting on all cylinders. It took a while for it to get running smoothly

[Q:] You were President when SHA met in Williamsburg (January 1968). Was it Ivor Noël Hume who invited the SHA to Williamsburg?

Yes, it was. Well, I took over as president from Cotter in Williamsburg. Noël Hume got up at the Dallas meeting when we voted to form the SHA and invited everyone to come for the first annual meeting at Williamsburg. Since we had met in Dallas in January, we decided to hold the future annual meetings in January. One of the reasons for that decision was that a

lot of the good time slots had been preempted by annual meetings of other societies, and we did not want to meet in the summer when a lot of people would be out in the field.

Yes, Cotter was the first president [1967], and at the business meeting in Dallas it was decided that the President would serve for only one year, which I think is kind of bad as you hardly get into office and you are out. Perhaps it should be two years.

[Q:] Therefore you were President for 1968 and up to the meeting in Tucson. Did you help to plan the meeting in Tucson or was that mostly Fontana?

I do not recall doing much toward planning the Tucson meeting.

[Q:] Did you run the Elections and Nomination Committee for that year?

I cannot remember. I cannot remember if the policy of having the immediate past president chair the nominations committee had been established at that early date or not. There have been so many different committees in so many different organizations that they all blur.

[Q:] Did Williamsburg (1968) and Tucson (1969) seem successful as meetings?

Yes, absolutely. Williamsburg was a success and everybody was delighted with the meetings. There were some interesting personal glitches which you perhaps know about and why not mention them. What happened is that Cotter was corresponding with Noël Hume about the upcoming meeting in Williamsburg [January 1968—the first official SHA Annual Conference]. Jack was up in Philadelphia and Noël was down in Virginia; in fact, I have copies of some of their correspondence, and I guess that in Noël's mind Jack seemed to be trying to take over planning the meeting, trying to make too many decisions and not leaving enough autonomy for Noël down in Williamsburg. So finally one day Noël just writes a letter to Jack and tells him "OK, you take over the meeting." Noël Hume did not come to the meeting in Williamsburg [RLS, "Oh, he did not attend?!"]. No, he sat in his house several miles out of Williamsburg and sent word that because of icy roads he could not get into town.

[Q:] There were no problems like that in Tucson, I take it?

No, the only problem in Tucson was the hotel [RLS, "The Santa Rita Hotel."] with cockroaches running all over the place.

Looking back to the Williamsburg meeting, one of the things I wanted to tell you, and it should go in the record, is that Noël Hume put on a wonderful banquet. He arranged for that part of the meeting and it set a precedent which was followed for several years in SHA but I guess has now disappeared. He selected a banquet theme based on 18th century banquets in Williamsburg. So, in Tucson Bunny Fontana decided to do something like it locally, and he got a bunch of Papago [Tohono O'odham] Indians and they were barbequing all these things, whatever they were, opossums or something, all sorts of amazing things, and a lot of people who ate it got sick. But it was certainly an interesting meal, a real anthropological experience. Then the following year when we met in Bethlehem [1970] with Vincent Foley, you probably did not go to that meeting [RLS, "No, I did go to that one in Bethlehem and the earlier one in Tucson."], he replicated a banquet for George Washington in the 18th century, with a roasted pig with an apple in its mouth, and all sorts of things. Later we went to Minneapolis in January [1973 St Paul] and had what the voyageurs would have eaten in a banquet arranged by Alan Woolworth. There was a tradition of having these historic banquet meals for a while which has now disappeared.

[Q:] John Cotter was the first President of the SHA, you followed him in office (1968), and John H. Rick succeeded you in office (1969). What was Cotter like as president and what do you think were his primary accomplishments in office? How and when did you meet Rick—before Dallas?—and how did he do as president?

Cotter's main problems as president stemmed from the fact that everything was new. He was conscientious about his responsibilities and was determined to establish the necessary operational procedures to get the society off the ground. There were crises to face, including the resignation of Glenn Little as editor, a problem that Cotter solved by editing the first volume of *Historical Archaeology* himself. I described his involvement with planning the first annual meeting at Williamsburg and the resulting friction that developed between he and Noël Hume.

In my opinion he did a creditable job with a very difficult assignment. My only criticism is that, in trying to ensure that everything went well, he may have taken on too many chores himself. He might have saved himself a lot of work and a few headaches if he had delegated more authority to others instead of trying to handle so many details himself.

After working out details by mail, in the early spring of 1965 I signed a contract with Canada to do the work at Signal Hill, Newfoundland that summer. At the SAA meeting in April, John Rick, Parks Canada's chief archaeologist, sought me out and introduced himself; then we discussed my upcoming fieldwork at Signal Hill. He visited my dig that summer, and I saw him in Ottawa several times over the next few years.

[Q:] Vincent P. Foley was the sixth SHA President (1972) but he served under you as the Secretary-Treasurer (1968–1970). When did you get to know Foley and how was he as Secretary-Treasurer?

Vince was very organized and competent and did a good job as secretary-treasurer. I believe I met him for the first time at the first SHA annual meeting in Williamsburg in January 1968.

[Q:] During the early years of the society there were three journal editors: J. Glenn Little III, David Armour, and John D. Combes. When did you first get to know these fellow officers and what is your impression of them as editors of *Historical Archaeology*?

I never met Little to my recollection, and of course he resigned [due to a heart attack] before getting Vol. 1 into print, so he really did no editing on the journal. I think I corresponded with Armour while he was editing Vol. 2, but I don't remember meeting him face to face. And I really have no opinion about Combes' performance as editor.

[Q:] Since you were deeply involved in the founding of the SHA and oversaw its early growth, how do you compare the SHA today in regard to its accomplishments and problems?

That is hard to comment on. I guess one of my problems is that I am too old and I can remember the good old days [laughter] when you went to a meeting and there were just a few people there, and there was one slate of papers, not concurrent sessions. By the end of the meeting almost everybody got to know everybody else. You sat around and there were not any tours or that kind of thing—not that the tours are not nice, in fact, I enjoy them—but it was just a different time and a different feeling, and you sat around in a hotel like this and talked about archaeology all night until the sun would came up next morning. That was the one opportunity you had to get together and communicate with your colleagues from all over. I am talking about regional meetings and even the SAA in the early days. But today the meetings have gotten so big, with all these concurrent sessions with hundreds of papers, and you see all these people milling around and you know about one percent of them; in fact, no one in the room knows more than one percent of them [laughter]. It is just a different thing. I have seen that change with both the SAA and the SHA as I go to both of their meetings pretty regularly every year.

[Q:] You did not become less involved with the Society for American Archaeology once the SHA had formed?

No, not at all.

[Q:] Are you optimistic about the future of the SHA as a society?

Yes, surely.

[Q:] In 1968 you moved from SMU to the Midwest and you were at Illinois State University in Normal for sixteen years. Why did you make that move?

When Judy and I left Dallas to go to Washington for a Smithsonian fellowship in the fall of 1967, we had to decide, since we owned a house in Dallas, whether we wanted to rent it out or sell it. For several reasons I had been thinking about moving on from SMU to some other place—one reason being that there are some negative things about SMU I would prefer not to get into here—but another reason was that at that time universities all over the country were building anthropology departments, and

they were just hiring people like crazy, offering you all kinds of goodies to move from one place to another. I went to a meeting somewhere, it must have been the SAA meeting that spring of 1968, where I met a sociologist from Illinois State University who was recruiting for someone to start an anthropology program there. He asked me to send in a resume, and I did, then I visited the campus, and they made me one of those offers you just could not turn down to come and organize an anthropology program. In fact, when we moved to Normal, I had no idea we would stay long. But they offered me a full professorship with tenure, a six-hour teaching load, graduate assistants, a much larger salary than I was making at SMU, and all kinds of perks, including the floor of a building to turn into an archaeology lab. So we moved to ISU and gave it a shot.

When we first went there, we did not like Normal, Illinois too much. I liked it better than Judy, but she would threaten to leave every Thursday and sometimes on Tuesdays and Sundays too. So when I retired 16 years later, I said OK now it is time to leave, she would not leave! We would go out and get in the car and drive to Arizona, back to Texas, and down to Florida and look for a place, but then go back to Normal and stay. And we are still there.

[Q:] You were the founder of the anthropology section of a joint department and then it split later into two departments?

Not exactly. It started as a sociology-anthropology department, but then they added social work and we had three divisions in there for awhile; but then social work split off and got its own department. One of the problems was we were all set to have a separate anthropology department about 1970. I had talked to the dean about that before I went to Normal, and he had agreed to support a separate department once we got it going. After a couple of years we were doing very well and had a lot of students, so I went back to the dean, and he said OK. We drew up the proposal for a separate department, but about that time all the hippies showed up and they started all these marches and confrontations on the campus. One day a bunch of students physically removed the university president from his office and occupied it themselves. The president announced that faculty didn't have to hold regular class meetings, but could go outside on the quad, get on a soapbox, and make political speeches if they chose to. This was going on all over the country. So the citizens of Illinois eventually said, OK if this sort of stuff is going to go on at state universities, then we are going to stop supporting them with our tax money. In response the legislature simply put a moratorium, a flat moratorium, on any expenditures for any new programs. You could not even offer a new course for two or three years at any state university. So they cut us off at the pass. By the time the legislative restrictions were removed, the country was in a recession and there were no funds for setting up a separate department. Now after all these years they are in the process again of trying to get a separate anthropology department.

[Q:] When you moved to Illinois State University did you continue to teach the seminar in historical archaeology, every year?

Yes, every year. I might add that at ISU I continued my practice of involving students in looking for "lost" historic sites. We made several excursions looking for the site of La Salle's Fort St. Louis, on the Illinois River near present-day Peoria, established in 1680, but we never did find it. Years before, I had inventoried

FIGURE 5. 1984 crew at the Laurens site, southern Illinois, first location of French Fort de Chartes, built in 1719. Left to right: Ed and Judy Jelks; ISU historian Carl Ekberg; ISU students Martin Wyckoff, Ed Safiran, Dave Waletschek, Dave Miller, and Keith Barr; Illinois State Historic Preservation Agency archaeologist Margaret Kimball-Brown; Illinois State Museum archaeologist Terry Martin; Bill Potter. (Courtesy of the Department of Sociology and Anthropology, Illinois State University, Urbana.)

the artifacts found by Glen Evans of the Texas Memorial Museum in 1950 at the site of La Salles's Fort St. Louis, established on the Texas coast in 1685, so I had a long-standing interest in La Salle's colonizing efforts.

In 1983 ISU history professor Carl Ekberg and I did identify the first site of Fort de Chartres built by the French in 1719 on the Mississippi in southern Illinois (the fort was later moved to another location). This identification involved study of contemporary documents, a magnetometry survey conducted by physics professor John Weymouth of the University of Nebraska, old aerial photos in the files of the Army Corps of Engineers, and, of course, on-site archaeological exploration.

[Q:] Who were some of the students you produced?

We had a lot of students who stayed in archaeology and some of them did very well. For example, Bob Sonderman, you know Bob I think, is the National Park Service archaeologist for the Capital District in Washington. Chip Smith is the head archaeologist for the Department of the Army now, and Deborah Hull-Walski is the collections manager for the anthropology collections at the Smithsonian's Museum of Natural History. Mike Wiant is curator of anthropology at the Illinois State Museum. Mark Esarey is Illinois State Archaeologist. Rose Schilt is with the Bishop Museum in Hawaii. Ron Deiss, Joe Phillippe, Mary McCorvie, Ed Safirin, Steve Rogers, Judi Jackson, Alan Westover, and several ex-students work as archaeologists or historians for state and federal agencies. Floyd Mansburger owns a successful CRM firm, and a number of others are employed by CRM outfits. We have them scattered all over, and a lot of these are primarily historical archaeologists.

[Q:] Was the program at ISU a Master's program?

Yes, a Master's program. Some students went on to get a Ph.D. at other universities, but most of them stayed with the MA degree.

[Q:] Was it during this period that you worked at West Point Military Academy and was that the ISU Fieldschool? What was the ISU Fieldschool doing in New York state?

Yes and that was 1971. Well, at the 1971 annual SHA meeting Pinky Harrington came up to me and told me that this colonel from West Point had come to the meeting looking for someone to do some archaeological work at the academy. They were getting ready for the Bicentennial in 1976 several years ahead and wanted some archaeological data to use as a basis for restoring some of the original Revolutionary War period fortifications. They had come to Pinky and he did not want to do it, or could not do it, for some reason. He recommended me, and asked if I would be interested. So I talked to the colonel at the meeting and later went over to West Point on a preliminary visit, which was quite an experience in itself, and talked with the superintendent there and decided to accept. I set the project up as a field school. Archaeologists do not do that much today, but combining contract work with field schools had worked for me over the years. I had a contract to do the work, the students supplied the labor and got the minimum wage plus course credit, and I wrote a report, and that was the end of that project, and everybody was happy.

[Q:] Was the West Point Project one season?

Yes, one season. They wanted me to come back the next season but something had come up, I do not remember what it was now, that kept me from going back, not that I did not want to because we had enjoyed the summer there. But Pinky went back the second year and continued the work that I had begun.

[Q:] Was that Constitution Island?

Yes, it was Constitution Island. That was where I worked at West Point.

[Q:] What was the Midwestern Archaeological Research Center at ISU?

That was the archaeological research center I started at Illinois State. We did mainly contract work.

[Q:] So, it was a CRM set up. Does it still exist?

No. It died on the vine after I left ISU.

[Q:] What were the dates for the existence of the MARC at Illinois State?

FIGURE 6. Jelks taking picture from improvised photo tower, Constitution Island, West Point Military Academy, 1971. ISU students holding lines: facing camera, left to right, Christie Williams, Lee Minnerly, Stephanie Santmeyers; back to camera, Steve Rogers. (Courtesy of Department of Sociology and Anthropology, Illinois State University, Urbana.)

When I went there I swore I would not get involved in doing contract archaeology, because as I mentioned earlier I done fieldwork full-time for 15 years for the River Basin Surveys. Although not contract as such, it was the same game. You had to go out and dig a site, write a report and meet all the deadlines, and it just went on and on and on until finally you just got tired of that routine. In Illinois they were building a lot of highways, so one day Chuck Bareis at the University of Illinois told me that they just had to have more help with the programs and asked me to help. We could contract on Phase I, Phase II and Phase III on a section of the interstate highway down toward St Louis. But I said, "No, I am not going to do it." But I had all these students at ISU, and they heard about it, and they started to ding dong me about it so they could go out make wages and get field experience. So in a moment of weakness I said, "OK."

We started out doing prehistoric work, and it was while we were doing this work that I saw all these old farmhouses that were just being bulldozed down. So I got in touch with Benny Keel at the NPS office in Atlanta who had oversight over the highway work. He came to Illinois and checked out the situation and made the Illinois Department of Transportation include study of historic sites in the highway rights of way. That is how it got started.

[Q:] What year was this work started?

I moved to ISU in 1968, so it was probably 1972 or 1973, somewhere along in that period. I finally got the state to fund historical archaeology in the CRM programs, and I was handling virtually all of that work in Illinois, using my students. We still had the prehistoric work continuing and it was more than I could handle alone. So we set up two divisions, and I hired Fred Lange to come in and take over the management of the historic division and David Carlson, who had just gotten his Ph.D. from Northwestern, to take over the prehistoric work. The way the research center was organized was that I was director, Carlson supervised all the prehistoric CRM, and Fred Lange did all the historic sites. That went on for several years; in fact, a lot of the kids I have been talking about who are now at the Army Corps of Engineers, the Smithsonian, the NPS, the State of Illinois, and other places, went through that program and got a lot of their field and lab experience there.

When I retired in 1983 we looked for a new MARC director and hired Vergil Noble, but he left after three or four years. Then Charles Rohrbaugh took over for a couple of years. Chuck Orser replaced Rohrbaugh as MARC director, but as it turned out he decided to go in a different career direction. Initially he was doing local CRM stuff but then got into more exotic historical archaeology and did research in Portugal, then in Brazil, and then in Ireland, where he has developed a successful on-going program, taking students over to Ireland for the last five or six years. So with Orser heavily involved in other research, the MARC was discontinued.

[Q:] When you were at SMU and initially when you moved to Illinois State was the period when the "New" or Processual Archaeology emerged in America. When did you become aware of it as a movement and what was your reaction to it?

I remember Lew Binford giving a paper at an SAA meeting in the 1960s which generated a lot of interest in the audience. I guess I just gradually became aware that there was this group of which Binford was the bellwether, if that is the right term; he was the guru. Bob, you were involved in that also. Were you one

of the Processual Archaeology types? [RLS. "Not really. Two or three times removed, sort of."] I also knew of some of the work that Jim Deetz had done, but he insists that he was never a "New Archaeologist." I just gradually became aware of the movement

Of course, I am old enough to have witnessed the roots of the movement in Walt Taylor's "A Study of Archaeology," published in 1948. I knew Walt, had been in the field with him several times, and had talked with him about a lot of this stuff. J. Charles Kelley, one of my mentors at UT, was a classmate of Taylor at Harvard, so I heard a lot about the beginnings of the idea of a scientific archaeology, anthropological and processual, even back in those days, the late 1940s. I witnessed the whole thing, saw it come and have seen it go, or it seems to be going in large part, let's put it that way.

[Q:] Was your reaction mostly positive or mostly negative?

Some of both. I felt from the beginning and still feel that there were some very positive things about Processual Archaeology, but there also were many negatives. Among the positive things is the idea that archaeologists should be more rigorous and more scientific in their approach. By scientific I mean following formal procedures like the hard sciences, so called, are wont to do.

I think archaeologists need to be more rigorous. I think that is all to the good. But on the down side, the New Archaeology put so much emphasis on cultural process, removed from the empirical field data by three or four levels of inference, that we ended up with a lot of students going through their education without being trained in how to go out and collect empirical data in the first place. Anyway that is my view of Processual Archaeology. I see some good and some bad in it, like in anything else.

I guess I am so old, Bob, that you might even call me a Pre-Processual Archaeologist. But as I started out in zoology I was trained to take a very rigorous approach to doing research, and there are certain things you should do. For one thing, all of your empirical observations should not only entail careful note-taking but also be reproduced and made available to your colleagues. A lot of the literature of the "New Archaeology," and this is just my opinion, talks about processual models of various kinds, but does not include the empirical data upon which these interpretations were based, so how was one able to evaluate the models?

You may remember when Stanley South wanted to collect empirical data from several sites to illustrate his pattern recognition, he combed the literature and could not find much empirical field data in the literature. He used my Signal Hill report as one example because I had put all the data in the report.

So that is my major criticism of the New Archaeology: they got too far away from the empirical data. I consider myself a dirt archaeologist—not an armchair archaeologist—and I feel that there are certain procedures based on theoretical and methodological principals that should always be followed when digging a site, and they apply to historical archaeology, prehistoric archaeology, biblical archaeology, or any type of archaeology. I do not think such basic things are being taught in universities much anymore, or at least not as much as they used to be.

[Q:] As you have always been interested in the patterning found within an individual archaeological site, do you think W. W. Taylor's "conjunctive approach" was an influence on you?

Yes, except I never knew for certain what the "conjunctive approach" was! And I do not think anyone else knew what it was. As I said, I was in the field several times down in Mexico and on the Texas border with Walt Taylor, and I used to talk with him about this question, and he was never able to explain it to my satisfaction. His idea was right, his fundamental idea was right, but he never explained how to do it in the field. You were not around at that time, but you may understand that what Taylor did was to say "OK, here are all these leading American archaeologists," including A. V. Kidder, Frank H. H. Roberts, Emil Haury, James Griffin, and others who were the pre-eminent prehistorians of the period in North America, and Taylor said, "OK, all you guys claim to be anthropologists"—he just listed them all one by one—and he said "you have degrees in anthropology and what you are doing is not

anthropology but historiography," which by Taylor's definition was purely descriptive and did not get into cultural process. He told them they had to do anthropology, and he would tell them how. But he never did! He never finished or published the promised reports on work he had done at Archaic sites in northern Mexico in which he was to demonstrate the conjunctive approach.

I remember one time about 1953 when Alex Krieger and I went down to Mexico because archaeologists from the National Museum in Mexico had found this very interesting cave with a bunch of prehistoric burials thrown into it [Candeleria Cave], and they were pulling all these skeletons out. Walt Taylor, who was living in Mexico City at the time, heard about the site and showed up there. We were sitting around the camp talking, and Krieger said to Taylor, "Well, Walt, how is your great report coming along, your magnum opus?" Taylor said, "Well, I got twelve hundred pages done," and he paused and said, "it is quadrupled spaced." [All laugh] He worked on that report for many years but never finished, or at least never published it.

Taylor came to Austin about 1948 while I was a graduate student there before I started to work for Stephenson, and he was looking for a graduate student to come out to Santa Fe and assist him in putting together this great report, and he offered me the job. The student would get junior author credit and everything. I had the good sense not to go. Many years later, about 1971, when I needed another archaeologist at Illinois State, I hired Jonathan Reyman, brand new Ph.D. from Southern Illinois University, where he had been a student of Taylor. He had just spent a whole summer, maybe more than that, maybe a whole year, out in Santa Fe working with Taylor on that report. So when Jonathan came to ISU he was all excited because they just about had that report ready, a great big massive two or three volume thing by Walter W. Taylor, Jr. with Jonathan Reyman as junior author. He kept waiting, and he would write to Taylor and Taylor would write back, and this went on for 12 years or so until Jonathan finally came to realize that nothing was going to happen. And Jonathan also learned that he had been the latest of a series of students over the years that Taylor had hired to help him with the report. Anyway, that is just a little story.

Taylor was a very bright guy and had some very original ideas, but he made the mistake of telling the leading American archaeologists, "You all do not know what you are doing and I am going to tell you how to do it." So no matter what he published they were ready to jump right on him.

[Q:] You were not only one of the founders of the SHA but in the 1970s you were one of the people who helped to set up the Society of Professional Archaeologists (SOPA) and very recently the Register of Professional Archaeologists (ROPA). How did that come about?

I have what I think is the unique experience of having chaired the organizational meetings of two major archaeological societies: SHA and SOPA.

With the rise of CRM, anybody could say "I am an archaeologist," so the people who needed to write contracts with archaeologists did not know who was qualified or was not qualified to do professional work. Rex Wilson, then the chief NPS archaeologist, approached me and Bob McGimsey at a SAA conference in the early 1970s and said, "I am going to tell you right now boys that either the profession organizes a certification program for recognizing qualified archaeologists, or the federal government is going to do it." That scared the be-Jesus out of a lot of people and led to the Airlie House Conference of 1974. Initially the conference was to talk about certification as the only issue, but other issues were added to the agenda later.

Recommendations coming out of the Airlie House conference led to the appointment of an SAA committee that turned out to be the instrument that formed SOPA.

[Q:] What was the Airlie House Conference? When was it called, who chaired it, what historical archaeologists attended, and was it successful?

Sponsored by the SAA and financed by the National Park Service, this conference was organized by Bob McGimsey and was held at Airlie House, a conference center in Virginia, in 1974. There were four or five different committees, each of which met separately and considered a separate issue. I was on the com-

mittee with Ray Thompson (chair), Jim Judge, McGimsey, Stuart Struever, and Fred Wendorf that explored the possibility of certifying archaeologists. This committee recommended that the SAA establish and administer a register of certified archaeologists.

Acting on that recommendation, the SAA Executive Board appointed an Interim Committee on Professional Standards (Jesse Jennings, Richard Woodbury, Charles Cleland, Stuart Struever, and Bob McGimsey) charged with the responsibility for making preparations to establish the registry. The Interim Committee drafted a document setting forth steps for establishing a registry. After a lot of debate at the 1975 SAA meeting and elsewhere, a ballot was sent out to the SAA membership, which voted about three to one in favor of establishing a registry that would be separate from the SAA and would be open to anyone (not only SAA members).

The Interim Committee was enlarged to include representatives from the SHA and the AIA as well as the SAA. The final committee, consisted of me as chair, Jane Buikstra, Charles Cleland, Hester Davis, James Hester, Jesse Jennings, Tom King, Bill Lipe, Bill McDonald, Bob McGimsey, and Stuart Streuver. We met at the University of Arkansas in January 1976 and, after a week of discussion, decided to form the Society of Professional Archeologists as an independent society because the SAA had backed off from sponsoring such a society. We elected officers at that time and prepared a report to the SAA executive board, which I, as first SOPA president, presented at the next SAA annual meeting in the spring of 1976. The SAA executive board thanked the committee for establishing SOPA and urged all qualified SAA members to join the new registry.

Back to your questions about the Airlie House conference, I do not remember who was on all the different work groups, nor the different issues they addressed. The proceedings of the conference containing all these details have been published. I do remember that Stan South was on one of the groups, and there may well have been other historical archaeologists there too. I believe that the conference was successful in the sense that there was thorough airing of several important issues facing the archaeological community; and it led, of course, to the formation of SOPA, which in turn led ultimately to the creation of the RPA.

[Q:] How important was Bert Salwen in regard to SOPA and also on the federal level to establish professional standards?

I really do not recall what Bert's involvement was. He was not on the Interim Committee that established SOPA, but he was always a strong supporter of having formalized professional standards. What influence he may have had at the federal level I do not know.

[Q:] What was the reaction of the general archaeological community, say between 1976 and 1980, to the founding of SOPA?

There was a distinct division in the archaeological community between the supporters and the opponents of SOPA. There may have been a large group that had no opinion one way or another, but it was my impression that most archaeologists took a position on one side or another. There were a lot of people on each side of the issue.

[Q:] To return to the creation of SOPA. In 1976, the founding year, you were the first SOPA President (elected or appointed?) and of the 12 Directors 4 (Charles Cleland, Hester Davis, yourself, and Bert Salwen) were either historical archaeologists or fellow travelers. You were succeeded in office in 1977 by Chuck Cleland. Stanley South became SOPA's first Secretary-Treasurer. Also in 1977 the number of Directors had contracted to five, three of whom (John Cotter, Kathleen Gilmore, and Bert Salwen) were historical archaeologists. Finally by 1979, when Carl Chapman was President, half of the eight member Board of Directors (Cleland, Gilmore, Bruce Rippeteau, and Lyle Stone) were again historical archaeologists and Cotter was, I believe, the first SOPA Grievance Coordinator. It seems to me that considering the number of historical archaeologists compared to the number of prehistorians in North America in the mid-1970s that this record is an astonishing showing. How do you explain the high visibility of historical archaeologists in the formation of SOPA

Regarding the four you mention among the first directors, two (Hester Davis and I) are

at least as much prehistorians as historical archaeologists, and Cleland has done a lot of prehistoric research too, I believe. Salwen is the only one who could be considered strictly an historical archaeologist. The committee that established SOPA had representatives on it of the SHA, the AIA, and ASCA, so there were several people with historical archaeological experience involved with SOPA from the beginning. I really have no explanation for the large number of historical archaeologist directors during Chapman's tenure as SOPA president unless the chair of the nominating committee (and I have no idea who that was) was partial to historical archaeologists for some reason.

[Q:] Currently the Register of Professional Archaeologists (RPA) is co-sponsored by the SAA and the SHA (as well as the AIA). Why was this not done in 1976, and was there any difference in the reaction of the SAA and the SHA to the establishment of SOPA?

Some of the most outspoken critics of SOPA in the early years were officers of, or leaders within, the SAA. It was their opposition that forced the SAA's decision not to sponsor a registry of professionals, despite the three-to-one favorable vote of the membership. One of their arguments was that legal complications might lead to dire consequences, even possibly to bankruptcy of the SAA.

I made a trip to New York while I was SOPA president and talked to officers of the AIA, who were quite favorable to the concept of registering professionals; but without the leadership of the SAA they were not prepared to take action on their own. I believe the same was true of the SHA leadership at that time.

In short, it is my impression that a few influential officers and leaders within the SAA mounted a successful campaign to keep the SAA uninvolved, and without SAA leadership, the other societies did not go along.

The problem of identifying archaeologists who meet minimal professional standards of education and experience has been building up over the years since SOPA was formed in 1976 to address that need. Two or three years ago—for the second time after twenty-odd years—the SAA leadership decided that something had to be done to identify professionals, and they began to talk about establishing a register. Several people said, "Hey, wait. SOPA already has the mechanism for doing that. Do you want to just scrap SOPA and start over from scratch?" After some discussion the SAA decided to go ahead with a registry, using SOPA's Code of Ethics and Standards of Work Performance as a model and inviting the SHA and the AIA to be co-sponsors. So, that is how it happened.

[Q:] Looking back over the twenty year existence of SOPA what were its accomplishments and what were its failings? Why in 1998 was it necessary to replace SOPA with RPA

SOPA's main accomplishments were:

1. specification of minimal educational and experiential requirements for recognition as a professional archaeologist,

2. formulation of the first comprehensive code of ethics and standards of work performance for professionals, together with procedures for enforcing the code and standards,

3. maintenance of a directory of archaeologists who met the professional standards and who subscribed to the code and standards,

4. serving as a model that was adopted by the major American archaeological societies when they jointly established the Register of Professional Archaeologists.

[Q:] Let me ask you some concluding questions. Looking back over the whole history of historical archaeology as a discipline what do you think are its major accomplishments but also what do you think are its continuing problems?

Well, I think first of all that doing archaeology at historic sites, if you call that historical archaeology, is a perfectly legitimate pursuit. And I think, I am certain of it, that The Society for Historical Archaeology's existence has had a lot to do with the acceptance of this fact by the profession, as well as by government agencies. In other words, historical archaeology has come to be recognized as an important part of the overall archaeological agenda. The SHA has certainly played a role in bringing that about. It has provided a focal point for historical archaeologists to rally around and push for what they think should be done.

[Q:] What do you think are some of the continuing problems of the discipline of historical archaeology?

Well, a lot of the problems are those that apply to the whole discipline of archaeology. The CRM thing has become very big in both prehistoric and historical archaeology, and no one knows quite what to do with it. I find it hard to think of problems that are specific to historical and not prehistoric archaeology. One of the things that is visible in historical archaeology, but again not limited to it, are the underwater treasure salvors, and certainly that is a problem. I do not know what to do about it and neither does anyone else.

[Q:] What about the argument that if you have documents why do archaeology?

I have heard that argument but not from any historical archaeologists. It is obvious that the documents do not tell you about everything that went on in the past, and sometimes they tell it wrong. But again going back to my position as a staunch supporter of empirical field observation, which does not lie provided you make your observations carefully and objectively, reasonable inferences based on what you see in the field sometimes contradict what you see in some of the historical documents. You sometimes can use archaeological data to correct errors in written documents. Historical archaeology augments our knowledge beyond what is recorded in documents, and that is the standard answer I would give.

[Q:] Do you think that historical archaeology is inferior, or holding second place, to general prehistoric studies?

No. Historical archaeology studies different peoples than does prehistoric archaeology: that is the only difference except for the availability of historical records for the one and not the other.

[Q:] Has the situation gotten better?

Yes. As I said earlier, my experience in Illinois a few years ago was that most prehistorians did not want to have anything to do with historic sites. Now some of the prehistorians are doing historical archaeology. John Walthall for one. I have seen the general acceptance of historical archaeology locally, but I do not really have an eye on what is going on nationally and internationally, except for the substantial increase in the number of publications in historical in recent years. You and I both, and Judy too, went to that conference in London last year [joint meeting of the SHA and the Society for Postmedieval Archaeology], and that indicates what our colleagues across the pond are doing.

[Q:] When you look across your whole career would you primarily classify yourself as an historical archaeologist?

No. I consider myself an archaeologist who has used archaeological methods and techniques to study several difference cultures of the past, including some for which there are related contemporary documents. If I had to declare myself as one or the other—and that would be a silly, useless exercise—I would have to come down on the side of prehistory, simply because that is what I have done mostly. I was trained by prehistorians, and have spent two or three as much time on prehistoric research as on historical. This is reflected both in my field research, my publication record, and my teaching career, which included more courses on prehistoric, or on general method and theory, than on historical archaeology. I do not mean by saying that to in any way diminish my interest in, and enthusiasm for, historical archaeology. I feel very strongly about that interest.

[Q:] Do you think that it is in any way negative that most students today in historical archaeology have little to do with prehistoric archaeology as they tend to be exclusively historical archaeologists?

It should not make any difference in my mind as long as they receive proper training in the basics of conducting archaeological research. Archaeology is archaeology, no matter what culture area or time period one chooses to specialize in.

I used the term "dirt archaeologist" earlier for the generic archaeologist, but there is another term that has been kicked around. Some years ago, as far as I know published for the first time in Europe, was the concept of "archaeography" and "archaeology" as counterparts to the terms "ethnography" and "ethnology." Just as ethnographers go out and collect empirical data about existing peoples and use those data for ethnological studies, so do archaeographers observe cultural manifestations that people left behind that can be used for synthetic processual models of cultural dynamics (archaeology? or

paleoethnology?). I sometimes in my classes said that archaeologists perform autopsies on the cadavers of past cultures.

So it does not matter if you are an historical archaeologist or a prehistoric archaeologist, there is a right way to study the archaeological record, and there are many wrong ways to study it. I think there is a set of very sound fundamental principals that should underlie all field procedures. I spent years trying to teach these principles to a couple of generations of students and to impress on them that the important thing is to know how to dissect and observe the anatomy of the cultural cadaver in an objective, scientific way.

There are certain basic things that must be done. For one thing you cannot go out there and dig a bunch of random squares comprising four percent of the surface area of a site and come up knowing very much about the anatomy of that site. That is not a valid statistical sample because it does not reveal how a site is structured, how the geological components and cultural components are articulated in the ground. Those must be exposed and observed objectively if inferences about extinct peoples are to be valid.

I feel that archaeography—if you want to use that term to refer to the scientific collection of empirical observations on the archaeological record—is fundamental and must be kept clearly separated from synthetic processual modeling, which is done as a later phase of research.

Incidentally Jim Deetz gave a keynote address at an SAA meeting, maybe 12 or 15 years ago, where apparently independently of the people in Europe who had preceded him on this, he came up with the term "archaeography," synonymous with the European usage of the term. Binford made the same distinction but without using that term. Walt Taylor did the same back in 1948, using the term historiography as approximately synonymous with what I am here calling archaeography. Willey and Phillips in 1955 who promulgated the famous dictum that "archaeology is anthropology or it is nothing," also distinguished between modeling of cultural process (that is, doing ethnological studies of peoples who are not here anymore) and the collection, identification, and ordering of empirical data. Some one has to do this groundwork at the descriptive level, or there will be no sound empirical data on which to base models of cultural process

[Q:] Is it equally important to be trained as an anthropologist?

No. Of course not. To construct *anthropological*, processual models, Yes. But not to do "archaeography." Look at all our Classical Archaeologists and our Biblical Archaeologists. I would hate to think that all of those guys do not know what the hell they are doing. Of course they know how to dig. Or most of them do, just as most (but by no means all) anthropological archaeologists know how to dig a site properly. Like reasoning on any subject, your final conclusion depends on the premise you start out with. If you start out with Willey and Phillips' dictum, "archaeology is anthropology or it is nothing," obviously you have to know anthropology or you are not doing archaeology by that definition. But even so you still have to do the "archaeography" part.

Those are my views on archaeology.

[RLS] *Then this is a good place to stop.* [EJ] I think so.

Thank you for the interview and for being allowed to follow you through a half century of the history of the field.

Curtis D. Tunnell

A Conversation with Kathleen Kirk Gilmore

Introduction

The Society for Historical Archaeology's first female president and the first female recipient of the J. C. Harrington Award, Kathleen Gilmore, is widely recognized as the leading authority on Spanish colonial archaeology in Texas. After receiving a Bachelor of Science in Geology at the University of Oklahoma and working as a geologist for several years, Kathleen took a recess from professional activities while she and her husband, Bob, raised a family of four girls. When the girls were grown, Kathleen returned to a long-standing but latent interest in archaeology to earn master's and Ph.D. degrees at Southern Methodist University. She was adjunct professor at the Institute of Applied Sciences at the University of North Texas from 1975 to 1990.

While a graduate student at SMU, she became interested in the 17th- and 18th-century Spanish missions of Texas, especially the sites of several missions and presidios whose exact locations had become lost. When she found archaeological field evidence of the three San Xavier missions and presidio, she formulated a rigorous method for combining documentary and archaeological data to demonstrate an historic site's location. She then used the San Xavier project as a test of the method and as a subject for her master's thesis.

Other historic sites on which Kathleen has done documentary and field archaeological research include San Sabá, Rosario, San Ildefonso, and Concepción missions; Las Amarillas and Loreta presidios; La Salle's Fort St. Louis; and the French fort at English Turn on the Mississippi near New Orleans. Over the years, she has developed expertise in the typology of both Spanish and French colonial ceramics and has researched the ceramics from the above sites and many others, including the *Belle*, La Salle's ship whose remains have recently been located

and excavated in Matagorda Bay by the Texas Historical Commission.

The interview took place on 11 April 2001 at Victoria, Texas, near the site of La Salle's ill-fated, late-17th-century Fort St. Louis and Loreta Presidio, which was built on the ruins of the French fort by Spaniards in the early-18th century. Both Kathleen and Curtis had been working for many months as part-time consultants at the site on excavations that were being conducted by the Texas Historical Commission under the direction of James E. Bruseth.

Two days after the interview, Curtis died without warning, the victim of a massive heart attack. Ed Jelks transcribed and edited the tapes.

Curtis's questions and comments are italicized.

The Interview

Kathleen, let's start with a little bit of biographical background on you. When and where were you born, what were your parents' names, where did you go to school, and so forth?

I was born in Altus, Oklahoma, 12 November 1914, way back there. My mother, Jesse Horton, was a native of Mississippi and my father, Rufus Patrick Kirk, a native of North Carolina. They moved to southwestern Oklahoma, probably during a very lush year when my father saw the plains full of beautiful high grass, and my parents thought it was an ideal place to live. As time went on, they realized it wasn't the best place in the world. When I was twelve, we moved to Tulsa, Oklahoma. I have an older sister, now deceased, and a younger brother. I went to school in the Tulsa schools and, later, attended the University of Tulsa for three years before graduating from the University of Oklahoma.

OK, so you all were living in Tulsa then at the time you went to college.

That's right. When I was thirteen in Tulsa, I read an article about "The Lost Civilization of the Mayans"; remember, this was some time ago. I was very interested in it, so I took a course in geology in my senior year with the idea that there was something I could learn about antiquities. Later when I got to the University of Tulsa, I decided to do the same thing. This was during the depression, and money was very tight at that time. I knew that I would have to make some money and support myself. So I thought, well, I'll major in geology. I did not want to be a secretary. I did not want to teach. Those were the two occupations, almost always the only occupations, that were open to women at that time.

When I majored in geology, I was advised to go to the University of Oklahoma because they had a very fine school in petroleum geology. Also, at that time, Tulsa was known as the oil capital of the world. Since then, I think it has deteriorated somewhat. But going to the University of Oklahoma then, I had a bachelor of science degree in geology.

When I got out of school with a BS degree, a friend of mine who had taken stenographic discipline, so to speak, for two years in college was making $125 a month. Well, I went out with a bachelor's degree in geology and finally got a job with an independent oil operator plotting well logs, but I was making $80 a month. I thought, "Oh wow, I got in the wrong profession."

During school, I had worked at my cousin's hospital (he was an orthopedist), the Bone and Joint Center, in Tulsa in the evenings from 5 until 10 o'clock for twenty-five cents an hour. That helped in those times as money was scarce. Things cost maybe one tenth as much as they do now, so the pay wasn't quite as bad as it sounds.

At any rate, trying to find work, make some money, and go to college was very difficult because the male students could always get jobs, which was very hard to take sometimes. They could mow the grass, they could be locker boys, they could be water boys, they could work in the library. They could do all kinds of things, but not the female students. There was hardly any work for the female students.

Finally, I was able to get a job in the library at the University of Tulsa, again at twenty-five cents an hour. I was able to quit the job at my cousin's hospital in the evenings. That was a help. Then, I got a small scholarship to the University of Oklahoma. Later, when I was having a difficult time getting a job as a geologist, I decided I had to go to business

FIGURE 1. Kathleen Gilmore with Ross Fields recording a "pothole" at Tilson Mound Site (now named Horace B. Cabe Site), Bowie County, Texas, 1979.

school. It practically broke my heart. I was never any good at shorthand and not very good at typing.

I worked for the American Association of Petroleum Geologists in Tulsa, which is the headquarters, as an editorial assistant or assistant to the editor. That was a confining and a very detailed job. However, I learned a great deal, and the experience was helpful later on when I was writing reports in archaeology. I stayed there a year and then went to Houston, which was the booming oil center at the time, to find a job.

I took the city directory and looked at the oil companies in the different buildings. I'd written up a vita and went floor by floor. Well, I left out a little thing: I did go back to night school at the University of Tulsa to study micropaleontology. So, I did have some skills along that line besides what I knew about petroleum geology. Finally, I was offered a job by Humble Oil Company in a stenographic pool. The geologist who had offered me the job said most of the stenographers couldn't even spell "geologist." He was pretty excited to find a person who knew a little bit about, well, shorthand and typing and could spell geologist. But

I looked at that stenographic pool and almost threw up, "uhhh!"

Finally, after the offer of several jobs, I went to Corpus Christi with Superior of California as a typist. There was a geologist and a scout in the office, and I typed up the well reports. I tend to say it was an exciting time for me because I had never lived on the water before. As time went on, I left that job for one in Houston with Standard of Kansas where I'd interviewed the year before and then stayed there until I married.

How did you and Bob meet?

Actually, first I knew him slightly in high school and then dated him when I was at Oklahoma University. He and a friend of his came to OU. I had a date with his friend, and Bob had a date with my friend, but later on we got together. When I was working in Corpus Christi, he proposed, and I said, "I don't want to get married now." But World War II was coming along, and I decided to go ahead and get married.

We were married Christmas Day 1940. I'd come home from Corpus Christi, and he'd come home from Okemah, Oklahoma—a small, very small oil town where he was stationed with Shell Oil Company. We were to move to Okemah, and I had a list of things I was going to do there. I was afraid it was going to be quite a boring time. Also, I had been told that I'd probably never have any children, so I was trying to figure out what I could do in Okemah. One thing I planned to do was learn how to work on an automobile. I never got around to that, thank goodness.

I quit my job with Standard of Kansas. In the meantime, when Bob had come to Houston to see me, he had driven back with my boss from Standard of Kansas, a geologist. My boss asked me about Bob, and he said that a new company in Dallas, De Golyer and McNaughton [Petroleum Engineers], an oil evaluation firm, was looking for a young petroleum engineer. He wondered if Bob would be interested. Well, of course, I was ecstatic because that meant I didn't have to live in Okemah, Oklahoma. Bob also decided it'd be a pretty good deal.

Bob was a practicing geologist?

He was a petroleum engineer. But we both took micropaleontology together at night at the University of Tulsa when we were dating. In between, I was engaged to another guy in California, but when he called me up, he said, "You've got two minutes. I've got my stop-watch on you." And so I thought, "well, you rascal!" I cut him off.

How did you get such an independent spirit at an early time when a lot of women accepted their role in society as such, but you didn't do that. You took geology in order to do something different.

I have no idea. Maybe it's genetic. My mother was quite an independent person, and that's probably where it came from. My sister's somewhat the same way, but mom had wanted to be a medical doctor. There were many medical doctors in her family, but she was too bound by tradition. Being a southern woman, it would have been very difficult for her to go into medicine. That's probably part of it. And maybe just personality, something on that order. Who knows?

So, you all moved to Dallas then?

Yeah, moved to Dallas. But they were building power plants and that sort of thing around the country at the time, and De Golyer and McNaughton had a lot of geologists besides engineers. Then Bob worked on the soil foundations and drilling holes, well core holes, to be sure that the foundations were all right. He did that most of the time during the war. It was called a strategic occupation ... I've forgotten the exact term. Then during those times, we had four daughters—Betsy, Judy, Pat, and Sally. They're in chronological, alphabetical order. I didn't realize until someone told me. We lost Betsy in 1993. It was very difficult for us. Now we have the three daughters and four grandchildren.

When our youngest daughter was 12 and the others were away from home in college or such, one of Bob's friends in Houston with Humble—I had told him of my interest in archeology—said, "Well, we've just got through doing some radiocarbon dates for the Dallas Archaeological Society. Why don't you join that?" I had no idea that there were such things, but I looked it up and joined. Lloyd Harper, King Harris, oh, a lot of the other "old timers" were in the society. King Harris ran it pretty well with some help from his wife, Inus Marie. All in all, it was a very interesting, interested group. They were trying to teach the people that joined to be people who picked up artifacts with something in mind, who documented where they got them and what they got.

Then SMU decided to establish a department of anthropology, and Fred Wendorf came to SMU to establish the department. He had been in New Mexico and was working with the state, but he got interested in the African scenario, along with Tony Marks and some other people. He brought them all to SMU. Then I decided to go to school and applied for graduate school.

A question on the graduate school application said, "Why do you want to go to graduate school?" I put down there, "Well, I wanted to go into archaeology and the best way to do that, I thought, was to go to school." I had to take the GRE, and I probably made the lowest grade ever in math by a person ever admitted to graduate school. I'm not going to tell you what it was. I'm still that way. Bob was a fine mathematician, being an engineer, and the girls mostly have been too, but it's never been one of my good qualities. I'd say, "Bob, I want to make a third of this oatmeal recipe and it calls for a cup, how do I get it." He'd say, "It's very simple. Do this." But I wouldn't do it; I would always ask him.

FIGURE 2. Kathleen Gilmore and Doug Markwell excavating a burial at San Francisco Mission, San Xavier Complex, Milam County, Texas, 1968.

You joined the Dallas Archaeological Society. What about the Texas Archeology Society?

I found out about that, of course, later. I believe the first meeting was in Victoria. I went to the field school at the Gilbert Site before the Victoria meeting because I had not met Dee Ann [Story] or Mardith Schuetz or any of those. Ed Jelks and Mott Davis were at the Gilbert Site, so then the meeting was after that in 1962 or 1963. The field school lasted for three weeks. There was one week that one archaeologist had charge, the next week another one, and the third week another one. I think it was Jelks, Schuetz, and Story—no, Mott Davis had charge one week, I believe. It was a very exciting time for me to be able to learn all of that. The field school was not far from Dallas. At the time, I was still very much tied to my family and felt like I couldn't spend too much time away. So, I spent maybe one or two nights there, and then drove back and forth to Dallas. It was dry in Raines County, meaning no sale of alcoholic beverages. I'd take orders going to Dallas and bring stuff back. When Dee Ann was at the school, she said, "Well, here's five dollars. Get me a bottle of wine. I don't care about quality. Just get the most that you can for five dollars." Which I did. But that was a very good time.

The Gilbert Site was an historic Indian village of the contact period.

Well, a little later—as I remember, around the 1730s—a very interesting site, lots of artifacts.

It was represented in the documents, the Spanish documents, I guess.

Well, no it wasn't. Now, there was a site at Lake Tawakoni that Father Calahorra had visited. LeRoy Johnson and Ed Jelks had worked on the documentary material as well as the site, I believe, at that time. I don't know actually whether anyone ever really tried to look up any archival material on the Gilbert Site. At that time, it was sort of the beginnings of historical archaeology in Texas. Lots of people didn't know how to handle it.

I remember a little article I wrote for *The New Handbook of Texas* on historical archaeology. Erik Reed had said in the late 50s that he wasn't sure whether historical archaeology should be called archaeology at all—that he thought archaeology included only prehistoric materials. So, we were getting into the beginnings of historical archaeology, and I was not sure that I wanted to go into it. But with the Gilbert Site and other things that were happening, I decided the field wasn't too bad. I did my dissertation on the Caddoan material in the Lake Palestine area. I thought at the time that the Caddo was what I was most interested in. But I decided that it was the mission period and the contact period I liked the best.

Ed Jelks had been real interested, at that same time, in some of the historic sites, hadn't he? He was an influence on me, I know, at that time.

Well, and Ed influenced me a great deal. But, of course, he had come to SMU, and he was, of course, one of my major professors, along with Fred Wendorf. That's the way that people change, I think. Other people influence them and they become interested in different kinds of things. But Ed was very helpful to me, and I wrote my master's thesis at SMU on the San Xavier Missions. You [Curtis] and Ed were instrumental in getting me the job of the excavation.

On the San Xavier Missions, you really got involved in all of the documentation—the Spanish documents and things of that sort.

That's right. But after that, it didn't look like documentation was what I was interested in; however, I still was working on my Ph.D. at SMU on the Caddoan sites. Finally, I got my degree in 1973. In the meantime, I had done some work at San Augustine, at the Mission Delores de los Ais, where Father Margil spent his last days. It was very difficult to find that mission. We had the spot pretty well, but we couldn't find any structural remains.

Meantime then, Parks and Wildlife had offered me a job at Mission Rosario, a site that they had owned for some time but had never done any excavation or testing there. One time, Raiford Strickland, a restoration architect, came out to the site where we were digging. I had smoothed off an area and had some artifacts that I had left in situ to plot. So Raiford came to the site, and he said, "Look! Look at that!" and took out his penknife and popped up the artifact. It was no longer in situ.

FIGURE 3. Kathleen Gilmore excavating a cabin on the Collin McKinney farm near the site of a French military outpost at Roseborough Lake, Bowie County, Texas, 1976.

He, Raiford, had been at Rosario before World War II. Raiford and Roland Beard—he was there before Roland Beard—had, I believe, been in charge of some of the large units who were laborers at the site under Strickland and Beard together or separately, I'm not sure how that actually worked. But Raiford had decided that it would be nice to reconstruct Mission Rosario—I call it *con*struct because you cannot *re*construct it if there's not anything much left of it. He had reconstructed Presidio la Bahia to the Texas Revolutionary Period, not the Spanish period with Katherine O'Connor's help. Of course, it would be a job for him if Rosario were *con*structed.

There were some foundations and things.

Yes, quite a few remains actually: the compound wall and a staircase, some other walls, but I was not at all in favor of doing any kind of construction or reconstruction. I still am not, although I think some valuable information could be obtained from a little more exploration within the compound walls.

At the San Xavier missions, you found some structural evidence, but it wasn't stone construction or anything.

Right. The local word was that a school building in the small town of San Gabriel across the river from the mission area had been built of stones from the missions—there were three missions and a presidio. But we found no evidence of stone at all. The name of the mission where we dug was San Francisco de Horcasitas Mission. The group lumped together were called the San Xavier missions. On top of the hill, and marked in the ground, was a setting trench about 20 cm wide with posthole molds, probably about a cubit—which is about 18 in. from elbow to the wrist, an old measurement that goes back to the Egyptians. These posts were spaced about that or a little less, and they were offset, so that one post and the next post were offset a few, maybe 10 cm, and then another post in line with the first one and so forth. For a while I assumed, presumed, that wattles or branches could be woven around those and then daubed, plastered, on each side or either side or neither, whatever the situation asked for. The trench was traced with some blank spaces to the size of the church noted by Father Dolores, the resident priest. I used a map with Jelks's help and LeRoy Johnson who had decided and measured very carefully how much a league was. They had decided with good background material that a league was 2.63 miles, so I used that in my calculations to try to find these missions.

You found all three missions. And you found artifacts at each site?

Right. San Ildefonso—by the way, Bolton [H. R. Bolton, the historian] had placed these missions and the presidio at certain places on the San Gabriel River, but his location was not actually demonstrated. That was one of the problems with that area—to demonstrate where each of these missions and the presidio had been. A land survey had been made during the early life of the missions by the Spaniards. San Ildefonso was fairly easy because there were a lot of artifacts, and it was on a small hill—not where Bolton had predicted. Then the mission Candelaria, which was near the presidio, was pretty nebulous. But we finally found some artifacts there—Abo for one thing, a majolica type—but we were actually finding the structural remains for Candelaria.

The presidio was on the river. But the Spanish survey didn't say the presidio was on the river. The survey said it was a surveyed-out area, that the presidio was so many *varas*

from Candelaria. I had measured that with a standard measure of 33 in. per *vara* and had come up with a spot on the San Gabriel River that was just that area. But I could not believe that the Spaniards would put up a building or structure on a river that they knew flooded. The survey had noted that there was flood debris that high up.

Later on, we made a few little tests there in that area and, sure enough, there were enough artifacts to be able say that it was the site of the presidio. The measurement the Spaniard had made from Candelaria to where we found the artifacts was almost exactly right. I had to eat my words on that one. But that happens, you know. Then Rosario.

You did excavation work there?

Yes. I left the San Augustine project to Jim Corbin who had accepted a position at Stephen F. Austin University in Nacogdoches, and he was close by.

Oh, had you all found the mission?

No. There were some bare, empty burial pits, and I dug a trench across the road. We had worked on some pretty good documentary material, but still I was limited to one area there at San Augustine and finally got permission to put a trench across the road. It looked like there was more material over there. So, I left it to Jim Corbin. Later, across the road, he did find some structural evidence of the mission. Since then, the local residents have done a wonderful job of putting up a small museum, a research museum, at the site—not on it but at it—with a walking tour of the town. The town of San Augustine has worked very hard for many years to get that to come to fruition.

Then Rosario—excavations had been done there before World War II under WPA auspices with large crews of CCC personnel. Some pictures from that era show huge piles of back dirt. So the first season there, it seemed like the best thing to do was to record what had been done in the past and see what the possibilities were to get more information. We found their trenches very easily because the strata are of different colors, and we could easily tell whether the strata had been overturned or not and where the mixtures were. But we could not find any notes that had been made during the WPA times.

There was only one sheet of notes that Roland Beard had made.

Strickland had said that they had closed the site, the explorations at the site, in three days at the beginning of the war. They had stored the notes in a barn, and a hurricane had come along at some later date and had destroyed the notes. It's hard to know what to believe because I think it's possible copious notes were never made.

There were quite a few pictures. Strickland had some that he gave to me, and I have since had them filed at the Texas Historical Commission. I spent three seasons there and did quite a bit of work, wrote a two-volume report that Parks people tell me they are using to make the site ready for viewing by the public. Texas Parks and Wildlife—or it's now Parks—had several planning meetings. I was involved with some of the last. Of course, I am not a parks specialist, but we all had, most of us, input into what we thought would make an adequate and informative presentation for the public.

On each one of these sites that you've been working on, like San Xavier and Dolores and Rosario, you've been doing the archival work—studying the Spanish documents and all of that. So, you have become very familiar with the Spanish colonial literature.

Well yes, because during the time of my self-education in historical archaeology, it seemed to me that the thing to do was to do the background work, the archival work first. This is a little different approach from prehistoric archaeology, because historical archaeology has records to go on. These records may be flawed, and most of them are, because it's the human condition that flaws these things. The perspective of individuals, of one individual, will have a completely different story of a happening that was viewed by another individual as well.

Those things have to be taken into consideration when you are looking at the archival material. Some of the priests, missionaries, and the whole hierarchy had reasons to get money to help with their pet projects like converting the Karankawa or the Apaches or whatever. So you have to look at what each one said with a little bit of a raised eyebrow, then you take as many documents as you can find about each situation and compare those records. Then you use the facts that have the most correlations—maybe not necessarily as the true facts but the one that are the most likely to be correct.

I got my Ph.D. while I was working on Rosario. I wasn't going to walk across the stage, but my youngest daughter was at home, and Bob wanted me to attend the ceremony. So, I went to Dallas. Every time I come back, I feel like I look terrible—sunburned and wrinkled and hair awry—so I had to go to the beauty shop. I called my hairdresser, but she could not take me. I called another beauty shop in the area. The beauty operator said, "We just can't do a thing; we don't have any room today." I thought, well, heck, I would go ahead and pull a little rank. And I said, "Well, I just have to go today. This is Dr. Gilmore, and I really need to get in there." The operator gasped, "Uhh, well, I'll call you back." She called in a few minutes and, sure enough, she found somebody to take me. If your Ph.D. is no good for anything else, it certainly will get you a hair appointment. I like to tell that story every once in a while.

Anyway, Bob bought a magnum of, let's see, Dom Perignon, French champagne. After we got home, we all had a glass of champagne, and it wasn't very good. I don't know what was the matter with it, but we had this whole celebration situation full of bad champagne. And then I hopped back to the airport and went back to work. But it was all right. It was fun. Now let's see, what came next?

That would have been in the early 1970s, sometime around in there when The Society for Historical Archaeology was organized?

I think it was 1967 or 1966. I had gone to the Central States Archaeological Society; it was in St Louis, Missouri. Several of us were talking archaeology in somebody's room, and I don't remember exactly who all was there—Ed Larrabee and I think maybe Ed Jelks, and I'm not sure who else was there. I'm sure somebody knows, and it's probably in that first journal of The Society for Historical Archaeology.

But anyway, we were sitting around talking about how so many of us were doing historical archaeology. Larrabee was talking about glass goblets. Then Williamsburg, of course, was being reconstructed and there was historical archaeology there. So somebody said, "Well, we need to have an organization to get together." And I said, "Well, let's get it done." And Jelks said, "Well, OK, let's get it done." And Larrabee said, "OK, let's get it done." We were all in full agreement.

After we got back to SMU—I was still in graduate school—Ed got busy and, with Norma Hoffricter's help, wrote to a lot of the people he knew who were doing historical archaeology. I helped a little, but I didn't do as much work as they did. All those archaeologists got together at SMU in one big meeting and formed The Society for Historical Archaeology.

As I remember, there was a big argument among the grammarians about whether it should be "historic" or "historical" archaeology. The word came out as historical. Ever since then, I have realized why it is historical and not historic.

The first meeting was in Dallas, and it's been going great guns ever since. I was the president in 1978. That was the year of the big ice storm in Dallas. We were without electricity for three or four days. We cooked with gas on the fireplace and outside on a gas furnace. But, finally, the sun came out, and ice was still on the trees. That was the day I was to leave for Nashville—I was to be at the meeting as president of the society. The sun was shining on the ice on the trees, a truly magnificent sight. Bob borrowed a four-wheel drive to take me to the airport. We started a couple of hours ahead of time, creeping down the highway.

But I got to Nashville with hair trouble again—I have trouble with beauty shops as anyone can tell by looking at me. I couldn't wash my hair—no hot water and no beauty shop. I had to do something. A friend had a hair dryer, and said she would help me with getting my hair washed and rolled up and looking halfway decent anyway. So, again, a problem with beauty shops.

It was an interesting year as president. We had one project: we were to formulate a definition of historical archaeology and what it meant for the Society of Professional Archeologists. We needed that definition for membership applicants to SOPA, but we needed it for SHA as well. So, I got together a group in Dallas to work on that. There were about six or eight of us, and we formulated a definition that was, for a while, in the bulletin of the society journal,

and we used it for SOPA. Since then, it has been reworked and is now in better condition. We were struggling along trying to do the best we could.

Later on, Rosario then took a while. In the meantime, I had gone to the University of North Texas as an adjunct professor at the Institute of Applied Sciences. Scott Hayes was there as an archaeologist. Later on, Reid Ferrin came—he's still there. I retired from there in 1975. I was 59 when I got my Ph.D.

What was next? You worked on the Fort St. Louis project?

Yes. Well, what I did, in fact, was to analyze the artifacts or, at least, to describe the artifacts that Glen Evans had dug at 41VT4, which is the site of Fort St. Louis and Presidio Loreta la Bahia. The publication was 1974, I believe. But at that time, Bolton had been out there in 1914 and had said there was blue and white pottery on the ground, but he didn't really conclusively give any definition that it was the site of Fort St. Louis.

FIGURE 4. Kathleen Gilmore at the site of La Salle's Fort St. Louis in Texas, Victoria County, 2001.

And there had been a lot of controversy continuing for years as to whether or not that was the site ...

Well, lots of it because, for one thing, they had only Joutél's journal of his experiences at the site, and that was about all we had to go on. But he had said that it was on the Cow River, and, of course, *la vaca* in Spanish is "the cow." But, of course, that's Spanish, and many people thought it was on the Lavaca River.

Then you, Curtis, as the executive director of the Historical Commission, wanted me to decide, as best I could, whether this actually was the site of Fort St. Louis. Analyzing the ceramics, it looked like there was one set of earthenware of green glaze, which was manufactured in France. So, the report I wrote was entitled, "The Probable Site of La Salle's Fort St. Louis in Texas."

Then you called me some time later, about 1986, and said that the report was OK, and that Father Habig, archivist, priest, had said that, of course, it was not the *probable* site, it *was* the site. So I thought, well, good night, maybe I better be more positive about that. I was pretty green when I wrote that report, was nervous about making very definite statements. So, I went back and got a piece of the green-glazed ceramics—earthenware—and sent it to Canada where detailed studies of French ceramics had been made. Gerard Gussat wrote back, sent the sherd back, and said that it definitely was of French origin from the Santonge area near La Rochelle. Then I wrote another article, a brief account of the historical background, published in the *Bulletin of the Texas Archeological Society*, saying I considered that Site 41VT4 was without a doubt the site of Fort St. Louis and Presidio La Bahia. I had no reason to doubt it at all.

You had the French material from the right period, and you had all the Spanish material from the right period too. From the documents, you knew that both of those had been on the same site.

That's right. And that was one demonstrated factor, too, that here we had two sites, one on top of the other. We knew from historical material that the Spaniards loved to show—we call it the law of dominance—that they had conquered the French or were going to or wanted to or whatever.

They had built the presidio on top of the French settlement. We knew that. They did that in Mexico where the Spaniards built a church on top of the Aztec's buildings in Mexico City, and they did it in many, many places. Then, after that, well, I had tried to get excavation testing at the site, but the landowners were not conducive to it at all because the traffic would have to go right through their ranch. But, also, the ranch owner had agreed to protect it. However, he really didn't do it, and because the site is right on the river, on the Garcitas Creek, people could come up in a boat and, using metal detectors, probably got many, many of the artifacts off the site.

Later on, in 1996, La Salle's ship, the *Belle*, was discovered on Matagorda Peninsula. I had suggested that it was about in the place where they found it, and, of course, one of the documents had very clearly said where it was. And then the same year, just after we had done most of the excavation of the *Belle*, we found the cannon. Metal detectors were rampant on the site, and one of the scavengers apparently had discovered a cannon and had sense enough to call the Historical Commission. You and some others went to the site, with permission of course, and dug up the eight cannon that had been buried by the Spaniards when they had discovered the French settlement site.

Thank goodness, Evans had gotten a big collection from the site back in 1950 before a lot of the metal detecting was done.

Right. And that is evident, too, in the report I published that described those artifacts. The sherds were larger and there were many more metal artifacts. I was thinking about that later, and I thought, "Oh my gosh, I said where the site was in that report, and I might have been instrumental in promoting some of those metal-detector people."

I don't think so.

Well, OK, it's too late now anyway. So that's the way it goes. But we should be careful about that. I did a project at English Turn south of New Orleans. After La Salle's settlement attempt aborted, Louis XIV didn't want to follow up on La Salle's plan. But around 1700, however, Lemoyn Iberville and his brother Bienville were sent to establish a colony on the Gulf coast of

Texas. They established Mobile. Along with them were the two Talon boys and the priest, Le Clercq who had witnessed La Salle's murder [The three had been residents at Fort St. Louis in Texas].

Bienville was sent over to the Mississippi River, and he was sailing up the Mississippi when a British boat came up. They were at a place called now English Turn. It was named that because Bienville said, "Turn back, English." And they turned back without a word. Later on, New Orleans was established a little bit upstream.

There's a bend in the Mississippi River where the wind changes, and as long as sailboats were being used, they had to stop at this particular place and wait for a favorable wind to take them on upriver. So, the French had built a fort at this turn and one across from it because that's where the ships had to pause. Well, the Corps of Engineers were getting ready to revet an area there at the turn because, of course, that's where the river erodes it pretty badly. They were trying to keep it from eroding so much. They wanted to see if there were any remains that needed to be preserved at the French fort. Also, there was a later fort there from about 1812.

We did a lot of documentary work on it first and considered that we had enough documentary work—what it looked like, where it was—and excavations started. However, the river refused to go down for us; we were flooded most of the time and had lots of water to contend with. We did a fair amount of excavation and found some brick remains, but it turned out that those were the remains of the 1812 fort. And we did not find actual remains of the French fort, although we did quite a bit of documentary work on it and even on the area around—a very interesting area as far as the plantations and early life in the Mississippi River Valley, with the sugar cane plantations, indigo, and actually the plain old plantation life.

Then later on, the Corps called me and asked about what I thought about revetting the site. Having had Bob for a husband who was continually saying, "Don't forget the living people," I decided that, not finding the remains of the fort and very little of the 1812 fort, it could be revetted. I may have made some people provoked by that, but yet I couldn't see that enough remains were there to preserve.

It may be that the French fort had eroded into the river.

It's entirely possible because the one across the river apparently had eroded into the river. And the flood plain was so wide that you could tell it meandered all over this wide flood plain. With the traffic on the river like it is, I think they almost had to revet it. So, I did tell them that. But it was an interesting time with, well, a little bit of a different culture there in Plaquemine Parish, Louisiana, that was a "one-man show" until not long ago.

Did you do a lot more documentary research on that?

Yes, in a publication for the Corps. And it's an interesting situation down there.

You also did some more work at the presidio at San Sabá, didn't you?

Oh well, very little. That was the very first report I ever wrote, for an archaeological report. We were looking for the mission that had been burned by the Indians. A group of Indians composed of Caddo, Wichita, and other tribes. This was the one time that a number of tribes got together and were able to beat the Spaniards.

You were unsuccessful in actually finding the mission at that time, but your conceptual model put it there, didn't it?

Right. Well, I was convinced, though—maybe I get convinced too easily—that it was pretty much in that area where it was found. It was reasonable that it was. But there was no evidence on the ground anywhere, and it was only after the ground, the area, was cleared and the rains washed the material up there. All the infrared, metal detector things did not work on that site. There were hardly any artifacts, and, as far as we know, it hadn't really been collected from. We have no evidence anyway or no artifacts around. Of course, it's possible that we just don't know about that.

That was a fairly short-term establishment anyway.

Nine months. Although it would have been nice to have a little sealed context from that. Then in 1995 I was honored by being presented with the J. C. Harrington Award by The Society for Historical Archaeology for contributions

FIGURE 5. Kathleen Gilmore, Jim Bruseth, and Kay Hindes at La Salle's Fort St. Louis in Texas, Victoria County, 2001.

to historical archaeology. I felt like I didn't deserve it because I wasn't sure what kind of contributions I had really made. But I was very, very honored in receiving that award.

It was very well deserved—all your work and contributions. Now let's talk a little bit about some of the other people in The Society for Historical Archaeology, like James Deetz or some other people that you may have known through the years and been associated with.

Well, Deetz, who died fairly recently, was a very interesting character. He said one time he never paid income tax, and I should have gotten back with him and asked him how he got away with that because I'd like to not pay it either. Deetz became president of the society, I believe about the third president, when the current president [Vincent Foley] had to resign. Deetz had a hard time showing up at committee meetings.

He was a law unto himself. When he was asked to do comments on a symposium or be a commentator, he would always agree to do it. But you'd go to the symposium, and Deetz would comment on what had happened, but, unfortunately, his comments had nothing to do with the symposium. So it was really kind of funny when somebody would say, "Oh, I'm going to go hear what Deetz has to say about this symposium." And I'd say, "Well, it won't do you any good. He won't say anything about it."

He was one of the people who was really dedicated to historic type archaeology.

He certainly was very dedicated and did some wonderful work. He worked so long there at Plymouth and also with the missions in California. I don't know what he was doing in the latter part of his life. But he made lots of contributions. His dissertation was about the change on the Plains from a matrilineal to a patrilineal society when the horse began to be a major part of the Plains culture. He had a very good thesis there and demonstrated it pretty well—a very interesting paper.

Who were some other people who served as president? Ed Jelks? He had done work at Jamestown.

Yes, under John Cotter. Now, Cotter might have been at that first meeting; I'm not sure, but I'll bet he was. Anyway, I believe Cotter was the first president maybe. He was a very dedicated historical archaeologist as well, did the work at Jamestown. J. C. Harrington was a very personable man. I only met him a couple of times. They called him Pinky. He was red-headed and a high-energy type person.

Actually, I was at that meeting, that first meeting at SMU because of my association with Ed Jelks. You know, I had been working with Ed for quite a few years at that time, and he invited me to come up for that, but I don't have a lot of recollection of that meeting. But Ed was certainly enthusiastic about forming, I know, The Society for Historical Archaeology. Did Ed ever serve as president?

Yes, he did. And he also was awarded the Harrington Medal. He was about, maybe third, fourth, somewhere president in there. I was the first female president, also the first female to get the Harrington award.

Bernard Fontana has been one of the people that has worked on historic sites in the Southwest. Was he in the society? Do you remember him?

Yes, he was. "Bunny" was an early president, among the first six, I think. He's not a groupie, really; he very seldom attended the meetings. He was a Harrington awardee as well, and he made lots of contributions to historical archaeology. He's interested in the missions near San Xavier del Bac in Arizona. And the Southwest Missions Research Center—he does lots of documentary work for it and also book reviews for the Gran Qivira Conference. Actually, he organized the Gran Qivira Conference that I go to irregularly.

I know Art Woodward did a lot of work on the trade goods that the historic period. Was he ever associated with the society?

I think that he was not, as I remember. And he died not too long after that, I think. But he had several publications. He was at the Amon Carter Museum in Fort Worth for a while, doing research there, and he had a few little classes, but I didn't attend any. He finally moved down to southern Arizona where he died.

John Goggin? I don't know when Goggin died. But he was real active studying Spanish pottery and everything

I never knew Goggin, but he was a pioneer. Of course, the Listers also did a lot of study, Florence Lister especially. She started it while Bob Lister was still working with prehistoric archaeology. But he got involved with the majolica and other ceramics of the period. They did work on the subway excavations in Mexico City. And that's a big publication. Florence is still writing and publishing. Bob was doing tours for Crow Canyon Research Center in New Mexico, northern New Mexico, not too far from Mesa Verde. Bob and Florence had bought a place at Mancos Park near Fort Bliss. He was leading a trip there for Crow Canyon, and he raised up his hand and died.

Florence wrote me a letter—and I imagine that she wrote this to many people—saying Bob died a poetically appropriate death doing the things that he wanted to do. I thought that was very nice. They were very lovely people.

Bob and I were in Bristol [England] for a ceramics conference some years ago, which the Listers attended along with other people from the United States. We used to visit some of the cathedrals. Florence, having been an art history major, knew about the historical architecture—the Norman base and those sorts of things. We bought a bottle of wine, some cheese, and sat by the Westminster Abbey on a bench. A very nice time.

You've also been to France, haven't you, to some of the pottery-making areas?

Yes. I went with Jim Bruseth. We visited the Santonge area, the Chapelle des Pots, where the green-glaze material was made, and it is distinctive. Some of the potters are still there. The clay is light colored with iron oxides in it—hematite, limonite, and magnetite—so the clay, then, bakes into a very distinctive body of the ceramics. We visited Rouen, where La Salle was from and also Henri Joutél. The museum there has many, many vessels of faience because Rouen was one of *the* places where faience was made, and the museum collected many fine examples of it. We saw La Salle's home there or the site of the home; it's gone. It was very exciting. Then we went to La Rochelle and went from there to the Santonge area where we saw the two pillars on the bay at La Rochelle that La Salle sailed to—again a very exciting sight—almost as exciting as 41VT4 where La Salle had tread.

Did you all collect any pottery samples or anything from any of those pottery areas to compare with the stuff you were getting on the site?

Yes, we did from the Santonge area. And what we will do is use some of those for neutron activation as well as thin sectioning, so we can compare even the ones that Evans excavated as well as those that we've excavated. That ought to make a really good comparative study.

By the way, Mr. Marle, one of La Salle's colonists who was on his way back to France and drowned in the Red River, had three musket balls in his chest. I think that would make a very good comparative study for your study of the other musket balls. It would be interesting to find out whether he might have been shot in France or at the site or before they got to the site. Or really, whether you could determine anything from it.

Were they all the same size? Do you remember?

No. I never did see them. A. T. Jackson dug them up in 1933. They should be at TARL [Texas Archaeological Research Laboratory]. He was buried in a small mound by the chief's house. From the document, it is very obvious where he was buried. So, when Terán was on the Red River in 1691, he had a map drawn of the area and on that map is labeled "The chief's house," and there is a small mound behind it with a cross on it, standing up.

Jackson found one adult in the small mound by the chief's house and about six children. But all these years, it was always thought that the mound was an Indian burial. We analyzed the documents and the burial. Goldstein and Bill Maples had done the measurements, and there were very good photographs of a skull, but we couldn't find the skull anywhere. Gil King, the forensic anthropologist, determined that the probability was very good that it was a European.

We had most of the postcranial skeleton, not all of it. But King was able to use those measurements to do some statistical analysis. Some people don't agree with the results and say that we were a little bit too quick to judge. But all the evidence comes together—the documentary evidence, the forensic analysis. Well, of course, I could make a definite statement, which I probably shouldn't do, but I will—it was Mr. Marle.

And I wrote some people—he was from La Briei, which now is a suburb of Paris. Patty Lemay had a phone book from Paris with all the Marles. I wrote to all the Marles; there were twelve, and got some good answers back. One man whose family, probably, the drowned man belonged to intimated Mr. Marle's name must have been Jean Pierre. It was a very common name in that family, a common name in France. If we do find out that we can do some DNA, it would be interesting to have Marle done this way.

And Joutél, the journalist of the expedition, said that Marle was one of the prime men of his party. Now, a person can be shot in the chest without hitting an organ, a vital organ, and live for quite some time. It's been documented. Maybe, but I doubt very seriously if he could have lived more than a year with those musket balls in his chest. He probably died in 1687.

He also had a broken arm. I suspect most of that happened on the expedition, either when they were rescuing material from the *l'Aimable* or some other reason. But the journalist said very little about, well practically nothing about, any quarrels or any contentious activity at the site, which is interesting because you know that they must have been feuding with each other.

What is the number of that site where he was found?

Bowie County—it's the Kaddohadacho—right there at the Ely Moore site. And it's definitely shown on Teran's map.

I'm going to make a search for those three musket balls. I'll let you know if I can find them.

Oh, do, because I think that would be really interesting to know where they came from.

It might. The musket balls there are primarily of three sizes. It would be interesting to see if one of those—by far the greatest volume of musket balls is of one size—are that size, you know. That would be circumstantial evidence.

Joutél had pistols with him, Joutél the diarist, and, I believe, a bigger gun as well, a flintlock maybe, along with other things, so there were pistols at the site.

You're working on the ceramics from the Belle?

That's right. I had hoped that perhaps the material that we were working with at the *Belle* might indicate what was loaded on a ship for a settlement or a long cruise, but I decided after looking at them that this was not the case with the *Belle*—that it had been reloaded, unloaded, and reloaded with La Salle's goods for a trip around the coast when it was wrecked. Of course, it didn't make a trip around the coast, and the sailors who left the ship took off most of La Salle's belongings. When they found a boat, I guess an Indian canoe, stranded on the shore, they took most of that back to the site. And also the Spaniards who discovered the wreckage of the *Belle* took some of—must have taken some of the—material. I can't see anybody getting on a wrecked ship and not salvaging some of the material. So, I had to discard that idea, but yet it does indicate some of the things that were needed.

Probably the bulk of some of their material went down with the l'Aimable, *don't you imagine? So, they had a smaller amount of stuff on the* Belle. *And it wasn't representative necessarily of all the things they brought.*

Right, not at all. However, the few stoneware jars on the *Belle* and the very little stoneware in the collection that Evans made from the site in 1950, and very little stoneware from the site seems to indicate a lot of it wasn't being used. Greg Waselkov had found that most of the stoneware at that date was used on ships and very little for utilitarian use on shore, which is

interesting. Very little faience was on the *Belle*. Most were small jars, but the finish was a beautiful finish on all of them, not crackled at all. No decorated ceramics at all, either earthenware or faience, which is somewhat curious. To interpret that is speculative because we don't know whether the decorated material was too costly for La Salle to have on his expedition or whether it was not being made. Now I suspect that some of the decorated earthenwares were not being made at that particular time, pre-1685 when the vessels were loaded. Because in Canada and at Louisbourg (the Fortress of Louisbourg where Kenneth Barton has analyzed the earthenwares), most of the coarse earthenwares were decorated. Barton could even categorize them by their decorations, whereas we have no decoration at all. I'm not sure because I haven't seen everything from the site that has been excavated thus far, but I don't believe there is any decorated earthenware. That's interesting.

Have you been to some of the sites in Canada?

Well, not many. No, I went to a meeting, a SHA early meeting in Ottawa and drove to Quebec City in a blizzard. I stopped at a motel in Montreal right on the highway where lots of people were stranded, and it was a kind of a fun time because the motel owner came around and gave everybody free drinks, and everybody had a very fine time. So I have not been.

What about Mexico where they make the majolica, have you ever visited any of the sites?

Well, I've been to Puebla. That's a very interesting town, of course, because that was where the guilds came from Spain and settled in. Most of the churches and missions there and in the surrounding area are tiled on the outside—the towers are tiled, and some of the entire buildings are tiled. And probably the paintings on the outsides of the buildings are tiled like at San José [18th-century-mission in Texas] and even at Mission Rosario [Texas]. There were murals in the chapel in the church and also diamond [design] paintings on the tower's staircase, which was probably the bell tower. But these murals represent tiles that probably are copying Puebla. As a matter of fact, the murals that we did find at Rosario are called, according to one of the architects, the Puebla urn style. The mural has an urn in a space with columns of three colors and lunates, which alternates with another space of the same design. So, that's known as the Puebla urn. And, of course, they used lots of it in the interior. But the colonial potteries there in Puebla are hard to find, according to the Listers who have done work there too.

It's just amazing how much of that majolica was brought up to Texas. It would have had to be of some importance to be brought across the rivers and such. There must be thousands of broken pieces just from Presidio la Bahia, which was not occupied very long.

Right. And they brought it by carts, I think, because at the mission Refugio, the last mission established in Texas, there's a document, a letter from one of the priests or missionaries, talking about how things were not going right. And he said the mail hadn't come, and the cart with clay for the potter had not come. It looked as if they were shipping all kinds of things from Mexico. That one quote there gives us a little indication of the bias in the pottery because although that's a volcanic material—it contains volcanic material at Puebla—the material they were getting, the local clay, would not contain volcanic material. But if they were getting it from Mexico, it would. So, you've got a little bit of a problem there with trying to decide the clay sources.

You're going to also do an entire excavation analysis of thin sections of some of the Spanish pottery from Fort St. Louis, aren't you?

Yes. We haven't found somebody to do it yet, but we have it all set up, ready to go.

And the French as well as the Spanish, for comparative purposes.

What about The Society for Historical Archaeology? Do you foresee it continuing to gain in strength and membership?

Well, I do, certainly, because as time goes on, historical sites continue "to be made." However, there's a lot of work being done in 19th century archaeology. Of course, a lot of things have been documented that late, and yet usually more things can be found out from the ground. But I don't know whether 20th century archaeology will ever be as popular, say, as 16th, 17th, and 18th century, where we don't know as much. Also, I expect that some of the approaches may change through time of how to do 20th century archaeology, or late-19th century.

There's a difference, I've found, between the focus of prehistoric archaeologists and historical archaeologists. I think it's the difference between induction and deduction. Prehistoric archeologists will excavate the material, then interpret it. Usually historical archaeologists do the documentation and then interpret their excavations from the documentary material, which is really no big deal, but, yet, it is a difference in approach.

Do you continue to go to The Society for Historical Archaeology meetings?

Well, yes. I didn't go last year, but it's going to be in Mobile this coming year, and they're having a sort of a get-together to talk about missions—a kind of an open meeting, and that should be interesting. I may join that group.

I think you should. You're the grande dame of Texas missions.

[Laughter.] Well, thank you.

Darby C. Stapp

An Interview with Roderick Sprague

Roderick Sprague and Darby Stapp

Introduction

Roderick (Rick) Sprague is one of the founding members of The Society for Historical Archaeology, a two-term president of the SHA, and the only member to receive both the J. C. Harrington Medal for lifetime contributions to the field of historical archaeology and the Carol V. V. Ruppé Distinguished Service Award in recognition of volunteer service to the SHA.

Sprague is one of the pioneers of historical archaeology in the Northwest and is well known for his work on burials and historic grave goods, beads, buttons, the fur trade, industrial archaeology, and the typology and classification of both artifacts and sites. He was instrumental in supporting the passage of the Native American Graves Protection and Repatriation Act (NAGPRA) while president of the SHA. His book *Burial Terminology: A Guide for Researchers* (2005) is a cornerstone for work in mortuary archaeology. Now retired and professor emeritus at the University of Idaho, Sprague trained successive generations in historical archaeology methods and materials during his more than 30-year tenure at Idaho, including a number of the field's leading scholars. For further information on his career and contributions, see "J. C. Harrington Award 2000: Roderick Sprague" (Karlis Karklins 2000).

135

This interview with Sprague was conducted by Darby C. Stapp, a former student of Sprague's at Idaho, as a product of the SHA History Committee, chaired by Richard Veit. The History Committee is interviewing and recording the personal reflections of influential members of the society on the origins, history, and operations of historical archaeology and the SHA. As the SHA moves toward its 50th anniversary, *Historical Archaeology* looks forward to publishing more of these interviews and providing the opportunity these personal perspectives offer SHA members to reflect on how we have gotten to where we are as well as what might lie ahead.

References

KARLIS KARKLINS
    2000 J. C. Harrington Award 2000: Roderick Sprague. *Historical Archaeology* 34(4):1–6.

SPRAGUE, RODERICK
    2005 *Burial Terminology: A Guide for Researchers.* AltaMira Press, Lanham, MD.

J. W. JOSEPH, EDITOR
HISTORICAL ARCHAEOLOGY

Sprague Interview: 12 October 2006

This is Darby Stapp, and I am here with Roderick Sprague in Moscow, Idaho, as part of the SHA's oral history effort. It is 12 October 2006. My first question for you, Rick, is when did you first start to think about historical archaeology as something that you wanted to do?

SPRAGUE: It is difficult to pin down a specific time, but certainly the summer of 1967, I believe, when I was digging burials on Ford Island (Washington) was one of the important events. There was a ranch on the island that was going to be flooded, so everything on the ranch that was still left was going to be on the bottom of the reservoir. In my spare time, which I had a lot of, I started taking apart a wagon and saving smaller parts, analyzing what the parts looked like, trying to get a better idea of what you would find if you were to find the remains of a wagon. I began to realize that there was a need for this, and, incidentally, one of my major interests has been artifacts and their location in contrast to theory, which we

can talk about later. I also began to realize that prehistory was a limited resource and watching it going under water, be bulldozed by the Corps of Engineers and other destructive activities, I began to realize that we needed to start looking at some of the more-recent material. By using that original material, I gave an invited paper on post-1800 American Indian sites at the zero or organizational meeting at Rice University. I developed an interest in talking with other people; I had become interested in historical archaeology talking to Bunny Fontana when we were both at the University of Arizona. He was working on Johnny Ward's ranch, and I stopped by every day and looked at things he was trying to identify and occasionally would be able to identify them, having lived for much of my life on a farm. So there was a series of events that came together, and I think it was after that zero meeting that I realized we do need an historical society, we do need our own society, we do need to have our own identity and that I was observing colleagues who had some bitterness about the way in which the Society for American Archaeology treated what they called "tin can archaeology." It was a matter of self-awareness and pride in what we were doing. Fortunately, this attitude has changed for the better through time.

Tell me about historical archaeology at Arizona at that time.

SPRAGUE: There were a few of us who in 1964 to 1967 had an interest in historical archaeology, people like Jim Ayres and Bunny Fontana, who talked to each other like regular students and colleagues do. Bunny was on the faculty by then. We would use him, the staff of the museum, and interested archaeologists, and we became interested in historical archaeology amongst ourselves as a group. About that time, Art Woodward showed up in Patagonia, Arizona, south of Tucson. We talked to Art when he was up at the Arizona Historical Society, helping them set up the displays, things like that, and he was convinced, probably mostly by Bunny, to teach a course in historical archaeology. It had about 10 people in it. Bunny wasn't registered, but he certainly came in for many of the lectures. Jim Ayres and I were probably the two most excited about having a course in historical archaeology. It was a very interesting and unique course. It was certainly something that we all needed and enjoyed, and Arthur Woodward was very generous and was always willing to open up his library for student research.

What was Art Woodward's background and interests?

SPRAGUE: He had worked on the East Coast, but much of his career he was the curator of the Los Angeles County Museum. He often played the part of the mountain man and specialized in mountain man artifacts, publishing on such objects as Green River knives. He analyzed beads for my master's thesis while I was still at Washington State University. His dating of beads in California strongly influenced my dating in the Northwest.

He wrote for fur-trade artifact publications.

SPRAGUE: Yes.

Was this the first course in historical archaeology in North America?

SPRAGUE: I don't know. I don't know whether John Cotter did one earlier or not. I don't think anyone has ever pursued that. I've heard both called the earliest, so it's hard to tell.

What made you go to the University of Arizona?

SPRAGUE: Oh that was a decision that came when I was applying to several schools, and I wanted to stay in the West. I applied to Berkeley, Arizona, and New Mexico. Berkeley gave me a scholarship; Arizona gave me a teaching assistantship; and New Mexico rejected me with a postcard. I had visited the University of Arizona when I was in the Army at Fort Bliss in El Paso, Texas. I had an opportunity to see it and to know what it was. I liked the campus and Emil Haury was friendly.

Was there any historical archaeology at Washington State College?

SPRAGUE: No.

Did you experience any of the National Parks Service historical archaeology in the Northwest during those early years?

SPRAGUE: No, I never observed any of the work that Louis Caywood did, except after the fact.

Didn't you start in the early 1950s?

SPRAGUE: Right. One of the other factors in my interest in historical archaeology was my master's thesis. A series of graves was removed by a class under Richard Daugherty at Washington State. It was within the town of Asotin, Washington, and was historic in date. It had a lot of glass beads, brass buttons, and decorative objects like that. I ended up, after I came back from the Army, in writing that up as a master's thesis at Washington State. It was definitely historic and gave me an interest in historical archaeology. Doug Osborne had recently published his *Bureau of American Ethnology, Bulletin* 166, which served as a model, mostly positive, for analyzing the historic trade goods.

Interesting.

SPRAGUE: The McNary Dam excavation and his beads and historic artifacts had been analyzed by Art Woodward, so I got Art Woodward's address and sent him the beads to be analyzed—a string of which he removed (unknown to me) and showed up in his class.

Who were some of the people that influenced you as you developed into an historical archaeologist?

SPRAGUE: It wasn't as a matter of faculty-student as much as peers, fellow graduate students at Arizona. Whatever work was done in Washington State, there was no one interested in historical archaeology. Allan H. Smith was interested in ethnographic material and cultural, which certainly helped. At Arizona, again there was no one on the faculty who was interested in it. Bunny Fontana, as I said, was on the staff of the museum and normally didn't teach. There were really no professionals at the time who were really interested in historical archaeology in the West.

At one point in my career, the National Park Service arrived to review the State Historic Preservation Office (SHPO) program in Idaho. One of the official complaints was that I had never been a student on an historical archaeological field school and that I never had any supervised experience digging on an historical site. This was a serious and formal complaint by an NPS employee who had previously worked for me. Of course our response was that this was a ridiculous statement to make because I was teaching the course yearly, had taught the first field school of historical archaeology in the Northwest, and thus how could I have taken the course? I found this a ridiculous, turn of events.

So where did you go from Arizona?

SPRAGUE: I returned to Washington State to work in the laboratory as their sole archaeologist.

Washington State College?

SPRAGUE: By then it was Washington State University … .

Ok. How did the University of Idaho job come about?

SPRAGUE: Alfred W. Bowers had been here for a number of years, and when he retired, they tried to replace him with bits and pieces. Finally the dean of the College of Letters and Science realized they were going to have to replace Bowers with a full-time position. One who was interviewing for the position was Deward E. Walker, Jr., who convinced the dean that he needed two people, and so I became the other one. So Deward Walker and I both left Washington State University because we saw no future in our positions there and came over to Idaho only ten miles away. The dean who hired us had lived most of his life on the Nez Perce Reservation and was very much in sympathy with anthropology.

Since you mentioned the word "dean," I did have a question regarding deans in general. Is it the job that makes deans the way they are or do they arrive that way?

SPRAGUE: In my experience, they arrive that way. The dean that hired us was probably the second-best one I had worked under at Idaho. The best I ever worked under was a chemist who understood anthropology as a science. The two other, in humanities, had absolutely no idea what anthropology was all about and resented our research money.

Do you ascribe to any particular theoretical orientation in historical archaeology? How would you describe your theoretical orientation?

SPRAGUE: My feeling on theory in historical archaeology is that there's not a large enough body of data to be yet worrying about theory. Theory seems to be something that comes and goes; it's cyclical; you have one theory around and then you have some new wonderful theory that appears. Let's figure out first how we're excavating sites, what we're digging up, and what it dates to and then start worrying about the theory. We don't have solid terminology for the materials we recover. We don't always present them in a way they can be compared. I have strong feelings on this—that theory is premature in historical archaeology, and we're wasting paper talking about theory. It is doing us no good and is confusing the younger students.

Wow.

SPRAGUE: That will never be a popular view.

To me the various orientations simply provide ways to discuss what you found. It seems to me they're all kind of relevant; they're all kind of useful at some level to describe what you found. I don't know why they have to be competing. What direction would you say historical archaeology needs to go?

SPRAGUE: It's obvious that we need to work more on terminology, classification, maybe typology in some areas.

You are arguing the "building block" scenario.

SPRAGUE: Yes. To figure out where we are and what we're doing with what, start worrying about what came out of the ground today, not what kind of capitalism you are talking about, U.S., English, German, French, Japanese. I forgot who it was who said it, but I just feel there is a lot of wasted effort spent upon changing theory that doesn't do any good anyway.

As you look back at the history of historical archaeology in America, can you talk about how you've seen it develop? Do you feel that it is a long continuum or can you kind of put it into stages?

SPRAGUE: I think that it has been a fairly even flow of development. I think it's maturing, but it's a long way from being totally mature. I think The Society for Historical Archaeology is the most representative of the group and maturity of the field. The journal, under Ronn Michael, has become a very, very scholarly journal and has grown in content, grown in amplitude, and it's become an important journal in archaeology. It is not recognized enough I think by the prehistorians.

What was your involvement in the SHA, and what do you think of the development of the society? What has your role been over the years?

SPRAGUE: Well I became very involved when I was elected secretary-treasurer. It was one job in those days, and it was a fairly primitive system. We used an Addressograph for sending out the journals and the newsletter, which I had to get printed. We didn't have contracts; we just took them to the local printer and said, "here, give us the lowest rate you can," and then had to take them to the post office. Get the accounts, answer the complaints, and all of that was volunteer labor.

Would that have been in the late 1960s?

SPRAGUE: That was right after it started, starting with Volume 2. Then I served on the Editorial Board for a number of years, which was not a lot of work, but then I became reviews editor, which I held for some terrible number of years, like 20 years. That was a job that had to be developed into a system and an organization created, so that we were getting good reviews

from people who were dependable. I think that I had only one really angry, oh well, two, really angry authors who felt they were done dirt by their reviewer. In one case, it was simply the reviewer's reactions to something that was portraying a racial group, and she was a bit sensitive. The other one was an unfortunate situation that came down to a matter of personalities. That was one issue that should have never happened, and if I would have known what had happened earlier, I would have never allowed that person to do the review.

You mean they had a conflicting relationship that you were unaware of when you set up the review?

SPRAGUE: Yes, I was not aware of the conflict.

We're talking about authors getting upset about the reviews that were published in the journals.

SPRAGUE: Yes

Only two cases that you heard about?

SPRAGUE: Only two cases. One of the interesting things about being the reviews editor was at one point the women's conference objected to the fact that there weren't enough women reviewing books, and I showed very, very clearly two things: number one was that I was getting more women—a higher percentage of women—reviewing books than the previous book reviews editor who was a women and, secondly, that I was getting a higher percentage of women reviewing the books than there were women in the society. Once I gave them those statistics, I heard nothing, not even a thank you. Book reviews editor is a thankless job, so I was happy to finally leave it.

Book reviews are my favorite part of journals.

SPRAGUE: I think the policy of the SHA to not publish them, to only have them on the Web, is a very serious, serious error.

I wondered what happened to the reviews in the journal. What additional jobs did you hold?

SPRAGUE: I was dumb enough to run for president twice. The first time made sense. It was pretty much my turn. I tried to do a good job. The next time, some of the membership felt the two nominated candidates weren't experienced enough, and they asked me run as a write-in. Unfortunately, I won.

Was your name even on the ballot of the running? I don't remember.

SPRAGUE: It was. It was kind of a situation that you have enough people suggest that you be nominated, and you get nominated along with those from the Nominations Committee.

So there were actually three people running?

SPRAGUE: Yeah there were three people running, and I was told I got over 50%.

So did it do away with the Nominations Committee? The Nominations Committee comes up with the candidates and somebody or some group didn't feel like they were qualified.

SPRAGUE: That is essentially it.

Do you think it would be appropriate to talk about the names of those reviewers, I mean of the author and the reviewer of that incident that you were just discussing?

SPRAGUE: No, I don't. The only other thing that I have really enjoyed about the society is that I have been recognized. I got the Harrington award then I got the Ruppé award. So far, I am the only person dumb enough to do enough volunteer work to get both of them. Being president twice and getting both of those awards shows you that I don't have the ability to say "no" ... I appreciate it very much that the society has recognized my efforts.

Feels good?

SPRAGUE: Yeah.

Nice to be recognized for your efforts. What role are you playing today in the society?

SPRAGUE: Virtually nothing. I am still on the History Committee. [Since this interview I have also resigned as parliamentarian and from the Editorial Advisory Committee.]

Can you talk about some other key people in the society that have played an instrumental role in building the society over the years?

SPRAGUE: Oh that's a serious question.

Ok we're not going to work on that question, because if you don't mention everybody and somebody reads it that wasn't mentioned, they want to know why they weren't mentioned.

SPRAGUE: Yeah.

That's not what it's about. Did you attend the January 1967 formation meeting in Dallas, Texas?

SPRAGUE: Yes, I did. I gave a paper there.

Oh the zero meeting. I didn't understand what that term was. I meant to ask you. That was the first?

SPRAGUE: That was the organizational meeting.

Organizational meeting?

SPRAGUE: Yup.

You guys call it the zero meeting?

SPRAGUE: Yeah. I think Bill Adams started that.

Who was there? What was the atmosphere and what did you think about the meeting? What do you remember about that meeting?

SPRAGUE: My memory of that meeting was that there was a great deal of enthusiasm, and it was very positive. The papers were quite varied and showed the range of what the society could do. It showed the range of time periods, approaches, theoretical approaches, and it was mostly attended by those who had a desire to do something with this concept of historical archaeology. Most of those who were involved in the organization of the society continued to work in the society. There were few who had conflicts with the meeting time. One, originally from the Northwest, was Edward Larrabee, who just recently died. He was very interested in historical archaeology and had done some in the Northwest and then went to teach at a school where registration was the same time as the society meeting, year after year, so that he and his wife, Susan Kardas, simply didn't become involved in the society meetings.

How many people were there?

SPRAGUE: I don't know.

How many sessions? Were they concurrent sessions?

SPRAGUE: No, there were very few papers actually, in terms of the meeting.

Who made the effort to organize and send up announcements and papers? Who organized it?

SPRAGUE: You really have to look at the first issue of *Historical Archaeology* to get the whole story and also the interview of Ed Jelks … .

Ok. Let's talk about the processual archaeology movement of the 1960–1970s and the postprocessual archaeology movement of the 1980–1990s. One thing that I like about postprocessualism is the idea that the bias of the researcher kind of dictates how they go about doing things. I like it when people talk about who they are, what they're interested in, how they view what they are doing. I think that is pretty useful. The idea that there is no purely objective approach seems reasonable.

SPRAGUE: I would certainly say that it was a move forward. You're dealing with people, and people have their own biases, their interests, their own reactions to what they find. You have to consider who did it; it's nonsense to think people can think like a computer, simply record the material.

Can you point to some major accomplishments that historical archaeology has made to society?

SPRAGUE: Well I think its major contribution thus far has been the fact that it has shown that there is, indeed, a component in human culture that has to be dug out of the ground—that history is written by the winners. Also, history has always been interested in the big man theory. Historical archaeology seems to concentrate more on the culture of the individual person.

So you are saying that you can have the best-documented site, maybe even tons of oral history, and you would still argue that material culture in the ground is going to inform you a little bit more about what went on there?

SPRAGUE: Maybe even a great deal more.

Maybe even a great deal more. How important has the SHA been to the rise and success of historical archaeology as a discipline?

SPRAGUE: I don't think there would be any discipline of historical archaeology without the society.

How do you think the society has evolved and changed over the last three decades?

SPRAGUE: The thing I see changing the most is the attitude of "what the society can do for me" and, to paraphrase Kennedy, more of an attitude of "what can the society do for me, rather then what can I do for the society." The major problem with The Society for Historical Archaeology at the moment is that nobody seems to have any fiscal responsibility. They're willing to take all the activities and work, like organize meetings, and give it to the management people who are doing everything for money. It's to their advantage to have the cost go up, and I've seen no concern about this from the people who we're electing. In the election personal comments, printed in the *Newsletter*, the only person who had more than a phrase about the fiscal problems was one candidate. I think she was running for the Underwater Board; she was from Portland. She gave a whole paragraph to the fiscal problems of the society. None of the others seem to have the faintest idea. First, Tef Rodeffer quit, and then Ronn Michael was off the board, so there was no one concerned about making money and keeping a bank balance. I would say the greatest concern that some of us have is that the society is going to go bankrupt or have incredible dues increases ... .

What do you see as the role of a professional society?

SPRAGUE: I think the major function of any professional society, in my experience, should be the collection and dissemination of information to the membership and to the public. If it doesn't lead to that, it really shouldn't be taken out of the dues of the member. If the board wants to meet twice a year, let them pay for getting to the midyear meeting, like we did when I was on the board, instead of putting them up in a fancy hotel. There is much less volunteerism in most societies, at least the ones I'm familiar with. I would say that the Society for Industrial Archeology is functioning like SHA did in the earlier days. Other than the fact they don't know how to spell "archaeology," they are a good bunch of people. There is an historical reason why they use the etymologically incorrect spelling because of the influence of the Smithsonian on the formation of the society. They haven't gone overboard trying to be another Society for American Archaeology. They accept the fact that the membership is going to be smaller, the influence on archaeology is going to be smaller, and they are happy with it. I worry when board members of the SHA look to see how SAA does something. The fact the SHA and SAA are different is because they are different, so don't worry about it.

What other organizations have been important to historical archaeology?

SPRAGUE: It's quite varied because each person has their own special concern. If you're interested in theory, maybe work in *American Antiquity* is valuable to you. I dropped my membership years ago because it didn't tell me anything helpful. I started membership in things like the Early American Industries Association and the Council on the America's Military Past (CAMP), which was formerly called the Council on Abandoned Military Posts. I think societies that you belong to are based on what your interests are, what in historical archaeology you want to do.

What about the relationship with the English group of the Society for Post-Medieval Archaeology?

SPRAGUE: Yes, I belong.

How would you characterize that group?

SPRAGUE: I see some cross-fertilization, more on the East Coast and more in ceramics, but I definitely get something out of it. I find that the Australasian Society for Historical Archaeology is one of the more useful for me because it is based on colonial exploitation, which we are investigating in the western United States. I have more colleagues in Australia then I do in England, for example.

What were some of your first archaeological projects in the Northwest, following the cemetery work?

SPRAGUE: First, I had two major projects, running concurrently. In the spring was the Lake Roosevelt project, which included some prehistory, but it was mostly historical archaeology at Fort Colvile (the proper spelling for the HBC post) where we worked in the very nasty spring weather. It was tough to get people to work. We even took people out of the Kettle Falls city jail to work on crews. It was interesting work, and it was archaeology that should have been done before the dam flooded, but in those days all you really cared about was the prehistory. So it was almost a pristine site. The Kettle Falls Coulee Dam project lasted five years. In the summer, we were working on the San Juan Islands for the Park Service. The Bureau of Reclamations was providing the funds for Lake Roosevelt, but the San Juan National Historical Park was a Park Services project for the development of the national park. We worked at the English Camp, which the Park Service tried to change its name and called it British Camp but eventually got, quite correctly, shot down. American Camp, San Juan town, and the Hudson's Bay Company Bellevue Farm were the other sites we worked on out there. It was a pleasant eight-year project.

Those years were?

SPRAGUE: 1970 through 1977. It was pure historical archaeology and, I think pretty good work. Before the report was completed, the Park Service ran out of money, but we still produced a thousand-page final report with numerous authors.

What other projects were there?

SPRAGUE: We had work at Cataldo Mission for the state of Idaho. I had one very small but good season to get some idea of what was going on, then I let a former faculty member have it for the second season, and all he did was prehistory, in spite of what was stated in the proposal and contract. Since then, it's been less rushed and less salvage orientated. Several seasons on Forest Service mining sites, and we both have worked at Silver City, Idaho.

I want to talk about the Joso Trestle construction camp, a fairly large construction camp in the teens of the 20th century. It was a bit of a fight for you, wasn't it, to get funding for that?

SPRAGUE: Yeah, the work we did at Joso Trestle construction camp was due to work that was going on at a Corps of Engineers fish hatchery. They were getting water out of the impoundment that was supposed to protect the Marmes site [the Marmes family pronounces it as Marmes not Marmz]. It turned out that the water inside the impoundment was cleaner than the water on the outside in the reservoir, so they laid a pipeline from Marmes Rockshelter down to the flat land along the Snake River. That placed it right on top of the construction camp where the Washington State SHPO said, "no, we're not going to do that; we're not going to waste good archaeological money on any historical sites but Hudson's Bay Company sites."

How interesting, Washington SHPO?

SPRAGUE: The Corps of Engineers' colonel's wife wanted to go out and do archaeology, so corps funds were made available for the Joso Trestle construction camp. A great deal of new information was discovered during the excavation and historical research.

So the opposition was not with the corps?

SPRAGUE: No it was not with the corps.

Interesting.

SPRAGUE: It was with the Washington SHPO. Washington State has a strange system where the SHPO is not the same as the state archaeologist. The state archaeologist is under the SHPO, and they get into conflicts when they don't agree. This is still happening with different players.

I worked at the Joso Trestle construction camp there and read the report that Pricilla Wegars produced. So I wonder, how you did feel after the project? You fought to do the work, and you recovered a lot of material, a lot of information. Would you say it was definitely worth doing?

SPRAGUE: Oh yeah. You ask how I feel. I feel vindicated that I had made an issue of it. I had known of the site since 1964 when I was still at Washington State University. I was right near the site when working on the Palus Burial site and walked over it several times and saw the potential of it. I felt vindicated by the results that came out of it. Pricilla and I did a lot of newspaper research and other background for it. The evidence we found in the ground was much that you just wouldn't know otherwise. I mean the fact that they were playing early 78 rpm phonograph records just doesn't seem like something you would expect. We learned a lot about what they were eating, smoking, drinking. We sure found evidence of the Hawaiian divers who worked in the caissons that were in the Snake River for the foundation work. There was a lot of good evidence of what went on out there that we never would have guessed or even speculated … .

This question kind of leads to the issue of social consciousness. Do you agree that you have some kind of social consciousness and where did it come from, do you think?

SPRAGUE: I think, for the most part, it came from my parents. I'm a second generation PhD. I think I gained from my father an interest in all science; he was a plant pathologist/botanist. I still subscribe to *Science*, which he started me with, and it would probably be the last journal I ever cancel because you even learn the latest archaeology from *Science*. It's a powerful lobby. My mother was a schoolteacher. She was a women's liberation voice long before there was such a thing. I remember her making comments that, "I'm not a housewife; I'm not married to a house; I'm a homemaker." That was in the late 1930s. They were strong Republicans when Roosevelt was in, but that was mainly because my dad worked for the federal government. I know my mother was still very liberal, toward the end, and did not approve of what the Grand Old Party was doing. So I come from a family who was fairly conscience of social inequity. They were very, very upset with the Japanese internment during World War II. Both of my parents went to school with Wanapum Indians at White Bluffs, Washington, and my mother taught them at Beverly, Washington, in her first job.

How has working with American Indians affected you or changed you?

SPRAGUE: I think the major effect, outside of the burial issue, was it made me realize that you don't have to do everything today. It was an appreciation of time and energy. I think it also made it much easier for me and my family to spend a year in Inner Mongolia, PRC. Again change didn't happen fast, or it didn't happen at all. Patience is definitely a virtue in working with American Indians. As far as the question of burial repatriation is concerned though, we're talking about what happened at Idaho 15 years before NAGPRA was enacted as a matter of respect for the Indian people. They were quite concerned about what would happen to their ancestors, and I had some experiences that have been written up elsewhere, but made

me very conscious of the need for repatriation. I've been a little astounded that some federal agencies have taken NAGPRA as a way to slow down repatriation. It was done within six months before NAGPRA, and the most recent one that I have experience with under NAGPRA took 40 years—longer than there has been a NAGPRA law.

It feels a little awkward to talk about, say, burials with historic items, grave goods. I hope that was the right term. Julie Longenecker was just telling me how useful your recent book on burial terminology is. We should talk about this because it is common to have historic items interred with people. I did my master's thesis on historic items found in American Indian graves, but it doesn't feel right to talk about the historical archaeology of Indian interments, and yet we've learned a lot about things from those items. Do you support the idea of reburying the items just as we do the remains?

SPRAGUE: I support whatever the people involved, the descendants, want. Sometimes they don't want them reburied; they want to keep them in a museum.

Would some people not want them even studied?

SPRAGUE: Yeah, definitely. The only way that happens is if the descendants are the first ones there. I mean if they do the excavation and reburial.

Well just the notion of reburying collections, I know the Washington SHPO has taken a hard stance of oversight of the collections, and those will not be reburied in terms of archaeological type collections. Which I'm not sure if that seems a little extreme.

SPRAGUE: It's very extreme in my estimation; more, it's morally wrong.

Even for prehistoric site studies?

SPRAGUE: If it's clearly the ancestors of the modern descendants who are making the decisions of that particular tribe, I say yes … .

Well just one or two questions to wrap up this session. You'll want your break anyway to talk about our other business. I have a question from Sasquatch, "do you believe in me, and have we ever met in the woods?"

SPRAGUE: I believed absolutely in the concept of you. There are too many tribes who discuss you, and there are too many people who see what they view as evidence of you. I don't think we can deny the fact that there is a concept of a Sasquatch, but whether you really exist as a creature or not, I don't know. Just expressing the fact that we should study you has certainly not done my career any good.

Sprague Interview – 17 October 2007

This is Darby Stapp, and I am here with Rick Sprague again on 17 October 2007. We're doing a follow-up interview to our previous one for The Society for Historical Archaeology, interviews with former presidents of the society. We're going to start today by talking about one of the shifts in the nature of The Society for Historical Archaeology and the role its members play, specifically what Rick calls volunteerism. So you've noticed a shift at some point?

SPRAGUE: Yeah, it hasn't been dramatic at any particular point, but it has been a tendency. It has moved, I think, to a pretty serious level, and one of the factors in this, I think, is the fact we now have a management company managing our activities. They want more money, so they have us out getting more money. Cost of registration for meetings goes up; cost of annual dues goes up. Yet at the same time, people are not volunteering to do their travel on their money like they used to. The board used to pretty much pay its own way to midyear meeting for example. This is now paid by the society. Such things as proofing of the journal is now a paid position, and I can speak to that because I was one of the first who was paid. What I was getting paid was nothing compared to the amount of work I was doing. Decisions were made by the editor on issues that are now being made by the paid proofreader. So that we're more and more passing duties down to paid employees of the society rather than volunteers making the decisions through

committees and figuring out what the society members want. The board seems quite willing to let the management people make decisions the board used to make. I see this as a mistake in the operation of the society. It's costing more and we're getting less. So much of it was done on a volunteer basis, especially the meetings. Now we have small groups priced out of the book room, people who cannot afford to pay the fee. This is contrary to the objectives of the society. I am concerned that what I see is a change in the wrong direction, at least in terms of volunteer help within the society.

That has far more implications than just economics. It costs more to be a member or go to a meeting, and it's changing the whole nature of the society, I guess.

SPRAGUE: Yeah, I feel it is.

Members don't have ownership in the society any longer, maybe.

SPRAGUE: Yeah, that's one way of looking at it.

You think someone else is going to take care of that, and I just have to pay my dues, and what am I going to get? I would imagine that's kind of a trend of societies in general.

SPRAGUE: I fear that it probably is. It's going to be tough. We're going to have to start electing people to the board who are more concerned about the way things are running than the recent boards have been. There have been people on each board who have been concerned and have tried, but they have been a minority for quite a number of years now.

If you're basically talking about the younger generation coming up that are filling these roles, and I don't have a lot of broad experience with younger professionals, but the ones I do know have a far different attitude than my generation. I am sure my generation was far different from yours, but you know they say things like, "I'm not going to conferences if I have to spend my own money" or "I'm not writing this paper if I'm not going to be paid to write this paper; I'm not going to work for free." You know, it's shocking really, some of things I hear people say. They want to get paid for every hour they work. If someone is not going to pay them to go to a conference, they're not going. I have hardly ever been paid to go to a conference.

SPRAGUE: You go to a conference for the scholarly interchange, the social interaction that you also develop over the years.

Oh absolutely. Networking, but also the intellectual stimulation.

SPRAGUE: There is certainly no obligation for anyone to pay you for this, which is to your benefit, completely.

It's part of being a professional. Some won't join a society if the company won't pay of it. Can you believe it?

SPRAGUE: Yup.

I have been meaning to write something to the students in the student section of American Anthropological Society about the value of going to conferences. Just what we said, networking. You go and hear all these ideas. You get a little break from work. I always come back super charged up with all kinds of ideas. So I want to tell these younger people, go to any conference you can, join the professional societies. The networking alone is worth it.

SPRAGUE: Just the attitude toward the journal, the fact that people feel they don't need to subscribe. To me, this tells us things are changing. Electronic form is not as good. Its simply isn't a permanent document you can hold in your hand and read and reread, and that's what people are losing. As I have already said to you, I think taking the book reviews and making them strictly electronic is a serious mistake. There are people in the society who agree, but they don't seem to be those who have any power in terms of decision making.

That was done so they could have more research articles?

SPRAGUE: That was the theory.

I learned more from the reviews than I do from the research articles a lot of the time, mostly because I read them.

SPRAGUE: I would have to agree.

What are the types of articles you do enjoy reading in HA?

SPRAGUE: As I already said, I feel that we're spending too much print on theory and not enough on the basic facts of our time periods. This is why I enjoy writing and reading articles on artifact groups.

Like George Miller has done with ceramics, is that right?

SPRAGUE: Exactly.

He has really dug in there and tried to get the building blocks, the nuts and bolts.

SPRAGUE: Exactly. This is what we need more of. George has taken data, such as prices of various ceramics, and made sense out of this and drawn more conclusions than all the theory that you can gather up.

So he's managed to get the different documentary and archaeological data and merge them, truly integrate them. He has derived information from them.

SPRAGUE: Yeah, he's found the data in the artifacts, both those he's dug up and those that are out there in the literature and made sense of them.

There seems a general pattern, that is, you get the historical overview, you get the archaeological finds, and that's kind of it. It's been tough in the field I think to make meaningful insight from archaeological materials. To go beyond what's already known in history and that's an age-old question for us.

SPRAGUE: I don't think it's an important issue anymore. It's so clear that archaeology can bring new facts, new information.

That leads to new questions.

SPRAGUE: That leads to the greater study of the time period being studied and adds an element to the history that history is simply incapable of doing itself. That used to be a hot question, but I think it's pretty much gone by the wayside.

That may be with historic archaeologists. I don't know about historians, if they recognize the value of archaeology.

SPRAGUE: In my lifetime, I have seen some major improvement.

It seems that we have a good artifact paper or two in each HA journal issue.

SPRAGUE: We don't in any of the thematic issues. For someone on the West Coast, the thematic issues are usually just a thorough waste. They are usually based on Boston, or New York, or Philadelphia with lots of theory. They are not what some of us are looking for and need.

I have noticed quite a few thematic issues.

SPRAGUE: That was started to create more issues per year and was largely successful, but like I say, I'm not enthralled by the content of many of them.

Have they been having a pretty steady stream of manuscripts submissions?

SPRAGUE: Pretty much, yeah. Ronn Michael always had. He followed the principle that I follow in another journal that you always want to have enough material ready to go to pay off the debt of subscriptions. In other words, a year's issues should always be in reserve. I'm not in contact with the editing of the journal now, but that was certainly a policy in the past.

The editor position is still volunteer?

SPRAGUE: Yeah, and it's a big job if done right.

Do you think that the lack of submissions on artifact typology and those types of manuscripts is a reflection of the research being done across the country—that there is not a lot of that going on anymore, or is it just not reaching the publication format?

SPRAGUE: I think, its part of the phenomenon that actually put it in print. In the introduction to a book in which I said, that if I had to make a choice of saving all master's theses or all dissertations in historical archaeology, and I might add anthropology in general, it would take no time at all for me make a decision that I would save the master's theses.

Wow, that's a great line.

SPRAGUE: They have the data, the irreplaceable knowledge. Whereas the dissertations are filled with a bunch of worthless theory that you have to throw in to get your degree. I'm talking from the position of someone who has been there.

Yeah. Well, that is one thing I appreciated about Schuyler, He didn't subscribe to that. He just thought it should be a good study. So I wasn't forced to try to make some grand theoretical type of paper. Although I have employed his concept of historical ethnography. Seemed to be a smart thing to do.

SPRAGUE: Yeah.

Since we've been speaking of typology-type issues, I had some interactions with Bill Lockhart of the bottle group.

SPRAGUE: Oh yeah.

In Alamogordo, New Mexico.

SPRAGUE: Yeah, a very knowledgeable person.

I don't know him, but I was impressed when I sent him the table of the bottles from the Hanford construction camp. Days later, he came back said we learned a couple new things from this because of that tightly dated site. So they have a pretty active group, and that's the kind of thing you're talking about, what we need.

SPRAGUE: Yeah.

I suppose we have ceramic groups and all that. It seems that we need to have greater reference material for artifact typology and. . . .

SPRAGUE: Classification.

Classifications and dating, it's a hodgepodge.

SPRAGUE: Yeah.

Out of date, out of print.

SPRAGUE: Spread all over.

You may know someone did something in 1985 and that's it. I guess that's a reflection of the diversity of the material culture. One would think you would have some standard encyclopedias or something, or artifact types that you can pull off the shelf and answer some of these basic questions.

SPRAGUE: That's one of the efforts of Left Coast Press with their new series.

Well, hopefully.

SPRAGUE: I think they will be successful.

People need it?

SPRAGUE: Yeah, it's a much-needed part of the total program.

When you ran for president the first time, what year was that?

SPRAGUE: 1976.

Did you start thinking of things that you wanted to achieve during your presidency?

SPRAGUE: At that time it was pretty much a caretaker job, trying to keep things running smoothly. You get a lot of correspondence that probably nowadays is done by the managers. For the most part, it was trying to expand the functions of the society. Especially publications, I think that was the central theme, publications and to do a good job.

At that time there just wasn't a lot of literature I imagine.

SPRAGUE: No there wasn't any surplus. The second time as president in 1990 was really a time in which I was trying to be more of an Eisenhower, just take care of things and stay out of trouble. While I did have a good body of support, I felt that I was in a position where I had to be careful and not step on too many toes since I was a third-party candidate. One of the things I felt I did accomplish was to get The Society for Historical Archaeology to support NAGPRA. We were the only major archaeological society in the United States that did fully support NAGPRA. This was partly because we are dealing with late burials and historic burials. The later the burial, the more likely you'll be offending relatives, social political groups, or racial groups. So it was something I was pleased to push and did. Much of the antagonism in the society came directly from a few people strongly involved in the Society for American Archaeology.

What were some of the debates within the society over the years, some of the big ones that kind of put people into camps? Were there many, or were there some?

SPRAGUE: There were very few. I think one of the things that made me willing to work so hard for the SHA was the lack of conflict, the friendly nature of the meetings. There weren't private conferences in the halls, trying to figure out how to stop this or that. The society has been very, I think, very open and very friendly in its interactions. I see some clouds on the horizon where there's going to be some problems in the future between volunteer management and professional management and that does worry me.

Right. The intellectual debates, say from the Stanley South camp, to the, I guess, Mary Beaudry type of movements have all stayed at a professional level.

SPRAGUE: Oh I think so. I think much more than the average academic groups. Stan South and I, for example, have some interesting disagreements, but we've had fun doing it and are good friends.

That's good.

SPRAGUE: We've enjoyed each other's input.

Doesn't seem like we've had a lot of one-on-one debates in historical archaeology like have characterized prehistory.

SPRAGUE: No, I don't think so.

I mean the good intellectual kind of debate, I guess.

SPRAGUE: There have been clean, friendly, intellectual debates. I don't think there's been any vicious debates, except perhaps for one review mentioned above that did not follow the procedure I had established of sending reviews to the author before sending them to *HA*.

Schuyler is always good for throwing a few zingers in here and there.

SPRAGUE: I think that's one of his functions. I've known Bob since he was an undergraduate, so I appreciate what he is, where he is coming from. This is why I was willing to recommend you to him for your doctorate.

That was a great experience. No question about going back there and going to school like that, taking classes, and getting to know him. He's a fun guy. Julie [Longenecker] and I would have lunch with him about every day at the University Museum. It was good.

SPRAGUE: It is because of Bob that this series of tapes is being recorded and transcribed for *Historical Archaeology*.

Thanks, Rick. This concludes our interviews for the SHA.

DARBY C. STAPP
PACIFIC NORTHWEST NATIONAL LABORATORY

J. W. Joseph

An Interview with
Stanley A. South

FIGURE 1. Stan South discusses excavations at Bethabara during the final meeting of the Conference on Historic Site Archaeology, Winston-Salem, North Carolina, 1978. J. W. Joseph is on the far right. Photograph courtesy of Linda Carnes-McNaughton.

Introduction

Stanley A. South is one of the foundational figures in historical archaeology. South's *Method and Theory in Historical Archaeology*, published by Academic Press in 1977, introduced processual archaeology to the young discipline and provided a number of important concepts that would shape the development of the field, including the mean ceramic date formula, *terminus post quem*

concept, and pattern recognition. In his search for patterning, South also provided historical archaeology with a uniform classification system for the analysis of historic artifacts.

A participant in the SHA's formative meeting in Dallas in 1967, it was South who made the motion that the new organization be named "The Society for Historical Archaeology" (*Historical Archaeology* 1967:3); he, along with Charles Fairbanks and Arnold Pilling formed the inaugural editorial advisory board for the SHA's journal *Historical Archaeology*. Stan South was one of the first to organize the field, having established the Conference on Historic Site Archaeology out of the Southeastern Archaeological Conference (SEAC) in 1960. The Conference on Historic Site Archaeology was a regional forerunner to the SHA and would remain a key resource for the development of historical archaeology in the southeast until it merged back into SEAC in 1982.

South published 15 volumes of the *Conference on Historic Site Archaeology Papers* from 1965 through 1980, providing a series of collected papers that contains many of the important articles in the field. A one-man press and editor extraordinaire, South used the revenues generated from the *Conference Papers* to publish 50 theses and dissertations as *Volumes in Historical Archaeology*, as well as 16 volumes of *Historical Archaeology in Latin America*. A complete listing of these publications may be found at <http://www.cas.sc.edu/sciaa/hapubs.html>.

South's publications in historical archaeology are voluminous and wide ranging. He has served as one of the historians of the field, authoring several articles on the history of historical archaeology as well as editing *Pioneers in Historical Archaeology* (1994) and penning his autobiographical journal *An Archaeological Evolution*, in 2005. In addition to his site studies and works on scientific archaeology, he was also an early proponent of public archaeology and site interpretation. Beyond *Method and Theory*, his major publications include the edited volume *Research Strategies in Historical Archaeology* (1977), and the books *Historical Archaeology in Wachovia* (1999), and *Archaeological Pathways to Historic Site Development* (2002).

South has published articles in the *Conference on Historic Site Archaeology Papers*, *American Antiquity*, *Historical Archaeology*, *South Carolina Antiquities*, *North Carolina Archaeology*, as well as other journals, and has contributed to multiple edited books. His authorship of *Research Manuscripts* for the South Carolina Institute of Archaeology and Anthropology is encyclopedic. His profound influence on the field was recognized by his receipt of the SHA's J. C. Harrington Award in 1987, the fifth year in which the award was presented.

I had the pleasure of working with Stan for several seasons at Santa Elena, as well as being his student while an undergraduate at the University of South Carolina. As a teacher, Stan would come into class and pull from his pocket some obscure object that he had found in the gutter on his walk to school. He would challenge us with the question that drove his career: What is it? For Stan South, figuring out what objects were, how they functioned, who used them, when they were made, where they came from, and how they fit into the cultural system were the fundamental questions of historical archaeology. His work has given us many of the answers to these questions as well as the tools we need in our own quests.

References

HISTORICAL ARCHAEOLOGY
  1967 Beginnings. *Historical Archaeology* 1:1–22.

SOUTH, STANLEY A.
  1977 *Method and Theory in Historical Archaeology*. Academic Press, New York, NY.
  1999 *Historical Archaeology in Wachovia: Excavating Eighteenth-Century Bethabara and Moravian Pottery*. Kluwer Academic/Plenum Publishers, New York, NY.
  2002 *Archaeological Pathways to Historic Site Development*. Kluwer Academic/Plenum Publishers, New York, NY.
  2005 *An Archaeological Evolution*. Springer, New York, NY.

SOUTH, STANLEY A. (EDITOR)
  1977 *Research Strategies in Historical Archaeology*. Academic Press, New York, NY.
  1994 *Pioneers in Historical Archaeology*. Plenum Publishing, New York, NY.

South Interview, 14 July 2008

I am Joe Joseph with the SHA History Committee. It is 14 July 2008 and I am with Stanley South in Columbia, South Carolina. Stanley, we're looking forward to your thoughts on your life and career in historical archaeology. If you could start us with the beginnings—when did you come into archaeology as a career? Was it when you were in college?

SOUTH: I was at Appalachian State Teachers College in the 1940s, when my wife Jewell and I would go out on weekends and at lunchtime to collect arrowheads and pottery in those mountain valleys where Native Americans used to live. ... I would catalog all the things we found and made a little movie of Jewell and me sitting in bed at night cataloguing pottery and arrowheads and making a record of them.

Later I contacted Joffre Coe at the University of North Carolina and he showed me the form used to properly record things archaeologically. So that acquaintance with him and my interest in collecting Native American objects was an early inspiration to become an archaeologist.

Later I went to Chapel Hill and trained under Joffre Coe to get my master's in anthropology. While I was there he agreed to hire me at Town Creek Indian Mound when I graduated. ... Howard Sergeant was then at Town Creek. He was an archaeologist from the Southwest. He had placed four posts on top of the temple mound because Joffre wanted to someday rebuild the temple.

When I got to Town Creek I asked Joffre two or three times when were we going to get around to building that temple. He said we would get around to it someday. I was anxious to do it and couldn't wait to get started. So I went out and I rented a chainsaw and started cutting down pine trees on Mr. Frutchey's property. He was a great supporter of Joffre's work who gave me permission to cut the poles. I had 55-gallon drums cut in two and welded together to make big vats to conserve pine logs with pentathiazole. With the help of Ed Gaines I put the roof on the temple and built the walls of cedar poles.

In my weekly report I had said I started cutting trees for use in the temple. The next week I reported we had begun putting some of the posts in the ground. So I just dropped clues along the way to keep him informed of what I was up to. I didn't want to cut him totally out of the picture [laughs]. When he came for a visit he was pleased with what I had done. I said I hope it's okay, and he replied that he figured we'd do it someday [laughs]. He said: You might as well go ahead since you're so anxious to do it, so I did. That was my first fascinating experience at interpreting different lifeways from the archaeological record for the enjoyment and education of the visiting public at places like Town Creek.

Did you learn historical archaeology at UNC or is that—

SOUTH: Historical archaeology? No [laughs]! After I'd been at Town Creek two years and had built the temple, I got an offer from Archives

& History. ... My supervisor, Sam Tarlton, was interested in Brunswick Town, an 18th-century town ruins located on Orton plantation. The owners, James Sprunt, through the urging of Charles Lee, had donated the town site to the state, and Tarlton had tried to hire Charles Fairbanks to come up from Florida to direct that site. He knew Fairbanks was one of the very few archaeologists in those days who paid any attention to historical archaeology. Others were Pinky Harrington, John Griffin, and a few others. I used to count them on one hand [laughs] at the time I got into the field. Now of course there's lots more [laughs] who have entered the field of historical archaeology.

As it turned out, they didn't have enough money to hire Fairbanks so they asked me as a second choice. I asked Joffre Coe about taking that job and leaving Town Creek to move into historical archaeology. He said: Well, if you want to end your career in archaeology I guess you could do that [laughs].

But I didn't take his advice that seriously because I had read about archaeologists excavating King Tut's tomb and other classical archaeology sites. I was fascinated by the fact that here in America in North Carolina, we had a ruin of a whole town that had never been excavated. To me that was a great challenge. It was just too exciting and tempting to turn down. Joffre had never pushed historical archaeology at all and his attitude about historical archaeology was reflected in that statement saying that I would end my career in archaeology if I went into that field.

At that time historical archaeology was a stepchild to Native American archaeology and historical archaeologists had to plug in 10-minute papers into Southeastern Archaeological Conference meetings. So they didn't have much time to report what they wanted to say. You could tell that whenever someone gave a paper on historical archaeology the attendance in the room would drop, leaving only a few who would hang around to hear what historical archaeology was about.

When you were working at Brunswick were you teaching yourself how to dig historic sites? Were you talking with others?

SOUTH: Joffre had made a clear case for *schnitting* (shovel shaving) off the clay surface and revealing the stains of the different colors of the soil from the Native American sites. His field methods were excellent. I was well aware of the detail needed to conduct scientific field research. When I first visited Town Creek with Jewell when we were at Appalachian, I met Ernest Lewis as he troweled with Ed Gaines. ... They were down on their knees troweling off numbered features, and keeping everything separate. That inspired me to realize that I'd like to spend the rest of my life recording these little clues from the past on a Native American site and trying to come up with the truths about past cultures reflected in those few little clues left for us to unravel. That was a wonderful challenge for me.

I realized that some of us cared enough about the past, and [*laughs*] were willing to work hard and dig hard, to try to uncover the past from little nails, pennies, thimbles, and musket balls. Each artifact, when you researched it, opened up a whole new exploratory world of curiosity, research and discovery.

At that time you would have had to have researched a lot of the material objects yourself. I mean there weren't many publications.

SOUTH: Oh yeah, when I was at Brunswick Town I would go to the library and look up books on antiques and came to realize what a rich asset that the historical record was to understanding the past. In the Native American record there are ethnographies and other written accounts of how the Native Americans lived, that were used to tie into the archaeological record. But with historical archaeology there were more abundant written records and original documents that opened up a fuller understanding of how artifacts were used at different times to understand past culture process.

I see archaeology as the search for the truth. I have in my pocket a gold coin that I had struck a while back that addresses that search for understanding about the past and search for the truth. My parents raised me in the Methodist church. But when I was 13 years old I began singing in the choir and sung there for many years. I'd sit up there and look out over the audience and listen to the preacher, look at those stained glass windows, and listen to what he was saying. A lot of the things he said made sense but a lot of it urged us to not explore into the truth of the world around us. So my skepticism and aversion to religious dogma came from the age of 13. That exposure every Sunday to those sermons admonishing people to take what they read on sheer faith and not inquire beyond that, pushed me into science, where no such dogma is present in the search for truth.

Many years later I had a gold coin struck, which I carry. On one side it has the date of my birth, 1928. It says, "Religion: Life is God's will. Don't question it." On the other side is 2008, the year I had it struck. It says, "Science: Seek life's truths to set you free." That is my basic philosophical belief.

When I got into the field of historical archaeology, as I mentioned, it was a stepchild to Native American archaeology. I could see there was a need for the introduction of scientific methods into historical archaeology such as had previously been the case in Native American archaeology. Some of the historic pit profiles looked like potholes. So there was not the refinement that was coming to be associated with Native American sites methodology. By the time I came along in the 50s there was a great interest in better methodology. I saw it as a field that needed better methodological and theoretical underpinning, so I took that ball and ran with it at Brunswick Town where I dug my first historic site.

So you for historical archaeology, and Lewis Binford and others in prehistoric archaeology kind of defined a new archaeology—processual archaeology. Did that come out of your desire to see archaeology become more scientific?

SOUTH: Lew Binford and I were classmates at Chapel Hill. He was more into the theoretical end of things and I was more into digging and discovery. I wanted to get my shovel in the ground and demonstrate I could dig a straight profile. Lew and I were good friends in those days and we would stay up most of the night sometime discussing an issue brought out by someone's article. We would dig out the problem, point out the mistakes and faults, and chuckle at their foibles, an interaction that stimulated both of us.

Then he went to Michigan. I had applied to go there also, but then my wife, Jewell, had a car wreck with my 1939 Ford, ricocheting off of a truck, then hit a deputy sheriff's car. So I had to pay for the truck, the load of coal it dumped, the deputy sheriff's car, and my car. That put me back so far financially that I never made it to Michigan for my doctorate. But Lew went on and made a name there when he started publishing. When I entered archaeology I would read about his new processual archaeology and the theory underwriting it. I wasn't impressed with it at that time because it seemed remote from refining field methods, lithics, and potsherds, so I didn't read much of his stuff.

When I was at Brunswick Town, obsessed with digging that classic lost city, I began publishing the results. When I began analyzing the meaning of the cultural material I had found, everywhere I turned there was an article by Lew Binford. It was then I realized he had something important to say to the field of archaeology, and I had better find out what he was talking about.

So, after some years of not reading his stuff, I was at the stage of trying to translate some of the methodology I had developed at Brunswick Town into a broader processual picture, and came to the view that Lew had already been into from the very beginning. We reestablished our friendship at that time, because by then I was as much a fan of his as many others in the field were at that time and since.

Many resisted that as I had, because of past archaeological tradition. Even in Native American archaeology people resisted his processual approach. But it made such good sense once you got into it and realized that he was asking the same questions I'd been asking about past cultures. We were trying to figure out what the processes were that caused people to use their environment and adapt to it. I was as interested in these processes as Lew was. So once that clicked [laughs], and I realized where he was going, I got on the bandwagon and rode along with him on the journey to explore culture pro-

cess in an in-depth manner and explain how they produced the revealed archaeological record.

Binford and I dug together during a survey of the Roanoke Rapids Basin, which was my first archaeological site. I hired him for 75¢ an hour, and my wife, Jewell, for the same. Joffre Coe got a grant from the VEPCO, Virginia Electric Power Company, which was building a dam across the Roanoke River to make electricity. We found 74 sites in that basin. Later, when I got converted to historical archaeology [laughs], Joffre hated to see me leave the field.

I had found a rich pottery-period site on the Roanoke, and when Joffre visited it he said: Don't quit digging here because you find something interesting at the top. Keep digging down until you hit water. I said I would do that before I left, because I knew that was one of his rules. So I dug from the high bank of the Roanoke down to the water level and got down about eight feet deep and found the Savannah River level, a stratified brown level you could see in the profile. I dug on below that and found what I called the Halifax level, characterized by little white chert spear points notched on the sides, with ground bases, in association with notched ax heads.

I knew they dated earlier than the Savannah River projectile points, so I named it for the county where I was digging, calling it the Halifax point. Joffre came up and visited and was pleased that I had dug down to make that discovery. When he went back home he told his wife, Sally, I told him dig down until he hit water because I think the site he's on is stratified. He had it in his mind from the time he saw the site, but didn't share his suspicion with me [laughs]. He knew from what he saw.

Joffre was not the kind to spill out what he was thinking to you. He would not spill his guts and not quit talking out like I do. He was very noncommittal, and when you asked him a question he would say: What do you think the answer is? That made you think. He made Lew Binford think, he made Benny Keel think, he made Roy Dickens think, he made others think that came through his mill if they were truly interested in learning archaeology.

His mantra was [*laughs*]: Figure it out for yourself—and I thought, that's the craziest way of teaching I ever heard of. I wanted him to feed me the answers. But he didn't do it. He would say: What do you think about that? And I'd tell him, and he'd tell me I should read this or that source, and I'd be a little better informed.

Several times I accused him of being a left-handed teacher. But he was a teacher that kept all he knew to himself and made you go out and root hog or die to get the answers [*laughs*]. That's what some of us did, because we wanted to impress this shut-mouthed teacher with the fact that we could go out and research the question and come up with our own answers. That sometimes frustrating method was a great inspiration to many of us privileged to deal with him and be inspired by his ability to encourage you to learn on your own [*laughs*].

Now that I've gotten older I appreciate that approach to learning, but I still have to blurt out what I think I know, so have never been able to use his technique. He told me once that when I started teaching, I would find in a classroom full of students, most wouldn't care much about anything I had to say. But if there were one or two who listened carefully, they would be the ones to become archaeologists in the future. That kind of left-handed philosophy paid off for him, and it paid off for those of us who were able to study under him. That perspective on research paid off for me in the field of historical archaeology, which is something he was never very excited about [*laughs*].

If he'd have taught it, you wouldn't have learned it as well as you did being required to research the answer on your own.

SOUTH: That's right. I just transferred his research perspective on method and theory into a new field, a new database.

Now when did you come to South Carolina and the institute?

SOUTH: I came to South Carolina in 1969. In North Carolina I was making $9,400 a year at Town Creek Indian Mound in '58, and I was transferred to dig at Brunswick Town for the same thing. By the late 1960s, they wanted to transfer me to Raleigh to be an administrator. I didn't want to go, but they transferred me anyway. I was there for two years. At a meeting, I talked with John Combs, assistant director at the University of South Carolina Institute of Archaeology and Anthropology and asked if they had another job in South Carolina. He said he didn't think I'd be interested, but I told him I didn't want to be an administrator. I wanted to stay in the field of archaeology.

He talked with Bob Stephenson at the time who was the director. And Bob hired me, offering $14,500, which was a nice increase over what I was making in North Carolina. But before I left North Carolina I went into my supervisor's office in the Department of Archives and History. I said, I'll stay here if you'll pay me what they're offering me in South Carolina. He said: No, we can't pay you that kind of money. And besides that, we don't need an historical archaeologist in North Carolina. We have Joffre Coe at UNC, who we can consult with as needed.

So I came here and started digging at Charles Towne Landing, and that put me to discovering another lost town [*laughs*]. That was the beginning of another exciting adventure. From there, on a contract basis, I went back up to North Carolina to dig at Bethabara, another lost Moravian town. I was directed to get back to archaeology at Brunswick Town, so I hired Gary Stone in my absence to complete my contractual work at Bethabara and at the Fifth House in Old Salem.

When I was at Brunswick Town, interest in the field of historic sites was growing. Sam Tarlton, my supervisor, sent me out to different sites where they were interested in a house or a site, where I'd do a one-day project. I'd go back and write a report on it, because I was determined to report everything I did. That's always been a rule of mine. If you're going to take somebody's money and do the digging, conduct the analysis, and do the research to make some sense out of it, it ought to be published. It shouldn't just be put in a file somewhere. It should be disseminated to the visiting public to the sites, or to laypeople or students interested in archaeology. That's why I've published hundreds and hundreds of articles and a dozen-or-so books trying to share what I have learned through the archaeological research experience.

Now when Bob Stephenson brought you to the institute, was that specifically to work at Charles Towne Landing?

SOUTH: Oh yeah. He did that.

So he knew he needed an historical archaeologist?

SOUTH: Right. The State of South Carolina's Tricentennial Commission was established with money from the state to develop some of the better-known historic sites commemorating the early settlement of the state. They worked out an agreement with the Warings, the owners of the property at Charles Towne Landing, to turn it over to the state and let the state operate it. Bob Stephenson heard from John Combs that I was interested and he had made me an offer to come dig at Charles Towne Landing.

I dug there for a year, finding the palisade around the town on Albemarle Point across from the later site of Charleston. The commission hired an architect who designed the museum to be on top of where I had discovered the palisade that once protected the town in 1670. I strongly objected to that saying putting the museum there would destroy that valuable archaeological resource. I suggested they put the museum somewhere else. They got rid of that architect and hired another one who planned it further back.

The commission then asked me to take a look at the site where the new museum was planned, to be sure there were no ruins there. I dug and found a square 200 ft. Mississippian moundless ceremonial center with a temple in the middle. The compound had two stockades around the outside with square ground sheds on the inside, in the Southeast Creek tradition, along with pots and many wonderful things.

I jumped back into Native American archaeology where the training under Coe had served me well as it had in historical archaeology. With that discovery, I wanted to move the proposed museum site again, but that caused a controversy. A member of the commission said:

This ground mole is going to find something everywhere we put him to digging. And I said [*laughs*]: That's the name of the game as far as I'm concerned. I didn't expect to find it, but revealed it through the mitigation process. I argued that it was there, and we should not destroy the evidence, but rather, to interpret it. But the commission voted to destroy it, so I had to salvage what I could.

Recently, I wrote an account of that moundless ceremonial center which was recently published. So Charles Towne Landing turned out to have a lot of excitement for me and the sponsors. It combined history, historical and Native American archaeology, and historic site development, as well as educating the public. That is the essence of archaeology research.

Then I went to Ninety Six, South Carolina to explore and discover another lost town. There I found the palisade around the town dating from the French and Indian War, and the Revolutionary War fortifications, excavated the jail, and recovered other valuable data that had waited two centuries to be revealed.

There were seven different fortification and town sites [*laughs*] I found at Ninety Six, the discovery and development of which was a big major block of work that I did there toward understanding what went on there and where. It is now a national park, and I've always wanted to go back to do more archaeology where it is badly needed.

The stockade around the town had two neat little bastions about eight feet across. I wanted to go there with a grant and put posts back, so when people come to visit they would see the town enclosure, because they don't see a whole lot there now. They see the Holmes Fort parapet I constructed when I was there and marked the location of the blockhouse inside the Holmes Fort. I wanted to go there and show that town—that earlier stockade around the town—but I never was able to and I couldn't convince the National Park Service to put money into it. They did erect a log blockhouse at Holmes Fort, which adds to the interpretation of that site, but the stockade around the town was never replaced in its original position which I had found.

It is my hope that maybe someone, someday, can get up there with a grant to replace posts in the postmolds I found for the fort around the town. Then visitors could visually see where the town was and how small it was during the French and Indian War. They do see the later Holmes Fort up on top of the hill and the embankment at the Star Fort, built by the British when they took over the place during the Revolution, so their impression is primarily that of a later period than the town of Ninety Six.

Visitors can still see the embankment of the Star Fort built to defend the town against General Nathanial Greene's American army during the Revolution. There is a tremendous amount of history there, but the emphasis has been on the history rather than the archaeology since I left. I just feel like I went through there like a flash in the pan pointing out and mapping those treasures [laughs] in the ground for some later archaeologist to rediscover. But, decades and decades later the Park Service hasn't grabbed the ball and run with it, but that takes research, and they prefer to interpret a site at the point where they took it over. But there's so much more opportunity there for enriching the Ninety Six site far beyond where it is now. Perhaps long after I am dead some Park Service administrator with vision and an interest in research will look at my maps of the site and take up the interpretive and reconstructive effort I began as a result of the archaeological discoveries I made.

You established the Conference on Historic Site Archaeology. Can you tell me about what it was that started bringing historical archaeologists together to start talking about forming that association, and later the Society for Historical Archaeology?

SOUTH: When the Southeastern Archaeological Conference met in Chapel Hill in 1960, I wanted to present a paper on my work at Brunswick Town. I was told they could give me only 10 minutes, while everyone else had 30 minutes. When I got up to give my 10-minute summary, I was asked by the chairman to limit my talk to 5 minutes. So I got up and took as long as I felt like I needed until they started hammering the gavel for me to sit down. That emphasized to me the chances of giving a paper

on historical archaeology at the Southeastern Conference was nil. That's when I knew I had to start a conference on historic site archaeology. In 1960, I wrote a letter to colleagues Fairbanks, Goggin, and several others interested in historical archaeology, suggesting we meet the day before the Southeastern Conference.

First conference was in Florida. And to my surprise, about 20-some people attended the day before the SEAC meeting. A number of those were Native American specialists who were also interested in historical archaeology. They showed up, and some of the old-timers showed up, and we had a good conference and I was pleased with it. I announced we would be holding that every year the day before SEAC met.

That continued for a number of years, until we met one year in Memphis. Jimmy Griffin came in to sign up. He hadn't sent in his hotel reservation. He assumed there would be a room there for him. He was the guru of Southeastern archaeology. He was told the hotel was full because a lot of people attending the Conference on Historic Site Archaeology had signed up the previous day, so he had to go to another hotel. He didn't like that.

At the SEAC business meeting they voted to ask me not to meet with them anymore because it took the rooms. That vote divorced the Conference on Historic Site Archaeology from the Southeastern Conference. The first meeting on our own was held in Asheville, where we had a good attendance. There were 30-some people there as I remember. We kept meeting at different places throughout the Southeast at a time of our own choosing in the years to follow.

When the Society for American Archaeology met in Dallas, Texas, word went out that those of us interested in historical archaeology should be there to help create a society for historical archaeology. Ivor Noël Hume was there from Colonial Williamsburg. There was a long debate over the name of the new Society for Historical Archaeology. So the issue of a name was finally settled.

I announced I would continue to hold my regional Southeastern Conference on Historic Site

Archaeology. Each year I would announce to those presenting papers to turn their paper in to me to publish in the *Conference on Historic Site Archaeology Papers*, and 16 volumes were published. But there came a time when we held a CHSA in Winston-Salem, and nobody submitted a paper to be published because they wanted to present it to the more prestigious national SHA journal—*Historical Archaeology*. That's when I drew an end to the Conference on Historic Site Archaeology.

I was going to turn the publication money I had accumulated for publication over to SHA. But the more I thought about it, the more I thought I would just continue to publish submitted papers and master's theses and dissertations. I began publishing those and have now published 50 volumes through the publication budget from the Conference on Historic Site Archaeology which no longer exists.

Most all the early papers are available for $10 each, with thicker master's theses and dissertations costing more, given 2009 publication costs. There's a lot of value in those 50 volumes, still waiting for those interested in learning what's being done in research in the field of historical archaeology. The proceeds go to my Historical Archaeology Research Fund at the USC Educational Foundation.

Didn't you also publish a number of theses and reports on Latin American subjects?

SOUTH: Yeah. Meanwhile as a sideline [*laughs*], I was invited by Nelsys Fusco Zambetogliris, an archaeologist in Uruguay, to give the keynote address at the first Historical Archaeology in Latin America Conference, a decade after my CHSA effort in North America.

I went there and gave that keynote address and found out there were a number of people there interested in doing historic site archaeology. But the same thing prevailed there that had prevailed in the earlier years here—that is, they were mainly interested in uncovering archaeological sites representing Native American cultures living there before Europeans came. If some archaeologist said they wanted to learn about the Portuguese, or the Spaniards, or the French, or

others that were settling in that area, they were looked upon strangely for that. Those at that conference said there was a great need to get their historic site archaeology papers published.

They prevailed upon me to make an announcement that I would begin a series of papers called *Historical Archaeology in Latin America*. I agreed to pay for them and ship them to Latin American countries for colleagues to buy. I was naïve about crossing international borders with things to sell, and discovered there was an insurmountable difficulty because the only way I could ship them would be to ship them free. But I would have to pay the postage from my Historical Archaeology Research Fund.

I started receiving papers in Portuguese, Spanish, and English. Then I published 16 volumes of *Historical Archaeology in Latin America,* shipping 10 volumes to a representative for each country to be handed out free to their colleagues. But then I began to run out of money in my research fund and had to cease the publication of that series.

I had many volumes left over, so I contacted a colleague in Argentina, Andrés Zarankin, who I'd met in Uruguay and had given a talk for him at his university in Argentina. I told him I had 16 of the volumes to be shipped to anyone who would pay the $55 cost of postage. A few of my South American colleagues have taken advantage of that offer to avail themselves of those publications.

I put an announcement in the SHA journal saying that they were available and received one or two orders from people in North America. My advice to young people is to learn Spanish, Italian, German, and other languages to expand your field of knowledge. Meanwhile I'm still enjoying research and publishing in historical archaeology as I always have.

The book I'm writing now is on 20th-century artifacts from my house. Joe, you have seen in my house boxes of stuff packed all over. What I did was photograph the things I had pack-ratted in my house and cellar over my lifetime, mostly over the last 50 years, including heirlooms from my parents and my grandparents. I photographed all of them and put together two books. The first book is to be published by Eliot Werner Publications. It is called *Talking Artifacts: The Twentieth-Century Legacy*. I hope I will complete editing it for him before the end of the year.

When I show the pictures to my colleagues they often don't recognize some of the objects. The name of the second book is *Twentieth-Century Artifact Function*. That's the one in which I discuss how the artifacts functioned in the past cultural system and the process involved in their usage. I have long used the 1897 Sears and Roebuck catalog as a basic reference, so why not have a household assemblage of 50 years or 100 years of the 20th century showing the typical accumulation of mundane things?

These are not the upper-class things emphasizing the current value such as seen on the *Antiques Roadshow* show. There they focus on the wealthy objects collected by the upper classes. At the end of the show they show people who brought a family treasure because it spoke to them about past family lifeways, but such objects are valued at very little because they do not represent the high price of things treasured by the upper classes. My book is not dedicated to those upper-class things but to those things found in the homes of the working-class people, along with things I rescued from the curb.

What do you think about the future of historical archaeology? I mean what are the questions that we should be asking about the 20th century?

SOUTH: Oh that's a good question. I quit subscribing to the journal *Historical Archaeology* many years ago because when I would open it up, the articles, they would focus on storytelling rather than data. I'm a storyteller, but I separate fiction from archaeology. This dichotomy became noticeable in the field as I disagreed with the position of Deetz and Leone in their emphasis on storytelling at the expense of searching through truth through archaeological science.

This resulted in the sponsors of the SHA meeting in Nashville setting up a panel to allow Deetz and me to discuss our differences. Deetz told about his perspective that scientific archaeology was not that beneficial because you never did know the final answer, so you might as well make up stories that go with the archaeology to make it more interesting. That concept had caught on at the SHA meeting in Charleston. The program chairman then was Leland Ferguson. He invited Deetz, Leone, Binford, and others to participate. As it turned out the storytelling concept caught on big.

That was a surprise to me, because I'd been pushing historical archaeology towards more rigorous and detailed scientific examination. I was pushing quantification, pattern recognition, and theory, urging archaeologists not to forget the distinguishing attributes of little nails, tacks, buttons, potsherds, and other artifacts reflecting past culture processes. They're as important as whole objects, which some archaeologists have emphasized in the past, toward understanding the processes that drive cultural evolution.

So do you think archaeology has gone too far into storytelling?

SOUTH: Oh yeah. A lot of that influence of Deetz and Leone and the storytelling phenomenon is still with us. It's nice to tell a story, but when you're dealing with an archaeological site you explain some of the things and how they functioned, and you get to a certain point where you don't know what happened within the specific family who dropped those objects. You don't know what the family was like. You don't know what the relationship between the parents and the children was. So what the storytellers are saying is enrich it with fiction. My response is that archaeological explanation does not need fiction to enrich it, because it then becomes fiction.

Leave the fiction for the classic fiction writers who do their research into the documents and archaeology, through which they find out what is known that characterizes a period. They create characters and put them into a story using the broader cultural context. Such novels do indeed help us to understand and explain the past. That contextual association, I believe, is perhaps what Deetz and Leone were talking about. My point of view has been to keep fiction and archaeology separate. Don't mix them and call them archaeology. Call it a fictional novel which can also make a contribution to knowledge.

For example, fiction writers produce some of the best stuff on the Civil War you can imagine, but the story is fiction. The facts are real and authentic based on truth. My feeling is that archaeology ought to draw the line and say what archaeology is and what fiction is. Some may say I'm an old-fashioned, out-of-date codger with an attitude. But when I read articles I find that some are not oriented toward discovering the factual truth within the archaeological record.

Recently SHA turned out an issue containing only one photograph of an artifact in the whole volume. That prompted me to think we are at the stage now where archaeologists can forget all those little bits and pieces of culture and just ignore them. The absence of informative data in some articles is sometimes covered by saying: The usual mid-18th-century assemblage was found, but here's the story. Somewhere there ought to be a good line drawn between science and fiction, but in my opinion, that is not a very popular idea in historical archaeology today [laughs].

Do you think in some way we've become too popular? In your generation there were few historical archaeologists and you were discouraged from being one, and now maybe there are so many archaeologists that they're running short of sites to dig.

SOUTH: You see, one of the problems I had with historical archaeology journals and publications in the past is that they only reported what they found and didn't move into the processual explanation of what processes caused it. They didn't move into the anthropology much. So when Deetz and Leone said we need to make archaeological science more human through storytelling to appeal to the general public, it made sense that some young archaeologists throw storytelling into the breech.

I must be too old-fashioned for the new historical archaeology that's being published as archaeology now. That's not to say that a few archaeologists are not still hanging in there milking ever iota of data they can from the archaeological record. The current explosion of historical archaeology in the contract end of the field has taken over for economic reasons and wags the tail of the pure

research. It seems to me that contract clients are saying we don't want the magnum opus of this site. We just want a report where we can check a box when the Feds ask if they have a report written on it. Then they can stick that report in the file and it never sees the light of day. There are, however, some contract archaeologists who take it on themselves to insist on publishing the results using the motivation of sharing what they learned with colleagues and future generations. Then they'll dig it out and research it and publish their results on their own time. Carl Steen is an archaeologist concerned with doing just that.

My earliest experience, which I'll share with you now and then shut up, was with my grandmother. She used to come to my dad on weekends saying: Austin take me for a drive out on the Blue Ridge Parkway. We would go out there and she'd say: Oh, there's a chimney! Stop here! And dad would sit in the car with mama and talk, while I would go with grandma down to the site where the chimney was located. And she would say: Looky, here's the spring. I'm going to clean it out. So she cleaned out the spring. She pulled out a piece of a 19th-century transfer-printed bowl and asked me if I knew why that bowl was in there.

Then she began her story: Well there was a little girl who lived in that house where the chimney stands. Her mama handed her a bowl with butter wrapped in wax paper and told her to put the bowl in the spring with a rock on the butter to hold it down to keep it from floating. So grandma said the little girl came to the spring, but tripped right before she got there and broke the bowl. But, she put the butter in the spring and put a rock on it anyway.

I didn't realize until I was an archaeologist [laughs], and started writing about my past influences, that it was Grandma Casey who programmed me to have an appreciation for the past, the little pieces of broken dishes and how they functioned in the past household. That also gave me an early introduction to the storytelling which Deetz and Leone have emphasized. My grandma was tying storytelling into discovery to make it more interesting. Her storytelling was indeed interesting, but as an archaeologist I have trouble mixing that wonderful world of fictional storytelling with archaeological science [*laughs*]. Grandma would be the first to insist storytelling was not science! I find that storytelling cocktail intoxicating and seductive, but the quest for scientific truth prevents me from imbibing it.

Now talk to me about Method and Theory in Historical Archaeology. *What—*

SOUTH: *Method and Theory?*

Yes. What were your driving thoughts when you were preparing that book?

SOUTH: Several of those chapters in that book had been papers I'd published elsewhere prior to that. I took some of those papers with me to Virginia when I was invited to go to Winterthur to give a talk. I showed some of the papers to Stuart Struever. After he read them he said I should publish them in a book. On the way back from that conference on the train I sat there and outlined a book. That outline was used to write my *Method and Theory in Historical Archaeology* book using papers I had written, plus a few new chapters.

As I thought about how I would milk the data the idea of the cow chart came to me, and I drew the first draft during that train ride. Later I did the pig chart, the chicken chart, and the global illustration in the front there [*laughs*]. I was trying to put the archaeological process into a broad perspective to show how broader interpretation could emerge from the database of archaeology. I was interested in reaching for the public to share what we think we know. That is probably what Deetz and Leone were trying to get across with their emphasis on storytelling, because a lot of the archaeology we write about is boring except to archaeologists focused on discovering the truth in a scientific manner. But we also have a responsibility to translate our science in a manner that is understandable to the average visitor to historic sites.

It seems to me that one of the things so influential about Method and Theory *was that you standardized ways of looking at sites. You gave us the Mean Ceramic Date Formula. So now when somebody is talking about the age of their site they aren't just saying I think this is early*

19th century or maybe it's around the late 18th century, they have a way to run a more reliable date range. And you did the pattern analysis and developed different pattern profiles for sites, also widely used.

SOUTH: Right.

What influenced you to think about applying those types of mathematical statistical applications to archaeological sites and data?

SOUTH: What impressed that on me was I thought that at Brunswick Town I had an opportunity to compare one ruin with others to see what the percentage relationship was between the various classes of artifacts. In order to do that you have to count them, not simply make guesses. That's why it was shocking to me when Noël Hume said: I don't count sherds. To me that was heresy [*laughs*]. But he told me he thought such counting was anthropological idiocy [*laughs*], because he knew we anthropologists counted things from Native American sites, and I had done it on historic sites as well.

When I got all those counts together from the Brunswick Town ruins I published the resulting profiles in my *Method and Theory in Historical Archaeology* book. The patterned relationship between ruins was so similar it was amazing. Which meant to me that the acquisition process for the ceramic types for those middle-class families along the Street on the Bay in Brunswick Town was part of the world cultural system at that time.

I asked Noël Hume if he would send me quantitative counts that were comparable from sites he had dug so I could see if they matched the pattern of the 18th-century artifact counts from Brunswick Town. He said he didn't have such counts. He said they glued together the bottles and ceramics but didn't count sherds. He was mainly interested in the whole pieces. I felt I had to have a basic bottom line for comparing excavated collections. I couldn't just say I'm going to count bottles and that's it. I said I'm going to count fragments of everything. And so I did.

That pattern raised another question: What about a slave house where somebody doesn't have that much money, and they only get heirlooms and old dishes that are replaced by newer dishes brought into their homes through their owner's contact with the world trade network? Well one of the first sites in America on historical archaeology was by a Florida archaeologist, Ripley Bullen, who dug and reported on a slave house in 1944, called Black Lucy's Garden. He pointed out that the excavated things were likely from the main house and were handed down to Black Lucy. That early example of historical archaeology addressed cultural questions I've always been fascinated by.

I found that one or two of the Brunswick Town sites I dug had been occupied after the Revolution when the town had been burned by the British. However, some of the house sites were reoccupied. Maybe the house wasn't that burned or whatever, and they were able to reoccupy it. They contained pearlwares and some later creamwares and transfer-printed wares. The patterns from those ruins allowed me to demonstrate the value of ceramic analysis through counting sherds, to demonstrate ruins with different periods of occupation. You can see those patterned relationships in my *Method and Theory* book. There you have percentages from a later period that you don't get in the others that were burned. So teasing out these little differences, to me seemed like one of the important functions that archaeologists should be involved with. That's where I began to focus my whole book on trying to point out the need to look at patterned artifact associations beyond the local level, to the broader world cultural system.

When I submitted the manuscript to the editor of Academic Press to be published, I got a letter back saying they were glad to publish my book and had sent it to their printer in California, with instructions to edit out all those animal charts: the pig chart, chicken chart, and cow chart. Those explanatory charts were going to be eliminated as not appropriate to a professional book. I immediately sent him a telegram saying for him to return the manuscript to me. I told him that when that book was published, it would contain those illustrations they considered superfluous and inappropriate. The editor conceded and the book was published with those charts intact.

I'm saddened to see so many papers writing about the theoretical this and the theoretical that without supporting data to underwrite the theory. Not that I'm against theory. Theory is the bridge from the database into the broader explanation. You have a theory, then you dig the next site with the questions raised by that theory to test it. But you need to test it with the archaeological data. You shouldn't just throw out theories anymore than you should simply avoid the data in order to tell a good story.

On the other hand, many articles today simply tell you what they found and may even give you some counts and tell a story. But then they'll throw out a theory to try to explain it and I ask: Where has it been tested? That's part of the scientific process, that constant inductive, deductive scientific process that keeps some of us trying to seek the truth. What we think we know today is not necessarily going to prove true tomorrow, but we continue that search.

J. W. JOSEPH
NEW SOUTH ASSOCIATES
6150 EAST PONCE DE LEON AVENUE
STONE MOUNTAIN, GA 30083

Vergil E. Noble

A Conversation with Charles E. Cleland

Charles E. Cleland, *right*, with Vergil E. Noble.

Introduction

Charles E. ("Chuck") Cleland is a familiar fixture at SHA conferences, having attended just about all of them since the organizational meeting held at Dallas in 1967. In fact, he is among the very few founding members who still regularly attend the annual conference. Cleland continues to be an active scholar, though he retired from teaching more than a decade ago, and he is often called upon to contribute his unique historical perspective and sage advice in the governance of our scholarly organization.

Trained in zoology, Cleland had his first flirtation with archaeology while a graduate student at the University of Arkansas. Upon completion of his master's degree, he enrolled in the anthropology program at the University of Michigan to pursue a doctorate under the formidable James Bennett Griffin. Later, as a professor of anthropology at Michigan State University, Cleland personally built an outstanding program in historical archaeology at a time when very few academic institutions had any involvement with the emerging discipline. Over the ensuing years, scores of students received their graduate degrees under his capable direction, and most emphasized historic sites research in their studies. Many of them also emulated his example in the realm of "archaeopolitics," contributing their talents to the governance of SHA and many other professional organizations.

By virtue of his standing as a past-president of the society (1973), and as a recipient of the prestigious J. C. Harrington Medal (2002), the SHA History Committee selected Cleland to be the subject of an oral history intended to trace the outlines of his distinguished career and the evolution of our discipline. Given the length and breadth of his professional life, comprising nearly five decades and varied intellectual interests, such an undertaking would not be a simple task, but that challenge and distinct honor fell to me. Accordingly, I conducted several recorded interview sessions with Chuck while attending the Conference on Historical and Underwater Archaeology held at the Fairmont-Royal York Hotel in Toronto, 7–11 January 2009. What follows is an edited transcript of those wide-ranging conversations. A fuller summary of Charles E. Cleland's many academic achievements is reported in the published testimonial for his 2002 Harrington Medal (*Historical Archaeology* 36[4]:1–9).

Let's begin with your childhood, Chuck. I know that both of your parents were physicians. Did they try to steer you toward medicine as a child?

CLELAND: No, but they certainly did steer me toward science. For example, every Thanksgiving my mother would take out the turkey heart, slice it open, and show me the ventricles and the auricles, and show me where the veins went and the arteries, and then we'd do the gizzard. I was constantly exposed to the idea of investigating things, and I was very interested in how things worked.

I remember once my dad told me, "If you want to be a famous scientist, you can do that fairly easily. All you have to do is ask the right kind of question." I said, "Like, what makes tree bark brown?" And he said, "Yes, that would be a very good question."

We would take trips to museums in Pittsburgh and Philadelphia, and I was always fascinated with what I found there—not archaeology, per se,

but fossils and insects: natural history.

And you moved around quite a bit, because your father was in the service.

CLELAND: He was in the Army Air Corps, and between about 1942 and '45 we moved often. I went to many schools—six or eight of them over several years. And my first-grade experience was unique, because I was the only Anglo in a neighborhood school in Clovis, New Mexico.

I suppose those relocations exposed you to a wide range of people. Was that when you developed an interest in cultural diversity?

CLELAND: I don't think that I did back then. I was more influenced by the diversity of the natural environment. At one point we lived in a small cabin high in the Rockies west of Colorado Springs. I had free rein to climb, and fish, and explore, and it was great. My interest in anthropology came much later.

But I understand that there was an aptitude test you took with interesting results.

CLELAND: I think that I was a freshman in high school, and my father was already starting to wonder what I would do with my life. So he found a psychologist and had me tested for my occupational aptitude. To everyone's surprise there were two professions indicated in which I would be successful: one was to be a plumber, and the other one was to be an archaeologist.

And what did your parents think of that?

CLELAND: Well, it was fairly confounding. There was no way that they were going to let me be a plumber—though, had I become a plumber, I certainly would have made more money than as an archaeologist. Of course, being an archaeologist was, then as it is today, something that parents just can't imagine would be a way for a child to make a living.

And you had no real interest then.

CLELAND: My first inkling of any interest in archaeology was while reading an adventure book as a child. Some kids found an Indian treasure hidden behind a waterfall in a cave, and I thought that was pretty neat. Needless to say, my career didn't bear such fruit.

Then you went off to college in the natural sciences.

CLELAND: I majored in biology at Denison University [Ohio]—with a less than sterling record, I might add.

But you made it through.

CLELAND: I did make it through, and I did well in the biology part, but there were other problems here and there. I wasn't a very serious student, I'm afraid, and my background wasn't horribly solid, because I had changed schools so often. My "readin', and 'ritin', and 'rithmetic" left something to be desired.

Yet you decided to pursue a graduate degree.

CLELAND: When I graduated with a B.A. degree there was a military draft. I had gone through Air Force ROTC and was interested in flying. I applied for Marine Corps aviation, but I couldn't pass the eye test. So there was a distinct possibility that I would be drafted into the army, and at the same time I had decided to continue in school.

I was interested in studying parasitology, and one of my professors at Denison helped me locate this parasitologist at the University of Arkansas. So I applied to Arkansas and was accepted. When I got there and met with that professor, who turned out to be an old and crusty fellow, he talked to me for about five minutes and said, "My advice to you, son, is that you should join the army." I thought, "Well, I'm here precisely because I don't want to join the army!"

As it turned out, I was hired as a field researcher in wildlife management, which was a program run through the zoology department sponsored by the state game and fish commission. I had a wonderful time, because I had free run of the Ozarks, dealing with squirrels, and turkeys, and other animals—doing research, which I really loved.

I loved it to a degree, but I began to question whether I wanted to do it for a living. At

one point, a zoology professor asked me if I wanted to go to a wild turkey conference in Memphis—thinking at first that he was talking about whiskey, of course. [*laughter*] At any rate, I went, and there were wildlife managers from all over. They were talking about problems in reestablishing turkey populations, which is now one of the great success stories in American wildlife management. It occurred to me, though, that wildlife managers don't really manage animals; they have to manage people, because that's where the problem comes. So I found it, in the end, fairly frustrating.

And, by chance, you ran into a man named Bob [Charles R.] McGimsey.

CLELAND: I did. That was very much by chance. It sobers one when you think how turns in your career can happen just out of the blue. I was wandering through the little museum that they had at Arkansas, and I met this young professor, not too much older than I was. It was Bob McGimsey, and he had just arrived from Harvard—this would have been around 1959 or '60. I started talking to him about my problem, and he said that he might be able to help.

He said, "So, you're majoring in zoology; I guess they teach you how to identify animal bones, don't they?" I said, "Yes, they do," which was somewhat of a fib. So he said, "Well, I could give you a job if you're interested in working on animal remains from archaeological sites and, if you *are* interested in doing that, maybe you could work that up for your master's thesis."

Having no better alternative, I took the offer. I ran directly to the library and started checking out books on mammalian osteology, avian osteology, and so forth. Over the weekend I taught myself how to identify animal bones, or at least got a good start on it.

I ended up working with animal remains from the bluff shelters found along waterways of northwestern Arkansas. They were in with collections gathered during the WPA [Works Progress Administration] under almost no methodology. The artifacts were just grubbed out of these dry rock shelters—but *spectacular* material! I like to say that my first day in archaeology was definitely the best, getting to see all those wonderful things.

Was your involvement then out of an academic curiosity, or did you simply want a job?

CLELAND: Sure, I wanted a job. But I did soon realize, once I got started, that I could contribute a great deal to understanding the materials. For example, there were all these deer mandibles, and I aged them according to wildlife specifications. Then I charted those on an age curve, and I could see that it was a typical predator curve: a lot of very young animals, a lot of very old animals, and very few mature animals. The bones, of course, had resulted from human hunting, but showed the same results that you would get if it were wolves hunting. By looking at the ecological preferences of the species that were represented, I also could say quite a lot about the prehistoric environment and ecology, the diversity of hunting patterns, and that kind of thing.

Back then I was probably at the forefront in developing ethnozoology as a part of archaeology. For quite a few years in the early '60s, I was one of the few people in the country doing more than just providing a list of species, which was common at the time. I wanted to see what those bones could tell us.

You did a master's thesis on the subject. Was that in zoology, or was it in anthropology?

CLELAND: Actually, at that point in time the zoology department and the anthropology department at Arkansas were linked. Bob McGimsey, who was my thesis director, was in the anthropology department, but I got my degree in zoology. The other members of my committee were all zoologists.

Was [now-retired Arkansas State Archaeologist] Hester Davis there at the time that you met McGimsey, or did she come later?

CLELAND: She was there. In those days we called her "Rusty," because she had red hair. She was a good friend, and she was very helpful. Hester took me out to visit a number of archaeological sites—the first excavations I had ever seen—and

helped to instruct me on what went on in the field. I found it very interesting, but that was as far as it went.

So I knew Hester Davis and Bob McGimsey very well, and I continued to have a close association with them for many years—particularly as part of their push to pass the historic preservation legislation, to start up SOPA [Society of Professional Archaeologists], and other things. Bob was a mentor to me in the sense that he got me introduced around and appointed to national committees.

I find it interesting that the genesis of American cultural resource management came out of Arkansas in those years, and that those two people still are very active today.

CLELAND: And their close ally was [the late] Carl Chapman up in Missouri. One shouldn't forget that Carl was very influential in all this, too.

In those days archaeology was a very small discipline and, when I went to [the University of] Michigan to study with Jimmy [James B.] Griffin, almost all of the people I knew in archaeology had passed through Michigan or were associated with Jimmy in some way. He and Bob knew everyone and were doing all the organizing, and I worked into that mix.

How is it that you landed in Ann Arbor?

CLELAND: In 1960, the legislature of Arkansas passed a law that said that people teaching at state institutions could not belong to, or contribute to "subversive" organizations. The administration required that everybody list their organizations, and I had two "bad" ones: the NAACP [National Association for the Advancement of Colored People] and the Congress of Racial Equality [CORE]. Remember those were the days when Little Rock Central High School was being desegregated under the eye of the federal military, and I felt inclined to support that effort.

Because of my contributions to those organizations, I was fired from my teaching assistantship in the zoology department. That was pretty bad, because I had a wife and family, and I didn't know what I was going to do. My master's thesis was nearly finished, and then one day in the spring Bob McGimsey called me into his office.

Bob said, "I've just been to the SAA meetings," and he explained that was the Society for American Archaeology, which was news to me. "I saw Professor Griffin from the University of Michigan, and he's just got a big grant from NSF [National Science Foundation] to work on the prehistoric ecology of the Lake Huron basin. He was asking around to see if anybody was doing ethnozoology, or paleoecology, and I mentioned you."

Several weeks later my phone rang and a voice said, "Mr. Cleland? This is James Griffin at the University of Michigan. I understand that you can identify animal bones from archaeological sites." I said, "Yes, sir, I can do that," this time with some confidence. So he said, "How would you like to come here and get a Ph.D. in anthropology?"

Well, I thought for a minute, and I said to myself, "Jeez, I've never had a course in anthropology. I don't even know what anthropology is." But having nothing better on the horizon, I said that I would like to do it. So I applied and, since my academic record had improved, I got in. I moved to Ann Arbor in the summer of 1960 and was immediately involved in a field program in the Saginaw basin. It was my first field experience.

How did that impress you?

CLELAND: I loved it; I really did. I liked everything about field research. Of course, I wasn't very good at it—didn't know much about it, but I learned pretty fast. The field project was under the direction of an advanced graduate student, Mark Papworth, and he was very skillful. Plus, the crew included other graduate students in archaeology who knew what they were doing. So I learned pretty quickly how to do the basic things: run a transit, shovel, and trowel, and all the other skills that one needs.

So Griffin had this huge NSF grant. Did he assign various aspects of the program to different students?

CLELAND: Yes. We had three or four sites going in the Saginaw Valley and a big project up at the Juntunen site on Bois Blanc Island in the Straits of Mackinac. Griffin showed up that summer at the site I was working on, and we were introduced. He said, "I need you to come down to Ann Arbor and take a Suburban from the motor pool up to the crew on Bois Blanc Island." I didn't even know where that was, but he told me where I needed to go—up to Sheboygan to take the ferry. So I was about to leave, and I said, "Professor Griffin, how am I supposed to get back?" He replied, "You've got a thumb, don't you? Hitchhike! You'll get to see the country that way."

So I delivered the vehicle and stayed around there four or five days. I just loved northern Michigan, and I decided that, if I was going to be a real archaeologist, I would like to work in the northern Great Lakes.

Griffin was a giant of North American archaeology, and he could be a very intimidating sort. What was it like to study under him?

CLELAND: He had an encyclopedic memory of the archaeology of the eastern United States. You could hand him a potsherd from anywhere east of the Mississippi—and a lot of places west, too—and he could tell you within 50 years when it was made and all about it. I've seen him do it, literally. He knew the details of hundreds and hundreds of sites, not only from reading but also because he had visited many of them over the years.

He was very demanding of his students and, as you mentioned, very intimidating. It went on day and night. Every coffee break was a seminar. He'd turn to you and say, "What do you think of the new radiocarbon dates that have just come in from the Lamoka Lake site in New York?" You were expected to comment and, if you weren't within the acceptable range of his conceived "truth," you got it.

That was the learning atmosphere we had. He taught a course called "The Archaeology of the Eastern United States." It was a seminar for graduate students, and it was 10 hours a day of work—day in, day out. He would call on you and say, "Today we're studying the late Archaic period, and what do you know about it, Mr. Noble?" You'd start out, go state by state, and try to give all the details correctly—sites, artifact types, and dates. You'd look over and see his eyebrows bobbing up and down, and he's getting red in the face. Then he'd say, "Well, you don't believe what Bill Ritchie has to say about that pottery up there in New York, do you?" It was like that, intimidating.

I notice that you use terms like "Professor Griffin" and "Mr. So-and-So." Was he a very formal person?

CLELAND: No, he called me "Charles," actually. You know, he very seldom would praise a student. I remember distinctly the few occasions that he did. After I had left grad school, I was giving a paper at a meeting, and he came up afterwards and said, "Well, Charles, that was a rather good paper." I didn't know what to say. I had never heard him say anything like that. I recall that in my paper I likened the development of late Woodland pottery to one of Walt Disney's slow-motion films of a flower blooming. It was a more qualitative kind of a development, and he liked that.

Griffin had a tremendous number of very bright students, almost all of whom went on to distinguished careers. Who were some of the people you went to school with at Michigan?

CLELAND: The two most senior students were Mark Papworth and Lewis Binford, who were there through my first several years in Ann Arbor. There was Dick Yarnell, who was doing ethnobotany; he and I worked fairly closely together. Henry Wright was an undergraduate student at Michigan then, but he participated fully with the grad students in all of our activities. There were many other very smart people there and an interesting dynamic.

That was the cradle of the New Archaeology in those people. It was all "new archaeology" to me in those days, of course, and somewhat different from what developed later. It had an emphasis on the quantitative dimension of research and the science of trying to put the archaeological material into a cultural context. It was a very different approach from that of most of our professors, who had been trained in a different time.

Was Griffin terribly sympathetic toward that trend?

CLELAND: No, he wasn't sympathetic at all. I can remember one time I was taking a course from Leslie White—or maybe it was Elman Service or Marshall Sahlins, and we were studying tribes, bands, and chiefdoms. In Griffin's seminar we were studying the Mississippian, and I said some things about a site representing a typical chiefdom because it had certain dimensions. I can remember Griffin shaking his head and saying, "I don't want to hear about chiefdoms; I want to hear about pottery!" That was his forte: artifacts. Griffin understood the new theories, but that's not what he was interested in teaching.

You were particularly taken with Leslie White's teachings on cultural evolution and called upon them in "The Crisis of Identity in Historical Archaeology" [1968], which you wrote some years later with a former classmate, Jim [James E.] Fitting. Were you trying to pull anthropology more into historical archaeology?

CLELAND: I think that we were voicing a concern about whether historical archaeology was going to be developing as a science, with its basis in anthropology, or if it was going to develop in the humanities, with its basis in history. It was a tension that we felt very acutely in those early years.

You mentioned Binford earlier. He worked with Moreau Maxwell in 1959 at the Straits of Mackinac on the initial excavations at Fort Michilimackinac, 50 years ago. Do you know how that came about?

CLELAND: That was a little before my time, but I knew both Maxwell and Binford very well and heard about events later. Maxwell was at Michigan State, 60 mi. down the road from Ann Arbor. At that time Max was in a combined sociology/anthropology department, and they didn't have any graduate students in archaeology. Maxwell developed this program, starting in '59, at Fort Michilimackinac, which has been going every year since and must certainly be the oldest ongoing excavation in historical archaeology. Max called Griffin and said, "I need an experienced guy to do this work," so Griffin talked to Binford. While all the rest of us were working on the Lake Huron Project in the Saginaw Valley, or at the Juntunen site, Lew was up at Fort Michilimackinac.

I remember we were all somewhat astounded at this, because in those days there weren't many historic site excavations. Lew came back with all these artifacts that were totally unknown to us. He was a very imaginative guy, very smart, and he worked out the pipestem dating formula that winter. I remember him being elated about the results he was getting from his statistical work.

So you were all very aware of historical archaeology, but somewhat mystified by it then.

CLELAND: One of the things that I learned from Griffin was never to speak disparagingly about your program, or your professors, or your fellow students, and we never did. So now I'm going to say something a little bit negative, but I don't want to put it in that sense.

I respected Jimmy Griffin highly; I think he was a great person and a great archaeologist. But, I remember, once Jim Fitting and I were working on a site from the Detroit River corridor. It was a prehistoric site, but it had a 19th-century component. So we had all these transfer-printed plates, and we had them spread out on the table with the other artifacts. We knew Arnold Pilling at Wayne [State University in Detroit], and we knew that he worked with this kind of material. So we knew that it was a legitimate kind of archaeology, but we didn't know anything about it.

We were looking at this collection and trying to figure out what to do with it. Griffin walked in and asked, "What are you guys doing?" We told him that we were trying to work with the ceramics, and he said, "Throw that crap in the wastebasket!"—turned on his heels and walked out. So that was his attitude about historical archaeology.

There were two avenues [toward historical archaeology] that were open at Michigan. There was Lew Binford, working with historic materials from the fort, and then there was George Quimby, who was at the Field Museum [in Chicago]. He was a very good friend of Griffin, and he used to show up quite regularly at the museum in Ann Arbor.

We students all had ideas that differed from Griffin's interpretations, but we couldn't argue with him, because we didn't know enough. Quimby did. He'd come to those coffee breaks we had, and Griffin would be asking us his questions or discussing things, and George would say, "Oh, Jimmy, that's not right." Then they'd have a big argument. George could throw the archaeological data back and forth as well as Griffin could, so I came to have a great deal of respect for him.

One of the things that George was interested in, of course, was early historic Indian materials. He knew a lot about trade silver, iron axes, beads, and that kind of thing. That was legitimate with Griffin, too, because it defined the terminal date of prehistory.

Quimby became your very close friend and colleague. Can you tell me something of his influence on your thinking, or just a good story about George?

CLELAND: He was very influential on my thinking because we had many good, productive conversations about historic Indians and the fur trade. George was very knowledgeable about both archaeology and ethnology. In 1938 or '39, he took a trip up to James Bay [at the south end of Hudson Bay] with George Stanley, who was a geologist, to study glacial phenomena. He visited several Cree Indian villages along the shore, and George said that it was very much like Michigan would have been in the 18th and 19th centuries. He felt that he had experienced the past first hand, and he had a lot of great insights as a result.

So George was doing ethnoarchaeology before it had a name.

CLELAND: He was. When I published my book, *Rites of Conquest* [University of Michigan Press, 1992], I sent him a signed copy of it. He called me after reading it and said, "This is the new ethnoarchaeology." I really appreciated that comment, because it was exactly what I was trying to do.

At any rate, a good story: I remember once we had a crew working over at the Norton Mounds near Grand Rapids. There was a long drive that came into the mound group, and we were working on top of this mound digging. We saw an enormous limousine turn in and come slowly up the road—drove right to the base of that mound where we were working. The window rolled down, and George Quimby stuck his head out— quite unexpected, of course: "Hey, guys! How ya doin'? Mind if I visit you for a while?"

It turned out that George had borrowed the limousine of his boyhood friends, the Bissell brothers of the Bissell carpet-sweeper family in Grand Rapids. He borrowed the limo and the chauffeur—and a huge bar, which he brought along in the trunk of the car. Before we knew it, the chauffeur was serving us martinis and other drinks. We had quite an afternoon visiting with George.

So, you finished your research and wrote your dissertation. Do you have any comments about that research and how it fits into the greater scheme of things?

CLELAND: My dissertation was called *The Prehistoric Animal Ecology and Ethnozoology of the Upper Great Lakes Region* [1966]. It was very esoteric. I tried to reconstruct environmental change using the animal bones, and faunal populations, and other data to do that. Then I outlined a series of subsistence changes through time. At the time it was a rather unusual study, and it was cited "zillions" of times. It's still cited by people that I know haven't actually read it [since it's been out of print for many years].

I look at my dissertation as a jumping off point for a lot of other things that I did later. In the first few years of my career I was pretty much devoted to doing faunal analysis. Eventually, like most other things that I did, I grew bored with it and moved on.

And you moved on to Michigan State, of all places.

CLELAND: I did. During the time I was working on my dissertation, I worked on a side project involving some dog skeletons that Moreau Maxwell at Michigan State [MSU] had excavated on the south coast of Baffin Island. The use of dogs was of some concern in the chronology up there, defining one difference between pre-Dorset and Dorset cultural developments. So the question

was, were these the skeletons of wolves, were they dogs, what were they? I was able to say definitively that they were dogs. So, by working through those problems with Maxwell, I got to like him and know him.

He called me one day and said, "I'm going on a Fulbright to Denmark, and I wonder if you would be interested in coming here and filling in for me while I'm gone. You can be an instructor in anthropology and curator in the museum." I thought that would be good, so I said I would do it. This was while I was finishing my dissertation. In fact, I still had some of my comprehensive exams to take, too, while I was teaching at MSU in the fall of 1964.

So, yes, I went to work at Michigan State and stayed there, as it turned out, throughout my career. When Maxwell came back from his tour in Denmark, the anthropology department at Michigan State was formed, and he became its chair. That opened a vacancy, and I had been in his old position for year, so I was hired.

For a new Ph.D., what was it like to confront those new responsibilities and challenges?

CLELAND: One thing I recall is that I had never taught a class of any kind, never ever, because I went through my Ph.D. program on a research assistantship; I was never a teaching assistant. Suddenly, I was asked to teach an introductory class that had 200 students in it, and I was petrified. I worked hard to get my lectures going—these, I think, were 10-week courses at the time. And I distinctly remember that, by the end of nine weeks, I had taught absolutely all the anthropology that I knew—and I still had a week to go. But it got better over time.

The other thing is that Maxwell, before he left for Denmark, had started the archaeology program at Michilimackinac, and I inherited that from him. It was suddenly under *my* directorship.

I remember very well the first time I was in the museum, where the archaeological collections were kept, and pretty much all we had then were the artifacts from Michilimackinac—French and British materials. I wandered through there, pulling out drawers and looking at the collection, and having no idea what any part of it was. I didn't know a gunflint from a gunlock. I didn't know anything about the ceramics, and I was just beside myself. [I wondered] how can I direct a project if I don't know the material culture—if I don't know anything about the historical circumstances of the site?

I soon came to the conclusion that I couldn't and that I had to get help. I managed to finagle a graduate assistantship and advertised the position widely. There were several applicants, and the best of those clearly was Lyle Stone, who was then a graduate student with Rey [Reynold J.] Ruppé at Arizona State. Lyle was originally from Nebraska, and he had actually excavated some historic forts there. He knew what he was doing, and he knew historic artifacts, so I hired him.

Lyle showed up—I believe it must have been in '65, and he became my first graduate student at Michigan State. I feel to this day that Lyle taught me much more historical archaeology than I taught him; I know that's true. I remember going through the cabinets with Lyle—he would be pointing out this and that—and then later visiting the site with him, talking about field strategy. I was learning from him all the time.

I tried to keep that pattern with other students that came to MSU. Pat Martin, for example, came in after having excavated down at Arkansas Post; he taught me things. Henry Miller came in, and he taught me about faunal material from the Chesapeake Bay area. And Bill Lees came in, eventually, and he had been excavating in the Carolinas. It was quite a dramatic group. Now, I haven't mentioned you, Vergil, because you had been an undergraduate there.

Right. All I could teach you was what I'd learned from you. [laughter]

CLELAND: But I'd like to think that, in working with all the bright students that came through MSU over the years, I learned nearly as much from them as they learned from me.

It was very much an atmosphere like I suppose yours was in graduate school. All the students were interacting constantly, working on various things, and you coordinated it all.

CLELAND: Yes, and that's something I picked up from Griffin. When you have a lot of graduate students involved in different things, and particularly different field programs, as a professor you want to get them field experience. You want to get them experience in directing a crew, teaching students in the field—all the aspects. I used to involve them in doing the budgets, going over to talk to the people in the administration building, all aspects of it.

I spent most of my summers in those years traveling from one site to another, talking to the student field directors and doing other things—trying to make sure that all was running smoothly and everybody was happy, that each site was excavated in such a way that the questions we had could be answered.

One of your other colleagues on the faculty in the early days at MSU was Jim [James A.] Brown. He also worked at Michilimackinac for a while in the late '60s. How did he get involved?

CLELAND: One of the things that we were trying to do in those years was to build a program, and you can't build an archaeological program with one person. You have to have diversity of opinions. Jim had, theretofore, worked on prehistoric sites. He was very well known, a very established scholar. Jim, perhaps because of his contact with Lew Binford at [the University of] Chicago, wanted to work at Michilimackinac, and I was happy to have him doing it.

When you think of those early years, we had some great leadership at the straits—Maxwell first, a very well-respected archaeologist. We had Lew Binford, certainly one of the smartest guys in the field. We had Lyle, and we had Jim Brown, and Jim, as I said, was superb. So that was a very good start to the field program up there.

When you started at MSU, the historical archaeology there was almost exclusively geared toward French colonial archaeology. How did that program evolve?

CLELAND: It was a gradual process of building expertise and student interests beyond the French colonial period. Of course, that was a major component at Michilimackinac. Later, we had a large project at Fort Ouiatenon in northern Indiana on the Wabash [River, near Lafayette]. Both Judy Tordoff and you, Vergil, were participants in that, and also Terry Martin. All of you worked up your dissertations on that site.

That led to a certain expertise of working with fortifications. Ultimately, we worked at the site of Fort Brady in Sault Ste. Marie, which was an American site, and much later at Fort Gratiot in Port Huron, which was also an American military site—War of 1812 era. Lee Minnerly was involved with Fort Brady, and Mark Esarey with the site down on the end of Lake Huron—the Fort Gratiot site. Marcy Gray also wrote a report on National Park Service excavations that had been done by others at Fort Vancouver in Washington.

In addition, there were several field projects in St. Ignace on the north side of the straits.

CLELAND: Yes, that's true—the Marquette Mission site and the large Huron Indian village it served. We worked on that for a period of a decade or so, going back on several different occasions. It was a very interesting site and one that led ultimately into a museum enterprise that we were instrumental in designing, and other cultural tourism projects.

Lyle Stone, in fact, did the initial investigations.

CLELAND: He did. There was also some work done there by the State of Michigan [directed by James E. Fitting] in the early years. Then, of course, you and Sue [Schacher] Branstner worked on the site, and a number of other graduate students.

There were some other Indian sites in St. Ignace—cemetery sites we investigated. There was the Gros Cap site that we worked on somewhat, and then the Lasanen site, which was a 17th-century burial site.

Lasanen was believed to be a Feast of the Dead ceremonial site, was it not?

CLELAND: Yes. It was a series of small ossuaries, very rich in artifacts of the period. It was a very important site. I did a [1971] publication on it with the cooperation of student researchers, both

graduate and undergraduate, who wrote parts of the report.

We also moved into some other kinds of historic sites—the Mill Creek site comes to mind, on the south side of the Straits of Mackinac. It was an early American sawmill, and later a farm, in support of the fort out on the island—Fort Mackinac. Pat Martin ultimately wrote that up for his dissertation.

Were you involved with the Fletcher site investigations?

CLELAND: I was involved with that site, but I was more politically involved with it than archaeologically involved. That site was a mid- to late-18th-century French-Indian burial site, and it was revealed by dredging along the Saginaw River near Bay City. I had a crew up in northwest Michigan that summer, digging prehistoric sites, and we kept getting word through the grapevine that people were finding all these skeletons, and trade kettles, and guns, and so forth, down in Bay City.

Finally, we got a request to go down and try to do something about it. It was just a terrible mess; there were pothunters in there going to work, but we finally got the site under control. I believe that summer Moreau Maxwell came in later with a crew of MSU students and worked on it. Subsequently, Jim Brown was there with a crew. It was a pretty spectacular site, too. Of course, that material has all been repatriated. Bob Mainfort did his dissertation on the burial complex at that site.

The only other thing that comes to mind from that period is some work that Margaret Kimball Brown did.

CLELAND: Yes, Margaret had previously worked on sites in Illinois related to the Kaskaskia, the Peoria, and others, and she had some materials that had been excavated down there. She did a study on the archaeological evidence for acculturation. I think that may be a fairly full catalog of the upper Great Lakes sites.

Then, in the 1980s, the program changed direction, and a new generation of students began work at MSU.

CLELAND: Yes, we had a major new project down on the Tombigbee Waterway [near West Point, Mississippi]. That project entailed the excavation of three antebellum town sites [Colbert, Barton, and Vinton] along the waterway, which were supposedly going to be impacted by a huge channelization of the Tombigbee River. We were in the field down there for three full years, with generous funding, and we had 75 people in the field for most of that time. Lee Minnerly, who had worked previously at the straits and at Fort Brady, was in overall charge of operations, assisted by Mike Polk, who was the field director coordinating excavations at the three town sites. We also had an archives research team and an oral-history team in addition to the field and laboratory personnel.

How did it come about that Michigan State was working in the Deep South?

CLELAND: By the 1980s, we had developed a good national reputation for training students in historical archaeology. The National Park Service out of Atlanta, which had the main responsibility for pulling off the work along the Tombigbee along with the Corps of Engineers, wanted to get one institution to do all the historic site work. They also wanted an educational component to the project, and there weren't too many institutions around the country at that point with the capability to field such a huge project.

Ultimately, the project had a million-and-a-half dollar budget, so it was huge in that era. Several of our students, like Kim and Steve McBride and Leah [Allen] Rogers, got their dissertation or thesis research out of that project. There were other MSU grad students there who didn't do their theses or dissertations on Tombigbee topics, like Dean Anderson and Judy Tordoff, and students from other universities, like Bob Sonderman and Debbie Hull-Walski. All of them, though, got very good experience and learned a great deal. I know that I came out of it with a much more sophisticated view of what historical archaeology should be about, and I think that the students who worked on the Tombigbee Project did, too.

Of course, it was a very, very difficult project administratively. I dealt with the university end of it, and Lee Minnerly dealt with the field end.

The park service and the corps insisted that we do the project in four different phases. We had to do a report for each completed phase, and then a proposal for each new phase, before the next phase could start. This created all kinds of budgetary nightmares, because we had a local laboratory down there, dozens of housing units rented, cars leased, and so forth. The government would stop making payments as soon as we put each phase report in, and then they waited until we got the next proposal approved before starting up payments again.

It was a very difficult situation for us, and we were continually going into arrears. The university had to cover for us—they weren't very happy about that. It all worked out in the end, of course, but getting there was difficult. The excavations were very productive, and I very much enjoyed working down there. Tef [former SHA secretary/treasurer Stephanie H.] Rodeffer was the park service person overseeing our project. I enjoyed working with her, even though the scheme of management was not what either of us would have desired.

The academic program at Michigan State had always been rather informal, but you later created several courses related to historical archaeology.

CLELAND: Probably it was in the '70s I realized that this catch-as-catch-can kind of education was not going to sustain a program. So I designed two courses in historical archaeology: one was a theory course, basically a graduate seminar, and the other one was a material culture course, which dealt with the whole spectrum of historic artifacts. Those were offered each year, and it wasn't long before we had a good cadre of students that were capable of handling not only historic site archaeology, but they were also getting training in prehistoric archaeology. We were turning out very well-rounded students that could handle any job.

In fact, I recall your insistence that you did not turn out historical archaeologists; you turned out North American archaeologists.

CLELAND: Yes, that was our goal—and I don't think an unreasonable one.

175

One part of your career that I don't know much about is the period after I left Michigan State in 1983. What happened from then through the time of your retirement?

CLELAND: I retired in 2000, so there's a period of time there, but sometime in the early '90s I sensed that my interests were shifting toward ethnohistory. I talked to the chairman of my department and said, "Look, I'd like to do less archaeology and more ethnohistory," and that change was agreed upon.

I tried to make that transition, but unfortunately—or fortunately, depending on your perspective, I couldn't quite pull it off, because we still had a lot of students in our historical archaeology program. We had a lot of field projects going and potential field projects, which they needed for their theses and dissertations. I was the only one willing at that time, during the '90s, to continue with the field work and sponsor the students involved with those projects—people like Eric Perkins and Paul Demers.

But I did form an ethnohistory interest group at the university, which had people from both history and anthropology in it. Further, I began to teach, in the '90s, graduate seminars in ethnohistory and on the relationship between cultural anthropology and history. I found that to be an awful lot of fun and very enjoyable. I still, by the way, continued to teach courses in both prehistory and historical archaeology.

I also had the idea during that period that since most archaeologists were then employed in the private sector, and since that was the market for our students, and since those firms required much different skills out of their employees than was a traditional part of the training in archaeology, then we ought to be turning out students that knew something about management—something about budgets, something about how to make their way in the world of business. We got some of my colleagues together, and we roughed out a program to train cultural resource people for their jobs.

Regretfully, that wasn't a very successful venture. The cultural anthropologists [on the department faculty] saw it as something they might be able to horn in on, so they wanted to turn it into an applied anthropology program in which cultural resource management would be a subpart. I think that is the main reason why it didn't succeed. I mean, archaeologists were the ones that had the employment market, and we had a very strong idea of what the skills set should be for that market. The others didn't really have anything but an amorphous idea that there might be government employment for cultural anthropologists.

I do remember that, as part of setting up that program, we had a very interesting session in which we brought back to the campus some of our former students who were employed in a whole spectrum of archaeological jobs in government and the private sector. We asked them to discuss what kind of skills they thought people needed to take advantage and to succeed in the new environment of archaeology during that era and continuing into this. I think that we faculty members had our eyes opened, frankly, because we began to see that we weren't doing a very good job of training people.

While I think that the degree program designed around that concept was not successful, I think that, individually as advisors, we tried to see from then on that people—if they were planning to work in the contract business—would have the skills that they needed. In that way it did succeed.

One thing not often acknowledged or widely known is that your first student, Lyle Stone, was also one of the first people to go off and start a business in archaeology.

CLELAND: And at the time I thought he was nuts! [*laughter*] He had a very good job with the Mackinac Island State Park Commission on a site that he knew very well. We were all very excited that he was working there and were looking forward to continuing the cooperation between our university and the commission with Lyle in place.

One day, suddenly, he came around and announced that he was quitting. I said, "What are you going to do?" He said, "I'm going to move back to Arizona, and I'm going to start a private contracting business." I said, "Lyle, you'll be starving to death in six months. There's just not enough work."

Well, he certainly proved us all wrong. I know that he had a real struggle with some of the professionals in the state of Arizona and with the Arizona State Museum. They didn't want to see a private contractor coming in, doing business on their turf. Lyle stuck it out; he did good work; he had high professional standards, lots of integrity, and he built a very, very successful business.

So I think that we were all amazed by this new development. Of course, that was just the beginning trickle out of the floodgate.

Soon after Lyle Stone arrived at MSU, you and he went down to Ed [Edward B.] Jelks's conference in Dallas in 1967, which was the genesis of the SHA.

CLELAND: Yes, we did. The year before that there was a meeting of some kind in St. Louis, probably it was an SAA conference, and I couldn't go. I was busy, and I asked Lyle to represent us. When Lyle came back he said, "I need to talk to you about something. I ran into Ed Jelks down there, and Ed and I got talking."—there were some others involved, too—"Ed wants to have a conference to talk about forming a new discipline, historical archaeology. I think this is something we want to support."

I certainly agreed with that, because you didn't have to dig too far to see that a lot of the work being done in historical archaeology then was not very good. On the other hand, I really didn't see historical archaeology as being much different from prehistoric archaeology in method and theory, though there was a different set of artifacts that people had to master. I was somewhat ambivalent about it, but I agreed with Lyle that it was something we ought to support as an institution.

I would say also that, at that time in the mid-'60s, archaeology was diversifying very rapidly. All kinds of new specialties were developing, and clearly historical archaeology was a potential discipline with its own body of material culture and its own theory, and particularly its own methods. Or at least I could see that as a potential.

Even though you had not yet developed a strong research interest in historical archaeology of your own, you had an interest in the theoretical bent of the emerging discipline and wanted to have an influence on it.

CLELAND: Yes. I think at that point I was, as I've already said, interested in keeping a scientific and anthropological component in historical archaeology. On the other hand, I had enough experience by then to see that the use of documents was a very powerful methodological component of historical archaeology that prehistoric archaeology did not have. As Maxwell, my mentor at Michigan State, often said to me, "The thing about historical archaeology is that it's got to make sense, because you have documents that the artifacts and the interpretations have to square with." It wasn't that I was in any way anti-history. I simply thought that historic documents had to be used to ask broader questions, and I still believe that.

Did you perceive then that you were going to be drawn into the leadership of this new organization?

CLELAND: No, I had no idea that would happen. But I was good friends with Ed Jelks, and he was the mover and shaker. He and I, over the years, often talked, and plotted, and strategized about not only how to develop historical archaeology, but how to bring professionalism into archaeology through SOPA and the RPA [Register of Professional Archaeologists] later on.

Those two threads: If I contributed anything when the field started to diversify, I, as well as others, supported the foundations for historical archaeology. Then, a little bit later, when we saw the need for professional ethics in archaeology, we also supported that. Those were my interests, and I hope those are the interests I helped bring to this profession.

Before we move on to your long service in the SHA, tell me a bit about your role in the founding of SOPA and its successor, the Register of Professional Archaeologists.

CLELAND: SOPA was formed in '76 at a meeting of the Society for American Archaeology at St. Louis. I remember participating in a small ceremony that took place at the top of Monk's

Mound [at Cahokia Mounds State Historic Site, across the Missouri River in Illinois]. There was a small group of us appointed as a committee of the SAA to study some way to codify ethics, research standards, and to bring that into practice.

We had met down in Fayetteville, at the University of Arkansas, for several weeks, I believe, and we hammered out what was to be the basic structure of SOPA. Then we went to work on the SAA and tried to get them to adopt it. We couldn't get SAA to act on this committee recommendation, so that day on Monk's Mound we just said that we'd had it: "We'll break away and form our own organization." And we did. That was SOPA, and it struggled along for quite a long time.

After Ed Jelks, I was the second president of SOPA, in 1977 and 1978. Later, I was elected to be the grievance coordinator of SOPA, between 1981 and 1983—right before my last term on the SHA board. SOPA Grievance Coordinator was, frankly, a very onerous position and very difficult. I had a great number of complaints to investigate, and it was almost a full-time job for me. Fortunately, my institution let me work on it.

Because of those grievance procedures, SOPA was doing the job it was designed to do, but it was not gaining the numbers that it would have to have in order to make it a strong professional organization. Some of us began to think of ways that we might be able to make SOPA evolve into something stronger. That happened in the early '90s. There was a committee formed, on which I was the SHA representative. This committee was going to try to do something about SOPA—to broaden its base, to make it stronger, and, especially, to increase its membership. SOPA was stable, but it wasn't gaining new members very fast. We thought that, for it to be successful, we had to do something to increase membership.

We had a meeting in St. Louis with reps from SAA, SHA, and AIA [Archaeological Institute of America]—and maybe some other organizations, as well. We had some pretty tough discussions, and I'm proud to say that I sketched out a new structure on a piece of tablet paper. My suggestion was that a new organization be created—not really an organization, but a register. It would

have the same enforcement powers and the same code as SOPA, but it would be an institution that was jointly supported by AIA, SHA, and SAA. That was finally agreed to after some negotiation among those sponsors, and the modern Register of Professional Archaeologists was formed.

Coincidentally, our current SHA president-elect [now president], Bill Lees—one of your former students, was the last president of SOPA and the first president of the RPA.

CLELAND: He was, yes, and he did a very good job in that transition, which I can guarantee was difficult. We had to abolish SOPA and start up RPA. We had to do that without disrupting the whole flow of professionalism, keeping all the organizations on board and happy, and interfacing with the new board. I know it was a trial for Bill, but he did a great job with it.

As for your unexpected leadership role in the SHA, you ultimately ended up on the board of directors several times, chaired many committees over the years, and served as president of the organization in 1973. I presume that you saw many changes during those years.

CLELAND: I did—terrific changes. In retrospect, I think that this organization has been a fantastic success. It's developed with a lot of integrity and a lot of enthusiasm. This was an organization, of course, that was [an entirely] volunteer organization for many years, and I think that spirit is still there. I hope it always will be, because I think that's what makes the SHA very strong—the fact that people participate and pitch in.

During that time there was a tremendous growth in the discipline and diversification of interests. You were in the middle of all that as it was going on. Did you actively try to steer things in one way, or let it run its own course?

CLELAND: "Archaeopolitics" was alive and well then, just like it is now—maybe more so. There was always tension in the early years between SHA and SAA, and I don't think that the SAA was really happy to see a new organization grow up and flourish. Not that there was any formal resistance, but we had to struggle somewhat to have a voice, say, in Washington with bills that were passed. But since I knew McGimsey and Chapman, and the people who were working on that other side, I could have a foot in both camps.

I remember lobbying on the National Historic Preservation Act [of 1966] and on the UNESCO Convention on antiquities. We had a council on which the SAA, SHA, and AIA were all represented. I appeared before a senate committee when I was president of SHA, testifying for all archaeologists in the country. That was pretty nice—not in a personal way, but for the fact that we had diverse archaeological interests coming together and speaking with one voice. That was very good.

As archaeology diversified, during the '60s and '70s, historical archaeology got caught up with the underwater group. It didn't come out of SHA, but we had common interests. After a few years of association there was some movement in the underwater community to separate from SHA, particularly when I was president in 1973.

Some of the underwater people, like Barto Arnold and George Fischer, approached me and said, "What are we going to do about this?" I liked the idea that underwater archaeology had come quite a ways during our early association, particularly in the development of ethical positions, so I thought they should stay.

I got a little education in those matters, by the way, because one of the early SOPA committees I served on was trying to set standards for underwater survey. I was at a meeting down in Austin, and the people involved in the original Gulf of Mexico oil-lease surveys also were there. We were trying to decide what constituted an adequate survey of bottomland sites with side-scanning sonar, and so forth. There I began to understand what the underwater archaeologists were trying to do.

So, in 1973, I met with the underwater folks and argued strongly that they ought to remain in SHA, and they decided to do that. I felt like that was a good contribution I made, trying to keep them with the SHA where I believed they belonged, because our [mutual] emphasis was on the preservation of sites. Our emphasis was on developing appropriate theory and methodology

to deal with major kinds of questions, not just recovering artifacts.

What else stands out in your mind from the time you were SHA president?

CLELAND: [*laughs*] Well, in some ways this organization was much easier to govern in those days, because there weren't a lot of committees. The board would meet and make its decisions, and things ran fairly smoothly. I say "fairly." I recall that I was past-president during the year that James Deetz was president, and it was discovered midway through his term that he wasn't a paid-up member of SHA [for that year]. That caused a bit of a problem, and I had to run a few meetings in his absence, but it all worked out.

Things were much simpler. Unfortunately, in those days people would be appointed to head a committee, and they would look on it as an honor rather than a working assignment. That was difficult. Things have now become much more businesslike.

We have had various controversies in the discipline and the society, and you were right in the thick of some. Is there anything that you would like to set down for the record?

CLELAND: Yes, I would talk about one, which was very troubling to me, personally, but part of the history of SHA. That had to do with a situation that occurred when I was elected to my second term on the SHA board, starting in 1982. I was just about to go to my first meeting [of the incoming board], and I was accosted in the hall by several of my friends who were underwater archaeologists.

They asked me if I knew that the incumbent SHA president was involved with an underwater salvage company and explained that this had to do with the wreck of the *Wydah* in Boston Harbor. And they said, "Do you remember when you came to talk to us back about 10 years ago about us staying in SHA? How you were going to put emphasis on ethics and the preservation of sites? Now, at this meeting, there have been two board meetings, and nobody on the old board has mentioned this problem. We think that it's a really bad problem, and we want *you* to bring it up."

I didn't particularly want to do it. I found it very disturbing. But I went to that board meeting and, after discussing some of the normal business, I finally brought the matter to the attention of President [Edwin "Ted"] Dethlefsen. I was relieved to find that a lot of other people on the board were upset with this situation, too. Some knew of it, but nobody else had raised it.

I respected Ted very much, on the basis of his previous work, and I thought that he was a great guy and a great president for the society. But he made the argument then that I think we still, unfortunately, hear today, that if you don't cooperate with treasure salvors data will be lost. But it was the position of SOPA, and the position of the underwater people, that it's the sites that we should protect. If we cooperate with the salvors we only lend legitimacy to a project aimed only at retrieving artifacts, perhaps with little regard for the site itself.

Anyhow, after considerable discussion—and some argument—we adjourned, and several days later President Dethlefsen resigned. I always felt very bad about it. Nevertheless, I thought it was something that needed to be done—not just because we had to keep faith with our underwater colleagues, but because, in the broader sense, we needed to establish good ethics within our own profession. That's something that stands out in my mind as a very difficult time.

Aside from less-pleasant experiences, you also formed many close friendships with colleagues over the years through the SHA. At the risk of offending somebody for not being mentioned, do any of your colleagues stand out as being particularly important influences?

CLELAND: Oh, gosh, there are so many that I feel uncomfortable mentioning any of them. But I would say this: I feel that, just as I learned from many of my students, I also learned from many of my colleagues—not so much by listening to formal papers, but by chatting about their projects and their views about various theoretical and methodological issues. I'm not saying that I never attended a paper, you understand. [*laughter*]

Of your own work in historical archaeology, where

do you think that you might have made some important substantive or theoretical contributions?

CLELAND: Let's leave out the word "important" and leave that for posterity to judge—which they will, anyhow. [*laughter*]

Let me say that I've had some fairly serious transitions in my career. I started out as a prehistorian. I pretty much exclusively did prehistoric archaeology for 10 years or so. I liked prehistoric archaeology; I still like prehistoric archaeology; I still do prehistoric archaeology. But then I discovered historical archaeology and enjoyed that very much. And from that, I think that I took away a love of working with historical documents—in the context of historical archaeology, first, and in the context of ethnography, second.

In that latter sense, I tried to master the documentary record relating to Indian tribes of the upper Great Lakes during the late 18th and the 19th century through modern times. That knowledge I applied to another field, which is the law and trying to work with native tribes in pursuing their rights under various Indian treaties.

In fact, you gave testimony in some important landmark trials.

CLELAND: I did—most all of them in the Great Lakes region—hunting and fishing cases, reservation boundary issues, sovereignty issues, environmental issues, some criminal cases. In all of those instances, I was an expert witness in ethnohistory, and I enjoyed it very much.

I suppose that your earlier performance as the SOPA grievance coordinator immersed you in legalities that later proved useful in those litigations related to Indian treaty rights.

CLELAND: Yes, it's strange the way your experience later comes to bear on things. I used to get kidded when I was SOPA's grievance coordinator that I was practicing law without a license. In some respects I really was, because the hearings were quasi-judicial processes. I traveled to hearings with SOPA's very good lawyer, and he taught me how to take depositions and how to question people in a hearing. That held me in good stead when I got involved with the expert witness work that I later did for the Great Lakes tribes.

It's a very different experience explaining things to lawyers, I suppose.

CLELAND: It is. You know, in a sense, writing for the law and for the courts can be much more demanding. When you're writing for a group of professional colleagues, you can assume a certain body of knowledge that everyone would accept. When you're writing for the law, for a judge who doesn't know anything about the material, you can't assume that at all. You can't assert that a certain artifact, for example, has a certain use. You have to document that conclusion for them.

Unlike most of our research in archaeology, your work had impacts on peoples' lives today—serious impacts on their livelihoods.

CLELAND: Yes, it has. This all came about because of my dissertation dealing with paleoecology and the subsistence practices of native people. I finished that in '66, and one day, in 1974 or '75, I got a call from a young woman attorney who worked for one of the northern Michigan tribes. She said to me on the phone, "I've been reading your dissertation, and I find it fascinating." I thought, "My goodness, what is this about?" I couldn't imagine that anybody would have thought it was "fascinating," let alone a lawyer. [*laughter*]

She drove all the way down from Sault Ste. Marie to East Lansing to talk to me about my dissertation, we met, and she told me, "Our tribe has a lawsuit with the State of Michigan. We're gill-net fishermen, and the State of Michigan is claiming that Indians learned to gill net from the French."

But my dissertation research showed pretty clearly that, at least by A.D. 1000, Indians were using gill nets in the Great Lakes. It had been an independent, indigenous invention. The tribe was very anxious that I come to court and present that evidence. I did; they won the right to fish and, ultimately, they got control over all the commercial fishing in the upper Great Lakes—in the treaty waters, and it was an enterprise that was worth millions of dollars annually to tribal fisherman.

In fact, that was a case where the federal government was suing in behalf of the tribal people against the state for limiting federal agreements with the native tribes, was it not?

CLELAND: Yes, that's correct. That was true not only in the Michigan case, but subsequently in Wisconsin and through central and eastern Minnesota. Those were all separate treaties, but they were all treaties that guaranteed Indians the right to usufruct activities—whether hunting, fishing, or gathering, in the territories they ceded to the United States. That was part of the quid pro quo for all this land the federal government acquired.

Soon after that happened, the states and territories began telling the tribes, "Wait a minute. We own the resources and, therefore, you have to buy a license from us." Indians always protested that, and they never believed it. However, the states did arrest and prosecute them, and then confiscated their equipment. Ultimately, as the tribes became more sophisticated in the 1960s, and some young attorneys went to law school from the tribes, they became more belligerent about this—trying to establish those rights that they believed they had. The federal government, after the tribes had initiated the lawsuits, came in on their side and said, "These treaties are agreements between the Indian people and the United States of America. Some of you states didn't even exist when those agreements were made."

So, in some small measure, through my work those rights have now been reestablished. They're very important rights to native people, because they are a very important part of their sovereignty, their jurisdiction, and other kinds of issues that give them status with state and local governments.

You were involved with at least one case in Canada, were you not?

CLELAND: I was involved with several cases in Canada. One was a criminal prosecution for fishing, which was in the eastern part of Lake Superior under the Huron-Robinson Treaty of 1850. Another one had to do with the Sarnia First Nation across from Port Huron, Michigan, on the other side of the St. Clair River, which was a land claim.

Much of that expert-witness work was done late

in your career. While a lot of people might begin to coast toward retirement, you were getting a lot busier. Even in retirement you continue to write and do research, including a major synthesis on treaty rights [Faith in Paper: The Ethnohistory and Litigation of Upper Great Lakes Indian Treaties, *University of Michigan Press, 2010*].

CLELAND: I convinced myself, I guess, that the story of this treaty litigation in the Great Lakes needed to be told. Then I further convinced myself that I was the only one who could tell it, because, of all of the attorneys and witnesses involved in those various cases, I participated in all of them—knew all of the actors and the issues. So I decided that I had to write it.

It's an interesting story. I hope that people will read the book and understand the saga. But, in order to write it, I couldn't continue to do the expert-witness work, so I had to "re-retire." I retired from that, and I've finished the book. Now I have to find something else to do!

Though it's been 10 years since you retired from teaching, you continue to come to the SHA meetings and stay active in the organization.

CLELAND: Well, this is where my friends are—and my former students, who are also my friends. I very much enjoy coming annually to see them, and visit with them, and learn of what they're doing. I think I'll continue to come to SHA meetings as long as I can contribute something. I don't see any end to that.

You were present at the creation of historical archaeology as an organized discipline. What has impressed you as being very fruitful research, and where do you think that we might have gone astray over the years?

CLELAND: I guess I would say that perhaps one of my disappointments is how slowly a body of theory has developed in historical archaeology. If you compare the content of historical archaeological journals with the prehistoric journals, I think that you would conclude that there are many fewer theoretical articles. I don't know why that is, because I think that historical archaeology has very fruitful avenues to pursue.

Of course, I've written about this before. I think that the emphasis on historic specifics has been far too strong to suit my tastes.

I recall that the great French sociologist, Emile Durkheim, said that the study of culture is often taken up with an assumption that it's guided by human choices—this is a paraphrase, of course. He said that events cannot be understood without understanding the underlying cultural principles that are behind the actions of individuals, and that you can't understand the latter without understanding the former. One of my teachers at Michigan, Leslie White, wrote an essay along similar lines called "Man's Control over Civilization: An Anthropocentric Illusion" [1948].

Perhaps it's a phenomenon of funding, or historical tourism, but I believe that we still put too much emphasis on individuals and events in historical archaeology. To me, it should be the other way around: how did cultural phenomena influence events and people in producing certain outcomes? So I've been particularly taken over the years by studies that have a very broad scope and ask very broad questions—or at least have a problem-oriented research perspective.

I call to mind a study done, I think, by the State of Pennsylvania relating to farmsteads, and it's based on the proposition that farmsteads are parts of a large network that includes urban settings. You can't understand land tenure; you can't understand production or prices on a farm unless you know that there's another part of it—a market part. I also admire Jim [James E.] Ayres's work with logging communities in Utah and Wyoming, in which he's looking at logging as a big areal system in which the product and supplies are moving through corporate units. Field operations are all networked together.

That kind of approach seems to me to be very productive, and it does not have its emphasis on who occupied the cabins or farmsteads, or even exactly when they were occupied. Instead, it deals with systemic issues. There have been plenty of studies along those same lines in urban archaeology and many other fields.

Do you have any thoughts about where we ought

to be going, either as an organization or as a discipline, in the coming years?

CLELAND: I think that I would like to see us give more attention to the "Big Picture" and ask the more complicated questions. While more difficult and more costly, they're enormously more productive in terms of what we can contribute.

Any other closing observations?

CLELAND: No. I'd just like to thank you for spending the time to help me through this maze.

It's a long and distinguished career to summarize in a few hours' conversation, but I think we've done well.

CLELAND: I hope so. I've had fun.

Daniel G. Roberts

A Conversation with Ronald L. Michael

There is nothing typical about the way in which Ronald L. Michael came to embrace archaeology as a profession, nor in the way in which he pursued his career. From a very early age he had an interest in American history and later developed interests in anthropology and industrial technology that he ultimately parlayed into two advanced degrees and a 36-year teaching career at a university in Pennsylvania that many think is in California. His bachelor's and master's degrees are from schools in North Dakota that offered virtually no archaeology or anthropology courses. Undaunted, and together with his mentor at the University of North Dakota, Ronn created a master's curriculum combining anthropology and history practically from scratch, and along the way received a teaching certificate that allowed him to teach various subjects most anywhere in North Dakota. After receipt of his master's degree,

and although he maintained a strong interest in history and his thesis was on the fur trade in North Dakota's Red River Valley, he had little firsthand experience in historical archaeology. But three summer stints as a ranger/historian with the National Park Service at Grand Portage National Monument in Minnesota changed all that, and he went on to receive his doctorate at Ball State under the mentoring of archaeologist B. K. Swartz, Jr. Yet even his doctorate and dissertation topic were unusual: rather than the typical Ph.D., he received the Ed.D., and rather than the usual narrative dissertation his dissertation was a comprehensive, annotated archaeological bibliography that is still used throughout the state of Indiana today.

After receipt of his Ed.D. degree, Ronn began a long and productive teaching career at California University of Pennsylvania, where he developed and creatively taught a number of highly unusual courses on various technological processes, and he founded and managed his own consulting company for two decades simultaneously with his teaching. But it is his work as the longtime editor of *Historical Archaeology* that best defines Ronn to most historical archaeologists.

When Ronn took over the editorial responsibilities for the society's journal, publication of *Historical Archaeology* was nearly two years in arrears. He quickly went about the task of marshalling old and new manuscript submissions to bring the journal up to date, which he accomplished in only one year. Although the first volume to bear his name as editor was volume 12, in reality he put together the previous volume almost single-handedly. By 1980, he had caught up and began making plans to issue the journal twice a year instead of only once. Amazingly, within a year, the journal was published with two numbers each year, and by 1990 it had become a quarterly publication, which it still is today. Along the way, Ronn also revived the dormant *Special Publications* series, which saw seven volumes published before it morphed into a yearly thematic volume; initiated a very useful bibliographic series called *Guides to* the *Archaeological Literature of the Immigrant Experience in America*, which has five volumes published to date; developed relationships with several university presses; and brought the society's publishing programs into the digital age.

The position of editor in the Society for Historical Archaeology is filled on an appointed, three-year renewal basis rather than an elected one. Every three years, Ronn would signify his willingness to continue on, and every three years the president and board of directors would recognize Ronn's talents and reappoint him. Frankly, it was his job for life if he wanted it, he was that good, but after 27 years at the editorial helm Ronn finally made the hard decision to retire in 2004. Quite a run for a small-town boy from the Midwest who had little exposure to historical archaeology until he was well along in his career in, er, well, historical archaeology.

During his highly productive career, Ronn was also busy doing other things besides tending to the society's publishing programs. He routinely had a teaching load of three or four courses at California University of Pennsylvania and for many years directed the university's archaeology program. In order to provide a ready outlet for his advanced students to gain hands-on experience in applied archaeology, in 1977 he founded his own consulting firm, NPW Consultants, Inc., which for 20 years was a cultural resources force to be reckoned with in Pennsylvania and the surrounding states.

Meanwhile, in 1978 he began an eight-year tenure on the Commonwealth Historic Preservation Board, chairing the Pennsylvania National Register for Historic Places Review Committee for six years, and, in 1981, he was a founding member of the Pennsylvania Archaeological Council, the commonwealth's first and only professional organization, and served three consecutive two-year terms as the organization's first president. And Ronn didn't limit his editing talents to the Society for Historical Archaeology—for more than 25 years he also served as editor of *Pennsylvania Archaeologist*, the quarterly journal of the Society for Pennsylvania Archaeology and one of the best state archaeological journals in the country.

Ronn has been happily retired to his farm in southwestern Pennsylvania for several years now. To hear him tell it, he is now doing what he always wanted to do: planting trees, clearing trees and brush, mowing grass, and doing various other daily chores that keep him physically fit and looking a good 10 to 15 years younger than he really is. However, he still maintains frequent contact through email and by telephone with his many friends and colleagues in the profession, and rarely fails to attend the society's annual conference. I caught up with Ronn on 7 January 2010, in a suite at the society's annual meeting at Amelia Island Plantation, Florida, and thoroughly enjoyed conducting the following interview.

I'd like to start by asking how and when you first got interested in archaeology.

MICHAEL: My interest in archaeology first came about when I was at Jamestown College in Jamestown, North Dakota. There was no anthropology program at Jamestown College at that time, but at the end of my senior year I had gotten a job with the National Park Service as a seasonal ranger/historian at Grand Portage National Monument, Grand Portage, Minnesota. Although I was a physics major and graduated with a physics degree, I actually had a double major in history because, at some point in my four years as an undergraduate student, I realized I didn't want to end up in a lab for the rest of my life. And so I got a job at Grand Portage, not really knowing what to expect. Alan Woolworth of the Minnesota Historical Society was in charge of a field crew under contract to the National Park Service doing archaeology at the fur-trading post. This really intrigued me, and I spent a lot of time talking to Alan and his wife Nancy, and some of the crew, about what they were doing.

When I left that fall to go to the University of North Dakota to begin a master's program in history, I inquired about the possibility of combining archaeology with history. My mentor, a gentleman by the name of Elwyn Robinson, who was a well-known northern plains historian, long since deceased, got me into the anthropology program at North Dakota where there was a freshly minted Ph.D. anthropologist from the University of Missouri by the name of Raoul Anderson, who left North Dakota in 1966 for Memorial University, St. John's, Newfoundland, where he became well known for his whaling-community research. For some reason he was taken by the fact that I had an interest in both archaeology and history. The program offered no real courses for me to take, so Anderson designed some reading courses for me. I don't know if he realized he almost killed me, but he gave me a reading list of 10 books every week for four semesters, which taught me in a real hurry how to use book reviews, learn how to look up topic sentences, and things like that. We discussed all 10 books each week.

When I finished my master's degree, my goal was not to find a job in historical archaeology. When I had begun at the University of North Dakota, I realized that it would take me two years to finish my master's degree. So I enrolled in what at that time was called a fifth-year professional-education program, which would lead to a teaching certificate. So, with this teaching certificate in hand, I was certified to teach high-school history and physics in North Dakota and elsewhere. I started looking for high-school history-teaching jobs, mainly in suburban Chicago and was offered a few, except they were for teaching physics and coaching tennis, which I didn't want to do. So again, my mentor at the University of North Dakota, Dr. Robinson, came through by saying, "I just heard from the president of a small college in Wisconsin. Would you be interested in a teaching job in that kind of environment?" And that was the first time I had ever given any consideration to college teaching, and so I went for the interview and was hired at Lakeland College, outside of Sheboygan, Wisconsin. I would teach history, but I still had to coach the men's tennis team.

What year was this?

MICHAEL: This would have been 1965. By the time I arrived at Lakeland, I had spent three summers at Grand Portage. During the summer before I started at Lakeland, Alan Woolworth was there again, and so I became more interested in archaeology, although I didn't do any actual excavation. Once I started teaching at Lakeland College, I realized I was interested in going beyond a master's degree, but I still wanted to combine anthropology and history. So I started contacting graduate schools, including the universities of Michigan, Illinois, and

Wisconsin at Milwaukee, as well as Northern Illinois University. Eventually I applied to all of those schools and was accepted at each of them, but it was only at Northern Illinois and Wisconsin at Milwaukee where it seemed they were interested in letting me try to combine anthropology with history.

In the meantime, one of my colleagues at Lakeland was finishing his doctorate at Ball State University. He informed me they had a doctoral program with a lot of flexibility. It was a history department program, but it allowed you to take courses in a variety of different disciplines. He put me in contact with the history department chair. I explained to him what I would like to do, and he provided me with contacts among the anthropology faculty, including Dave Scrutin and B. K. (Ben) Swartz, Jr. So, I applied to Ball State because they really seemed enthusiastic about what I wanted to do. They also offered me a nice fellowship, $3,600.00 a year, which was a lot of money at that time. I started classes in the fall of 1967. Ray White, who was a Western historian, was my history advisor, and Ben Swartz was my anthropology advisor. And so that's the way I got started in historical archaeology.

It sounds to me that the seeds of historical archaeology were really planted in your first summer at Grand Portage.

MICHAEL: They were. In fact, I forgot to say earlier that I wrote my master's thesis at the University of North Dakota on the fur trade of the Red River valley of North Dakota. At Grand Portage I read practically every book and fur trade journal the National Park Service had in their library. From that reading it was clear little research had been done on the fur trade along the Red River. My thesis was all historical, as at that time no historical archaeology had been done in the river valley, not even in Winnipeg, Manitoba.

What was your dissertation topic at Ball State?

MICHAEL: Well, my dissertation topic was very strange. I had to satisfy Ben Swartz, who had a reputation with graduate students of not being easy to get along with. He alienated his students more than anything else, and I believe I was the only student of his that ever got through the program. I approached him with various historical archaeology topics, and he had no interest in any of them. However, he had an interest in bibliographies, and I had known that for some time. In fact, I had done a few annotated bibliographies for him, just because he wanted them, and I needed him "to be on my side." And so I did the only thing I could get him to agree to for my dissertation topic—a complete annotated bibliography of all archaeological literature in the state of Indiana "since year one." This didn't appeal to me to any great extent, but nevertheless, I started going through all the old publications in Indiana. I spent days down at the Indiana State Archives in Indianapolis going through everything relating to archaeology and history, including everything that Glenn Black had done. And that was my dissertation. It was the strangest dissertation you could ever think of. However, it's amazing how many people have come up to me and mentioned how useful the bibliography was in their research.

It seems to me that you were nearly in an intellectual vacuum at Ball State in regard to historical archaeology.

MICHAEL: Aside from Jim Keller at the University of Indiana, I didn't run into anybody, while at Ball State, anywhere in Indiana that knew anything about historical archaeology, and at the time Kellar wasn't particularly enthusiastic about it. There was an archaeology program in Indiana State University at Terre Haute, but they knew nothing about historical archaeology. There was nobody, absolutely nobody in historical archaeology. I got to know several prehistorians in the region through Ben Swartz, including Jimmy Griffin, but there were no historical archaeologists anywhere in the vicinity.

That's an interesting story. You really were sort of independently developing as a historical archaeologist.

MICHAEL: Yes, but I didn't know it at the time. In fact, when I went out to look for a job, my initial job offers had nothing to do with historical archaeology, because nobody was hiring historical archaeologists. They just offered history jobs.

Can you tell us why your doctorate is a doctorate of education rather than a doctorate of philosophy?

MICHAEL: At Ball State, at this time, you could take your doctorate either as a Ph.D. or an Ed.D. If you took it as a Ph.D. you had to pass two different language tests, but if you took it as an Ed.D, you could substitute statistics for one language. And so I decided to do the latter. I decided I didn't need two foreign languages in order to do research, so that's the reason I ended up with an Ed.D.

So, you were awarded your doctorate of education in 1969. Is that correct?

MICHAEL: Yes, I finished in 1969, but I went through graduation in the spring of 1970. The only reason I mention this discrepancy is because the formal records of Ball State show my graduation date to be 1970. But, all the papers were signed in the fall of 1969.

In the meantime, before you actually had your degree in hand, were you job hunting?

MICHAEL: Yes, in the spring of 1969, all of us who were going to be finished that year were counseled by the history department faculty. And they were very good, providing tips on how to get a job, and they helped us put vitas together and edited them. Using department funds, the department chair sent our vitas to all the colleges and universities in the United States. He just blanketed the whole country with them. And I had several responses. In particular, I was home for lunch one day, and the phone rang. The lady said she was calling from California State College and mentioned the department chair who wanted to talk to me.

This call was made on the basis of the blanket mailing?

MICHAEL: Yes, the blanket mailing only. I had not applied to this school. I never heard of this school. In fact, I remember thinking she was calling from Sacramento or somewhere in California. I knew nothing about specific colleges and universities in Pennsylvania. Indiana, where I was living then, was the farthest south and east that I had ever lived. So, the department chair got on the phone, told me that he had received my vita, and asked me to come for an interview. His name was Phil Jack. But since I had never heard of the school and I was just about ready to accept an offer at Eastern Kentucky University, I wasn't really very interested in further interviews. I do remember asking Phil Jack questions about the program. He explained they were trying to develop a new anthropology program with a focus in archaeology instead of cultural anthropology. They already had three archaeologists on staff, although one was going to be leaving, and they wanted to replace him with a historical archaeologist.

That was pretty forward thinking way back in 1969.

MICHAEL: Yes, it really was. They knew nothing, really, about historical archaeology. However, since it was a six-hour drive just to get there for an interview, I can remember asking him on the telephone, "What are my chances of you offering me a job if I come for an interview?" Obviously you don't want to say that if you want a job, but I didn't need another offer, as I already had several, and I especially didn't need it at some place that I had never heard of.

A bit forward of you, I'd say.

MICHAEL: Yes, but his immediate reply back was that if I was as good in person as I was on paper they would probably offer me the job. So, that intrigued me. I made the trip, and when I got there, they put me up in a small downtown hotel, where I had a room above a bar. When I got up the next morning, the morning of the interview, my car was covered with coal soot. Where I lived, coal was going out of fashion, but in California, Pennsylvania, coal was still king. And my car was all black, and I was not happy. But I went for the interview which was with an archaeologist, a historian, and the department chair. We spent several hours in the morning talking, and then they excused me and asked me to come back after lunchtime; when I did, only the department chair was there, and he said, "We'd like to invite you to join the faculty." That really surprised me. He also said I needed to go talk to the president of the university, because it was the president who would decide the money part of the offer. The faculty

had the authority to decide who to hire, but it would be up to the president to tender the money offer. I was advised by Phil Jack to say how much money I wanted, which of course stunned me. Because California State College (as it was called at that time) is wholly owned by the Commonwealth of Pennsylvania, university employees collectively bargain by commonwealth law, and, as a result, there are salary schedules for each job title. I knew how much I had been offered elsewhere, and being young and naïve, I looked at the salary schedule and chose a sum that was beyond anything I had been offered elsewhere. Phil Jack told me that if it's too much money the president will tell you so, but if it's less than he would be willing to pay you, he will *not* increase his offer. When I talked to the president, I told him what I'd like for a starting salary, and he said, "That's fine." I then had to confess that I would not have my degree in hand, because I could not defend my dissertation until fall. I assured him it would be done, but I said I understand that it's often necessary to pay a person less until they actually have the degree in hand. He said, "No, that's okay, I trust you." And so I got the salary I requested. The deal was actually better than that, because California State College at that time was on a trimester system, and since they had a big archaeology program during the summer, I was unconditionally guaranteed a third semester each year, which gave me 30% more money. So it was an offer I could not refuse. I went back to Ball State and told my advisor what I was offered as a nine-month salary, and he said I would be making more than he was making, which was a little embarrassing. I let another person on my committee know what I was offered, and I'll never forget that his whole facial expression changed when I told him the amount. So, that's how I came to California State College, now California University of Pennsylvania.

It sounds like you were really impressive in your interview, or they were really desperate.

MICHAEL: I've often wondered how or why this happened. I never could figure out why I got hired at such a high salary. I did find out a couple months after starting at California that the college was short of people with doctorates and would shortly be up for accreditation review, but they clearly didn't have to pay the kind of money they paid me to get such people. In fact, I was hired as an associate professor, a higher rank than where I should have been hired.

That's unheard of.

MICHAEL: I only had two real years of college experience at Lakeland College. In order to hire me as an associate professor, I had to have five years teaching experience. When I came back from talking to the president, I remember very clearly that the department chair said, "We have to find some more teaching experience in your background to put on your application to the state." And I thought to myself, "I don't know where you're going to find this experience." I was only 27 years old. But he asked had I ever been a Boy Scout leader, and I had. Then he asked, "Did you ever teach Sunday school?" And, well, I had, and together we found other "teaching" experience in my background. I left that interview and headed back to Ball State convinced that the state would not accept my application with the "ginned up" teaching experience. But, within two weeks, I had a letter of appointment with everything approved.

Talk about being in the right place at the right time.

MICHAEL: That's exactly right. It was nothing more than being in the right place at the right time. I don't know what they really saw in my vita because I hadn't done a whole lot at that time. I guess whatever I said in the interview was exactly what they wanted to hear. And so, when I got to California, even though I didn't know what to anticipate, having already taught in college, I wasn't intimidated. All I knew was that I would be teaching mainly archaeology.

This would have been the fall of 1969?

MICHAEL: Yes, fall of 1969.

So, you got through this incredible interview process and, let's be frank, lucked out.

MICHAEL: No question about it that I lucked out, and I continued to luck out. Instead of just running a historical archaeology field school, which

had been the plan, health issues arose with Bill Womsley, the senior anthropologist/archaeologist who was supposed to be in charge. Consequently, I was asked to run the entire field school by Phil Jack, both prehistoric and historical archaeology. Furthermore, Phil also asked me to take over coordination of the Master's of Arts in Social Sciences program. So, by the end of my first year at California, I was in charge of running both the historical and prehistoric field schools, plus a master's program. Shortly thereafter, and for the next 10 years, I was also a member of the college graduate council.

Sounds like you were doing everything. What were the other faculty members doing?

MICHAEL: Well, some of them didn't do much, which became a point of contention in later years. After I was there for six or seven years, I was asked to run for department chair, which I did not want to do because I already had plenty to do. I was part of a 30-faculty social science department at that time, and fortunately I did not get voted in as chair, and several of my colleagues came up and apologized for not voting for me because they were afraid that I would expect them to do too many things. This was an absolute relief because, as I said, I did not want any part of it. The university provost had told me I wouldn't like the job, although he noted I would likely find it easy, but annoying. The point is, California State College provided me with every opportunity to do almost anything I wanted.

So going back to the summer of 1970, where were the two archaeological field schools held?

MICHAEL: I picked a 19th-century stagecoach tavern along the National Pike (present-day US 40) for the historical archaeology field school, and the prehistoric field school was held at a big late-prehistoric village close to the college, where the field school had been held for the past couple of years. The previous archaeology was done by Bill Womsley, who was a Ph.D. student of Bill Sanders at the Penn State University. In 1970 another of Sanders's Ph.D. students, Joe Marino, directed the prehistoric archaeology field school, and he decided that we were dealing with a huge mound where the

Aztecs had once been, and it caused an absolute furor. I got a call from Don Dragoo at the Carnegie Museum of Natural History, in Pittsburgh, who wanted to know what was going on down there. Barry Kent, the Pennsylvania state archaeologist also became involved because he had gotten calls from all kinds of people about what nut was attributing a late-prehistoric village site in Pennsylvania to the Aztecs. The situation was especially sensitive for Barry Kent because he, Marino, and Womsley had all graduated with Ph.D's, from Penn State within a few years of each other. Attempts to temper Marino's words and actions met with minimal success that summer, but he never again participated in any of the university's archaeology field programs.

It appears the college followed through with their intention to emphasize archaeology.

MICHAEL: Yes, they did follow through. We had access to the students in the Ph.D. program at the University of Pittsburgh. That's how I came to know Ron Carlisle, who was a Pitt student working on his master's degree at the time. He came to work for me as a field supervisor. Ron and other field supervisors were mostly students of Jim Richardson. At about the same time, Jim Adovasio came to Pittsburgh and began to excavate Meadowcroft Rockshelter, after California State College declined the invitation to excavate it.

So you and your students actually had first reported Meadowcroft Rockshelter?

MICHAEL: Not exactly. Meadowcroft was a previously known prehistoric site on a family farm owned by Albert Miller. Miller had a strong interest in history and archaeology, and had convinced staff at the Carnegie Museum to test the site. They did test it, concluding that it didn't have much research potential.

Is that right?

MICHAEL: Yes, it's well known that Carnegie wrote off the site; I think the staff later found this to be quite embarrassing. I don't remember who did the testing, but that's what the Carnegie opinion was. California State College

thus had an opportunity to test and excavate the site, but it was just too hard for us to get to. The commute was a lengthy drive over several hilly, winding roads, and we had students who could only work in the field half a day because of their class schedules. The college would not allow us to set up a field camp to take the students overnight, so we simply weren't able to accommodate our students at Meadowcroft. The property owner had collected numerous artifacts from the site and was quite persuasive. He felt strongly that the site had more research potential than the Carnegie Museum staff had projected. We were interested in doing additional study at the site, but we just couldn't accommodate our field-school students.

So you actually had the right of first refusal to excavate Meadowcroft Rockshelter and passed on it? I understand you then recommended the project to Jim Adovasio?

MICHAEL: Yes, and we were very happy to do so because we had become good friends with Jim, and we could not have done the rockshelter the justice it deserved, using it as a training site for undergraduate students. Adovasio's training with Jesse Jennings at Utah had focused on rockshelter excavations in the West.

You have no regrets turning down an opportunity to excavate the now world-famous Meadowcroft Rockshelter?

MICHAEL: No! If the truth be known, I was having fun teaching every day. I was given a lot of freedom, enough freedom that I could have hung myself in the process. I wasn't particularly excited by the thought of a rockshelter excavation, because it's a difficult type of site to research. I was more interested in other prospects at that time. The first year I was at the university I was asked to apply to the National Science Foundation for a Student Science Training Program grant. The previous year the staff had applied for the same grant, but it had been denied. The grant would allow us to bring highly motivated academic students from across the country to campus for a summer field program. We were in the midst of trying to build a strong, large, field program and trying to excavate a rockshelter wasn't a good fit for us at that time. We were successful in obtaining the NSF grant. We were also getting a fairly large number of field school students from other universities, including the University of Pittsburgh. Prior to Advasio operating a field school at the rockshelter, Pitt had no local/regional archaeology field schools. At the time we probably had the largest regional archaeology field school. During the early to mid-1970's we normally had six professional staff assigned to our field schools and would enroll 75 to 100 students each summer through our two six-week-long sessions, and we were operating both a prehistoric and a historic field school in each six-week session.

How many years did you run the field school?

MICHAEL: I ran the field school from the fall of 1969 through 1985.

Fifteen-plus years is a long time.

MICHAEL: Yes, and after a while, I became tired of it. It took a lot of energy, and by then I was doing so many other things. In fact, in 1978 I established a corporation to undertake compliance archaeology, hiring mainly our field-school graduates. It was time for somebody else to run the university field schools.

What were you focusing on in your teaching at this time?

MICHAEL: When I came to California, much to my surprise, I was given all upper-division archaeology classes to teach, with the exception that every student at California University at that time had to take a course entitled World Culture. So, for the first three years, if I remember correctly, I was teaching two sections of World Culture each semester. Our total teaching load was four classes or 12 semester hours.

That's a pretty heavy teaching load.

MICHAEL: That was the state-system requirement in Pennsylvania and still is the same today. For the first several years, I would teach two classes in World Culture, and two upper-division archaeology classes. Then I began teaching graduate research and writing methods

in the graduate program that I was coordinating. We put a research methods course in the program that was subject specific, so I started teaching that once a year. I still continued to teach upper-division courses. Slowly the World Culture courses were phased out, so after a while, I didn't have to teach them any longer, and I thereafter had a three-hour load reduction and thus only taught nine hours each semester.

Were most of your students local? What kind of students were they, and how many of them went on to practice archaeology as a profession?

MICHAEL: At California, the majority of the students, probably 90%, were from southwestern Pennsylvania. We did have some students from Maryland, New York, and New Jersey. Interestingly, in spite of the predominance of local students, I'd say probably two-thirds of our anthropology majors were not from Pennsylvania. For some reason, archaeology and anthropology did not appeal much to local students as a career choice. I think part of the reason for this was because they were first-generation college students, and most families were employed in the steel or coal industry and were not oriented to a profession like anthropology/archaeology. Parents and students were more interested in a major that would lead to an instant job at the end of the four-year degree. During my earlier years at the university, the majority of the students were majoring in some kind of a teaching program; it changed through the years as public-school teaching jobs diminished.

A reasonable number of our anthropology graduates went into graduate programs, but not always anthropology graduate programs. I don't know how many of them finished, but our very first anthropology major, who graduated two years after I arrived there, later got his Ph.D. and taught in the Alabama university system. His name was Harry Holstein, and he's now retired. We also had several that went into historical archaeology at the master's level, including Mary Zylowski, Mark Wittkofski, Mark Henshaw, and Arron Kotlensky. The school did a poor job of tracking graduates in any program. They didn't provide funds for us for such research, so we never really tracked graduates who enrolled in Ph.D. programs.

Another woman who went on to get her master's degree and completed almost all work for a Ph.D. and is working successfully, at a high level, in the CRM field is Denise Grantz. I know there are several other practicing archaeologists with master's degrees, but how many finished their Ph.D.'s I just don't know. We had a fair number of graduate students at California who received a master of arts degree with an emphasis in CRM and worked or are working in that field. A couple of those graduates are working in the museum-management field, e.g., Kelly Cosgrove.

What was the typical class size that you taught?

MICHAEL: Well, in the early years, we were told we would have about 35 students. We didn't have large auditorium facilities in the newly built building where I taught and had an office and where our lab was located. There were three classrooms that would hold about 200 students, but in anthropology we didn't have any classes that size. Most of our classes were no larger than 30, but most of my classes were even smaller because they were upper-division classes and were with students who were specifically interested in anthropology.

As I mentioned earlier, our field-school classes were some of our largest classes. A lot of students, from widely varying majors, were attracted to these field schools, but for some reason this didn't translate into our anthropology program attracting large numbers of majors. Over the years, we had some very good students in the field programs, most of whom were not anthropology majors. Students frequently took the field school as an elective in their major or sometimes just as a free elective.

Tell us about your early interest in 18th- and 19th-century technology, and how you eventually used this interest and knowledge quite effectively in your teaching.

MICHAEL: As a youngster, my family moved around a lot. My father was in aircraft communications with the federal government, and I got to live in a number of different places. I was born in Ohio, went from there to Chicago, then to Detroit, to central Michigan, and then to North Dakota. From a young age, my father told me that I was inquisitive and a good observer. I would carefully watch adults do their daily tasks, and as a youngster growing up about 200 mi. north of Detroit, we had a neighbor who lived a lifestyle that was more like that of the late 19th century than anything else. I spent a lot of time with him. He was a man in his 70s, a retired lumberjack, and he was very friendly to me, although all the other neighborhood kids were scared to death of him. He was a very nice man and would let me tag along as he worked at home, let me observe what he was doing, and so on. He had chickens that he would butcher, planted a large garden with simple tools and horses, and repaired all types of equipment. A short distance away from his house and my home was a general repair garage, where they did auto-body and welding work, and I'd hang out there, learning to understand the technology of welding. In addition, I had a friend whose father owned a farm-implement supply store about two blocks away from my house. I spent a lot of time at this store, sometimes helping, but mostly just watching the men work. The people who worked there were very nice. I'm sure I asked more questions of them than they had ever heard anyone ask. All those experiences spurred my interest in technology, simple technology, how things worked and how you used tools, and so forth. My father had shown me the crafts of carpentry, plumbing, and electrical work as a youngster, and as I got older I was always very fascinated with that type of thing.

When I was at Grand Portage, the Park Service was reconstructing part of the facilities, and they were squaring felled logs with felling axes, broad axes, and adzes, so I got the opportunity to learn to do that. This wasn't part of my job, but when I showed an interest and was willing to spend some free time to do it, the craftsmen were glad to have me work with them to learn their craft. When it got closer to the American Bicentennial in 1976, I began tying technology into our historical archaeological field schools. The students and I would sit around at lunchtime and talk about the artifacts that we had been finding, and the students, of course, had a lot of questions about the technology, how the artifacts were made, how they functioned, etc.

We'd also talk about the plants that had been growing across and around the site where we were working and how the people would use those plants. It was either in 1974 or 1975 that some of the field-school students approached me after the field school concluded, asking whether we could develop a class where they could learn more about 18th- and 19th-century technology.

I had never really given such a class a whole lot of thought. At that time, curriculum development in colleges was very loose in the sense that all kinds of courses were being developed, unusual types of courses, so developing a class like this wouldn't have been unreasonable. So I introduced such a class to the group of students who asked for it. I don't remember now what subjects I initially selected, but I structured the class so that each week we would change subjects. We met for three hours one night each week for the 15-week semester. I had a reading component to the class, and this was just at the time when the first Foxfire books had been published. I used the first two Foxfire volumes and a few other things, such as Eric Sloane's book *Reverence for Wood*. About one-third of each class was spent discussing the reading assignment, which would relate in some way to what we would do as a hands-on activity that evening. Then the other two-thirds of the class would be devoted to the hands-on activity, e.g., tinsmithing, blacksmithing, candle dipping, corn-broom making, cider pressing, shingle splitting, log hewing, and butter churning.

So that's the way the technology class got started. I had anticipated that I would teach it only once, but when it came time to set the curriculum for the following year, a group of students petitioned the dean to offer the class again. The upshot is I taught it at least once a year until I retired in 2005. It attracted a wide cross section of students on campus. I had to restrict the class size because our lab space was such that I couldn't take any more than 25 students. We had the use of a loading ramp right beside our building, and I could take some activities outdoors, such as blacksmithing. But ultimately I had to quit blacksmithing because the fire department showed up too frequently. The problem was that if the wind was wrong, the smoke from the blacksmithing forge would draw into the air vents

of the classroom building. After our forge smoke filtered into all the classrooms and the students were evacuated from the building one day, the dean decided that teaching blacksmithing wasn't feasible any longer.

How did you procure the necessary raw materials for the technology class?

MICHAEL: Most of the time I procured the necessary raw materials for the class myself. I would charge the students a $5 flat fee that netted about $125, and I would go to a dairy and buy cream for butter churning, to a farm to procure field corn, to a welding or machine shop to get steel for blacksmithing, and to a lumber mill to buy logs. For the most part, I'd get red oak for shingle splitting, and I would have a log cut up into the length that I wanted, put it in my pickup truck, and away I went. We made wooden shingles. I had made a couple of English-style shaving horses years ago to practice using a draw knife, something I had learned to use as a youngster. So I took one of the shaving horses to the university so students could dress the shingles they had hand split. For log hewing I'd set the log in the front of the classroom on blocks and demonstrate the use of a felling ax to score the log, a broad ax to square the log, and an adze to smooth off the broad-ax marks. It was kind of a demonstration, but the students could then actually engage in the activities. We did wood turning with a foot-powered counterbalanced wooden lathe I'd built. Students used the lathe until the university put a drop ceiling in our lab, and the lathe wouldn't fit in the room. I had located a 19th-century broom-making machine and lacing vise in the adjacent county and bought it so the class could make corn brooms. I grew some of the broom corn we used but bought most of it from a regional supplier.

I changed the weekly subjects until eventually I found what worked best in a classroom setting and were crafts that the students liked to do. For candle dipping I had a big pot of wax. If you've ever dipped candles, you know that you have to wait between dips until they cool, so I'd have 25 students lined up around the perimeter of the room, walking around slowly, just about the right pace to dip candles. In all, it took about one and one-half hours to dip a set of candles. One week we would dip candles, the next week we would do tinsmithing and make a traditional candleholder. I had gotten the basic tinsmithing tools from the college industrial arts department, so we had all the equipment we needed. We also dyed yarn and fabric using natural plant material that the students would collect for the dyestuff.

I know of no other classroom setting where students could get this kind of instruction.

MICHAEL: I never met anybody who taught anything like it, either.

It must have been a really unique experience for the students.

MICHAEL: Through the years I've had more contact with former students relative to that class than any other class I taught. In addition, a lot of in-service teachers took that class so they could use the concepts learned in their public-school teaching. There were people who went on and did all kinds of things, but they remembered that class. Just this past summer, I was at a theater performance in a neighboring town and a woman came up to me and said, "I bet you don't remember me," and, of course, I didn't, but she had been in that class, noting how much she enjoyed it and remembered the projects, and that she was sharing portions of it with her young son.

When did you decide to get into the consulting archaeology business and establish NPW Consultants, Inc.?

MICHAEL: That happened as a result of trying to develop a CRM program through the university. About a decade after the first U.S. cultural resource laws were passed in the 1960s, there were situations where we could take contracts at the university, and we did. We had U.S. Department of Agriculture, Soil Conservation Service, and Pennsylvania Department of Transportation contracts by about 1975 or 1976, and contracts with strip-mining companies after the passage of the Surface Mining Control and Reclamation Act of 1977. We were successfully doing these types of contracts through the university for a two- or three-year period until one of our clients went

bankrupt. At that point, our contracts at the university were being administered in the name of the Student Association, Inc., a legal entity of the school, and, structurally, where the school decided it was better to handle contracts. I cannot tell you why they were administered this way, other than I was told the decision was based on legal advice.

In the bankruptcy case, the Student Association didn't want to pay the students who had worked on the project, even though the students had written contracts with the Student Association. I was told that the Student Association wasn't going to pay the student workers because the association wasn't getting paid. I said, "You can't do that, you don't have to pay me for my time, but you need to pay the students." And they absolutely wouldn't pay them, and I said, "I'll get the bankruptcy papers and you can file in bankruptcy court, you might get a little money back." They wouldn't even do that. I got the papers, and they refused to even file. I said, "This is never going to happen again. I'm not going to have the students not be paid for the work they do." So I set up a fictitious company named National Pike West Associates in June 1977 and incorporated a few months later as NPW Consultants, Inc. I was living along the National Pike (US Route 40), west of Uniontown, so the name came naturally. From then on I hired students outside of the university structure.

Even though the university continued to give me a lot of flexibility, and they liked it when a faculty member would engage in professional activities that would bring positive feedback to the university, I had become disenchanted and wanted to secure an academic appointment elsewhere. But the academic job market had virtually collapsed in the early to mid-1970s, so in order to leave, I would have had to take a $15,000 to $20,000 annual pay cut. I decided that with my young family I simply could not do that. Not only were the circumstances of my hire strange, but within a very short period of time I had been given merit increases, I had been given tenure, and at the end of five years I held the rank of full professor. By the end of seven years I was at the top of the Pennsylvania university system salary scale and remained there until I retired, which made it very difficult financially to leave. So, I developed a better archaeology structure that paid students regularly, at the higher end of the regional CRM pay scale, and on time. In a nutshell, that's what drove me to set up a separate corporation.

So, it was really for your students, not you, that you set up this new business?

MICHAEL: That's correct. Initially, I had absolutely no interest in running a business, but after the first two years I concluded that the corporation was a much better structure for CRM work than the university. I ran the corporation for just over 20 years, during which time most of the employees were university students. They weren't all anthropology majors because the work ethic of some people was simply better than others. That is, I found I could get some of the top academic students in other fields who were eager to have summer work doing something interesting. I vividly remember Pennsylvania State Archaeologist Barry Kent saying to me many times, "Why don't you quit teaching and just do contract work, because essentially you're doing two fulltime jobs." I was, in fact, doing two jobs. It about drove me into the ground because I did everything for NPW. I did all the financial books, I did all the payroll, I did everything. I typically had a three-day teaching schedule at the university, including one night class. I would have two days free during the week, but I also taught morning classes. There were a couple semesters where I ended up teaching a class at 1 o'clock, but normally I was done at 11 o'clock, sometimes noon. I would get to the university between six and six-thirty in the morning, with my first class at eight o'clock, so I would get a lot of work done before that class, when few faculty, administrators, or students were on campus. When I had the corporation then I could come home and make the necessary business phone calls, do needed paperwork, write proposals, etc., until about nine o'clock most evenings. The structure of the state system required me to inform the president of the school, in writing, what I was doing. The president was very supportive because I was participating in many campus activities, was doing extensive public relations work for the school, was giving numerous public talks about our university archaeology field projects, was engaged in considerable professional activity, rarely missed teaching my classes, and always made myself available to students.

He considered it moonlighting?

MICHAEL: Well, I guess he did, but since I was doing just about everything the university wanted me to do—field schools, talks to outside groups, public relations, scheduling, editing, and such—I was bringing more positive attention to the school than other department faculty members and practically any faculty member at the school, so the fact that I was running the corporation as a full-time business on the side was acceptable to the administration. It caused conflict and jealousy with my colleagues in the department but not with the administration. However, there came a point in time that NPW had so many contracts and so much work to do that I didn't have much of a personal life. I would finish with business late at night, go to bed, and get up early the next morning. Literally, that's all the time there was. I sacrificed my health and everything else, and that's when I decided that part of it had to go. So I closed down NPW.

Can you estimate how many projects you did during those 20 years?

MICHAEL: Somewhere close to 300.

That's a lot of projects, nearly 15 a year.

MICHAEL: It was a very nice situation, I guess an envious situation, because unlike a private CRM firm where you had to support a permanent staff of people, where you had to take contracts you might not really want, I had the luxury of doing what I wanted. I could say yes or no to working for clients, I didn't need to take the work. My livelihood was not tied to the business. Professionally, it occasionally created some tension because, while I wouldn't bid on certain projects, I would go after certain other projects, and because of the way we were structured, I could usually get the work.

You mean your costs were low?

MICHAEL: Our overhead was low, which made us less expensive. For about half the years I was in business I bid on very little. The work was mainly repeat business, largely for the various utility companies that sole sourced the work to us.

That's very nice when you can get it, as they say.

MICHAEL: Yes, but it also causes some hard feelings with competitors who are trying very hard to sustain a business. But from my perspective, it was a lot of fun. I discovered that I could do all right managing that type of enterprise. I did not like the bookkeeping part of it, but I guess I did all right at it. I didn't delegate much because it was just easier to do it myself. I did enjoy the management end of it, especially the interaction with clients, although some clients more so than others.

How did you wind up so heavily involved in the natural-gas industry?

MICHAEL: It happened because of one large gas transmission company, CNG Transmission Corp., out of Clarksburg, West Virginia. We were hired by them, actually kind of by default, after someone at CNG decided the morality of the crew and supervisor of a previous consulting company was unacceptable to them. CNG's environmental manager was a religious person and a very nice gentleman, and we became good friends. NPW did most if not all of their cultural resources work for over a decade. And, like so many industries, word of mouth is frequently one of the best marketing tools. As a result, we began to get other gas transmission work. The CNG environmental manager left the company, moving to Washington Gas Light (Washington, D.C.) and so then we had the CNG work plus the Washington Gas Light work. We did projects in the Washington, D.C., and Maryland Eastern Shore areas. We then tied in with Baltimore Gas and Electric and gradually built up a lot of repeat customers in the industry. And that worked out very nicely. We also worked for Consolidation Coal Co. (Consol Energy—America's largest coal producer), which was headquartered very close to us, and the environmental manager had graduated from California University and liked the university. I also did some pro bono work for him through the university. I felt as a public servant being paid by the Commonwealth of Pennsylvania I had an obligation to help a lot of different types of businesses with their cultural resources needs, because it was the early years of the CRM regulations and small companies had practically

nowhere to turn for advice. So, at the university, I would simply provide consulting services gratis, which led to paying work on a number of occasions. The university administration really liked the fact that I'd do that. I'd go out and meet with local business owners, and the feedback to the university was very positive.

How did you get involved in editing, and when did you first realize editing might be one of your callings? How did you become editor for the Society of Pennsylvania Archaeology (SPA)?

MICHAEL: I had no aspirations to be an editor, absolutely never thought about it! In 1972, the SPA was looking for an editor. Phil Jack, who hired me at the university, came to me and said, "How about if we lobby for you to be editor of the *Pennsylvania Archaeologist*? The department and college will support you totally." And I knew at that time I had the unconditional support of the top administration of the university, since he and the university president were good friends, having for a number of years been history faculty colleagues at the college. So it was Phil Jack who actually lobbied for me. He submitted my name, I didn't do anything. I don't know what he did, but at the society's annual meeting the board of directors voted, and the next thing I knew I was editor of *Pennsylvania Archaeologist*.

Do you remember who was on the SPA Board or who the president was at that time?

MICHAEL: No, I know the person who really wanted the editorship, but didn't get it. However, I honestly don't remember who was on the board at the time. It was 1972, and I was new enough to Pennsylvania I really didn't know a lot of those people well. For some reason, I had the support of John Cotter, who wasn't real active in the SPA but had a lot of influence in Pennsylvania archaeological circles.

How did you know what to do when you first took over the editorship?

MICHAEL: Frankly, I didn't know what to do. I had no journalism background and had never done any editing, except for my own manuscripts. The university employed a printer, a very eccentric gentleman, who I had become friends with because of our field-school brochures and some other media needs. I spent a lot of time with him because he knew the printing industry. I also spent a lot of time talking on the telephone with Schuyler Miller, a member of the SPA, a former SPA editor and an employee of Fisher Scientific Corporation in Pittsburgh, who was in charge of putting together the massive Fisher Scientific catalog.

So between talking to Miller and the printer, I learned a lot about the publishing industry in a hurry. At that time, I had to paste up the galleys and do everything else by myself. I retained the printing firm in Michigan that had the journal printing contract when I took over. I kept them because I didn't know anything about choosing printers, and it was easier to go with a known quantity. I would send everything to them. I learned how they wanted copy marked up, I learned how to use proofreading marks, which I had no experience with, and I would copy edit everything and send it to the printer. When I received the proof sheets I would have a pair of scissors and a Scotch-tape dispenser, and literally create the pages of the journal by cutting and taping. Copies of those pasted-up pages were what I sent to authors to proofread. After entering all corrections on the original galley pages, I would then ask the printer if, aesthetically, everything looked "all right." And so that's the way I learned to put out a scholarly journal. We also mailed the journals from the university, so I had to get student volunteers together so we could package and label all the envelopes. I'd then bring my pickup truck to the university and haul the mail bags to the California post office and bulk mail the journal.

Editing isn't a bad job unless you receive manuscripts that are just not of publishable quality from established archaeologists. I'll never forget getting a horribly written manuscript from a very well-known New York archaeologist. This person was near the end of his professional career, had published several books, and had substantial stature in the field. I didn't know what to do with the manuscript, so I called Jim Fitting, who was still in Michigan at that time, and said, "Jim, what do I do?" Fitting knew this person well too, so he said, "You send it

back to him, tell him it's a piece of crap, and have him fix it." And I thought, oh my God, I can't do this, this will be the end of me, so I spent an enormous amount of time copyediting the paper, and I sent it back. A few weeks later the manuscript comes back with a letter which I'll never forget. This person was effusive in his praise that I had spent the time to fix his paper and said that throughout his entire career writing was his main shortcoming and that he constantly struggled with it. He found that most editors were not interested in helping him and truly appreciated the time I had spent.

Those kinds of notes make it all worthwhile.

MICHAEL: They do, they do. And from that time forward I knew that no matter who it was I could do the same thing, even if the person had considerable stature in the field.

It's amazing how many established archaeologists are surprisingly poor writers.

MICHAEL: I don't think it's restricted to archaeologists. The New York archaeologist had relied on editors all his life to make his work publishable. Within several years of beginning as the SPA editor, I found that I could essentially rewrite any manuscript and still have it read as if it had been written by the paper author. As SPA editor, it was generally easier and quicker to rewrite a poorly written paper from an avocationalist than trying to force the author to do the rewrite when they lacked the skills to accomplish the task. The avocationalist would have the most important part of the paper—the content. I could, without too much effort, add the necessary structure to the manuscript so that it was a publishable paper.

I imagine it becomes routinized to some extent.

MICHAEL: Yes, it does, it becomes very routinized. It took time, but it wasn't hard to do.

Did you do any other editing during this period?

MICHAEL: I was approached by the Eastern States Archaeological Federation to edit their bulletin. I said I really wasn't very interested, but I said I would do it nevertheless, and I think I did that for two or three years. About that same point in time I was approached by the Council for Northeast Historical Archaeology about editing their journal, *Northeast Historical Archaeology*, which I did for a few issues. Even though it had never crossed my mind that I wanted to do any editing, all of a sudden I was doing quite a bit of it. I guess what appealed to the folks at *Northeast Historical Archaeology* was the fact that I had put *Pennsylvania Archaeologist* back on track, having taken the reins of editor when publication of the journal was several years in arrears, and *Northeast Historical Archaeology* was behind in its publishing schedule when I accepted the editor job.

They also must have thought you had connections.

MICHAEL: I guess they did. What was important to me with *Pennsylvania Archaeologist* was to have a better journal and to get it published on time. To me that made all the difference in the world, and once I was able to do this, I realized we couldn't issue a quarterly because we weren't getting that many manuscripts. So what we did for many years was combine issue numbers, numbers one and two together, and numbers three and four.

My experience as editor of *Pennsylvania Archaeologist* opened doors for me in the profession that otherwise never would have been opened, because I began to know large numbers of people. When you're the only person seeking reviewers and you have to call people you don't know, you get to know them rather quickly. You pick up the phone and go from there, and as a result I met an awful lot of people. I do cherish those acquaintances.

How did you come to be selected the editor of *Historical Archaeology*?

MICHAEL: In 1978, the SHA was looking for a new editor because the journal was behind in its publication schedule. Kathleen Gilmore was president of the society and appointed Jim Ayres (immediate past-president) to chair a committee to look for a new editor. I believe they advertised it, they had a piece in the society's newsletter, and that's how I found out about it. *Historical Archaeology*, by that time, was the

journal that I actually was interested in editing, so I put together a proposal and sent it to Jim, who I did not know at the time. Actually, I believed my chances of being selected as the SHA editor were slim.

This was in 1978?

MICHAEL: Yes, 1978. I was appointed somewhere around March 1978. SHA's mid-year board meeting was in Tucson in April of 1978, and that was the first meeting I attended as editor. I only knew a few of the board members. At the meeting I was informed that shortly I would receive from the former editor, John Combes, the necessary materials, though nobody knew what they consisted of. Shortly thereafter, I realized I could not continue editing the *Bulletin* for the Eastern States Archaeological Federation, *Northeast Historical Archaeology*, and *Pennsylvania Archaeologist*, and also do *Historical Archaeology*, so it was an easy decision for me to give up the *Bulletin* and *Northeast Historical Archaeology*. I felt that I should keep my hand in *Pennsylvania Archaeologist* because, being in Pennsylvania, it was an entrée to a lot of different things, and I didn't mind doing it. Of the journals I was doing, it was probably the most enjoyable at that time, although *Northeast Historical Archaeology* was also fun to edit.

This was after you submitted your proposal?

MICHAEL: Yes, it was after I submitted the proposal, was selected by the committee, and appointed by the president as SHA editor that I got invited to the meeting. I don't remember the exact timing of when I got the letter saying they had selected me as editor, but the next meeting was the mid-year meeting in April of 1978, so that's when I actually took over. Upon returning home after the meeting I waited for my package from John Combes to arrive, and when it did, it was frightening because the expectation was that I would get the journal caught up real soon. What I found in the box were unreviewed manuscripts! I didn't have the circle of contacts that I needed to be able to get the papers reviewed quickly. Also, I could see that the task I was facing was more grim than expected. I needed help! So I enlisted the help of Ron Carlisle, because at that time he was working with me in the university field-schools program. For several years Ron handled preparing about one-third of the manuscripts. Finally, Ron's other commitments forced him to resign as my associate editor. I then enlisted the help of Donna Seifert, and we worked together for several years before I added other associate editors.

When you took over from Combes, it was an annual publication?

MICHAEL: Yes, once a year.

And when did you go to twice a year?

MICHAEL: Again, I don't recall. I'd have to go to the shelf and look up dates. Our goal was to expand to more than one issue, which we did in a relatively short time. [Editor's note: The transition to biannual publication took place in 1981.]

Tell us more about those early days, and how you corrected a situation that was getting pretty intolerable to the members.

MICHAEL: There were an awful lot of members who were annoyed because they weren't getting the journal on time, and this was the only thing they thought they were paying for. Before the box arrived from Combes, I believed that the next issue was pretty much set to be sent to a printer, but I quickly found that absolutely nothing was set to go. Combes used an editorial advisory committee, so I talked to the members, Chuck Cleland, Stan South, and Paul Schumacher, about how the process worked. At that time, this small committee reviewed *all* submitted manuscripts. And I realized that it was probably not the best approach to rely on the same small group of people to review absolutely everything. We needed to match reviewer expertise with the content of the submissions, so I separated out the editorial advisory committee from the manuscript readers. I wanted an editorial advisory committee that would do exactly what the word says, advise, and I wanted a functioning committee because I needed additional expertise. I felt that the committee should be composed of people who had some stature in the field, and I also thought it was important to maintain SHA-board support by involving current and former

board members. So I started building an editorial advisory committee with those types of people.

With regard to manuscript reviewers, I had decided that, like I had been doing with *Northeast Historical Archaeology*, I wanted to have a minimum of three reviewers for every manuscript, with no exceptions. I had intended from the very beginning to listen to the reviewers. I felt that was important if I was going to ask people to review manuscripts, that I needed to respect what they had to say. If I didn't want their opinion, I shouldn't have bothered to ask for it to start with. In this way, it wasn't so much my making the decision of whether we would publish or not publish a given manuscript as much as it was the reviewers. If two of the three reviewers agreed the manuscript should be published, I typically went with that opinion. I always started by calling a person and asking if they would review the manuscript. I felt it extremely important from my own experience of submitting manuscripts for publication that the reviews should be done in a timely fashion. I had had manuscripts of my own out for review for a year or more and I found that to be totally unacceptable. So I set up guidelines that were very structured, asking people if they could review something within 30 days, asking them for an honest answer if they couldn't meet that deadline. I'd rather know it up front that I wasn't likely to receive comments within my stated 30-day window rather than having to browbeat a reviewer into getting comments to me after the 30-day period of time. This system worked quite well. Authors appreciated it, I think reviewers appreciated it knowing that they had a set timeframe, and if they didn't meet the timeframe they were going to get a telephone call. And they also seemed to appreciate that I would respect what they had to say. I was looking for their critical evaluations, and I would utilize them in my decision-making process. There were authors early on that would "bug us," asking why I didn't accept their manuscript for publication, but I had the expert reviewers' comments to fall back on. At times, it was very difficult to get authors to accept that, but that's really the way it worked. Ron Carlisle and I worked very hard the first several months to get through the manuscript backlog. The first issue under my editorship was shipped in 1978, so we got caught up within a year, and that helped a lot to gain the board's support.

I remember when the journal got caught up, and I thought that was great.

MICHAEL: I thought that was the most important thing to do while still maintaining the quality of it. The next goal was to expand to a biannual publication with the ultimate goal of being a quarterly. At that time, nobody knew whether it would ever happen. We were not getting enough quality manuscripts. We knew that we did not want to publish site reports, and we wanted to publish material that would appeal to a more national audience. From the very beginning, when I became editor, it was always difficult to get theoretical submissions. As editor, if I had one disappointment, it was not being able to publish more theoretical pieces. We even tried soliciting theoretical pieces, with only limited success.

Slowly the number of submissions picked up. We were able to go from an annual publication to a biannual in 1981, to a quarterly in 1990. To switch to the quarterly, we also had to expand the editorial staff, so I appointed several new associate editors, because as we got more and more manuscripts, we needed more people to oversee the review process. I think you were added as an associate editor around that time.

Yes, I was.

MICHAEL: An expanded group of associate editors was not foreign to me because it had been successful for me with *Pennsylvania Archaeologist*. So I expanded the SHA editorial staff to keep up with the increasing number of manuscript submissions. I made sure I put people on the committee who I knew would deliver, possessed the necessary manuscript evaluation and editing skills, and were familiar with the field of historical archaeology, and I found it to be a very good group with which to work. When I would consult with them on various subjects I would get excellent feedback, and they worked together, I think, as a group quite well over a long period of time. Unfortunately, there were times when manuscripts just weren't coming in, so we hit upon the idea of publishing thematic issues, never thinking that

the thematic issues would become really popular with society members. Inserting a thematic issue within a quarterly journal structure is not something that other journals were typically doing at the time. But after we started doing this, we found that thematic issues had a lot of support from our members because many of these issues were useable in a classroom setting, since they focused on a single subject. It wasn't planned that we'd publish thematic issues; we came out with thematic issues because we couldn't initially produce a quarterly publication otherwise, and even today the thematic issues are still popular with the members. We also spent a lot of time, off and on, trying to solicit manuscripts, but we never had much success with that. We tried targeting good papers or sessions presented at the SHA annual meeting—we had people from the editorial advisory committee sitting in on paper sessions quite frequently—but this approach wasn't altogether successful.

Another problem with that approach is that you can be accused of favoritism in the procedure you use to select the paper or sessions.

MICHAEL: That's always a risk if you solicit, and some people think soliciting excuses them from having their paper vetted, and that by soliciting you make a promise that it will be published. I always felt that we just could not do this. I knew as an editor you have the prerogative to do that, but I did not feel that publishing unreviewed papers was appropriate. I had made a commitment to myself as well as to others that we would have manuscripts peer reviewed before they would be published, and I know that I lost several manuscripts from prominent people in the field because I wouldn't accept a paper without subjecting it to peer review. A few authors wouldn't submit a solicited manuscript to the journal under those conditions, and that was just the way it was.

When I solicited peer-review comments in my role as associate editor, I was constantly amazed at the incredible knowledge some people had about certain topics.

MICHAEL: Yes, the detailed comments that some reviewers provided were incredible, but occasionally you'd get a review letter that didn't say much. I always tried to make it clear that a review is absolutely worthless unless you provide critical feedback. There are some well-known people in our profession who didn't review critically, and I would tell them we can't use you as a reviewer because you provide no feedback to the author. I promised the author that we would provide feedback to him or her, and if you can't provide a candid, detailed review you won't be helping the author. Some would change the way they wrote a review, some preferred just not to review, and some indicated they just did not have the time to write the review. I respected knowing up front when someone was not going to do the review for whatever reason, and I didn't call on that person again.

Would you agree that your work as journal editor is your most significant professional contribution?

MICHAEL: Yes, I guess it is. Although editing became a very rewarding experience for me, I realized at some point in time that my own publishing just wasn't going to continue. There weren't enough hours in my life, what with teaching full time and doing other things at the university, running the corporation, and editing. It was a sad decision for me to make, but it wasn't a real hard decision, because I realized that I was making a greater contribution to the profession as a managing editor than I ever would as an author.

Whether that was true or not, you certainly made major contributions, but the important thing I'd like to observe is that it takes a very selfless person to do what you did, and you are to be commended for it.

MICHAEL: I enjoyed editing and meeting people, the contacts, the interactions, and being able to see a profession evolve. Historical archaeology was still a very young profession at the time I became editor, and being able to be involved for as long as I was, seeing our profession evolve, seeing the journal evolve, I'm glad to say I was part of it.

Yes, you were a major part of it.

MICHAEL: And the professional opportunities that it gave me were extremely rewarding. We spent a lot of time and effort on working with first-time authors and people publishing for the first time in a national or international journal, reassuring them that their writing could be published and we would work with them to get it published. We told them that addressing the review comments may appear to be daunting, but the reviewers are positive that if you can make most of the recommended changes, the piece will be much improved. And we would also assure them that we really did want to publish their paper. It's not that we're being critical to get rid of you, we actually want to publish your work, and if you are ready to work with us, then we'll work with you to help make a good paper even better. We will get you through the process. It was very rewarding to see some young professionals get published in a national or international venue for the first time and to read what they had to say. They sometimes did not express to me that they were pleased to accomplish this, but we knew they were, and it was very enjoyable to see some of those same people go on and become respected members of our profession.

Did you get as much pleasure out of teaching?

MICHAEL: I liked to work with students. I found the administration part of it to be easy, but I also found it to be annoying. At the university I was not a good meeting person. I did not want to run a department. To have to sit through meeting after meeting after meeting in that kind of structure just annoyed me. I spent 10 years attending meetings as a member of the university graduate council early in my career, and I finally said I can't tolerate these meetings any longer. I just find that sitting through meetings wastes my time for the most part. I can interact with two or three people and we can get something done. I much prefer to do that. But working with students and being able to see a student evolve from an unsophisticated freshman to a mature graduate can be extremely rewarding.

Grading, however, was something that I just hated to do. I never graded on a curve, and a lot of my students weren't very happy as a result. If everyone in the class earns Cs, then you're all going to get Cs. My grades were low in comparison to colleagues, but I felt that my students should be asked to meet a certain standard, and when they didn't I wouldn't reward them with a contrived grade. Some of my best students were not anthropology majors. They would come from the natural sciences or some other field. I found that they would respect you if you had well-defined expectations of them and would spend the preparation time if you're willing to work with them. I found working with students under these conditions, and seeing them mature and go on, a very pleasant thing. Although I enjoyed it immensely, I don't think I'm as good at teaching as I am at management.

I think a lot of your students would probably disagree with that assessment.

MICHAEL: Well, I think I was always relatively good at establishing rapport with students in a classroom setting. I never seemed to have a problem with talking to students on the subject and keeping their attention. When push comes to shove, I suppose teaching was my first love. That's why I have maintained contact with some students since I retired.

What kind of contact?

MICHAEL: I mainly work with international students that I'd come into contact with in the social science graduate program. Toward the end of my career, I worked with several African and Latin American undergraduate students, and I've had contact with some of them since my retirement. International students have a lot of problems or concerns that other students don't have. They have the same kinds of problems that a typical student does, but, in addition, because they're not close to home, because they have visa issues, because of language, and because they don't know the culture, they need somebody that they can talk to, that understands their problems, and that they can ask for help and advice. I enjoy helping to fulfill that role with international students.

Well, I think we're just about at the end of this really fascinating conversation, so I'd like to ask, if you could do anything differently in your career, what would it be?

MICHAEL: I haven't lost a lot of sleep over that question, but I have thought about it. When I started college, I was really serious. I was going to become a physicist, and that was that. After I graduated with a B.S. degree and changed career paths completely, I guess I had a guilty conscience for awhile. This was primarily due to the fact that there were five physics majors that graduated the same year, and not one of us went on in physics, although four of the five earned doctorates. One became an astronomer, one a mathematician, and one got his Ph.D. in English. The fifth student earned a master's degree, but I don't know in what field. After I finished graduate school, I had an opportunity to go back to Jamestown College, and I asked our physics mentor, "Doesn't it make you feel strange that all five of us abandoned physics?" And his answer surprised me, to say the least.

What did he say?

MICHAEL: He said, "No, that's one of the best compliments I ever had, because all of you have become very successful in your chosen fields, and you all have my science training in common. Knowing that I must have trained you all well, even if it was in a different field than the one you chose to follow, is the ultimate compliment." And through the rest of my life I have thought about that comment and have never had any regrets about leaving physics as a result.

As far as any other regrets go, I don't have any. Because I didn't have etched-in-stone goals, I didn't fail in that sense. I was amazed, first of all, that I never ended up teaching in a public school, and instead I started out teaching college. I really liked that teaching experience and instinctively knew soon after starting to teach at Lakeland College that I wanted to go on to get my doctorate. I did not, however, anticipate that it would lead in the direction that it did. I felt that it would probably be more in the field of history. When I left Ball State and went to California State College—as it was called at the time—I never, ever, could have pictured that federal legislation would have been passed creating the cultural resource industry, allowing me to establish a consulting business, and I never could have pictured myself doing editing. I never realized until later in my career that so many things would come so naturally to me, that there were so many different things that I enjoy. And so, when I look back and try to think what I should or could have changed, I don't know what it would have been. Initially, one thing that I had wanted to do was to stay at California only for a few years and go on to a larger school. In retrospect, I think that I probably made the right decision to stay. I don't think I would have had the same latitude had I left for a larger university—the publishing expectations would have been totally different at a larger university.

How many years were you at California?

MICHAEL: From 1969 until 2005, 36 years. I'm certain that, had I left California for a larger university, I would have been forced to devote a substantial amount of time to research. I wouldn't have had the time to do the editing and run NPW. I also doubt that I would have found that the administration of a larger university would have afforded me the flexibility, the time, to do the editing that I did, because I wasn't fulfilling the academic expectation of publishing original research. So my career took a different path, and I have absolutely no major regrets. There were times with the editing, when I was under time pressure, that I probably wasn't as kind to somebody as I should have been, knowing that I had to meet a tight deadline, so I do regret instances such as that.

Do you consider any of your work to be a legacy?

MICHAEL: Well, I suppose the body of journals is a legacy of a sort.

There's no doubt about that. But I think that some of your students would also say that your teaching is an important legacy as well.

MICHAEL: I do understand that. There are students, though, that would probably disagree. The student that found my tests too hard, my assignments too long, my expectations too high, and my unwillingness to compromise my ideals is likely to totally disagree with the statement. And there were plenty of those students through the years. For me a teaching legacy is hard to evaluate. How do you measure your legacy? By the number of students who obtained advanced degrees? By the number of students who have become anthropology professionals? By the number of students who maintain communication with you? If I had taught at a university where I largely worked with graduate students, I think measuring my legacy might be easier. Having taught largely undergraduate students I don't have a large body of master's or Ph.D. students in the profession that are tangible evidence of my teaching success or legacy.

Over time, having periodically considered the legacy issue, I've come to understand or accept that my teaching legacy can be better measured by the highly praiseworthy comments I received from academically talented students, the comments from more-typical college students that they really enjoyed how I exposed them to subjects they knew nothing about and how well I was able to explain concepts to them, and the comments from graduates about how many things they still remember from a class I taught. I also believe my teaching legacy can be evaluated from comments of graduates, years after their graduation, relative to how much they have used something I taught and how much I contributed to their present career situation. I typically don't dwell on comments from graduates as to how much I contributed to their being able to obtain their present job, but when I hear a comment, as I did recently in a restaurant, from a Pennsylvania county district attorney that I was his mentor, it does feel good, and when you think about it, that is part of my teaching legacy. Of course, there is the young lady I failed in class who ends up being my son's grade-school teacher, or the young man to whom I gave a D grade that becomes the high-school principal where my wife teaches—those are my legacies too!

Quite possibly, though, my greatest teaching legacy was being able to provide support and advice to young women, who had been reared in a cultural environment where women were typically treated as inferior to men, that they had value, were intelligent, could have meaningful and significant professional careers, and could feel good about themselves and have strong self-worth. To hear from a number of my former students years later about how important that support had been to them probably has been my greatest teaching reward. Soon after arriving in southwestern Pennsylvania, as I taught sections of the course titled World Culture, I discovered how poorly many area women were treated by men of all ages. Quite accidentally I began to indicate what I had observed and began, in the classroom setting, to provide encouraging support to the women students. I did so primarily because of my disgust of the male behavior I was observing, but I soon learned from the woman students how much they appreciated my classroom support and advice.

My editing and CRM work have also contributed substantially to my teaching legacy. I wouldn't have been nearly as good a teacher had it not been for my editing and CRM work.

Did your students know much about your editing responsibilities?

MICHAEL: Some of the undergraduate students knew about my editing, some of them knew quite a bit about the editing, but most of them didn't because it's not something that a professor would normally discuss with students. A lot of what I did in editing carried to the classroom because it gave me the contacts with people in the profession. More of my work in CRM transferred to the classroom, because of its practical application, and it's applied anthropology, but most undergraduate students just weren't aware of my professional editing. They would sometimes come into my office and see the publications that I had edited, on the shelves and around my office, and look at them. Some of them would ask questions, because collectively the journals extended across many shelves and together impressed students because they were so numerous. A few would ask questions, but I really don't think many of them knew much about what I was doing, except for the graduate students in the research methods and writing course I taught for over 30 years. Those students really benefitted from my editing experience, and over the years I've frequently heard from those students after they were established in their careers that the methods and writing class I taught was probably their most useful graduate class.

Well, I think that brings us to the end of the interview, and we have the perfect opportunity to thank you for your many, many years of dedicated service to the society as editor, and also a personal thank you from me for the 16 years of working with you as an associate editor. I enjoyed those years immensely.

MICHAEL: Well, as you know, a big part of the editorial process is getting to work with talented people, the editors, associate editors, and the authors themselves. Getting to know talented and dedicated people, working with them in this way, is one of the most rewarding aspects of the job and certainly makes all those volunteer hours worthwhile. I worry that the younger generation does not have the same volunteer spirit and commitment. I used to get asked often, "Why do you volunteer so much of your time?" And I always answered, "Because you get so much in return." But it's personal and I enjoyed it, and I thank you for your comments, but it was my pleasure to do it, it really was.

Acknowledgments

I'd like to thank my long-time administrative assistant at John Milner Associates, Inc., Margy Schoettle, for cheerfully and most ably transcribing the spoken to the written word, and for enduring several editorial review episodes. I'd also like to thank John Milner Associates, Inc. for providing the time and resources that enabled both of us to complete this interview for and with Ronn.

DANIEL G. ROBERTS

The Odyssey of a Transatlantic Archaeologist: Conversations with Ivor Noel Hume. Volume 47, Number 4 (2013): 144-166. By Henry Miller.

Henry M. Miller

The Odyssey of a Transatlantic Archaeologist: Conversations with Ivor Noël Hume

Introduction

Ivor Noël Hume is one of the founders of historical archaeology. He was born in London in 1927 and educated at Framlingham College, Suffolk, and St. Lawrence College, Kent. After service in the army during World War II, he returned to London. From 1949 to 1957 he worked as archaeologist for London's Guildhall Museum, with the responsibility of recovering archaeological finds being revealed by the many construction projects associated with London's rebuilding after the war. In this effort, he became one of the first to recognize the significance of postmedieval remains in England and helped found the new field of study now called historical archaeology. Early on, his talent for presenting the findings of archaeology and communicating their significance to the public became apparent. His first books on the topic were published in the 1950s: *Archaeology in Britain* (1953) and *Great Moments in Archaeology* (1957).

Noël Hume's experience with London's early modern sites and artifacts attracted the attention of J. C. Harrington, which in turn led to him becoming chief archaeologist for the Colonial Williamsburg Foundation at Williamsburg, Virginia, in 1957. Thus began a career in the United States that spans more than five decades (Figure 1). He rose to become director of archaeology in 1964, resident archaeologist in 1973, and foundation archaeologist in 1983. Noël Hume retired from this position at the end of 1987, but continued service as consulting archaeologist and curator of the Winthrop Rockefeller Archaeological Museum from 1988 to 1992. Not a retiring type, Noël Hume then embarked upon equally significant research projects, such as the search

for Sir Walter Raleigh's Roanoke Colony, and has continued writing.

While at Williamsburg, he directed many archaeological investigations within the historic town, including excavations at the Coke-Garrett House, 1959; the Anthony Hay Cabinet Shop, 1960–1961; the Travis House site, 1962–1964; the Custis House site, 1963; Captain Orr's Dwelling, 1964; Wetherburn's Tavern, 1965–1966; Prentis Store, 1969; the Chiswell site, 1970; the Public Hospital site, 1972–1973 and 1980–1981; and the James Anderson House, 1974–1975. These were museum projects with the purpose of providing data to guide restoration efforts and interpretation. He also directed the initial excavations at Carter's Grove in 1970–1971. Perhaps best known of Noël Hume's many excavations is the discovery and study of the early-17th-century settlement of Martin's Hundred at Carter's Grove, 1976–1983. This plantation complex, largely destroyed in the 1622 Algonquian Indian uprising, yielded valuable insights about the first decades of English settlement in America and provided key evidence later used to help interpret Jamestown. Martin's Hundred attracted widespread public attention and increased public recognition for both historical archaeology and the 17th-century era, being reported in the popular book *Martin's Hundred* (1982a). Projects outside Colonial Williamsburg include excavations in Virginia at Rosewell Plantation, 1957–1959; Tutter's Neck, 1960–1961; the Challis pottery kiln site, 1961; Clay Bank, 1962–1963; and Mathews Manor, 1964–1965 (Noël Hume 1966); the Amelung Glass Factory, 1962–1963, in Maryland; and Fort Raleigh in North Carolina, 1991–2001.

Throughout his career, Noël Hume has striven to bring archaeology and history to the public using his impressive speaking and writing talents. This includes delivering countless public lectures around the world and publication of numerous articles and booklets about archaeology and artifacts, all specifically intended for visitors. For this purpose, he created the popular and still in print "Colonial Williamsburg

Figure 1. Ivor Noël Hume excavating a well at the Custis site, 1963. (Courtesy, Colonial Williamsburg Foundation.)

Archaeology Series" and published eight of its booklets between 1969 and 1983. Among the 17 nonfiction books he has published thus far are *Here Lies Virginia* (1963), *All the Best Rubbish* (1974), *The Virginia Adventure: Roanoke to Jamestown* (1994), *In Search of This and That* (1996), *If These Pots Could Talk* (2001a), and *Something From the Cellar* (2005b). A biography entitled *Belzoni: The Giant Archaeologists Love to Hate* was released in 2011. He has also authored three works of fiction, including an historical novel *Civilized Men: A James Towne Tragedy* (2005a), and one play, "Smith! Being the Life and Death of Cap'n John" (2007).

Presenting history and archaeology to the public through film and museum exhibits was another of Noël Hume's major goals. He wrote a number of movie scripts, including *Doorway to the Past* (1969), one of the first efforts to present historical archaeology to the public via film. It won the Cine Golden Eagle at Washington, D.C.,

in 1970, and the Chris Statuette (top award in the social studies category) at the 18th Columbus Film Festival the same year. A decade later, he wrote and was onscreen narrator of *Search for a Century*, the Colonial Williamsburg Foundation's film on archaeology at Carter's Grove. Completed in 1980, it won a gold medal at the 24th Annual Film and TV Festival, New York, 1981; the Cine Golden Eagle Award in 1981; and later the Palme d'Or at the International Festival of Archaeology and Ethnology at the Louvre, Paris.

Planning and building museum exhibits is another aspect of Noël Hume's career, beginning with exhibits at the Guildhall Museum in the 1950s. In the United States, he designed a 1957 exhibit on historical archaeology for the Colonial Williamsburg Visitor Center and later created an exhibit on the relationship of archaeological finds to colonial life at the Anderson House in Williamsburg (1974). Other major exhibits include "Searching for Another Century" at the

National Geographic Society, Washington, D.C. (1980–1981), and the design and creation of the Martin's Hundred exhibit in the Winthrop Rockefeller Archaeological Museum at Carter's Grove, Virginia (1989–1991).

Noël Hume played a central role in the formation of the scholarly discipline of historical archaeology, participating in the founding meeting of the Society for Historical Archaeology in 1967 and organizing the first annual conference. He published two volumes that have had a deep and enduring influence on the emerging field: *Historical Archaeology* in 1969, and *A Guide to Artifacts of Colonial America* (1970). *Historical Archaeology* was the first volume dedicated to this topic to be published and provided a methodological guide for historical site excavations and analysis. It continues to yield practical insights about excavating and feature recognition for students (Noël Hume 1969a). The more prominent *Guide to Artifacts* is a treatise that almost instantly became and remains one of the key resources for artifact identification and analysis of historical sites worldwide. From his work in Britain, Noël Hume developed the first refined chronology for 17th- to early-19th-century glass bottles, published in 1961. His knowledge of artifacts (ceramics, glass, hardware, clothing accoutrements, and so forth) has aided numerous researchers over the years in identification and dating of finds, and his published artifact contributions include volumes such *Early English Delftware from London and Virginia* (1977) and *If These Pots Could Talk* (2001a). Noël Hume has authored over 100 articles and reports on archaeology, history, material culture, and crafts in England and America. In 2010, he published his autobiography, entitled *A Passion for the Past: The Odyssey of a Transatlantic Archaeologist*.

These many contributions have been recognized by numerous organizations. They include honorary doctorates from the University of Pennsylvania (1976) and the College of William and Mary (1983). In 1991, he received the J. C. Harrington Medal in Historical Archaeology, the highest award of the Society for Historical Archaeology. And in 1992, he received the prestigious Officer of the British Empire (O.B.E.) from Her Majesty Queen Elizabeth II at Buckingham Palace in recognition of his many services to British cultural interests while working in the United States.

To summarize, Ivor Noël Hume helped guide the development of historical archaeology, has been a leader in bringing history and archaeology to the public, and his work has influenced generations of archaeologists. As William Kelso wrote in nominating Noël Hume for the Society for Historical Archaeology's J. C. Harrington Award: "If J. C. Harrington is the 'father' of Historical Archaeology as Noël himself has often remarked, then Ivor Noël Hume surely must be its 'godfather.'"

The following is a composite of several interviews, conducted by Henry M. Miller in August 2008 and February 2010 at Mr. Noël Hume's home overlooking the James River near Williamsburg, along with more recent email exchanges.

Interview

MILLER: *How did you begin in archaeology?*

NOËL HUME: I started as an archaeologist for the city of London for seven years, never having intended to be an archaeologist at all. After leaving the army at the end of the war, I got a job as assistant stage manager for the J. Arthur Rank organization, which produced shows in those days, and I decided that since I had already written plays when I was at school, I thought I wanted to be a playwright. So I worked in theater for four years, at various theaters that were mostly repertory companies, and things like that. So it was in 1945 that I got my first job working in the theater. Troops began coming back after the war, and many of them were really experienced in the theater and looking for jobs, so jobs were becoming harder to find. So I spent my time going from theatrical agent to agent, but that is a lot of work and you don't get jobs that fast. So I had been listening to the BBC and heard about a man named Robin Green who went down to the Thames at low tide and found antiquities in the exposed mud, and I thought, well, I have nothing else to do, why don't I go and do that, and so I did. And from doing that, I got to know Adrian Oswald, who was really the father of historical archaeology in London, and I took the things I found to him.

In the summer of 1949 I worked with him on the Bankside Power Station site (now the Tate Modern Gallery), which was being built, and learnt the craft of archaeology, historical archaeology, from him as he showed me the importance of stratigraphy and the relationship of artifacts to the strata, and so forth. But he was in charge of the whole City, that is, the city within the old walls, the original square mile of London, not out of London, not in the county, but he had the whole of the City. Now, building and construction after all the destruction from the war was just beginning, and he as the head of the Guildhall Museum was responsible for the recovery of antiquities in the City, which he couldn't possibly handle by himself, and so he asked me whether I could help. I had been working as a volunteer for him, going out on sites, washing pots, and so on and so forth, while waiting for my big theatrical break. And in the middle of September 1949, Adrian said, "Would you care to have a job at the museum?" Now I had no experience, and so I said yes to have it as a fill in until something better comes along. About a week later, Adrian got pneumonia and left the museum and never came back, which left me, the new employee, as the city's sole ... I guess I was the archaeologist, the collection's curator, the whole smear!

There was ... it is a long story ... at that time formal excavations were being done in the city by a man named W. F. Grimes, who was director of the London Museum. And the London Museum was anxious to take over the city of London's [Guildhall] museum. This was a hostile takeover attempt, and so the librarian at the Guildhall, who was head of the library and the museum, said to me, "We have got to save the museum." The library board was made up of men who were businessmen, civic-minded people, but had no interest in archaeology or antiquities, or anything like that. So he said, "You have got to make those people interested. We have got to get publicity," and so he instructed me to do so. And I fortunately knew a man named Rene Cutforth who was a BBC commentator, and so whenever I found anything, the BBC was there. Trailing along behind the BBC was the Associated Press and everybody else. And so I was getting all the publicity they wanted, and we were finding all sorts of exciting things. But this did not go

down at all well with Grimes and his excavations because he was just digging little trenches and not finding much, or not being able to interpret what he found.

And here was I on building sites which had been stripped and lots of stuff turning up from every time period, so my universe was infinitely wider than his, and everybody was saying in the profession: "Who the hell is this? Who is this guy? Where did he come from?" So I got involved in controversy. But fortunately Adrian Oswald remained a close friend, and he kept warning me about what Grimes was trying to do. He wanted to get me fired, and he also wanted to get the Guildhall Museum, because now the museum was as well known as the Museum of London, but there was a battle going on and I found myself in the middle of it. ... Much later, in 1975, the merger of the Guildhall with the London Museum was made. The time was then right, and I think the Museum of London should be ranked high among Britain's postwar cultural accomplishments. So ... working for the Guildhall is how I got into archaeology.

How long did you work there?

NOËL HUME: I stayed as the Guildhall field archaeologist for seven years. In 1950 Pinky Harrington, Jean Carl "Pinky" Harrington, came to England, having just finished work on the Glasshouse at Jamestown for the National Park Service, and he was looking for anybody who knew anything about 17th-century glass. Well, I had decided that if I was going to stay in this archaeology business, I should deal with materials that nobody else was dealing with. And the realization of that came out of looking at a site I was working on at Walbrook in the City, which had three charcoal bands across it, the bottom one most likely from looting and burning during the uprising of A. D. 61, the second one was the Hadrianic fire of about A. D. 120, and then the third one, right near the top, was the Great Fire of 1666. And I realized that I could not be a Roman specialist because I just didn't have the background for it, so therefore I chose to focus upon the centuries that nobody was interested in then. You know, everybody was keen on the Romans.

And there was no archaeological interest at the time in what we would now call the early modern or postmedieval era?

NOËL HUME: None at all. Except for Adrian Oswald and me. So Oswald was working on his pipes, and I decided that I would focus on the postmedieval period, primarily trying to arrive at a chronology of something in the same way that Adrian was trying to sort out the evolution of the clay tobacco pipe. So I decided that, well, since some wine bottles are actually dated, and as I knew that they evolved, I didn't know quite how, or at what speed, but anything that was underneath the Great Fire was prior to 1666, and anything that cut through it, pits and wells and things like that, were after it. Pretty simple. And I also realized that archaeology is really an incredibly simple use of logic, and if you don't have that, you don't do very well.

That is so very true.

NOËL HUME: And so I started to develop a chronological series of the evolution of wine bottles, which was later published in the Corning Museum of Glass studies in 1961. But the thing was that Harrington came to the museum at the time that I was working on 17th-century glass bottles. Actually, I wasn't there, but my primary volunteer assistant, Audrey Baines, who became my wife, she was there to help him. Harrington was really interested in finding out about glass bottles and tasting good malt whiskeys—that was his primary interest in coming to England. So anyway, Pinky [Harrington] went off around the country drinking the whiskey, and I saw him briefly when he came back to London on his way to America. And that, I thought, was that!

I should inject at this point that Audrey knew a hell of a lot more about archaeology than I did. She had a B.A. degree in Roman history and archaeology, and was then working on a master's thesis on Roman coffins, so she was essentially a Romanist. She had been a student of Sir Mortimer Wheeler. He was a very eccentric fellow, and he had three students at the Institute of Archaeology in London. He went off to India and left his students to go to the British Museum and work under a man named

Bruce Mitford, whom she didn't like. So she came as a volunteer to me. She had also previously volunteered for Grimes, so Audrey had a background in the academic side of archaeology that I did not have. We were married in September 1950. But she saw Harrington and helped him, and what happened was that five years went by. Colonial Williamsburg then said wouldn't it be neat to bring somebody from England to give this whole thing a sort, and so Harrington was then in Richmond as the regional federal Park Service archaeologist, and so they asked him if he knew of anybody in England who knew about 18th-century artifacts, and he remembered me. Now I don't recall that meeting. It's a funny thing that some of the most important moments of one's life you don't remember. I don't recall Harrington's visit to the Guildhall Museum or to London.

So anyway, Harrington says, "Why don't you ask Noël Hume to come over? Half the artifacts you find in Williamsburg are broken bottles and he is a specialist in broken bottles, why don't you ask him to come and write up the bottles?" I had never heard of Williamsburg. I thought American history began at Plymouth. So the offer was made for me to come over for three months, and for Audrey to come over too. So we did. I was still responsible for the recovery of antiquities in the City at that point, working on excavations. I was very, very tired of commuting back and forth; we then lived in Wimbledon, outside London. You know, you would spend your day at a site, coated in mud, and then make your way back on the subway, and in those days you gave up your seat to ladies, so you spent your time hanging on a strap for hours back and forth, and this got pretty old after a while. So, when the offer came to come to America for three months, I gladly accepted it.

I found when I got here that Colonial Williamsburg knew virtually nothing about archaeology—at least the kind that I knew. They had been doing it since 1928 but the archaeologists were architects, although they were referred to in the documents as archaeologists, they were really architects, so their experience was not that relevant. They would dig up foundations, because that's what they were about, the business of reconstructing buildings, and it never occurred to anybody that there was any cultural material not directly related to the buildings that could or should be recovered.

Their first archaeologist was a man named Prentice [Van Walbeck] Duall. He was an interesting man. He came from Tucson, Arizona, and he had some experience in Spanish Mission architecture. But he was on his way to Egypt, he had made his real career in Egyptology, and so he only stayed a very short time, he only did a little work on the Wren Building and also the Governor's Palace; the Governor's Palace excavation was still going on when he left. And then a man named Jimmy Knight came along, and he was an architectural draftsman. Then there was also John T. Zaharov, a White Russian and a model maker and a difficult person, apparently. So these guys, who knew really nothing about artifacts, but could measure foundations, this was the team. After the Wall Street crash came, by 1933, Colonial Williamsburg decided the restoration was finished and they could get rid of them, so the archaeological people were fired and they went to the Park Service and worked at Yorktown. Then, when the Park Service started work at Jamestown, this team was shifted to Jamestown. So, after a while, the Park Service hired two previously trained archaeologists, one was H. Summerfield Day and the other was Alonzo Pond. Those two started really putting the archaeology in some sort of order. They also had an interest in artifacts. Day was the first person, not Harrington, to start studying the importance of the evolution of clay pipes [in the United States].

Really. And this was at Jamestown?

NOËL HUME: This was at Jamestown. But then, in charge of the architectural side at Jamestown was your guy, what's his name?

You mean Henry Chandlee Forman.

NOËL HUME: Yes, and Forman didn't like the anthropologists at all. He thought it was nonsense. And so eventually the Park Service tried to resolve it by deciding that the anthropologists would dig to within 3 ft. of any foundation, and, from then on, the architectural people would take

charge; so they had two WPA teams, Day and Pond had the archaeologists, and Forman had his architect team. Now the snag in this was that when you are digging, you don't always know when you are 3 ft. from a building, and so they actually came to blows, between the two crews, on this sort of DMZ line.

What a bizarre field situation.

NOËL HUME: And eventually Forman was fired and came to you (St. Mary's City, Maryland) and wrote his book (*Jamestown and St. Mary's: Buried Cities of Romance*, 1938). And then Harrington, whose background was initially to be an architect, he was an architectural draftsman, he had worked in the Southwest in archaeology, but he didn't know anything about colonial sites. He said he didn't even know where Jamestown was when he was hired. So then he came down to replace Forman, and I think this was 1936 or so. And anyway so he then becomes the big guy and really set people like Day aside and was the father of historical archaeology. In 1955, he wrote a seminal article, "Archaeology as an Auxiliary Science to American History," that was published by the American Anthropological Association (Harrington 1955). In it he argued that archaeology assisted history. It was a seminal wake-up call, except nobody actually woke up. So years go by and Harrington is whistling in the dark.

Then I come along and agreed with him. Prior to that, Jimmy Knight and such people had dug, but without recognizing the importance of artifacts or stratigraphy, and they dug little trenches diagonal to the lot lines, because that is how you find brick foundations. But the trenches were this wide [about 10 in.] and 6 ft. apart, a shovel's-width trench.

If it were anything other than a substantial and rather intact foundation, you would never see it with that method.

NOËL HUME: No, and no they didn't know anything about postholes or things like that. But they were finding foundations, and that is what they were supposed to do, and Jimmy Knight was supposed to do, and he did it pretty adequately, except for the artifacts, and most of the artifacts were thrown back into the trenches after they had dug them. But some were collected, if they were large or architecture-related, then they were kept.

So when I arrived there was a considerable collection of stuff, and what I found was a warehouse full of fish boxes which were full of unwashed artifacts, which included large boxes of broken wine bottles. So that is what I dealt with during that summer of 1956, but I also tried to talk with the man who was in charge of the architectural and historical research, Orin Bullock, a very nice man with a very nice bowtie. He was a wonderful guy but really did not have a grasp of archaeology, he was not an archaeologist. Orin's real interest was in the theater. He wanted to have a little theater established at Williamsburg, and he lived in Marot's Ordinary, which is now Shields Tavern, and had a theatrical evening once a month in his basement, which came to be known as "Bullock's Underground," and to which I was introduced. Well, they were not plays, only parts of plays because really the important purpose was drinking, especially bourbon, which prevented anyone from ever getting to the third act.

So, anyway, I went back to England having tried to instill in them the idea that archaeology was a cultural activity, not just an architectural activity. And they were building the new information center or reception center ...

For Colonial Williamsburg?

NOËL HUME: Yes, and they needed an exhibit built to interpret archaeology, which was the first attempt I had to show the architects and the public the importance of the relationship of artifacts to stratigraphy.

Was this while you were still a consultant or after you had started full time at Williamsburg?

NOËL HUME: He (Bullock) wanted this built, but I was still a consultant and had gone back to England, it was the time of the Suez Crisis, and I thought that was the end of it. But Orin was still obsessed with this little theater thing, so he arranged for me to come back to direct the little theater by getting me the job of heading up the archaeological program at Colonial Williamsburg.

I said there were a couple of things I needed, one was housing and the other was to get rid of the man who was then in charge of the (archaeology) lab for Colonial Williamsburg, and they said that would be done. But when I came back, it hadn't been done. They hadn't provided housing or taken care of the man whose name escapes me. So I was taking over, Jimmy Knight was still in the field, still digging his trenches, I had to get rid of that as delicately as I could, being a foreigner. And the man was Morrow B. C. Chambers. His background had been in the army at Fort Eustis, in charge of recording returning vehicles. So that was the experience he brought to the archaeology lab. And in those days, there was no air conditioning, so everybody sort of hunkered down and slept through the afternoon until it was time to go home, which was about four o'clock. So nothing was being accomplished. And I was this new broom, trying to sweep as clean as I could. Fortunately, there was one employee, whose name was John Van Ness Dunton, who was the conservator for the archaeological collection and did an extremely good job. He eventually went to the Fortress Louisbourg project in Nova Scotia and did conservation his whole career. John and I built this exhibit for the new information center, and that exhibit survived, I am not sure if it still survives, it went from place to place until the 80s when we redid the information center, that exhibit went to the state which they had at Yorktown and then after Yorktown was closed, it went to the Park Service.

It must have been one of the first, if not the first, permanent exhibits specifically showing the methods of historical archaeology in the United States **(Figure 2).**

NOËL HUME: Yes, I believe it was the first.

And you created it.

NOËL HUME: Yes, I built it with John's help. We wanted it to be behind glass, I did, but Orin, who was in charge, said that is not necessary. So one of the things we had was a Wendell Wilkie campaign button in a drain tile. Its purpose, along with other things, was to show how artifacts are used for dating. It didn't last two days before it was stolen. And we went through as many campaign buttons as we could find, and they were stolen one after

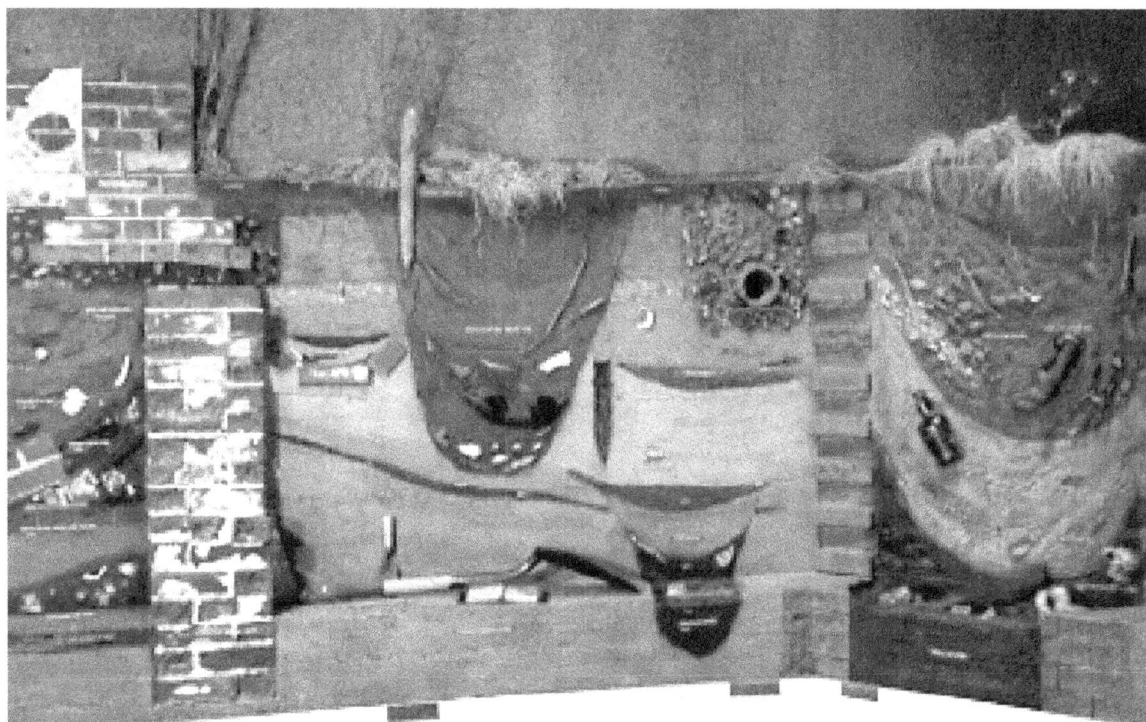

Figure 2. The first historical archaeology exhibit designed by Ivor Noël Hume and John Dunton for Colonial Williamsburg, 1957. (Photo by Ivor Noël Hume.)

the other, so finally, we put it behind glass, and it has been behind glass ever since. ... So anyway, that is how this whole thing began. And we went on from there.

So you came back in 1957 to begin work as a full-time archaeologist. What were the research program and public aspects of it like at that time? Was restoration still the real focus?

NOËL HUME: Oh yes. And restoration was all for the public ... and was filmed, and Colonial Williamsburg had made a big splash in 1955 with *The Story of a Patriot*, which still survives. And there was a man on the board called George Seaton, and George had an Oscar for *A Country Girl*, I believe it was, and so he pushed Colonial Williamsburg into filmmaking, which I was happy to do, and so I got along well with George. At about that same time, around 1960, Alfred Knopf, who was a major publisher after the war, was on the board at the Institute of Early American Culture, and Alfred said I ought to do a book, and I had already thought of such a book and had done it, and it was to be called "Williamsburg's

Buried Treasures." And Ed Kendrew, who was senior vice president and head of architecture, had come in with a very specific interest, and so everything focused on the architecture. So Ed said go ahead and write this book, but we have to check it through. So everybody checked it through, to the point that there was virtually no book left—an exaggeration, of course, but the shape of the book was muddied.

So this was the first book they were encouraging you to write.

NOËL HUME: Yes, and when it was finally shown to Carl Humelsine, who at that time was the president of Colonial Williamsburg, he said this is not what I had in mind, and I said it is not what I had in mind either. So it went on the shelf. So then Knopf asked about writing a book, and I said the only thing I had done was this book on Williamsburg, and so he read it, and said I think you should broaden this, the bones of a good book are here, but you should broaden it, and we will publish it. So that became *Here Lies Virginia* (1963).

And it was an extremely popular work.

NOËL HUME: Yes, it remained in print for the best part of 25 years.

Am I correct in thinking that this book brought the idea of combining history and archaeology to the public in a way that was new in a lot of respects?

NOËL HUME: I think, to the public, yes it was. And there was a spinoff from it from Jimmy Maloney, who ran the Williamsburg Pottery, which by then was growing and becoming almost a rival to Colonial Williamsburg as far as tourist interests. He had the idea that there ought to be a museum for historical archaeology in Virginia. He put up money, or was prepared to put up money, for it, the builder also said he would provide the land, so we had to have a committee appointed by the governor. But the chairman of that board was a vice president at the College of William and Mary, Melville Jones, and then the Department of Anthropology got wind of this and said you cannot have a museum of historical archaeology, it has to be a museum of all archaeology, and therefore the anthropologists would lead the way. And it foundered because of that, it never came off, and all we have is the prospectus for what it could have been. But eventually the state did put together an office for archaeology, a preservation office, and Bill Kelso was hired to do that. Bill Kelso had worked for me at Wetherburn's Tavern, so that is how his archaeological career began. And he became the commissioner of archaeology for the state, and he ended up with an office in the basement of the Wren Building.

And then it was said after the Bicentennial and the building of the Victory Center at Yorktown, that that building would then become the state's archaeological museum. This was proposed by Senator Hunter Andrews, and Hunter Andrews had all the power. He and his sidekick both said this is what we will do, but they never did. They allowed Bill Kelso's office to move into the Victory Center, but they were sort of on the fringe of it. So it all went in the wrong direction. So the history of archaeological exhibits and that sort of thing has really been sort of checkered.

I thought there needed to be a decent [archaeological] museum in Williamsburg. What I had inherited was the courthouse of 1770, which had exhibits that had been put in by the architects back in the 1930s, and basically they consisted of hinges, an entire wall of hinges arranged in a sort of sunburst. I tried to explain to Orin Bullock and other people that, really, people were not interested in a mass of hinges, but they could be made interested in hinges if you gave them a story, saying why this hinge is interesting because you have one at home like that, and what an H-L hinge is and so on. You go from what you have and what you know, then you cross your way back into the past. So then we were thrown out of there in the early 1970s, thrown out of the courthouse, because they were turning it into a visitor center, and so we took over the Anderson House on Duke of Gloucester Street. Actually [Edwin] Kendrew, until his retirement, had actually been very helpful to me in that he allowed me to use his basement at the Anderson House as an archaeological lab, because I thought it was improper to include other projects within the framework of Colonial Williamsburg. At the time I was doing excavations at Rosewell Plantation and had that material to study. The artifacts found on our extramural sites were best kept separate, which we did. So we had the lab in Ed's basement. When he retired, I then took over the house and tried to create an exhibit, I don't know if you ever saw it.

Yes, I did on several occasions.

NOËL HUME: I came up with the idea of a room, a traveler's room, which has all the artifacts in it as parallels for each item in the complete furnishings, which even Graham Hood, who was curator of the collections, said that this was the most authentic room in Williamsburg, and I think it probably was. We put it up in 1974. Incidentally, within weeks of my retiring, they destroyed it all, and turned the building into offices.

Your goal with that exhibit was to try and show the relationship between archaeological objects and colonial life?

NOËL HUME: That is what it was about. Showing the bed curtains, the chamber pots, and things like that. We had the little pieces of them from the archaeology in cases on the rail, with photographs beside the little pieces showing the section of the room (with the corresponding items). And it seemed to work. After taking them through that, we will then show you how we do it, and then they saw sketches of the well and things like that, stratigraphy, and finally, the last thing was about the blacksmith's activity, Anderson was a blacksmith, and they were about to start reconstruction of the blacksmiths' forges behind the building, and so this whole thing led to you going out and seeing what they were doing. And it worked, and it was highly praised actually.

Yes, it was effective.

NOËL HUME: But as I said, it was closed right after I retired.

But the idea of telling the public and teaching them and bringing them into the process is something that was rather new at the time in archaeology, wasn't it?

NOËL HUME: Yes, I think it was and, to some degree, it still is. Most archaeologists tend not to recognize their responsibility to the public. I think if you are going to dig up somebody's past, you'd better tell them about it.

So do you believe historians and archaeologists have an obligation to communicate their findings to the public as well as their colleagues?

NOËL HUME: Yes, I couldn't agree more. We are digging up the past of America, and America has the right to see what we did with it and to learn from it if they want to. The museum at Carter's Grove, the Martin's Hundred Museum, did you ever go through that?

Many times. In my estimation, it was one of the finest colonial archaeology exhibits yet created. We took every field-school class to it for years.

NOËL HUME: I thank you. You know it only had 200 artifacts in it.

It seemed like there were many more.

NOËL HUME: Every artifact was working. It had something to say, which carried it on to something else, whether it was art or armor or whatever it was, and it led you to the site. At most archaeological museums related to sites, you go to the site and then you see some stuff that was found there, and I always said that is the wrong way around. You should see the things, the stuff, get the feel for the site, and then see it. And that is what we did. And people loved it. And then Colonial Williamsburg sold it. It is one of the saddest stories in the history of Colonial Williamsburg. But they closed it in 2002 on the grounds that repairs were needed. I firmly believe, and there is some proof of it, that they intended to sell the property from the start. So the museum stayed shut for five years, meanwhile, the visitor center fell apart, and has since been torn down. ... (Figure 3).

The problem is that Carter's Grove did very well, visitation was good, but 85% to 90% of the ticket sales were sold at the visitor center downtown, and all the income from that went into the general fund. Ten percent of the tickets were sold actually at Carter's Grove and that 10% was credited to its budget. And in consequence, it looked as though it was losing money hand over fist. So when Colonial Williamsburg wanted to do some cutting, they said let's get rid of Carter's Grove. They knew this situation because I have seen a report on it, so they knew all along what was afoot.

The mansion and land were sold in 2008. The easement obtained by Colonial Williamsburg specifically stated that "[t]he building that housed the Winthrop Rockefeller Archaeological Museum and the recreated Wolstenholme Town interpretive structures may be demolished or modified at the Grantor's discretion." This has been done. All the Wolstenholme Towne reconstructions have been demolished, and the colonists' grave markers torn up and tossed down a ravine. Meanwhile, the 18th-century Carter's Grove mansion suffered damage from lack of repair and maintenance. The visitor center has been demolished and the museum emptied prior to its authorized destruction, though all the cases, lighting, and labeling are still in good order and could be reactivated if the artifacts were returned. The promised archaeological museum galleries in Williamsburg remain unbuilt, and the 17th-cenury artifacts languish deep in storage.

Figure 3. Ivor Noël Hume contemplating the fate of Martin's Hundred. (Photo by Glenn Farris, ca. 1994.)

It is a sad story about what was a major contribution to America's early history.

NOËL HUME: Yes, and it really doesn't do any credit to Colonial Williamsburg. The future should learn from the past, not just earn from it, and there is more to the past than 18th-century buildings. It is true that the 17th century is not relevant in restored and reconstructed Williamsburg; but there is much more to the colonial story than Queen Anne and the Georges, as the King Jameses and Charleses would no doubt loudly protest. So I have become rather cynical in my old age, but keep writing because, all along, I have really believed that our duty is to the public.

You published two of what can be described as the foundational volumes for the field, Historical Archaeology *and* A Guide to Artifacts of Colonial America. *What was the inspiration?*

NOËL HUME: There was a need to help people improve their excavation methods, demonstrate how to do historical archaeology, and a means of identifying the artifacts from it. At the time, nearly everyone was trained in prehistoric. Originally, my idea was to make it a single volume, but my editor at Knopf, Angus Cameron, decided otherwise. So *Historical Archaeology* about the methods and techniques, was published first in 1969, followed by *A Guide to Artifacts* the next year. The *Guide* really needs to be updated.

Perhaps, but it has served the field incredibly well and continues to do so. One of the big problems we face today with artifacts and sites is their preservation, both from land and underwater.

NOËL HUME: Yes, and the problems are not the same. On land we need to protect everything we possibly can. Although, if we started trying to save every place that somebody did something at some time, there wouldn't be any room for anybody at all. So you have to be selective. And that is what I said back when we were discussing this archaeological museum for the state, trying to establish a policy that one really should be selective. "Pinky" Harrington once said to me, he said, "pick the battles you can win," and that was good advice. In my early start, I was running around all over the state, digging at Rosewell and places like that, and got terribly upset when people destroyed sites. And Pinky said just do what you can do, and do it well. And that was really my attitude.

I get into trouble these days with underwater archaeology. I have rashly, perhaps, allied myself with the deepwater salvage people in the belief that if they can, if they have machinery, which they do, which will remove objects from shipwrecks and record objects from the ships from 2,000 ft. down, where divers cannot reach, we can learn things. If they raise the money to do this, and I know one company that I talked with, Odyssey [Marine Exploration], it costs $37,000 a day to keep a ship on station, so they have to get money, and someone has to get something back for it. And they say they want to be able to sell artifacts, the duplicates, to the public. They may have millions of dollars in 50¢ pieces and such stuff. So the archaeological profession says this is disgraceful, nobody should ever sell an artifact. No one should make money off archaeology. So I say, "What about your salaries? Aren't you making money off archaeology?" And so my position is, if we can get some information from these deep-sea wrecks, and the quality of the work is extremely high, far higher than anything that is done in the shallow diving, the high-quality mapping, photometric mapping, and photomosaics of the ships, which are lying at a great depth, not just in mud but sitting on the bottom more or less to some degree intact. If we can learn about them, what's wrong with getting these people to do it? But the archaeological profession says, "Hell no."

It is a very difficult ethical issue because we do not wish to encourage looting.

NOËL HUME: No, of course not. The archaeology has to be done right. But it's about selling artifacts. That is a different issue.

Well, there is a lot of ethical debate about artifacts, from land or sea, who owns them, who has access to the knowledge that they yield, what we decide to curate, so it is a very complex and sensitive topic.

NOËL HUME: It really is, but I contend that if you have 1,000 coins that are exactly the same, and you intend to sell 500 of them to recover the cost of getting them, recovery, conservation, and all, I think that is the price of doing business. And that is the price of our being enriched by the ability to study those coins. And if those coins have been photographed and reported and studied by numismatists and half preserved in a collection, then the rest are not as important, and they do enable the project to go forward. At one time, I know, in England when one had a broken up mosaic, little bits of tesserae, you sold these pieces to the public to be able to raise funds to keep the project going. It's simply practical common sense. But that doesn't have anything to do with ethics, you can argue all sorts of ways about that.

I venture to add that when the Society for Historical Archaeology bans Odyssey's curators from delivering papers at its conferences and has their reports removed from the book tables—all in the name of ethics—then the priests of ethics need to review their religion in the light of common sense and modern reality.

Well, I agree that this is a very challenging subject. Thank you for your perspective on it. Looking at what we save and decide to permanently curate, in an important sense, all archaeology is sampling. We rarely dig every part of a site and do not save every object we excavate, often only retaining a sample of specific materials.

NOËL HUME: Of course, at Williamsburg, I kept everything.

Well, I mean things like brick fragments, bits of mortar or shell, other such things, you only take enough, perhaps the whole ones or a percentage to have a good sample for curation, at least for some categories of material.

NOËL HUME: Right. Now in England, I remember at St. Alban's Verulamium I went to their lab and found that they were only keeping the tops, the rims and the bases of the pots they found, none of the other pieces were being saved. They discarded them. And there was no such thing as cross-mending in those days. I was the person who invented cross-mending.

Really?

NOËL HUME: Yes

There was no cross-mending being done for analysis by anyone?

NOËL HUME: No, there was no cross-mending there, nor any being done over here either.

But that is such a vital step in the analysis and the deciphering of an archaeological site. So you introduced that method?

NOËL HUME: Yes, I was the first person to do that. It is simple when you think about it, isn't it? And you know that is how you determine this part of the site relates to that part of the site, this layer to that layer, and so forth. That is where a key part of the story is told, in the cross-mendng, but no one did it. ... I started that in England and brought it here. From the beginning, I was seeing beyond the artifact. When you talk about cross-mending, you mean it's broken and the pieces are scattered. And interpretation rests in bringing that scattering back together, and therefore the association of the provenience numbers that mend, because you recorded them, is important, and out of that comes the story. That's why I am not a prehistorian, because there isn't any story. [*laughter*] There really isn't.

Well it normally does take a different approach.

NOËL HUME: Yes, it is an entirely different approach to the past. I have a myopic view when talking about one person doing something. And the aim is trying to reach out to that one person. When you are talking about cultures, Middle Woodland or whatever it is, you really don't see the person as clearly. And when it comes to the public, the catalyst or the desire is to see the person. That is what makes history into historical archaeology.

What about that idea of the artifact as being as valuable as, even comparable, to a word in a document. Historians don't typically feel as comfortable working with objects as they do something in writing, but you helped us to understand that objects are as significant, if not more so.

NOËL HUME: Yes, you see that historians for decades really didn't get along with the anthropologists. They speak different languages, and so the jargon of anthropology, particularly the idea of cultures, which are broad, is intriguing, but historians want to narrow it down to this and that, and anthropologists don't do that, they can't do that, and, therefore, what they can do is not appreciated as much as it should be by historians. ... I was once at a talk given by Bill Kelso at UCLA on Jamestown. But the anthropologists thought it was nonsense. This is not us. Here you have the anthropologists not liking the historians and the historians not liking the anthropologists. And I don't see this being entirely overcome.

In the same way, I have always been supportive of the amateur. I don't think it matters if you do a job well whether you are paid for it or not. Amateurism does not mean amateurish. And this is where archaeology comes from. All the great people of the past were amateurs. People who did research on artifacts, like numismatists and people like that, wrote copious volumes on every conceivable aspect and yet none of them were paid for this. They were simply amateurs. And I have found that with the 17th-century groups like the Sealed Knott Society in England, the reenactment group, they do some very good work. Someone takes an interest in shoemaking or building construction, and they write little papers about what they have learned. They ... are deeply interested in the history and make contributions. The sad thing is that they are not really encouraged by museums because museums are run by professionals, and so people who do perfectly good work wind up being pushed aside. It is the same thing with this underwater thing. I think to refuse to allow papers to be read by people who are underwater archaeologists but amateurs is wrong. One should encourage the amateurs to learn how to do it well, but not just tell them you cannot do it, at least in my opinion.

Certainly, some of the most talented excavators I have worked with are people who have been doing it for 20 or 30 years as volunteers and have amassed a huge amount of expertise. Are they important in the public sphere also because they talk with other people and generate interest?

NOËL HUME: Right, and I think if you can get people, kids, interested through field schools and things of that sort, they may grow up to be legislators who can vote you money, or at least can influence legislators. It all can fit together. But archaeologists are not so good at writing reports. If they write them, they are not particularly interesting, and no one reads them, and they know that no one reads them, but they know they have to do it.

I was asked while writing my autobiography by a reviewer, "What is the significance of archaeological reports? Why do people write archaeological reports?" They were specifically asking about Carter's Grove. And why did Audrey and I write this very long report? I said because we had to. It's part of the job. Everything you find needs to be analyzed, and we were fortunate in that we had support with money from Colonial Williamsburg and especially from National Geographic to do

it thoroughly. But I said that is not the real end product. The real end product was the book I did on Martin's Hundred. ... I felt there was a story to be told and the public ought to know what it is. And so I did the book which had nothing to do with Colonial Williamsburg, and then we made the movie, which to my astonishment won the gold prize in Paris.

This is the film **Search for a Century?**

NOËL HUME: Yes. These were outreach kind of things and, basically, we were doing these before anybody else was. Nowadays, Colonial Williamsburg does these electronic field trips and things like that which are wonderful, but in those days they didn't. But having come at it from the theater, I had that interest and took the whole thing full circle.

You are a playwright and have authored at least 18 volumes, along with many other publications. If you had to choose which of those you are most proud and are favorites, which would they be?

NOËL HUME: I think probably the novel I wrote, *Civilized Men: A James Towne Tragedy* (2005a). It is about Lord Delaware's year here in 1610 and its ties to history. I am a great supporter of the Indians, and so the person in the book asks, "Who were the civilized men, the English or the Indians?" I tried to show that the English were as barbarous as those they called savages. That is one of my favorite books. And the one I wrote on antiques back in the 1970s—*All the Best Rubbish*. It didn't do very well, only went into a second edition. Then I did *1775*, and that was an attempt in the late 1960s to show how you could take all the little pieces of history—documents, letters, newspaper quotes, ads, and things like that—to fit them together to reconstruct a year (Noël Hume 1967). And that I suppose is one of my best. But a reviewer who was up in Chicago raised the question: "Should archaeologists try to write history?" And his conclusion was "not necessarily."

Archaeologists have to write reports. They have to do their thing because it may be that out of their report something more useful will emerge, and it may lead somewhere. But why publish every archaeological report? If nobody is going to read it, what is the point? It takes a lot of money and comes to $30,000 or $40,000 to put it into print, and then you have a warehouse full of unsold copies. So why do that? Providing you don't skip the report, so that the report exists, and so it is available in libraries. Colonial Williamsburg's reports, they are not published but were written. But all through my career there, I was writing something else—little booklets.

You mean things like **Wells of Williamsburg** *(Noël Hume 1969b),* **Williamsburg Cabinetmakers** *(Noël Hume 1971), and so forth?*

NOËL HUME: Yes, that's right. I was trying to get those things out fairly quickly to appeal to the visiting public. And I called them "thumber books," which meant that if you put the pictures right to the edge of the page and somebody flipped through it, [they would conclude] it must be worth a buck. And it worked. They are still in print, although no longer for a buck.

That seems a splendid way of rapidly bringing the results of the research to the public and in a way they could readily understand and appreciate.

NOËL HUME: Yes, and if you wanted to refer at the backs of each one of them, there were the numbers, measurements, and numbers of the objects, because I don't think the average person who reads the caption wants to read the sizes and such details.

In developing that series, did you have support, or was it a struggle to get them published?

NOËL HUME: No, I don't ever recall having a problem. If I said I wanted to do it, I did it. At least until I wanted to do a booklet on the museum at Carter's Grove, about that collection and what it meant. And the then vice president in charge of education said that is ridiculous, if you haven't said what needs to be said in the exhibit, then the exhibit is a failure, so what is the point? So, I said, some people like to take it home. So that one was written but never published.

You once wrote that the archaeology leads the researcher, and it is not the other way around. I thought that was an interesting expression, and could you elaborate a bit on that?

NOËL HUME: I don't think you should do archaeology for the sake of doing archaeology. If you have an important question to ask, and archaeology will answer it or try to answer it, then it is worth doing. But I am opposed to going out and digging into sites for no better reason than the fact that you have a field school that can dig it. And then it never gets finished.

So archaeology is a catalyst. For example, like oyster shells we found were a catalyst, [they can take] you back into history and from them you can study the transportation and use of oysters over the centuries, from Roman times on. It opens the door, but it isn't often that the archaeology really precedes historical inquiry.

You have really merged colonial history and archaeology. Since you began your work, archaeology has dramatically increased our knowledge about colonial and postcolonial America. Martin's Hundred was certainly one of the pivotal projects of your career as well as in historical archaeology. What were the greatest challenges and greatest satisfactions of that project?

NOËL HUME: The ability, unexpectedly, to study a large area. The archaeology I did in Williamsburg was half-acre lots, so it was very intent on small blocks. At Martin's Hundred, we were seeing families, the whole layout of the fort, the village, the cemeteries, we really saw those people in a perspective we had never seen before (Figure 4). And I think that was the real importance of it. I think that Bill Kelso's work at Jamestown, by the time he is through with it all, will far eclipse what we did at Martin's Hundred. But it was a start. For example, our work on the fort at Martin's Hundred really opened the door to reassessing the fort at Jamestown. Its construction recorded by Strachey, which matched what we had found, then became more relevant to the interpretation of Jamestown (Noël Hume 2001b, 2009). The problem at Jamestown was that the Park Service had misread Strachey's account and got measurements that were much too small. He had said the curtain wall was 300 on this side, 300 ft. on that side, and roughly 340 or 380 on the other, but the Park Service took those three measurements to be the fort. They didn't realize that a curtain wall is only a stretch of walling between two flankers or redoubts, towers, or whatever, and so when you put those in there, and figure out how much room you need for a *saker*, 15 ft. with its carriage and stuff, when you add that in, the thing grows immensely. And finding the size of the flanker really changed the thinking about the fort at Jamestown. So although the importance of Martin's Hundred was later in time than Jamestown, having done that first and interpreting what was found and what could be said about Jamestown, this worked backwards to accurately interpret its documents. At that time, it [the Jamestown Fort] was supposed to be out in the river.

Certainly, in terms of history, Martin's Hundred brought the 17th century to the public mind in a way that perhaps had not been done since 1957 with Jamestown's celebration.

NOËL HUME: Yes, I think that about Martin's Hundred, especially because we had National Geographic backing. That came about in a strange way in that we were sent down there to dig looking for the 18th century and then fell into the 17th century. We had done Site A, which was Governor Harwood's plantation site and house, we werc due to pack up, the season was over, and Colonial Williamsburg wanted to have land to put

exhibits on during the Bicentennial because they thought there would be so many people coming there, which didn't work out in the end.

But the chairman emeritus of the National Geographic Society came down, and Carlisle Humelsine (then president of Colonial Williamsburg) called me up and said they are staying with us but it's no good. They are staying with us but he has come on the wrong weekend, can you do something? Take him down to the site, show him some stuff, don't you have some slides you can show him? I said all right, so he and his wife came down on a Saturday, and they sat silently through my presentation, and I said well that's it. But he was actually impressed and, as it turned out, the Geographic stayed with us for five years, funding the excavation, and they did two articles on it, and they had never done two articles on anything so close together (Noël Hume 1979, 1982b). After I wrote the first one, and it became the number-one choice of people or readers' choice for the year, and then two years later we did a second one, and it did it again. And then we had the exhibit (at National Geographic headquarters), which I was told that three quarters of a million people saw it in Washington. And it was all that public

Figure 4. The Martin's Hundred fortification under excavation. (Photo by Ivor Noël Hume, 1978.)

interest and people coming down to Carter's Grove saying, "When can we get to see this Wolstenholme site?" and Winthrop Rockefeller had recently died, and he had an interest in Carter's Grove, so four million dollars of his legacy started that museum. But it would never have happened had it not been for the prior publicity and public interest that was generated by Geographic. So it is amazing how things go around, you never know how things are going to work out.

So that unplanned Saturday morning slide show really paid a large dividend.

NOËL HUME: It truly did, indeed.

You have worked in museums your whole career, basically, and how do you see public archaeology and history in museums? Are they the critical places where the public comes in contact with our past?

NOËL HUME: They can be. Of course it depends upon the different age levels. When we were designing the museum for Carter's Grove, I said we need to have a stratigraphic section, which will enable kids to see where a posthole starts and where it stops, and so forth. And the committee said nonsense, nobody will want to see that. But I did it anyway, and the kids spent more time studying that thing than adults, because they have minds that are growing, and inquiring minds tend to level off when they get to their 20s. I found that people have a really quite limited attention span. I went around the army museum at Chelsea, England, with a stop watch, seeing people looking at videos. And I found out that the average person will sit in front or stand in front of a video for four minutes and no longer. And you show them another video, and another video, and another, by the time you get to the inevitable another after another, they're pressing the button, taking one look, and going on. So you have to take that into consideration. So when we did Martin's Hundred, and I had my barrel spiels [barrels with audio presentations] all around it, they had a place on the top which told you how long the spiel was, so you would say it's two minutes, three minutes, or if it was four minutes you had a bench to sit on. But you knew it was finite, you pressed the button, and it's going to be over in three minutes. So you made a conscious

decision. After a while, people started stealing the little labels off the barrels, and the then director said there is no point in putting them back, they cost more than a dollar a piece, so let's take them all off, and so they did.

That was a very interesting arrangement, because to get the public interested you had a museum where they were first introduced to the site, then they saw the artifact exhibit, and then you led them out onto the landscape of the original Wolstenholme Towne as a tour route.

NOËL HUME: Right. And I think it worked. We first outlined the site with posts and strings around them, colored strings for the fort, buildings, and it really just looked like a forest of toothpicks. And I was coming down to the site one day and woman was coming back shaking her head saying, "The Park Service hasn't done a very good job with that." I didn't disillusion her.

But shortly thereafter, I was in Egypt and saw the site of Dendera, which has a curtain wall around it, the yard, and the wall was made of mud brick, and much of it had gone down to about 3 ft. high, but the gates were of Aswan granite and still intact, so you have a high gate standing above the walls. And I was there shortly after dawn and saw the sun strike it, and realized that the shadows cast by the sun outlined the thing and said, "That is what we are going to do at Carter's Grove." And that is what we did, with the gate at the fort and walls, gables of buildings, and so forth (Figure 5).

Today, we still hear people proclaim: "I hate history, it is so boring." Never have you been accused of making history boring. Based on your experience, what would you recommend archaeologists do to better present the remarkable stories of our past?

NOËL HUME: Approach it from this end. Don't expect people to take large leaps in time. If you can take them back to what your father had, your grandfather had, perhaps a Civil War photograph, tintypes, things like that, I think that helps you to get involved because it matters, there is a connection. The first thing you have to do is get the public to think it matters to them, and if it doesn't, you've got no hope. So that has always been my feeling. Like the thing with those hinges at Colonial Williamsburg, if you show them one hinge, then show why you are showing them one hinge. The same way at Carter's Grove, we show a thing that is smaller than a drill bit and show them why, because it is part of a garter, the garter fits onto a pair of britches, and then you have a person. And all these larger things come out of very small things. But you have got to explain to people in very short order, due to limited attention spans, why you think, why I think it is important. And it may be that if I am convinced it is important, and can tell them it is important, they will believe it.

I, once, when I was young and stupid back then, went to a museum in Rochester, in Kent, where they had a row of Samian terra-cotta bowls [a Roman redware], and the label said, "This is the kind of bowl a Roman centurion ate his gruel out of." And I thought that's kind of neat, I can see that man sitting, with his bowl on his lap, with his helmet, inside of the room. This came alive. Then I went back to our own museum, the Guildhall, and saw a similar bowl, and the label said "Trajan-Hadrian, Terra Sigillata, Dragendorff, Form 36." And I said, "Why do we put these incomprehensible labels on objects," and my boss, the curator, said, "Young man," he said, "it discourages small boys from coming in and breathing on the cases." And that was the attitude of the curators. [*laughter*].

Amazing! You have touched upon a very important point here, because so much of academic history focuses upon abstract or highly specific topics, and sometimes the human person seems to be left out of it, whereas in working with the public one needs to make a conscious effort to link with people. Your example is a perfect illustration of that. The person needs to be brought in.

NOËL HUME: Yes, in battles, when you look at the plan in a textbook with the little blue line here and little red line over there, you don't hear the battle, you don't even feel it, it is just something hard to grasp. But if you go there, that is why I

Figure 5. The fort interpretation at Martin's Hundred, showing the gate, wall line, and the guard tower, with Carter's Grove Plantation in the background. (Photo by author, 1995.)

think reenactors are so good, they have tremendous enthusiasm for what they do, but they also open the door to the public, and I think that is all for the good.

I think Plymouth (Plantation) does an extremely good job. It was Deetz who was responsible for that. When I first went up there years ago, and I tend not to go to the visitor centers, I do that later, the wrong way around, but I saw a class of African American kids from Boston going through there, and they were entranced by what they were seeing. The people were in a time frame from 1620 to 1627, and their language was geared to the period, sort of, and I couldn't understand how these kids were so entranced with this stuff. The answer was that they had been through the visitor center to start with and seen the film which told them about the language, told them about the parameters of what these people used, and so they had become part of it, they had played into the play. So I thought that was a lesson for me, that if you prepare the public for what they are going to see, then they will enjoy it and understand in a way they would not do otherwise. I think that is very important.

Your drama background clearly had a big influence on your ability to present history to the public.

NOËL HUME: I am afraid that it did.

And that was for the good. But you also used it in writing films, because one of the first movies made, I believe, that tried to present historical archaeology was your Doorways to the Past *(1970). It attempted to show the public the way daily life became the archaeological record. Was that a project that you dreamed up and produced?*

NOËL HUME: Yes, and it was premiered at the American Anthropological Association annual meetings that were held in New Orleans, and the anthropologists booed it. They just thought that it was ridiculous to have people dressing up as in the past and trying to tie archaeology into this. They just thought it was nuts. I never forgot that! But it did receive two documentary awards and is still available in DVD over 40 years later.

It did prove popular and has been used in teaching for decades.

NOËL HUME: Yes it has. My favorite scene is the last one, my great achievement, where there is a button that comes off a young girl's sweater, and it rolls across the floor, and it falls between the floorboards, and then we cut to a shot under the floorboards, and we see the button lying there on a brick, and slowly over time dust covers it and the cobwebs grow, and it becomes archaeological. The snag to that was that no one ever watches the credits, so very often when it is shown in schools they cut it off before it gets there. So I thought that one of my greatest strokes of brilliance, but it doesn't go for much.

Well it certainly shows the tie between life and archaeology for both students and adults. In doing archaeology, you have always talked about the importance of first doing historical background work, of trying to gain a sense of the history, of what might be there.

NOËL HUME: Yes, you won't be digging if you did not have a good reason to dig, and if you didn't have the reason, you didn't have the background, so it all has to fit together. There will always be thoughts, search lines that come out of the archaeology, but you should do your basic research first.

But I know that at Carter's Grove we found evidence of the potting industry there, we didn't know who the potter was, and it was not until several years after the excavation was finished that a letter was found signed by "Thomas Ward, Pot Maker," in which he was discussing an Indian attack after the massacre of 1622, in 1628, which was a localized attack and beaten off. But it is recorded nowhere except in Thomas Ward's letter. So therefore, a page of Martin's Hundred history came to us only from the history and not from the archaeology. And if we had that in hand earlier, we might have looked slightly differently at the site.

But it also could be that the most important piece of information comes from your study of what you found in the ground, which then leads you in one direction as opposed to another. It's a jigsaw puzzle. That is a terribly trite thing to say, but it is true, and the picture becomes clearer as the pieces are put together. And then when you have the picture, you can see beyond the picture to what it means.

Yes, and much of assembling the pieces occurs in the lab. Many of the public do not realize that, they think archaeology mostly occurs in the field.

NOËL HUME: No, no, no! The fieldwork is the easy part. [*laughter*]

That's not what many think, but it is true. Now, you have done so many projects and important studies over the years; which of those you have done would you say have been the most rewarding?

NOËL HUME: Archaeologically in the field, I would say the Martin's Hundred Project. And we got a huge amount of public interest, which is really the payoff for archaeology. Now of course, Colonial Williamsburg has sold it, saying that the 400 years of history that can be told on that site isn't in our area of interest.

Let's look back for a moment to the 1960s, when you were conducting excavations on a wide variety of sites, and there was a rather significant meeting in Dallas that led to the founding of the Society for Historical Archaeology. What are your memories of that meeting?

NOËL HUME: It really began with a meeting at the Smithsonian Institution hosted by the historian "Wid" [Wilcomb] Washburn to try and set up a Department of Archaeology there. He gathered many prominent archaeologists and anthropologists, but they never were able to pull off the new department. But one of the proposals from the meeting was to formally create an international society for historical archaeology. A year later, in January of 1967, Ed Jelks hosted a meeting at Southern Methodist University in Dallas to form the society. We discussed many weighty issues, such as the name, what to call ourselves— fellows, directors, and so forth. Perhaps my major contribution there was that I was the one who put the *a* in archaeology as the proper spelling and argued for "historical." The major objection to

the spelling was from Pinky Harrington because the Park Service still does it with only an *e*, even today. And the name was debated. It was first called "historic sites archaeology," and the Park Service talked about historic, and my feeling was that—what is historic? What is important in history? And important in history to whom? Something can be very important to me in history but not to anybody else. So I urged them to focus upon "historical," as within the period of historic time, rather than historic. If you are going to take it at the national level, Gettysburg is historic, but maybe a little skirmish here on the James River would be important to the county, and they would call it historic, but in the broad scheme of things, it isn't. So there was much debate over an adjective and a letter.

I was made a director and given the responsibility of hosting the society's very first annual meeting, to be held at Williamsburg. I should say that, at the same time, a comparable society was being formed in England, and I was appointed the first vice president from America. But the name historical did not work so well there, as "historical" in Europe goes back to classical times. Since England already had a Society for Medieval Archaeology, it was decided to call the new one the Society for Post-Medieval Archaeology. I think the links between the British and American societies have provided many benefits. The British society immediately moved in the direction of publishing studies on specific sites and artifact categories, thereby becoming a source of good practical archaeological knowledge. But the American society gradually became more theoretical and political in orientation, which is not wrong, but it does offer less of the practical knowledge needed by archaeologists.

So has the field developed in the way you envisioned it would?

NOËL HUME: I think it has become more culturally anthropological and much more theoretical, it's not site specific. Those are good things you can talk about in the classroom, and it does provide the basis for teaching and argument. What I would like to see is much more of the site-specific stuff published. But if you are talking about issues ... such as the social place of women in the 18th century, it's more theoretical and doesn't have as much to do with actual digging in the ground. It's certainly important, but it's history, and I don't think it advances archaeology, which is said to be, if you believe Webster, about the material remains of humans' life and activity. Just thinking about it isn't enough.

Would you recommend that a young student go into archaeology today?

NOËL HUME: I really wouldn't.

You would not?

NOËL HUME: No, The departments of archaeology don't really exist, with rare exceptions. They are departments of anthropology. And departments of history, where archaeology should be a natural arm, generally speaking, do not want archaeologists. Or they don't have places and tenure for archaeologists. So even years ago, shortly after I retired, I learned that Colonial Williamsburg called the archaeological department "the Gypsies," because they were here today, gone tomorrow. And that's no way to make a career. Archaeology is a service, in my mind, it is not the end product. It provides a service to historians, anthropologists, artists, whatever. And so basically embarking on a career that involves archaeology should start by being absorbed in those disciplines, and then using archaeology as a tool, an outreach, an adjunct. But to say I am going to be an archaeologist, I want to be an archaeologist, you have to try and find out what it is they mean by that. So I don't think there is a safe future, a few happy years certainly, but there comes a point when the happy years get a little creaky, and it's then you start wondering about things like pensions, health care, and that sort of thing. Archaeologists, unless they are in a department or a university, simply do not have that kind of security.

But cultural resource archaeology does give good employment, although it often means moving frequently.

NOËL HUME: Yes, so they really are gypsies, they follow the roads, and that is a shame because there are some very good people. But there just are not enough permanent jobs to go around, and I think that unless the economy suddenly picks up, there are going to be fewer jobs. Archaeology is not essential. It is often seen as unnecessary by budget creators. States have to cut, counties have to cut, universities have to cut, so archaeology isn't in the mainstream.

That is a long-term problem and one we always fight. But isn't that why bringing it to public attention, as you consistently have done, is so valuable and perhaps even essential for generating that greater level of popular support we must have?

NOËL HUME: Yes, I think that it is, and this is why we did a field school at the public hospital in 1972. I brought together 28 social-studies teachers for that. We made the mistake of paying them [*laughs*] instead of having them pay us, and that was a naive mistake. But the purpose was to get those teachers to go back to their classes and use archaeology, the logic of archaeology, in their teaching, in the hope that when their kids grew up, they would have sufficient interest in archaeological work and an understanding of archaeological work to support it, and even vote for it in the General Assembly.

That was a farsighted idea. Now, I would like to ask this question. How would you describe your career, as an archaeologist or an historian?

NOËL HUME: I don't know what I was. I still don't know what I was. You know, I called archaeology "the handmaiden of history," I think I coined that phrase (Noël Hume 1964). And it is. In most cases, it expands history and it dots the i's and crosses t's, you know. In some cases, as at Roanoke, you haven't got anything else but the archaeology. So there the archaeology takes precedence, but I always feel that history is what it is all about. But history lies. You can't always believe what you are getting from somebody's letters. There is a bias. Basically I suppose I became an historian, a social historian who uses the artifacts to illuminate and expand what we think we know. ... But as much as anything, Henry, I am an antiquarian, a fellow of the Society of Antiquaries of London. Artifacts are central to archaeology, and the more we know about them the better.

Do you think historical archaeology has a future?

NOËL HUME: Yes, of course. But I think in the long haul it will be espoused as much by dedicated good amateurs as academics.

I am surprised at that.

NOËL HUME: They can use archaeology to enrich their own lives to some degree but also that of their locality. So if there is something interesting to be found in a county, the whole county benefits from it. Making a discovery in a rural area, or in a city, creates an interest in history, which may relate to archaeology but makes people more aware of their past, and I think that is very, very important.

So you see it serving as local stimulation to help people look at their surroundings, their environment, and perhaps better recognize the history that lies within it?

NOËL HUME: That's right. They are masters of their environment, unless they happen to be the Park Service. [*chuckles*] So they are the protectors of the history, and if they do not care, it goes away, it is going every day. So it is very much that the future of archaeology lies in localities and its history, rather than the broad scope of, say, Neolithic studies, that are not as site specific. But you can be fairly myopic on a plantation site or a house site and do it completely and well, take as long as it takes, and all you really inject into it is a sore back. [*laughs*] But you pull out a whole lot more than a sore back, I should say.

An effort that gives something back to the public?

NOËL HUME: That is right. After all, the past belongs to the people.

Would it be accurate to summarize that what you have striven to do over your career is give the past back to the people?

NOËL HUME: Yes I have. Yes, I really have.

Thank you so much.

References

FORMAN, HENRY CHANDLEE
1938 *Jamestown and St. Mary's: Buried Cities of Romance.* Johns Hopkins University Press, Baltimore, MD.

HARRINGTON, J. C.
1955 Archaeology as an Auxiliary Science to American History. *American Anthropologist* 57(6):1,121–1,130.

NOËL HUME, IVOR
1953 *Archaeology in Britain*, unauthorized ed., 1971 (destroyed). Foyle, London, UK.
1957 *Great Moments in Archaeology,* Phoenix House, London, UK. (Swedish edition, 1962; Danish edition, 1964.)
1961 The Glass Wine Bottle in Colonial Virginia. *Journal of Glass Studies* 3:90–117. Corning, NY.
1963 *Here Lies Virginia.* Alfred A. Knopf, New York, NY. (New edition, 1994.)
1964 Archaeology: Handmaiden to History. *North Carolina Historical Review* 41(2):214–225.
1966 Mathews Manor: Preview of a Major Archaeological Discovery *Antiques* 90(6):832–836.
1967 *1775: Another Part of the Field.* Alfred A. Knopf, New York, NY. (British edition, Eyre & Spottiswood, London, UK, 1968.)
1969a *Historical Archaeology; A Comprehensive Guide.* Alfred A. Knopf, New York, NY. (Norton Library paperback edition, 1975.)
1969b *The Wells of Williamsburg: Colonial Time Capsules.* Colonial Williamsburg Archaeological Series, No. 4. Williamsburg, VA.
1970 *A Guide to Artifacts of Colonial America.* Alfred A. Knopf, New York, NY. (Vintage Books edition, 1991.)
1971 *Williamsburg Cabinetmakers: The Archaeological Evidence.* Colonial Williamsburg Archaeological Series, No. 6. Williamsburg, VA.
1974 *All the Best Rubbish; Being an Antiquary's Account of the Pleasures and Perils of Studying and Collecting Everyday Objects from the Past.* Harper and Row, New York, NY.
1977 *Early English Delftware from London and Virginia,* Colonial Williamsburg Occasional Papers in Archaeology, Vol. 2. Williamsburg, VA.
1979 First Look at a Lost Virginia Settlement. *National Geographic Magazine* 155(6):734–767.
1982a *Martin's Hundred,* Alfred A. Knopf, New York, NY. (British edition, Victor Gollancz, 1982; Delta Books paperback edition, 1983; University of Virginia Press edition, 1990.)
1982b New Clues to an Old Mystery. *National Geographic Magazine* 161(1):52–77.
1994 *The Virginia Adventure: Roanoke to James Towne: An Archaeological and Historical Odyssey.* Alfred A. Knopf, New York, NY.
1996 *In Search of This and That: Tales from an Archaeologist's Quest.* Colonial Williamsburg Foundation, Williamsburg, VA. (Second printing 1997.)
2001a *If These Pots Could Talk.* University of New England Press, Hanover, NH.

2001b William Strachey's Unrecorded First Draft of His *Sea Venture* Saga. *Avalon Chronicles* 6:57–88.

2005a *Civilized Men: A James Towne Tragedy*. Dietz Press. Richmond, VA.

2005b *Something from the Cellar: More of This and That*. Colonial Williamsburg Foundation, Williamsburg, VA.

2007 Smith! Being the Life and Death of Cap'n John. Manuscript, Ivor Noël Hume, Williamsburg, VA.

2009 *Wreck and Redemption: Williams Strachey's Saga of the Sea Venture and the Birth of Bermuda in a Newly Discovered Manuscript*. Port Hampton Press, Hampton, VA.

2010 *A Passion for the Past: The Odyssey of a Transatlantic Archaeologist*. University of Virginia Press, Charlottesville.

2011 *Belzoni: The Giant Archaeologists Love to Hate*. University of Virginia Press, Charlottesville.

Noël Hume, Ivor, and Audrey Noël Hume

2001 *The Archaeology of Martin's Hundred*. University of Pennsylvania Museum, Philadelphia.

Henry M. Miller
Historic St. Mary's City
St. Mary's City, MD 20686

Part II: Memorials

MEMORIAL: Adan Eduardo Treganza, 1916-1968. Volume 3 (1969): 85-86. By Paul J. F. Schumacher.

IN MEMORIAM

Adan Eduardo Treganza – 1916-1968

PAUL J. F. SCHUMACHER

Adan E. Treganza was born in Salt Lake City, Utah, on December 27, 1916, to Alberto Owen Treganza and Antoinette Kaufman Treganza. While still in his youth, the Treganza family moved from Utah to Florida, and then to Lemon Grove, San Diego County California. From his father who was a licensed architect and amateur ornithologist, as well as a talented artist, Adan inherited his interest in the outdoors and in birds and wildlife, as well as his fine ability to draw. He illustrated his own reports with a great finesse.

After his graduation from public school, he started at San Diego State College and transferred during his sophomore year in 1937 to the Anthropology Department of the University of California at Berkeley, receiving his B.A. degree in 1940. He continued there for graduate work, with a hiatus during the war when he worked in a local shipyard as a welder. In 1947 he was appointed instructor in the Department of Geology & Geography at San Francisco State College. He received his Ph.D. from the University of California at Berkeley in 1950. During the latter part of his graduate years, he taught summer sessions at the Universities of New Mexico and Washington, and was a teaching assistant at Berkeley.

From this start, he developed over the years the entire anthropological program at San Francisco State College which eventually became a full-fledged department offering an M.A. degree in anthropology. He was the departmental head and chairman over these years.

Treganza was not just an archaeologist or an anthropologist, he was a humanist — the Universal Man. In his teaching, his fieldwork, and his research, this aspect of the man could be seen and felt. His vitality, interest, and constant curiosity gave an effervescence to his being, and this he transmitted to the people who surrounded him. He constantly encouraged his students, friends, and colleagues. Yet, every man was his peer — farmer and rancher, bulldozer operator and local Indian, scholar and politician. He walked easily amongst the humblest and the highest. To everyone he was known as "Trig".

He loved the outdoors and nothing was more pleasurable to him than to be camping out and living off of the land — whether trapping game, tickling fish as the Indians did, or preparing a clam chowder dinner for 60 people from mollusks he had collected along the seashore, embellishing it with a delicious salad of watercress, miner's lettuce, and mushrooms which he had gathered. He knew his birds (*Ardea herodias treganzi* was named after his father), and he was always collecting dead animals for his comparative faunal laboratory collection.

Trig's interest in anthropology covered the entire spectrum of man's existence on earth from Early Man through the proto-contact and contact period, the living Indian, and the European cultural period. He was well known for his historical archaeology research into the 16th-Century landing of Sir Francis Drake and Ceremeno on the north coast of California, having excavated for numerous years at Point Reyes National Seashore, California, and at many other Marin County sites containing Chinese porcelain and European contact material. In California he excavated the Olema

Lime Kilns (at Point Reyes), Fort Ross, Mission San Francisco de Solano, Vallejo Adobe in Petaluma, and William B. Ide Adobe in Red Bluff. In Washington, he excavated at the British Camp (Pig War Site) on San Juan Island. Treganza was in constant demand as a talented speaker at schools and meetings, and before numerous California County Historical Societies. He collaborated closely with the American Historical Society, the California State Parks system, the National Park Service, and the California Historical Society. In 1960 Trig gave a field course in archaeological techniques in Agrigento, Sicily. Recently, he was active as a planning consultant with the newly constructed Oakland Public Museum. He was a member of and presented papers to the Society for Historical Archaeology at the 1968 Williamsburg, Virginia, meeting, as well as the Society for American Archaeology, and the Society for California Archaeology.

On September 19, 1968, Adan Treganza died in Berkeley, California, of a coronary. He had suffered from a heart problem for a number of years, but he was active and vital to the very end. He is survived by his widow, Mrs. Marion V. Treganza, his son, Marco Treganza, and four sisters. The museum at San Francisco State College which he started is now called the Adan E. Treganza Museum of Anthropology and Archaeology, and a San Francisco State College Memorial Fund has been established in his name. A selected bibliography on Trig's historical archaeology follows.

TREGANZA, ADAN E., AND ROBERT F. HEIZER
   1944   Mines and Quarries of the Indians of California. *California Journal of Mines and Geology,* Vol. 40, July 1944, No. 3.

TREGANZA, ADAN E., AND STUDENTS
   1950   Excavations at English Camp, San Juan Island, Washington. (Field notes, reports, artifact list, photos, & maps). July 1950.

TREGANZA, ADAN E.
   1951   Old Lime Kilns Near Olema: 1951. *Geologic Guidebook of San Francisco Bay Counties. Bulletin 154,* pp. 65-72. State of California, Department of Natural Resources, Division of Mines.
   1954   Sonoma Mission: An Archaeological Reconstruction of the Mission San Francisco, Solano Quadrangle. 1954.
   1954   Fort Ross: A Study in Historical Archaeology. *Reports of the University of California Archaeological Survey* No. 23, Jan. 15, 1954.

   1957   The Examination of Indian Shellmounds within San Francisco Bay with Reference to the Possible 1579 Landfall of Sir Francis Drake — 1957. Manuscript for Robert H. Power, Nova Albion Explorations. Published by the Reporte Publishing Co., Vacaville, California, 1957.
   1958   Archaeological Investigations of the Vallejo Adobe, Petaluma Adobe State Historical Monument. 1958. Manuscript for California State Parks & Recreation.
   1958   Archaeological Investigations at the William B. Ide Adobe, Red Bluff, California. 1958. Manuscript of California State Parks & Recreation.
   1958   The Examination of Indian Shellmounds within San Francisco Bay with reference to the possible 1579 Landfall of Sir Francis Drake: Second Season, Oct. 1958. Manuscript for Robert H. Power, Nova Albion Explorations.
   1959   The Examination of Indian Shellmounds on the Tomales & Drakes Bay Area with Reference to the 16th Century Historic Contacts. Manuscript for the California State Parks & Recreation. 1959.
   1959   Archaeological Sites in the Point Reyes National Seashore Project. Manuscript for the National Park Service. October 1959.
   1960   *The Indian Story of Point Reyes.* National Park Service publication of Point Reyes National Seashore Land Use Survey. Feb. 1960.

- - - -, and MARTIN H. HEICKGEN
   1961   Salvage Archeology in the Black Butte Reservoir Area, Glenn County, California, 1961. Manuscript for National Park Service 1961. Published as S.F.S.C. Anthropology Museum *Occasional Papers* No. 2, 1969.

   1963   An Archaeological Survey of the Aboriginal and Early Historic Sites of Lassen Volcanic National Park, California. Manuscript for National Park Service. 1963.
   1964   Archaeological Investigations at Bolenas Bay, California. Manuscript prepared for Aubrey Neasham, Western Heritage Inc. 1964.

- - - -, and TOM F. KING
   1968   Archaeological Studies in Point Reyes National Seashore, June 1968. To be published as Treganza Anthropology Museum *Occasional Papers* No. 6.

MEMORIAL: Charles C. Di Peso, 1920-1982. Volume 17, Number 2 (1983): 106-111. By Donna J. Seifert.

MEMORIALS

Charles C. Di Peso, 1920–1982

Charles C. Di Peso died of cancer on 20 November 1982, at the Tucson Medical Center. Di Peso served for 30 years as Director of the Amerind Foundation, a non-profit research center in Dragoon, Arizona, devoted to the study of Native American culture history. His work on the prehistoric and early historic peoples of southern Arizona and northern Mexico is well known and respected. Di Peso belonged to many professional organizations, including the Society for Historical Archaeology, of which he was a founding member. His participation in the Society and in the profession will be greatly missed.

Di Peso was born on 20 October 1920, in St. Louis, Missouri to Charles Corradino and Emma Klein Di Peso and grew up in Chicago Heights, Illinois. While still in high school, Di Peso was invited by Paul S. Martin of the Chicago Field Museum of Natural History to participate in an archaeological project in Colorado. The experience confirmed an interest in archaeology, which he pursued at Beloit College, working as a student assistant under Paul S. Nesbitt, director of Beloit's Logan Museum. In 1941 Di Peso again joined Paul Martin on a Field Museum expedition, this time the Pine Lawn, New Mexico, project.

Di Peso graduated from Beloit in 1942 with a B.A. in Anthropology and a B.S. in Geology, and in June he married Frances Teague. From 1942 to 1946 Di Peso served in the United States Air Force as a First Lieutenant, Pilot, and Instructor in Advanced Training Course and Instrument Flying. After the war, he went back to archaeology as the Phoenix City Archaeologist. Following a brief hiatus (during which he earned a B.F.T. at the American Institute of Foreign Trade in Glendale, Arizona) Di Peso again returned to archaeology, beginning graduate work at the University of Arizona and accepting in 1948 a position with the Amerind Foundation. Di Peso was promoted to Archaeologist-in-Charge in 1950 and became the Foundation's Director in 1952, the position he held until his death.

Di Peso received his M.A. in Anthropology from the University of Arizona in 1950 and his Ph.D. in 1953. According to Emil W. Haury, his graduate advisor, Di Peso was the first Ph.D. in Anthropology at the University of Arizona, preceeding his classmate, Joe Ben Wheat, only because degrees were awarded in alphabetical order.

At the Amerind Foundation Di Peso began an ambitious series of projects, designed to reconstruct the culture history of the native peoples of the American Southwest and North Mexico, the geographical area he later defined and called the Gran Chichimeca. His first major publication (1951) reported his excavations at the Babocomari village site, a late prehistoric site in the San Pedro River drainage of southeastern Arizona. In this first work, as in those that followed, Di Peso presented detailed reporting of the data (with emphasis on artifact use or function) and some controversial interpretations of those data. In order to include the contact and historic periods in the San Pedro sequence, Di Peso next excavated Sobaipuri Indian sites, dating from A.D. 1400 to 1700. The work is especially important to the literature of the historic Southwest. Few reports at this time (1953) provided such detailed information on historic artifacts or devoted so much attention to pertinent historical documents, and the work provided some of the first excavated information on a Spanish presidio site (Santa Cruz de Terrenate).

Di Peso next turned to the Santa Cruz river valley, where he excavated the Paloparado site, which he identified as the historic Pima village of San Cayetano del Tumacacori. In his published report, Di Peso presented what he called an "archeohistoric reconstruction" of the culture history of the Pimaria Alta based on documentary sources, oral tradition, and archae-ological evidence. The data from the excavation are described thoroughly and organized by categories, emphasizing the function of artifacts in the context of native culture (rather than by strictly material categories—stone, bone, ceramics, etc.) in an effort to reconstruct village life. Di Peso's approach, integrating historical, ethnographic, and archaeological sources, is an important contribution. In addition to reporting the excavation and the archeohistoric recon-struction, Di Peso proposed a reinterpretation of Pimaría Alta culture history, which did not pass unnoticed. Di Peso restricted the use of the name Hohokam to an intrusive population out of Mexico, which moved into the area around 1000 A.D. The resident Ootam (a new term for the ancestors of the Upper Pima, previously identified as Hohokam) co-existed with eventually expelled the Hohokam between A.D. 1250 and 1300. At the Paloparado site, Di Peso identified two distinct occupations, a Hohokam and an Upper Pima (late Ootam), the latter of which was contacted by the Spanish and came to be called San Cayetano.

Di Peso returned to the San Pedro River valley for additional excavation to further amplify the history of southern Arizona. In the report Di Peso presented archaeological evidence for the occupation of the Reeve Ruin site by a western Pueblo people and discussed Pueblo-Ootam cultural contacts.

Di Peso's best known and certainly most ambitious work was in the Casas Grandes valley of northwestern Chihuahuha, Mexico. The research was a joint project of the Amerind Foundation and the Instituto Nacional de Antropologia e Historia of Mexico. After 15 years of work, Di Peso and his colleagues published their results in the eight volumes of *Casas Grandes: A Fallen Trading Center of the Gran Chichimeca*. Di Peso proposed the term Gran Chichimeca for the geographical area of the southwestern United States and northern Mexico to replace the term Greater Southwest. In the first three volumes, Di Peso presented the culture history of Casas Grandes (Paquimé) from 10,000 B.C. through the beginning of Apache raids in 1686 on the mission at the site, San Antonio de Padua de Casas Grandes. Throughout his discussion, Di Peso emphasized the impact of external cultural contacts, expecially trade contracts with the native people of the south. For each period, Di Peso presented a historical narrative of the Gran Chichimeca and contemporaneous Mesoamerica, along with detailed archaeological evidence, organized according to functional categories as in his previous publications. Volumes Four through Eight of the series, co-authored with John B. Rinaldo and Gloria Fenner, provided a very detailed catalogue of architectural data and artifacts in the traditional format, organized by material. The work is clearly a major contribution to the literature of the area, and Di Peso's extensive use of Spanish documents and attention to historic architecture and artifacts make the work a major resource for scholars of Spanish Borderlands ethnohistory and archaeology.

Though his work was often controversial, Di Peso's contribution to his profession did not go unacknowledged. He was awarded the Alfred Vincent Kidder Award for achievement in American archaeology by the American Anthropological Association in 1959, was made a fellow of Sigma Xi in 1961, and was awarded a Doctor of Science degree in 1970 by his undergraduate school, Beloit College. He served as President of the Society for American Archaeology in 1972–1973. In 1975, following the publication of the Casas Grandes volumes, Di Peso received the Governor's Commendation from the State of Chihuahua, Mexico, for his investigations at Casas Grandes, and a Special Award for Excellence from the Border Regional Library Association (El Paso, Texas) for the publication itself. Di Peso held many executive positions and appointments, including a position on the Board of Governors of Cochise College for nearly 20 years. In recognition of his service, the College Learning Resource Center was dedicated as the Charles Di Peso Library.

In 1981 Di Peso had surgery for stomach problems and was told he had cancer. For the following year, he continued to work, nearly completing the manuscript on his investigations at Wind Mountain, a prehistoric site he believed to be a Casas Grandes satellite on a trade route from Casas Grandes to Mesa Verde. (The Amerind Foundation plans to complete and publish the report.) At the time of his death, Di Peso was planning a new research project in the Gila River valley.

Di Peso is survived by his wife, Frances, his sons Charles and David, two grandchildren, and his sister. Memorial contributions in his name may be made to the Amerind Foundation, Inc., P.O. Box 248, Dragoon, Arizona 85609, or to the American Cancer Society.

DONNA J. SEIFERT

Acknowledgements: I have drawn freely from information provided by Patric H. Beckett, Gloria Fenner, Rex Gerald, Emil W. Haury, and the Amerind Foundation.

BIBLIOGRAPHY

1945 Pueblo Grande. City of Phoenix, *Thunderbird* 3(14).

1946 The Vanished People. In *Pueblo Grande Parcher Guide* pp. 14–16.

1949 Preliminary Report of a Babocomari Indian Village. *The Kiva* 14(1–4):10–14.

1950a A Guaraheo Potter. *The Kiva* 16(3):1–5.

1950b Painted Stone Slabs of Point of Pines, Arizona. *American Antiquity* 16(1):57–65.

1951a The Babocomari Village Site on the Babocomari River. Southeastern Arizona. *Amerind Foundation Publications* No. 5. Dragoon, Arizona.

1951b A Ball Court Located on the San Pedro River in Southeastern Arizona. *American Antiquity* 16 (3):257–60.

1952 The Location of Santa María del Populo: A Seri Mission Founded in the San Miguel River Valley in the Year 1678. Ms. on file, Department of Anthropology, University of Arizona, Tucson; Library of The Amerind Foundation, Dragoon, Arizona.

1953a The Clay Figurines of Acambaro, Guanajuato, Mexico. *American Antiquity* 18(4):388–89.

1953b The Clay Monsters of Acambaro. *Archaeology* 6(2):111–14.

1953c Clovis Fluted Points from Southeastern Arizona. *American Antiquity* 19(1):82–85.

1953d The Sobaipuri Indians of the Upper San Pedro Valley, Southeastern Arizona. *Amerind Foundation Publications* No. 6. Dragoon, Arizona.

1954 The Life of Father Kino. *Tucson Daily Citizen* January 9—April 17.

1955 Two Cerro Guamas Clovis Fluted Points from Sonora, Mexico. *The Kiva* 21(1–2):13–15.

1956a An Archaeological Classification of Culture Contact Situations. In Seminars in Archaeology: 1955. Edited by Robert Wauchope, *Society for American Archaeology, Memoir* 11; and *American Antiquity* 22(2):1–30.

1956b The Upper Pima of San Cayetano del Tumacacori. *Amerind Foundation Publications* No. 7. Dragoon, Arizona.

1956c Review of Highway Salvage Archaeology, Vol. I, edited by Fred Wendorf. *American Antiquity* 21(3):326–27.

1956d Letter in "Notes and Documents." *New Mexico Historical Review* 31(3):248–51.

1956e The Coming of the Apache de Gila. *Tucson Daily Citizen*, Fiesta de Los Vaqueros edition.

1956f Review of: The Material Culture of Pueblo Bonito, by Neil M. Judd. *American Anthropologist* 58(1):200–01.

1957 A Tubular Stone Pipe (?) from Sonora. *American Antiquity* 22(3):288–90.

1958a The Reeve Ruin of Southeastern Arizona. *Amerind Foundation Publications* No. 8. Dragoon, Arizona.

1958b Western Pueblo Intrusion Into the San Pedro Valley. *The Kiva* 23(4):12–16.

1959a El Enfoque Arqueohistórico. In *Esplendor del México Antiguo*, edited by Raúl Noriega, Carmen Cook de Leonard, and Julio Rodolfo Moctezuma, Vol. 2, pp. 671–86. México, D.F.

1959b Review of: Excavations, 1940, at University Indian Ruin, Tucson, Arizona, by Julian D. Hayden. *American Antiquity* 25(1):140–41.

1960 Recent Excavations at Casas Grandes (Chihuahua). *Katunob* 1(4):47–48.

1961a *Exploraciones Arqueologicas en Casas Grandes*. Paper presented at Mesa Redonda

Sobre Problemas Antropológicos de México y Centro América, Noveno Reunión, Chihuahua, 1961.

1961b Padre Francisco Eusebio Kino. In *Encyclopaedia Britannica*, (Vol. XIII:402–03).

1962 Review of: Prehistoric Agriculture at Point of Pines, Arizona, by Richard B. Woodbury. *American Anthropologist* 64(2):440–41.

1963a The Archaeologist and the Pre-Colonial Borderlands. Ms. on file, Library, The Amerind Foundation. Dragoon, Arizona.

1963b Cultural Development in Northern Mexico. In Aboriginal Cultural Development in Latin America: An Interpretative Review, edited by Betty J. Meggers and Clifford Evans. *Smithsonian Institution, Smithsonian Miscellaneous Collections* 46(1):1–15.

1964a Northern Mexico, A.D. 100–1150. Paper presented at the Arizona Academy of Science Symposium on Southwestern Prehistory, Arizona State University, April 4, 1964. Ms. on file, Library, The Amerind Foundation, Inc. Dragoon, Arizona.

1964b Review of: Chapters in the Prehistory of Eastern Arizona, I, by Paul S. Martin *et al. American Antiquity* 29(4):530–31.

1965 The Clovis Fluted Point from the Timmy Site, Northwest Chihuahua, Mexico. *The Kiva* 31(2):83–87.

1966a Preliminary Archaeological Explorations of Casas Grandes, Mexico. Ms. on file, Library, The Amerind Foundation. Dragoon, Arizona.

1966b *Preliminary Report on the Excavations at Casas Grandes*. Paper (slide talk) given at Society of American Archaeologists meeting.

1966c The Archaeological Explorations at Casas Grandes. For El Paso Archaeological Society, 1964. Ms. on file, Amerind Foundation, Dragoon, Arizona.

1966d Archaeology and Ethnohistory of the Northern Sierra. In *Archaeological Frontiers and External Connections*, edited by Gordon F. Ekholm and Gordon R. Willey, in *Handbook of Middle American Indians*, Vol. 4, edited by Robert Wauchope, pp. 3–25. University of Texas Press, Austin.

1966e Man in the Spanish Borderlands. Ms. on file, Library, Amerind Foundation. Dragoon, Arizona.

1967 *The Amerind Foundation*. Dragoon, Arizona. Brochure.

1968a The Correlation Question in General Archaeological Perspective for Northern Mesoamerica and Beyond. *Proceedings: 37th International Congress of Americanists, Buenos Aires, 1966* 3:23–27.

1968b Casas Grandes and the Gran Chichimeca. *El Palacio* 75(4):45–61.

1968c Casas Grandes, A Fallen Trading Center of the Gran Chichimeca. *The Masterkey* 42(1):20–37.

1968d The Role of the Museum in Adult Education. *Western Museums Quarterly* 5(1):10–13.

1968e Review of: Dendrochronology in Mexico, by Stuart D. Scott. *American Anthropologist* 70(2):417–18.

1969a The Prehistoric People of Northern Chihuahua Challenge Aridity. Ms. on file, Library, The Amerind Foundation. Dragoon, Arizona.

1969b Review of: Earl Morris and Southwestern Archaeology, by Florence C. Lister and Robert H. Lister. *Arizona and the West* 2(3):270–71.

1971a Casas Grandes. In *Encyclopaedia Britannica*, (Vol. V:8).

1971b Casas Grandes Water Control System. *The Cochise Quarterly* 1(1):7–11.

1971c Use and Abuse of Southwestern Rivers: The Pueblo Dweller. In Hydrology and Water Resources in Arizona and the Southwest. *Proceedings American Water Resources Association, Arizona Section, and Arizona Academy of Science, Hydrology Section, Meetings, 1971* 1:381–96.

1972 Review of: The Southwestern Journals of Adolph F. Bandelier, 1883–1884, edited and annotated by Charles H. Lange and Carrol L. Riley. *American Antiquity* 37(3):459–60.

1973a Handbook for the Position of President. Society for American Archaeology. Ms. on file, Library, The Amerind Foundation, Dragoon, Arizona.

1973b 3-Dimensional Records in the Spanish and Mexican Periods. *El Palacio* 78(4):2–13.

1973c Review of: 1) The Seri Indians of Bahia Kino & Sonora, Mexico, by W. J. McGee. 2) New Trails in Mexico: Travels Among the Papago, Pima, & Cocopa Indians, by Carl Lumholtz. And 3) The Last of the Seris of Mexico, by Dane Coolidge and Mary R. Coolidge. *Arizona and the West* 15(2):196–197.

1974a Commentary. In Art and Environment in Native America, edited by Mary Elizabeth King and Idris R. Traylor, Jr. *The Museum, Texas Tech University, Special Publications* 2:9–10.

1974b Geography and Demography. *Encyclopedia of Indians of the Americas*, Vol. I, *Conspectus and Chronology*, edited by Keith Irvine, pp. 143–158. Scholarly Press. St. Clair Shores, Michigan.

1974c Narrative of Paquimé. Ms. on file, The Amerind Foundation, Dragoon, Arizona.

1974d Casas Grandes: A Fallen Trading Center of the Gran Chichimeca. *Amerind Foundation Publications* No. 9, Vols. 1–3. Dragoon, Arizona.

1975a Father Eusebio Francisco Kino, S. J., Comes to Cochise County. *The Cochise Quarterly*. 5(2,3):5–6.

1975b *Prehistoric Adaptations of the Casas Grandes Valley in the Mid-Eleventh Century*. Paper prepared for the Society for American Archaeologists Annual Meeting, 1975, Dallas, Texas. Ms. on file, Amerind Foundation, Dragoon, Arizona.

1975c Problems of Site Photography. In Photography in Archaeological Research, edited by Elmer Harp, Jr., pp. 211–222. *School of American Research, Advanced Seminar Series.* University of New Mexico Press, Albuquerque.

1975d *Casas Grandes and the Chaco Canyon Cultures.* Paper presented at the Pecos Conference, 1975, Salmon Ruins, New Mexico. Ms. on file, Amerind Foundation, Dragoon, Arizona.

1975e The Museum Hidden in the Rocks. *American Indian Art Magazine* 1(1):7–8.

1976a Art as a Key to Prehistory in the Southwest. *El Palacio* 82(1):2–8.

1976b Foreword in *Across the Chichimec Sea, Papers in Honor of J. Charles Kelley,* edited by Carroll L. Riley and Basil C. Hedrick. Southern Illinois University Press, Carbondale.

1976c That Other Revolution. *Archaeology* 29(3): 186–93.

1976d The Sobaipuris: Defenders of the San Pedro Valley Frontier. In *Views on the Military History of the Indian-Spanish-American Southwest, 1598–1885,* pp. 20–30. U.S. Communications Command, Fort Huachuca, Arizona.

1976e Gila Polychrome in the Casas Grandes Region. *The Kiva* 42(1) 57–63.

1977a Review: Seri Prehistory. The Archaeology of the Central Coast of Sonora, Mexico, by Thomas Bowen. *Man, The Journal of the Royal Anthropological Institute* 12(1):184.

1977b Review: The Mesoamerican Southwest: Readings in Archaeology, Ethnohistory; and Ethnology, edited by Basil C. Hedrick, J. Charles Kelley, and Carroll L. Riley. *American Anthropologist* 79(2):499.

1977c Casas Grandes Effigy Vessels. *American Indian Art Magazine* 2(4):32–37,90.

1977d *The Northern Sector of the Mesoamerican World System.* Paper presented at Clements Seminars 1977, Summer, Fort Burgwin Research Center, Taos, New Mexico. Ms. on file, Amerind Foundation, Dragoon, Arizona.

1978a Review: Mimbres Painted Pottery, by J. J. Brody. *New Mexico Historical Review,* 53(3): 276–78.

1978b Review: Jewelry of the Prehistoric Southwest, by Jernigan. *Man, The Journal of the Royal Anthropological Institute* 14(1):169–71.

1979a Culture Change in Northern Mexico: The Bureaucratic Conquest of the Gran Chichimeca, A.D. 1540-A.D. 1600. Paper presented at the Symposium, "Mesoamerican Communities from Proto-Historic to Colonial Times: Models of Culture Change," *Acts of the XLIII International Congress of Americanists, 1976, Paris, France* (Vol. VII).

1979b Roots of the New Tradition. *Juan Quezada,* brochure of California State University, Fullerton. pp. 10–22.

1980a Prehistory: O'otam. In *Southwest,* edited by Alfonso Ortiz, *In Handbook of North American Indians,* Vol. 9, edited by William C. Sturtevant, pp. 91–99. Smithsonian Institution, Washington, D.C.

1980b Prehistory: Southern Periphery. In *Southwest,* edited by Alfonso Oritz, in *Handbook of North American Indians,* Vol. 9, edited by William Sturtevant, pp. 152–61. Smithsonian Institution, Washington, D.C.

1980c Review: Tarahumara, Where Night is the Day of the Moon, by Bernard Fontana; photographs by John P. Schaefer. *American Indian Art Magazine* 5(3):69,71.

1980d The Hohokam and the O'otam. In Current Issues in Hohokam Prehistory, edited by David Doyel and Fred Plog, pp. 224–230. *Arizona State University, Anthropological Research Papers* 23. Paper given at 43rd Annual Mtgs. of Society for American Archeology, Tucson, May 4–6, 1978.

1980e Macaws . . . Crotals . . . and Trumpet Shells. *Early Man* 2(3):4–11.

1980f Problemas Anthropologicos Reales y Su Relacion a La Historia de Las Americas. *Revista de Historia de America* 90:99–102.

1981a The Rio Grande as seen from Casas Grandes. Presented at the 1977 Pecos Conference Symposium. *Archeological Society of New Mexico, Anthropological Papers* 6:23–41.

1981b *Hispanic Impact and Regional Developments: Arizona.* Paper presented at Annual Meetings of Society for Historical Archaeology, January 4–7, 1981, in press.

1981c The Amerind Foundation. *American Indian Art Magazine* 6(2):46–51.

1981d Review: The Apaches, by Worcester. *Arizona and the West* 23(2):183–84.

1981e Review: Ceramic Sequence in Colima: Capacha, An Early Phase, by Isabel Kelly, in press.

1981f Review: An Unusual Basket-Handle Bowl from Central New Mexico, by Jonathan E. Reyman. *Pottery Southwest,* in press.

1981g Hohokam Artifacts. Paper presented at Hohokam Symposium, Heard Museum, April 25, 1981. Ms. on file, Amerind Foundation, Dragoon, Arizona..

1981h History of the Gran Chichimeca. Ms. on file, Amerind Foundation, Dragoon, Arizona.

1981i Structure of the Eleventh Century Casas Grandes Agricultural System. Paper presented at the Annual Meetings of the Society for American *Anthropological Institute* 14(1):169–71. Ms. on file Amerind Foundation, Dragoon, Arizona. *University of Arizona Anthropological Papers*, in press.

1981j *Displaced Native Americans of the Gran Chichimeca*. Paper presented at Society for American Archaeology, April 30-May 3, Philadelphia. Proceedings, in press.

1981k Gran Chichimeca. In *Historia General y Americana*. Instituto Panamerica de Geografia e Historia, Organization of American States. Venezuela, in press.

1981l *The Northern Sector of the Mesoamerican World System (revised)*. Paper given at 1980 Meetings of Society for Historical Archaeology and Conference on Underwater Archaeology, Jan 8–12, Albuquerque, New Mexico, in press.

1981m "Discussion" from Protohistoric Conference, Tempe, Arizona, March 23, 24, 1979. In The Protohistoric Southwest, Northern Mexico and the American Southwest, A.D. 1450–1700. *Anthropological Research Papers, Arizona State University* No. 24.

1981n Review: Material Culture: Styles, Organization, and Dynamics of Technology. Heather Lechtman and Robert Merrill, editors. *American Anthropology* 83(4):968–70.

1981o Prehistoric Trade Routes. *Arizona Highways* 57(10):12–13.

1982 Review: Snaketown Revisited, a Partial Cultural Resource Survey, Analysis of Site Structure and an Ethnohistorical Study of the Proposed Hohokam-Pima National Monument, by David Wilcox, Thomas R. McGuire and Charles

Sternberg. University of Arizona, October 1981, Archaeological Series #155. *The Kiva*, in press.

Di Peso, Charles C., and Daniel Shaw Matson
1965 The Seri Indians in 1692 as Described by Adamo Gilg, S. J. *Arizona and the West* 7(1):33–56.

Di Peso, Charles C., John B. Rinaldo, and Gloria J. Fenner
1974 Casas Grandes: A Fallen Trading Center of the Gran Chichimeca. *Amerind Foundation Publications*, No. 9, Vols. 4–8. Dragoon, Arizona.

Di Peso, Charles C., Renato Rosaldo, and Robert R. Anderson
1961 *Index to El Archivo de Hidalgo del Parral, 1631–1821*. Arizona Silhouettes, Tucson.

Di Peso, Charles C., and Arthur Woodward
1962 Watercolors and Drawings from the John Russell Bartlett Papers (1850–1852) in the John Carter Brown Library, Brown University. Ms. on file, Amerind Foundation, Dragoon, Arizona.

Documentary and Educational Film Scripts

Sponsored by the Harmon Foundation,
Ray Garner Productions

1948 Point of Pines
1949 Betatakin
1950 Los Niños
1951 The Sierra Madre

Presented by The Reading Laboratory, Inc., Content Materials Division, in cooperation with The Archaeological Institute of America, Archaeological Perspectives on Man.

1974 The Gran Chichimeca: Casas Grandes and the People of the Southwest.

MEMORIAL: Iain C. Walker, 1938-1984. Volume 19, Number 1 (1985): 106-110. By Olive R. Jones.

MEMORIALS

Iain C. Walker, 1938–1984

Iain Walker was born in Edinburgh, Scotland on January 13, 1938. He studied prehistoric archaeology at the University of Edinburgh and received his M.A. from that University in 1961. For his Master's thesis he studied the Neolithic and Bronze ages in Nairn, Moray and Banff, three counties in north-east Scotland. In 1962 Walker moved to Canada, working as an archaeologist at the Fortress of Louisbourg, Nova Scotia, a major restoration project undertaken by the Canadian government. While working on this 18th century French fortress, Walker became interested in clay tobacco pipes, a topic which absorbed much of his subsequent research endeavours. In 1966 he transferred to the Historic Sites Division in Ottawa from where he excavated various sites in eastern Canada. In May 1967 he was awarded a Canada Council Doctoral Fellowship for the University of Bath, England, to study the clay tobacco-pipe industry. During the two years at Bath he made an exhaustive analysis of manufacturing techniques used to make pipes, and visited surviving factories in Britain, the Netherlands, Belgium and Germany as well as museums in those countries and in France. While Walker's doctoral work centered on the Bristol pipe industry he also investigated the history of pipe manufacture in Europe, Great Britain and North America, of overseas trade in pipes, and of the social and economic factors affecting the clay tobacco-pipe industry.

Late in 1969 Walker returned to Ottawa where he became Head of Artifact Research and worked on his PhD which he received in 1973. He held several other positions with Parks Canada: Staff Archaeologist (1974–1977), Acting Head of Historical Resources Impact Assessment (1977–1978) and Head of Publications (1978–1979). By the late 1970s Walker had become interested in a career in management and in 1979 he joined the Archaeological Survey of Canada, National Museum of Man, Ottawa, as Head of the Collections Management Section. In 1983, however, he was again back in archaeology as Head of the Historical Archaeology Program in the National Museum's History Division. This was the first such position at the National Museum and Walker's first task was to oversee the excavations at the two sites for Canada's new National Museum and the new National Gallery.

Iain Walker's published work on clay tobacco pipes attests to his integrated research approach, his attention to detail and his understanding of the various forces at work in the production and use of a specific group of artifacts. As well as his dissertation, published in 1977, Walker leaves behind more than 20 articles and papers on the manufacture and trade of the clay tobacco pipe. He considered no detail, no fact too insignificant to be investigated as thoroughly as was humanly possible. Those of us who have had the privilege of working with or under Iain learned many valuable research skills from him as well as a deep respect for knowledge.

Apart from his work with clay tobacco pipes, Walker is best known for his eloquent and literate defence of the "historicalist" view of historical archaeology in North America. He had little patience with those who took neither the time nor the trouble to learn their historical facts or to understand the nature of scientific evidence or scientific laws before heading into the forests of theory and hypothesis. Iain enjoyed his skirmishes against the barbarian hordes of New Archaeologists sweeping through those forests.

An early supporter of the Society for Historical Archaeology, Walker was also active in the Council for Northeast Historical Archaeology, the Ottawa chapter of the Ontario Archaeological Society, and the Conference on Historic Site Archaeology. He was elected a Fellow of the Society of Antiquaries in Scotland in 1961 and a Fellow of the Society of Antiquaries in London in 1980.

Iain Walker died of cancer in Ottawa, 6 May 1984. He is survived by his wife Llyn de Sansoucy Walker of Greely, Ontario, by his mother and brother, both of whom live in Edinburgh and by many friends and coleagues who will miss his wit and stimulating conversations.

Olive R. Jones

Bibliography

1961a   The Prehistory of Nairn, Moray and Banff in the Neolithic and Bronze Age. *University of Edinburgh Department of Preshistoric Archaeology, Thirteenth Annual Report* (1960–61):6–9.

1961b   The Prehistory of Nairn, Moray and Banff in the Neolithic and Bronze Ages: The Study of an Area. M.A. thesis, University of Edinburgh.

1962a   [Note on a possible Clava cairn in Strath Dearn]. *Discovery and Excavation, Scotland, 1961*:33–34.

1962b   [Note on a possible jadeite axe from Galloway]. *Discovery and Excavation, Scotland, 1961*:35.

1963   (with J.C. Wallace) A Cinerary Urn Cemetery at Easter Culbeuchly, near Banff. *Proceedings of the Society of Antiquaries of Scotland* 94 (1960–61):317–20.

1963a   [Note on a bronze spearhead from Banff]. *Discovery and Excavation, Scotland, 1962*:23–24.

1963b   [Note on a beaker from Nairn]. *Discovery and Excavation, Scotland, 1962*: 36.

1963c   Preliminary Report, Excavations at King's Bastion, Fortress of Louisbourg, September to December 1962. Ms. on file, Fortress of Louisbourg, Louisbourg, Nova Scotia.

1964a   [Note on a halberd from Nairnshire. *Discovery and Excavation, Scotland, 1963*:39.

1964b   An Unpublished Beaker from Nairnshire. *Proceedings of the Society of Antiquaries of Scotland* 95(1961–62):305–06.

1964c   Two Decorated Axes from the Laich of Moray. *Proceedings of the Society of Antiquaries of Scotland* 95 (1961–62):306–07.

1964d   Excavation Report on Well found in Basement of United Church, Louisbourg, N.S., Autumn 1962. Ms. on file, Fortress of Louisbourg, Louisbourg, Nova Scotia.

1965a   The Clava Cairns. *Proceedings of the Society of Antiquaries of Scotland* 96 (1962–63):87–106.

1965b   Some Thoughts on the Harrington and Binford Systems for Statistically Dating Clay Pipes. *Quarterly Bulletin, Archeological Society of Virginia* 20(2): 60–64.

1965c   Archaeological Report on the North Half of the Chateau, Fortress of Louisbourg, N.S. Ms. on file, Fortress of Louisbourg, Louisbourg, Nova Scotia.

1966a   TD Pipes—A Preliminary Study. *Quarterly Bulletin, Archeological Society of Virginia* 20(4):86–102.

1966b   Clay Pipes from Louisbourg. *Eastern States Archeological Federation Bulletin* 25(May):14–15.

1966c   A Pipemaker's Mark from Gouda, The Netherlands—Then and Now. *American Antiquity* 31 (5, pt 1):747–48.

1966d   [Montreal clay pipes.] *Gazette*, Montreal, 5 October 1966, p. 6.

1966e   Dating from Modern Bottles. *El Palacio* 73(3):40; correction in 74(1):47.

1966f   The Laigh of Moray. *Northern Scot Christmas Number* (Dec.):25, 27–28.

1966g   Chateau St-Louis: Archaeological Furnishings Report, Part 1, vol. 8, Clay Tobacco Pipes. Parks Canada. Microfiche Report Series No. 19.

1966h   Fortress of Louisbourg: Archaeological Report on Revetted Glacis of the King's Bastion. Ms. on file, Fortress of Louisbourg, Louisbourg, Nova Scotia.

1967a   [Quebec City clay pipes.] *Quebec Chronicle-Telegraph*, Quebec City, 3 April 1967, p. 4.

1967b   Clay Pipes from the Fortress of Louisbourg, Nova Scotia, Canada. *The Conference on Historic Site Archaeology Papers 1965–1966*:96–99.

1967c   Clay Pipes from Louisbourg. *Archaeology* 20(3):186–93.

1967d   The Council for Canadian Archaeology: A Comment. *Anthropologica* 9(1):91–95.

1967e   The Counties of Nairnshire, Moray and Banffshire in the Bronze Age—Part I. *Proceedings of the Society of Antiquaries of Scotland* 98(1964–66):76–125. (Chalmers-Jervise Prize Essay 1965.)

1967f   Some Objects from Nairnshire, Moray and Banffshire in the British Museum. *Proceedings of the Society of Antiquaries of Scotland* 98(1964–66):312–15.

1967g   Excavation with Backhoe. *Ontario Archaeology* Publication Number 10 (June 1967):12–17.

1967h   Excavations at Fort Malden, Amherstburg, Ontario, 1966. Ms. on file, Parks Canada, Ottawa, Ontario.

1967i   Excavations at the Alleged Wintering Site of Dollier-Galinée in 1669–70, Port Dover, Ontario—1966. Ms. on file, Parks Canada, Ottawa, Ontario.

1968   (with Audrey S. Henshall) Three Beakers from the Cawdor Area, Nairnshire. *Proceedings of the Society of Antiquaries of Scotland* 99(1966–67):225–56.

1968a   Historic Archaeology—Methods and Principles. *Historical Archaeology 1967* 1:23–34.

1968b   Statistical Methods for Dating Clay Pipe Fragments. *Post-Medieval Archaeology* 1(1967):90–101.

1968c   Eastern of Roseisle: A Forgotten Site in Moray. In *Studies in Ancient Europe: Essays Presented to Stuart Piggott*, edited by J.M. Coles and D.D.A. Simpson. pp 95–115, Leicester University Press.

1968d   Reviews of *English Clay Tobacco Pipes*, by A. Oswald and ''The Making of Clay Pipes in Leicester,'' by J.A. Daniell (offprint from *Transactions of the Leicester Archaeological and Historical Society*). *Industrial Archaeology* 5(3):300–02.

1968e   Comments on Clyde Dollar's 'Some Thoughts on Theory and Method in Historical Archaeology'. *The Conference on Historic Site Archaeology Papers 1967* 2(pt 2):105–23.

1969   (with Llyn de S. Walker) McDougall's Clay Pipe Factory, Glasgow. *Industrial Archaeology* 6(2):132–36, 139–41, 145–46.

1969a   Ford Family of Pipemakers. *The London Archaeologist* 1(2):47–48.

1969b   Review of *On The Trail of the Iroquois Indian* by G. Elmore Reaman. *Post-Medieval Archaeology* 2:213–14.

1969c   Beakers from Easter Gollachy, near Buckie, Banffshire. *Proceedings of the Society of Antiquaries of Scotland* 100(1967–68):188–90.

1970a   The Pipe Makers. pp 100–05 in *The Upper Ottawa Valley* by C.C. Kennedy, Renfrew County Council, Pembroke, Ontario.

1970b   The Crisis of Identity—History and Anthropology. *The Conference on Historic Site Archaeology Papers 1968* 3:62–69.

1970c   Comments on Garry Wheeler Stone's 'Ceramics in Suffolk County, Massachusetts, Inventories 1680–1775'. *The Conference on Historic Site Archaeology Papers 1968* 3:99–111.

1970d   Dating and the Clay Pipes from the Galphin Trading Post at Silver Bluff, South Carolina. *The Florida Anthropologist* 23(4):159–62.

1971a   Note on the Bethabara, North Carolina, Tobacco Pipes. *The Conference on Historic Site Archaeology Papers 1969* 4:26–36.

1971b   The Manufacture of Dutch Clay Tobacco-Pipes. *Northeast Historical Archaeology* 1(1):4–17.

1971c   An Archaeological Study of Clay Pipes from the King's Bastion, Fortress of Louisbourg. *Canadian Historic Sites: Occasional Papers in Archaeology and History* 2:55–122.

1971d   Nineteenth-Century Clay Tobacco Pipes in Canada. *Ontario Archaeology* Publication Number 16:19–35.

1971e   A Clay Tobacco Pipe from Bath. *Somerset Archaeology and Natural History* 114:100.

1971f   A Chichester Tobacco-Pipe Maker. *Post-Medieval Archaeology* 4(1970):167.

1971g   (ed) Notes on Historical Archaeology. *Northeast Historical Archaeology* 1(2):46–47.

1971h   Ecclesiastical Archaeology—A Review Article. *Industrial Archaeology* 8(4):392–97.

1972a   Some Notes on the Westminster and London Clay Tobacco-Pipe Makers' Guild. *Transactions of the London and Middlesex Archaeological Society* 23 (pt 1):78–89.

1972b   (ed) Notes on Historical Archaeology. *Northeast Historical Archaeology* 2(1):62–64.

1972c   Sir Walter Raleigh Pipes. *Quarterly Bulletin, Archeological Society of Virginia* 26(4):161–64.

1972d   Comments on Stanley South's 'Evolution and Horizon as Reavealed in Ceramic Analysis in Historical Archaeology'. *Conference on Historic Site Archaeology Papers 1971* 6:127–57.

1972e   *The Bristol Clay Tobacco-Pipe Industry.* City Museum, Bristol (1971).

1973a   Reviews of *Fifty Years a Potter*, by W. Fishley Holland and *BIAS Journal* vols 1–3 (1968–70). *Historical Archaeology 1972* 4:116–18.

1973b   Note on a London Pipemaker. *Transactions of the London and Middlesex Archaeological Society* 23(Pt 2):214.

1973c   *Cajote*—A Franco-African Word for a Smoking Pipe? *West African Journal of Archaeology* 3:239–43.

1973d   Three Somerset Pipemarkers. *Somerset Archaeology and Natural History* 116(1972):114–115.

1973e   Note on a Wiltshire Pipemaker. *Wiltshire Archaeological and Natural History Magazine* 67(1972):163.

1973f   Aspects of the Clay Tobacco-Pipe Industry from the Point of View of the Manufacturing Techniques and of the Changing Patterns of Trade and Smoking, and with Particular Reference to the Industry in Bristol. Ph.D. thesis, University of Bath.

1974a   Notes on Eight Gloucestershire Pipemakers. *Transactions of the Bristol and Gloucestershire Archaeological Society* 92:139–44.

1974b   Note on a Hereford Pipemaker. *Transactions of the Woolhope Naturalists' Field Club* 40(pt 3, 1972):388–89.

1974c   Binford, Science, and History: The Probabilistic Variability of Explicated Epistemology and Nomethetic Paradigms in Historical Archaeology. *The Conference on Historic Site Archaeology Papers 1972* 7:159–201.

1974d   Etude archéologique des pipes en terre provenant du bastion du Roi à la forteresse de Louisbourg. *Lieux historiques canadiens: cahiers d'archéologie et d'histoire* 2:59–131. (Translation of 1971c).

1975a   The Counties of Nairnshire, Moray and Banffshire in the Bronze Age, Part II. *Proceedings of the Society of Antiquaries of Scotland* 104(1971–72):71–120.

1975b   Cooking in a Skin. *Antiquity* 49(195):216–17.

1975c   The American Stub-Stemmed Clay Tobacco-Pipe: A Survey of Its Origins, Manufacture, and Distribution. *The Conference on Historic Site Archaeology Papers 1974* 9:97–128.

1975d   A Dunkirk-Made Clay Pipe from the Fortress of Louisbourg, Nova Scotia. *Post-Medieval Archaeology* 9:231–33.

1975e   European Smoking-Pipes. In *The Archaeology of Benin* by G. Connah, pp 235–36, 163 Clarendon Press, Oxford.

1976a   The Potential Use of European Clay Tobacco-Pipes in West African Archaeological Research. *West African Journal of Archaeology* 5(1975):165–93.

1976b   Churchwarden Clay Tobacco-Pipes and the Southorn Pipemaking Family of Broseley, Shropshire. *Post-Medieval Archaeology* 10:142–49.

1976c   Gallipots. *The London Archaeologist* 3(1):23.

1977a   [Comments on clay pipes]. pp 62–63 in *Mansion in the Wilderness: The Archaeology of the Ermatinger House* by C.S. Reid, Research Report no 10 (February 1977), Ontario Ministry of Culture and Recreation, Toronto; *repeated in* "Clay Pipes in the Upper Great Lakes: The Ermatinger Assemblage" *Northeast Historical Archaeology* vol 5 no 1–2 (Spring 1976) by C.S. Reid, pp 6–9.

1977b   *Clay Tobacco-Pipes, with Particular Reference to the Bristol Industry. (History and Archaeology* 11), Department of Indian and Northern Affairs, Ottawa (4 vols).

1978a,b   "Historic Archaeology—Methods and Principles." Chapter 25 (pp 208–15) and "Binford, Science, and History: The Probabilistic Variability of Explicated Epistemology and Nomothetic Paradigms in Historical Archaeology." Chapter 27 (pp 223–39). *Historical Archaeology: A Guide to Substantive Contributions*, R.L. Schuyler ed, Baywood Publishing Company, Farmingdale, New York. (Reprints of 1968a, 1974c).

1978c   Review of *Fort Stanwix: History, Historic Furnishings, and Historic Structure Reports* by J.F. Luzader, L. Torres, and O.W. Carroll. *APT Bulletin* 10(1):79–81.

1978d   Alternative Uses for Clay Tobacco Pipes and Tobacco Pipe Fragments: Some Notes. *Historical Archaeology* 10(1976):124–27.

1979   (with P.K. Wells) Regional Varieties of Clay Tobacco-Pipe Markings in Eastern England. pp 3–66 in *The Archaeology of the Clay Tobacco Pipe. I. Britain: The Midlands and Eastern England*, P. Davey ed (British Archaeological Reports, British Series 63), Oxford.

1979   Whither Industrial Archaeology?. *Industrial Archaeology* 13(3, Autumn 1978):196–217.

1980   The Central European Origins of the Bethabara, North Carolina, Clay Tobacco-Pipe Industry. pp 11–69 in *The Archaeology of the Clay Tobacco Pipe. IV. Europe I*, P. Davey ed (British Archaeological Reports, International Series 92), Oxford.

1981a   Clay Tobacco-Pipes from Yuquot, British Columbia. pp 93–102 in *The Yuquot Project, Volume 3 (History and Archaeology* no 44). Environment Canada, Ottawa.

1981b   Pipes en terre de Yuquot en Columbie-Britannique. pp 99–110 in *Fouilles à Yuquot, volume 3 (Histoire et archéologie* no 44). Environement Canada, Ottawa. (Translation of 1981a).

n.d.   Nineteenth-Century Clay Tobacco-Pipes in Canada. *The Archaeology of the Clay Tobacco Pipe*, forthcoming volume, P. Davey ed (British Archaeological Reports), Oxford.

MEMORIAL: Charles Herron Fairbanks, 1913-1984. Volume 19, Number 2 (1985): 122-124. By Kathleen Deagan.

MEMORIALS
Charles Herron Fairbanks, 1913–1984

Charles H. Fairbanks, one of the country's pioneers in historical archaeology, died in Gainesville, Florida, on 7 July, 1984. He had a significant influence on a generation of historical archaeologists through his initiation of the archaeology of disenfranchised groups, through his strong commitment to rigorous graduate training, and through his effective integration of science and humanism in archaeology.

Charles Fairbanks was born in Bainbridge, New York in 1913. As a young man he attended Swarthmore college and later the University of Chicago, where he received his first formal training in Anthropology and published his first archaeological paper (The occurrence of coiled pottery in New York State, *American Antiquity*, 1937).

While at Chicago, he was a student of Fay Cooper-Cole, who sent him to work on the Tennessee Valley Authority archaeological projects from 1937–1938. It was there that Charles Fairbanks began his long and distinguished career in southeastern archaeology. After graduating with the AB degree from Chicago in 1939, he left for Ocmulgee National Monument in Macon, Georgia, where he worked as an archaeologist until 1943. During his five years at Macon, Charles Fairbanks played an important role in the development of the rigorous and painstaking field methodology that was an important contribution of the depression era Works Progress Administration archaeological programs. He subsequently brought this precision to the historical archaeology of the southeastern United States and to a generation of students in that region.

The years between 1943 and 1945 were spent in the United States Army, and in 1946 Charles Fairbanks resumed his archaeological career as Superintendent of Fort Frederica National Monument, Georgia. At Frederica his excavations at the Hawkins-Davidson houses were an important stage in the development of recovery and interpretive methods in historical archaeology. Although he left Frederica in 1948 to resume his graduate studies at the University of Michigan, his involvement in Frederica archaeology both directly and through his students, continued throughout his life.

At Michigan, Charles Fairbanks studied with James B. Griffin and became part of the Michigan-trained group of archaeologists who subsequently were to become very influential in the development of both historic and prehistoric archaeology in the southeastern United States. After receiving his Ph.D. in 1956, he began his teaching career at Florida State University. While at FSU he developed his interest in Spanish colonial archaeology, an area in which he was to become a leading figure. In 1963, Charles Fairbanks left Florida State to assume the position of chairman of the Anthropology Department at the University of Florida. During his eight years as chair, he oversaw the initiation of M.A. and Ph.D. programs in Anthropology, the growth of the faculty from three to 11 members, and the establishment of the department as one of the major graduate programs in the country for southeastern prehistory and historical archaeology. During this time he initiated and developed active programs or research in Spanish colonial archaeology and the ethnohistory of Florida's native groups, he pioneered the archaeology of slavery and of plantations, and introduced the concept of "backyard archaeology" in historic sites. In 1976 he was named Distinguished Service Professor of the State University system of Florida, and retired as Distinguished Service Professor Emeritus in 1983.

His early involvement in historical archaeology is reflected in his participation in professional societies. He was a founding member of the Society for Historical Archaeology, was on the first Board of Directors, was the Society's fourth president, and the first recipient of the J.C. Harrington award for outstanding contribution to the field of historical archaeology.

As a teacher, Charles Fairbanks directed more than 20 M.A. students and 11 Ph.D. students. His style was a combination of personal concern, rigorous standards, staunch loyalty, and occasional towering rages. It mesmerized his students and inspired great affection as well as a healthy respect for both his scholarship and his opinions. The annual Charles H. Fairbanks Armadillo Roast, which celebrates his birthday, is in its fifteenth year, and is a major social event and academic homecoming for a considerable number of historical archaeologists.

Charles Fairbanks was a thorough and uncompromising scholar, as well as an uncompromising man of principle. He was inherently fair, giving equal consideration to colleagues and students, to hired workers and interested amateurs, and to men and women. Once committed, he could be relied upon completely as an ally and supporter, but he had little patience for bureaucratic red tape, or for what he considered to be restrictive or unnecessary formality. Both true and apocryphal tales of Chuck's uninhibited dealings with red tape and formalities are swapped regularly in more than one archaeological field camp. He was a man of direct physical action who was also ceaselessly observant of and curious about the natural and cultural worlds. To those of us fortunate enough to have been his students, he gave a truly holistic and anthropological view of the world and its workings.

Chuck is survived by his wife of 43 years, Evelyn Timmerman Fairbanks, a son Charles, daughter Marie, one grandchild, and a great many colleagues and students who miss his help and opinions, and who continue to be inspired by his example and his work.

Kathleen Deagan

BIBLIOGRAPHY OF CHARLES HERRON FAIRBANKS.

1937 The Occurrence of Coiled Pottery in New York State. *American Antiquity* 3:178–179.

1938 The Kirksville Site. *The Missouri Archeologist* 4(2):np.

1940 Classification Problems of Southeastern Archeology in Relation to Work in the Tennessee Valley. *Readings of the Society for Georgia Archaeology* 2.

1940 "Salt Pans" from the Southeast. *American Antiquity* 6(1):65–67.

1941 Indoor Archeology. in Prehistoric Cultures of the Southeast. *National Park Service Popular Studies Series, History, 4. Washington. pp. 27–32.*

1941 Hunting 500 Years Ago. Regional Review National Park Service Region one, 6(1–2):3–6. Richmond.

1942 The Taxonomic Position of Stallings Island, Georgia. *American Antiquity* 7(3):223–231.

1946 The Kolomoki Mound Group, Early County, Georgia. *American Antiquity* 11(4):258–260.

1946 The Leake Mounds, Bartow County, Georgia. *American Antiquity* 12(2):126.

1946 The Macon Earthlodge. *American Antiquity* 12(2):94–108.

1948 Fort Frederica National Monument. *Emory University Quarterly* 4(1):8–14.

1949 A General Survey of Southeastern Prehistory. in *the Florida Indian and his Neighbors.* Winter Park. pp. 55–76.

1950 A Preliminary Segregation of Etowah, Savannah and Lamar. *American Antiquity* 16(2): 142–151.

1952 Creek and Pre-Creek. in the *Archeology of Eastern United States,* edited by J.B. Griffin. Chicago, University of Chicago Press. pp. 285–300.

1953 The Protohistoric Creek of Georgia. *Southeastern Archeological Conference Newsletter* 3(3):21–22.

1954 1953 Excavations at Site 9 HL 64, Buford Reservoir, Georgia. *Florida State University Studies* 16:1–26.

1955 The Abercrombie Mound, Russell County, Alabama. *Early Georgia* 2(1): 13–19.

1956 The Excavation of the Hawkins-Davidson Houses, Frederica National Monument, St. Simon's Island, Georgia. *Georgia Historical Quarterly* 40(3): 213–229.

1956 Archeology of the Funeral Mound, Ocmulgee National Monument Georgia. *National Park Service Archeological Research Series Number Three.* Washington, D.C.

1957 Ethnological Report, Florida Seminole. 300 pp. Mimeographed.

1957 Ethnological Report on Royce Area 79 (Creek, Chickasaw, Cherokee) 250 pp. Mimeographed.

1958 Ocmulgee Check Stamped Pottery. *Prehistoric Pottery of the Eastern United States.* University of Michigan Museum Publication, Ann Arbor.

1958 Some Problems in the Origin of Creek Pottery. *The Florida Anthropologist* 11(2): 53–64.

1958 Anthropology and the Segregation Problem. in The Negro in American Society; *Florida State University Studies* 28:1–18. Tallahassee.

1959 Additional Elliot's Point Complex Sites. *The Florida Anthropologist* 12(4):95–100.

1961 Comment on Joffre L. Coe's "Cherokee Archaeology." in Symposium on Cherokee and Iroquois Culture. *Bureau of American Ethnology Bulletin* 180:63–65. Washington.

1962 The Check-Stamped Series. *Southeastern Archeological Conference Newsletter* 9(1): 10–16.

1962 A Peripherally Punched Card System for Pottery Types. *Southeastern Archaeological Conference Bulletin* 8: 24–28

1962 European Ceramics from the Cherokee Capital of New Echota. *Southeastern Archaeological Conference Newsletter* 9(1):10–16

1962 Late Creek Sites in Central Alabama. *Southeastern Archeological Conference Newsletter* 9(1):

1962 The Contribution of the Amateur. *The Florida Anthropologist* 15(1): 13–20.

1962 Excavations at Horseshoe Bend, Alabama. The Florida Anthropologist 15(2): 41–56.

1962 A Colono-Indian Ware Milk Pitcher. *The Florida Anthropologist* 15(4): 103–106.

1963 Defendant's requested finding of fact, objections to Petitioners proposed findings, and brief. Before the Indian Claims Commission, Seminole Indians vs. The United States, Dockets # 73 & 151. Summary of Fairbank's testimony pp. 29–67. U.S. Department of Justice.

1964 Ethnohistoric Report on the Biloxi, Pascagoula and Adjacent Tribes. U.S. Department of Justice.

1964 (editor with I. Rouse and W. Sturtevant) *Indian and Spaniard: Selected Writings of John Goggin.* Coral Gables: University of Miami Press.

1964 Early Occupations of Northwestern Florida. *Southeastern Archeological Conference Bulletin* 12(1):27–30.

1964 Underwater Historic Sites on the St. Marks River. *The Florida Anthropologist* 17(2):44–49.

1965 Proposed Antiquities Law. *The Florida Anthropologist* 18(1):63–64.

1965 Gulf Complex Subsistence Economy. *Southeastern Archeological Conference Bulletin* 13(2): 57–62

1965 The Paleo-Indian Era: Distribution of the Finds. *Southeastern Archeological Conference Bulletin* 13(2): 11–12

1965 Excavations at the Fort Walton Temple Mound. *The Florida Anthropologist* 18(4):239–264.

1965 Florida's New Antiquities Law. *The Florida Anthropologist* 18(3):155–160.

1966 A Feldspar Inlaid Ceramic Type from Spanish Colonial Sites. *American Antiquity* 31(3):430–432.

1968 Early Spanish Colonial Beads. *Conference on Historic Sites Archeology Papers* 2:3–22.

1968 The Archeological Contribution to Urban Studies. in *Urban Anthropology: Research Perspectives and Strategies* edited by E. Eddy. *Southern Anthropological Society Proceedings.* 2. Athens, pp. 16–23.

1968 Florida Coin Beads. *the Florida Anthropologist* 21(4):102–105

1970 Archeology and History of Coastal Georgia. in *Conference on the Future of the Marshlands and Islands of Georgia.* edited by D. Maney, F. Marland and C. West. Atlanta. pp. 35–45.

1971 with R. Ascher. Excavation of a Slave Cabin, Georgia, U.S.A. *Historical Archaeology* 5:3–17

1972 The Cultural Significance of Spanish Ceramics. in *Ceramics in America* edited by I. Quimby. Charlottesville: University of Virginia Press. pp. 141–174.

1974 Comment on "Red, Black and White, Ethnohistory in the Southeast." *Proceedings of the Southern Anthropological Society,* 5: 67–55.

1974 *Ethnohistorical Report on the Florida Indians* Commission Findings, Indians Claims Commission. New York: Garland Press.

1975 The Kingsley Slave cabins in Duval Country, Florida. *Conference on Historic Sites Archeology Papers* (1972) 30–59.

1975 Spanish Artifacts at the Fortress of Louisbourg, Cape Breton Island. *Conference on Historic Sites Archeology Papers* 1974: 30–59.

1976 From Missionary to Mestizo: Changing Culture of Eighteenth Century St. Augustine. in *Eighteenth Century Florida and the Caribbean.* edited by S. Proctor, Gainesville: University Presses of Florida. pp. 88–99.

1976 Spaniards, Planters, Ships and Slaves: Historical Archaeology in Florida and Georgia. *Archaeology* 29 (3): 164–172.

1976 Backyard Archaeology as a Research Strategy. *Conference on Historic Sites Archeology Papers,* 1976:133–139.

1978 The Ethnoarchaeology of the Florida Seminole. in *Tacachale: Essays on the Indians of Florida and Southeastern Georgia during the Historic Period* edited by J.T. Milanich and S. Proctor. Gainesville: University Presses of Florida. pp. 120–149.

1980 The Archaeology of Slavery. *Early Man.*

1980 *Florida Archaeology* (with J.T. Milanich). New York: Academic Press.

1983 Historical Archaeological Implications of Recent Investigations. *Geoscience and Man* 23:17–26.

1984 The Plantation Archaeology of the Southeastern Coast. *Historical Archaeology* 18:1–14.

MEMORIAL: Bert Salwen. Volume 24, Number 1 (1990): 104-109. By Nan A. Rothschild.

MEMORIAL
Bert Salwen, 1920–1988

Bert Salwen, Professor of Anthropology at New York University and considered by many to be the "father" of urban archaeology, died unexpectedly on Christmas Day 1988, in his Greenwich Village home. He was 68 years old. Bert will be remembered as a pioneer, in a new archaeological field. He will also be remembered for his personal characteristics, for his love of archaeology, for his modesty and integrity, his honesty, humor, and lack of pretension, and for his warmth.

At the time of his death, Salwen was deeply involved in New York University's joint program in history and historical archaeology which he had created. It is one of the few genuinely interdisciplinary programs in this field, and although relatively new, its students have already produced a number of Master' theses and PhD dissertations. Salwen was also in the final stage of completing a report on the first major archaeological excavation in Greenwich Village, the Sullivan Street site, analyzing the artifactual material and documentary evidence from the Village's first, suburban phase of development.

Salwen compressed a great deal of archaeology into a 30-year second career. His first profession was that of engineer; he worked in aircraft and machine design and as a contractor for 15 years. His engineering background was useful to him later on, and was always visible in his drafting, his meticulous fieldwork, and his comfort with straightforward, basic quantitative analysis. But Bert became fascinated with archaeology, as an amateur, and in 1957 entered the Columbia University PhD program in the Department of Anthropology.

In a recent interview, Salwen acknowledged that William Duncan Strong had the greatest influence on his intellectual development at Columbia; this can be seen in Salwen's later interest in the Contact period, and in his concern with archaeological field technique. Strong was responsible for Bert's first professional field work experience, as an assistant to Carlyle Smith, working in South Dakota. Richard Woodbury, Ralph Solecki, and Morton Fried were also important academic influences at Columbia. Jacques Bordaz and Jerome Jacobson were studying archaeology there during the same period of time.

His first full-time faculty position was at Bennington College, where Salwen taught for three years. In 1966 he went to New York University to join a new department that was being organized with a focus on Urban Anthropology. He was Director of Graduate Studies at NYU for many years, and served as Acting Chair for several years. He was committed to field training as an essential part of the archaeology program and taught a summer field class for 21 of the 25 summers between 1962 and 1987, with spring and/or fall classes in some of those years also. Although he concentrated his field research in New York, he did fieldwork in 10 other states (including Alaska), plus the District of Columbia. Students who participated in these field schools will always remember his fierce insistence on technical excellence, the familial quality (and fun) of group life, and his harmonica playing.

Salwen was committed to students. This can be seen in the many papers he wrote with them. He was always teaching archaeology, formally or informally, and his enthusiasm gave him a Pied Piper quality that is probably responsible for a number of careers in archaeology. He taught graduate, undergraduate, and high school students, and when he was a consultant to the United States Department of the Interior he designed and taught basic archaeology training programs for non-archaeologist federal managers. These are still being taught today, following his guidelines.

Salwen's first and continuing research interest was the prehistoric Northeastern United States. His dissertation integrated Rhodes Fairbridge's work on post-Pleistocene sea level changes with data from a series of archaeological sites, in order to address archaeological site formation processes. It remains a standard reference in coastal studies. He wrote extensively about the period of European-Indian contact in southern New England (cf., *The Handbook of North American Indians* 15, 1978), and conducted excavations at Fort Shantok, Connecticut, and Fort Ninigret, Rhode Island. As an archaeologist who was committed to the salvage of information from threatened sites, and who became involved in local projects, it was probably inevitable that Salwen began to work in urban settings. In 1970 he excavated the remains of the original Dutch stockade in Kingston, New York, and after that worked in a variety of cities, in a series of projects around historic houses (The Wycoff House, the Van Campen Inn, the Adriance House, and the Vander-Ende Onderdonk site, to name just a few). He also observed the urban research of archaeologists in such cities as New York, San Francisco, Boston, Atlanta, and Albany, and consulted with many scholars from abroad in a wide range of cities in Europe, Great Britain, and Asia. He began to think about the nature of urban archaeology and the contribution that archaeologists could make to the understanding of cities. He considered both pragmatic and theoretical issues: What were the limits of the urban site (building, block, or city)? Should we simply be doing archaeology *in* the city or should we try to do the archaeology *of* the city? What kinds of materials could be included in urban archaeological analysis and did they all have to come from below the ground?

Salwen began to learn history, taking courses in historiography and archival research. He also wrote about the distinction between method and theory, noting that too much of archaeology was simply method and technique, and that as such it was equivalent to ethnography, being essentially descriptive. He suggested that our theory should come from anthropology, history, and other social sciences, allowing us to generate significant research questions related to the processes and phenomena of urban settlement. He and his students have been very involved in urban excavations, particularly in New York City. He was always willing to share his extensive knowledge and experience in urban settings with others doing similar research and was involved in many panel discussions on the conduct of urban archaeology.

Almost from the beginning of his career as an archaeologist Salwen was concerned with the accelerating rate of destruction of the archaeological record. He expressed his concern in several ways. As an individual he was an outstanding spokesman for archaeological resources, communicating problems and precipitating action in a variety of contexts, through his enthusiasm and insight. He was also active in many organizations involved with environmental protection legislation at federal, state, and local levels. He worked as a consultant to the U. S. Environmental Protection Agency and the United States Department of Interior, helping to develop federal policy, writing guidelines and regulations, and developing standards for archaeological research.

He also participated in, and in many cases, helped to found a number of archaeological organizations dedicated to preservation. In 1980–1981, he served as President-Elect and President of the Society for Historical Archaeology, during which time the Harrington Medal was struck and issued for the first time. He also served as president (and was a founding member) of the New York Archaeological Council, and Professional Archaeologists of New York City. He was one of the incorporating directors of the Society for Professional Archaeologists and a Senior Director of the National Preservation Institute. He was also a board member of the Coordinating Council of National Archaeological Societies, the Association for Field Archaeology, the Council of Northeastern Historical Archaeology, and the Society for Ethnohistory. In 1983 he was awarded the Annual Conservation Award from ASCA. He was an active member of many organizations: (AAA, SAA, AAAS, the New York Academy of Sciences, the New York State Archaeological Association, and a number of other state and local organizations.

Salwen is survived by his wife Sarah Bridges, an archaeologist; five children, Peter, Nancy, Joshua, Ethan, and Sarah Frances; and a grandson, James.

Nan A. Rothschild

BIBLIOGRAPHY OF BERT SALWEN

PUBLICATIONS:

1960 The Introduction of Leather Footgear in the Pueblo Area. *Ethnohistory* 7(3):206–38. Bloomington, Ind.

1961 Article: Anthropology and Archaeology. In *World Scope Yearbook for 1960*, pp. 69–71. World Scope Publishers. New York.

Article: Archaeology. In *Collier's Yearbook for 1960*, pp. 69–71. Crowell-Collier Publishing Corp., New York.

1962 Sea Levels and Archaeology in the Long Island Sound Area. *American Antiquity* 28(1):46–55. Salt Lake City. (Reprinted in, *In Search of Man: Readings in Archaeology*, Ernestine L. Green, ed., pp. 149–58. Little Brown & Co. Boston.)

Field Notes: I.B.M. Site, Port Washington, L.I., N.Y. *New York State Archaeological Association, Bulletin* 25:7–9. Ossining, N.Y.

Article: Anthropology and Archaeology. In *World Scope Yearbook for 1961*, pp. 69–71. World Scope Publishers. New York.

Article: Archaeology. In *Collier's Yearbook for 1961*, pp. 69–72. Crowell-Collier Publishing Corp. New York.

1963 The Reliability of Andre Thevet's New England Material. *Ethnohistory* 10(2):183–85.

Article: Archaeology. In *Collier's Yearbook for 1962*, pp. 76–78. Crowell-Collier Publishing Corp. New York.

(with Timothy J. O'Leary) A Bibliography of the Publications of William Duncan Strong. *American Anthropologist* 65(5):1107–11.

1964 Article: Archaeology. In *Collier's Yearbook for 1963*, pp. 136–38. Crowell-Collier Publishing Corp. New York.

1965 Archaeological Survey of the Hercules Powder Company Properties Near Lewes, Delaware. *Archaeological Society of Delaware, Bulletin*, n.s., 4:14–36.

Article: Archaeology. In *Collier's Yearbook for 1964*, pp. 106–7. Crowell-Collier Publishing Corp. New York.

1966 European Trade Goods and the Chronology of the Fort Shantok Site. *Archeological Society of Connecticut, Bulletin* 34:5–39.

(with Ann Harvey) A Stratified Ceramic Sample from the Muskeeta Cove Site. *Nassau County Museum of Natural History, Research Newsletter* 1. Seaford, N.Y.

Sea Levels and the Archaic Archaeology of the Northeast Coast of the United States. *Coastal Research Notes* 2(2):9–10.

Article: Archaeology. In *Collier's Yearbook for 1965*, pp. 99–101. Crowell-Collier Publishing Corp. New York.

1967 A Comment on Emery and Edwards' "Archaeological Potential of the Atlantic Continental Shelf." *American Antiquity* 32(4):546–47. Salt Lake City.

Article: Archaeology. In *Collier's Yearbook for 1966*, pp. 99–101. Crowell-Collier & MacMillan, Inc. New York.

1968 Muskeeta Cove 2: A Stratified Woodland Site on Long Island. *American Antiquity* 33(3):322–40.

Article: Archaeology. In *Collier's Yearbook for 1967*, pp. 121–23. Crowell-Collier Educational Corp. New York.

1969 A Tentative "In Situ" Solution to the Mohegan-Pequot Problem. In The Archaeology and History of the Connecticut Valley Indian, Wm. R. Young, ed., pp. 81–88. *Springfield Museum of Science, Publications*, n.s., 1(1). Springfield, Mass.

Article: Archaeology. In *Collier's 1969 Yearbook*, pp. 107–9. Crowell-Collier Educational Corp. New York.

1970 Archeological Resources. In *Comprehensive Water and Related Land Resources, Connecticut River Basin: Appendix O, A Report of History and Environment*, pp. O-213–O-277. U.S. Dept. of the Interior, National Park Service. Philadelphia.

Cultural Inferences from Faunal Remains: Examples from Three Northeast Coastal Sites. *Pennsylvania Archaeologist* 40(1):1–8.

Article: Archaeology. In *Collier's 1970 Yearbook*, pp. 109–11. Crowell-Collier Educational Corp. New York.

1971 Human Paleoecology. *Conservation Educator* 3(3):3,6,9.

Article: Archaeology. In *Collier's 1971 Yearbook*, pp. 109–11. Crowell-Collier Educational Corp. New York.

1972 Test Excavations at the Zipser Lower Field Site, Warren County, New Jersey. *Archaeological Society of New Jersey, Bulletin* 28:1–15.

(with Ann Ottesen) Radiocarbon Dates for a Windsor Occupation at the Shantok Cove Site, New London County, Connecticut. *Man in the Northeast* 3:8–19.

1973 Archaeology in Megalopolis. In *Research and Theory in Current Archaeology*, Chas. L. Redman, ed., pp. 151–63. Wiley-Interscience. New York.

(with Ralph S. Solecki and Jerome Jacobson) Archaeological Reconnaissances North of the Brooks Range in Northeastern Alaska. *University of Calgary, Dept. of Archaeology, Occasional Papers* 1.

1974 Article: Archaeology. In *Funk and Wagnalls Encyclopedia Yearbook*, pp. 73–74. Funk and Wagnalls. New York.

(with Sarah Bridges) The Ceramics from the Weeksville Excavations, Brooklyn, New York. *Northeast Historical Archaeology* 3(1):4–29.

(with Sarah Bridges) Note on "The Ceramics from the Weeksville Excavations." *Northeast Historical Archaeology* 3(2):8.

(with Sarah Bridges and Joel Klein) An Archaeological Reconnaissance at the Pieter Claesen Wyckoff House, Kings County, New York. *New York State Archaeological Association, Bulletin* 61:26–38.

Wall Map: Indians of Connecticut. Hearne Map Co. Detroit.

1975 Post-Glacial Environments and Cultural Change in the Hudson River Basin. *Man in the Northeast* 10:43–70.

1977 (coeditor with Walter S. Newman) Amerinds and their Paleoenvironments in Northeastern North America. *New York Academy of Sciences, Annals* 288. New York.

(with Sarah Bridges) Cultural Differences and the Interpretation of Archaeological Evidence: Problems with Dates. In Current Perspectives in Northeastern Archaeology: Essays in Honor of William A. Ritchie, Robt. E. Funk and Chas. F. Hayes III, eds., pp. 165–73. *New York State Archaeological Association, Researches and Transactions* 17(1).

Introduction. In Early Papers in Long Island Archaeology, G. Levine, ed., pp. xi–xiii. *Readings in Long Island Archaeology and Ethnology* 1. Stony Brook, N.Y.

1978 (with Geoffrey Gyrisco) Archeology of Black American Culture: An Annotated Bibliography. *11593* 3(1). Office of Archeology and Historic Preservation, Heritage Conservation and Recreation Service. Washington, D.C. (Reprinted in *Archaeological Perspectives on Ethnicity in America*, R.L. Schuyler, ed., pp. 76–85. Baywood Publ. Co. Farmingdale, N.Y.)

(with Susan Mayer) Indian Archaeology in Rhode Island. *Archaeology* 31(6):57–58. New York.

Indians of Southern New England and Long Island. In *Handbook of North American Indians* 15, Bruce G. Trigger, ed., pp. 160–89. Smithsonian Institution. Washington, D.C.

Archaeology in Megalopolis: Updated Assessment. *Journal of Field Archaeology* 5(4):453–59.

1979 Archaeology: Partnership in Historic Preservation. *Journal of Field Archaeology* 6(3):365–66.

1980 (with Sarah Bridges) Weeksville: The Archaeology of a Black Urban Community. in *Archaeological Perspectives on Ethnicity in America*, R.L. Schuyler, ed., pp. 38–47. Baywood Publ. Co. Farmingdale, N.Y.

1981 (with Sarah Bridges and Nan Rothschild) The Utility of Small Samples from Historic Sites: Onderdonk, Clinton Avenue, and Van Campen. *Historical Archaeology* 15(1):79–94.

1982 Urban Archeology: The Past is Waiting to be Uncovered. In *Cities: The Forces that Shape Them*, Lisa Taylor, ed., p. 43. Cooper-Hewitt Museum, Smithsonian Institution. New York.

Foreword. In *Archaeology in Urban America*, Roy S. Dickens, Jr., ed., pp. xiii–xvii. Academic Press. New York.

(with Geoffrey Gyrisco) Urban Archaeology: A Selected Bibliography. *North American Archaeologist* 3(3):259–70.

An Anthropologist Looks at Preservation. *Livability Digest* 2(3):36–38. (Issues in Urban Archeology, Robt. H. McNulty, ed.)

1983 Indians of Southern New England and Long Island. In *Connecticut Archaeology: Past, Present, and Future*, R.E. Dewar, K.L. Feder, and D.A. Poirier, eds., pp. 79–115. Univ. of Connecticut, Dept. of Anthropology, Occasional Papers. Storrs, Conn.

(with Lucianne Lavin) The Fastener Site: A New Look at the Archaic/Woodland Transition in the Lower Housatonic Valley. *Archeological Society of Connecticut, Bulletin* 46:15–43.

Has Historical Archaeology Survived the Bicentennial? An Inquiry into the Development of Historical Archaeology in the United States. *Northeast Historical Archaeology* 12:3–6.

Comments: Goals, Methods, and Accomplishments in Army Archeological Resources Management. *American Society for Conservation Archaeology, Proceedings*, pp. 63–66.

(Participant) Gomez Foundation of Mill House: Seminar at the Mill House, February 20, 1983. Transcript. Gomez Foundation for Mill House.

1985 Comments [Evaluative Chapter]. In *Urbanization and Social Change in Historical Archeology*, Nan Rothschild, Joan Geismar, and Diana Wall, eds., pp. 219–21. American Archeology, Vol. 5, No. 3. Albuquerque, N.M.

1986 (coeditor with Anne-Marie Cantwell) Status Report of the SAA's 1984 Northeast Regional Conference. In *Regional Conferences Summary Report*, Cynthia Irwin-Williams and Don D. Fowler, eds., pp. 78–95. Society for American Archaeology, Special Publication. Washington, D.C.

The Development of Historical Archaeology in the Coastal New York/Southern New England Region. In *The Historical Archaeology of Long Island: Part 1. The Sites.* Gaynell Stone and Donna Ottusch-Kianka, eds., pp. 10–12. (Readings in Long Island Archaeology and Ethnohistory, Vol. 7.) Suffolk County Archaeological Association. Stony Brook, N.Y.

Submitted for Publication:

The Development of Contact Period Archaeology in Southern New England and Long Island. (for Symposium volume, Brown University Conference on Contact Period Archaeology. Providence, R.I.)

REPORTS SUBMITTED TO CLIENTS AND CONTRACTING AGENCIES:

1960 (with Charles W. Ward) *Test Excavations of Two Sites in the Tocks Island Reservoir Area, New Jersey.* To

National Park Service, Northeast Region. Philadelphia.

1964 (with Peter H. Cousins) *Report on an Archeological Survey of Seven Water Control Areas in Vermont and New Hampshire.* To National Park Service, Northeast Region. Philadelphia.

1966 *Archeological Survey of Six Water Control Areas in Connecticut and Massachusetts, 1965.* To National Park Service, Northeast Region. Philadelphia.

1967 *Report on Test Excavations at Archaeological Sites in the Hop Brook, Black Rock, and Sucker Brook Reservoir Basins, Connecticut.* To National Park Service, Northeast Region. Philadelphia.

1971 (with Sarah Bridges) *Preliminary Report of Archaeological Field Work, Clinton Ave. No. 1 Site, June 14 to June 23, 1970.* To Kingston Historic Landmarks Commission (under grant from N.Y. State Council on the Arts). Kingston.

(with Sarah Bridges) *Report on an Archaeological Survey in the Murderers Creek Drainage, Greene County, New York.* To United States Properties, Inc. Athens, N.Y.

1972 (with Sarah Bridges) *Archaeological Survey in the Murderers Creek Drainage, Greene County, New York: Supplementary Report Number One.* To United States Properties, Inc. Athens, N.Y.

1974 *Report of an Archaeological Reconnaissance in the Cromline Creek Flood Control Area, Chester, Orange County, New York.* To U.S. Soil Conservation Service. Syracuse, N.Y.

(with John Vetter) *Report on an Archaeological Reconnaissance of Fire Island, Suffolk County, New York.* To Jack McCormick & Associates, Inc. (for National Park Service.)

1975 (with John Vetter) *Report on an Archaeological Reconnaissance of the Long Island Lighting Company's Jamesport Property, Suffolk County, New York.* To Long Island Lighting Company.

(with Lorraine Williams and Bruce Eberle) *Preliminary Report: 1974 Archaeological Investigations at the Isaac Van Campen House, Sussex County, New Jersey.* In association with New Jersey State Museum. (for National Park Service.)

(with Joel Klein and Hetty Jo Brumbach) *Report of an Archaeological Reconnaissance of Five Sections of the Guilderland Sewer System, Albany County, New York.* To Town of Guilderland. Guilderland, N.Y.

(with Brenda Lockhart) *Report on the Second Archaeological Reconnaissance of the 15-Inch Mohawk River Interceptor Sewer Project, Schenectady, New York.* To Schenectady County Planning Department. Schenectady.

1976 (with Lorraine Williams) *Final Report: 1974 Archaeological Investigations at the Isaac Van Campen House, Sussex County, New Jersey.* To National Park Service. Philadelphia.

1978 (General Editor) *Survey of the Archaeological Resources of New York State: Pilot Study.* Prepared by the New York Archaeological Council for the Division for Historic Preservation, N.Y. State Office of Parks and Recreation. Albany.

1983 (with Arnold Pickman) *Analysis of Archaeological Resources in the Vicinity of the Barney Circle Freeway Modification Project.* To National Preservation Institute. Washington, D.C.
Preliminary Assessment of Archaeological Resources of the Proposed International Trade Center, Washington, D.C. (for D.C. Planning Board.)

1984 *Cultural Resources Assessment, U.S. Navy Surface Action Group Homeporting Project, Stapleton and Fort Wadsworth, Staten Island, N.Y.* To Tippetts-Abbett-McCarthy-Stratton, New York, for inclusion in environmental impact statement.

1985 National Register Nomination: Fort Shantok Archaeological Site, Montville, Connecticut. For Connecticut Historical Commission. Hartford.
Appendix C: Cultural Resources Report. In *Environmental Impact Statement, Hudson Ridge Development, Ossining, N.Y.* To RPPW, Inc. Tarrytown, N.Y.

1986 (with Eugene Boesch and Arnold Pickman) *Report on Investigations of the Archaeological Potential of the Bloomingdale Woods Project Area, Staten Island, New York: Background Research and Reconnaissance Level Survey.* To RPPW, Inc. Tarrytown, N.Y.

1987 *Report on Spring 1987 Test Excavations at the Jacob Adriance House Site (Queens County Farm Museum), Bellerose, Queens County, New York.* To Queens County Farm Museum. Floral Park, N.Y.
(with Eugene Boesch) *Report on a Phase 1b Archaeological Survey of the Prospect Point Development Property, Ossining, Westchester County, New York.* To RPPW, Inc. Tarrytown, N.Y.
(with Leonard Bianchi) *Documentary Study of the Archaeological Potential of the Melrose Commons Development Project Area, Borough of the Bronx, New York City.* Prepared for the NYC Public Development Corporation. New York.

REVIEWS:

1960 The Stony Brook Site and Its Relation to Archaic and Transitional Cultures on Long Island (William A.Ritchie). *American Anthropologist* 62(4):728–29.

1961 Preceramic and Ceramic Cultural Patterns in Northwest Virginia (C.G. Holland). *American Anthropologist* 63(2):444–45.

1963 From Cabot to Cartier (Bernard G. Hoffman). *American Anthropologist* 65(2):447–48.

1969 Debert: A Palaeo-Indian Site in Central Nova Scotia (George F. MacDonald). *American Anthropologist* 70(6):1231–33.

1970 The Orringh Stone Tavern and Three Seneca Sites of the Late Historic Period (Charles F. Hayes III). *Historical Archaeology* 4:111–12.

1971 Delaware's Buried Past: A Study of Archaeological Adventure (C.A. Weslager). *American Antiquity* 36(3):376–77.

1974 Archeology in the Upper Delaware Valley: A Study of the Cultural Chronology of the Tocks Island Reservoir (W. Fred Kinsey III). *American Anthropologist* 76(4): 958–60.

1976 First Americans (Film) (Craig Fisher). *American Anthropologist* 78(2):359–60.

1981 Indian New England Before the Mayflower (Howard S. Russell). *William and Mary Quarterly*, July, pp. 517–19.

1982 Foundations of Northeast Archaeology (Dean R. Snow, ed.). *American Scientist* 70(4):428.

ABSTRACTS OF PAPERS:

1963 Midden Analysis: Examples from the Northeast Coast. *Eastern States Archaeological Federation, Bulletin* 22:12.

1966 Post-Pleistocene Changes in the Northeastern Coastline. *Eastern States Archaeological Federation, Bulletin* 25:8–9.

1967 Muskeeta Cove: A Stratified Woodland Site on Long Island. *Eastern States Archaeological Federation, Bulletin* 26:15.

1969 Subsistence Patterns and Faunal Remains. *Eastern States Archaeological Federation, Bulletin* 27 & 28: 13–14.

Memorial

REYNOLD J. RUPPÉ, 1917–1993

Reynold J. Ruppé at the end of a long dive in search of drowned terrestrial sites, Gulf of Mexico, 1975. (Photo by Carol V. Ruppé.)

Reynold J. Ruppé, professor emeritus in the Department of Anthropology at Arizona State University and its founding chair, died on Saturday, 30 October 1993, at his home in Tempe; he was 76 years old. More than any other single individual, Rey Ruppé was responsible for establishing the Department of Anthropology at ASU and for building its graduate program into one of national standing.

The older of two children born to Matilda Anna Onufrey and Reynold J. Ruppé, Rey was born on 15 October 1917 in Hellertown, Pennsylvania, though he was to grow up in New Jersey. He was a U.S. Army veteran of World War II, originally trained in the ski troops, who saw combat with the infantry in Europe. At the close of hostilities, Ruppé was assigned to the War Crimes Branch (1945–1946), interrogating captured German officers. After the war, he received his formal education at the University of

Historical Archaeology, 1994, 28(3):1–6.
Permission to reprint required.

New Mexico (B.A., 1949) and at Harvard (Ph.D., 1953); both degrees were granted in anthropology (prehistoric archaeology).

After seven years (1953–1960) on the faculty at the University of Iowa, then the State University of Iowa, during which time he was appointed Iowa's first State Archaeologist (1959–1960), Ruppé was hired by ASU as chairman of its Department of Sociology and Anthropology. Arizona State College had just become Arizona State University, as a result of a statewide plebiscite and subsequent act of the state legislature, following years of bitter opposition by the partisans of the University of Arizona. Having left Iowa frustrated by his lack of state support, Ruppé arrived at ASU in 1960 only to find himself the head of a troubled unit, riven by internal disputes and in need of direction.

A condition Ruppé placed on his acceptance of the appointment was that the combined Department would eventually be separated into two autonomous units. After a lapse of two years, the university administration kept its promise and created a Department of Anthropology in 1962. Ruppé chaired the Department from its inception until 1973, guiding it through a period of unprecedented growth in faculty lines and in the development of its graduate programs. Upon the latter he had placed the highest priority, gaining authorization to start a Master of Arts program in 1963, followed by approval of a doctoral program in 1968.

Thanks to Rey's initial efforts, the graduate degree program in anthropology has since become one of ASU's finest. At this writing, 290 M.A.s and 84 Ph.D.s have been awarded by the Department, and ASU anthropology graduates are now employed at some of the most prestigious research institutions in the country. Moreover, in 1993 a Society for American Archaeology survey ranked ASU's 25-year-old archaeology doctoral program fourth in the nation.

Rey Ruppé was particularly successful at program building, and during his tenure as chair the number of full-time anthropology faculty increased from two to 17. Indeed, Ruppé recruited, as freshly-minted assistant professors, most of the cohort of senior faculty on staff today. Once they were hired, and always contingent upon performance, Ruppé felt it incumbent upon a department chair to provide the kind of physical and social environment in which faculty members could develop their intellectual skills to their maximum potentials. Ruppé paid close attention to those important intangibles, building a solid foundation that has been strengthened all the more by subsequent chairs. He also worried about tangible things, like where to house the growing Department.

From 1962 to 1973, the Department occupied a suite of offices in the Social Sciences Building, now home to the College of Liberal Arts and Sciences. By the late 1960s, however, a lack of space was becoming a major problem and, through a sustained effort of five years' duration, Ruppé convinced the university administration to grant the Department new space. Anthropology thus was allocated to the old Fine Arts Building—a large, three-story, neoclassical structure built in 1914.

Rey's initial reaction to this bequest was one of dismay, since the building was known to be in a poor state of repair. Recognizing its potential, however, he convinced the ASU administration to gut the structure and completely renovate it at a cost of approximately $1 million. The resulting structure, which the Department has occupied since 1973, is now viewed as one of the most functional physical plants in the country, extensively redesigned—largely by Ruppé himself—with the needs of a growing anthropology program in mind.

Ruppé was equally adept in the conduct of his archaeological research. His career spanned more than four decades, beginning with excavations in Colorado in 1946 and continuing on to field work in New Mexico, Iowa, Arizona, and Florida. He carried out that research, moreover, on both land and sea. In the course of his diverse career, then, Rey Ruppé was able to make significant contributions to North American archaeology in three distinctly different areas.

First, he conducted pioneering field research in several regions of the American Southwest and Midwest that had received little attention by archaeologists prior to the 1940s and 1950s. With his long-time friend and colleague, A. E. Dittert, Ruppé surveyed, tested, and excavated pithouse villages and pueblo communities on Cebolleta Mesa, west-central New Mexico (1948–1952), which formed the basis for his doctoral dissertation, awarded in 1953 and published in 1990 as a Garland "classic." The research was significant for its early, innovative use of systematic survey methods and for its perspective on long-term culture change, spanning pre-pottery horizons to the modern Pueblo of Acoma. It was also remarkable for its close collaboration with the Acoma community—a collaboration that Dittert continues today.

During his tenure at Iowa, when he was the only practicing archaeologist in the state, Ruppé conducted ethnoarchaeological field work among the Mesquakie Indians. He also established a successful summer field school program in Midwestern archaeology that investigated sites in western and southeastern Iowa with minimal institutional support. The latter work addressed the regional culture history of Iowa, especially in regard to the diverse range of prehistoric architectural features, ceramic types, and lithic assemblages present. As the first State Archaeologist for Iowa, and one of the first in the country, Ruppé accomplished much despite the limited resources afforded him during his brief tenure of office. Rey was tireless in advocating archaeology and instrumental in developing early cultural resource management practices in that state.

Second, Ruppé contributed to making the archaeological survey a standard research method in North American field work. In 1966, he published a seminal paper in *American Antiquity,* titled "The Archaeological Survey: A Defense," in which he justified the importance of survey data to a wide range of research questions. He also argued that survey data not only supplemented excavation data, but provided new kinds of information on regional processes and demographic trends. The essay reflected his experiences doing field work in New Mexico, in Iowa, and in Arizona's Salt River valley and on its Navajo Reservation.

Ruppé carefully considered different survey types and methods, including subsurface detection procedures, and the potential biases that result from the adoption of different survey strategies. His publication proved to be very timely, as a younger generation of archaeologists was then beginning to rethink the efficacy of traditional field methods in the American Southwest. Encouraged by the compelling defense Ruppé crafted of the problem-oriented survey as more than a simple prelude to excavation, Fred Plog and others developed new survey strategies that specifically addressed "processual" questions on a regional scale and advanced systematically-designed surveys as integral components of archaeological research designs.

Third, and of particular relevance to this journal, Ruppé contributed to the study of coastal archaeology with his research on drowned terrestrial sites and sea level transgressions. The latter years of his long career were devoted to addressing the archaeological implications of post-Pleistocene eustatic rise on prehistoric coastal populations. Arguing for the early and intensive use of coastal habitats by foraging peoples, Ruppé hypothesized that inundated coastal settlements should be common components of the underwater landscape of continental shelves.

Beginning in 1973, and continuing throughout the 1980s, Ruppé initiated an underwater archaeological program in western Florida, where the broad, gently-sloping shelf afforded ideal conditions for the preservation and detection of drowned sites. The 1973–1976 interval was spent excavating the Venice Beach site, a shell midden located at depths of 1–2 m off Florida's west coastal city of Venice. Subsequent research focused on survey methods for detecting other submerged settlements on the outer shelf. His experiments with mechanical corers, side-scan sonar, and subbottom profilers eventually led to the discovery of 30 drowned sites in the vicinity of Venice Beach. Ruppé subsequently received a major National Science Foundation grant in 1986 to generate a catalog of subbottom profiler "signatures" for the identification of underwater sites off the west Florida coast, depending upon site structure, site constituents, and local marine geomorphology.

As an active field researcher whose broad interests are demonstrated above, Ruppé was a member or a fellow of many learned societies. Among the more prominent professional organizations to which he belonged were the American Association for the Advancement of Science, the American Anthropological Association, the Society for American Archaeology, the Society for Historical Archaeology, and the International Oceanographic Foundation. A founder of the Advisory Council on Underwater Archaeology, Rey served as its first chair (1976–1981) and remained an influential member.

From 1979 through 1980, Ruppé was Senior Archeologist for the Bureau of Land Management, Outer Continental Shelf Office, in New Orleans. He also served on the editorial boards of several journals, including a seven-year term (1953–1960) editing the *Journal of the Iowa Archaeological Society,* and was a long-time member of the Board of Trustees of the Heard Museum (1967–1980).

Although Rey Ruppé will be remembered as the architect of ASU's Anthropology Department, and for the various contributions he made to North American archaeology, perhaps his most enduring accomplishment was the guidance, motivation, and friendship he extended to countless students at the University of Iowa and at Arizona State University. Rey's charismatic personality could inspire even the most skeptical graduate student to recognize the importance of regional survey, or excite an undergraduate to register for a course on underwater archaeology in land-locked Arizona! His door was always open to students and colleagues alike. This junior author remembers fondly the late afternoons when students, one by one, would slip into his office. In his Johnny-Carson persona, Rey would ask us to "move down the couch" to make room for the next visitor who had come to seek advice from the "grand old man."

Ruppé retired in 1985 and two years later, on the occasion of the 25th anniversary of the founding of the Department, a volume of essays by 25 friends, colleagues, and former students was published to honor him. The *ASU Anthropological Research Paper* No. 38, *Coasts, Plains and Deserts,* reflects in title and content the three major contexts of Rey's archaeological research career: his longstanding interest in underwater archaeology, his early field work in Iowa, and his southwestern research both before and after his arrival at ASU. The *festschrift* is testimony to the high regard in which he was held by the archaeological profession.

Reynold J. Ruppé is survived by his wife of 49 years, Carol V. Ruppé; also surviving are his daughter, Tricia Ruppé Durden, and son, Larry Ruppé, grandchildren Reynold Ruppé Durden and Georgia Carolyn Durden, and sister Matilda Ann Ruppé. Memorials can be made as contributions to The Ruppé Prize in Archaeology, care of the ASU Foundation, Arizona State University, Tempe, Arizona 85287-0904.

GEOFFREY A. CLARK
KENT G. LIGHTFOOT

BIBLIOGRAPHY OF REYNOLD J. RUPPÉ

DITTERT, A. E., JR., AND R. J. RUPPÉ
1951 The Archaeology of Cebolleta Mesa: A Preliminary Report. *El Palacio* 58(4):116–129. Santa Fe, New Mexico.
1952 The Development of Scientific Investigation of the Cebolleta Mesa Area, Central-Western New Mexico. *The Kiva* 18(1–2):13–18. Tucson, Arizona.

GALINAT, W. C., AND REYNOLD J. RUPPÉ
1961 Further Archaeological Evidence of the Effects of Teosinte Introgression in the Evolution of Modern Maize. *Botanical Museum Leaflets* 19(8):1–61. Harvard University, Cambridge, Massachusetts.

LIGHTFOOT, KENT G., AND REYNOLD J. RUPPÉ
1980 Oyster Carrying Capacity at Venice, Florida, Two Thousand Years Ago. *Bulletin of the Bureau of Historic Sites and Properties* 6:47–60. Tallahassee, Florida.

Ruppé, Reynold J.

1953   The Present Status of Iowa Archaeology. *Journal of the Iowa Archaeological Society* 3(2–3):16–24. Iowa City.

1954a   An Archaic Site at Olin, Iowa. *Journal of the Iowa Archaeological Society* 3(4):12–15. Iowa City.

1954b   *The Mesquakies of Iowa.* Federated Women's Clubs of Iowa, Iowa City.

1955a   Archaeology Students Excavate Prehistoric Indian Village near Cherokee. *On Iowa,* September:4–5.

1955b   The Earliest Indians of Iowa. *The Iowan* 3(4):24–27.

1955c   The Woodland Indians of Iowa. *The Iowan* 3(5):16–19, 47.

1955d   Mississippian Cultures Dominate Iowa. *The Iowan* 3(6):16–19.

1955e   Iowa Indians in Turmoil. *The Iowan* 4(1):34–37.

1955f   Cherokee and Turin, Iowa: Archaeological Excavations Reveal More Knowledge about Prehistoric Man. *SUI Staff Magazine* 6(2):16–20, 30–31. Iowa City.

1955g   Archaeological Investigation of the Mill Creek Culture of Northwestern Iowa. *Yearbook of the American Philosophical Society, 1954*:335–339. American Philosophical Society, Philadelphia.

1956a   Review of *Paa-ko. Archaeological Chronicle of an Indian Village in North-Central New Mexico,* by Marjorie F. Lambert; and *The Physical Type of the Paa-ko Population,* by Spencer L. Rogers. *American Antiquity* 22(2):203–204.

1956b   Iowa Archaeology I: The Earliest Indians of Iowa. Reprint of 1955 article. *Journal of the Iowa Archaeological Society* 5(2–3):2–10. Iowa City.

1956c   Iowa Archaeology II: The Woodland Indians of Iowa. Reprint of 1955 article. *Journal of the Iowa Archaeological Society* 5(2–3):11–17. Iowa City.

1956d   Iowa Archaeology III: Mississippian Cultures Dominate Iowa. Reprint of 1955 article. *Journal of the Iowa Archaeological Society* 5(2–3):19–26. Iowa City.

1956e   Iowa Archaeology IV: Iowa Indians in Turmoil. Reprint of 1955 article. *Journal of the Iowa Archaeological Society* 5(2–3):27–32. Iowa City.

1957a   An Occurrence of Marion Thick Pottery in Iowa. *Newsletter of the Iowa Archaeological Society* 23:4. Iowa City.

1957b   Discover Ancient Lore in Mound. *The Iowan* 5(3):20–21, 50.

1960   The Westwood Site: A Middle Woodland Burial Mound. *Journal of the Iowa Archaeological Society* 9(3):20–23. Iowa City.

1961   North American IV—Anthropology. *Encyclopaedia Britannica,* pp. 363–367. Encyclopaedia Britannica, Chicago, Illinois.

1963   Pioneers in Southwestern Anthropology. *Journal of the Arizona Academy of Science* 2(2):135–137.

1965   Review of *Studies at Navajo Period Sites in the Navajo Reservation District,* assembled by James J. Hester and J. L. Shiner. *American Antiquity* 31(1):126–127.

1966a   The Archaeological Survey, a Defense. *American Antiquity* 31(3):313–333.

1966b   Review of *Excavations at Snaketown: Material Culture,* by Emil W. Haury, E. B. Sayles, and Nora Gladwin. *American Antiquity* 31(6):884–885.

1974   Review of *Underwater Archaeology,* by P. E. Cleator. *Undersea Biomedical Research* 1(3):302–303.

1978a   Underwater Site Detection by Use of a Coring Instrument. Paper presented at the 11th Annual Meeting of the Society for Historical Archaeology and 9th Conference on Underwater Archaeology, San Antonio, Texas.

1978b   Underwater Site Detection by Use of a Coring Instrument. In Beneath the Waters of Time: Proceedings of the Ninth Conference on Underwater Archaeology, edited by J. Barto Arnold III. *Texas Antiquities Commission Publication* No. 6:119–121. Austin, Texas.

1979a   Ground Truth Testing of Remote Sensing Signals. Paper presented at the 12th Annual Meeting of the Society for Historical Archaeology and 10th Conference on Underwater Archaeology, Nashville, Tennessee.

1979b   Sea Level Change as a Variable in Colonial American Archaeology. Paper presented at the 12th Annual Meeting of the Society for Historical Archaeology and 10th Conference on Underwater Archaeology, Nashville, Tennessee.

1980a   The Archaeology of Drowned Terrestrial Sites. *Bulletin of Historic Sites and Properties* 6(1):35–45. Tallahassee, Florida.

1980b   Sea Level Rise and Caribbean Prehistory. Proceedings of the Eighth International Congress for the Study of the Pre-Columbian Cultures of the Lesser Antilles, edited by S. Lewenstein. *Arizona State University Anthropological Research Papers* No. 22:331–337. Tempe, Arizona.

1980c   An Assessment of the Marine Archaeological Survey Program: Bureau of Land Management Outer Continental Shelf Program. Paper presented at the 45th Annual Meeting of the Society for American Archaeology, Philadelphia, Pennsylvania.

1980d   An Assessment of Marine Survey Archaeology. Paper presented at the 13th Annual Meeting of the Society for Historical Archaeology and 11th Conference on Underwater Archaeology, Albuquerque, New Mexico.

1980e Drowned Terrestrial Site Archaeology: The Fifth Season. An Assessment of Marine Survey Archaeology. Paper presented at the 13th Annual Meeting of the Society for Historical Archaeology and 11th Conference on Underwater Archaeology, Albuquerque, New Mexico.

1981a Sea Level Change as a Variable in Colonial American Archaeology. *The Realms of Gold: Proceedings of the Tenth Conference on Underwater Archaeology*:195–201. W. A. Cockrell, editor. Fathom Eight Publications, San Marino, California.

1981b Shipwreck Archaeology. *Science* 184:813.

1981c Underwater Site Detection by Use of a Coring Instrument. Paper presented at the 46th Annual Meeting of the Society for American Archaeology, San Diego, California.

1982a An Assessment of Cultural Resource Surveys on the Outer Continental Shelf. Prepared by Reynold J. Ruppé. Submitted to U.S. Department of the Interior, Bureau of Land Management, New Orleans, Louisiana.

1982b Review of *Archeology Under Water: An Atlas of the World's Submerged Sites,* by Keith Muckelroy; *Texas Legacy from the Gulf,* by Dorris L. Olds; *An Underwater Archeological Magnetometer Survey and Site Test Excavation Project Off Padre Island, Texas,* by J. Barto Arnold III; *The Nautical Archeology of Padre Island: The Spanish Shipwrecks of 1554,* by J. Barto Arnold III and Robert Weddle; and *Documentary Sources for the Wreck of the New Spain Fleet of 1554,* by David McDonald and J. Barto Arnold III. *American Anthropologist* 84(4):941–942.

1982c Geophysical Remote Sensing as an Aid to Underwater Site Survey. Paper presented at the 15th Annual Meeting of the Society for Historical Archaeology and 13th Conference on Underwater Archaeology, Philadelphia, Pennsylvania.

1983a Predictive Models for Locating Underwater Cultural Resources on Outer Continental Shelves. *Proceedings of the Alaskan Marine Archaeology Workshop, Alaska Sea Grant Report* 83–9:3–24. University of Alaska, Fairbanks.

1983b Continental Shelf Archaeology. Poster presented at the 16th Annual Meeting of the Society for Historical Archaeology and 14th Conference on Underwater Archaeology, Denver, Colorado.

1984a Geophysical Remote Sensing as an Aid to Underwater Site Survey. *Proceedings of the Thirteenth Conference on Underwater Archaeology*:47–50. Donald H. Keith, editor. Fathom Eight Publications, San Marino, California.

1984b Predictive Modeling and Drowned Terrestrial Sites. Paper presented at the 17th Annual Meeting of the Society for Historical Archaeology and 15th Conference on Underwater Archaeology, Williamsburg, Virginia.

1986a Technologies for Underwater Archaeology and Maritime Preservation. In *Technologies for Prehistoric and Historic Preservation—Executive Summary.* Office of Technology Assessment, Washington, D.C.

1986b Testing Predictive Models for Location of Drowned Terrestrial Sites on the Continental Shelf. Paper presented at the 19th Annual Meeting of the Society for Historical Archaeology and 17th Conference on Underwater Archaeology, Sacramento, California.

1987 Review of *Quaternary Coastlines and Maritime Archaeology: Towards the Prehistory of Land Bridges and Continental Shelves,* edited by P. M. Masters and N. C. Flemming. *American Antiquity* 52(2):429–431.

1988 Review of *Coastal Erosion and Archaeological Resources on National Wildlife Refuges in the Southeast,* by Susan E. Garrett. *Historical Archaeology* 22(1):128–130.

1988 The Location and Assessment of Underwater Archaeological Sites. In *Wet Site Archaeology,* edited by Barbara A. Purdy, pp. 55–68. Telford Press, Caldwell, New Jersey.

1990 *The Acoma Culture Province: An Archaeological Concept.* Garland, New York.

RUPPÉ, R. J., AND A. E. DITTERT
1952 The Archaeology of Cebolleta Mesa and Acoma Pueblo: A Preliminary Report Based on Further Investigation. *El Palacio* 59(7):191–217. Santa Fe, New Mexico.

1953 Acoma Archaeology: A Preliminary Report on the Final Season in the Cebolleta Mesa Region, New Mexico. *El Palacio* 60(7):259–273. Santa Fe, New Mexico.

[While he served as Editor of the *Journal of the Iowa Archaeological Society* (1953–1960), Reynold J. Ruppé wrote a regular column, titled "Archaeological Chats," and contributed many anonymous incidental pieces not included here. Conference papers include only those presented since 1978. —Memorials Editor]

Memorial

CARLYLE SHREEVE SMITH, 1915–1993

Carlyle Smith demonstrating his marksmanship with a percussion pistol at Talking Crow, 1951. (Photo by Roger Grange.)

Carlyle Shreeve Smith died 13 December 1993 in Kansas City, Missouri. Smith was among the founding members of the Society for Historical Archaeology and the 1989 recipient of its most prestigious award, the J. C. Harrington Medal for Contributions in Historical Archaeology. He was also widely known for his archaeological field work in New York, the Plains, and the Pacific.

Smith carried out 23 major research grants from many funding sources. He served as Assistant Editor for the Plains for *American Antiquity* (1949–1955) and edited the *University of Kansas Publications in Anthropology* (1969–1973); Smith also was an Advisory Editor for the *North American Archaeologist* from 1978 until his death. He served on the National Research Council (1961–1964) and the Kansas Historical Sites Board of Review (1970–1983).

Carlyle ("Carl") Smith was born in Great Neck, Long Island, New York, on 8 March 1915 to Harold William Smith and Lulu Arrandale, née Allen. His early education was oriented towards foreign languages, and he ultimately knew Latin, French, German, Spanish, and Norwegian. He earned his A.B.

Historical Archaeology, 1994, 28(3):7–14.
Permission to reprint required.

from Columbia College in 1938 and was awarded the Ph.D. from Columbia University in 1949. Carl's interest in archaeology began as a high school student when he carried out archaeological work on Long Island that would later be incorporated into his doctoral research. His archaeological work in New York began in 1932 and continued intermittently to 1947.

Carlyle began his contacts with Clark Wissler and other leading anthropologists at the American Museum of Natural History while still in high school. Later, he learned ethnology from the likes of Gene Weltfish and Alexander Lesser. Others who greatly influenced Carl in college included William Duncan Strong, Ralph Linton, and geologist Alfred Lobeck.

Strong introduced Carl to field work in the Plains through excavations in North Dakota and extensive travels in 1938. His interest in the Plains continued, and he became a WPA unit supervisor at the Lovitt site in Nebraska in 1939. He also assisted in the excavation of Ash Hollow Cave. Carlyle, George Metcalf, and Ralph Solecki visited many other sites that year, including Talking Crow—the site that would later become the scene of some of his major work in the Plains.

The summer of 1940 was spent assisting Mary Butler of Vassar College with her work in the Hudson Valley. Upon completion of his assignment for Butler, he went to Louisiana for nine months in 1940–1941. There he learned pottery type and seriation concepts as a WPA laboratory supervisor for George Quimby.

Carlyle married Judith Pogany in 1942. During the early part of World War II, Carl worked as an inspector of engine parts in the Ranger Aircraft Engines factory. He was then inducted into the U.S. Army Air Force in 1943, serving in Greensboro, North Carolina, as a corporal and technical instructor in air photo interpretation and map reading.

In spite of his wartime military duties, Carlyle managed to publish three papers on Long Island archaeology during this period. Discharged in 1946, he returned to Columbia to work on his doctorate. Carl's dissertation, *The Archaeology of Coastal New York,* was published by the American Museum of Natural History in 1950. His research became the foundation for prehistory in that part of New York, and it is still cited today.

Smith began his most intensive work in the Plains in 1947, when appointed assistant professor of anthropology and assistant curator, Museum of Natural History, at the University of Kansas in Lawrence. He was to spend the remainder of his career at KU, during which time he taught countless students and prepared numerous archaeological and ethnological museum exhibits. Carlyle was promoted to associate professor and associate curator in 1954 and then to professor and curator in 1960. In 1968 he became professor and research associate in the new Museum of Anthropology and, finally, professor emeritus and curator emeritus upon retirement in 1981.

His early KU archaeological expeditions were unusual for the time, running counter to the prevailing attitudes about crew composition. Not only did Carlyle take his wife and children to the field, but he also routinely included women in his field crews. Indeed, years later he was fond of pointing out that women in those days were not even supposed to be seen in university vehicles!

Carlyle excavated numerous sites in Kansas between 1947 and 1980 and worked intensively in the River Basin Salvage programs in South Dakota and Kansas from 1950 to 1978. His work at Talking Crow and related sites in South Dakota embodies Carl's most significant contribution to Plains prehistory. That multi-component site demonstrated continuity between the Central Plains Tradition and later periods in Arikara archaeology. Moreover, Smith's work at the site demonstrated the unity that can be achieved between archaeologists and native peoples. Carlyle's training and skills in ethnology helped foster good local relations while excavating at the site, and he was given the honorary name *Kangi-ia-wakan,* Holy Crow Voice or ''Talking Crow,'' by the Dakota in a ceremony at Fort Thompson.

During this time almost every excavation in the Missouri Valley produced a new cultural complex. Accordingly, Carl defined numerous new ceramic types, and his seriations, based on stratigraphy at Talking Crow, were important in the development of regional culture history. Articles, papers at meetings, and discussions at the "accidental" Plains conferences—held in the Silver Spur Bar in Pierre, South Dakota—kept his colleagues apprised of the data. He further extended exposure of his work to international congress audiences in Costa Rica, Austria, Mexico, Spain, France, and the former Soviet Union. Carl's very extensive work at Talking Crow produced mountains of material, and the final publication appeared in 1977.

Smith was invited to join Thor Heyerdahl's Norwegian Archaeological Expedition to Easter Island and the East Pacific in 1955–1956, which opened a new mini-career in Pacific archaeology. He contributed extensively to the reports on this field work and, in 1963–1964, Carlyle carried out an additional excavation at the Pekia site on Hiva Oa, Marquesas Islands, French Polynesia.

Carlyle's expertise in that exotic area led to an invitation from Lindblad Travel to serve as shipboard lecturer and guide on a cruise to Easter Island in 1967. That was the start of yet another facet of Carl's career and led to a total of 19 cruises as lecturer and guide to the Pacific and Mediterranean for Lindblad Travel, the Norwegian American Line, Prudential Lines, and the Royal Viking Line.

At an early age in New York, Smith became interested in the history and development of firearms, and he pursued his firearms research both professionally and recreationally. Carlyle developed a superb personal collection of period firearms, all restored to operating condition. Consequently, his students in the field and in the course he taught on the subject at KU had the unique opportunity for firsthand experience with such important historic trade materials. Carl even had a small cannon in his collection and was skilled in firing concrete-filled orange juice cans at logs floating on the Missouri River! His research on firearms and their identification was Carlyle's primary contribution to historical archaeology, with at least 23 of his publications falling into that category. He was a unique resource archaeologist— generous with his time and effort in identifying gun parts sent to him; scholarly, thorough, and punctual in his responses to colleagues.

Not limited to collections research, Carlyle excavated some Historic-period sites and components in the river basin projects, as well as at the Riggs House in Lawrence, Kansas, which produced evidence of the 1863 Quantrill raid. He also excavated the Kansas Monument site, an important Historic-period Pawnee village, integrating prehistory and historical archaeology. Carlyle later extended his gunflint research to include both field and archival work in France (1960) and Italy (1964).

Carlyle's ill health slowed his active field work after 1966, but it was improved through bypass surgery in 1972. He retired from his regular faculty appointment on 31 December 1980, but continued as a lecturer and guide on cruise ships. His improved health after the surgery also enabled him to continue his writing and publication, as well as his great fondness for personal travel. Unfortunately, Carl was unable to recover from another such operation in December 1993.

Carlyle Smith's valuable contributions to archaeology earned him three significant honors. His pioneering research in Long Island archaeology was recognized when "The Carlyle S. Smith Archaeological Laboratories" at the Nassau County Museum of Natural History, Garvies Point, Glen Cove, Long Island, New York, was named for him in 1967. Carlyle's lasting contributions to South Dakota archaeology also were recognized with the Doctor of Humane Letters, *honoris causa,* awarded him in 1979 by the University of South Dakota. Furthermore, as noted previously, in 1989 the Society for Historical Archaeology bestowed on him its highest honor, the J. C. Harrington Medal for Contributions in Historical Archaeology.

Carlyle Shreeve Smith is survived by his wife Judith, son Evan, daughter Pamela, and grandchildren Nathan Mannella Smith, David Allen Creed, and Andrew Jacob Creed. At this writing, a memorial fund is yet to be established in his name. Details will be announced in the SHA *Newsletter* when they are made final.

ROGER T. GRANGE, JR.

[I have drawn upon materials provided by Judy Smith and Alfred Johnson. —RTG]

Roger T. Grange, Jr.

BIBLIOGRAPHY OF CARLYLE SHREEVE SMITH

Mulloy, William, Arne Skjölsvold, and Carlyle S. Smith
1964   Easter Island: Reply to Barthel's Review. *American Anthropologist* 66(1):148–149.

Smith, Carlyle S.
n.d.   Fort Thompson, Shannon, and Campbell Foci. Anonymous and undated mimeograph, attributed to Carlyle Smith, on file, Midwest Archeological Center, National Park Service, Lincoln, Nebraska.
1942   Review of *Two Sites on Martha's Vineyard,* by Douglas Byers and Frederick Johnson. *American Anthropologist* 44(1):125–127.
1944a   Clues to the Chronology of Coastal New York. *American Antiquity* 10(1):87–98.
1944b   Notes on the Archaeology of Long Island. *Bulletin of the Massachusetts Archaeological Society* 5(4):56–59.
1946a   The Sondergaard Burial Site. Manuscript on file, Nebraska State Historical Society, Lincoln.
1946b   Manhasset Rock. Manuscript on file, Department of Anthropology, American Museum of Natural History, New York.
1946c   A Stone Effigy from Long Island. *American Antiquity* 11(3):200–201.
1946d   Review of *Excavation at the Old Lyme Shell Heap,* by A. A. Praus; *The Indian River Village Site,* by E. H. Rogers; and *The South Woodstock Site,* by A. A. Praus. *American Antiquity* 11(4):271–273.
1947a   Review of *An Early Site in Cayuga County, New York,* by William A. Ritchie. *American Antiquity* 12(3):195–196.
1947b   A Resumé of the Archaeology of Coastal New York. *Newsletter of the Archaeological Society of New Jersey* 16:15–18.
1947c   An Outline of the Archaeology of Coastal New York. *Archaeological Society of Connecticut Bulletin* 21:3–9.
1949a   Review of *Grassy Island: Archaeological and Botanical Investigations of an Indian Site in the Taunton River, Massachusetts,* by Frederick Johnson and Hugh M. Raup. *American Antiquity* 14(3):235–236.
1949b   Archaeological Investigations in Ellsworth and Rice Counties, Kansas. *American Antiquity* 14(4):292–300.
1949c   Archaeological Research at the University of Kansas, 1946–1947. *Proceedings of the Fifth Plains Conference for Archaeology:* 29–30. J. L. Champe, compiler. *Laboratory of Anthropology Note Book* 1. University of Nebraska, Lincoln.
1949d   Two Pottery Collections from the State of Kansas. *Proceedings of the Fifth Plains Conference for Archaeology:* 81–84. J. L. Champe, compiler. *Laboratory of Anthropology Note Book* 1. University of Nebraska, Lincoln.
1949e   Fieldwork in Kansas, 1949. *Plains Archaeological Conference Newsletter* 2(4):5–6. Lincoln, Nebraska.
1950a   European Trade Material from the Kansas Monument Site. *Plains Archaeological Conference Newsletter* 3(2):2–9. Lincoln, Nebraska.
1950b   The Pottery from the Kansas Monument Site. *Plains Archaeological Conference Newsletter* 3(4):79. Lincoln, Nebraska.
1950c   The Archaeology of Coastal New York. *Anthropological Papers of the American Museum of Natural History* 43(2):91–200. New York.
1950d   Climate and Archaeology in Kansas. *Proceedings of the Sixth Plains Archaeological Conference, Anthropological Papers* 11:98–99. University of Utah, Salt Lake City.
1951a   Pottery Types from the Talking Crow Site, Fort Randall Reservoir, South Dakota. *Plains Archaeological Conference Newsletter* 4(3):32–41. Lincoln, Nebraska.
1951b   Floyd Schultz, 1881–1951. *American Antiquity* 17(1):49.
1951c   Review of *Preliminary Appraisal of the Swanson Site, 39BR16,* by W. R. Hurt, Jr. *American Antiquity* 17(1):75.
1951d   Archaeological Investigations at the Talking Crow Site (39BF3) in Fort Randall Reservoir, South Dakota, 1950. Prepared by University of Kansas, Lawrence. Submitted to National Park Service and Smithsonian Institution, River Basin Surveys, Lincoln, Nebraska.
1952a   Archaeology in the Vicinity of New York City. *Proceedings of the 29th International Congress of Americanists,* Part 3:131–135.
1952b   Review of *A Survey of Indian River Archaeology, Florida,* by Irving Rouse; and *Chronology at South Indian Field, Florida,* by Vera Masius Ferguson. *American Anthropologist* 54(2):254–256.
1952c   Supplementary Data on the Talking Crow Site in Fort Randall Reservoir, South Dakota: A Report to the National Park Service on Archaeological Investigations in 1951. Prepared by University of Kansas, Lawrence. Submitted to National Park Service, Lincoln, Nebraska.
1953a   Talking Crow, 1952. A Report to the National Park Service on the Third Season at Site 39BF3. Prepared by University of Kansas, Lawrence. Submitted to National Park Service, Lincoln, Nebraska.
1953b   Digging up the Plains Indian's Past. *University of Kansas Alumni Magazine* 52(4):4–5.
1954a   Cartridges and Bullets from Fort Stevenson, North Dakota. *Plains Anthropologist* 1:25–29.
1954b   A Note on Fort Massapeag. *American Antiquity* 20(1):67–68.

1955a An Analysis of the Firearms and Related Specimens from Like-A-Fishhook Village and Fort Berthold I. *Plains Anthropologist* 4:3–12.

1955b Revised Chronology for the Archaeology of Coastal New York. *Nassau County Archaeological Society Bulletin* 1(1): 4–5.

1955c Review of *Report of the Investigation of the Thomas Riggs Site, 39HU1, Hughes County, South Dakota*, by W. R. Hurt, Jr. *American Anthropologist* 57(2):375.

1957 The East River and Windsor Aspects—A Reply. *American Antiquity* 23(2):170–171.

1958a Pottery Types from Talking Crow Site. Manuscript on file, Midwest Archeological Center, National Park Service, Lincoln, Nebraska.

[1958b] Excavation of Certain Sites in Tuttle Creek Reservoir, Kansas, June–August 1957. Prepared by University of Kansas, Lawrence. Submitted to National Park Service, Lincoln, Nebraska.

1959a Reconstructing a Plains Indian Earth Lodge. In *The Archaeologist at Work*, edited by Robert F. Heizer, pp. 113–133. Harper and Row, New York.

1959b Review of *Arqueología chilena: contribuciones al estudio de la región comprendia entre Arica y la Serena*, edited by R. P. Schaedel. *American Anthropologist* 61(1):164.

1960a The Temporal Relationships of Coalescent Village Sites in Fort Randall Reservoir, South Dakota. *Actas del XXXIII Congreso Internacional de Americanistas, Tome II*:111–123; figs. 1–3. San Jose, Costa Rica.

1960b An Anthropological Conclusion Found in an Unusual Context. *Plains Anthropologist* 5(9):28.

1960c Thor Heyerdahl *og Sugga Bok. Verdende Gang* 288:3. Oslo, Norway.

1960d Cartridges and Bullets from Fort Stevenson. Appendix in Archeological Investigations at the Site of Fort Stevenson (32ML1), Garrison Reservoir, North Dakota, by G. Hubert Smith. *Bulletin* 176. Smithsonian Institution, Bureau of American Ethnology. *River Basin Surveys Papers* 19:232–236.

1960e Defense, Hunting and Other Subsistence Activities. In The Archeology of a Small Trading Post (Kipp's Post, 32MN1) in the Garrison Reservoir, North Dakota, by Alan R. Woolworth and W. Raymond Wood. *Bulletin* 176. Smithsonian Institution, Bureau of American Ethnology. *River Basin Surveys Papers* 20:267–269.

1960f Experiments in Checking Documented Dates Against Dates Derived from Trade Goods. Prepared by University of Kansas, Lawrence. Submitted to National Park Service, Lincoln, Nebraska.

1960g Experiments in Checking Documented Dates Against Dates Derived from Trade Goods. In Indian Trade Guns, edited by T. M. Hamilton. *Missouri Archaeologist* 22:25–27.

1960h Two 18th Century Reports on the Manufacture of Gunflints in France. In Indian Trade Guns, edited by T. M. Hamilton. *Missouri Archaeologist* 22:4–49.

1960i Review of *The Indian Journals, 1859–62*, edited by Leslie A. White. *Journal of the Central Mississippi Valley American Studies Association* 1(1):44.

1960j Review of *The Stony Brook Site and Its Relation to Archaic and Transitional Cultures on Long Island*, by William A. Ritchie. *American Antiquity* 26(1):131.

1961a A Temporal Sequence Derived from Certain *ahu*, Report 2. In Reports on the Norwegian Archaeological Expedition to Easter Island and the East Pacific, 1955–1956. Vol. 1, Archaeology of Easter Island, edited by Thor Heyerdahl and Edwin N. Ferdon. *Monographs of the School of American Research and the Kon-Tiki Museum* No. 24, Pt. 1:181–219. Santa Fe, New Mexico, and Stockholm, Sweden.

1961b Two Habitation Caves, Report 4. In Reports on the Norwegian Archaeological Expedition to Easter Island and the East Pacific, 1955–1956. Vol. 1, Archaeology of Easter Island, edited by Thor Heyerdahl and Edwin N. Ferdon. *Monographs of the School of American Research and the Kon-Tiki Museum* No. 24, Pt. 1:257–271. Santa Fe, New Mexico, and Stockholm, Sweden.

1961c The Maunga Auhepa House Site, Report 6. In Reports on the Norwegian Archaeological Expedition to Easter Island and the East Pacific, 1955–1956. Vol. 1, Archaeology of Easter Island, edited by Thor Heyerdahl and Edwin N. Ferdon. *Monographs of the School of American Research and the Kon-Tiki Museum* No. 24, Pt. 1:277–286. Santa Fe, New Mexico, and Stockholm, Sweden.

1961d Tuu-ko-ihu Village, Report 7. In Reports on the Norwegian Archaeological Expedition to Easter Island and the East Pacific, 1955–1956. Vol. 1, Archaeology of Easter Island, edited by Thor Heyerdahl and Edwin N. Ferdon. *Monographs of the School of American Research and the Kon-Tiki Museum* No. 24, Pt. 1:287–289. Santa Fe, New Mexico, and Stockholm, Sweden.

1961e The Poike Ditch, Report 16. In Reports on the Norwegian Archaeological Expedition to Easter Island and the East Pacific, 1955–1956. Vol. 1, Archaeology of Easter Island, edited by Thor Heyerdahl and Edwin N. Ferdon. *Monographs of the School of American Research and the Kon-Tiki Museum* No. 24, Pt. 1:385–391. Santa Fe, New Mexico, and Stockholm, Sweden.

1961f Radio-Carbon Dates from Easter Island, Report 17. In Reports on the Norwegian Archaeological Expedition to Easter

Island and the East Pacific, 1955–1956. Vol. 1, Archaeology of Easter Island, edited by Thor Heyerdahl and Edwin N. Ferdon. *Monographs of the School of American Research and the Kon-Tiki Museum* No. 24, Pt. 1:393–396. Santa Fe, New Mexico, and Stockholm, Sweden.

1961g   Review of *An Introduction to Kansas Archaeology,* by Waldo R. Wedel. *American Antiquity* 26(4):570–571.

1962   Identification of French Gun Flints. *Yearbook of the American Philosophical Society, 1961:*419–423. Philadelphia, Pennsylvania.

1963a   Time Perspective Within the Coalescent Tradition in South Dakota. *American Antiquity* 28(4):489–495.

1963b   An Outline of Easter Island Archaeology. *Asian Perspectives* 6:239–234.

[1963c]   Survey of Archaeological Resources of Milford Reservoir, Kansas, 1963. Prepared by University of Kansas, Lawrence. Submitted to National Park Service, Lincoln, Nebraska.

1965a   Test Excavations and Surveys of Miscellaneous Sites on the Island of Rapa Iti, Report 5. In Reports on the Norwegian Archaeological Expedition to Easter Island and the East Pacific, 1955–1956, Vol. 2, edited by Thor Heyerdahl and Edwin N. Ferdon. *Monographs of the School of American Research and the Kon-Tiki Museum* No. 24, Pt. 2:77–87. Santa Fe, New Mexico, and Stockholm, Sweden.

1965b   The Burial Complex on the Island of Rapa It, Report 6. In Reports on the Norwegian Archaeological Expedition to Easter Island and the East Pacific, 1955–1956, Vol. 2, edited by Thor Heyerdahl and Edwin N. Ferdon. *Monographs of the School of American Research and the Kon-Tiki Museum* No. 24, Pt. 2:89–95. Santa Fe, New Mexico, and Stockholm, Sweden.

1965c   An Archaeological Hoax in the Marquesas. *American Antiquity* 30(3):355.

1965d   Review of *The Experimental Earthwork on Overton Down, Wiltshire, 1960,* edited by P. A. Jewell. *American Antiquity* 30(4):519–520.

[1965e]   Survey of Clinton Reservoir, Kansas, Spring 1965. Prepared by University of Kansas, Lawrence. Submitted to National Park Service, Lincoln, Nebraska.

[1965f]   Intensive Excavation of Several Small Plains Woodland Sites in Perry Reservoir, Kansas, June–August 1965. Prepared by University of Kansas, Lawrence. Submitted to National Park Service, Lincoln, Nebraska.

1966a   Collection of Specimens of Worked and Unworked Flint in Alto Adige, Italy. *Year Book of the American Philosophical Society, 1965:*624–625. Philadelphia, Pennsylvania.

1966b   The Incorporation of Religious Dogma, Dogma, Doctrine and Taboo in Legal Codes. . . . *Playboy* 13(4):62–65.

1966c   Une baïonnette en forme de couteau de chasse de la Manufacture Imperiale de Ningenthal. *Bulletin Bi-Mestriel les Arquebusiers de France* No. 17:7–11. Paris.

1967a   Early Russian Weapons. *Guns Review* 7(11):402. London.

1967b   Review of *The Black Partizan Site,* by W. R. Caldwell. *Plains Anthropologist* 12(38):420–421.

1968   Review of *Prehistoric Culture in Oceania,* edited by I. Yawata and Y. H. Sinoto. *Science* 162:1378–1379.

1969a   Review of *Indian Life on the Upper Missouri,* by J. C. Ewers. *American Anthropologist* 71:319–320.

1969b   Review of *Big Bend Historic Sites,* by G. H. Smith. *American Antiquity* 34:335–336.

1970a   Archaeological Investigations at Pekia, Hiva Oa, Marquesas Islands. *VII-me congrès internationale des sciences anthropologiques et ethnologiques, Moscou (3 aout–10 aout 1964)* 9:52–55. Academy of Sciences, U.S.S.R. Moscow.

1970b   Review of *The La Roche Site,* by J. J. Hoffman. *American Antiquity* 35:399–400.

1970c   Review of *The Shermer Site (32EM10),* by James E. Sperry. *American Anthropologist* 72(5):1186–1187.

1970d   Review of *Early Indian Trade Guns: 1625–1775,* by T. M. Hamilton. *Plains Anthropologist* 15(49):233–234.

1971   Review of *Island at the Center of the World: New Light on Easter Island,* by Sebastian Englert. *American Anthropologist* 3(6):1416–1417.

1972a   Firearms, Gunflints, Ammunition, and Military Gear from Like-A-Fishhook Village. In Like-A-Fishhook Village and Fort Berthold, Garrison Reservoir, North Dakota, by G. H. Smith. *National Park Service Anthropological Papers* No. 2:80–88. Washington, D.C.

1972b   Firearms, Ammunition, and Military Gear from Fort Berthold I. In Like-A-Fishhook Village and Fort Berthold, Garrison Reservoir, North Dakota, by G. H. Smith, *National Park Service Anthropological Papers* No. 2:108–111. Washington, D.C.

1974a   Review of *Tree Ring Dating and Archaeology in South Dakota,* by Ward F. Weakly. *Plains Anthropologist* 19[1](66): 319–320.

1974b   Archaeological Excavations at the Stricker Site (39LM1), Big Bend Reservoir, South Dakota, 1959. Prepared by University of Kansas, Lawrence. Submitted to National Park Service, Lincoln, Nebraska.

1975a   The Stricker Site. *Plains Anthropologist* 20[1](1):1–5.

1975b   Review of *Archéologie d'une vallée des îles Marquises: Évolution des structures de l'habitat à Hane, Ua Huka,* by Marimari Kellum-Ottino. *American Anthropologist* 77(3):692.

1977   The Talking Crow Site, a Multi-component Earthlodge Village in the Great Bend Region, South Dakota. *University of Kansas Publications in Anthropology* No. 9. Lawrence.

1978a Prefatory Comments on Long Island Archaeology. *Readings in Long Island Archaeology and Ethnohistory* 2:x–xi.

1978b William Thomas Mulloy, 1917–1978. *Plains Anthropologist* 23[1](82):337–339.

1978c Archaeological Research at the University of Kansas, 1946–1947. *Proceedings of the Fifth Plains Conference for Archaeology,* compiled by J. L. Champe, pp. 29–30. Reprint of 1949 publication. J and L Reprints, Lincoln, Nebraska.

1978d Two Pottery Collections from the State of Kansas. *Proceedings of the Fifth Plains Conference for Archaeology:*81–84. J. L. Champe, compiler. *Laboratory of Anthropology Note Book* 1, University of Nebraska, Lincoln. Reprint of 1949 publication. J and L Reprints, Lincoln, Nebraska.

1979 Review of *Les fusils de traité en Nouvelle-France, 1690–1760,* by Russel Bouchard. *Historical Archaeology* 12:110–111.

1980a Review of *The Eighth Land,* by Thomas Barthel. *Pacific Affairs* 52(4):766–767.

1980b Floyd Schultz, 1881–1951. Edited and abridged reprint of 1951 obituary. In *Discussion Leader's Guide for Neshnabek: The People,* by Donald Stull and James Divney, p. 23. University of Kansas Press, Lawrence.

1982a Review of *Ceramic Classification in the Middle Missouri Subarea of the Plains,* by Craig M. Johnson. *Plains Anthropologist* 27(1):96.

1982b Documented Dates versus Dates Derived from Trade Goods. In *Indian Trade Guns,* edited by T. M. Hamilton, pp. 243–246. Retitled reprint of 1960 article. Pioneer Press, Union City, Tennessee.

1982c 18th Century Manufacture of French Gunflints. In *Indian Trade Guns,* edited by T. M. Hamilton, pp. 147–158. Retitled reprint of 1960 article. Pioneer Press, Union City, Tennessee.

1983a Review of *The Modernisation of Easter Island,* by J. Douglas Porteous. *Pacific Studies,* Spring Issue.

1983b The Life and Work of Carlyle Shreeve Smith. Oral history transcript on file, K.U. Retirees' Club, University of Kansas, Lawrence.

1992 Carlyle S. Smith, KU Years: 1947–1980. In Archaeology at the University of Kansas: Williston–Eiseley–Spaulding–Smith, edited by Marlin F. Hawley. *Kansas Anthropologist* 13(1–2):58–72.

SMITH, CARLYLE S. (TRANSLATOR AND ANNOTATOR)

1960k Report on the Art of Making Gunflints (fire flint); by Citizen Dolomieu, in the Year 5 (1796–1797). Translation of 1797 French article. In Indian Trade Guns, edited by T. M. Hamilton. *Missouri Archaeologist* 22:50–61.

1960l Extract from a Report by Citizen Salivet on the Making of Gunflints in the Departments of Idre and Loir-et-Cher; by F. P. N. Gillet-Laumont: With an Indication of Some Other Places Where They Are Made Also. Translation of 1797 French article. In Indian Trade Guns, edited by T. M. Hamilton. *Missouri Archaeologist* 22:62–69.

1982d The Art of Making Gun Flint; by Citizen Dolomieu, in the Year 5 [1796–1797]. In *Indian Trade Guns,* edited by T. M. Hamilton, pp. 161–174. Retitled reprint of 1960 article. Pioneer Press, Union City, Tennessee.

1982e Extract from a Report by Citizen Salivet on the Making of Gun Flints in the Departments of Idre and Loir-et-Cher; by F. P. N. Gillet-Laumont. In *Indian Trade Guns,* edited by T. M. Hamilton, pp. 176–185. Retitled reprint of 1960 article. Pioneer Press, Union City, Tennessee.

SMITH, CARLYLE S., AND MARTIN BEHRENS

1974 Das Amerikanische *Springfield,* Gewehr, *Model* 1855. *Deutsches Waffen Journal:*135–141, 254–259. Schwabisch Hall.

1977 Der Skandal um den *Hall-North*-Karabiner, *Model* 1843. *Deutsches Waffen Journal:*1036–1041. Schwabisch Hall.

1980 La Grosse Carabine Système Delvigne. *Deutsches Waffen Journal:*1134–1139. Schwabisch Hall.

1981 Die Kammerbuchse der Bersaglieri. *Deutsches Waffen Journal:*528–534. Schwabisch Hall.

1983 Das *Remington*-Gewehr der *New York State* Miliz. *Deutsches Waffen Journal:*182–187, 302–307. Schwabisch Hall.

SMITH, CARLYLE S., AND W. H. BIRKBY

1962 A Preliminary Report on Archaeological Investigations in the Melvern Reservoir, Osage County, Kansas, 1962. *Kansas Anthropological Association Newsletter* 8:33–36.

SMITH, CARLYLE S., AND ROGER T. GRANGE, JR.

1954 The Spain Site, 39LM301, A Winter Village in Fort Randall Reservoir, South Dakota. Prepared by University of Kansas, Lawrence. Submitted to National Park Service, Lincoln, Nebraska.

1958 The Spain Site (39LM301), a Winter Village in Fort Randall Reservoir, South Dakota. *Bulletin* 169. Smithsonian Institution, Bureau of American Ethnology. *River Basin Surveys Papers* 11:79–128.

SMITH, CARLYLE S., AND THOR HEYERDAHL

1961 Itinerary and Organization of the Norwegian Expedition. In Reports on the Norwegian Archaeological Expedition to Easter Island and the East Pacific, 1955–1956. Vol. 1, Archaeology of Easter Island, edited by Thor Heyerdahl and Edwin N. Ferdon. *Monographs of the School of American Research and the Kon-Tiki Museum* No. 24(1):15–19. Santa Fe, New Mexico, and Stockholm, Sweden.

SMITH, CARLYLE S., AND ALFRED E. JOHNSON
1963   The Two Teeth and Cadotte Sites. Report on file, University of Kansas, Lawrence.
1964   Archaeological Investigations at the Two Teeth Site (39BF204) and Sites in the Skunk Island Area, Big Bend Reservoir, South Dakota. Prepared by University of Kansas, Lawrence. Submitted to National Park Service, Lincoln, Nebraska.
1968   Two Teeth Site. *Publications in Salvage Archaeology* 8. Smithsonian Institution, River Basin Surveys, Lincoln, Nebraska.

SMITH, CARLYLE S., AND G. HUBERT SMITH
1972   Firearms, Gunflints, and Ammunition from Fort Berthold II. In Like-A-Fishhook Village and Fort Berthold, Garrison Reservoir, North Dakota, by G. H. Smith. *National Park Service Anthropological Papers* No. 2:163–165.

[Museum staff at the University of Kansas, Lawrence, are now seeking support to identify and catalogue Smith's papers on file. Additional notes by Smith are present in the files of the Nebraska State Historical Society, Lincoln. Furthermore, during his term as Assistant Editor for the Plains Area (1950–1955), Carlyle S. Smith also contributed 17 ''Notes and News'' columns in *American Antiquity.* —Memorials Editor]

Memorial

KENNETH EARL KIDD, 1906–1994

Kenneth Earl Kidd, at home on the occasion of his 75th birthday, 21 July 1981.

Kenneth E. Kidd, a pioneer of North American historical archaeology, died on 26 February 1994, in Peterborough, Ontario. The importance of both his methodological and intellectual contributions to the discipline of historical archaeology were formally acknowledged in 1985, when Ken was awarded the third J. C. Harrington Medal in Historical Archaeology by the Society for Historical Archaeology (*Historical Archaeology* 19(2):1–4). His commitment to systematic field research and careful scholarship has had a profound influence upon a generation of archaeologists.

Ken Kidd was born in Barrie, Ontario, in 1906. He studied history and English at the University of Toronto, and received his Honors B.A. from that institution in 1931. This was followed by a year at the Ontario College of Education and a brief teaching career at the Mohawk Institute in Brantford, Ontario. His experience at the Institute prompted him to become a lifelong advocate for the education of Native American peoples and the amelioration of their social condition.

In 1935, Ken began his 30-year association with the Royal Ontario Museum of Archaeology, Toronto, when he accepted a junior appointment in the Department of Ethnology. That same year, he returned to the University of Toronto to undertake graduate work, earning his M.A. degree in anthropology and

Historical Archaeology, 1995, 29(1):1–9.
Permission to reprint required.

history. Ken subsequently received a graduate scholarship and took a year's leave of absence from the Royal Ontario Museum in 1938 so he could pursue anthropological studies at the University of Chicago. By 1956, he had achieved the rank of Joint Curator of Ethnology at the Royal Ontario Museum.

Ken Kidd first engaged in archaeological fieldwork in 1937, and during his long museum career he was to direct the excavation of numerous historic and prehistoric sites. Most notable was his 1941–1942 work on the remains of the early 17th-century Jesuit Mission of Sainte-Marie-among-the-Hurons, located near Midland, Ontario. The first extensive excavation of an historic site in Canada, it was a pioneering model of field method in North American historical archaeology. When Ken's full descriptive and interpretive report on the Ste.-Marie excavations was published in 1949, it was the premier scientific and comprehensive archaeological report of its type in North America. The monograph, which has been reprinted several times, is still considered an important reference.

Acknowledging at the time that he was working in a virtual comparative vacuum, Ken's attention to detail led him to a lifelong study of European trade goods found on native sites in North America. Through that experience he developed a special interest in the production and dating of glass beads, and out of Ken's basic research have sprung essential references widely used by both historical and contact-period archaeologists. Perhaps the most important product of that research was the development of a bead classification system for field archaeologists, which he and Martha Ann Kidd published in 1970 (English) and 1972 (French).

Apart from his work on historic materials and sites, Ken is also remembered for his prehistoric research. By the late 1940s, he had become the leading authority on the native past in Ontario—and, perhaps, Eastern Canada—and was invited to write the first synthesis of Ontario prehistory for James B. Griffin's classic *Archaeology of Eastern United States,* published in 1952. Ken also introduced underwater archaeology and promoted studies of rock art in Canada. The latter undertaking, initiated in 1957, has been characterized as the first of its purview on the continent.

In recognition of his prominent career as an archaeologist and ethnohistorian at the Royal Ontario Museum, Ken Kidd was asked in 1964 to found and become Chair of the Department of Anthropology at Trent University, Peterborough, Ontario. Until his final retirement in 1973, Ken emphasized the teaching of historical archaeology, and in Canada his courses on the subject were prototypical. Today, due to Ken's efforts, Trent has become one of the larger departments of anthropology in Canada and one of the few that offers courses in historical archaeology at the M.A. level.

Moreover, in 1968–1969, Ken developed the Indian-Eskimo Studies Program—now the Native Studies Department—at Trent. That special course of study was designed to facilitate the university education of Canada's native peoples through a selective curriculum and an appropriate setting. A North American precedent, the program has served as a model for similar academic departments at other Canadian universities.

During his lifetime Ken was a member of, and held offices in, several professional organizations in Canada, America, and abroad. Apart from his active involvement as a founding member of the Society for Historical Archaeology, which he later served as a director (1973–1975), Ken was vice-president of the Society for American Archaeology (1957–1958) and an honorary life member of that society. A Fellow of the American Anthropological Association, he was also a member of the American Ethnological Society. Further afield, he was a Fellow of the Royal Anthropological Society and a member of both the Royal Geographical Society and the International Congress of Americanists. Ken was also closely associated with a number of avocational archaeological and amateur heritage organizations.

As a pioneer in ethnohistory, visual anthropology, and material culture studies, Ken was the recipient of numerous honors. He was commended by the General of the Order of the Society of Jesus in Rome for his work at Ste.-Marie (1950) and shortly thereafter received a Guggenheim Memorial Fellowship (1951–1952) to study European trade goods found on native sites. He also was awarded the Cornplanter

Medal (1970) for his outstanding Iroquoian scholarship. This medal, presented by the Cayuga County Historical Society of Auburn, New York, previously had been given to such luminaries as the Rev. William M. Beauchamp, Dr. Reuben Gold Thwaites, John B. Hewitt, Arthur C. Parker, Prof. Frederick Houghton, and Dr. William A. Ritchie.

In later years, Ken was awarded an Honorary Curatorship in the Department of Ethnology at the Royal Ontario Museum (1981), the Trent University Eminent Service Award (1983), the J. C. Harrington Medal in Historical Archaeology (1985), the Society for American Archaeology's Award for Outstanding Contributions to American Archaeology (1985), and a Doctor of Laws *honoris causa* from Trent University (1990). The crowning achievement of his distinguished career came in 1993, when he received the Commemorative Medal for the 125th Anniversary of the Confederation of Canada. This final award was bestowed by the Right Honourable Ramon John Hnatyshyn, Governor General of Canada, in recognition of Ken's significant contributions to compatriots, community, and Canada.

Ken is survived by his wife, Martha Ann Kidd, of Peterborough, Ontario, and by numerous relatives, colleagues, and students who will miss his informative verbal forays into the many facets of the past, his opinions, and his help. A self-effacing pragmatist who held that the ultimate objective of education is to create a better world, he has set for us an example that will be hard to follow.

BIBLIOGRAPHY OF KENNETH EARL KIDD

DEWDNEY, SELWYN, AND KENNETH E. KIDD
  1962   *Indian Rock Paintings of the Great Lakes.* University of Toronto Press, Toronto.
  1967   *Indian Rock Paintings of the Great Lakes.* Second edition. University of Toronto Press, Toronto.

KIDD, KENNETH E.
  1927   Printemps. *Il Voc Collegi* (Spring 1926):19. Barrie Collegiate Institute, Barrie, Ontario.
  1937   The Education of the Ontario Indian. *Canadian School Journal* 15(1):7–8. Ontario School Trustees' and Municipal Councillors' Association, Toronto.
  1940   Review of *The Tale of the Nativity as Told by the Indian Children of Inkameep, British Columbia,* by Anthony Walsh. *The School, Elementary Edition* 29(4):315. Ontario College of Education, Toronto.
  1941a *Outline Guide to the Middle American Collections.* Royal Ontario Museum of Archaeology, Toronto.
  1941b Excavation at Old Fort Ste. Marie. *Martyrs' Shrine Message* 5(3):10–12. Martyrs' Shrine, Midland, Ontario.
  1941c Fort Ste. Marie Excavations. *Monthly* 5(2):45. University of Toronto, Toronto.
  1941d The Excavation of Fort Ste. Marie. *The Canadian Historical Review* 22(4):403–415.
  1942a An Historic Site Is Excavated. *The School: Secondary Edition* 30(8):712–715. Ontario College of Education, Toronto.
  1942b Indian Arts and Crafts (in Canada). *Boletín Indigista* 11(2):11–12.
  1942c The Excavations at Fort Ste. Marie. *Martyrs' Shrine Message* 6(2):14–16, 18. Martyrs' Shrine, Midland, Ontario.
  1942d Fort Ste. Marie, an Ancient Shrine. *Martyrs' Shrine Message* 6(2):7. Martyrs' Shrine, Midland, Ontario.
  1943a The Architecture of Sainte Marie. *Journal of the Royal Architectural Institute of Canada* 20(5):71–73.
  1943b The Excavation of Fort Ste. Marie. Canadian Historical Review, *Proceedings* 8:54–55.
  1943c The Architecture of Ste. Marie. *Martyrs' Shrine Message* 7(3):4–6. Martyrs' Shrine, Midland, Ontario.
  1944   The Secrets of Fort Sainte Marie. *Martyrs' Shrine Message* 8(3):4, 18. Martyrs' Shrine, Midland, Ontario.
  1946   The Wanderings of Kane. *The Beaver* Outfit 277, December:3–9.
  1947a A Finger Ring 300 Years Old. *Martyrs' Shrine Message* 11(2):32. Martyrs' Shrine, Midland, Ontario.
  1947b Review of *Conrad Weiser, 1696–1760: Friend of Colonist and Mohawk,* by Paul A. W. Wallace. *Canadian Historical Review* 28(2):206–207.
  1948a The Excavation of a Huron Ossuary. *Bulletin of the Society for American Archaeology* 1. University of Toronto, Toronto.
  1948b A Prehistoric Camp Site at Rock Lake, Algonquin Park, Ontario. *Southwestern Journal of Anthropology* 4(1):98–106.
  1949a *The Excavation of Ste. Marie I.* University of Toronto Press, Toronto.
  1949b The Identification of French Mission Sites in the Huron Country: A Study in Procedure. *Ontario History* 41(2):89–94.
  1949c Some Notes on Historic Huron Pottery from Orr Lake, Ontario. *Bulletin of the Society for American Archaeology* 2:5–7.
  1949d Review of *Native Designs of British Columbia,* by Indian Arts and Welfare Society, Victoria, B.C. *Canadian Forum* 28(336):239. University of Toronto, Toronto.

1950 Orr Lake Pottery: A Study of the Ceramics of an Early Historic Huron Site. *Transactions of the Royal Canadian Institute* 28(2):165–185.

1951a *Canadians of Long Ago: The Story of the Canadian Indian.* Longmans, Green, Toronto.

1951b Burial of an Ojibwa Chief, Muskoka District, Ontario. *Pennsylvania Archaeologist* 21(1–2):3–8.

1951c Fluted Points in Ontario. *American Antiquity* 16(3):260.

1951d Paul Kane: A Sheaf of Sketches. *Canadian Art* 8(4):166–167.

1951e Excavations at Fort Ste. Marie, 1941–1943. *Martyrs' Shrine Message* 15(2):44–47. Martyrs' Shrine, Midland, Ontario.

1952 Sixty Years of Ontario Archaeology. In *Archaeology of Eastern United States,* edited by James B. Griffin, pp. 71–82. University of Chicago Press, Chicago, Illinois.

1953a The Excavation and Historical Identification of a Huron Ossuary. *American Antiquity* 18(4):359–379.

1953b Review of *Papiers contrecoeur et autres documents concernant le conflit Anglo-Français sur l'Ohio de 1745 à 1756,* by Fernand Grenier. *Pennsylvania Magazine of History and Biography,* October:481–482. Philadelphia.

1954a Some Brief Notes on the History of Archaeological Development in Ontario. The Archaeological Society of Central New York, *Bulletin* 9(2):15–17.

1954b Trade Goods Research Techniques. *American Antiquity* 20(1):1–8.

1954c A Woodland Site Near Chatham, Ontario. *Transactions of the Royal Canadian Institute* 30(2):141–178.

1954d A Note on the Palaeopathology of Ontario. *American Journal of Physical Anthropology* 12(4):1–6.

1954e Fashions in Tobacco Pipes Among the Iroquois Indians of Ontario. Royal Ontario Museum of Archaeology, *Bulletin* 22:15–21. Toronto.

1954f Glass Trade Beads from Dutch Hollow. In Dutch Hollow, an Early Historic Period Seneca Site in Livingston County, New York, edited by William A. Ritchie. *Researches and Transactions of the New York State Archeological Association* 13(1):38–43. Also published in *Rochester Museum of Arts and Sciences, Research Records* 10.

1955a Paul Kane, Painter of Indians. Royal Ontario Museum of Archaeology, *Bulletin* 23:9–13. Toronto.

1955b The Royal Ontario Museum. *Archaeology* 8(12):76–81.

1955c Review of *Dutch Hollow: An Early Historic Period Seneca Site in Livingston County, New York,* by William A. Ritchie. *American Antiquity* 21(2):190–191.

1956a A Brief Study of the Human Remains from the Krieger Woodland Site in Southwest Ontario. *Pennsylvania Archaeologist* 26(1):15–26.

1956b Serpent Mounds Excavation. *Ontario History* 48(4):187–188.

1957a Some Recent Accessions in the Department of Ethnology. Art and Archaeology Division, Royal Ontario Museum, *Bulletin* 26:21–23. Toronto.

1957b Trading into Hudson's Bay. *The Beaver* Outfit 288, Winter:12–17.

1958 Review of *A Survey of the Aboriginal Populations of Quebec and Labrador,* by Jacob Fried. *Man* 81(80–85):72.

1960a A Dugout Canoe from Ontario. *American Antiquity* 25(3):417–418.

1960b Ethnological Field Work and Accessions. *The Annual:* 70–74. Art and Archaeology Division, Royal Ontario Museum, Toronto.

1960c A Peruvian Water Jar. *The Annual:*75–76. Art and Archaeology Division, Royal Ontario Museum, Toronto.

1960d Review of *Maya Hieroglyphic Writing,* by Eric Thompson. *Queen's Quarterly* 67(2):325–326. Queen's University, Kingston, Ontario.

1960e Review of *Birdstones of the North American Indian: A Study of These Most Interesting Stone Forms, the Area of Their Distribution, Their Cultural Provenience and Possible Uses and Antiquity,* by Earl C. Townsend, Jr. *Ethnohistory* 7(4):419–421.

1961a The Cloth Trade and the Indians of the Northeast During the Seventeenth and Eighteenth Centuries. *The Annual:* 48–56. Art and Archaeology Division, Royal Ontario Museum, Toronto.

1961b Review of *Archaeological Excavations at Jamestown Colonial National Historic Park and Jamestown National Historic Site, Virginia,* by John L. Cotter. *American Journal of Archaeology* 65:90–91.

1962a Note on Scattered Works of Paul Kane. *The Annual:* 64–68. Art and Archaeology Division, Royal Ontario Museum, Toronto.

1962b Review of *Cabot to Cartier: Sources for a Historical Ethnography of Northeastern North America, 1497–1950,* by Bernard Hoffman. *William and Mary Quarterly* 19(3):466–467.

1963a Archaeological Investigations in Quetico Park, 1963. *Transactions of the Royal Canadian Institute* 34(2):106–110.

1963b Rock Paintings—An Ontario Heritage. *The Ontario Naturalist* 1(2):26–28.

1963c Review of *River Basin Surveys Papers: Interagency Archaeological Program,* Nos. 15–20, edited by H. H. Roberts, Jr. *Plains Anthropologist* 8(20):135–137.

1963d Review of *No Stone Unturned: An Almanac of North American Prehistory,* by Louis A. Brennan. *Man* 63(31–35):29.

1963e Review of *Essays in Precolumbian Art and Archaeology,* by Samuel K. Lothrop et al. *Queen's Quarterly* 70(1):158–159. Queen's University, Kingston, Ontario.

1964a Some Approaches to the Problems of Identifying Historical Materials. In *Diving Into the Past,* edited by June Holmquist and Ardis Hillman Wheeler, pp. 44–48. Minnesota Historical Society, St. Paul, Minnesota.

1964b Reviews of *Evolution of the Oldest House,* by Frederick C. Gjessing et. al.; and *Search for the Cittie of Raleigh,* etc., by Jean Carl Harrington. *American Antiquity* 30(2):232.

1964c Review of *The Iroquois Book of Rites,* edited by Horatio Hale and with an introduction by William N. Fenton. *Ethnohistory* 11(1):64–65.

1965a Birch Bark Scrolls in Archaeological Contexts. *American Antiquity* 30(4):480–483.

1965b Review of *Davidson Black, a Biography,* by Dora Hood. *Canadian Forum,* December:209. University of Toronto, Toronto.

1966 Review of *Indian Trade Goods,* by Arthur Woodward, edited by Emory Strong. *Archaeology* 19(2):149.

1967 Archaeological Field Work at Trent University. *Archaeological Newsletter* 22:1–2. Royal Ontario Museum of Archaeology, Toronto.

1968a Review of *Indian Culture and European Trade Goods,* by George Irving Quimby. *American Antiquity* 33(2):56.

1968b Review of *Firearms, Traps and Tools of the Mountain Men,* by Carl P. Russell. *The Beaver* Outfit 299, Winter:56.

1968c Archaeological Work at Trent University, 1976. *Archaeological Newsletter* 31:1–2. Royal Ontario Museum, Toronto.

1969a Historical Site Archaeology in Canada. *Anthropology Papers* 22. National Museum of Canada, Ottawa.

1969b Review of *An Early Historic Niagara Frontier Iroquois Cemetery in Erie County, New York: Archaeology and Physical Anthropology of the Kleis Site,* by Marion E. White. *American Anthropologist* 71(5):971–972.

1970 *The Excavation of Ste. Marie I.* Reprint of 1949 edition. University of Toronto Press, Toronto.

1972 Contact Material from the Dawson Site. In *Cartier's Hochelaga and the Dawson Site,* edited by James F. Pendergast and Bruce G. Trigger, pp. 327–332. McGill-Queen's University Press, Montréal.

1973a *The Excavation of Ste. Marie I.* Reprint of 1949 edition. Published for Historic Sites Branch, Ontario Ministry of Natural Resources, Toronto. University of Toronto Press, Toronto.

1973b Demolish Our Old Buildings? Then Burn Traill's Books Too! *Peterborough New Paper,* 3 April:6. Peterborough, Ontario.

1977 Les fouilles au Parc Cartier-Brébeuf, Québec, 1959. In *Histoire et archéologie* 10:137–205. Direction des lieux et des parcs historiques nationaux, Parcs Canada, Environnement Canada, Ottawa.

1979a Glass Bead-Making from the Middle Ages to the Early 19th Century. *History and Archaeology* 30. National Historic Parks and Sites Branch, Parks Canada, Environment Canada, Ottawa.

1979b La fabrication des perles de verre, du Moyen Age au début du XIXe siècle. *Histoire et archéologie* 30. Direction des lieux et des parcs historiques nationaux, Parcs Canada, Environnement Canada, Ottawa.

1980 The Excavation at Cartier-Brébeuf Park, Québec City, 1959. *History and Archaeology* 10:93–141. National Historic Parks and Sites Branch, Parks Canada, Environment Canada, Ottawa.

1981a A Radiocarbon Date on a Midéwiwin Scroll from Burntside Lake, Ontario. *Ontario Archaeology* 35:41–44.

1981b Tradition and the Canadian Indian. Reviews of *Salish Weaving,* by Paula Gustafson; *Gathering What the Great Nature Provided: Food Traditions of the Gitksan,* by the People of 'Ksan; *The Covenant Chain: Indian Ceremonial and Trade Silver,* by N. Jaye Fredrickson and Sandra Gibb; and *The Life and Art of Jackson Beardy,* by Kenneth James Hughes. *The Journal of Canadian Studies* 16(3–4):222–225.

1983a Problems in Glass Trade Bead Research. *Proceedings of the 1982 Glass Trade Bead Conference, Rochester Museum and Science Center Research Records* 16:1–4. Charles F. Hayes III, editor. Rochester, New York.

1983b The Dating of Cutlery Objects for the Use of Field Archaeologists. Parks Canada, National Historic Parks and Sites Branch, *Microfiche Report Series* 46. Ottawa.

1986 Blackfoot Ethnography. *Manuscript Series* 8. Alberta Culture, Historical Resources Division, Archaeological Survey of Alberta, Edmonton.

1989 The Jebb Family of Simcoe County. *East Georgian Bay Historical Journal* 5. East Georgian Bay Historical Foundation, Elmvale, Ontario.

1994 The Phoenix of the North. In *Pioneers in Historical Archaeology: Breaking New Ground,* edited by S. South, pp. 49–66. Plenum Press, New York.

KIDD, KENNETH E., AND MARTHA ANN KIDD
1970 A Classification System for Glass Beads for the Use of Field Archaeologists. *Canadian Historic Sites: Occasional Papers in Archaeology and History* 1:45–89. National and Historic Parks Branch, Department of Indian Affairs and Northern Development, Ottawa. Reprinted in 1983 in Proceedings of the 1982 Glass Bead Conference. *Rochester Museum and Science Center, Research Records* 16:219–257. Charles F. Hayes III, editor. Also reprinted in part in 1991 in *Glass Trade Beads in the Northeast,* by Gary Fogelman, pp. 12–33. Fogelman Publishing, Turbotville, Pennsylania.

1972   Classification des perles de verre à l'intention des archéoloques sur le terrain. *Lieux historiques canadiens: Cahiers d'archéologie et d'histoire* 1:47–92. Direction des parcs nationaux et des lieux historiques, Ministère des affaires Indiennes et du Nord Canadien, Ottawa.

KIDD, KENNETH E., EDWARD ROGERS, AND WALTER A. KENYON
1964   A Brief Bibliography of Ontario Anthropology. *Occasional Paper* 7. Art and Archaeology Division, Royal Ontario Museum, Toronto.

Unpublished Manuscripts of Kenneth Earl Kidd

BUEHLER, ALFRED, AND KENNETH E. KIDD
1962   A Bibliography on Beads. Mimeographed manuscript on file, Corning Museum of Glass, Corning, New York.

KIDD, KENNETH E.
1926   Narrative About a Trip Down the Ottawa River. Manuscript in possession of Martha A. Kidd, Peterborough, Ontario.
1936a   A Month Among the Blackfeet of Alberta. Manuscript (93–011, Box 8) on file, Trent University Archives, Peterborough, Ontario.
1936b   Notes on a Blackfoot Buffalo Pound (2 pp. + missing plates). Manuscript (93–011, Box 17) on file, Trent University Archives, Peterborough, Ontario.
1942–   Kenneth E. Kidd Diaries. Tapes in possession of Martha A. Kidd, Peterborough, Ontario. Manuscripts on restricted file,
1956   Trent University Archives, Peterborough, Ontario.
1949   Memorandum to the Director Regarding the Annual Report (2 pp.); Antiquities Law in Ontario (1 p.); Memorandum Accompanying Recommendations re. An Antiquities Law in Ontario (7 pp.); and Comments Upon Last Draught re. Antiquities Act (3 pp.). Manuscript (93–011, Box 16) on file, Trent University Archives, Peterborough, Ontario.
1951   Suggestions for Excavating Indian Sites. Mimeographed manuscript on file, Division of Art and Archaeology, Royal Ontario Museum of Archaeology, Toronto.
1955   Journal of a Trip to Quetico Park, Ontario, and Adjacent Regions. Manuscript in possession of Martha A. Kidd, Peterborough, Ontario.
1956   Diary of K. E. Kidd's Trip Through Northwestern Ontario with the Department of Lands and Forests Fur Recording, 4–10 June 1956 (18 pp.). Manuscript (93–011, Box 17) on file, Trent University Archives, Peterborough, Ontario.
1957   Glass Trade Beads in the Northeast: Their Technology, History, Classification and Archaeological Utility (xi + 139 pp. + tables and appendices). Manuscript (80–030, Box 12, Folder 5) on file, Trent University Archives, Peterborough, Ontario.
1959a   Excavations on the St. Charles River, Québec City, August 1959. Manuscript in possession of Martha A. Kidd, Peterborough, Ontario.
1959b   Native Requirements and the Cloth Trade in the Northeast, 1500–1750 (27 pp.). Manuscript (93–011, Box 17) on file, Trent University Archives, Peterborough, Ontario.
1961   The Sketches of Paul Kane (127 pp.). Manuscript (92007, Box 1) on file, Trent University Archives, Peterborough, Ontario.
1963   The Technology and Nomenclature of Glass Beads (81 pp.). Manuscript (80–030, Box 11) on file, Trent University Archives, Peterborough, Ontario.
1977   Glass Bead-Making in Western Europe Since the Middle Ages (146 pp. + figures). Manuscript (80–030, Box 11) on file, Trent University Archives, Peterborough, Ontario.
1980   Helping to Shape the Future of Peterborough. Manuscript in possession of Martha A. Kidd, Peterborough, Ontario.
1982   Outline Draft of a Trade Goods Bibliography (4 pp.). Manuscript (93–011, Box 17) on file, Trent University Archives, Peterborough, Ontario.
1984a   Comments on Early Methodism. Manuscript in possession of Martha A. Kidd, Peterborough, Ontario.
1984b   The Sources of Contemporary Native Indian Art. Manuscript (93–011, Box 8) on file, Trent University Archives, Peterborough, Ontario.
1985   The Sources of Contemporary Native Art in Canada (35 pp.). Manuscript (93–011, Box 16) on file, Trent University Archives, Peterborough, Ontario.
1987   Obituary: Richard B. Johnston (1930–1987). Manuscript (93–011, Box 8) on file, Trent University Archives, Peterborough, Ontario.
1987   Notes for an Article on Wilfred Jury. Manuscript in possession of Martha A. Kidd, Peterborough, Ontario.
1988a   Daniel Ferguson Kidd. Manuscript in possession of Martha A. Kidd, Peterborough, Ontario.

1988b William Livingston Kidd. Manuscript in possession of Martha A. Kidd, Peterborough, Ontario.

1989a C. T. Currelly, Museum Founder. Manuscript in possession of Martha A. Kidd, Peterborough, Ontario.

1989b Some Recollections on the Jebb and Kidd Families. Manuscript in possession of Martha A. Kidd, Peterborough, Ontario.

1990 Review of *A Selected Bibliography of Historical Artifacts, 1760–1920,* by Mary Margaret Smith and Heinz W. Pyszczyk. Manuscript on file, Archaeological Survey of Alberta, Alberta Culture and Multiculturalism, Historical Resources Division, Edmonton, Alberta.

1992a Notes for a proposed paper on K. E. Kidd's work as an archaeologist. Manuscript in possession of Martha A. Kidd, Peterborough, Ontario.

1992b Outline for proposed book, entitled An Illustrated Social History of the Indians of Canada, 1821–1923. Manuscript in possession of Martha A. Kidd, Peterborough, Ontario.

1992c Cloth in the Montréal Merchants' Records. Manuscript in possession of Martha A. Kidd, Peterborough, Ontario.

1992d Textiles in the Montréal Merchants' Records. Manuscript in possession of Martha A. Kidd, Peterborough, Ontario.

1992e Textiles: Made-Up Goods in the Montréal Merchants' Records. Manuscript in possession of Martha A. Kidd, Peterborough, Ontario.

1992f Notes to Accompany My Plan of Grandfather Jebb's Cookstown House. Manuscript in possession of Martha A. Kidd, Peterborough, Ontario.

1992g The Martins of Carrickfergus. Manuscript in possession of Martha A. Kidd, Peterborough, Ontario.

1992h Mary Josephine Jebb. Manuscript in possession of Martha A. Kidd, Peterborough, Ontario.

n.d.a Royal Gifts and Traders' Trinkets (15 pp.). Notes to accompany slide talk on Indian trade goods. Manuscript (93–011, Box 8) on file, Trent University Archives, Peterborough, Ontario.

n.d.b Beads in the Montréal Merchants' Records. Manuscript in possession of Martha A. Kidd, Peterborough, Ontario.

n.d.c Silver in the Montréal Merchants' Records. Manuscript in possession of Martha A. Kidd, Peterborough, Ontario.

n.d.d Taped interviews and tapes of reminiscences. Tapes in possession of Martha A. Kidd, Peterborough, Ontario.

n.d.e Glass Beads Among the Indians of Northeastern North America, 1500–1760: Their Nature, History, Uses and Archaeological Significance (122 pp. + notes). Manuscript (80–030, Box 11) on file, Trent University Archives, Peterborough, Ontario.

n.d.f The Adze (3 pp.); Awls (4 pp.). Manuscripts (93–011, Box 8) on file, Trent University Archives, Peterborough, Ontario.

n.d.g Thoughts on Native Education in Canada (29 pp.). Manuscript (93–011, Box 8) on file, Trent University Archives, Peterborough, Ontario.

n.d.h Mitla and Monte Albán. Unfinished manuscripts (93–011, Box 8) on file, Trent University Archives, Peterborough, Ontario.

n.d.i The French on the St. Lawrence (23 pp.). Manuscript (93–011, Box 8) on file, Trent University Archives, Peterborough, Ontario.

n.d.j The Indians and French in Canada (22 pp.). Manuscript (93–011, Box 8) on file, Trent University Archives, Peterborough, Ontario.

n.d.k French Iron Trade Goods. Manuscript (93–011, Box 8) on file, Trent University Archives, Peterborough, Ontario.

n.d.l A Brief Bibliography of the Archaeology of Ontario (20 pp.). Manuscript (93–011, Box 8) on file, Trent University Archives, Peterborough, Ontario.

n.d.m A Statistical Analysis of Trade Axes. Manuscript (93–011, Box 8) on file, Trent University Archives, Peterborough, Ontario.

n.d.n Visit to See Paul Kane Sketches in Winnipeg, 1954 (7 pp.). Manuscript (93–011, Box 8) on file, Trent University Archives, Peterborough, Ontario.

n.d.o European Trade Goods as Artifacts (13 pp.). Manuscript (93–011, Box 8) on file, Trent University Archives, Peterborough, Ontario.

n.d.p Holon Chan, The Mayan Indian Boy (46 pp. + missing illustrations). Manuscript (93–011, Box 8) on file, Trent University Archives, Peterborough, Ontario.

n.d.q Metalware Trade Goods (185 pp.). Manuscript (93–011, Box 8) on file, Trent University Archives, Peterborough, Ontario.

n.d.r Arts of Ancient Mexico (4 pp.); The Arts of Ancient Peru (2 pp.). Manuscripts (93–011, Box 8) on file, Trent University Archives, Peterborough, Ontario.

n.d.s Notes on a Collection from Pass Lake, Ontario (4 pp. + illustrations). Manuscript (93–011, Box 8) on file, Trent University Archives, Peterborough, Ontario.

n.d.t The H. W. Howes Collection from Cactus Lake, Saskatchewan (5 pp.). Manuscript (93–011, Box 8) on file, Trent University Archives, Peterborough, Ontario.

n.d.u A New World to Discover (4 pp.). Manuscript (93–011, Box 8) on file, Trent University Archives, Peterborough, Ontario.

n.d.v   Some Observations on the History of the Ethnological Collections in the Royal Ontario Museum, Especially as They Derived from the Old Provincial Museum of Ontario (9 pp.). Manuscript (93–011, Box 8) on file, Trent University Archives, Peterborough, Ontario.

n.d.w   Catalogue of Raymond Willis Collection of Paul Kane Sketches in the Royal Ontario Museum (37 pp.). Manuscript (92–007, Box 1) on file, Trent University Archives, Peterborough, Ontario.

n.d.x   Annotated Illustrations of Forks in the Sheffield City Museum Collections. Manuscript (93–011, Box 3) on file, Trent University Archives, Peterborough, Ontario.

n.d.y   Annotated Illustrations of Knives in the Sheffield City Museum Collections. Manuscript (93–011, Box 3) on file, Trent University Archives, Peterborough, Ontario.

n.d.z   Annotated Illustrations of Table Knives in the Sheffield City Museum Collections. Manuscript (93–011, Box 3) on file, Trent University Archives, Peterborough, Ontario.

n.d.aa   Annotated Illustrations of Spoons in the Sheffield City Museum Collections. Manuscript (93–011, Box 3) on file, Trent University Archives, Peterborough, Ontario.

n.d.bb   Annotated Illustrations of Scissors in the Sheffield City Museum Collections. Manuscript (93–011, Box 3) on file, Trent University Archives, Peterborough, Ontario.

n.d.cc   Annotated Illustrations of Razors in the Sheffield City Museum Collections. Manuscript (93–011, Box 3) on file, Trent University Archives, Peterborough, Ontario.

n.d.dd   Notes on Butcher and Other Knives. Manuscript (93–011, Box 3) on file, Trent University Archives, Peterborough, Ontario.

n.d.ee   Sheffield City Museum Collections: Specimens Examined and Measurements. Manuscript (93–011, Box 3) on file, Trent University Archives, Peterborough, Ontario.

n.d.ff   Miscellaneous Illustrations and Notes on Knives, Forks, and Spoons. Manuscript (93–011, Box 3) on file, Trent University Archives, Peterborough, Ontario.

n.d.gg   Lists of Cutlers: French and English. Manuscript (93–011, Box 3) on file, Trent University Archives, Peterborough, Ontario.

n.d.hh   Lists of Cutlers and Marks. Manuscript (93–011, Box 3) on file, Trent University Archives, Peterborough, Ontario.

n.d.ii   History of Ethnology Department at Royal Ontario Museum. Manuscript (93–011, Box 3) on file, Trent University Archives, Peterborough, Ontario.

n.d.jj   Archaeology and the Royal Ontario Museum: A Personal Perspective (8 pp.). Manuscript (93–011, Box 17) on file, Trent University Archives, Peterborough, Ontario.

Conference Participation of Kenneth Earl Kidd

1942   Ste. Marie in the History of Ontario and of Canada. Lecture given at the Royal Canadian Institute, Toronto, Ontario.

1945   Problems of Ethnological Research in Iroquois Area (Canada). Discussion led by William N. Fenton at the First Annual Conference on Iroquois Research, Red House, New York.

1948   Excavations at Ossossané. Discussion led by James B. Griffin at the Fourth Annual Conference on Iroquois Research, Red House, New York.

1951a   Some General Observations on Ossuaries. Paper presented at the Seventh Annual Conference on Iroquois Research, Red House, New York.

1951b   European Trade Goods Distributed to the Indians of Canada. Paper presented at the Annual Meeting of the Eastern States Archaeological Conference.

1953   Trade Goods Research Techniques. Paper presented at the Eighteenth Annual Meeting of the Society for American Archaeology, Urbana, Illinois.

1958   Ethnohistorical Aspect of Archaeology on the Canadian Frontier. Paper presented at the Fifty-Seventh Annual Meeting of the American Anthropological Association, Washington, D.C.

1959   Native Requirements and the Cloth Trade in the Northeast, 1500–1750. Paper presented at the Fifty-Eighth Annual Meeting of the American Anthropological Association, Mexico City.

1963a   Chair of ''Historical Research and Identification'' Session. Conference on Underwater Archaeology, Minnesota Historical Society, St. Paul, Minnesota.

1963b   Some Approaches to the Problem of Identification of Historical Materials. Conference on Underwater Archaeology, Minnesota Historical Society, St. Paul, Minnesota.

1963c   Historic Sites Archaeology in Ontario. Paper presented at the Twenty-Eighth Annual Meeting of the Society for American Archaeology, Boulder, Colorado.

1965a Chair of "The Function of a Fur Trade Research Centre" Session. North American Fur Trade Conference, St. Paul, Minnesota.

1965b The Functions of a Fur Trade Centre. Paper presented at the North American Fur Trade Conference, St. Paul, Minnesota.

1967 Progress in Archaeology. Address to the Annual Meeting of the Ontario Archaeological Society, Toronto, Ontario.

1969 Discussant: "Glass Trade Beads, 2" Session. Second Annual Meeting of the Society for Historical Archaeology, Tucson, Arizona.

1971a The Beginnings of Rock Art Studies in Canada. Paper presented at the Second Annual Meeting of the Canadian Rock Art Association, Saskatoon, Saskatchewan.

1971b The Training of Anthropologists—Retrospect and Prospect. Roundtable discussion chair, Sixth Annual Meeting of the Canadian Sociology and Anthropology Association, St. John's, Newfoundland.

1973 Vandalism in Rock Art Sites in Canada. Paper presented at the Fourth Annual Meeting of the Canadian Rock Art Association, Peterborough, Ontario.

1977 Masonry Architecture in the Early French Regime. Paper presented at the 10th Annual Meeting of the Society for Historical Archaeology, Ottawa, Ontario.

1978 Some Problems in Trade Bead Research. Paper presented at the 11th Annual Meeting of the Canadian Archaeological Association, Québec City, Québec.

1983 The Burden of Sisyphus. Paper read before the Fortnightly Club, Trent University, Peterborough, Ontario.

1984a The Sources of Contemporary Native Indian Art. Paper presented at the Symposium on Canadian Indian Art, Art Gallery of Ontario, Toronto, Ontario.

1984b It's Time to Reminisce. Paper presented at the 15th Annual Meeting of the Canadian Rock Art Association, Peterborough, Ontario.

SUSAN M. JAMIESON

[Susan Jamieson acknowledges with gratitude that Martha Ann Kidd kindly lent considerable assistance in compiling this definitive bibliography of her late husbands's writings, including reference to his several family histories, and the Society owes Mrs. Kidd our sincere thanks. In addition to Professor Kidd's formal works, he annotated a series of cards, *Forty Indians of Canada Postcards*, illustrating specimens in the ethnological collections of the Royal Ontario Museum. The ROM issued the cards at Toronto, ca. 1958.—Memorials Editor]

Memorial

JOHN H. RICK, 1934–1993

John H. Rick on holiday at Mt. Rushmore, South Dakota, 1988. (Photo by DiAnn Herst.)

When John Rick passed away suddenly on Christmas Eve of 1993, friends and colleagues in the fields of historical archaeology and heritage preservation lost an effective and indefatigable supporter, and one whose professional life was dominated by the compulsion to build and maintain solid organizations based on high standards of research and publication. Adding poignancy to his untimely death was our knowledge that he had been expected to appear at the 1994 Conference on Historical and Underwater Archaeology in Vancouver, B.C., to accept the SHA's Award of Merit on behalf of Parks Canada for distinguished contributions to the field of historical archaeology.

Between 1959, when he obtained his M.A. in anthropology from the University of Toronto, and 1961, when he joined what is today Parks Canada as its first full-time archaeologist, John spent two seasons

Historical Archaeology, 1995, 29(4):1–3.
Permission to reprint required.

excavating at Tikal, Guatemala, for the University of Pennsylvania Museum. He worked for a time as an assistant field director for the North Dakota State Historical Society, as an instructor for the University of North Dakota's archaeological field school, and as a specimen analyst at the University of Florida's zooarchaeological lab. In between, he acquired experience in archaeological survey work for the Saskatchewan government and on various digs with the Royal Ontario Museum.

When he was recruited by Parks Canada in 1961, John was handed a daunting mission best expressed, with only modest exaggeration, as, "Add water and stir. We need archaeological capability on a nation-wide scale—fast." To its credit, Parks gave John his lead, and his energy, commitment, and indomitable debating ability did the rest. By 1967, after six years of recruiting, and occasionally directing field excavations personally, he was chief of an expanding division with a laboratory, large artifact collections, and a growing pool of staff experience with sites that ranged from 17th-century settlements on the Atlantic Coast to late 19th-century police posts in the Canadian West. The vexing problems of jurisdiction over underwater sites and the challenge of recording and studying materials from wrecks had, by this time, become a constructive preoccupation for John, and the Parks Canada underwater archaeology unit was already on its way to becoming a recognized leader in that specialty.

In 1967, John assumed enlarged responsibilities as Chief of Research, managing Parks Canada's activities in historical research, architectural history, and publishing, as well as the operations of the Archaeological Research Branch. Later still he conceived and pushed through the creation of a conservation laboratory that became one of the best in Canada. He supported a strong publishing role for all research disciplines in Parks, and in the 1960s launched three ongoing series of professional publications. John continued in this complex role until 1981, with the additional duty of providing functional guidance on research matters to the five Parks Canada regional offices that had been created between 1974 and 1979, each with its own archaeological staff and historical research unit.

John's tireless work was recognized by the profession at large in 1969, when he was elected as the third president of the Society for Historical Archaeology. He subsequently strongly encouraged his staff to take an active role in the Society, with the result that a number of individuals did exactly that, two going on to become presidents, themselves.

In 1981, John branched out into strikingly different areas, accepting assignments in the varied areas of environmental assessment, policy writing, and strategic planning, both in Parks Canada and in its then-parent department, Environment Canada. The reasons had to do with the very qualities that had made him an effective leader and innovator in the research disciplines. John was above all a builder, a creator of things organizational, moving ahead restlessly, devising rigorous standards, cajoling heterogenous researchers into interdisciplinary cooperation, pushing staff to professional accomplishments they had not known were within their capacities, and establishing new units and techniques as the national historic sites system expanded and Parks Canada's archaeological, conservation, and historical research tasks became more voluminous. When the economic recession that began to invade Canada in the later 1970s deepened into the pervasive governmental retrenchment of the 1980s, Parks's research units suffered along with other parts of the program. But because they were solidly established and working to capacity, they were at least safe from crippling cutbacks. Growth was over, though, and the means no longer existed to conquer new worlds. While he returned to Parks Canada from time to time to address crucial cultural resource issues, John spent most of the last decade of his life pursuing his second area of interest: the analysis of global environmental and socioeconomic issues.

John's contribution to the field of historical archaeology, like his accomplishments in the broader areas of cultural resource management, lies in having had the faith and having kept it. Historical archaeology, no less than other professions, knows little of national or geographical boundaries. When he began his work in Parks Canada in 1961, it had no archaeological equipment beyond the shovels stored in maintenance sheds, and the discipline itself was still in its infancy in Canada. The staff John built up had an international composition, with all the exciting intellectual ferment that rising young professionals intermingled with seasoned hands can create in a virtually new world.

Of course, the task he undertook was not always easy. Parks generally endorsed John's incisively eloquent calls for good equipment, careful excavation, reputable publications, and well-funded studies of material culture. However, even enlightened bureaucracies harbor bean counters, and they descended periodically on the research branches, acronym-clad crusaders determined to prove—their crystal balls to the contrary—that management is a science and that the research units, staffed with people who often acted as if they might be enjoying their work, must be a costly and unnecessary luxury. In the 1960s came "program management evaluation," followed by "management by objectives" (MBO), then "zero-based budgeting" (ZBB), and latterly "value for money" ("Why can't you sell the artifacts, or just rebury them?"). Each time, John answered the evaluators and auditors with his carefully sculptured but unemotional and remorselessly logical prose. Usually he won hands down, because no one knew how to refute such a resolutely rational debater—quite aside from the fact that John was a big man with unwavering eyes and a disconcertingly commanding presence.

In standing firm, John Rick did the world of research a great favor, leaving the largest heritage agency in Canada with the means to practice informed, knowledge-based cultural resource management. Thanks to his vision and energy, the value of both historical and native-site archaeology to the understanding and preservation of heritage is now as firmly planted in the consciousness of Parks Canada's nationwide staff as the foundations of our many excavated national historic sites are embedded in the soil.

MAX SUTHERLAND

[Karlis Karklins deserves thanks for facilitating the development of this memorial to his late colleague.—Memorials Editor]

BIBLIOGRAPHY OF JOHN H. RICK

RICK, JOHN H.
  1968   Review of "The Excavation of Fort Pic, Ontario," by Patricia L. Gall. *Historical Archaeology* 2:123–124.
  1969   President's Page: Man and Superman. *Historical Archaeology* 3:1–2.
  1970   Archaeological Investigations of the National Historic Sites Service, 1962–1966. *Canadian Historic Sites: Occasional Papers in Archaeology and History* 1:9–44.
  1980   Excavations at Cartier-Brébeuf Park, Quebec City, 1962. *History and Archaeology* 10:143–155.

ZACHARCHUK, WALTER, AND JOHN H. RICK
  1969   The Mallorytown Wreck. *Historical Archaeology* 3:7–11.

Memorial

ARNOLD REMINGTON PILLING, 1926–1994

Arnold R. Pilling, Crescent City, California, Fall 1967. (Courtesy of George L. Miller.)

Arnold Pilling was a founder of the Society for Historical Archaeology and its first Secretary-Treasurer. He was born 23 October 1926, in Berkeley, California, the same city where he later would take his bachelor's and doctor's degrees in anthropology. Arnold received his Ph.D. from the University of California at Berkeley in 1958 with a dissertation entitled *Law and Feud in an Aboriginal Society of North Australia*. In addition to his studies at Berkeley, he spent a year of graduate work at University College in London, England, and a year at the University of Sydney in Australia. Heavily influenced by Alfred L. Kroeber's approach to anthropology, Arnold Pilling considered himself first and foremost an anthropologist in the Boasian tradition.

Historical archaeology was just one of Arnold's many areas of research. Throughout his career he maintained a strong interest in Australian aborigines; the Yurok and other Native American groups of northwestern California; the Amish in Pennsylvania, Ohio, and Indiana; and more generally in ethnohistory and linguistics. Some of his later research concentrated on African-American archaeology and gay/lesbian topics in social anthropology. Those diverse areas of research in many ways contributed to

Historical Archaeology, 1995, 29(4):4–10.
Permission to reprint required.

the development and expansion of his central pursuits in historical archaeology and English ceramics for which we best remember him.

Robert Heizer was a major influence upon Arnold's interests as a student of archaeology. While an undergraduate, he worked on several California site surveys and excavations under Heizer's direction. Consequently, an early interest in historical archaeology would develop out of excavations at two central California sites—a Russian settlement excavated in 1949 and a Spanish mission investigated in 1955. Back then, very little historical archaeology was taking place in California, so Arnold had to teach himself about the historic ceramics he was finding.

When Arnold wanted to do a directed study of Spanish majolica in connection with his developing involvement in California mission sites he had to take the course through the art history department, since his mentors in anthropology did not consider the subject to be anthropological. His personal research into English ceramics, on the other hand, may have been spurred by the fact that some of his ancestors had emigrated from England where they had worked in the Staffordshire potteries. Once in America, they would establish the Gladding, McBean and Company pottery at Lincoln, California, not far from Sacramento.

Arnold's interest in historical archaeology turned yet another direction in 1954, while doing ethnographic fieldwork among the Tiwi on Bathurst Island in Australia. During that time he had the opportunity to conduct preliminary archaeological work at Fort Dundas (1822–1924) on Melville Island, Northern Australia. It is also worth noting that, given its early date, the research Arnold performed in Australia was probably the first historical archaeology done on that continent.

Wayne State University in Detroit hired Arnold Pilling in January 1957 as a lecturer in anthropology, and by 1970 he had been promoted through the ranks to full professor. For almost 40 years he taught a variety of courses, ranging from the history of anthropological theory to courses on Native Americans, as well as historical archaeology. He was active in the affairs of the Department of Anthropology until his death on 27 October 1994. Arnold also served in those years as Director of the Wayne State University Museum of Anthropology, which he founded in 1959.

Many students at Wayne State received their first exposure to historical archaeology by taking Arnold's Saturday field classes or by working as volunteers in the anthropology museum. He was one of the first historical archaeologists to concentrate on urban sites, and archaeological research at Wayne State during the late 1950s through the 1960s focused almost exclusively on the salvage of sites being destroyed by construction in downtown Detroit. Back in 1962, when the Detroit Bank and Trust Company was planning to build a new headquarters, its proposed location was on the site of Fort Lernault, a fortification built by the British in 1778. Through his own efforts, Arnold was able to secure some funding from the bank for salvage excavations prior to construction, but the funding was small by today's standards.

In fact, most of the salvage excavations Arnold conducted in downtown Detroit were unfunded, which meant the work was done on a voluntary basis by students and local amateurs. Moreover, access to the sites for research was often dependent on the good will of the construction crews. A high level of camaraderie developed around those projects, where crews had to make do with minimal equipment and work under highly variable and at times adverse conditions, such as just in front of the bulldozers! I recall that during one winter's excavation of a ceramic importer's dump site, we had to deal with large, frozen blocks of clay and sherds, which we thawed by leaving them behind the tailpipe of a university station wagon left running for that purpose.

Containers in the Wayne State University Museum consisted of whatever could be scrounged at Arnold's behest, as funding for curation was even more scarce. One student worked in a large Detroit hospital, which was an excellent source of various cardboard boxes that had held medications and hospital supplies; Demerol® boxes were our favorite for storing artifacts. We also used a lot of heavy, clear plastic sheeting from discarded oxygen tents as dust covers for our storage areas.

The world of unfunded, make-do archaeological salvage work was changed by the introduction of environmental laws, which provided funding for testing and excavation of threatened sites. Much was gained by those laws, but some things were also lost. Without funding and deadlines, one was free to change one's objectives in the study of collections. The cost of living in Detroit in the 1960s was very low, of course, making this type of archaeology possible. I doubt we could ever go back to that again with the same results. Because of those salvage excavations, however, several of Arnold's students were already trained and ready when archaeology became a routine part of the development process in the Detroit area under the new laws.

Years of salvage excavations by the WSU Museum of Anthropology built up a fine collection of English ceramics, which have been well used in providing students a strong exposure to the typology and chronology of these wares. In addition, Arnold donated a large part of his personal library to the Anthropology Museum, and his field notes have been given to the Walter P. Reuther Archives of Labor History and Urban Affairs of Wayne State University. As a result, he leaves behind a resource legacy that will continue to serve students and researchers for years to come.

Teaching was one of Arnold's greatest gifts. He had a wonderful way of telling stories and presenting material in a historical perspective, which made his lectures a pleasure to attend. Arnold rarely used notes in presenting his classes and was fully capable of going off on tangents in response to questions during class. One might be fooled by the lack of lecture notes into thinking that his lectures were not organized. However, I realized the solid foundation of his ''off-the-cuff'' style while sitting in on his Saturday lecture on ceramics a year after having been through the class. When I later compared my notes from both lectures, the basic outline of organization had remained the same despite new information being introduced.

Arnold was a bibliophile and played an active role in ordering out-of-print books for the University library. It was difficult to come up with a topic upon which he did not have some information or reference suggestions. In addition, Arnold always was available to listen to students or colleagues with research problems, willingly offering suggestions on sources or approaches.

Some students shied away from Dr. Pilling, because he was a tough grader on term papers and particularly tough on grammatical and spelling errors. It was widely known that his grading habits often resulted in the need for multiple drafts of a paper, and I, for one, can remember getting back papers marked ''D+, do you wish to rewrite?'' But while he was a stern task master, he was rarely judgmental, and Arnold often spent large amounts of his time working with students on their writing, as well as on their research. Those of us fortunate enough to have had Arnold Pilling as a mentor gained a great deal from the experience.

GEORGE L. MILLER

BIBLIOGRAPHY OF
ARNOLD REMINGTON PILLING

HART, C. W. M., AND ARNOLD R. PILLING
    1960   *The Tiwi of North Australia.* Henry Holt, New York.
    1977   *The Tiwi of North Australia.* Fieldwork edition. Holt, Rinehart, and Winston, New York.

HART, C. W. M., ARNOLD R. PILLING, AND JANE C. GOODALE
    1988   *The Tiwi of North Australia.* Holt, Rinehart, and Winston, New York.

PILLING, ARNOLD R.
    1948a   Archaeological Survey of Northern Monterey County. California Archaeological Survey Manuscripts 106. University of California, Berkeley.
    1948b   The Vaqueros Province. California Archaeological Survey Manuscripts. University of California, Berkeley.
    1949a   Recording Local Collections. In *A Manual of Archaeological Field Methods,* edited by Robert F. Heizer, pp. 58–60. National Press, Milbrae, California.
    1949b   Structural Remains. In *A Manual of Archaeological Field Methods,* edited by Robert F. Heizer, pp. 43–44. National Press, Milbrae, California.

1950a   Recording Local Collections. In *A Manual of Archaeological Field Methods,* edited by Robert F. Heizer, pp. 59–61. Revised edition. National Press, Milbrae, California.

1950b   Structural Remains. In *A Manual of Archaeological Field Methods,* edited by Robert F. Heizer, pp. 44–45. Revised edition. National Press, Milbrae, California.

1950c   The Archaeological Implications of an Annual Coastal Visit for Certain Yokuts Groups. *American Anthropologist* 52:438–440.

1951   The Surface Archaeology of the Pecho Coast, San Luis Obispo County, California. *Masterkey* 25:196–200.

1952a   The British Museum Collection from near Avila, California. *American Antiquity* 18:169–172.

1952b   California Mission Maiolica. California Archaeological Survey Manuscripts 139. University of California, Berkeley.

1955a   Relationships of Prehistoric Cultures of Coastal Monterey County, California. *Kroeber Anthropological Society Papers* 12:70–87.

1955b   Glazed Ceramics—Relationships in California (Farallon Island). California Archaeological Survey Manuscripts 231. University of California, Berkeley.

1957a   Australia. *Asian Perspectives* 2:151–177.

1957b   An Incised Pebble from Lassen County, California. *Reports of the California Archaeological Survey* 38:6. University of California, Berkeley.

1958a   Australia. *Asian Perspectives* 3(1):98–111.

1958b   Recording Local Collections. In *A Guide to Archaeological Field Methods,* edited by Robert F. Heizer, pp. 102–103. National Press, Palo Alto, California.

1958c   Structural Remains. In *A Guide to Archaeological Field Methods,* edited by Robert F. Heizer, p. 71. National Press, Palo Alto, California.

1959a   Archaeology. In Palaeopathology of a California Archaeological Site, by James G. Roney, Jr. *Bulletin of the History of Medicine* 33(2):100.

1959b   Local History and Local Archaeology. *Detroit Historical Society Bulletin* 16(1):4–10.

1961a   Genetic Change among the Tiwi of North Australia. Paper presented at the 10th Pacific Science Congress.

1961b   Six Archaeological Sites in the Detroit Area, I. *The Michigan Archaeologist* 7:13–30.

1961c   Six Archaeological Sites in the Detroit Area, II. *The Michigan Archaeologist* 7:33–54.

1962a   *Aborigine Culture History: A Survey of Publications 1954–1957.* Wayne State University Press, Detroit, Michigan.

1962b   A Historical Versus a Non-historical Approach to Social Change and Continuity among the Tiwi. *Oceania* 32(4):321–326. Sydney, Australia.

1962c   Some Questions on Taos Dancing. *Ethnomusicology* 6(2):88–92.

1962d   Statistics, Sorcery, and Justice. *American Anthropologist* 64:1057–1059.

1963a   Aranda. *Encyclopedia International,* Vol. 1, p. 515. Grolier, New York.

1963b   Australian Aborigines. *Encyclopedia International,* Vol. 1, pp. 223–225. Grolier, New York.

1963c   Cultural Material on the 585-Foot and 605-Foot Beach Lines of the Western Shore of Lake St. Clair. *The Michigan Archaeologist* 9:15–16.

1963d   Review of *Chicago Area Archaeology,* edited by Elaine A. Bluhm. *American Antiquity* 28:406–407.

1963e   Review of *I, the Aboriginal,* by Douglas Lockwood. *American Anthropologist* 65:1152–1153.

1963f   Review of *World of Wakara,* by Conway B. Sonne. *Western Folklore* 22(1):63–64.

1964a   Cushman's Wolf Lake Site, Jackson County, Michigan. *The Totem Pole* 47(2–3).

1964b   Matriarchy. In *A Dictionary of the Social Sciences,* edited by Julius Gould and William Kolb, pp. 416–417. Free Press of Glencoe, Toronto.

1964c   Moiety. In *A Dictionary of the Social Sciences,* edited by Julius Gould and William Kolb, pp. 436–437. Free Press of Glencoe, Toronto.

1964d   Patriarchy. In *A Dictionary of the Social Sciences,* edited by Julius Gould and William Kolb, p. 458. Free Press of Glencoe, Toronto.

1964e   Review of *An Archaeological Survey of Mutau Flat, Ventura County, California,* by Hal Eberhart and Agnes Bierman Babcock. *American Antiquity* 30:119–120.

1964f   Tasmanians. *Encyclopedia International,* Vol. 17, p. 517. Grolier, New York.

1964g   Torres Strait Islanders. *Encyclopedia International,* Vol. 18, p. 167. Grolier, New York.

1965a   An Australian Aboriginal Minority: The Tiwi See Themselves as a Dominant Majority. *Phylon* 26:305–314.

1965b   Fort Lernoult Excavations. In *Wayne State University Department of Sociology and Anthropology, Museum of Anthropology,* pp. 6–17. Report to Dean Martin Sterns for the period between 1 May 1962 and 30 April 1963. On file, Wayne State University, Detroit, Michigan.

1965c   Pontchartrain Hotel Excavations. In *Wayne State University Department of Sociology and Anthropology, Museum of Anthropology,* pp. 17–20. Report to Dean Martin Sterns for the period between 1 May 1962 and 30 April 1963. On file, Wayne State University, Detroit, Michigan.

1966a   Life at Porter Site 8, Midland County, Michigan. *The Michigan Archaeologist* 12:235–248.

1966b   Fort Pontchartrain to Pontchartrain Hotel. *Proceedings of the Second Annual Michigan Junior Science and Humanities Symposium 1966:*19–29.

1967a   Skyscraper Archaeologist: The Urban Archaeology in Detroit. *Detroit Historical Society Bulletin* 23(8):4–9.

1967b   International Conference on Historic Archaeology, 6–7 January 1967, at Southern Methodist University, Dallas, Texas, U.S.A. *Current Anthropology* 9:231–232.

1968a   Southeastern Australia: Level of Social Organization. In *Man the Hunter,* edited by Richard B. Lee and Irven DeVore, pp. 138–145. University of Chicago Press, Chicago, Illinois.

1968b   A Use of Historical Sources in Archaeology: An Indian Earthworks near Mt. Clements, Michigan. *Ethnohistory* 15:152–202.

1969a   Six Archaeological Sites in the Detroit Area, I. Reprint of 1961 article. In Selections from *The Michigan Archaeologist,* Vols. 1–10, assembled by James E. Fitting. *Michigan Archaeological Society Special Publications* 1:121–138. Ann Arbor.

1969b   Six Archaeological Sites in the Detroit Area, II. Reprint of 1961 article. In Selections from *The Michigan Archaeologist,* Vols. 1–10, assembled by James E. Fitting. *Michigan Archaeological Society Special Publications* 1:139–160. Ann Arbor.

1969c   Vancouver Collection from Trinidad, California, as Described in the Notes of Arnold R. Pilling, December 1969. Manuscript on file, Humboldt County Collection, Humboldt State University, Arcata, California.

1970a   Introduction. In *Diprotodon to Detribalization: Studies of Change Among Australian Aborigines,* edited by Richard A. Waterman and Arnold R. Pilling, pp. 1–48. Michigan State University Press, East Lansing.

1970b   Changes in Tiwi Language. In *Diprotodon to Detribalization: Studies of Change Among Australian Aborigines,* edited by Richard A. Waterman and Arnold R. Pilling, pp. 256–274. Michigan State University Press, East Lansing.

1973   The Area of Mound Road and 7 Mile Road on July 27th, 1973. Report prepared by Department of Anthropology, Wayne State University, Detroit. Submitted to Office of the State Archaeologist, Bureau of History, Michigan Department of State, Lansing.

1974a   Dating Early Photographs by Card Mounts and Other External Evidence: Tentative Suggestions. *Image* 17(1):11–16.

1974b   Eight Historic Artifacts from 4-Mnt-12. *Monterey County Archaeological Society Quarterly* 4(1).

1975   Eight Historic Artifacts from 4-Mnt-12. *Monterey County Archaeological Society Quarterly* 4(2):1–5.

1977   Land Use Histories of Detroit's Early Areas. In *The Detroit Consortium: A Model for City/University Collaboration on Urban Concerns,* edited by Otto Feinstein and John J. Munsial, pp. 119–120. Center for Urban Studies, Wayne State University, Detroit, Michigan.

1978a   Glazed Earthenware. In *The Knife River Phase,* by Donald J. Lehmer, W. Raymond Wood, and C. L. Dill, pp. 358–365, 414–415, 439–441, 444–447. Report prepared by Department of Anthropology and Sociology, Dana College, Blair, Nebraska, and American Archaeology Division, University of Missouri, Columbia (contract number C3537[68] and purchase orders A-3514[75] and A-3521[78]). Submitted to Interagency Archaeological Services, U.S. Department of the Interior, Denver, Colorado.

1978b   Yurok. In *Handbook of North American Indians,* edited by William Sturtevant. Vol. 8, *California,* edited by Robert F. Heizer, pp. 137–154. Smithsonian Institution, U.S. Government Printing Office, Washington, D.C.

1979   Native American Religious Rights: Constitutional Considerations. *Indian Historian* 12(1):13–19.

1980   Southeastern Michigan. In *Phase II Completion Report for the Conference on Michigan Archaeology: Major Problem Orientations in Michigan Archaeology, 1980–1984,* edited by James W. Mueller. Report No. R-2134 on file, Commonwealth Associates, Inc., Jackson, Michigan.

1981a   Linked Riverfront Parks Project: St. Aubin Park, Land Use History. Report prepared by Department of Anthropology, Wayne State University, Detroit. Submitted to Office of the State Archaeologist, Bureau of History, Michigan Department of State, Lansing.

1981b   Marinea/Lagoon Alternative: Chene Park Land I and II, Land Use History. Report prepared by Department of Anthropology, Wayne State University, Detroit. Submitted to Office of the State Archaeologist, Bureau of History, Michigan Department of State, Lansing.

1981c   Sacred Sites: Some Cross-cultural Questions. *Archaeology Resource Center Newsletter* 5(4):3.

1982a   A Cultural Resource Inventory, Southeastern Michigan: Phase I, Michigan Historical Division Grant S81-160, Completion Report. Report prepared by Department of Anthropology, Wayne State University, Detroit. Submitted to Office of the State Archaeologist, Bureau of History, Michigan Department of State, Lansing.

1982b   Detroit: Urbanism Moves West; Palisaded Fur-trade Center to Diversified Manufacturing City. *North American Archaeologist* 3:225–242.

1982c   Preface. In *Chilula: People from the Ancient Redwoods,* by Robert G. Lake, Jr., pp. xi–xv. University Press of America, Washington, D.C.

1982d   Chilula Concept of Confession and Sickness. In *Chilula: People from the Ancient Redwoods,* by Robert G. Lake, Jr., pp. 154–156. University Press of America, Washington, D.C.

1982e   Chilula War Story on Round Valley. In *Chilula: People from the Ancient Redwoods,* by Robert G. Lake, Jr., pp. 149–154. University Press of America, Washington, D.C.

1985   Protective Recovery and Testing at Deer Lake Site, 20MT119.F.S. CRI No. 09–04–03–200: Final Report. Report prepared by Department of Anthropology, Wayne State University, Detroit. Submitted to Office of the State Archaeologist, Bureau of History, Michigan Department of State, Lansing.

1986a   Dating Photographs. In Ethnohistory: A Researcher's Guide, edited by Dennis Wiedman. *Studies of Third World Societies, Publication* 35:167–226. College of William and Mary, Williamsburg, Virginia.

1986b   Euro-American Glazed Ceramics and Glass. In Papers in Northern Plains Prehistory and Ethnohistory: Ice Glider 320L110, edited by W. Raymond Wood. *South Dakota Archaeological Society, Special Publication* 10:113–137, 203–215. Sioux Falls.

1988   Anthropology's Culture and Personality School and Homosexuality: A Review Article. *Society of Lesbian and Gay Anthropologists Newsletter* 11(1):19–22.

1989a   Lost Caption #1. *News from Native California* 2(6):7.

1989b   Alexander Smith Taylor, Early California Ethnologist: An Update. Paper presented at the Fifth Annual California Indian Conference, Humboldt State University, Arcata, California.

1989c   Teaching about Homosexuality: Lesbian and Gay Issues and the Anthropology Curriculum. Paper presented at the 88th Annual Meeting of the American Anthropological Association, Washington, D.C.

1989d   Review of *Crossroads of Continents: Cultures of Siberia and Alaska,* by Aaron Crowell. *Choice* 26:1718.

1989e   Review of *Trail to Heaven: Knowledge and Narrative in a Northern Native Community,* by Robin Ridington. *Choice* 26:1369.

1989f   Review of *To Fish in Common: The Ethnohistory of Lummi Indian Salmon Fishing,* by Daniel L. Boxberger. *Choice* 27:352.

1989g   Review of *The Curtain Within: Haida Social and Mythical Discourse,* by Marianne Boelscher. *Choice* 27:522.

1989h   Review of *Archaeological Perspectives on the Battle of the Little Bighorn,* by Douglas D. Scott, et al. *Choice* 27:542.

1989i   Yurok Aristocracy and Great Houses. Special Issue: The California Indians. *American Indian Quarterly: Journal of American Indian Studies* 13(4):421–436.

1990a   Review of *Buying Back the Land: Organizational Struggle and the Aboriginal Land Fund Commission,* by Ian Palmer. *American Anthropologist* 92:221–222.

1990b   Review of *End of an Era: Aboriginal Labour in the Northern Territory,* by Ronald M. Berndt and Catherine H. Berndt. *American Anthropologist* 92:221–222.

1990c   Observer Sexual Orientation, Fieldwork Rapport, and Data Collection on Homosexuality and Hermaphroditism. Paper presented at the 89th Annual Meeting of the American Anthropological Association, New Orleans, Louisiana.

1990d   Northwest California Indian Gender Classes: ''Those Who Could Not Marry,'' ''Those Men Who Have Never Been Near a Woman,'' and ''Women Who Do Men's Things.'' *Society of Lesbian and Gay Anthropologists Newsletter* 14(2):15–23.

1990e   Review of *Tracing Archaeology's Past: The Historiography of Archaeology,* by Andrew L. Christenson. *Choice* 28:1358.

1990f   Yurok of Northwest California: Some Sub-Classes of Males and Females; Men and Women Who Could Not Marry. Sixth International Conference on Hunting and Gathering Societies. *Hunting and Gathering Societies: Changing Peoples, Changing Theories. Precirculated Papers and Abstracts* 1:59. University of Alaska, Fairbanks.

1991a   Australian Local and Regional Histories as Anthropological Works. *Reviews in Anthropology* 18:17–27.

1991b   Review of *Conversations with Claude Lévi-Strauss,* by Claude Lévi-Strauss and Didier Eribon, translated by Paula Wissing. *Choice* 28:1815–1816.

1991c   Review of *A History of Archaeological Thought,* by Bruce G. Trigger. *Winterthur Portfolio* 26(1):81–82.

1991d   Northwest California Indian Gender Classes: ''Those Who Could Not Marry,'' ''Those Men Who Have Never Been Near a Woman,'' and ''Women Who Do Men's Things.'' Paper presented in plenary session, ''Gender in Native California: A Tribute to Arnold R. Pilling,'' organized by Lee Davis, at the Seventh Annual California Indian Conference, Sonoma State University, Rohnart Park, California.

1991e   Uses of Photographs in Diachronic Anthropology. Paper presented at the 90th Annual Meeting of the American Anthropological Association, Chicago, Illinois.

1992a   Homosexuality among the Tiwi of North Australia. In *Oceanic Homosexualities,* edited by Stephen O. Murray, pp. 25–31. Garland, New York.

1992b   Review of *Voices of the First Day: Awakening in the Aboriginal Dreamtime,* by Robert Lawlor. *Choice* 29:1792.

1993a   Cross-Dressing and Shamanism among Selected Western North American Tribes. Paper presented at the 92nd Annual Meeting of the American Anthropological Association, Chicago, Illinois.

1993b   Review of *Gay Ideas,* by Richard D. Mohr. *Choice* 30:1507.

1994a   Review of *To the American Indian: Reminiscences of a Yurok Woman,* by Lucy Thompson. *Journal of California and Great Basin Anthropology* 14(2):254–260.

1994b   Review of *Economics and the Dreamtime: A Hypothetical History,* by N. G. Butin. *Choice* 31:1620.

[1996a]   Use of Photographs in Diachronic Studies. In *Diachronic Anthropology,* edited by Joseph Chartkoff, Walter Randolph Adams, and David Rindos. Academic Press, New York, in press.

[1996b] Euro-American Occupation: British Period. In *Michigan Archaeology,* edited by John Halsey. Cranbrook Institute Press, Bloomfield Hills, Michigan, in press.

PILLING, ARNOLD R., AND RICHARD K. BEARDSLEY
    1948   Notes on Various Collections from Monterey County. California Archaeological Survey Manuscripts 26. University of California, Berkeley.

PILLING, ARNOLD R., AND MARK C. BRANSTNER
    1982   The Collot Map. Report on file, Bureau of History, Michigan Department of State, Lansing.
    1985   The Collot Map, Part II. Report on file, Bureau of History, Michigan Department of State, Lansing.

PILLING, ARNOLD R., AND GORDON L. GROSSCUP
    1992   Dating Mexican Photographic Post Cards. Paper presented at the 91st Annual Meeting of the American Anthropological Association, Washington, D.C.

PILLING, ARNOLD R., GORDON L. GROSSCUP, AND GEORGE L. MILLER
    1967   Nineteenth-Century Glazed Ceramics in Michigan and Elsewhere: Part 2, Archaeological Evidence. *Coffinberry News Bulletin* 14:60–70.

PILLING, ARNOLD R., AND GEORGE L. MILLER
    1967a   Nineteenth-Century Glazed Ceramics in Michigan and Elsewhere: Part 1, Rationale. *Coffinberry News Bulletin* 14:49–56.
    1967b   Nineteenth-Century Glazed Ceramics in Michigan and Elsewhere: Part 3, Other Types of Evidence. *Coffinberry News Bulletin* 14:77–82.

PILLING, ARNOLD R., AND PATRICIA L. PILLING
    1970   Cloth, Clothes, Hose, and Bows: Nonsedentary Merchants among the Indians of Northwestern California. *Proceedings of the 1970 Annual Spring Meetings of the American Ethnological Society:*97–119. University of Washington Press, Seattle.

PILLING, ARNOLD R., AND DAVID TEETER
    1981   Review and Reproduction of the Archaeological Reports of Wayne State University: Michigan History Division Grant S81–125; Completion Report. Prepared by Department of Anthropology, Wayne State University, Detroit. Submitted to Office of the State Archaeologist, Bureau of History, Michigan Department of State, Lansing.

PILLING, PATRICIA L., AND ARNOLD R. PILLING
    1989   Jews of Del Norte County, California: The Wolfe Morris Family. *Western States Jewish History* 21:122–131, 239–247.

RIDDELL, FRANCIS A., CHESTER CHARD, AND ARNOLD R. PILLING
    1953   Chipped Stone. In The Archaeology of the Napa Region, edited by Robert F. Heizer. *University of California Anthropology Records* 12:261–265, 290–294. Berkeley, California.

SHOSHANI, JEHESKEL, ARNOLD R. PILLING, AND HENRY T. WRIGHT
    1989   Kessell Side-notched Point: First Record for Michigan. *Current Research in the Pleistocene* 6:22–24. Center for the Study of Early Man, University of Maine, Orono.

SHOSHANI, JEHESKEL, HENRY T. WRIGHT, AND ARNOLD R. PILLING
    1990   Ecological Context of Two Early Archaic Projectile Points from Michigan: A LeCroy and a Kessell Point Recovered at 20OK394. *The Michigan Archaeologist* 36:1–20.

WATERMAN, RICHARD A., AND ARNOLD PILLING (EDITORS)
    1970   *Diprotodon to Detribalization: Studies of Change Among Australian Aborigines.* Michigan State University Press, East Lansing.

[The National Anthropological Archives, Smithsonian Institution, curates a set of Arnold Pilling's research notes relating to their manuscript collection of George Gibb's mid-19th-century observations on Klamath River and Humboldt Bay, California, peoples. Pilling catalogued the Harry Roberts photographic collection deposited at the Humboldt State University Library in Arcata, California, which contains numerous historic images of northwestern California natives, principally Yurok. Of course, most of Arnold Pilling's unpublished manuscripts and papers are housed at Wayne State University in Detroit, Michigan.— Memorials Editor]

MEMORIAL: J.C. Harrington, 1901-1998. Volume 32, Number 4 (1998): 1-7. By George L. Miller.

Memorial

J. C. HARRINGTON, 1901-1998

J. C. Harrington, 1965.

Jean Carl Harrington passed away the 19th of April 1998 in Richmond at the age of 96 years. Many date the beginning of historical archaeology with Harrington's work for the National Park Service at Jamestown in 1936. He was better known as Pinky by his friends and colleagues. This nickname was given to him when he was a graduate student at the University of Chicago in the 1930s. His nick name came from his red hair and the bright shade of pink that he turned when exposed to the sun. In an autobiography written for his family, Pinky stated that "My first name has been a nuisance and annoyance all my life." On his birth certificate he was listed as female, which he had to correct later. From grad school on, he went by Pinky or J. C. Harrington.

Pinky, the son of teachers, was born in Millbrook, Michigan on 25 October 1901. Later his father became a school superintendent which took Pinky's family to a number of small Michigan towns including Scottville, Ypsilanti, Vasser, and Albion. As a teenager, Pinky held a great variety of part time jobs including a paper boy, a janitor, a picture framer, a repairer of hand cranked phonographs, a highway flagman, some secretarial work for a high school faculty member, and for one summer he was a bell hop at the Kellogg Sanitarium in Battle Creek, Michigan. His high school annual said "Most Likely to Keep Busy." This work pattern continued when he attended Albion College. His jobs while in college included working in an iron foundry, a patent medicine plant, hand coloring glass projector slides, operating a movie projector, and some secretarial work for a professor.

After completing a two-year pre-engineering program at Albion College, Pinky attended the Massachusetts Institute of Technology in Boston for a year to take courses in the architectural school. Pinky's interest in architecture grew out of his abilities as a draftsman. He completed his bachelor's degree at the University of Michigan in Architectural Engineering in 1924. Throughout his college career, Pinky was active in Sigma Nu Fraternity.

Part of the Architectural Engineering program at the University of Michigan involved a requirement that students spend a summer working in an architect's office or carrying out an architecture related research project. For his project, Pinky, in the summer of 1923, joined the School for American Research in Santa Fe to make measured plan drawings of old Spanish mission churches. Working under the direction of an archaeologist, Pinky and another architecture student, recorded Gran Quivira and eight other mission churches from Acoma to Ranchos de Taos. At Gran Quivira, he met Edgar L. Hewett and his excavation crew, who included Anna Shepard. After finishing the missions recording project, he worked for the New Mexico Highway Department for a month to earn his train fare back to Michigan. He lived in the Old Governor's Palace in Santa Fe with two Hopi Indians, one being Fred Kaboti the artist, who became a lifelong friend. This experience gave him an interest in archaeology and a love for the state of New Mexico.

After graduating from the University of Michigan in 1924, Pinky moved back to New Mexico and took a job with the New Mexico Highway Department and later with a mining company. Neither of these jobs was related to architecture. In New Mexico he fell in with the archaeology and museum crowds that he had met earlier. Among the sites he visited was Pecos, where Alfred Kidder was excavating. He worked in New Mexico for a couple of years before returning East to be close to his family after the death of his sister. Pinky took a position with an architect in South Bend, Indiana. That job came to an end in 1932 because of the Great Depression which gave Pinky time to reconsider his career path. He decided to go into archaeology and became a graduate student at the University of Chicago under Fay-Cooper Cole and Robert Redfield. Some of his fellow graduate students included Jesse Jennings and Robert (Stu) Neitzel, Horace Minor, and Joffre Coe. While at Chicago, an opportunity came for Pinky to join an expedition funded by the Carnegie Institution of Washington for a site survey across the Yucatan Peninsula with J. Eric Thompson. That experience was described by Pinky in his article "The Mules Knew the Way," which was published last year in *Historical Archaeology* (31[4]:5-14). Pinky finished the requirements for a Master's degree in 1935, and passed his written comprehensive exams for his doctorate the following year. Soon after that he was running a major excavation at Jamestown for the National Park Service. He never got around to writing a dissertation.

In 1936, Pinky was approached by the National Park Service to work at Jamestown. Excavations there had begun using Civil Conservation Corps workers. Conflict had developed, however, between the architects and the archaeologists in a dispute over who would dig what. The architects were to excavate the building foundations up to an area three feet out from the walls. The rest of the site was to be excavated by the archaeologists. Apparently this led to a rather acrimonious situation with crews almost coming to blows. The National Park Service decided to look for an archaeologist with an architecture background. Harrington fit the bill. When first approached, Pinky said that he was not interested in working for the government and that he did not see much future excavating something that was only 300 years old. The National Park Service sent him a form asking what the minimal acceptable salary would be and Pinky sent it back asking for "$600 more than he though he would ever earn." They offered him the position at that salary, and he accepted. He had to look up Jamestown on the map to see where he was going to be working.

In 1937 Virginia Hall Sutton, a fellow student at the University of Chicago, was employed as a Ranger Historian at Jamestown. Pinky and Virginia were married in 1938. Virginia was the first female Ranger ever hired by the National Park Service. The Harringtons have always worked as a team in sharing their interest in archaeology and using each other as a sounding board. When Pinky arrived at Jamestown, the excavations were sealed off from the public with high board fences. He and Virginia had the fences taken down and began public tours of the sites as well as working out interpretations of the sites for visitors. One of the goals of excavation at Jamestown was to provide work for young unemployed males through the Civil Conservation Corps. This meant that excavation took place at a hectic pace until the beginning of World War II.

In 1938 Pinky finished the excavation of the May-Hartwell site and wrote it up that winter. This was the only Jamestown site to have a complete site report, however, the National Park Service had little interest in publishing the report because they said that they were "not a research institution; that its function was to preserve and interpret." It would not be until 1950 that one of Pinky's reports on Jamestown Island would be published. It was on the excavation of the brick kiln which was published in *The Virginia Magazine of History and Biography*. To overcome this problem, Pinky and Virginia along with other National Park Service employees joined together to found the Eastern National Park and Monument Association in 1948. Virginia Harrington was the first treasurer of the organization. This organization provided funding for publishing postcards and pamphlets on the history and archaeology of National Parks and Monuments. Several of Pinky's archaeological reports were published by the Eastern National Park and Monument Association. Anyone looking through Pinky's publications will be impressed with the wide variety of magazines and journals that he used to reach a broad audience. Today we have national and regional journals which provide readily available places to publish our research. This has been a major improvement, however, we are not reaching the wide audience that Pinky was reaching back in the 1940s and 1950s.

Excavations at Jamestown came to a stop during World War II and Pinky was made Acting Park Superintendent, a position he held until 1946. After the war, Pinky went on to become the Eastern Regional Archeologist for the National Park Service, a position he held until he retired in 1965. With the 1946 promotion, the Harringtons moved to Richmond where they raised a daughter and son. During Pinky's 30 years with the National Park Service, he ran or managed 30 projects in the Eastern Region and 12 outside his region. Among the better known are the Jamestown Glass Works, Fort Raleigh, Fort Necessity, Fort Frederica, Fort Smith, Arkansas Post, and the Appomattox Court House. After retiring, Pinky and Virginia went on to excavate several sites for the Church of Jesus Christ of the Latter-Day Saints (Mormons) in Nauvoo, Illinois, including the Mormon Temple and the Times and Seasons excavated by Virginia Harrington while Pinky was excavating, the Brigham Young Site, and the Edwin Webb Blacksmith shop. After four summers of excavation in Nauvoo, they went on to excavate on Constitution Island for West Point Military Academy.

One of Pinky's major contributions was his article "Dating Stem Fragments of Seventeenth and Eighteenth Century Clay Tobacco Pipes," which was published by the Archaeological Society of Virginia in 1954. Pinky had observed that white clay pipe stem fragments from 17th century sites had larger stem holes than those from 18th century sites. He measured the pipe stem bore diameters from several sites using steel drill bits that were calibrated in 64ths of an inch. These data were presented in a series of histograms that clearly showed that the bore diameter of the pipe stems decreased over time. Lewis Binford took Pinky's data and converted them into a regression formula which is still used to date collections of pipe stem fragments.

In 1952 Pinky published "Historic Site Archaeology in the Unites States," which appeared in a volume dedicated to Fay-Cooper Cole entitled *Archaeology of Eastern United States*. This was the first summary of the field of historical archaeology and some of the problems it faced in the early days when there were very few archaeologists who were excavating historical sites not of the contact period. This was followed in 1955 with the article "Archaeology as an Auxiliary Science to American History" which examined some of the contributions that historical archaeology could make to our understanding of the past. This is one of the earliest articles on historical archaeology in the *American Anthropologist*. Later, in 1965, Pinky published a significant booklet for the Society for State and Local History entitled *Archaeology and the Historical Society*. This was the first publication to give many people outside of archaeology some idea of the types of questions that could be addressed by the emerging field of historical archaeology.

Pinky and Virginia Harrington were very active in helping organize The Society for Historical Archaeology at the first meeting in 1967. As the Society matured and felt the need to recognize those that had made significant contributions to the field, they created the J. C. Harrington Medal in Historical Archaeology in 1982. The first medal was struck in silver and presented to Pinky at the 1982 meeting in Philadelphia. The rest of the metals were struck in bronze. Presentation of the medal at our annual meetings has been an event of great importance and a wonderful vehicle for remembering the major contributions made by J. C. Harrington to the development of historical archaeology.

All of the above contributions fall short in letting us know what Pinky Harrington was like. I had the good fortune to be his lab manager for three years in Nauvoo, Illinois which gave me some insights into Pinky. He was always very organized and well prepared. For example, he gave me all of the information I would need to write this obituary several years ago. Nothing was ever said about writing the obituary, but we had an understanding that I would be the one to write it. His excavations were very orderly, as were his field notes and drawings which were models of clarity. Pinky did not like clutter or disorder. He and Virginia lived simple lives with minimal material possessions. When he retired from the National Park Service, he gave away most of his professional library. After their family was raised, the Harringtons sold their house and moved into an apartment in Richmond which made it easier to travel and take on projects like Nauvoo. After retirement, Pinky and Virginia traveled to more than 101 countries visiting archaeological and historical sites. One of their favorite tours was the single malt distilleries in Scotland. They had a very nice collection of single malt scotches to share with their guests.

Pinky did not bear fools well. One summer, in Nauvoo, we were putting up a sun shelter over a feature that Pinky was getting ready to draw. A crew member was holding one of the shelter poles waiting for instructions. Pinky said "Well Jack, we could do three things here: you could tie the pole off; you could let it fall; or you could hold it up for the rest of the day. What do you think we ought to do Jack?" His responses encouraged those working for him to find solutions before being asked some questions that would point out the obvious. Pinky was a modest man. He was hired by Nauvoo Restoration in Illinois because of his reputation. The person advising the restoration told him that he was one of the top three archaeologists in the United States. Pinky heard the guides at Nauvoo telling groups of tourists that he was one of the top three historical archaeologists but asked them to stop doing so because he felt that it was improper. He rarely talked about himself and one had to ask direct questions to get him to divulge his role in the development of the field. This was not due to shyness, he was a very focused person and generally concentrated on what was to be done at the moment and what needed to be done to complete whatever project was at hand. The National Park Service was very fortunate to have Pinky Harrington to develop their program. This was recognized in 1952 when they gave him the Citation for Distinguished Service from the Office of the Secretary of the Interior. This award is usually given to high ranking government officials or as a posthumous award to recognize major contributions. One wonders what Pinky's contribution would have been if he had been a university professor. Clearly he would have had students, however, he may not have ever discovered historical archaeology, which would have deprived the field of historical archaeology of a founding father.

GEORGE L. MILLER

BIBLIOGRAPHY OF
J. C. HARRINGTON

PUBLISHED WORKS

HARRINGTON, J. C.

1938   Report on the Excavations of Mount Bo1:1. *The Missouri Archaeologists* 4(1):1-11.

1940   Partnership at Jamestown. *The Regional Review* 5(2-3):3-6.

1946   Interpreting Jamestown to the Visitor. *The Museum News*, 24(11):7-8.

1949   America's First Glass Factory. *Antiques* 56(5):361-363.

1949   The Finding of Fort Raleigh. *Southern Indian Studies* 1(1):18-19.

1949   Archaeological Exploration of Fort Raleigh. *The North Carolina Historical Review* 26(2):127-149.

1950   Seventeenth Century Brickmaking and Tilemaking at Jamestown, Virginia. *The Virginia Magazine of History and Biography* 58(1):16-37.

1951   Some Delft Tiles Found at Jamestown. *Antiques* 59(1):36-37

1951   Tobacco Pipes from Jamestown. *Quarterly Bulletin, Archaeological Society of Virginia* 5(4):1-8.

1951   An Olde Iron Sickle from Fort Raleigh, North Carolina. *The Iron Worker* 15(3):12-15.

1952   *Glassmaking at Jamestown.* The Dietz Press, Richmond, VA.

1952   Historic Site Archaeology in the United States. In *Archaeology of Eastern United States*, edited by James B. Griffin, pp. 335-344. University of Chicago Press, Chicago.

1953   Archaeology and Local History. *Indiana Magazine of History* 49(1):69-79.

1954   Fort Necessity—Scene of George Washington's First Battle. *Journal of the Society of Architectural Historians* 13(2):25-27.

1954   Fort Raleigh, 1585. *Journal of the Society of Architectural Historians* 13(4):27-28. Reprinted 1955 in *Southern Architect*, June:19-21.

1954   The Metamorphosis of Fort Necessity. *The Western Pennsylvania Historical Magazine* 37(3 & 4):181-188.

1954   Dating Stem Fragments of Seventeenth and Eighteenth Century Clay Tobacco Pipes. *Quarterly Bulletin of the Archaeological Society of Virginia* 9(1)10-14.

1955   Archaeology as an Auxiliary Science to American History. *American Anthropologist* 57(6):1121-1130.

1956   Evidence of Manual Reckoning in the Cittie of Raleigh. *The North Carolina Historical Review* 33(1):1-11.

1957   *New Light on Washington's Fort Necessity: A Report on the Archaeological Explorations at Fort Necessity National Battlefield Site.* Eastern National Park and Monument Association, Richmond, VA.

1957   The Tools of America's First Glass Blowers. *The Chronicle of the Early American Industries Association* 10(1):2.

1959   Some Lessons from Archaeology. In *The Present World of History*, pp. 70-75. The American Association for State and Local History, Nashville, TN.

1962   Search for the Cittie of Raleigh. Archeological Excavations at Fort Raleigh National Historic Site, North Carolina. National Park Service, *Archeological Research Series* No. 6. Washington.

1965   *Archaeology and the Historical Society.* The American Association for State and Local History, Nashville, TN.

1966   *An Outwork at Fort Raleigh. Further Archeological Excavation at Fort Raleigh National Historic Site, North Carolina.* Eastern National Park and Monument Association, Richmond, VA.

1967   The Manufacture and Use of Bricks at the Raleigh Settlement on Roanoke Island. *The North Carolina Historical Review* 44(1):1-17.

1968   Review of *Post-Medieval Archaeology*, Vol. 1, No. 1. *Historical Archaeology* 2:115-116.

1972 *A Tryal of Glasse-The Story of Glassmaking at Jamestown*. Revision of *Glassmaking at Jamestown*. The Dietz Press, Richmond, VA.

1976 The Puzzle of Washington's Fort Necessity. *Archaeology* 29(3):178-185.

1977 The Churchyard Wall at Christ Church. *Discovery* 9(2):7-10

1979 Romans Battery: Early Revolutionary War Fortifications. *Pennsylvania Archaeologists* 49(3):31-41.

1979 The Importance of Interpretation in Historical Archaeology. *North American Archaeologist* 1(1):75-84.

1984 *Archaeology and the Enigma of Fort Raleigh*. The Division of Archives and History, State of North Carolina, Raleigh, NC.

1984 Jamestown Archaeology in Retrospect. In *The Scope of Historical Archaeology* edited by David G. Orr and Daniel G. Crozier, pp. 29-51. Occasional Publications of the Department of Anthropology, Temple University, Philadelphia, PA.

1994 From Architraves to Artifacts. *Pioneers in Historical Archaeology: Breaking New* Ground, edited by Stanley South, pp. 1-14. Plenum Press, New York.

1997 The Mules Knew the Way. *Historical Archaeology* 31(4):5-14

HARRINGTON, J. C., ALBERT C. MANUCY, AND JOHN GOGGIN

1955 Archaeological Excavations in the Courtyard of Castillo de San Marcos, St. Augustine, Florida. *The Florida Historical Quarterly* 34(2):101-141. Reprinted by St. Augustine Historical Society, *Bulletin* 1. St. Augustine, FL.

HARRINGTON, VIRGINIA AND J.C. HARRINGTON

1971 *Rediscovery of the Nauvoo Temple*. Nauvoo Restoration Inc., Salt Lake City, UT

MANUSCRIPT REPORTS

HARRINGTON, J. C.

1936-38 Jamestown Archeological Project, Narrative Reports. Manuscript, curator's office, Colonial National Historical Park, Jamestown, VA.

1937 Jamestown Archeological Project, Policies and Objectives, General Long-Range Program Recommendations. Final Revision. Manuscript, curator's office, Colonial National Historical Park, Jamestown, VA.

1938 Colonial National Historic Park, Jamestown Archeological Project, Progress Report, Archeological Field Work, 1938 Season. Manuscript, library, Colonial National Historical Park, Yorktown, VA.

1938 Summary of Documentary Data on the William May-Henry Hartwell Property Preparatory to its Excavation. Manuscript, NPS files, Colonial National Park, Jamestown, VA.

1939 Monthly Narrative Reports and Technicians' Reports-1939. Manuscript, curator's office, Colonial National Historical Park, Jamestown, VA.

1940 Monthly Narrative Reports and Technicians' Reports, 1940. Manuscript, curator's office, Colonial National Historical Park, Jamestown, VA.

1940 Archeological Report May-Hartwell Site, Jamestown, Virginia. Manuscript, permanent file, Colonial National Historical Park, Yorktown, VA.

1940 Field and Laboratory Guide for Recording Archeological Data, revised edition. Manuscript, Colonial National Historical Park, Jamestown, VA.

1940 Archeological Site Report on Occaneechee Island, Virginia; Theme: Woodland Pattern, Siouan Tribes of the Middle Atlantic Area; Mecklenburg County, Virginia. Manuscript, permanent file, Colonial National Historical Park, Yorktown, VA.

1940 Monthly Report for the Superintendent for the Jamestown Archeological Project for September, 1940. Manuscript, curator's office, Colonial National Historical Park, Jamestown, VA.

1941 Monthly Report for the Superintendent for Jamestown Archeological Project. Manuscript, curator's office, Colonial National Historical Park, Jamestown, VA.

1941 Archeological Report, Exploratory Excavations in Unit A, Jamestown Island, Virginia. Manuscript, permanent file, Colonial National Historical Park, Yorktown, VA.

1941   The Elay-Swann Report, Jamestown Island, Virginia. Preliminary Historical Study and Archeological Report on the 1937 Exploratory Excavations. Manuscript, Colonial National Historical Park, Yorktown, VA.

1941   Preservation vs. Restoration of Historic Sites. Manuscript, curator's office, Colonial National Historical Park, Jamestown, VA.

1941   Monthly Narrative Report for the Jamestown Archeological Project. Manuscript, permanent file, Colonial National Historical Park, Yorktown, VA.

1942(?) The Appendix. Includes data upon the composition of various kinds of glass made in the Early Colonial period of the United States of America. Manuscript, curator's office, Colonial National Historical Park, Jamestown, VA.

1942   Stabilization of Structure 6, Jamestown Island, Virginia. Manuscript, curator's office, Colonial National Historical Park, Jamestown, VA.

1942   Yorktown Artifacts and Museum Materials Stored, February, 1942 in the Jamestown Archeological Laboratory, Jamestown Island, Virginia. Manuscript, artifacts information file, Colonial National Historical Park, Yorktown, VA.

1942   Progress Report on the 1941 Excavations in the Grounds of the Association for the Preservation of Virginia Antiquities, Jamestown Island, Virginia. Colonial National Historical Park, Jamestown, Special Report. Manuscript, curator's office, permanent file-Yorktown, No. 740-02, Colonial National Historical Park, Jamestown, VA.

1947   Archeological Investigations at Grace Church, Yorktown, Virginia. Manuscript, permanent file, Colonial National Historical Park, Yorktown, VA.

1949   Mr. V. C. Swicker's file on Dr. Walter J. Sparks. Includes Correspondence on Colonial American Glass. Manuscript, curator's office, Colonial National Historical Park, Jamestown VA.

1949   Archeological Exploration of the Area to be Used for Sewage Disposal Field in the Grounds of the Association for the Preservation of Virginia Antiquities, Jamestown Island, Virginia. Manuscript, permanent file-Yorktown No. 740-02., Colonial National Historical Park, Yorktown, VA.

1949   Preliminary Report, Archeological Explorations at Glass House Point, Jamestown, Virginia. Manuscript, curator's office, Colonial National Historical Park, Jamestown VA.

1950   The Jamestown Glass Factory, Pictorial Record of the Archeological Excavations. Manuscript, curator's office, Colonial National Historical Park, Jamestown VA.

1951   Records for the Stabilization of Structure 6, Jamestown Island, Virginia. Manuscript, Colonial National Historical Park, Jamestown VA.

1953   Report on Stabilization of Structure 31, Jamestown, Virginia. Manuscript, permanent file Yorktown No. 740-03, Colonial National Historical Park, Yorktown, VA.

1963   Report on Archeological Testing at Fort Raleigh. Manuscript, Cape Hatteras National Seashore, Manteo, NC.

1965   Salvage Exploration at For Raleigh: 1963-1965. Manuscript, Cape Hatteras National Seashore, Manteo, NC.

1967   Archaeological Excavations at the Wilford Woodruff Site (106-1). Manuscript, Nauvoo Restoration Inc., Salt Lake City, UT.

1968   Archaeological Excavations at the Brigham Young Site (126-2). Manuscript, Nauvoo Restoration Inc., Salt Lake City, UT.

1969   Archaeological Excavations at the Webb Blacksmith and Wagon Shop (127-4). Manuscript, Nauvoo Restoration Inc., Salt Lake City, UT.

1972   Report on the Excavations of Revolutionary War Fortifications on Constitution Island, West Point Military Academy. Manuscript, West Point Military Academy Archives, West Point, NY.

1987   Digging up My Past. Manuscript, autobiography written for the Harrington family and held by the family.

HARRINGTON, J. C. AND CONRAD BENTZEN

1941   Monthly Narrative Reports and Archeological Technician's Reports. June-December 1941: Harrington, and February 1941-January 1942: Bentzen. Manuscript, Colonial National Historical Park, Jamestown VA.

MEMORIAL: John L. Cotter, 1911-1999. Volume 33, Number 4 (1999): 6-18. By Daniel G. Roberts.

Memorial

JOHN L. COTTER, 1911-1999

John L. Cotter, one of the pioneers of North American historical archaeology, died on 5 February 1999 after a short battle with lymphoma. He had celebrated his 87th birthday two months prior to his passing and his 58th wedding anniversary the day before. He is survived by his wife, Virginia Tomlin Cotter, a daughter, Jean Spaans, a son, Laurence, three grandsons and one great-granddaughter.

John Lambert Cotter was born on 6 December 1911, in Denver, Colorado, the only surviving offspring of John Aloysius Cotter and Bertha Becker Cotter. He was christened John Aloysius Cotter, Jr., but later (1936) legally changed his middle name to Lambert. His father had a job installing PBXs (private branch exchanges) throughout the west, thus young "Jack," as he was called in those days, moved many times in his early years. Between 1912 and 1930, he variously lived and went to school in Denver; Butte, Helena, and Livingston, Montana; Spokane, Washington; and La Mesa, California. In June 1930, John graduated from East Denver High School (where he was a classmate of H. Marie Wormington) as a National Honor Society student. He had also been the editor of his high school newspaper "The Spotlight," and this experience led him to his first paying job, working the night shift in the summer of 1930 for the Associated Press at the Rocky Mountain News office in Denver. At this point in his life, John had every expectation of pursuing journalism as a career but, as fate would have it, this was not to be.

In September 1930, with a one-half year tuition scholarship in hand, John enrolled at the University of Denver where he began coursework in English and journalism. He soon began to sour on journalism as a career and, by chance, took a course or two in anthropology. At that time, the Anthropology Department at the University of Denver consisted of one man, E. B. Renaud. Renaud ran an archaeological field school every summer in the Santa Fe area, and John enrolled in the summers of 1932 and 1933. By the beginning of his second field school season, the archaeology "bug" had bitten and John switched his major to anthropology. In 1934 he was awarded his Bachelor of Arts degree in anthropology. That summer, he got his first paying job in "archaeology," working in Weld County, Colorado at a fossil bed excavation for the Colorado Museum of Natural History. He also continued his studies and was awarded the Master of Arts degree in anthropology from the University of Denver in June 1935. His thesis, *Yuma and Folsom Artifacts*, is essentially a treatise on the then-known distributions of Paleoindian artifact types in the Rocky Mountain west.

During this period John met Jesse D. Figgins, Director of the Colorado Museum of Natural History. In the summer of 1935, Figgins asked John if he would head a field party for the Colorado Museum of Natural History at the Lindenmeier Site, a Folsom site located in Larimer County, Colorado. Here, John worked alongside Frank H. H. Roberts, who was in charge of another field party at Lindenmeier under the auspices of the Smithsonian Institution. Through his acquaintance with Roberts, he met other well-known archaeologists and anthropologists, including Edgar B. Howard and Frank Speck, both from the University of Pennsylvania in Philadelphia. With the help of Speck, John landed a Harrison Fellowship at the University of Pennsylvania, and he enrolled there in the fall of 1935 to pursue his doctorate in anthropology as an unpaid graduate assistant to Speck, taking courses with both Speck and A. Irving Hallowell.

In the summer of 1936, Howard asked John if he would head up an excavation at the Clovis type-site, and John readily said "yes." So, together with C. T. R. Bohannon, John drove to New Mexico from Philadelphia in Bohannon's 1928 Ford roadster to work at Clovis, where he served as chief-of-party in Howard's absence. He wound up the field season of 1936 back at Lindenmeier working with the Smithsonian party, and completed a second field season at Clovis in the summer of 1937 under Howard's direction. Upon his return to Penn that fall, Howard magnanimously asked John if he would like to write up the results of the two field seasons at Clovis. This led to John's first professional publication, a report on the 1936 field season entitled "The Occurrence of Flints and Extinct Animals in Pluvial Deposits Near Clovis, New Mexico," published in 1937 in the *Proceedings of the Academy of Natural Sciences of Philadelphia*. It was followed by a report on the 1937 field season, published in the same *Proceedings* in 1938. It was also during this period that John met Virginia Wilkins Tomlin, Howard's secretary, who was later to become John's wife.

Meanwhile, John had completed his doctoral coursework at Penn, took his oral examinations and, in his own words, "busted them flat" (Roberts 1999:13). Through his connections with Jesse Figgins, who by then had moved to Lexington, Kentucky, John was offered a job working for William S. Webb under the auspices of the Works Progress Administration (WPA) in Kentucky. John accepted, and in the winter of 1937 he moved to Lexington. Shortly after his arrival, John was sent to Island, Kentucky, where he headed up a crew of about 40 out-of-work coal miners excavating a small burial mound. By the fall of 1938, John had been named State Supervisor of the Survey, and he moved back to Lexington where, working with William G. Haag, his job was to coordinate as many as 250 men on 11 WPA field teams excavating sites throughout Kentucky. He also traveled at least once to the WPA office in Washington to hand-process the paperwork necessary to keep the Kentucky projects going, and to keep the men on the crews continuously employed.

In early 1940, John was told that a Civil Service application he had submitted in 1936 had been accepted, and he took a job with the National Park Service that, in various positions and assignments, was to last for the better part of four decades. His first assignment was at Tuzigoot National Monument in Clarkdale, Arizona where he was placed in charge of the archaeological collection, interpretation, and conservation as a "lone post custodian." On 4 February 1941, John Cotter and Virginia Wilkins Tomlin were married in Prescott, Arizona, and set up housekeeping in a small apartment that was part of the museum premises at Tuzigoot. In March 1943, the Cotters' first child, Jean, was born in Jerome, Arizona. John continued his work at Tuzigoot, spending much of his time with National Youth Administration (NYA) youngsters reconstructing and stabilizing the walls of the ruins there. In the fall of 1943, John was inducted into the U.S. Army.

After sending his wife and young daughter home to Philadelphia where they stayed with Virginia's mother and father, John spent 17 weeks in infantry training at Camp Roberts, California. Upon completion of infantry training, John was assigned to Company F, 357th Infantry Regiment of the 90th Division and sent to Exmoor, Devon, where staging for the invasion of Europe was held. Six days after the initial Normandy invasion, John's regiment was deployed into action on-shore, and several days later he was badly wounded in the left leg, for which he was later awarded the Purple Heart. After a period of rehabilitation in England, John continued his military service in the Armed Forces Institute in Paris, where his duties consisted of training instructors how to instruct others. This was followed by a full year in London at the Armed Forces Institute-European Theater of Operations, where he worked on the staff that processed the correspondence of GIs in the field who were trying to complete their schooling. Upon completion of his military service in December 1945, John returned home, where he resumed his National Park Service career at Tuzigoot.

After spending more than a year back at Tuzigoot, and presiding over the birth of his second child, Laurence, at Cottonwood, Arizona, John was transferred in July 1947 to the Natchez Trace Parkway at Tupelo, Mississippi. As Archeologist-in-Charge, he worked at the Hopewellian Bynum Site with John M. Corbett, with whom he later co-authored a major report entitled *Archeology of the Bynum Mounds, Mississippi*, published by the National Park Service in 1951. John also worked at Emerald Mound, the Gordon Site, the Mangum Site, and on a Chickasaw burial during this period, and published several reports of his findings. These reports, for the most part, were completed between 1949 and 1951.

In July 1951, the Cotters moved to Bladensburg, Maryland after John was assigned as Acting Chief Archeologist of the National Park Service in Washington, ironically taking Corbett's place in that role while the latter finished his military service. John served in this position for two years, during which time he was principally involved with policy-making for the Park Service. He also managed to get in a bit of field time during this stint, when he took annual leave in 1952 to excavate at the Van Cortland Manor House on the Hudson River for John D. Rockefeller, Jr. Aside from his earlier excavation of the Chickasaw burial at Natchez Trace, this was John's first hands-on experience in historical archaeology.

In July 1953, John was transferred to Colonial National Historical Park, where he was assigned as Chief Archeologist of excavations at Jamestown in anticipation of the 350th anniversary of that settlement in 1957. In this role, John followed in the footsteps of J. C. "Pinky" Harrington, who had excavated at Jamestown for several seasons in the 1930s and 1940s. At Jamestown, John worked with Edward B. Jelks, Joel Shiner, B. Bruce Powell, J. Paul Hudson, and Louis R. Caywood, among others. It was during this period that the Cotters bought their first house, in Williamsburg, in 1954. In all, John excavated approximately seven miles of trenches at Jamestown, and authored or co-authored several publications on the results, culminating in the publication of *Archeological Excavations at Jamestown, Virginia,* produced by the National Park Service in 1958. The Archeological Society of Virginia published an updated version of his monograph in 1994, and it was this pioneering work at Jamestown in the 1950s that launched John on his way in the newly emerging sub-discipline of historical archaeology.

In July 1957, John was transferred yet again, this time back "home" to Philadelphia, where he was named Regional Archeologist of the Northeast Region. Shortly after his arrival in Philadelphia and some 20 years after his initial departure, John became acquainted with Loren Eiseley, who was on the faculty of the University of Pennsylvania. With Eiseley's encouragement, in the fall of 1957 and at the age of 46, John once again enrolled in Penn's doctoral program. Utilizing weekends, evenings, and leave time to full advantage, John took courses with Alfred Kidder, Ward Goodenough, and Irving Hallowell, who was still at Penn 20 years after John last took coursework with him in 1937. In June 1959, having completed his new suite of courses, passed his oral examinations, and revised his Jamestown publication to be accepted as his dissertation, John was awarded his Ph.D. in anthropology.

Meanwhile, John was still pursuing his full-time career with the Park Service. In this role, he administered dozens of archaeological projects in the Park Service's Northeast Region, which covered nearly one-third of the country, from Virginia to Maine, and Michigan to Missouri. Under John's administration such noted northeastern archaeologists as Jacob Gruber, Barbara Liggett, Vincent Foley, Herbert C. Kraft, Daniel G. Crozier, Edward S. Rutsch, and W. Fred Kinsey III worked under contract in various Park Service holdings in the Northeast Region. Being headquartered in Philadelphia, much of John's attention was focused on Independence National Historical Park, and he conducted or administered numerous archaeological investigations there over a period of more than a decade.

Shortly after he received his doctorate the irrepressible Cotter began another chapter in his life, one that later was to bring him further recognition as one of the pioneering founders of North American historical archaeology. In 1960, Anthony Garvan, who was on the Penn faculty in the Department of American Civilization, invited John to teach a course in historical archaeology. This course, variations of which John taught (or occasionally co-taught with David G. Orr) for 19 years, is now widely recognized as the first course in historical archaeology taught in an American university. It also included field sessions at some of the notable historic landmarks in the Philadelphia region, including Valley Forge, Fort Mifflin, and several locally significant historic houses, estates, and institutions. One of these field sessions resulted in a 1988 publication co-authored with one of John's students and two of his colleagues entitled *The Walnut Street Prison Workshop*. Amazingly, John was able to juggle his teaching with his full-time Park Service job, largely by taking annual leave from the Park Service and conducting field sessions on weekends and whenever he could fit them in. Several well-established historical archaeologists, including Betty Cosans-Zebooker, Paul Huey, and Garry Wheeler Stone, among others, were first introduced to historical archaeology through John's classes. Ironically, John did not believe he was a very good teacher, saying in a recent interview (Roberts 1999:39) "the fact of it is that I was a rotten teacher. . . ." Modesty was one of John's most endearing character traits and in spite of his contention, legions of former students and colleagues would respectfully but adamantly disagree with this self-effacing appraisal.

During the 1960s John found time to engage in several other professional activities, his demanding schedules at the Park Service and at Penn notwithstanding. In 1962 he began work on a bibliography of historic sites archaeology which, in its initial version, was published in microfiche by University Microfilms, Inc. in 1966. This bibliography was greatly expanded over the years with the help of William D. Hershey, Roderick Sprague, and Ronald L. Michael, and it can now be found on line at the SHA's website. John also found time during this period to produce a little-known but extremely useful booklet entitled *Handbook for Historical Archaeology, Part I*, privately published by John in 1968. This booklet provided a compendium of information on artifact types that the archaeologist was likely to encounter on historic archaeological sites. Much to his everlasting regret, he never found the time to follow up this initial effort with "Part II." John also found time in the mid-to-late 1960s to have a major hand in the founding of The Society for Historical Archaeology. Indeed, he was the first president of the society and the second editor of the journal *Historical Archaeology*. He also produced a small booklet entitled *Above Ground Archaeology*, published in 1974. This booklet was written to promote an appreciation for artifacts and memorabilia by the American public.

In 1977, after a 35-year career interrupted only by military service, John retired from the National Park Service. Given the Park Service's enduring penchant for periodic reorganization, and aside from his stints at Tuzigoot, Natchez Trace, and Jamestown, John served the NPS in several capacities, including Acting Chief Archeologist in Washington (1951-1953); Regional Archeologist, Northeast Region (1957-1970); Archeologist, Eastern U.S., Eastern Service Center (1970-1972); Archeologist, Denver Service Center, based in Philadelphia (1972-1974); and Regional Archeologist, Mid-Atlantic Region (1974-1977). In 1979, John officially retired from the faculty at Penn, having held the title of Adjunct Associate Professor in the Department of American Civilization for 19 years. He also held the title of Curator in American Historical Archaeology, University of Pennsylvania Museum from 1972 until 1980, and Curator Emeritus thereafter until his death. In the latter capacity John still maintained an office at Penn and worked half-days there, taking care of correspondence, writing, and counseling students until about a week before he died.

In 1983, Daniel G. Roberts and Michael Parrington joined forces with John and began work on *The Buried Past: An Archaeological History of Philadelphia,* ultimately published in 1992 by the University of Pennsylvania Press. This book synthesized all of the major historic archaeological research undertaken in the Philadelphia region through 1989, and built upon a little-known unpublished manuscript written by John in 1967 (Cotter 1967). The published book, while updated to include more than 20 years of additional archaeological research in Philadelphia, nevertheless bears the unmistakable *imprimatur* of John's earlier unpublished effort.

In addition to the books and monographs noted above, John published more than 130 articles and reviews on a wide variety of topics during his career. In his later years he was a regular contributor to *Archaeology* Magazine's Forum series. Based on the positive responses to *The Buried Past,* he and David Orr in 1994 began planning *The Archaeology of Great American Cities* series which, as the title implies, is to be a series of books on the archaeology of several American cities published by the University of Pennsylvania Press. Volumes for New York, Denver, Boston, Washington, St. Louis, Mexico City, and San Francisco were planned to be written by specialists and edited by Cotter and Orr. At the time of John's passing, the volume on Denver was nearing completion. In his later years John also took an interest in gerontology from an anthropological perspective; one of his last publications, appearing in the *Occasional Papers of the Association of Senior Anthropologists,* is entitled "Keeping in Focus Before and After Retirement." In keeping with this interest in gerontology, John served for several years as a member or officer of the resident's association council of the retirement community in Philadelphia where Virginia and he lived since 1984.

John was an active supporter of a great many professional organizations and societies throughout his career. He became a Charter Member of the Society for American Archaeology in 1935 and a Life Member of The Society for Historical Archaeology in 1984. He also became a member of the Society of Professional Archaeologists (SOPA) at a time when it was not fashionable to do so, and when he hardly needed the credential. He was an ardent supporter of the transformation of SOPA to the Register of Professional Archaeologists (RPA). He was a Fellow of the American Association for the Advancement of Science and the American Anthropological Association, a Stockholder in the Athenaeum of Philadelphia, and a Life Member of the Archaeological Institute of America. He also served as an editorial advisor for *Archaeology* Magazine from 1967 until his death. He was a Charter Member of the Society for Industrial Archaeology, and actively supported the National Trust for Historic Preservation and more than a dozen regional, state, and local organizations. In short, John deeply believed in his chosen profession and allied fields, and his long-term support of so many organizations amply demonstrated this commitment.

In recognition of his long and distinguished career, John was the recipient of numerous awards and honors. Among the most noteworthy are the J. Alden Mason Award of the Society for Pennsylvania Archaeology (1974); the Outstanding Service Award of the National Park Service (1977); the David E. Finley Award for Outstanding Achievement in Historic Preservation in the United States bestowed by the National Trust for Historic Preservation (1978); the Out-of-State Archaeologist of the Year Award presented by the Archaeological Society of Virginia (1984); and the J. C. Harrington Medal in Historical Archaeology of The Society for Historical Archaeology (Anonymous 1984). He was also honored by the publication of a *festschrift* 15 years ago (Orr and Crozier 1984) which brought together in one volume 11 papers by former students and colleagues. In celebration of his 80th birthday in 1991, John was the guest of honor at a symposium at the University of Pennsylvania Museum, entitled *Digging Philadelphia: The Archaeology of a City* in which several of his colleagues presented papers. Moreover, in recognition of his pioneering teaching achievements and for his "equally important life-long record of involvement with and enthusiastic support for each new generation of people entering the discipline" (Schuyler 1999:2), The Society for Historical Archaeology named the John L. Cotter Award in Historical Archaeology in his honor at its 1999 annual meeting in Salt Lake City. Shortly after his death the National Park Service established an award in John's name "to recognize a specific archeological project within a unit of the National Park System, conducted by Park Service staff, permitee, or consultant, and guided by senior Park Service staff archeologist(s), each fiscal year . . ." (National Park Service 1999).

John's career came full-circle in a fitting way, almost as if he had choreographed it. Just three days after his death, on 8 February 1999, his last publication, *Clovis Revisited: New Perspectives on Paleoindian Adaptations from Blackwater Draw, New Mexico*, co-authored with Anthony T. Boldurian, went to press, bringing his career-long passion for Paleoindian manifestations in the Americas to completion. Remarkably, John was able to see a mock-up of the book's cover, since published by the University of Pennsylvania Museum in April 1999, only hours before he died. His comment on seeing the cover was "Marvelous!" (A. T. Boldurian pers. comm. 1999).

While John most certainly was deeply passionate about the past, he never lost sight of the relevance of both the present and future. In 1967, in the aforementioned unpublished monograph on Philadelphia's archaeology, he (Cotter 1967[Preface]:2) had this to say about perspective, in which he somewhat prophetically anticipated the post-processual heyday of the late 1980s and 1990s:

> Perspective is heady stuff in this life and not for the good and easy man or matron who sees life as the same today, yesterday, and forever. . . . The products of the present are the archaeological specimens of the future, and all this growth and change in nation and city is a matter of history. Future centuries will further document the record (always reinterpreted by new generations in their own perspective) with archaeology. For artifacts and tastes and activities so revealed do not lie. The more accurately they are interpreted, the better the future can verify the past.

John was blessed with an intellect that at once was poetic as well as visionary. In 1967, at a time when few American archaeologists were contemplating archaeology in and of the city (with all due respect to the late Bert Salwen and a few others), he had this to say about the nature of cities and urban archaeology (Cotter 1967[V]:1):

> Of all the jungles which have ever hidden the works of man, the most formidable is the concrete jungle. This peculiarly human blight upon the land . . . lives by devouring itself continually. There is never a moment when some part of it is not being battered by iron balls, shattered, bulldozed and carted away until leveled, only to be gouged deep into the earth beneath and a new growth encouraged to reach into the air. . . . New growth is doomed from birth to vanish before newer growth, which in turn gives way to the newest growth . . . [but] among the roots of this jungle of metals and masonry, between deep multiple cellars, interrupted constantly by subways, utility conduits, sewers, street foundations and sunken expressways, are interspersed remnants of the past. Here a stone bridge 30 feet beneath the surface still spans a fossil creek which was filled in two centuries ago, [and] there a well, dry since the Revolution and choked with the debris of the last days of the 18th century . . . [in] its neat, circular brick casing.

John's career spanned more than six decades, and his archaeological and anthropological interests were as broad as his career was long. His dedication to excellence inspired several generations of students and fellow professionals, and his many contributions to his chosen profession reflected his wide-ranging interests. Moreover, he was a modest, generous, and compassionate man who always enjoyed sharing his vision of the world with others, and always with a smile on his face and a twinkle in his eye. He was also a consummate gentleman and a gentle and genteel man, an ardent optimist who viewed each day as another opportunity to learn and a master at challenging others never to cease learning. As testimony to his passion for learning, John's voluminous compilation of notes taken at lectures, conferences, and field trips throughout his life has become the stuff of legend among those who knew him well. In his own words, "I've always been a witness rather than a creator. . . . I have always been fascinated with observing, first, how people in prehistory and history . . . lived their various lifeways, and second, how anthropologists and archaeologists have responded to . . . interpretative challenge" (Roberts 1999:40).

John's love of poetry, and in particular the poetry of T. S. Eliot, was never far from his thoughts as he wrote about archaeological topics. He concluded his 1967 unpublished manuscript with the following passage (Cotter 1967[XVI]:5):

The scientist can explain it all, but he too often writes a labored language. The poet must be as perceptive and as precise as the scientist, only he must express himself with supreme clarity and communicate universally. The final word for the archaeologist has been said with beauty by T. S. Eliot in his Four Quartets:
"We shall not cease from exploration
And the end of all our exploring
Will be to arrive where we started
And know the place for the first time."

There can be no more fitting epitaph for the richly textured life and career of John L. Cotter than this, his favorite stanza by his favorite poet.

ACKNOWLEDGMENTS

I gratefully acknowledge the assistance of several people in helping me compile information on the life and career of John L. Cotter. First, to Virginia Tomlin Cotter, Laurence Cotter, and Jean Spaans, my heartfelt gratitude for taking the time to review and correct errors in the manuscript at a time when they were still grieving their loss. To Helen Schenck, my thanks for tracking down the photograph of John from the University of Pennsylvania Museum archives. The photograph is used through the courtesy of University of Pennsylvania Museum of Archaeology and Anthropology, H. Fred Schoch, photographer. Allen Cooper made available to me a listing of John's unpublished reports from his National Park Service career, and the accompanying bibliography could not have been completed without this huge assist from Allen. David Orr kindly provided me with information on the Park Service's newly established award in John's name, and made several suggestions to improve the accuracy of the manuscript. Likewise, Anthony Boldurian reviewed and made corrections to the manuscript and, although we had never met until after John's death, our shared reminiscences of a close friend and colleague provided us both with strength and comfort over the ensuing months. Rebecca Yamin also reviewed the manuscript and made several suggestions for its improvement. Margy Schoettle expertly assisted me with word processing and editing chores, a not so insignificant task considering the sheer number of bibliographic entries that encompass John's career. Finally, I am grateful that I had the opportunity to know and work closely with John for more than a decade. He was an unparalleled source of personal and professional inspiration for me, and I will forever remember his unfailing courtesy, generosity, sense of humor, and wise counsel.

REFERENCES

ANONYMOUS
1984 J. C. Harrington Medal in Historical Archaeology: John L. Cotter, 1984. *Historical Archaeology*, 18(2):1-3.

COTTER, JOHN L.
1967 The Friendly Underground: An Archaeological View of Philadelphia. Manuscript, University of Pennsylvania Museum of Archaeology and Anthropology, Philadelphia.

NATIONAL PARK SERVICE
1999 Proposal: An Annual Award in Recognition of Dr. John L. Cotter's Contributions Toward Professional Archeology Within the National Park System. Manuscript, Valley Forge National Historical Park, Valley Forge, PA.

ORR, DAVID G., AND DANIEL G. CROZIER (EDITORS)
1984 *The Scope of Historical Archaeology: Essays in Honor of John L. Cotter*. Laboratory of Anthropology, Temple University, Philadelphia, PA.

ROBERTS, DANIEL G.
1999 A Conversation with John L. Cotter. *Historical Archaeology*, 33(2):6-50.

SCHUYLER, ROBERT L.
1999 John L. Cotter Award in Historical Archaeology. *Historical Archaeology*, 33(2):1-5.

Daniel G. Roberts

BIBLIOGRAPHY OF JOHN L. COTTER

PUBLISHED WORKS

COTTER, JOHN L.

1937 The Occurrence of Flints and Extinct Animals in Pluvial Deposits Near Clovis, New Mexico: Part IV, Report on Excavations at the Gravel Pit, 1936. *Proceedings of the Academy of Natural Sciences of Philadelphia*, 89:1-16. Philadelphia, PA.

1937 Introduction to Early Man. *Frontiers* 1(1). Philadelphia, PA.

1937 Digging—The Search for the First American. *Frontiers*, 2(1):16-18. Philadelphia, PA.

1937 The Significance of Folsom and Yuma Artifact Occurrences in the Light of Typology and Distribution. Philadelphia Anthropological Society, *Twenty-Fifth Anniversary Studies*, pp. 27-35. Philadelphia, PA.

1938 The Occurrence of Flints and Extinct Animals in Pluvial Deposits near Clovis, New Mexico: Part VI, Report on Field Season of 1937. *Proceedings of the Academy of Natural Sciences of Philadelphia*, 90:113-117. Philadelphia, PA.

1945 Tuzigoot National Monument. In Arizona's National Monuments. *Southwestern Monuments Association Popular Series*, 2. Santa Fe, NM.

1948 Archeological Survey of Bynum Site, Chickasaw County. *The Journal of Mississippi History*, 10(2):116-118.

1949 Archeological Survey of Emerald Mound. *The Journal of Mississippi History*, 11(1):65-66.

1949 Archeological Survey of the Natchez Trace Parkway. *Southern Indian Studies*, 1(2).

1950 The Miller Pottery Types in Review. *Southern Indian Studies*, 2(1):25-29.

1950 Prehistoric Peoples Along the Natchez Trace. *The Journal of Mississippi History*, 12(4):231-237.

1951 Review of *Ancient Man in North America* by H. M. Wormington. *American Anthropologist*, 53(1):117-118.

1951 Dr. Monette's Observations on Emerald Mound. *The Journal of Mississippi History*, 13(1):31-40.

1951 Stratigraphic and Area Tests at the Emerald and Anna Mound Sites. *American Antiquity*, 17(1):18-32.

1951 Review of *The Wulfing Plates—Products of Prehistoric Americans* by Virginia Drew Watson. *American Antiquity*, 17(2):160.

1952 The Mangum Plate. *American Antiquity*, 18(1):65-68.

1952 The Gordon Site in Southern Mississippi. *American Antiquity*, 18(2):110-126.

1953 Review of *A Bone Industry from the Lower Bann* by C. Blake Whelan. *American Anthropologist*, 55(2):276.

1953 Review of *Early Man in the Eden Valley* by John H. Moss. *American Journal of Archaeology*, 57:52-53.

1953 Salvaging Prehistory. In *Story of Our Time for 1953*, pp. 302-304. The Grolier Society.

1954 Indications of a Paleo-Indian Co-Tradition for North America. *American Antiquity*, 20(1):54-57.

1954 Review of *The Jonathan Creek Village, Site 4, Marshall County, Kentucky* by William S. Webb. *American Antiquity*, 20(2):182-183.

1955 Archeological Progress at James Citty, on Jamestown Island. *Quarterly Bulletin of the Archeological Society of Virginia*, 10(1).

1955 Indians and Pioneers, America's First Tourists. *National Parks Magazine*, 29(121):75.

1956 Winter Archaeology: To Freeze or Not to Freeze. *American Antiquity*, 22(2):180.

1957 Excavations at Jamestown, Virginia. *Antiquity*, 31(121):19-24.

1957 Jamestown: Treasure in the Earth. *Antiques*, 71(1):44-46.

1957 Rediscovering Jamestown. *Archaeology*, 10(1):25-30.

1958 Archeological Excavations at Jamestown, Virginia. National Park Service, *Archeological Research Series*, 4. Washington, DC.

1959 Review of *The Pool and Irving Villages: A Study of Hopewell Occupation in the Illinois River Valley* by John C. McGregor. *American Anthropologist*, 61(2):336-337.

1960 Digging an Historical Shrine: Philadelphia's Independence Park. *Expedition*, 2(3):28-32.

1960 Review of *Indians of the High Plains from the Prehistoric Period to the Coming of Europeans* by George E. Hyde. *The William and Mary Quarterly*, 17(3):417-418.

1961 Review of *The Archeology of the Childersburg Site, Alabama* by David L. DeJarnette and Asael T. Hansen. *American Antiquity*, 26(4):573-574.

1961 Review of *Hidden America* by Roland Wells Robbins and Evan Jones. *Archaeology*, 14(3):121-122.

1961 Foreword to Symposium on Salvage. *Archaeology*, 14(4):230.

1962 Commentary on *The Paleo-Indian Tradition in Eastern North America* by Ronald J. Mason. *Current Anthropology*, 3(3):250-252.

1962 Perils and Pleasures of Historic Sites Archaeology. *Southeastern Archaeological Conference Newsletter*, 9(1):46-49.

1962 Report on the Symposium on Pleasures and Problems of Historic Sites Archaeology. *Eastern States Archaeological Federation Bulletin*, 21(11-12).

1962 Compiler, Symposium on Historic Sites Archaeology. *American Antiquity*, 27(4):207-609.

1962-1970 Compiler, Current Research: Northeast. *American Antiquity*.

1963 Review of *The Fort at Frederica* by Albert C. Mauncy. *American Antiquity*, 28(3):404.

1963 Review of *The Quest for Nonsuch* by John Dent. *Archaeology*, 16(1):66.

1963 Review of *Johnny Ward's Ranch: A Study in Historic Archaeology* by Bernard L. Fontana and J. Cameron Greenleaf. *Archaeology*, 16(4):301.

1963   Commentary on *The Upper Palaeolithic and the New World* by E. F. Greenman. *Current Anthropology*, 4(1):69-70.

1964   Review of *Here Lies Virginia, An Archaeologist's View of Colonial Life and History* by Ivor Noël Hume. *Archaeology*, 17(3):212-213.

1965   Review of *Trade Castles and Forts of West Africa* by A. W. Lawrence. *Archaeology*, 18(4):316.

1965-1981   Editor, Current Research: Northeast. *Newsletter of The Society for Historical Archaeology*.

1966   *Bibliography of Historical Sites Archaeology*, University Microfilms, Ann Arbor, MI.

1966   Commentary on *Pre-Folsom Estimates of the Age of Man in America*. *American Anthropologist*, 68(1):196-198.

1966   Review of *A 1715 Spanish Treasure Ship* by Carl J. Clausen. *American Antiquity*, 31(4):591-592.

1967   Progress on a Chapbook and Bibliography for Historical Sites Archaeology. *The Conference on Historic Site Archaeology Papers 1965-1966*, (1):15-18.

1968   Current Historic Sites Archaeology in Pennsylvania and New Jersey. *Bulletin of the Philadelphia Anthropological Society*, 19(2):2-4.

1968   *Handbook for Historical Archaeology, Part I*. John L. Cotter, Wyncote, PA.

1968   Editor, *Historical Archaeology 1967*, Annual Publication of The Society for Historical Archaeology, Philadelphia, PA.

1968   Review of *Industrial Archaeology: An Introduction* by Kenneth Hudson. *American Anthropologist*, 70(2):422.

1968   Review of *Iroquois Culture, History, and Prehistory*, Elizabeth Tooker, editor. *American Antiquity*, 33(4):520-521.

1968   Review of *Late Paleo-Indian and Early Archaic Manifestations in Western Kentucky* by Martha Ann Rolingson and Douglas W. Schwartz. *Pennsylvania Archaeologist*, 36(1-2):72.

1968   Preserving Our Heritage. *Archaeology*, 21(3):214-215.

1968   Review of *Novgorod The Great: Excavations at the Medieval City, 1951-62* by M. W. Thompson. *Archaeology*, 21(3):239-240.

1969   Review of *The Art and Architecture of Medieval Russia* by Arthur Voyce. *Archaeology*, 22(2):159-160.

1969   Review of *Historical Archaeology* by Ivor Noël Hume. *American Anthropologist*, 71(6):1215-1216.

1969   Review of *Old Buildings, Gardens and Furniture in Tidewater Maryland* by H. Chandlee Forman. *Archaeology*, 22(3):241-242.

1970   Review of *Colonial Williamsburg Display*. *Technology and Culture*, 11(3):417-427.

1970   Review of *Settlement Archaeology* by K. C. Chang. *Archaeology*, 23(3):265-266.

1970   Review of *Conceptions of Kentucky Prehistory* by Douglas W. Schwartz. *Archaeology*, 23(4):348.

1970   Review of *Historical Archaeology* by Ivor Noël Hume. *Archaeology*, 23(4):353-354.

1970   Trends in Historical Archaeology: Education and Conservation. *The Conference on Historic Site Archaeology Papers 1968*, 3(1):38-42.

1970   Review of *Archaeology and Wetherburn's Tavern* by Ivor Noël Hume and *The Wells of Williamsburg, Colonial Time Capsules* by Ivor Noël Hume. *Historical Archaeology*, 4:109-110.

1971   Review of *Barbarian Europe* by Gerald Simons and The Editors of Time-Life Books. *Archaeology*, 24(1):88.

1971   Review of *Northeast Historical Archaeology, The Journal of the Council for Northeast Historical Archaeology*, Vol. I. *Historical Archaeology*, 5:127-128.

1972   Archaeological Sites, Important National Resources. *Archaeology* 25(2):152-153.

1972   Review of *The Cultural History of Marlborough, Virginia: An Archaeological and Historical Investigation of the Port Town for Stafford County and the Plantation of John Mercer, Including Data Supplied by Frank M. Setzler and Oscar H. Darter* by C. Malcolm Watkins. *Archaeology*, 25(3):243-244.

1972   Review of *Foundations of Pennsylvania Prehistory*, Barry C. Kent, Ira F. Smith III, and Catherine McCann, editors. *The Pennsylvania Magazine of History and Biography*, 96(4):526-528.

1972   Review of *A Guide to Artifacts of Colonial America* by Ivor Noël Hume. *Archaeology*, 25(3):240-241.

1972   Review of *Surveying and Mapping: A Manual of Simplified Techniques* by Robert F. G. Spier. *Technology and Culture*, 13(1):114.

1973   Review of *Public Archeology* by Charles McGimsey III. *Archaeology*, 26(2):148.

1973   Review of *Contemporary Archaeology: A Guide to Theory and Contributions*, Mark P. Leone, editor. *Archaeology*, 26(4):312.

1974   *Above Ground Archaeology*. Booklet sponsored by the American Revolution Bicentennial Commission on behalf of the Society for American Archaeology. Washington, DC.

1974   Above Ground Archaeology. *American Quarterly*, 26(3):266-280.

1974   Review of *Beginner's Guide to Archaeology: The Modern Digger's Step-by-Step Introduction to the Expert Ways of Unearthing the Past* by Louis A. Brennan. *Archaeology*, 27(1):76.

1974   Review of *Research and Theory in Current Archaeology*, Charles L. Redman, editor. *Archaeology*, 27(4):287-288.

1976   After the Dig is Over: Abstracted Symposium Articles. *Notebook of The Institute of Archaeology and Anthropology 1974*, 6:1.

1976   Historical Archaeology: An Introduction. *Archaeology*, 29(3):150-151.

1976   Architecture at Jamestown: Seventeenth Century and Beyond. *Archaeology*, 29(3):152-163.

1976   Review of *Fort Michilimackinac 1715-1781: An Archeological Perspective on the Revolutionary Frontier* by Lyle M. Stone. *Archaeology*, 29(3):210.

1976   Review of *Folk Housing in Middle Virginia: Structural Analysis of Historic Artifacts* by Henry H. Glassie. *Archaeology*, 29(4):282-283.

1977 Collecting and Archaeology. *Archaeology,* 30(3):207.

1977 Continuity in Teaching Historical Archaeology. In Teaching and Training in American Archaeology: A Survey of Programs and Philosophies, pp. 100-107. Southern Illinois *University Museum Studies Research Records,* 10. Carbondale.

1978 Archaeology and Material History: A Personal Approach to Discovery of the Past. In *The Study of American Culture: Contemporary Conflicts.* Luther S. Luedtke, editor, Chapter 5. Everett-Edwards, Deland, FL.

1978 Review of *Camden: A Frontier Town in Eighteenth Century South Carolina* by Kenneth E. Lewis. *American Anthropologist,* 80(3):744.

1978 Premier Establishment Français en Acadie: Sainte Croix. *L'Dossiers de Archéologie,* 27:60-71.

1978 Symposium on Role of Archaeology in Historical Research: Summary and Analysis. In *Historical Archaeology: A Guide to Substantive and Theoretical Contributions.* Robert L. Schuyler, editor, Chapter 5. Baywood Publishing Company, Farmingdale, NY.

1979 Archaeologists of the Future: High Schools Discover Archaeology. *Archaeology,* 32(1):29-35.

1979 Review of *Drayton Hall: Preliminary Archaeological Investigations at a Low Country Plantation* by Lynne G. Lewis. *Historical Archaeology,* 12:108-109.

1980 Review of *Captain Jones's Wormslow: A Historical, Archaeological, and Architectural Study of an Eighteenth-Century Plantation Site Near Savannah, Georgia* by William M. Kelso. *Journal of American History,* 67:123-124.

1980 Excavating Ben Franklin's House. *Early Man,* 2(2):17-20.

1981 Review of *Frontiers in the Soil: The Archaeology of Georgia* by Roy S. Dickens, Jr. and James L. McKinley in collaboration with James H. Chapman and Leland G. Ferguson. *Archaeology,* 34(5):74-75.

1981 The Upper Paleolithic—However It Got Here, It's Here (Can the Middle Paleolithic Be Far Behind?). *American Antiquity,* 46(4):926-928.

1983 Commentary on the Paleo-Indian Tradition in Eastern North America—20 Years Later. *Archaeology of Eastern North America,* 11:15-18.

1983 Review of *Martin's Hundred* by Ivor Noël Hume. *American Historical Review,* February:170-171.

1985 The History of Sporting America. *Expedition,* 27(2):57-61.

1989 Of Warps and Wormholes (Forum). *Archaeology,* 42(2):80.

1989 Freud's Magnificent Obsession (Forum). *Archaeology,* 42(5):84.

1989 Publishing: The Bottom Line—Challenges and Innovations. *The Society for Historical Archaeology Newsletter,* 22(2):19-22.

1990 Cryptoarchaeology (Forum). *Archaeology,* 43(3):80.

1990 Review of *Interdisciplinary Investigations of the Boott Mills, Lowell, Massachusetts, Vol. II: The Kirk Street Agents' House,* Mary C. Beaudry and Stephen A. Mrozowski, editors. *North American Archaeologist,* 11(1):85-90.

1991 Update on Natchez Man. *American Antiquity,* 56(1):36-39.

1993 Review of *The Art and Mystery of Historical Archaeology: Essays in Honor of James Deetz,* Anne Elizabeth Yentsch and Mary C. Beaudry, editors. *Bulletin of the History of Archaeology,* 3(2):23-25.

1993 Historical Archaeology Before 1967. *Historical Archaeology,* 27(1):4-9.

1993 Kentucky Memoir: Digging in the Depression. *Archaeology,* 46(1):30-35.

1993 Preface: The Historical Archaeology of 17th-Century Virginia. In The Archaeology of 17th-Century Virginia, Theodore R. Reinhart and Dennis J. Pogue, editors. *Archeological Society of Virginia, Special Publication,* 30. Richmond.

1994 Archaeological Memoir of the Natchez Trace. *Mississippi Archaeology* 29(1):1-16.

1994 Archaeology at Independence National Historical Park. *Pennsylvania Archaeologist,* 64(1):52-64.

1994 Beginnings. In *Pioneers in Historical Archaeology: Breaking New Ground,* Stanley South, editor, pp. 15-25. Plenum Press, New York.

1994 Foreword to Descriptive Analyses and Taphonomical Observations of Culturally-Modified Mammoths Excavated at "The Gravel Pit" Near Clovis, New Mexico in 1936, by Jeffrey J. Saunders and Edward B. Daeschler. *Proceedings of the Academy of Natural Sciences of Philadelphia,* 145:1-28. Philadelphia, PA.

1994 Republication of Archeological Excavations at Jamestown, Virginia (1958), with additions. *Archeological Society of Virginia Special Publication,* 32. Richmond.

1994 The Triumph of Fossil Homo (Forum). *Archaeology,* 47(1):84.

1995 Bert Salwen—A Recollection. In *From Prehistory to the Present: Studies in Northeastern Archaeology in Honor of Bert Salwen,* Nan A. Rothschild and Diana di Zerega Wall, editors. *Northeast Historical Archaeology,* 21-22:218-220.

1995 Review of *Historical Archaeology of the Chesapeake,* Paul A. Shackel and Barbara J. Little, editors. *The Pennsylvania Magazine of History and Biography,* 119(3):283-285.

1995 Review of *A Patch of Land Owned by the Company: Historical and Archaeological Investigations of House Lots #117/119 Main Street, Eckley Miners' Village, Eckley, Pennsylvania* by Stephen G. Warfel. *North American Archaeologist,* 16(1):68-70.

1995 You *Can* Take It With You (Forum). *Archaeology,* 48(4):80.

1996 Keeping in Focus Before and After Retirement. *Association of Senior Anthropologists Occasional Papers,* 1(1):35-42.

1997 Antique Archaeologists (Forum). *Archaeology,* 50(1):88.

1997 An Unsinkable Story (Forum). *Archaeology,* 50(3):80.

1997 Historical Archaeology: A Retrospective. *The Review of Archaeology,* 17(2):5-9.

1998 A Bibliography of Historical Archaeology in North America, North of Mexico. <http://www.sha.org/cot2intr.htm>.

1998 Obituary, Jean Carl Harrington. *Newsletter of the American Anthropological Association,* 39(6):28.

1998   Remembering 1948 (Forum). *Archaeology,* 51(5):100.

1998   Jamestown: A Personal Reminiscence. *Expedition,* 40(3):17-26.

1999   Commentary on Jamestown. *CRM,* 22(1):3.

BOLDURIAN, ANTHONY T., AND JOHN L. COTTER
1999   *Clovis Revisited: New Perspectives on Paleoindian Adaptations from Blackwater Draw, New Mexico.* University of Pennsylvania Museum of Archaeology and Anthropology, Philadelphia.

COTTER, JOHN L., AND JOHN M. CORBETT
1951   Archeology of the Bynum Mounds, Mississippi. National Park Service, *Archeological Research Series,* 1. Washington, DC.

COTTER, JOHN L., D. H. DAY, J. I. KLEIN, AND J. S. POLLAK
1977   Comment on Turnbaugh. *American Antiquity,* 42(4):637-638.

COTTER, JOHN L., AND WILLIAM D. HERSHEY
1971   Recent Publications in Historical Archaeology. *Historical Archaeology,* 5:131-134.

COTTER, JOHN L., AND J. PAUL HUDSON
1957   *New Discoveries at Jamestown, Site of the First Successful English Settlement in America.* National Park Service, Washington.

COTTER, JOHN L., AND EDWARD B. JELKS
1957   Historic Site Archaeology at Jamestown. *American Antiquity,* 22(4):387-389.

COTTER, JOHN L., ROGER W. MOSS, BRUCE C. GILL, AND JIYUL KIM
1988   *The Walnut Street Prison Workshop.* The Athenaeum of Philadelphia, Philadelphia, PA.

COTTER, JOHN L., AND DAVID ORR
1975   Historical Archaeology of Philadelphia. *Historical Archaeology,* 9:1-10.

COTTER, JOHN L., DANIEL G. ROBERTS, AND MICHAEL PARRINGTON
1992   *The Buried Past: An Archaeological History of Philadelphia.* University of Pennsylvania Press, Philadelphia.

MANUSCRIPTS AND UNPUBLISHED REPORTS

COTTER, JOHN L.
1935   Yuma and Folsom Artifacts. Masters thesis, University of Denver, Denver, CO.

1950   Excavation of Fill Area Between Bridge House and Charcoal House (Operation 1), Hopewell Village Archeological Work. Report, Hopewell Furnace National Historic Site, Elverson, PA, and Independence National Historical Park, Philadelphia, PA.

1950   Cross-Section Tests of the West Head Race (Operation 2), Hopewell Village Archeological Work. Report, Hopewell Furnace National Historic Site, Elverson, PA, and Independence National Historical Park, Philadelphia, PA.

1954   Field Observation, Visitor Needs and Interpretive Methods at Fort McHenry. Report, Fort McHenry National Monument and Historic Shrine, Baltimore, and Independence National Historical Park, Philadelphia, PA.

1954   Report on Archeological Investigation in the Neck-of-Land Area Near Jamestown, Virginia. Report, Colonial National Historical Park, Jamestown, VA, and Independence National Historical Park, Philadelphia, PA.

1954   Report on Stabilization Work at Jamestown, 1954 (Structure Nos. 6, 31, 32 and 87). Report, Colonial National Historical Park, Jamestown, VA, and Independence National Historical Park, Philadelphia, PA.

1955   Comments on Exhibit Plan, Jamestown Visitor Center. Report, Colonial National Historical Park, Jamestown, VA, and Independence National Historical Park, Philadelphia, PA.

1956   Completion Report: Jamestown Archeological Explorations, 1954-56. Report, Colonial National Historical Park, Jamestown, VA, and Independence National Historical Park, Philadelphia, PA.

1956   West House Area Archeological Investigations, April 2 Through 13, 1956: Final Report. Report, Independence National Historical Park, Philadelphia, PA.

1957   The Aborigines of Jamestown Island. Report, Colonial National Historical Park, Jamestown, VA, and Independence National Historical Park, Philadelphia, PA.

1957   Archeological Report on Yorktown Sewer. Report, Colonial National Historical Park, Jamestown, VA, and Independence National Historical Park, Philadelphia, PA.

1957   Excavations at Jamestown, Virginia, Site of the First Permanent English Settlement in America. Report, Colonial National Historical Park, Jamestown, VA, and Independence National Historical Park, Philadelphia, PA.

1957   Summary Report of Archaeological Explorations at Jamestown, 1901-1957. Report, Colonial National Historical Park, Jamestown, VA.

1958   Archeological Excavations at Jamestown, Colonial National Historical Park and Jamestown National Historic Site, Virginia. Report, Colonial National Historical Park, Jamestown, VA, and Independence National Historical Park, Philadelphia, PA.

1958   Archeological Tests, Hopewell Village National Historic Site: 1. Garden Area of Ironmaster's House, 2. Parking Lot Extension, 3. Entrance to Charcoal House. Report, Hopewell Furnace National Historic Site, Elverson, PA, and Independence National Historical Park, Philadelphia, PA.

1958   Archeological Tests for Oven at the Bryan House, Gettysburg, June 10 and 11, 1958. Report, Gettysburg National Military Park, Gettysburg, PA, and Independence National Historical Park, Philadelphia, PA.

1959   Archeological Explorations at the Barn Site, Hopewell Village National Historic Site, April 27-28, 1959. Report, Hopewell Furnace National Historic Site, Elverson, PA, and Independence National Historical Park, Philadelphia, PA.

1959   Report on the Reconstruction of the Historic Flagstaff, Fort McHenry National Monument and Historic Site. Report, Fort McHenry National Monument and Historic Shrine, Baltimore, and Independence National Historical Park, Philadelphia, PA.

1960   Store Excavation and Road Tests, Hopewell Village, April 4 Through 8, 1960. Report, Hopewell Furnace National Historic Site, Elverson, PA, and Independence National Historical Park, Philadelphia, PA.

1961   Report of Archeological Investigation, Hopewell Village Structure 39, Charcoal Kiln, April 30, 1961. Report, Hopewell Furnace National Historic Site, Elverson, PA, and Independence National Historical Park, Philadelphia, PA.

1961   Report on Location of Brick Drain Under Fort McHenry Courtyard. Report, Fort McHenry National Monument and Historic Shrine, Baltimore, and Independence National Historical Park, Philadelphia, PA.

1962   Independence Square Wall-Corners; 5th & 6th, Walnut Street. Report, Independence National Historical Park, Philadelphia, PA.

1964   Archaeological Observations in the Basement of the East Wing Building, Independence Hall: Sub-Floor Walls. Report, Independence National Historical Park, Philadelphia, PA.

1964   Archaeological Report on the Investigation of a Brick Vault Catchment, "Cistern No. 2," Beneath the Cement Floor, Basement of Old City Hall. Report, Independence National Historical Park, Philadelphia, PA.

1964   Observations of Back Hoe Test Area of Supposed 1819 Road and Preliminary Archeological Report on Store and Gun House and Stable and Store House Sites. Report, Independence National Historical Park, Philadelphia, PA.

1965   Observations of Excavation for Removal; New Foundation and Reconstruction of a Section of the South Wall East of Steps of Second Bank. Report, Independence National Historical Park, Philadelphia, PA.

1966   Archaeological Appendix C in Historic Structures Report II on Independence Hall. Report, Independence National Historical Park, Philadelphia, PA.

1966   Archaeological Observations During the Preparation of the Gun Shed and Storehouse, the Tavern, and the 1814 Hospital for Interpretation. Report, Independence National Historical Park, Philadelphia, PA.

1966   Archaeological Observations on the Kitchen Excavation, Fort Building "E" (Fort McHenry). Report, Fort McHenry National Monument and Historic Shrine, Baltimore, MD, and Independence National Historical Park, Philadelphia, PA.

1966   Archeological Report on Preliminary Tests at the Orangerie, Hampton. Report, Hampton National Historic Site, Hampton, VA, and Independence National Historical Park, Philadelphia, PA.

1966   Man Full of Trouble: The Story of Philadelphia's Oldest Inn. Manuscript, University of Pennsylvania Museum of Archaeology and Anthropology, Philadelphia.

1966   Preliminary Report on Archaeological Investigations at the Pennsylvania Encampment at Valley Forge, July-October 1966. Report, Valley Forge National Historical Park, Valley Forge, PA, and Independence National Historical Park, Philadelphia, PA.

1967   The Friendly Underground: An Archaeological View of Philadelphia. Manuscript, University of Pennsylvania Museum of Archaeology and Anthropology, Philadelphia.

1969   Archeological Summary on Franklin Court. Report, Independence National Historical Park, Philadelphia, PA.

1969   Fort Mifflin Archaeological Feasibility Study. Report, University of Pennsylvania Museum of Archaeology and Anthropology, Philadelphia.

1970   Archaeological Investigations at the Snyder House, Gettysburg National Historical Park. Report, Gettysburg National Military Park, Gettysburg, PA, and Independence National Historical Park, Philadelphia, PA.

1972   Further Observations on the Hut 9 Excavation. Report, Valley Forge National Historical Park, Valley Forge, PA, and Independence National Historical Park, Philadelphia, PA.

1972   Saugus Archaeological Collection Examined and Inventoried at Harpers Ferry, May 31-June 2. Report, National Park Service, Boston MA.

1973   Observations of Utility Trench for Evidence of Archeological Features and Artifacts, Hopewell Village National Historic Site, Nov. 19-23. Report, Hopewell Furnace National Historic Site, Elverson, PA, and Independence National Historical Park, Philadelphia, PA.

1974   Archeological Observations on Grounds of 704 Market Street, Philadelphia, Two Doors West of the Graff House, 700 Market Street. Report, Independence National Historical Park, Philadelphia, PA.

1974   Construction-Related Cleanup of Franklin Court Archeology. Report, Independence National Historical Park, Philadelphia, PA, and Valley Forge National Historical Park, Valley Forge, PA.

1975   Archaeological Investigation of Waynesborough: A Field Exercise by the Students of the University of Pennsylvania. Report, University of Pennsylvania Museum of Archaeology and Anthropology, Philadelphia.

1976   Harriton Archaeological Tests: Summary Report. Report, University of Pennsylvania Museum of Archaeology and Anthropology, Philadelphia.

1977   An Archaeological Feasibility Study of Grumblethorpe. Report, University of Pennsylvania Museum of Archaeology and Anthropology, Philadelphia.

1979   Summary Report on Archaeology of Franklin Court. Report, Independence National Historical Park, Philadelphia, PA.

BLADES, BROOKE S., AND JOHN L. COTTER

1977   The South Fork Dam Sluice Culvert at Johnstown Flood National Memorial. Report, Johnstown Flood National Memorial, Johnstown, PA, and Independence National Historical Park, Philadelphia, PA.

1978   Archaeological Test Excavations at the Hare House Site, Petersburg National Battlefield. Report, Petersburg National Battlefield, Petersburg, VA, and Independence National Historical Park, Philadelphia, PA.

COTTER, JOHN L., AND BROOKE S. BLADES

1977   Completion Report: George Washington Birthplace National Monument. Report, George Washington Birthplace National Monument, VA, and Independence National Historical Park, Philadelphia, PA.

1977   Preliminary Archaeological Investigation; Washington and Brooks Site. Report, Independence National Historical Park, Philadelphia, PA.

COTTER, JOHN L., AND JOSEPH H. HALL IV

1979   The Wyck Site: An Archaeological Feasibility Study, July-August, 1979. Report, University of Pennsylvania Museum of Archaeology and Anthropology, Philadelphia.

COTTER, JOHN L., AND LEE H. NELSON

1958   Addendum to Archeological Report by G. Hubert Smith, Archeologist, 1958. Report, Independence National Historical Park, Philadelphia, PA.

COTTER, JOHN L., B. BRUCE POWELL, AND LEE H. NELSON

1965   Summary of Archeological Cooperative Work at the North and South Entrances of Independence Hall and in Front of East Wing Building. Report, Independence National Historical Park, Philadelphia, PA.

COTTER, JOHN L., AND STUDENTS

1967   Physick House Garden Archaeological Tests. Report, University of Pennsylvania Museum of Archaeology and Anthropology, Philadelphia.

1969   Philadelphia's Urban Renewal and the Loss of Heritage: The Federal Building Site. Report, University of Pennsylvania Museum of Archaeology and Anthropology, Philadelphia.

1975   Ridley Creek State Farm Project: Excavation of the Water Supply System and Sawmill Complex. Report, University of Pennsylvania Museum of Archaeology and Anthropology, Philadelphia.

1978   Archaeological Excavations at Grumblethorpe: The Ice House Test by Partial Excavation. Report, University of Pennsylvania Museum of Archaeology and Anthropology, Philadelphia.

1978   An Archaeological Feasibility Study of the Grange in Haverford Township, Pennsylvania. Report, University of Pennsylvania Museum of Archaeology and Anthropology, Philadelphia.

HARRIS, WILLIAM A., AND JOHN L. COTTER

1966   Historic Structures Report (Part 1): Administrative and Archeological Data Sections, Orangerie, Hampton National Historic Site. Report, Hampton National Historic Site, Hampton, VA, and Independence National Historical Park, Philadelphia, PA.

NELSON, LEE H., AND JOHN L. COTTER

1964   East Wing Sidewalk Well Report. Report, Independence National Historical Park, Philadelphia, PA.

RONSHEIM, ROBERT P., AND JOHN L. COTTER

1961   Historic Structures Report (Part I): Historical and Archeological Data Sections, Charcoal Kiln Ruins. Report, Hopewell Furnace National Historic Site, Elverson, PA, and Independence National Historical Park, Philadelphia, PA.

Daniel G. Roberts

MEMORIAL: James Fanto Deetz, 1930-2000. Volume 38, Number 2 (2004): 103-123. By Marly R. Brown, III.

Memorial

James Fanto Deetz, 1930–2000

On Saturday, 25 November 2000 historical archaeology lost one of its brightest lights, a scholar who did more than anyone of his generation to define the scope of the field and place it securely within the fold of anthropology. James Deetz's passing barely two months shy of his 71st birthday also silenced one of the most talented teachers ever to grace the halls of America's universities. His final battle with a chronic illness brought his family members and close friends to his bedside in Charlottesville. Nearby at Jim's sister's house, his children tried to celebrate Thanksgiving, the holiday whose traditions their father had so cleverly exposed in his 1969 essay "The Reality of the Pilgrim Fathers" (Deetz 1969). The irony of the timing of his passing was not lost on Jim's friends. One headline written a week after his death read simply, "Pilgrim scholar Deetz dies after his holiday."

Less than a month before he died, we had been treated to his further debunking of the Pilgrim myth in the first chapter of Jim's last book, *The Times of Their Lives: Life, Love, and Death in Plymouth Colony* (Deetz and Deetz 2000). Written with his second wife, Patricia Scott Deetz, *The Times of Their Lives* reflects on the results of the most important archaeological and historical research he did there in the 1960s and early 1970s. With the assistance of his wife and some of his University of Virginia (UVA) graduate students, Jim was able to expand on his original work and take care of some important unfinished business. We are fortunate that so much of his work is now also accessible to us online at the wonderful *Plymouth Colony Archives* Web site created and maintained by Chris Fennell and supported by UVA. There, too, can be found an extensive collection of information about Jim's career.

In this final book, Jim also recounted what surely must have been some of the "times of his life." At least they seem that way to someone like me who shared so intimately in them. His account is enlivened by reminiscences of celebrations of Thanksgivings past, such as the 1971 Turkey Day when the Deetz family hosted several busloads of Native Americans who were in Plymouth to observe their National Day of Mourning. He also used the published work of the well-known playwright and actor Sam Sheppard to further engage us in his analysis of what Plymouth meant to him and what it means to us today as a memorial landscape. Sheppard was one of Bob Dylan's many camp followers on the 1976 tour known as the Rolling Thunder Review. It was the bicentennial year, and what better place to begin a national tour than the "birthplace of America." Sheppard's trenchant commentary on the tour's first stop in Plymouth provided Deetz with a useful counterpoint for his own interpretation of the Plymouth experience.

The gathering in the fort with Bob Dylan and Joan Baez occurred in the year of Jim's last Thanksgiving celebration at Plymouth.

But partying with famous folkies in what many of us considered "the other village" was not what made Jim Deetz's tenure in Plymouth memorable, nor was it his revisionist take on the Pilgrim's first Thanksgiving. Between 1967 and 1978, Jim created the most exciting living history museum ever—the outdoor reconstruction known as Plimoth Plantation devoted to the Pilgrims of 1627 and later embracing their Wampanoag neighbors. He built Plimoth on the back of careful archaeological and historical research, undertaken by a dedicated group of historians and interpreters who increasingly embraced Deetz's vision of a Pilgrim village peopled by the very individuals known to have lived there, dressed in the most accurate of period clothing, even speaking in the dialects of their English county of origin.

Role-playing, as this interpretive strategy was called then (or character interpretation as it is more commonly known today), would not be fully implemented until after Deetz left the plantation, but his flair for the dramatic was clearly in evidence by the early 1970s. Major life events such as marriages became the centerpiece for living history pageants, in which visitors were treated to reenacted rituals involving hundreds of costumed employees and volunteers. In the summer of 1973, an earthfast house was raised in the village. Based on archaeological discoveries at the Allerton site and planned with the help of friend and colleague Henry Glassie, this reconstruction inspired countless efforts at other outdoor museums, including the one that I work for, Colonial Williamsburg. Like many other events in the village in those days, the house raising became a "happening" that visitors and participants alike will never forget.

Deetz's impact on the world of living history museums may have been a surprise for some who saw him foremost as a "new archaeologist," a scholar purportedly more interested in hypothesis testing than role-playing. But this flair for the dramatic in the interpretation of the past would not have surprised his classmates at Fort Hill High School in Cumberland, Maryland. James Deetz was born in Cumberland in 1930 to John Harold Deetz and Catherine Fanto Deetz. He and his younger sister, Barbara, spent their entire childhood there. Although he became known around town for his bird watching and butterfly collecting, by the time he was a senior in high school, Jim's lepidopterist pursuits had to make room for his thespian pretensions. By senior year he had become the school's most prominent leading man, a member of both the Fort Hill High Players and a National thespian. He went to Harvard in fall 1948 to prepare for medical school, not drama school, but no one who had the pleasure of experiencing Jim in front of a lecture hall podium would ever doubt his acting skills.

Harvard, Back to Harvard, and Harvard Again

Deetz did not stay with his pre-med concentration long, switching to anthropology after a very stimulating introductory course in the subject and a very disappointing grade in chemistry. J. O. Brew, director of the Peabody Museum and Jim's main mentor throughout his time at Harvard, set him up with his first excavation. In June 1950 he became a member of Don Lehmer's field crew at the Dodd site in South Dakota, a project sponsored by the Missouri River Basin Survey run out of Lincoln, Nebraska. Jim stayed on into the fall and as a result was drafted (the Korean War had broken out the same month he had left to join the excavation crew).

He joined the Air Force in early 1951 and found his undergraduate education interrupted for five years. He served all over the country, but his most difficult posting was in Greenland. While there, Deetz kept up his interest in anthropology in two ways. He took an extension course on California Indians through the University of California Extension Service, and he initiated his own excavation of a recently abandoned village site. As he once told me, the extension course came in handy when, during his PhD orals, Clyde Kluckhohn asked him to name all the tribes in California, starting with San Diego and the coast and going north, coming down the valley, and then back up the Sierra. Jim succeeded and sometimes felt a need to ask at least one comparable question to his own PhD students during their orals.

Deetz's excavation was not so successful. Although it didn't damage his subsequent career, his Greenland dig created an international incident at the time, not having the proper permission from the king. I asked him why he would risk offending the Danish government and he told me,

> You had to have been there, but if you're stuck with 10 other guys in a shack on a mountaintop for a year, half of which is always dark and the other half is always daylight, you've got to find something to do. Well, I'm a bird-watcher, so I watched the birds, and I collect butterflies, so I collected the only butterfly that was there, so I had one butterfly and that was that, and then I found this site down by the fjord (James Deetz, 26 August 1989, Berlekey, CA, pers. comm. [interview with Marley Brown]).

Deetz was hard at work plotting caribou bone element distributions before his project was shut down by two investigating archaeologists sent up from the War College (Jim described his effort as "doing a kind of pre-Binford whatever"). He carefully mapped the bones on the site in relation to the house pits and then reconstructed them in a vacant barracks building. His undoing came when the Danish liaison officer was invited to an exhibit he mounted in the base theatre. Soon thereafter, the Danish officials lodged a formal protest with Washington.

During his four years in the Air Force, Deetz also met and married his first wife, Eleanore Joanne (Jody) Kelley. They married in 1953 upon his return from Greenland and started their family when Jody gave birth to eldest son James Christian (Jamey) in 1954. Deetz returned to Harvard after his discharge from the Air Force in January 1955. To get ready for his return to school, Deetz went to see Hal Movius. Jim was both surprised and pleased to be remembered after a five-year absence. Movius became his advisor, and that spring Deetz began "reading everything he could get his hands on" in anticipation of finishing up his undergraduate studies. He took classes from A. V. Kidder, Earnest Hooton, and Leslie Spier, which he remembered as being "pretty amazing. Anybody who had a course from Leslie Spier, it was like saying you had a course from Louis Henry Morgan" (Deetz, 1989, pers. comm.). He characterized much of this course work as "the most painful recitation of classic, mid-thirties trait listing. Very Boasian but with no integration" (Deetz, 1989, pers. comm.). Although Jim led me to believe that he found the emphasis of so many of his Harvard classes, both before and after the Korean War, to be "regrettable" in their exclusive attention to traits and sequences, he learned them well. Lecture notes from his classes on archaeology during the 1960s reveal that Deetz most certainly shared in some aspect of this approach in his teaching.

As he was finishing up his bachelor's degree, Deetz found other helpful faculty at Harvard. He began to spend more time with Gordon Willey, and it was Willey who persuaded him to stay at Harvard for his PhD. Deetz was planning to go to Arizona, but Willey assured him that the department would find money to support his graduate study. During his senior year he worked with William H. Howells, for whom he was a teaching assistant, and maintained his close association with J. O. Brew. As Jim recollected, Brew, as director of the Peabody, was always willing to see people in his office, "but he never really saw you in his office, he walked in and he walked out and you followed him out and you stood in the front hall and talked" (Deetz, 1989, pers. comm.). Often in the group standing around at the Peabody while Jim chatted with Brew would be fellow students Clifford Geertz and Dell Hymes. Jim officially received his bachelor's degree from Harvard in June 1957 (cum laude) and, true to his promise, Willey helped Deetz secure fellowships so that he could stay on and do his dissertation. That same year, his second son, Joseph Dayton (Joey), was born, joining an elder sister, Antonia (Toni), born the year before.

After graduating, Deetz returned to the Missouri River Basin Survey in summer 1957. He spent the first part of the summer on Herbert Smith's crew, searching for an 18th-century French fort but finding only a modern reservation-era house (ca. 1920). I once asked Jim if this first foray into the modern period of historical archaeology had any influence on his career. His response was, "Yeah, it had a negative impact. I swore I'd never do it again" (Deetz, 1989, pers. comm.). Luckily for Deetz, he was able to transfer across the river to a crew being led by fellow Harvard graduate student Bill Irving, excavating the large multi-component site known as Medicine Crow. As Deetz tells it, Irving wasn't interested in the Middle-Missouri components. He turned the earth lodges over to Jim, so he could pursue a much earlier occupation with intact hearths.

Deetz returned to the site the next summer to complete this project. In his approach, he was able to call on the techniques learned under Lehmer's supervision during the summer of 1950. Deetz also recalled a conversation he had had with a fellow crewmember from that first summer on the Missouri, Frank Livingstone, who went on to study sickle-cell anemia. As they were working on one of the later Arikara-period lodges, Livingstone made a casual observation about how pottery with certain designs seemed to be clustered in different structures. This idea stuck with Jim, although he would not recall it in detail until the artifacts from his second summer of excavation at Medicine Crow had been shipped back to Cambridge.

Early in fall 1958, Deetz began to examine the ceramics from later phases at Medicine Crow. It dawned on him that, as he described it, "something is going on here. I thought a little more about what Frank said and then one day the light went on in my head" (Deetz, 1989, pers. comm.). Quite excited by his discovery, Jim approached the first person he saw, who happened to be Clyde Kluckhohn: "I grabbed Clyde and dragged him out there and I showed him what I thought was going on and for the first time we actually had a conversation where I could understand him and he could understand me. And he managed to get me some money to pay for the computer time" (Deetz, 1989, pers. comm.).

Jim needed to call in a number of favors to get help from some students at the Massachusetts Institute of Technology who had access to a mainframe the "size of a city block." They would run his data from Medicine Crow whenever there was free time, often in the middle of the night. He took the printouts and worked the data until he had defined the trends through time in the association of design attributes that became the basis for his ideas about changing residence patterns (and, by inference, changing descent systems). Based on the work he did during his second year of graduate study, Deetz produced a dissertation entitled "An Archaeological Approach to Kinship Change in Eighteenth Century Arikara Culture" (Deetz 1960a), for a committee composed of Kluckhohn, Brew, Howells, and Stephen Williams. The latter was his official advisor by virtue of being the full-time North American archaeologist on the faculty when Deetz submitted his dissertation in spring 1960. Though he had completed his dissertation by mid-1959, he had to wait until 1960 to defend. He was awarded his doctoral degree in June of that year, just about five years after he had returned to Harvard for his junior year.

One day during early spring 1959, while Deetz was engrossed in his analysis of the Medicine Crow ceramics, Brew came out of his office and yelled up to the Peabody's mezzanine level to get Jim to come down to meet someone. The visitor was Harry Hornblower, who along with Brew, Ripley Bullen, John Howland Rowe, Chester Chard, and others, had been a member of the Harvard Excavator's Club in the early 1940s. Harry was looking for someone to advise on the construction of an Indian camp to be put in the Pilgrim village at Plimoth Plantation, the museum established on his family's estate in Chiltonville, Massachusetts.

Jim went down to check out Plymouth over the next weekend, and after meeting most of the plantation staff, he agreed to move his family down to one of the houses owned by the plantation opposite the Plymouth town beach. Taking the trip that summer were Jim and his wife and their four children. Second daughter Kristen (Cricket) had been born early that year. Once settled in the beach house, Jim contributed to the design of the plantation's Indian camp but put most of his effort into his first real excavations on historic sites — sites associated with families of the "Pilgrim Fathers."

The most interesting of these was the Joseph Howland site located in the Rocky Nook section of nearby Kingston, Massachusetts. Jim was taken to the site by a local amateur archaeologist, Arthur Vantangoli, who would become one of the plantation's most valuable archaeological volunteers. When asked how he decided where to dig, Jim observed that he "just put a hole beside the big stone with a bronze plaque on it" (Deetz, 1989, pers. comm.). Soon confronted with some pieces of a Westerwald-type stoneware mug, Jim recalled, "I thought somebody had busted a beer stein there that they had brought back from Munich" (Deetz, 1989, pers. comm.)

Deetz readily admitted that he began the excavation of the Howland site lacking "an intimate familiarity with the artifacts." But he soon caught up, using such sources as Ivor Noël Hume's *Here Lies Virginia* (1963) and John Cotter's synthetic report on the Jamestown excavations (1958). Jim published two articles about the site, both published by the Howland Family Association's newsletter *Howland Quarterly* in 1960 (Deetz 1960b, 1960c). These two articles, really his first publications, show the same concern for phasing and chronology that so occupied Deetz in his analysis of the ceramics from the Arikara phase of Medicine Crow. Stratigraphic controls were in place, and Deetz paid special attention to the problem of separating fill from actual occupation deposits, much as he had learned from Don Lehmer at the Dodd site. Nonetheless, he was able to adapt J. C. Harrington's approach to pipestem dating (Harrington 1954) to the problem of chronology at the Howland site and used the pipes to divide a 75-year occupation span into three phases. Almost 30 years later, Deetz would return to pipestem dating and offer other innovative applications of the Harrington technique: first to discover periodicities in site occupation spans at Flowerdew Hundred (Deetz 1987a) and, subsequently, to help in understanding the occupation sequence at an early Dutch fort in South Africa (Schrire et al. 1990).

In choosing to emphasize pipestems and the implications of "bimodality" in their distribution at the Howland site, Deetz was simply engaging in the kind of pattern recognition that made him such a brilliant archaeologist. He is rightly credited with some very innovative work in his study of stylistic motifs appearing on Arikara ceramics. In fact, his interpretation of the Arikara evidence in terms of changing residence patterns was the first of its kind to appear, predating dissertations on similar phenomena within southwestern pueblos by several years (Longacre 1963; Hill 1965). Using today's popular parlance, it can be said that Deetz's interpretation of Arikara ceramics and their spatial and temporal dynamics was a striking example of practice theory applied in the context of Contact period archaeology.

As Deetz once reminded me, his dissertation came out in 1960, and it delved deeply into descent systems and kinship terminology. By the time his dissertation was published in 1965, much had changed, including the dissemination of the work on Broken K Pueblo and Carter's Ranch (Hill 1965). Deetz credited an extensive prepublication review of his manuscript by Irving (Ben) Rouse for the shift in emphasis from descent systems to residence, the latter viewed as a direct representation, to use his words, of "the proceedings of social interaction" (Deetz, 1989, pers. comm.). Rouse also steered him away from unilocality to multilocality in his understanding of the breakdown of what had formerly been for the Arikara an "orderly process of interaction," a normal routine that had progressively broken down under the pressures of contact.

The Santa Barbara Years (Summers Back East)

During 1959 and 1960, the Deetz family joined "the summer people" of Plymouth as Jim directed excavations at the Howland site. But after he received his doctorate, Deetz's career moved into high gear. He was hired to teach at the University of California at Santa Barbara and Jim's transition from graduate student to faculty member was quick and far-reaching. He became professionally active in a way he had consciously avoided as a graduate student. He established his reputation as a brilliant teacher of undergraduates. Right after arriving in Santa Barbara, Deetz joined colleagues Roger Owen, Jack Chilcott, and Tony Fisher in teaching a National Science Foundation-sponsored summer institute for high school teachers, a kind of program that he would return to in earnest at his last major field project at Flowerdew Hundred in the late 1980s and early 1990s.

The institute on the campus of the Midland School greatly altered his career because among its most eager participants was Edwin (Ted) Dethlefsen, a biology teacher at Midland. Ted and Jim became good friends. When Ted decided he wanted to continue his education, Jim helped him get into the PhD program at Harvard. They also used work they did together during summer 1961 at the site known as Alamo Pintado, an historic Chumash village site, as the basis for their first co-authored article on the use of soil chemistry in archaeology (Deetz and Dethlefsen 1963). Deetz also published a brief note on a pictograph from this site in a 1964 volume of *American Antiquity* (Deetz 1964). It was the second collaboration between Deetz and Dethlefsen, however, that attracted all of the attention.

Deetz has described the details of their mutual discovery at the Concord, Massachusetts, cemetery at length "down to the brand of ale that he and Ted were drinking" (Deetz 1989:ix–xiv). Jim had returned to Harvard to teach during the 1963 summer session. Dethlefsen was his teaching assistant. One hot afternoon they were "cooling their heels" in the Concord cemetery, and Ted pointed out to Jim how the styles of decoration on different stones seemed to change with time. From the beginning Deetz saw the gravestone studies as a kind of "experimental historical archaeology." He and Dethlefsen shared authorship on a very important series of articles published between 1965 and 1971. Deetz formulated most of the substantive analysis and wrote all of the papers. His two favorites were the first paper on the Doppler Effect (Deetz and Dethlefsen 1965) and the last on the subregional manifestation of stylistic variability (Deetz and Dethlefsen 1971). He admitted to me that a colleague told him, after hearing his ideas about how the position of the observer seemed to influence the workings of seriation, that, "hey, man, that's the Doppler effect" (Deetz, 1989, pers. comm.). After applying the formula and, as he recollected, "seeing how nicely it fit," he said "I used to think for awhile that it was one of those cases where human behavior might follow some kind of principle defined primarily out of the physical world" (Deetz, 1989, pers. comm.). Deetz and Dethlefsen's final co-authored gravestone publication gave Jim an opportunity to disabuse himself of such heresy. In that paper, he presents a set of structural principles to account for the localized stylistic transformations he had traced in several cemeteries, principles that were more in line with the linguistically inspired interpretation he was turning to at the beginning of the 1970s.

During his tenure on the faculty at Santa Barbara (he began as instructor of anthropology in fall 1960 and left as a full professor in 1967), Deetz was instrumental in helping build a small department into a very important one. Recruitment of distinguished faculty, including Albert Spaulding from Oregon and Tom Harding from Michigan, continued and culminated in a major transfer of talent from Michigan to Santa Barbara, bringing Loring Brace and Elman Service to campus. These were years of exceptional colleagueship for Jim, a time when close friends were made and much productive collaboration occurred. In addition to the summer institute, Deetz joined Roger Owens and Anthony Fisher in putting out a collection of sources on Native Americans (Owens et al. 1967) and reported on the value of "simulated" archaeological sites for teaching excavation techniques in an article written with lifetime friend John (Jack) Chilcott (Chilcott and Deetz 1964), who later joined the faculty at the University of Arizona.

The Chilcotts and Owens also provided the Deetz kids with excellent companionship, and friendships made in those years among various children endured the subsequent relocation of all the families. And in the Deetz case, the family continued to grow. Jim and Jody welcomed three more children into an increasingly crowded house in Montecito, California. Sons John Eric (Eric), William Geoffrey (Geoff), and Joshua Andrew (Josh) were born in 1960, 1962, and 1963, respectively, and daughter Cynthia (Cindy) came along in 1964.

During his Santa Barbara years, Deetz also discovered that he owned some very interesting and valuable Indian baskets, acquired in antique stores in and around Cambridge while he was still in graduate school. Once in Santa Barbara, he figured out that one of them was Chumash. Wanting to know more, he found help in the person of Lawrence (Larry) Dawson, then a curator at the Lowie Museum at the University of California at Berkeley. Jim met Larry at a Southwestern Anthropological Association meeting, and their collaboration was very productive, resulting in an exhibit on Chumash art and a survey of Chumash basketry (Dawson and Deetz 1964, 1965). Deetz put some of his newly gained insights about basketry into the introductory book he was writing in summer 1966. He also incorporated lessons and case studies into the book from all the excavations he had worked on up to that point, including the highlights of his 1963 summer season at La Purisima Mission in Lompoc, California.

Deetz took on the California project at the request of Fritz Riddell of the Department of Parks and Recreation. With the help of a very able crew, including two people who would follow him to Plymouth the next year, Deetz oversaw an impressive program of excavation and interpretation. His careful recording and analysis of La Purisima's Indian barracks yielded important insights into differential rates of change in gender-based productive activities among Indian neophytes, while close attention to some artifacts recovered from the tanning vats produced a compelling example of what today would be called creolization (Deetz 1963:186–189; 1967:114, 116).

Published by Doubleday in 1967, Deetz's *Invitation to Archaeology* became an instant classic, a book that effortlessly introduced basic concepts, such as stratigraphy and seriation for the first-year student, and presented a complex model of the relationship between behavioral patterning and assemblage variability that took advantage of all of his prior research. This book also introduced a brand-new linguistic model for the manufacture of artifacts, one whose origins reach back to the several linguistics courses he took at Harvard but that was directly inspired by conversations he was having with friend Loring Brace and colleague Margaret Mead.

He had come to know Mead during her term as a visiting scholar at Santa Barbara. Jim credited Douglas Oliver, another former Harvard professor of his, with the introduction to the Doubleday editor. Oliver had already written an introduction to cultural anthropology (Oliver 1964) and thought Deetz would do a good job with a similar volume on archaeology. Deetz and the Doubleday editor agreed, and Jim sat down and wrote the book in four weeks. He sent in the manuscript and then realized, as he put it, "my God, they have my manuscript and I don't have a contract. I hope they're honest." It turned out they were. *Invitation to Archaeology* was a top best seller of such academic texts for more than a decade.

The Brown/Plymouth Years or Back and Forth on Route 44

Deetz also credited Oliver with his move in 1967 from Santa Barbara to Brown University. As Jim told it,

> Doug knew they were looking for an archaeologist and he gave them my name and he kept saying to me when he'd see me at meetings, well you ought to think about Brown. Then Reagan was elected [governor] and we were young and idealistic and dumb, and we had all these protests and thought, well what the hell. Times have changed. We went back to Plymouth (Deetz, 1989, pers. comm.).

Of course, Deetz was no stranger to Plymouth, even during his seven years at Santa Barbara. He had spent several summers there, along with a sabbatical year at Harvard during academic year 1965–66. In fact his archaeological adventures during one of these summers, 1966, is chronicled in the well-known hit film *Colonial Six*.

During its run, this film made by Plimoth Plantation was the only introduction to the techniques of historical archaeology available for the classroom. The site itself, associated with Major John Bradford, was not very interesting, but the film held up very well over the years. Because Jim had kept up his close association with the plantation, it came as no surprise that the arrangement negotiated to bring him back to serve on the Brown faculty included a half-time appointment at the plantation. After a year, the museum's director, David Freeman, offered Deetz the position of assistant director, wanting him to be responsible for research, exhibits, and visitation.

Jim immediately took action to improve the exhibits. As he recalled the plantation in those years, "It was terrible. Mannequins in all the houses. Red metal foil embers, rubber fish, sawdust corn-meal. And what struck me was that the visitors would spend something like 45 seconds in each house. I mean there was nothing to see" (Deetz, 1989, pers. comm.). It took Jim some time to implement the kind of changes he had in mind, in part because of the opposition of members of the Society of Mayflower Descendants. Among those he brought in to help were Cathy Gates and Dick Humphrey, who had been instrumental in the success of his work at La Purisima.

Gates was put to the task of detailed furnishings research, with the goal of identifying the kinds of objects that should be in the houses. Probate inventories figured prominently in this research, as did the results of excavations stretching back to Harry Hornblower's efforts with the Excavator's Club. With assistance from historian John Demos at Brandeis, Deetz also initiated a systematic program of population reconstitution or mass biography. Without access to computers, all of this research was compiled with the help of a byzantine (by modern standards) system of punch cards. Jim also hired someone steeped in the techniques of role-playing to begin the process of training interpreters. In three years there was a noticeable change in the physical appearance of the village, living history was increasingly in evidence, and historical research sponsored by the plantation began to appear in a series of important publications by soon-to-be-prominent historians (Rutman 1967; Demos 1970).

As Jim took to his job at the plantation, he became, as he put it, "completely turned on to what amounts to American studies, which is not surprising because clearly the plantation was a very integral part of what American studies would be. And that came from first reading Glassie's book *Pattern in the Folk Material Culture of the Eastern United States* [Glassie 1968] and meeting him on Halloween night 1969" (Deetz, 1989, pers. comm.). Running into Henry Glassie at the American Studies Association meeting in Toledo, Ohio, was a memorable event for Deetz and they got along famously from the very beginning. Jim recalled, "actually for the first 10 minutes *Pattern in the Material Culture of the Eastern United States* met *Invitation to Archaeology* because we had each read the other's book" (Deetz, 1989, pers. comm.). They sat together at the banquet, "right up by the head table and after the dinner was over the program chair stood up and said 'We will now hear six papers on Walt Whitman,' and the two of us looked at each other and without saying a word, stood up, walked out, followed by a bunch of grad students, and headed to the bar" (Deetz, pers. comm., 1989). Hearing this account of their behavior at their first meeting banquet together gave me a much better understanding of my subsequent experiences sitting with Henry and Jim at various SHA banquets during the 1970s.

If his responsibilities at the plantation exposed him to brand-new audiences, such as those attending his panel at the American Studies Association, his faculty position at Brown brought Deetz into contact with an undergraduate community eager for interaction with a teacher of his caliber. The sherry hours with Jim as a guest were standing room only in 1968, and the popularity of his introductory course was such that they had to move his lectures to the largest auditorium available, Pembroke's Alumnae Hall. Where once a roomful of 90 would have been noteworthy, a lecture class of 350 was commonplace for Deetz (these numbers may seem small compared to what he achieved both before and after at much larger universities, but this was Brown, after all).

Right away Deetz attracted the interest of students who would go on to study anthropology at the graduate level. A number of his Brown undergraduates have become very prominent archaeologists in their own right, but, interestingly, many are not historical archaeologists. By the early 1970s, as well, Deetz had recruited a small corpus of graduate students. The ranks swelled in fall 1973 when a large class entered whose collective identity did much to create the sense of a distinctive Brown graduate program in historical archaeology. There is no question that this group of Brown students identified with a set of common goals and strove to accomplish them in their individual scholarship. Deetz was able to reproduce at Brown the great success he enjoyed at Santa Barbara, with the added benefit of doctoral students who had not been present there, at least in anthropology. What is so impressive, though, is the fact that he would do so twice more, having similar impact on the students at Berkeley and at UVA. This track record is clear testimony to his exceptional skills as a teacher at all levels.

Beyond the courses that had become standards for him, such as introductory prehistory and physical anthropology and archaeological methods, Deetz developed a brand-new offering, reflecting his turn towards American studies. First taught in fall 1971, American Material Culture drew a good-size class for an upper-level undergraduate lecture course. He used his and Glassie's books, along with a new reader he had just compiled for Little Brown. This new book, *Man's Imprint from the Past* (Deetz 1971), brought together all of Jim's favorite articles on what he considered to be the essentials of archaeological method. Putting these classics such as Spaulding's "The Dimensions of Archaeology" and Brew's "The Use and Abuse of Taxonomy" together with case studies of gravestones, vernacular architecture, and historic ceramics really worked.

Word got around, and enrollments for this class grew rapidly. Not only was this course the basis for his next major book, *In Small Things Forgotten*, published in 1977, American Material Culture became a staple course offering for Deetz throughout the remainder of his teaching career. Thousands of Berkeley and UVA students joined the hundreds from Brown who would experience this wonderful synthesis of America's material legacy. Jim kept changing the content as his own interests and fieldwork opportunities expanded. As time went by, he also incorporated more monographs by historians, a selective list that included books he admired for their analytical innovation or interpretive insight (e.g., Boyer and Nissenbaum 1974; Morgan 1975).

Although he found material culture studies and later museology to be subjects worthy of teaching during his time at Brown, Deetz did not forget about fieldwork. In the 10 years he was at the plantation, the archaeology lab was always active. There were notable excavations such as the Wellfleet Whaling Station and Tavern in 1968, the Allerton site in 1971, and, of course, Parting Ways in 1975 and 1976, along with many efforts that did not meet with as much success. Prior to writing *In Small Things Forgotten,* Jim produced two important syntheses of what archaeology had revealed about Plymouth's colonial period material life, one dealing with vernacular buildings and the other with foodways.

In a 1972 paper written for Winterthur's "Ceramics in America" conference, Deetz first laid out his cognitive model of cultural development during the colonial period (Deetz 1972). He did so, however, in a paper that can otherwise be read as a spoof on the excesses of what Kent Flannery called the "Law and Order" school (Flannery 1973). Much as he had done for the Medicine Crow artifacts in the second-floor space in the Peabody, Deetz laid out the ceramics recovered from Plymouth assemblages in the plantation lab and looked for patterns in ware type distributions and vessel form ratios. He promoted the concept of foodways as the most useful framework for understanding the changes he saw in these materials (Deetz 1972). His advocacy of the foodways model for historical archaeology was further evidence of the impact that the discipline of folklore was having on his scholarship, an influence that came both from Glassie and from Deetz's own efforts to breath new life into the Pilgrim village. Jay Anderson, whose University of Pennsylvania dissertation on Stuart yeoman foodways provided Deetz the still-cited definition of this subject, also set up the cooking interpretation at the plantation (Anderson 1971). Anderson collaborated with Deetz on a revisionist account of what the Pilgrims really ate for their Thanksgiving dinner (Deetz and Anderson 1972).

With the publication of *In Small Things Forgotten* (Deetz 1977), Deetz repeated the successes of his first modest paperback. He used this book to define his perspective on historical archaeology and characterize its basic concepts and techniques as he had been teaching them. More importantly, he laid out his new synthesis of early-American material culture, one he had been working towards since his first lecture on the topic in fall 1971. In fact, he used a manuscript version of his book as a text the last year he taught American Material Culture at Brown, and it has become quite a collector's item, all the more so because Jim's class in 1977 was his last on the subject at Brown University. As Jim described it, "1977 was one big watershed year. I wrote *In Small Things Forgotten*, and anytime you write a book it is a stunning experience and you pull it all together and say this is where I am. And that was the year I went off to William and Mary. I went out to Flowerdew and got interested in that and was hired by Berkeley" (Deetz, 1989, pers. comm.).

Deetz accepted the position of Eminent Scholar in the Department of Anthropology at the College of William and Mary in spring 1977. That August when Jim and his wife packed up the family for the trip to Williamsburg, their van had two more passengers. In 1975 his youngest daughter Kelley had been born, and the next year daughter Cricket presented Jim with his first grandchild, Hartman Hunawa Deetz. Hartman and Kelley joined the eight older kids for the move to Virgina, where they found themselves in a rental about half the size of their Plymouth house. His teaching at William and Mary expanded Deetz's following among undergraduates, persuading still more to go on to graduate work.

His presence in Williamsburg also brought him into much closer contact with the community of Chesapeake historical archaeologists, whose work he had been admiring from a distance for so many years. Jim had always recommended Cotter's report on Jamestown and the collections there held a great fascination for him. He also got to know Bill Kelso, then commissioner of archaeology for the Commonwealth of Virginia, and had a chance to visit many of the important sites that Kelso and his staff were excavating. But his most important site visits during that year occurred at Flowerdew Hundred, where Southside Historic Sites, Inc., had been excavating for several years. Professor Norman Barka, who had invited Jim to come to Williamsburg, graciously included him in many of Southside's activities that year, and Jim made an important connection with David Harrison, the man who owned the property on which Flowerdew Hundred was located. As it turned out, the draw of Flowerdew would ultimately be too strong to resist.

Berkeley Beckons

At the end of his academic year in Williamsburg, Deetz had a tough decision to make. Three schools wanted his services. He had been offered a teaching position at the University of California at Berkeley. William and Mary also made a bid, and Brown matched the offers. Jim and the family decided to head back to the West Coast. Jim Deetz had been given countless offers over his years at Brown. Some were clearly tantalizing and gave him pause; others he simply ignored. I asked him often in those days why he didn't use these situations to his advantage and ask Brown for more money. His reaction was one of disgust at the very idea. He believed that such jockeying was lacking in honor, and he made his disapproval of such behavior clear to his students. He did not take the job at Berkeley for the money. It was time for a change and the opportunity for good colleagueship in the company of so many distinguished anthropologists was too good to pass up, even though leaving his many friends in Plymouth was painful.

The move to Berkeley gave Jim the opportunity to develop a new graduate training program but in the context of a much larger and more-established department. There was no doubt that the department fully covered the four fields, and among Berkeley's large and distinguished faculty, Jim would find many colleagues whose friendship was more reminiscent of the relationships he developed during his years at Santa Barbara. It also did not take Jim long to attract a large following of students. In his early years at Berkeley, many of his most talented undergraduates were encouraged to stay on for graduate work, but he also accepted several students from his Brown/Plymouth network. He needed a place to train them, a need that soon brought him back to the Chesapeake and Flowerdew Hundred.

For a few years, however, Deetz trained students in fieldwork at the site of Somersville, a late-19th-century coal-mining town in the hills about an hour north of Berkeley. When he initiated this project, he had just taken over the directorship of the Lowie Museum, a post he would hold for eight years (1979–1987). He was able to recruit a number of the museum's long-time staff members to help out on the project, and with the assistance of some of his first graduate students, Deetz mounted a program of excavation that featured more than 200 undergraduates working in coordinated teams of a dozen under the supervision of more experienced undergraduates and graduate students. Done over several years, the Somersville excavation examined the dynamics of interaction among households in a multiethnic community. It is also one of the few archaeological projects ever to be featured in *TV Guide* (Deetz 1980), a prelude to the first broadcast of the PBS program *Other People's Garbage*.

Flowerdew Hundred became the place where Jim Deetz fully developed his talents as a teacher of field schools. He ran an undergraduate program at Flowerdew beginning in summer 1981 and held several successful summer institutes funded by the National Endowment for the Humanities there in the late 1980s and early 1990s. Jim started the long-term field project at Flowerdew Hundred explicitly to train his undergraduate and graduate students. Several hundred Berkeley undergraduates went through the program, as did more than 100 university faculty members. Towards the end, Flowerdew began to serve as a sort of "spa" for some of the latter, and Deetz harbored the idea of establishing a program specifically for archaeologists who, as he put it, "were on the verge of burnout and needed to get back on track." As he demonstrated summer after summer at Flowerdew, Deetz had the ability to reach any and every student, no matter where they might have been in their careers. No doubt he would also have been successful if he had ever acted on the idea to establish a summer program for weary and discouraged veterans.

No one who participated in the Flowerdew summer school will ever forget the experience. In addition to the digging, there were the outstanding meals prepared by son Geoff, who, like other of Jim's kids, had turned into a culinary artist. There was also the music. No matter who was sitting in, Jim could always be counted on to break out his old-time banjo, and those who knew him well will never forget that look of steely determination on his face as he concentrated on his clawhammer technique. Another of the excitements of Flowerdew was the all-too-frequent early morning appearance of another kind of "rolling thunder review," only these concerts didn't feature Bob Dylan and Joan Baez.

It was part of Jim's plan for the research to be reported on mainly by his graduate students, and indeed several excellent dissertations came out of the Berkeley field school at Flowerdew. But Jim also had his own chances to reflect on the significance of the research undertaken there. His first effort was detailed in an article published in 1987 (Deetz 1987a) and then presented more broadly in the 22 January 1988 issue of *Science* (Deetz 1988a). Based on a playful exercise with some of his students and Flowerdew staff, Deetz returned to the kind of analysis that had intrigued him in examining the pipestems from the Howland site 30 years before. The result was an application of the Harrington pipestem dating formula that measured the intensity of site occupation spans. Using the Harrington histograms, Deetz was able to establish temporal patterns in the duration of site occupation that could be examined spatially to see if there were any trends related to aspects of areal and regional settlement dynamics. Deetz recalled that, after reading his article in *Science*, "Pinky Harrington wrote me a letter, which characteristically I didn't answer. But he told me, 'Gee, finally, after all these years somebody finally used it for the purpose that I designed it for'" (Deetz, 1989, pers. comm.).

Towards the end of his tenure on the Berkeley faculty, Deetz completed a book on the work at Flowerdew. Published by University Press of Virginia in 1993, *Flowerdew Hundred: The Archaeology of a Virginia Plantation, 1619-1864* functions much like Deetz's earlier books (Deetz 1993). It distills the essence of his thinking over the time that had elapsed since his last book, in this case more than 15 years. Although many of his arguments derive from his maturing conception of the relationship between the written and material records (the key dynamic underlying his ideas about the importance of folklife studies to historical archaeology), this book cannot be fully appreciated without some background on the research he conducted in South Africa, research interests that began to form almost immediately after he arrived in the country in fall 1984. He had gone there to teach historical archaeology as visiting professor of anthropology at the University of Capetown, a posting suggested to him by an old friend and colleague, Nick van der Merwe.

The Beginnings of Comparative Colonial Archaeology

Deetz's visits to South Africa, beginning with his first teaching experience at Capetown in the early 1980s, helped to usher in the current interest in the global scale of comparative research among many historical archaeologists. One of the basic tenets of historical archaeology set forth in *Flowerdew Hundred* is, "Historical archaeology is international in scope and must adopt an international comparative method to be of maximum value" (Deetz 1993:163). Deetz first made this point in a little paper he presented at the 1986 meeting of The Society for Historical Archaeology in Sacramento, titled "Some Issues of Scale in Historical Archaeology." This paper draws attention to the parochialism inherent in the practice of historical archaeology and through examples drawn from his previous work as far back as La Purisima and from what were then very recent observations from South Africa, Deetz advocated assemblage-level artifact comparisons at the global scale. He saw these exercises not only as an entry point into important aspects of the international economy but as a way of understanding significant differences in the meaning of objects as they were incorporated into the lives of both those who did the colonizing and those who were colonized. Much like the four levels of behavior he presented in *Invitation to Archaeology* in 1967, his Sacramento paper identified similar levels or scales at which comparison became valuable, once the global or international perspective was adopted.

That first trip to teach at Capetown clearly stimulated Jim to write down these ideas, which he first made clear in print in 1988 (Deetz 1988b). Deetz also more than accomplished the purpose that van de Merwe had in mind when he extended the invitation to teach in South Africa. Jim met archaeologists Carmel Schrire and Martin Hall, who had already begun to do research on historic sites there, and he established the first course in historical archaeology at the University of Capetown.

Over the next several years, he returned several times, on one occasion to work with Carmel in her excavation of Oudepost, the Dutch fort in the far Western Cape. Carmel has gone on record about how important Jim's advice was to the success of her project. They collaborated on the analysis of the artifact assemblage, notably extending the Harrington technique to Dutch pipes (Schrire et al. 1990).

As interested as he was in the Dutch, Deetz wasn't comfortable with initiating a major research project on people whose language and culture were so unfamiliar. Instead, through Simon Hall of the Albany Museum, he was introduced to Grahamstown and the Eastern Cape province. As he once described the opportunity to me, "more than anywhere I've ever seen, the Eastern Cape gives us a situation that's just perfect in that 5,000 English were dumped in there at one time with little follow-up immigration. Planted in place, they put together a world very quickly, which was more English than not" (Deetz, 1989, pers. comm.). Jim was able to take advantage of this new research opportunity with the help of Berkeley students, both undergraduate and graduate.

He conducted three seasons of fieldwork in the Grahamstown area, the most productive being at the site of Salem Hall, where he collaborated with his Berkeley graduate student Margot Weiner. Other of his students also went to South Africa with Jim's encouragement or through the contacts he had established with Carmel Schrire and Martin Hall (for example, Markell et al. 1995). There is no question that Deetz's many visits to South Africa to do fieldwork, teach, and consult over more than a decade were a major catalyst for the development of that country's research program in historical archaeology.

During one of these trips in spring 1988, Jim, along with Colonial Williamsburg chief curator Graham Hood, delivered the keynote address at the annual meeting of the South African Museums

Association being held that year in Stellenbosch. There he met Patricia (Trish) Scott, who had traveled to the meeting from her home in Grahamstown. Scott had recently received her MA in History and was looking for an opportunity to get back into museum work (at the time she was on the senior administrative staff of Rhode University). Over the next several years, they developed a very productive professional relationship as well as a personal one (Jim had separated from first wife, Jody, in 1983). For the next seven years, Deetz pursued his research on the British settlement of the Eastern Cape and continued his summer program at Flowerdew. His made his last trip to South Africa in 1993.

A Final Cross-Country Move

The early 1990s were an extremely busy time for Jim. He was completing his fieldwork in the Eastern Cape, running his very successful field program at Flowerdew Hundred, and completing the manuscript that was published as *Flowerdew Hundred* in 1993. His life became even more complicated when he was offered an endowed chair at UVA in 1993. Although David Harrison, the sponsor of his work at Flowerdew Hundred, had been discussing such an arrangement with Jim for some time, the negotiations weren't finalized to everyone's satisfaction until that year. Deetz came out in fall 1993 as a visiting professor of New World studies and occupied the chair the next fall, becoming the Harrison Professor of Historical Archaeology at the University of Virginia in 1994. He held this position until his death. Also in 1994, Deetz was appointed a trustee at Plimoth Plantation, renewing what became a most productive relationship with the museum he had helped create 25 years before.

As part of his negotiations with UVA, Deetz was able to secure the transfer of several of his graduate students who had just started working with him at Berkeley as well as the appointment of Patricia Scott as a research associate in the anthropology department. During Jim's years in Charlottesville, Scott would become a key collaborator on his research and teaching, and on his final book. After Jim was divorced in 1997, she became his second wife. With her help, and with the help of a new generation of students, Jim was able to return to a project that had so fascinated him in the late 1960s when he was busy remaking the 1627 Pilgrim village: the historical ethnography of 17th-century Plymouth Colony.

Very soon after he had come to Brown, Deetz began recruiting graduate students to work on Plymouth Colony records. One of the first master's theses he supervised was a study of the "wayward Pilgrim," modeled after Kai Erickson's classic study of social deviance in Massachusetts Bay Colony (Erickson 1966). He also encouraged several of his colleagues in the Brown anthropology department to work with the Plymouth material, and he established a long-term relationship with John Demos at Brandeis. Demos would provide the students to work on the plantation's biographical reconstruction of Plymouth Colony's population.

Despite all of the excellent primary research done under his overall direction between 1967 and 1978, in both the documents and in the ground, Deetz still had much he wanted to do. Some of this work was accomplished through seminars at Berkeley. One of his most popular was the class he ran on the analysis of probate inventories. By 1987 he and his students had developed a very innovative technique for interpreting the use of space with room-by-room inventories, which Jim reported on at that summer's Dublin Seminar on New England Folklife (1987b). But he did not return to the Plymouth data in earnest until he had become established at UVA.

Beginning in fall 1996, Jim began to teach a series of seminars on the general topic of historical ethnography. Some were what are called freshman seminars, designed to give new undergraduates an intensive introduction to a specific subject along with an opportunity to practice their writing skills. Others were upper-level classes that benefited greatly from the participation of his graduate students. He used these classes, among the last he was to teach, to pull together many of the ideas he had been entertaining for nearly three decades. The result is his last book, *The Times of Their Lives: Life, Love, and Death in Plymouth Colony*, written with his wife Trish and published the year he died (Deetz and Deetz 2000). The last chapter recounts his perspective on the history of the plantation and the role he played in making it what it became—a truly outstanding example of the outdoor living history museum.

Of course, upon his relocation to Charlottesville, Deetz was that much closer to the property where he had been running field schools for more than a decade. He did continue the Flowerdew program for a few more years, two summers as a joint Berkeley/UVA program and finally, the last two summers, as a UVA class. In summer 1995, however, one of his graduate students made what turned out to be the final discovery at Flowerdew, the site of the windmill. This find fulfilled Harrison's quest to locate the earliest windmill in the American colonies, and so he brought an end to the wonderful field program he had sponsored for more than 30 years.

But Deetz did not stay out of the field long. Having begun his classes on the Plymouth Colony material, he decided to return to the Plymouth area. In the current fashion of the day, he chose to reassess or rediscover the archaeology that someone else had done many years before, in this case excavations of the John Howland site done by architect Sidney Strickland in 1937. Over two summers, 1998 and 1999, Jim's graduate students and a UVA field school re-exposed and properly mapped foundations first excavated 60 years before. Jim's reinterpretation of the site is one of his last such analyses (Deetz and Deetz 2000:240–245), and it exhibits the same kind of careful, step-by-step inference that his earlier site accounts contain (e.g., Deetz 1963).

That fall, failing health forced Jim out of the classroom for what would be his last class, ending close to 40 years of undergraduate and graduate instruction. Fortunately, he was in better health the next summer when his youngest daughter Kelley was married in Williamsburg. Nearly his entire family was able to be at the wedding, a group that included all of his children and most of his grandchildren. It was great to see them all together one last time.

And Finally—On a Personal Note

For the heading of his chapter on gravestones in his book *In Small Things Forgotten*, Jim took a line from one of the many epitaphs he enjoyed: "Remember me as you pass by." Jim chose to be buried among family members in St. Peter's Cemetery in the little town of Westernport, Maryland, about 25 mi. south of his birthplace in the far western panhandle of the state. It is fair to say, that aside from a special effort to pay homage to Jim, most of us won't be passing by his gravestone any time soon, if at all. But we will remember him, all of us, just the same. The memory may simply take the form of seeing a citation in a journal article or book placed there to stereotype Deetz's writings as the work of a "structuralist," "new archaeologist," or any number of other inaccurate labels. Or the memory may come from the opposite experience, an encounter with *The Times of Their Lives* or *In Small Things Forgotten* that leads to a serious and rewarding exploration of his scholarly contributions to the fields of historical archaeology, American studies, and, most significantly, anthropology.

But for those of us fortunate enough to have been a student of Jim Deetz, anywhere along the way (Harvard, Santa Barbara, Brown, William and Mary, Berkeley, Capetown, UVA), we will all remember his brilliant mind and his amazing presence in the classroom. This presence could be a captivating one. Jim rescued many a lost undergraduate from four years of indifference. At his funeral in Williamsburg on a chilly Saturday morning, I gazed up from my pew and saw a long line of young people, all dressed in black, looking lost and forlorn. It made me sad at first but then I realized they wouldn't be there, so visibly in mourning, if not for Jim's brilliance as a teacher and mentor and his warmth and openness as a person. Some were his serious students. Others were probably just fans.

In a way I was envious. In 1996 he presented me with a copy of his revised *In Small Things Forgotten* and wrote in the front, "For all the good times, Cheers, Jim." My closest times with him had been in the past and they were, indeed, some of the very best times of my life. But regardless of how often we saw one another in later years, the opportunity to learn something new, or just to think about things in a different way, was always there. A mental spark from Jim was such a great pleasure, in large part because it was always a two-way street for him.

It is difficult for me to imagine the practice of historical archaeology without Jim Deetz. I know he had strong opinions about what was happening to the field. In fall 1994, Steve Mrozowski and I organized a session for the Washington, DC, SHA meetings on historical archaeology and the culture concept. Program chair Henry Miller found the topic to be a compelling one and decided to make it the plenary session for that year's meeting. I asked Jim to put together his thoughts on the subject as the keynote. Although the paper he wrote was never published, I think it is important for us to consider most seriously what Jim had to say (with some help from his friend Henry Glassie) at the 1995 plenary:

> What is the current status of the concept of culture; is it still healthy, or rather is it suffering from some terminal affliction, or even worse, has it met with what some would see as a timely demise? There are those who have already erected the grave marker with what seems an almost morbid, and certainly, cynical satisfaction. Remember Kent Flannery's Old Timer, who was forced into early retirement because he believed in culture? I must admit that I find this situation both sad and deeply alarming. Leaving aside the simple fact that behavior can be seen as a product of culture, regardless of which of the many definitions we choose to employ, such a perspective is a reflection of a century or more of thoughtful insight. Are we really prepared to jettison the works and thoughts of people such as E. B. Tylor, Franz Boas, A. L. Kroeber, Leslie White, or Claude Levi-Strauss, to name but a very few? I think not, and would suggest that what might make better sense would be to create parallel and separate agendas, one for those who find the culture concept useful in reaching some basic understandings of the human condition, and the other for those who choose behavioral explanations
>
> Another problem that I see ... is a fixation on words, almost for their own sake. One can spot such writing with even the most superficial skimming of text—situated knowledge, masking, negotiation, deconstruction, everyday life, hegemony, embedded, to privilege. This liberal sprinkling of text with fashionable words and phrases, like jimmies on an ice cream cone, lead to what Henry Glassie aptly called a "verbal gyre through which criticism descends into cynicism, self complaint permutes into self fascination, political responsibilities evaporate into elitist abstractions, interest in the world is replaced by interest in the academical, and righteous action, numbed by paradox, stops."
>
> Well, folks, I still have a healthy interest in the world, real or not, and like the Old Timer, I still believe in culture, whether it is fashionable to do so or not (Deetz 2001).

The profession of historical archaeology has been fortunate to have among its long-term practioners a scholar like Jim Deetz who will be remembered for his commitment to anthropology and for his ability to communicate the significance of archaeology to all audiences. Jim's gifts were on display every time he went into the classroom, every time he sat down and got to work on his well-worn typewriter, and every time he kneeled down to have a closer look at a soil stain or artifact in the ground.

ACKNOWLEDGMENTS

Over two days in late August 1989, Jim Deetz and I sat in the living room of his house in the Berkeley hills talking about his career up to that point, an interview encouraged by my colleagues and fellow Deetz students, Mary Beaudry and Anne Yentsch (who were putting together what is now fondly referred to as the Deetzschrift). The results of that conversation, patiently transcribed from cassette by my former secretary, Nan Reisweber, didn't make it into a volume, but they are the source of Jim's voice in this memorial essay. I have also drawn on material gathered for my 1997 Harrington Award presentation, based on another formal interview with Jim, who by that time had moved his living room to Charlottesville, Virginia. On that occasion, we focused on identifying various photographs that chronicled his life, which had been graciously provided to me by eldest daughter Tonia Rock, by Gene Prince and Maria Franklin, and by Jim himself. The final version of this memorial could not have been prepared without the contribution of Jim's wife, Patricia Scott Deetz, son Eric Deetz, daughter-in-law Anna Agbe-Davies, and son-in-law Seth Mallios. Chris Fennell, who helped bring Jim into the Internet age, gave an earlier draft a thorough reading and has been very supportive throughout the preparation of this memorial essay, which has also benefited from review and comment by Greg Brown, Andy Edwards, and Kathleen Bragdon. Finally, in his capacity as memorial editor, Bill Lees helped me bring this essay to completion. I thank him for giving me this assignment and for his persistence in seeing it through to completion. Any errors in this portrait of Jim Deetz's career are, of course, my responsibility alone.

REFERENCES

ANDERSON, JAY
1971 *"A Solid Sufficiency:" An Ethnography of Yeoman Foodways in Stuart England.* Doctoral dissertation, University of Pennsylvania, Philadelphia. University Microfilms International, Ann Arbor, MI.

BOYER, PAUL, AND STEPHEN NISSENBAUM
1974 *Salem Possessed: The Social Origins of Witchcraft.* Harvard University Press, Cambridge, MA.

COTTER, JOHN L.
1958 Archeological Excavations at Jamestown Virginia. *U.S. National Park Service Archeological Research Series,* No. 4. Washington, DC.

CHILCOTT, JOHN H., AND JAMES F. DEETZ
1964 The Construction and Uses of a Laboratory Archaeological Site. *American Antiquity,* 29(3):328–337.

DAWSON, LAWRENCE E., AND JAMES DEETZ
1964 *Chumash Indian Art.* Exhibit Catalogue, Art Gallery, University of California, Santa Barbara.
1965 A Corpus of Chumash Basketry. *UCLA Archaeological Survey Annual Report,* pp. 193–275. Department of Anthropology, University of California, Los Angeles.

DEETZ, JAMES
1960a An Archaeological Approach to Kinship Change in Eighteenth-Century Arikara Culture. Doctoral dissertation, Department of Anthropology, Harvard University, Cambridge, MA.
1960b Excavations at the Joseph Howland Site (C5), Rocky Nook, Kingston, Massachusetts, 1959: A Preliminary Report. *Howland Quarterly,* 24(2&3):1–12.
1960c The Howlands at Rocky Nook: An Archaeological and Historical Study. *Howland Quarterly,* 24(4):1–8.
1963 Archaeological Investigations at La Purisima Mission. Archaeological Survey, Department of Anthropology, *Annual Report 1962–63.* University of California, Los Angeles, pp. 161–241.
1964 A Datable Chumash Pictograph from Santa Barbara County, California. *American Antiquity,* 29(4):504–506.
1967 *Invitation to Archaeology.* Natural History Press [Doubleday] for The American Museum of Natural History, Garden City, NJ.
1969 The Reality of the Pilgrim Fathers. *Natural History,* 78(9):32–44.
1972 Ceramics from Plymouth, 1620–1835: The Archaeological Evidence. In *Ceramics in America,* Ian M. G. Quimby, editor, pp. 15–40. University Press of Virginia, Charlottesville.
1977 *In Small Things Forgotten: The Archaeology of Early American Life.* Doubleday, Anchor Press, New York.
1980 Other People's Garbage. *TV Guide,* 10 May:33–34.
1987a Harrington Histograms Versus Binford Mean Dates As a Technique for Establishing the Occupational Sequence of Sites at Flowerdew Hundred, Virginia. *American Archaeology,* 6(1):62–67.
1987b Plymouth Colony Room-by-Room Inventories, 1633–1684. Manuscript abstracted in Early American Probate Inventories. *Dublin Seminar for New England Folklife Annual Proceedings,* vol. 12:182. Boston.
1988a American Historical Archaeology: Methods and Results. *Science,* 239:362–367.
1988b Material Culture and World View in Colonial Anglo-America. In *The Recovery of Meaning: Historical Archaeology in the Eastern United States,* Mark P. Leone and Parker B. Potter, Jr., editors, pp. 219–233. Smithsonian Institution Press, Washington, DC.
1989 Foreword. In *Cemeteries and Gravemarkers: Voices of American Culture,* Richard E. Meyer, editor, pp. ix–xiv. UMI Research Press, Ann Arbor, MI.
1993 *Flowerdew Hundred: The Archaeology of a Virginia Plantation, 1619–1864.* University Press of Virginia, Charlottesville.
2001 Cultural Dimensions of Ethnicity in the Archaeological Record. Keynote Address, 28th Annual Meeting of The Society for Historical Archaeology, Washington, DC, 1995. In *The Plymouth Colony Archive Project,* Patricia Scott Deetz and Christopher Fennell, editors. University of Virginia, Charlottesville. <http://etext.lib.virginia.edu/users/deetz/Plymouth/JDeetzmem6.html>.

DEETZ, JAMES (EDITOR)
1971 *Man's Imprint from the Past: Readings in the Methods of Archaeology.* Little, Brown & Co., Boston.

DEETZ, JAMES, AND JAY ANDERSON
1972 The Ethnogastronomy of Thanksgiving. *Saturday Review of Science,* November:29–38.

DEETZ, JAMES, AND PATRICIA SCOTT DEETZ
2000 *The Times of Their Lives: Life, Love, and Death in Plymouth Colony.* W.H. Freeman, New York.

DEETZ, JAMES, AND EDWIN S. DETHLEFSEN
    1963   Soil pH As a Tool in Archaeological Site Interpretation. *American Antiquity*, 29(2):242–243.
    1965   The Doppler Effect and Archaeology: A Consideration of the Spatial Aspects of Seriation. *Southwestern Journal of Anthropology*, 21(3):196–206.
    1971   Some Social Aspects of New England Colonial Mortuary Art. In Approaches to the Social Dimensions of Mortuary Practices, James A. Brown, editor, pp. 30–38. *Memoirs of the Society for American Archaeology*, no. 25.

DEMOS, JOHN
    1970   *A Little Commonwealth: Family Life in Plymouth Colony.* Oxford University Press, Oxford, England.

ERIKSON, KAI T.
    1966   *Wayward Puritans: A Study in the Sociology of Deviance.* John Wiley & Sons, New York.

FLANNERY, KENT V.
    1973   Archaeology with a Capital "S." In *Research and Theory in Current Archaeology*, Charles Redman, editor, pp. 47–53. John Wiley & Sons, New York.

GLASSIE, HENRY
    1968   *Pattern in the Material Folk Culture of the Eastern United States.* University of Pennsylvania Press, Philadelphia.

HARRINGTON, J. C.
    1954   Dating Stem Fragments of Seventeenth- and Eighteenth-Century Clay Tobacco Pipes. *Quarterly Bulletin of the Archaeological Society of Virginia*, 9(1):9–13.

HILL, JAMES NEWLIN
    1965   *Broken K: A Prehistoric Society in Eastern Arizona.* Doctoral dissertation, The University of Chicago. University Microfilms International, Ann Arbor, MI.

LONGACRE, WILLIAM ATLAS
    1963   *Archaeology As Anthropology: A Case Study.* Doctoral dissertation, The University of Chicago. University Microfilms International, Ann Arbor, MI.

MARKELL, ANN, MARTIN HALL, AND CARMEL SCHRIRE
    1995   The Historical Archaeology of Vergelegen, an Early Farmstead at the Cape of Good Hope. *Historical Archaeology*, 29(1): 10–34.

MORGAN, EDMUND S.
    1975   *American Slavery, American Freedom: The Ordeal of Colonial Virginia.* W.W. Norton, New York.

NOËL HUME, IVOR
    1963   *Here Lies Virginia: An Archaeologist's View of Colonial Life and History.* Alfred Knopf, New York.

OLIVER, DOUGLAS L.
    1964   *Invitation to Anthropology.* Natural History Press, Garden City, NY.

OWEN, ROGER C., JAMES J. F. DEETZ, AND ANTHONY D. FISHER (EDITORS)
    1967   *The North American Indians: A Sourcebook.* Macmillan, New York.

RUTMAN, DARRETT B.
    1967   *Husbandmen of Plymouth: Farms and Villages of the Old Colony, 1620–1692.* Beacon Press, Boston, MA.

SCHRIRE, CARMEL, JAMES DEETZ, DAVID LUBINSKY, AND CEDRIC POGGENPOEL
    1990   The Chronology of Oudepost I, Cape, As Inferred from an Analysis of Clay Pipes. *Journal of Archaeological Science*, 17(3):269–300.

BIBLIOGRAPHY OF JAMES F. DEETZ

Compiled by Patricia Scott Deetz and Christopher Fennell

PUBLISHED WORKS

CHILCOTT, JOHN H., AND JAMES F. DEETZ
    1964   The Construction and Uses of a Laboratory Archaeological Site. *American Antiquity*, 29(3):328–337.

1977   The Construction and Uses of a Laboratory Archaeological Site. In *Experimental Archaeology*, Daniel Ingersoll, John E. Yellen, and William MacDonald, editors, pp. 252–268. Columbia University Press, New York. Reprinted from 1964 *American Antiquity* edition.

DAWSON, LAWRENCE [E], AND JAMES DEETZ
1964   *Chumash Indian Art.* Exhibit Catalogue, Art Gallery, University of California, Santa Barbara.
1965   A Corpus of Chumash Basketry. *UCLA Archaeological Survey Annual Report*, pp. 193–275. Department of Anthropology, University of California, Los Angeles.

DEETZ, JAMES
1958a   The Archaeology of Western Mexico. Middle American Archaeology Seminar Papers (Anthropology 211), Vol. 1, pp. 1–58. Manuscript, Department of Anthropology, Harvard University, Cambridge, MA.
1958b   A Brief History of the Discovery of Neanderthal Man. Papers on Neanderthal Man (Anthropology 202). Manuscript, Department of Anthropology, Harvard University, Cambridge, MA.
1960a   An Archaeological Approach to Kinship Change in Eighteenth-Century Arikara Culture. Doctoral dissertation, Department of Anthropology, Harvard University, Cambridge, MA.
1960b   Excavations at the Joseph Howland Site (C5), Rocky Nook, Kingston, Massachusetts, 1959: A Preliminary Report. *Howland Quarterly*, 24(2&3):1–12.
1960c   The Howlands at Rocky Nook: An Archaeological and Historical Study. *Howland Quarterly* 24(4):1–8.
1962   Abstract of an Archaeological Approach to Eighteenth-Century Arikara Kinship Change. *Abstracts in New World Archaeology*, vol. 2, Society for American Archaeology.
1963a   Archaeological Investigations at La Purisima Mission. *Annual Report of the Archaeological Survey, Department of Anthropology, University of California, Los Angeles, 1962/1963*, pp. 161–241.
1963b   Style Change in New England Colonial Gravestone Design: An Experiment in "Historic Archaeology" (Archaeological Materials and Techniques). Manuscript, Department of Anthropology, Harvard University, Cambridge, MA.
1964   A Datable Chumash Pictograph from Santa Barbara County, California. *American Antiquity* 29(4):504–506.
1965a   The Dynamics of Stylistic Change in Arikara Ceramics. *Illinois Studies in Anthropology*, No. 4. University of Illinois Press, Urbana.
1965b   Old Tools As New Tools. *Anthropology Curriculum Study Project Newsletter*, 4:6–7. Chicago, IL.
1966   Stone Tools, Anthropology Curriculum Study Project. Excerpt in *Origins of Humanness: Patterns in Human History*, Edwin Dethlefsen, editor, pp. 74–84. Macmillan & Co., New York.
1967   *Invitation to Archaeology.* Natural History Press [Doubleday] for The American Museum of Natural History, Garden City, NJ.
1968a   Cultural Patterning of Behavior As Reflected by Archaeological Materials. In *Settlement Archaeology*, Kwang Chih Chang, editor, pp. 31–42. National Press Books, Palo Alto, CA.
1968b   The Inference of Residence and Descent from Archaeological Data. In *New Perspectives in Archaeology*, Lewis R. Binford and Sally Binford, editors, pp. 41–48. Aldine Press, Chicago, IL.
1968c   Late Man in North America: Archaeology of European Americans. In *Anthropological Archaeology in the Americas*, Betty J. Meggers, editor, pp. 121–130. Anthropological Society of Washington, Washington, DC.
1969a   Hunters in Archaeological Perspective. In *Man the Hunter*, Irven DeVore and Richard Lee, editors, pp. 281–285. Aldine Press, Chicago, IL.
1969b   The Reality of the Pilgrim Fathers. *Natural History*, 78(9):32–44.
1970a   Archaeology As a Social Science. In Current Directions in Archaeology, *Bulletin of the American Anthropological Association* 3(3), pt. 2:115–125.
1970b   A New World Viewpoint. In *Introductory Readings in Archaeology*, Brian M. Fagan, editor, pp. 10–13. Little, Brown & Co., Boston.
1970c   Prehistoric Social Systems. In *Introductory Readings in Archaeology*, Brian M. Fagan, editor, pp. 339–347. Little, Brown & Co., Boston.
1971a   The Historic House Museum: Can it Live? *Historic Preservation*, 23(1):50–54.
1971b   Late Man in North America: Archaeology of European Americans. In *Man's Imprint from the Past: Readings in the Methods of Archaeology*, James Deetz, editor, pp. 208–218. Little, Brown & Co., Boston. Reprint of 1968 edition in *Anthropological Archaeology in the Americas*.
1971c   Must Archaeologists Dig? In *Man's Imprint from the Past: Readings in the Methods of Archaeology*, James Deetz, editor, pp. 2–9. Little, Brown & Co., Boston.
1972a   Archaeology As a Social Science. In *Contemporary Archaeology: A Guide to Theory and Contributions*, Mark P. Leone, editor, pp. 108–117. Southern Illinois University Press, Carbondale. Reprint of 1970 edition in *Bulletin of the American Anthropological Association*.
1972b   Ceramics from Plymouth, 1620–1835: The Archaeological Evidence. In *Ceramics in America*, Ian M. G. Quimby, editor, pp. 15–40. University Press of Virginia, Charlottesville.
1974   A Cognitive Historical Model for American Material Culture, 1620–1835. In Reconstructing Complex Societies—An Archaeological Colloquium, Charlotte B. Moore, editor, pp. 21–29. *Supplement to the Bulletin of the American Schools of Oriental Research*, 20.
1976a   Black Settlement: Plymouth. *Archaeology*, 29(3):207.

1976b What Is Archaeology? In *The Evolution of Human Adaptations: Readings in Anthropology*, John J. Poggie, Jr., Gretel H. Pelto, and Pertti J. Pelto, compilers, pp. 26–39. Macmillan, New York.

1977a Archaeology As a Social Science. *ASA Journal* 1(2):5–14. Reprint of 1970 article in *Bulletin of the American Anthropological Association*.

1977b *In Small Things Forgotten: The Archaeology of Early American Life*. Doubleday, Anchor Press, New York.

1977c Material Culture and Archaeology—What's the Difference? In Historical Archaeology and the Importance of Material Things, Leland Ferguson, editor, pp. 9–12. The Society for Historical Archaeology. *Special Publication Series*, no. 2. California, PA.

1978a Archaeological Investigations at La Purisima Mission. In *Historical Archaeology: A Guide to Substantive and Theoretical Contributions*, Robert L. Schuyler, editor, pp. 160–190. Baywood, Farmingdale, NY. Reprint of excerpts of 1963 edition of *Annual Report of the Archaeological Survey, Department of Anthropology, University of California, Los Angeles, 1962/1963*.

1978b A Cognitive Historical Model for American Material Culture, 1620–1835. In *Historical Archaeology: A Guide to Substantive and Theoretical Contributions*, Robert L. Schuyler, editor, pp. 284–286. Baywood, Farmingdale, NY. Reprint of 1974 article in *Supplement to the Bulletin of the American Schools of Oriental Research*.

1978c Late Man in North America: Archaeology of European Americans. In *Historical Archaeology: A Guide to Substantive and Theoretical Contributions*, Robert L. Schuyler, editor, pp. 48–52. Baywood, Farmingdale, NY. Reprint of 1968 article in *Anthropological Archaeology in the Americas*.

1979 Plymouth Colony Architecture: Archaeological Evidence from the Seventeenth Century. In *Architecture in Colonial Massachusetts: A Conference Held by the Colonial Society of Massachusetts, September 19 and 20, 1974*, pp. 43–59. The Colonial Society of Massachusetts, Boston [Distributed by the University Press of Virginia].

1980a Guessing Who Came to Dinner. *Canadian TV Guide*, 17 May:27–28.

1980b Other People's Garbage. *TV Guide*, 10 May:33–34.

1980c A Sense of Another World: History Museums and Cultural Change. *Museum News*, 58(5):40–45.

1981 The Link from Objects to Person to Concept. In *Museums, Adults, and the Humanities: A Guide for Educational Programming*, Zipporah W. Collins, editor, pp. 24–34. American Association of Museums, Washington, DC.

1982 Households: A Structural Key to Archaeological Explanation. *American Behavioral Scientist*, 25(6):717–724.

1983a The Artifact and Its Context. *Museum News*, 62(1):25–26.

1983b Scientific Humanism and Humanistic Science: A Plea for Paradigmatic Pluralism in Historical Archaeology. In Historical Archaeology of the Eastern United States: Papers from the R. J. Russell Symposium, Robert W. Neuman, editor. *Geoscience and Man*, 23:27–34.

1987a Harrington Histograms Versus Binford Mean Dates As a Technique for Establishing the Occupational Sequence of Sites at Flowerdew Hundred, Virginia. *American Archaeology*, 6(1):62–67.

1987b Plymouth Colony Room-by-Room Inventories, 1633–1684. Manuscript abstracted in Early American Probate Inventories. *Dublin Seminar for New England Folklife Annual Proceedings*, vol. 12:182. Boston.

1988a American Historical Archaeology: Methods and Results. *Science*, 239:362–367.

1988b History and Archaeological Theory: Walter Taylor Revisited. *American Antiquity*, 53(1):13–22.

1988c *Invitation to Archaeology*. Japanese translation. Tuttle-Mori Agency, Inc., Tokyo.

1988d Material Culture and World View in Colonial Anglo-America. In *The Recovery of Meaning: Historical Archaeology in the Eastern United States*, Mark P. Leone and Parker B. Potter, Jr., editors, pp. 219–233. Smithsonian Institution Press, Washington, DC.

1989a Archaeography, Archaeology, or Archeology? *American Journal of Archaeology*, 93(3):429–435.

1989b Foreword. In *Cemeteries and Gravemarkers: Voices of American Culture*, Richard E. Meyer, editor, pp. ix–xiv. UMI Research Press, Ann Arbor, MI.

1989c *In Small Things Forgotten: The Archaeology of Early American Life*. Doubleday, New York. Reprint of 1977 edition.

1990 Landscapes As Cultural Statements. Prologue in *Earth Patterns: Essays in Landscape Archaeology*, William M. Kelso and Rachel Most, editors, pp. 1–4. University Press of Virginia, Charlottesville.

1991 Introduction: Archaeological Evidence of Sixteenth- and Seventeenth-Century Encounters. In *Historical Archaeology in Global Perspective*, Lisa Falk, editor, pp. 1–9. Smithsonian Institution Press, Washington, DC.

1992 Foreword. In *Cemeteries and Gravemarkers: Voices of American Culture*, Richard E. Meyer, editor, pp. ix–xiv. Utah State University Press, Logan, UT. Reprint of 1989 UMI Research Press.

1993 *Flowerdew Hundred: The Archaeology of a Virginia Plantation, 1619–1864*. University Press of Virginia, Charlottesville.

1994 Foreword. In *A Chesapeake Family and Their Slaves: A Study in Historical Archaeology*, by Anne Elizabeth Yentsch, pp. xviii–xx. Cambridge University Press, Cambridge.

1995 *Flowerdew Hundred: The Archaeology of a Virginia Plantation, 1619–1864*. University Press of Virginia, Charlottesville. Reprint of 1993 edition.

1996 *In Small Things Forgotten: An Archaeology of Early American Life*, expanded and revised version of 1989 edition, originally published in 1977. Anchor Books, Doubleday, New York.

1997a Introductory Archaeology: An Identity Crisis in the Temple of Doom. In *The Teaching of Anthropology: Problems, Issues, and Decisions*, Conrad P. Kottak, Jane J. White, Richard H. Furlow, and Patricia C. Rice, editors, pp. 232–238. Mayfield, Mountain View, CA.

1997b Preface. In *Archaeology at Monticello*, by William M. Kelso, pp. 11–13. Thomas Jefferson Memorial Foundation, Charlottesville.

1998 Discussion: Archaeologists As Storytellers. In Archaeologists As Storytellers, Adrian Praetzellis and Mary Praetzellis, editors. *Historical Archaeology,* 32(1):94–96.

1999 Archaeology at Flowerdew Hundred. In *"I, Too, Am America": Archaeological Studies of African-American Life,* Theresa A. Singleton, editor, pp. 39–46. University Press of Virginia, Charlottesville.

DEETZ, JAMES J. F.
1963 Basketry from the James Abels Collection. *Museum Talk,* 38(2):17–23.

DEETZ, JAMES, AND JAY ANDERSON
1972 The Ethnogastronomy of Thanksgiving. *Saturday Review of Science,* November:29–38.

DEETZ, JAMES, AND PATRICIA SCOTT DEETZ
2000a Rocking the Plymouth Myth. *Archaeology,* 53(6):16–17.
2000b *The Times of Their Lives: Life, Love, and Death in Plymouth Colony.* W. H. Freeman, New York.
2001 *The Times of Their Lives: Life, Love, and Death in Plymouth Colony.* Anchor Books, Random House, New York. Reprint of 2000 W. H. Freeman edition.

DEETZ, JAMES, AND EDWIN [S.] DETHLEFSEN
1963 Soil pH As a Tool in Archaeological Site Interpretation. *American Antiquity,* 29(2):242–243.
1965 The Doppler Effect and Archaeology: A Consideration of the Spatial Aspects of Seriation. *Southwestern Journal of Anthropology,* 21(3):196–206.
1967 Death's Head, Cherub, Urn and Willow. *Natural History,* 76(3):29–37.
1971 Some Social Aspects of New England Colonial Mortuary Art. In Approaches to the Social Dimensions of Mortuary Practices, James A. Brown, editor. *Memoirs of the Society for American Archaeology,* vol. 25. *American Antiquity,* 36 (3), pt. 2:30–38.
1972 Death's Head, Cherub, Urn and Willow. In *Contemporary Archaeology: A Guide to Theory and Contributions,* Mark P. Leone, editor, pp. 402–410. Southern Illinois University Press, Carbondale. Reprint of 1967 edition in *Natural History.*
1977a Death's Head, Cherub, Urn and Willow. In *Man's Many Ways: The Natural History Reader in Anthropology,* Richard A. Gould, editor, pp. 88–93. Harper & Row, New York. Reprint of 1967 edition in *Natural History.*
1977b The Doppler Effect and Archaeology: A Consideration of the Spatial Aspects of Seriation. In *Experimental Archaeology,* Daniel Ingersoll, John E. Yellen, and William MacDonald, editors, pp. 133–144. Columbia University Press, New York. Reprint of 1965 article in *Southwestern Journal of Anthropology.*
1978 Death's Head, Cherub, Urn and Willow. In *Historical Archaeology: A Guide to Substantive and Theoretical Contributions,* Robert L. Schuyler, editor, pp. 83–89. Baywood, Farmingdale, NY. Reprint of 1967 edition in *Natural History.*

DEETZ, JAMES, AND PATRICIA E. SCOTT
1995 Documents, Historiography, and Material Culture in Historical Archaeology. In The Written and the Wrought: Complementary Sources in Historical Archaeology. Essays in Honor of James Deetz. Mary Ellin D'Agostino, Elizabeth Prine, Eleanor Casella, and Margot Winer, editors. *Kroeber Anthropological Society Papers,* 79:110–115. Kroeber Anthropological Society, Berkeley, CA.

DETHLEFSEN, EDWIN, AND JAMES DEETZ
1966 Death's Heads, Cherubs, and Willow Trees: Experimental Archaeology in Colonial Cemeteries. *American Antiquity,* 31(4): 502–510.
1967 Eighteenth-Century Cemeteries: A Demographic View. *Historical Archaeology,* 1:40–42.
1977 Death's Heads, Cherubs, and Willow Trees: Experimental Archaeology in Colonial Cemeteries. In Passing: The Vision of Death in America, Charles O. Jackson, editor, pp. 48–59. *Contributions in Family Studies,* vol. 2. Greenwood Press, Westport, CT. Excerpted from 1966 *American Antiquity* edition.
1998 Experimentacion Arqueologica en Cementerio Colonial: Disenos de Calaveras, Querubines y Sauces [cover title: Arqueologia Experimental en Cementerios Coloniales], Jaime Miasta Gutierrez, translator, pp. 31–55. Translation of 1966 *American Antiquity* edition of Death's Heads, Cherubs, and Willow Trees: Experimental Archaeology in Colonial Cemeteries. *Lecturas "Emilio Choy,"* no. 15. Universidad Nacional Mayor de San Marcos, Seminario de Historia Rural Andina, Lima, Peru.

EKHOLM, ERIK, AND JAMES DEETZ
1970 Wellfleet Tavern. *Natural History,* 80(7):48–57.

SCHRIRE, CARMEL, JAMES DEETZ, DAVID LUBINSKY, AND CEDRIC POGGENPOEL
1990 The Chronology of Oudepost I, Cape, As Inferred from an Analysis of Clay Pipes. *Journal of Archaeological Science,* 17(3):269–300.

SCOTT, PATRICIA E., AND JAMES DEETZ
1990 Building, Furnishings, and Social Change in Early Victorian Grahamstown. *Social Dynamics,* 16(1):76–89.

WINER, MARGOT, AND JAMES DEETZ
1990 The Transformation of British Culture in the Eastern Cape, 1820–1860. *Social Dynamics: A Journal of the Centre for African Studies, University of Cape Town*, 16(1):55–75.
1992 The Transformation of British Culture in the Eastern Cape, 1820–1860. *Kroeber Anthropological Society Papers*, 73/74: 41–61.

WINER, MARGOT, PATRICIA SCOTT, AND JAMES DEETZ
1991 Buried Treasure: Household Archaeology in the Eastern Cape. *Phoenix: Magazine of the Albany Museum*, 4(2):5–13.

EDITED WORKS

DEETZ, JAMES (EDITOR)
1971 *Man's Imprint from the Past: Readings in the Methods of Archaeology.* Little, Brown & Co., Boston.

OWEN, ROGER C., JAMES J. F. DEETZ, AND ANTHONY D. FISHER (EDITORS)
1967 *The North American Indians: A Sourcebook.* Macmillan, New York.

PUBLISHED ONLINE

DEETZ, JAMES
2001 Cultural Dimensions of Ethnicity in the Archaeological Record. Keynote Address, 28th Annual Meeting of The Society for Historical Archaeology, Washington, DC, 1995. In *The Plymouth Colony Archive Project*, Patricia Scott Deetz and Christopher Fennell, editors. University of Virginia, Charolttesville. <http://etext.lib.virginia.edu/users/deetz/Plymouth/JDeetzmem6.html>.

DEETZ, JAMES, AND PATRICIA SCOTT DEETZ
2000 Seventeenth-Century Timber Framing. In *The Plymouth Colony Archive Project*, James Deetz, Patricia Scott Deetz, and Christopher Fennell, editors. University of Virginia, Charlottesville. <http://etext.lib.virginia.edu/users/deetz/Plymouth/framing.html>.

DEETZ, JAMES, AND EDWIN S. DETHLEFSEN
2001 Death's Head, Cherub, Urn and Willow, reprint of 1967 edition in *Natural History*, with 19 additional illustrations from the James F. Deetz Archaeological Slide Collection (maintained by J. Eric Deetz). In *The Plymouth Colony Archive Project*, Patricia Scott Deetz and Christopher Fennell, editors. University of Virginia, Charlottesville. <http://etext.lib.virginia/users/deetz/Plymouth/deathshead.html>.

DEETZ, PATRICIA SCOTT, AND JAMES DEETZ
1998 Vernacular House Forms in Seventeenth-Century Plymouth Colony: An Analysis of Evidence from the Plymouth Colony Room-by-Room Probate Inventories 1633–85. In *The Plymouth Colony Archive Project*, James Deetz, Patricia Scott Deetz, and Christopher Fennell, editors. University of Virginia, Charlottesville. <http://etext.lib.virginia.edu/users/deetz/Plymouth/folkhouse.htm>.

FESTSCHRIFTS IN HONOR OF JAMES DEETZ

D'AGOSTINO, MARY ELLIN, ELIZABETH PRINE, ELEANOR CASELLA, AND MARGOT WINER (EDITORS)
1995 The Written and the Wrought: Complementary Sources in Historical Archaeology. Essays in Honor of James Deetz. *Kroeber Anthropological Society Papers*, no. 79. Kroeber Anthropological Society, Berkeley, CA.

YENTSCH, ANNE ELIZABETH, AND MARY C. BEAUDRY (EDITORS)
1992 *The Art and Mystery of Historical Archaeology: Essays in Honor of James Deetz.* CRC Press, Boca Raton, FL.

Marley R. Brown III

MEMORIAL: George Irving Quimby, 1913-2003. Volume 38, Number 2 (2004): 124-132. By Charles E. Cleland and Virgil E. Noble.

Memorial

George Irving Quimby, 1913–2003

George Quimby at the wheel of a sailing schooner, Hudson Bay, 1939. (Photo courtesy Ed Quimby, previously published in Quimby 1993 and 1994.)

George Irving Quimby succumbed to pneumonia-related causes on 17 February 2003 in Seattle, Washington, at the age of 89. With his passing, historical archaeology lost one of its last true pioneers, a major scholar of international repute, and a prolific contributor to the literature of our discipline. Beyond his well-earned status as a leading figure in the profession, George was a loving husband and devoted father, as well as a dear friend and mentor to three generations of archaeologists. His ready wit and treasure trove of vivid stories on the early years of American archaeology, including those derived from his own remarkable adventures, were fascinating attractions that none could resist.

Born on 4 May 1913, George spent his childhood in Grand Rapids, Michigan. His lifelong sense of adventure as well as his abiding interest in Native Americans emerged early in life. At age six, having read about the Seminoles of Florida in *National Geographic*, he loaded his wagon with soap bars and headed south to trade with them as the pioneers had done. George was discovered that night in a barn some four miles from home, tired but undaunted. His subsequent travels as a young man, though, would take him much farther afield, immersing him in landscapes that later significantly informed his understanding and interpretations of the past.

While a teenager, George spent three summers sailing a wooden schooner on the upper Great Lakes (at times, by his own accounts, running whiskey from Canada during Prohibition). In summer 1939, as an assistant to geologist George M. Stanley, he canoed along the eastern coast of Hudson Bay, mapping glacial landforms and correlating them with archaeological sites—an experience that George would later recall as being like a trip in a time machine. He also lived in the Deep South, as a Works Progress Administration (WPA) archaeological field director in 1939–1941, while America emerged from the Great Depression. In each of these diverse places, George observed many small communities that, as he put it, "were more typical of the 19th century than of the 20th, ... scenes more familiar to my ancestors than to my descendants" (Quimby 1994:116–117).

George Quimby completed a BA in anthropology at the University of Michigan in 1936 and his MA at the same institution in 1937, having studied under James B. Griffin, who would become a lifelong friend. He then enrolled in the graduate program at the University of Chicago but cut short his studies for work with the WPA after James A. Ford offered him a job while attending the first Southeast Archaeological Conference at Birmingham, Alabama, in 1938. Once, when asked in casual conversation why Quimby had not continued to study for his PhD, Griffin answered matter-of-factly that there simply was not anyone who knew enough to give George a comprehensive exam.

With the WPA Archaeological Survey on the campus at Louisiana State University in Baton Rouge, he met Helen Margery Ziehm, then an art student majoring in sculpture, and they were married in 1940. When his position was eliminated in July of 1941, the couple moved to western Michigan, where Quimby briefly held the position of director at the Muskegon County Museum.

In 1942, Quimby's Chicago contacts paid off when Chief Curator Paul S. Martin offered him a position at the Field Museum of Natural History in Chicago, where he advanced from assistant curator to curator of North American archaeology and ethnology in 1954. Until he left the Field Museum in 1965, he conducted research on the archaeology and material culture of such far-flung locales as the upper Midwest, the Southeast, the Southwest, the Aleutian Islands, Alaska, and the Kamchatka Peninsula of Siberia. Along with Martin and fellow curator Donald Collier, Quimby also introduced several courses in museum methods that were taught at the Field Museum through the University of Chicago.

Quimby's comprehensive knowledge of North American archaeology served him well when in 1947 he joined Martin and Collier in publishing *Indians before Columbus: 20,000 Years of North American History As Revealed by Archaeology*. The book was one of the first comprehensive surveys of American prehistory and stood as a standard text on the subject until the application of radiocarbon dating provided an accurate chronology for prehistoric cultural developments. Likewise, his book *Indian Life in the Great Lakes 11,000 B.C. to A.D. 1800*, published in 1960, was the first systematic treatment of that region's archaeology. Unlike most of the archaeological books of the era, this one did not end with the advent of European contact but took the reader well into the early Historic period that had long intrigued him.

In fact, it is worth noting that Quimby's very first publications in the late 1930s dealt with the analysis of historic material culture, specifically the use of European trade items and particularly silver ornaments for dating archaeological deposits. In 1966, he summarized the culmination of almost 30 years of research on the fur trade and its material culture in *Indian Culture and European Trade Goods: The Archaeology of the Historic Period in the Western Great Lakes Region*. This book was his best known and, perhaps, most significant contribution to historical archaeology, and scholars of the fur trade today still frequently refer to it.

One chapter in that book, "The First European Trade Ship on the Western Great Lakes," is particularly remarkable for its early consideration of maritime history in an archaeological text. During his 23 years at the Field Museum, Quimby had developed an academic interest in the search for LaSalle's *Griffin* and, though not a diver, was a strong advocate for scientific underwater archaeological research. Indeed, he was a participant at the first Conference on Underwater Archaeology held at St. Paul, Minnesota, in 1963, which some authorities mark as the catalyst for the creation of the Advisory Council on Underwater Archaeology.

Quimby announced in 1965 that he had accepted an appointment as full professor of anthropology at the University of Washington with a joint appointment as curator of ethnology at its Thomas Burke Memorial Washington State Museum. He privately noted at the time that it was his first real teaching position and that he enjoyed starting at the top. Certainly it was a novel career change, not only because of the regular teaching duties he would assume but also in the total departure from his Midwestern roots and experience. As he himself explained, "A person should do something radical—once every 25 years."

In Seattle, Quimby turned his attention and considerable energies to the Northwest Coast and its native cultures, and he was soon named director of the Burke Museum in 1968. Bringing to the job a clear commitment to professionalism, in short order Quimby reorganized and modernized the museum into a first-class institution, which emphasized indigenous cultures of the Pacific Rim and was devoted to both research and public education. Not limiting his efforts to the confines of his own institution, he was also instrumental in developing one of the very first interdisciplinary academic programs in museology in North America, established at the University of Washington in 1972. He also lent his assistance and encouragement to the Makah Nation in their efforts to create a museum of tribal heritage.

Quimby's demanding administrative and teaching duties, however, did not interfere with his own scholarly research. Urged on by an insatiable curiosity, he continued to investigate and publish on new topics in archaeology and ethnohistory: the fur trade of the Pacific Northwest, native art of Northwest Coast tribes, and underwater archaeology in Puget Sound. He also took a keen interest in ethnographic film and collaborated on the award-winning restoration of photographer Edward Curtis's 1914 silent classic, *In the Land of the War Canoes*, re-released in 1973.

George Quimby assists Makah craftsman Steve Tyler in carving a traditional single-log cedar canoe, Makah Tribe Archaeological Laboratory, Neah Bay, Washington, 1977. (Photo by Ed Quimby.)

In addition to his scholarly output, Quimby gave much of himself to the profession, serving the Society for American Archaeology as its secretary (1948–1952) and president (1957–1958), and he twice served The Society for Historical Archaeology as a director (1971–1973 and 1975–1977). In return, his colleagues honored him in many ways over the years. Among the outstanding tributes paid to him in later life was a retirement festschrift, *Lulu Linear Punctuated: Essays in Honor of George Irving Quimby*, edited by Robert C. Dunnell and Donald K. Grayson in 1983 (Anthropological Papers, Museum of Anthropology, University of Michigan, No. 72, Ann Arbor), the coveted J. C. Harrington Medal in Historical Archaeology, presented by SHA in 1986, and SAA's Distinguished Service Award in 1989. Perhaps most notable, Grand Valley State University, located near his hometown in Michigan, recognized Quimby's numerous contributions by awarding him an Honorary Doctorate of Humane Letters in 1992 and has since established a memorial fund in his name to assist deserving students.

In a career that spanned seven decades, George Irving Quimby authored more than 170 publications, including many that were written for the general public—a practice whose time has now come in our profession, but which he anticipated by a half-century. He also gave countless papers at conferences, well into his late 70s, and could frequently be spotted roaming the meeting halls in his trademark bow tie or talking with students about their common research interests in the hotel lounge. Having made an indelible mark in the fields of archaeology, museology, and ethnohistory, George will be best remembered for his engaging and often impish personality, with which he could quickly bring calm to a tense faculty meeting or put an awestruck student immediately at ease.

Surviving George are his wife of 62 years, Helen Ziehm Quimby of Seattle; his daughter, Sedna Helen Quimby Wineland, of Boulder, Colorado; sons G. Edward, John E., and Robert W. Quimby of Seattle; and five grandchildren.

For those of us who were fortunate enough to know George Quimby, his passing does not so much evoke a sense of sadness but, rather, a reason to celebrate his life and remarkable character. Where archaeologists gather, glasses will be raised to George for generations to come. What will be missing is that certain twinkle in his eyes, a wry grin, and a twist at the tip of his mustache, all of which would let you know that there was a real whopper coming!

REFERENCE

QUIMBY, GEORGE I.
  1994 Historical Archaeology As I Saw It: 1935–1970. In *Pioneers in Historical Archaeology: Breaking New Ground*, Stanley South, editor, pp. 113–124. Plenum Press, New York.

BIBLIOGRAPHY OF GEORGE IRVING QUIMBY

Single-authored publications by Quimby are alternately attributed to George I. Quimby, George I. Quimby, Jr., or George Irving Quimby in the original. Co-authored references are cited in this bibliography as attributed in the original publications.

The Field Museum of Natural History in Chicago for a time (ca. 1943–1965) was called the Chicago Natural History Museum. To avoid confusion, citations herein consistently refer to the Field Museum, regardless of the particular title page imprint.

BINFORD, LEWIS R., AND GEORGE I. QUIMBY
  1963 Indian Sites and Chipped Stone Materials in the Northern Lake Michigan Area. *Fieldiana: Anthropology* 36(12):277–307. Chicago, IL.
  1972 Indian Sites and Chipped Stone Materials in the Northern Lake Michigan Area. In *An Archaeological Perspective*, Lewis R. Binford, editor, pp. 346-372. Seminar Press, New York. [Reprint of 1963 version published in *Fieldiana: Anthropology*, 36(12):277–307.]

CASTEEL, RICHARD W., AND GEORGE I. QUIMBY
  1975a Introduction. In *Maritime Adaptations of the Pacific*, Richard W. Casteel and George I. Quimby, editors, pp. 1–4. Mouton, The Hague.

CASTEEL, RICHARD W., AND GEORGE I. QUIMBY (EDITORS)
  1975b *Maritime Adaptations of the Pacific*. Mouton, The Hague.

COLLIER, DONALD, AND GEORGE I. QUIMBY, JR.
  1945 Review of *The Fort Ancient Aspect, Its Cultural and Chronological Position in Mississippi Valley Archaeology*, by James Bennett Griffin. *American Anthropologist* 47(1):142–146.

FORD, JAMES A., AND GEORGE I. QUIMBY, JR.
  1945 The Tchefuncte Culture, an Early Occupation of the Lower Mississippi Valley. *Memoirs of the Society for American Archaeology*, 2.

GRIFFIN, JAMES B., AND GEORGE I. QUIMBY
  1961a The McCollum Site, Nipigon District, Ontario. In Lake Superior Copper and the Indians: Miscellaneous Studies of Great Lakes Prehistory, James B. Griffin, editor, pp. 91–102. *Anthropological Papers, Museum of Anthropology, University of Michigan*, 17. University of Michigan, Ann Arbor.
  1961b Prehistoric Copper Pits on the Eastern Side of Lake Superior. In Lake Superior Copper and the Indians: Miscellaneous Studies of Great Lakes Prehistory, James B. Griffin, editor, pp. 77–82. *Anthropological Papers, Museum of Anthropology, University of Michigan*, 17. Ann Arbor.

HOLM, BILL, AND GEORGE I. QUIMBY
  1980 *Edward Curtis in the Land of the War Canoes: A Pioneer Cinematographer in the Pacific Northwest*. Thomas Burke Memorial Washington State Museum Monograph 2. University of Washington Press, Seattle.

MARTIN, PAUL S., GEORGE I. QUIMBY, AND DONALD COLLIER

1947 *Indians before Columbus: 20,000 Years of North American History Revealed by Archaeology.* University of Chicago Press, Chicago, IL.

1975 *Indians before Columbus: 20,000 Years of North American History Revealed by Archaeology,* paperback edition. University of Chicago Press, Chicago, IL.

QUIMBY, GEORGE I.

1937 Notes on Indian Trade Silver Ornaments in Michigan. *Papers of the Michigan Academy of Science, Arts, and Letters,* 22: 15–24. Ann Arbor.

1938 Dated Indian Burials in Michigan. *Papers of the Michigan Academy of Science, Arts, and Letters,* 23:63–72. Ann Arbor.

1939a Aboriginal Camp Sites on Isle Royale, Michigan. *American Antiquity,* 4(3):215–223.

1939b European Trade Articles As Chronological Indicators for the Archaeology of the Historic Period in Michigan. *Papers of the Michigan Academy of Science, Arts, and Letters,* 24:25–32. Ann Arbor.

1940a The Manitunik Eskimo Culture of East Hudson's Bay. *American Antiquity,* 6(2):148–165.

1940b Notes and News—Southeast Area. *American Antiquity,* 5(3):238.

1940c Some Notes on Kinship and Kinship Terminology among the Potawatomi of the Huron. *Papers of the Michigan Academy of Science, Arts, and Letters,* 25:553–563. Ann Arbor.

1941a The Goodall Focus, an Analysis of Ten Hopewellian Components in Michigan and Indiana. *Indiana Historical Society Pre-history Research Series,* 2(2):63–161.

1941b Hopewellian Pottery Types in Michigan. *Papers of the Michigan Academy of Science, Arts, and Letters,* 26:489–494. Ann Arbor.

1941c Review of *Bulletin of the Texas Archaeological and Paleontological Society,* 12. *American Antiquity,* 7(2):194–195.

1942a Indian Trade Objects in Michigan and Louisiana. *Papers of the Michigan Academy of Science, Arts, and Letters,* 27: 543–551. Ann Arbor.

1942b The Natchezan Culture Type. *American Antiquity,* 7(3):255–275.

1943a The Ceramic Sequence within the Goodall Focus. *Papers of the Michigan Academy of Science, Arts, and Letters,* 28: 543–548. Ann Arbor.

1943b Review of *Irene Mound Site, Chatham County, Georgia,* by Joseph Caldwell and Catherine McCann. *American Antiquity,* 8(4):405–406.

1943c A Subjective Interpretation of Some Design Similarities between Hopewell and Northern Algonkian. *American Anthropologist,* 45(4):630–633.

1944a Aleutian Islanders, Eskimos of the North Pacific, Helen Z. Quimby, illustrator. *Field Museum Anthropology Leaflet,* 35. Field Museum of Natural History, Chicago, IL.

1944b Review of *A Selected Bibliography of American Indian Archaeology East of the Rocky Mountains,* by John Otis Brew. *American Antiquity,* 10(2):218.

1944c Some New Data on the Goodall Focus. *Papers of the Michigan Academy of Science, Arts, and Letters,* 29:419–424.

1945a Periods of Prehistoric Art in the Aleutian Islands. *American Antiquity,* 11(2):76–79.

1945b Pottery from the Aleutian Islands. *Fieldiana: Anthropology,* 36(1):1–13. Chicago, IL.

1946a Natchez Social Structure As an Instrument of Assimilation. *American Anthropologist,* 48(1):134–136.

1946b The Possibility of an Independent Agricultural Complex in the Southeastern United States. In *Human Origins: An Introductory General Course in Anthropology, Selected Readings, Series 31,* pp. 206–210. University of Chicago Press, Chicago, IL.

1946c The Sadiron Lamp of Kamchatka As a Clue to the Chronology of the Aleut. *American Antiquity,* 11(3):202–203.

1946d Toggle Harpoon Heads of the Aleutian Islands. *Fieldiana: Anthropology,* 36(2):14–24. Chicago, IL.

1947a Archaeology, Western Hemisphere. In *1947 Britannica Book of the Year,* pp. 66–68. Encyclopaedia Britannica, Chicago, IL.

1947b Archaeology, Western Hemisphere. Ten Eventful Years. In *Encyclopaedia Britannica,* vol. 1, pp. 153–154. Chicago, IL.

1947c The Prehistory of Kamchatka. *American Antiquity,* 12(3):173–179.

1948a Archaeology, Western Hemisphere. In *1948 Britannica Book of the Year,* pp. 59–62. Encyclopaedia Britannica, Chicago, IL.

1948b Culture Contact on the Northwest Coast, 1785–1795. *American Anthropologist,* 50(2):247–255.

1948c Notes and News—Executive Committee Decisions. *American Antiquity,* 14(2):160.

1948d Prehistoric Art of the Aleutian Islands. *Fieldiana: Anthropology,* 36(4):77–92. Chicago, IL.

1948e Review of *Man in Northeastern North America,* Frederick Johnson, editor. *American Anthropologist,* 50(3):525–527.

1949a Archaeology, Western Hemisphere. In *1949 Britannica Book of the Year,* pp. 58–60. Encyclopaedia Britannica, Chicago, IL.

1949b Excavations. In Cochise and Mogollon Sites, Pine Lawn Valley, Western New Mexico, Paul S. Martin, John B. Rinaldo, and Ernst Antevs, editors, pp. 26–33. *Fieldiana: Anthropology,* 38(1):1–232. Chicago, IL.

1949c A Hopewell Tool for Decorating Pottery. *American Antiquity,* 14(4):344.

1949d Notes and News—Meetings of the Society. *American Antiquity,* 15(2):176.

1950a Archaeology, Western Hemisphere. In *1950 Britannica Book of the Year*, pp. 54–56. Encyclopaedia Britannica, Chicago, IL.

1950b Changes in Cultures of United States Indians. *Field Museum of Natural History Bulletin*, 21(9):6–7. Chicago, IL.

1950c "Old Iron" for Treasured Furs: Indian Trade in the 1700's. *Field Museum of Natural History Bulletin*, 21(12):9–10. Chicago, IL.

1951a The Medora Site, West Baton Rouge Parish, Louisiana. *Field Museum of Natural History, Anthropological Series*, 24: 81–135. Chicago, IL.

1951b Natchez Archaeology. *Southeastern Archaeological Conference Newsletter*, 3(3):22–24.

1951c Plains Indians Record Their Story in Pictographs. *Field Museum of Natural History Bulletin*, 22(8):4–5. Chicago, IL.

1951d Sailor Anthropologists of the 18th Century, Mr. De La Perouse, 1799. *Field Museum of Natural History Bulletin*, 22(2): 6–7. Chicago, IL.

1952 The Archaeology of the Upper Great Lakes Area. In *Archaeology of the Eastern United States*, James B. Griffin, editor, pp. 99–107. University of Chicago Press, Chicago, IL.

1953a Indians Had a Lake Level Problem 60 Centuries Ago. *Field Museum of Natural History Bulletin*, 24(2):6–7. Chicago, IL.

1953b Natchez Archaeology—A Tribute to the Natchez for Their Seeming Consistency in the Production of the Fictile Fabric. *Southeastern Archaeological Conference Newsletter*, 3(3):22–24. Baton Rouge, LA.

1954a Cultural and Natural Areas before Kroeber. *American Antiquity*, 19(4):317–331.

1954b Discovered: A Possible Tecumseh Portrait. *Field Museum of Natural History Bulletin*, 25(9):3. Chicago, IL.

1954c *Indians of the Western Frontier: Paintings of George Catlin*. Field Museum of Natural History, Chicago, IL.

1954d The Old Copper Assemblage and Extinct Animals. *American Antiquity*, 20(2):169–170.

1954e Pawnee Concept of Eternity: Soul Villages in Sky. *Field Museum of Natural History Bulletin*, 25(8):7. Chicago, IL.

1954f Rare Portrait of Indian Preserved in Museum. *Field Museum of Natural History Bulletin*, 25(3):2. Chicago, IL.

1955 Reply to Aschmann's Comment [on Quimby 1954a]. *American Antiquity*, 20(4):378–379.

1956a The Locus of the Natchez Pelvis Find. *American Antiquity*, 22(1):77–79.

1956b Pawnee. In *Encyclopaedia Britannica*, vol 17, p. 408. Chicago, IL.

1957a The Archaeology of Environment. *Field Museum of Natural History Bulletin*, 28(7):4–5, 7). Chicago, IL.

1957b The Bayou Goula Site, Iberville Parish, Louisiana. *Fieldiana: Anthropology*, 47(2):87–170. Chicago, IL.

1957c Dating the Past: Upper Great Lakes Area. *Field Museum of Natural History Bulletin*, 28(6):6–7. Chicago, IL.

1957d An Old Copper Site at Menominee, Michigan. *Wisconsin Archaeologist*, 38(2):37–41.

1957e An Old Copper Site? at Port Washington. *Wisconsin Archeologist*, 38(1):1–5.

1957f Prehistoric Hunters: Upper Great Lakes Area. *Field Museum of Natural History Bulletin*, 28(5):6–7. Chicago, IL.

1958a Fluted Points and Geochronology of the Lake Michigan Basin. *American Antiquity*, 23(3):247–254.

1958b Late Archaic Culture and the Algoma Beach in the Lake Michigan Basin. *Wisconsin Archaeologist*, 39(3):175–179.

1958c Mastodons and Men in the Upper Great Lakes Area. *Field Museum of Natural History Bulletin*, 29(7):6–7. Chicago, IL.

1958d New Evidence Links Chippewa to Prehistoric Culture. *Field Museum of Natural History Bulletin*, 29(4):7–8. Chicago, IL.

1958e Silver Ornaments and the Indians. *Miscellanea Paul Rivet Octognario Dicata, XXXI Congreso Internacional de Americanistas*, Part I, pp. 317–337. Universidad Nacional Autonoma de Mexico, Mexico, D.F.

1959a Feast of the Dead Released Hurons' Souls. *Field Museum of Natural History Bulletin*, 30(7):4–6. Chicago, IL.

1959b Lanceolate Points and Fossil Beaches in the Upper Great Lakes Region. *American Antiquity*, 24(4):424–426.

1959c The Old Copper Indians and Their World. *Field Museum of Natural History Bulletin*, 30(1):4–5. Chicago, IL.

1959d Postscript to George M. Stanley's Review of *Geology of the Great Lakes*, by Jack L. Hough. *American Antiquity*, 25(2): 279.

1959e Review of *Late Pleistocene Geochronology and the Paleo-Indian Penetration into the Lower Michigan Peninsula*, by Ronald J. Mason. *American Antiquity*, 24(3):327.

1959f Upper Lakes Farmers and Artists, 100 B.C. *Field Museum of Natural History Bulletin*, 30(3):6–7. Chicago, IL.

1960a Burial Yields Clews to Red Ochre Culture. *Field Museum of Natural History Bulletin*, 31(2):5. Chicago, IL.

1960b Habitat, Culture, and Archaeology. In *Essays in the Science of Culture in Honor of Leslie A. White*, Gertrude E. Dole and Robert L. Carneiro, editors, pp. 380–389. Thomas Y. Crowell Co., New York.

1960c *Indian Life in the Upper Great Lakes 11,000 B.C. to A.D. 1800*. University of Chicago Press, Chicago, IL.

1960d Rates of Culture Change in Archaeology. *American Antiquity*, 25(3):416–417.

1960e Review of *Birdstones of the North American Indian*, by Earl C. Townsend, Jr. *American Antiquity*, 25(3):430.

1961a Cord Marking Versus Fabric Impressing of Woodland Pottery. *American Antiquity*, 26(3):426–428.

1961b Old Copper Artifacts from Chicago. In Chicago Area Archaeology, Elaine A. Bluhm, editor, pp. 34–36. *Illinois Archaeological Survey Bulletin*, 3. Urbana.

1961c The Pic River Site. In Lake Superior Copper and the Indians: Miscellaneous Studies of Great Lakes Prehistory, James B. Griffin, editor, pp. 83–89. *Anthropological Papers, Museum of Anthropology, University of Michigan*, 17. Ann Arbor.

1961d Review of *The American Heritage Book of Indians*, by William Brandon. *Chicago Tribune Magazine of Books*, 12 November. Chicago, IL.

1961e Review of *Ethnographic Bibliography of North America*, 3rd edition, by George Peter Murdock. *American Antiquity*, 27(1):119.

1961f Review of *Ishi in Two Worlds: A Biography of the Last Wild Indian in North America*, by Theodora Kroeber. *Chicago Tribune Magazine of Books*, 19 November. Chicago, IL.

1961g Review of *Prehistoric Copper Mining in the Lake Superior Region*, Roy W. Drier and Octave J. DuTemple, editors. *Michigan History*, 45(4):377–378.

1962a The Age of the Oconto Site. *Wisconsin Archeologist*, 43(1):16–19.

1962b Alexander Henry in Central Michigan, 1763-1764. *Michigan History*, 46(3):193–200.

1962c The Old Copper Culture and the Copper Eskimos, an Hypothesis. In Prehistoric Cultural Relations between the Arctic and Temperate Zones of North America, John M. Campbell, editor, pp. 76–79. *Arctic Institute of North America, Technical Paper*, 11. Calgary, Alberta.

1962d Omaha Kinship Terminology and Spruce-Fir Pollen. *American Antiquity* 28(1):91–92.

1962e Review of *The Archaeology of Carajou Point*, by Robert L. Hall. *Journal of the Illinois State Historical Society*, Winter: 421–422.

1962f A Year with a Chippewa Family, 1763-1764. *Ethnohistory*, 9(1):217–239.

1963a A Brief Note on the Codex Canadiensis. *Ethnohistory*, 10(4):396–397.

1963b The Gros Cap Cemetery in Mackinac County, Michigan. *Michigan Archaeologist*, 9(4):50–57.

1963c Late Period Copper Artifacts in the Upper Great Lakes Region. *Wisconsin Archeologist*, 44(4):193–98.

1963d A Maple Sugar Camp 200 Years Ago. *Field Museum of Natural History Bulletin*, 34(3):6–7. Chicago, IL.

1963e A New Look at Geochronology in the Upper Great Lakes Region. *American Antiquity*, 28(4):558–559.

1963f Review of *Indian Rock Paintings of the Great Lakes*, by Selwyn Dewdny and Kenneth E. Kidd. *American Journal of Archaeology*, 67(1):114–115.

1964a European Trade Objects As Chronological Indicators. In *Diving into the Past: Theories, Techniques, and Applications of Underwater Archaeology*, June D. Holmquist and Ardis H. Wheeler, editors, pp. 48–52. Minnesota Historical Society, St. Paul.

1964b The *Griffin*. *Field Museum of Natural History Bulletin*, 35(5):3–5. Chicago, IL.

1964c The Stony Lake Mounds, Oceana County, Michigan. *Michigan Archaeologist*, 10(1):11–16.

1965a Exploring an Underwater Indian Site. *Field Museum of Natural History Bulletin*, 36(8):2–4. Chicago, IL.

1965b An Indian Earthwork in Muskegon County, Michigan. In Papers in Honor of Emerson Greeman, James E. Fitting, editor. *Michigan Archaeologist*, 11(3–4):165–169.

1965c Plains Art from a Florida Prison. *Field Museum of Natural History Bulletin*, 36(10):2–5. Chicago, IL.

1965d Underwater Archaeology in Lake Michigan. *Field Museum of Natural History Bulletin*, 36(6):2–4. Chicago, IL.

1965e The Voyage of the *Griffin*: 1679. *Michigan History*, 49(2):97–107.

1966a The Dumaw Creek Site: A Seventeenth-Century Prehistoric Indian Village and Cemetery in Oceana County, Michigan. *Fieldiana: Anthropology*, 56(1):1–91. Chicago, IL.

1966b *Indian Culture and European Trade Goods: The Archaeology of the Historic Period in the Western Great Lakes Region*. University of Wisconsin Press, Madison.

1966c Review of *American Indian Tomahawks*, by Harold L. Peterson. *Pacific Northwest Quarterly*, 57(2):89–90.

1966d Review of *Artists of the Old West*, by John C. Ewers. *American Anthropologist*, 68(6):1585.

1966e Review of *Underwater Archaeological Techniques, a Review of Marine Archaeology: Developments during Sixty Years in the Mediterranean*, Joan du Plat Taylor, editor. *Science*, 152(3718):58.

1967a Curtis and the Whale. *Pacific Northwest Quarterly*, 58(4):141–144.

1967b The Indian Tribes of the Upper Great Lakes Region. In *The North American Indians: A Source Book*, Robert C. Owen, James J. F. Deetz, and Anthony D. Fisher, editors, pp. 576–580. Macmillan, New York.

1968a Archaeology. In *Encyclopedia Americana*, Vol 1, pp. 186–208. New York.

1968b Habitat, Culture, and Archaeology. In *Man in Adaptation: The Biosocial Backgrond*, Yehudi A. Choen, editor, pp. 291–296. Aldine, Chicago, IL.

1968c Hawaiians and De Meurons in the Upper Great Lakes. *Michigan Archaeologist*, 14(3–4):167–169.

1968d A Northwest Coast Artifact from Northern Wisconsin. *Wisconsin Archeologist*, 49(4):172–175.

1968e Review of *A Pictographic History of the Oglala Sioux*, by Amos Bad Heart Bull and Helen H. Blish. *American Anthropologist*, 79(4):840.

1969a Adventures in Good Eating East of the Cascades 1810–1821. *Puget Soundings*, January, pp. 12–13. Junior League of Seattle, Seattle, WA.

1969b Review of *O-kee-pa: A Religious Ceremony and Other Customs of the Mandans*, by George Catlin, John C. Ewers, editor. *Pacific Northwest Quarterly*, 60(1):37–38.

1970a Asians among Indians in the Early Northwest. *Pacific Search*, 4(25). Seattle, WA.

1970b *Indian Culture and European Trade Goods: The Archaeology of the Historic Period in the Western Great Lakes Region*, paperback edition. University of Wisconsin Press, Madison.

1970c James Swan among the Indians: The Influence of a Pioneer from New England on Coastal Indian Art. *Pacific Northwest Quarterly*, 61(4):212–216.

1971a Humor among the Treaty Makers and Fur Traders or *Joe Miller's Joke Book* in the Pacific Northwest. *Ethnohistory*, 18(3): 267–271.

1971b *Indian Life in the Upper Great Lakes 11,000 B.C. to A.D. 1800*, paperback edition. University of Chicago Press, Chicago, IL.

1971c Review of *Shipwrecks and Archaeology: The Unharvested Sea*, by Peter Throckmorton. *American Anthropologist,* 73(6): 1398.

1972 Hawaiians in the Fur Trade of North-West America, 1785–1820. *The Journal of Pacific History,* 7:92–103. Canberra, Australia.

1976a Comment on Differential Artistic Productivity in the Eskimo Culture Tradition. *Current Anthropology,* 17(2):216–217.

1976b An Exotic Campsite in East Hudson's Bay. *Historical Archaeology,* 10:121–123.

1977a George I. Quimby. *The Teocentli,* 81:13. Knoxville, TN.

1977b Women of the Lower Columbia River in the Early-Nineteenth Century. In For the Director: Research Essays in Honor of James B. Griffin, Charles E. Cleland, editor, pp. 230–241. *Museum of Anthropology, University of Michigan, Anthropological Papers,* 61. Ann Arbor.

1978a *Indian Culture and European Trade Goods: The Archaeology of the Historic Period in the Western Great Lakes Region.* Greenwood Press, Westport, CT. Reprint of 1970 edition published by University of Wisconsin Press, Madison.

1978b Review of *A Classification System for Glass Beads for the Use of Field Archaeologists,* by Kenneth E. Kidd and Martha A. Kidd. *Canadian Journal of Archaeology,* 2:169.

1978c Trade Beads and Sunken Ships. In *Archaeological Essays in Honor of Irving B. Rouse,* Robert C. Dunnell and Edwin S. Hall, Jr., editors, pp. 231–246. Mouton, The Hague.

1978d Yankee Artist, James Madison Alden in Washington Territory 1854. *Pacific Northwest Quarterly,* 69(1):31–33.

1979a A Brief History of WPA Archaeology. In The Uses of Anthropology, Walter Goldschmidt, editor, pp. 110–123. *American Anthropological Association Special Publication,* 11.

1979b Review of *A. F. Kashevarov's Coastal Explorations in Northwest Alaska,* James W. VanStone, editor [*Fieldiana: Anthropology,* 69]. *Pacific Northwest Quarterly,* 70(4):182.

1979c Review of *E. W. Nelson's Notes on the Indians of the Yukon and Innoko Rivers, Alaska,* James W. VanStone, editor [*Fieldiana: Anthropology,* 70]. *Pacific Northwest Quarterly,* 70(4):182.

1980 The Wife of Portsmouth's Tale, 1813–1818. *Pacific Northwest Quarterly,* 71(3):127–130.

1982a Edward S. Curtis and Visual Anthropology. *Society for the Anthropology of Visual Communication Newsletter,* 10(2): 5–6.

1982b Robert S. Neitzel: Appreciation and Reminiscences. In Robert S. Neitzel: The Great Sun, Jeffrey P. Brain and Ian W. Brown, editors, pp. 30–32. *Lower Mississippi Survey Bulletin,* No. 9. Peabody Museum, Harvard University, Cambridge, MA.

1984 Review of *A Guide for Historical Archaeology in Illinois,* Charles E. Orser, Jr., editor. *Historical Archaeology,* 18(1): 116.

1986 Japanese Wrecks, Iron Tools, and Prehistoric Indians of the Northwest Coast. *Arctic Anthropology,* 22(2):7–15.

1987 George I. Quimby. *The Teocentli,* 90:23. Knoxville, TN.

1988 George Quimby Remembers Hudson Bay, 1939. *The Beaver: Exploring Canada's History,* 68(4):17–28. Winnipeg, Manitoba.

1990 The Mystery of the First Documentary Film. *Pacific Northwest Quarterly,* 81(2):50–53.

1991 That Earthy Farm Smell. In "And Stuff Like That There": In Appreciation of William G. Haag, Jon L. Gibson, Robert W. Neuman, and Richard A. Weinstein, editors, p. 189. *Louisiana Archaeology,* 18. Louisiana Archaeological Society, Lafayette. Imprinted for LAS membership year 1991 but copyrighted 1995.

1993 A Thing of Sherds and Patches. *American Antiquity,* 58(1):7–21.

1994 Historical Archaeology As I Saw It: 1935–1970. In *Pioneers in Historical Archaeology: Breaking New Ground,* Stanley South, editor, pp. 113–124. Plenum Press, New York.

QUIMBY, GEORGE I., AND CHARLES E. CLELAND

1976 James Bennett Griffin: Appreciation and Reminiscences. In *Culture Change, and Continuity: Essays in Honor of James Bennett Griffin,* Charles E. Cleland, editor, pp. xxi–xxxvii. Academic Press, New York.

QUIMBY, GEORGE I., AND JAMES B. GRIFFIN

1961 Various Finds of Copper and Stone Artifacts in the Lake Superior Basin. In Lake Superior Copper and the Indians: Miscellaneous Studies of Great Lakes Prehistory, James B. Griffin, editor, pp. 103–117. *Anthropological Papers, Museum of Anthropology, University of Michigan,* 17. Ann Arbor.

QUIMBY, GEORGE I., AND H. S. HARRISON

1965 Material Culture. In *Encyclopaedia Britannica,* vol. 14, pp. 1054–1155. Chicago, IL.

QUIMBY, GEORGE I., BILL HOLM, AND DAVID GERTH (PRODUCERS)

1973 *In the Land of the War Canoes: Kwakiutl Life on the Northwest Coast,* restored re-release of 1914 silent film, originally titled *In the Land of the Head-Hunters: A Drama of Primitive Life on the Shores of the North Pacific,* Edward S. Curtis, director and cinematographer. University of Washington Press, Seattle. Copyrighted 1972 but usually cited by its 1973 release date.

1979 *The Image Maker and the Indians: Edward Curtis and His 1914 Kwakiutl Movie,* documentary film. University of Washington Press, Seattle.

1992 *In the Land of the War Canoes: Kwakiutl Life on the Northwest Coast*, videotape release of Quimby et al. 1973. Milestone Film & Video, Harrington Park, NJ.

2000 *In the Land of the War Canoes: Kwakiutl Life on the Northwest Coast*, DVD release of Quimby et al. 1973, includes Quimby et al. 1979 short subject. Milestone Film & Video, Harrington Park, NJ.

QUIMBY, GEORGE I., AND JAMES D. NASON

1976 Comment on H. Russell Bernard's review of *Maritime Adaptations of the Pacific. Reviews in Anthropology*, 3(5):567–569.

1977 New Staff for a New Museum. *Museum News*, 55(5):50–52.

QUIMBY, GEORGE I., AND ALBERT C. SPAULDING

1957 The Old Copper Culture and the Keweenaw Waterway. *Fieldiana: Anthropology*, 36(8):189–201. Chicago, IL.

QUIMBY, GEORGE I, AND ALEXANDER SPOEHR

1950 Historic Creek Pottery from Oklahoma. *American Antiquity*, 15(3):249–251.

1951 Acculturation and Material Culture. *Fieldiana: Anthropology*, 36(6):107–147. Chicago, IL.

RITZENTHALER, ROBERT, AND GEORGE I. QUIMBY

1962 The Red Ocre Culture of the Upper Great Lakes and Adjacent Areas. *Fieldiana: Anthropology*, 36(11):243–275. Chicago, IL.

SWADESH, MORRIS, GEORGE I. QUIMBY, EMIL W. HAURY, GORDON F. EKHOLM, AND FRED EGGAN

1954 Symposium: Time Depths of American Linguistic Groupings. *American Anthropologist*, 56(3):361–377.

TAPED INTERVIEW

1989 *Bringing the Past Alive* [videotape]. Donna LaFleur, director; Ann Ramenofsky, producer. Louisiana State University, Department of Geography and Anthropology in cooperation with Louisiana Public Broadcasting and with a grant from the National Endowment for the Humanitites, Baton Rouge. 1989 public interview with George I. Quimby and William G. Haag on WPA and other New Deal era archaeological projects in the lower Mississippi River valley.

Charles E. Cleland
Vergil E. Noble

MEMORIAL: Carol Varley Ruppé, 1923-2003. Volume 39, Number 4 (2005): 5-8. By Donna J. Seifert.

Memorial

Carol Varley Ruppé 1923–2003

The Society for Historical Archaeology lost a devoted member, and archaeologists lost a dear friend on 4 November 2003 with the passing from this life of Carol Varley Ruppé. Carol spent many years organizing the book room at SHA's annual conference. She was a friend of my family in Iowa in the 1950s, and it was in the book room that our paths again crossed years later. To those who knew her, she was a cheery lady who enjoyed her work. Her childhood giggle, remembered by Girl Scout pal Virginia, mellowed into the smoky chortle known to archaeologists who gathered at her home or took a seat beside her in the SHA book room. Carol successfully joined her lifelong interest in anthropology with her pragmatic choice of career in librarianship to become a master at connecting students and scholars with information.

Carol (Helen Carolyn Varley) was born 22 February 1923 to Mildred Reed Varley and Brian Jennings Varley in Menlo, Iowa. Carol's family moved to Chicago, where her brother, Brian Reed Varley, was born. The Varleys lived first in the Ravenswood neighborhood; in 1933, they moved to a house on New England Avenue in the Elmwood Park neighborhood. Carol attended Sayre School from the sixth through the eighth grade. She was active in her Girl Scout troop, which met in the basement of the Congregational Church, and went to Camp Juniper Knoll in Elkhorn, Wisconsin, with friends from her troop.

In 1936 the Varleys moved to Denver, Colorado, where she was a frequent visitor to the nearby Denver Museum of Natural History. Carol went to East High School, graduating in 1940. In fall 1940, Carol began her undergraduate work at the University of New Mexico, majoring in anthropology and joining Alpha Delta Phi sorority. Freshman Audrey Richard (Dittert) also began her training in anthropology that year, and senior Florence Cline (Lister) completed hers. Because of appendicitis and illness, Carol had to return in 1944 to her parent's home in Denver without finishing her degree, working as a telephone operator after her recovery.

She met Reynold J. Ruppé while he was stationed at Camp Hole, Colorado, where he was training to become a ski trooper. Rey transferred to the air force and then to the infantry. In October 1944, shortly before he was to leave for Europe, Rey was sent to Camp Van Doren, Mississippi. Carol traveled by bus to nearby Baton Rouge, Louisiana, to visit Rey and to get married. She went back home to Denver, and Rey went to France.

Carol returned to the University of New Mexico to finish her bachelor of arts degree in anthropology in 1945. During this year, she spent time with a group of young women in Albuquerque whose husbands were stationed at Kirtland Air Force Base. The women knew their husbands were training for a secret mission, but it was only after the men suddenly left on this mission that they learned their husbands belonged to the crew of the *Enola Gay*.

After the surrender of Germany, Rey remained in Europe, serving as a clerk in Wiesbaden, Germany, assisting in the preparation of cases to be tried at Nuremberg. When Rey returned in 1946, Carol and Rey moved to Gunison, Colorado, so Rey could work on his undergraduate degree at Western State College. After about a year, Carol persuaded him to move to Albuquerque, where Rey completed his bachelor of arts degree in anthropology at Carol's alma mater, the University of New Mexico, in 1949.

They temporarily left the Southwest for Harvard University in Cambridge, Massachusetts, so Rey could begin work on his doctorate, while Carol worked at the engineering library. Winters were spent in Cambridge, but summers were spent back in the Southwest, surveying the Cebolleta Mesa pueblo sites with colleague A. E. Dittert (who married Carol's college friend Audrey Richard). In the winter of 1952–1953, Rey finished his dissertation in Denver.

In 1953, Rey joined the faculty at the University of Iowa. They moved to Iowa City and purchased a house on a terrace above the Iowa River (classified as a beach cottage in the tax rolls), beginning lengthy and extensive renovations. Weekends were often spent in eastern Iowa with Carol's grade-school friend from Chicago, whose home had the luxuries of a functioning kitchen and bathroom. Carol returned the favor many times over in the following years, when the same friend made frequent trips to Iowa City for all-day visits to the pediatric clinic at the university hospital. Carol looked after the younger siblings, saving them from hours of boredom in the clinic waiting room.

Carol and Rey's daughter, Patricia Ann, was born in 1954, and their son, Lawrence Reed, followed in 1956. During the mid-1950s, Carol and her young children spent the summers in Denver with her parents. She pursued a master's degree at the University of Denver while Rey ran field schools in Iowa. In 1959, the University of Denver awarded Carol a Master of Arts in Librarianship and Information Management. As the children grew older, the whole family spent summers together at archeological field schools at sites in southeastern and western Iowa. Many archaeologists practicing today worked at or visited these excavations.

Carol returned to library work during her years in Iowa City, taking a position at the Iowa City Public Library. She also developed friendships with women in the Mesquakie community at Tama, Iowa, where she and Rey did ethnographic research. Carol learned to select and gather wetland vegetation to weave mats and to construct wickiups. One evening, her Mesquakie friends asked Carol to dance with them at a powwow. She hesitated, saying she really should not, but the Mesquakie women assured her that since it was night, no one would notice a white woman dancing with the Indians. Carol spent a lot of time with those women; her Mesquakie friends hosted a baby shower for her as the birth of her first child approached.

In 1960, Rey was asked to chair the Department of Sociology and Anthropology at Arizona State University in Tempe. Carol and her family left the beach cottage on the Iowa River and moved back to the Southwest. In 1962, Carol began working a part-time position at the university's Hayden Library, later moving to full-time and becoming the chair of the reference department, the position she held until her retirement in 1986. She specialized in developing the collection for anthropology, and department members quickly learned that Carol could help them find whatever they needed or she would ensure that the library acquire it. She prepared numerous resource guides, several of them focusing on Native American arts and ethnology. In recognition of her contributions to the university, in 1983 Carol was awarded the ASU Presidential Award for Service.

In 1962, Carol began her work as a volunteer with the Heard Museum in Phoenix. For years, she worked at the museum's library on Tuesday afternoons, focusing on developing the library's holdings and on building the Native American Artists Resource Collection. With the first staff librarian, Mary Graham, Carol collected information in the field to develop a collection that now includes files on 23,000 Native American artists. She was awarded the Heard Museum Guild Outstanding Library Volunteer Award in 1999. Long after her retirement from her position at the Hayden Library in 1986, Carol continued to volunteer at the Heard library just because she liked it. Only when she was no longer able to come to the library, in the fall of 2003, did she retire from the Heard. On 15 January 2004, shortly after her death, the Board of Trustees of the Heard Museum adopted a resolution recognizing her 41 years of service.

Carol also shared her expertise in collection development with the Desert Botanical Garden in Phoenix, where she volunteered in the library. Memorial services for both Rey (1993) and Carol (2003) were held at the garden.

The Society for Historical Archaeology was also the beneficiary of Carol's special skill of connecting scholars with sources. Carol proposed the concept and organized the first book room at the SHA annual conference in Charleston, South Carolina, in 1975. Under her guidance, the exhibit grew to be one of the most popular components of the conference. The book room became a destination for nearly all participants and the place where one could always find Carol. She continued to organize the book room until 1988, well into her professional retirement. Even after she handed over the responsibilities, she continued to come to the conference and could often be found in the book room visiting with old friends and browsing through the new publications. During the last year of her life, Carol continued her mission of connecting researchers with resources through her work on the *International Handbook of Underwater Archaeology*, serving as the volume's co-editor.

SHA recognized Carol's years of service to the society with the creation of the Carol V. Ruppé Distinguished Service Award, which was announced in 1990 and presented to her at the annual conference in Tucson, Arizona. The award recognizes outstanding service to the society. It has been presented to date to only four other members, as the level of service Carol devoted to the society is rarely matched.

Carol was well known to historical and underwater archaeologists, and many still note her absence while visiting the book room at the annual meeting. Her outstanding service to the society will long be remembered by those fortunate enough to have known her, and meeting participants who never even knew Carol will benefit from her contributions to the society for years to come.

ACKNOWLEDGMENTS

The author wishes to acknowledge the generous assistance of Carol's colleagues, friends, and family: Lawrence Babits, Marilynn Bubb, Jane Conrow, Audrey Dittert, Sylvia Gaines, Keith Kintigh, Mario Nick Klimiades, William Lees, Ronald Michael, Michael Rodeffer, Stephanie Rodeffer, Lawrence Ruppé, Patricia Ruppé, Robert Schuyler, Marsha Schweitzer, Richard Seifert, Virginia Spikins Seifert, Brenda Shears, Barbara Stark, Reed Varley, and Linda Williams.

DONNA J. SEIFERT

MEMORIAL: Norman F. Barka, 1938–2008. Volume 43, Number 2 (2009): 1-8. By Richard Veit.

Memorial

Figure 1. Norman Barka on boat, Guana Island, British Virgin Islands 1999. (Photo by Mark Kostro.)

Norman F. Barka 1938–2008

On 29 April 2008, Norman F. (Forthun) Barka, a stalwart in the field of historical archaeology, died at the age of 70. At the time of his passing, he was professor emeritus in the Department of Anthropology at the College of William and Mary. He had taught there for 39 years, retiring in 2004. Barka is survived by his wife of 28 years, Patricia Kandle; his three sons, Eric T. Barka, Daniel J. Barka, and David N. Barka; two grandchildren; and Anne G. McBride of Washington State, his wife by a previous marriage.

Norman Barka, known as Norm to his friends and Stormin' Norman to many of his students, first evinced an interest in archaeology as a young man growing up in Chicago. His parents, Scandinavian immigrants, encouraged the archaeological interests of their precocious son. Norm aspired to be the next Howard Carter and was drawn to movies with archaeological themes, such as Boris Karloff's *The Mummy*. Even before he had graduated from high school he was working as a research assistant for the Smithsonian Institution. His first paying job in archaeology was digging a Mandan site along the Missouri River (Robertson 2008). When he was only 20 years old, he participated in the Smithsonian Institution's excavation of the Russell Cave in Alabama.

Norm attended Beloit College in Wisconsin for his undergraduate degree, graduating in 1960 with a Bachelor of Arts in Anthropology. During his formative years, he worked on sites in Mexico, Georgia, Washington State, Wisconsin, New York, and Canada. These experiences would serve him well later in life as he trained dozens of graduate and undergraduate students with diverse interests.

Barka's graduate work was completed at Harvard University where he took courses under the noted Paleolithic archaeologist Hallam Movius. His talents were unmistakable, and Movius held on to some of his work, including a paper titled "The Significant Traits of the Main Developmental Stages of Pre-Urban Culture in Mesopotamia, Egypt, and at Jericho" (Barka 1961). It was during this period (1961–1964) that Barka's interest in the then nascent field of historical archaeology developed. It may have started when he began working on early French sites in Canada. He was exceptionally productive during this period. In 1964, he published a bibliography on historic sites archaeology, titled *Some Sources for Use in the Interpretation of Historic Sites*. The following year he completed his dissertation on the historical archaeology of Portland Point in New Brunswick, Canada, from 1631 to 1850 (Barka 1965).

In 1965, Barka began his teaching career at the College of William and Mary in Virginia. He and his friend and colleague Nathan Altschuler were largely responsible for the founding of the Department of Anthropology, a program that has gone on to become one of the best-known training grounds for historical archaeologists in the United States.

In 1979, the College of William and Mary began offering the Master of Arts in Anthropology with a concentration in historical archaeology. Barka served as graduate director for more than 20 years, shepherding dozens of students through the program and training them in excavation and artifact analysis. He also participated in the creation of William and Mary's doctoral program and saw it welcome its first crop of graduate students before he moved into retirement (Brown 2005).

After a diverse array of early field experiences, Barka focused his interests on the archaeology of French colonial sites. Later, at William and Mary, he established himself as an expert in comparative colonialism, doing work in the Chesapeake, Netherlands Antilles, especially St. Eustatius, and later on in Bermuda and Guana in the British Virgin Islands. In all of these areas, he made significant contributions, both by training students and through thoughtful publications.

In 1966, he discovered the Poor Potter's site. Thanks to his fine work, it is one of the most meticulously excavated colonial potteries in North America (Figure 2). The site's name does not

Figure 2. Norman Barka crouched next to a kiln at the Poor Potter Site in Yorktown, Virginia. (Photo courtesy of College of William and Mary, Williamsburg, Virginia.)

reflect any lack of skill on the part of the potter, rather it is drawn from a letter by Virginia's Governor William Gooch who sent reports to England's Board of Trade about American manufactures and in 1732 noted the presence of a poor potter in the colony (Barka 2004:15). The statement was obviously made to confound the Board of Trade as Barka's excavations revealed two well-preserved kilns and the scattered and broken wares of a very talented potter on property once owned by William Rogers. That Barka's excavation of the site is still relevant today, 35 years after his initial excavation, speaks volumes for his meticulous craftsmanship. He and his students dug there until 1981 (Barka 2004:23).

In 1971, Barka, following up on the work of avocational archaeologist Leverette Gregory, identified the site now known as Flowerdew Hundred in Prince George's County, Virginia (*Time Magazine* 1972). He and his colleagues from William and Mary, particularly Charles Hodges and Andrew Edwards, would work there until 1978, although excavations continued after that under the direction of James Deetz and others (Deetz 1995:xi). One of the first English plantations in the New World, Flowerdew consists of a series of archaeological sites located on the grounds of a working farm owned by investment banker David A. Harrison III. Excavating there, Barka found armor and other traces of early settlement, including the remains of a cruck house, a form of earthfast dwelling. His work there foreshadowed later work by Ivor Noël Hume at Martin's Hundred and William Kelso at Jamestown. When Flowerdew Hundred was discovered, it was the only known enclosed settlement associated with the settlement period in colonial Virginia.

One of Barka's well-known publications, the article "Impermanent Architecture in the Southern American Colonies," co-authored with Cary Carson, William M. Kelso, Garry Wheeler Stone, and Dell Upton, built on the knowledge of earthfast structures he gained at places like Flowerdew (Carson et al. 1981).

Later, Barka expanded his research interests to include the colonial Caribbean. In 1981, he began digging in the Netherlands Antilles on the small but historically important island of St. Eustatius (Figure 3). Known colloquially as the Golden Rock for the wealth that accrued to the island's merchants through trade, St. Eustatius or Statia gained fame on 16 November 1776 when Governor Johannes de Graaff returned the salute of the American brig-of-war *Andrew Doria*. Archaeologically the site is one of the richest in the Americas, and although geographically small, it contains such an assortment of ruins and archaeological features reflecting its 18th-century prosperity that it has been dubbed a New World Pompeii (Dethlefsen et al. 1982).

Statia provided an ideal field laboratory for Barka. Over a nearly two-decade period, he regularly returned there with students in tow, excavating forts and warehouses, even discovering one of the first synagogues in the New World.

After Statia, Barka continued to develop his interest in comparative colonialism. In 1993, he began collaborating with his friend Edward Harris in the study of Bermuda's first forts. Among his most significant discoveries were the two towers of the diminutive Smith Fort, dating from 1613 (Harris 2002:12). During this period, he also dug the Captain's House at King's Castle, Bermuda. This is arguably the oldest standing English house in the Americas. Later still, Barka did survey work on St. Martin and Guana in the British Virgin Islands.

In addition to his teaching, scholarship, and fieldwork, Barka was a dedicated supporter of The Society for Historical Archaeology. After years of regularly attending meetings, he became an officer in the society. In 1979 he joined the Board of Directors as president-elect, serving the next year as president. In 1984, he organized a highly successful conference in Williamsburg, Virginia, setting a new attendance record for the society. His greatest accomplishment, however, may have been serving as *SHA Newsletter* editor for the society for 20 years from 1982 until 2002. During this time, he edited 81 newsletters! His record of editorial fortitude is unlikely to be matched. Under his oversight, the *Newsletter* matured from a mimeographed reporting of recent events to a much more substantial regular publication. For his hard work, he was rewarded with the SHA's Carol V. Ruppé Distinguished Service Award in 2001.

Speaking about his career in archaeology at the SHA's 2000 conference in Quebec City, Norm stated simply, "It's what I always wanted to be. In the end, historical archaeology is fun, an

Figure 3. Norman Barka in the sugar factory on Guana Island, British Virgin Islands, 2003. (Photo by Chuck Meide.)

enjoyable way of life. I have been very fortunate in feeling that my job is not really a job. It is just something I do and think about for 24 hours a day" (Barka 2005). With the passing of Norman Barka, historical archaeology has lost a meticulous researcher, gifted scholar, and a talented teacher and mentor. Perhaps most importantly we have lost someone who made historical archaeology fun.

Acknowledgments

I gratefully acknowledge the assistance of several individuals who helped me compile information on the life and career of Norman Barka. I particularly appreciate the assistance shown by Marley R. Brown III, Grant Gilmore, Shannon Mahoney, Frederick Smith, and Robert Schuyler. Mahoney was able to secure a number of early photographs of Norm Barka, one of which appears with this memorial. I am grateful for having had the opportunity to study with Norman Barka who encouraged my interests in historical archaeology and, particularly, in gravestone studies. His dry wit and interest in early American material continue to inspire me as I am sure they do numerous former students.

References

BARKA, NORMAN F.
    1961   The Significant Traits of the Main Developmental Stages of Pre-Urban Culture in Mesopotamia, Egypt, and at Jericho. Manuscript, Harvard University Archives, Cambridge, MA.

1964   Some Sources for Use in the Interpretation of Historic Sites. Manuscript, Tozzer Library, Harvard University, Cambridge, MA.

1965   Historic Sites Archaeology at Portland Point, New Brunswick, Canada, 1631–1850 A.D. Doctoral dissertation, Department of Anthropology, Harvard University, Cambridge, MA.

BROWN, MARLEY R. III
2001   Carol V. Ruppé Distinguished Service Award: Norman F. Barka, 2001. *Historical Archaeology* (35)4:4–7.

2005   Speech on the Retirement of Norman Barka. Manuscript on file with the author.

CARSON, CARY, NORMAN F. BARKA, WILLIAM M. KELSO, GARRY WHEELER STONE, AND DELL UPTON
1981   Impermanent Architecture in the Southern American Colonies. *Winterthur Portfolio* 16(2–3):135–196.

DEETZ, JAMES
1995   *Flowerdew Hundred, the Archaeology of a Virginia Plantation 1619–1864.* University of Virginia Press, Richmond.

DETHLEFSEN, EDWIN, STEPHEN J. GLUCKMAN, R. DUNCAN MATHEWSON, AND NORMAN F. BARKA
1982   Archaeology on St. Eustatius: The Pompeii of the New World. *Archaeology* 35(2):8–15.

HARRIS, EDWARD
2002   Archaeological Advances in Bermuda. *SHA Newsletter* 35(1):10–12.

ROBERTSON, ELLEN
2008   Archaeologist Norman F. Barka Dies. *Richmond Times Dispatch,* 4 May <http://www.inrich.com/cva/ric/news/sunday. apx.-content-articles-RTD 2008 08040256.html>. Accessed 2 July 2008.

TIME MAGAZINE
1972   Treasures of Flowerdew. *Time Magazine* (20 Nov.) <http://www.time.com/time/magazine/article/0,9171,712205,00. html>. Accessed 2 July, 2008.

Bibliography of Works by Dr. Norman Barka

Compiled by Shannon Mahoney, Mark Kostro, and Andrew Edwards

ALTSCHULER, NATHAN, EDWARD AYRES, NORMAN BARKA, AND ARTHUR BARNES
1979   Interpretation of Flowerdew Hundred, Virginia. Manuscript, Southside Historical Sites, Inc., Williamsburg, VA.

BARKA, NORMAN F.
1961   The Significant Traits of the Main Developmental Stages of Pre-Urban Culture in Mesopotamia, Egypt, and at Jericho. Manuscript, Harvard University, Cambridge, MA [undergraduate paper].

1964   Salvage Excavations, 1963, at Peter Pond National Historic Site, near Prince Albert, Saskatchewan (Sturgeon Fort No. 1). In *Saskatchewan Museum of Natural History Annual Report*, pp. 1–3. Saskatchewan Department of Natural Resources, Regina, Canada.

1964   Some Sources for Use in the Interpretation of Historic Sites. Manuscript, Harvard University, Cambridge, MA.

1965   Historic Sites Archaeology at Portland Point, New Brunswick, Canada, 1631–c.1850 A.D. Doctoral dissertation, Department of Anthropology, Harvard University, Cambridge, MA.

1968   Destruction of Archaeological Data. *Quarterly Bulletin of the Archaeological Society of Virginia* 23(2):98–100.

1968   A Polished Stone Pipe from Lancaster County. *Quarterly Bulletin of the Archaeological Society of Virginia* 23(1):50–51.

1970   The Excavation of the La Coupe Site in Eastern New Brunswick. Manuscript, National Historic Sites Service, Department of Indian Affairs and Northern Development, Ottawa, Canada.

1973   The Kiln and Ceramics of the "Poor Potter" of Yorktown: A Preliminary Report. In *Ceramics in America*, Ian E. G. Quimby, editor, pp. 291–318. University Press of Virginia, Charlottesville.

1976   The Archaeology of Flowerdew Hundred Plantation: The Stone House Foundation Site, An Interim Report. Manuscript, Southside Historical Sites, Inc., and Department of Anthropology, College of William and Mary, Williamsburg, VA.

1976   Archaeology of the Yorktown Battlefield, Yorktown, Virginia. Yorktown Research Series Report, No.1. Manuscript, Southside Historical Sites Inc., and Department of Anthropology, College of William and Mary, Williamsburg, VA.

1978   The Archaeology of Fort Lennox, Ile-aux-Noix, Quebec, 1964 season. History and Archaeology, No. 20. Manuscript, Parks Canada, National Historic Parks and Sites Branch, Department of Indian and Northern Affairs, Ottawa.

1978   Archaeology of George Washington Birthplace, Virginia. Manuscript, Southside Historical Sites Inc., and Department of Anthropology, College of William and Mary, Williamsburg, VA.

Richard Veit

1978 Archaeology of the Nelson, Smith, and Ballard Houses, Yorktown, Virginia. Yorktown Research Series Report, No. 3. Manuscript, Southside Historical Sites Inc., and Department of Anthropology, College of William and Mary, Williamsburg, VA.

1980 The First Annual Report, Archaeological Investigations, Yorktown Pottery Factory, Virginia. Manuscript, Department of Anthropology, College of William and Mary, Williamsburg, VA.

1981 The Second Annual Report, Archaeological Investigations, Yorktown Pottery Factory, Virginia. Manuscript, Department of Anthropology, College of William and Mary, Williamsburg, VA.

1985 *Archaeology of St. Eustatius, Netherlands Antilles: An Interim Report on the 1981–1984 Seasons.* St. Eustatius Archaeological Research Series Report, No. 1. Department of Anthropology, College of William and Mary, Williamsburg, VA.

1985 Book Review: "American Stonewares, The Art and Craft of Utilitarian Potters" by Georgeanna H. Greer. *Historical Archaeology* 19(2):138–139.

1986 *Archaeology of the Government Guest House, St. Eustatius, Netherlands Antilles: An Interim Report.* St. Eustatius Archaeological Research Series Report, No. 2. Department of Anthropology, College of William & Mary, Williamsburg, VA.

1987 *Archaeological Investigations of the Princess Estate, St. Eustatius, Netherlands Antilles: An Interim Report on the Supposed Jewish Mikve.* St. Eustatius Archaeological Research Series Report, No. 3. Department of Anthropology, College of William and Mary, Williamsburg, VA.

1987 *The Potential for Historical Archaeology Research in the Netherlands Antilles* Archaeological-Anthropological Institute of the Netherlands Antilles, Report No. 4, Curacao.

1988 *Archaeology of the Jewish Synagogue Honen Dalim, St. Eustatius, N.A.: An Interim Report.* St. Eustatius Archaeological Research Series Report, No. 4. Department of Anthropology, College of William and Mary, Williamsburg, VA.

1988 *The Second Season of Archaeological Investigations of the Government Guest House, St. Eustatius.* St. Eustatius Archaeological Research Series Report, No. 5. Department of Anthropology, College of William and Mary, Williamsburg, VA.

1988 *The Simon Doncker House: Archaeological Exploration of the Yard.* St. Eustatius Archaeological Research Series Report, No. 6. Department of Anthropology, College of William and Mary, Williamsburg, VA.

1990 *Archaeological Investigations of Structure 4, Government Guest House, St. Eustatius, Netherlands Antilles.* St. Eustatius Archaeological Research Series Report, No. 6. Department of Anthropology College of William and Mary, Williamsburg, VA.

1990 Review of *Artifacts of the Spanish Colonies of Florida and the Caribbean, 1500–1800, Volume 1, Ceramics, Glassware, and Beads* by Kathleen Deagan. *American Antiquity* 55(2):435.

1990 The Potential of Historical Archaeology in the Netherlands Antilles. In *Proceedings of the Eleventh International Congress for Caribbean Archaeology,* Agamemnon Gus Pantel Tekakis, Iraida Vargas Arenas, and Mario Sanoja Obediente, editors, pp. 393–399. La Fundacion Argueologica, Antropologica e Historica de Puerto Rico. La Universidad de Puerto Rico, Recinto de Rio Piedras, Puerto Rico.

1991 *Archaeological Investigations of Battery Concordia St. Eustatius, Netherlands Antilles.* St. Eustatius Archaeological Research Series Report, No. 7. Department of Anthropology College of William and Mary, Williamsburg, VA.

1991 *The Final Structural Report, Government Guest House Complex, St. Eustatius.* St. Eustatius Archaeological Research Series Report, No. 8. Department of Anthropology, College of William and Mary, Williamsburg, VA.

1991 The Merchants of St. Eustatius: An Archaeological and Historical Analysis. *Proceedings of the Thirteenth International Congress for Caribbean Archaeology,* Jay Haviser, editor, pp. 384–392. Archaeological-Anthropological Institute of the Netherlands Antilles, Curaçao.

1992 *The Archaeological Survey of Ebenezer Sugar Plantation, Philipsburg, St. Maarten.* St. Maarten Archaeological Research Series Report, No. 2, Department of Anthropology, College of William and Mary, Williamsburg, VA.

1993 *Archaeological Survey of Sites and Buildings, St. Maarten, Netherlands Antilles: I.* St. Maarten Archaeological Research Series Report, No. 3. Department of Anthropology, College of William and Mary, Williamsburg, VA.

1993 The Archaeology of Piersey's Hundred, Virginia, Within the Context of the Muster of 1624/5 In *Archaeology of Eastern North America: Papers in Honor of Stephen Williams,* J. Stoltman, editor, pp. 313–336. Mississippi Department of Archives and History, Jackson.

1994 *The Archaeological Survey of Sites and Buildings, St. Maarten, Netherlands Antilles: II.* St. Maarten Archaeological Research Series Report, No. 4. Department of Anthropology, College of William and Mary, Williamsburg, VA.

1995 *The Country Estate of Governor Johannes DeGraaf: Preliminary Investigations.* St. Eustatius Archaeological Research Series Report, No. 9. Department of Anthropology, College of William and Mary, Williamsburg, VA.

1995 St. Eustatius: Entrepot on the Golden Rock. Manuscript, Department of Anthropology, College of William and Mary, Williamsburg, VA.

1996 Citizens of St. Eustatius, 1781: A Historical and Archaeological Study. In *The Lesser Antilles in the Age of European Expansion,* Robert L. Paquette and Stanley L. Engerman editors, pp. 223–238. University Press of Florida, Tallahassee.

1996 *Archaeology of the Dutch Elite: The Country Estate of Johannes de Graaff.* St. Eustatius Archaeological Research Series Report. Department of Anthropology, College of William and Mary, Williamsburg, VA.

1996 The Historical Archaeology of Virginia's Golden Age: An Overview. In *The Archaeology of Eighteenth-Century Virginia*, T. Reinhart, editor, pp. 1–46. Spectrum Press, Richmond, VA.

1998 *Archaeology of Belvedere Plantation: The Boiling House*. St. Maarten Archaeological Research Series Report, No. 5. Department of Anthropology, College of William and Mary, Williamsburg, VA.

2001 Review of *John Dwight's Fulham Pottery, Excavations 1971–79* by Chris Green. Archaeological Report, No. 6. In *Ceramics in America*, Robert Hunter, editor, pp. 247–249. University Press of New England, Hanover, NH.

2001 Time Lines: Changing Settlement Patterns on St. Eustatius. In *Island Lives: Historical Archaeologies of the Caribbean*, P. Farnsworth, editor, pp. 103–141. University of Alabama Press, Tuscaloosa.

2004 Archaeology of a Colonial Pottery Factory: The Kilns and Ceramics of the "Poor Potter" of Yorktown. In *Ceramics in America*, Robert Hunter, editor, pp. 15–47. University Press of New England, Hanover, NH.

BARKA, NORMAN F. (EDITOR)
1969 *Bibliography of the Virginia Indians*. Archeological Society of Virginia, Richmond.

BARKA, NORMAN F., AND NORMAN ALTSHULER
1976 *Archaeological, Historical, and Cultural Study of Flowerdew Hundred Plantation, Virginia*. Manuscript, Southside Historical Sites, Inc., and Department of Anthropology, College of William and Mary, Williamsburg, VA.

BARKA, NORMAN F., EDWARD AYRES, AND CHRISTINE SHERIDAN
1984 *The "Poor Potter" of Yorktown: A Study of a Colonial Pottery Factory: Colonial National Historical Park, Virginia*, 3 vols. Yorktown Research Series Report, No. 5. U.S. Department of the Interior, National Park Service Denver Service Center, Denver, CO.

BARKA, NORMAN F., AND ANNE BARKA
1976 *Archaeology and the Fur Trade: The Excavation of Sturgeon Fort, Saskatchewan*. History and Archaeology Report, No. 7. Parks Canada, National Historic Parks and Sites Branch, Department of Indian and Northern Affairs, Ottawa.

BARKA, NORMAN F., AND MARLEY R. BROWN III
1989 A Phase II Evaluation of Cultural Resources within the Proposed York River Crossing Alternatives. Manuscript, William and Mary Center for Archaeological Research, Department of Anthropology, College of William and Mary, Williamsburg, VA.

BARKA, NORMAN F., AND JUNIUS FISHBURNE, JR.
1978 Archaeological, Historical, and Cultural Study of Two Seventeenth-Century Sites at Flowerdew Hundred, Virginia. Manuscript, Southside Historical Sites, Inc., and Department of Anthropology, College of William & Mary, Williamsburg, VA.

BARKA, NORMAN F., AND EDWARD C. HARRIS
1994 The 1993 Archaeological Investigations at Castle Island, Bermuda. *Bermuda Journal of Archaeology and Maritime History* 6:1–80.

1998 Archaeology of Daniel's Island Fort, Bermuda. *Bermuda Journal of Archaeology and Maritime History* 10:90–106.

1999 The Archaeology of Paget Fort: Bermuda's First Fort. *Bermuda Journal of Archaeology and Maritime History* 11:1–24.

BARKA, NORMAN F., EDWARD C. HARRIS, AND HEATHER M. HARVEY
1996 Archaeology of the King's Castle Island, Bermuda: The 1994 and 1995 Seasons. *Bermuda Journal of Archaeology and Maritime History* 8:1–29.

BARKA, NORMAN F., EDWARD C. HARRIS, AND PATRICIA L. KANDLE
1999 Guana Island Archaeological Project, The Sugar Factory (GN1): A Report on the First Season. Manuscript, Department of Anthropology, College of William and Mary, Williamsburg, VA.

BARKA, NORMAN F., AND THORLEY, J. PALIN
1979 *The Archaeology of Kiln 2, Yorktown Pottery Factory, Yorktown, Virginia*. Yorktown Research Series Report, No. 4. Department of Anthropology, College of William and Mary, Williamsburg, VA.

BARKA, NORMAN F., AND DOUGLAS SANFORD
1976 *The Archaeology of Highland (Ash Lawn), Albemarle, Virginia*. Manuscript, Southside Historical Sites Inc., and Department of Anthropology, College of William and Mary, Williamsburg, VA.

BARKA, NORMAN F., AND SUE SAUNDERS
1990 *A Preliminary Study of Welgelegen, St. Maarten, Netherlands Antilles*. St. Maarten Archaeological Research Series Report, No. 1. Department of Anthropology, College of William and Mary, Williamsburg, VA.

Richard Veit

BARKA, NORMAN F., AND CHRIS SHERIDAN
1977 The Yorktown Pottery Industry, Yorktown, Virginia. *Northeast Historical Archaeology* 6(1–2):21–32.

CARSON, CARY, NORMAN F. BARKA, WILLIAM M. KELSO, GARRY WHEELER STONE, AND DELL UPTON
1981 Impermanent Architecture in the Southern American Colonies. *Winterthur Portfolio* 16:135–196.

DETHLEFSEN, EDWIN, NORMAN F. BARKA, STEPHEN J. GLUCKMAN, AND R. DUNCAN MATHEWSON
1981 Historical Archaeology and Documentary Silence: A Case for the Spade. In *Underwater Archaeology: The Challenge before Us,* Gordon P. Watts, Jr., editor, pp. 225–231. *Proceedings of the Twelfth Conference on Underwater Archaeology.* Special Publication No. 2. Fathom Eight, San Marino, CA.

DETHLEFSEN, EDWIN S., STEPHEN J. GLUCKMAN, DUNCAN R. MATHEWSON, AND NORMAN F. BARKA
1979 A Preliminary Report on the Historical Archaeology and Cultural Resources of St. Eustatius, Netherlands Antilles. Manuscript, Department of Anthropology, College of William and Mary, Williamsburg, VA.
1982 Archaeology on St. Eustatius: The Pompeii of the New World. *Archaeology* 35:15–28.

EDWARDS, ANDREW C., AND NORMAN F. BARKA
1979 The Archaeology of Upper Wolfsnare, Virginia Beach, Virginia. Manuscript, Southside Historical Sites Inc., and Department of Anthropology, College of William and Mary, Williamsburg, VA.

EDWARDS, ANDREW C., CHRISTIE R. SMITH, CHARLES G. TROUP, AND NORMAN F. BARKA
1977 An Archaeological Survey of Gunston Hall Plantation. Manuscript, Southside Historical Sites, Inc., and Department of Anthropology, College of William and Mary, Williamsburg, VA.

HUNTER, ROBERT R., NORMAN F. BARKA, PATRICIA L. KANDLE, AND MARLEY R. BROWN
1986 A Phase I Archaeological Survey of the Proposed Ware Creek Reservoir Area, James City and New Kent Counties, Virginia. Manuscript, Department of Anthropology, College of William and Mary, Williamsburg, VA.

KANDLE, PATRICIA L., AND NORMAN F. BARKA
1986 Phase I Archaeological Survey of Section II Development Lafayette Faily-Lafayette Elderly Complex, Longhill Road, James City County, Virginia. Manuscript, Department of Anthropology, College of William and Mary, Williamsburg, VA.

MCCARY, BEN C., AND NORMAN F. BARKA
1977 The John Smith and Zuniga Maps in the Light of Recent Archaeological Investigations along the Chickahominy River. *Archaeology of Eastern North America* 5:73–86.

ROBINSON, GARY G., NORMAN F. BARKA, ANNE BARKA, AND ROBERT R. HUNTER
1989 A Cultural Resource Planning Overview of the Proposed Route 29 Project, Project 6029-005-122, PE100 and 6029-118-107, PE101, Amherst and Campbell Counties, Virginia. Manuscript, William and Mary Center for Archaeological Research, College of William and Mary, Williamsburg, VA.

TROUP, CHARLES G., ARTHUR G. BARNES, AND NORMAN F. BARKA
1978 The Potts and Wilson Iron Forge/Foundry, Patowmack Canal, Great Falls Park, Virginia. Manuscript, Southside Historical Sites Inc., and Department of Anthropology, College of William and Mary, Williamsburg, VA.
1979 The Samuel Briggs Grist Mill, Patowmack Canal, Virginia, Great Falls Park, Virginia. Manuscript, Southside Historical Sites Inc., and Department of Anthropology, College of William and Mary, Williamsburg, VA.

RICHARD VEIT

MEMORIAL: Kathleen Kirk Gilmore, 1914-2010. Volume 44, Number 4 (2010): 1-7. By Jim Bruseth, Kay Hindes, and Tamra L. Walter.

Memorial

Kathleen Kirk Gilmore, 1914–2010

FIGURE 1. Kathleen Kirk Gilmore at the site of La Salle's Fort St. Louis in Texas, Victoria County. (Photo courtesy of the Texas Historical Commission, 1997.)

On 18 March 2010, Kathleen Kirk Gilmore, a leading figure in Texas Spanish- and French-colonial archaeology, died at the age of 95. At the time of her passing, Gilmore was actively working on a book about the 18th-century Spanish captain Felipe de Rábago y Terán, who commanded the San Xavier and San Sabá missions in central Texas. Despite her age and troubling physical ailments, Gilmore remained active in historical archaeology until the very end of her life. Gilmore is survived by daughters Judy Gilmore Lepthien and Pat Gilmore, brother Rufus P. Kirk, five grandchildren, and three great-grandchildren.

Gilmore began her professional career not as an archaeologist but as a geologist. Although she was fascinated by archaeology as a young girl, she was discouraged from entering the field. Instead she pursued a college education in geology—a decision made during the depths of the Great Depression to ensure employment in the burgeoning oil-exploration business (Tunnell 2003:5). Upon graduation from the University of Oklahoma with a B.S. in geology, however, Gilmore found it difficult to find work in the male-dominated petroleum geology field. Faced with a need to make a living, Gilmore entered business school, and learned shorthand and typing.

Gilmore's first job with an oil company came in the late 1930s, when she moved to Houston to work as a stenographer for Humble Oil Company (Tunnell 2003:5). Although Gilmore hated the job, the company was happy to find a typist who knew geological terms. She eventually moved up to work in the oil fields, which she did until 1940 when she married Robert Gilmore, also a petroleum geologist.

After raising a family of four daughters, Gilmore decided finally to pursue her dream of becoming an archaeologist. She joined the Texas Archeological Society (TAS) and the Dallas Archeological Society to learn about the discipline. In 1962 she attended the TAS's first field school, when the historical Native American Gilbert site was excavated. There she learned how to conduct field excavations under the direction of Ed Jelks, who was to become her mentor and lifelong friend. The Gilbert site was excavated at a time when historical archaeology was in its infancy, and the experience instilled in Gilmore a keen interest in historical-period sites, where documentary evidence could be used to understand the archaeological record better.

In 1963, Gilmore entered the newly created graduate program in anthropology at Southern Methodist University (SMU). During the fall of 1966, she attended a graduate seminar in historical archaeology taught by Ed Jelks, then teaching at SMU. Based on her work in this course and after Jelks's encouragement, she developed a passion for locating and investigating Texas Spanish-colonial archaeological sites using primary source documents (Gilmore 1969:1). In 1967 she published her first historical archaeological report, based on fieldwork conducted at Presidio San Luis de las Amarillas and a search for the nearby Mission Santa Cruz de San Sabá, both in central Texas (Gilmore 1967). In this report, she developed a process for using historical documents to formulate a conceptual model of what was to be expected in the archaeological record. This was a methodology that she would use throughout her career to guide her archaeological investigations.

Her next field project occurred a year later when she sought to locate the sites associated with the San Xavier mission complex. The complex consisted of the San Ildefonso, Nuestra Señora de la Candelaria, and San Francisco Xavier de Horcasitas missions, and the San Francisco Xavier de Gigedo presidio (Figure 2). Following her methodology of studying the documentary records to formulate a model, Gilmore proposed where the sites should be located. She field tested the model and found all three missions, and possibly the presidio (Gilmore 1969). This project became the topic of her master's thesis at the Department of Anthropology at SMU (Gilmore 1968).

Gilmore next became involved in some early contract archaeology work, conducting excavations on Caddoan sites at Lake Palestine (Anderson et al. 1974) and investigating a shell midden at Lake Wallisville (Gilmore 1974a). She wrote about the work at Lake Palestine in her doctoral dissertation (Gilmore 1973b).

The work on Caddoan sites at Lake Palestine caused Gilmore to think for a time that she wanted to pursue Caddoan archaeology as her focus, but it was not long before she was back in historical archaeology. Curtis Tunnell, then Texas state archaeologist, and Jelks, then at Illinois State University, suggested to Gilmore that she analyze artifacts that had been collected from excavations at Fort St. Louis, the site of Robert Cavelier, Sieur de La Salle's ill-fated Gulf Coast colony.

In 1685 La Salle had landed on the central Texas coast in an attempt to establish a French colony to control trade along the Mississippi River. Not realizing that he had missed the Mississippi by more than 400 mi., he constructed a small fortification near the modern town of Victoria, Texas. After a few years La Salle was assassinated by his men and the colony failed. Historians had long speculated on the location of the colony, but without conclusive proof the location of the site remained in dispute. In 1950 the Texas Memorial Museum conducted excavations at the Keeran site, on a ranch along Garcitas Creek in southeast Texas. The work, directed by Glenn Evans, recovered several thousand artifacts, but no analysis was completed and a report was not written. Tunnell and Jelks thought that the artifacts from the site might answer the question of whether the site was the location of Fort St. Louis.

Gilmore took on the project. After analyzing the artifacts, she published her study of the Keeran site, entitling it *The Keeran Site: The Probable Site of La Salle's Fort St. Louis in Texas* (Gilmore 1973a). In her report she noted that some green-glazed ceramics found were "probably of French derivation" (Gilmore 1973a:36). Some years later, she reflected on her tentative conclusions about the Keeran site as "probably" the location of Fort St. Louis. She sent one of the green-glazed ceramics

FIGURE 2. Kathleen Kirk Gilmore and Doug Markwell excavating a burial at Mission San Francisco, Milam County, Texas. (Photo by Robert Gilmore, 1968.)

to Gerard Gusset at Parks Canada. He replied that the sherd was definitely of French origin, and was from the Saintonge region of southwestern France. Gilmore wrote a new paper, titling this one as, more definitively, *La Salle's Fort St. Louis in Texas* (Gilmore 1986), declaring her new confidence that the Keeran site was indeed the location of the French colony.

Gilmore's next major Spanish colonial excavation was in 1973–1974 at Mission de Nuestra Señora del Rosario. This mission was established in 1754 and closed in 1806. Her work—focused inside the walled compound and identified several stone building foundations (Gilmore 1974b, 1974c). She identified several construction phases of the mission that matched archival documents about the development and ultimate decline of the site.

In 1974 Gilmore accepted an appointment as adjunct professor of archaeology and research archaeologist with the Institute of Applied Sciences at the University of North Texas in Denton. This position allowed her to continue to work on a variety of historical archaeology projects in Texas. Much of her Texas work involved CRM projects in which she would direct the historical archaeology. She did this for investigations at Lakeview Lake, Granger Reservoir, North Fork Reservoir, and Lake Ray Roberts. She also established and directed the Red River Archaeology Project, a program to conduct surveys and other research into archaeological sites along the Red River of Texas and Oklahoma. She had long felt that the archaeology of this portion of the Red River, crossing east–west across the southern plains, had received too little attention. This important work brought more attention to the area's rich archaeological heritage.

Two investigations took Gilmore to other states. In 1978 she conducted survey and testing in North Carolina at the Single Brothers industrial complex in Old Salem; and in 1981 she undertook archaeological testing in Louisiana at Fort St. Leon, the location of both a French and an American fort at English Turn on the Mississippi River.

In addition to her own projects, Gilmore was a consultant on many projects conducted by other investigators. Starting in the mid-1990s she worked with Jim Bruseth as a research consultant on the excavation of the shipwreck *La Belle*. *La Belle* was a ship lost in 1686 by La Salle along the Texas coast. The ship was discovered in 1995 by the Texas Historical Commission (THC) and excavated in 1996–1997 inside a steel cofferdam with the seawater pumped out (Bruseth and Turner 2005). Then in 1999, the THC undertook a major reexcavation of Fort St. Louis, with the fieldwork continuing until 2002. This work fully supported Gilmore's earlier finding that the Keeran site was the location of La Salle's Fort St. Louis. Further archaeological evidence for La Salle's French fort was found, along with the remains of Nuestra Señora de Loreto en la Bahía, a Spanish presidio built over the French fort. During both projects, Gilmore was a constant source of guidance and inspiration. A particularly memorable experience for the senior author was traveling to France with Gilmore to visit places where ceramics and other artifacts excavated had been made.

Beginning in 1993, Gilmore served as the lead consultant to a team of archaeologists and researchers, including one of the junior authors (Hindes), in an effort to locate the site of the Mission Santa Cruz de San Sabá, the Spanish mission on which she had first reported in 1967. Relying heavily on Gilmore's previous archival research and field search, the team rediscovered the site of the mission, known as the "Missing Mission of Texas," in an alfalfa field east of Menard, Texas. Gilmore's contributions to the project were enormous, including financial support for the search, which she later termed "Mission Impossible."

In 1997 and 1998, Gilmore also served as project advisor to the TAS archaeological field investigations at the site of 41VT10, the second location of Mission Espíritu Santo de Zúñiga, in Victoria, Texas. Officially founded in 1722, the mission was moved in ca. 1725 from Garcitas Creek to a site on the Guadalupe River in current-day Victoria City Park. One of the highlights of the field investigations was a visit to the site by Ed Jelks, reuniting the two friends and colleagues.

In her last years, Gilmore conducted archival research on presidios in Texas with emphasis on places that Rábago y Terán had commanded. The Texas Presidios Project, which Gilmore initiated and supported, focused on recovering documents from archives in Spain, Mexico, and Italy. In 2008 she traveled to Seville to work in the Archivo General de Indias. Working with a translator and paleographer, Gilmore slowly translated documents that chronicled Rábago y Terán's activities at both Presidio San Xavier and Presidio San Sabá. Intrigued by the accounts of Rábago y Terán's contemptible behavior, she began writing a book based on this research. Although not complete at the time of her passing, the book will be published posthumously using Gilmore's lengthy notes and detailed research. While Rábago y Terán was a major focus of the Texas Presidios Project, the research Gilmore helped to support is also yielding valuable information regarding many of the forts established by the Spanish in the 18th century.

Gilmore served in several elected positions and received numerous honors during her lifetime. She served as president of the TAS in 1982–1983, and of the Council of Texas Archeologists in 1975. In 2003 she became the first recipient of the THC's Curtis D. Tunnell Lifetime Achievement Award, for outstanding service to Texas archaeology. Five years later, on her 40th anniversary of conducting archaeological excavations in Texas, she was honored by Governor Rick Perry with the THC's Governor's Award for Historic Preservation (Figure 3).

The Society for Historical Archaeology (SHA) was also a great passion of Gilmore's. In the late 1960s she took part in the initial planning meeting held to discuss forming a society, and subsequently she helped Jelks and others establish the organization (Tunnell 2003:10–11). In 1978 she also served as the SHA's first female president, and in 1995 she was awarded SHA's prestigious J. C. Harrington Award.

Gilmore's passion for archaeology inspired her to become a major philanthropist. She established the Bob and Kathleen Gilmore Endowment for Spanish and French Colonial Archeology in Texas, with the Friends of the Texas Historical Commission. This fund provides grants to researchers who study the archaeology of the colonial period in Texas, thus continuing Gilmore's legacy.

Professional and avocational archaeologists in Texas and across the nation will miss the advice and inspiration of Dr. Kathleen Kirk Gilmore.

FIGURE 3. Kathleen Kirk Gilmore receiving the Governor's Award for Historic Preservation from Texas governor Rick Perry, with Steve Tomka and Larry Oaks looking on. (Photo courtesy of the Texas Historical Commission, 2008.)

References

ANDERSON, KEITH M., KATHLEEN GILMORE, OLIN F. McCORMICK III, AND E. PIERRE MORENON
  1974 *Archaeological Investigations at Lake Palestine, Texas.* Southern Methodist University, Contributions in Anthropology, No. 11. Dallas, TX.

BRUSETH, JAMES E., AND TONI S. TURNER
  2005 *From a Watery Grave: The Discovery and Excavation of La Salle's Shipwreck,* La Belle. Texas A&M University Press, College Station.

GILMORE, KATHLEEN KIRK
  1967 *A Documentary and Archaeological Investigation of Presidio San Luis de las Amarillas and Mission Santa Cruz de San Saba, Menard County, Texas.* State Building Commission Archaeological Program, Report No. 9. Austin, TX.
  1968 The San Xavier Mission: A Study in Historical Site Identification. Master's thesis, Department of Anthropology, Southern Methodist University, Dallas, TX.
  1969 *The San Xavier Mission: A Study in Historical Site Identification.* State Building Commission Archaeological Program, Report No. 16. Austin, TX.
  1973a *The Keeran Site: The Probable Site of La Salle's Fort St. Louis in Texas.* Texas Historical Commission, Office of the State Archaeologist, Report No. 24. Austin.

1973b *Caddoan Interaction in the Neches Valley, Texas.* Doctoral dissertation, Department of Anthropology, Southern Methodist University, Dallas, TX. University Microfilms International, Ann Arbor, MI.

1974a *Cultural Variation on the Texas Coast: Analysis of an Aboriginal Shell Midden, Wallisville Reservoir, Texas.* Texas Archaeological Survey, University of Texas, Research Report No. 44, Part 1. Austin.

1974b *Mission Rosario Archeological Investigations 1973.* Texas Parks and Wildlife Department, Parks Division, Historic Sites and Restoration Branch, Archaeological Report No. 14, Part 1. Austin.

1974c *Mission Rosario Archeological Investigations 1974.* Texas Parks and Wildlife Department, Parks Division, Historic Sites and Restoration Branch, Archaeological Report No. 14, Part 2. Austin.

1986 La Salle's Fort St. Louis in Texas. *Bulletin of the Texas Archaeological Society* 55:61–72.

TUNNELL, CURTIS D.
2003 A Conversation with Kathleen Kirk Gilmore. *Historical Archaeology* 37(2):4–18.

Bibliography of Works by Kathleen Gilmore

Complied by James E. Bruseth and Timothy K. Perttula

ANDERSON, KEITH M., KATHLEEN GILMORE, OLIN F. McCORMICK III, AND E. PIERRE MORENON
1974 *Archaeological Investigations at Lake Palestine, Texas.* Southern Methodist University, Contributions in Anthropology, No. 11. Dallas, TX.

BRUSETH, JAMES E., JEFFREY DURST, AND KATHLEEN GILMORE
2004 Curtis Tunnell and the Discovery of the Palisade Trench at Presidio La Bahía. *Bulletin of the Texas Archeological Society* 75:71–84.

GILMORE, KATHLEEN KIRK
1967 *A Documentary and Archaeological Investigation of Presidio San Luis de las Amarillas and Mission Santa Cruz de San Saba, Menard County, Texas.* State Building Commission Archaeological Program, Report No. 9. Austin, TX.

1967 A Microscopic Study of Certain Pottery Types and Clays in the Southern Plains. In *A Pilot Study of Wichita Indian Archeology and Ethnohistory*, Robert E. Bell, Edward B. Jelks, and W. W. Newcomb, compilers, pp. 221–230. National Science Foundation, Washington, DC.

1968 The San Xavier Mission: A Study in Historical Site Identification. Master's thesis, Department of Anthropology, Southern Methodist University, Dallas, TX.

1969 *The San Xavier Mission: A Study in Historical Site Identification.* State Building Commission Archaeological Program, Report No. 16. Austin, TX.

1973 *Caddoan Interaction in the Neches Valley, Texas.* Doctoral dissertation, Department of Anthropology, Southern Methodist University, Dallas, TX. University Microfilms International, Ann Arbor, MI.

1973 *The Keeran Site: The Probable Site of La Salle's Fort St. Louis in Texas.* Texas Historical Commission, Office of the State Archaeologist, Report No. 24. Austin.

1974 *Cultural Variation on the Texas Coast: Analysis of an Aboriginal Shell Midden, Wallisville Reservoir, Texas.* Texas Archaeological Survey, University of Texas, Research Report No. 44, Part 1. Austin.

1974 *Mission Rosario Archeological Investigations 1973.* Texas Parks and Wildlife Department, Parks Division, Historic Sites and Restoration Branch, Archaeological Report No. 14, Part 1. Austin.

1974 *Mission Rosario Archeological Investigations 1974.* Texas Parks and Wildlife Department, Parks Division, Historic Sites and Restoration Branch, Archaeological Report No. 14, Part 2. Austin.

1978 Spanish Colonial Settlements in Texas. In *Texas Archeology: Essays Honoring R. King Harris*, Kurt D. House, editor, pp. 132–145. Southern Methodist University Press, Dallas, TX.

1979 The Single Brothers' Industrial Complex: Research Plan, Old Salem, North Carolina. *Conference on Historic Site Archaeology Papers* 13:76–108.

1980 Mission Dolores de los Ais, Historical Background and Field Investigations, 1972–73. In *Mission Delores de los Ais*, James E. Corbin, Thomas C. Alex, and Arlan Karlina, editors, pp. 223–276. Stephen F. Austin State University, Papers in Anthropology No. 2. Nacogdoches, TX.

1982 So Shall Ye Reap: The San Xavier Missions. *La Tierra* 9(1):2–10.

1983 *Caddoan Interaction in the Neches Valley, Texas.* Reprints in Anthropology, Vol. 27. J & L Reprint, Lincoln, NE.

1984 The Indians of Mission Rosario. In *The Scope of Historical Archaeology: Essays in Honor of John L. Cotter*, David G. Orr and Daniel G. Crozier, editors, pp. 163–191. Temple University, Laboratory of Anthropology, Philadelphia, PA.

1986 *French-Indian Interaction at an 18th Century Frontier Post: The Roseborough Lake Site, Bowie County, Texas.* Institute of Applied Sciences, North Texas State University, Contributions in Archaeology No. 3. Denton.

1986 La Salle's Fort St. Louis in Texas. *Bulletin of the Texas Archaeological Society* 55:61–72.

1988 The Beginnings of Historical Archeology in Texas. *The Record* 42(3):107–108. Dallas, TX.

1989 The Indians of Mission Rosario for the Books and from the Ground. In *Colombian Consequences, Vol. 1, Archaeological and Historical Perspectives on the Spanish Borderlands West,* David Hurst Thomas, editor, pp. 231–244. Smithsonian Institution Press, Washington, DC.

1990 Spanish Padres and French Fusils: Spanish and French Approaches to Native Peoples in Texas. *Heritage* 8(2):2–14. Austin, TX.

1991 An Archeological Footnote to History. *Bulletin of the Texas Archeological Society* 60:303–324.

1992 French-Spanish-Indian Interaction in Colonial Texas. *Bulletin of the Texas Archeological Society* 63:123–133.

1995 Archeology of Spanish and Mexican Colonialism in Texas: A Guide to the Literature. In *The Archaeology of Spanish and Mexican Colonialism in the American Southwest,* James E. Ayers, compiler, pp.103–133. Society for Historical Archaeology, Ann Arbor, MI.

1996 A. C. Saunders Site. In *The New Handbook of Texas,* Vol. 1, Ron Tyler, editor, p. 1. Texas State Historical Association, Austin.

1996 Early European-Indian Ceremonies on the Red River. *Journal of Northeast Texas Archaeology* 7:1–2.

1996 Historical Archaeology. In *The New Handbook of Texas,* Vol. 3, Ron Tyler, editor, pp. 632–633. Texas State Historical Association, Austin.

1996 Nuestra Señora del Rosario Mission. In *The New Handbook of Texas,* Vol. 4, Ron Tyler, editor, p. 1,073. Texas State Historical Association, Austin.

1996 San Francisco Xavier de Gigedo Presidio. In *The New Handbook of Texas,* Vol. 5, Ron Tyler, editor, pp. 848–849. Texas State Historical Association, Austin.

1996 San Francisco Xavier de Horcasitas Mission. In *The New Handbook of Texas,* Vol. 5, Ron Tyler, editor, p. 849. Texas State Historical Association, Austin.

1996 San Luis de las Amarillas Presidio. In *The New Handbook of Texas,* Vol. 5, Ron Tyler, editor, pp. 866–867. Texas State Historical Association, Austin.

1998 Treachery and Tragedy in the Texas Wilderness: The Adventures of Jean L'Archeveque in Texas (A Member of La Salle's Colony). *Bulletin of the Texas Archeological Society* 69:35–46.

2005 People of La Salle's Last Expedition. *Bulletin of the Texas Archeological Society* 76:107–121.

2007 French Ceramics from the Keeran Site (41VT4):1950 Excavations. In *French Colonial Pottery: An International Conference,* George Avery, editor, pp. 297–308. Northwestern State University Press, Natchitoches, LA.

GILMORE, KATHLEEN KIRK, AND NORMA HOFFRICHTER
1964 Preliminary Investigations, L. O. Ray Site, Delta County, Texas. *The Record* 19(1):3–17. Dallas, TX.

GILMORE, KATHLEEN KIRK, AND OLIN MCCORMICK
1980 *Red River Archaeological Project, Phase I.* Institute of Applied Sciences, North Texas State University, Denton.
1982 *Red River Archaeological Project, Phase II.* Institute of Applied Sciences, North Texas State University, Denton.

GILMORE, KATHLEEN KIRK, AND VERGIL NOBLE
1983 *Archaeological Testing at Fort St. Leon (16PL35), Plaquemines Parish, Louisiana.* Institute of Applied Sciences, Contributions in Archaeology No. 2, North Texas State University. Denton.

GILMORE, KATHLEEN KIRK, AND NANCY REESE
n.d. *Ceramics from the Wreckage of La Salle's Ship* La Belle. Texas Historical Commission, Report. Austin. Forthcoming.

HINDES, V. KAY, MARK R. WOLF, GRANT D. HALL, AND KATHLEEN KIRK GILMORE
1995 *The Rediscovery of Santa Cruz de San Sabá, A Mission for the Apache in Spanish Texas.* Texas State Historical Foundation, Austin, and Texas Tech University, Lubbock.

PERTTULA, TIMOTHY K., AND KATHLEEN K. GILMORE
1988 *Archaeological Survey Along Mill Race Creek and Tributaries, Wood County, Texas: 1987–1988.* Institute of Applied Sciences, Contributions in Archaeology No. 6, University of North Texas. Denton.

STORY, DEE ANN, BYRON BARBER, ESTALEE BARBER, EVELYN COBB, HERSCHEL COBB, ROBERT COLEMAN, KATHLEEN GILMORE, R. K. HARRIS, AND NORMA HOFFRICHTER
1966 Indian Artifacts: Pottery Vessels. *Bulletin of the Texas Archeological Society* 37:112–187.

JIM BRUSETH
ARCHEOLOGY DIVISION
TEXAS HISTORICAL COMMISSION
AUSTIN, TEXAS 78711

KAY HINDES
OFFICE OF HISTORIC PRESERVATION
CITY OF SAN ANTONIO
1901 S. ALAMO
SAN ANTONIO, TEXAS 78283

TAMRA L. WALTER
DEPARTMENT OF SOCIOLOGY, ANTHROPOLOGY,
AND SOCIAL WORK
TEXAS TECH UNIVERSITY
2500 BROADWAY
LUBBOCK, TX 79409

MEMORIAL: Roderick Sprague, 1933–2012. Volume 46, Number 4 (2012): 1-7. By Ronald L. Michael.

Memorial

Roderick Sprague 1933–2012

Recently the SHA lost one of its founders, and the greater anthropological community had to say farewell to a special person. You begin to realize how special the person was when the chief of a Native American tribal government appears at his memorial service to express what he had meant to the tribe's people and the importance of his friendship.

Roderick Sprague was born on 18 February 1933, in Albany, Oregon, and died on 20 August 2012, in Moscow, Idaho, following several years of debilitating health. He was the youngest of three children of Roderick Sprague and Mary Willis Sprague (both deceased). He is survived by two older sisters: Anne Geaudreau of Oldtown, Idaho, and Arda Rutherford of Prescott, Arizona; his wife, Linda Ferguson Sprague, Moscow; and four children: Roderick IV and Katherine K. Sprague (her partner Tabitha) from a previous marriage, and Frederick L. Sprague (his wife Dawn and son Jack) and Alexander W. Sprague (his wife Rebecca and son Phineas) from his current marriage.

Rick Sprague lived most of his life in Idaho, Washington, and Oregon, although part of his youth had been fondly spent in North Dakota, where his father was a federal agricultural agent. He received his bachelor's and master's degrees in anthropology from Washington State University, served two years in the U. S. Army (honorably discharged with the rank of E-5), and received his Ph.D. in anthropology from the University of Arizona, Tucson. He worked at Washington State University as a research archaeologist for three years before going to the University of Idaho in 1967 as an assistant professor of anthropology. Within a year and a half of his arrival he became chairman of the Department of Sociology/Anthropology and director of the Laboratory of Anthropology. After 12½ years the two positions became too much for one person and the two units were separated. He chose to remain the director of the Laboratory of Anthropology, but continued to teach anthropology part-time, including summer archaeological field schools. He spent a sabbatical year in 1986–1987 teaching at Inner Mongolia University as the first participant in the University of Idaho's exchange with that institution.

Rick did field work in Idaho, Washington, Oregon, Alaska, Arizona, Montana, and Prince Edward Island. He received both the University of Idaho Library Faculty Award for Outstanding Service and the Sigma Xi Published Research Paper Faculty Award in 1986, and the Phi Kappa Phi Distinguished Faculty Award for Research in 1996. In 2000 he was honored with the J. C. Harrington Medal, the highest international award in historical archaeology, and in 2004 he received the Carol Ruppé Service Award, both given by the Society for Historical Archaeology. He currently remains the only member to receive both of these awards and the only member to serve two terms as president of the society.

During his career Rick published over 130 scientific papers, articles, and book reviews, and also authored over 100 unpublished reports to agencies, specializing in historical archaeology, culture-change theory, and artifact analysis, including such areas as glass trade beads and buttons. He conducted research and burial excavations at the request of 10 different American Indian tribal governments in the Plateau, Great Basin, and Northwest Coast, with repatriation a standard procedure many years prior to the enactment of the federal Native American Grave Protection and Repatriation Act. Legal work for five different Northwest tribes and two tribes outside of the area involved testimony in Fifth District Federal Court on five occasions, including one case before the U.S. Supreme Court, as well as testimony before various state and federal legislative bodies.

Editorial duties involved 40 years as senior coeditor for the *Journal of Northwest Anthropology* (*JONA*, formerly *Northwest Anthropological Research Notes*), 96 of the 98 issues of the *University of Idaho Anthropological Reports*, 20 years as review editor for *Historical Archaeology*, as well as serving on numerous editorial advisory boards. Rick was extremely proud of his volunteer service to the Society for Historical Archaeology. Following is a list of offices, committee positions, and contributions he made to the society.

Offices and Committees

Regional Coordinator for Research, Northwest, 1968–1977
General Program Chairman, 2nd annual meeting, 1969, Tucson
Director, 1970–1971
Secretary-Treasurer, 1971–1974 (a three-year term plus a "Truman" year to put
    the Secretary-Treasurer and Editor on different three-year cycles)
President, 1976 (plus the usual President-Elect and Past-President positions)
Historical Archaeology Reviews Editor, 1977–1997
Editorial Board Member, 1977–2008
Parliamentarian, 1984–2008
Archivist, 1987–1998
President, 1990 (plus the usual President-Elect and Past-President positions)
Associate Copy Editor, 2002–2008
Committees—far too many to list but history committee at the time of his death

Additionally, he spent five "long" years preparing the Cotter bibliography for posting on the SHA website.

After retirement Rick continued to live in Moscow, Idaho, with his wife Linda. He was designated professor emeritus of anthropology and director emeritus of the Laboratory of Anthropology at the University of Idaho. He continued to conduct research and serve as an expert witness for Northwest tribes.

Besides so generously giving of his time and integrity to the SHA and *JONA*, Rick was passionate about supporting and keeping track of the careers of his many graduate students. Only a couple of months prior to his death, as his health was in serious decline, he took steps to ensure that one of his early graduate students, Karlis Karklins, was nominated for the SHA Carol Ruppé

Distinguished Service Award. He also faithfully attended paper presentations of his former students at professional meetings.

Rick was a friendly and fun-loving person. He had time to talk to all who wanted to talk to him. I remember him many times finishing a conversation with one person and walking over to a friend to ask whether they knew the person with whom he had been talking. He never hesitated to talk to a stranger and help that person in any way he could. He enjoyed social conversation, and little delighted him more than being able to sit down with former students and/or friends, have a beer or two, and discuss just about any subject.

Rick felt strongly that his *Historical Archaeology* memorial not include material that had previously been published concerning his life and work. Having been an editor and copy editor for many years he simply believed that it was unnecessary to repeat what had already been said. Additional information may be found in Sprague (1994), Karklins (2000), Michael (2004), Allen and Michael (2008), and Stapp (2009).

References

ALLEN, REBECCA, AND RONALD L. MICHAEL
  2008 Forty Years of Historical Archaeology, 1967–2007. *Historical Archaeology* 42(2):8–16.

KARKLINS, KARLIS
  2000 J. C. Harrington Award 2000: Roderick Sprague. *Historical Archaeology* 34(4):1–6.

MICHAEL, RONN
  2004 Carol V. Ruppé Distinguished Service Award: Roderick Sprague. *Historical Archaeology* 38(4):8–9.

SPRAGUE, RODERICK
  1994 Bead Typology: The Development of a Concept. In *Pioneers in Historical Archaeology: Breaking New Ground*, Stanley South, editor, pp. 85–100. Plenum Press, New York, NY.

STAPP, DARBY C.
  2009 An Interview with Roderick Sprague. *Historical Archaeology* 43(2):135–149.

Bibliography

*Major, important, or influential works.

BIES, MICHAEL, AND RODERICK SPRAGUE
  1979 San Juan Island Artifact Summary 1977 and 1978. In *Miscellaneous San Juan Island Reports, 1977–1978*, pp. 75–100. University of Idaho Anthropological Manuscript Series, No. 54. Moscow.

BORESON, KEO, CRAIG E. HOLSTINE, GROVER S. KRANTZ, AND RODERICK SPRAGUE
  1985 *The Burials at 45CH296, Chelan County, Washington*. Eastern Washington University Reports in Archaeology and History, No. 100-40. Cheney.

FERGUSON, LINDA, MARY GIDDINGS, DUANE MARTI, AND RODERICK SPRAGUE
  1975 Three Late Wagons from 45 SJ 295, the Hudson's Bay Company Bellevue Farm Site, San Juan Island, Washington. In *Miscellaneous San Juan Island Reports 1971–1973*, pp. 223–243. University of Idaho Anthropological Research Manuscript Series, No. 16. Moscow.

FIELDER, GEORGE, AND RODERICK SPRAGUE
  1974 *Test Excavations at the Coeur d'Alene Mission of the Sacred Heart, Cataldo, Idaho, 1973*. University of Idaho Anthropological Research Manuscript Series, No. 13. Moscow.

GUNSELMAN, CHERYL, AND RODERICK SPRAGUE
  2003 *A Buried Promise: The Jefferson Peace Medal. *Journal of Northwest Anthropology* 37(1):53–90.

GURCKE, KARL, MICHAEL BIES, THOMAS M. J. MULINSKI, RODERICK SPRAGUE, CAROLINE CARLEY, JULIA LONGENECKER, AND PRISCILLA WEGARS
  1982 *Nez Perce National Historical Park Archaeological Excavations, 1979–1980*. University of Idaho Anthropological Research Manuscript Series, No. 70. Moscow.

KARKLINS, KARLIS, AND RODERICK SPRAGUE
    1972 Glass Trade Beads in North America: An Annotated Bibliography. Historical Archaeology 6:87–101.
    1980 *A Bibliography of Glass Trade Beads in North America. South Fork Press, Moscow, ID.
    1987 A Bibliography of Glass Trade Beads in North America, First Supplement. Promontory Press, Ottawa, ON.

LAHREN, S. L., AND RODERICK SPRAGUE
    1994a Final Report for the Multi-phase Testing for California Bar Site, Lemhi County, Idaho. Report to Meridian Gold Company, Salmon, MT, from Lahren Associates, Dillon, MT.
    1994b Leesburg, Idaho Stabilization Project: Archaeological Excavation for Concrete Stabilization Pads. Report to Meridian Gold Company, Salmon, MT, from Lahren Associates, Dillon, MT.

LOHSE, E. S., AND RODERICK SPRAGUE
    1998 *History of Research. In Handbook of the American Indians, Vol. 12, Plateau, Deward E. Walker, Jr., editor, pp. 8–28. Washington, DC.

PAVESIC, MAX G., MARK G. PLEW, AND RODERICK SPRAGUE
    1979 A Bibliography of Idaho Archaeology, 1889–1976. Northwest Anthropological Research Notes, Memoir No. 5. Moscow.

ROBINSON, WILLIAM J., AND RODERICK SPRAGUE
    1965 *Disposal of the Dead at Point of Pines, Arizona. American Antiquity 30(4):442–453.

RODEFFER, MICHAEL J., STEPHANIE H. RODEFFER, AND RODERICK SPRAGUE
    1972 Nez Perce Grave Removal Project. University of Idaho Anthropological Research Manuscript Series, No. 5. Moscow.

SAPPINGTON, ROBERT LEE, AND RODERICK SPRAGUE
    1989 Archaeological Investigations at Lyon's Ferry State Park, on the Lower Snake River, Franklin County, Washington. Report to U.S. Army Corps of Engineers, Walla Walla District, Walla Walla, WA, from Laboratory of Anthropology, University of Idaho, Moscow.

SPRAGUE, RODERICK
    1960a Archaeology of the Sun Lakes Area of Central Washington. Washington State University, Laboratory of Anthropology, Report of Investigations, No. 6. Pullman.
    1960b Burial Patterns of the Lower Snake River Region. In Archaeological Excavations in the Ice Harbor Reservoir, 1959, R. D. Daugherty, author, pp. 4–11. Washington State University, Laboratory of Anthropology, Report of Investigations, No. 3. Pullman.
    1961 Review of The Archaeologist's Notebook. Kiva 27(2):31–32.
    1963 Glass Beads. In Highway Salvage Archeology, Lava Beds, National Monument: Final Report, B. K. Swartz, author, pp. 90–91. Manuscript, National Park Service, Tucson, AZ.
    1964 Inventory of Prehistoric Southwestern Copper Bells: Additions and Corrections I. Kiva 30(4):18–24.
    1965 Descriptive Archaeology of the Palus Burial Site. Washington State University, Laboratory of Anthropology, Report of Investigations, No. 32. Pullman.
    1967a *A Preliminary Bibliography of Washington Archaeology. Northwest Anthropological Research Notes 1(1). Reprinted 1968 in Washington State University, Laboratory of Anthropology, Report of Investigations, No. 43. Pullman.
    1967b Post-1800 Historical Indian Sites [Dallas organizational meeting]. Historical Archaeology 1:70.
    1968a *The Meaning of Palouse and the Identification of the Palloat Pallah Indians. Idaho Yesterdays 12(2):22–27.
    1968b Papers Presented at the First Twenty Annual Meetings of the Northwest Anthropological Conference, 1948–1967. Northwest Anthropological Research Notes 2(1):123–134.
    1968c A Suggested Typology and Nomenclature for Burial Analysis. American Antiquity 33(4):479–485.
    1969 Excavations at the Roma Site, Prince Edward Island, 1968. University of Idaho Anthropological Research Manuscripts Series, No. 1. Moscow.
    1970a *Editorial on Sasquatch. Northwest Anthropological Research Notes 4(2):127–128.
    1971a Addendum on Beads. In A Bison Jump in the Upper Salmon River Valley of Eastern Idaho, B. Robert Butler, author, p. 13. Tebiwa 14(1):4–32.
    1971b Annotated Bibliography of Lake Roosevelt Archaeology. Washington Archaeologist 15(1):2–24.
    1971c Burial Pattern Relationships between the Columbia and Canadian Plateaus. In Aboriginal Man and Environments on the Plateau of Northwest America, Arnoud H. Stryd and Rachel A. Smith, editors, pp. 183–196. Students' Press, Calgary, AL.
    1971d Review of Astor Fort Okanogan. American Anthropologist 73(4):934–935.
    1971e Review of Canadian Historic Sites: Occasional Papers in Archaeology and History. Historical Archaeology 5:128–129.
    1972a The first of 90 University of Idaho, Laboratory of Anthropology, Letter Reports, produced every year from 1972 to 1998.
    1972b Glass Trade Beads. In The Archaeology of Pass Creek Valley, Waterton Lakes National Park, Brian O. K. Reeves, author, pp. 252–253. National Historic Sites Service, Manuscript Report, No. 61. Ottawa, ON.
    1972c Mission San Antonio Glass Trade Beads. In Excavations at Tes-haya, Donald M. Howard, author. Monterey County Archaeological Society Quarterly 2(1). Carmel, CA.

1973a *Chapter 9. The Pacific Northwest. In *The Development of North American Archaeology*, James Fitting, editor, pp. 250–285. Doubleday, New York, NY.

1973b Location of the Pig Incident, San Juan Island, In *Miscellaneous San Juan Reports, 1970–1972*, pp. 17–38. University of Idaho Anthropological Research Manuscript Series, No. 7. Moscow.

1974 *American Indians and American Archaeology [invited editorial]. *American Antiquity* 39(1):1–2.

1975a *The Development of Historical Archaeology in the Pacific Northwest. *Northwest Anthropological Research Notes* 9(1):6–19.

1975b *Recommendations for Historical Archaeology at Fort Egbert, Alaska*. University of Idaho Anthropological Research Manuscript Series, No. 18. Moscow.

1975c Review of *Historical Archaeology in Northwestern North America*. *Historical Archaeology* 9:90–91.

1976 The Submerged Finds from the Prehistoric Component, English Camp, San Juan Island, Washington. In *The Excavation of Water-Saturated Archaeological Sites (Wet Sites) on the Northwest Coast of North America*, pp. 78–85. National Museum of Man, Archaeological Survey of Canada Mercury Series, No. 50. Ottawa, ON.

1977 The Field Notes of Arthur G. Colley, San Juan Island, 1919–1926. In *Miscellaneous San Juan Island Reports 1912–1926, 1975*, pp. 63–69. University of Idaho Anthropological Research Manuscript Series, No. 38. Moscow.

1978a *Nez Perce Grave Recovery, Lower Granite Dam Reservoir, 1973–78*. University of Idaho Anthropological Research Manuscript Series, No. 47. Moscow.

1978b Review of *Kanaka Village/Vancouver Barracks, 1974*. *Pacific Northwest Quarterly* 69(4):189–190.

1979 The First Archaeological Excavation in Whitman County was Historic. *Bunchgrass Historian* 7(1):23–24. Colfax, WA.

1980a Metal Cleaning for Whom: Archaeologist, Curator, or Descendants. *Idaho Archaeologist* 4(2):7–8.

1980b The Relationship between the Carved Stone Heads of the Columbia River and the Sasquatch. In *Manlike Monsters on Trial*, M. Halpin and M. M. Ames, editors, pp. 229–234. University of British Columbia Press, Vancouver.

1981 *A Functional Classification for Artifacts from 19th and 20th Century Historical Sites. *North American Archaeologist* 2(3):251–261.

1982a Bibliographies of Greater Northwest Archaeology. *Quarterly Review of Archaeology* 4(1):6–7.

1982b The Preservation of Written and Printed Archaeological Records. *Northwest Anthropological Research Notes* 16(2):206–211.

1983a Rock Art Studies on the Columbia River. *Quarterly Review of Archaeology* 4(3):2.

1983b *Tile Bead Manufacturing. In *Proceedings of the 1982 Glass Trade Bead Conference*, Charles F. Hayes III, editor, pp. 167–172. Rochester Museum and Science Center, Research Records, No. 16, Rochester, NY.

1984a *A Check List of Columbia Basin Papers. *Northwest Anthropological Research Notes* 18(2):256–259.

1984b The Father of Oregon Prehistory on Film. *Quarterly Review of Archaeology* 5(2):16.

1984c Glass Trade Beads. In *A Nineteenth Century Ute Burial from Northeastern Utah*, Richard E. Fike and H. Blaine Phillips II, editors, pp. 69–70. Utah Bureau of Land Management, Cultural Resource Series, No. 16. Salt Lake City.

1985a *Glass Trade Beads: A Progress Report. *Historical Archaeology* 19(2):87–105. Reprinted in 1991 and 2000 in *Approaches to Material Culture Research for Historical Archaeology*, Society for Historical Archaeology, Ann Arbor, MI.

1985b Historic Artifact Analysis. In Phase II Testing of Four Sites on Cassimer Bar and Testing and Evaluation of Site 45 OK 74, Denise Carlevato, author. Report to Douglas County PUD, Wenatchee, WA, from Western Heritage, Inc., Olympia, WA.

1985c Identification of Archeological Research Topics and Questions for the Downtown Seattle Transit Project [project participant]. Report to Parsons, Brinckerhoff, Quade, & Douglas, Seattle, WA, from Hart Crowser and Associates, Seattle.

1986a *Ng Ka Py Vessel Terminology. *Asian Comparative Collection Newsletter* 4(2):insert.

1986b A Possible Prosser T-Hole Bead from Japan. *Bead Forum* 8:10–11.

1986c Review of *Adobe Walls*. *Pacific Historian* 30(3):81.

1987a The Descriptive Archaeology of Nat Cave, 45-GR-100. *Tebiwa* 23:1–8.

1987b *Participant contribution to *Proceedings of the Conference on Reburial Issues*. Society for American Archaeology and Society of Professional Archeologists, Washington, DC.

1987c *Plateau Shamanism and Marcus Whitman. *Idaho Yesterdays* 31(1&2):55–56.

1988a Bead Analysis, a Contribution to *Archaeological Testing at Ice House Lake*, Rick Minor, author, pp. 52–55. Heritage Research Associates Report, No. 76. Eugene, OR.

1988b Bead Analysis, Appendix B. In *Further Archaeological Testing at 45SA16, Skamania County, Washington*, Rick Minor, author, pp. 45–49. Heritage Research Associates Report, No. 67. Eugene OR.

1988c More on Tile Beads. *Bead Forum* 13:3–4.

1989a The Fenstermaker Bead Collection. *Bead Forum* 14:6–8.

1989b Glass Trade Beads. In *Curation Manual for the Archaeological Collections from 45AS11, North Bonneville, Washington*, Kathryn Toepel, editor, pp. 75–80. Heritage Research Associates Report, No. 81. Eugene, OR.

1989c Review of *A Study of Five Historic Cemeteries at Choke Canyon Reservoir, Texas*. *Historical Archaeology* 22(2):131–132.

1989d Review of *The History of Beads from 30,000 B.C. to the Present*. *Beads* 1:95–96.

1989e Rock Art Studies on the Columbia River. In *The Interpretation of Prehistory: Essays from the Pages of the Quarterly Review of Archaeology*, pp. 146–148. *Review of Archaeology* 10(1):146–148.

1989f The Structure of Anthropological Research Units. *Thunderbird* 9(4):2–3. Corvallis, OR.

1990a *Archaeological Footnotes. In *Journals of the Lewis and Clark Expedition*, Vol. 7, Gary E. Moulton, editor. University of Nebraska Press, Lincoln.

1990b Glass Trade Beads. In *An Overview of Investigations at 45SA11: Archaeology in the Columbia Gorge*, Rick Minor et al., authors, pp. 156–158. Heritage Research Associates Report, No. 83. Eugene, OR.

1990c Historical Archaeology and the Chinese of Silver City. In *They Came to Owyhee, Owyhee Outpost #21*, Dale M. Grey, editor, pp. 47–55. Owyhee County Historical Society, Murphy, ID.

1990d Obituary of Alfred W. Bowers. *Anthropology Newsletter* 31(8):5.

1991a *A Bibliography of James A. Teit. *Northwest Anthropological Research Notes* 25(1):103–115.

1991b Ceramic Cones [I]. *Asian Comparative Collection Newsletter* 8(3):5–6.

1991c Description of Glass Beads, 10-CW-4. In *Archaeological Investigations at the Clearwater Fish Hatchery Site (10-CW-4), North Fork of the Clearwater River, North Central Idaho*, Robert Lee Sappington, author, pp. 86–87. University of Idaho Anthropological Reports, No. 91. Moscow.

1991d Foreword. In *Mandan Social and Ceremonial Organization*, 2nd edition, Alfred W. Bowers, author, pp. iii–v. University of Idaho Press, Moscow.

1992 Review of *Scientific Research in Early Chinese Glass. Beads* 4:69–72.

1993a A 1937 Government View of Indian Beadworking Ability. *Bead Forum* 22:11–13.

1993b *American Indian Burial and Repatriation in the Southern Plateau with Special Reference to Northern Idaho. *Idaho Archaeologist* 16(2):3–13.

1993c Chinese Cones: II. *Asian Comparative Collection Newsletter* 10(3):5.

1994a *Bead Typology: The Development of a Concept. In *Pioneers in Historical Archaeology: Breaking New Ground*, Stanley South, editor, pp. 85–100. Plenum Press, New York, NY.

1994b Glass Bead Inventory. Appendix C. In *An Assessment of Archaeological Resources within the Proposed Sahhalie Condominiums Project Area, Seaside, Clatsop County, Oregon*, Rick Minor, author, pp. 116–120. Heritage Research Associates Report, No. 167. Eugene, OR.

1994c A Note from 1887 on Glass Beadmaking. *Bead Forum* 24:5–6.

1995a Chinese Cones: III. *Asian Comparative Collection Newsletter* 12(2):6.

1995b Classification of Historic Trade Beads. In *Archaeology of the Cape Creek Shell Midden, Cape Perpetua Scenic Area, Central Oregon Coast*, Rick Minor and Ruth L. Greenspan, authors, pp. 107–111. Coastal Prehistory Program, University of Oregon, Eugene.

1995c Classification of Glass Beads. In *Archaeological Investigations for the Port of Siuslaw Norpal Street Project, Florence, Oregon*, Rick Minor, author, pp. 27–30, 65–82. Heritage Research Associates Report, No. 182. Eugene, OR.

1996 *An Anthropological Summary of the Coeur d'Alene Tribe's Occupation of the Coeur d'Alene Lake Area. Manuscript, Coeur d'Alene Tribe, Plummer, Idaho. Written testimony in Coeur d'Alene Tribe vs. State of Idaho, District Court, Coeur d'Alene, ID.

1997a The Historic Period. In *Results of Archaeological Investigations at Kam'-nak-ka, Kooskia National Fish Hatchery, Middle Fork of the Clearwater River, Northcentral Idaho*, R. Lee Sappington, author. University of Idaho Anthropological Reports, No. 98. Moscow.

1997b Review of *The Sasquatch in Alberta. Cryptozoology* 16.

1998a *The Literature and Locations of the Phoenix Button. *Historical Archaeology* 32(2):56–77

1998b *Palouse [Palus]. In *Handbook of the American Indians*, Vol. 12, *Plateau*, Deward E. Walker, Jr., editor, pp. 352–359. Washington, DC.

1999a *An Anthropological Summary of the Dependence of the Coeur d'Alene Tribe upon Coeur d'Alene Lake. Manuscript, Coeur d'Alene Tribe, Plummer, Idaho. Written Testimony in United States vs. ASARCO et al., District Court, Coeur d'Alene, ID.

1999b *Ceramic Cones: IV and Final. *Asian Comparative Collection Newsletter* 16(2):insert.

1999c A Review of Stability of Southern Plateau Burial Practices [The Ancient One/Kennewick Man]. Manuscript, Confederated Tribes of the Umatilla Indian Reservation, Cultural Resources Protection Program, Mission, OR.

2000 Exposure Route Footnotes for Coeur d'Alene Subsistence Scenario. Report to Coeur d'Alene Tribal Council, Plummer, ID, from Terragraphics Environmental Engineering, Moscow, ID.

2001a *An Extended Bibliography of Anthropology and Historical Archaeology for the Pre-1943 Hanford/White Bluffs Area. Pacific Northwest National Laboratory Report, No. 13948. Richland, WA.

2001b *Testimony before NAGPRA Committee, 18 November, Cambridge, MA, on the Relationship of Spirit Cave Man to the Fallon Paiute-Shoshone Tribe in the Area of Burial Practices. Decision favorable [BLM thus far has refused to obey the decision].

2002 *China or Prosser Button Identification and Dating. *Historical Archaeology* 36(2):111–127.

2004 *Incised Dentalium Shell Beads in the Plateau Culture Area. *Beads* 16:51–68 [published 2007].

2005a *Burial Terminology: A Guide for Researchers. AltaMira Press, Lanham, MD.

2005b *Canoes and Other Water Craft of the Coeur d'Alene. *Journal of Northwest Anthropology* 39(1):41–62.

2005c Northwest Graduate Studies Concerning Beads. *Bead Forum* 46:3–5.

2006 A Glass Bead Rattlesnake Bracelet. *Bead Forum* 48:5–6.

2007 A Glass Bead Rattlesnake Bracelet [Reprint in color of original in *Bead Forum* 48:6]. *Bead Forum* 50:insert.

2008 *Coeur d'Alene Burials. *Journal of Northwest Anthropology* 42(1):71–84.

SPRAGUE, RODERICK (EDITOR)

1970b George L. Howe and the Antiquarian. *Northwest Anthropological Research Notes* 4(2):166–222.

1971f Field Notes and Correspondence of the 1901 Columbia Museum Expedition by Merton L. Miller to the Columbia Plateau. *Northwest Anthropological Research Notes* 5(2):201–232.

1983c *San Juan Archaeology, 2 vols. University of Idaho, Laboratory of Anthropology, Moscow, ID.

Sprague, Roderick, and Walter H. Birkby
1970   Miscellaneous Columbia Plateau Burials. *Tebiwa* 13(1):1–32.
1973   *Burials Recovered from the Narrows Site (45OK11), Columbia River Washington.* University of Idaho Anthropological Research Manuscript Series, No. 11. Moscow.

Sprague, Roderick, and John D. Combes
1966   *Excavations in the Little Goose and Lower Granite Dam Reservoirs, 1965.* Washington State University, Laboratory of Anthropology, Report of Investigations, No. 37. Pullman.

Sprague, Roderick, and An Jiayao
1990   *Observations on Problems in Researching the Contemporary Glass Bead Industry of Northern China. *Beads* 2:5–13.

Sprague, Roderick, and Grover S. Krantz (editors)
1977   *The Scientist Looks at the Sasquatch.* University of Idaho Press, Moscow.
1979   *The Scientist Looks at the Sasquatch, II.* University of Idaho Press, Moscow.

Sprague, Roderick, and Daniel S. Meatte
1992   The Idaho Archaeological Conference, 1973–1991. *Northwest Anthropological Research Notes* 26(1):57–71.

Sprague, Roderick, and Jay Miller
1979   *Burial Relocation Survey, Chief Joseph Reservoir, 1977–78.* University of Idaho Anthropological Research Manuscript Series, No. 51. Moscow.

Sprague, Roderick, and Thomas M. J. Mulinski
1980   *Ancestral Burial Relocations, Chief Joseph Dam, 1979.* University of Idaho Anthropological Manuscript Series, No. 63. Moscow.

Sprague, Roderick, and Michael J. Rodeffer
1989   The Bloody Point Archaeological Investigations. *Overland Journal* 7(3):26–28.

Sprague, Roderick, and Aldo Signori
1963   *Inventory of Prehistoric Southwestern Copper Bells. *Kiva* 28(4):1–20.

Striker, Michael, and Roderick Sprague
1993   *Excavations at the Warren Chinese Mining Camp Site, 1989–1992.* University of Idaho Anthropological Reports, No. 94. Moscow.

Turnipseed, Donna, Michael Striker, and Roderick Sprague
1994   *Florence Tells Her Secrets.* University of Idaho Anthropological Reports, No. 96. Moscow.

Walker, Deward E., Jr., and Roderick Sprague
1998   *History until 1846. In *Handbook of the American Indians*, Vol. 12, *Plateau*, Deward E. Walker, Jr., editor, pp. 138–148. Washington, DC.

Wegars, Priscilla, and Roderick Sprague
1981   *Archaeological Salvage of the Joso Trestle Construction Camp, 45-FR-51, Lower Monumental Project.* University of Idaho Anthropological Research Manuscript Series, No. 65. Moscow.

Wegars, Priscilla, Roderick Sprague, and Thomas M. J. Mulinski
1983c *Miscellaneous Burial Recovery in Eastern Washington, 1981.* University of Idaho Anthropological Research Manuscript Series, No. 76. Moscow.

Sprague's bibliography also includes ca. 100 manuscripts, but in his written instructions to me, the bibliography presented here is "as complete as I would want it for SHA." Those ca. 100 works are archived at the Fort Walla Walla Museum, Walla Walla, Washington.

Ronn L. Michael

Memorial

Daniel G. Roberts 1947–2014

Cultural resource management (CRM), historical archaeology, and public archaeology lost a major voice on 24 May 2014 when Daniel G. Roberts passed away from prostate cancer coupled with the long-term effects of Parkinson's disease. In addition to serving as a pioneer in the fields of CRM and public archaeology, Dan Roberts was also an author, editor, former Society for Historical Archaeology (SHA) Board member, long-time *Historical Archaeology* Associate Editor, and a tireless volunteer for the avocational and professional societies supporting archaeology. He was a mentor to members of a generation of historical archaeologists working in CRM, who heeded his call to publish their work and share it with the public. The SHA's award for public archaeology is given in his name.

Dan Roberts was born on 12 October 1947 at Philadelphia's Hahnemann Hospital and was the only child of Ada Eleanor Wahl and Daniel Baird Roberts. He was educated at the William Penn Charter School, a Quaker school, attended Quaker meeting, and tried to bring the Quaker values of piety, simplicity, and pacifism with him through life. Dan learned the game of golf while at Penn Charter, joined the school's golf team, and rose to first position and captain by his senior year (1965). The school won the highly competitive Inter-Academic League Championships in Dan's junior and senior years, with Dan one of the few self-taught golfers in the league.

In the eighth grade he visited the University Museum at the University of Pennsylvania and became enamored with Egyptology and archaeology; he would read C. W. Ceram's *Gods, Graves, and Scholars*, James Michener's *The Source*, and similar popular studies of archaeology. Dan graduated from high school intent on pursuing a degree in archaeology, and his advisor recommended Beloit College in Wisconsin. He applied, was accepted, and began his undergraduate studies at what was then one of the top undergraduate anthropology programs in the country. Dan studied with Robert J. Salzer, William S. Godfrey, and Marco Bicheria, and worked with Salzer on a 14-week field school on the Northern Lakes Project in northern Wisconsin. Graduating in 1969, Dan worked as a sometimes-paid/sometimes-volunteer field technician on projects in Kentucky, Illinois, and Wisconsin. Returning home in 1971, Dan found work with Barbara Liggett at the National Park Service excavations at Franklin Court, as well as excavations at Budd's Row in Society Hill and Gorgas Mill in Mount Airy. While working as a field tech, he also drove a cab to make "real" money. In 1973 he went to work with the Pennsylvania Historical and Museum Commission on surveys along the Susquehanna River. Ready to begin the next stage of his career, with a primary interest in lithic technologies at that time, Dan applied to and was accepted by Idaho State University (ISU). In the fall of 1974 he drove to Pocatello, Idaho, to begin his graduate education with full tuition and a research assistantship.

At ISU, Dan fell under the tutelage of Robert Butler and worked with Butler on ISU CRM contracts. For his M.A. thesis he sample surveyed 300,000 ac. of Bureau of Land Management land along the Tetons, camping on the desert floor as he and his team moved from one sample zone to the next. Butler taught Dan to write logically and professionally and to critique others' work fairly, and he taught Dan that archaeological knowledge is mostly made up of ideas rather than facts. Dan used his survey of the Bureau of Land Management lands as his thesis topic and graduated in 1976 with an M.A. in anthropology with an emphasis in CRM, certainly one of the first graduate degrees given in CRM, since the term had only been coined in 1974.

While at ISU, Dan began collecting vintage paperback books. Over time, he would amass a collection of more than 60,000 books, one of the largest vintage collections in the country. Dan became a well-respected collector and scholar of pulp fiction and published articles in *Paperback Quarterly* and the *Paperback Parade.*

Dan continued work with ISU after graduation, excavating at the Wasden site near Idaho Falls, an important prehistoric cave site, where he discovered a Folsom point in a cluster of mammoth bones, the first artifact discovery that proved Paleoindians had hunted mammoth. Dan applied for a newly created position of assistant curator at the ISU Museum and was hired for the job, where he would have worked for Bob Butler. However, the Idaho State Legislature cut funding for education in the 1976 budget and the position was eliminated. With his work at the Wasden site completed, Dan was left high and dry in Pocatello and returned home to Philadelphia.

Colleagues in Pennsylvania informed Dan that an architecture firm known as National Heritage Corporation might be hiring an archaeologist. Dan interviewed with Alex Townsend at National Heritage and was offered the position as the number-two archaeologist in a two-person shop. Townsend had been the second archaeologist hired by National Heritage, and Dan was the third in the firm's history. In 1977 National Heritage Corporation changed its name to John Milner Associates (JMA). However, Dan was frustrated with the management structure and project development in the archaeology program at JMA and decided that he needed to pursue his Ph.D. He applied and was accepted into Southern Methodist University's doctoral program with the understanding that he could pursue Southern Plains prehistory as a dissertation topic. When he arrived in Dallas in early 1978, however, he discovered there had been a shift in the program's emphasis and only doctorate research on Israel or Egypt would be accepted. Dan stayed for the winter semester and then returned East, where he went back to work for Alex Townsend at JMA.

Dan worked on a variety of projects with JMA in the late 1970s and early 1980s, many of which were components of architectural restorations. However, he saw the opportunity to grow JMA's cultural resource program, and in 1982 Dan was promoted to be JMA Director of Archaeology. He actively marketed JMA's cultural resource program and began to develop a strong department of talented archaeologists and historians. The early 1980s was an period when CRM was becoming institutionalized in government contracting, and under Dan's leadership JMA grew into one of the nation's largest and most prominent CRM firms. Dan's approach to CRM emphasized commitment to the resources and the community; he published extensively on CRM projects, as well as on the CRM process, and encouraged JMA staff to follow his lead. At that stage in the history of CRM, publication was largely seen as the domain of those in academia, and Dan's efforts helped promote a broader shift in the field and the recognition that CRM could be research archaeology as well as contract archaeology. Dan published in national, peer-reviewed journals, such as *Historical Archaeology*, *American Archaeology*, and *Archaeology*, as early as 1984. He emphasized consultants' obligation to disseminate and publish the results of their work and wrote an article on that subject in the *SHA Newsletter*. JMA's cultural resource staff became his extended family; he encouraged them in their research and publications, always offering a strong editorial eye to their efforts. Dan's colleagues were his students, and historical archaeologists who worked with him include Jo Balicki, Wade Catts, Charles Cheek, Tom Crist, John McCarthy, Mike Parrington, Tom Wheaton, Rebecca Yamin, myself, and others.

While Dan's interests through graduate school had emphasized prehistory, his research focus at JMA shifted to historical archaeology. This shift was a product of two factors. First, JMA was an architectural firm, and many of Dan's early projects focused on providing archaeological input to architectural topics associated with building restorations, as well as recovering archaeological data from new construction locations on historical sites. JMA was also based in the oldest historically, continuously occupied portion of the nation, and hence historical sites were far more common in the Middle Atlantic and Northeast than they had been in the West. Although trained in prehistory, Dan tackled historical archaeology with the same self-direction he had applied to golf. He sought out the advice and friendship of two prominent Pennsylvania historical archaeologists, John Cotter at the University of Pennsylvania and Ronn Michael at Indiana University of Pennsylvania. Cotter, one of the founders of historical archaeology, was a National Park Service archaeologist who worked at Jamestown and who would join the faculty of the University of Pennsylvania. Cotter had first met Dan when he was a technician on the Franklin Court excavations in 1971. Cotter gladly shared his thoughts on historical archaeology, as well as his research in Philadelphia, when Dan reached out to him.

Together, Cotter and Roberts decided that the work that had been conducted in Philadelphia could educate the public on historical archaeology's contribution to the knowledge of history. With Cotter and Michael Parrington, Dan coauthored *The Buried Past: An Archaeological History of Philadelphia*, which was published by the University of Pennsylvania Press in 1992 and was awarded the Antoinette Forrester Downing Award of the Society of Architectural Historians. Always one to repay his debts, Dan subsequently published an interview with John Cotter, as well as Cotter's memorial in *Historical Archaeology* in 1999. In 2007, Dan and David Orr published an anthology of Cotter's work, *Witness to the Past*, through the Society for American Archaeology (SAA) Press with support of the SHA.

Dan met Ronn Michael at the 1979 SHA annual meeting in Nashville. Michael was then the editor of *Historical Archaeology*, a position he held for 27 years, and also editor of *Pennsylvania Archaeology*. Michael brought Dan in as an associate editor of *Pennsylvania Archaeology* and noted that Dan took particular pleasure in working with avocational archaeologists to turn their work into publication-quality articles. Dan would subsequently become an associate editor with *Historical Archaeology*, a position he held from 1988 until 2004. Dan considered Michael his mentor and used him as a sounding board for discussions on project and business management, and the business of CRM, which Michael also engaged in through his own firm, NPW Consultants. A historian of the field of historical archaeology, Dan's interview with Ronn Michael was published in *Historical Archaeology* in 2012.

Dan's growing interest in historical archaeology and urban archaeology would lead to JMA's involvement in the excavation in 1983 and 1984 of Philadelphia's First African Baptist Church Cemetery, a landmark cemetery-relocation project. Working on the project, Dan insisted that there be public outreach and the opportunity for members of Philadelphia's African American community to visit the excavations and learn about their collective past through archaeology. This occurred at a time when most CRM work was done behind a fence and agencies were reluctant to invite the public to witness cemetery excavations. Working closely with Dick Tyler, the head of the Philadelphia Historical Commission, Dan implemented a program of public archaeology, including site tours, that was very well received by Philadelphia's African American community. He went on to publish articles on the benefits of public outreach, encouraging other archaeologists to follow his lead. Dan and JMA's work at First African Baptist Church Cemetery would lead to other African American cemetery relocations, including the Tenth Street Cemetery in Philadelphia, and ultimately to involvement in New York City's African Burial Ground Project, another nationally recognized cemetery project with a strong public outreach element.

While best known for his work on historical cemeteries, Dan worked on a broad range of historical sites with JMA, from urban domestic occupations to industrial sites to military conflict sites, and for clients ranging from pipeline companies to private developers, to state transportation departments, and to federal agencies, particularly the National Park Service, General Services Administration, and U.S. Army Corps of Engineers.

Dan's service to professional archaeology associations was unparalleled—he was on the board of the Society for Historical Archaeology from 2002 to 2004 and an associate editor of *Historical Archaeology* from 1988 to 2004; on a variety of committees with both the SHA and the SAA; on the Register of Professional Archaeologists (RPA) Grievance and Standards Board (1991–1993); vice president (1997–2002) and president (1987–1989) of the Pennsylvania Archaeological Council; and associate editor of the Society for Pennsylvania Archaeology's *Pennsylvania Archaeology* from 1988 to 2004. He was one of the founders of the American Cultural Resource Association (ACRA), hosting ACRA's first board-of-directors meeting at JMA's offices in West Chester, reviewing ACRA's by-laws and constitution, and serving on the ACRA Board of Directors from 1995 to 2003, and as vice president from 1997 to 1998 and 2001 to 2003. His service to ACRA was recognized by receipt of the ACRA Director's Award in 2011. His stature in the field was such that he was selected as a member of the Advisory Council on Historic Preservation's National Task Force on Archaeology, representing four national associations: the SHA, SAA, ACRA, and RPA.

Dan rose through JMA to serve as a vice president, ultimately becoming the firm's president in 2006 before retiring at the end of 2010. He was honored with a session devoted to his work at the 2007 SHA conference in Williamsburg and with a memorial gathering of colleagues and friends in West Chester on 12 October 2014. Throughout his career, Dan operated with the philosophy that we as archaeologists all share the same objectives—to bring consideration of the past into planning for the future—and that we all have an obligation to share our work with both our colleagues and the public.

Dan is survived by his wife of 19 years, B. J. Titus, his co-workers at JMA, and all of us who were fortunate to know him as a colleague, mentor, advisor, and friend.

Acknowledgments

Dan hired me as assistant archaeologist at JMA in 1984. After working on various field projects I was brought into JMA's lab and then promoted to a desk in the main building. JMA's office, then at 309 North Matlack Street, West Chester, Pennsylvania, was located in an historic house, and my desk was in a closet off Dan's office. I passed his desk daily, and Dan and I would have frequent conversations, and at the end of the workday Dan and I would discuss his interactions with clients and staff, as well as his approach to various proposals and projects, seeking feedback and teaching me the management side of CRM. His mentorship of my career in CRM would resume in 1988 when Dan convinced his colleagues at JMA to provide financial and managerial support for a new CRM company, New South Associates, that Tom Wheaton, Mary Beth Reed, and I were creating. JMA would be a shareholder in New South until 2006, and Dan and I would continue our conversations on historical archaeology, public outreach, and CRM through the years. Dan's colleagues at JMA, past and present, shared their memories, as did Ronn Michael and Vergil Noble, and I appreciate their thoughts. Recognizing that his time was coming to an end, Dan left an autobiographical summary of his early life. All of us who had the good fortune to work with him will work to carry his voice into the future.

Bibliogrp hy

ANTHONY, DAVID W., AND DANIEL G. ROBERTS

1990 Recent Archaeological Discoveries in the Lehigh Hills of Eastern Pennsylvania. *Proceedings of the Lehigh County Historical Society* 39:296–311.

COTTER, JOHN L., DANIEL G. ROBERTS, AND MICHAEL PARRINGTON

1992 *The Buried Past: An Archaeological History of Philadelþi a.* University of Pennsylvania Press, Philadelphia.

CRIST, THOMAS A. J., AND DANIEL G. ROBERTS

1996 Engaging the Public through Mortuary Archeology: Philadelphia's First African Baptist Church Cemeteries. *CRM* 10:5–8.

CRIST, THOMAS A. J., DANIEL G. ROBERTS, REGINALD H. PITTS, JOHN P. MCCARTHY, AND MICHAEL PARRINGTON

1997 The First African Baptist Church Cemeteries: African-American Mortality and Trauma in Antebellum Philadelphia. In *In Rememb ance: Archaeology and Death*, David A. Poirier and Nicholas F. Bellantoni, editors, pp. 19–49. Bergin & Garvey, Westport, CT.

JOSEPH, J. W., AND DANIEL G. ROBERTS

2001 Visual Effects and Cell Towers: A Different Point of View. *ACRA Edition* 7(3):1,6–7.

NOBLE, VERGIL E., AND DANIEL G. ROBERTS

2004 SHA's "Ethical Principles": A Dissenting Opinion. *Society for Historical Archaeology Newsletter* 37(2):8–9.
2005 Continuing the Dialogue on SHA's Ethical Principles. *Society for Historical Archaeology Newsletter* 38(1):12–14.

PARRINGTON, MICHAEL, AND DANIEL G. ROBERTS

1984 The First African Baptist Church Cemetery: An Archaeological Glimpse of Philadelphia's Early Nineteenth Century Free Black Community. *Archaeology* 37(6):26–32.
1990 Demographic, Cultural, and Bioanthropological Aspects of a Nineteenth-Century Free Black Population in Philadelphia, Pennsylvania. In *A Life in Science: Pap rs in Honor of J. Lawrence Angel*, Jane E. Buikstra, editor, pp. 138–170. Center for American Archeology Scientific Papers No. 6. Kampsville, IL.

ROBERTS, DANIEL G.

1976 *Final Repr t on the 𝟗   Camas Creek-Little Grassy Archaeological Survey.* Idaho State University Museum of Natural History, Pocatello Archaeological Report No. 5. Pocatello.
1982 The Archeology of Groundbreaking. *Dodge National Forum* 5(2):5–7.
1984 Management and Community Aspects of the Excavation of a Sensitive Urban Archaeological Resource: An Example from Philadelphia. *American Archeology* 4(3):235–240.
1987 The History and Archaeology of Immanuel Episcopal Church, New Castle, Delaware. *Pennsylvania Archaeologist* 57(1):1–33.
1989 The Obligation to Document: A Consultant's View of Archaeological Reporting and Publishing. *Society for Historical Archaeology Newsletter* 22(3):9–10.
1997 Methods of Overhead Transmission Line Construction and Prevention of Disturbance to the Archeological Record: An Example from the Pennsylvania Piedmont. In *The Sixth International Symps ium on Environmental Concerns in Rights-of-Way Management*, J. R. Williams, J. W. Goodrich-Mahoney, J. R. Wisniewski, and J. Wisniewski, editors, pp. 261–272. Elsevier Science, New York, NY.
1999a A Conversation with John L. Cotter. *Historical Archaeology* 33(2):6–50.
1999b Memorial: John L. Cotter. *Historical Archaeology* 33(4):6–18
2000a Compliance Archaeology in Pennsylvania: The Long and the Short of It. *Journal of Middle Atlantic Archaeology* 16:269–274.
2000b From the Desert of Southeastern Idaho to the Consulting World of the East Coast. *National Association for the Practice of Anthropl ogy Bulletin* 20(1):12–14.

ROBERTS, DANIEL G. (EDITOR AND COMPILER)

1985 *Archaeological Resources of the Piedmont and Coastal Plain of Southeastern Pennsylvania, Contribution to the Comprehensive State Plan for the Conservation of Archaeological Resources*, Vol. 2. Pennsylvania Historical and Museum Commission, Harrisburg.
1994 Pennsylvania Archaeology: A Retrospective: A Compilation of Revisits to Early Archeological Projects by Several Notable Pennsylvania Archeologists. *Pennsylvania Archaeologist* 64(1):1–69.

ROBERTS, DANIEL G., AND DAVID BARRETT

1984 Nightsoil Disposal Practices of the Nineteenth Century and the Origin of Artifacts in Plowzone Proveniences. *Historical Archaeology* 18(1):108–115.

ROBERTS, DANIEL G., AND JOHN P. McCARTHY
1995 Descendant Community Partnering in the Archaeological and Bioanthropological Investigation of African American Skeletal Populations: Two Interrelated Case Studies from Philadelphia. In *Bodies of Evidence: Reconstructing History through Skeletal Analysis*, Anne L. Grauer, editor, pp. 19–36. John Wiley & Sons, New York, NY.

ROBERTS, DANIEL G., AND DAVID G. ORR (EDITORS)
2007 *Witness to the Past: The Life and Works of John L.C otter.* SAA Press, Washington, DC.

ROBERTS, DANIEL G., AND MARK B. SANT
1983 A Preliminary Replicative Analysis of Teshoa Flake Production. *Pennsylvania Archaeologist* 53(1&2):28–41.

ROBERTS, DANIEL G., AND ARTHUR SPIESS (EDITORS)
2003 The Neal Garrison Paleoindian Site, York County, Maine. *Archaeology of Eastern North America* 3: 733.

ROBERTS, DANIEL G., RICHARD J. WEBSTER, BETTY J. COSANS, JULIE MARTIN-CUSHMAN, AND SCOTT WASHBURN
1981 *Resource Protection Plan: A Framework for Decision-Making in Protecting the Cultural Resources of the Pennsylvania/Delaware River Coastal Zone.* Pennsylvania Historical and Museum Commission, Harrisburg, and Cee Jay Frederick Associates in association with John Milner Associates, West Chester, PA.

WEED, CAROL S., AND W. KEVIN PAPE (EDITORS)
1997 Changing Directions: A Roundtable Discussion [panel discussion with Daniel G. Roberts, Ellen Armbruster, Kurt W. Carr, Susan Levitt, and Lynne Sebastian]. *Society for American Archaeology Bulletin* 15(1):18–20,35; 15(2):18–20.

J. W. JOSEPH

Memorial

James Edward (Jim) Ayres 1936–2015

James Edward (Jim) Ayres died at his Tucson home on 10 March 2015 after a brave battle against leukemia. He was born on 30 September 1936, in Eau Claire, Wisconsin, to Wayne and Alice (Gutow) Ayres, and in 1944 the family moved to Colorado. Jim graduated from high school in Evanston, Wyoming, in 1955; served in the U.S. Air Force for four years, where he worked in the areas of security and intelligence; and received a bachelor's degree in anthropology from Fresno State College in 1963 and a master's degree in anthropology from the University of Arizona in 1970. He is survived by his wife of 43 years, Marianne F. (Kay) Ayres, and three brothers—Larry, Bill (also an archaeologist), and Jon.

Jim is only the second person to be honored by the Society for Historical Archaeology (SHA) with both the J. C. Harrington Medal in Historical Archaeology (2008) and the Carol V. Ruppé Distinguished Service Award (2014); the other was Jim's close friend Roderick Sprague. Essays in *Historical Archaeology* detail Jim's deep and lasting contributions to the historical archaeology of the American West, for which he was awarded the Harrington Medal (Cleland and Majewski 2008), and his sustained and truly outstanding record of service to the SHA, for which he received the Ruppé Award (Noble 2014). While these publications will certainly serve as a permanent record of Jim's accomplishments, I hope to focus the lens on Jim's life in a slightly different direction in this memorial. According to *Merriam-Webster's Collegiate Dictionary* (2008:774), the noun "memorial" is "something that keeps remembrance alive." In this memorial, I hope to capture some of what I believe Jim might wish us to remember about his life and his career, and what to keep alive during our own professional and personal journeys, based not only on his curriculum vitae, but also on personal impressions and the moving obituary prepared by his wife Marianne and his close friend Marlesa (Marcy) Gray (Gray and M. Ayres 2015).

Historical Archaeology, 2015 49(4):1–11.
Permission to reprint required.

Jim was tireless in promoting the value of historical archaeology within the anthropological and archaeological establishment, and to the public. He did this through the jobs he held, his teaching and work with students, his research and publications, his volunteer service to SHA and other organizations, and his civic engagements. As noted in his obituary:

> Jim was a pioneer in [the] historical archaeology of the West and remained active in the field until shortly before his death. He was one of the first archaeologists in Arizona to recognize the importance of historical-period sites and research to fleshing out the entire continuum of human existence in the American Southwest. (Gray and M. Ayres 2015)

Until relatively recently, historical archaeology in Arizona has been viewed as almost entirely secondary to the state's admittedly rich and varied prehistoric archaeological record. When Chuck Cleland and I wrote the essay about Jim as Harrington Medalist in 2008, we primarily focused on his historical archaeological accomplishments, which was appropriate, as the award was given by SHA. Perhaps it would have been more accurate to say that he promoted the value of all the components that somehow make up an holistic research approach to historical archaeology, i.e., field archaeology, material culture studies, documentary research, oral history, ethnography, and the built environment. The numerous projects in which he was involved afforded him insight into an enormous range of functional site types and material classes. His resume includes over 120 publications, including peer-reviewed articles, cultural resource management (CRM) reports, editorials, historic contexts, synthetic overviews, and a research guide to conducting historical archaeology in Arizona, for which he served as lead compiler. As of 2013, it was in its sixth, revised edition. Jim's work on railroad-related sites, the Chinese in Arizona, and Native American archaeology is especially significant.

It was critically important to him that longitudinal studies be carried out whenever possible, and that all research meet the absolute highest standards. Two examples of his personal research stand out as examples of his tenacity. From the 1960s onward, he spent many summers recording and re-recording historical period logging sites in the Uinta Mountains of Utah, documenting the changes that occurred in the conditions of the sites over half a century. Over the course of 15 years, Jim indexed all Tucson's English-language newspapers published during the period from 1870 to 1911; the index will be published posthumously and will be an invaluable research tool for historians and archaeologists. The day before he died, the Arizona Historical Society (AHS) wrote to Jim, honoring him for his monumental work and said that the room where he conducted his research at the AHS would, upon publication of the index, be publicly renamed in his honor. Sadly, Jim died unaware of this singular honor.

Downtown Tucson, Arizona, was one of many cities where significant portions of the architecturally and archaeologically rich historic core was virtually obliterated by urban renewal in the 1960s and 1970s. From 1967 to 1979, during his time at the Arizona State Museum (ASM), Jim directed the Tucson Urban Renewal Archaeological Project, working tirelessly with others in a salvage setting to record and recover as much as possible given limited time and resources. Several important publications resulted from the project, particularly Jim and others' work on the Chinese in Tucson. However, it personally saddened Jim that more research has not been conducted on the extensive collections from the project curated at ASM.

I suspect that his experiences on the Tucson Urban Renewal Project and in various positions at ASM spurred his serious concerns about and involvement with historic preservation at the state and local levels. From 1979 to 1981, he served as Arizona State Historic Preservation Officer (SHPO) and, from 1981 to shortly before his death, worked either as an independent consultant or as an employee for many Arizona firms, as well as for the National Park Service, on projects in Arizona, California, Colorado, Utah, and New Mexico. The bibliography included with this memorial provides glimpses into his work history. For example, after his time as Arizona SHPO, from ca. 1982 to 1985 he worked on many projects with Lyle M. Stone as an employee of Lyle's company, Archaeological Research Services, Inc.

Jim frequently taught classes on historical archaeology and material culture, mostly in adjunct, *ad honorem* positions, at both Arizona State University (ASU) (1981–1998) and the University of Arizona (UA) (1963–1965, 1972–1979, 1999–2013). Jim's teaching filled a void for students at these institutions. One of his students at ASU, Carol Griffith, went on to become deputy state historic preservation officer in the Arizona State Historic Preservation Office, and in that position she led many important initiatives to improve the practice of historical archaeology in the state. At UA, where I have an adjunct position, I was fortunate to team teach with Jim and serve on graduate student committees with him on a number of occasions, and it was always a very positive experience. Constantly thinking of ways to help students, the summer before his death he donated most of his library of materials on historical archaeology to the Department of Anthropology at Fort Lewis College in Durango, Colorado.

Sometimes Jim's dedication to his profession came at the price of his personal life. In an anecdote shared by Marianne Ayres with Marlesa Gray (2015, pers. comm.), during part of his tenure as instructor at ASU and while he was also working simultaneously in CRM, he maintained an apartment in Tempe where he would stay from Sunday through Thursday of each week. At that time, Marianne was head of nursing in the emergency room at University Medical Center, Tucson, so she could not join him in Tempe. Jim made friends with a florist in Tempe and often brought bouquets of flowers to Marianne when he would return home on Thursday evenings.

Jim believed that professionalizing our field and mentoring students and recent graduates was the way to encourage them to pursue lives of scholarship and service, regardless of where they would ultimately work (academia, government, private sector, or a museum). He was involved with the Society of Professional Archeologists (SOPA) from its inception in 1976 and served as SHA representative to SOPA from 1988 to 1993. When SOPA became the Register of Professional Archaeologists in 1998, he continued as a member until his death. He served two terms on the SHA Board of Directors: 1972–1975 and 1992–1995, and was president of the society in 1977. He was a regional editor for the *SHA Newsletter* for 28 years (1971–1999), an associate editor for *Historical Archaeology* (1988–1993), and served as a member of the Editorial Advisory Committee (EAC) and its subsequent morphs from 1978 until his death. Originally, the SHA Dissertation Prize (renamed by the SHA board in 2011 as the Kathleen Kirk Gilmore Dissertation Award) competition was run as a subcommittee of the EAC (Dissertation Prize Subcommittee), of which Jim was a member from 2001 to 2011 and chair from 2003 to 2011. He also served as an advisory editor for *North American Archaeologist* and for *Abstracts in Anthropology*. He took his editorial work very seriously and believed that research must follow technical and substantive standards, and that this should be reflected in both technical and synthetic writing. He was as exacting when he reviewed others' work as he was when evaluating his own.

Jim's record of service began when he was at Fresno State College studying for his undergraduate degree in the 1960s. There he became involved with the Fresno County (California) Historical Society and served on its board of directors and as curator of the Roedding Park Museum. Subsequently, in addition to his service for SHA and other professional organizations, he was a tireless member of state and local boards, commissions, and committees focused on preservation, and also served as an advisor to the National Trust for Historic Preservation for Arizona and on the International Centre Committee for the Advisory Council on Historic Preservation. Some of his more unusual involvements were as an archaeological consultant to the UA Office of Arid Lands Studies and as a member of the Arizona State Landmarks Committee, the Rangeland Resource Team for Southern Arizona for the Bureau of Land Management, the Governor's Commission on Arizona Environment, and the Pima Association of Governments Transportation Enhancement Task Force. His expertise was even sought by a local Tucson federal credit union, where he served for six years as a member of the loan review committee.

He became involved anywhere he could increase the visibility of and educate people about historical archaeology and historic preservation. Raising the awareness of the public and public officials about the importance of historical archaeology was a personal mission for him, but his "pitch" was always holistically presented as part of the preservation whole. He had a way of luring others into lives of volunteer service. When his term on the Tucson–Pima County Historical Commission (T–PCHC) ended, he personally recruited me, and I am still serving there. He also urged me to become involved with other things in the state, and we overlapped on the SHA board when he served his second term. He inspired me with his close attention to the society's budget and his support of initiatives that would benefit students and young professionals in the field.

Jim was obsessed with understanding material culture and the technologies behind it, and he spent countless hours researching all the major material classes we encounter as historical archaeologists, and compiled resources to aid in his own work, but also to share with others when he taught classes or workshops. Quite simply put, he loved learning and pursued it voraciously throughout his life. Although his favorite conference was undoubtedly the SHA's annual conference on historical and underwater archaeology, his travels around the world, accompanied by his beloved wife Marianne, always included visits to museums, historic sites, and points of cultural interest. I am sure both familial loyalty and curiosity took them to Easter Island, where his sibling Bill was working on an archaeological project, but the lure of seeing something new and exciting was the deciding factor when they attended the Vernacular Architecture Forum (VAF) held in 2003 at Saint-Pierre and Miquelon, which is technically part of France (off the coast of Canada). VAF is dedicated to the appreciation and study of ordinary buildings and landscapes—just the kind of thing that would benefit a curious historical archaeologist trying to look at the field holistically.

His contributions were acknowledged publicly through the numerous awards he received, not just the Harrington Medal and the Ruppé Award from SHA, but state and local awards as well. It is a testament to his innate modesty about such things that the list of awards he received is on the last page of his 16-page 2013 resume. His SHA awards have already been mentioned. In May 1995, the T–PCHC honored him with the Alene Dunlap Smith Award (now the Alene Dunlap Smith and Paul Smith Award) for his high level of dedication and a long-term commitment toward supporting and promoting historic preservation in Tucson and Pima County. At the state level (Arizona), he received a Governor's Award for Historic Preservation in 1995, the Award in Public Archaeology in the Professional Archaeologist Category from the Governor's Archaeology Advisory Commission in June 2008, and a Governor's Centennial Award in Historic Preservation in March 2012. In 2015 Jim was posthumously honored by the Arizona Archaeological and Historical Society, which he served as president from 2004 to 2007, with the Byron Cummings Award. The Cummings Award is given for outstanding contributions to knowledge in anthropology, history, or a related field of study pertaining to the southwestern United States or northwestern Mexico.

A memorial to Jim would be incomplete without a few words about him as a friend and colleague. Jim could be gruff and exacting at times, and that is how some will remember him. He had the knack for conveying the gist of an issue, even if his delivery often ruffled feathers. It was very difficult for him to suffer fools. He had close friends that he had known for many more years than he knew me (which is going on 25 years), but we both lived in Tucson. Once he identified something in you that he approved of and connected with, you suddenly found yourself involved in things you had never dreamed of doing. I have participated in many of the same boards, committees, and commissions in which he had been involved, and, while I have certainly learned a great deal from these experiences, I hope I have given something back as well. (He would often remind me if I had not considered something, but we could disagree respectfully, and at times we did.) He was a dependable and honorable colleague. If he promised something to you, he got it to you without fail. Many of us have our own personal memories of Jim, and I am sure they vary widely. He loved to smoke a good cigar, enjoy excellent food and wine (as well as fine tequila), and travel. Jim enjoyed visiting with friends, telling stories, and knowledgably discussing a wide range of subjects, especially at the SHA annual conference, when he and his buddies would get together and "hold court," usually in the hotel bar. A man of many interests and an independent spirit, Jim was a member of the Sigma Xi "companions in zealous research," as well as a fellow of the Explorers Club.

He was a thoughtful and generous friend. I shared many a meal with him, Marianne, Marcy Gray, and other friends. He would drive across town every few weeks from his office to mine to show me an artifact he was wondering about, bring a tidbit from his newspaper research that he thought would interest me, or just drop off copies of the latest investment newsletter he had received, in the hopes that I might benefit from paying more attention to this type of thing. He was a very busy man, but always made time to listen to a concern or offer advice. On holidays and birthdays, I would always receive a special bottle of wine he and Marianne had selected for me or a unique gift brought back from their travels. One summer, Marcy Gray and I visited him in Wyoming and toured high-altitude logging camps with him and Marianne. I admired a walking stick he was using to great advantage during our strenuous hikes. That Christmas he presented me with my own, made from a local tree and perfectly proportioned for my height. It even has a bronze label affixed with the place and dates of our trip. Jim and I frequently attended meetings or presented workshops together in Arizona or neighboring states (laden with boxes of artifacts to use for teaching and reams of printouts), and I treasure the time I spent with him when we could have leisurely conversations on topics that ranged from our life stories to politics, to historical archaeology and historic preservation.

Looking at Jim's resume, you would notice the many overlapping date ranges for his work experiences. He always seemed to be juggling many obligations, but perhaps he saw them as necessary opportunities that could not be missed or delegated. By his own admission he was often overcommitted, but these conflicting projects were just one more piece in the puzzle that made up the historical archaeology of the American West. When we spoke by telephone in the fall of 2013, after he had learned from his doctors about the severity of his illness, he said he was not really angry about the prognosis. Instead, he regretted that there was so much left to be done that he would not have time to finish.

So, how do we keep remembrance alive? All of us have different ways of promoting historical archaeology to the discipline's many potential audiences. I think Jim's example emphasizes this and shows that, over a lifetime, we each have the potential to make a real difference, no matter how far we advance along the *cursus honorem*. His career and contributions show that one can and should work to achieve a balance between making choices that enhance one's own individual career (he did have over 120 publications) and choosing to "pay forward" through service and scholarship with a purpose. He volunteered for so many things because he believed he could make a difference, and he encouraged others to do the same.

Although I am deeply honored to have been asked to write this memorial for Jim, I struggled mightily with it. I knew I could get the details relatively correct, but would he approve of my commentary and choices of what to emphasize? I finally decided to insert a little of my own subjectivity and go beyond the details in an attempt to convey just how much he did to support and bolster the field of historical archaeology. His view of the field, as something broader than explicitly taught, is refreshing but challenging. Whether you were Jim's close friend or colleague, an acquaintance, or did not know him at all, I invite you to think about what Jim's life shows us about our possibilities and responsibilities.

References

CLELAND, CHARLES E., AND TERESITA MAJEWSKI
    2008 J. C. Harrington Medal in Historical Archaeology 2008 James Edward Ayres. *Historical Archaeology* 42(2):15

GRAY, MARLESA, AND MARIANNE AYRES
    2015 In Memory of James Edward Ayres. Obituary for James Ayres. Book of Memories, Adair Funeral Home <http://www.adairfuneralhomes.com/book-of-memories/2083/ Ayres-James/obituary.php>. Accessed 25 July 2015

MERRIAM-WEBSTER'S COLLEGIATE DICTIONARY
    2008 ²Memorial *n*. In *Merriam-Web ter's Collegiate Dictionary*, 11th edition, p. 774. Merriam-Webster, Springfield, MA.

NOBLE, VERGIL
    2014 Carol V. Ruppé Distinguished Service Award 2014: James Edward Ayres. *Historical Archaeology* 48 2):94 1.

Bibliogrp hy

This bibliography represents nearly all of James Edward Ayres's work, and includes all but a few of the CRM and historic preservation reports he authored, coauthored, or to which he contributed. A number of people—Vincent Alascia, Marianne Ayres, Dale S. Brenneman, David E. Doyel, Suzanne Griset, Diana Hadley, and Lyle M. Stone—helped me to locate essential citation information, and I am very grateful to them.

AYRES, JAMES E.

196 An Archaeological Reconnaissance of the Boyce Thompson Arboretum, Arizona. Manuscript, University of Arizona, Arizona State Museum Library, Tucson.

196 The Central California Colony. *Fresno Past and Present* 7(2):2.

196 A Summary of Archaeological Sites in Maricopa County, Arizona. Manuscript, University of Arizona, Arizona State Museum Library, Tucson.

196 A Clovis Fluted Point from the Kayenta, Arizona Area. *Plateau* 8 4):768

196 A Prehistoric Farm Site near Cave Creek, Arizona. *Kiva* 3(3 :106 11.

1970a An Early Historic Burial from the Village of Bac. *Kiva* 8 2):4448

1970b Two Clovis Fluted Points from Southern Arizona. *Kiva* 8 3 :121+24.

1971a Buildings and Bottles. *Southern Arizona Genealogical Society Bulletin* 6 3 :48.

1971b Use and Abuse of Southwestern Rivers: The Desert Farmer. In *Hydrology and Water Resources in Arizona and the Southwest: Proceedings of the 9 Meetings of the Arizona SectionA merican Water Resources Assn. and the Hydrology Section–Arizona Academy of Science: Ap il3 9 Temp , Arizona*, Vol. 1, pp. 339. Arizona Academy of Science, Tempe.

1974 Arizona. In *Preservation in the States*, n.p. National Trust for Historic Preservation, Board of Advisors, Annual Report 1973-4. Washington, DC.

1975 Archaeological Reconnaissance of the Gila River Indian Reservation, Final Report. Report to Gila River Indian Community, Sacaton, AZ, f rom Arizona State Museum, Tucson.

1975 Cultural Values in the Wilderness: The Historical Perspective. In *The Wilderness and Cultural Values: A Symps ium*, Dee F. Green, editor, pp. 89. U.S.D.A. Forest Service, Southwestern Region, Archeological Report, No. 7, pp. 89. Albuquerque, N M.

1975 Arizona. In *Preservation in the States*, n.p. National Trust for Historic Preservation, Board of Advisors, Annual Report 1974-5 Washington, DC.

1976 Arizona. In *Preservation in the States*, pp. 767. National Trust for Historic Preservation, Board of Advisors, Annual Report 1975-6P reservation Press-National Trust for Historic Preservation, Washington, D C.

1978 Archaeological Report: Preliminary Report of Ex avations at TUR 1:6 (the Cordova House). In *The Restoration of La Casa Cordova*, J . B. Hunt, c ompiler and editor, pp. 137. J unior League of Tucson, Tucson, AZ.

1979 Archaeological Investigation in the Art Center Block: A Brief Summary. In *Master Plan for the Tucson Museum of Art*, Appendix2. J ames Gresham and Associates, Tucson, AZ.

198 Foreword [to Mex can Lead-Glazed Earthenware, Mark R. Barnes, author]. In *Spni sh Colonial Frontier Research*, Henry F. Dobyns, e ditor, p. 91. C enter for Anthropological Studies, S panish Borderlands Research No. 1. Albuquerque, N M.

198a An Archaeological Examination of an Historic Railroad Agent's House, Tempe, Arizona. Report to City of Tempe, Community Development Department, Redevelopment and Housing Division, Tempe, AZ, from Archaeological Research Services, Tempe, AZ.

198b Archaeological Survey of Golden Spike National Historic Site and Record Search for Promontory, Utah. Report to National Park Service, M idwest Archaeological Center, L incoln, N E, f rom Arizona State Museum, Tucson.

198 Archaeological Survey and Evaluation of Structural Components of the Roosevelt Power Canal. Report to Salt River Project, P hoenix AZ, f rom Archaeological Research Services, Tempe, AZ.

198 Historic Logging Camps in the Uinta Mountains of Utah. In *Forgotten Places and Things: Archaeological Persp ctives on American History*, Albert E. Ward, editor, pp. 251–255. Center for Anthropological Studies, Contributions to Anthropological Studies, N o. 3 Albuquerque, N M.

198a The Anglo Period in Archaeological and Historical Perspective. *Kiva* 49(& 4):2233.

198b Appendix B: Historic Site Inventory. In *An Archaeological Assessment of the Middle Santa Cruz River Basin, Rillito to Green Valley, Arizona, for the Props ed Tucson Aqe duct Phase B. Central Arizona Project*, Jon S. Czaplicki and James D. Mayberry, authors, pp. 101+21. University of Arizona, Arizona State Museum, Cultural Resource Management Division, Archaeological Series, N o. 16. Tucson.

198c Archaeological Concerns and Techniques. In *Adob : Practical and Technical Asp cts of Adob Conservation*, James W. Garrison and Elizabeth F. Ruffner, e ditors, pp. 1922. H eritage Foundation of Arizona, P rescott.

198d *Rosemont: The History and Archaeology of Post-8 Sites in the Rosemont Area, Santa Rita Mountains, Arizona*. University of Arizona, Arizona State Museum, Cultural Resource Management Division, Archaeological Series, No. 147, Vol. 3 Tucson.

198 Preliminary Report on the Annecy Project: Ex avations in Entreverne, Chevaline, and D'Here, near Annecy, France, Summer 198M anuscript, Arizona State University, D epartment of Anthropology, Tempe.

1989 Post-Fire Assessment of Historic Sites, Yellowstone National Park, 198 Report to National Park Service, Rocky Mountain Region,D enver,C O,f rom James Ayres, Tucson, AZ.

1990 *Historical Archaeology at the Tucson Community Center.* University of Arizona, Arizona State Museum, Cultural Resource Management Division, Archaeological Series,N o. 18. Tucson.

1991a Historical Archaeology in Arizona and New Mexico. *Historical Archaeology* 26 3 :183

1991b Historic Investigations of the Wilkerson Ranch Sites, Greenlee County, Arizona. Report to Mr. Jeff Menges, Morenci, AZ, and Bureau of Land Management,S afford District,S afford, AZ,f rom SWCA Environmental Consultants, Tucson, AZ.

1992 Chair's Message. In *State of Arizona Historical Advisory Commission Annual Repr t 9 9* , p 3 Arizona Department of Library, Archives and Public Records,P hoenix

1993 Chair's Message. In *State of Arizona Historical Advisory Commission Annual Repr t 9 9* , p. 3 Arizona Department of Library, Archives and Public Records,P hoenix

1993 Historic Artifacts. In *Archaeological Investigations near Nogales, Arizona, and Site Testing at the Buena Vista Ranch Site, AZ EE:9 9 ASM),*R obert B. Neily,a uthor,pp. 7276S tatistical Research, Technical Report,N o. 93 21. Tucson, AZ.

1993 Historic Materials. In *The Chihuahua Lake Basin to the Chihuahua Desert: Archaeological Studies along the Arizona Interconnection Project Transmission Line Corridor, Data Recovery Repr t,* J. Simon Bruder, editor, pp. 5 1295 16 Zuni Archaeology Program,R eport,N o. 37,a nd Zuni Archaeology Program,R esearch Series,N o. 7. Pueblo of Zuni,N M.

1993 Historic Use of the Project Area. In *In the Shadow of South Mountain: The Pre-Classic Hohokam of La Ciudad de Los Hornos, 19 Excavations Part II,* Mark L. Chenault, Richard V. N. Ahlstrom, and Thomas N. Motsinger, editors, pp. 58S WCA Environmental Consultants, Archaeological Report,N o. 93 9. Tucson, AZ.

1993 J. C. Harrington Medal in Historical Archaeology: Bernard L. Fontana 1993 *Historical Archaeology* 27(3 :13

1994a The Archaeology of Chinese Sites in Arizona. In *Origins and Destinations: 4 Essays on Chinese America,* Munson A. Kwok and Ella Yee Quan, editors, pp. 489. Chinese Historical Society of Southern California and UCLA Asian American Studies Center,L os Angeles.

1994b Chair's Message. In *State of Arizona Historical Advisory Commission Annual Repr t 9 9* , p. 3 Arizona Department of Library, Archives and Public Records,P hoenix

1994c *A Cultural Resources Inventory of the Imp ovements to Business-0 in Quartzsite, Arizona.* Cultural & Environmental Systems, Technical Series,N o. 6. Tucson, AZ.

1995 Chair's Message. In *State of Arizona Historical Advisory Commission Annual Repr t 9 9* , p. 3 Arizona Department of Library, Archives and Public Records,P hoenix

1995 History of Columbine, Colorado. In *Archaeological Testing and Data Recovery at the Columb ne Townsite and Farwell Ditch, Routt County, Colorado,* John D. Goodman II and Mark L. Chenault, editors, pp. 574. SWCA Environmental Consultants, Archaeological Report, No. 95 76D urango,C O.

1995 Introduction. In *The Archaeology of Spni sh and Mexican Colonialism in the American Southwest,* James E. Ayres, compiler, pp. 12. Society for Historical Archaeology, Guides to the Archaeological Literature of the Immigrant Epe rience in America, No. 3C alifornia,P A.

1995 Report on Archival Research of Historical Foundations at AZ EE:1:3 (ASM), In *Archaeological Test Excavations at the Green Valley Electrical Sub tation Portion of AZ EE:1 3 (ASM) for Tucson Electric Power Compny in Green Valley, Pima County, Arizona,* Jeffrey T. Jones, author, Appendix C, pp. 68. Old Pueblo Archaeology Center, Archaeology Report,N o. 95 3 Tucson, AZ.

1996 Artifacts from AZ DD:4:212. In *Archaeological Testing and Mitigation at Four Sites on the Santa Rita Sp ings Prop rty Developm ent in Green Valley, Pima County, Arizona,* Jeffrey T. Jones, author, pp. 50. Old Pueblo Archaeology Center, Archaeology Report,N o. 5 Tucson, AZ.

1996 Chair's Message. In *State of Arizona Historical Advisory Commission Annual Repr t 9 0* , p. 2. Arizona Department of Library, Archives and Public Records,P hoenix

1996 Little Appreciated and Long Forgotten: Guayule Farming in Southern Arizona 1916922. In *Archaeological Testing and Mitigation at Four Sites on the Santa Rita Sp ings Prop rty Developm ent in Green Valley, Pima County, Arizona,* Jeffrey T. Jones,a uthor,pp. 4950 ld Pueblo Archaeology Center, Archaeology Report,N o. 5 Tucson, AZ.

1996 Standard Timber Company Logging Camps on the Mill Creek Drainage, Uinta Mountains, Utah. *Proceedings of the Society for California Archaeology* 9:17948.

1997 Chair's Message. In *State of Arizona Historical Advisory Commission Annual Repr t 9 9* , p. 2. Arizona Department of Library, Archives and Public Records,P hoenix

1998 Chair's Message. In *State of Arizona Historical Advisory Commission Annual Repr t 9 9* , p. 2. Arizona Department of Library, Archives and Public Records,P hoenix

1999 History of Esmond Station. In *Class III Archaeological Survey of a 9 Acre Parcel and Access Right-of-Way West of Houghton Road, Tucson, Pima County, Arizona, and Documentation of Historic Buildings on the Parcel,* Morgan Rieder, author,pp. 8 1. Aztlan Archaeology, Technical Report,N o. 99-19. Tucson, AZ.

2001a Agua Caliente: Life of a Tucson-Area Ranch. In *Archaeological Investigations at Roy P. Drachman Agua Caliente Park: The Whip ail Site and Agua Caliente Ranch,* Kevin D. Wellman and Mark C. Slaughter, authors, pp. 71123 SWCA Environmental Consultants,C ultural Resource Report,N o. 00-03 Tucson, AZ.

2001b Fontana, Bernard L. (193) . In *Encyclop dia of Archaeology, History and Discoveries,* Tim Murray, editor, pp. 3031. ABC CLIO,S anta Barbara,C A.

2001c Historical Artifact Analysis. In *Archaeological Investigations at Roy P. Drachman Agua Caliente Park: The Whip ail Site and Agua Caliente Ranch*, Kevin D. Wellman and Mark C. Slaughter, authors, pp. 12548 and Appendix E, pp. EE 93 SWCA Environmental Consultants,C ultural Resource Report,N o. 00-03 Tucson, AZ.

2001d Pantano: The Development and Influence of a Small Railroad Community. *Archaeology Southwest* 1(4):8

2002 Agua Caliente: The Life of a Southern Arizona Ranch. *Journal of Arizona History* 4(4):092.

200a Assessment of River Road as a Historic Route of Travel. In *Cultural Resources Survey and Historical Assessment for the River Road Expns ion and Realignment b tween Camp ll Avenue and Alvernon Way, and the Binghamp on Pub ic Park Developm ent in Pima County, Arizona*, Janet H. Parkhurst, Eric J. Kaldahl, James E. Ayres, and Allen Dart, authors, pp. 8 8O ld Pueblo Archaeology Center, Technical Report,N o. 2001.005 Tucson, AZ.

200B A Brief History of Mining and Ranching on Middle Pinto Creek. In *The Carlota Cop r Mine Archaeological Project, Volume 4 Part 1 Historic Site Descrip ions*, John D. Goodman II, Jean H. Ballagh, and Douglas R. Mitchell, editors, pp. 178. S WCA Environmental Consultants,C ultural Resources Report,N o. 97-191. Tucson, AZ.

2004a Historical Artifact Analysis. In *Eligib lity Testing at the Valencia Homestead (AZ AA:6] ASM]) and at a Historical Airfield (AZ AA:16:362[ASM]) in the Southeastern Margin of the Avra Valley, Pima County, Arizona*, Jennifer Levstik and Mary Charlotte Thurtle, authors, pp. 28. Tierra Right of Way Services, Tierra Archaeological Report, No. 2003 49. Tucson, AZ.

2004b President's Message [A monthly two-page column for the Arizona Archaeological and Historical Society]. *Glyphs* 6 1(.

2005 President's Message. *Glyphs* 6 712) ,6 1(.

2006 President's Message. *Glyphs* 6 712) ,5(1(.

2007 President's Message. *Glyphs* 5(712) ,8 12) .

0 Chillson's 1910 Sketch of "The Old Mission" at Caborca,S onora,M ei co. *SMRC Revista* 4(2):1016

AYRES, JAMES E. (COMPILER)

1995 *The Archaeology of Spni sh and Mexican Colonialism in the American Southwest*. Society for Historical Archaeology, Guides to the Archaeological Literature of the Immigrant Ewe rience in America,N o. 3C alifornia,P A.

AYRES, JAMES E. (CONTRIBUTOR)

198 A Plan for Archaeological Investigations at Historical Dam Construction Camps in Central Arizona, A. E. Rogge and Cindy L. Myers, editors. Report to U.S. Bureau of Reclamation, Arizona Projects Office, Phoenix, from Dames & Moore, Phoenix AZ.

1994 *The Historical Archaeology of Dam Construction Camp in Central Arizona, Vol. 1 Synthesis*, A. E. Rogge, Melissa Keane, and D. Lorne McWatters, authors. Dames & Moore Intermountain Cultural Resource Services Research Paper, No. 10. Phoenix AZ.

1996 *Anthropl ogical Studies of Land Use, Sub istence, Settlement and Technology in the Mineral Creek Mining District and Cop r Butte Region of the Drip ng Sp ings Mountains*. Cultural & Environmental Systems, Southwest Cultural Series, No. 20. Tucson, AZ.

AYRES, JAMES E., AND RICHARD CIOLEK-TORRELLO

9 Historical Period Artifacts. In *Pit House, Presidio, and Privy: 0 Years of Archaeology and History on Block 0 Tucson, Arizona*, Richard Ciolek-Torrello and Mark T. Swanson, editors, pp. 277419. Statistical Research, Technical Series, No. 6 Tucson, AZ.

AYRES, JAMES E., CAROL GRIFFITH, AND TERESITA MAJEWSKI (COMPILERS)

2013 *Historical Archaeology in Arizona: A Research Guide*, Si h edition, ewa nded and revised from the 2001, 2007, 2008 2009, and 2010 editions, with contributions by the Historical Archaeology Advisory Committee, Thomas Jones, and Archaeological Consulting Services. Arizona State Parks, State Historic Preservation Office, Historical Archaeology Advisory Committee [formerly SHPO Advisory Committee on Historical Archaeology],P hoenix

AYRES, JAMES E., WILLIAM LIESENBIEN, LEE FRATT, AND LINDA EURE

198 Beer Bottles from the Tucson Urban Renewal Project, Tucson, Arizona. Manuscript, RG5 Sg3 Series 2, Subseries 1, Folder 220. Arizona State Museum Archives, Tucson, AZ.

AYRES, JAMES E., AND JANET H. PARKHURST

2005 Mining and Mining Towns in Southern Arizona. In *Cross-Cultural Vernacular Landscap s of Southern Arizona: A Field Guide for the Vernacular Architecture Forum 0 h Anniversary Conference, Tucson, Arizona, 0* , Laura H. Hollengreen and R. Brooks Jeffrey,e ditors,pp. 718. Vernacular Architecture Forum, Tucson, AZ.

AYRES, JAMES E., A. E. ROGGE, EVERETT J. BASSETT, MELISSA KEANE, AND DIANE L. DOUGLAS

1992 Humbug! The Historical Archaeology of Placer Mining on Humbug Creek in Central Arizona. Report to U.S. Bureau of Reclamation, Arizona Projects Office, Phoenix, from Dames & Moore, Phoenix, AZ.

AYRES, JAMES E., A. E. ROGGE, MELISSA KEANE, DIANE L. DOUGLAS, EVERETT J. BASSETT, DIANE L. FENICLE, CINDY L. MYERS, BONNIE J. CLARK, AND KAREN TURNMIRE
　　1994　*The Historical Archaeology of Dam Construction Camp in Central Arizona, Vol. 2 : Sites in the Roosevelt Dam Area.* Dames & Moore Intermountain Cultural Resource Services Research Paper,N o. 11. Phoenix AZ.

AYRES, JAMES E., AND GREGORY R. SEYMOUR
　　1993　*Life on a 9 Homestead: Historical Archaeological Investigations of the Brown Homestead on the Middle Agua Fria River, Yavapai County, Arizona.* SWCA Environmental Consultants, Anthropological Research Paper, No. 2. Tucson, AZ. [Revised version of 1990 report to U.S. Bureau of Reclamation, Phoenix AZ, from SWCA Environmental Consultants, Tucson, AZ.]

AYRES, JAMES E., AND LAURIE V. SLAWSON
　　1993　*Archaeological Investigations at Vulcan Camp Historic Mining on the Vulcan and Prince Rup rt Claims in the Pima Mining District.* Cultural & Environmental Systems,S outhwest Cultural Series,N o. 13 Tucson, AZ.
　　1994a　*Archaeological Investigations North of Mob le, Arizona. A Limited Testing Program at AZ T:5 2 (ASM).* Cultural & Environmental Systems, Technical Series,N o. 46 Tucson, AZ.
　　1994b　*Archaeological Investigations in the Silver Bell Mining District: AZ AA:0 3 a Mexican-Occup ed Mining Camp* Cultural & Environmental Systems,S outhwest Cultural Series,N o. 14. Tucson, AZ.
　　1994c　*Archaeological Monitoring at Roy P. Drachman Agua Caliente Regional Park, Pima County, Arizona.* Cultural & Environmental Systems, Technical Series,N o. 45 Tucson, AZ.
　　1994d　*A Cultural Resources Overview of the Cienega Creek Natural Preserve in Pima County, Arizona.* Aztlan Archaeology, Technical Report,N o. 94-1. Tucson, AZ.
　　9　*Archaeological and Historical Investigations of Blocks 5 and 6 in the Florence Townsite, Arizona.* Aztlan Archaeology, Archaeological Series,N o. 1. Tucson, AZ.

AYRES, JAMES E., AND MATTHEW A. STERNER
　　1997　Artifact Analysis. In *Archaeological Investigation of Historic Blocks 0 and 3 The Main Gate Monitoring and Data-Recovery Project, Tucson, Arizona*, Matthew A. Sterner, author, pp. 49-122. Statistical Research, Technical Series, No. 6. Tucson, AZ.

AYRES, JAMES E., AND LYLE M. STONE
　　1982a　An Archaeological Survey of Proposed Home Construction Sites on the Colorado River Indian Reservation, Yuma County, Arizona. Report to Colorado River Indian Tribes,P arker, AZ,f rom Archaeological Research Services, Tempe, AZ.
　　198b　Archaeological Evaluation of a Sewer Line Replacement Project at Prescott, Yavapai County, Arizona. Report to John Carollo Engineers,P hoenix AZ, Archaeological Research Services, Tempe, AZ.
　　198　Historic Period Cultural Resources. In *An Archaeological Assessment of the Middle Santa Cruz River Basin, Rillito to Green Valley, Arizona, for the Props ed Tucson Aqe duct Phase B, Central Arizona Project*, Jon S. Czaplicki and James D. Mayberry, authors, pp. 63–78. University of Arizona, Arizona State Museum, Cultural Management Division, Archaeological Series,N o. 16. Tucson.

BRUDER, J. SIMON, EVERETT J. BASSETT, PATRICK M. O'BRIEN, JAMES E. AYRES, AND A. E. ROGGE
　　1990　Cultural Resources Technical Report for the MCI Fiber Optic Cable Project: Rialto, California to Phoenix Arizona and Tucson, Arizona to El Paso, Tex s: Arizona, New Mex co and Tex s Segments. Report to MCI Telecommunications Corporation,R ichardson, TX,f rom Dames & Moore,P hoenix AZ.

CHENAULT, MARK L., KIRK ANDERSON, AND JAMES E. AYRES
　　1991　*Archaeological Testing at a Portion of La Ciudad de Los Hornos: The Sup rstition Freeway and Priest Drive Locale (AZ U:9 8 ASM).* SWCA Environmental Consultants, Archaeological Report,N o. 91-10. Tucson, AZ.

CZAPLICKI, JON S., JAMES D. MAYBERRY, AND JAMES E. AYRES
　　1983　Future Research in the Phase B Area. In *An Archaeological Assessment of the Middle Santa Cruz River Basin, Rillito to Green Valley, Arizona, for the Prop sed Tucson Aqe duct Phase B, Central Arizona Project*, Jon S. Czaplicki and James D. Mayberry, authors, pp. 87. University of Arizona, Arizona State Museum, Cultural Resource Management Division, Archaeological Series,N o. 16. Tucson.

DOUGLAS, DIANE L., A. E. ROGGE, KAREN TURNMIRE, MELISSA KEANE, AND JAMES E. AYRES
　　1994　*The Historical Archaeology of Dam Construction Camp in Central Arizona, Vol. C . Sites at Other Dams along the Salt and Verde Rivers.* Dames & Moore Intermountain Cultural Resource Services Research Paper,N o. 13P hoenix AZ.

FENICLE, DIANE L., JAMES E. AYRES, EVERETT J. BASSETT, CINDY L. MYERS, A. E. ROGGE, MELISSA KEANE, AND DIANE L. DOUGLAS
　　1994　*The Historical Archaeology of Dam Construction Camp in Central Arizona, Vol. B : Sites in the New Waddell Dam Area.* Dames & Moore Intermountain Cultural Resource Services Research Paper,N o. 12. Phoenix AZ.

GARRISON, JAMES, JAMES WOODWARD, SUSAN WILCOX, ROBERT TRENNERT, AND JAMES AYRES
   199 *Transcontinental Railroading in Arizona: A Context for Preserving Railroad Related Properties.* Arizona State Parks Board, State Historic Preservation Office, Phoenix.

GILMORE, KEVIN P., AND JAMES E. AYRES
   1997a Culture History of the Rocky Mountain Arsenal. In *Archaeological Investigations and Cultural Resources Management Plan for the Archaeological Resources of the Rocky Mountain Arsenal, Adams County, Colorado,* Bonnie J. Clark, editor, pp. 248S   WCA Environmental Consultants, Archaeological Report, No. 96 110. Denver, CO.
   1997b Results of Archival Research. In *Archaeological Investigations and Cultural Resources Management Plan for the Archaeological Resources of the Rocky Mountain Arsenal, Adams County, Colorado,* Bonnie J. Clark, editor, pp. 49-72. SWCA Environmental Consultants, Archaeological Report, No. 96 110. Denver, CO.
   1997c Material Culture. In *Archaeological Investigations and Cultural Resources Management Plan for the Archaeological Resources of the Rocky Mountain Arsenal, Adams County, Colorado,* Bonnie J. Clark, editor, pp. 84-3.   SWCA Environmental Consultants, Archaeological Report, No. 96 110. Denver, CO.

HEUETT, MARY LOU, AND JAMES E. AYRES
   1993 *An Archaeological Testing Program at AZ U:5 5 (ASM) in Florence, Arizona.* Cultural & Environmental Systems, Technical Series, No. 9. Tucson, AZ.

HULL-WALSKI, DEBORAH A., AND JAMES E. AYRES
   199 The Historical Archaeology of Dam Construction Camps in Central Arizona, Vol. 3 Laboratory Methods and Data Computerization. Report to U.S. Bureau of Reclamation, Phoenix Area Office, Phoenix, AZ, from Dames & Moore, Phoenix AZ.

LONGACRE, WILLIAM A., AND JAMES E. AYRES
   196 Archaeological Lessons from an Apache Wickiup. In *New Perspectives in Archaeology,* Sally R. Binford and Lewis R. Binford, editors, pp. 1-19.   Aldine, Chicago, IL.

MABRY, JONATHAN B., JAMES E. AYRES, AND REGINA L. CHAPIN-PYRITZ
   1994 *Tucson at the Turn of the Century: The Archaeology of a City Block.* Center for Desert Archaeology, Technical Report, No. 92-10. Tucson, AZ.

MAJEWSKI, TERESITA, AND JAMES E. AYRES
   1997 Toward an Archaeology of Colonialism in the Greater Southwest. *Revista de Arqueología Americana* 12:8

O'BRIEN, PATRICK M., A. E. ROGGE, AND JAMES E. AYRES
   1990 Historic Archaeological Excavations at China Alley: A Preliminary Report of Data Recovery Fieldwork in Phoenix's Chinatown. Manuscript, Dames & Moore, Phoenix AZ.

QUINN, KATHLEEN, AND JAMES E. AYRES
   198 An Archaeological Survey of the Red Mountain Ranch Property Located near Mesa, Maricopa County, Arizona. Report to Game Creek Properties, Redwood City, CA, from Archaeological Research Services, Tempe, AZ.

ROGGE, A. E., JAMES E. AYRES, AND EVERETT J. BASSETT
   1998 Archaeological Investigation at Cleveland Camp, Grant County, New Mexico. Report to Bayard Mining Corporation, Price, UT, Mining Remedial Recovery Company, Helper, UT, and Viacom International, Salt Lake City, UT, from Dames & Moore, Phoenix AZ.

ROGGE, A. E., JAMES E. AYRES, EVERETT BASSETT, DIANE FENICLE, CINDY L. MYERS, AND DEBORAH A. HULL
   198 Archaeological Perspectives on the Social History of Construction Camps. In Historical Archaeological Investigations at Dam Construction Camps in Central Arizona Second Annual Report, A. E. Rogge and Cindy L. Myers, editors, pp. 99-121. Report to U.S. Bureau of Reclamation, Arizona Projects Office, Phoenix, from Dames & Moore, Phoenix, AZ.

ROGGE, A. E., MELISSA KEANE, BRADFORD LUCKINGHAM, JAMES E. AYRES, PAMELA PATTERSON, AND TODD W. BOSTWICK
   1992 *First Street & Madison: Historical Archaeology of the Second Phoenix Chinatown.* Dames & Moore Intermountain Cultural Resource Services Research Paper, No. 9. Phoenix AZ.

SEYMOUR, GREGORY R., AND JAMES E. AYRES
   1991 *An Archaeological Survey of Approximately 0 Acres of Tonto National Forest Land near Miami, Gila County, Arizona.* SWCA Environmental Consultants, Archaeological Report, No. 91-29. Tucson, AZ.

SLAUGHTER, MARK C., AND JAMES E. AYRES
   1991 *An Archaeological Survey of 15 Acres and Surface Analysis of Two Historic Sites near Clifton, Greenlee County, Arizona.* SWCA Environmental Consultants, Archaeological Report, No. 91-3 Tucson, AZ.

SLAUGHTER, MARK C., R. THOMAS EULER, AND JAMES E. AYRES

1990 Archaeological Test Ex avations at Four Historic Sites and a Survey of Two Historic Sites near San Jose, Graham County, Arizona. Report to State of Arizona Department of Administration, Phoenix Arizona Department of Corrections, Phoenix and Bureau of Land Management,S afford District,S afford, AZ,f rom SWCA Environmental Consultants, Tucson, AZ.

SLAWSON, LAURIE V., AND JAMES E. AYRES

1992 *Cop r Mining, Railroading, and the Hellhole of Arizona: Archaeological Investigations in the Silver Bell Mining District.* Cultural & Environmental Systems,S outhwest Cultural Series,N o. 12. Tucson, AZ.

1994 *Archaic Hunter-Gatherers to Historic Miners: Prehistoric and Historic Utilization of the Silver Bell Mining District.* Cultural & Environmental Systems,S outhwest Cultural Series,N o. 16 Tucson, AZ.

STONE, LYLE M., AND JAMES E. AYRES

1982 A Description and Evaluation of Archaeological Resources, San Bernardino Ranch National Historic Landmark, Cochise County, Arizona. Report to Johnson Historical Museum of the Southwest, Sun City, AZ, from Archaeological Research Services, Tempe, AZ.

198 An Evaluation of Historic Cultural Resources in Relation to the Central Arizona Water Control Study. Report to U.S. Bureau of Reclamation, Arizona Projects Office, Phoenix, from Archaeological Research Services, Tempe, AZ.

198 An Archaeological and Historical Evaluation of Proposed Redevelopment Parcels on Blocks 6, 5 and 9. Report to City of Tempe, Redevelopment and Housing Division, Community Development Department, Tempe, AZ, from Archaeological Research Services, Tempe, AZ.

SWANSON, MARK T., AND JAMES E. AYRES

1992 Historical Archaeology of the Channel Gateway Project. In *Life in the Ballona: Archaeological Investigations at the Admiralty Site (CA-LAN-J and the Channel Gateway Site (CA-LAN-9 h)*, Jeffrey H. Altschul, Jeffrey A. Homburg, and Richard S. Ciolek-Torrello,a uthors,pp. 37412. S tatistical Research, Technical Series,N o. 3 Tucson, AZ.

TERESITA MAJEWSKI

Memorial

Stanley A. South 1928–2016

STANLEY SOUTH AT CHARLES ToMWNE LANDING, SOUTH CAROLINA, 2000.
(PHOTO BY MICHAEL STONER, SOUTH CAROLINA INSTITUTE OF ARCHAEOLOGY AND ANTHROPOLOGY.)

Stanley A. South, one of the pioneers of historical archaeology, a founder and early officer of the Society for Historical Archaeology, the organizer of the Southeastern Conference on Historic Sites Archaeology, one of the leading figures in the "new archaeology," and a prolific and persuasive author and editor, passed away on 20 March 2016 at the age of 88. Stan referred to himself as a "mountain groundhog" (South 2005:1), but for other historical archaeologists he was simply a mountain, a prominent figure that dominated the landscape of the discipline.

Stan South was born on 2 February 1928 in the Appalachian mountain town of Boone, North Carolina. He was raised in Watauga County in a household that supported and encouraged both the arts and education. Growing up in the mountains, he was exposed to rural life on family farms as well as life in the town of Boone and was aware of the social, cultural, and economic differences between town and farm, his first recognition of culture. Stan was interested in the world beyond the mountains and, at the age of 13, on his own, he rode his bike from the mountains to Charleston on the South Carolina coast, a one-way distance of roughly 300 mi. His interest in the world at large led him to graduate from high school three years early and attempt to join the military, but he failed the physical because of a punctured eardrum. Instead, Stan enrolled at Appalachian State Teachers College (ASTC), now Appalachian State University, pursuing a degree in education. After finishing his freshman year, he enrolled in the navy. As Stan was completing his training, it was announced that the A-bomb had been dropped on Hiroshima, Japan, and hence the war was drawing to a close. Following his discharge in 1946 and with the support of the GI Bill, he enrolled in the Southwest Photo Arts Institute in Dallas, Texas. In that same year, with a photography certificate in hand, he returned to ASTC as a sophomore at the age of 18.

Stan became a photographer for the ASTC student paper and yearbook while pursuing his education. In his senior year, he met Jewell Barnhardt, whom he would subsequently marry; the couple had three children, David, Robert, and Lara. Jewell shared and supported Stan's interest in archaeology, as did David in later years. Following graduation Stan became a junior high school sciences and social-studies teacher. The social-studies curriculum required teaching about American Indians, but the textbook assigned to Stan's class did not have a section on Indians. This gap led to an interest in learning about American Indian life, and Stan and Jewell began exploring Watauga County to find American Indian sites and artifacts. Stan took artifacts they found to Douglas Rights, author of The American Indian in North Carolina. Rights identified one of the projectile points as a Hardaway Point and advised Stan to contact Joffre Coe at the University of North Carolina (UNC), as Coe had recently named the point based on its recovery from a site of the same name. Coe introduced Stan to the UNC Research Laboratory of Anthropology and informed him of the need to record his finds carefully. Stan and Jewell continued to survey Watauga County over the next year, with Stan preparing a report on their findings. By now hooked on archaeology and with a report that demonstrated his interest and ability to Coe, Stan applied and was admitted to the graduate program at UNC Chapel Hill.

While studying with Coe, Stan directed archaeological work on a number of sites, most notably the Gaston and Thelma sites for the Virginia Electric Power Company's Roanoke Rapids hydroelectric reservoir on the North Carolina/Virginia border. The work included the survey of the reservoir as well as excavations at the Gaston site, where Jewell and classmate Lewis Binford assisted him. Stan's work on the stratified Gaston site was reported in Newsweek as well as in the North Carolina newspapers. Planning on pursuing his Ph.D. in anthropology, Stan and his classmate, Lew Binford, had applied to and been accepted by the University of Michigan's Department of Anthropology, home to James Griffin and Leslie White. However, Jewell crashed the Souths' car into a coal truck, totaling the car, damaging the truck, and causing it to lose its load of coal. Once Stan had paid for the damage, the load of coal, Jewell's medical bills, and the police citation, his savings were exhausted and plans for doctoral work cancelled.

Having completed his master's degree, Stan took a job with North Carolina State Parks to work at Town Creek, an American Indian site he had visited with Coe, who had worked there extensively. At Town Creek, Stan worked with Ed Gaines on excavation of the site, as well as on an interpretive reconstruction for the public of the priests' house and temple house. His interest in the house reconstruction brought him into contact with Charles Fairbanks, who had directed excavations of the earth lodge at the Ocmulgee National Monument. Stan heard Fairbanks speak on excavations of the Hawkins-Davidson houses and historical archaeology at the 1956 Southeastern Archaeological Conference (SEAC) and began paying more attention to the few papers and publications then being produced on historical archaeology. In 1957, Sam Tarleton, Stan's boss at the time, contacted him about a new historic state park that was being established on the Cape Fear River. Tarleton told Stan that Fairbanks had been offered the job as archaeologist for the site and asked him to write a letter of support for Fairbanks's file, which Stan did. Fairbanks, however, declined the job offer to remain at the University of Florida, and Tarleton, in turn, offered the job to Stan. Stan sought the advice of his mentor, Joffre Coe, who said: "If you want to end your career in archaeology, I suppose you should take it" (South 2005:106). Stan took the job despite Coe's opinion, becoming the archaeologist at the Brunswick Town historic site.

Brunswick Town would prove to be pivotal in Stan South's career. It introduced him to the then-emergent field of historical archaeology, and it was the first in what would prove to be a lifelong emphasis on the archaeology of lost towns. Building on the emphasis Joffre Coe placed on taxonomy and typology, Stan's excavations focused on material culture, to which he added Leslie White's concepts of the science of culture. He interacted with the few other historical archaeologists then active in the field, visiting Ivor Noël Hume at Colonial Williamsburg to learn more about British historical ceramics and publishing, in 1959, Description of the Ceramic Types at Brunswick Town. At Brunswick Town, South developed the mean ceramic date, his historical artifact classification system, and artifact patterning, all of which would become hallmarks of the field.

As Stan communicated with other archaeologists interested in historic sites, he encountered disinterest and discouragement from prehistoric archaeologists regarding the value of this work. When he contacted Joffre Coe, who at the time was chair of the 1958 SEAC Conference, requesting the opportunity to present his work on Brunswick Town, Coe refused to add him to the program, noting that SEAC was primarily interested in "Indian Archaeology." The following year, Stan requested travel funding from his boss, Sam Tarleton, to attend the SEAC Conference, but Tarleton refused on the grounds that he worked in the state's Historic Sites Department, which did not justify going to an Indian conference. This led Stan to organize the Conference on Historic Sites Archaeology. Writing to his colleagues in the field, he noted that

we historic sites archaeologists are often looked upon by our fellow anthropologists as a kind of bastard researcher—half archaeologist and half historian. ... We will always remain a breed apart from our colleagues' work on the American Indian. As a result ... we are not represented in the programs of the existing archaeological conferences. ... I would like to suggest the formation of the Historic Sites Archaeological Conference that would meet each year to present a program based on problems encountered by historic sites archaeologists in the excavation and analysis of their data. (South 2005:112)

Beginning in 1960, what became known as the Conference on Historic Sites Archaeology met the day before SEAC in the same town and hotel. These co-location meetings continued until the Tuscaloosa, Alabama, meeting in 1976. There, prominent archaeologist James Griffin arrived at the conference hotel without a reservation, only to find that there were no hotel rooms available. Griffin advised the SEAC directors that "the historic sites people have taken all the rooms," and, as a result, SEAC informed Stan that the CHSA was no longer allowed to meet in conjunction with SEAC. CHSA continued to hold annual meetings on its own through 1982. Stan published the conference papers each year, and the Conference on Historic Sites Archaeology Papers were an early and extremely important outlet for historic sites studies. However, the 1982 conference generated no contributed papers, which led Stan to bring the conference to an end.

Since it was tied to SEAC in the beginning, the CHSA also emphasized historic sites in the southeastern U.S., but the emergence of the discipline nationally led to the formation of another organization. Stan met with other historical archaeologists in Dallas in 1967, during which the Society for Historical Archaeology (SHA) was created. In his autobiography, Stan noted that much of the discussion centered around whether the new society should be "for" or "of" "historic" or "historical" archaeology, and whether archaeology should be spelled with or without the second a. Stan argued that "historic" implied the field itself was historic if not connected to the word "sites," and that "historical" was the correct term, thus giving the SHA its name.

Stan continued to work on North Carolina historic sites and parks, which included the lost towns of Russellborough and Bethabara, as well as Fort Fisher and Brunswick Town. Living in Raleigh, South became engaged in the sixties art culture of the area, applying his hand to poetry, painting, photography, sculpture, ceramics, and music. Poetry would remain a passion throughout his later years. While his creative capabilities were clearly on display, scientific archaeology remained South's favored endeavor. In 1966, he took on a contract assignment from Glen Little, president of Contract Archaeology, Inc., that led him to work outside North Carolina at the Paca House in Maryland. Back in North Carolina, he was contacted by John Combes regarding the South Carolina Tricentennial Commission's desire to excavate the original site of Charleston, Charlestowne Landing, in preparation for the South Carolina Tricentennial in 1970. Replying that he might be interested, Stan subsequently received an offer from Robert Stephenson, director of the South Carolina Institute of Archaeology and Anthropology (SCIAA), to join Combes in the survey of Charlestowne Landing. Stan worked on the project on a leave of absence from North Carolina Historic Sites, but returned from the first season of fieldwork to be told that he was a "loose cannon," who should curtail his out-of-state work efforts and focus on administration rather than archaeology. After turning in his report on the exploratory work at Charlestowne Landing, Stan received a job offer from Bob Stephenson to serve as an archaeologist with the SCIAA on a permanent basis. He accepted the offer, shunning administration to keep his hand in the archaeology game while moving on to the fluorescence of his career in South Carolina.

At Charlestowne Landing, Stan employed a large-scale site-excavation approach and the kind of reconstruction he had learned at Town Creek. The opening of large excavation blocks and shovel shaving, "schnitting," their surfaces to identify cultural features, guided the reconstruction of the town's palisade. These excavations also encountered a moundless American Indian ceremonial site on the proposed location of the visitors' center, and Stan lobbied the Tricentennial Commission to preserve the site by modifying the project plans. When the find was reported on the Huntley-Brinkley national nightly news, with Chet Brinkley noting the irony that an American Indian site was being destroyed for the construction of a visitors' center, the commission dug in its heels. They were determined not to be influenced by northern media and refused to modify the plans.

Working with Stephenson at the SCIAA provided Stan the support and platform to expand his publications and research. Stephenson established both the Research Manuscript Series (RMS) geared to professional archaeologists and the Notebook geared to the public, and Stan was a frequent contributor to both; in fact, his 1969 report, "Exploratory Archaeology at the Site of the 1670–1680 Charles Towne on Albemarle Point in South Carolina," became the first publication in the RMS. Stephenson subsequently established the Anthropological Studies series, for more in-depth publications aimed at both the description and interpretation of significant sites, and Stan's Palmetto Parapets, published by the institute on his work at Fort Moultrie in 1974, was also the first in that series. With Stan's growing resume of publications in the RMS, Notebook, and the Conference on Historic Sites Archaeology Papers, he achieved recognition as one of the significant voices of historical archaeology. In 1974 he was invited to attend a Society for American Archaeology seminar on report writing and, while there, interacted with Stuart Struever, consulting editor for the Studies in Archaeology Series from Academic Press. Struever asked South if he was interested in preparing a book on historical archaeology for the series, and Method and Theory in Historical Archaeology, published in 1977, was the result.

Method and Theory was a landmark publication in which South relayed his thoughts on historical archaeology as a scientific discipline and his concepts of artifact patterning, material culture patterning, dating material culture, and the archaeological perspective on historic sites and cultures. Along with Noël Hume's Guide to the Artifacts of Colonial America, it was, and still is, found on the shelves of every historical archaeologist.

Hosted by the SCIAA, Stan saw the 1975 SHA conference in Charleston, South Carolina, as an opportunity to promote scientific archaeology—the conference theme was "Toward Archaeological Science through the Material Remains of Culture" (South 2005:284). Stan tasked Leland Ferguson, a recent addition to the institute staff, to chair a session in which scientific and humanistic archaeology would be compared and contrasted. Ferguson's session, entitled "Historical Archaeology and the Importance of Material Things," featured talks by Lewis Binford, James Deetz, Leland Ferguson, James Fitting, Henry Glassie, Mark Leone, and William Rathje. It was subsequently published by the SHA as Special Publication Number 2. Much to Stan's chagrin, humanism, led by Glassie, Deetz, and Leone's presentations, held sway over the audience, as opposed to science, which Stan acknowledged in his introduction to the volume.

Stan went on to work on a number of historic sites in South Carolina including the Revolutionary War–era star fort at Ninety Six, the Pawley House, and Fort Moultrie, and he also conducted a survey with Michael Hartley of 18th-century sites along the rivers near Charleston. In 1978, he began work at his last lost town—Santa Elena. Stan's interest in Santa Elena had been piqued in 1958 when he was working at Town Creek with Joffre Coe. Coe had noted that copper found in some of the Town Creek burials could have originated either from the Spanish at Santa Elena or possibly from the French Charlesfort. Charlesfort (1562–1563) was established by the French along the South Carolina coast, and a fortification at the tip of Parris Island—the Marine Corps Training Center—had been excavated by Major Osterhout in the 1920s and identified as the French Charlesfort. Santa Elena was established in 1566 as the first capital of Spanish Florida in what would become South Carolina; it was in existence from 1566 to 1587 and abandoned following conflict with local American Indians in 1576. The town was burned, but the Spanish returned in 1577 to rebuild the town and fort that remained until 1587. The Spanish constructed three forts at Santa Elena—San Felipe I, San Felipe II, and San Marco—and there was discussion and debate in the historical community over whether the fortification identified by Osterhout was actually Charlesfort or one of Santa Elena's fortifications.

In 1978, Bob Stephenson of the SCIAA received a call from Joseph Judge, senior associate editor of National Geographic, who was planning to do an article on 16th-century Spanish La Florida and was requesting permission to send either Charles Fairbanks or Kathy Deagan to Parris Island to look for evidence of Santa Elena. Stephenson replied that if anyone was going to search for Santa Elena, it would be Stan South and the institute. South thus applied to the Marine Corps for permission to conduct an archaeological survey to search for Santa Elena and submitted a proposal to the National Geographic Society to fund it. The Marine Corps approved his proposal, but the National Geographic did not fund it, stating that he had not provided evidence that Santa Elena existed at the end of Parris Island, which was, of course, what the survey sought to determine.

In response, Stan launched a largely volunteer effort to survey the end of Parris Island, working with his family (notably his wife, Jewell, who did the recording, and sons, David and Robert, who assisted with the excavations), friends, and two SCIAA technicians, Mike Harmon and Joe Joseph, who Stephenson had agreed to fund. Stan laid out a grid of 3 ft. excavation squares to begin the survey. The excavations recovered a number of early-20th-century Marine Corps artifacts, as well as other historical materials, but nothing conclusively identified as Spanish. However, both South and Joseph excavated units that exposed a dark feature deposit, and to determine its extent and width they both began slot trenches from their units to reach the feature's outer edge. The two excavated feverishly, racing to find the opposite edges of the feature, while also recognizing that the feature was extensive. Once the edges were reached, it became clear that they had discovered a ditch roughly 14 ft. wide. Stan recognized the ditch as a fortification moat and laid out additional units to map the moat's presence further. While excavating Square 34, David South encountered pottery in the feature fill, which he cleaned and photographed in situ. It proved to be the neck of a Spanish olive jar, which led Stan to conclude that they had found Fort San Felipe and the town of Santa Elena. The story made national news, and National Geographic funded further work on the site. This began Stan's work at Santa Elena, the major excavation of his career.

From 1979 to 1985, Stan worked on Fort San Felipe, Fort San Marcos, Santa Elena's last fort, and two lots that were subsequently identified as belonging to Santa Elena's governor from 1580–1587. He returned to Santa Elena in 1991 with Chester DePratter as codirector, a partnership that continued until 2007. In 1993, they discovered a Spanish pottery kiln on the periphery of the site, and in 1996 they announced the discovery of French Charlesfort, which was found buried beneath Spanish Fort San Felipe. In all, Stan directed nearly 30 excavation projects at Santa Elena. During these busy years, Stan was not content to work on only a single site. He also directed projects at the Bartlam Pottery at Cainhoy near Charleston, and new investigations at Charles Towne Landing and Ninety Six, sites that he had worked on in the 1970s.

Stan South was a man of tremendous energy who was totally committed to his research. During his entire career as an archaeologist, he worked full weekdays and every evening and weekend, with only occasional time off to see a doctor or take his worn out automobiles to the shop. Toward the end of his life, he focused on clearing out his backlog of unfinished work. He published the edited volume, Pioneers in Historical Archaeology: Breaking New Ground, in 1994. His final report on excavations at the town of Bethabara and the Moravian pottery came out in 1999 when he was 71 years old. In 2002, be published his final report on Charles Towne Landing. In 2005, he published a memoir, An Archaeological Evolution, covering his life and work, and also his M.A. thesis, a work that had contributed important data for Joffre Coe's volume, The Formative Cultures of the Carolina Piedmont. He edited and published his final report on his excavations at Brunswick Town, North Carolina, in 2010. With funds left over from the CHSA, he started, edited, and funded a new series, Historical Archaeology in Latin America, that published a series of Latin American historical archaeological studies that Stan edited and printed and then shipped to colleagues in South America for distribution. Through all those years, he continued his field research, wrote reports, published numerous papers and articles, and, of course, wrote poetry. Then, in 2012, he compiled and published Recording the Journey: An Annotated Vita, a 60-page volume. And then, after nearly 60 years of writing and publishing, Stan set aside his pen and wrote no more.

Over the course of his long career, Stan received many honors due to his lifetime dedication to historical archaeology:

1979 Distinguished Alumnus Award, Appalachian State University
1984 Halifax Resolves Award, Historic Halifax Restoration Association
1987 J. C. Harrington Medal, Society for Historical Archaeology
1993 R. L. Stephenson Lifetime Achievement Award, Archaeological Society of South Carolina
1997 Honorary Doctor of Humanities Degree, University of South Carolina
1999 Order of the Palmetto, State of South Carolina

2006 Old North State Award, State of North Carolina
2003 Lifetime Achievement Award, Southeastern Archaeological Conference
2008 Major G. Osterhout Archaeological Stewardship Award, Historic Beaufort Foundation
2010 Golden Shield Award, Daughters of Founders and Patriots of America

Stan's wife and early partner in the field, Jewell, died of cancer in 1980, the same year in which Stan went through quintuple bypass surgery and was advised he had roughly four years to live. Stan married Linda Hunter in 1981 and Janet Reddy in 1991, but neither of these later marriages took. Stan is survived by his children, David, Robert, and Lara, and his grandchildren.

In April 2016, the Santa Elena Foundation opened the Santa Elena History Center in Beaufort, South Carolina. The center and its exhibits are the direct result of Stan's decades of work at the Charlesfort–Santa Elena National Historic Landmark. Visitors to Beaufort can now learn about the site's history and archaeology. Stan did not live to see the opening of this center, but he would have been especially proud to have this part of his life story told in a museum setting and to see the archaeological past brought to the public, one of the constant verses in the poem of Stan South's life.

Reference

SOUTH, STANLEY A.
    2005   An Archaeological Evolution. Springer, New York, NY.

J. W. JOSEPH
CHESTER B. DEPRATTER

Part III:
Harrington Awards

The J. C. Harrington Medal In Historical Archaeology

By the early 1970s archaeological scholarship in America had been irreversibly transformed and expanded by the addition of a subject matter radically different from the traditional study of prehistory. Historical archaeology, with roots that ultimately extend in an unbroken line to early investigations of the contact period and National Park Service work on famous Euroamerican sites, has emerged as a separate and firmly established discipline. A national society of almost 2,000 members, a number of smaller but active regional groups exclusively devoted to the field, recognition in the undergraduate and graduate curricula of many leading universities and colleges, numerous new and on-going field projects each year, and a growing literature of pertinence to anthropology, history, and American Studies are all indicators of the "coming of age" of American historical archaeology.

In recognition of the significance and future potential of the discipline, the Board of Directors of the Society for Historical Archaeology at its January 1981 meeting in New Orleans ordered the creation of a medal to honor those scholars who have made outstanding contributions to the field. The medal is named in honor of Jean Carl Harrington, one of the founders of historical archaeology in this country. His career and numerous accomplishments have been detailed in the March 1982 *Newsletter of the Society for Historical Archaeology*. The first copy of the medal was struck in silver to distinguish it from all future issues, which will be in bronze, and at a surprise ceremony during the 1982 General Business Meeting in Philadelphia it was bestowed on its namesake. After being introduced by President Bert Salwen, Harrington was formally presented the medal by the first president of the society, John L. Cotter.

The J. C. Harrington Medal in historical archaeology is a bronze medallion almost three inches in diameter. The face carries the names of the award and the society encircling a scroll which bears an inscription (*Beyond The Strictly Historical*) taken from Harrington's 1952 pioneer synthesis of historic site archaeology in America. The design emphasizes Harrington's precocious position, now endorsed by all, that documentary research is of equal importance, along with excavation and artifact analysis, to a complete historical archaeology. The reverse side presents a tri-partite motif honoring fieldwork. It represents both the discipline as a whole and Harrington's individual career. The Eastern seacoast and immediate hinterland are symbolized in the ground plans of two of the most famous sites he excavated, as are the opening and closing phases of the colonial world—Cittie of Ralegh (1585) and Fort Necessity (1754). The 19th century settlement of the interior and opening of the West are, in turn, represented by the outline of the foundations of the Mormon Temple at Nauvoo, uncovered by both Harrington and his wife, Virginia, as well as others, between 1962 and 1969.

The medal was designed by Stanley South, one of the finest scientific illustrators in American archaeology. The face is executed in raised lettering while the three archaeological plans on the reverse are cut into the surface of the antique bronze.

Future recipients of the J. C. Harrington Medal will be selected on an annual basis, provided a qualified candidate is available. A rotating committee chaired by the SHA Immediate Past President and his four predecessors will designate those scholars to be honored and presentations of the medals, which are housed at the American Anthropological Association headquarters in

Robert L. Schuyler

Washington, D.C., will occur at the General Business Meeting of the Society for Historical Archaeology.

ROBERT L. SCHUYLER
PRESIDENT
SOCIETY FOR HISTORICAL ARCHAEOLOGY

J. C. Harrington Medal: Face and Reverse Sides (Photograph courtesy of the University Museum, University of Pennsylvania).

J. C. Harrington Medal in Historical Archaeology: Charles H. Fairbanks, 1983. Volume 17, Number 2 (1983): 1-3.

J. C. Harrington Medal in Historical Archaeology

CHARLES H. FAIRBANKS

1983

Charles H. Fairbanks was honored at the 1983 annual SHA meetings in Denver, Colorado, as the first recipient to receive the Society's J. C. Harrington medal in recognition of his contributions to the field of historical archaeology.

Fairbanks' formal training in Anthropology began at the University of Chicago, from which he received the A.B. degree in 1939. As a student at Chicago, he was exposed to the teaching and research of such influential anthropologists as Fay Cooper-Cole, Robert Redfield, Radcliffe-Browne, Harry Hoijer, and Thorne Deuel. Cole, however, was his primary source of guidance, and it was he who sent Fairbanks to gain some of his first professional experience with the Tennessee Valley Authority in 1937–1938. In 1939 after graduating from Chicago, Fairbanks went to Ocmulgee National Monument, Macon, Georgia, as an archeologist.

During his five years at Macon he worked on the sites of the Creek earthlodge and on the funeral mound, which was later to become the topic of his dissertation. One of the contributions to American archaeology in general made by the large, government sponsored Works Project Administration excavations was the development and refinement of a rigorous and painstaking field methodology. Fairbanks had a significant part in this development and subsequently brought this precision to some of the earliest historical archaeology in the East.

It was also in Macon that Chuck Fairbanks met Evelyn Adams Timmerman, to whom he was married in 1941. Evelyn was introduced early to the rigours of being married to an archaeologist. It was on their wedding day, in fact, that young park archaeologist Fairbanks was summoned to give a tour of the Mounds to Dr. Margaret Mead, who happened to be in the area. Fairbanks gave the tour and made it to the wedding on time. Forty-one years later, Evelyn has seen first hand—and lived at—a respectable portion of the archaeological sites and academic institutions of Florida and Georgia.

Fairbanks spent three years, 1943 to 1945, in the Army, but continued his archaeological career after his military service at Frederica, Georgia, one of the early major historic sites to be excavated in the Southeast. Fairbanks was the Park superintendent and archaeologist at Frederica from 1946 to 1948, and his excavation at the Hawkins-Davison House there was an important event in the development of recovery, recording, and interpretive methods on historic sites. His involvement—and that of his students—has continued at Frederica to the present day.

From Frederica Fairbanks went to the University of Michigan to do graduate work in Anthropology. There he became involved with James B. Griffin and the group of archaeologists—formerly at Chicago—who were subsequently to play a major developmental role in historic and prehistoric southeastern archaeology. While pursuing his graduate studies, Fairbanks returned to Ocmulgee National Monument where he developed the museum and park exhibits.

After receiving his Ph.D. from Michigan in 1954, he began his teaching career at Florida State University. His approach to student training has been that of complete—but supervised—involvement of his students in all phases of archaeological research including publication of the final results. Like his teacher, Fay Cooper-Cole, he maintains a personal interest in the welfare of the students. While at FSU he trained students on several historical sites, including Horseshoe Bend, Alabama, and Fort St. Marks near Tallahassee. Also in Florida, surrounded by such colleagues as John Griffin, Hale Smith, and John Goggin, Fairbanks began his lifelong involvement in Spanish colonial studies.

In 1963 Fairbanks left FSU to assume direction of the Anthropology department at the University of Florida, then headed by John Goggin. During Fairbanks' eight years as chair, the department developed M.A. and Ph.D. programs, grew from a faculty of 3 to 11, and established a national reputation as one of the first programs of graduate study in historical archaeology. In 1976 Fairbanks was named a Distinguished Service Professor of the State System of Florida. During the early years in Gainesville, he also was a founding member of the Society for Historical Archaeology, served on its first Board of Directors, and was the Society's fourth president.

At the University of Florida Fairbanks maintained his active involvement in historical archaeological research and the ethnohistory of Florida's native groups. The archaeology of slavery and plantation life was initiated, and his pioneering study of slave life at Kingsley Plantation, Florida, took place in 1967 and 1968. This was followed by his work with Robert Ascher on Cumberland Island, Georgia, and later by the work at Butler Plantation on St. Simon's Island, Georgia. Through his continuing involvement in this area, and the work of his students trained at these sites, his influence in this area of historical archaeology has extended throughout the United States.

His role as a leader in Spanish colonial archaeology has also continued to this day through his research and the work of his students in mission sites, Spanish domestic sites, and material studies. "Backyard archaeology" as a research strategy for historical archaeology was introduced with his initial work in 1972 in St. Augustine. That research has also been continued since then through the work of his students. More recently, the project at Puerto Real, Haiti, under his direction has initiated processually-oriented, systematic historical research in the Spanish Caribbean.

Students have been a continuous feature of Fairbanks' career since 1954. He has directed more than 20 masters and 11 doctoral students, a majority of whom have concentrated in historical archaeology. His role in encouraging women in archaeology should also be noted. During the 1960's and early 1970's—when opportunities for women archaeologists were somewhat more limited—Fairbanks provided support and encouragement for equal numbers of men and women students. Seven of his 11 Ph.D. graduates, in fact, have been women.

One student-initiated Florida institution that cannot go unmentioned is the Annual Charles H. Fairbanks Armadillo Roast. Now in its twelfth year, the Armadillo Roast is put on each year by the students in honor of Fairbanks' birthday. Each roast has an official T-shirt, and an entire assemblage of them is now highly collectible.

Through his work over the last four decades, Charles Fairbanks has brought to the field of historical archaeology a unique and workable integration of scientific methods and humanistic perception. Because of this, because of his pioneering work in the archaeology of disenfranchised historic groups, and because of his direct influence on the present generation of historical archaeologists, he has been awarded the 1983 J. C. Harrington award for outstanding contribution to the field of historical archaeology.

J. C. Harrington Medal in Historical Archaeology

JOHN L. COTTER

1984

John L. Cotter was honored at the 1984 annual SHA meetings in Williamsburg, Virginia, as the second recipient to receive the Society's J. C. Harrington medal in recognition of his contributions to the field of historical archaeology.

Cotter's initial introduction to archaeology bagan at the University of Denver where he was awarded the A.B. degree in anthropology in 1934. During his Denver residence Cotter, a native Coloradan, participated in two significant prehistoric excavations. In 1934/35 he was a member of the Denver Museum of Natural History field crew at the Lindenmeier Paleo Indian site in western Colorado and remained for one additional season in 1935/36 under the direction of the Smithsonian Institution. Subsequently, Cotter was the chief of the research team which investigated the Clovis Type site under the sponsorship of the Academy of Natural Sciences, Philadelphia, Pennsylvania. Cotter published some of the results of his work in two articles of the *Proceedings of the Philadelphia Academy of Natural Sciences* in 1937 and 1938. After receiving his M.A. at the University of Denver in 1935, Cotter enrolled in the Anthropology Department at the University of Pennsylvania where he was influenced by Frank Speck and other members of the University Museum staff.

Cotter left Pennsylvania for a position as state supervisor of the archeological survey of Kentucky in 1938 and this work occupied him until 1940. In this capacity he gained valuable experience in the then blossoming field of governmental archaeology, knowledge which served Cotter well throughout his career. He entered the National Park Service in 1940 as an archaeologist/manager of Tuzigoot National Monument (a pueblo site) in Arizona and by this act began a nearly four decades of service in that agency. Cotter's duties there included maintenance, interpretation, research, and administration. When he led a tour, for example, it was necessary to close the small museum!

Cotter had met his wife, Virginia Wilkins Tomlin, at the Academy of Natural Sciences in Philadelphia, and their Tuzigoot experiences form some of their early marital memories. Virginia, trained as a classical scholar, responded well to the anthropologist's world and has prospered in it ever since.

During the Second World War, Cotter served in the 357th Infantry Regiment during the Normandy Invasion and later assisted in Army educational programs in London and Paris. After the conclusion of the war, he returned to the National Park Service as an archaeologist in charge of the Natchez Trace Parkway archaeological investigation program. This project involved the early utilization of developmental impact strategies and Cotter's survey of the Parkway mitigated the construction component of the park. Among the sites investigated by Cotter were the Bynum mounds, a complex of southern Hopewellian structures, and an historic Chickasaw settlement on the Trace. Cotter's exposure to the latter constituted his first experience on an historic site and began a career of specializing in such investigations. He also worked on the Emerald Mound, an extensive 13th century A.D. temple mound located near Natchez, Mississippi. Throughout this assignment, Cotter was successful in treating large scale survey archaeology as an integral part of development.

After a short term as acting Chief Archaeologist for the National Park Service in Washington, Cotter was placed in charge of the archaeological excavations at Jamestown, Colonial National Historical Park, from 1953–1957. Cotter's direction of this work was the most challenging archaeological assignment undertaken during his tenure with the National Park Service. Ably assisted by Edward Jelks, Joel Shiner, and others, Cotter proceeded from the earlier work of J. C. Harrington. Laboring under a tight time frame, Cotter excavated a sizeable portion of the town. This work stimulated a whole new generation of historical archaeologists and helped spur interest in tidewater Virginia archaeology.

Cotter's subsequent career with the National Park Service was one primarily concentrated on historical archaeology. As regional archaeologist for the Northeast and later the Mid-Atlantic Region, he championed the new field of study and was one of its most eloquent spokesmen. During the fifties, sixties, and seventies, Cotter formulated historical archaeological programs for the Park Service and worked hard to carry them to fruition. At the University of Pennsylvania, Cotter returned and finished his Ph.D. and began immediately to teach historical archaeology as a separate discipline. His first course, taught in 1960, must be considered as being among the first course of its kind offered in the United States. Cotter continued to teach this course in the American Civilization Department until his "full" retirement in 1979. We must place "full" in quotation marks since Cotter retired earlier in 1972 and then came back under the rubric of a "re-hired annuitant."

Cotter's academic work at the University of Pennsylvania centered on an anthropological approach to American Studies which in turn strongly influenced the American Civilization Department. His teaching generated twelve Ph.d. dissertations and about two dozen Master's theses. He has published over 100 articles and reviews on historical archaeology and anthropology. Additionally, as an ardent bibliographer, Cotter has assembled a vast listing of all works appropriate to the field since 1966. This project is currently being computerized and hopefully will be published. W. G. Hershey has aided Cotter in his effort for most of its recent history.

Cotter's support for the Society for Historical Archaeology as a co-founder, first president, and first editor, is well known. Throughout the history of the SHA, John Cotter has been an enthusiastic sponsor, member, and officer. John Cotter's career has demonstrated a broad based approach to cultural history. During the United States Bicentennial, for example, he published a widely distributed booklet entitled "Above Ground Archaeology." He has consistently supported a flexible stance for both historical archaeology and the study of American material culture. Because of this, and in consequence of his contributions to the study of historical archaeology, and because of his positive influence on two generations of historical archaeologists, he has been awarded the 1984 J. C. Harrington award for outstanding contributions to the field.

J. C. Harrington Medal in Historical Archaeology

KENNETH E. KIDD

1985

The Society for Historical Archaeology selected Kenneth E. Kidd to be the third recipient of the J. C. Harrington medal.

Kenneth Kidd was born in Barrie, Ontario, in 1906 and grew up on the family farm in Simcoe County. Kenneth Kidd began his University training in History and English and received his Honors B.A. from the University of Toronto in 1931. He then entered the Ontario College of Education where he earned a Specialist's Certificate in 1932 and, upon graduation, taught at the Mohawk Institute, Brantford, Ontario. The Institute was the first residential school in Canada for Six Nation's Indians. In 1935 Kenneth Kidd joined the staff of the Royal Ontario Museum (ROM) of Archaeology as a secretary in the Department of Ethnology, to begin a lifelong association with that institution. At that time, Ethnology at the ROM was really Anthropology for it embraced all branches of that science so far as they affected museum activity. After the mid-thirties, however, archaeology gained prominence.

Ken Kidd soon returned to the University of Toronto to begin graduate work in Anthropology and History and in 1936 did field work among the Blackfoot Indians of Alberta, collecting material for his thesis. In the twenties and thirties, anthropology was a very young discipline in Canada and the single professorship in the country was held by Thomas F. MacIlwraith at the University of Toronto.

Kidd's first exposure to archaeology was at Chaco Canyon where he attended the University of New Mexico Summer Field School in 1937. The following year he went on his first Canadian dig, at a late prehistoric site at St. Thomas, Ontario, led by Philleo Nash from the University of Toronto and during the next season he directed his own excavation in Algonquin Park, the first of many to follow.

These were the beginnings of scientific archaeology in Ontario, and the first attempts to bring it before the public. The results of the ROM's field work were always promptly displayed in the galleries, public lectures were given of the summer's activities, and a museum news letter began to circulate in May 1962.

The Government of Ontario responded and made the generous grant of $3000 for all the archaeological summer projects of the museum. As you may surmise, the field worker's wages in the thirties and forties were paid for by food and tent, air and sunshine and the excitement of discovery.

In the fall of 1941, the director of the ROM, Charles Currelly, stopped Ken Kidd in the corridor one day and told him point blank, as was his habit, that come spring Kidd would have to go to Midland to dig up a 17th century mission site.

The site in question was Ste Marie I, built by the Jesuits in 1639 and a center of their activities among the Huron Indians until its destruction in 1649.

The excavation lasted about eight months—was the first of its kind in Canada—and was a pioneering effort in the methodology and field techniques in historical archaeology.

Ken Kidd recognized the nature of the difficulties and wrote in the report on the site, *The Excavation of Sainte Marie I,* with characteristic modesty. ''Since the amount of historical archaeology which has been done in North America is still rather inconsiderable, each fieldworker has had to devise many of his own procedures, while following in general established techniques. This certainly has been true of work at Ste. Marie.''

The procedures that Kidd devised have stood the test of time and his monograph on the pioneering historical excavation in America is a model of archaeological research, analysis, and style.

Some years later, in 1950, Ken Kidd received a Letter of Commendation from the General of the Jesuit Order in Rome. Ste. Marie One has now been restored, not entirely as the excavator would have hoped, but is a major North American reconstruction nonetheless.

Some time before the excavation of Ste. Marie, in the fall of 1938, Ken Kidd had taken a leave of absence from the ROM to accept a scholarship at the University of Chicago. While in residence at International House, he met Martha Maurer. Martha, who was also doing graduate work at the time, at the Art Institute of Chicago, had been warned by her great Aunt to stay away from International House because she might meet and marry a foreigner. That warning obviously went unheeded, for Ken and Martha were married on 9 October 1943.

In 1947 Kidd began the excavation of the historic ossuary at Ossassané, near Midland, Ontario. This is the only Indian ossuary that has a reasonably exact date and has yielded a wealth of material goods and the remains of almost 500 individuals. In 1836, the Jesuit Jean de Brebeuf was at the scene of the ceremonies, which lasted almost a week, and recorded them in considerable detail.

By the late 1940s Ken Kidd had become the leading authority on eastern Canadian prehistory and was asked to write a chapter on Ontario in the first synthesis of Northeastern Archaeology by James Griffin, *Archaeology of Eastern United States*. Kidd's contribution ''60 Years of Ontario Archaeology'' is the earliest overview of the prehistory of the province.

In 1951 Kidd received a Guggenheim Memorial Fellowship for the study of European goods traded to the Indians during the early period of contact. Not much was known at the time about European technology of the 17th and 18th centuries that produced the artifacts found on Indian and European sites and Ken and Martha Kidd spent much of 1951 and 1952 traveling through New England, New York, and Pennsylvania visiting museums, private collections, and archives.

In 1956 the Kidds went on a similar quest, this time to the museums and archives in Great Britain, France and Germany, as well as Denmark and Sweden. In 1960 they added Italy, Spain and the Netherlands to their research network.

They returned with sheaves of notes, photocopies, photographs, and drawings and Ken set about organizing this material for publication—between a multitude of curatorial duties at the museum.

The publications that resulted from Kidd's study of early contact trade and domestic artifacts have become essential references in the discipline. They include *Trade Goods Research,* 1954; *Historic Site Archaeology in Canada,* 1969; *A Classification System for Glass Beads for the Use of Field Archaeologists* (with Martha as co-author), 1970; *The Manufacture of Glass Beads from the Middle Ages to the Beginning of the XIXth Century,* 1979; *A Study of Cutlery for the Use of Field Archaeologists,* 1982. Kidd's museum research on this subject was so wide-ranging that a few more papers are being readied for publication.

In the same context should be mentioned Kidd's continuing interest in Paul Kane, many of whose ethnographic paintings and sketches are housed at the ROM. Paul Kane, like George Catlin in the United States, traveled across Canada in the middle of the 19th-century and made a visual record of native life and material culture. Kidd published several papers on Kane's wanderings and sketches.

In 1954 Kidd became the curator of Ethnology at the ROM. In 1956 he was made a member of the Council of the Champlain Society and in 1957 was elected Vice President of the Society for American Archaeology.

During his years at the ROM, Ken Kidd not only personally excavated sites, did extensive research on historic trade goods, guided the growing department of Ethnology, but he initiated and started a number of programs and projects, some of which have grown to international significance, such as the Royal Ontario Museum program in British Honduras, now Belize. Kidd also coordinated the excavation of the Serpent Mounds near Peterborough, Ontario (1956 to 1960) and initiated a program of ethnological research in the Patricia District at Round Lake (1958 to 1959).

Although not a swimmer himself, Kidd introduced underwater archaeology in Canada and pioneered the systematic field recording of Indian rock art in the Great Lakes area. The results of this program, which began in 1957 and continued for four seasons, appeared in *Indian Rock Paintings of the Great Lakes,* in 1962, which Kidd co-authored with Selwyn Dewdney. This work continued the field observations with ethnohistorical research to provide the first account of the range, diversity and significance of native rock art.

In the mid 1960s the Government of Ontario was expanding the university system of the province and Ken Kidd was asked to establish the Department of Anthropology at the newly founded Trent University in Peterborough.

After 30 very active years at the Royal Ontario Museum, at a time when most curators quietly begin to daydream of retirement, Ken Kidd embarked on a second career and, in 1964, became the founding chairman of the Anthropology Department at Trent University.

Ken planned the foundations of the new department with great care and foresight so that now it is one of the few in Canada that has such a wide range of coverage of anthropology and an active graduate program in *Archaeology and Art of the Americas.*

In 1968 Kidd developed and initiated the *Indian and Eskimo Studies Programme* at Trent, the first in Canada, which now flourishes successfully as The Native Studies Department and which has come to serve as a model for similar departments at several other universities in the country.

The goal of this bold experiment was to facilitate the university education of the native community—in terms of a selective curriculum and an appropriate setting. The establishment of this program at Trent is the culmination of Kidd's lifelong interest in the native people of the Great Lakes—their historic past as well as their present condition. It should be noted that Ken Kidd is the only Canadian recipient of the Cornplanter Medal, given in 1970 by the Cayuga Museum of History and Art in recognition of his contributions to native studies.

Today, Ken Kidd divides his time between continuing research on historic trade goods and helping individual native students achieve their potential in modern society.

Throughout a career that now spans 50 years, in his pioneering studies in historical archaeology, material culture, and ethnohistory, Ken Kidd always sought to bring exactness to scholarship, precision to field work, and clarity to writing. These are also the qualities he passed on to his students.

But what is equally significant is that all of these accomplishments and achievements have been pervaded by a deep sense of humanity and an abiding faith in the individual and his worth.

J.C. Harrington Medal in Historical Archaeology

GEORGE IRVING QUIMBY

1986

George Irving Quimby was honored at the 1986 meeting of the Society for Historical and Underwater Archaeology in Sacramento, California, as the fourth recipient of the society's J. C. Harrington medal in recognition of his outstanding contributions to historical archaeology.

George Quimby was born in 1913 in Grand Rapids, Michigan, where he spent his boyhood. Quimby has written that he was raised in a community where people and artifacts of the Victorian and Edwardian era were an important part of the physical and social environment and were therefore a stimulus for his lifelong interest in the past. As a young man Quimby became an accomplished sailor of wind driven vessels; this and his sailing adventures on the Great Lakes in the early 1930s provided knowledge and experience which served him well as an archaeologist and as an enthusiastic supporter of underwater and marine research.

After graduating from the University of Michigan in 1936, where he concentrated on anthropology, Quimby pursued graduate studies in anthropology at both the University of Michigan and the University of Chicago. During this time he undertook research on historic artifacts from Michigan Indian and fur trade sites. He became particularly interested in trade silver which was the subject of his first professional article in 1937.

During the late 1930s Quimby participated in a number of excavations and expeditions where he learned the archaeological trade and met the small group of professors and students who formed the core of the emerging discipline of American archaeology. Of particular note is his trip to East Hudson's Bay in 1938. Here he not only met and interacted with Cree Indians who were still active fur traders but also collected archaeological materials from Eskimo sites on the Belcher Islands which he published in *American Antiquity* in 1940.

In that same year Quimby joined the Louisiana Archaeological Survey as a supervisor for the Work Project Administration's archaeological program. Along with a number of prehistoric sites Quimby excavated the Bayou Goula site, which featured a historic Indian occupation dating from the period 1723 to 1739. He recognized that French artifacts from Bayou Goula, the Fatherland site in Mississippi, and those from Fort St. Joseph in Michigan were very similar and thus supported the article he had written in 1938 on European trade articles as chronological indicators for archaeology of the Historic Period in Michigan. In 1942 Quimby presented an article elaborating further on the similarity of historic artifacts in these two regions of New France.

In 1940 Quimby met and married Helen Ziehm of Pine Bluff, Arkansas, who was a student at Louisiana State University. In 1942 they moved to Chicago where Quimby joined the staff of the Field Museum of Natural History where he ultimately became Curator of North American Archaeology and Ethnology. During his tenure at the Field Museum Quimby conducted archaeological field work in the southwest and Great Lakes region and was responsible for the care and exhibition of the Field Museum's huge ethnographic collections.

The book, *Indians Before Columbus*, which Quimby coauthored with Paul Martin and Donald Collier in 1947, was an immensely popular summary of northern American prehistory and was the authoritative source for this subject for nearly a decade. Although concentrating primarily on prehistoric archaeology in the 1940s and 1950s, Quimby undertook a study of the relationship between historic creek pottery in Georgia and Oklahoma with Alexander Spoehr and studied some historic sites on Lake Superior with James Griffin.

This latter experience rekindled Quimby's interest in historic artifacts and ethnohistory and he began a detailed study of the fur trade of the Great Lakes region. This research culminated in his book, *Indian Cultures and European Trade Goods*, which was published in 1966. This book, in addition to his earlier work on the prehistory of the region, *Indian Life in the Upper Great Lakes 11,000 B.C. to A.D. 1800*, established Quimby as the preeminent authority on the archaeology of the northern midwest.

In 1965 Quimby accepted an appointment at the University of Washington where he became Professor of Anthropology and Curator of Ethnology at the Thomas Burke Memorial Washington State Museum. Turning his attention to the Pacific Northwest, Quimby found familiar themes for his research and published several ethnohistorical studies on the Astoria fur trade. In Seattle Quimby was instrumental in reorganizing an amateur scuba club for the purposes of organized underwater research. Among other projects, this group was instrumental in the investigation of the wreck of the clipper ship, *Warhawk*.

Quimby became Director of the Burke Museum in 1968. Under his direction the museum underwent tremendous growth, including the development of a graduate program in museology. During the next decade, Quimby, along with his colleague Bill Holm, produced two highly acclaimed ethnographic films, *In the Land of the War Canoes*, and *The Image Maker and the Indians: Edward Curtis and his 1914 Kwakurth Movie*, as well as a well received book on Edward Curtis.

Quimby retired as director with the Burke Museum in 1983 and continues to actively pursue his research and writing as Professor Emeritus. Throughout his long and distinguished career Quimby has been an imaginative and productive scholar. He has been instrumental in directing our attention to problems of substance in the relationship between Indians and Euro-Americans. As a student, researcher, teacher, and administrator, Quimby has always taken a holistic view of the past and demonstrated through his work that specialized knowledge of archaeology and ethnohistory can speak to our understanding of broader human issues. Perhaps most importantly, Quimby has approached archaeology with good humor. From his example we learn that serious scholarship should also be great fun.

J. C. Harrington Medal in Historical Archaeology

Arthur Woodward

1987

Arthur Woodward died in Tucson, Arizona on January 24, 1986. He was 87 years old. With his passing, historical archaeology lost one of its true pioneers and most colorful practitioners.

He was born in Des Moines, Iowa, on April 18, 1898 of "fiddle-footed ancestry," as he liked to say, "who began in New England and ended in California over a period of some two hundred years." After a stint with the 20th Regular Infantry during World War I, Woodward studied history under Herbert E. Bolton and anthropology under Alfred E. Kroeber at the University of California at Berkeley. In 1922 he headed east where his first important paying job was as a reporter for the *New York Evening Journal*. This was followed by a brief time as a member of the research staff of the Museum of the American Indian, Heye Foundation, in New York. In 1925 he moved to work as a curator at the Los Angeles County Museum.

During World War II, Woodward served with the Office of Strategic Services, opening the first O.S.S. offices in Los Angeles. He was then attached to the U.S. Navy and spent three months on Admiral Richard Byrd's staff in the Southeast Pacific on a top secret presidential mission.

After retiring from an interrupted 25-year stint as Chief Curator of History and Anthropology at the Los Angeles County Museum, in 1961 the University of Arizona awarded him an honorary doctorate (Litt. D.). He relocated to southern Arizona, building a home and library in the rural community of Patagonia. From there he commuted regularly to Tucson and the University of Arizona where in the spring semester of 1964 he inaugurated a course in historical archaeology, one of the first such courses offered in the United States. He proved himself in that one-semester offering to be a walking, talking encyclopaedia, one who, without benefit of notes, happily turned the pages for his awe-stricken students. Like the content in his many dozens of books and articles, subjects ranged from porcupine quill work and Indian houses in Southern California to Indian uses of the silver gorget, Mexican pottery making, and Indian trade goods.

Woodward was well known in California mission circles for his work as a member of the Advisory Committee for the restoration of Mission La Purisima Concepción. He was once chairman of the Los Angeles Landmarks Committee and in 1935 he was the historian and archaeologist accompanying a National Park Service expedition to the missions of northern Sonora, Mexico. His account of that trip was translated into Spanish and published under the auspices of the Governor of Sonora in 1983 as *Misiones del Norte de Sonora: aspectos históricos y arqueológicos.*

Art Woodward wrote the pioneer work, *A Brief History of Navajo Silversmithing* (1938); the section on Spanish-period artifacts in Charles C. DiPeso's *The Sobaipuri Indians of the Upper San Pedro River Valley, Southeastern Arizona* (1953); and *Indian Trade Goods* (1967). Subjects on which he was among the country's leading experts and about which he wrote articles included antler implements; Karok dance paraphernalia; shell work of California Indians; Aztec feather working; the use of coral in the Southwest; catlinite; glass beads; wampum; California Mexican-period costume; horse furniture; Green River knives; Spanish and Mexican brands; ox carts and other horse-drawn wheeled vehicles; Spanish-period military paraphernalia; and much more.

By the time of his death in 1986, Woodward had put together a private library of more than 24,000 volumes, all of which were given to the Arizona Historical Society in Tucson. He also left behind thousands of note cards and photographs of a wide range of museum specimens from all over the world, everything from glass beads to silver gorgets.

Although he was a Renaissance man who failed to differentiate conceptually among history, anthropology, and archaeology, much less historical archaeology, Woodward's influence on the course of historical archaeology cannot be measured. Those who were fortunate enough to have taken or audited his course in 1964, to say nothing of the hundreds of people who had occasion to consult with him or simply to listen to him in conversation, have included countless dozens of persons whose own careers and contributions to historical archaeology were shaped by those moments.

In the eulogy delivered by a relative at the wake Art had prearranged for the occasion, those present were told Art had been asked before his death how he wanted to be remembered among his relatives, friends, and colleagues. His answer, with the twinkle in his eye: was: "As that old bastard!"

He will always be remembered, and loved, by all who knew him as "that old bastard," but also as one of the fathers of historical archaeology.

Bernard Fontana

J. C. Harrington Medal in Historical Archaeology: Stanley A. South, 1987. Volume 21, Number 2 (1987): 1-5. By Leland Ferguson.

J.C. Harrington Medal in Historical Archaeology

STANLEY A. SOUTH 1987

At this time, when Stanley South is receiving the most prestigious award our profession has to offer, I think it is appropriate to lay out, in his honor, another pattern in the fabric of historical archaeology. Naturally, it will be called the "Stanley South Pattern."

In creating this pattern I have deviated from a few of the axiomatic rules of pattern making. For example, I have not counted, that is quantified, anything. I have not even looked for Stanley's age; it is enough to say that he was born on Ground Hog Day. I have not created any "Groups" or "Classes," nor have I computer frequencies. No percentages were calculated and, therefore, I have no tables of percentage relationships that "reveal the 'Stanley South Pattern.' " What is even more unorthodox about this pattern is that I have tried not to let the facts interfere with the truth.

In putting this review together, it seemed that some of the most valuable sources might be Stan's colleagues who were starting out in the new field of historical archaeology at about the same time he was. I imagined calling Jim Deetz and Ivor Noel-Hume to ask for their comments on the highlights of Stan's career.

I first call Deetz. "Hello, Jim. This is Leland Ferguson." We exchange small talk, and then I tell him about Stanley's receiving the award and ask what he thinks are the highlights of Stan's career.

Without hesitation, Jim replies,"Oh, that's easy. You know, Leland, Stan's mean ceramic date formula has been used all over the world, wherever there were English Colonies. And his pattern construction has been very popular, and I think those things are major contributions. But I really think that the apex of Stanley's career, so far, was a few years back at that SHA meeting in Nashville when he read his poetry! Stan's understanding of deep structure as represented by that poetry made me feel that one day he really would get at the minds of the people he studies.

"Actually," he says, "Stan's poetry is not all that far from Mark Leone's archaeology!"

Stanley's poetry? Deetz thought that Stanley's poetry would yet lead him to his major contribution and the zenith of his career? He should see his painting. I was sure that Noel-Hume would have something more orthodox to say.

The telephone rings, and I can tell it is Noel-Hume who answers. "Hello, Noel?" (I'm very informal in my imagination), "this is Leland Ferguson."

"Who—?"

"Leland Ferguson, from the University of South Carolina."

There is an unsettling pause, then,"Oh, the young fellow with the Colono-Indian pottery."

"Yes," I reply, "that's me." Again, we pass a few pleasantries. We talk about Colono-Indian Ware and Colono Ware. I tell him about the award and say, "I wondered if you would tell me a few of the things that you think are the major contributions of Stanley's career."

Silence at the other end of the phone. Then Noel-Hume replied, "His major contributions?"

"Yes," I say. "You know, his best work."

Noel-Hume pauses some more, and then repeats, "His best work?"

"Yes," I say.

"Well, I've been completely through Stan's book. Now what was the title?"

Method and Theory in Historical Archaeology?" I offer.

"Yes," he says, "that's the one. Theoretical Archaeology. A few years ago, I went completely through that book, and . . . ugh, I liked the photographs, I found the illustrations to be . . . humorous, the tables were nicely done, and, knowing Stanley, I expect that all of those percentages were calculated correctly."

I listen. "Is there anything else?"

"Oh," he answers, "I think that as a graduate student he did some fine work in prehistory. And," he continues, "we did learn some valuable things about colonial North Carolina from the excavations he conducted at Brunswick Town and Bethabara. I remember," (he's reminiscing now), "Stan used to come up to Colonial Williamsburg with boxes full of sherds. He wanted to know about the types and dates of all kinds of ceramics, and I did my best to help him. I think that was when he was working on that formula. You know, the one that gives you a date you already know. That is you should know it if you know your ceramics and the archaeological context well enough." We end our conversation talking about the Savannah meeting.

Well, I thought, those were pretty interesting conversations, but there won't be enough to the Stanley South Pattern if I rely on only the stuff I got from those two fellows. Poetry? Illustrations? Amusing? I guess Noel-Hume was referring to the pig chart and the chicken chart.

I began to go over Stanley's life and career myself, trying to keep the faith that I would recognize a pattern. I asked myself, "Would it help to try being hypothetico-deductive?" No, I decided it would be more productive, not to mention fun, to be "particularistico-inductive." (By the way, "particularistico-inductive" is a new hyphenated word which I am donating, in Stan's honor, to methodoligical and theoretical archaeology). I decided to think about specific events, the specific elements of the pattern; I guess it could be called a "bill of historical particulars" of Stan's career. I had his vita, and there were many, many stories. Stories hang about Stanley like moss on a live-oak tree. I thought, perhaps, those stories together with the vita . . . well, that they would reveal a pattern.

Stanley South was born in the mountains of North Carolina. His father was a Democratic politician, the clerk of court in Watauga County, and his mother ran a guest house for summer tourists. From the time he was four years old and refused to take off his cowboy boots to go to bed, Mrs South knew this child was going to have a "mind of his own" (her euphemism for "bull headed").

It was not long after he started wearing cowboy boots that Stanley learned how to review and put red felt-tipped pen marks all over archaeological papers, and he learned it from a chicken! Stanley grew up on a mountainside overlooking the town of Boone. His grandmother lived a little farther up the mountain, and he often went to visit her in her little home.

Now, like most people in the mountains, Stan's grandmother had a fence around her house, and inside this fence was a big, and very bad, Dominecker Rooster. This rooster liked tow-headed, five-year-old boys—they "made his day." Trip after trip as he raced through a gauntlet of beak, and feathers, and talons, Stanley would end up crying on the porch.

Stanley's grandmother told him to call her when he was at the gate; but, although only five, Stanley was embarassed to have his grandmother have to escort him by a chicken. So one day Stanley decided to end it. He and this bird were going to have it out. On his way up the path to grandma's he picked up a big, heavy rock—a "Dominecker Rock." Breathing deeply, he boldly opened the gate and walked right through, just like he was going into the church yard. The dominecker saw the little boy and made his rush. Stanley waited, waited, and when the rooster was almost to him he let him have it with the rock, right on the head. The rooster fell into a limp pile of speckled feathers.

Stanley's grandmother had heard the commotion and was now on the porch. "Stanley Austin! My rooster! You've killed my rooster! You've killed my rooster!" Stanley was frightened, and tears were streaming down his little face. He didn't really mean to kill the rooster. But, there he was, limp in the dust.

Then, just as Stan was beginning to think that his grandmother was going to whip him for the very first time, the rooster moved. He slowly and drowsily got up, shook his feathers and began walking drunkenly around the yard. He survived! Stanley escaped the whipping, and from that point on, Stanley and the Dominecker had a good relationship of mutual respect.

Over the years, many of us have received Stanley's criticism of our archaeological reports. Papers have been returned from Stanley with red pen marks calling for references all over the pages and crimson epistles spilling down the margins. Receiving these blood-red reviews we have felt like we were hit over the head with a "Dominecker Rock." Nevertheless, we've recovered, and we have learned from Stanley's criticism. Moreover, we have developed a great respect for this man who stands firmly, and with a big rock, behind his convictions—another part of the Stanley South Pattern.

When he was eleven, Stanley began working toward a career goal that carried through to his college years. However, it wasn't historical archaeology, it wasn't even collecting arrowheads. At eleven years of age, six-foot-tall Stanley South began singing on the radio under the stage name "Wee Willie." Every Saturday, Stanley was down at the studio of Boone's WAUG, and every Saturday he entertained the Carolina mountains with songs like "Jeannie with the Light Brown Hair" and "Drink to Me Only with Thine Eyes."

Following "Wee Willie" was another program by one of Stan's chums known as "The Blind Wonder." After Stanley had thirty minutes of bringing the best in popular music to the mountains, his blind friend would come on and sing simple mountain songs while he accompanied himself with three chords on a guitar. Stanley felt sorry for his friend because he had to sing those old fashioned songs. Unlike Stanley he couldn't see to read music, and Stanley knew that poor Doc Watson didn't have much of a future in the music business. But Stanley—now Stanley could read music and he was on his way!

By the time he was seventeen years old, Stanley had completed one year of college and was enlisted in the United States Navy. It was World War II and, through some type of sophisticated intelligence gathering system, the Japanese must have learned that Stan was on his way: For, just after he completed boot camp and was ready to go overseas, they surrendered. (Maybe they had heard about the chicken.)

Returning as one of the youngest veterans of the War, Stanley resumed his career in music by studying music education at Appalachian State Teachers College in his home town. His education continued smoothly until his junior year and a course in musicology. This was a course in which the students covered the basics, that is the "nomothetic laws" of music: notes, scales, keys, transposition. Now Stanley was a solor singer. He sang in his own key and "reading music" to him was being able to tell if the notes went up or down, or, fast or slow. In this course the professor wanted him to understand how all these things fit together, and what was more he had to listen to music and write the score. Stanley tried. He tried, but he couldn't do it. He decided to switch majors. His switch led him to elementary education and then to work as a professional photographer, and finally to study archaeology in graduate school.

In looking over the whole sequence of events, I have come to another conclusion about the Stanley South Pattern. I think we can say that we now have a book entitled *Method and Theory in Historical Archaeology* because Stanley could not understand method and theory in music!

Stanley entered archaeology as a graduate student at the University of North Carolina. At that time, archaeology meant prehistoric archaeology, and Stanley's mentor Joffre Coe sent him to the Roanoke Rapids Basin on the border between North Carolina and Virginia to cut his archaeological teeth. Stan's late wife Jewel used to joke that this project almost ended their marriage.

Now before your imaginations run away with you on how the marriage almost ended, let me tell you about the project. The Roanoke basin was located in a very remote region of the coastal plain, and Stanley had limited gear and only small tents to establish a camp. It was really roughing it, and Jewel was holding her own. But then another graduate student, Lewis Binford, came up to help with the project. The three of them, Stanley, Jewel, and "Big Lew" began working together.

Okay, if you haven't guessed Jewel's problem already, imagine, just imagine the energy, the enthusiasm, the ebullience of Stanley South and Lewis Binford as second year graduate students! Jewel said that these two masters of archaeological communication talked nothing but archaeology, archaeology, archaeology. This pit, that level, Guilford Points, Halifax Points, cultural evolution, Leslie White, Louis Henry Morgan! They talked archaeology from the time they woke up in the morning, through the work day, over supper and into the night and on into the night. And Jewel was stuck with these two guys! She couldn't get away! It is testimony to her mettle and perserverance that she survived that ordeal of enthusiasm.

Out of that energy, enthusiasm and ebullience, Stanley produced his master's thesis, *A Study of the Prehistory of the Roanoke Rapids Basin: 1959.* It included the archaeology of the Gaston site, and it was a major contribution to the archaeology of the Atlantic coast. This thesis looks like about three or four normal theses stacked on top of one another; and using Stanley's thesis, as well as the results of other excavations, Joffre Coe was able to put together what is perhaps the most widely used publication on prehistoric archaeology of the Middle Atlantic States: *Formative Cultures of the Carolina Piedmont.* With his thesis, Stan demonstrated the exuberance for archaeology that would characterize the rest of his career.

Following graduate school Stan went to work as archaeologist for the North Carolina Department of Archives and History. His first assignment was as site manager and archaeologist at Town Creek Indian Mound where, in addition to excavating and running the park, he reconstructed a Mississippian-style temple atop the mound. It was in 1958 that Stan became an historical archaeologist, when he was transferred by Archives and History to excavate and manage the eighteenth century site of Brunswick Town and Civil War Fort Fisher. Local archaeological legend has it that upon occasion of this momentus transfer Joffre Coe said, in his droll manner, "Well, it looks like Stanley's left archaeology to dig around old house foundations."

Perhaps when he made the switch, Stanley didn't realize the changes that were in store. While he was at Town Creek, he regularly received time off to attend the Southeastern Archaeological Conference. In the fall after his move to the historical sites, Stan once again prepared to attend the Conference. His supervisor saw his preparations and said, "No!" Stanley asked why, and he was told that since he was *now* doing *historical archaeology* and since SEAC was a conference on *prehistoric archaeology* that he couldn't have time off to attend.

Of course, there was no conference on historic site archaeology to attend. So Stanley stayed home. But not the next year. Before the next SEAC meeting, Stanley quietly (that is as quietly as Stanley can be) made arrangements for a meeting of historical archaeologists to be held the day before the SEAC, and he went in and told his boss that this year they were having an historical archaeological conference! Might he have time off to go? He did, and in 1960 the *Conference on Historic Site Archaeology* was founded.

In total impact on the field, founding this conference was perhaps the most important contribution of Stanley's career. Through the Conference, historical archaeologists had a forum and a means for publication. Stanley organized every meeting, he kept track of all the finances and every year he collected, edited and published the proceedings, fifteen volumes in all. The Conference was the first historical archaeological organization in the country. It laid much of the groundwork for the Society for Historical Archaeology.

The more recent aspects of the Stanley South Pattern are much more widely known than those of earlier days. For many years now, Stan has been a Senior Archaeologist and Research Professor of Anthropology at the South Carolina Institute of Archaeology and Anthropology. From that position he has worked diligently to do his part in forging the new field of historical archaeology. Among his many excavations have been work at Charles Towne Landing, the Revolutionary War forts of Ninety-Six and Fort Moultrie, and the sixteenth century Spanish ciudad of Santa Elena. In addition to many, many papers and reports, Stanley has written one book (now in its third printing), edited another and served as Editor for books in the Academic Press series, Studies in Historical Archaeology. He was a contributor to the Airlie House Conference that established goals and guidelines for public service archaeology, and he has served the profession in a variety of other ways.

While doing all of this archaeological work, there is another part of Stanley's career that should be included in the pattern. In recent years, Stan has become a popular teacher in the graduate program at the University of South Carolina. However, throughout the years I have known him, Stan has always been a teacher. He couldn't help it. Stanley has always been willing to talk, read or write archaeology at any time, at any place, with anyone who was interested. With thousands of people, he has discussed projects, read reports and made his comments—comments that have, above all, called for scientific rigor in conducting archaeology. Moreover, as younger archaeologists have embarked upon their careers, Stanley has been there with support and encouragement as well as constructive criticism. It seems the appropriate time for me to say "Thanks, prof' " from all of us.

In conclusion: The Stanley South Pattern is energetic, industrious, productive, rigorous and critical. It is collegial, supportive, poetic, folksy, amusing and occasionally stubborn. Stnaley has enthusiastically given himself to our field. In the colorful and complicated fabric of historical archaeology, the Stanley South Pattern stands out as a significant part of the warp around which the weft of everyday archaeology has been woven. Moreover, I want to say that I know Stanley will have a good comeback to any critics who come up and say, "You know, Stan, Leland was right in the title of that review, *you really have warped historical archaeology.*"

Leland Ferguson

J. C. Harrington Medal in Historical Archaeology: Edward B. Jelks, 1988. Volume 22, Number 1 (1988):1-4. By Michael D. Wiant.

J.C. Harrington Medal in Historical Archaeology

EDWARD B. JELKS 1988

Edward B. Jelks was honored at the 1988 annual Society for Historical Archaeology (SHA) meetings in Reno, Nevada, as the sixth recipient to receive the Society's J.C. Harrington medal in recognition of his contributions to the field of historical archaeology.

Edward Jelks was born in Macon, Georgia, in 1922, lived in Hollywood, Florida, from 1923 to 1929, then he moved with his family to Texas. His curiosity about the past developed in central Texas, where as a youth he occasionally found artifacts while hunting and fishing.

Jelks began his university training as a pre-med student at the University of Texas, Austin, in 1939, but his undergraduate studies were interrupted when he enlisted in the Navy at the outbreak of World War II. As a Hospital Corpsman, he supervised the operating room staff of Acorn Red One, a field hospital on Guadalcanal that handled Navy and Marine casualties during the fall and winter of 1942–1943. After serving four years in the Navy, he returned to Austin and married Juliet Christian. For over 40 years Judy has accompanied Ed on many field projects and has been an indispensable partner in every facet of his archaeological research.

Ed began his formal training in anthropology as his minor field of study when he resumed his undergraduate training in Austin in 1945. He was particularly stimulated by G. C. Engerrand, an archaeologist experienced in European and Mexican prehistory. After completing a B.A. in English in 1948, Ed's interest in archaeology prompted him to begin graduate work in anthropology at the University of Texas. He studied mainly under J. Charles Kelly, Thomas N. Campbell, and Gilbert McAllister.

In 1950 after completing his M.A. course work, Jelks accepted a position as Robert L. Stephenson's assistant at the Austin office of the Smithsonian's River Basin Survey (RBS) project. During his first professional field season he participated in the excavation of the Stansbury site, an historic Indian village located on the Brazos River in central Texas. Jelks conducted documentary research on Stansbury and identified it as the 18th-century Quiscat Village of the Tawakoni instead of the 19th-century village of the Towash as it had been previously identified.

This experience stimulated Ed to develop a rigorous approach for identifying documented sites of uncertain location, which combined archaeological and documentary data. His approach involved the apriori construction of a detailed conceptual model from documentary and archaeological data that predicted which artifacts and other archaeological remains should be found at a particular site and the techniques for delineating the geographical areas where the site should be found. Using this method Jelks, his students, and collaborators have identified the archaeological remains of a number of historically documented sites, including Indian villages and Spanish missions in Texas, the site of the first Ft. de Chartres in Illinois, and Redoubt No. 10 at Yorktown, Virginia. In addition, he has traced routes of several expeditions including those of Spanish explorers in Texas and of Mormons in Illinois in 1834.

In 1951 Jelks became the Director of the RBS office in Austin. During the next two years, he and his staff surveyed several planned reservoirs and excavated numerous sites. Jelks was accompanied by Alex Krieger on many of these projects, and he profited greatly from Krieger's insight about archaeology and the past, as well as from discussions about field and analytical problems with other prominent archaeologists like James Ford. It was also at this time that Ed worked in the field with E. H. Sellards and Glen Evans at a number of Paleo-Indian sites, including Blackwater Draw, Lubbock Lake, and Friesenhahn Cave.

Concern with the organization of the immense amount of material recovered during these projects and others fostered the development of the Texas Handbook of Archeology compiled by Dee Ann Suhm, Ed's part-time office assistant, Alex Krieger, and Ed. First published in 1954 and revised in 1962, this monograph is one of the most comprehensive typologies of prehistoric and historic Native American artifacts and continues to be a standard reference.

In 1953, Ed was transferred to the National Park Service (NPS) when they assumed administrative responsibility for the RBS. Funding shortfalls led to the closing of the Austin office from 1954 through 1956 and Ed was transferred by the NPS to Virginia. In Virginia he served as John Cotter's assistant during exploratory excavations at Jamestown, where he was assigned to excavate a number of major features. While in Virginia, he conducted exploratory excavations at Yorktown Battlefield, locating and identifying components of the U.S. and French defensive earthworks of the Battle of Yorktown. Of particular note was his discovery of Redoubt No. 10, a key position whose capture turned the tide of battle in favor of the Americans. Because of his work at Jamestown and Yorktown, Jelks in 1982 was presented the Historic Preservation Award by the Association for the Preservation of Virginia Antiquities.

Ed returned to Austin in 1956 to reopen the River Basin Survey office. However, in 1958, the NPS permanently closed the office, opting instead to contract for rescue archaeological services. Coincidentially, at about the same time the University of Texas established a Ph.D. program in anthropology. Ed resigned from the National Park Service and entered the program but continued to work full-time on contract archaeology projects as organizer and director of the Texas Archeological Salvage Project (now the Texas Archeological Survey). During the 15 years (1950 through 1953 and 1956 through 1969) in which Ed directed salvage archaeology in Texas and Louisiana, a prodigious amount of archaeology was accomplished. Surveys were conducted at over 40 planned reservoirs, and more than 100 sites were excavated, 30 of which he personally supervised. The sites spanned a broad spectrum of aboriginal cultures: Paleo-Indian, Archaic, post-Archaic, and Historic Indian sites. In addition, several 18th- and 19th-century Spanish Colonial sites and a number of early to mid-19th century western pioneer sites were excavated. In all, over 150 rescue archaeology reports were written under Ed's direction; he authored or coauthored dozens of them, and edited all of them. Several dozen of these reports have been published. In recognition of part of this work, in 1984 Jelks was given the Clarence H. Webb Award for Contributions to Caddoan Archeology.

Jelks was awarded a Ph.D. in 1965, the first Ph.D. in anthropology in the University of Texas program. That same year, after 15 years of full-time field research, he began a teaching career at Southern Methodist University (SMU). His seminar in historical archaeology, first taught in 1966, was one of the earliest at any university. Kathleen Gilmore, a former SHA president, and Ned Woodall, the current president of the Society of Professional Archaeologists (SOPA), were both in that 1966 seminar.

In 1967, Jelks and Arnold Pilling, of Wayne State University, organized a conference on historical archaeology and invited 15 outstanding historical archaeologists to meet concurrently with the conference to consider the possibility of starting an international historical archaeology society. Pilling chaired the conference which met at SMU, while Jelks chaired the committee of 15. The committee's recommendation to form the Society for Historical Archaeology was acted upon by those attending the general conference. Ed served as the second president of the society in 1968.

Full-time teaching responsibilities did not curtail Ed's field work. Between 1965 and 1969, he conducted excavations and field studies at many historic sites in Texas including a number of historic Indian sites (especially of the Wichita tribes), Ft. Lancaster, a mid-19th century U.S. Army post on the Pecos River, at several 18th-century Spanish Colonial sties, at Ft. Leaton, a 19th-century frontier site in western Texas, and at Washington-on-the-Brazos, the center of Stephen F. Austin's colony and site of Texas' Declaration of Independence from Mexico. During the summers of 1965 and 1966, the Canadian government funded his excavations at Signal Hill National Historical Park, a British military post of the 1790–1860 period at St. John's, Newfoundland.

Jelks left SMU in 1968 and spent seven months at the Smithsonian Institution as a Research Fellow working on a typology of English, French, and Spanish colonial ceramics. That year he became Professor of Anthropology at Illinois State University (ISU), a position he held until he retired in 1984. At ISU he served as Acting Chairman of the Department of Sociology and Anthropology (1974–1975) and as Coordinator for Anthropology (1968–1974). During Jelks' tenure, ISU's Anthropology program expanded dramatically. His teaching skills and additions to the curriculum attracted many students. Particularly popular were his seminar in historical archaeology and the summer field school expeditions organized by him and Judy. Among the field school sites were Revolutionary War fortifications at West Point Military Academy's Constitution Island and the Grand Village of the Kickapoo in Illinois. In 1978 Ed and Judy, under contract with the Trust Territory of the Pacific Islands, carried out the first historical archaeology in the Marshall Islands, at a 19th-century copra plantation on Likiep Atoll.

In 1980 Jelks established the Midwestern Archaeological Research Center (MARC) at ISU in response to the expansion of contract archaeology in Illinois. The MARC program has focused primarily on historical archaeological sites and standing structures. Ed has long been an outspoken advocate of the significance of 19th and 20th century Euroamerican sites, which traditionally were ignored by cultural resource managers and contract archaeologists. His efforts did much to make protection of such historic sites standard procedure in both Illinois and Texas. Jelks served as MARC's Director until his retirement.

For many years Jelks has actively advocated the establishment of institutionalized archaeological standards, ethical codes, and professionalism. He was on the Society for American Archaeology's (SAA) Standards and Ethics Committee in the 1950s, he participated in the Airlie House conference on certification in 1974, and he chaired the SAA committee whose members formed the Society for Professional Archeology (SOPA) in 1976, and served as SOPA's first president. He currently serves on the American Association for the Advancement of Science's Professional Society Ethics Group and is on the editorial board of their quarterly newsletter.

Ed's research interests are most aptly described as diverse, but there are several prominent themes. He has a long-standing interest in artifact classification that includes work on European ceramics, French trade goods, and prehistoric lithics and ceramics. In 1961, he and Lathel Duffield devised a classification system and terminology for glass trade beads that has found wide acceptance. While serving as an alternate U.S. member of the History Commission of the Pan American Institute of Geography and History, he organized the Archaeology Work Group, which he chairs and which has met annually since 1981. The Commission recently published a standardized, multilingual set of terms for describing pottery decorations that is designed for computerization in English, Spanish, French, and Portuguese.

A common theme in many of Ed's writings and lectures is the importance of rigorous methods for interpreting the significance of *where* things are located in the archaeological record. He has developed a general methodology for analyzing and interpreting intrasite contexts and for inferring past human behavior from contextual data.

His long standing interest in statistics is reflected by his M.A. thesis (1952), which compares the horizontal distribution patterns of artifact types in unstratified sites. Later (1975), he wrote an important paper on the misuse of random sampling in archaeology in which he points out how nonjudgemental samples of archaeological sites has led to serious errors of interpretation. It is also noteworthy that in 1974 he and a sociologist coauthored a book on statistical probabilities in the game of bridge—the first such study ever done using computerized data—which has led many players to adjust the way they bid certain hands.

Ed continues to actively pursue his research and writing, with the support and assistance of Judy. They have recently finished compiling and editing a dictionary of North American archaeological terms which will be published in April 1988.

Edward Jelks has contributed significantly to the advancement of archaeology in general and particularly of historical archaeology, a field in which he is one of the pioneers. His contributions include advances in the methods of historical archaeology and in the conservation of historical remains. He played a leading role in the founding of the Society for Historical Archaeology. He has provided field, laboratory, and classroom training for many students who now pursue careers in archaeology, including a number who specialize in historical archaeology. For these accomplishments he has been awarded the 1988 J.C. Harrington award for outstanding contributions to the field of historical archaeology.

MICHAEL D. WIANT

J. C. Harrington Medal in Historical Archaeology: Carlyle Shreeve Smith, 1989. Volume 24, Number 4 (1990): 1-3.
By Roger T. Grange, Jr.

J. C. Harrington Medal in Historical Archaeology

CARLYLE SHREEVE SMITH 1989

Carlyle Shreeve Smith was born on March 8, 1915, in Great Neck, New York. His family was long resident in the area, and a tidewater grist mill built by an ancestor in 1710 still stands as a National Register site. In his youth Carlyle developed a deep interest in the material objects of the past, a fascination fueled by contact with Francis Bannerman Sons, a company which still deals in military surplus from all time periods and places. Carl began studying, collecting, and restoring firearms when he was 13. That hobby developed into professional expertise in firearms identification, a hallmark of his contributions to historical archaeology.

Carlyle had decided on a career in archaeology by the time he entered high school and took materials he excavated from local sites on Long Island to Nels Nelson at the American Museum. These specimens ultimately appeared in his Ph.D. dissertation. He was an avid student of history, literature, French, German, and Latin, later adding Norwegian to his language skills.

Carlyle did his undergraduate work at Columbia College of Columbia University where he took ethnology courses from Gene Weltfish, Alexander Lesser, and Ralph Linton. He was introduced to archaeology at historic sites by William Calver and Ralph Solecki. William Duncan Strong took him on the Columbia University Expedition to North Dakota in 1938, the year of his graduation, and he was "hooked" on Plains Archaeology.

Carl began graduate work in 1938/39 at Columbia. He increased his archaeological field experience working with A.T. Hill in a WPA archaeological field unit in Nebraska. He continued field work in 1940/41 in New York and served under George Quimby in Louisiana where he directed the excavation of the Bayou Goula site.

During World War II Smith worked for a time in the pre-Pearl Harbor aircraft industry and married Judith Pogany. He was offered a project to find and excavate Fort Pitt but World War II and Selective Service intervened, and he went instead to serve in the Army Air Force. After the war he completed his dissertation and received his Ph.D. from Columbia in 1949.

Carlyle's dissertation research, "The Archaeology of Coastal New York," has been recognized by the naming of "The Carlyle S. Smith Archaeological Laboratories" at the Nassau County Museum of Natural History, Garvies Point, Glen Cove, Long Island, New York.

Carl joined the faculty at the University of Kansas in Lawrence in 1947 as Curator of the Division of Anthropology of the Museum of Natural History, a post he held until 1968. He was also Professor of Anthropology until his retirement in 1980 when he became both Professor and Curator Emeritus. Carlyle made significant improvements in both museum and academic aspects of Anthropology at KU.

At the University of Kansas Carlyle Smith embarked on an extended period of work in Plains archaeology, and excavated the Kansas Monument site, a significant Pawnee village of the early 19th century. The specimens included vast amounts of trade goods and firearms and drew upon all of Carlyle's expertise in the identification of artifacts of Euro-American origin.

During the 1950s Smith was involved in salvaging archaeological data from sites to be inundated in the series of dams which obliterated the Missouri River from Nebraska to Montana. It was an exciting time when each site excavated produced a new culture or period. Carl spent three seasons at the Talking Crow site near Fort Thompson, South Dakota, where he defined several key ceramic types. His seriations, based on this significant stratified site, were very important to the culture history of the area. The recreational reconstruction of a scale model of an excavated house became an experiment widely publicized in "The Archaeologist at Work." Carl's ethnological skills meant good local relationships, and the Dakota at Fort Thompson ceremonially named him *Kangi-ia-wakan*, Holy Crow Voice or Talking Crow.

Carlyle Smith excavated many important prehistoric and protohistoric sites in South Dakota: Spain Site, Two Teeth, and Stricker are prominent examples. It is notable that Bert Salwen, honored with the Harrington Medal this same year, was Carlyle's field assistant at the Stricker site. Carlyle's inclusion of women as equal members of his field crews was exceptional in that period. He was honored for his contributions to Plains Archaeology with the award of Doctor of Humane Letters, *Honoris causa*, by the University of South Dakota in 1979.

A shift in pattern began in 1955 when Carlyle joined Thor Heyerdahl's expedition to Easter Island. Carl dated artifacts, did research on the Poike Ditch, studied the *ahu* ceremonial platforms, and made a mold of one of the large statues. Always interested in historic sites, he visited Pitcairn Island where the mutinous crew of the *Bounty* settled. Carl and Judy returned to the Pacific in 1963 where he carried out a program of archaeological research at Pekia, a ceremonial site on Hiva Oa in the Marquesas.

In later years Carlyle's health limited his ability to continue rigorous field work but not his teaching and writing. Then he began a new career lecturing on archaeological subjects and serving as a guide on cruise ships where he brings to the general public a new awareness of the past. He has made at least 19 such voyages and returned to Easter Island many times.

Smith excavated several historic sites in the Plains. In addition to Kansas Monument, there were historic components at most sites in South Dakota. He excavated the Deerfly site, a 19th-century cabin near the prehistoric Spain Site, which many others would have abandoned once its age had been determined. In Lawrence, Kansas, his historical archaeology class excavated evidence of Quantrill's 1863 raid. Nearly a third of Carlyle Smith's publications are on historical archaeology topics especially dealing with firearms identification.

Carlyle's interest in firearms led him to historical research and translation of documents on gunflint manufacture which he coupled with field work at gunflint production sites in France and Italy. Carlyle also developed and offered courses in historical archaeology and in the evolution and history of firearms. His students in the classroom, as well as those in the field, were always given hands-on experience with working examples of flintlocks and other historical firearms. He is probably the only archaeologist capable of firing a bracket around a log in the Missouri River with his own cannon!

In the 1950s and '60s, before there was a Society for Historical Archaeology, Carlyle Smith was one of the very few archaeologists who could identify the firearms, gunparts, cartridges, and bullets found in historic sites like Kansas Monument or Like-a-Fishhook Village. He generously shared his knowledge with his colleagues. He was sought out time after time to identify these fragments. Sometimes these efforts resulted in publications with a by-line but more often than not are marked only by a brief acknowledgment of his contribution. The Society for Historical Archaeology particularly honors Carlyle Smith for these efforts which contributed to the early development of historical archaeology which he always has treated as a vital part of the discipline.

ROGER T. GRANGE, JR.

J. C. Harrington Medal in Historical Archaeology: Bert Salwen, 1990. Volume 24, Number 4 (1990): 4-8. By Joel I. Klein.

J.C. Harrington Medal in Historical Archaeology

BERT SALWEN 1990*

Bert Salwen was born on New York's Upper West Side in 1920 and grew up in suburban Queens during the Great Depression. Although his own family was comfortably off, he was very much aware of the suffering of the poor and underprivileged around him. This awareness was heightened by listening to conversations between his conservative Republican father and his liberal Democrat mother. His father was a school teacher, shop teacher, and volunteer basketball coach, as well as a businessman. His mother was active in Jewish self-help organizations like the Hadassah. Between them, they instilled in Bert, through their example, a concern for the rights of all individuals, regardless of their status.

Bert received a Bachelor of Science degree in mechanical engineering from Columbia University in 1941, and was immediately employed as a design engineer working on autogyros for helicopters, and later for small gliders for low level bombing raids. During the nine years Bert spent working in the

*Photograph by Ethan Salwen

aeronautics/defense industry he observed inequities in the way people were treated, and he became actively involved in civil rights and human rights activities. Eventually he was fired for union activities at the plant where he was working—an action which he fought before the National Labor Relations Board and eventually won.

By the early 1950s Bert was living in Trenton, driving an egg and poultry route to support his family, and still very much involved in fighting for social justice. When six black youths were framed for a murder, he joined in and helped win reprieves from the gas chamber. The case is still remembered as the Trenton Six. At the same time Bert ran for the office of Mercer County Freeholder and was responsible for what to this day is the only legal challenge of the Subversive Activities Control Act of 1950. Not all of Bert's activities were of the same level of importance. I can remember him speaking with equal enthusiasm of his attempts to organize the employees at the Trenton plant of the Trojan prophylactic company. All of this was going on at the height of the reign of Senator Joseph McCarthy, and as you can well imagine, his activities did not go down well with his neighbors. On one occasion a cross was burned on the lawn of his house. On another, several gunshots were fired through his kitchen windows. Worst of all, his eldest son Pete was ostracized by his peers.

When construction began on Levittown, Pennsylvania, Bert, who had been trained as a cabinetmaker by his father, went to get work as a carpenter. The employment test was very practical. Bert was asked to take a hammer, a saw, and a 2 × 4 and build a sawhorse. Bert was an engineer, and his father had taught night school shop classes and had been an amateur cabinetmaker. By watching what others were doing he managed to pass the test.

It was while living in Trenton and working in Levittown that Bert came, rather late in life, to archaeology. I have heard several versions of the story that ignited his interest, but the one I like the best—which I suspect has suffered some elaboration over the years—is as follows. His son Pete, who was studying the Leni Lenapi Indians in the fourth grade, developed a passionate desire to find some arrowheads like the ones in the museum. After some initial reluctance Bert agreed to drive Pete out into the nearby countryside where they found some farm fields and began to walk over them. They found some interesting looking pieces of stone and pottery and took them to the New Jersey State Museum where they left them with the secretary in the Bureau of Archeology and Ethnology. About a week later, Bert received a postcard from the museum. "Come pick up your rocks," it said.

Not one to be easily deterred from a task once he had set out to do it, Bert spent the next several weekends walking fields and bringing his finds to the museum. The result was always the same—a postcard with the same "come pick up your rocks" message. After this had gone on for some time, the secretary at the museum, who by this time had quite a collection of Salwen rocks in her desk drawer, took pity on Bert. On his next visit to the museum she said, "If you really want to find some good things, follow State Street until you see a big red barn, turn left, go one mile until you can see the river, walk into the field on the right, and dig down about 18 inches."

Bert followed her directions, which led to the heart of what was to become the Abbot Farm National Historic Landmark, walked around and collected some more pieces of stone which he promptly returned to the museum. A week later the postcard arrived. This time, however, the message was different. It read, "Please stop by the Museum to pick up the Salwen collection—one projectile point, a stemmed knife, and three fragments of Woodland pottery." This Bert promptly did. He remarked to the secretary that this stuff was really interesting and asked where one went to learn more about it. The secretary replied, "First, you have to study anthropology."

Within a relatively short time Bert had relocated to New York City and enrolled as a graduate student at Columbia. Under the tutelage of Duncan Strong and Ralph Solecki he began to develop the skills and knowledge of archaeological fieldwork and analysis that would serve him the rest of his life.

Everyone who has ever worked in the field with Bert knows him to have been the consummate field archaeologist. Bert's fieldwork experiences while at Columbia included a stint in South Dakota under the direction of Carlyle Smith, working for the Smithsonian River Basin Survey program. This was followed by a major expedition to the North Slope of Alaska with Ralph Solecki. As a trained engineer Bert understood the need for precision in recording data. However, Bert also possessed that sixth sense about where to dig.

I remember the first time I met him. I was a senior enrolled in a spring field class at CCNY. We were excavating at the Goodrich site on Staten Island. Sharing the site with us were field schools from Columbia and NYU. One afternoon, after work at the site had been going on for several weeks, I had occasion to walk over to the portion of the site where the NYU crew was digging. In the space of several minutes I saw more artifacts recovered than the Columbia and CCNY crews had found to date. Clearly, this was the guy who knew where the goodies were. I also noticed that the NYU trenches seemed to have walls that were just a little bit straighter.

Bert's sixth sense about archaeology manifested itself in other ways. He once confided to me that at a meeting of the Society for American Archaeology at Yale University, during a lunchtime walk through the New Haven green, he bent over and picked up a small-stemmed projectile point. Everyone accused him of having dropped it down his pants leg—something which, in later years, many a developer was facetiously to accuse him of doing at the construction sites.

Bert was nearing completion of work on his doctorate when an opportunity became available to accept a position in the Anthropology Department at Bennington College. Bert's Columbia classmate Morton Klass had been teaching at Bennington and one day received a message that some arrowheads had been found during the construction of a local highway. Prof. Klass along with some colleagues and as many students as they could find, none, students or faculty, with any experience in archaeology, ran out to the site. As Mort described it, "We dug—from early in the morning until late at night we dug—and we found absolutely nothing." The next day the highway came through. Later that week, Mort had occasion to talk to Bert, and he asked Bert what he should have done. Bert went on at great lengths about the laws that could have been called on and the procedures that should have been followed. After taking it all in, Mort said, "Bert—we dug all day long—all day long in the hot sun—and we found nothing—absolutely nothing. How can you stand it?" "Well it's like this," Bert answered. "You have to develop the right temperament. Let me tell you what I do. I drive around until I see a farm, a place that looks interesting. I stop and ask the farmer for permission to walk around. I spend a couple of hours walking around. Sometimes I make some surface finds, sometimes I see a place that I'd like to come back to, and sometimes I just have a pleasant walk in the sun." Mort was so impressed that he convinced Bennington to hire Bert to come to Vermont to solve all of that state's archaeological problems—which Bert did in short order.

About the same time, Bert completed his doctoral dissertation, which is still a basic reference on the relationship between sea level change and archaeological sites. In 1966 he returned to New York to join the new anthropology department at New York University. From the time he joined the department at NYU Bert was actively involved in its development and evolution. He served over the course of his career at various times as Acting Chairman and Director of Graduate Studies, and was a founder of NYU's joint Ph.D. program in history and historical archaeology. The latter was a source of great satisfaction to Bert. It represented the culmination of a long-term goal truly to integrate the disciplines and departments of history and anthropology in a form that was meaningful to both.

In his roles as teacher, advisor, and administrator, Bert always treated students, undergraduate and graduate, as people who had rights. Bert was always there whenever a student was having a problem with the university administration. He would never advocate or support breaking rules, but whenever possible he would find a way to bend them if the result was a fair resolution of a problem. Bert's concern for the professional development of his students is typified by the number of his publications with students as co-authors.

Although Bert's primary training was in cultural anthropology and prehistory, his interest in historical archaeology came naturally, developing out of his work at Fort Shantok, Connecticut, where he was studying the effects of European contact on Native American populations. The transition from prehistorian to prehistoric/historic archaeologist was natural for Bert. After all, as he put it, archaeology was "the study of behavior in the absence of the behavior." Whether one was studying a prehistoric site or a historic one, the ultimate goals were the same.

During his early years at NYU, Bert became involved in the excavation of a number of prehistoric and historic sites. One of these was in Kingston, New York. Working with the State Historic Sites Bureau, Bert found, under a sidewalk on Green Street, the remains of the 17th–century stockade constructed by Peter Stuyvesant. Think about it, under the sidewalk! From that time on, one of the things that could get him angrier than almost anything else was when someone would say, "There can't be anything left there—it's all been disturbed by modern construction."

It was at about the same time that Bert began to put his old political savvy to work for the cause of historic preservation. He was one of the founders, along with Marion White, of the New York Archaeological Council, the first of the state professional councils. It was not long before NYAC was involved in a lawsuit charging the New York State Historic Preservation Officer, the U.S. Environmental Protection Agency, and 50 some odd municipalities with violating the provisions of Section 106 of the National Historic Preservation Act.

The New York SHPO and the U.S. EPA were no match for two seasoned anthropologists who had challenged Joe McCarthy. An out-of-court settlement resulted in EPA agreeing to conduct cultural resources surveys on all their construction grant projects. It would no longer be sufficient for some local official to say the location of a proposed sewage treatment plant was all disturbed. The burden was now on that official to prove that it was, not on the archaeologist to prove that it was not. The result was that hundreds of surveys were undertaken, and, not incidentally, hundreds of archaeologists were ultimately employed.

Bert's belief that he could find evidence of past behavior in the most unlikely places never wavered. What area could be more disturbed than downtown Manhattan? Bert was up to the challenge, and even more important, he was willing to look for archaeology where no one else would—under sidewalks, in vacant lots, under paved streets and parking lots, even on sites where large office buildings had been demolished. The results include the Stadt Huys Site and the Telco Block, Hanover Square, and Sullivan Street sites. All of these became the focus of major excavations carried out by Bert's students, always under Bert's sometimes official, and some times unofficial, watchful eye. All too often Bert stayed in the background. A much published photo of the Stadt Huys excavations does not include Bert. Featured in the photo are Mayor Ed Koch, Principal Investigator Nan Rothschild, field director Diana Wall, and New York City Landmarks Commission chairman Kent Barwick. Bert was busy taking the picture. A large part of the reason that the subject of urban archaeology—not just archaeology in the city, but the archaeology of the city—is such a large part of our discipline today is because of the pioneering principles set forth by Bert Salwen.

Bert was always able to communicate his enthusiasm for archaeology and the need to protect cultural resources to everyone. His annual summer field schools are legend. They included—in addition to his many seasons at Fort Shantok and Shantok Cove, Connecticut—work at Fort Ninigret in Rhode Island; work at historic and prehistoric sites in the Delaware Valley; work with the National Trust for Historic Preservation at Drayton Hall, South Carolina, and Lyndhurst, New York; and work in Danville, Virginia, and Virginia City, Nevada.

Bert used to say that he did not publish enough. Perhaps he felt that way because he was busy making sure that there would be sites around for the rest of us to publish on. Throughout his career he worked to change the way our discipline functions in the political arena. As the president of the New York

Archaeological Council, the Professional Archaeologists of New York City, and our own Society; as a member of the boards of directors of the Society of Professional Archeologists, the American Society for Ethnohistory, the Association for Field Archaeology, and the Council on Northeast Historical Archaeology, Bert worked to ensure the passage and continued enforcement of laws to protect archaeological sites.

Bert was not content, however, with preaching to the converted. For more than 10 years he served as an official and unofficial consultant to numerous federal, state and local governmental agencies. One of the accomplishments of which he was especially proud was his development and participation in a Department of the Interior archaeological training course for non-archaeologists with responsibility for managing cultural resources. Ten years later, these courses are still being given throughout the United States. His work on developing archaeological standards for the Outer Continental Shelf environmental review program, and with the Office of Technology Assessment earned for Bert the annual Conservation Award of the American Society for Conservation Archaeology. Bert was that rare person among archaeologists. He was someone who spent as much time looking ahead to the future as he did looking back into the past.

Bert Salwen died suddenly on Christmas Day 1988. At the time he was enthusiastically making plans to attend the SHA annual meeting last year in Baltimore, because a number of his colleagues (all former students) were giving papers. This is part of Bert's professional and personal legacy—a population of professionally active archaeologists whose lives and careers were touched and, more often than we realize, shaped by Bert. The SHA has come a long way since Bert served as the Program Chairman for the third SHA annual meeting in Bethlehem, Pennsylvania—the first annual meeting with concurrent sessions, two. Historical archaeology is what it is today in large measure as a result of Bert.

JOEL I. KLEIN*

J. C. Harrington Medal in Historical Archaeology: Ivor Noël Hume, 1991. Volume 26, Number 2 (1992): 1-2. By William M. Kelso.

J. C. Harrington Medal in Historical Archaeology
IVOR NOËL HUMME 1991

The Society for Historical Archaeology awarded the 1991 J. C. Harrington Medal in Historical Archaeology to Ivor Noël Hume at the annual meeting of the Society for Historical Archaeology Conference on Historical and Underwater Archaeology in Richmond, Virginia.

"Noël" has had a long and distinguished career. He was born in London in 1927 and educated at Framlingham College, Suffolk, and St. Lawrence College, Kent. After serving in the Indian Army in 1944, from 1949–1957 he was the archaeologist responsible for the recovery of antiquities for the Guidhall Museum, as post-war London was rebuilt. At a time when salvage programs focused on Romano-British remains, Noël began to develop a keen interest and unique expertise in the artifacts from the "layers above," that is, objects dating from the post-medieval years that most everyone else in

England ignored. It was that special curatorial knowledge combined with his years of experience with British stratigraphic field methods that led the Colonial Williamsburg Foundation at Williamsburg, Virginia, to consult with him and where he soon became Chief Archaeologist (1957–1964). Noël had also become known for a special ability to communicate the discoveries and value of archaeology to the public, having published *Archaeology in Britain* (1953) and *Great Moments in Archaeology* (1957).

His long-standing and outstanding career at Colonial Williamsburg almost spanned four decades during which time he was also named Director of Archaeology, 1964–1983; Resident archaeologist, 1973–1986; and Foundation archaeologist, 1986–1988 (retired). In fact, his retirement is in name only as he has been currently engaged as Winthrop Rockefeller Archaeological Museum curator, 1988–1992. Historical and intense field research of the Anthony Hay shop, Wetherburn's Tavern, and the Public Hospital in Williamsburg stand out as examples of how well the two disciplines of history and archaeology can guide restoration and reconstruction work in a museum setting. It was also under the direction of Noël Hume that field studies of rural life at Carter's Grove turned up 17th-century Martin's Hundred which—owing to Noël's writing, public speaking and media talents, and the National Geographic Society—practically became another American household word. His publication of *Martin's Hundred* (1982) was, in fact, only the latest of a series of significant publications in historical archaeology which included: *Here Lies Virginia* (1963), *Historical Archaeology* (1975), *A Guide to Artifacts of Colonial America* (1970), and *Early English Delftware from London and Virginia* (1977). Indeed, the reference work *Guide to Artifacts* has become a bible for historical archaeologists working on British-American sites worldwide.

Noël Hume is also a Research Fellow for the Smithsonian Institution, and he received honorary degrees in Humane Letters from the University of Pennsylvania in 1976 and the College of William and Mary in 1983. He has always been active in the field of historic preservation, serving on Boards of Directors of the Virginia Historic Landmarks Commission and the Institute of Early American History and Culture.

But even beyond his extraordinarily successful career and many accomplishments in the field, it is especially fitting that the Society for Historical Archaeology's 1991 J. C. Harrington Medal in Historical Archaeology go to Noël; he was one of the leading forces in organizing the SHA in Dallas in 1967 and, in fact, first coined the term "Historical Archaeology," insisting on the "al" in "historical" and the "a" in "archaeology." If J. C. Harrington is the "father" of Historical Archaeology as Noël himself has often remarked, then Ivor Noël Hume surely must be its "godfather".

WILLIAM M. KELSO

J. C. Harrington Medal in Historical Archaeology
BERNARD L. FONTANA 1993

The Society for Historical Archaeology awarded the 1993 J.C. Harrington Medal in Historical Archaeology to Bernard L. Fontana at the annual meeting of the Society for Historical Archaeology Conference on Historical and Underwater Archaeology in Kansas City, Missouri.

Dr. Bernard L. (Bunny) Fontana has been honored for 35 years of contributions to historical archaeology and fields related to it. This is the second Harrington Medal award I have presented; the first was for Arthur Woodward whose biographical sketch was written by Dr. Fontana, and now the second is for Bunny himself. It is a genuine honor to be able to present a survey, albeit a brief one, of Dr. Fontana's

Historical Archaeology, 1993, 27(3):1–3.
Permission to reprint required.

long and distinguished career in anthropology, of which historical archaeology has been one small but significant part.

Fontana was born 7 January 1931 in Oakland, California, and spent his formative years there. In 1948 he entered the anthropology program at the University of California at Berkeley, where, among other things, he served as research assistant to Robert Heizer and Teaching Assistant to Charles Brant. He graduated with a B.A. in 1953. Upon completion of his degree, and with the pressing interests of Uncle Sam to be satisfied, he joined the Army for a two year stint. He spent most of his military career in Alaska. In 1955, with his service obligation completed, he applied for and was accepted into the Ph.D. program at the University of Arizona, Tucson, where he received his degree in 1960.

It is difficult to pinpoint exactly when Bunny first became interested in historical archaeology but it was while he was a graduate student. During this period, he and fellow graduate student William Robinson became interested in locating a site that contained evidence of continuous occupation from the prehistoric period into the historic. At that time, to close the "gap" between the prehistoric and the historic periods was a research problem pursued, or at least talked about, by several Southwestern archaeologists. Stimulated in this search during a graduate seminar, they began excavations at San Xavier del Bac south of Tucson in the Spring of 1958. As it turned out, they did not find the connection they sought, but rather late 18th-century remains. This effort was published by William Robinson in 1963 as "Excavations at San Xavier del Bac, 1958" in *The Kiva*.

As a result of the seminar and of the excavation project, Fontana as senior author, William Robinson, Charles Cormack, and Ernest Leavitt, Jr., published a book entitled *Papago Indian Pottery* in 1962. This study drew together for the first time virtually everything available about the subject to that time, while also providing a detailed description of contemporary Papago pottery-making. It has achieved the status of a regional classic and is still the only reliable source available about Papago (Tohono O'odam) pottery.

In part because of his desire to stay in Tucson after receiving his Ph.D. in 1960, he found a job as Field Historian at the University of Arizona Library, a position he held for two years.

About the time work on the Papago pottery book was completed, another excavation was begun at the Johnny Ward's Ranch site south of Tucson near the Mexican border. Informed that this site was in reality a Spanish mission, Fontana, John Greenleaf, and others began excavations on Sundays in late 1960 and completed them in early 1961. They quickly and disappointedly recognized that the site was a 19th-century ranch house, not a mission. With this discovery the site became somewhat less interesting to them, but all agreed that they had to complete the project. The resulting report, "Johnny Ward's Ranch," was published in *The Kiva* in 1962. Up to this time, no historic site other than those of the Spanish period had been excavated and reported in Arizona.

A thorough history of the site plus detailed technological studies of nails, tin cans, other metal, glass, and ceramics made the report a useful reference. The report was a genuine pioneering effort in that it was the first to take late 19th-century interchangeable parts-type artifacts and treat them seriously. At the same time, work on this project changed Fontana's way of looking at archaeology; and needless to say, it changed the views of many others as well. This report became very well known and was, and still is, widely cited. In fact, in certain historical archaeological circles it is probably as well known as the Bible.

In 1962, Fontana became Ethnologist at the Arizona State Museum, a position he held until 1977. During his tenure at the Museum, he continued his interest in historical archaeology. It was during these years that much of this work in ethnology, ethnohistory, and historical archaeology was accomplished.

The 1960s decade was a period of definition of historical archaeology, and Bunny was an active contributor to this dialogue. Among other articles, he wrote "On the Meaning of Historic Sites Archaeology" for *American Antiquity* in 1965; and in 1968 he wrote "Battles, Buckets, and Horseshoes: The Unrespectable in American Archaeology" for the *Keystone Folklore Quarterly*, which resulted from the important Smithsonian Conference on Historical Archaeology held in that year. Also in 1968 he described a collection of excavated artifacts from Magdalena, Sonora, Mexico, in a short article in *Historical Archaeology* entitled, "Bottles and History: The Case of Magdalena de Kino, Sonora, Mexico." This study represented the first time artifacts of the late 19th and early 20th centuries had been reported for a Mexican site.

In the Spring of 1964 Arthur Woodward taught the first historical archaeology class at the University of Arizona; Fontana sat in on the course and found his interest in the subject further excited. Later he created his own course which he taught from 1966 to 1972. This innovative and lively class, which had a humanistic orientation, served to expose students to the subject and encouraged several of them to make a career in the field.

In 1964 he and William Robinson planned an excavation at Guevavi, an 18th-century Spanish mission ruin near Nogales, Arizona. The project, carried out on winter weekends over a two-year period, resulted in a report written by Robinson in 1976 entitled "Mission Guevavi: Excavations in the Convento," published in *The Kiva*.

Dr. Fontana has served the Society for Historical Archaeology well over the years; he was involved with the founding of the Society and has been an enthusiastic promoter of it. He was elected to the Board of Directors at the 1967 meeting for a term that expired in 1971. That position was given up when he was elected in 1969 to serve as the Society's fourth president in 1970.

After about 1970 Bunny's direct involvement with historical archaeology was diverted more and more towards ethnohistory and ethnology, although historical archaeology continued to be of interest to him. Reasons for the diversion included a four-year stint as editor of the journal *Ethnohistory* (1969–1972), directing the Doris Duke American Indian Oral History Project (1967–1975), and co-founding the Southwest Mission Research Center in Tucson at the University of Arizona (1965). In 1967 he assumed responsibility for the Center's newsletter. Bunny packed this publication with information and made it eminently readable, a newsletter rarity. It increasingly demanded more and more of his available time; he resigned as editor in 1992.

In 1977 Bunny left the Arizona State Museum to once again become the Field Historian for the University Library and also to serve as Special Assistant to the President of the University.

He "retired" in 1990 but continued his historian duties at a 49 percent effort until 1992, when he actually retired from the University. It is ironic, perhaps, and it certainly says something about his abilities and skills, that he was hired twice for the same job, especially when we consider that he did not have a degree in history, and in fact other than a mandatory undergraduate class or two, never had formal exposure to the subject.

Finally, over the years many individuals have expressed interest in Dr. Fontana's nickname, "Bunny." It was given him at a very early age, and it has surivived for nearly 60 years. I am certain, that if it did not create at least one embarrassing situation for him, it did cause occasional confusion. At least one student's wife asked the question, "What do you mean you are going on a dig with 'Bunny'? And who is she anyway?"

JAMES E. AYRES

J. C. Harrington Medal in Historical Archaeology
KATHLEEN KIRK GILMORE 1995

Kathleen Kirk Gilmore was born in Altus, Oklahoma, moved to Tulsa as a child, and graduated from high school there. She got her first job while a junior in high school as switchboard operator at the Tulsa Bone and Joint Clinic, where she received the munificent salary, by Great Depression standards, of 25 cents an hour. Saving her money for a couple of years, she was barely able to finance her freshman year at the University of Tulsa.

But she needed to find a part-time job if she was going to continue at the university after that first year, and all the campus jobs at that time normally went to male students. Never one to be intimidated by protocol, Kathleen showed her feminist tendencies for the first time—but by no means for the last time—when she badgered the university library into giving her a job.

She had had a long-standing interest in archaeology, sparked by reading about the ''lost cities of the

Historical Archaeology, 1995, 29(2):1–3.
Permission to reprint required.

Maya'' at the age of 13; and when she discovered a collection of ethnographic artifacts on the library's fourth floor she was strongly tempted to major in archaeology. However, upon reflection, she decided that such a course was impractical because the cost was beyond her means. Besides, her main interest was American prehistory and the only brand of archaeology available at most universities at the time was classical. Furthermore, most jobs for female archaeologists were in museums and Kathleen wanted to get out and DIG.

So she followed a more practical course. With a $250 loan from the Tulsa Town Club she transferred to Oklahoma University where she earned a B.S. degree in the university's prestigious geology department.

But who would hire a female geologist with a B.S. degree when all the jobs for geologists were in the field, prospecting for likely formations, drilling wells, and the like? This was considered men's work where women would be out of place; and superstitious oilworkers considered it very bad luck for a female even to step on a derrick floor.

Stifling her feminist resentment, Kathleen learned to type and take shorthand, after which she landed a job in Tulsa with a small independent oil operator, where she got to do a bit of geology, drew maps, plotted well logs, and even was permitted to visit a drilling rig or two.

But her employer soon went broke, after which Kathleen found a job with the American Association of Petroleum Geologists as editorial assistant for their *Bulletin*. This was too tame for her, however, so she quit her job and moved to Houston—center of the oil business—to seek something better. After a month or so of pounding the pavement, she got several offers—mainly because she could type, the degree in geology being only of incidental importance. Still it was nice to have options to choose from, so she decided to accept an offer from the Superior Oil Company of California to type field reports in their Corpus Christi office.

After nine months in Corpus Christi, she was offered, and took, a job back in Houston with the Standard Oil Company of Kansas. In 1940 she married Bob Gilmore, a former classmate at the University of Tulsa, and a year later they moved to Dallas where Bob was hired as a petroleum engineer with DeGoyler and MacNaughton.

During World War II there was a demand for women to replace male geologists who were called to the war effort, so Kathleen went to work for Atlantic Oil Company, doing well log analysis and running the sample lab. With the end of the war and the birth of the first of four girls, she quit her job and devoted her energies to raising her daughters.

When an archaeology curriculum was initiated at Southern Methodist University in Dallas in 1964, Kathleen was one of the first in line to register. She earned her doctorate in anthropology there in 1973.

A major field project of the historical archaeology seminar that I taught at SMU in 1967 was an effort to locate the sites of the three San Xaviér missions, established and operated for a few years in the mid-18th century by Spanish missionaries in east-central Texas. After abandonment their exact locations had become lost to memory, but surviving documents indicated with virtual certainty that they were located a short distance from one another along modern-day Brushy Creek.

After putting together a model of what we should expect to find at the mission sites (18th-century Hispanic ceramics, etc.), we sallied forth to Brushy Creek and broke up into teams, each of which was assigned to examine likely places. When the teams regrouped several hours later, Kathleen produced a sack of sherds her team had found in a vegetable garden behind a farmhouse. Most of the sherds were recent, but among them were several good 18th-century Puebla Blue-on-white Majolica sherds—precisely the kind of indicators we were looking for.

Kathleen's excitement at finding evidence of a lost Spanish mission led to an abiding passion that she pursued over the years: establishing the locations of ''lost'' historic sites by discovering their archaeological remains.

In 1969, with funding from the Texas State Historical Commission, she got down to serious fieldwork at the San Xaviér missions. There she found archaeological evidence to verify the locations of all three missions and the associated military garrison. This project became the topic of her M.A. thesis.

In addition to the San Xaviér complex, she has worked with colleagues in their successful search for the San Sabá mission. Other Spanish Colonial sites in Texas where she has conducted fieldwork include Rosario Mission, Nasoni Mission, Amarillas Presidio, and Loreto Presidio, the latter built on the ruins of LaSalle's ill-fated Fort St. Louis of 1685.

Talk about your late bloomers! It would be hard to find anyone who has blossomed more spectacularly than Kathleen. In 1974 she became a research archaeologist and adjunct professor in the Institute of Applied Sciences at the University of North Texas in Denton, embarked on two decades of research and teaching, and earned national recognition as an authority on Spanish Colonial archaeology, as well as a leading light in Texas archaeology, both historical and prehistorical.

During her 16 years at North Texas—she took early retirement in 1990—Kathleen trained a generation of students both in the classroom and in the field. Her feminist instincts bore fruit during this time and she became a greatly admired role model to her female students, a number of whom were inspired to follow her example to successful careers in archaeology.

Kathleen has published extensively on her Spanish Colonial fieldwork and documentary research, including site reports on the San Xaviér, Rosario, Santa Cruz de San Sabá, and Dolores de los Ais missions; also on the Presidio San Luís de las Amarillas and Fort St. León. Her synthetic publications on French-Spanish-Indian interactions and on Caddoan prehistory are widely recognized as major contributions to the discipline.

In addition to her research and teaching, Kathleen has made substantial contributions to her profession through service to archaeological and historical associations. She has been president of the Society for Historical Archaeology, president of the Texas Archeological Society, and president of the Council of Texas Archaeologists. She has served on the Texas Board of Review, which reviews and recommends nominations to the National Register of Historic Places, and on the board of directors of the Texas Historical Foundation. She has been on too many committees to mention here.

Kathleen played an important role in the birth of the SHA in January 1967, when Arnold Pilling and I organized a meeting of 15 people we considered to be among the leading historical archaeologists to consider the possibility of establishing a society devoted to historical archaeology. SMU sponsored the meeting, and Kathleen, a graduate student at the time, made most of the local arrangements for the meeting, as well as for a concurrent conference at which two days of formal papers on historical archaeology were presented. It was at this conference that the SHA was founded. Especially memorable was a party that she and Bob hosted at a private club atop a Dallas skyscraper.

After retirement, Kathleen and Bob have divided their time between their homes in Dallas and Santa Fe, and in traveling the world. Kathleen also finds time to continue her research interests in Spanish Colonial archaeology.

It is altogether fitting that the signal honor of being the first woman to receive the prestigious J. C. Harrington medal falls to an outstanding researcher, teacher, and mentor, a staunch supporter of feminine rights, truly a lady and a scholar: Kathleen Kirk Gilmore.

EDWARD B. JELKS

J. C. Harrington Medal in Historical Archaeology
JAMES DEETZ 1997

In describing his own career, James Deetz picked the year 1948 as a place to begin, observing that it was not only the year he graduated from high school, but also the year he went off to Harvard College from his hometown of Cumberland, Maryland. He was, to use his words, "an early case of affirmative action, providing for the admission of hillbillies to Ivy League institutions." At Harvard, Jim changed from premed to anthropology in his freshman year, and embarked on a period of undergraduate and graduate training in anthropology at Harvard, interrupted only by four years of service in the United States Air Force during the Korean War.

Before he enlisted in the Air Force, Jim spent a long field season working for Don Lehmer salvaging sites slated to be drowned by the construction of the Oahe Dam on the Missouri River. After returning to Harvard to complete his undergraduate studies—he received his B.A. *cum laude* in 1957, Jim spent more time working on the River Basin Survey, notably at the Medicine Crow site, also in the Missouri River drainage. This project would form the basis of his Ph.D. dissertation, entitled *"An Archaeological Approach to Kinship Change in Eighteenth Century Arikara Culture,"* which he submitted in 1960. That fall he began his university teaching career with an appointment as Assistant Professor of Anthropology at the University of California at Santa Barbara.

The same year that Jim did dissertation fieldwork in South Dakota, 1958, he met Harry Hornblower II, the man who would introduce him to the archaeology of "the Pilgrims" and to the world of outdoor living history museums. Harry's family had donated the land to establish Plimoth Plantation, an outdoor reconstruction devoted to telling the story of the Pilgrims in the year 1627, just prior to their dispersal through what became Plymouth Colony. He needed someone to advise him on Native American exhibits, and he turned to his old friend John Otis Brew for advice. Brew, who was also Deetz's mentor at Harvard, put the two men together, forever changing the nature of Jim's career as an anthropological archaeologist, and profoundly altering the way that the Pilgrims would come to be understood by the American public in the years ahead.

J. O. Brew, a recognized pioneer in early historic sites archaeology, had known Harry Hornblower since the latter's undergraduate days just before World War II when Hornblower was a Harvard undergraduate, digging on the early house sites of Pilgrims in the Plymouth area along with fellow members of the Harvard Excavators Club. It was just such a site, the Joseph Howland house in Kingston, Massachusetts, that brought Jim Deetz into the field of North American colonial archaeology. His excavation there in 1959 was undertaken while he was completing his very innovative analysis of Arikara ceramics from the Medicine Crow site. At the same time he was using an IBM mainframe computer to discover "stylistic coherence" on over two thousand rim sherds from central South Dakota, Deetz was using a set of 1/64-in. drill bits to date the pipe stems that would help him establish an occupation sequence for the Howland site.

After Jim's faculty appointment at Santa Barbara he became a "bicoastal" archaeologist, dividing his summers between Plymouth, where he, wife Jody, and growing family stayed in a beach house owned by Plimoth Plantation, and Santa Barbara, where he worked on several excavations in Santa Barbara County, most notably at Mission La Purísima in Lompoc, California. The first half of the 1960s was very important to Deetz's career. He began friendships and collaborations with colleagues that in some cases still continue. He attracted a loyal and talented group of students at Santa Barbara, as well as earned a huge following through his very popular introductory courses. He also taught on several occasions at his alma mater, and it was during one of these teaching stints, in the summer of 1963, that Jim discovered gravestones in the Concord, Massachusetts, cemetery.

During this period, his doctoral dissertation on the Arikara, which was published by the University of Illinois Press as *The Dynamics of Stylistic Change in Arikara Ceramics*, caught the eye of a number of prehistorians who were doing similar kinds of studies in the American Southwest, trying to link principles of social organization with artifact patterning at the attribute level. Deetz's case study correlating ceramic design to residence patterns, and by inference to rules of descent and kinship terminology, was presented in a number of forums, including a very important symposium at the 1965 annual meeting of the American Anthropological Association in Denver. This symposium was later published in 1968 under the editorship of Lewis and Sally Binford as *New Perspectives in Archaeology,* a book that became required reading for "New Archaeologists" everywhere.

Through this and other unintended associations, Jim Deetz became for some a poster boy for "New Archaeology," though in presentation and content his work was in direct contrast to the stridency that characterized the archaeological rhetoric of the early 1960s. Mislabeled or not, Deetz joined a group of American archaeologists who became internationally known for their contributions to the general theory of anthropological archaeology, a reputation based on their apparent success at discovering patterning in archaeological data that reflected changes in domains of past human behavior of interest to students of ethnography and ethnology. Jim Deetz would soon add to his general reputation in anthropological archaeology when he and Ted Dethlefsen published their first account of the dynamics of stylistic change evident in gravestone design motifs from a large sample of New England cemeteries.

The first gravestone paper was published in 1967, the year that I met Jim Deetz for the first time, when he lectured on this subject to the introductory cultural anthropology course I was taking at Brown. Another of my teachers, Doug Anderson, had brought Deetz to my attention a year before, when the deal to bring him from Santa Barbara to Brown had been negotiated. I had never heard of James Deetz and, always having been a literal learner, I immediately wanted to know if he was mentioned in our textbook, the first volume of Gordon Willey's (1966) *An Introduction to American Archaeology*. Deetz was nowhere to be found in the text or bibliography. As a first-semester sophomore just deciding to major in anthropology, I had yet to understand the reasons for Doug Anderson's excitement. Deetz's arrival the next academic year as a professor in Brown's then-Department of Sociology and Anthropology quickly changed all that, marking the beginning of an important new chapter in his career, and a significant one for the development of the field.

The next fall, Deetz offered the introductory course in human prehistory for the first time at Brown, a course that would become one of the largest and most popular lecture courses offered at the school in that period. We used his newly-published introductory text, *Invitation to Archaeology*, one of the most innovative books of its kind ever published. In addition to using materials from the various projects he had been working on since 1958 to explain and illustrate basic concepts and techniques in archaeology, Jim developed an explicit linguistic model for artifact manufacture and use that formalized his thinking about what he termed "the mental template." In this chapter, written in 1966, Deetz anticipated his adoption of a more explicit structuralist approach to material culture in the early 1970s. These ideas began to crystallize as he developed a new course, *American Material Culture*, which he first offered in the fall of 1971, but his pursuit of this approach had received a major boost two years before when he was introduced to Henry Glassie, a folklorist who had himself just turned to structuralism as a model for understanding folk material culture.

It is fair to say that the friendship and collaboration between Deetz and Glassie was one of the major influences on the development of material culture theory during this period. Their ideas had a substantial impact on archaeological theory in general, on historical archaeology, and on the research of a range of scholars engaged in the new specialty of material culture studies. Although Deetz introduced some explicitly structuralist ideas such as "the Georgian mindset" in his 1972 analysis of ceramics and foodways in the area of Plymouth Colony, his book, *In Small Things Forgotten: The Archaeology of Early American Life*, published in 1977, is a culmination of his thinking and teaching during the early 1970s. It fully develops his structuralist interpretation of American material culture, which as he acknowledges owes much to the work of Glassie.

The same year that *In Small Things Forgotten* was published, Deetz left Brown and spent a year teaching at the College of William and Mary. He never returned to his teaching position at Brown, but spent the summer of 1978 putting his affairs in order at Plimoth Plantation. In late August of that year, he and his family returned to California, where Jim joined the faculty in the Department of Anthropology at the University of California at Berkeley. This move brought to a close a very productive decade at Plimoth Plantation, where Deetz had made so many fundamental changes in the way that the lives of the Pilgrims were interpreted to the public. As Assistant Director between 1967 and 1978, Deetz had transformed Plimoth Plantation from a mannequin-furnished commemoration of the *Mayflower* passengers to a vibrant living history museum replete with accurately-costumed character interpreters engaged in the nitty-gritty of daily life. What is more, he extended this approach to the interpretation of the local Native Americans, the Wampanoags, with their blessing and assistance. Very soon after it was developed, the Indian village at Plimoth Plantation was staffed and administered by local Native Americans, one of the first such programs of its kind in the United States.

When he departed for California, Deetz also left behind the fledgling *Parting Ways Museum of African American Ethnohistory*, an organization devoted to interpreting a small settlement of former slaves, freed after their service in the Revolutionary War and granted nearly one hundred acres of land on the outskirts of Plymouth. Excavations of this community began in the summer of 1975, with a crew made up of local African-American kids who were discovering their heritage with support from a bicentennial grant administered by the town. Although the museum never materialized, this project did much to advance the cause of African-American archaeology as an important area of research within historical archaeology, research that in this case was pursued expressly for the purpose of engaging the local minority community in the interpretation of its own past. Now such programs are commonplace, but Jim Deetz began promoting these efforts more than 25 years ago, long before "social responsibility" and "public outreach" became widely shared imperatives among the archaeological profession.

In leaving New England, Deetz also ended an important chapter for many of us who had been his graduate students at Brown. Although he would remain our advisor and mentor, the program in historical archaeology at Brown would never be the same. But he very quickly attracted a number of new Ph.D. students, including several recruited from the undergraduate program in anthropology at Cal, and others who followed him west. He began to train this new crop of students primarily through research at Flowerdew Hundred farm in Prince George County, Virginia, a property with which he had become acquainted during his year as a visiting professor at William and Mary. He also turned in earnest to projects that took advantage of the interface between historical archaeology and folklife studies. Closest to Berkeley was his multiyear project at the abandoned coal-mining town of Somersville, California. Somewhat further away, Jim worked with a team from the American Folklife Center to document traditional lifeways in Paradise Valley, Nevada. Twenty years after his first job in the University of California system, Jim Deetz was once again dividing his research time between the two coasts.

Soon, however, he went international, expanding his active research territory to include South Africa, which he first visited in 1984. For the remainder of the 1980s, Deetz, brought graduate and undergraduate students from Berkeley to the Eastern Cape, where they worked on a number of research projects in cooperation with various South African colleagues. During this same period, he kept his summer program at Flowerdew Hundred active as well, running a series of very popular summer institutes for college teachers and a Cal field school. A number of Ph.D. dissertations have been produced from this work, and Deetz himself produced a published synthesis of his work at Flowerdew in 1993. This book, like others he has done, brought together many of the ideas he had been developing through his teaching and other writing in the prior decade.

Jim Deetz had one more cross-country move to make. In the fall of 1993, he accepted an endowed chair at the University of Virginia, leaving some students behind and bringing others with him as he had done when he moved to Berkeley from Brown 15 years earlier. Shortly after his arrival in Charlottesville, Deetz undertook a major revision of his classic *In Small Things Forgotten*, one which incorporated some of the most significant results of his research in the Chesapeake, notably his ideas about African-American cultural development in the region. At Virginia, Jim has again demonstrated his extraordinary skills as a teacher. His undergraduate offerings have attracted a large following, and he has assembled an outstanding group of doctoral students.

Still, Jim Deetz has reached that stage in his career where he is entitled to reflect on his accomplishments and wonder how others in the profession perceive him. Several years ago he remarked that "after 30 years in the business, I have first been a culture historian, then a New Archaeologist, then a structuralist, and now apparently, a passionate post-structuralist. The fact is, I am not doing things that differently from the way I did in the '60s. I don't think I have changed at all; the transformations have been in the way my work has been perceived by others. Fine! What goes around comes around, but I cannot help but wonder what kind of an archaeologist I will be in the year 2000."

The millennium is still a few years away, but The Society for Historical Archaeology has gone on the record with its collective perception of Jim Deetz, awarding him the 1997 J. C. Harrington Medal, an honor richly deserved by a scholar and teacher who has done more than any other single member of his generation to make historical archaeology a credible pursuit within the discipline of anthropology.

Aside from being a Harrington Medal winner, what kind of archaeologist will Jim Deetz be in the year 2000? It is hard to say. He has recently indicated that his digging days are over, but he is a long way from retirement. Jim has much to look forward to, both professionally and personally. The nine children he and Jody raised have produced 17 grandchildren. Jim and his second wife, Trish Scott, are hard at work on a new book, which interestingly enough takes him back to Plymouth to renew research on probate records he began over 30 years ago. Most importantly, Jim Deetz still has a great group of graduate students, who like those before them will make their contributions to the field in any number of ways. This will certainly be one of his most important legacies, and I know I speak for all of his students, past, present, and future, when I say, "Congratulations, Jim Deetz, and thank you for all that you have done and will do for us and for the discipline of anthropological archaeology."

Marley Brown III

J. C. Harrington Medal in Historical Archaeology: George F. Bass, 1999. Volume 33, Number 4 (1999): 1-5. By Kevin J. Crisman.

J. C. Harrington Medal in Historical Archaeology

George F. Bass 1999

George F. Bass may be unique among the distinguished archaeologists who have been awarded the J. C. Harrington Medal in Historical Archaeology by The Society for Historical Archaeology. He began his career over forty years ago working on Bronze and Iron Age sites in the eastern Mediterranean. Since that time George has expanded his research to include sites dating to the classical and medieval periods, but with the exception of brief forays into the waters of the Caribbean and North America, he has remained an Old World archaeologist working on sites pre-dating the renaissance. Even if his own excavations have had little to do with the early-modern period, George Bass has nevertheless had a profound impact on the field of historical archaeology, and more particularly its sub-field in the Americas, underwater or nautical archaeology. This Harrington medal honors George for his pioneering work in shipwreck archaeology, for his tireless efforts to promote professional, ethical underwater archaeology around the world, and for his role in creating educational and research institutions that have advanced the study of seafaring in the historical period.

At first glance George's formative years would appear to give little hint of what the future held in store for him. He was born in South Carolina, the son and grandson of professors of English literature. Growing up as he did in a household filled with great books (and he had read of all of Shakespeare's works by the time he was 14), it is perhaps no surprise that when he enrolled at Johns Hopkins University in Baltimore, Maryland in the fall of 1950 he chose to major in English literature. Following in the footsteps of his father and grandfather, George envisioned a career as a professor of English literature at a college or university.

Other influences were at work during his youth, however, influences which ultimately decided his choice of professions. One of these was a fascination with the water and exploring what lies beneath it. This interest led George and his brother to attempt to build a submarine out of wood; luckily for all concerned, this craft was never completed and launched. Another early influence was his uncle Dr. Robert Wauchope, a professor of archaeology who served as the head of the Middle American Research Institute at Tulane University. Wauchope conducted extensive excavations of Mayan sites, appeared in *National Geographic*, and, according to George, seemed to live an adventurous and exotic life seeking out traces of ancient civilizations in the jungles of Central America. Finally, during a break from university classes in the spring of 1952, George and several of his university friends took an informal tour of classical-period archaeological sites in Italy and Sicily, an excursion that awakened a strong interest in the ancient civilizations of the Mediterranean.

Infected by the archaeology bug, George abandoned English literature after graduating from Johns Hopkins in 1955 and spent the next two years attending the American School of Classical Studies in Athens, where he participated in excavations at Lerna, a Bronze Age site in Greece and at Gordion, an iron age site in Turkey. Lerna and Gordion sealed his decision to become a classical archaeologist. After two years of service as a lieutenant in the United States Army, George began Ph.D. studies in Classical Archaeology under Dr. Rodney Young at the University of Pennsylvania in 1959.

That first year at the University of Pennsylvania was pivotal, both for George and for the development of underwater archaeology as a discipline. By 1959 scuba equipment had been around for over a decade and a half, diving was becoming an ever-more-popular sport, and the underwater world was now more accessible to exploration than ever before. Scuba technology had opened up a vast new arena for archaeological research, particularly for the study of shipwrecks, but professional archaeologists in the Old World and the New World had yet to attempt an underwater excavation that matched the professional standards of a land excavation. Some even doubted that it could be done. In 1959 journalist Peter Throckmorton approached Rodney Young at the University of Pennsylvania with news of an exciting underwater discovery he had made that summer: the wreck of a late Bronze Age vessel sunk off the coast of Turkey, near Cape Gelidonya. Dr. Young recognized the potential of the wreck to shed light on ancient seafaring and trade, and asked his new graduate student if he would be willing to learn how to dive and then direct the excavation. George agreed to take on the project and the rest, as they say, is history.

The excavation of the Bronze Age wreck at Cape Gelidonya in 1960 set the example for future underwater archaeological research: the digging and recording was carried out by diving archaeologists rather than professional divers, the locations of all finds were carefully plotted on the seabed prior to removal, and after careful analysis of the site the results were widely published in professional journals. A detailed final report was presented in the December 1967 volume of the *Transactions of the American Philosophical Society*. The Cape Gelidonya project proved that there was no reason why underwater sites should not be excavated using the same rigorous archaeological standards applied to terrestrial sites. It also demonstrated that shipwrecks can provide unique perspectives on seafaring practices, maritime trade, and naval warfare, information that might not be available from any other source. For those of us here in 1999, nearly forty years after Cape Gelidonya, the archaeological worth of shipwrecks seems self-evident, but in 1960 this was a new and unproven concept.

The 1960s saw George complete his Ph.D. and become a tenured professor in the Classical Archaeology Department at the University of Pennsylvania and an associate curator in the University Museum. He built upon his earlier success at Cape Gelidonya by directing a series of ambitious projects in Turkish waters, including shipwreck surveys and the excavations of two wrecks at Yassi Ada (Flat Island), one of them dating to the 7th century and the other to the 4th century A.D. This work served as a training ground for a number of scholars who went on to distinguished careers in nautical archaeology, including Frederick Van Doorninck, David Owen, Cynthia Eiseman, and Stuart Swiny. The work in Turkey in the 1960s also provided the opportunity to invent and refine the tools and techniques which have since become commonplace in underwater surveys and excavations.

George's other accomplishments during this time include overseeing the building of the world's first private research submarine, the *Asherah*, and directing the first side-scan sonar survey to locate an ancient wreck in the Mediterranean.

One of George's defining characteristics as an archaeologist is his commitment to publishing the results of his work in both scholarly and popular journals, and thereby share the underwater discoveries with as wide an audience as possible. He has also published a series of books that have introduced the discipline of nautical or underwater archaeology to other scholars and to the public. The first book of this type, published in 1966, was entitled *Archaeology Under Water*, and was produced by Praeger as part of the Ancient Peoples and Places series. Six years later, in 1972, George edited *A History of Seafaring Based on Underwater Archaeology*, a magnificent, color-illustrated volume published by Thames and Hudson of London and Walker and Company of New York. *A History of Seafaring* subsequently appeared in French, German, Italian, Dutch, and Swedish editions. In these two books George's holistic approach to the study of seafaring is apparent: both discuss wrecks, harbors, and submerged archaeological finds from every period and geographical locale, and four of the twelve chapters in *A History of Seafaring* are devoted to wrecks of the post-medieval period.

In the 1970s George made two decisions that would directly advance the study of shipwrecks and submerged sites. The first of these was his decision in 1973 to give up the tenured faculty position at the University of Pennsylvania and to strike out on his own by creating a non-profit institution devoted to the support of research in nautical archaeology. Initially known as the *American Institute of Nautical Archaeology*, the organization's name was subsequently shortened to the *Institute of Nautical Archaeology* (INA). The mission of the institute is extraordinarily open ended. Quite simply, its goal is to seek out significant examples of shipwrecks from every century of human history, to study them, and publish the results and thereby increase our understanding of seafaring through the ages and its effect on the development of cultures. Ancient shipwrecks in Turkish waters have continued to be a focal point of INA research, but since its formation the institute has sought to carry out its wider mission by sponsoring archaeological projects around the world.

The second key decision came in 1976. By that time George was convinced that if the institute were to achieve its goals it would not only have to carry out its research mission but also take an active role in training future generations of nautical archaeologists. This meant joining in a partnership with a major university. In 1976 George accepted an offer from Texas A&M University in College Station, Texas to start a nautical archaeology graduate program within the Anthropology Department. The program initially offered only a Master's degree, but expanded to include a doctoral degree in 1988. Faculty members originally consisted of George Bass, Frederick Van Doorninck, and J. Richard Steffy; in 1978 Donny L. Hamilton joined the Nautical Program to teach conservation and historical archaeology. Over time the faculty has expanded, and now consists of seven professors, three of whom have specialized in the study of historical-period sites.

The Institute of Nautical Archaeology celebrated its 25th anniversary last year and the Nautical Archaeology Program at Texas A&M has been in existence for 23 years. The word "symbiotic" probably best describes the relationship between the two entities. The academic program offers students laboratory courses in artifact conservation, ship construction and reconstruction, as well as seminars that examine developments in seafaring in the ancient Mediterranean, medieval Europe, and the post-medieval world. The INA provides students with fieldwork opportunities, and in turn has greatly benefitted from student participation in the research and publication of its results. Graduates of the Texas A&M Nautical Program can be found working in maritime museums, in archaeological research institutions, in contract archaeology companies, in state- and national-level archaeological management offices, and as faculty at universities.

The Institute of Nautical Archaeology has continued to study bronze age, classical, and medieval sites in Turkey, and the institute recently expanded its Turkish headquarters with the construction of an administrative and research complex in Bodrum. Of more relevance to the J. C. Harrington medal, however, is the work that the institute and the nautical archaeology program have carried out on historical-period wrecks and submerged sites in the Americas and elsewhere around the world. These projects have taken many forms, including full-scale excavations, test excavations, surveys, and collaborative efforts with other research institutions. The following is a summary of some of the research that has taken place.

The Institute of Nautical Archaeology's involvement in Central America and the West Indies has been quite extensive over the past two decades. In 1979 George and nautical student Donald Keith taught a one-month course in nautical archaeology at the University of Mexico, which led to a two-year collaborative study with the Mexican Department of Underwater Archaeology on a 16th-century wreck at Cayo Nuevo in the Bay of Campeche. At the same time nautical archaeology graduate student Roger Smith carried out an extensive survey for shipwrecks in the Cayman Islands. Other I.N.A. surveys in the Caribbean included a search for wrecks on Pedro Bank off the south coast of Jamaica and a multi-year search for the remains of two caravels beached on the north coast of Jamaica by Columbus during his fourth and final voyage to the New World.

In 1981 Dr. Donny Hamilton commenced a ten-year program of excavation and research on the remains of Port Royal, Jamaica, the notorious port of pirates which sank beneath the sea during an violent earthquake in June of 1692. It would be no exaggeration to say that Port Royal is among the most significant English colonial sites yet excavated in the western hemisphere. Students participating in Hamilton's Texas A&M field schools uncovered the floors and fallen walls of numerous buildings, along with thousands of objects which were part of the everyday lives of Port Royal's inhabitants. Conservation and analysis of the finds continues at Texas A&M, but thus far the site has provided material for over a dozen theses and dissertations.

A second major research initiative in the 1980s looked at the nature of ships and seafaring during the early stages of European exploration of the New World. Between 1982 and 1983 Don Keith and several associates excavated the Molasses Reef Wreck in the Turks and Caicos Islands, a vessel that is among the earliest known examples of a 16th-century European ship of discovery and colonization. This wreck proved to be the catalyst for the formation of a research team, composed principally of Texas A&M Nautical Program students, to comb through Spanish archives and to examine other examples of 16th-century vessels. Among its many accomplishments the team carried out test excavations of the Highborn Key Wreck in the Bahamas and conducted surveys in Panama.

The Institute of Nautical Archaeology researchers have been active in North America over the past quarter century as well. During the era of the American bicentennial in the 1970s three Revolutionary War wrecks were investigated in INA-sponsored projects, including the American privateer *Defense* in Penobscot Bay, Maine, and the Cornwallis Cave Wreck and the Royal Navy frigate *Charon* at Yorktown, Virginia. Other North American projects have included the excavation and study of a late 18th-century sloop in South Carolina, the Clydesdale Plantation Vessel, an endeavor directed by Dr. Frederick Hocker, and a collaborative effort with Dr. Paul Johnston of the Smithsonian Institution to record the remains of the 19th-century propeller-driven steamship *Indiana* in Lake Superior. Since 1990 Lake Champlain has been a focus of institute research, and here Nautical Program field school students have documented the remains of eleven wrecks including a unique horse-propelled ferry boat, an intact 19th-century schooner, and two War of 1812-era naval vessels.

Institute of Nautical Archaeology work on post-medieval wrecks has not been limited to the western hemisphere. The wreck of a late 17th-century Portuguese frigate, the *Santo Antonio de Tanna* was excavated by staff member Robin Piercy at Mombasa, Kenya between 1975 and 1980. More recently, nautical program alumni Dr. Cheryl Ward and Douglas Haldane have completed their investigation of the remains of an 18th-century Islamic merchant vessel at Sadana Island, Egypt. The institute is also currently engaged in a multi-year shipwreck survey in the Azores in collaboration with Portuguese nautical archaeologists.

As this review of projects suggests, the Institute of Nautical Archaeology and the Nautical Archaeology Program at Texas A&M have busy over the last quarter century. If George has not been directly involved in the study of historical-period shipwrecks in recent years, he has nevertheless continued to take a leading role in promoting nautical archaeology in the Americas. In 1983 he recognized that while much research had been carried out on shipwrecks of the western hemisphere, there was no single, comprehensive book on the subject. He set out to correct this deficiency by editing *Ships and Shipwrecks of the Americas*, a book published by Thames and Hudson in 1988. Ten years after publication this book is still the best single source on the archaeology of seafaring in the Americas, and, I might add, it was recently re-issued in a paperback edition. George has also been active in the protection of shipwrecks in the United States, by writing journal articles that have attempted to put the treasure-hunting versus archaeology debate in perspective and by testifying before United States House and Senate committees during the debate over the passage of the Shipwreck Protection Act.

George remains as committed to the advancement of nautical archaeology today as when he began his work at Cape Gelidonya nearly forty years ago. He continues to teach graduate and undergraduate classes at Texas A&M University, and is serving his second term as president of the Institute of Nautical Archaeology. Even as he is completing the final publication on a 10th-century A.D. Islamic wreck he is organizing the institute's next excavation in Turkey, a 5th-century B.C. merchant vessel.

It is safe to say that no other single person has had as much influence on the development of the field of nautical archaeology as George F. Bass. For his efforts to promote professional, and ethical archaeological research, his devotion to students, his dedication to publishing and his encouragement to others to publish, and for his philosophy that all shipwreck sites, whether ancient, medieval, or early modern, have something to tell us about the human seafaring past, George is hereby honored by his colleagues in The Society for Historical Archaeology.

Kevin J. Crisman

J. C. Harrington Medal in Historical Archaeology

Roderick Sprague 2000

Roderick Sprague was born in Albany, Oregon, on 18 February 1933, and spent the first eight years of his life in Corvallis. His father was a plant pathologist for the U.S. Department of Agriculture attached to the Department of Botany at Oregon State College (now University). Rick's mother had been a school teacher from the age of 18, but stopped teaching for 20 years while she raised Rick and his two older sisters. She later returned to school and received a Master's in counseling.

Shortly before the start of World War II, the family moved to Mandan, North Dakota, his father having been transferred to the Northern Great Plains Experiment Station. North Dakota was a good place to be during the war because it was essentially unaffected. Rick's father was not only too old to get drafted, but he was classified as being in an essential job so could not volunteer.

During the war, meat (among other things) was rationed and shotgun shells were completely unavailable. The experiment station, however, had problems with ringneck pheasants getting into the experimental wheat plots so Rick's dad was issued shotgun shells to keep their numbers down. Rick hates pheasant meat to this day!

Historical Archaeology, 2000, 34(4):1—6.
Permission to reprint required.

During his grade-school days, Rick often hitchhiked to the capitol, Bismarck, which was only six miles away. There he would visit the State Historical Museum with its extensive collections of Indian and pioneer artifacts. Even closer to Mandan was the state (now national) park that included Fort Lincoln from whence Custer left on his ill-fated last adventure, Fort McKeen, a later military post, and the Mandan Indian Slant village. George Will was excavating at the Native site and Rick would ride his bike out to it and watch them excavate by the hour. Rick's first collecting was undertaken in a reasonably scientific manner with maps and artifact labels in the dump of Fort McKeen. It is interesting to note that even then his interest was in historical-period materials.

Rick's interest in the local Indians was more with the living. Mandan was the division point on the Northern Pacific Railroad, hence trains stopped here longer than at most stations while they changed crews and let people off to eat non-dining-car food. To take advantage of this long stop, the local Mandan group met every passenger train and danced in formal dress. They collected coins from the crowd, especially from the troop trains during the war. After several years of watching as often as he could, the dancers knew Rick and even occasionally talked to him. This experience clearly affected his relationships with other tribes in later years. He learned to watch and listen without talking or intruding into their lives and learned to appreciate their culture and problems.

In 1947, the family moved back West when Rick's dad was offered a research and teaching job at Washington State College (now University) in Pullman, Washington. Rick attended Pullman High where he filled out a form for Washington State in which they asked for his interests. He put down anthropology and, as a freshman, he got Richard D. Daugherty as an advisor. Daugherty totally ignored Rick's intended major of agricultural engineering and kept putting him into classes which eventually led to a major in anthropology. The classes taught by the two social anthropologists, Allan H. Smith and William W. Elmendorf (both deceased in the last year), turned Rick on to ethnography.

Rick went on his first dig at McGregor Cave in the summer of 1952 with Daugherty and five other male students. This site was within a mile of the later and more-famous Marmes rockshelter. The cave was filled with roof fall and perishables, mostly cordage and worn-out mats used to line storage pits. It was a horrible experience and should have turned off anyone even thinking about archaeology. It was during a field trip that summer that Rick first met Luther Cressman, one of the Northwest's great anthropologists (and Margaret Mead's first husband). During the rest of his undergraduate career, Rick continued to work summers on a farm where he drove a crawler tractor and bucked bales, two reasons why his back is so bad today.

After graduating from WSC (now WSU), Rick worked on his Master's degree. WSC did not have a Master's in anthropology so he started in sociology with the guarantee that it would be anthropological in nature. In spite of making satisfactory progress on his graduate degree and being married, Rick was drafted into the Army at the age of 26 and sent to Fort Carson, Colorado, in December. Rick's second eight weeks of training was at Fort Bliss (a real misnomer) where, as Honor Graduate (a distinction he did not even know existed until five minutes before graduation), he was kept on post for the remainder of his two years. Texas Western College (now University of Texas, El Paso) provided some archaeological collections to see and Rick enjoyed his off-duty time in Juarez drinking cheap–but very good–beer.

Upon returning to Pullman, Sprague renewed his degree at Washington State University which could now be in anthropology as this degree had been instituted. After a year of additional class work and the writing of a thesis, T. Stell Newman and Rick received the first two Master's in anthropology presented by WSU. Again, it is interesting to note that Stell and Rick both went into historical archaeology. Stell's life and career were cut short by an automobile accident while working as an NPS archaeologist in the Pacific islands.

Rick spent the next year working to earn enough money to go on for a Ph.D. His job at the university was figuring chi squares on a rotary calculator. He spent a year doing what now takes about ten minutes on a computer. By then Rick's first son, Roderick IV, had been born. That summer Sprague field directed a burial dig on a Snake River island. All of the remains of a ranch on the island were going to be flooded so he spent his evenings completely taking apart a farm wagon and other equipment to familiarize myself with the various metal parts. After that summer, Rick headed to Tucson to enroll in the University of Arizona doctoral program. Rick now gets some pleasure out of the fact that Berkeley and U of A offered him assistantships while the University of New Mexico, with only a post card, totally rejected the identical application.

Sprague had gone to U of A largely because he wanted to work with Edward Spicer in the area of culture change. This turned out to be a less-than-rewarding experience but Emil Haury was so supportive and easy to work with that Rick went back into archaeology. Other important people at Arizona in anthropology besides Haury were Fred Hulse, Ed Dozier, Robert Hackenberg, and Harry Getty (all deceased except Hackenberg who recently retired from the University of Colorado, Boulder). Within the Tree-Ring Laboratory, Bryant Bannister was also very supportive.

Historical archaeology was not held in high esteem at Arizona. Bunny Fontana, Arizona State Museum Ethnologist, was in the process of finishing his Johnny Wards Ranch report and Rick and he often discussed specific artifacts. Fellow graduate student Jim Ayres also shared an interest in historical archaeology but a friendship did not develop until about 1963 when they both took Arthur Woodward's Historical Archaeology course, the first time he taught it. Several future members of the SHA took that class.

After four years of course work, well beyond what was required to graduate, Rick returned to WSU to direct the excavation of 260 Palus Indian burials for the Corps of Engineers. This dig served as part of Sprague's dissertation along with archaeological, ethnohistorical, and ethnographic descriptions of Plateau burial practice, plus a review of burial terminology and Palus ethnography. Rick finished and defended his dissertation at the U of A in 1967. By then Haury had retired and Ray Thompson took over as his chairman. At this time Rick's only daughter, Kathy, was born.

Sprague took over operation of the WSU salvage program on the Snake River the next year. This involved Park Service funds distributed through Paul Schumacher, another good friend and an old-time historical archaeologist. All of the equipment that had been built up by the salvage program over the years was suddenly shifted to a non-salvage program. This, along with Rick still being treated as a graduate student by his fellow faculty, resulted in his deciding to move on. He and another young and "too aggressive" member of the department, Deward Walker, moved as a team nine miles away to the University of Idaho in Moscow in the fall of 1967.

At Idaho they were in a huge and unmanageable department of Social Science along with sociology, political science, history, and strangely, philosophy. After a year, they had convinced the dean to separate off anthropology along with sociology. After one semester as chairman, Walker quit and left Sprague as chair. Sprague agreed to take it for the rest of the year and finally got rid of the job 12½ years later. Walker moved to the University of Colorado the following year and Rick started the long process of hiring people to fill a department that had not benefited from the growth typical of other land grant universities in the post-war salvage archaeology period.

One of the first decisions was to emphasize historical archaeology because WSU, only nine miles away, did not. The second decision of Walker and Sprague was to not maintain a collection of American Indian skeletal material. These two decisions determined the direction of the department for the next thirty years.

The department had an agreement with the Nez Perce Tribe that was expanded eventually to all Plateau tribes within the United States that if any Native skeletal material were found, it would be analyzed within six months and then returned to the tribe for reburial. In that way they would not have to bother with burials. This was a serious miscalculation as it resulted in their being called in any time skeletal material was found because they did what the tribes wanted. It was NAGPRA 25 years before NAGPRA and a lot faster and more efficient. This program also resulted in a dramatic increase in the number of osteometric analyses and several theses based on these data. The reburial projects have become smaller with time but they still provided weekend work for students and continue to the present.

The first summer at Idaho, Rick did not have a field school program established so through his friendship with Jervis Swannack from the University of Arizona he was asked to direct the new Parks Canada excavations at the Roma site on Prince Edward Island. This introduced Rick to a whole group of Parks Canada researchers including John Rick, Pierre Nadon, and DiAnn Herst.

For many years, the only historical archaeology being done in the Northwest below the international border was done by the University of Idaho. Long-time programs such as the San Juan Island, Fort Colvile, and Spalding/Fort Lapwai programs all began in 1970. The San Juan Island, Washington, project was a NPS program that utilized a field-school environment for the archaeology required to develop the new park. Work at English Camp, American Camp, San Juan Town, and the Hudson's Bay Bellevue Farm trained over 150 students and provided material for over a dozen theses. In addition to theses, there were annual reports covering nine years and a final summary report which only covered about half of the data collected, but was still over 1000 pages long. During this time period Rick became single again but often had his two children with him during the summer field season.

The fifth year of the project, which was the second year of work at American Camp, Rick returned to the island married to his former field lab director, Linda Ferguson. Linda wrote the annual artifact summaries for several years and analyzed the nine years of ceramics for her thesis. Those last several summers on San Juan Island with Linda were the best field seasons of Rick's career.

The Lake Roosevelt project was in a less idyllic place and time of year. The cold, early spring was when the draw downs occurred and the Columbia River in this area was filled with Canadian filth. The work was a mixture of prehistoric and historic work at old HBC Fort Colvile. Much of the prehistoric work was on Hays Island where, if your boat motor died, so did you going over Kettle Falls. In spite of the weather, Sprague managed to drive the 150 miles each weekend and find students eager to work and take on thesis projects.

Other historic work has included Spalding and Fort Lapwai on the Nez Perce Reservation. A project in downtown Boise in the Chinese section was also conducted by the University within sight of Boise State University. In recent years, the projects for summer work have been less-well funded and not nearly as large, but more relaxed and enjoyable. Several mining camp excavations and surveys in Idaho have included Silver City, Sawtooth City, Florence, and three seasons at a Chinese site in Warren. On many of these projects, with the exception of San Juan Island and Warren, Sprague served as principal investigator while other staff members or advanced graduate students served as directors or field directors. One of Rick's sociology colleagues once accused him of printing his own money to support students because there was so much of it. Rick took that as a compliment.

Meanwhile, back at the lab, the work as department head and lab director were becoming too much for one person so Rick hired an out-of-work Ph.D. graduate from WSU, Ruthann Knudsen. Ruthann took over the routine salvage work and the operation of the site survey. After a few years, she left for a job in industry at twice the pay so Rick made a deal with the central administration where he would retire as department head but stay on as Lab Director. The laboratory would become an independent unit and any salary savings that were incurred the central administration could have. It was now possible for Rick to devote most of his energy to the operation of the lab.

The teaching he performed was now almost entirely historical archaeology with a course on Plateau ethnography every other year. It was an ideal teaching situation. All of his courses were double listed with WSU anthropology as well as the U of I and WSU history departments. The mixture of students was great. In later years, the WSU students were taught by interactive TV and, on occasion, even Idaho State University in Pocatello was included. Since U of I and WSU faculty can serve as full-fledged members of each other's graduate committees, Sprague had an opportunity to have many of the WSU Ph.D. students in his historical archaeology classes, students such as Bill Adams, Dave Brauner, and Tim Riordan. With the establishment of an historical archaeology Ph.D. in the UI history department, several individuals have completed the program including Priscilla Wegars, Herman Ronnenberg, and Annalies Corbin. Rick has served as the chairman for over 60 Master's theses, half in historical archaeology and including such society members as Caroline Carley, Nick Fielder, Karl Gurcke, Jonathan Horn, Keith Landreth, Smoke Pfeiffer, Karl Roenke, Steve Phillips, Linda Sprague, Darby Stapp, Donna Turnipseed, Dick Waldbauer, Bob Weaver, and of course, the Canadian crowd: Pierre Beaudet, Serge Rouleau, Willis Stevens, and Karlis Karklins.

Rick's dedication to teaching and research have not gone unnoticed. He received the University of Idaho Library, Faculty Award for Outstanding Service in 1986, and was named Outstanding Professor by Phi Kappa Phi in 1996. The following year the Boise State University Senior Award in Anthropology was named the "Roderick Sprague Award." The J. C. Harrington Award is a fitting addition to this list.

Sprague's involvement with the Society for Historical Archaeology goes back three decades. He was at the founding meeting in 1967, and has been to all but two of them since. The first absence, in 1987, was unavoidable as Rick was in Inner Mongolia as a Visiting Scholar at the time. The second time was when his back failed him and he couldn't travel to the 1992 meeting in Jamaica. This will always be a sore point with him and Linda.

Since joining the society in 1968, Sprague has held numerous societal positions including Regional Coordinator for Research, Northwest (1968-1977), Board of Directors (1970-1971), Secretary-Treasurer (1971-1974), Review Editor (1977-1997), Parliamentarian (1984-present), and Archivist (1987-1998). He has been on the Editorial Board since 1977, and is the only person to have served as President on two different occasions (1976 and 1990). This involvement reflects Rick's strong interest in and dedication to the society and the discipline of historical archaeology.

Editorial duties have been a continuing part of Sprague's work load; not only the usual editing of lab reports and theses but also of several journals and serials. These include *Northwest Anthropological Research Notes* (Associate Editor and Editor; 1967 to the present), *American Antiquity* (Assistant Editor for Current Research, Northwest; 1968-1981), *University of Idaho Anthropological Reports* (Editor; 1968-1997), *Anthropological Monographs of the University of Idaho* (Series Editor; 1970 to present), *Abstracts in Anthropology* (Advisory Editor, Northwest; 1973-1990), *North American Archaeologist* (Associate Editor for Northwest Historical Archaeology; 1977-present), and *Quarterly Review of Archaeology* (Northwest U.S. Contributing Editor; 1983-1993). He is currently the society's copy editor.

While Rick's research interests are many, he is particularly fond of beads. It was while working on his Master's that Rick first encountered these little baubles. Knowing little about them himself, he sent off a sample to Arthur Woodward who was well versed in trade goods. Seeing their research potential, Rick subsequently began a lifelong study of beads with emphasis on those made using the Prosser process. Having kindred interests, Rick and I met at the SHA conference in Washington in 1971. This led to the publication of *A Bibliography of Glass Trade Beads in North America* which we co-authored. With typical generosity, he let me be the senior author to give my CV a boost. We have been friends ever since and I highly value our friendship.

Since retirement, Rick has kept busy doing the research and writing he enjoys so much. Research not supported by contracts but done for pleasure has involved bells (even prehistoric Southwest copper bells), buttons, and especially beads, both glass and ceramic, largely with Karlis Karklins and more recently also with Lester Ross. Other areas of interest which Rick has recently published on include the history of anthropological research in the Northwest, especially historical archaeology, bibliographies, and a study of Rick's ethnographic father figure, James A. Teit. Serving on the editorial board of the Plateau volume of the *Handbook of American Indians* resulted in a chapter on the Palus Indians and another (as co-author) on the history of Plateau anthropological research. A current effort is to bring together over a dozen authors in a book on the subject of Plateau burials. Recent writing on previous archaeological work in Skagway, Alaska, for the National Park Service has been rewarding for Rick because his grandfather was a newspaper man there during the gold rush and Rick's father was born in Skagway in 1901. Sprague's personal work in recent years has also turned to doing more to support the tribal view on repatriation with court appearances in Nebraska, Montana, Washington, and Idaho. Expert witness work for the Yakama, Nez Perce, Kootenai, and Coeur d'Alene tribes has taken a major portion of his time. This work has been more ethnographic than archaeological. Rick's interests have obviously rubbed off on his youngest son, Alex, who–ignoring his father's advice–is majoring in anthropology. Fred, his oldest son from his second family, has wisely heeded his father's advice.

The Society for Historical Archaeology has always been a source of pleasure to Roderick Sprague and it is rewarding to know that the society has seen fit to present the J. C. Harrington Medal to him for his achievements in the field of historical archaeology. I can think of no better person to be so honored on the threshold of the new millennium. I can only hope that his achievements and dedication to research, education, and this society will inspire others to similarly give unselfishly of themselves to further both our profession and society in the 21st century.

KARLIS KARKLINS

J. C. Harrington Medal in Historical Archaeology

Roberta S. Greenwood 2001

I am pleased and honored to present just a little of the justification for the presentation of the J. C. Harrington Medal to Roberta S. Greenwood. Hard work, professional contributions, and sheer longevity are the usual criteria for this award, but in this case you must also add educator and advocate. Bobby was and is a teacher. I do not use the word in the formal academic sense, but more from a personal perspective. When I first went to work for Bobby in 1974, I did not realize that my fellow workers and I had become enrolled in the University of Greenwood. We were introduced to the Ventura Mission site, given background and objectives, instructed, and deployed. While we worked there was always her presence on the site, unhurried but purposeful. She would walk among the units, features, wash racks, and laboratory, giving explanation and direction to the tasks at hand. Discussions on the site were encouraged. You felt empowered after speaking with her. She paid attention and most importantly, you knew it. Looking back on that initial experience I realize how lucky we were.

She gave us the framework to do good work and perhaps more importantly, the challenge and ability to think critically about what we were doing and the endless horizons that such thinking could open for us. She has always remained responsive to requests for instruction whether from scouts or as guest lecturer at many universities.

Bobby learned to shovel while growing up in Massachusetts. She was already a writer-editor of her high school paper, regional editor for a horse magazine, a college editor of *Mademoiselle*, and an author of prize-winning short fiction. She learned to wear jeans while majoring in economics at Wellesley College. Completing her degree early, she enrolled at Boston University in the field of public administration, and went to work at the Research Center for Group Dynamics at MIT. After moving to Los Angeles in 1948, she spent two years at the Haynes Foundation researching and writing a history of organized labor. All very formative, but still not an archaeologist.

While on leave to raise two daughters, she pursued a youthful interest in Egyptian art and history by enrolling in an evening extension course on Old World culture history at UCLA with Clem Meighan. Her term paper for this course was published in *Archaeology* magazine, and she went back to graduate school in archaeology. The rest is history. In her second year, Dr. Meighan suggested that she take temporary leave from the Ph.D. program to assume direction of the Browne Site, subsequently published in 1969 as SAA *Memoir*, No. 23," The Browne Site: Early Milling Stone Horizon in Southern California." She then excavated a coastal village in Ventura where Cabrillo landed in 1542, and after this, she directed the work at Diablo Canyon that established a chronology for the central coast of California (*9000 Years of Prehistory at Diablo Canyon, San Luis Obispo County, California,* 1972), and designed and installed an interpretive exhibit at the PG&E Visitor Center. From there she went to important work on the Channel Islands for the National Park Service that foreshadowed many prevailing theories. She was an innovator in promoting otolith analysis, standardizing volumetric reporting of shellfish remains, identification of wear patterns on ground stone, and was using a power shaker and wash racks with pressure regulators and attached hot shower 40 years ago. She could always figure out a way to get things done even before cell phones and digital everything.

She never made it back to school. As her work was increasingly recognized, the state selected her to try to find a long-lost outpost of Ventura Mission, located anywhere along a stretch of proposed new highway. And she did (*The Chapel of Santa Gertrudis,* 1968, Pacific Coast Archaeological Society 4[4]:1–59). This was her first published contribution in historical archaeology, although it should be said that the associated Native American remains were given the same attention as historical materials had been given in her prehistoric excavations. During the 1970s between field surveys and research studies, she undertook two summers of work at the first location of Ventura Mission (*3500 Years on One City Block,* 1975 and *The Changing Faces of Main Street,* 1976, both published by the Ventura Redevelopment Agency). This was also her first encounter with a Chinese collection, experience enhanced by studies in El Paso, Napa, San Diego, Phoenix, San Luis Obispo, Los Angeles, and remote areas of China itself. Other important fieldwork, historical research, and laboratory analyses were carried on at the Warm Springs Dam, New Melones Lake project, Prado Basin, and the Eastside Reservoir, each a broad federal undertaking with a commitment over several years. She has always emphasized the multi-disciplinary aspect of archaeology, and was applying NAA and XRF assays to ceramics from adobe sites, 20 years ago.

I think what differentiates Bobby from many others is that she applies her boundless curiosity and persistence in research without bias. She extracts the maximum information from an antique Chinese porcelain, the Mexican pottery from the first Ortega chili factory, or the divided plate from a 20th century fast-food lunchroom. The methods and resources vary but the attention and objectives remain the same. She demonstrated her feeling of obligations to the public at Santa Gertrudis as far back as 1966, with interviewing and being interviewed for the media. At Ventura Mission, she brought City officials and students to the site often and made regular presentations to the City Council. The Sunday site tours were even advertised in Los Angeles papers. Through her efforts, the site was preserved, an historical park developed instead of the projected high-rise, and a muffler shop on the property turned into an on-site museum. That project also demonstrated that intact and significant resources *can* survive directly under the pavement or successive buildings right on Main Street, a crusade she has led ever since. This work stimulated a whole generation of historical archaeologists throughout California. From the missions of southern California to the gold fields of the 49ers, she assembled teams and taught the lessons needed to conduct and think through the tasks and challenges of historical archaeology. She continued to expand our knowledge of not only what historical archaeology was but what it could do. And she has done it all: National Register nominations, HABS and HAER documents, broad thematic overviews, studies of some 34 adobe structures at last count, and not least, convincing public agencies at all levels to do what the laws require. She has never shrunk from controversy, and always enjoys being in the field. She is a very hands-on leader at the site, in the laboratory, and with that big red editorial pen.

Her work on Chinese-American sites was a fundamental thrust to add to the strictly historical, and interpret the unwritten. The excavation at Los Angeles Chinatown was another example of community outreach, involvement, and continuing public benefit. Members of the Chinese Historical Society were invited to the site and taught to assist in the laboratory; in turn, the Society was reinvigorated, she assisted them in obtaining landmark status for the old cemetery, reacquiring the property and rehabilitating and rededicating the 1887 shrine. She persuaded the client to donate the entire collection from Los Angeles Chinatown to the Society which now maintains permanent and traveling displays of the artifacts. Her book presenting both the historical research and archaeological interpretations received the Lloyd Cotsen award for a distinguished publication (*Down by the Station,* UCLA Institute of Archaeology, 1993) and has become a standard reference. I think the majority of us can appreciate the effort and work that went into convincing those contractors and officials that this was a necessary and legitimate science.

She has also served the profession as an elected or appointed officer in the SCA, ASCA, SAA, SOPA, and the *North American Archaeologist.* Bobby's support for The Society for Historical Archaeology on the Board of Directors, the Editorial Advisory Committee, and as representative to SOPA and general gadfly, is well known. Her enthusiasm and her inability to say no, enhance her contributions to the profession. Roberta Greenwood's career is based on hard work, dedication, self-sacrifice, and an enthusiasm for archaeology. With an unusually broad background, a world traveler—Renaissance woman—she can still out dig, out survey, and out think a lot of us, but her ultimate legacy will be her influence on past and current generations of historical archaeologists. Because of this, and in consequence of her contributions to the study of historical archaeology, she has earned the 2001 J. C. Harrington award for outstanding contributions to the field.

JOHN M. FOSTER

J. C. Harrington Medal in Historical Archaeology

Charles E. Cleland 2002

There is a just a touch of irony in this celebration of Chuck Cleland's remarkable career because, over the past three decades, I have heard him emphatically and repeatedly declare that he is not an historical archaeologist—or any other sort of narrow, topical specialist. Throughout his professional life, Chuck has styled himself, first and foremost, as an anthropologist who pursues whatever lines of evidence are relevant to his broad interests. His research domain has never been circumscribed by temporal or regional boundaries, nor has he ever been inclined toward investigating the particulars of specific persons, places, or events. Rather, Chuck has sought to examine the processes of cultural adaptation in order to improve our understanding of how we as a species come to cope with our changing environment.

It is precisely that universal perspective that has made his occasional forays in the field of historical archaeology important ones. Moreover, for 35 years he ably taught several generations of students now active in the field of historical archaeology and played a pivotal role in the governance of our society, thus effecting lasting influences on the growth and development of our discipline. Accordingly, despite Chuck's unassuming disclaimers, the Society for Historical Archaeology has chosen appropriately and wisely in its selection of Charles E. Cleland as this year's recipient of its most prestigious award—the J. C. Harrington Medal in Historical Archaeology.

Before I actually met Chuck Cleland, as an undergraduate anthropology major in September 1972, I was already well aware that he was a figure of considerable standing on the campus at Michigan State University (MSU). After all, he held the impressive titles of professor in the Department of Anthropology and curator of anthropology at The Museum. I also learned that he was then president-elect of the Society for Historical Archaeology, a title that failed to impress me at the time, but for which I have come to have a much greater appreciation. The most striking thing about the man on first meeting, however, was that he was not at all the stodgy academic I was expecting. To the contrary, Chuck was then only 36 years old and sporting faded blue jeans, worn moccasins, and a full beard turned flaming red from fieldwork in the summer's sun. He looked to me more like a typical graduate student of the 1970s, hardly one's image of a senior faculty member!

For him to have come so far at a relatively young age would perhaps suggest the ambitious pursuit of a career focused on clear goals, but that was hardly the case. To the contrary, Chuck's rapid rise probably owed more to a generalizing strategy toward professional development marked by a truly exceptional adaptability to changing circumstances. Further, his rise was consistent with his willingness to take occasional risks when others might chose to follow a more conventional course of action.

Born in Kane, Pennsylvania, on 2 February 1936, Charles Edward Cleland is the eldest child of Margaret Elizabeth (Mason) and Charles E. Cleland. His parents were both doctors who met while in medical school at the University of Pittsburgh and later settled in the rural, northwestern corner of the state to open a joint practice. There they raised a family that in time would also include a daughter, Margaret Mason, and a second son, John Matthew (Jock). Although his roots are in small-town America, Chuck's father and mother instilled in him an appreciation for the world beyond their hearth and nurtured an abiding love of both science and the humanities. Chuck's eyes also were opened at an early age to cultural diversity unknown in Kane, and most rural midwestern communities, thanks to his father's frequent changes of duty station as a doctor called to active service in World War II. The war years carried the Cleland family to distant corners of the United States, and Chuck learned far more from his life on the road than from his attendance at six different grade schools during those turbulent times.

Back in Kane, after his father went overseas to serve with the air corps in the Pacific, Chuck at first struggled to overcome the spotty formal education he had received while moving about the country. He made substantial strides through his high school years, however, and even learned that he would be well suited to working either as a plumber or as an archaeologist. An aptitude test administered in the 10th grade had offered those seemingly disparate options, presumably on the basis of some required talents they hold in common, but neither his guidance counselor nor his parents were enthused with those prospective vocations. Life as a tradesman was simply out of the question for someone destined for college practically from birth, whereas a career in archeology—then as now—seemed wholly impractical. Consequently, by his senior year, Chuck hoped to make something of the many hours he had spent peering though his father's microscope and enrolled as a biology major at Denison University, a small liberal arts institution in central Ohio that his mother had attended.

Upon completion of his B.A. in 1958, Chuck decided to seek an advanced degree at the University of Arkansas, where he initially hoped to study parasitology. Before departing for Fayetteville, however, he wed Mary Gayley, who had been a classmate in high school. With new challenges to face, starting graduate school seemed an exhilarating prospect. Like many graduate students, though, he eventually would become disenchanted with his studies and began to have second thoughts about his choice of careers.

Once at Arkansas, Chuck settled into the zoology department and began writing his master's thesis, "The Re-introduction of the Wild Turkey into the Ozark Highlands," contemplating a career in wildlife management. Chuck soon came to the dismaying realization, however, that such work had less to do with managing wildlife and more to do with accommodating his fellow human beings. At this same time, Arkansas was in the throes of impassioned racial tension over the attempted integration of Central High School in the capital city, Little Rock. The state legislature, irritated with federal law enforcement efforts in Arkansas, in turn responded by passing its own law prohibiting state employees from holding memberships in "subversive" organizations such as the Congress on Racial Equality and the National Association for the Advancement of Colored People. Thanks to his liberal upbringing, Chuck was a card-carrying member of both CORE and the NAACP, and he was summarily fired from his teaching assistant position in 1959.

Uncertain of his future at the age of 23, Chuck happened into a chance encounter that proved pivotal in defining the direction his life would take. In the small museum on an upper floor of the campus administration building, he met Charles R. (Bob) McGimsey III, a young professor recently arrived from Harvard to start up an archaeology program at Arkansas. Upon learning that Chuck was a zoology graduate student, McGimsey asked whether he could identify animal bones derived from excavations. Moreover, he told Chuck that such a skill would be worth a paying job in the museum laboratory and could be the basis of an interesting thesis project. Not one to let a promising opportunity slip away, Chuck answered without hesitation that he had extensive training in the identification of animal bone—and then hastened off to the library, where he gathered up every book he could find on the subjects of mammalian and avian osteology. Before long, thanks to diligent study, Chuck could truthfully claim that he knew almost as much as anyone in the country about the subject.

Under McGimsey's capable guidance, though still a zoology student, Chuck began work on his new thesis, "Animal Remains of the Ozark Bluff Shelters." He also took his first course in archaeology, which at last put his assigned tasks in a broader context. Later he would meet Hester Davis, hired by McGimsey in 1959 to help build the archaeology program at Fayetteville. From modest beginnings, the program they started eventually would grow to be the Arkansas Archaeological Survey, which has ably served as a model for statewide field research programs throughout America. Chuck's introduction to archaeology at Arkansas was all too brief, but the influence of McGimsey and Davis on his thinking was considerable, and, in later years, the three would again join forces in the cause of establishing and maintaining professional standards for archaeology.

By spring 1960, Chuck first learned the delights of fatherhood with the birth of his daughter, Elizabeth Ann (Lisa). His thesis was near completion, but now with a young family to consider, Chuck again found himself at a crossroads. Again, fate intervened—this time in the person of James B. Griffin, the "grand old man" of eastern U.S. prehistory. At the SAA meetings that year, Griffin learned from McGimsey of Chuck's ability to identify animal bones, which by that time he had developed into a genuine talent. Griffin allowed that he could use such a person on his research team, so he called Chuck and invited him to pursue a doctorate in anthropology at the University of Michigan (U of M). Not entirely sure what he was getting into, but figuring it was bound to lead to something better, Chuck and his family were soon off to Ann Arbor.

Before the academic year began, Chuck had the opportunity to experience his first summer of excavations at the Feeheley site, a late-Archaic site in the Saginaw Valley of Michigan. With that experience for inspiration, Chuck was truly excited about his new graduate career and began his studies in earnest that fall. Having never taken a course in anthropology, at first, of course, he felt ill-prepared and deficient, feelings rather reminiscent of his grade school days in Kane. Chuck again proved himself to be a quick study, however, and before long he was enjoying the lectures of such luminaries as Elman Service, Eric Wolf, and Marshall Sahlins. Even the formidable Leslie White enthralled Chuck, who saw immediately that White's theories of cultural evolution fit well with what he had already learned about the natural world. In fact, Chuck so thoroughly enjoyed the teachings of Leslie White that he sat in on White's course The Evolution of Culture three times!

Equally important to Chuck's growing enthusiasm for his studies derived from his office environment at the Museum of Anthropology, where he interacted frequently with faculty researchers such as Griffin, Emerson Greeman, Art Jelenik, and the ethnobotanist Volney Jones. He was also one of a large cohort of bright, energetic, and deeply committed graduate students who challenged and encouraged one another to explore new ways of thinking about the human condition. The synergy of their learning environment must have been truly marvelous, with every coffee break as stimulating as any formal seminar. Almost every one of those graduate students went on to distinguish themselves in academia.

All of Chuck's excavation experience in graduate school was on prehistoric sites, such as the Holcombe Beach site, Spider Cave, and the Norton Mounds. He clearly enjoyed the excitement of archaeological fieldwork and its unconventional lifestyle. The state of Michigan was still relatively unknown archaeologically in those days, with only a handful of researchers actively pursuing field opportunities in the state, and so every new project added tremendously to a developing body of knowledge. Griffin placed senior graduate students in charge of excavations at various locations every summer and spent much of his time traveling from site to site, offering programmatic oversight as well as keen insights into the meaning of their finds. This was a style of research administration that Chuck himself would adopt in later years to good effect.

Chuck first came to recognize the potential for doing archaeological research on the historic period while a student in Ann Arbor, though it was hardly an emphasis of the U of M program. Griffin's close friend George Quimby, then at the Field Museum in Chicago, was particularly interested in understanding the dramatic changes introduced to American Native populations during the time of European contact, and Chuck began a long professional relationship with Quimby out of a mutual interest in the contact period. Chuck also followed closely the progress of MSU's continuing excavations at Fort Michilimackinac, which Moreau S. Maxwell had initiated in 1959 with assistance from another U of M graduate student, Lewis Binford.

Griffin had recruited Chuck specifically to analyze data derived from his 1960–1964 National Science Foundation research project on the correlation between prehistoric cultural complexes and the post-Pleistocene ecologies of the upper Great Lakes, which produced doctoral dissertation topics for Chuck and several others. Chuck's dissertation, "The Prehistoric Animal Ecology and Ethnozoology of the Upper Great Lakes Region," developed several original concepts concerning human subsistence strategies, particularly the focal-diffuse model, which he would develop further in a series of important articles later in his career. Before completing his degree, however, Chuck had been given the chance to teach at MSU in 1964, while Maxwell was in Denmark as a Fulbright scholar.

Upon Maxwell's return to campus in 1965, he became head of the new anthropology department, which had just broken away from its traditional connections with sociology. That reassignment left a vacancy at The Museum, where Maxwell had held an appointment as curator. Chuck soon found himself curator of anthropology at age 29, with the promise of promotion from instructor to assistant professor upon completion of his degree, which came to pass the next year. Maxwell's strong desire to build the fledgling department gave Chuck the opportunity to develop a program of field research in the upper Great Lakes, and he turned out to be a capable organizer who accomplished much with meager resources. He quickly formed an alliance with the small department at Western Michigan University, and the two universities, thereafter, conducted a series of joint field schools on sites in northern Michigan with shared personnel and equipment.

Coincident to Chuck's new curatorship at The Museum, came the addition of a son, Joshua Charles, to his family. Chuck recalls this 1965 event as spot of joy in an otherwise difficult period of his life. Although his future was now more certain, the demands on his time had become considerable with the need to prepare lectures for large introductory courses, while organizing and conducting an expanding program of field and laboratory research. Further, he was still in the final stages of studying for his comprehensive exams and completing his dissertation. As it so often happens with young academics, Chuck's marriage suffered under this added strain, and the couple began to grow apart; in time they would separate and ultimately divorce.

In that same year, Chuck recruited Lyle Stone, who had been one of Ray Ruppé's students at Arizona State, specifically to take over the research at Fort Michilimackinac after Maxwell began to refocus his interests on Arctic prehistory. Having worked at several fortification sites on the Great Plains, Stone was a natural to manage and analyze the growing museum collections derived from that important 18th-century site and to continue the excavations into new areas. He also became Chuck's first doctoral student, completing one of the earliest dissertations based on historical archaeology in 1970.

In January 1967, Ed Jelks hosted the founding meeting of the Society for Historical Archaeology, which had the official title of "International Conference on Historic Archaeology," on the campus of Southern Methodist University at Dallas. Chuck attended the small meeting and presented a paper entitled "Analysis of Economics and Natural Environment," in keeping with his attraction to the interplay between human populations and the world around us. He also took part in the first official SHA business meeting, though he was not a member of the special organizing committee chaired by Jelks.

That committee made several recommendations related to the naming and purpose of our society, and general discussion of each subtle nuance appears to have been both prolonged and lively. Aside from the well-known controversy over semantic distinctions between the terms "historic" and "historical," there was also considerable debate over whether to include the Old World as part of our legitimate disciplinary realm. According to the minutes from that meeting, in light of the recommended temporal emphasis on periods of "Exploration and Settlement, Contact Aboriginal, Colonial, National Development, and Modern," Cleland expressed the view that "the New World should be specified, for 'Colonial' was clearly a term related to the New World." This seems an oddly narrow view of the Era of European Expansion, at least for Chuck, but perhaps it can be forgiven in the context of an "international" conference that included only North American participants, most of them from the United States!

Chuck's commitment to the emergent discipline was now on the rise, and he would soon co-author an article with Stone on the Erie Canal system, which would be published in the first volume of *Historical Archaeology* (1:63–70, 1967). Chuck also teamed up with Jim Fitting, a former classmate from the U of M, to write "The Crisis of Identity: Theory in Historic Sites Archaeology," which they presented at Stan South's Conference on Historic Site Archaeology later in 1967 (*The Conference on Historic Site Papers*, 1968, Vol. 2, Pt. 2, pp. 124–138). Influenced heavily by the teachings of Leslie White, and still cited today, that paper was a seminal contribution to the early debate over whether our discipline should be principally grounded in anthropology or history.

As a consequence of Chuck's growing involvement in historical archaeology, MSU began to acquire a reputation for research in the newly christened field of study. More graduate students were drawn to the department, and perhaps half of those who studied with Chuck took an interest in the early-historic period. Emphasis of the research program in the late 1960s and early 1970s was entirely on Native American and European sites associated with the interior fur trade, such as the Lasanen and Mill Creek sites at the Straits of Mackinac and Fort Ouiatenon in Indiana. It would eventually expand, however, to include much later American fortifications, such as Fort Brady and Fort Gratiot in Michigan and, in the early 1980s, several 19th-century town sites in Mississippi that would be affected by federal undertakings along the Tennessee-Tombigbee Waterway. Throughout the 1980s and 1990s, historic period fieldwork also took place intermittently at the Marquette Mission site in St. Ignace, Michigan, and at several other locations in the extreme northern parts of the state.

This is not to say that Chuck turned his back entirely on prehistory. To the contrary, he also attracted a number of excellent students to MSU whom he directed through various prehistoric research projects, including some that specifically came to work with him on topics related to the analysis of animal remains from archaeological sites. Indeed, in the 1990s, Chuck at last managed to combine his many varied interests in a multiyear survey project on islands within the St. Mary's River, which forms the border between the U.S. and Canada at the eastern end of Michigan's Upper Peninsula. Field investigations on Lime Island, Drummond Island, and elsewhere enabled him to work with students interested in middle- and late-Woodland problems as well as those who sought to examine early-Historic industrial sites and fortifications.

From time to time, Chuck continued to write articles on historical archaeology, often inspired by particularly interesting facets of his students' field research. Among those were his 1970 article "Comparison of the Faunal Remains from French and British Refuse Pits at Fort Michilimackinac: A Study in Changing Subsistence Patterns" (*Canadian Historic Sites: Occasional Papers in Archaeology and History* 3:7–23, Ottawa), his 1972 *American Antiquity* (37[2]:202–212) article "From Sacred to Profane: Style Drift in the Decoration of Jesuit Finger Rings," and "Merchants, Tradesmen, and Tenants: The Economics of the Diffusion of Material Culture on a Late-Nineteenth Century Site," which he published in the journal *Geoscience and Man* (23:35–44) in 1983.

It should be noted that for many years, the historical archaeology program at MSU consisted only of field opportunities and, much like Chuck's own experience at U of M, the constant interaction of students working at The Museum. Indeed, in the early days, Chuck probably learned more about historical archaeology from some of his students who had come to MSU with considerable practical experience than he was able to teach them about the subject. By the mid-1970s, however, he had developed two much-needed additions to the departmental curriculum: Method and Theory in Historical Archaeology and The Practice of Historical Archaeology, which was basically a lab practical in material culture analysis, known fondly as the "pots and pans" class. Those were arguably among the earliest formal courses in historical archaeology offered at any American university, and they were the core of the program for many years, supplemented only by independent study seminars and course work in history, geography, urban planning, and other related disciplines.

It was also in this period of professional growth that Chuck's personal life took a marked turn for the better with the help of Nancy Nowak who was pursuing a course of study in ethnobotany. The two met on a field project in northern Michigan and married in 1975. Their complementary interests and mutually supportive companionship have now sustained them through more than a quarter-century together, with Nancy frequently contributing to Chuck's research over those years. What's more, Nancy and Chuck had two daughters, Elena Mason (Ellie) in 1977 and Katherine Pearce (Katie) in 1980, who have added considerable pleasure to their lives.

Throughout much of his teaching career, Chuck also held a joint appointment in the Department of Racial and Ethnic Studies. In that capacity, he taught periodic seminars in ethnohistory and contemporary Native American issues, inspiring graduate students from several other departments to study under his guidance. Combining this subject matter with his interest in human subsistence, Chuck also entered a realm of research that would occupy him through much of his later career—namely, the origins and evolution of native fishing practices. Not only did that research lead to a number of important academic publications, most notably his 1982 *American Antiquity* (47[4]:761–784) article "The Inland Shore Fishery of the Northern Great Lakes: Its Development and Importance in Prehistory," it also led to dramatic changes in the lives of contemporary native peoples.

Chuck's ethnohistorical research was directed, like all of his research, by a desire to understand adaptation and change in the context of cultural traditions and history. His ability to meld documentary and archaeological evidence helped produce narrative accounts and interpret historic events in the light of evolving federal Indian policy. The research also led to his involvement with the landmark court case, *U.S. v. Michigan*, in which the federal government sued the state in support of tribal treaty rights. Along with other expert witnesses, Chuck gave testimony in U.S. Federal Court that ultimately led to victory for the United States in its quest to affirm fishing rights granted to tribes in Michigan under the 1836 treaty. In 1979, that decision was upheld by the U.S. Court of Appeals.

He soon became a much-sought-after consultant on treaty rights, eventually working on behalf of better than a dozen Great Lakes bands in Michigan, Minnesota, Wisconsin, and Canada. One notable case in 1994, *Mille Lacs Band of Ojibwe v. Minnesota*, asserted the right of band members to hunt and fish free of state law on lands ceded in Minnesota and Wisconsin under the Treaty of 1837. Although decided in favor of the band, the state pursued a lengthy appeals process, with the case ultimately going to the U.S. Supreme Court in 1999. Liberally citing Chuck's research, the justices rendered a majority opinion concurring with the lower court decision.

Indeed, every trial for which Chuck served as a witness was eventually resolved in favor of the tribe whose treaty rights were in question. That is not to say, however, that they were all easy victories. The case of *Crown v. Agwa*, for example, involved criminal charges against an Ojibwe fisherman charged with violating provincial game laws, despite his claim that the Superior-Robinson Treaty of 1850 gave him certain rights to fish. The defendant was convicted at trial, and that decision was subsequently upheld on appeal. The Canadian Supreme Court, however, ultimately affirmed the larger right of Canadian Indians to their treaty provisions under the new Canadian Constitution.

All of this research has lead to a spate of major publications in the past decade that form the capstone of Chuck's academic career. These include more than a half-dozen articles on his various ethnohistorical studies as well as two important books: *Rites of Conquest: The History and Culture of Michigan's Native Americans* (University of Michigan Press, Ann Arbor, 1992) and *The Place of the Pike (Gnoozhekaaning): The History of the Bay Mills Community* (University of Michigan Press, Ann Arbor, 2001). Moreover, I have it on good authority that other major contributions to the literature are in the works, now that Chuck has more time to write, that is, when he is not excavating with a few volunteers on a late-Archaic site not far from his retirement home in northern Michigan.

It remains for us to examine the larger impact that Chuck Cleland has had on this discipline of historical archaeology and the profession of archaeology in general. As we have seen, Chuck's early substantive and theoretical writings include several well-known articles, but he continues to provide authoritative commentary on historical archaeology's current status and future direction, such as his lead article, "Historical Archaeology Adrift?" in last year's journal Forum (*Historical Archaeology*, 35[2]:1–8). More important to the profession, however, have been his frequent efforts on behalf of our discipline through political action.

Chuck, as I have already noted, participated in the founding meeting of the Society for Historical Archaeology in 1967. The next year, he served an interim term on the board of directors before being elected to a full three-year term in 1970. In 1972, he returned to serve on the board, as president-elect, prior to beginning his term as our seventh president in 1973. Most of our past presidents have gladly retired from "archaeo-politics" upon completing their duties in this demanding office, but Chuck would again return to the board a decade later in 1982 for another term as a director.

During those many years on the SHA board, Chuck was a persistent voice of reason in society deliberations, and his efforts to advance both intellectual and practical causes were well known and widely respected. As president, he managed the society capably during a period of rapid growth and argued for the continued association of terrestrial and underwater archaeology in the society, when some thought that separation of the two was preferable and inevitable. In those years, the practice of historical archaeology began to coalesce into a distinct discipline, but Chuck was also determined to see that all of archaeology should join other pursuits as a true profession, like medicine and the law.

Toward that end, beginning in 1974, Chuck was a member of the Society of American Archaeology's Committee on the Recovery of Archaeological Remains, serving with his early mentors from Arkansas, Bob McGimsey and Hester Davis, and nine others, who later liked to think of themselves as the "Dirty Dozen." For all intents and purposes, the committee essentially seceded from the SAA and founded the Society of Professional Archeologists in 1976. Chuck was elected successor to Ed Jelks, as SOPA's second president (1977–1978), and later served twice on the board of directors (1986–1988 and 1993–1995) as the SHA's elected representative, defeating yours truly for that honor in the 1993 election.

He would later be instrumental in advocating the transformation of SOPA into the Register of Professional Archaeologists, which occurred in 1998 and, subsequently, has nearly tripled in size under sponsorship of SHA, SAA, the Archaeological Institute of America, and, most recently, the American Anthropological Association. His most important contribution to the cause of professionalism in archaeology, however, is without doubt the two years he served as SOPA's grievance coordinator (1985–1987). In that crucial position, Chuck faced the challenges of investigating allegations of professional misconduct in several extremely sensitive cases. In that capacity, he employed considerable skill and finesse to negotiate settlements among parties, earning a reputation as a firm but fair defender of professional integrity as well as the integrity of SOPA's disciplinary procedures. Even today, under the Register of Professional Archaeologists, grievance coordinators still may call upon Chuck's wise counsel whenever dealing with particularly troublesome cases.

Finally, there are Chuck's academic progeny—the many students who have gone on to make careers in historical archaeology and the broader profession. He is justifiably proud of his four children, of course, but Chuck's extended family also includes the impressive number of graduate students he guided to degree completion over the past 35 years. Through 1999, as he was preparing for retirement, he had signed off as committee chair on 12 master's theses as well as 25 doctoral dissertations, and another ten students were then nearing the end of their degree programs. Of the nearly 50 students whose committees he chaired, no fewer than 20 are now principally involved with historical archaeology, whether they work in academia, government, museums, or private business. Further, most of the other students at MSU who concentrated on prehistoric archaeology, even those directed by other faculty members, were first introduced to the essentials of historical archaeology under Chuck's tutelage.

It is also worth noting that many of Chuck's students also have emulated his long dedication to professional service. Seven have served on the SHA board of directors, and three of those went on to election as president. In fact, there has been at least one Cleland student on the SHA board in every year since 1990, and four of his former students ably hosted our annual conferences in the past decade.

Most of the other major professional societies have similarly benefited from the contributions of Chuck's students, including the Society for Industrial Archaeology, the Society for Archaeological Sciences, the Society for American Archaeology, the American Cultural Resources Association, the Society of Professional Archeologists, and its successor the Register of Professional Archaeologists. In short, Chuck Cleland leaves the archaeological profession a living legacy that will continue to have extensive and recognizable influences on our discipline well into the 21st century.

In his keynote address at the 1981 SHA conference at New Orleans, Chuck offered up his vision of what historical archaeology needed to do in order to achieve its full potential. Indeed, he has regularly returned to that theme whenever called upon to provide sage commentary on the state of the art, witness his 1987 paper "Questions of Substance, Questions that Count" (*Historical Archaeology*, 22[1]:13–17, 1988) from the Savannah Plenary Session and his 2001 journal Forum already mentioned.

Of the many propositions Chuck put forth 20 years ago, sadly, few have yet been fully realized by the discipline. He set our goals high, and we continue to strive toward them. Chuck's closing statement, however, still stands out in my mind. He said that our ultimate mission as researchers should be "to push intellectual frontiers, to make more mistakes, to improve models, to advance theory." In so doing, he acknowledged the risks taken each time one of us offers a new interpretation of the past as we boldly venture, in J. C. Harrington's words, "beyond the strictly historical."

Chuck Cleland has persistently challenged us to pose questions that count, imploring us to seek answers that expand upon our understanding of the human condition. He has also helped lead us toward an elevated sense of professionalism as we endeavor to follow his example. In a career that now spans parts of five decades, Chuck has been the recipient of many accolades, including the Distinguished Faculty Award from Michigan State University in 1978 and the Distinguished Service Award from the Society of Professional Archeologists in 1991. To those high honors, we are privileged to add one more, and I suspect he will quietly treasure it above all others.

For the outstanding role he has played in making historical archaeology a distinct and vital field of inquiry on a global scale, the SHA proudly honors Charles E. Cleland with the J. C. Harrington Medal in Historical Archaeology.

VERGIL E. NOBLE

J. C. Harrington Medal in Historical Archaeology: Merrick Posnansky, 2003. Volume 38, Number 2 (2004): 1-6.
By Christopher R. DeCorse.

J. C. Harrington Medal in Historical Archaeology

Merrick Posnansky 2003

Merrick Posnansky is the quintessential Africanist, having conducted research on Stone Age, Iron Age, and Historic period sites over much of the continent and provided both context and critical appraisal for researchers studying the African Diaspora. He has published almost 200 monographs, articles, book chapters, and reviews, and trained a generation of African and Africanist archaeologists. Merrick's work in developing museums and academic programs in Kenya, Uganda, Ghana, and the United States marks him as one of the leading scholars of his generation. As a mentor, he is both a model and an inspiration to his students. In recognition of his work in historical archaeology and for his continuing role in teaching a new generation of scholars, it is appropriate that we honor him with the J. C. Harrington Medal in Historical Archaeology.

Despite his contributions to Africa and historical archaeology, Merrick's training and his initial research focused on British prehistoric archaeology. The tenth of 11 children, Merrick became interested in the study of the past as a child. At one point, inspired by a lecture by a curator from the British Museum, he decided he would study numismatics. Fortunately, the lecturer told him there was only one job available—and it was taken. But he also suggested that Merrick look at broader fields like archaeology and museum studies. These fields were to remain central to Merrick's career.

Although he was interested in archaeology, it was not offered at the University of Nottingham, and Merrick's undergraduate degree was in history and geography. He did, however, have his first taste of archaeology, working at several excavations beginning with a Mesolithic site in 1948. It was also during this period that he participated, accidentally, in his first historical archaeological project—digging a 2-ton stone out of a hillside near Burnley, Lancashire, which was believed to be part of a Bronze Age cemetery. In fact, the feature proved to be associated with 19th-century potato storage pits. Interestingly, the project was directed by Frank Willett who later also become well known as an Africanist.

More successful, was Merrick's work on the medieval tile works of Lenton Priory, which was located on the University of Nottingham campus. This was done by the University of Nottingham, Students' Archaeological Society, which Merrick had formed in autumn 1951. Merrick also worked on the analysis of the material, which was subsequently published (Swinnerton, Chalmers, and Posnansky 1956).

Notably, one of the first lectures sponsored by the new Students' Archaeological Society was by Grahame Clark, a driving force in the increasingly prominent archaeology program at Cambridge. Following graduation from Nottingham, Merrick completed a postgraduate diploma in prehistoric archaeology at Peterhouse, Cambridge, at that time, the only postgraduate program aside from the PhD that was offered. His year at Cambridge was important in introducing him to Africa through the teaching of Miles Burkitt, whose pioneering research in Southern Africa was a stimulus to many other Africanist archaeologists, including J. Desmond Clark and Brian Fagan. Burkitt's ability to inspire excitement about the study of the past (Fagan 2001:15–16) can be seen in Merrick's own career. At Cambridge, Merrick was also taught by Charles McBurney and Grahame Clark. He maintained these Cambridge contacts, and they proved of primary importance in his decision to work in Africa.

Merrick retuned to the University of Nottingham for his PhD, which he completed under the supervision of H. H. Swinnerton (who was actually a geologist). Merrick's research dealt with the Pleistocene chronology and prehistoric archaeology of the English East Midlands. While his dissertation covered some of the archaeology of more recent periods, the subsequent publications primarily focused on the Paleolithic (Posnansky 1963).

In 1955, Merrick conducted a salvage excavation of the Lamport Post Mill in Northamptonshire (Posnansky 1956). Initial investigation suggested that the site was Bronze Age barrow, but excavation revealed the footings of two post mills—one medieval (late-13th to early-15th centuries) and the other, 17th century. The dating of the site was aided by the innovative use of clay tobacco pipes, which were then being studied by Adrian Oswald, the son of Felix Oswald who had established the archaeological museum where Merrick worked as a volunteer at Nottingham university. Although not dating to the Bronze Age, the mill was the first of its kind excavated, and the site was noted as one of the most important archaeological discoveries of the year in the London *Times*. The report continues to be cited in reviews of postmedieval British archaeology (Crossley 1990).

As a new PhD, Merrick received a letter from Grahame Clark asking if he would be interested in working as a warden for the Royal National Parks of Kenya, an opportunity Merrick was delighted to seize. He arrived in Africa in 1956, where he worked closely with Louis Leakey (Posnansky 2002a: 432). Although this was the colonial era, it would be erroneous to collectively view Merrick's work and that of all of his contemporaries as colonialist. To do so would be to simplify their objectives and research concerns (Robertshaw 1990:78). Like much of sub-Saharan Africa, East Africa was still very poorly known archaeologically in the mid-20th century. The early hominid discoveries at Olduvai Gorge were still several years in the future. Nevertheless, much of the work in eastern Africa focused on human origins and the Stone Age. Merrick published the first excavation report on the classic early-Stone Age site of Olorgesailie, later excavated by the late Glynn Isaac (Posnansky 1959a, 1959b; Morell 1995:275). However, Merrick also worked on more recent Iron Age sites (Posnansky 1967a) and Masai burial mounds (Posnansky 1968a), and he visited many of the coastal Swahili sites, which were then being excavated by James Kirkman and Neville Chittick. These were Historic period sites, known from Arabic sources dating back to the early second millennium A.D. Merrick's exposure to this diversity of sites contributed to the broad perspective that characterizes his writing.

Merrick moved to Uganda in 1958 as curator of the Uganda Museum (Posnansky 2002a:432). There he brought the Uganda Antiquities Service under the museum, excavated the 19th-century forts of Emin Pasha and Samuel Baker, and put Ugandan rock art on the map (Posnansky and Nelson 1968). He transferred to the newly established British Institute of History and Archaeology in Eastern Africa (later the British Institute of Eastern Africa) in 1962, and he ran the Kampala Office for two years. Notably, from the onset, the institute's research orientation was on the Iron Age and later prehistoric period (Robertshaw 1990:87–88). With the institute's move to a central office in Nairobi, Merrick chose to join the University College of East Africa at Makerere where he had already been offering the first archaeology courses in East or Central Africa, beginning in 1962. He also helped draw up planning documents for university archaeology courses in Kenya, Tanganyika (later Tanzania), and Ethiopia.

Merrick's archaeological research in Uganda is characterized by an increasing focus on the more recent African past. His work at Bigo (Posnansky 1969a) and Bweyorere (Posnansky 1968b) dealt with the archaeology of the settlements but also dealt with the methodological concerns of reconciling oral traditions with information gleaned from excavation (Posnansky 1966, 1967b; Schmidt 1990). Recognizing the important contribution of African oral traditions, Merrick referred to this work as historical archaeology (Posnansky 1959a, 1959b). Significantly, this was before the widespread acceptance of the value of oral sources in African historical studies. Indeed, in the late 1950s some scholars still disparaged the idea of African history as worthy of study or saw the archaeological record as largely unconnected to modern African societies (Posnansky 1998). The view that oral sources as well as written records define the discipline of historical archaeology continues to typify the perspective of the majority of African and Africanist scholars.

While in Uganda, Merrick met and married Eunice Lubega, the first African woman to graduate with a university degree in East or Central Africa. Given the social climate of the time, the marriage was unusual. Eunice accompanied Merrick on innumerable trips to archaeological sites, museum collections, and meetings, including a two- or three-week trip to look at sites in Kenya, Tanganyika, and northern and southern Rhodesia that passed as a honeymoon. Merrick acknowledges her tolerance with appreciation. Merrick and Eunice have three daughters Sheba, Tessa, and Helen, all of whom have vivid memories of family trips to archaeological sites.

In 1967, Merrick moved to Ghana as a professor and chair of the Archaeology Department at the University of Ghana, Legon, where he remained for nine years. In Ghana, he developed both undergraduate and graduate curricula, making Legon the largest archaeological program in sub-Saharan Africa with six fulltime faculty. During the 1960s and early 1970s, Legon was a focal point of African studies and many historians, anthropologists, and archaeologists visited or taught in the various programs on the campus.

In Ghana, Merrick's research dealt with sites of the second millennium A.D. known through oral traditions. He initiated the West African Trade Project, an umbrella for a number of projects aimed at examining regional trade patterns (Posnansky 1973). Merrick's principal field research was on the archaeology and ethnoarchaeology of Begho in central Ghana. Begho, which reached its peak between the 15th and the 18th centuries, typifies the African trading communities of the forest-savanna ecotone. It was divided into four quarters, the names of which were recalled in the oral traditions of the modern village of Hani. Merrick continued to conduct ethnoarchaeological work at Hani for almost three decades, making this one of the longest running projects of its kind (Posnansky n.d.).

Merrick also stimulated work on the coastal Ghanaian sites associated with the European trade. The numerous forts and castles had been the focus of previous work. Indeed, A. W. Lawrence, first professor of archaeology at the University College of Achimota (later to become the University of Ghana), had focused on the European trade posts of Ghana and West Africa (Kense 1990; Lawrence 1963). However, unlike previous researchers, Merrick's interest was on the transformations in African societies during the era of the Atlantic trade, not the architectural histories of the European monuments. With Merrick's inspiration, the *Coastal Survey of 1969* examined all of the African settlements located adjacent to European trade posts (Golden 1969; Posnansky 1969b, 2002b:

47). He participated in excavations at Sekondi in 1970 and in the dungeons of Cape Coast Castle in 1973 (Simmonds 1973). Although limited, the latter still provides the only direct archaeological information on enslaved Africans from an African context.

In late 1975 and early 1976, Merrick, in collaboration with the late Albert Van Dantzig, uncovered traces of ill-fated Fort Ruychaver (Posnansky and Van Dantzig 1976). Founded by the Dutch in 1654, 87 km up the Ankobra River, this small lodge was intended to expand trade into the interior gold producing regions. It stands as one of the few attempts made by the Europeans to establish an outpost in the African hinterland. Though initially successful, the venture ended in 1658 when the Dutch West India Company commander blew himself up in a conflict with the local African chief. Archaeological research confirmed the location of the fort and provided some indication of the building's size and construction. The publication calls attention to the potential for historical archaeological research in Ghana, including African sites such as Elmina.

Merrick moved to the Department of History at UCLA as a full professor in 1977, where he remained until he accepted early retirement in 1994. His appointment in a department of history reflects the historically close disciplinary connections between history and archaeology in African studies. In addition to his teaching responsibilities in history and anthropology, Merrick served as chair of the Archaeology Interdepartmental Program (1979–1981), director of the Institute of Archaeology (1984–1987), and director of the James S. Coleman African Studies Center (1988–1992).

At UCLA, Merrick introduced the first undergraduate class in historical archaeology, a course that became one of the largest undergraduate courses of its kind in the country. He continued to teach this course, with excellent enrollment, five years after retirement. Merrick also trained many history and archaeology graduate students, including many who went on to complete dissertations on the historical archaeology of Africa, the Caribbean, and the United States.

Merrick's research, rooted in the pragmatics of developing culture historical sequences for poorly known regions of Africa can be characterized by what some historians of archaeology have called traditional or normative archaeology. In general, the New Archaeology of the 1960s made limited in roads in African archaeology. This was, perhaps, in part because of the limited data available for much of the continent and, as a result, a focus on site identification and chronology building. However, it is equally significant that the majority of the American and British archaeologists that worked in Africa, including Merrick, were either trained by or greatly influenced by the work of J. Desmond Clark and not the purveyors of the New Archaeology (see Posnansky 2002a:432–434; Robertshaw 1990:86).

Merrick's methodological reliance on nonarchaeological source material and ethnoarchaeological research, coupled with an appreciation of the cultural context in which social systems operated, prefigured the thrust of many post-proccessual analyses of the 1980s and 1990s. For graduate students at UCLA, Merrick thus made an appealing counterpoint to Jim Hill—who often taught the archaeological research methods course and who espoused a rigidly Hempelian, scientific, processual approach to archaeology. It is not surprising that many Americanist historical archaeologists, as well as Africanists, selected Merrick as an advisor.

Merrick's own research interests widened as he looked at historical archaeology in an increasingly broad perspective, including the material record of diasporic African populations. His review of historical archaeology in sub-Saharan Africa, presented at the 1984 Historical Archaeology conference and subsequently published in *Historical Archaeology*, surveyed the majority archaeological research then undertaken on sites where context was provided by documentary sources, including the settlements of the west African savanna and east African coast recorded in Arabic sources, as well as post 15th-century European coastal sites (Posnansky and DeCorse 1986). The article is notable in that Merrick had conducted research on or visited many of the sites discussed.

In terms of studies of the African Diaspora, Merrick's article "Towards an Archaeology of the African Diaspora," published in 1984, outlines both the potential and methodological pitfalls faced in making trans-Atlantic connections. His calls for the integrated study of both sides of the Atlantic and for greater collaboration between American researchers and scholars working in Africa are equally pertinent today (Posnansky 2002b).

Merrick has also maintained his long-standing interest in museums, beginning with his curatorship of the Uganda Museum in 1958. His recognition of the value of contemporary African art, concern for the training of African museum curators, and interest in the preservation of Africa's cultural resources continues today (Posnansky 1996, 1998). Apart from the countries where he himself worked, Merrick trained and influenced museum professionals over much of the continent. In recognition of his contributions, he was awarded the Leadership Award of the Arts Council of the African Studies Association (Posnansky 1998).

Merrick's ability to make connections and facilitate his students' work is a pervasive aspect of his career. The preliminary contacts, academic relations, and personal connections he made throughout the world facilitated research by a host of graduate students. Many students Merrick trained went on to play important roles in developing other programs in Africa, the Caribbean, and the United States. Merrick was a mentor to many of the first-generation African archaeologists who, in turn, have been important in establishing archaeology and museum programs in Uganda, Kenya, Tanzania, Benin, Togo, Ghana, and Zambia, as well as Jamaica. Reflecting on African archaeology, it is indeed possible for Merrick to say "African archaeology has come of age" (Posnansky 1982). A consequence of these wide-ranging connections is that Merrick's students constitute the core of a still-small group of historical archaeologists who have done substantive work on both sides of the Atlantic. Merrick has consistently viewed his role as educator and mentor as more important than his career as an archaeologist. Our collective appreciation for Merrick's efforts is reflected in the festschrift volume (11) of the *African Archaeological Review*, published by his students in 1993.

And so, Merrick, we honor you with the J. C. Harrington Medal in Historical Archaeology for professional contributions but also in recognition of your role as a mentor, colleague, and friend.

REFERENCES

CROSSLEY, DAVID
    1990 *Post-Medieval Archaeology in Britain.* Leicester University Press, New York.

FAGAN, BRIAN
    2001 *Grahame Clark: An Intellectual Life of an Archaeologist.* Westview Press, Boulder, CO.

GOLDEN, BERNARD
    1969 Coastal Survey: 1969. Manuscript, Department of Archaeology, University of Ghana, Legon., Africa.

KENSE, FRANÇOIS J.
    1990 Archaeology in Anglophone West Africa. In *A History of African Archaeology*, Peter Robertshaw, editor, pp. 135–154. Heinemann, Portsmouth, NH.

LAWRENCE, A. W.
    1963 *Trade Castles and Forts of West Africa.* Jonathan Cape, London.

MORELL, VIRGINIA
    1995 Ancestral Passions: The Leakey Family and the Quest for Humankind's Beginnings. New York, Simon and Schuster.

POSNANSKY, MERRICK
    1956 The Lamport Post Mill. *Journal of the Northamptonshire Natural History Society and Field Club,* 33:66–79.
    1959a A Hope Fountain Site at Olorgesailie, Kenya Colony. *South African Archaeological Bulletin,* 14:83–89.
    1959b The Progress and Prospects in Historical Archaeology in Uganda. In Discovering Africa's Past, pp. 31–39. *Uganda Museum Occasional Papers,* no. 4. Kampala.
    1963 The Lower and Middle Paleolithic Industries of the English East Midlands. *Proceedings of the Prehistoric Society,* 29(12): 357–394.
    1966 Kingship, Archaeology, and Historical Myth. *Uganda Journal,* 30:1–12.
    1967a Excavations at Lanet, Kenya 1967. *Azania,* 2:89–114.
    1967b The Iron Age in East Africa. In *Background to Evolution in Africa,* Walter William Bishop and J. Desmond Clark, editors, pp. 629–649. University of Chicago Press, Chicago, IL.
    1968a Cairns in the Southern Part of the Kenya Rift Valley. *Azania,* 3:181–187.
    1968b The Excavation of an Ankole Capital Site at Bweyorere. *Uganda Journal,* 32:165–182.
    1969a Bigo bya Mugenyi. *Uganda Journal,* 33:125–150.

1969b Myth and Methodology, the Archaeological Contributions to African History. *University of Ghana, Legon, Open Lecture Series*. Ghana Universities Press, Accra.

1973 Aspects of Early West African Trade. *World Archaeology*, 5(2):149–162.

1982 African Archaeology Comes of Age. *World Archaeology*, 13:345–358.

1984 Toward an Archaeology of the Black Diaspora. *Journal of Black Studies*, 15(2):195–205.

1996 Coping with Collapse in the 1990s: West African Museums, Universities, and National Patrimonies. In *Plundering Africa's Past*, Peter R. Schmidt and Roderick J. McIntosh, editors, pp. 143–163. Indiana University Press, Bloomington.

1998 Acceptance of the Arts Council of the African Studies Association Leadership Award. Paper presented at the 11th Triennial Symposium on African Arts, New Orleans, LA.

2002a Working with J. Desmond Clark. In J. Desmond Clark, An Archaeologist at Work in African Prehistory and Early Human Studies, Teamwork and Insight, Kathy Schick and Nicholas Toth, editors, pp. 432–444. *University History Series*. Regents of the University of California, Berkeley.

2002b Revelations, Roots, and Reactions—Archaeology and the African Diaspora. *Ufahamu*, 29(1):45–63.

n.d. Processes of Change—A Longitudinal Ethno-Archaeological Study of a Ghanaian Village: Hani 1970–1998. *African Archaeological Review*, in press.

POSNANSKY, MERRICK, AND CHRISTOPHER R. DECORSE
1986 Historical Archaeology in Sub-Saharan Africa: A Review. *Historical Archaeology*, 20(1):1–14.

POSNANSKY, MERRICK, AND CHARLES NELSON
1968 Rock Paintings and Excavations at Nyero. *Azania*, 3:147–166.

POSNANSKY, MERRICK, AND ALBERT VAN DANTZIG
1976 Fort Ruychaver Rediscovered. *Sankofa*, 2:7–18.

ROBERTSHAW, PETER
1990 The Development of Archaeology in East Africa. In *A History of African Archaeology*, Peter Robertshaw, editor, p. 78–94. Heinemann, Portsmouth, NH.

SCHMIDT, PETER
1990 Oral Traditions, Archaeology, and History: A Short Reflexive History. In *A History of African Archaeology*, Peter Robertshaw, editor, pp. 252–270. Heinemann, Portsmouth, NH.

SIMMONDS, DOIG
1973 A Note on the Excavations in Cape Coast Castle. *Transactions of the Historical Society of Ghana*, 14(2):267–297.

SWINNERTON, HENRY H., WALTER R. CHALMERS, AND MERRICK POSNANSKY
1956 The Medieval Tile Works of Lenton Priory. *Transactions of the Thoroton Society,* Vol. 60.

Christopher R. DeCorse

J. C. Harrington Medal in Historical Archaeology: Kathleen A. Deagan, 2004. Volume 38, Number 4 (2004): 5-7.
By Bonnie G. McEwan.

J. C. Harrington Medal in Historical Archaeology

Kathleen A. Deagan 2004

Kathleen A. Deagan was honored at the 2004 annual meeting of The Society for Historical Archaeology in St. Louis, Missouri, as this year's recipient of the J. C. Harrington Medal for her contributions to the field of historical archaeology.

Born in Norfolk, Virginia, Deagan is the daughter of a U.S. Navy meteorologist. Her family lived on Navy bases around the world, and she attended twenty-two different schools before entering college. Deagan has suggested that her early predisposition to anthropology resulted from having spent much of her youth figuring out the social organization of her constantly changing schools.

In 1966, Deagan's father was transferred to the Navy hurricane squadron in Jacksonville, Florida, and she enrolled as an undergraduate at the University of Florida. After taking classes in prehistory and American Indians, with Charles Fairbanks, and an archaeological field school, directed by the charismatic Jerald Milanich, she decided to major in anthropology. As a doctoral student in the early 1970s, Deagan became involved in the long-term research program in St. Augustine initiated by Fairbanks and John Griffin. Fairbanks had been advocating a shift from monumental structures to backyard archaeology, and the first of these investigations was at the 18th-century residence of an Indian woman, Maria de la Cruz, who was married to a Spanish soldier. The site provided ideal historical parameters for Deagan to initiate the archaeology of *mestizaje* (European-Indian intermarriage and cultural admixture) while creating a social history for poorly documented segments of St. Augustine society. It also marked the beginning of her interdisciplinary approach to research and her lifelong interest in the processes underlying the development of the Hispanic-American cultural tradition.

After completing her doctoral degree at the University of Florida in 1974, Deagan was hired as an assistant professor at Florida State University and continued her research aimed at defining social attributes and their archaeological correlates for St. Augustine's 18th-century population. Five years later, she turned her attention to 16th-century sites, interpreting these in reference to their well-documented 18th-century counterparts. Deagan's study of the 16th-century community began with an innovative auger survey to delimit the early settlement. By plotting the distribution of materials from the colonial town and its hinterland, she was able to determine the physical evolution of the community. Deagan also archaeologically documented one of the more devastating realities of colonization; the earliest sites were defined by the presence of pure Timucua pottery, while later sites contained gradually higher proportions of tribally mixed ceramics, revealing the rapid decline of the indigenous population and the relocation of other native peoples into the area. The results of this survey were so successful that the methodology has been emulated throughout the Spanish colonial research community.

In 1982, Deagan left Florida State University and joined the faculty at the Florida State Museum (now the Florida Museum of Natural History) at the University of Florida. She immediately assumed responsibility for the Puerto Real project in modern-day Haiti that had been initiated by Fairbanks a few years earlier. Puerto Real (1503–1578) was one of 13 original settlements established by Nicolás de Ovando on Hispaniola, and Deagan had long recognized the potential of the earliest Caribbean sites for her study of colonialism and the development of the modern world. For the next seven years she not only directed annual work at Puerto Real but, in 1983, also began her search for the nearby settlement of La Navidad (also known as En Bas Saline) where Columbus's ship, the *Santa Maria*, ran aground in 1492. Periodic work at La Navidad continues to this day.

At the University of Florida, Deagan met and married internationally renowned wildlife ecologist Larry Harris and became a caring stepmother to his four children. Marriage and family did not slow Deagan's pace. Rather, Harris invigorated her intellectual curiosity and reshaped some of her ideas through their shared interests in natural and cultural systems. Deagan and Harris have a remarkable relationship in their marriage, their professional lives, and among family and friends.

In 1989, Deagan expanded her research to the modern-day Dominican Republic to investigate La Isabela (1493–1498), Columbus's first permanent settlement in the New World. As the only wholly 15th-century European settlement in the Americas, La Isabela represented the ideal context to investigate plants, animals, pathogens, social institutions, and technologies initially introduced on the American landscape, and the roots of the adaptive strategies she had documented at later sites. In 1995, once the La Isabela project was well underway, Deagan initiated work at Concepción de la Vega (1496–1562), another of the earliest cities in Spanish America located in the interior of the present day Dominican Republic.

Despite her very active research program in the Caribbean during the 1980s and 1990s, Deagan has always maintained projects in St. Augustine. In 1986, she embarked on fieldwork at Ft. Mosé, the first legally sanctioned free black town in the Americas. The attention she brought to this site resulted not only in the state's acquisition of the property but also in one of the most successful traveling exhibits in the country. Deagan has continued work at the Fountain of Youth Park and Nombre de Dios, investigating the initial settlement of Pedro Menéndez de Avilés and St. Augustine's first and most complex mission community.

Using impeccable field techniques, Deagan has methodically amassed an extraordinary database from which she has formulated the outlines of a Spanish colonial adaptive strategy that incorporates gender, socioeconomic variables, and ethnicity—broad patterns with regional variations that she has explored throughout the Americas. She has also engaged in a scholarly investigation of American Indians and Africans in Euramerican cultural development as well as their profound contributions to New World colonial life and Latin American culture today.

When she determined that available typological tools were inadequate, Deagan addressed Spanish material culture systematics. Initially drawing on the ceramic studies of Fairbanks, John Goggin, and

Florence and Robert Lister, Deagan has spent the past 20 years conducting comprehensive research on Hispanic material culture. This ongoing study has resulted in the publication of two encyclopedic reference volumes, with a third one in progress.

Students have been a significant feature in all of Deagan's research projects. She has taught as many as three field schools a year, sometimes alternating in different countries. These sojourns have become legendary for their rigor, for their immersive approach to all things archaeological, and for the remarkable number of her students who have gone on to become professional archaeologists. To this day, Deagan teaches one of the finest archaeological field schools in the country, and most of her students remember having highly influential educational experiences with her. They also remember her special field school traditions such as cooking wonderful dinners (usually Minorcan clam chowder) for the crew before midterm exams, fun nights on the town with her graduate supervisors, and, of course, the famous end-of-semester proms that have kept St. Augustine's thrift stores in business over the years.

Those who have been fortunate enough to have her as a major professor owe her a lifelong debt as a mentor and friend. While at FSU, Deagan had dozens of master's students; as of 2002 at the University of Florida she had served on 55 graduate committees and chaired 8 PhDs and 10 MAs. Countless students have been supported by the more than 50 major research grants she has been awarded.

In much the same way that she has selflessly guided and supported students, Deagan has reached out to archaeologists throughout Latin America and Europe. She has always made a special effort to help those in underserved Latin American and Caribbean countries who have limited access to resources through her frequent visits, consultations, workshops, and donated publications. On many occasions she has invited students and scholars from around the world into her home for extended periods of time while they conducted research, attended conferences, and completed coursework. She is unquestionably one of historical archaeology's finest international ambassadors.

Kathleen Deagan's efforts throughout the years have enriched and facilitated the work of others by example, generosity, and unmatched intellectual contributions. Her publication record is nothing short of phenomenal and includes 10 books, 35 major articles, and 18 chapters in books. Her most recent two-volume set (with José María Cruxent) on the history and archaeology of La Isabela was awarded the 2003 outstanding book award by the Society for American Archaeology. Other scholarly achievements have been recognized through awards by numerous institutions and organizations over the years. Deagan was named Distinguished Research Curator at the Florida Museum of Natural History in 1995, Alumna of Outstanding Achievement by the University of Florida in 1997, and awarded a Distinguished Research Professorship by the University of Florida Research Foundation in 1999.

Over the past 25 years, Deagan has also been committed to professional service and has served as an elected officer for the Florida Archaeological Council, Southeastern Archaeological Conference, and the Society for American Archaeology. She has been an active member of SHA throughout her career as newsletter coordinator for the Southeast (1979–1984), board member (1980–1983), Editorial Advisory Committee member (1983–1999), president-elect (1984), and president (1985). Currently, she is an important political face of archaeology as the chair of the Florida Humanities Council (2002–2005).

In recognition of three decades of extraordinary scholarship, student training, and professional service, Kathleen Deagan has been awarded the 2004 J. C. Harrington Medal for her outstanding contributions to the field of historical archaeology.

BONNIE G. MCEWAN

1

J. C. Harrington Medal in Historical Archaeology

Marcel Moussette 2005

The Archaeologist Who Came in from the Cold

Marcel Moussette's life and work resemble a river whose nature changes while essentially remaining the same through time. This may seem a tired metaphor, but when the St. Lawrence River is as important as it has been for Marcel in his personal and professional evolution, it is the only metaphor that can be used to grasp the full depth of his achievement. This is especially true when "St. Lawrence River" is said in French: *fleuve*, meaning a mighty watercourse flowing into the sea. No English equivalent exists for *fleuve* and this, too, is appropriate, as Marcel's contribution to scholarship has been almost exclusively in French. Only Marcel could tell us if this is a political gesture, but its importance as a cultural statement is there for the whole world to see. For all of us, his work is a benchmark of the intellectual maturity of historical archaeology, as the concepts and substance of our discipline flow into other cultural universes.

A hallmark of Marcel's work is depth—depth of detail, depth of understanding—deep structures that lead us to comprehend the richness of social life. It is easy and appropriate to add breadth—breadth of subject, breadth of explanation—to Marcel's qualities. Together, depth and breadth can be conjugated in both French and English as *context*, and Marcel has always maintained the importance of this approach in his research as well as in his teachings.

The importance of context goes back to his early life.

Marcel was born and raised in La Prairie, a small town founded as a Jesuit mission in the 17th century on the south shore of the St. Lawrence, facing Montréal across the Lachine Rapids. He spent his childhood with both feet in the current, fishing, swimming, and playing. Many recurring themes in Marcel's work have resonances with this time and place. La Prairie is next door to the Iroquois community of Kahnawake (Caughnawaga), renowned for a church bell reputedly taken from Deerfield, Massachusetts, in the infamous 1704 raid. Was one of Marcel's ancestors in that raiding party? Perhaps not, but his own forays into American intellectual territory lead me to believe it is possible! La Prairie and Kahnawake have intermingled during their 330 years of existence, hybrids of French and Iroquoian cultures. Marcel's continuing interest in the mutual influence of European and Amerindian cultures on each other, evident in his early work as a biologist and predominant in his recent work on the symbolism of religious medallions, is perhaps a consequence of the proximity of these two communities. His father worked in La Prairie's brickyards, which may be the inspiration for his deep interest in ceramics, processes for fabricating objects and, ultimately, in the fabrication of meaning.

Marcel began his studies, as he did his career, as a biologist studying fishing in the St. Lawrence. He was no ordinary biologist and could easily have been mistaken for an ethnographer as he studied the history of the industry and conducted fieldwork with traditional fisher folk. This research resulted in a publication on fishing technologies from the Contact period up to the 20th century (*La pêche sur le Saint-Laurent, répertoire des méthodes et des engins de capture*, Boréal Express, 1979), and it was to herald Marcel's great interest in material culture within a larger cultural system. It is not surprising to see that he continued his studies as an ethnologist and historian in the anthropology department of the Université de Montréal and then the history department of Université Laval. His doctoral research, based on material from Parks Canada's large-scale archaeological project, the Forges de Saint-Maurice, addressed a subject that warmed the hearts of all those who read it: the history of domestic heating in Canada, published as *Le chauffage domestique au Canada* (Presses de l'Université Laval, 1983).

Marcel's specialty has always been material culture—he is one of the foremost specialists on French material culture in North America. He worked from 1968 to 1980 with Parks Canada, first in Ottawa as a field archaeologist and analyst and then in Québec City as director of the Québec region's material culture division. It was while working in Ottawa that Marcel met his lovely and charming wife, Jane Macauley, and became the father of two sons.

One of his achievements as an applied archaeologist was directing the development of guides for classifying finds from Parks Canada's numerous projects according to material and function. This was a huge step towards understanding the voluminous material coming from projects such as the Forges de Saint-Maurice, the Fortifications of Québec City, and Beaubassin, to mention only the better-known sites. This was done at a time when comparable endeavors were being undertaken in the United States (remember, this was the heyday of New Archaeology) and when nothing similar existed in French. It allowed a young generation of scholars to sink their teeth directly into archaeology without first having to go through language training. The guides also permitted easy and efficient communication within that community, as they soon became the standard instruments for historical archaeology in French Canada. They continue to be used to this day, though they have undergone several revisions to take new discoveries and growing sophistication into account. Marcel continues to oversee the production of material culture guides (*Identifier la céramique et le verre anciens au Québec: guide à l'usage des amateurs et des professionnels*, Michel Brassard and Myriam Leclerc, CÉLAT, 2001). Marcel has given much thought to the complex meaning of objects, and his approach to material culture has gone far beyond typologies, extending to the analysis of their context ("L'objet archéologique, réceptacle et générateur de sens," *Paléo-Québec*, 1995, 23:3–15).

He published an analysis of coarse earthenwares from Place-Royale in Québec City and a report on excavations at Champlain's Habitation during a brief 15 months as a freelance consultant after leaving Parks Canada in 1980. The published results of these projects (*Les terres cuites communes des maisons Estèbe et Boisseau*, Collection Patrimoines, Ministère de la Culture et des Communications, dossier 51, 1996; *Le site de l'Habitation de Champlain à Québec*, Ministère des Affaires culturelles, dossier 58, 1985, with Françoise Niellon) are essential references for archaeologists studying the French Régime in North America.

When Marcel joined the faculty of Université Laval in 1981, he instigated a field school at the Intendant's Palace site in Québec City. This project, which ran from 1982 to 1991, sustained a large number of master's theses, and it was a particularly fertile training ground for numerous students. His 1994 monograph, *Le site du Palais de l'intendant à Québec, génèse et structuration d'un lieu urbain* (Septentrion), explores the relationship between structural changes that occurred there over three and a half centuries and the various meanings attributed to the site by the inhabitants of Québec City. It is an excellent example of the use of contextual archaeology to study the multiple universes of an archaeological site, and it remains a seminal work on urban archaeology. Marcel's influential article on the site, published in *Historical Archaeology* ("The Site of the Intendant's Palace in Québec City: The Changing Meaning of an Urban Space," 1996, 30(2): 8–21) opens a window on this rich project. The Intendant's Palace project produced many other articles, many of which are unknown, as they are published in French. It is for that reason that full references are included here.

Marcel's most recently published research is the result of years of patient work begun on the Intendant's Palace site but ranging over the vast territory of New France—one-third of North America—that was administered from this site during the French colonial period. This research examines the dual symbolism of religious medallions used as tools of acculturation by the French and accepted as tokens of their own cultural identity by Amerindians, and it aptly shows the depth of his inquiry. At Marcel's plenary session address at the 2002 meetings in Mobile, Alabama ("An Encounter in the Baroque Age: Amerindians and French in North America"), he ably expounded on the hybridization of European and Native American ideologies as witnessed in the use of baroque art styles. Several articles develop this theme in depth: "Des couteaux pour la traite des fourrures," *Material History Review/Revue d'histoire de la culture matérielle,* 2000, 51:3–15; "Les médailles religieuses, une forme de l'imagerie baroque en Nouvelle-France," *Les cahiers des Dix,* 2001, 55:295–329; "Les garnitures de fusils de traite des magasins du roi à Québec: un autre chemin de l'univers baroque en Amérique du Nord," *Archéologiques,* 2001, 14:50–78; "Archéologie d'une rencontre. Les univers dualistes français et amérindiens dans l'Amérique septentrionale des XVIIe et XVIIIe siècles," *Recherches amérindiennes au Québec,* 2002, 32(1):13–27.

In 1987, Marcel returned to the St. Lawrence River, where, until 1998, he directed a research project on an early agricultural site—l'île aux Oies. This research program has greatly expanded perceptions of the 17th-century rural world by documenting in detail insular subsistence patterns and their influence on land use during the early French Regime. This project demonstrated the research potential of rural seigneuries and farmsteads that had been largely overlooked by Québec archaeologists ("Il nous reste un passé à creuser. Pour une archéologie du monde rural du XVIIe siècle," *Interface,* 1995, 16(3):18–29). His soon-to-be-published monograph, covering 12 years of research on this project, will be for the deep structure of meaning for agricultural sites what the Intendant's Palace site was for urban archaeology. He has, at the same time, directed several seasons of field schools in his hometown of La Prairie.

The ecumenical nature of Marcel's work has been recognized by his peers in Québec. He was a member of the provincial Cultural Properties Commission from 1983 to 1986. As such, he played an instrumental role in directing the protection and development of the province's heritage resources. From 1985 to 2002, he was co-coordinator for the Memorandum of Agreement for archaeological research between the City of Québec and Université Laval. He has assumed similar responsibilities in a Memorandum of Agreement between the City of La Prairie and Université Laval since 2000. These agreements have fostered the training of hundreds of undergraduate students and dozens of graduate students in historical archaeology. In 1997, he was accepted as a member of *La société des Dix* (The Group of Ten), an exclusive multidisciplinary intellectual society founded in 1935. His inaugural essay ("Un héros sans visage: Champlain et l'archéologie," *Les cahiers des Dix,* 2000, 54:13–44) addressed the thorny question of the populist archaeological fascination for the tomb of the founder of New France, Samuel de Champlain.

William Moss

This debate steeled positions in Québec through the 19th and 20th centuries in much the same way as metal detectorists are the subject of controversy in this new century. Marcel's key role in developing historical archaeology in Québec and Canada was recognized by The Society for Historical Archaeology when it presented him its Award of Merit in 2000. Most recently (August 2003), he was elected as the director of the CÉLAT, an inter-university research center uniting 30 scholars from five different universities in subjects as various as literature, art history, sociology, semiotics, history, anthropology, and, of course, archaeology. His role as director of an interdisciplinary research center goes beyond strictly disciplinary research to combine the strengths of its component social sciences.

I have known Marcel Moussette as a teacher, a mentor, a colleague, and a friend. We have lived in the same neighborhood for more than 25 years, so I have seen him very frequently and in many different contexts. I often run into him on the street, where he may be talking to a student, a colleague, someone who has found bottles in their back yard, or an artist looking for inspiration from someone known for his coherent worldview. Marcel is such a well-known personality that even his former neighbors, the local Hell's Angels chapter, would ask him for advice. I do not know if their questions were strictly limited to archaeology, but, elsewhere, I do know that he has lectured on the subject for a grassroots initiative called "The People's University." His outreach is real and constant, and it comes in many forms. You probably haven't read his two novels—yes, they are only in French—but you may have heard the French-language versions of Canadian folk-rock singer Bruce Cockburn's songs translated by Marcel, some of his other lasting contributions to Canadian cultural life.

I know of no endearing faults (nor of annoying ones), only of many personal and intellectual qualities. His greatest intellectual quality is certainly his insatiable curiosity, while his greatest personal quality is without a doubt his humaneness, evident through his respect for others and his great generosity. He is patient, levelheaded, attentive, wise, and, above all, modest. For all of this, Marcel is greatly appreciated by his students and hotly sought after as a thesis director (he has directed 39 master's students and 5 doctoral). He is proficient and generous with advice on subjects as diverse as literature, child-raising, hiking equipment, or speed skating. I know he has been of succor to colleagues, friends, and students in life crises on many occasions.

Marcel is able to apply the substance of his work to everyday life. One example comes from his intellectual interest for heating systems. Marcel and I were in a restaurant one freezing winter day. It was –30 outside, and that is either Centigrade or Fahrenheit when it gets that cold. A person, perhaps a man but too bundled-up to tell, came in and walked by. Marcel remarked that the bundle was dragging a "cloud of cold" with it through the restaurant. It was all too true. This remark inspired another analogy that rings true for the Laurentian valley as well as for the spread of historical archaeology into new cultural universes. It will also serve as my conclusion: the recognition that Marcel Moussette receives today from The Society for Historical Archaeology marks his coming in from the cold. Thank you, Marcel, for warming our hearts and minds.

WILLIAM MOSS

J. C. Harrington Medal in Historical Archaeology

Donald L. Hardesty 2006

Donald Lynn Hardesty was born 2 September 1941 in Terra Alta, West Virginia, to Ezra J. and Mary Aidren Jenkins Hardesty. Don's father clerked in the local store and worked as a coal miner. From 1943 through 1945 the family lived part of the time in Baltimore, Maryland, while Ezra Hardesty was employed in a defense plant. Before leaving for Maryland, the family bought a small farm in Bear Wallow, 2-1/2 miles from Terra Alta and lived there until 1959. After World War II, Don's father went to work for the Uptegraf Manufacturing Company, which built industrial

electrical transformers. When the plant moved to Somerset, Pennsylvania, in 1959, so did the Hardesty family.

After Don graduated from Terra Alta High School in 1959, he moved to Washington, DC, at first living with an uncle. He got a job at the National Bureau of Standards and then located to the District of Columbia near Chevy Chase, Maryland. Don worked at the bureau for three years, taking night classes in electrical engineering at George Washington University. He learned about archaeology by visiting the Smithsonian Institution on weekends, particularly the National Museum of Natural History, and by reading. He decided archaeology was more interesting than electrical engineering and applied to the universities of New Mexico, Arizona, and Kentucky. He was accepted at all three but chose the University of Kentucky where he encountered Douglas K. Schwartz, then a young associate professor who was developing a local archaeological program, running a small museum, and serving concurrently as an associate dean.

Schwartz, who had done his dissertation research on the archaeology of the Grand Canyon, had begun a project to excavate archaeological sites on the Unkar Delta in the bottom of Grand Canyon, an epic undertaking in southwestern archaeology since the crew and all supplies had to be shuttled from the South Rim to the canyon bottom and back by helicopter. Don took classes from Schwartz with fellow students Robert Dunnell (also a refugee from West Virginia) and Lee Hanson. (Dunnell went on to get a PhD at Yale and had a long and eminent career in southeastern archaeology and teaching at the University of Washington; Hanson became a prominent National Park Service archaeologist.)

From 1962 through mid-1964, Hardesty and Dunnell did archaeological fieldwork in southwestern and eastern Kentucky, initially under Schwartz's direction until Schwartz left to become director (later president, now president-emeritus) of the School of American Research (SAR) in Santa Fe. After moving to SAR, Schwartz continued the Grand Canyon project, and Hardesty was a crew chief during the major excavations in 1967.

Hardesty graduated from the University of Kentucky in 1964 and entered the anthropology graduate program at the University of Oregon (U of O), taking his first archaeology seminar under Albert Spaulding. Later, the inimitable Don Dumond became his dissertation advisor. In 1967, Dumond sent Hardesty off to Mexico to help U of O architect George Andrews record the Classic-period Maya site of Comalcalco in the State of Tabasco. Hardesty continued to pursue Mesoamerican archaeology in graduate school and as late as 1974 worked at the post-Classic Maya site of Utatlan in the western highlands of Guatemala with a team from SUNY-Albany.

Meanwhile, Hardesty had become interested in physical anthropology. He attended the International Seminar on Methods in Human Biology at Wayne State University in Detroit, Michigan, right after the riots of 1967–1968, an interesting and dicey time to be in Motown, but he still needed a dissertation topic. Hardesty had finished his course work, received an MA in 1967, taken his doctoral comprehensive exams, and was ABD by spring 1968. Ecological anthropology was just becoming a major focus in American anthropology, growing out of the earlier cultural ecology of Julian Steward. Hardesty did his dissertation on that topic, completed in 1972, which was the basis for his *Ecological Anthropology* (1977). In spring 1968, a phone call led him to Nevada.

Warren d'Azevedo had been brought to the University of Nevada (after 1968 the University of Nevada, Reno, or UNR) in 1963 to start an anthropology program. By 1967–1968, the nascent department was moving toward splitting off from sociology and broadening its curriculum. Someone was needed who could teach physical anthropology. D'Azevedo called Verne Dorjahn at U of O, who recommended Hardesty. He was hired on a one-year appointment for the 1968–1969 academic year.

The appointment was made permanent in May 1969 (contingent on his finishing a dissertation), and Don had found a fiancée. On 29 August 1969, Donald Lynn Hardesty married Susan Bennett, of Reno, Nevada, the daughter of Henry (Chick) and Maria Zimbalist Golet Bennett. Susan was a horsewoman, an artist, and an avid bridge player, considerably talented and skilled at all three. She gave up the horses but remains an artist, an avid Giants baseball fan, and a gracious spouse and helpmate to Don, nearly 37 years (and counting) as of this writing.

By 1971 Hardesty was turning his interests from Mesoamerica to the Great Basin. He had undertaken an archaeology project in the Lava Beds area of southern Oregon, including some of the redoubts built by the Indians during the so-called Modoc War of 1872–1873. It was his first foray into Great Basin historical archaeology. Don Hardesty and his UNR colleagues have made the Great Basin the central focus for their researches in prehistoric and historical archaeology, ethnography, linguistics, ethnohistory, and ecological anthropology of the various ethnic populations who have lived therein at various times. These populations include Native Americans as well as Chinese, Basques, Mexicans, and members of the numerous ethnic groups from northern and western Europe who came to the region after about 1820. When the department initiated a doctoral program in 1988, the focus was expanded to the American West, including Mexico, to better reflect the range of faculty and student research. A major part of that program has been Hardesty's historical archaeology track, which continues to attract students from across the country.

In 1973, Don ran his first archaeological field school in Little Valley, a high mountain valley on the east side of the Sierra Nevada between Reno and Carson City. The area had been logged during the Comstock boom times, and he focused on a sawmill and a logging camp. In January 1974, he gave his first paper at a professional meeting on the Little Valley work at the annual meeting of The Society for Historical Archaeology in Oakland, California. Paul Schumacher of the National Park Service heard the paper and encouraged Don to continue to develop historical archaeology in the Great Basin. As SHA members know, Schumacher had a long-standing interest in historical archaeology and was aware that cultural resource management (CRM) was then aborning. After the now-legendary meeting on conservation archaeology in Denver, Colorado, in December 1974, CRM quickly came to dominate American archaeology, particularly in the West. Hardesty soon found no lack of contracts available to support various historical archaeology projects. He completed work in Little Valley and began excavation of two Pony Express stations, Cold Springs and Sand Springs, as well as the Rock Spring Overland Stage and Telegraph station in west-central Nevada in 1976–1978.

In the meantime, he finished his justly famed *Ecological Anthropology*, first published in 1977 and widely used for many years as a textbook. In 1979 it was translated and published in Spanish and, later, in Chinese (2003). In a long series of important papers published between 1972 and the present, Hardesty has expanded and enriched his theoretical approach to ecological anthropology and its salient applications to general anthropology,

demography, environmental change, and historical archaeology. These publications led to his appointment from 1977 to 1987 to the prestigious international directorate for arid lands ecosystems of the UNESCO Man and the Biosphere program.

He did not really commit himself fully to historical archaeology until fall 1978, which he spent with Stan South, Ken Lewis, and others at the University of South Carolina, working at Middleton Place Plantation near Charleston. Hardesty began to put together the methods he had learned in prehistoric archaeology with those of South and his colleagues and applied them in the Great Basin. Increasingly, his ecological anthropology theoretical orientation led him to think about the American western frontier, particularly the mining frontier, in new and fruitful ways. Since 1980, he and his graduate students have applied historical archaeological and ecological anthropology methods and theories to investigate the industrial, social, and cultural histories of mines, mining districts, and mining towns in the Great Basin at (among other sites) Cortez, Candelaria, Shermantown, Island Mountain, Treasure City, Unionville, and especially Virginia City as well as in the Mojave Desert at Fort Irwin and Joshua Tree National Park. More recently, he and his students have invaded Alaska to investigate Klondike era Gold Rush sites and early military communications systems.

In 1993, in cooperation with the Nevada State Historic Preservation Office, Hardesty and his students initiated an ongoing program of public archaeology in Virginia City involving dozens, indeed hundreds, of volunteers ranging from school children to well-trained avocational archaeologists. Thousands of tourists who came to Virginia City seeking the mythical Bonanza of television fame eagerly watched, instead, the meticulous excavation of 19th-century saloons and other cultural features. By 1990, Hardesty and his students also began investigating 1930s homesteads and sites at which various gender and ethnic issues could be defined through the excavation and documentation of various sites from Lake Tahoe to eastern Nevada and on to Colorado and Montana. All of this has been fodder for a long series of thoughtful and groundbreaking papers in which Hardesty has fruitfully ruminated about mining frontiers and mining history, not only in the American West but also in Europe and elsewhere.

Then there is the Donner Party. As all those who teach anthropology 101 know, nothing grabs the attention of college students and the general public like incest and cannibalism. In 1987, Hardesty began excavations at Donner Party sites in the Sierra Nevada. There is no record of incest (so far), but the legends are plentiful of anthropophagy during the terrible winter of 1846–1847 that the Donners and their compatriots spent snowbound in the mountains. In 1997 Hardesty published *The Archaeology of the Donner Party* with contributions by colleagues (University of Nevada Press, Reno), the first summary of the archaeological evidence relating to the tragedy.

Don Hardesty's entire academic career from 1968 to the present has been at the University of Nevada-Reno, beginning as a temporary instructor and becoming a full professor in 1980. In 2005 he was named the Mamie Kleberg Professor of Historic Preservation and Anthropology. He has been department chair three times: 1973–75, 1984–86, and 2004 to the present. He also served as acting dean of the Graduate School in 1989–1990. The university has, quite appropriately, honored him with its two most prestigious awards for active faculty—a UNR Foundation Professorship, 1994–1996, and the UNR Outstanding Researcher of the Year Award, 2001. External awards include the Rodman Paul Award from the Mining History Association for outstanding scholarship in mining history in 2000.

In addition to his regular teaching, Hardesty was a major lecturer/seminar leader in the University of Nevada-Reno Continuing Education Program in Heritage Resources Management from its inception in 1987 until 2004. As the program's founding director, I appreciated not only Don's skills as an instructor but his advice about the development and management of the program. His and Barbara Little's 2000 *Assessing the Archaeological Significance of Historic Sites* (Altamira Press, Walnut Creek) is one of several significant publications that grew out of that program and is widely used across the country in both academic and CRM contexts.

Hardesty has served on innumerable university committees. His statewide service includes the Editorial Board of the Nevada Historical Society

Quarterly, 1979–1986; the University of Nevada Press Advisory Board, 1993–1997; the State of Nevada Advisory Board for Historic Preservation and Archaeology, 1977–1993; and the State Board of Museums and History, 1993–present.

Hardesty's national and international service has been exemplary. In addition to his contributions to the UNESCO Man and the Biosphere program, he also served as archaeology theme editor for UNESCO's *Encyclopedia of Life Support Systems*. Since 1980 he has been a consulting archaeologist for the National Park Service and the Historic American Engineering Record on a series of projects. He has served The Society for Historical Archaeology (SHA) well, as president in 1987 and as a member of the Board of Directors in 1981–1983 and again in 1986–1988. He also has served on the Editorial Board of *Historical Archaeology* since 1986 and as an associate editor from 1988 to 2004.

On a personal note, I particularly appreciated his being president of SHA in 1987, since I was then president of the Society for American Archaeology, and we could talk archaeo-politics in the hallway between our offices. We talked mostly about the historic shipwrecks legislation which all of us were working on at that time. In addition to his SHA duties, Hardesty served the Society of Professional Archaeologist (SOPA) on the Executive Board, 1986–1988; the Nominations Committee, 1990–1992; and the Standards Board, 1993–1994. He was president of the Register of Professional Archaeologists (RPA) in the critical period when SOPA was metamorphosing into RPA, 2000–2001. As if this were not enough, he also served on the Mining History Association Executive Council, 1990–1992, and was the association's president in 1999.

Finally, and most importantly in Don's eyes, there are his students. He has taught hundreds of undergraduates over the years in courses reputed to be "hard, but boy it's interesting," as one undergrad opined. As of December 2005, Don has graduated 26 master's and 5 doctoral students. He has found monies for assistantships and field research for nearly all of them. They have been privileged to have him as a mentor and as a role model of what a scholar should be. His UNR compatriots are privileged to have Don Hardesty as a colleague and friend.

The professions of historical archaeology and anthropology, as well as the general and scholarly publics, are privileged to have a wise and innovative scholar who has helped us know more about the lives and times of those who lived in the American West and beyond.

DON D. FOWLER

J. C. Harrington Medal in Historical Archaeology: William M. Kelso, 2007. Volume 41, Number 2 (2007): 1-4. By Carter L. Hudgins.

J. C. Harrington Medal in Historical Archaeology

WILLIAM M. KELSO 2007

Bill Kelso left his native Ohio in 1963, the year he completed an undergraduate degree in history at Baldwin-Wallace College, to enroll in a graduate program in early American history and culture at the College of William and Mary. He has, except for a brief stint in Georgia, lived and worked in Virginia ever since. Bill has said that reading a *National Geographic* article about the 1957 excavations at Jamestown on a cold March day in his college library inspired his path to Virginia where it might, he thought, be possible to blend his two passions, archaeology and early American history. Williamsburg was exactly the right place to combine those interests. Kelso wrote a master's thesis on shipbuilding in 18th-century Virginia, but he also met, and soon worked for, Ivor Noël Hume. Summer field seasons from 1964 to 1966, one of them excavating the site of Williamsburg's 18th-century Public Hospital, launched a career in historical archaeology that now spans five decades.

As a graduate student at William and Mary, Kelso visited Jamestown where he, like other visitors, was told that the site of the 1607 fort and subsequent settlement there had eroded into the James River. Something about that explanation did not ring true, and in 1993, with permission to explore an area almost precisely where J. C. Harrington had conducted some of the last archaeological work he pursued at Jamestown, Kelso found that James Fort and almost everything that colonists had built, burned, torn down, and thrown away was still there, buried just inches beneath commemorative statues to John Smith and Pocahontas. Kelso's work at Jamestown has continued for more than a dozen years. Those excavations will likely be his last, and they are likely to be the accomplishment for which he will best be remembered. Kelso's discovery of James Fort is, however, only the most recent of a string of notable achievements that have punctuated his career in historical archaeology since its start in the early 1960s. His successes and contributions to historical archaeology range from the bureaucratic, when he served as Virginia's first state archaeologist and established programs that continue to this day; to the methodological, when he pioneered many of the techniques of open area excavation that archaeologists working in the Chesapeake now take for granted; to the evangelical, when he inspired the establishment of permanent archaeological research programs at historic sites such as Mount Vernon and Monticello. Along the way, Kelso helped train a younger generation of archaeologists who have moved from his field crews to university and research programs of their own. Alumni of his projects and classes (through the School of Architecture at the University of Virginia and the Department of History at the College of William and Mary) all benefited from the collaborative approach he learned in the first years of his own career.

For several years after completing his master's degree, Bill taught history at James Blair High School in Williamsburg where he was also its successful football coach. The summer months were reserved for archaeology with Colonial Williamsburg. Not many years of part-time archaeology passed before he decided in 1967 to leave the classroom (and briefly, Virginia) to work as a staff archaeologist with the Georgia Historical Commission in Savannah, Georgia.

Among other projects, he explored an early-18th-century fortified house at Wormslow Plantation. His work in Georgia produced important glimpses of the settlement strategies employed in establishing the youngest of America's 13 British mainland colonies (*Captain Jones's Wormslow: A Historical, Archaeological, and Architectural Study of an Eighteenth-Century Plantation Site near Savannah, Georgia,* University of Georgia Press, Athens, 1979). Bill also had a chance to dust off an old set of skills—moonlighting as a place kicker for a semiprofessional football team. Bill's Georgia years gave him an opportunity to complete a PhD at Emory University.

Kelso returned to Virginia in 1970 to accept a position with Colonial Williamsburg as field director for what today would be called an archaeological resources assessment of Carter's Grove Plantation. There was little, at that time, in the way of technical manuals or research designs to guide how best to assess potential archaeological resources within a parcel that contained many hundreds of acres, and many of the techniques he employed foreshadowed the CRM repertoire that emerged in the following decades.

On the heels of this project, Kelso began a project on an adjacent plantation, Kingsmill, that would occupy him for much of the next decade and that would, among other important results, yield insights into the evolution of settlement patterns in Virginia from the early-17th to the early-19th centuries (*Kingsmill Plantation, 1619–1800: Archaeology of Country Life in Colonial Virginia,* Academic Press, New York, NY, 1984). Significant among the findings at Kingsmill were several dozen earthfast structures whose analysis provided much of the data woven into the seminal essay, of which Kelso was a coauthor with historian Cary Carson, archaeologist Gary Wheeler Stone, and architectural historian Dell Upton: "Impermanent Architecture in the Southern American Colonies" (*Winterthur Portfolio* 16 [1981]:135–196). Important for its interpretation of the emergence of a distinctive regional architecture in the early Chesapeake, the influence of this frequently cited essay has extended well beyond Virginia and Maryland. It challenged how historians and architectural historians describe the domestic architecture of early America and explain its origins and evolution.

Kelso's work at Kingsmill and Carter's Grove also provided an early opportunity for him to investigate broad issues in the recovery and interpretation of historical landscapes, a topic that he pursued aggressively during his tenure as director of archaeology at Thomas Jefferson's Monticello and Poplar Forest, Jefferson's retreat in Bedford County, Virginia. While at Monticello, Kelso organized a conference in 1986 that resulted in a collection of essays to which he contributed "Landscape Archaeology at Thomas Jefferson's Monticello," one of nearly a dozen essays through which he explored the meaning of landscapes, both formal and informal (*Earth Patterns: Essays in Landscape Archaeology*, William M. Kelso and Rachel Most, editors, University Press of Virginia Charlottesville, 1990; also "Landscape Archaeology and Garden History Research," in *Journal of Garden History,* John Dixon Hunt, editor, pp. 31–57, 1993; and "Landscape Archaeology: A Key to Virginia's Past," in *Eighteenth Century Life* 8(2):159–169, 1983). His 1997 book *Archaeology of Thomas Jefferson's Monticello: Artifacts of Everyday Life in the Plantation Community* (Thomas Jefferson Memorial Foundation, Charlottesville, Virginia) provides access to the excavations that explored Mulberry Row, the complex of houses and gardens that housed the enslaved Africans who made Thomas Jefferson's elaborate lifestyle possible.

Kelso has focused the last dozen years on Jamestown where he has served as director of archaeology for the Association for the Preservation of Virginia Antiquities (APVA) *Jamestown Rediscovery* project. Since undertaking the excavation of the 1607 James Fort, he has reported the results of his work there through a series of technical reports and booklets published annually between 1995 and 2000 and summarized in *Jamestown Rediscovery 1994–2004* (APVA/ Preservation Virginia, Richmond, 2004). *Jamestown, The Buried Truth* (University of Virginia Press, Charlottesville, 2006) supersedes these earlier publications. While it is early to weigh the significance of the research presented in these books, it is already clear that the work at Jamestown challenges long-standing notions about the character of life during the colony's first decades. Discussion of the implications of what has been discovered at Jamestown will stretch well into the future. An important part of that discussion will be further consideration

of the tension inherent in nearly everything that happened at Jamestown between "being English" and becoming something else—not yet "American" and not yet "Virginian" but, nevertheless, distinct. Kelso suggests that process is "American inventing itself."

Kelso's legacy in the archaeology of early Virginia will extend far beyond his work at Jamestown and will benefit his successors in numerous ways. During his tenure as commissioner of archaeology from 1971 until 1979 for the Virginia Historic Landmarks Commission, then Virginia's state historic preservation office, Bill actively pursued projects in which he could engage, directly or through the media, the broad public that he understood shared his enthusiasm for archaeology. Resulting popular interest, gained through exhibits, press coverage, and documentary films in the late 1970s and during his work at Monticello, established a pattern that Bill replicated at Jamestown with programs prepared for the History Channel, the Discovery Channel, National Geographic Explorer, as well as a number of PBS programs. All of them have raised public interest in Jamestown and in historical archaeology in general. This ability to address both popular audiences and specialists may, in time, turn out to be Bill's most important legacy. His deft touch with public audiences also led to constructive alliances with local and state political officials who led efforts to introduce zoning and permitting regulations that provided additional protection for archaeological resources. Certainly, Virginia is for historical archaeology far more hospitable and supportive than it was before Bill began to lobby for the administrative and research programs that continue to energize archaeological research in the Commonwealth. The public with whom he worked also included developers, a constituency whose members emerged, surprisingly, in some portions of Virginia as partners in some of the most important archaeological projects undertaken in the last quarter of the 20th century.

Bill's accomplishments have already earned wide acclaim. Baldwin-Wallace College awarded him an honorary doctorate in 2002, the year he delivered the commencement address for his undergraduate alma mater and was named a distinguished alumnus by Emory University. The Virginia Press Association named him "Virginian of the Year" in 2005, an honor that followed his election as Fellow of the Society of Antiquaries.

Kelso's professional reputation, as understood through his publications, occupies a significant place in historical archaeology. His publications are widely cited and often assigned in both undergraduate and graduate courses. He is among that very small band of historical archaeologists whose research David Hurst Thomas and other chroniclers of the history of archaeology have deemed important enough to weave into their histories of our craft. Kelso's essays and books have been, and will continue to be, essential to the continuing dialogues about the recovery and interpretation of historical landscapes, about the antecedents and evolution of domestic architecture in early America, about the architecture and material culture of plantation slavery, and, of course, about Jamestown and the beginnings of English settlement of North America.

In his free time, Bill plays guitar and banjo with bluegrass bands styled "Ever Who Shows Up" and "Gas Money," distinctive for their floating composition of musician friends from the Williamsburg area. He has long been a dedicated runner, remains an avid football fan, and fishes more now that he resides on Jamestown Island. Bill restored a 19th-century mill when he worked at Monticello and is now restoring a 19th-century cabin near Charlottesville. His wife, Ellen, a retired teacher who plays bass for the bands, is the self-proclaimed "mayor of Jamestown (population 2). She and Bill, who share the small cottage with their two basset hounds, have two children, Libbie and Marty, as well as four grandchildren. "Godspeed Cottage" (named after one of the ships, *Godspeed*, that delivered some of Jamestown's first colonists) is a stone's throw from the recently excavated west wall of James Fort.

Kelso's discovery and subsequent excavation of the fort and the structures that crowded early-17th-century Jamestown are sufficient to secure him a place of honor in the history of historical archaeology in North America. It is, however, the scope of his long career as well as the breadth of his scholarly writing for which he so well deserves the Harrington Award. Thanks to the extensive laboratories and financial support systems Kelso has built at Jamestown, analytical studies of the data retrieved thus far will continue well into the future. As they do, it will, one suspects, become more and more clear that Bill owes much to Pinkie and the work he conducted at Jamestown more than half a century ago. Bill, more than any of us, works daily in Harrington's professional and intellectual shadow and nothing, one guesses, will honor William Kelso and his accomplishments more than being named 2007 recipient of The Society for Historical Archaeology's J. C. Harrington Award.

CARTER L. HUDGINS

J. C. Harrington Medal in Historical Archaeology: James Edward Ayres, 2008. Volume 42, Number 2 (2008): 1-5. By Charles E. Cleland and Teresita Majewski

J. C. Harrington Medal in Historical Archaeology

James Edward Ayres 2008

James Edward Ayres's long career in archaeology has been dominated by difficult and continual struggles to promote the value of historical archaeology within the archaeological establishment and with the public. Perhaps his battles have something to do with Ayres working in the American West, particularly Arizona, where prehistoric archaeology and its spectacular material culture are so well entrenched, but perhaps it is due to his insistence that archaeologists take a considerably broader perspective of the past. Throughout his career, he has tirelessly advocated for the preservation of the archaeological record in all its dimensions, insisted that the highest research standards be applied to all archaeological sites, and especially argued that historical period sites and material culture must hold a place of special importance in explicating the past.

His publications are numerous and varied. Ayres has written about sites, material culture, and historical topics from the Spanish colonial period through the 20th century. His works on the historical archaeology of Native Americans in Arizona, vernacular architecture, mining, logging, urban archaeology, and the archaeology and history of the Chinese in Tucson have become classics. Few archaeologists have contributed as significantly to historical archaeological scholarship in cultural resource management reports in the western United States.

While it is true that many of us in The Society for Historical Archaeology (SHA) share Ayres's values, his career is replete with examples of how he fought to establish historical archaeology as a respected profession. The acceptance that our discipline now enjoys with the public as well as the other branches of archaeology is, to no small degree, due to his firm professionalism and tenacity. It is for these qualities—his unflagging service to SHA, his commitment to the profession of historical archaeology, and his broad-ranging and lasting scholarly contributions—that James Edward Ayres is awarded the J. C. Harrington Medal in 2008.

Jim was born in Eau Claire, Wisconsin, on 30 September 1936. His father, Wayne, was a farmer who worked in several localities in the Eau Claire area. In 1943, the family moved to eastern Colorado, where Wayne managed one of his uncle's ranches. In the ensuing years, the Ayres family moved back and forth between Colorado and Wisconsin several times, but they settled permanently in Evanston, Wyoming, in 1950. Here Wayne started a new job as an independent logger in the high country of the Uinta Mountains along the Wyoming and Utah border. Wayne's new career was very much a family affair, involving his four sons and their mother, Alice, all of whom worked side by side in the woods. Because he was too young to handle the very heavy chain saws of that era, Jim spent summers removing limbs from fallen trees with an ax. This was not only physically demanding work but also lonely as well. Jim did not always appreciate spending the summers of his teenage years in the isolation of the family's lumber camp.

Jim graduated from Evanston High School in 1955 and immediately joined the U.S. Air Force. After basic training, he worked in the USAF Security Service, an electronic-intelligence-gathering organization. After a busy and exciting four years in intelligence work, Jim enrolled at Fresno State College in California, where he received a B.A. in Anthropology in 1963. During his undergraduate years, he become involved in his first archaeological fieldwork through a project in central California. This experience led him to decide upon a career in archaeology, and in 1963 he began graduate work in anthropology at the University of Arizona, where he earned a master's degree in 1970.

At the University of Arizona, two pioneers in historical archaeology influenced Jim: Arthur Woodward, who introduced him to the discipline, and Bunny Fontana, who taught him the importance of documentary research. Jim now joins both of these mentors as a fellow recipient of the J. C. Harrington Medal. As a graduate student, Jim got involved with the anthropology department's Grasshopper Archaeological Field School, for which he was hired as the assistant director (1965–1967). During the same period, he was assistant archaeologist at the Arizona State Museum (ASM) in Tucson. An outgrowth of his work at Grasshopper was his pioneering and often reprinted 1968 article with William Longacre, "Archeological Lessons from an Apache Wickiup" (*New Perspectives in Archeology*, S. R. Binford and L. R. Binford, editors, pp. 151–159, Aldine, Chicago), one of the first forays into the historical archaeology and ethnoarchaeology of Native Americans. The article was based on a paper presented at the Society for American Archaeology meeting in 1966.

In 1967, it became apparent that urban renewal plans for the downtown area of Tucson would threaten the archaeological record that documented the community's founding and development from its Spanish roots through the 1920s. In cooperation with the Tucson Urban Renewal Office and demolition contractors, Jim organized an archaeological salvage program to recover as much data from these occupations as possible. Eventually, Jim, along with 150 university student volunteers, excavated 200 privies, wells, trash dumps, and other features, recovering more than one million artifacts. In those days, the Tucson Urban Renewal Project (TUR) provided the only avenue available for undergraduate archaeological field training at the University of Arizona. Because the project was badly underfunded and involved huge collections of historical period artifacts, it was not a popular project with some of the staff at ASM. Nonetheless, Jim's project was among the first and largest archaeological urban renewal projects in the entire nation and the first of its type to receive funding from the U.S. Department of Housing and Urban Renewal. TUR also produced some of the best information on the Spanish colonization of the American Southwest as well as the early Chinese and Anglo-American communities of Tucson.

In 1970, Jim was promoted to associate archaeologist at ASM and in 1978 became head of its research division. He held this post until 1979, when he resigned to become Arizona's State Historic Preservation Officer (SHPO), a position he held until 1981. He later became an adjunct faculty member in the Department of Anthropology at Arizona State University (ASU) and subsequently an adjunct lecturer in the anthropology department at the University of Arizona. In both cases, he often provided the only instruction available to students interested in historical archaeology. His courses drew, and continue to draw, large enrollments.

It can certainly be said that Jim has always viewed his teaching as a professional responsibility and a service to students, rather than as a career path or as a means of supporting himself financially. Teaching was a duty he assumed in addition to many other competing responsibilities. He and Teresita Majewski frequently team-teach classes and seminars in historical archaeology, and several times per year they go on the road with hands-on workshops on historical period material culture and documentary research, which have been presented at Arizona Site Stewards meetings, Arizona state historic preservation conferences, meetings of the Arizona SHPO's Historical Archaeology Advisory Committee, and other state-level archaeological venues. Jim is determined to introduce professionals and avocational archaeologists alike to the full range of historical period material culture so that sites dating from the contact period onward can be correctly identified, dated, and interpreted. He is also keenly aware of the value of curated collections, and students in his most recent seminar on historical period material culture analyzed artifacts related to a mid-19th-century military post that had been sitting untouched in storage for almost 40 years at ASM. The outcome of this analysis will be a publication featuring the research conducted by the students.

Over the years, Jim has shown a deep commitment to The Society for Historical Archaeology, serving on the Board of Directors (1972–1975 and again 1992–1995), as president in 1977, as a member of the Editorial Advisory Committee for *Historical Archaeology* (1978–present), as an associate editor for the journal (1988–1993), and as a member of the Dissertation Prize Subcommittee (2001–present) and as chair since 2003. Besides serving on many other SHA committees, he has represented SHA on the Society of Professional Archeologists (SOPA) board (1983–1987) and on the Advisory Council for Historic Preservation's International Centre Committee (1975–1982).

His professional service does not end with SHA. Other professional organizations have benefited from his participation. For example, he was the secretary-treasurer of the American Society for Ethnohistory (1971–1979), a member of SOPA's Membership Committee in 1976 and 1977, president of the Arizona Archaeological and Historical Society (2004–2007), board member on the chapter and state levels of the Arizona Historical Society (1998–2003), and advisor from Arizona to the National Trust for Historic Preservation (1973–1982). Since 1988, he has served as an advisor emeritus to the trust, a position that attests to his wealth of knowledge in historic preservation.

While serving on the Arizona SHPO's Advisory Committee on Historical Archaeology since its inception in the late 1990s, he contributed to a statewide context for identifying, documenting, and evaluating historical period refuse deposits. Jim is the lead compiler (with Carol Griffith and Teresita Majewski) of *Historical Archaeology in Arizona: A Research Guide*, an online publication of the Arizona SHPO that is updated frequently <www.pr.state.az.us/partnerships/shpo/archyguide. pdf>. He feels strongly about volunteer projects such as these, because they provide the background for the appropriate scholarly treatment of archaeological resources from the historical period.

On the local level, Jim has been involved in countless preservation activities. An excellent example is his service on the Tucson-Pima County Historical Commission as member (1990–1998) and chair (1992–1998). Because Tucson is a certified local government, the commission is the body responsible for addressing review of city and other projects, especially those in National Register districts. In his years on the commission, he constantly worked to raise awareness of Tucson's rich historical archaeological heritage to the level where it clearly became an important concern for city and county officials and administrators. This awareness is especially crucial given the rapid growth of the city and its environs over the past decades. His work on the commission's Plans Review Subcommittee, which is tasked with reviewing projects proposed in city historic districts and National Register districts, honed his approach to preservation of architectural resources and their importance to a comprehensive approach to considering historical archaeological sites in his own research. In 1995, Jim's contributions to historic preservation in its many forms at both the local and state levels were recognized when he received the commission's highest accolade, the Alene Dunlap Smith Award for his contributions to historic preservation, as well as the coveted Arizona Governor's Award for Historic Preservation.

It should be emphasized that Jim's considerable work with professional organizations as well as his research and teaching commitments were undertaken without the security of tenure or even full-time employment. For much of his career, Jim assumed these responsibilities while scrambling for contracts, working on underfunded research projects, or teaching for minimum wage or as a volunteer. By these means and under these difficult conditions, he managed to make a profound contribution to the field of historical archaeology and to many young people interested in the discipline. Jim Ayres set an excellent standard for all his fellow archaeologists.

After completing his service as Arizona SHPO in 1981, Ayres began working as an archaeological consultant in earnest, participating in projects for Aztlan Archaeology, Inc.; Dames & Moore, Inc.; Archaeological Research Services, Inc.; Old Pueblo Archeology Center; Desert Archaeology, Inc.; Statistical Research, Inc.; SWCA, Inc.; the National Park Service; and ASM, among others. As an archaeological consultant, Jim has conducted historical archaeology, documentary research, and material culture analysis at a wide variety of site types throughout the western United States (Arizona, California, Colorado, New Mexico, and Utah) and on ASU's Annecy Project in east-central France.

Key projects completed by Ayres as a consultant include his work on mining, specifically his investigations of the Rosemont Mining District south of Tucson, where his research focused on the technology and operational challenges of mining and the ethnicity of the miners who lived and worked there and was published in 1984 (*Rosemont: The History and Archaeology of Post-1880 Sites in the Rosemont Area, Santa Rita Mountains, Arizona*, Archaeological Series No. 147, Vol. 3, Arizona State Museum, University of Arizona, Tucson). He has also investigated placer mining at Humbug Creek in central Arizona, copper mining and railroading in the Silver Bell Mining District near Tucson, and copper mining and ranching on Middle Pinto Creek in east-central Arizona.

Ayres also made significant contributions to one of the largest archaeological projects ever undertaken in the Southwest, funded by the Bureau of Reclamation's Regulatory Storage Division (Plan 6) of the Central Arizona Project, which focused on eight dams in the central portion of the state. He and Deborah Hull-Walski were in charge of designing and implementing the analysis of material culture recovered from construction camps associated with the eight dams. Many Apache men helped to build the Roosevelt Dam, and they lived in the associated camps with their families. His analysis of the artifacts used by the Apaches and their non-Native American coworkers provided fascinating insights into the use and reuse of artifacts as well as our abilities to associate material culture with specific ethnic groups. He contributed as author or editor to most of the reports in the multivolume series, published in the late 1980s and early 1990s, and entitled, *Historical Archaeological Investigations at Dam Construction Camps in Central Arizona*, Dames and Moore, Phoenix. Volume 3, *Laboratory Methods and Data Computerization*, coauthored with Hull-Walski, contains illustrations of more than 1,500 marks on glass, ceramics, metal, and other materials. Of all the volumes in the series, this one is found on the shelves of all historical archaeologists in Arizona and used constantly for reference when conducting artifact analysis.

Ayres has also consulted frequently on the history and historical archaeology of railroads. In 1989, he contributed to *Transcontinental Railroading in Arizona: 1878–1940: A Context for Preserving Railroad-Related Properties,* a historic context study submitted by Janus Associates of Phoenix to the Arizona SHPO; has completed in-depth historical archaeological and historical studies of Pantano and Esmond Station, two railroad communities near Tucson; and inventoried the Promontory townsite within Golden Spike National Historic Site in Utah.

Ayres's consulting work has also focused on ranches, homesteads, and townsites. From material culture analysis and historical research conducted for the Agua Caliente Ranch project, Pima County, Arizona, he was able to provide critical information used in reconstructing the architectural, landscape, and occupational history of the site (see his 2002 article "Agua Caliente: The Life of a Southern Arizona Ranch," *Journal of Arizona History* 43:309–342). Throughout the years, Ayres has become familiar with the material culture and documentary record of the Chinese who came to the West in the late 1800s, primarily to work on the railroads. His experience with Chinese material culture is extensive, beginning with the TUR excavations in downtown Tucson. His 1994 publication "The Archaeology of Chinese Sites in Arizona" (*Origins and Destinations: 41 Essays on Chinese America,* Chinese Historical Society of Southern California and UCLA Asian American

Studies Center) provides an overview of the archaeology of the Chinese who lived throughout Arizona, working on ranches and in mining camps and urban communities.

Throughout the years, Ayres has published synthetic pieces that summarize the state of historical archaeology in the Southwest, ranging from the Spanish Conquest through the early-20th century. These have become key resources for understanding the development of historical archaeology in this region: "The Anglo Period in Archaeological and Historical Perspective," *Kiva* 49:225–232, 1984; "Historical Archaeology in Arizona and New Mexico," *Historical Archaeology* 25(3):18–23, 1991; *The Archaeology of Spanish and Mexican Colonialism in the American Southwest* (compiler), Guides to the Archaeological Literature of the Immigrant Experience in America, No. 3, The Society for Historical Archaeology, 1995; and "Toward an Archaeology of Colonialism in the Greater Southwest" (with Teresita Majewski), *Revista de Arqueología Americana* 12:55–86.

Another example of Ayres's level of commitment to the field and to understanding the past is his decades-long study of the logging industry and its buildings, structures, and artifacts in southwestern Wyoming and northeastern Utah. He started documenting lumber camps in the Uinta Mountains in the 1960s, and today, roughly 40 years later, he spends most of the summer months continuing to locate, map, photograph, and record camps and their layouts, functions, and relationships to the environmental areas. His research focus has been on the changing nature of the architecture and the ethnicity of the loggers who occupied these camps. The insights he has gained into the formation processes of the archaeological record through longitudinal study of these sites are unparalleled. Glimpses of his findings were offered in two publications: "Historic Logging Camps in the Uinta Mountains of Utah" (*Forgotten Places and Things: Archaeological Perspectives on American History*, Albert Ward, editor, Contributions in Anthropological Studies, No. 3, Center for Anthropological Studies, Albuquerque, 1983) and "Standard Timber Company Logging Camps on the Mill Creek Drainage, Uinta Mountains, Utah" (*Proceedings of the Society for California Archaeology* 9:179–182, 1996). He is currently writing up the results of this ongoing study.

Besides his own personal history with logging, Jim is spending much of his time on this project because many of the camps are being disturbed by vandals, have succumbed to destruction by fire, or have simply fallen into oblivion because the USDA Forest Service is indifferent toward the study and preservation of these important resources. On this and other of his projects, Jim has had the invaluable assistance of his dear wife, Marianne, whom he married in 1986. Whenever Jim is found measuring an old building, you can be sure Marianne is at the other end of the tape. Both authors of this tribute have been fortunate enough to visit Jim and Marianne during the summer in Wyoming to enjoy their hospitality and visit some of the logging camps.

Significantly, Ayres has continually demonstrated throughout his career the potential importance of sites that seem to have been written off by others—isolated homesteads, ranches, mining towns, sites occupied by historical period Native Americans, and of course, logging camps. In investigating these sites, he has shown himself not only to be a master of 19th- and early-20th-century material culture but also a relentless researcher of archival and oral historical sources. A project that clearly illustrates his interest and expertise in documentary research is his painstaking reading and indexing of more than 300 topics of relevance to historical archaeology that appear in the four Tucson newspapers dating from 1870 to 1912. He recently received a grant to have these materials prepared for publication so that they can be of use to other researchers.

This brief summary of the career of Jim Ayres has only touched upon his deep and lasting contributions to the historical archaeology of the American West, for which he has received the J. C. Harrington Medal. For more than 40 years, he has focused on promoting historical archaeology through tireless service as well as broad-ranging and lasting scholarly contributions. For Jim, service and scholarly contributions are inextricably linked in a circle of cause and effect. He has never been a self-promoter, but his work has inspired countless others to pursue service and scholarship in historical archaeology.

CHARLES E. CLELAND AND TERESITA MAJEWSKI

J. C. Harrington Medal in Historical Archaeology

Robert L. Schuyler 2009

Robert L. Schuyler was honored at the 42nd annual SHA meetings in Toronto, Canada, as the 2009 recipient of the J. C. Harrington Medal in recognition of his outstanding contributions to the field of historical archaeology.

Bob's interest in archaeology can be traced back to his earliest years in New Haven, Connecticut. After a brief seduction by dinosaurs (based on their size, not their brains) and astronomy (based on a false hope of meeting aliens), he proclaimed by the fifth grade that he was going to be an archaeologist. He never changed that decision. Although he came from a working-class background—neither of his parents went to high school and he was the only child out of four siblings to go to college—he was born into a supportive New England urban environment. New Haven had an excellent public school system and was home to the Yale Peabody Museum of Natural History. These institutions, reinforced by stories in the *National Geographic Magazine*, created an image in Bob's mind of archaeology as the study of ancient civilizations. In Sheridan Junior High School, however, he expanded this view to include both world prehistory and the broader field of anthropology.

In 1957 Bob spent the summer with his older sister in Los Angeles, and on the fourth of July visited Arizona. He explored pueblo ruins, such as Walnut Canyon National Monument near Flagstaff, and fell in love with the Southwest. Returning home, he joined the New Haven Chapter of the Archaeological Society of Connecticut. Under Lyent W. Russell, a physics instructor at Yale and leader in the society, Bob excavated on Grannis Island, a prehistoric site on the Quinnipiac River. Before he graduated from James Hillhouse High School, Bob had also joined the Society for American Archaeology and was able to attend the SAA 25th-anniversary founding meeting (May 1960) at the Hotel Taft in New Haven. He saw many of the doyens of American archaeology—Junius Bird, Jesse Jennings, Waldo Wedel, Gordon Willey, and others—but especially went to meet the Arizona contingent. He heard Raymond H. Thompson speak on black-on-white wares and shook hands with "Doc" Haury. By 1960 he had decided to be an anthropologist and a Southwestern prehistorian, and so he only applied to one college, the University of Arizona in Tucson.

During his four years (1960–1964) as an undergraduate, Bob got an excellent grounding in general anthropology. Thompson was central as his archaeology advisor, but Bob also studied with Emil W. Haury, Frederick Hulse (physical), Edward H. Spicer (cultural), and Edward P. Dozier (linguistics). In Introductory Anthropology 1A, under Hulse, Bob had an advanced doctoral student as a teaching assistant, Roderick Sprague. In 1963, after attending the University of Arizona Archaeological Field School on its first season at Grasshopper Pueblo, he was introduced to Binfordian processual archaeology by a new faculty member, William A. Longacre. He partially but not totally endorsed this "New Archaeology." His earlier discovery of culturology and cultural evolution in the works of Leslie White enabled him to see both the inherent strengths and limits of this movement. In 1964 Bob graduated *magna cum laude* with departmental honors, and he wrote the first senior honors thesis in anthropology at Arizona.

After another year (1964–1965) in Tucson as a graduate student on a National Science Foundation Fellowship, he shifted his interests back to his earlier focus on ancient but complex societies. He planned on doing a comparative study of Mesoamerican and Indus Valley civilizations and in 1965 he started doctoral work at Harvard University. In Cambridge he studied Maya civilization under Gordon R. Willey. Because of intellectual and personal conflicts, both he and his fellow graduate student Mark P. Leone left Harvard after one year. They actually spent only one semester on campus, serving as junior field assistants during the spring on Willey's Maya Seibal Project in the Peten lowlands of Guatemala. Earlier in the fall semester, however, Bob took classes at Harvard with a visiting associate professor from the University of California at Santa Barbara, James Deetz. Bob enrolled in Deetz's archaeology seminar and also helped him with his cemetery-gravestone survey by inventorying the Newburyport, Massachusetts, burial ground. With Deetz's support and letters from Arizona, Bob received the last teaching fellowship at UCSB for 1966–1967.

The new anthropology department at Santa Barbara was on a secondary UC campus, but its chair, Charles J. Erasmus, set out to make the department visible as a center for both the New Archaeology and evolutionary cultural anthropology. By the mid-1960s he had partially succeeded. Under Erasmus's plan, Deetz, Lewis and Sally Binford, and Albert C. Spaulding had been or were being hired, along with Claude Warren, Bill Allen, and Brian Fagan. For cultural anthropology, Thomas G. Harding, a young evolutionary scholar from Michigan, and Elman R. Service arrived, while, after Schuyler left, Leslie White retired there as professor emeritus.

Such a potent mix reinforced by national political events, including the election of Ronald Reagan as governor of California, caused continuing perturbations on the campus and in the department. Between 1967 and 1969, when he completed the in-residence part of the program, Bob went through three different advisors/dissertation chairs: Deetz, who left for Brown at the end of Bob's first year, Spaulding, and finally Brian Fagan. His doctoral dissertation, "Archaeological Perspectives in Historical Archaeology," was not completed until 1974, five years after he had taken his first academic appointment.

Bob's transition from Mesoamerican archaeology to historical archaeology occurred at UCSB, but it was a slow and complex process. It actually took place after Deetz left Santa Barbara but was complete by 1968. The establishment of The Society for Historical Archaeology was also an important influence. In summer 1967 Bob served as a junior project archaeologist on excavations at the historic Fortress of Louisbourg in Canada.

His first academic appointment at the University of Maryland in College Park, another newly formed department of anthropology, lasted only one year. That year (1969–1970) saw the violent climax of opposition to the war in Vietnam exploding onto campuses across America. Bob took a leadership role as chair of the Student Strike Committee (although he was a faculty member) and as an officer in DRUM, the Democratic Radical Union of Maryland. These groups organized resistance on the College Park campus, which was soon under siege by the state police and the Maryland National Guard, and helped to launch demonstrations into Washington, DC. By the end of the year, although he had started a limited testing program on contact Native American sites along the Potomac River, he was of too much interest to local authorities, the FBI, and the university central administration, so, like so many before him in the Chesapeake, he took the Underground Railroad (actually Amtrak) north.

In a process of academic musical chairs involving people (Mark Leone, Mel Thurman, and Bob Schuyler) and institutions (University of Maryland, Princeton, and City College of New York), Bob ended up in his second but first permanent position at CCNY under its founding chair, Diane Sank. It was at City College (and slightly later at the CUNY Graduate Center) that for the first time Bob had a stable base from which he could build his professional career in historical archaeology. This base was duplicated and expanded when he moved in 1979 to the University of Pennsylvania.

Schuyler's contributions to historical archaeology, which span four decades, fall into three interrelated categories: scholarship, education, and the simple but continuing building of the discipline.

His scholarly contributions can be reviewed by entering through a predictable side door—politics. In 1976 at the Eastern States Archaeological Federation (ESAF) bicentennial meetings in Columbus, Ohio, Schuyler presented a keynote address, entitled "Images of America: The Contribution of Historical Archaeology to National Identity" (*Southwestern Lore* 1976). Some have looked back on this article as one of the opening attempts to use the history of the discipline to examine historical archaeology itself as a socio-political phenomenon. He assessed historical archaeology in 1976 while a much more senior scholar, Jimmy Griffin, evaluated prehistoric studies. Schuyler did not please the bicentennial audience when he pointed out the nationalistic and hegemonic nature of the field's contributions as a materializing of a mythical past. Griffin also did not go over well when he told the audience: "You like banner stones, you like arrowheads, but you don't much like living Indians." Schuyler was however congratulated by one person attending the conference—Griffin. At the same time, Schuyler always points out that he also made statements in the same paper like the following:

> Such research [the study of minorities, workers, women, etc.] will certainly expand in the years ahead but its purpose should not simply be the generation of alternate images of our national heritage. In fact, objective archaeological data will probably be no more palatable to an ethnic minority than it will to a ruling majority. All cultures are based on mythologies which have little to do with historical fact... (p. 37).

For Schuyler, archaeology—general archaeology—is a science, a social science (not a physical or natural science), and, of course, it is interpretive. It is neither a political cause nor an attempt to liberate anyone, even from his or her own "false consciousness." Its purpose is to understand the human past, both in its own terms and from a contemporary, objective, scientific perspective. In order to enhance these goals within historical archaeology, it is necessary to understand its disciplinary history and its current socio-political setting. Schuyler has been, along with a few colleagues like Sprague, a major advocate for such studies. In 1998 he created "Images of the Past," a column for the *SHA Newsletter* that attempts to preserve visual elements of that history. This column, with strong support from previous editors, Norman Barka and William Lees, is one of the most popular sections in the current *Newsletter*.

The second important scholarly contribution, beyond trying to get the field to study its own origins and development, has been to ask the most fundamental question of all: What is historical archaeology? In 1970 Schuyler published a definitional article, "Historical and Historic Sites Archaeology as Anthropology: Basic Definitions and Relationships," (actually written in 1969) that attempted to answer this question and resolve some basic approaches and relationships to general scholarship. In this well-known paper Schuyler defined what is now called historical archaeology as "the study of the material manifestation of the expansion of European culture into the non-European world starting in the 15th century and ending with industrialization or the present ... ." Historical archaeology is defined not by its methodology (which is basically the same across all of archaeology) nor by the presence or absence of written sources. Many archaeologies of history have nothing to do with this field. Historical archaeology is defined by its subject matter—a major phase in human culture history which exists because "a set of underlying patterns and processes created the historical entity it is studying."

Over the next decade Schuyler, and others, worked on this definition. He attempted to move it beyond its overly historicalist and New World frameworks onto a broader processual foundation, recognizing the centrality of the archaeology of Europe itself, the truly global nature of the field (all peoples, all cultures, all civilizations), and fully incorporating the 19th and the 20th centuries. He came to define historical archaeology as the study of the modern world: its emergence between A.D. 1400 and 1600, its successful and permanent establishment between 1600 and 1800, and the transformation of this modern world system by the continuing processes of industrialization between 1800 and the present. So-called "globalization" is simply the most recent phase in a 500- to 600-year-long cultural evolution.

If historical archaeology is correctly defined as the archaeology of the modern world, then what is its proper housing or location within general scholarship? This is the third basic scholarly issue that has concerned Schuyler across his career. Is historical archaeology an autonomous, stand-alone discipline? No. Is it part of an autonomous discipline of archaeology? It could be and has been but should not be. Is it an interdisciplinary field? Certainly not. Indeed, the very concept of "interdisciplinary studies" in general is one of the repeating "bad pennies" that keeps cropping up in modern scholarship. A key strength of current research is the ability of *different, separate* disciplines to explore the same subject from equally valid but different perspectives. For example, a sociological vs. and anthropological study of the University of Pennsylvania as an example of American higher education at the start of the 21st century would undoubtedly yield very different results.

Historical archaeology could be and on rare occasions has been a subfield of a number of disciplines including archaeology, history, folklore, geography, or even historical sociology. Schuyler's advocacy has been that the field is best situated and most productive as an integral specialization within anthropological archaeology. Why anthropology? Its central culture concept, strong empirical fieldwork tradition, comparative methodology, relativistic inclusion of all human cultures, equal attention to material culture, and, finally, the fact of cultural evolution move historical archaeology naturally under the aegis of this broader field.

In the 1970s this position led him to participate in an early history vs. anthropology debate within the field. In 1978 he edited the first sourcebook centered in part around this issue. *Historical Archaeology: A Guide to Theoretical and Substantive Contributions* was a sourcebook, not a reader. He purposely excluded any new items, reprinting only classic programmatic statements and classic case studies issued between 1900 and the late 1970s. His selections (35 items) were quite successfully inclusive, except he could not get permission from Krauss Reprints to include the Johnny Ward's Ranch site report.

For the next decade, perhaps 15 years, this volume served as the introduction for most people entering the discipline. It has sold more than 15,000 copies and is still in print; indeed, it now has a second life as a basic text for teaching the history of the field.

Another general scholarly contribution was Schuyler's early emphasis on the global nature of the field's subject matter. Several people had made this world observation as early as the January 1967 conference in Dallas. Building on this discussion, Schuyler clearly underlined it in his sourcebook. In 1972 he had already created a "Global" section in the *SHA Newsletter* in an attempt to cover research outside of North America and Western Europe. This column, reporting on work in Latin America, Africa, Eastern Europe-Russia, Asia and Oceania, ran until 1980 when more focused regional *Newsletter* sections made it unnecessary.

Before attempting to define the discipline, highlight its history, firmly place it within general scholarship, and emphasize its global scale [the only archaeology to have such a scale], Schuyler joined with all historical archaeologists in his final contribution to scholarship. Across four decades he supported the continuing attempts to expand the legitimate horizons of and topics within historical archaeology. Initially he started with a very traditional research topic, contact period 17th–18th century Native American sites along the Potomac River. Immediately, however, he shifted into new territory. He was a pioneer in studying the archaeology of ethnicity and race, especially free African American communities. Between 1971 and 1973 he excavated Sandy Ground, an African American oystering town on Staten Island. Large areal surveys and specific site excavations explored this distinctive community's archaeological history. As Theresa Singleton has pointed out, Schuyler was one of the first investigators to move beyond a search for Africanisms and redirect the study of African-Americans to understanding them as an integral group (or groups) within American history. The Sandy Ground Project eventually became William Askin's doctoral dissertation, and Schuyler went on to edit the first volume on such minority groups: *Archaeological Perspectives on Ethnicity in America: Afro-American and Asian American Culture History* (1980).

From the archaeology of ethnicity he moved on between 1974 and 1977 to explore an industrial urban setting in Lowell, Massachusetts, one of the first planned industrial cities in America. Then he went back to the American West in 1980 to explore another industrial but specialized community, Silver Reef, Utah, an ephemeral (1877–1890) mining town. More recently he has continued this love of the American West by studying an eastern frontier in southern New Jersey. A marginal region, lightly settled by Anglo-American colonists who focused primarily on extractive industries, particularly iron and glass, until opened by the arrival of the railroad to more intensive settlement, the Pine Barrens of central and southern New Jersey are a striking parallel to the American Far West. His study of Vineland, New Jersey, and its agricultural hinterland, initiated in 2001, is exploring an historic landscape that did not exist in 1860 but was fully formed by 1880. This project also represents a new topic—the archaeology of the 20th century.

Related to these scholarly contributions but forming a separate category, Schuyler has also been a major educator within historical archaeology. He has produced an impressive number of undergraduate, masters, and doctoral students. His activities in this category extend across multiple generations. The first generation is readily recognizable. These are the CCNY-CUNY cohort and include William Askins, Roselle Henn, Meta Janowitz, Jed Levin, Jerome Schaefer, and Edward Staski. Bob's relationship to this group is complex because some were his undergraduate anthropology majors at City College whom he sent on to graduate schools; others were graduate students at CUNY.

The second cohort is composed of University of Pennsylvania students. Schuyler moved to Philadelphia in 1979 where he became a member of the Department of American Civilization, with a secondary appointment in anthropology, and as a curator in the Penn Museum. This student list is longer and includes undergraduates who continued on in the field and masters as well as doctoral advisees:

Anna Agbe-Davies	Lorinda Goodwin	Olivia Ng
Rebecca Allen	Barbara Heath	Carol Nickolai
Amber Bennett	Audrey Horning	Elizabeth Norris
Carin Bloom	William Hunt, Jr.	Benjamin Pykles
Jane Busch	Patrice Jeppson	Elizabeth Ragan
John Chenoweth	J. W. Joseph	Mary Beth Reed
Minette Church	Lisa Kealhofer	Richard Schaefer
Brian Crane	Julia King	John Seidel
Kevin Crisman	Chana Kraus-Friedberg	Sheli Smith
Elizabeth Crowell	Martha Lance	Darby Stapp
Lu Ann De Cunzo	Orloff Miller	Richard Veit
Kevin Donaghy	Lynn Morand (Evans)	
Joel Fry	Jessica Neuwirth	

With 32 of his students having completed PhDs, Schuyler may hold that record in historical archaeology. This enormous human contribution has been recognized at the University of Pennsylvania. In 2004 Schuyler was selected for the SAS Dean's Award for Innovation in Undergraduate Teaching. More recently, in 2008 he was honored with a very difficult award to win at University of Pennsylvania: the Provost's Award for Graduate Education and PhD Mentoring. Currently Bob continues his contribution as an educator working with his active graduate students. This list includes masters and doctoral students:

Christopher Barton	Jill Bennett Gaieski
Lynsey Bates	Jordan Pickrell
Craig Cipolla	Teagan Schweitzer (R. Preucel, primary advisor)
Dawn Di Stefano	Janet Six
Kristen Fellows	Kyle Somerville

Bob's third and final contribution beyond scholarship and higher education is that of a simple but energetic builder of historical archaeology. He shares this goal with many of his colleagues and the primary environment in which he has built is that of scholarly organizations. He is a founding member, life member, or early member of almost all pertinent groups. For example, he is a founding life member of the Australian Society for Historical Archaeology (now the Australasian SHA) and a founding member of both the Association for Gravestone Studies and the Society for Commercial Archaeology. He has been quite active in several such organizations including the Council for Northeastern Historical Archaeology (CNEHA). When he became an executive officer in 1980, CNEHA was moribund. Its journal was not publishing; it had no formal new membership outreach; and meetings were held on Bear Mountain in the Hudson Valley, a location hard to get to except by car. Bob combined forces with Paul Huey, a long time and dedicated CNEHA member, and George Miller. They made themselves life members by putting together a few hundred dollars to create a "war chest." Then they forcefully brought the journal back on publication schedule, where it has (under a sequence of excellent editors and adequate manuscript flow) remained. They forced a change in venue to easily reached locations starting with the 1980 Albany meeting, and finally, they launched the first formal membership drive. The CNEHA is so successful today because of these efforts and the work of subsequent leaderships.

Finally, of course, Bob has been quite active in The Society for Historical Archaeology. He joined as it formed but could not attend the first formal meeting (Williamsburg 1968) as he was a poor graduate student on the West Coast. Fortunately, the SHA came west the next year. A delegation of students from UCSB and UCLA, including Bob, Mel Thurman, and Larry Spanne, drove to Tucson where Bunny Fontana and Rick Sprague organized the Second Annual Conference at the Santa Rita Hotel. It was a wonderful meeting, and Bob ran around touching base with all the pioneers in the field (Harrington, Cotter, Caywood, Woodward, among them), collecting information for his dissertation research. He went on to attend all SHA conferences except for two—a total of 39 meetings.

For almost 40 years he worked for the society. He first served under Paul Schumacher running the "Pacific West" section of the *Newsletter*, then his "Global" section, and now "Images of the Past." He has chaired the membership drive as well as the Inter-Societal, Awards, and History committees. He was the junior co-organizer with John L. Cotter for the 15th Annual Meeting in Philadelphia (1982). He joined the SHA Board in 1978 and served as president in 1983. Finally across these four decades, he has been a single-person membership drive as many now in the society know.

For all these reasons: scholarship, higher education, and loyal building up of historical archaeology as a discipline, The Society for Historical Archaeology selected Robert L. Schuyler as the 2009 recipient of the J. C. Harrington Medal in Historical Archaeology.

RICHARD VEIT

J. C. Harrington Medal in Historical Archaeology: Judith Ann Bense, 2010. Volume 44, Number 2 (2010): 1-7. By William B. Lees and Elizabeth D. Benchley.

J. C. Harrington Medal in Historical Archaeology

Judith Ann Bense

Judy Bense tells all who will listen that she was a walk-on at the University of West Florida (UWF) in 1980. The university in that year was barely 15 years old, had fewer than 5,000 students, and did not employ an archaeologist or anthropologist in any capacity. With characteristic optimism, Dr. Bense saw this as prerequisite for success. With tenacity and growing political acuity she built archaeology into a signature program for the university, and with great energy and passion reached out beyond west Florida to make significant contributions to archaeology and historic preservation in Florida, nationally, and through an organization that she truly loves, the Society for Historical Archaeology.

Although she was born in Morristown, New Jersey, Judith Ann Bense has long called west Florida home. The promise of a successful dairy farm caused parents Bud and Bette to move their two young children to Panama City, Florida in 1951 (a third child was born later in Florida). Family trips to historical state parks in the region may have been what sparked Judy's early interest in history and archaeology, proclaimed as early as eight years of age. She attended Panama City's Bay High School (the "Fighting Tornadoes") and graduated in 1963. For reasons that have eluded those involved, an unusually large number of Bay High graduates have gone on to become practicing archaeologists, including Jay Johnson (University of Mississippi), the late George Hicks (formerly chair of Anthropology, Brown University), Bennie Keel (National Park Service, retired), Keith Stephenson (University of South Carolina), Louis Tesar (Florida Bureau of Archaeological Research), and Martha Zierden (Charleston Museum).

On graduating from high school, Judy went straight on to college at Florida State University (FSU) intent on studying archaeology. At FSU she discovered that archaeology was a part of anthropology. She studied under David S. Phelps, who chaired her thesis work on the Late Woodland shell ring, Bird Hammock, in Wakulla County, Florida. Phelps later moved to East Carolina University and was instrumental in the search for Sir Walter Raleigh's Lost Colony. Also at FSU was Hale G. Smith who had founded the department in 1950 and was director of the historical archaeology program. His work on Spanish colonial sites in Florida predicted some of Judy's later work: She says of this, "I wound up chasing [him] all over Pensacola and northwest Florida because he did all these Spanish sites."

Judy completed her masters in March of 1969 and immediately took her first paid job in archaeology, working for six months as a crew chief for B. Calvin Jones of the Florida Division of Archives, History, and Records Management (predecessor of the Florida Division of Historical Resources) on the Interstate 10 survey through Tallahassee. With legendary intuition, Jones led the crew to several Spanish missions within the right-of-way. The crew consisted of day labor drawn mostly, as Judy recalls, from "Vietnam veterans in various stages of being out of the jungle and being shot at. They were fine."

From the I-10 project Judy went directly to doctoral study at Washington State University, arriving there in the fall of 1969. While an undergraduate at FSU, Judy had minored in geology, and she took that interest with her to Washington State to study geoarchaeology with Richard Daugherty, who was department chair, and the late Frank C. Leonhardy who served as her major professor. Her dissertation, *The Cascade Phase: A Study in the Effect of the Altithermal on a Cultural System,* utilized site data from a decade of excavations conducted along the lower Snake River which was being impounded for hydroelectric power. This huge compliance project was winding down when Judy arrived in Pullman, Washington, and she used site data to examine the effects of prehistoric climate change on the local Native American cultures.

At the time Judy completed her Ph.D. in 1972 when she was 27 years old, she was faced with a crossroads defined by family needs and by serious personal uncertainties about the culture of academic archaeology. Her father had passed away in 1967 shortly after seeing Judy receive her bachelor's from FSU, and her mother died suddenly in 1972 three months before she completed her Ph.D. With both parents gone, she felt the need to return to Florida to care for her elderly grandmother and great aunt, and be near her two younger brothers (Chris and Allan) who were immersed in their college educations. With this, and with a growing discontent with the covertly individualistic, competitive nature of archaeological scholarship that she had witnessed at major universities on opposite sides of the continent, Dr. Bense hung her new diploma at the family farm in Panama City. There she turned her attention away from academia and toward what she perceived to be a more refreshing, overtly competitive yet honest business world. For five years she focused on making a living and providing support for her family with a business focused on horses and dogs.

Her decision to put her academic training aside came at a time when the profession of archaeology in the United States was seated largely in major research universities and in government agencies at the federal and state levels. In Judy's intervening "horse and dog" years, the landscape of professional archaeology changed dramatically.

For an individual who proclaimed her desire to be an archaeologist at the age of eight, it is perhaps less than surprising that Judy did not stay away long. In 1977 she accepted an appointment as adjunct assistant professor at the Panama City Center of UWF and taught upper-level undergraduate classes at night. In the summer of 1977 she taught a field school at the Kings Point site on St. Andrews Bay. This was the first archaeological field school ever taught at UWF. One of her students was Bay High graduate Martha Zierden.

Of pivotal importance in Judy's career was attendance at the 42nd annual meeting of the Society for American Archaeology in New Orleans in the spring of 1977. There she reconnected with the Washington State crowd, including Bennie Keel, Leslie Wildesen, Ruthann Knudson, and Gerald Schroedl. They filled her in on the sea change that had swept American archaeology since 1972. In

1971, President Nixon had signed Executive Order 11593 that required federal agencies to ensure that historical and archaeological properties under their jurisdiction were preserved. Among other results, this executive order caused agencies to undertake major resource inventories and National Register evaluations of sites on property they managed. In 1974 the U.S. Congress passed the Moss-Bennett Act (Public Law 93-291) which amended and expanded the Reservoir Salvage Act of 1960 and required all federal undertakings to consider impacts to historical and archaeological properties. These developments established the groundwork for today's cultural resource management and by 1977 had created an incredible need for professional archeologists available to go to work. With this great influx of development- and management-based projects and a limited number of unaffiliated Ph.D.'s, Judy was well positioned to take advantage of this uncertain yet heady new world.

Bennie Keel, one of the many products of Bay High School, and a graduate of FSU and Washington State, had long been an acquaintance of Judy's. In 1977 he was chief of the National Park Service's Interagency Archaeological Services in Atlanta, and was well positioned to help Judy reenter archaeology on a full-time basis. He immediately set up Dr. Bense with a contract for a cultural resource reconnaissance of the St. Marks National Wildlife Refuge along the Apalachee Bay on the Florida Gulf Coast. This project was her first contract in archaeology, and fieldwork was undertaken during the semester break in the winter of 1977–1978. Bennie followed this project with a contract for a small mitigation project in Mobile, Alabama, and a large testing project of 58 sites along the Tennessee-Tombigbee Waterway in Mississippi.

"Tenn-Tom," as it was affectionately known, took Judy away from Panama City and into the business of professional archaeology, but this project also landed her back at a large research university. In 1978 she became senior research archaeologist at the Office of Archaeological Research, University of Alabama. At Alabama she completed the testing project for Interagency Archaeological Services and then undertook additional work on Tenn-Tom for the Mobile District of the U.S. Army Corps of Engineers. These were massive projects, involving extended periods of field work and large crews of both anthropology bachelor's graduates and unskilled laborers. But at Alabama she found the same negative internal atmosphere that she had experienced at FSU and Washington State, and liked it no better the third time around. She did not stay.

Dr. Bense looks back at her decision to leave Alabama as the biggest crossroads of her career. She wanted to teach and do research but she was not interested in doing this at a large university with an established program in archaeology with all its internal baggage and attitudes. She became determined to find a university setting where she could build a truly collegial team focused on the concept that students were the priority. She believed that if she could not find this place soon she would leave archaeology again, for good. She had come to realize that the only way to accomplish this dream was to find a smaller university setting where archaeology was non-existent—a place without the baggage, existing relationships, expectations, and politics that she had repeatedly seen at major research universities.

In 1979 Dr. Bense visited UWF and set the groundwork for a move to Pensacola. In exchange for bringing her Tennessee-Tombigbee contracts to UWF, the university agreed to establish a new anthropology bachelor's degree program with two faculty lines. From Judy's perspective, UWF was the perfect location to build a program that was based on teamwork and focused on students. The key attraction of UWF was, in fact, its lack of archaeology or anthropology; there was no status quo, no expectations, and no personal agendas to navigate. In 1980 Judy became a walk-on at the University of West Florida. The qualities that attracted her to UWF of course also presented immediate challenges as she sought to establish an archaeological research program on a campus not at all prepared for this type of endeavor.

In these early days of CRM, however, things were different, and as part of the contract came federal infrastructure support to purchase capital equipment. A new curation facility was also erected on campus funded by project overhead. The research unit was called variously the Office of Archaeological Research, the Office of Contracts and Grants, the West Florida Institute of Archaeology, and finally, the UWF Archaeology Institute. This building remained home to the archaeological research program for 17 years, and now houses the university printing office. In the 1990s, a modern new building with exhibit, lab, classroom, and office space was constructed to house the UWF Archaeology Institute. It sits prominently at the main entrance to campus.

While work associated with the Tennessee-Tombigbee project lasted through 1984 and established archaeology at UWF, with this massive project ending Dr. Bense immediately began to cast about for opportunities, which were not long in coming. This work included contracts with utilities and developers, and state historic preservation grants.

The year 1984 brought two projects that anchored the future of archaeology at UWF. In that year, construction of a new city hall building began in downtown Pensacola. Reports of the discovery by collectors and looters of amazing relics of the town's forgotten colonial history soon made their way to Judy, and she and her very first archaeology students salvaged some of what was quickly being destroyed. This experience revealed to Dr. Bense the vulnerability of the pristine archaeological deposits right in her front yard, and the high level of ignorance about their existence among well-educated and well-meaning community leaders. She immediately realized public and city officials needed to be educated about the importance of what was underground and how easily it could be lost. The presence of a new archaeology office on campus paved the way for years of scientific excavation within downtown Pensacola as urban renewal came to town. During this period the city and its residents came to realize that the remains of Pensacola's Spanish and British colonial history were well preserved just inches below the surface throughout much of downtown.

The massive urban archaeology work kicked off by the City Hall project brought Dr. Bense face to face with Spanish and British colonial archaeology. A career that previously had focused on prehistory was rapidly transformed to one anchored by a deep interest in the archeology of the Spanish colonial period. Dr. Bense refers to this immersion in historical archaeology as her second Ph.D., and it was the point at which she began to self-identify as an historical archaeologist.

In 1984 Dr. Bense also made a proposal to Gulf Power that paved the way for public archaeology at UWF. Construction of the new Gulf Power headquarters building had been announced for a piece of land east of downtown Pensacola—the location of a Middle Woodland period site and the historic African American neighborhood known as "Hawkshaw." Although it was under no obligation to do so, Judy proposed that Gulf Power conduct archaeological and historical investigations prior to construction, and make the results accessible to the public through programs, publications, and exhibits. Gulf Power agreed, and for the next two years the archaeology at Hawkshaw was very much in the public eye. In 1986, Gulf Power and Dr. Bense received the Department of the Interior's National Public Service Award in recognition of the Gulf Power project at Hawkshaw. This was the first time this award was bestowed for archaeology.

The visibility that Hawkshaw and the downtown projects brought to archaeology and the UWF illustrated to Judy the importance of the public in advancing archaeology, and as a consumer of archaeological research. It was at this point that she embraced what today is known as "public archaeology" (though in the 1980s this term referred to what we today call cultural resource management), and it has become an essential component of UWF archaeology, leading ultimately to the creation of the Florida Public Archaeology Network in 2005.

Over the next decades, archaeology in downtown Pensacola (the 1754–1763 Presidio San Miguel de Panzacola, the 1763–1781 British Fort of Pensacola, and the 1781–1821 Spanish Town of Pensacola) came to be expected, and public interest in, and knowledge of Pensacola's colonial heritage grew. Dr. Bense also undertook research on the well preserved 1698–1722 Spanish Presidio Santa María de Galve located on Naval Air Station Pensacola between 1995 and 1998; and the 1722–1752 Presidio Isla de Santa Rosa located on Gulf Islands National Seashore (first investigated by Hale Smith in 1964) between 2002 and 2004. These projects have formed the basis of Dr. Bense's research, and have also provided experience and thesis projects for innumerable undergraduate and graduate students.

Maritime archaeology at UWF can be traced back to 1989, when State Underwater Archaeologist Roger Smith taught a class on weekends during the spring semester, followed by UWF's first maritime archaeology field school that summer. The site investigated was the Dead Man's Island wreck, which had been reported during a terrestrial survey the previous summer. Investigated were the remains of a late-18th-century British sloop.

In the early 1990s, Roger Smith returned to Pensacola to conduct the Pensacola Shipwreck Survey for the Bureau of Archaeological Research (BAR). This survey resulted in the discovery of a 16th-century Spanish shipwreck in 12 ft. of water off downtown Pensacola's shoreline. The "Emanuel Point" wreck was one of several sunk in a hurricane in 1559, one month after the arrival of the settlement expedition commanded by don Tristán de Luna y Arellano. The BAR-conducted initial investigations of this wreck in the mid-1990s, and in 1997 a partnership between BAR and UWF led to the continued excavation of this wreck. Well-preserved remains of this vessel and fragments of its cargo were discovered during this work. Excavations were watched closely by an enthralled public and media.

The success of the Emanuel Point project convinced Dr. Bense to take the underwater heritage of Pensacola Bay under her wing and inspired her to add maritime archaeology to the research and academic program at UWF. In 1999, work was begun by UWF on what are probably the remains of the *Nuestra Señora del Rosario y Santiago Apostol*, a large frigate and former flagship of the Spanish Windward Fleet which had patrolled Gulf and Caribbean waters. The *Rosario* was lost in a 1705 hurricane shortly after arriving at Presidio Santa María de Galve (1698–1719), near the modern city of Pensacola, Florida. From these beginnings the UWF's graduate program, which offers maritime archaeology, has gained national respect in terms of research, public outreach, and student training.

Concurrent with the development of local archaeological research and the growing importance of public archaeology at UWF was the development of the academic program. In 1979 Dr. Bense had helped to design the original anthropology curriculum. In 1981, cultural anthropologist Terry J. Prewitt joined the faculty and assisted Judy in teaching classes for an undergraduate degree in anthropology in a department that was partnered with sociology (and chaired by a sociologist), and which, over the years, variously included other disciplines such as geography and environmental science. In 1983 Judy became visiting assistant professor of anthropology and in 1985 entered the tenure track as assistant professor. In that same year she was appointed as director of the Archaeology Institute. Judy received tenure in 1988 and became a full professor in 1994.

Recognizing that a graduate program in anthropology was unlikely as long as sociology controlled the department, Dr. Bense worked with Dr. William Coker, chair of the Department of History, to create a master's program in historical archaeology within that department. Dr. Bense taught the anthropology graduate classes in this program which was established in 1991 and had its first graduate in 1996.

In 2000, Dr. Bense became chair of the Department of Sociology and Anthropology. The following year, sociology was dropped from the department name, recognizing the much diminished role of sociology in the curriculum. In 2002 a master's in anthropology and in historical archaeology was established within the department.

In 2004 and 2005, Dr. Bense and others worked to establish legislation and obtain funding for the Florida Public Archaeology Network (FPAN). This program is housed at UWF and operates regional public archaeology centers throughout Florida, where public archaeologists are charged with raising awareness of Florida archaeology through public outreach, work with local government, and assistance to the Florida Division of Historical Resources. Together, the successes of the Archaeology Institute, Department of Anthropology, and FPAN have led to the recognition of anthropology as a signature program of the UWF.

In 2008, the sitting president of UWF resigned to take another position and Judy was nominated to serve for one year as interim president. After review of numerous applicants and interviews with a short list including Dr. Bense, the board of trustees appointed her as interim president effective 1 July 2008, hoping that she could do for the university what she had done for anthropology. The board of trustees has subsequently removed the "interim" from her title and has extended her appointment through 2012.

The J. C. Harrington Medal was established by the SHA in 1981 to recognize a lifetime of contributions to the discipline of historical archaeology focused on scholarship. It remains the highest honor bestowed by the society. In reviewing the career of Dr. Judy Bense, it is clear that while her scholarship alone is sufficient to qualify her for this honor, her contribution to the discipline extends well beyond the confines of her research.

Dr. Bense found historical archaeology in downtown Pensacola in the mid-1980s, and she found her professional home in the Society for Historical Archaeology after she joined in 1982 and attended her first conference in 1985 in Boston. She has served the society in a variety of roles, including a term on the board of directors (2001–2003) and as president (2005–2006). She has served on committees, including major and sustained involvement with the SHA Governmental Affairs Committee since 2001. In 2002 the society recognized her contribution to public archaeology with the Award of Merit.

A review of Dr. Bense's extensive record of presented papers and juried publications will reveal two major trajectories of thought during the past three decades: one related to public archaeology and the other related to the archaeology of Spanish colonial Florida. In fact, a closer examination of her contribution to public archaeology will reveal that it is, as has already been mentioned, firmly planted in the historical archaeology of Pensacola and West Florida. Her scholarship over the past three decades has more specifically been focused on the presidios of Pensacola, which, due to their different locations, provide a perfect seriation of Spanish colonial life in Florida. This research has resulted in two edited volumes (*Archaeology of Colonial Pensacola 1750–1821* in 1999, and *Presidio Santa María de Galve: A Struggle in Survival in 18th-Century Pensacola* in 2003) and a thematic volume of *Historical Archaeology* (2004), *Presidios of the North American Spanish Borderlands*. Her coffee-table book *Unearthing Pensacola*, published in 2006, was based on her immensely popular local public radio program of the same name. In addition to these major works in historical archaeology, Dr. Bense also published in 1994 a standard reference in southeastern archaeology, *Archaeology of the Southeastern United States: Paleoindian to World War II*.

Dr. Bense is currently two-thirds of the way towards completion of a synthetic monograph on the presidios of Pensacola, although her duties as UWF president have put this project on hold. Also on hold is a new research initiative on Mexico's Gulf Coast, where she has begun to investigate the 17th- and 18th-century communities from which the first permanent settlers to Pensacola were drawn. The testing phase of this project, conducted jointly with the Instituto Nacional de Antropología e Historia (INAH), showed the presence of extensive, well-preserved remains of this period.

Dr. Bense's contribution to scholarship in historical archaeology is also reflected in the strongly applied graduate program that she built at UWF starting in 1991, and her role as a mentor to many students who are now taking their places in the ranks of successful professionals and research scholars. The applied program at UWF requires a major commitment by students to a serious, local research regime, which Dr. Bense skillfully leveraged by allowing students to be involved in her research and to utilize resulting data for their thesis projects.

It is impossible to talk about Dr. Bense's contribution to scholarship without also talking about her ability in obtaining resources. Through a successful program of grantsmanship which goes back to her first years at UWF, and through successful program development in the Florida legislature, archaeology at UWF has grown from non-existent in 1980 to a program that is today a leader in Spanish colonial and historical archaeology, underwater archaeology, and public archaeology. Due to her efforts, the Department of Anthropology, Institute of Archaeology, and FPAN today employ 14 archaeologists.

Dr. Bense's leadership in historical archaeology and at UWF has also been recognized through her appointment to the Florida Historical Commission beginning in 2002 (chair since 2003), and to the board of the National Center for Preservation, Training, and Technology (chair since 2006). She has also received the Department of the Interior's National Public Service Award (the first ever given for archaeology), the Florida Legislature's Outstanding Performance and Achievement Award, UWF's Distinguished Teaching Award for 1994 and 2001 (selected by students), the Pensacola Pride Award, the Daughters of the American Revolution's National History Award Medal, the Florida Anthropological Society's Ripley P. Bullen Award, the Society for American Archaeology's Presidential Award, the SHA Award of Merit, and the Pace Award for Professional Leadership.

Since joining SHA in 1982, Dr. Bense has regularly contributed to the program of the annual conference. She has organized and chaired seven symposia and one workshop, and has presented a dozen or so research papers. She has also presented regularly at the meetings of the Southeastern Archaeological Conference and the Society for American Archaeology, as well as at venues such as the World Archaeological Congress and a wide range of regional, specialized, and one-time conferences. She has lent her service to the Society for American Archaeology on their Governmental Affairs Committee, between 1984 and 1999 (chair from 1995); the Southeastern Archaeological Conference as conference chair for the 1984 and 1999 meetings, and on the board of directors (1980–1985 and 1997–1999); the Florida Anthropological Society as second vice president (1992–1993); and the Florida Archaeological Council on the board of directors (1995–1997), Stewards of Heritage Awards Committee (chair 1994–1995), and Florida Archaeological Week Committee (1993).

By awarding Dr. Judith Ann Bense the 2010 J. C. Harrington Medal in Historical Archaeology at the Amelia Island, Florida conference, the Society for Historical Archaeology acknowledges its gratitude that Dr. Bense chose to leave the business of horses and dogs behind in 1977 and reenter the world of archaeology to which she has been so well suited. In so doing, by sheer ability and perseverance she has built precisely the sort of program of which she had dreamed. As president of UWF and past president of the Society for Historical Archaeology, she was among those dignitaries who this past year welcomed to Pensacola King Juan Carlos and Queen Sophia of Spain on the advent of the 450th anniversary of the first Spanish settlement of Florida in 1559. Judy told them about archaeology. They were fascinated and they were grateful, and, of course, Dr. Bense made certain that UWF students shared in the experience.

Acknowledgements

The authors would like to thank Della Scott-Ireton and Monica L. Beck for their thoughtful comments on earlier versions of this manuscript.

WILLIAM B. LEES AND ELIZABETH D. BENCHLEY

J. C. Harrington Medal in Historical Archaeology: María del Pilar Luna Erreguerena, 2011. Volume 45, Number 2 (2011): 1-6. By Margaret E. Leshikar-Denton and Toni L. Carrell.

J. C. Harrington Medal in Historical Archaeology

María del Pilar Luna Erreguerena

María del Pilar Luna Erreguerena (Pilar) is the recipient of the 2011 Society for Historical Archaeology (SHA) J. C. Harrington Medal in Historical Archaeology. In 1997, Pilar was recognized with an award of merit from the SHA for her work to that time. She has continued to devote her life to archaeology, most notably to the field of underwater archaeology in Mexico, which includes research, protection, management, and interpretation of prehistoric, pre-Columbian, and historical heritage sites, as well as to international advocacy for underwater cultural heritage (UCH). The J. C. Harrington Medal represents formal recognition by her peers of her pioneering and sustained achievements and contributions to the field. It is fitting that Pilar received this prestigious award at the SHA's annual conference in Austin, Texas, a location near the border with Mexico that provided Pilar's family members and Mexican friends and colleagues the best opportunity to attend and witness her receipt of this lifetime-achievement award. Texas is also the location from which two of Pilar's earliest colleagues and friends in underwater archaeology, Donald H. Keith, president of Ships of Discovery, and George F. Bass, founder of the Institute of Nautical Archaeology (INA) traveled and brought with them seeds of knowledge that encouraged her to devote her life to the protection and management of the world's UCH.

Pilar has done more than any other person to bring scientific underwater archaeology to Mexico. Former chief of the Submerged Resources Center of the U.S. National Park Service Daniel Lenihan expressed in his letter of support of Pilar for this award that

> while considering such fortunes of birth writ large in nations and small in individuals, it occurred to me that Pilar's parents showed prescience in picking the name. It means *firme* or *sustentadora*, in Spanish and translates its subtext well to the word "pillar" in English—that which offers firm, upright support for a superstructure, not unlike a national program which needs thoughtful, yet unwavering leadership.

She has labored unrelentingly at this task, often vigorously opposed, criticized, and even threatened by treasure hunters, bureaucrats, prejudiced scholars, and navy officers. Pilar had to win over literally scores of officials in Mexico's sprawling bureaucracy, ranging from oceanographers to admirals in the navy. Over the last three decades, Pilar and her team have been Mexico's sole defense against numerous all-out efforts by foreign treasure-hunting companies to search for and salvage shipwreck sites in Mexican waters. It has been a lonely struggle, and she has often been sustained by the moral support received from her international archaeology colleagues. Lenihan aptly expressed:

> It is my conviction that Mexico has played the key role historically in the growth of underwater archaeology in the New World. Since the work of Edward Thompson at Chichen Itza in 1907 that focused on Mexico all the conflicting forces of antiquarianism, romanticism, true archaeology and predatory nationalism—up to the modern day attentions of maritime treasure hunters—Pilar's home has been a centerpiece of the storm.

> I have watched Pilar over the years move carefully but with a certain stolid confidence and sure sense of purpose through rough seas in Mexican and international politics. She has maintained a staunch sense of what cannot be compromised away in the name of mature consensus. That trait has served historical archaeology well in Mexico specifically and Latin America generally.

> When opportunities arose to work with Pilar's team in Mexico, my response to eager subordinates who enjoyed working with their Mexican colleagues was usually—"find a way to do it, this place is really worth it." When asked why I felt so strongly, the answer was simple, "because Mexico is Mexico and because Mexico has Pilar."

Pilar is a native of Tampico, Mexico, with fluency in Spanish, English, French, and Italian, having studied languages and general culture at the Stella Viae School in Rome, Italy. She is the youngest of five children, born to Spanish parents, who had her baptized in the Cathedral of Tampico, between the Mexican and Spanish flags, on the anniversary of Columbus's arrival in the New World. Although they did not always understand her passion for the cause of UCH, her family faithfully encouraged her studies and supported her decision to pursue archaeology. She obtained her bachelor's degree in archaeology from the National School of Anthropology and History, and her master's degree in anthropological sciences from the National Autonomous University of Mexico.

Indeed, Pilar may have been destined to become an underwater archaeologist. She was born with a love of the sea; as a youth she loved to swim for hours, just for the pleasure of it. In her early twenties, she was the first person in Mexico to teach children with Down syndrome how to swim. In 1975, she won two championships in underwater navigation and two gold and four silver medals in an underwater techniques competition. That same year, she participated in her first underwater archaeology project at Chunyaxché Lagoon, Quintana Roo, Mexico, with Dr. Harold Edgerton under the direction of Dr. Nancy Farris. She returned to terrestrial work, and in 1978, while a young professional working on the excavations in downtown Mexico City, in the Templo Mayor of the former Aztec city of Tenochtitlán, she made a unique discovery, unearthing an enormous conch shell carved in precise detail without the use of metal tools, out of pink and gray andesite, a volcanic stone. The artifact is so unique and rare that in 1980 it became the central piece of the first exhibit of pre-Columbian art held in the National Palace of Fine Arts in Mexico City. Today it is prominently displayed at the Templo Mayor site museum and was also featured on the 10,000-peso bill.

As a student in the National School of Anthropology and History in the early 1970s, Pilar took an interest in underwater archaeology, realizing that Mexico has a tremendous variety and wealth of such sites, from cenotes in Maya ceremonial sites to shipwrecks along Mexico's Gulf, Pacific, and Caribbean coasts. By the late 1970s, she convinced the authorities of the National School of Anthropology and History to sponsor a series of lectures on and exercises in underwater archaeology. In the words of Donald Keith, "During this class we discussed how to grow underwater archaeology in México—which we quickly perceived was more than Pilar's professional ambition, it was her passion."

In 1979, Pilar traveled to Turkey to gain field experience with the INA under George Bass, working on two ancient shipwrecks from the Hellenic and Byzantine periods at Serçe Limani. It was a life-changing experience from which she emerged even more committed to the cause of underwater archaeology in Mexico. Long before traveling to Turkey, Pilar and three students prepared a proposal to create a program dedicated to underwater archaeology, and presented it to the general director of Mexico's National Institute of Anthropology and History (INAH). Historian Flor Trejo calls this the "foundational document" because it envisions all that has been completed so far and more that is still to be accomplished. It took Pilar eight years of lobbying and passion to succeed in convincing INAH to create the Department of Underwater Archaeology in 1980. She is the founder and has been the head of the department since that time, and has also served as a member of several of Mexico's archaeology and cultural heritage organizations.

During her career, Pilar has directed projects in Mexican marine and continental waters and has worked internationally not only in Turkey, but also in the Cayman Islands with Roger C. Smith (1980), Jamaica with Donny L. Hamilton (1983), and with Donald H. Keith in the Bahamas (1986) and Panama (1990) in fieldwork sponsored by Ships of Discovery. One of her main concerns has been to promote the participation and commitment of official and private institutions and specialists in other disciplines in underwater archaeology projects.

In the midst of these accomplishments, Pilar completed her master's thesis in 1982, entitled "Underwater Archaeology." She graduated cum laude, and her thesis was recommended for publication.

Among the first projects that Pilar initiated and carried out are the survey and test excavation of 16th- and 18th-century shipwrecks on Cayo Nuevo Reef in the Bay of Campeche (1979–1983); the survey and sampling projects in the Media Luna Spring (1981–1982); the relocation and test excavation of an early-16th-century shipwreck site in Bahia Mujeres (1983–1984, 1990); the survey of Chinchorro Reef (1984); the mapping of Maya "lighthouses" along the east coast of the Maya Peninsula (1984–1985), which led to a successive project on pre-Columbian aids to navigation (1985–1989); the cooperative mapping of the USS *Somers* with the U.S. National Park Service (1990); the relocation and test excavation of a 17th-century shipwreck near Isla Contoy (1994); and the study and conservation of shipwreck artifacts now housed in the museum of Garrafón, a state park on Isla Mujeres, all in Quintana Roo. Of that first project on Cayo Nuevo Reef, Donald Keith remarked:

> It could be argued that Mexican underwater archaeology was born during that first expedition to Cayo Nuevo in late November, 1979. Far from the classroom, it was not a simple, safe, learning exercise. It's just as well that we didn't know the Bay of Campeche is not a good place to be in winter. Pilar saw recovery of the bronze cannon as an opportunity to draw attention to her efforts to jump-start underwater archaeology in México, and was willing to lay everything on the line to stage a high-profile raid on Davy Jones' locker. It was the first of what eventually became three expeditions to Cayo Nuevo and the crucible in which Pilar's mettle was tested. For that matter, we were all tested—but Pilar had the most at stake. A lot of important people were looking over her shoulder.

In 1994, Pilar engineered an intensive master's level course in underwater archaeology offered through the National School of Anthropology and History and open only to applicants already holding or nearing degrees in archaeology or conservation. She invited colleagues Donald Keith, Jack Hunter, and Monica S. Hunter from the United States, and Steve Willis from Canada to teach and provide their insights into the practice of underwater archaeology. The first of its kind in Mexico, the course was a tremendous success and, as a result, Pilar's department was upgraded within INAH in 1995 to become the Underwater Archaeology Vice-Directorate. Its aims are to protect, preserve, research, and disseminate information about Mexico's submerged legacy.

Pilar's ongoing commitment to training new Mexican underwater archaeologists is evident. Every year she invites renowned specialists from different parts of the world to give minicourses and share their knowledge and experience with Mexican underwater archaeologists, as well as conservators, biologists, historians, students, divers, and fishermen, among others. Chris Amer, state underwater archaeologist of South Carolina, observed that "Pilar has been instrumental in bridging the gulf between professionals and watermen by engaging them in the process of discovery, identification, and registration of shipwrecks and other submerged cultural resources."

More recently a third course in underwater archaeology, "Research and Management in Underwater and Maritime Archaeology" took place in Campeche from 27 September to 8 October 2010. It was sponsored by UNESCO and INAH, and 20 countries in Latin America and the Caribbean were invited to send participants. Of these, 14 countries sent 27 professionals from the fields of archaeology, anthropology, law, conservation, cultural resource management, and undergraduate students in archaeology and conservation. One of the important outcomes was the creation of the regionwide Organización Latinoamericana de Arqueología Subacuática (Latin American Underwater Archaeology Organization); its goals are to establish a regional network of professional support and to work toward the adoption and implementation of the 2001 UNESCO Convention throughout the region. Matthew Russell, chair of the Advisory Council on Underwater Archaeology (ACUA), stated: "The international impact of INAH's projects is due to Pilar's practice of including students and scholars from across both Latin and North America in her research projects. This practice of promoting international cooperation has resulted in a coherent network of colleagues and collaborators spanning the western hemisphere."

Soon after becoming a vice-directorate in 1995, three major research projects were initiated: the 1630–1631 New Spain fleet research project; the Inventory and Diagnosis of Submerged Cultural Resources in the Gulf of Mexico; and the Underwater Archaeological Atlas for recording, studying, and protecting cenotes (sinkholes) in the Yucatan Peninsula. In recent times, three new projects have been initiated: research into a Manila galleon in Baja California, in cooperation with researchers from the United States; survey of two lagoons in the crater of the Nevado de Toluca volcano and its surroundings; and survey and recording of UCH at the Banco Chinchorro Biosphere Reserve in Quintana Roo, in conjunction with the official agency in charge of the natural patrimony, and further seeking its nomination as a World Heritage Site on the basis of natural and cultural criteria.

In 2003, the Underwater Archaeology Vice-Directorate initiated five special programs: (1) attention to public reports of cultural material findings, (2) dissemination of information about UCH, (3) training, (4) conservation of archaeological material recovered from submerged sites, and (5) agreements for national and international collaboration.

Perhaps as a result of growing respect in Mexican archaeological and scientific circles for Pilar's perseverance and success in the face of seemingly insurmountable obstacles, she has received accolades from INAH and her colleagues in Mexico. She has expanded her influence by actively consulting with other Central and South American nations, offering advice on how to establish programs to protect their submerged cultural resources. Dolores Elkin, director of the Underwater Archaeology Program in Argentina's National Institute of Anthropology, remarked in support of Pilar for this award:

> I first met Pilar Luna in Montevideo in 1994, when she was invited to lecture on underwater cultural heritage in the context of Uruguay's national archaeology conference. At that time there were virtually no maritime archaeologists in South America, so for many people, like myself, meeting Pilar became the first opportunity to have direct contact with someone who was actually doing underwater archaeology in Latin America. I was instantly impressed by this woman who was a pioneer in such a male-dominated environment as our region is, particularly in activities related with diving.
>
> Pilar's presence in Uruguay was also crucial for its impact on the general public: At that time the country's waters were being looted by treasure hunters, and Pilar's lectures, talks and mass media interviews allowed people to hear a totally different message with regard to sunken ships. Her contribution to Uruguay's public awareness on the protection of underwater cultural heritage was an extension of her struggle in her own country, Mexico, where she was fighting against various international salvage companies.
>
> Pilar's model was sufficient enough for me to decide to become involved in maritime archaeology and to try to follow her steps by learning to dive and by putting together a team which in due time could become capable of studying and protecting the underwater cultural heritage. In those first and not so easy years Pilar was a permanent source of encouragement and assistance: she sent people from her team to train us in underwater archaeological techniques here in Argentina, and she also invited members of our team to participate in maritime archaeology courses and fieldwork in Mexico.
>
> Fifteen years down the road it is therefore fair to say that, directly or indirectly, the achievements of the Argentinean Underwater Archaeology Program at the National Institute of Anthropology are, in many ways, thanks to Pilar Luna.
>
> Pilar's contribution to maritime archaeology in Latin America continues to take place through courses and other initiatives aimed at young archaeologists from various countries of the region.

Dolores Elkin is not the only woman to take inspiration from Pilar's example. Mark Staniforth, associate professor in the Maritime Archaeology Program at Flinders University in Australia, noted in his letter of support that "Pilar has been an important role model for the involvement of women in underwater archaeology, which is still a male-dominated area within historical archaeology. She has been generous in her support of and assistance to both colleagues and students ... and has created a lasting legacy."

Pilar led the Underwater Archaeology Vice-Directorate in increased participation in international forums held by organizations such as the SHA, the International Council on Monuments and Sites (ICOMOS), UNESCO, and the World Archaeological Congress. She is chair of the Underwater Archaeology Scientific Committee for ICOMOS Mexico, and one of the four international advisors for the National Geographic Society. A member of the ACUA since 1982, she is now an emeritus member. She has served on the ICOMOS International Committee on Underwater Cultural Heritage (ICUCH) since 1992, the Ships of Discovery Board of Directors since 1989, and the Waitt Institute for Discovery Advisory Committee since 2006. Pilar first attended an SHA conference in 1980, has continued to participate in subsequent conferences, and today serves on the SHA UNESCO Committee. Paul Johnston, curator of maritime history at the Smithsonian's National Museum of American History, summed it up when he wrote in support of Pilar's nomination that "she has been one of the strongest and most tireless international advocates of the preservation ethic in the area of underwater cultural heritage."

Pilar served on the Mexican delegation during development of the 2001 UNESCO Convention on the Protection of the Underwater Cultural Heritage. She was instrumental in Mexico's ratification of the convention on 5 July 2006. She continues to represent Mexico at the ongoing UNESCO States Parties Meetings on the 2001 convention, and served as vice-chairperson of the first meeting of the Scientific and Technical Advisory Body to the UNESCO States Parties, held in Cartagena, Spain, from 13 to 15 June 2010. In her letter of support for Pilar for the J. C. Harrington Medal, Lyndel V. Prott, former director of the Cultural Heritage Division of UNESCO wrote:

I first became acquainted with Ms. Luna during preparations in the early 1990s for the negotiation of the UNESCO Convention on the Protection of the Underwater Cultural Heritage 2001. At that time she impressed with her great experience and her insistence on the high standards required in underwater archaeology.

During the negotiations, she was one of the most active and influential figures. She often represented the interests of the Latin American States and she was a most knowledgeable source of information for those not experienced in underwater cultural heritage matters or in the administration of protective rules. She also proved to have considerable diplomatic skills, being able to persuade with both arguments and humour, and she showed considerable patience with those not familiar with the complexities of underwater archaeology, the law of the sea, and the diversity of national systems of maritime law.

I believe it is fair to say that, without her participation, the text of the Convention as adopted would not appear as it now does.

Pilar has presented numerous lectures, written articles, and given interviews in radio, television, and the popular press in an effort to create a national and international consciousness regarding the importance of submerged cultural patrimony in Mexico and beyond. These activities have included the scientific community, diving groups, fishermen, and the public. In supporting Pilar's nomination, Francisco Alves, head of Portugal's Nautical and Underwater Archaeology Branch, expressed his "admiration of her professional, scientific and leadership skills, her tremendous human personality, and her talent as an engaging and clear communicator." Pilar's most recent book (coedited with Margaret Leshikar-Denton), detailing aspects of the Mexican experience and more, is *Underwater and Maritime Archaeology in Latin America and the Caribbean* (Left Coast Press 2008). It was inspired by a symposium on the subject that was held at the Fifth World Archaeological Congress (WAC-5) held in Washington, D.C., in 2003. Lyndel Prott particularly commended the work:

This book has long been needed and is a very valuable demonstration of the variety and significance of the underwater heritage of this region. Its appearance contributes to the understanding and the debate on ratification of the

2001 Convention at a time when many States are working towards its acceptance. As such, it continues Ms Luna's significant contribution to the international protection of the underwater cultural heritage.

I believe that her work on the Convention will be seen to be of considerable historic significance, this Convention being the first universally applicable on this subject.

In support of Pilar, Robert Grenier, former chief of underwater archaeology at Parks Canada and past-president of ICOMOS ICUCH wrote of her innate wisdom:

I often had to rely on advice from respected colleagues in periods of crisis. None could equal Pilar as my most reliable advisor: her incredible judgement, her overall vision, her well balanced sense of values and her indefatigable rigor made her advice irreplaceable. No wonder that she could successfully face adversity in such a macho world from her own managers, powerful admirals, treasure hunters, colleagues and even her own team members. This reputation of successful continuity in her achievements against all odds raised her profile and helped her build this solid national team, and influence the development of UCH protection in the hemisphere and all over the Hispanic world.

Matthew Russell expresses the sentiments of many of Pilar's colleagues in highlighting that "through her international activities, Pilar serves as a powerful example of how a single, committed individual can influence national policies and steer a nation towards a preservation ethic. In this, she is a role model internationally for colleagues across the globe, who strive to protect archaeological sites underwater."

In spite of physical ailments, including a near-fatal bout with histoplasmosis acquired during a cave excavation in the Yucatán, and a back injury that occurred during the abandonment of a sinking ship, Pilar has succeeded because of her respectful, articulate, and professional manner, leading the way for a new generation of underwater archaeologists. Maybe one of her best qualities is her kindness and warm way of being with people and with life in general. Her favorite quote is from the Spanish poet Antonio Machado: "Walker, there is no road. You make the road while you walk." So it is with Pilar, whose hard-won legacy has opened the way in Mexico. The SHA proudly presents Pilar Luna Erreguerena with the J. C. Harrington Medal in Historical Archaeology.

MARGARET E. LESHIKAR-DENTON AND TONI L. CARRELL

J. C. Harrington Medal in Historical Archaeology: George L. Miller, 2012. Volume 46, Number 2 (2012): 1-8. By Silas D. Hurry.

J. C. Harrington Medal in Historical Archaeology

George L. Miller

George L. Miller is the recipient of the 2012 Society for Historical Archaeology (SHA) J. C. Harrington Medal in Historical Archaeology. This award was presented to George at the SHA's annual conference in Baltimore, in recognition of his pioneering work, lifetime contributions, and dedication to scholarship in historical archaeology.

The Early Years in the "Old Northwest"

George was born in Detroit, Michigan, in 1942. His early archaeological influences occurred while he was an undergraduate at Wayne State University in Detroit. His principal professors and mentors were the late Dr. Arnold Pilling and Dr. Gordon L. Grosscup. While at Wayne State, he had the opportunity to work with a number of other individuals at a variety of sites in the "Old Northwest." His first archaeological job was in 1965 as an excavator for the University of Michigan, Museum of Anthropology at the Custer Road Dump site on Mackinac Island. This was followed by laboratory experience under Dr. Pilling and Dr. Grosscup at the Wayne State University Museum of Anthropology.

In 1966, 1967, and 1968, Miller served as the laboratory person for the great J. C. ("Pinky") Harrington during the excavations at Nauvoo, Illinois, the town that the Mormons built in 1839 under the direction of Joseph Smith after being forced out of Missouri. The opportunity to work with "Pinky" and, equally important, Virginia Harrington had a great impact on George and forever colored the way he looks at archaeology. Between times, Miller had the chance to participate in a site survey with Dr. James Fitting in southern New Mexico under the auspices of the University of Michigan, Museum of Anthropology and to excavate at the Walker Tavern site in Cambridge Junction, Michigan. He subsequently undertook the analysis of the ceramics from the tavern with Dr. Grosscup.

In 1969, Miller began a long-term research relationship with a site in Portage County, Ohio. The Franklin Glass Works occupied George through the spring of 1970. While initially the crew chief, Miller became director of excavations in September of 1969. He wrote a history of the glassworks (published in 1987) and began the study of the ceramics—ceramics that have been studied much longer than the mere nine years the site was in operation. One of the early fruits of this analysis was George's first published article: "Time Expended for Archaeological Excavations vs. Technical Analysis of Artifacts from the Franklin Glass Works Site, Kent, Ohio" (Miller 1971b). George started fighting for adequate lab budgets early. In the same year, Miller (1971a) published an article that explored mean ceramic dating with 19th-century ceramics. This was George's most "South"erly foray.

George Miller Goes South

In the spring of 1972, Miller got his first fulltime archaeological position. He was hired by the St. Mary's City Commission (now the Historic St. Mary's City Commission) to set up and establish the archaeological lab and create processes for the study and treatment of artifacts from Maryland's first capital. He was hired by Garry Wheeler Stone and found himself in an incredibly rich intellectual environment. On staff at that time were Dr. Cary Carson, Alexander H. Morrison II, Dr. Lois Carr, Dr. Lorena Walsh, and Dr. Russell Menard. Among the "summer help" were myself, Henry Miller, Joanne Bowen, Mike Smolek, and Robert Keeler. George has said that each day at work was an intellectual feast, interacting with people who went on to revolutionize the entire area of "Chesapeake Studies." Miller directed the archaeology lab during the entire Watergate debacle. By his rule, the only radio that could be played in the lab had to be tuned to National Public Radio for the hearings.

While at St. Mary's City, George published his study of 19th-century ceramics from the Tole-Tabbs site, "A Tenant Farmer's Tableware: Nineteenth-Century Ceramics from Tabb's Purchase" (Miller 1974). Miller wrote, but did not publish, his first study of blue-edged earthenware with the wonderful topic sentence: "Who were the Blue Edgeware People?" At St. Mary's, George created the laboratory processes still used there, began an artifact conservation program, and introduced the staff to the idea of ceramic-vessel analysis, stressing that people used pots, not pieces. Also during this time, he began researching ceramic supply in the isolated Ohio Western Reserve, on which he published with Silas Hurry in 1983. In 1976, Miller celebrated the bicentennial of American independence by immigrating to Canada.

George Goes North

The cause of George's migration to Canada was to take a new job with Parks Canada in Ottawa, Ontario. Miller was employed as a material culture researcher under the direction of Olive Jones in the Glass Section. While there, he had the opportunity to work with Olive, Catherine Sullivan, and others on the *Parks Canada Glass Glossary* (Jones and Sullivan 1985), still the bible of glass-artifacts studies. Three other publications on glass and ceramics came from Miller's time at Parks Canada (Miller and Sullivan 1981; Miller and Pacey 1985; Miller and Jorgenson 1986). George has said that going to work at Parks Canada at that time was like attending a conference every day, surrounded by a range and wealth of material culture specialists. Miller also received a six-month fellowship to the Winterthur Museum, where he undertook a study of the Philadelphia ceramics and glass merchant George M. Coates, who was in business from 1817 to 1831 (Miller 1984). Following the fellowship, he organized a conference on marketing ceramics in North America in the 18th and 19th centuries. Five papers from that conference were subsequently published in

Winterthur Portfolio in 1984. Most notably, the research led to the 1980 publication of Miller's seminal study "Classification and Economic Scaling of 19th Century Ceramics" in *Historical Archaeology* (Miller 1980). This article has been reprinted both in Mary Beaudry's 1988 edited volume, *Documentary Archaeology*, and the SHA reader *Approaches to Material Culture Research for Historical Archaeologists* (Miller et al. 1991).

George Takes Williamsburg

In 1983, George Miller was lured back into the United States with a new job offer. This new position was as senior laboratory analyst under the direction of Dr. Marley Brown III. His work at Colonial Williamsburg involved helping to revise their computer cataloging system, improving the dating of artifacts, reviewing the analysis of reports, and teaching students. He was awarded two grants while at Colonial Williamsburg and completed major research projects on ceramic prices, index values, and chronologies. Miller also worked with numerous students writing their master's theses at the College of William and Mary.

During this period, Miller authored, coauthored, or contributed to 12 research articles, including "The Second Destruction of the *Geldermalsen*" (1987c). This article, which questioned the ethics of a museum dealing with underwater treasure hunters, was a significant contribution and a brave position to take when you are employed by one of the museums purchasing Chinese porcelain from the *Geldermalsen*. That article was subsequently reprinted twice by other journals, including the *Bermuda Journal of Archaeology and Maritime History* in 1990 and *Historical Archaeology* in 1992. Miller maintained a hectic pace of publication, both as a solo author and as a collaborative author. In 1986, George published "Of Fish and Sherds: A Model for Estimating Vessel Counts" in *Historical Archaeology* and, in 1987, "Origins of Josiah Wedgwood's Pearlware" in *Northeast Historical Archaeology.*

George Miller was awarded a two-year grant in December 1985 from the National Endowment for the Humanities (NEH) entitled "English Ceramics in America, 1760 to 1860: Marketing, Prices, and Availability." He directed two researchers working with merchants' records from Boston, Philadelphia, New York, and Williamsburg. As part of his research, George spent three months in Staffordshire working in the Wedgwood, Spode, and Minton archives.

Miller received a grant from Garrow and Associates of Atlanta, Georgia, in September of 1985 for research on the Staffordshire potters' price-fixing list of 1814. He was also awarded a three-month Winterthur Research Fellowship to the Winterthur Museum in Delaware in the fall of 1989. The research focused on defining the "market basket" of ceramics commonly available in country stores from 1780 to 1880. In 1990, Miller and Hunter published "English Shell Edged Earthenware: Alias Leeds Ware, Alias Feather Edge" in *Proceedings of the Thirty-fifth Wedgwood International Seminar.* In 1991, Miller received a six-month NEH/Winterthur Fellowship to the Winterthur Museum from July through December 1991 to continue this research.

The year 1991 saw publication of "A Revised Set of CC Index Values for Classification and Economic Scaling of English Ceramics from 1787 to 1880" in *Historical Archaeology* (Miller 1991a), which was subsequently reprinted in the second edition of *Approaches to Material Culture Research for Historical Archaeologists* (Brauner 2000) and later translated into Portuguese in 2009.

That same year, Miller began publishing a series of brief articles in the newsletter of the Council for Northeast Historical Archaeology (CNEHA) under the title: "Thoughts Towards a User's Guide to Ceramic Assemblages." The four-part series included "Part I: Lumping Sites into Mega-assemblages by Those That Cannot Tell Time" (Miller 1991b), "Part II: What Does This Assemblage Represent?" (Miller 1991c), "Part III: Breaking Archaeological Assemblages into Functional Groups" (Miller 1992), and finally "Part IV: Some Thoughts on Classification of White Earthenwares" (Miller 1993). These papers, which provide timeless guidance for material culture analysts focusing on ceramics, are available on the CNEHA website, <http://www.cneha .org/newsletters/millerguide.pdf>.

George in Delaware

In 1992, George Miller began a foray into the cultural resource management (CRM) world. He was employed as a material culture researcher by the Center for Archaeological Research at the University of Delaware under the direction of Dr. Jay Custer. While at the center, he created a computer catalog for glass and ceramic vessels, set up a computerized numbering system for the inventory control of artifacts from historical-period sites, and analyzed the artifacts from four sites ranging in date from the late 17th century into the early 20th century. His work involved training catalogers, historical archaeologists, and students. While at Delaware, Miller published with Rob Hunter "English Shell-Edged Earthenware" in *Antiques Magazine* (Hunter and Miller 1994).

In March 1993, George was awarded a one-year NEH grant, entitled "English and American Ceramics, 1846–1917: Prices, Index Values, and Chronology," which was an extension of his earlier work on ceramic prices. Much of this research subsequently fed into the article "War and Pots" (Miller and Earls 2008). In 1994, Miller and collaborators Ann Smart Martin and Nancy S. Dickinson published "Changing Consumption Patterns: English Ceramics and the American Market from 1770 to 1840" in *Everyday Life in the Early Republic,* published by the Winterthur Museum.

George in the Corporate World

In 1994, Miller left the quasi-commercial/quasi-academic world of the University of Delaware for the corporate world. He became the laboratory director for the archaeology section of URS Corporation in Burlington, New Jersey, where he remained until his retirement in 2008. He oversaw the artifact analysis for many CRM projects and continued to inspire and direct students. During this period, Miller authored or coauthored eight publications and began his deep involvement with the journal *Ceramics in America.* Miller had worked closely with Rob Hunter while at Colonial Williamsburg, and more collaborations continued. Significant articles from this period include his "All in the Family: A Staffordshire Soup Plate and the American Market" (Hunter and Miller 2001) and "How Creamware Got the Blues: The Origins of China Glaze and Pearlware" (Miller and Hunter 2001).

Miller continued collaborating and publishing in a range of venues. "Telling Time for Archaeologists," published in 2000 in *Northeast Historical Archaeology* with contributions by Patricia Samford, Ellen Shlasko, and Andrew Madsen, exemplifies George's penchant for meticulous research and is a "must read" for anyone conducting material culture analysis. This article led to a series of posters produced by URS for CNEHA.

While at URS, Miller worked closely with Terry Klein and Meta Janowitz. George and Meta were noted for their spirited discussions concerning pottery in its many forms. George and Terry collaborated on the important article: "A System for Ranking the Research Potential of Nineteenth- and Twentieth-Century Farmstead Archaeology in the Northeast" (Miller and Klein 2002). In this article, Miller and Klein proposed ways of evaluating the research potential of a ubiquitous type of site frequently found but seldom studied. Miller also returned, somewhat, to his roots, investigating the evolution of machine-made bottles.

In 1997, during his "URS period," George Miller collected his most significant "dish," his wife Amy Earls. Amy's friends assumed she had always wanted her own toby jug. George and Amy are both ceramics wizards who have also collaborated on significant publications.

George in Retirement

Retirement has found George Miller as active as when officially working. In 2008, he and Amy published a highly significant article entitled "War and Pots" in *Ceramics in America* (Miller and Earls 2008). The original paper had been presented at the 2007 Society for Historical Archaeology conference held in Williamsburg, Virginia. The essential thesis of this study is that external events led to major economic results, which can be seen in ceramics availability, selection, and use. This has been a reoccurring subtext in many of George's broader-scale investigations—seeing the big questions through the lens of broken pots. Pots are what archaeologists find, but people are what we want to study.

The year 2009 saw the publication with Rob Hunter of "Suitable for Framing: Decorated Shell-Edge Earthenware" in *Early American Life* (Hunter and Miller 2009). This article reached a very wide, popular audience, discussing what was an extremely common ceramic type that had first caught George's attention early in his career when he asked: "Who were the blue edgeware people?"

George's recent research has included more study of the advent of machine-made bottles and recent exploration of the production, cost, and distribution of cobalt, perhaps the most significant material used in the decoration of ceramics. Did cobalt cost affect how the potters decorated their wares? Wait until he publishes the article and be amazed.

George is also investigating a privateer prize cargo seized during the War of 1812 and auctioned off in Salem, Massachusetts, in 1813. It was not the ship that interested George, but rather the cargo. It included 250 crates of "Liverpool Ware" and assorted linens. The auction catalog contained a great amount of detail about the contents of those 250 crates that allowed Miller to analyze the assemblage much as he would an archaeological site, albeit one much better described and documented than anything found in the ground. So George is continuing to investigate the economic context of the War of 1812, a subject which also figured in his study with Amy of "War and Pots."

Mentoring Students and Reaching Out to the Public

One of George Miller's major and prolonged contributions has been in mentoring students who have matured into colleagues. George has been instrumental in directing students into research into the past that is not driven by the au courant theory. Several dissertations and theses have benefited from Miller's insights and enthusiasm, in spite of his never having a full-time academic job or an advanced degree. George worked directly with undergraduates at St. Mary's College of Maryland, undergraduates and graduate students at the College of William and Mary, a range of students at the University of Delaware, and most recently, graduate students at Temple University. Of course, many of these students went on for even more advanced studies, and they could depend on Miller to support them, push them farther than they wanted to go, and to provide insight that only comes with experience and dedication. Among the many students George mentored, many are now our colleagues. Just to mention a few, Ann Smart Martin, Patricia Samford, Nancy Dickinson, Ellen Shlasko, Meredith M. Poole, Andrew Madsen, Esther White, Robert Hunter, Mara Kaktins, Tony McNichol, and myself all benefited from our association with George.

With his many presentations of his seminar entitled "An Introduction to English Ceramics," George Miller has reached diverse audiences, ranging from college students to government agencies, professional organizations, and environmental and contract firms. George has given this presentation 60 times in 22 states. Venues have included 14 colleges and universities, 4 museums, 8 professional organizations, and 5 environmental and cultural resource firms.

George Miller has also reached out to the glass- and ceramics-collectors' world, where he has tried to move enthusiasts from the worship of "style" to an understanding of the underlying causal economics. His articles in the *Proceedings of the Wedgwood International Seminar*, *Antiques Magazine,* and *Ceramics in America* have brought the same rigor of research to new specialized and popular audiences.

George and his "Pun"ishing use of Language

George has long had a way with words. Some specific observations ensconced in his publications include "How Creamware Got the Blues" (Miller and Hunter 2001); "Pearlware did not replace creamware, decoration replaced creamware" (Miller and Earls 2008); "pearlware, that pigment of our imagination" (Miller and Earls 2008); and "Ode to a Lunch Bowl" (Miller 1986). George has always known how language can be used to advance a point or blunt an assault. He once spoke of "simple reductionist archaeology" and then added that he feared he had strayed "far south of his topic."

Sometimes Miller's wit has focused on the nature of the profession, specifically the pursuit of archaeology for profit and those who cut corners to achieve that end. George has imagined a CRM firm named Will, Bidlow, and Dolittle, Inc., whose corporate slogan is: "So the Present Can Earn from the Past." He actually envisioned the entire staff, which included the lithics specialist named Debby Tage and a business manager named Hiram Cheap.

Sometimes George Miller does not make a joke, but does make a point: "Overproduction and the resulting falling prices drove changing consumption patterns, not consumer demand." George always appreciates the need to see past the theory to the reality of the data and is not shy in pointing this out when others do not.

Sartorial George

George Miller has always made an unusual statement in his choice of attire. George invented casual Friday and then extended it to the entire week. A colleague once said Miller looked like a Bavarian tuba player, but Bavarian tuba players do not commonly wear sandals. Many have tried to emulate his sense of style, but few have succeeded. I have been told that when attending the rather formal American Ceramic Circle meeting in Philadelphia that his co-presenters, Ann Smart Martin and Patricia Samford, had to take George shopping so he actually would have a tie. George subsequently demonstrated his familiarity with ties by laundering it with his new outfit, dyeing all the clothes pink. But clothes don't make the man. Miller's sartorial signature at first disarms. Then he opens his mouth and we are totally disarmed intellectually. If sandals and suspenders catch our attention, it is the mind that we remember.

George and the Society for Historical Archaeology

George Miller is a charter member of SHA and attended the first meeting of the precursor of the SHA in Dallas in 1967. George served on the executive board of SHA from 1980 to 1982 and on the editorial advisory committee from 1983 to 1995. Miller was instrumental in beginning the series "A Reader from Historical Archaeology" with publication of *Approaches to Material Culture Research for Historical Archaeologists* in 1991 (Miller et al. 1991). He has presented 19 papers at annual meetings, 7 of which have been published. He has authored or coauthored 10 articles that have been published in the journal and has three book reviews also published there. George has long been a gadfly and conscience to the organization, especially about keeping prices down so students can participate. In 1973, at the annual business meeting, Miller inquired about the high cost of the registration fee for the conference. Rick Sprague explained that the fee, $12.50, was a result of the organization deciding it would no longer underwrite the expense of the banquet. It was Miller who taught me to always attend the business meeting—often the best theater and entertainment occurs in that *Robert's Rules of* [dis]*Order*–structured space.

Miller has been known to complain about the time of year we meet and the inclement weather that seems to follow us around. As detailed in a submission to the *SHA Newsletter*, George pointed out that in 1968 the second annual meeting, in Williamsburg, was beset with freezing rain; after the 1970 meeting in Bethlehem, Pennsylvania, heavy snow made travel home dicey; and at the 1973 conference in St. Paul, Minnesota, participants experienced arctic temperatures. The 1976 meeting in Philadelphia concluded with freezing rain. In fact, I recall driving back to Baltimore and being directed onto the highway median by Pennsylvania state troopers because of road conditions. The 1979 Nashville meeting was preceded by bad weather, causing many to miss the first day's sessions. In 1983, while Denver, Colorado, was ready for heavy weather, the rest of the world was not, leading to massive delays getting home, and who can forget Cincinnati in 1996 when numerous people were snowed in for days? The latter meeting stimulated George's complaint. (I fortunately took the advice of a wise man that had grown up across the river in Kentucky and left a day early.) Subsequent memorable meetings, weatherwise, include Corpus Christi, Texas, with ice storms, and more recently the less-than-warm weather of Amelia Island, Florida. Miller has suggested changing the time of year that SHA meets to something more appealing, but then we would all be on the beach like at the Kingston, Jamaica, conference in 1992. However, he always needs to remember that it was at an SHA conference in Washington, D.C., in 1995 that he met Amy—some good things do come from these conferences.

George Miller and the Discipline

From the birth of the discipline of historical archaeology with the Dallas meeting of 1967 through its maturation over the past 45 years, George Miller has contributed to our understanding of the past and has developed tools that measure in real ways the significance of artifacts. By stressing the use of potters' terminology and examining the value of decoration, Miller has grounded our studies of ceramics in a real world, not simply a collector's world. His long publication history and his willingness to teach students of all stripes have made a lasting contribution to our chosen area of study. George Miller has shown by example that understanding the past is not a simple mathematical equation but rather a thoroughgoing evaluation of data and what those data mean. George's outreach to many audiences demonstrates why we actually do archaeology. His ceramic seminars have reached countless students of material culture and broadened our audience in areas archaeologists seldom tread. His range of studies from ceramics to glass has enlightened the discipline and helped move our work into areas previously ignored. The "Telling Time" posters and his "Thoughts Towards a User's Guide to Ceramic Assemblages" have in clear English set standards for how archaeologists should think. His willingness to take on difficult subjects like the *Geldermalsen* has demonstrated a fierce determination to pursue what is right, not what is easy. In his retirement, Miller continues to contribute to historical archaeology. In my opinion, Pinky and Virginia Harrington would be proud.

References

BEAUDRY, MARY C. (EDITOR)
    1988   *Documentary Archaeology in the New World.* Cambridge University Press, Cambridge, UK.

HUNTER, ROBERT, AND GEORGE L. MILLER
    1994   English Shell-Edged Earthenware. *Antiques* 145(3):432–443.
    2001   All in the Family: A Staffordshire Soup Plate and the American Market. In *Ceramics in America*, Robert Hunter, editor, pp. 222–225. Chipstone Foundation, Milwaukee, WI.
    2009   Suitable for Framing: Decorated Shell-Edge Earthenware. *Early American Life* 40(4):9–19.

JONES, OLIVE, AND CATHERINE SULLIVAN
    1985   *The Parks Canada Glass Glossary.* With contributions by George L. Miller, Jane Harris, Ann Smith, and Kevin Lunn. Parks Canada, Ottawa, ON.

MILLER, GEORGE L.
    1971a The Application of the South Mean Ceramic Date Formula to a Nineteenth Century Site. *Conference on Historic Site Archaeology Papers* 6:193–194.
    1971b Time Expended for Archaeological Excavations vs. Technical Analysis of Artifacts from the Franklin Glass Works Site, Kent, Ohio. *Michigan Archaeologist* 17(2):91–95.
    1974   A Tenant Farmer's Tableware: Nineteenth-Century Ceramics from Tabb's Purchase. *Maryland Historical Magazine* 69(2):197–210.
    1980   Classification and Economic Scaling of 19th Century Ceramics. *Historical Archaeology* 14:1–40.
    1984   George M. Coates, Pottery Merchant of Philadelphia, 1817–1831. *Winterthur Portfolio* 19(1):37–49.
    1986a Ode to a Lunch Bowl: The Atlantic Lunch as an Interface between St. Mary's County Maryland, and Washington, D.C. *Northeast Historical Archaeology* 13:2–8.
    1986b Of Fish and Sherds: A Model for Estimating Vessel Populations from Minimal Vessel Counts. With an appendix by Meredith Moodey. *Historical Archaeology* 20(2):59–85.
    1987a History of the Franklin Glass Works, Portage County, Ohio. *Glass Club Bulletin of the National Early American Glass Club.* 152:3–9.
    1987b Origins of Josiah Wedgwood's Pearlware. *Northeast Historical Archaeology* 16:80–92.
    1987c The Second Destruction of the *Geldermalsen. American Neptune* 42(4):275–281.

1991a A Revised Set of CC Index Values for Classification and Economic Scaling of English Ceramics from 1787 to 1880. *Historical Archaeology* 25(1):1–25.

1991b Thoughts Towards a User's Guide to Ceramic Assemblages, Part I: Lumping Sites into Mega-assemblages by Those That Cannot Tell Time. *Council for Northeast Historical Archaeology Newsletter* 18:2–5.

1991c Thoughts Towards a User's Guide to Ceramic Assemblages, Part II: What Does This Assemblage Represent? *Council for Northeast Historical Archaeology Newsletter* 20:4–6.

1992 Thoughts Towards a User's Guide to Ceramic Assemblages, Part III: Breaking Archaeological Assemblages into Functional Groups. *Council for Northeast Historical Archaeology Newsletter* 22:2–4.

1993 Thoughts Towards a User's Guide to Ceramic Assemblages, Part IV: Some Thoughts on Classification of White Earthenwares. *Council for Northeast Historical Archaeology Newsletter* 26:4–7.

2000 Telling Time for Archaeologists. With contributions by Patricia Samford, Ellen Shlasko, and Andrew Madsen. *Northeast Historical Archaeology* 29:1–22.

MILLER, GEORGE L., AND AMY C. EARLS

2008 War and Pots: The Impact of Economics and Politics on Ceramic Consumption Patterns. In *Ceramics in America*, Robert Hunter, editor, pp. 67–108. Chipstone Foundation, Milwaukee, WI.

MILLER, GEORGE L., AND ROBERT R. HUNTER, JR.

1990 English Shell Edged Earthenware: Alias Leeds Ware, Alias Feather Edge. In *Proceedings of the Thirty-fifth Wedgwood International Seminar,* pp. 107–135. Birmingham Museum of Art, Birmingham, AL.

2001 How Creamware Got the Blues: The Origins of China Glaze and Pearlware. In *Ceramics in America*, Robert Hunter, editor, pp. 135–161. Chipstone Foundation, Milwaukee, WI.

MILLER, GEORGE L., AND SILAS D. HURRY

1983 Ceramic Supply in an Economically Isolated Frontier Community: Portage County of the Ohio Western Reserve, 1800–1825. *Historical Archaeology* 17(2):80–92.

MILLER, GEORGE L., OLIVE R. JONES, LESTER A. ROSS, AND TERESITA MAJEWSKI (COMPILERS)

1991 *Approaches to Material Culture Research for Historical Archaeologists: A Reader from Historical Archaeology.* Society for Historical Archaeology, California, PA.

MILLER, GEORGE L., AND ELIZABETH A. JORGENSON

1986 *Some Notes on Bottle Mould Numbers from Dominion Glass Company and Its Predecessors.* Parks Canada, Ottawa, ON.

MILLER, GEORGE L., AND TERRY H. KLEIN

2002 A System for Ranking the Research Potential of Nineteenth- and Twentieth-Century Farmstead Archaeology in the Northeast. *Northeast Historical Archaeology* 30 & 31:155–166.

MILLER, GEORGE L., AND ANTHONY PACEY

1985 Impact of Mechanization in the Glass Container Industry: The Dominion Glass Company of Montreal, a Case Study. *Historical Archaeology* 20(1):38–50.

MILLER, GEORGE L., AND CATHERINE SULLIVAN

1981 Machine-made Glass Containers and the End of Production for Mouth-blown Bottles. Parks Canada, *Research Bulletin* No. 171. Ottawa, ON.

SILAS D. HURRY

J. C. Harrington Medal in Historical Archaeology: Mary C. Beaudry, 2013. Volume 47, Number 2 (2013): 1-7. By Sara F. Mascia and Carolyn L. White.

J. C. Harrington Medal in Historical Archaeology

Mary C. Beaudry

Mary Carolyn Beaudry is the recipient of the 2013 Society for Historical Archaeology (SHA) J. C. Harrington Medal in Historical Archaeology. The award was presented to Mary at the SHA's annual conference in Leicester, United Kingdom, in recognition of her dedication to scholarship, innovative and pioneering work, commitment to mentoring students, and lifetime contributions in the field of historical archaeology.

Menu

Mary's wide-ranging interests in so many different areas are remarkable and impressive. One look at her curriculum vitae provides salient affirmation on her selection as the 2013 J. C. Harrington medalist. Her diverse research interests are reflected in her numerous publications and papers, as well as through the myriad courses she has offered to students over the years. She has influenced almost every historical archaeologist in some way—in her classroom, alongside her in the field, coauthoring a paper, being on a committee, serving with her for the SHA, or perhaps just by reading one of her many books or articles. From the first moment people meet her, they are exposed to an incredible intellectual ride with one of the principal architects of the discipline who has an exemplary record of scholarship, mentoring, and service.

In recent years, Mary has been exploring and teaching the anthropology of food, an interest that she has shared with many of her colleagues and students. Mary herself is an extraordinary banquet that we all have the privilege to enjoy.

Setting the Table

Mary Carolyn Beaudry came into this world with boundless energy and curiosity, further stimulated by her life as a child of a military family, moving from place to place. Her family eventually settled in Virginia, where her father worked at Fort Eustis, and her mother regularly brought her and her sisters on visits to nearby historic plantations and Colonial Williamsburg, offering her a glimpse of life in pre-Revolutionary America.

Amuse-Bouche or Appetizer

Mary's education was a mixed recipe that involved many ingredients. When she began her undergraduate study at the College of William and Mary, she was enrolled as an English major and aspired to become a writer. This choice of a potential profession comes as no surprise to her numerous colleagues and students who have had the privilege of reading her work. A colleague once described her articles on archaeology as demonstrating "literary elegance" (Evans 2012). This is a testament to her continued interest in exploring the written word throughout her career.

In 1970, Mary enrolled in Dr. Norman Barka's Introduction to Anthropology class in order to fulfill a college requirement. When Dr. Barka mentioned in class that he was excavating a shell midden at Maycock's Plantation and that students who were interested in volunteering on the weekends should speak with him after class, Mary jumped at the chance (Beaudry 2009a). One weekend, her fate changed with the introduction of a sharpened popsicle stick. The "tool," handed to her by Lefty Gregory, was to be used for the excavation of a Native American burial. As it turned out, the grave contained the remains of a young boy who was wearing a necklace of copper wire and glass beads. When Lefty explained to her that the necklace was European and dated to the 17th century, she was stunned. After inquiring whether archaeologists could study the historical period and not just prehistory, Mary was told that there was indeed a professional field for the study of historical archaeology. This revelation transformed Mary, and she immediately knew that she wanted to change course and become an historical archaeologist.

Along her educational path, Mary's insatiable curiosity about objects and their function was cemented during the many hours she spent in Dr. Barka's laboratory processing artifacts from Flowerdew Hundred. During the summer before her senior year, she was proud to have been offered a paid position working as a member of the field crew for the excavation at the Poor Potter's site in Yorktown. As the only female crew member, Mary felt in the spotlight when Dr. Barka insisted that she maintain perfectly vertical sidewalls, often stopping to check, measure, and make sure her sidewalls stayed true. The archaeologists and students who have since worked with Mary in the field know that she has never, ever, forgotten this attention to detail.

In 1972, Mary ventured north across the Mason-Dixon Line to study with Jim Deetz at Brown University. She once said that she found Deetz's work much more interesting than that of other archaeologists, so she conducted some research, found out where he was teaching, and applied to Brown with little expectation of admission. Of course, she was accepted.

During the 1970s, women were working toward expanding their influence in many professions. However, there were still many obstacles to surmount, as she and fellow student Anne Yentsch quickly learned. Women enrolled in archaeology courses at Brown were often selected to work with documents, while the male students went off to dig with Dr. Deetz. After her first year at Brown, she returned to Virginia, where she continued to focus on documentary research for several domestic sites, spurring her interest in probate inventories.

In her 1980 doctoral dissertation, *"Or What Else You Please to Call It": Folk Semantic Domains in Early Virginia Probate Inventories*, Mary combined both her intimate knowledge of Chesapeake material culture with her expertise in interpreting documentary evidence (Beaudry 1980a). As Mary later explained, the language used in probate records represents a "folk nomenclature," which is significant for interpreting and analyzing how the people who were using the vessels conceptualized them (Beaudry 1988:45). Her work from this period remains one of the most outstanding integrations of linguistic anthropology and archaeology. This is just a taste of the innovative and varied topics that Mary would focus on during the next three decades.

Soup

Following her successful dissertation defense, Mary was offered a job as assistant professor of anthropology at Boston University (BU). Shortly after she arrived, she was one of a few scholars hired to help build a new program in archaeology. Almost immediately, Mary began to acquire a large number of students and played a critical role in building a highly respected archaeology program. Her classes were always extremely popular, and not just because they were on occasion held in the nearby pub.

Much like Norm Barka before her, Mary quickly instituted "weekend excavations," where she invited her students to volunteer at archaeological sites in eastern Massachusetts. Many of these projects turned into papers, articles, theses, and dissertations for her students. In 1983, she requested that her students volunteer at the Paul Revere House. Upon arrival, each volunteer was presented with trowels and screens, and set to work. Over the next three decades, Mary provided her students with a variety of opportunities to learn and hone their field skills.

In 1985, Mary began to work with several colleagues at the Lowell Boott Mills in Massachusetts. This multiyear project reflected her wide-ranging interests in household makeup, material culture, corporate paternalism, oral histories, and historical documents. With her colleagues, the project produced in-depth information about the daily lives of individuals "living on the Boott" (Beaudry 1989). This landmark project also produced a detailed analysis of the landscape of the boardinghouse and the overseer's house by employing a comprehensive approach to the archaeology, intertwining various sciences, documentary evidence, and oral history (Mrozowski and Beaudry 1990). Rather than analyzing artifacts in a void, she encouraged the team to speculate how the people they were studying actually saw themselves and their possessions, without simply fitting them into predetermined categories. During this process, Mary became a consummate storyteller, sharing the past and the lives of the individuals that she unearthed with the world. In the end, she and her colleagues generated important information for the National Park Service to use in its management and interpretation of Lowell National Historical Park.

In 1988, Mary published the edited volume *Documentary Archaeology in the New World*, introducing the reader to the wealth of documentary resources available, as well as providing a guide to the innovative interpretation of historical archaeological materials. The volume also contains one of her most cited articles, "A Vessel Typology for Early Chesapeake Ceramics: The Potomac Typological System," which had originally appeared in *Historical Archaeology* in 1983 (Beaudry et al. 1983). POTS, as this work has been called, was a collaborative effort with several leading scholars working with material cultural in the Chesapeake. Concerned with the problem that varied names were used for the same vessel types in project reports throughout the region, Mary and her coauthors endeavored to categorize vessels in a manner that would "make the cultural dynamics behind them more accessible" (Beaudry et al. 2000:22–30). Mary's inclusion of this article in *Documentary Archaeology in the New World* provided a venue for this important work to reach a broader audience. While most historical archaeologists used documents in their research, Mary was a pioneer who encouraged colleagues and students to find ways to move beyond a simple reiteration of the information in documents and instead interpret the data that can be found in these vital resources.

The archaeological investigation at the Spencer-Peirce-Little Farm was another multiyear, multidisciplinary project that Mary undertook. Her interest in the diverse families that occupied the site over three centuries and their intimate connection with the house, their associated material culture, and, more importantly, the land, introduced those involved in the project to a delightful bounty of data to share at any dinner table.

Mary's love of language has always been evident when working with her students on a variety of projects. She often encouraged her students to coauthor papers with her for conferences. On one occasion she included the word "prosoprographically" in a coauthored paper. This was a word that the student had never seen before. Mary then informed her that as the second author, the student would have to deliver the paper at the conference. Needless to say, the student practiced the word over and over, sure that she was going to mispronounce one of Mary's gems. At the conference, Mary was there, front and center, encouraging the student, and, even when the word was inevitably mispronounced, Mary complimented her on the presentation. That kind of mentoring is rare and much appreciated by all of her students.

During the 1980s, Mary began to take on leadership roles in several professional associations. Below are just a few examples of her dedication and leadership in this capacity. She became the editor of the journal *Northeast Historical Archaeology*, making it into a first-rate, peer-reviewed publication. For her nearly two decades of work, the Council for Northeast Historical Archaeology presented her with its Award of Service. Mary has also excelled in her volunteer efforts for the SHA. She has served on a multitude of committees, including being one of the founders of the Women's Caucus (now the Gender and Minority Affairs Committee). Mary has also served the SHA as conference chair (1985), director (1986–1988), and president (1989).

There are very few individuals in the field who have had such a profound influence over the development of so many young archaeologists. Each of her students was encouraged to volunteer, and many have followed up by serving on the committees and boards of numerous regional and national associations dedicated to the field of historical archaeology. By her example, Mary truly instilled in her students the notion of service to their chosen field.

Like a gourmet chef, Mary has experimented in her "kitchen" with many aspects of historical archaeology. Her keen interest and enthusiasm have instilled in all of her students a curiosity for all segments of the human experience. She has given a new meaning to the term mentor in her roles as a professor, graduate-student advisor, dissertation advisor, and now as the chair of the Department of Archaeology at BU.

Main Course

Mary's care and devotion to education in archaeology is visible in so many threads of her work. Her interest in all things historical archaeological, when blended with a continual influx of students eager to engage in fresh lines of research, has been a recipe for creativity and innovation. Teaching and advising and otherwise interacting with multiple generations of students has, in Mary's own words, affected her intellectual growth and career path in many ways. Her openness to new ideas, her willingness to collaborate with students, and the plasticity of her thinking and writing has permitted an engagement with a wide variety of sites across time and space.

Mary has graduated 21 Ph.D. students and has served on 27 additional Ph.D. committees at BU and at many other universities. Her Ph.D. students include Myriam S. L. Arcangeli, Christa M. Beranek, Stephen A. Brighton, Alexandra A. Chan, Christopher A. Dixon, Julie H. Ernstein, Brent R. Fortenberry, Conrad M. Goodwin, Christina J. Hodge, Karen Anne Hutchins, David B. Landon, Ann-Eliza H. Lewis, Sara F. Mascia, Karen B. Metheny, Ruth Ann Murray, Travis G. Parno, Elizabeth S. Peña, Todd M. Reck, Gayle E. Sawtelle, Michelle M. Terrell, and Carolyn L. White. She has graduated 20 M.A. students in archaeology as well as in BU's Gastronomy Program. She has shepherded many undergraduate students through thesis research, chairing 12 honors committees while serving on many others.

After Mary was firmly established at BU, she began to extend her expertise more broadly, and from the 1990s through the present day she has engaged in research that has often focused on the household, but in many different contexts. She participated in numerous New England projects, ranging from excavations on Boston's Beacon Hill to smaller-scale excavations on assorted historical period house sites, often with her students. Massachusetts examples include excavations on Nantucket at the African Meeting House, the investigation of the 71 Joy Street privy in Boston, a survey of the Fairbanks House property in Dedham, and survey and testing at the Wakefield Charitable Trust Property in Milton. Farther afield, Mary worked in Scotland on the Flora McDonald Project on the island of South Uist with Dr. James Symonds, and she recently has been working on the island of Montserrrat with Lydia Pulsipher, Mac Goodwin, and Jessica Streibel MacLean.

Mary has published eight books, including *Findings: The Material Culture of Needlework and Sewing* (2006) and *Documentary Archaeology in the New World* (1988). She has collaborated with many colleagues on volumes addressing wide-ranging topics: *Archaeologies of Mobility and*

Movement (Beaudry and Parno 2013); material culture, *The Oxford Handbook of Material Culture Studies* (Hicks and Beaudry 2010); the transatlantic world *Interpreting the Early Modern World: Transatlantic Perspectives* (Beaudry and Symonds 2010); historical archaeology, *The Cambridge Companion to Historical Archaeology,* (Hicks and Beudry 2006); the Lowell excavations, *Living on the Boott: Historical Archaeology at the Boott Mills Boardinghouses in Lowell, Massachusetts* (Mrozowski et al. 1996); and a festschrift for James Deetz, *The Art and Mystery of Historical Archaeology: Essays in Honor of James Deetz* (Yentsch and Beaudry 1992).

She has published over 80 book chapters and articles in peer-reviewed journals along with 25 book reviews. She has presented over 115 papers at regional, national, and international conferences, and has given more than 80 public lectures to delighted audiences. Rather than offer a laundry list of Mary's contributions, we offer several perspectives on her work, through several examples, to demonstrate the breadth of her contributions as well as the depth of her influence in the field of historical archaeology.

Mary has an ability to tease out the interesting parts of a project and to take disparate pieces and place them at the center of broader questions within historical archaeology. For example, in 1996, a strange type of ceramic was recovered in several units along a fence line at the Spencer-Peirce-Little site. We (the field-school students, the teaching assistants, and Mary) called it "uglyware" or "wormy ware." Several years later, Mary published an article, entitled "A Pernicious Influence? Japanese Water Drop Ware" in *Ceramics in America* (Beaudry 2004b), about this funny type of ceramic—analyzed, explained, and contextualized. Her traplike mind has produced many moments like this, where a bit of what could be trivia is never quite released but, rather, marinates and becomes an element of something substantial.

Mary's career has never been one of excavate site, publish on said site, move to next site, and repeat. As a chef gathers influences from a lifetime of meals, each of Mary's projects has acted as an ingredient for present and future dishes. Like an excellent chef, Mary has been testing recipes along several themes throughout her career. Her work on households began in the 1970s, inspired by the work of the new social history, and she has returned to that topic throughout her career, publishing on her work at Lowell (Beaudry and Mrozowski 1988; Beaudry 1989, 1993) and Spencer-Peirce-Little (Beaudry 1998, 2001–2002), as well as reflecting her analysis on the household work of many others (Beaudry 1999, 2004a). Mary returns to these ideas and then places the theme on the proverbial back burner for a time in order to attend to other pots of projects and ideas. When the time is right, she returns to the stove to reinvent the recipe.

Her work on material culture began with her publication on spoons from the 17th-century Wampanoag burying ground at Burr's Hill in Warren, Rhode Island, reflecting Mary's interest in foodways as well as material culture (Beaudry 1980b). The focus on material culture and materiality is threaded through her publications, and Mary has catalyzed interest in materiality in the field, publishing on material culture (Cochran and Beaudry 2006), small finds (Loren and Beaudry 2006; White and Beaudry 2009), sewing and needlework (Beaudry 2009b, 2010b), as well as editing *The Oxford Handbook of Material Culture Studies* (Hicks and Beaudry 2010). She repeatedly pulls together the work of decades and reblends it to create an entirely new dish, as she has done with her work on the material culture of foodways, most recently with her article "Privy to the Feast: Eighty to Supper Tonight" (Beaudry 2010a).

Mary's work on telling the story of the past is yet another important category of research. In publications that use biography (Beaudry 2009b), narrative (Beaudry 1998), and microhistory (Beaudry 2008), she demonstrates through both theory and case studies that the order and sourcing of ingredients in the telling of the past make a difference. It is not just how we as archaeologists tell the story, but it is the angle and approach that matters and impacts what we can know about the past.

Historical archaeologists are indebted to Mary for the range of techniques she has brought to many themes in the field, sometimes cooking long, low, and slow, and other times using intense heat to make a particular point. Her repertoire includes themes of identity, documentary records, industrial archaeology, gender inequality, landscapes, urban archaeology, and method and theory. Her work has not only established these topics and ideas as essential to the field, but she has revisited and reinterpreted these themes, giving them a "modern twist," as they say on the cooking shows.

In what can seem effortless to those around her, Mary has produced important and influential scholarship across a number of themes. Many of her publications are synthetic, drawing together ideas from various disciplines while casting a critical eye on previous research and folding in her own work. She has always held fast to an image of historical archaeology as an anthropological endeavor that focuses on the *lives* of *people* in the past. One need only look over the range of publications in historical archaeology today to see her mark on the work of both established and emerging scholars, as well as on undergraduate and graduate students.

Mary was awarded the Harrington Medal at the SHA's 46th Annual Conference on Historical and Underwater Archaeology in the United Kingdom, which was most appropriate given her influence and reputation on the east side of the Atlantic. She taught as a visiting professor at the University of Sheffield and at Bristol University, was elected to the North American Fellowship of the Society of Antiquaries of London, served on the editorial boards of *Post-Medieval Archaeology* and the *Antiquaries Journal*, collaborated with many overseas colleagues, participated in many British conferences, and published with several British presses.

Mary C. Beaudry represents the best of our discipline. The SHA honors her as the 2013 recipient of the J. C. Harrington Medal in Historical Archaeology for her devotion to education, students, field methods, cultural resource management projects, and the Boston Red Sox, together with her record of scholarship, leadership, and service to historical archaeology.

References

BEAUDRY, MARY C.

1980a *"Or What Else You Please to Call It": Folk Semantic Domains in Early Virginia Probate Inventories.* Doctoral dissertation, Department of Anthropology, Brown University. University Microfilms International, Ann Arbor, MI.

1980b Spoons from the Burr's Hill Collection. In *Burr's Hill: A 17th Century Wampanoag Burial Ground in Warren, Rhode Island,* Susan G. Gibson, editor, pp. 72–78. Haffenreffer Museum of Anthropology, Brown University, Studies in Anthropology and Material Culture 2. Providence, RI.

1989 The Lowell Boott Mills Complex and Its Housing: Material Expressions of Corporate Ideology. *Historical Archaeology* 23(1):19–32.

1993 Public Aesthetics versus Personal Experience: Archaeology and the Interpretation of 19th-Century Worker Health and Well Being in Lowell, Massachusetts. *Historical Archaeology* 27(2):90–105.

1998 Farm Journal: First Person, Four Voices. *Historical Archaeology* 32(1):20–33.

1999 House and Household: The Archaeology of Domestic Life in Early America. In *Old and New Worlds,* Geoff Egan and R. L. Michael, editors, 117–126. Oxbow Books, Oxford, UK.

2001–2002 Trying to Think Progressively about 19th-Century Farms. *Northeast Historical Archaeology* 30&31:129–142.

2004a Doing the Housework: New Approaches to the Archaeology of Households. In *Household Chores and Household Choices: Theorizing the Domestic Sphere in Historical Archaeology,* Kerri S. Barile and Jamie C. Brandon, editors, pp. 254–262. University of Alabama Press, Tuscaloosa.

2004b A Pernicious Influence? Japanese Water Drop Ware. In *Ceramics in America,* Robert Hunter, editor, pp. 278–281. Chipstone Foundation, Milwaukee, WI.

2006 *Findings: The Material Culture of Needlework and Sewing.* Yale University Press, New Haven, CT.

2008 "Above Vulgar Economy": The Intersection of Historical Archaeology and Microhistory in Writing Archaeological Biographies of Two New England Merchants. In *Small Worlds: Method and Meaning in Microhistory,* James F. Brooks, Christopher DeCorse, and John Walton, editors, pp. 173–198. School of Advanced Research, Santa Fe, NM.

2009a This is How I Became an Archaeologist. Paper presented at the 42nd Conference on Historical and Underwater Archaeology, Toronto, ON.

2009b Bodkin Biographies. In *The Materiality of Individuality,* Carolyn L. White, editor, pp. 95–108. Springer, New York, NY.

2010a Privy to the Feast: Eighty to Supper Tonight. In *Table Settings: The Material Culture and Social Context of Dining in the Old and New Worlds AD 1700–1900,* James Symonds, editor, pp. 62–79. Oxbow Books, Oxford, UK.

2010b Stitching Women's Lives: Interpreting the Artifacts of Sewing and Needlework. In *Interpreting the Early Modern World: Transatlantic Perspectives,* Mary C. Beaudry and James Symonds, editors, pp. 143–158. Springer, New York, NY.

BEAUDRY, MARY C. (EDITOR)

1988 *Documentary Archaeology in the New World.* Cambridge University Press, Cambridge, UK.

Beaudry, Mary C., Janet Long, Henry M. Miller, Fraser D. Neiman, and Garry Wheeler Stone
1983   A Vessel Typology for Early Chesapeake Ceramics: The Potomac Typological System. *Historical Archaeology* 17(1):18–42.
2000   A Vessel Typology for Early Chesapeake Ceramics: The Potomac Typological System. In *Approaches to Material Culture Research for Historical Archaeologists*, David R. Brauner, editor, pp. 11–36. Society for Historical Archaeology, Uniontown, PA.

Beaudry, Mary C., and Stephen A. Mrozowski
1988   The Archeology of Work and Home Life in Lowell, Massachusetts: An Interdisciplinary Study of the Boott Cotton Mills Corporation. *IA, the Journal of the Society for Industrial Archeology* 14(2):1–22.

Beaudry, Mary C., and Travis G. Parno (editors)
2013   *Archaeologies of Mobility and Movement.* Springer, New York, NY.

Beaudry, Mary C., and James Symonds (editors)
2010   *Interpreting the Early Modern World: Transatlantic Perspectives.* Springer, New York, NY.

Cochran, Matthew D., and Mary C. Beaudry
2006   Material Culture Studies and Historical Archaeology. In *The Cambridge Companion to Historical Archaeology,* Dan Hicks and Mary C. Beaudry, editors, pp. 1–9. Cambridge University Press, Cambridge, UK.

Evans, Katherine
2012   The Life and Works of Dr. Mary Beaudry. Manuscript, Department of Anthropology, University of Massachusetts, Boston.

Hicks, Dan, and Mary C. Beaudry (editors)
2006   *The Cambridge Companion to Historical Archaeology.* Cambridge University Press, Cambridge, UK.
2010   *The Oxford Handbook of Material Culture Studies.* Oxford University Press, Oxford, UK.

Loren, Diana diPaolo, and Mary C. Beaudry
2006   Becoming American: Small Things Remembered. In *Historical Archaeology,* Martin Hall and Stephen W. Silliman, editors, pp. 251–271. Blackwell, Oxford, UK.

Mrozowski, Stephen A., and Mary C. Beaudry
1990   Archaeology and the Landscape of Corporate Ideology. In *Earth Patterns: Essays in Landscape Archaeology*, William M. Kelso, editor, pp. 189–208. University Press of Virginia, Charlottesville.

Mrozowski, Stephen A., Grace Ziesing, and Mary C. Beaudry
1996   *Living on the Boott: Historical Archaeology at the Boott Mills Boardinghouses in Lowell, Massachusetts.* University of Massachusetts Press, Amherst.

White, Carolyn L., and Mary C. Beaudry
2009   Artifacts and Personal Identity. In *The International Handbook of Historical Archaeology,* Teresita Majewski and David Gaimster, editors, pp. 209–225. Springer, New York, NY.

Yentsch, Anne Elizabeth, and Mary C. Beaudry (editors)
1992   *The Art and Mystery of Historical Archaeology: Essays in Honor of James Deetz.* CRC Press, Boca Raton, FL.

Sara F. Mascia
Carolyn L. White

J. C. Harrington Medal in Historical Archaeology: Theresa A. Singleton, 2014. Volume 48, Number 2 (2014): 1-8.
By Douglas V. Armstrong.

J. C. Harrington Medal in Historical Archaeology

Theresa A. Singleton

Theresa Ann Singleton is the recipient of the 2014 Society for Historical Archaeology (SHA) J. C. Harrington Medal in Historical Archaeology. The award was presented to Dr. Singleton at the SHA's annual conference in Quebec City, Canada, in recognition of her dedication to scholarship, innovative and pioneering work, commitment to mentoring students, and lifetime contributions in the field of historical archaeology.

A Path to Follow

The decision made by Theresa Singleton to pursue historical archaeology was important, as from that point forward she has quietly, yet decisively, conducted research and written many insightful works, while also serving as a trailblazing role model for generations of minority scholars. Theresa received her doctorate in 1980 from the University of Florida, having been advised by the first Harrington medalist, Charles Fairbanks. She has also been an active member of the SHA, serving as a board member (1992–1995), and also as a board member of the Southeastern Archaeological Conference (1988–1992). In April 2013, she was elected a member of the American Antiquarian Society in Worchester, Massachusetts, in recognition of her contributions to collection, preservation, and scholarship in American history.

This review of Singleton's contributions to historical archaeology provides a means by which those interested in the field may gain a deeper appreciation of the range of her contributions, which include not only formal publications, but public museum exhibitions and quality mentoring. Collectively, these qualities are the reasons Christopher Fennell and Harrington medalist Robert

Schuyler submitted materials in 2011 reflecting support from nearly 100 of her colleagues who stood behind her nomination for the Harrington Medal, an award of rich symbolic meaning. This collective action reflects Professor Singleton's high esteem within the historical archaeology community, the importance of her scholarly contributions, and her significant role as a pioneer. Harrington medalist Kathleen Deagan, who initially taught Theresa the basics of historical archaeology field techniques wrote: "Theresa has been a real pioneer in African American archaeology, and has inspired a very global vision of that enterprise" (Fennell and Schuyler 2011:3). J. W. Joseph describes Singleton's scholarly impacts, stating:

> Theresa's work in African American archaeology is extremely important and influenced the development and direction of the field. She has also developed strong museum-based public interpretative programs on African American history and archaeology that have further benefited the field and has supported and promoted African American archaeology from multiple states and forums (Fennell and Schuyler 2011:1).

Terrance Weik (2014, elec. comm.) pointed out to me that honoring Theresa with the Harrington Medal "is an important sign of diversification of archaeology and the growing presence of African American voices."

In my early years at Syracuse, when I was the only archaeologist on campus, I would regularly take refuge in the office of my senior colleague, John Langston Gwaltney, an African American cultural anthropologist and author of *The Dissenters: Voices from Contemporary America* (Gwaltney 1986). One day, Theresa's name came up in relation to the potential of historical archaeology and an event she was organizing with Fath Ruffins, John's friend and Theresa's boss at the Smithsonian Institution. John, who was always direct, blunt, yet encouraging, charged me with getting Theresa to come to Syracuse. It took some time, but with the assistance of Chris DeCorse, we convinced Theresa to join the faculty at Syracuse, where she has contributed significantly as a thoughtful colleague who never loses her cool, even when occasionally confronted by lower forms of academic politics. She is part of what makes our program so strong and cohesive, and I am glad to call her a close friend and colleague.

Formativ Years: The Value of Knowledg

Theresa Ann Singleton was born 15 April 1952 in Charleston, South Carolina. She was the fifth and youngest child of William Singleton and Helen North Singleton. Helen and William met when they were teaching at the same elementary school, hence education has always been at the center of Theresa's life. Surrounded by a family that valued education, her role model was her oldest sister Rosalind, who was outgoing and excelled in everything. Theresa excelled, but in a quiet and shy manner. Theresa was positively influenced by her maternal grandmother, Serena North, the only grandparent she knew. Her grandmother conveyed to Theresa the importance of having a career doing work she enjoyed, and she inspired Theresa to develop her personal fashion style. Theresa is a big fan of *Project Runway.* Her grandmother made many of Theresa's clothes, which she cherished and wore at every opportunity.

From kindergarten to her sophomore year in high school, Theresa attended Immaculate Conception School (ICS) in Charleston, as had her mother and all of her mother's sisters. Theresa's experiences in high school were uniquely hers, but mirror the changes and conflicts of the 1960s. The Oblate Sisters of Providence taught at ICS. The Oblates were a Roman Catholic order founded by women of African descent, some of whom had come to Baltimore as part of the refugee community from Haiti during and after the Haitian Revolution. In 1968, the Archbishop of Charleston merged ICS, the predominantly black Catholic high school, with Bishop England, the predominately white Catholic high school. Here Theresa was confronted by outright racism, as some of the white students made racist comments openly, and there was no effort on the part of the school's administration to check their behavior. This was a challenging environment, but Theresa managed to graduate with honors in 1970. Theresa received a scholarship to attend Trinity College, a predominantly white Catholic college in Washington, D.C. On reflection, given her experiences, she is not sure why she went there; she was already interested in museum studies, however, and thought that Washington, D.C., would be a good location. Moreover, her sister Rosalind lived there, as did numerous cousins—descendants of her grand-aunt, who migrated to Washington from South Carolina during the great migration of black Southerners in the early 1900s. During her first year, she took Trinity's only anthropology class and was captivated. The problem was, she was on scholarship at Trinity, so how was she going to take more anthropology? Fortunately for the field, the academic dean allowed her to create her own program of study and take anthropology classes at nearby Catholic University. She did well, graduating in 1974. In 1992, she would be asked by the president of Trinity College, Patricia McGuire, who graduated with Theresa in 1974, to give Trinity's commencement address.

Getting Started in Archaeology

In 1972, Theresa Singleton had her first experience in archaeology, a field school at the Paleo-indian Thunderbird site in Virginia that was directed by William Gardner from Catholic University. She enjoyed the field experience in archaeology, but was not excited about doing Paleoindian archaeology. Theresa heard about a field course in archaeology at Oxford University. Her parents agreed to pay for it, but she had to earn the airfare and spending money. After graduating, she worked three jobs up until the time she left for the trip. While in England, she visited sites like Stonehenge, and excavated at Grimes Graves, a Neolithic flint mine not far from Cambridge. She enjoyed the experience, but was resolved not to work at anymore lithic sites. She returned to South Carolina and began teaching in a public junior high school while she applied to graduate schools. Her father died in 1974, and she was considering schools near Charleston so that she could be near her mother. Fortunately, the SHA held its annual meeting in Charleston in January 1975. She went to the conference, where she met Charles Fairbanks. He strongly encouraged her to go to Florida, and told her that he would look out for her application. She was accepted and started at the University of Florida in September 1975. She describes her first year of graduate school as "intense" and was happy to get into the field for the spring and summer quarters.

Fairbanks recommended that she enroll in Kathleen Deagan's Florida State University field school at St. Augustine so she would have training in field methods specifically for historical archaeology. Deagan also worked with Theresa to define a master's project examining a barrel well and other 16th- and 17th-century contexts at the Joseph de Leon site (Singleton 1977). That summer, Theresa applied her newfound expertise in historical archaeology to sites on Sapelo Island, one of the barrier islands along the coast of Georgia (working with Ray Crook from her graduate cohort at Florida). During the first two weeks, they conducted test excavations at a sugar mill on Sapelo. Theresa would work the next four summers and the spring quarter of 1979 on the Georgia coast. Her investigation of Colonel's Island is described in a chapter exploring changing conditions of labor in the edited volume *Archaeology of Slavery and Plantation Life* (Singleton 1985a); see also Singleton (1985b, 1987). For her 1980 dissertation, Theresa investigated sites at the Butler Island rice plantation in 1978 and 1979. At its peak, the plantation had about 500 enslaved workers living in four separate settlements. The owner of Butler Island also owned a Sea Island cotton plantation on St. Simon's Island. In the 1950s, Butler Island became part of a waterfowl management area, and the practical objective of the project was to identify, locate, and test sites that should be avoided in creating habitats for the waterfowl. Theresa's dissertation also included an examination of the ways in which slave life on a rice plantation was similar to and different from that on the Sea Island cotton plantations on St. Simon's Island (Singleton 1980, 1986, 1992c).

Broadening Scope and Conducting Defining Scholarship

Singleton expanded her studies of rice plantations in coastal Georgia and presented her findings in broader comparative perspective in "An Archaeological Framework for Slavery and Emancipation," a chapter in Mark Leone and Parker Potter's volume *The Recovery of Meaning: Historical*

Archaeology of the Eastern United States (Singleton 1988a). Over the next few years, she wrote synthetic assessments of the role of archaeology in examining African American life in Southern plantation contexts in a range of archaeological and historical venues (Singleton 1988b, 1990a, 1990b, 1991a, 1991b, 1992a, 1992b, 1992c, 1994, 1995a, 1995b).

Theresa's work at Butler Island resulted in two unexpected outcomes that would have a lasting influence upon her future research and career decisions. First, her interaction with descendants of the enslaved people in the area made her realize that it was important to include them in archaeological research projects. Second, she began to appreciate the importance of making archaeological research accessible not only to descendants, but to the general public in formats like exhibitions, films, and publications geared toward lay audiences (Singleton 1984, 1986, 1988b, 1995a). She would contribute to organizing eight exhibitions, participate in making three films on archaeology, and publish eight articles and exhibit essays for popular consumption. One of her interviewees was Rudolph Capers, who as a boy had worked on rice fields in the area. Through her interviews she learned a great deal about the lifeways of the people now referred to as Geechee, but in the late 1970s they did not openly called themselves Geechee or Gullah. While she was writing her dissertation, she was awarded a Whitney M. Young Jr. Postdoctoral Fellowship that would allow her to gain museum experience at the Charleston Museum.

The state archaeologist, Lewis Larson, put Theresa in touch with Carole Merritt, who was developing an exhibition on the African American family in Georgia. Carole and Theresa came up with the idea of re-creating the hearth of one the excavated slave quarters at Butler Island and displaying some of the excavated artifacts that would allude to the formation of African American families during slavery. The exhibition, entitled Homecoming: Afro-American American Family Life in Georgia, opened in 1982 at the Atlanta Public Library. Working with Carole on the exhibition reignited Theresa's desire for a career in museums. Theresa taught briefly at the College of Charleston and at the University of South Carolina, and landed her first museum position at the South Carolina State Museum in 1983. She was hired to undertake background and object research for exhibitions planned for the history hall, such as one on the textile industry, part of which she used in her contribution to an exhibition on South Carolina quilts (Singleton 1985c).

In 1985, Theresa began working at the Smithsonian National Museum of American History, assembling a guide to all the historical materials related to African American life in the Smithsonian Institution's collections (with the exception of materials in the art museums). In 1988, she accepted her "dream job" as a curator in the Department of Anthropology at the National Museum of Natural History. She saw this as an opportunity to do both archaeology and museum work; unfortunately, a change in leadership at the museum combined with budget cuts eliminated her start-up funds for archaeology. While at the Smithsonian, she examined materials that had been collected at the New Orleans World and Cotton Exposition of 1885 and from the First Industrial Exposition of the Colored Citizens of the District of Columbia in 1886. She then organized the small exhibition Industry, Skill, Ingenuity: Southern Black Expositions 1880–1915, held in 1988 at the National Museum of American History.

While at the Smithsonian, she collaborated with Ronald Bailey, at that time the director of African-American Studies at the University of Mississippi, and together they won a National Endowment for the Humanities grant to organize a conference on African American archaeology called "Digging the Afro-American Past: Archaeology and the Black Experience," held in May 1989. This conference brought together a wide array of scholars and led to her founding the *African-American Archaeology Network Newsletter* in 1990, which is now known as the *African Diaspora Archaeology Newsletter* (<http://www.diaspora.illinois.edu/newsletter.html> and <http://scholarworks.umass.edu/adan/>). The conference was also the impetus for the publication of the edited volume *"I, Too, Am America": Archaeological Studies of African-American Life* (Singleton 1999a, 1999b). Shortly after the conference, she contributed to the development of a major exhibition on slavery organized by the Museum of the Confederacy—Before Freedom Came—which opened in 1991; and served as guest curator of the exhibition "Links in a Chain": The Significance of Black Labor, at the Charleston Museum in 1991 and 1992. In 1992, she developed a small exhibition of colonoware pottery at the Smithsonian with Mark Bograd—Pitchers, Pots and Pipkins: Clues to Plantation Life. Theresa and Mark Bograd also collaborated to compile a guide to the literature of the archaeology of the African diaspora for the SHA series, "Guides to the Archaeological Literature of the Immigrant Experience in America" (Singleton and Bograd 1995).

In 1990, she was invited to work with Lydia Pulsipher and Mac Goodwin at Galway Plantation on Montserrat, in order to collect archaeological data needed to fabricate a portion of a slave settlement on a sugar plantation for the Quincentenary exhibition. The exhibit, Seeds of Change, opened at the National Museum of Natural History in 1992. The work on Montserrat also whetted her appetite for working in the Caribbean, but first she traveled to West Africa.

Theresa met Chris DeCorse in 1991 at the SHA meeting in Richmond, and two years later they carried out a small survey project in coastal Ghana. Chris focused on the sites with European fortifications and Theresa on the nearby African villages. She conducted subsurface testing at one of the sites, the village of Eguafo. Two of Chris DeCorse's doctoral students, Sam Spiers and Gerard Chouin, would later undertake additional archaeological and ethnographical research at Eguafo. On that same trip to Africa, Theresa visited several sites in Benin and later published an article, "The Slave Trade Remembered on the Former Gold and Slave Coasts," in *Slavery and Abolition* (Singleton 1999c:150–169). Years later, the Africanist historian Robin Law told her he believes her article inspired a number of Africanists to pursue research on the memory of slavery in Africa. The article continues to be listed among the most frequently cited articles in the journal *Slavery and Abolition.*

It was the legendary archaeologist, Betty Meggers, a research associate in the Smithsonian's anthropology department, who came to Theresa in 1993 wanting to know about the archaeology of Africans in the Americas and particularly in Latin America. This conversation sparked Theresa's interest in the possibly of doing research in Cuba. In 1996, Theresa collaborated with an ethnographer to develop an ethnoarchaeological project focusing on Yoruba- and Fon-influenced Santeria sites near Havana and in the city of Matanzas. Unfortunately, the project was slowed by political and bureaucratic issues. Theresa's Cuban colleagues persuaded her to consider investigating coffee plantations. There were numerous coffee plantations in western Cuba, but no archaeological work had been conducted on them since the 1980s.

After a series of site visits, she began work at a former coffee plantation, Santa Ana de Viajacas, in 1999 (Singleton 2001c, 2005a, 2005c). The attraction of this site was the massive masonry wall built around a settlement of detached slave quarters known as *bohíos*. The wall enclosure became the lens through which Theresa conducted a study of slavery in an area, once the westernmost portion of Matanzas jurisdiction, with a large concentration of enslaved Africans, several significant slave uprisings, and numerous short-lived maroon settlements. Her research examines the master/slave social relation in a slave society characterized by considerable violence, resistance, and negotiated coexistence. She has published eight articles and book chapters on the project, and just completed a book manuscript on the subject that is now under peer review. The tentative title is *Behind a Wall Enclosure: An Archaeology of Slavery on a Cuban Coffee Plantation.*

In 1996, Theresa joined the faculty of the Department of Anthropology, Syracuse University, initially splitting her time between the Smithsonian and Syracuse. Since August of 2000, she has been at Syracuse full-time, and during this period she conducted the bulk of her research in Cuba (Singleton 2001c, 2003, 2005a, 2005c, 2007, 2008), while continuing to address issues of broad interest to the study of historical archaeology of the African diaspora (Bograd and Singleton 1997; Singleton 1996a, 1996b, 1997, 1998a, 1998b, 2001a, 2001b, 2005b, 2006, 2010a, 2010b, 2010d, 2011, 2013; Singleton and Bograd 2000; Singleton and Orser 2003; Singleton and Torres de Souza 2009).

At Syracuse University, Theresa Singleton has served on the committees of 29 Ph.D. students who have completed their degrees. She is currently on 17 Ph.D. committees, 9 of which are her advisees. The diverse research of these students spans the 17th–19th centuries temporally, and the United States, the Caribbean, Brazil, Mexico, and Peru geographically. Theresa's studies involve much more than archaeological investigations. She has spent considerable time learning about coffee production, particularly the ways coffee was produced in the Spanish Antilles. Because she was unable to visit coffee farms and mills in Cuba, she visited coffee production centers in the Dominican Republic.

In 2006, she began revisiting her earlier work on the Georgia coast. She has made several trips to the Georgia coast with the intention of developing a new field project. In 2008, she was invited to participate in a conference held in Savannah entitled "The Atlantic World and African American Life and Culture in the Georgia Lowcountry," and her contribution was published as a chapter, "Reclaiming the Gullah-Geechee Past: Archaeology of Slavery in Coastal Georgia," in Philip Morgan's 2010 edited volume, *African American Life in the Georgia Lowcountry: The Atlantic World and the Gullah-Geechee* (Singleton 2010c). More significantly, she has reconnected with the Geechee community. Later this year (2014) she will be participating in a homecoming celebration with the descendants of the enslaved people from Butler Island Plantation at Butler Island. To Theresa's surprise, several descendants of the enslaved community of Butler Island Plantation have read her dissertation and some of the articles she published on it.

Beyn d the Academy

All who know her will attest to Theresa's quiet, modest, and reserved disposition. As you get to know her, you will find that she is involved in a variety of interests beyond the university and museum, including antiquing, gardening, and jazz. When she was a teenager, Theresa's brother Billy introduced her to the jazz of Miles Davis, John Coltrane, and Mongo Santamaría. Working in Cuba and trips to the Dominican Republic revived her appreciation of jazz, particularly of Latin percussion. She has since become the number-one fan of Dominican percussionist and *rumbiero* (drummer for rumba) Victor Camilo.

Impact and Influence

Jamie Brandon emphasizes that Theresa's "work is foundational to those of us who do research on the African Diaspora and plantation South," and that "she has been an important role model for a new and growing generation of African-American archaeologists" (Fennell and Schuyler 2011:2). Deborah Rotman notes that Theresa's "work on the African diaspora has been inspirational" to analysts examining other subjects of culture group identities within historical archaeology generally (Fennell and Schuyler 2011:2–3).

Similarly, Akin Ogundiran attests that "Dr. Singleton's pioneering and trail blazing contributions in African-American Archaeology [have] helped [advance] the field of historical archaeology in general" (Fennell and Schuyler 2011:3). Martha Zierden further observes: "Besides all of her scholarly work, Theresa has always been willing to counsel archaeologists, individually and collectively, on appropriate and sensitive approaches to the field of African Diaspora studies" (Fennell and Schuyler 2011:3). Harrington medalist Merrick Posnansky points out the importance of Singleton's global vision, stating that she "is one of the few African American scholars to work in West Africa and learn about the research there at first hand. She has been an ambassador for our discipline" (Fennell and Schuyler 2011:3).

The SHA honors Theresa Ann Singleton as the 2014 recipient of the J. C. Harrington Medal in Historical Archaeology. Theresa has established a clear and broadened path for new generations of historical archaeologists to follow, and she has provided insights deeply rooted in the value of the pursuit of knowledge. She followed her grandmother's advice and selected a field of study that she enjoyed, and through her scholarly writings, museum exhibits, and quality mentoring has demonstrated the positive potential for diversity and creativity in the field of historical archaeology.

References

Bograd, Mark, and Theresa A. Singleton
  1997   The Interpretation of Slavery. In *Presenting Archaeology to the Public*, J. H. Jameson, Jr., editor, pp. 193–204. Altamira, Walnut Creek, CA.

Fennell, Christopher, and Robert L. Schuyler
  2011   Letter to the Society for Historical Archaeology Awards Committee, Nomination of Theresa A. Singleton for the J. C. Harrington Medal in Historical Archaeology, 21 October. Society for Historical Archaeology, Germantown, MD.

Gwaltney, John Langston
  1986   *The Dissenters: Voices from Contemporary America.* Random House, New York, NY.

Singleton, Theresa A.
  1977   The Archaeology of a Pre-Eighteenth Century House Site in St. Augustine. Master's thesis, Department of Anthropology, University of Florida, Gainesville.
  1980   *The Archaeology of Afro-American Slavery in Coastal Georgia: A Regional Perception of Slave Household and Community Patterns.* Doctoral dissertation, Department of Anthropology, University of Florida, Gainesville. University Microfilms International, Ann Arbor, MI.
  1984   The Slave Tag: An Artifact of Urban Slavery. In *Urban Archaeology in Charleston,* Nick Honerkamp and Martha Zierden, editors. Thematic issue, *South Carolina Antiquities* 16:41–66.
  1985a Archaeological Implications for Changing Labor Conditions. In *The Archaeology of Slavery and Plantation Life*, Theresa A. Singleton, editor, pp. 291–304. Academic Press, Orlando, FL.
  1985c Textiles in South Carolina. In *Social Fabric: South Carolina Traditional Quilts*, Laurel Horton and Lynn Myers, editors, pp. 5–10. McKissick Museum, Columbia, SC.
  1986   Buried Treasure: Rice Coast Digs Reveal Details of Slave Life. *American Visions* 1(2):35–39.
  1987   History and Historical Archaeology at Colonel's Island, Brunswick, Georgia. In *Archaeological Studies of a Marsh Island: The Cultural Occupation of Colonel's Island Georgia*, Karl T. Steinen, editor, pp. 29–62. West Georgia College Studies in the Social Sciences No. 26. Carrollton, GA.
  1988a An Archaeological Framework for Slavery and Emancipation, 1740 to 1880. In *The Recovery of Meaning: Historical Archaeology in the Eastern United States*, Mark P. Leone and Parker B. Potter, Jr., editors, pp. 345–370. Smithsonian Institution Press, Washington, DC.
  1988b Breaking New Ground. *Southern Exposure* 16(2):18–22.
  1990a The Archaeology of African American Life. *AnthroNotes* 12(2):1–4,14–15.
  1990b The Archaeology of the Plantation South: A Review of Approaches and Goals. *Historical Archaeology* 24(4):68–77.
  1991a The Archaeology of Slave Life. In *Before Freedom Came: African American Life in the Antebellum South*, Edward D. C. Campbell, Jr. and Kym S. Rice, editors, pp. 155–15. Museum of the Confederacy and University Press of Virginia, Charlottesville.
  1991b The Potential for African American Archaeology in Mississippi. *Mississippi Archaeology* 26 2):19–32.
  1992a Foreword. In *Traditional Gardens and Yards of African-Americans in the Rural South*, Richard Westmacott, author, pp. x–ix. University of Tennessee Press, Knoxville.
  1992b "Those Who Work Skillfully with Their Hands": African-American Artisans in South Carolina, 1700–1900. In *Conflict and Transcendence: African-American Art in South Carolina*, Lin Nelson-Mayson, editor, pp. 5–14. Columbia Museum of Art, Columbia, SC.
  1992c Using Written Records in the Archaeological Study of Slavery, an Example from the Butler Island Plantation. In *Text-Aided Archaeology*, Barbara Little, editor, pp. 55–66. CRC Press, Boca Raton, FL.
  1994   The African-American Legacy beneath Our Feet. In *African American Historical Places*, Beth Savage, editor, pp. 33–40. Preservation Press, Washington, DC.
  1995a An Archaeological Perspective on African American Artistic Production. *International Review of African American Art* 12(3):24–29.
  1995b The Archaeology of Slavery in North America. *Annual Review of Anthropology* 24:119–140.
  1996   Anthropology. In *Encyclopedia of African-American Culture and History,* 1st edition, Vol. 1, Jack Salzman, editor, pp. 143–151. Macmillan, New York, NY.
  1996   Plantation Life in the Southern United States. In *Oxford Companion to Archaeology,* 1st edition, Brian M. Fagan, editor, pp. 567–569. Oxford University Press, New York, NY.
  1997   Commentary: Facing the Challenges of a Public African-American Archaeology. In *In the Realm of Politics: Prospects for Public Participation in African-American and Plantation Archaeology*, Carol McDavid and David W. Babson, editors. Thematic issue, *Historical Archaeology* 31(3):146–152.
  1998a The Archaeology of African-American Life. In *Anthropology Explored: The Best of Smithsonian's AnthroNotes*, R. O. Selig and M. R. London, editors, pp. 205–215. Smithsonian Institution Press, Washington, DC.
  1998b Culture Contact and African American Identity in Plantation Archaeology. In *Studies in Culture Contact: Interaction, Culture Change, and Archaeology*, James G. Cusick, editor, pp. 172–188. Southern Illinois University, Center for Archaeological Investigations, Occasional Paper No. 25. Carbondale.

1999b An Introduction to African American Archaeology. In *"I, Too, Am America": Archaeological Studies of African-American Life*, Theresa Singleton, editor, pp. 1–17. University Press of Virginia, Charlottesville.

1999c The Slave Trade Remembered on the Former Gold and Slave Coasts. *Slavery and Abolition* 20(1):150–169.

2001a An Americanist Perspective on African Archaeology: Toward an Archaeology of the Black Atlantic. In *West Africa during the Atlantic Slave Trade: Archaeological Perspectives*, Christopher R. DeCorse, editor, pp. 179–184. Leicester University Press, London, UK.

2001b Race, Class, and Identity among Free Blacks in the Antebellum South. In *Race and the Archaeology of Identity*, Charles E. Orser, Jr., editor, pp. 196–207. University of Utah Press, Salt Lake City.

2001c Slavery and the Spatial Dialectics on a Cuban Coffee Plantation. *World Archaeology* 33(1):98–114.

2003 Archaeology and Material Culture of Santa Ana de Viajacas: A Coffee Plantation in Western Cuba. In *Proceedings of the XX International Congress of Caribbean Archaeology*, Vol. 2, Glenis Tavárez María and Manuel A. García Arévalo, editors, pp. 25–30. Museo del Hombre Dominicano and Fundación Garcia Arévalo, Santo Domingo, Dominican Republic.

2005a An Archaeological Study of Slavery on a Cuban Coffee Plantation. In *Dialogues in Cuban Archaeology*, L. Antonio Curet, Shannon L. Dawdy, and Gabino La Rosa Corzo, editors, pp. 181–199. University of Alabama Press, Tuscaloosa.

2005b Before the Revolution: Archaeology and the African Diaspora on the Atlantic Seaboard. In *North American Archaeology*, Timothy Pauketat and Diana Loren, editors, pp. 319–336. Wiley-Blackwell, Boston, MA.

2005c Investigando la vida del esclavo en el cafetal del Padre (Investigating slave life on the El Padre coffee plantation). *Gabinete de Arqueología Boletín* 4(4):4–13. Office of the Historian for the City of Havana, Havana, Cuba.

2006 African Diaspora Archaeology in Dialogue. In *Afro-Atlantic Dialogues: Anthropology in the Diaspora*, Kevin A. Yelvington, editor, pp. 249–287. School of American Research Press, Santa Fe, NM.

2007 Landscape, Archaeology, and Memory of Cuban Coffee Plantations. In *XXI Proceedings of the International Congress of Caribbean Archaeology*, Vol. 2, Basil Reid, Henri Petitjean Roget, and Antonio Curet, editors, pp. 655–663. University of the West Indies, School of Continuing Studies, St. Augustine, Trinidad & Tobago.

2008 Why Study Plantations? Lessons Learned from the Archaeology of Slavery and Plantations / ¿Por qué estudiar plantaciones? Lecciones aprendidas de la arqueología de la esclavitud y las plantaciones. In *Continuidd y camb o cultural en arqe - ología histó ica*, María Teresa Carrara, editor, pp. 28–36 Actas del Tercer Congreso Nacional de Arqueología Histó ica, Universidad Nacional de Rosario, Facultad de Humanidades y Artes, Escuela de Antropología, Rosario, Argentina.

2010a African Diaspora in Archaeology. In *The African Diaspora and the Disciplines*, Tejumola Olaniyan and James Sweet, editors, pp. 119–141. Indiana University Press, Bloomington.

2010b Archaeology and Slavery. In *Slavery in the Americas: Oxford History Handbooks*, Robert Paquette and Mark Smith, editors, pp. 02–24. Oxford University Press, New York, NY.

2010c Reclaiming the Gullah-Geechee Past: Archaeology of Slavery in Coastal Georgia. In *African American Life in the Georgia Lowcountry: The Atlantic World and the Gullah Geechee*, Philip Morgan, editor, pp. 151–187. University of Georgia Press, Athens.

2010d Slavery, Liberation, and Emancipation: Constructing a Post-Colonial Archaeology of the African Diaspora. *Handbook of Post-Colonial Archaeology*, Jane Lydon and Uzma Rizvi, editors, pp. 18–17. Left Coast Press, Walnut Creek, CA.

2011 Epilogue: Reflections on Archaeologies of Postemancipation from a Student of Slavery. In *The Materiality of Freedm : Archaeologies of Postemancipation Life*, Jodi A. Barnes, editor, pp. 27 282. University of South Carolina Press, Columbia.

2013 Reflexões sobre a arqueologia da diáspora africana no Brasil (Thoughts on the archaeology of the African diaspora in Brazil). *Vestigios: Revista Latino-Americana d Arqe ologia Histó ica* 7 1):211–219.

SINGLETON, THERESA A. (EDITOR)

1985b *The Archaeology of Slavery and Plantation Life*. Academic Press, Orlando, FL.

1999a *"I, Too, Am America": Archaeological Studies of African-American Life*. University Press of Virginia, Charlottesville.

SINGLETON, THERESA A., AND MARK D. BOGRAD

1995 *The Archaeology of the African Diaspora in the Americas*. Society for Historical Archaeology, Guides to the Archaeological Literature of the Immigrant Experience in America, No. 2. Tucson, AZ.

2000 Breaking Typological Barriers: Looking for the Colono in Colonoware. In *Lines that Divide: Historical Archaeologies of Race, Class, and Gender*, James A. Delle, Stephen A. Mrozowski, and Robert Paynter, editors, pp. 3–21. University of Tennessee Press, Knoxville.

SINGLETON, THERESA, AND CHARLES E. ORSER, JR.

2003 Descendant Communities: Linking People in the Present to the Past. In *Ethical Issues in Archaeology*, Larry J. Zimmerman, Karen D. Vitelli, and Julie Hollowell-Zimmer, editors, p. 143. Altamira, Walnut Creek, CA.

SINGLETON, THERESA, AND MARCOS ANDRÉ TORRES DE SOUZA

2009 Archaeologies of the African Diaspora: Brazil, Cuba, and the United States. In *International Handbook of Historical Archaeology*, Teresita Majewski and David Gaimster, editors, pp. 449–469. Springer, New York, NY.

DOUGLAS V. ARMSTRONG

J. C. Harrington Medal in Historical Archaeology: Douglas D. Scott, 2015. Volume 49, Number 2 (2015): 1-9. By William B. Lees and Vergil E. Noble.

J. C. Harrington Medal in Historical Archaeology

Douglas D. Scott

Douglas D. Scott is the recipient of the 2015 Society for Historical Archaeology (SHA) J. C. Harrington Medal in Historical Archaeology. The award was presented to Dr. Scott in January at the 48th Annual Conference on Historical and Underwater Archaeology in Seattle, Washington, in recognition of his lifetime contributions to scholarship in historical archaeology, pioneering work in battlefield and conflict archaeology, and in the application of archaeological methods to forensic studies, dedication to the mentoring of students and young professionals, and his collaborative approach to research.

Douglas D. Scott was born in Bethany, Missouri, on 17 July 1948. He was the first of two sons of Helena Frances (Dowell) and Edwin L. Scott. His family lived in and around Bethany until 1957, when his father accepted a job as vice president of a small bank in Independence, Kansas. Doug spent the next 10 years of his life in southeastern Kansas, graduating from Independence High School in 1966.

Challenged with a series of health issues in childhood that prevented him from normal outdoor play activities, Doug spent many hours haunting local libraries, reading whatever came to hand on archaeology and history, and talking with "old timers" about their memories of local history. Those early interests and readings made him decide at age six to be an archaeologist. To the amazement of his parents, he never wavered from the idea, and he kept his local and school librarians scrambling to find books on the subject.

Education and Early Career

While in high school, Doug volunteered on his first archaeological project in the summer of 1964. That experience, learning to shovel skim on an excavation for a reservoir salvage project in southeast Kansas for the Kansas State Historical Society (KSHS), was the catalyst that affirmed his determination to make archaeology a career. It was at the Elk City Reservoir Project that he met, for the first time, another Kansas boy, P. Willey, who went on to become a well-known physical anthropologist and professor at California State University, Chico. The two connected later in life at the Little Bighorn Battlefield and went on to collaborate on two books and a number of articles (Glenner et al. 1994; Scott and Willey 1995, 1996, 1997; Willey and Scott 1996; Willey et al. 1996; Scott et al. 1998).

After graduating from high school in 1966, Doug got his first paying job in archaeology as a shovel bum for the KSHS on the Elk City Reservoir Project. In 1967, he worked again for the KSHS at Perry Reservoir, where he received training in mapping and additional field techniques.

Doug decided he was not yet ready for the big college adventure when he graduated from high school and opted instead to attend Independence Community Junior College, where he graduated with an associate of arts degree in June of 1968. That summer he enrolled in the University of Kansas, Kansas State University, and Wichita State University Great Plains Archaeological Field School at White Cloud, Kansas. There he gained additional experience in excavation, mapping, and other field techniques. During this field school, he participated in the excavation of a Kansas City Hopewell site, a Woodland burial mound, and worked on his first historical period site, a Sac and Fox burial that was eroding out of a corn field (Scott 1976). He was hooked on historical archaeology after that. To put this in context, the SHA was officially formed and held its first annual meeting in Williamsburg, Virginia, that same year (Cleland 1993).

The fall of 1968 saw Doug enrolled at the University of Colorado as a junior. What would become a career-long dedication to professional service can be traced to his early years at Colorado, when he served in 1969–1970 as president of Anthropos, the undergraduate anthropology club.

In 1969, Doug attended the University of Colorado field school at Mesa Verde and surrounding areas. Since Doug had two years of paid dig experience and one field school already under his belt, he was assigned to work on independent crews excavating in Mancos Canyon on the Ute Mountain Reservation and conducting site survey on the Southern Ute Reservation, as well as at Mummy Lake on Chapin Mesa.

The summer of 1970 saw Doug as the field foreman at the Jurgens site near Kersey, Colorado, a Paleoindian bison-kill and -processing site. He graduated with his bachelor's in anthropology that June, then took a year off to establish residency in Colorado so that he could attend graduate school at an affordable cost. Doug began his graduate studies at the University of Colorado in the fall of 1971 and graduated with his master of arts in anthropology in 1973. In 1974, he was admitted to full membership in Sigma Xi.

Doug's master's thesis was on the archaeology of Fort Larned, Kansas, which at the time was undergoing restoration by the National Park Service (NPS) (Scott 1973, 1989). The restoration work at Fort Larned required a good deal of archaeology, and the NPS awarded contracts to the University of Colorado and Doug for that work from 1972 through 1974. The variety of features and buildings tested and excavated provided the basis for Doug's dissertation work, also at Colorado, which he completed in 1977 (Scott 1977).

At the conclusion of the 1974 Fort Larned work, and having completed all but his dissertation, the Oklahoma Historical Society (OHS) hired Doug as the curator of Fort Towson Historic Site in southeast Oklahoma. Doug's daughter Barbara was born in nearby Hugo, Oklahoma, in 1975. Though only at Fort Towson for a short while, he completed excavations and reports on two projects: the powder magazine and the commanding officer's quarters and privies (Scott 1975, 1983b). He also oversaw the accurate reconstruction of one of the barracks at nearby Fort Washita. It was at Fort Towson that he met University of Tulsa undergraduate anthropology majors William Lees and Tim Jones, both of whom volunteered on Doug's excavations in the summer of 1975. Another long-lasting friendship was formed with William, eventually resulting in collaboration on Civil War and Indian Wars battlefields in Oklahoma (Lees et al. 2001).

Department of the Interior

In the fall of 1975, Doug resigned from OHS to take a federal job in Colorado. He was hired as the first Bureau of Land Management (BLM) District Archaeologist in Colorado, stationed at Montrose. There he did a variety of cultural resource management (CRM) projects over the next eight years. One of his major accomplishments during that time was working with BLM State Archaeologist Gary Matlock and Bureau of Reclamation Archaeologist Ward Weakly to create, design, and secure funding for the Anasazi Heritage Center (AHC). The BLM created the AHC to house and interpret archaeological materials from the Dolores Archaeological Project and surrounding BLM lands (Scott 1983a). Today it is the headquarters for the Canyon of the Ancients National Monument and a premier museum and interpretative center in southwestern Colorado.

In 1983, an opportunity arose for Doug to move to the NPS Midwest Archeological Center (MWAC) in Lincoln, Nebraska. There he was a division chief for CRM work in what was then the Rocky Mountain Region, encompassing the states of North and South Dakota, Wyoming, Montana, Colorado, Utah, and part of Arizona. Doug worked on or supervised project work in most of the park units in those states. His greatest claim to fame was the happy byproduct of his 1983 move to the NPS, where his first project assignment was to assess archaeological needs following a range fire at Little Bighorn Battlefield National Monument, Montana, then called Custer Battlefield National Monument (Scott et al. 1989). The rest, as they say, is history. His work there, along with Melissa Connor and Richard Fox, captured the public imagination and the attention of the press, catapulting their archaeological work onto both the national and international stages. The incipient beginnings of the field of battlefield or conflict archaeology rolled out of the work at Little Bighorn. Doug continued doing battlefield archaeology by working at Little Bighorn every season for 23 years.

Doug also directed and assisted with numerous other battlefield and conflict-site investigations in the United States, England, Cuba, and Belgium. These included NPS projects, as well as other outside collaborative endeavors, such as the Washita Battlefield (now Washita National Historic Site) and Honey Springs Battlefield (OHS) with William Lees.

In another convergence, the work at the Little Bighorn and the discovery of soldiers' skeletal remains brought Doug and wife Melissa Connor into contact with Clyde Snow. Snow did an exceptional analysis of those remains, but also cajoled Doug and Melissa into taking the methods they had developed in battlefield recovery to the field of forensic science. Clyde's statement that they should take their methods to a "real" battlefield led them to work for Physicians for Human Rights (PHR) and the United Nations (UN) El Salvador Truth Commission (1992), the UN Truth Commission for Former Yugoslavia (1993), the UN International Criminal Tribunal for Former Yugoslavia (1996), the UN International Criminal Tribunal for Rwanda (1995 and 1996), the U.S. State Department on a case in northern Cyprus (1997), for PHR on the Greek side of Cyprus (1999), and for the Regime Crime Liaison Office in Iraq (2004 and 2006). Melissa shifted from prehistoric and historical archaeology to full-time forensic archaeology in 2000. She now directs the Forensic Investigation Research Station (FIRS) for Colorado Mesa University in Grand Junction.

In 1996, with an NPS reorganization, Doug became the program leader for the Great Plains at MWAC. He continued as a supervisory archaeologist working on and overseeing projects in parks in Kansas, Nebraska, Missouri, Minnesota, Arkansas, and the Dakotas. He also continued to work outside the Midwest Region, helping other parks and agencies when requested. Doug has worked in 15 different states and at 55 national parks, monuments, or historic sites.

Concurrent with his service to the Department of the Interior, Doug began a long relationship in 1984 with the University of Nebraska, Lincoln (UNL) that ended only after his retirement and move to Colorado. In various capacities, he taught classes, served on over 30 master's and doctoral committees, and helped direct several field schools in western Nebraska with UNL colleague Peter Bleed. Throughout his career he also lectured to public audiences, to avocational archaeological societies, and to business and professional groups. Notable here is his 1988 England lecture tour on the archaeology of the Little Bighorn, with presentations at Cambridge University; the Royal Military Academy, Sandhurst; Durham University; Sheffield University; the University of Newcastle upon Tyne; the London Borough of Havering; and the Manchester Borough of Staleybridge.

Doug retired from the NPS in January 2006 after 31 years, 4 months, and 23 days of credited service to the Department of the Interior. Since his retirement, Doug has stayed active in the field. With his move to Colorado he has become an adjunct instructor and visiting research scientist at Colorado Mesa University, and he continued his affiliation with UNL until 2012. He has also continued work in the forensic field, assisting Melissa with some casework for local law enforcement. In 2011, he helped direct excavations and the mapping for the Whistler, British Columbia, sled-dog animal welfare case with the British Columbia Society for the Prevention of Cruelty to Animals. Just a few months before receiving the Harrington Medal, he convinced a crew of aging colleague-volunteers to join him in the search for the Civil War camp of the 1st Colorado Volunteer Infantry at Fort Union National Monument, New Mexico.

Lifetime Achie▼ments

The J. C. Harrington Medal in Historical Archaeology recognizes a lifetime of contributions to the discipline centered on scholarship. The record of achievement by Dr. Douglas D. Scott amply qualifies him for this award. In fact, no other historical archaeologist comes close to matching the scope and quality of his considerable contributions to the specialty of 19th-century military-sites archaeology, particularly battlefield investigations and forensic archaeology with an emphasis on the analysis of firearms and ammunition used in conflicts.

During his many years in government service, Doug worked on a variety of sites in the Great Plains and Rocky Mountain West, and published widely on the results of those investigations. He has appeared in 28 television documentaries and written, coauthored, or coedited 11 books. Doug has an extensive resume of book chapters; peer-reviewed journal articles; encyclopedia entries; agency or organizational monographs; CRM reports; forensic archaeology and human rights, and firearms-related reports and publications; publications on military history and material culture; and book reviews. He has delivered close to 100 papers at scholarly meetings, about one-quarter of which were at SHA conferences.

Doug helped found the Colorado Council of Professional Archaeologists and served as its first president; he also was a founding member of the Nebraska Association of Professional Archaeologists, for which he later served as president. In addition, he served on the board of directors of the Plains Anthropological Society and was co-chair of the 3rd International Battlefield Archaeology Conference (Nashville, Tennessee). Most significant, perhaps, since joining SHA in 1972 Doug has served as the 1983 conference program chair (Denver, Colorado); chair of the Awards Development Committee (1988–1989), Procedures Manual Development Committee (1988–1995), and Ethics Committee (2000 and 2001); served on numerous other committees; was twice a member of the SHA Board of Directors (1987–1989 and 1998–2000); served as president-elect in 2005; and was the first two-year president in 2006 and 2007.

Most notable was his work on military fortifications, including Fort Towson, Fort Larned, Fort Laramie (Scott et al. 1992), and Fort Smith (Scott and Hunt 1998, 2000; Coleman and Scott 2003), and his work at more than 40 battlefield sites. In addition to Little Bighorn, he directed work at Big Hole Battlefield National Historical Site, Sand Creek National Historic Site (Scott 2000b; Greene and Scott 2004), Wilson's Creek National Battlefield (Scott 2000a, 2006a; Scott et al. 2007), Pea Ridge National Battlefield Park (Carlson-Drexler et al. 2008), and Monroe's Crossroads Battlefield (Belew and Scott 1997; Scott and Hunt 1998). His work at other battlefields, including collaborative work with additional organizations and colleagues, included Mescal Springs, Arizona; Milk Creek and Summit Spring, Colorado; Black Jack and Ivan Boyd Prairie, Kansas; Booneville, Centralia, Island Mound, and Moore's Mill, Missouri (Scott, Dasovich et al. 2014; Scott, Thiessen et al. 2014; Thiessen et al. 2014); Bear Paw, Montana (Scott 2001); Rush Creek, Nebraska (Scott et al. 2011); Glorieta, New Mexico; Honey Springs and Washita, Oklahoma; and Santiago de Cuba (Bleed and Scott 2005).

Doug's best-known efforts, however, relate to the Little Bighorn Battlefield, where George Armstrong Custer and his men met their end. Indeed, Scott has authored or coauthored some 50 publications on that site alone. In their preliminary report on the Little Bighorn, Doug and coauthor Richard Fox, Jr., first codified what is today accepted as the standard methodology for conflict archaeology (Scott and Fox 1987). Conflict archaeologists refer to this seminal work affectionately as "The Book." Doug has continued to refine the methodological approach to conflict archaeology, often in collaboration with other scholars, in many subsequent project-related and synthetic papers and publications. Doug's most recent book on Little Bighorn archaeology, *Uncovering History: Archaeological Investigations at the Little Bighorn* (Scott 2013), received the United States Literary Award in Anthropology/Archaeology in 2013, and in 2014 the Little Bighorn Associates John M. Carroll Book Award and the Custer Battlefield Historical and Museum Association G. Joseph Sills Book Award.

As the leading figure in conflict archaeology, Doug developed several innovative methods for the investigation of battlefield sites, especially related to the systematic use of metal detectors, electronic mapping techniques, and forensic analysis (Connor and Scott 1998; Scott 2006b, 2014a; Bleed and Scott 2011; Espenshade et al. 2012; Scott et al. 2012; Spude and Scott 2013). His work in historical archaeology has led him to become a technical advisor to the Association of Firearm and Tool Mark Examiners and a fellow of the American Academy of Forensic Sciences. His methods have been widely adopted by others in the field and serve as a model to a new generation of scholars engaged in such undertakings.

His contribution to conflict archaeology was not only innovative, but it was the foundation for the establishment of conflict archaeology as a respected part of historical archaeology (Fox and Scott 1991; Scott 1996, 2002, 2005, 2009, 2014b; Scott and McFeaters 2011). In his nomination testimonial, Steven Smith (2013) noted: "Doug Scott has done what Stan South did for the entire discipline of historical archaeology; that is raising conflict archaeology to a level of theoretical and methodological sophistication representative of a mature discipline that contributes significant insight into human conflict."

Whereas archaeologists had long excavated forts and fortifications, some of which were associated with battlefields, actual investigations of the battles themselves were deemed not suited to systematic archaeological inquiry, due to their scale and the dispersed nature of related archaeological data. Further, the tool that would become central to conflict archaeology—the metal detector—was associated with the unsystematic looting of sites and was not taken seriously as a tool of ethical archaeology. That all changed with Doug Scott and his amazing study of the Little Bighorn fight. Although Doug drew many collaborators into this and subsequent studies (one of his hallmarks as a professional), including metal-detector hobbyists previously scorned by professionals, he was the driving force in this study and in establishing a clear and effective method now ensconced within conflict archaeology. If the Harrington Medal's namesake is the father of historical archaeology, Doug is indeed the father of modern conflict archaeology.

Doug's success in battlefield archaeology was not due only to his identification of tools and development of a methodology, in his wide collaboration with other scholars, or in embracing expert volunteers. Key was his ability to showcase the interpretive power of the approach. Using sound scientific reasoning and teasing out sophisticated data from battlefield artifacts, Doug presented to the scholarly community compelling interpretations of events that addressed longstanding historical questions and that commented on questions of broad anthropological interest and importance. That he was a career public servant in the NPS probably compelled him to take the next important step, which was to offer a clearly understandable explanation of this scholarship and findings to the general public through publications and other media. In his Harrington testimonial, Peter Bleed (2013) noted: "Doug made scholars and the lay public excited about the role archaeology could play in understanding battles and past human conflicts. And as a result of Doug's research, historical archaeology grew and a new generation of scholars were drawn to the field."

Very much related to and growing out of his work on battlefields has been Doug's forensic studies. Perhaps most important among his forensic research projects has been the investigations he carried out at the behest of several international organizations. Applying archaeological methods, Doug aided with the disclosure of evidence in war crimes cases at locations around the globe. In addition to his reports of findings produced at mass graves and other sites, Doug was called upon to give expert testimony at trials and international tribunals, including, in 2006, the successful trial and conviction of Saddam Hussein for crimes against humanity perpetrated while he was leader of Iraq.

It is in Doug's nature, it seems, to collaborate and also to mentor students and young professionals. The number of practicing professional historical archaeologists who have been influenced by Doug, helped along the way, and who carry in their professional tool bags lessons learned from Doug is substantial. As W. Stephen McBride and Kim A. McBride (2013) said in their testimonial: "Doug has been a leader and mentor to many of us working on military sites. He has always been available to offer advice, comment on and edit articles and reports, and of course add a bit of Doug's humor when needed." P. Willey (2013) noted that "Doug's willingness to acknowledge accomplishments of his co-workers and tout their insights are renowned. ... His ecumenical outreach to many disciplines and scholars of diverse expertises sets high standards of inclusiveness."

Doug's work and research has been recognized repeatedly. He was elected a fellow of the Center for Great Plains Study in 1987. He received a literary medal from the Orders and Medals Society of America in 1997; a Certificate of Achievement, Intermountain Regional Office, NPS for the Sand Creek Project in 1999; an NPS CRM Award for the Sand Creek Project in 2001; and the Leslie Hewes Award (co-recipient with Peter Bleed) for the best social-science article published in Great Plains research in 2009. Doug was recognized in 2009 for his work with the PAST Foundation, receiving its Founder's Award and the Outstanding Service and Innovation Awards. The Department of the Interior honored him with its two highest awards: the Meritorious Service Award in 1999 and the Distinguished Service Award in 2002 for his career achievements, including the creation of the Anasazi Heritage Center and his work in battlefield and conflict archaeology. It is fitting, in light of his career achievements in scholarship, that the SHA—which has been Doug's professional home—be added to this list.

Dr. Douglas D. Scott's lifetime contributions to scholarship in historical archaeology are clear, significant, sustained, and deserving of recognition by the SHA by award of its highest honor: the J. C. Harrington Medal in Historical Archaeology.

References

BELEW, KENNETH, AND DOUGLAS D. SCOTT
    1997 Introduction. In *Cavalry Clash in the Sandhills: The Battle of Monroe's Crossroad, North Carolina, 0 March 6*, Kenneth Belew, author, pp. 1–12. Department of the Interior, National Park Service, Midwest Archeological Center and Southeast Archeological Center, Tallahassee, FL.

BLEED, PETER
    2013 Letter to William B. Lees in Support of Douglas D. Scott's Nomination for the J. C. Harrington Medal in Historical Archaeology, 1 November. University of West Florida, Florida Public Archaeology Network, Pensacola.

BLEED, PETER, AND DOUGLAS SCOTT
    2005 An Archeological Reconnaissance of the Battlefields of the Santiago Campaign of 1898. Manuscript, National Geographic Society, Washington, DC.
    2011 Context for Conflict: Conceptual Tools for Interpreting Archaeological Reflections of Warfare. *Journal of Conflict Archaeology* 6(1):43–45.

CARLSON-DREXLER, CARL G., DOUGLAS D. SCOTT, AND HAROLD ROEKER
2008 *"The Battle Raged ... with Terrible Fury": Battlefield Archaeology of Pea Ridge National Military Park*. National Park Service, Midwest Archeological Center, Technical Report No. 112. Lincoln, NE.

CLELAND, CHARLES E.
1993 The Society for Historical Archaeology and Its First Twenty-Five Years: Introduction. *Historical Archaeology* 27(1):3.

COLEMAN, ROGER E., AND DOUGLAS D. SCOTT
2003 *An Archeological Overview and Assessment of Fort Smith National Historic Site*. National Park Service, Midwest Archeological Center, Technical Report No. 87. Lincoln, NE.

CONNOR, MELISSA, AND DOUGLAS D. SCOTT
1998 Metal Detector Use in Archaeology: An Introduction. *Historical Archaeology* 32(4):73–82.

ESPENSHADE, CHRIS, DOUG D. SCOTT, PATRICK SEVERTS, SHELDON SKAGGS, TERRY POWIS, AND GARRETT SILLIMAN
2012 A Discussion of Standards for Metal Detecting. *Proceedings of the Advanced Metal Detecting for the Archaeologist Conference, Helen, Georgia*, Terry G. Powis, editor, pp. 5–13. Kennesaw State University, Department of Geography and Anthropology, Kennesaw, GA.

FOX, RICHARD A., JR., AND DOUGLAS D. SCOTT
1991 The Post Civil War Battlefield Pattern. *Historical Archaeology* 25(2):92–103.

GLENNER, RICHARD, P. WILLEY, AND DOUGLAS D. SCOTT
1994 Back to the Little Bighorn: Remains of a 7th Cavalry Trooper Recovered at Little Bighorn Battlefield in 1903 Provide a Glimpse of 19th Century Dental Practices. *Journal of the American Dental Association* 124(7):835–843.

GREENE, JEROME A., AND DOUGLAS D. SCOTT
2004 *Finding Sand Creek: History and Archeology of the 1864 Massacre*. University of Oklahoma Press, Norman.

LEES, WILLIAM B., DOUGLAS D. SCOTT, AND C. VANCE HAYNES
2001 History Underfoot: The Search for Physical Evidence of the 1868 Attack on Black Kettle's Village. *Chronicles of Oklahoma* 79(2):158–181.

MCBRIDE, W. STEPHEN, AND KIM A. MCBRIDE
2013 Letter to the Society for Historical Archaeology Awards Committee, Nomination of Douglas D. Scott for the J. C. Harrington Medal in Historical Archaeology, 12 November. Society for Historical Archaeology, Germantown, MD.

SCOTT, DOUGLAS D.
1973 The Archaeology of Fort Larned National Historic Site, Kansas. Master's thesis, Department of Anthropology, University of Colorado, Boulder.
1975 Archaeological and Historical Investigations at the Fort Towson Powder Magazine. *Chronicles of Oklahoma* 53(4):516–527.
1976 Ethnic Identification of an Historic Sac Burial from Northeastern, Kansas. *Plains Anthropologist* 21(72):131–139.
1977 *Historic Fact vs. Archaeological Reality, a Test in Environmental Reconstruction*. Doctoral dissertation, Department of Anthropology, University of Colorado, Boulder. University Microfilms International, Ann Arbor, MI.
1983a The Anasazi Heritage Center and the Dolores Project. *Conservation News, Rocky Mountain Regional Conservation Center* 1(1):3.
1983b Excavation of Officers Row 1975 Fort Towson Historical Site, Oklahoma. Manuscript, Oklahoma Historical Society, Oklahoma City.
1989 An Officer's Latrine at Fort Larned and Inferences on Status. *Plains Anthropologist* 34(123):23–34.
1996 Battlefield Archaeology of North America. In *The Oxford Companion to Archaeology*, Brian M. Fagan, editor, pp. 87–88. Oxford University Press, New York, NY.
2000a *Archeological Overview and Assessment for Wilson's Creek National Battlefield, Greene and Christian Counties, Missouri*. National Park Service, Midwest Archeological Center, Technical Report No. 66. Lincoln, NE.
2000b Identifying the 1864 Sand Creek Massacre Site through Archeological Reconnaissance. In *Sand Creek Massacre Project, Site Location Study, Volume 1*, National Park Service, author, pp. 74–144. National Park Service, Intermountain Regional Office, Denver, CO.
2001 *Archeological Reconnaissance of Bear Paw Battlefield, Blaine County, Montana*. National Park Service, Midwest Archeological Center, Technical Report No. 73. Lincoln, NE.
2002 Battlefield Archaeology. In *Encyclopedia of Historical Archaeology*, Charles E. Orser, Jr., editor, pp. 47–50. Routledge, New York, NY.
2005 The Archaeology of Battlefields. In *The Archaeology of War*, Mark Rose, editor, pp. 257–259. Hatherleigh Press, New York, NY.

2006a "A Stirring Effect on the Enemy": Civil War Archaeology of Sharp's Cornfield at the 1861 Battle of Wilson's Creek, Missouri. *Missouri Archaeologist* 66:77–92.

2006b Oral Tradition and Archaeology: Conflict and Concordance, Examples from Two Indian War Sites. *Historical Archaeology* 37(3):55–65.

2009 Studying the Archaeology of War: A Model Based on the Investigation of Frontier Military Sites in the American Trans-Mississippi West. In *International Handbook of Historical Archaeology*, Teresita Majewski and David Gaimster, editors, pp. 299–318. Springer, New York, NY.

2013 *Uncovering History: Archaeological Investigations at the Little Bighorn.* University of Oklahoma Press, Norman.

2014a Metal Detecting in Archaeology. In *Encyclopedia of Global Archaeology*, Claire Smith, editor, pp. 4836–4841. Springer, New York, NY.

2014b Reassessing the Meaning of Artifact Patterning. In *Battles and Massacres on the Southwestern Frontier: Historical and Archaeological Perspectives*, Ronald K. Wetherington and Frances Levine, editors, pp. 134–152. University of Oklahoma Press, Norman.

Scott, Douglas D., Peter Bleed, and Benjamin Bilgri
2011 Archaeological Investigations of the 1865 Rush Creek Battlefield, 25MO81, Morrill County, Nebraska. *Central Plains Archeology* 13(1):79–129.

Scott, Douglas D., Steven J. Dasovich, and Thomas D. Thiessen
2014 Archaeology of the First Battle of Boonville, Missouri, June 17, 1861. In *From These Honored Dead Historical Archaeology of the American Civil War*, Clarence R. Geier, Douglas D. Scott, and Lawrence E. Babits, editors, pp. 26–41. University Press of Florida, Gainesville.

Scott, Doug D., Chris Espenshade, Patrick Severts, Sheldon Skaggs, Terry G. Powis, Chris Adams, and Charles Haecker
2012 Advances in Metal Detector Technology and Applications in Archaeology. *Proceedings of the Advanced Metal Detecting for the Archaeologist Conference, Helen, Georgia*, Terry G. Powis, editor, pp. 33–54. Kennesaw State University, Department of Geography and Anthropology, Kennesaw, GA.

Scott, Douglas, and Richard Fox, Jr.
1987 *Archeological Insights into the Custer Battle: A Preliminary Assessment.* University of Oklahoma Press, Norman.

Scott, Douglas D., Richard A. Fox, Jr., Melissa A. Connor, and Dick Harmon
1989 *Archaeological Perspectives on the Battle of the Little Bighorn.* University of Oklahoma Press, Norman.

Scott, Douglas D., and William J. Hunt, Jr.
1998 *The Civil War Battle at Monroe's Crossroad, Fort Bragg North Carolina: A Historical Archeological Perspective.* Department of the Army, XVIII Airborne Corps and Fort Bragg, Fort Bragg, NC, and National Park Service, Southeast Archeological Center, Tallahassee, FL.

2000 *Archeological Investigations Conducted in Support of the Fort Smith Barracks/Courthouse/Jail Rehabilitation.* National Park Service, Midwest Archeological Center, Technical Report No. 68. Lincoln, NE.

Scott, Douglas D., and Andrew J. McFeaters
2011 The Archaeology of Historic Battlefields: A History and Theoretical Development in Conflict Archaeology. *Journal of Archaeological Research* 19(1):103–132.

Scott, Douglas D., Harold Roeker, and Carl G. Carlson-Drexler
2007 *"The Fire upon Us Was Terrific": Battlefield Archaeology of Wilson's Creek National Battlefield, Missouri.* National Park Service, Midwest Archeological Center, Technical Report No. 109. Lincoln, NE.

Scott, Douglas, W. E. Sudderth, and Christopher Schoen
1992 *Archeological Investigations of the 1874 Cavalry Barracks, Fort Laramie National Historic Site, Wyoming.* National Park Service, Midwest Archeological Center, Technical Report No. 16. Lincoln, NE.

Scott, Douglas D., Thomas D. Thiessen, and Steve J. Dasovich
2014 *A "Desperate and Bloody" Fight: The Battle of Moore's Mill, Callaway County, Missouri, July 8.* Missouri's Civil War Heritage Foundation, St. Louis, and National Park Service, American Battlefield Protection Program, Washington, DC.

SCOTT, DOUGLAS, AND P. WILLEY
1995 The Custer Battlefield National Cemetery Human Remains Identification Project. In *8 h Annual S mposium*, pp. 12–29. Custer Battlefield Historical and Museum Association, Hardin, MT.
1996 Custer's Men Took Names to Their Graves. *Greasy Grass* 12:20–28.
1997 Little Bighorn: Human Remains from the Custer National Cemetery. In *In Rememb ance: Archaeology and Death*, David A. Poirier and Nicholas F. Bellantoni, editors, pp. 155–171. Bergin & Garvey, Westport, CT.

SCOTT, DOUGLAS D., P. WILLEY, AND MELISSA CONNOR
1998 *They Died with Custer: The Sl d ers' S eletons from the Battle of the Little Bighorn.* University of Oklahoma Press, Norman.

SMITH, STEVEN D.
2013 Letter to the Society for Historical Archaeology Awards Committee, Nomination of Douglas D. Scott for the J. C. Harrington Medal in Historical Archaeology, 31 October. Society for Historical Archaeology, Germantown, MD.

SPUDE, CATHERINE HOLDER, AND DOUGLAS D. SCOTT
2013 NAGPRA and Historical Research: Reevaluation of a Multiple Burial from Fort Union National Monument, New Mexico. *Historical Archaeology* 47(4):121–136.

THIESSEN, THOMAS D., STEVE J. DASOVICH, AND DOUGLAS D. SCOTT
2014 Massacre and Battle at Centralia, Missouri, September 27, 1864: Historical and Archaeological Perspectives. In *From These Honored Dead Historical Archaeology of the American Civil War*, Clarence R. Geier, Douglas D. Scott, and Lawrence E. Babits, editors, pp. 26–56. University Press of Florida, Gainesville.

WILLEY, P.
2013 Letter to the Society for Historical Archaeology Awards Committee, Nomination of Douglas D. Scott for the J. C. Harrington Medal in Historical Archaeology, 20 November. Society for Historical Archaeology, Germantown, MD.

WILLEY, P., RICHARD A. GLENNER, AND DOUGLAS D. SCOTT
1996 Oral Health of Seventh Cavalry Troopers: Dentitions from the Custer National Cemetery. *Journal of the History of Dentistry* 44(1):3–14.

WILLEY, P., AND DOUGLAS D. SCOTT
1996 "The Bullets Buzzed Like Bees": Gunshot Wounds in Skeletons from the Battle of the Little Bighorn. *International Journal of Osteoarchaeology* 6(1):15–27.

WILLIAM B. LEES
VERGIL E. NOBLE

J. C. Harrington Medal in Historical Archaeology

Mark P. Leone

The 2016 Society for Historical Archaeology (SHA) J. C. Harrington Medal in Historical Archaeology was presented to Mark P. Leone at the 49th Annual Conference on Historical and Underwater Archaeology in Washington, D.C., in January. It is difficult to imagine historical archaeology scholarship that ignores the half-millennium impression of capitalism, evades the ways power is embedded in the most quotidian things, or does not acknowledge the political weight of archaeological practice. These have all been fundamental threads of Mark's work for more than 35 years. Mark has been a ceaseless advocate for a theoretically rich, intellectually ambitious, and politically relevant historical archaeology, examining a breadth of material, including formal gardens, historic sites, urban plans, mass-produced tableware, and African diasporan spirit bundles. Every Harrington recipient's story is, perhaps, a narrative about the scholarly communities that Harrington medalists have fostered, and Mark shares with nearly every Harrington recipient such a circle of colleagues. The collective creativity of that community of scholars has produced a quite distinctive archaeological voice that revolves around how historical archaeology can be an intervention in the way contemporary society is viewed.

Most historical archaeologists know Mark for the research he has directed in Annapolis, Maryland, beginning in 1981. The Archaeology in Annapolis Project was, in many ways, an adaptation of Mark's own training in the 1960s. Mark began his graduate work at the University of Arizona in 1963, and he was a student in 1964 in the second field school at Grasshopper Pueblo. That field school was directed by Raymond Thompson, who taught

Mark's first archaeology class at Arizona, and it included 2008 Harrington recipient Jim Ayres. A year earlier, the first field school at Grasshopper included 2009 Harrington Medalist Bob Schuyler. Not far away in Vernon, Arizona, the Field Museum's field school was directed by Paul S. Martin, who had over three decades of archaeological fieldwork experience in the American Southwest. By the early 1960s, Martin had become disaffected with much of his own descriptive research, and he became a convert to the New Archaeology, transformed by students and colleagues, including Bill Longacre. Lewis Binford's first doctoral student at the University of Chicago, Longacre was hired at the University of Arizona in 1964 and became Mark's advisor. Mark was among the first of Longacre's students, and Longacre secured him a post at Vernon.

The 1965 Vernon field school brochure championed the field school as "New Perspectives in Archaeology," reflecting immersion in the New Archaeology, and indicated that its mission was to train in "archaeology as anthropology," focused on the "scholarly ethnographic study of extinct cultures" (Mills 2005:74; Chazin and Nash 2013:334). Martin later argued that the Vernon field school was not focused on "teaching archaeological techniques," but was instead intended to "emphasize theory and method since these subjects are rarely dealt with in an academic context" (Chazin and Nash 2013:336). These field schools were philosophically ambitious, with Ezra Zubrow describing them as an "intellectual salon" (Chazin and Nash 2013:331). In 1968, the Vernon field school's staff of Fred Plog, Zubrow, and Mark hosted philosopher of science Thomas Kuhn as a guest lecturer alongside Leslie White, Robert McC. Adams, and Lewis and Sally Binford.

After completing his degree and publishing his doctoral analysis in *Science* in 1968 (Leone 1968), Mark became an assistant professor at Princeton University, and in 1972 he edited the collection *Contemporary Archaeology* (Leone 1972). Published a decade after Binford's "Archaeology as Anthropology," Leone's collection remains one of the most thorough surveys of the New Archaeology and gathers together nearly all the practitioners of 1960s anthropological archaeology: the 33 contributors include Martin, Longacre, Binford, Raymond Thompson, and Walter Taylor alongside their students, including James Deetz, Robert Schuyler, William Rathje, and Mark Leone. *Contemporary Archaeology* has since gone through five printings, but it came at a moment that the New Archaeology was itself transforming. Mark did not subsequently read the last rites over the New Archaeology, and his framework for conducting archaeology has remained persistently committed to scientific rigor. Nevertheless, Mark has advocated an archaeology consistently motivated by a commitment to social relevance, which was perhaps not part of many New Archaeologists' agendas.

The seeds for that interest in the political implications of archaeology had been planted in part by Lewis Binford's research on the material dimensions of ideology, and, during his tenure at Princeton, Mark was introduced to Marxian theory by his colleague Steve Barnett and Barnett's students. Marxism provided Mark a mechanism to extend the New Archaeology's intellectual foundations into the modern world and examine how archaeology functions in contemporary society. Perhaps the first test of this thinking came in Mark's work on Mormon material culture and economy, which included work on town plans, fences, and the new Mormon temple in Washington, D.C., near the University of Maryland, where he had moved in 1975 (Leone 1973, 1974, 1977). His paper examining the relationship between ideology and architecture at the Mormon temple appeared in the 1977 SHA Special Publication Series No. 2, *Historical Archaeology and the Importance of Material Things*, which was based on a 1975 SHA session. Mark, perhaps, did not imagine his analysis of the Mormon temple as his entry point into historical archaeology, but he legitimized it as historical archaeology because it "attempts to treat a piece of material culture in its whole social context" (Leone 1977:43). Mark recognized a view of archaeology that revolved around broadly defined materiality, acknowledging that the study "could also be called art history or architectural analysis or plain ethnography, but I am interested in calling it archaeology because it allows me to highlight the role of form—built, three dimensional form—in human behavior" (Leone 1977:43). In 1979, he published *The Roots of Modern Mormonism*, which synthesized his thinking on Mormon ideology and material culture (Leone 1979).

Within a few years of the 1977 volume, Mark was pressing the distinction between past and present, influenced by the work of Ian Hodder and his students at Cambridge, who argued that archaeological thought was an expression of contemporary society (Leone 1978a, 1978b, 1981b, 1982). Mark turned his attention to shallow notions of material culture, heritage, and relevance in public historical and archaeological scholarship, with much of that scholarship focusing on the interpretation of material culture in museums (Leone 1981c, 1983a, 1983b, 1989b, 1992, 1994a, 2008; Leone and Handsman 1989). In "Archaeology's Relationship to the Present and the Past," his contribution to the 1981 Richard Gould and Michael Schiffer volume *Modern Material Culture: The Archaeology of Us*, Mark accused archaeology of being boring, if not irrelevant, and laid the blame for this tedium at the feet of archaeologists, suggesting that "we are primarily concerned with accurate meaning and feel no obligation to notice the boredom our own interpretations communicate when made public" (Leone 1981a:12). For Mark, that tedium confirmed archaeology's irrelevance, and he argued that "when boredom accompanies archaeology, it is because the facts and the data are not tied to the present the way they should be" (Leone 1981a:13).

Armed with this commitment to examining how materiality and ideology shape historical and contemporary experience, Mark launched Archaeology in Annapolis in 1981. The project advocated a reflective public archaeology of contemporary social and material life, using excavation and material analysis to help community audiences rethink the roots of otherwise unrecognized modern practices. Mark argued for a public presentation of historical archaeology that is today relatively widely accepted: that is, archaeological sites provide exceptionally powerful spaces in which to conduct public archaeologies that involve rigorous ethnography, thorough documentary analysis, and community outreach (Leone 1994b). Yet, the heart of Archaeology in Annapolis was a very assertive critique of the city's romanticized historical narratives and shallow public scholarship. Archaeological research in Annapolis has attempted to intervene in heroic stories of the past and focused on narrating the underside of American democracy (Leone and Logan 1997; Leone, Delle et al. 1999; Leone, Matthews et al. 2002; Leone, Babiarz et al. 2005; Leone 2006b, 2009, 2010).

Among the most prominent of Mark's Annapolis studies was his 1984 analysis of the William Paca Garden, which examined how the American patriots rationalized their societal domination in beautiful formal gardens (Leone 1984); also see Leone (1987, 1988b, 1989a), Leone and Shackel (1987, 1990b), Leone and Hurry (1998), Leone and Gleason (2013a, 2013b), Leone and Pruitt (2015), and Leone, Harmon et al. (2005). Those gardens were interpreted as pleasurable diversions of Renaissance men, but Mark argued that they were, instead, material mechanisms that the Founding Fathers wielded to rationalize their power and prominence in American society. Mark's pronouncement that gardens were self-interested mechanisms of class inequality was an important contribution to landscape archaeology studies aspiring to press beyond description alone (Leone 1984). Yet, the focus on gardens and broader spaces of power struck a sour note with some observers who viewed archaeology as a search for fascinating things for adorning local historical narratives. Archaeology in Annapolis has had significant influence on historical archaeology in its advocacy of self-conscious and politicized archaeological practice; however, it has left little mark on Annapolis city planners and preservationists and, in some cases, has been actively dismissed. Some people were angered that Mark had the confidence to proclaim that celebratory local histories in places like Annapolis inelegantly evaded a complex and very un-American heritage, but the argument has resonated with scholars who negotiate similarly stale local stories of timeless national values and patriotism.

Archaeology in Annapolis followed a similar model developed at Vernon, with graduate students conducting research on various dimensions of the city's archaeological past. The earliest generation included Barbara Little and Paul Shackel, who both were students of Leone's former classmate Ezra Zubrow. Over the course of four field seasons, from 1983 to 1986,

Little directed field school excavations at the Green Print Shop; Shackel examined the material culture of modern discipline, completing his dissertation in 1987; and Parker Potter completed a dissertation on public archaeology and critical theory in 1989. Fifteen dissertations have been completed as part of Archaeology in Annapolis, and many of these have been published as monographs and peer-reviewed scholarship.

Mark coauthored the 1987 paper, "Toward a Critical Archaeology," with Potter and Shackel, and it remains perhaps the clearest statement of Mark's vision of critical thinking in historical archaeology (Leone, Potter et al. 1987); see also Leone (1986, 1991, 2003, 2006a, 2007a, 2007b, 2007c). Leone, Potter, and Shackel outlined an explicitly Marxian framework for "demystifying" how the past is constructed and the ways in which prosaic material things reproduce consequential ideologies. The paper's advocacy for public archaeology is perhaps now a settled issue, since most contemporary field practice embraces public interpretation, even if it remains cool to Marxian critical theory. The more important contribution of the paper may have been that it stood among a series of scholarly works that assertively turned the discipline's attention to capitalism (Paynter 1988; Johnson 1996; Orser 1996). In 1983, Mark had begun exploring the archaeology of the capitalist world when he delivered a series of lectures on materiality and capitalism during a trip to the United Kingdom. By 1988, the edited collection, *The Recovery of Meaning* (Leone and Potter 1988), included Mark's paper in which he argued that the Georgian order was properly understood as an expression of merchant capitalism (Leone 1988a, 1999). The paper aspired to extend James Deetz's famous argument for a Georgian worldview emerging in the 18th century, and Leone rooted that transformation in the social and material effects of 18th-century capitalist economics (Leone and Shackel 1990a).

Mark's advocacy of an historical archaeology focus on capitalism and the ways in which archaeologists can illuminate the roots of contemporary inequality became a central theme of his work. In 1993, he chaired the School of American Research Seminar, "Historical Archaeology of Capitalism," which was published as the edited collection, *Historical Archaeologies of Capitalism* (Leone and Potter 1999); see also Leone and Knauf (2015). In 1995, his *American Anthropologist* article, "A Historical Archaeology of Capitalism," reflected his evolving notion of the public politicization of archaeology and the ways historical archaeology might destabilize shallow notions of democracy and liberty. In the article he acknowledged that, "for a historical archaeology of capitalism to be possible, there would have to be dialogue with those who see knowledge about themselves as a way of dealing with their own oppression or victimization" (Leone 1995:261–262).

This interest in oppressed peoples reflected the project's research on African diasporan heritage, which began after Mark returned from teaching at the University of Cape Town, South Africa, in 1988. In 1990, Archaeology in Annapolis conducted its first African American archaeological research, work that eventually produced a series of studies on the materiality of African diasporan faith, the lives of free people of color, and postbellum African American life (Leone and Crosby 1987; Leone, Mullins et al. 1995; Leone and Fry 1999; Leone, Fry et al. 2001; Ruppel et al. 2003; Leone, Palus et al. 2006; Leone and Cuddy 2007; Deeley et al. 2013; Leone, Tang et al. 2013; Leone, Knauf et al. 2014; Leone and Tang 2014). Perhaps the best known of this scholarship examines the material remains of West African spirituality, identifying the complex material culture of African diasporan faith in captivity and freedom alike. In many ways, that work on African spiritualities spoke most clearly to Mark's interest in exploring how marginalized people negotiate capitalism. His 2005 study, *The Archaeology of Liberty in an American Capital: Excavations in Annapolis*, summarized the work conducted in Annapolis over more than 25 years, but, in many ways, it features the archaeological evidence of African faith (Leone 2005). The findings at a series of Annapolis sites (and subsequent analysis of comparable features elsewhere) have proven fascinating beyond archaeological circles because they so clearly unravel romanticized histories of captivity and underscore diasporan creativity and agency.

Mark's work has focused on the complications of American democracy, but his influence extends into global historical archaeology circles. He has been a tireless advocate for the discipline as a lecturer in places including South America, the United Kingdom, Western Europe, and Australia, and he served as a Fulbright Scholar in Chile in 2009. Yet, the legacies of Mark's scholarship may rest most significantly with the thousands of students whom he and his students have trained. Fifteen dissertations have been completed as part of Archaeology in Annapolis, with students hailing from institutions including the State University of New York at Buffalo, Brown University, Columbia University, the University of Massachusetts Amherst, the University of Virginia, and the University of Maryland, and legions more have trekked through their excavations and classrooms. The scholarship produced by Mark and Archaeology in Annapolis make the rather unremarkable Maryland capital exceptionally well understood from an historical archaeological perspective. Mark's wife, Nan Wells, and his daughter, Veronika Wells Leone, have been the heart of the circle of people supporting Mark and his scholarship, providing much of the stability that made his archaeology possible. As archaeologists we should not necessarily entertain the fantasy that Mark will be complacent with the state of the discipline, but it is a testimony to Mark's voice that we now consider historical archaeology a publicly engaged scholarship that can and should intervene in contemporary life.

References

CHAZIN, HANNAH, AND STEPHEN E. NASH
  2013   Moments, Movements, and Metaphors: Paul Sidney Martin, Pedagogy, and Professionalization in Field Schools, 1926–1974. *American Antiquity* 78(2):322–343.

DEELEY, KATHERINE H., STEFAN F. WOEHLKE, MARK P. LEONE, AND MATTHEW COCHRAN
  2013   West Central African Spirit Practices in Annapolis, Maryland. In *Kongo across the Waters*, Susan Cooksey, Robin Poynor, and Hein Vahnee, editors, pp. 240–247. University Press of Florida, Gainesville.

JOHNSON, MATTHEW
  1996   *An Archaeology of Capitalism*. Blackwell, Oxford, UK.

LEONE, MARK P.
  1968   Neolithic Economic Autonomy and Social Distance. *Science* 162(3858):1150–1151.
  1973   Archaeology as the Science of Technology: Mormon Town Plans and Fences. In *Research and Theory in Current Archaeology*, Charles L. Redman, editor, pp. 125–150. John Wiley & Sons, New York, NY.
  1974   The Economic Basis for the Evolution of Mormon Culture. In *Religious Movements in Contemporary America*, I. I. Zaretsky and Mark P. Leone, editors, pp. 722–756. Princeton University Press, Princeton, NJ.
  1977   The New Mormon Temple in Washington, D.C. In *Historical Archaeology and the Importance of Material Things*, Leland Ferguson, editor, pp. 43–61. Society for Historical Archaeology, Special Publication Series, No. 2. California, PA.
  1978a On Text and Interpretation. *Current Anthropology* 19(3):664–665.
  1978b Time in American Archaeology. In *Social Archaeology: Beyond Subsistence and Dating*, Charles L. Redman, Mary Jane Berman, Edward V. Curtin, William T. Langhorne, Jr., Nina M. Versaggi, and Jeffrey C. Wanser, editors, pp. 25–36. Academic Press, New York, NY.
  1979   *Roots of Modern Mormonism*. Harvard University Press, Boston, MA.
  1981a Archaeology's Relationship to the Present and the Past. In *Modern Material Culture*, Richard A. Gould and Michael B. Schiffer, editors, pp. 5–13. Academic Press, New York, NY.
  1981b Childe's Offspring. In *Symbolic and Structural Archaeology*, Ian Hodder, editor, pp. 179–184. Cambridge University Press, New York, NY.
  1981c The Relationship between Artifacts and the Public in Outdoor History Museums. In *The Research Potential of Anthropological Museum Collections*, A. M. Cantwell, J. B. Griffin, and Nan Rothschild, editors, pp. 301–313. New York Academy of Sciences, New York, NY.
  1982   Some Opinions about Recovering Mind. *American Antiquity* 47(4):742–760.
  1983a Method as Message. *Museum News* 62(1):35–41.
  1983b The Role of Archaeology in Verifying American Identity. *Archaeological Review from Cambridge* 2(1):44–50.
  1984   Interpreting Ideology in Historical Archaeology: Using the Rules of Perspective in the William Paca Garden in Annapolis, Maryland. In *Ideology, Representation and Power in Prehistory*, Christopher Tilley and Daniel Miller, editors, pp. 25–35. Cambridge University Press, New York, NY.

1986   Symbolic, Structural, and Critical Archaeology. In *American Archaeology Past, Present, and Future*, David Meltzer, Donald Fowler, and Jeremy Sabloff, editors, pp. 415–438. Smithsonian Institution Press, Washington, DC.

1987   Rule by Ostentation: The Relationship between Space and Sight in Eighteenth Century Landscape Architecture in the Chesapeake Region of Maryland. In *Method and Theory for Activity Area Research: An Ethnoarchaeological Approach*, Susan Kent, editor, pp. 604–633. Columbia University Press, New York, NY.

1988a The Georgian Order as the Order of Merchant Capitalism in Annapolis, Maryland. In *The Recovery of Meaning: Historical Archaeology in the Eastern United States*, Mark P. Leone and Parker B. Potter, Jr., editors, pp. 235–261. Smithsonian Institution Press, Washington, DC.

1988b The Relationship between Archaeological Data and the Documentary Record: Eighteenth-Century Gardens in Annapolis, Maryland. *Historical Archaeology* 22(1):29–35.

1989a Issues in Historic Landscapes and Gardens. *Historical Archaeology* 23(1):45–47.

1989b Keynote Address: Sketch of a Theory for Outdoor History Museums. *Association for Living Historical Farms and Agricultural Museums (ALHFAM), Proceedings of the 1987 Annual Meeting*, pp. 36–46. Smithsonian Institution Press, Washington, DC.

1991   Materialist Theory and the Formation of Questions in Archaeology. In *Processual and Postprocessual Archaeologies*, Robert W. Preucel, editor, pp. 235–241. Center for Archaeological Investigations, Carbondale, IL.

1992   Epilogue: The Productive Nature of Material Culture and Archaeology. In *Meanings and Uses of Material Culture*, Barbara J. Little and Paul A. Shackel, editors. Thematic issue, *Historical Archaeology* 26(3):130–133.

1994a An Archaeology of the DeWitt Wallace Gallery at Colonial Williamsburg. In *Museums and the Appropriation of Culture*, Susan Pearce, editor, pp. 198–212. Athlone Press, New York, NY.

1994b Overview of Archaeological Discoveries in Annapolis since 1981. In *The Historic Chesapeake: Archaeological Contributions*, Barbara J. Little and Paul A. Shackel, editors, pp. 219–229. Smithsonian Institution Press, Washington, DC.

1995   A Historical Archaeology of Capitalism. *American Anthropologist* 97(2):251–268.

1999   Ceramics from Annapolis, Maryland: A Measure of Time Routines and Work Discipline, with Assistance from Marian Creveling and Christopher Nagle. In *Historical Archaeologies of Capitalism*, Mark P. Leone and Parker B. Potter, Jr., editors, pp. 195–216. Kluwer Academic/Plenum, New York, NY.

2003   Where Is Culture to Be Found by Historical Archaeologists? Prologue. In *The Recovery of Meaning: Historical Archaeology in the Eastern United States*, expanded from 1988 edition, Mark P. Leone and Parker B. Potter, Jr., editors, pp. v–xxi. Percheron Press, New York, NY.

2005   *The Archaeology of Liberty in an American Capital: Excavations in Annapolis*. University of California Press, Berkeley.

2006a Foundational Histories and Power. *Archaeological Dialogues* 13(2):23–28.

2006b How the Landscape of Fear Works in Spring Valley, a Washington, D.C. Neighborhood. *City and Society* 18(1):36–42.

2007a Beginning for a Postmodern Archaeology. *Cambridge Archaeological Journal* 17(4):203–207.

2007b How to Work the Past: Middle Range Theory in Historical Archaeology. In *Expanding Method and Theory in Americanist Archaeology*, James Skibo, Michael Graves, and Miriam Stark, editors, pp. 21–39. University of Arizona Press, Tucson.

2007c The Role of Theory in Public Archaeology. In *Constructing Post-Medieval Archaeology in Italy: A New Agenda*, Sauro Gelichi and Mauro Librenti, editors, pp. 35–40. All' Insegna del Giglio, Florence, Italy.

2008   The Foundations of Archaeology. In *Ethnographic Archaeologies: Reflections on Stakeholders and Archaeological Practices*, Quetzil E. Castañeda and Christopher N. Matthews, editors, pp. 119–137. Alta Mira Press, Lanham, MD.

2009   Making Historical Archaeology Postcolonial. In *International Handbook of Historical Archaeology*, Teresita Majewski and David Gaimster, editors, pp. 159–168. Springer, New York, NY.

2010   *Critical Historical Archaeology*. Left Coast Press, Walnut Creek, CA.

LEONE, MARK P. (EDITOR)
   1972   *Contemporary Archaeology*. Southern Illinois University Press, Carbondale.

LEONE, MARK P., JENNIFER BABIARZ, AND CHERYL LAROCHE
   2005   The Archaeology of Black Americans in Recent Times. *Annual Reviews of Anthropology* 13(15):575–599.

LEONE, MARK P., AND CONSTANCE A. CROSBY
   1987   Middle-Range Theory in Historical Archaeology. In *Consumer Choice in Historical Archaeology*, Suzanne Spencer-Wood, editor, pp. 397–410. Plenum Press, New York, NY.

LEONE, MARK P., AND THOMAS W. CUDDY
   2007   New Africa: Understanding the Americanization of African Descent Groups through Archaeology. In *The Collaborative Continuum: Archaeological Engagements with Descendent Communities*, Chip Colwell-Chanthaphonh and T. J. Ferguson, editors, pp. 203–223. AltaMira Press, Lanham, MD.

LEONE, MARK P., JAMES DELLE, AND PAUL R. MULLINS
 1999 Archaeology of the Modern State: European Colonialism. In *Companion Encyclopedia of Archaeology*, Graeme Barker, editor, pp. 1107–1158. Routledge, New York, NY.

LEONE, MARK P., AND GLADYS-MARIE FRY
 1999 Conjuring in the Big House Kitchen: An Interpretation of African American Belief Systems, Based on the Uses of Archaeology and Folklore Sources. *Journal of American Folklore* 112(445):372–403.

LEONE, MARK P., GLADYS-MARIE FRY, AND TIM RUPPEL
 2001 Spirit Management among Americans of African Descent. In *Race and the Archaeology of Identity*, Charles E. Orser, Jr., editor, pp. 143–157. University of Utah Press, Salt Lake City.

LEONE, MARK P., AND KATHRYN L. GLEASON
 2013a Apprehending the Garden: Non-Destructive Approaches to Detecting Gardens. In *Sourcebook for Garden Archaeology: Methods, Techniques, Interpretations, and Field Examples*, Amina-Aïcha Malek, editor, pp. 97–126. Peter Lang, Bern, Switzerland.
 2013b William Paca's Gardens in Annapolis and on Wye Island, Maryland, US. In *Sourcebook for Garden Archaeology: Methods, Techniques, Interpretations, and Field Examples*, Amina-Aïcha Malek, editor, pp. 707–712. Peter Lang, Bern, Switzerland.

LEONE, MARK P., AND RUSSELL G. HANDSMAN
 1989 Living History and Critical Archaeology and the Reconstruction of the Past. In *Critical Traditions in Contemporary Archaeology*, Valerie Pinsky and Alison Wylie, editors, pp. 117–135. Cambridge University Press, New York, NY.

LEONE, MARK P., JAMES M. HARMON, AND JESSICA L. NEUWIRTH
 2005 Perspective and Surveillance in Eighteenth-Century Maryland Gardens, Including William Paca's Garden on Wye Island. *Historical Archaeology* 39(4):131–150.

LEONE, MARK P., AND SILAS D. HURRY
 1998 Seeing: The Power of Town Planning in the Chesapeake. *Historical Archaeology* 32(4):34–62.

LEONE, MARK P., JOCELYN KNAUF, AND AMANDA TANG
 2014 Ritual Bundles in Colonial Annapolis. In *Materialities of Ritual in the Black Atlantic*, Akinwumi Ogundiran and Paula Saunders, editors, pp. 198–215. Indiana University Press, Bloomington.

LEONE, MARK P., AND GEORGE C. LOGAN
 1997 Tourism with Race in Mind: Annapolis, Maryland Examines African-American Past through Collaborative Research. In *Tourism and Culture: An Applied Perspective*, Erve Chambers, editor, pp. 129–146. SUNY Press, Albany, NY.

LEONE, MARK P., CHRISTOPHER N. MATTHEWS, AND KURT JORDAN
 2002 The Political Economy of Archaeological Cultures. *Journal of Social Archaeology* 2(1):109–134.

LEONE, MARK P., PAUL R. MULLINS, MARIAN C. CREVELING, LAURENCE HURST, BARBARA JACKSON-NASH, LYNN JONES, HANNAH KAISER, GEORGE LOGAN, AND MARK WARNER
 1995 Can an African American Historical Archaeology Be an Alternative Voice? In *Interpreting Archaeology: Finding Meaning in the Past*, Ian Hodder, Michael Shanks, Alexandra Alexandri, Victor Buchli, John Carman, Jonathan Last, and Gavin Lucas, editors, pp. 110–124. Routledge, New York, NY.

LEONE, MARK P., MATTHEW M. PALUS, AND MATTHEW D. COCHRAN
 2006 Critical Archaeology: Politics Past and Present. In *Historical Archaeology*, Martin Hall and Stephen Silliman, editors, pp. 84–104. Blackwell, Malden, MA.

LEONE, MARK P., PARKER B. POTTER, JR., AND PAUL A. SHACKEL
 1987 Toward a Critical Archaeology. *Current Anthropology* 28(3):283–302.

LEONE, MARK P., AND ELIZABETH PRUITT
 2015 Archaeology of Telling Time: Plants and the Greenhouse at Wye House Plantation. In *Historical Archaeologies of Capitalism*, Mark P. Leone and Jocelyn Knauf, editors, pp. 103–125. Springer, New York, NY.

Paul R. Mullins

LEONE, MARK P., AND PAUL A. SHACKEL

1987   Forks, Clocks, and Power. In *Mirror and Metaphor: Material and Social Constructions of Reality*, Daniel W. Ingersoll and Gordon Bronitsky, editors, pp. 45–61. University Press of America, Lanham, MD.

1990a   The Georgian Order in Annapolis, Maryland. *Maryland Archeology* 26(1&2):69–84.

1990b   Plane and Solid Geometry in Colonial Gardens in Annapolis, Maryland. In *Earth Patterns*, William Kelso and Rachel Most, editors, pp. 153–167. University of Virginia Press, Charlottesville.

LEONE, MARK P., AND AMANDA TANG

2014   Definitions in Historical Archaeology: Enslaved African Americans Cultivating a Scientific Garden, Wye House, Maryland, USA. In *The Oxford Handbook of Historical Archaeology*, James Symonds and Vesa-Pekka Herva, editors. Oxford University Press, New York, NY. Oxford Handbooks Online <http://www.oxfordhandbooks.com/view/10.1093/oxfordhb/9780199562350.001.0001/oxfordhb-9780199562350-e-29>. Accessed 31 May 2016.

LEONE, MARK P., AMANDA TANG, BENJAMIN A. SKOLNIK, AND ELIZABETH PRUITT

2013   In the Shade of Frederick Douglass: The Archaeology of Wye House. In *Reclaiming Archaeology: Beyond the Tropes of Modernity*, Alfredo González-Ruibal, editor, pp. 220–232. Routledge, New York, NY.

LEONE, MARK P., AND JOCELYN KNAUF (EDITORS)

2015   *Historical Archaeologies of Capitalism*, 2nd edition. Springer, New York, NY.

LEONE, MARK P., AND PARKER B. POTTER, JR. (EDITORS)

1988   *The Recovery of Meaning: Historical Archaeology in the Eastern United States*. Smithsonian Institution Press, Washington, DC.

1999   *Historical Archaeologies of Capitalism*. Kluwer Academic/Plenum, New York, NY.

MILLS, BARBARA J.

2005   Curricular Matters: The Impact of Field Schools on Southwest Archaeology. In *Southwest Archaeology in the Twentieth Century*, Linda S. Cordell and Don D. Fowler, editors, pp. 60–80. University of Utah Press, Salt Lake City.

ORSER, CHARLES E., JR.

1996   *A Historical Archaeology of the Modern World*. Kluwer/Plenum, New York, NY.

PAYNTER, ROBERT

1988   Steps to an Archaeology of Capitalism. In *The Recovery of Meaning: Historical Archaeology in the Eastern United States*, Mark P. Leone and Parker B. Potter, Jr., editors, pp. 407–433. Smithsonian Institution Press, Washington, DC.

RUPPEL, TIMOTHY, JESSICA NEUWIRTH, MARK P. LEONE, AND GLADYS-MARIE FRY

2003   Hidden in View: African Spiritual Spaces in North American Landscapes. *Antiquity* 77(296):321–335.

PAUL R. MULLINS

Part IV:
Ruppé Awards

Carol V. Ruppé Distinguished Service Award. Volume 25, Number 3 (1991): 1-2. By Stephanie H. Rodeffer and Robert L. Schuyler.

Carol V. Ruppé Distinguished Service Award

At the 1989 Society for Historical Archaeology annual meetings in Baltimore, Maryland, the Board of Directors established a SHA Distinguished Service Award and named it in honor of Carol V. Ruppé. This special award recognizes individuals who have furthered the goals of the Society, either through a long and distinguished period of service or outstanding specific achievements. The award is named for Carol Ruppé, the SHA Bookroom Coordinator from 1975 to 1988, who created a unique opportunity to help the Society and its individual members grow. She has left a legacy of service and dedication to the Society that should be an inspiration for us all.

The founders of the Society established SHA in 1967 to "promote scholarly research in and the dissemination of knowledge concerning historical archaeology." Annual conferences were organized to provide forums for presenting and debating recent developments in the field. *Historical Archaeology*, first issued in 1967, became the primary publication outlet for research and the *Newsletter*, begun in 1968, disseminated information on current fieldwork and Society news. The amount and diversity of research on historic sites, and the resulting national literature, began to expand rapidly.

With a B.A. in Anthropology from the Univeristy of New Mexico and a 1959 M.L.S. degree from the University of Denver, Carol Ruppé combined the interests of archaeology and library science in one career. Through her librarian's eye she recognized the membership's need to have easy access to the growing body of literature published outside the auspices of the Society. She originated the idea of a bookroom at the annual meeting, where the latest in publications could be perused by the attendees at their leisure. With the encouragement of Robert L. Stephenson, General Chairman for the 1975 Conference, Ruppé developed, assembled, and managed this first bookroom at the Society's meeting in Charleston, South Carolina. Meeting participants were surprised, pleased, and soon clamoring for more. Through the years she greatly expanded the offerings of the bookroom to keep pace with the changing dimensions of the field. The SHA Bookroom evolved into a major information exchange center rather than the commercial book exhibits found at many scholarly conventions.

Development of the bookroom can best be characterized as creativity on a shoestring or the "painless sting." Carol is a masterful con artist who set the stage so skillfully that few could refuse. She recruited the participation of publishers and continually tried to identify and include *all* organizations with publications of interest to our members. She arranged free display space at the meeting for larger publishers who were normally charged $300 to $500 for the privilege. In return publishers often offered conference discounts and donated their sample copies to the host institution, thereby greatly enriching local libraries.

Ruppé professionally spent most of her full-time building library collections at Arizona State University (ASU) in Tempe. She joined their library staff on a part-time basis in 1962, and when she retired in 1988 she was Chair of the Reference Department. Her husband, Reynold J. Ruppé, had strongly supported her move into Library Science so as to avoid having two academic anthropologists in one family. Carol, in turn, introduced Ray to Underwater Archaeology when she took diving lessons. This divided career plan was not very complete, however, as she became the Anthropology Specialist in the Reference Section and built that collection into one of the finest in the Southwest. She also found ways to integrate the SHA Bookroom responsibilities into her position at Tempe, and the Society owes ASU acknowledgment for its continuing support. In 1983 Arizona State University granted Carol Ruppé its Presidential Award for Service.

As SHA Book Coordinator she and her staff were all volunteers. This pattern is also seen in her membership in the Guild for the Heard Museum in Phoenix. She built up their book holdings and helped to select the museum's first Librarian-Archivist. As a volunteer she still spends each Tuesday afternoon organizing their "Indian Artists Files." In a similar vein Carol recruited volunteers to help with various aspects of the SHA Bookroom. Depending on the circumstances, Carol tapped many members to lend a hand, a tool, or a bit of ingenuity to resolve a bookroom need or a logistical problem. In return she created a major reference center that warmly embraced the entire membership. Even though some days she answered the same question at least 50 times, her enthusiasm still bubbled over. Because she drew people to the bookroom it gradually became a place for reminiscences, business discussions, and a myriad of other small services. Carol took care of us all.

Carol Ruppé served for 14 years as Bookroom Coordinator and secured the continuation of this service by selecting and, over a two year period, training her successor, Lawrence E. Babits. We will never be able to fully measure the impact her 1975 idea has had on the Society and on historical archaeology, as she has offered the field opportunities to grow in a number of different ways. Many historical archaeologists have used the SHA Bookroom flyers and information to build their own institutional library holdings. Her influence on historical archaeology has truly been national. Ruppé's dedication and enthusiasm will serve as the standard by which future Distinguished Service Award recipients will be measured.

At the 1990 Annual Meetings in Tucson, Arizona, a surprise ceremony announced the creation of the Carol V. Ruppé Distinguished Service Award and presented it to its namesake. In the future an Award Committee comprised of the five SHA Past Presidents will select recipients for the award, a formal diploma under glass, as warranted.

STEPHANIE H. RODEFFER
ROBERT L. SCHUYLER

Carol V. Ruppé Distinguished Service Award
STEPHANIE HOLSCHLAG RODEFFER

When I was asked to be the presenter of the 1994 Society for Historical Archaeology Carol V. Ruppé Distinguished Service Award to Dr. Stephanie Rodeffer, I was both flattered and emotional. Emotional because, in various university classes I teach, I have for years used Tef Rodeffer as a role model of a highly successful career professional. I have frequently outlined for both women and men in those classes how Tef exemplifies, in the late 20th century, how women can be highly successful professionally yet give freely of their time to organizations in which they strongly believe and be a spouse in a warm and sharing marriage.

When I attended my first SHA board meeting in April 1978 it was my impression that Tef had been Secretary-Treasurer for several years. She seemed to know everything there was to know about the Society, and the Board members deferred to her for a variety of information. It was not until some months later that I realized she had assumed her position only several months before that April meeting.

Clearly from the moment Tef assumed the Secretary-Treasurer office she immersed herself in the affairs of the SHA and has never looked back. It is largely because of her diligence, understanding of fiscal matters, administrative talent, and ability to work effectively with persons of all personalities that the SHA has matured into one of the two most powerful scholarly archaeological societies in America. It is certainly no accident that the Society has grown and matured under her guardianship.

Historical Archaeology, 1994, 28(1):1–4.
Permission to reprint required.

Dr. Rodeffer began her anthropology career at the University of Kentucky from where she graduated in 1969, Phi Beta Kappa with High Distinction, and with Departmental Honors in Anthropology. Tef entered Kentucky with the intention of specializing in equitation. After a bout with peritonitis, subsequent corrective surgery, and an anthropology course or two, she changed her major—apparently some things are just meant to be. She entered Washington State University's Ph.D. program in anthropology as a National Defense Education Act (NDEA) Fellow in Fall 1969, was A.B.D. by December 1972, and was granted her doctorate in Spring 1975.

Tef's first archaeological field work was as a crew member on a 1967 University of South Carolina project on the Keowee River in the upper part of the state. During the summer of 1968, Tef served as a crew member on a Kentucky river basin project and participated in Southern Methodist University's (SMU) field school at the Ft. Burgwin Research Center near Taos, New Mexico. She returned to Ft. Burgwin in 1969 and 1970 to serve as an assistant in the archaeological field schools at Pot Creek Pueblo under the supervision of Dr. Fred Wendorf and Dr. Joel Shiner. Tef also participated in the analysis and write-up of materials from the Nez Perce Grave Removal Project under the supervision of Dr. Roderick Sprague in 1971 and 1972.

Tef met Michael Rodeffer on the Kentucky reservoir project in 1968, and they were married in September 1971. They moved to South Carolina in early 1973. That summer Tef taught anthropology at Montana State University and in the Fall joined the faculty at Lander College. Between 1974 and 1977, Tef directed two Lander College archaeological field schools at the Ninety Six Historic Site and participated in various other grant and contract projects at Ninety Six and around the state.

In 1977 Tef began a professional career with the National Park Service (NPS) in Atlanta, Georgia, where her organizational, administrative, and intellectual talents were quickly recognized by Dr. Bennie C. Keel who was Chief, Interagency Archaeological Services-Atlanta (Georgia). While at the Atlanta office Tef was acting chief in 1979–1980, but her greatest accomplishment and contribution to historical archaeology was securing equal status for historical alongside prehistoric archaeology in the Tombigbee Waterway Project. At that time the Tombigbee project was the largest budget archaeology project which the federal government had funded. Dr. Rodeffer not only secured equal project status for historical archaeology, but she managed the project historical research. Later, the research model which she developed was used as the research design for the Richard B. Russell Dam and Reservoir Project.

From 1980 through 1982 Tef was Archaeologist at the Southwest Regional office of HCRS in Albuquerque/Sante Fe, New Mexico, where she received a National Park Service Unit Award for excellence.

In 1982 she relocated to Philadelphia where she was an archaeologist in the Division of Cultural Programs in the Mid-Atlantic Region until 1984. In June 1984 she was appointed Acting Chief of the Preservation Planning Branch for the National Park Service, Mid-Atlantic office. Two years later, within months of the time when her husband, Mike, finally was able for the first time in about eight years to synchronize his archaeology career with that of Tef's and move to Philadelphia so they could live together normally, Tef was promoted to Chief of Interagency Archaeological Services' Branch at the National Park Service Western Regional office in San Francisco. Tef and Mike cheerfully moved to the Bay area. In August 1990 Tef was again rewarded for her administrative talents by the National Park Service when she was appointed Chief of the Museum Collections Repository at the Western Archaeological and Conservation Center in Tucson, Arizona.

As remarkable as her career with the National Park Service has been, it is in her volunteer service to the Society for Historical Archaeology that she has excelled to a level hard to comprehend. Few society members are aware of how unselfishly she has given of her time and for how many years she has given of huge blocks of her time. However, it is not only time which she has given to the SHA, but she has given her heart. Her service to the Society has not only been selfless but she has attended to the SHA interests as if the Society were part of her soul. She has, year after year, protected the Society's assets from assault by the SHA Board of Directors. Were it not for Tef the Society's financial position would not be rock-solid. She is the undisputed champion of honest, accurate, but cleverly prepared budgets—budgets that do not allow Board members to easily fund their pet projects by gobbling up needed general operating funds so that the Society is forced to deficit-spend by cutting into needed capital reserves.

In the same manner as she protects the Society's finances, she has a rare talent for being able to respond perfectly to every letter or query she receives from the membership. Tef graciously acknowledges letters of compliment and with a most deft pen responds to letters of complaint. Her ability through the years to reply promptly, fairly, and tactfully to disgruntled as well as outraged members has resulted in the Society receiving negligible negative correspondence. In this area we, as well as the National Park Service, are fortunate. It is not frequently that a scholarly society officer possesses the interpersonal skills that Tef brings to the SHA.

Despite the care which Tef gives to the Society's finances and correspondence, she also chooses to annually sacrifice an opportunity to listen to the various papers presented at the SHA annual meeting. From essentially the moment the Business office at the meeting is open, Tef occupies a chair beside the Business Manager or operates the office herself. Most SHA conference attendees likely believe she is paid to be present to sell Society publications, answer questions about dues, or generally act as the Society public relations officer. Like everything Tef does for the Society, she sells the SHA to anybody who will listen to her. She does not do this because she expects something in return. She promotes the SHA because she believes in its worth. And above all, she is not obligated by her job description as Secretary-Treasurer to give her time to the Society in this manner.

Why does Tef give so unselfishly of her time, talent, and energy to the SHA? Only she actually knows, but I suspect that it is because she loves to interact with people, strongly believes in the importance of historical archaeology to understanding our heritage, and feels that anything worth doing is worth doing well. In reviewing how she has served the Society, it is clear that it will be decades before another member will be able to amass a service record to match that of Stephanie Rodeffer. Her service to the Society even started before she was a member of any SHA committee or held an office in the organization. When Mike Rodeffer was Society Secretary-Treasurer, 1975–1977, Tef shared the work load by stuffing the SHA journal, *Historical Archaeology,* into envelopes and preparing it and the Society *Newsletter* for bulk mailing. I still vividly remember Tef describing a garage filled with Society publications where she sat on the floor stuffing envelopes and pasting on mailing labels as the hours of the night diminished.

Tef's first formal assignment for the Society was as membership chairperson from 1976 to 1979, and this job overlapped more than one year with her first term of office as the SHA Secretary-Treasurer. She assumed those responsibilities in 1978 and, as is well known, she was elected last fall to a fifth term of office. During those 16 years she has also annually chaired the SHA Budget Committee and has served on countless other SHA committees.

Nobody has ever put more of herself or himself into serving the SHA than Tef. In the early 1980s, when problems developed with the SHA Business office, Tef responded as if she were to blame for the difficulties and devoted untold unpaid hours to perform the duties of the business manager. Only when all the problems were solved, a new business manager selected, and the membership needs were totally satisfied was Tef happy. Her resolution to have the SHA run like a well-oiled machine has been perhaps the most significant factor in the Society's rapid maturation into a leading force in American archaeology. Tef normally stands quietly in the background smiling when the Society or any of its leaders are recognized for their contributions to historical archaeology, but without the thousands of hours of volunteer time and quality effort which she has unselfishly donated, the Society, its officers, board members, and the profession would not be smiling today. Dr. Stephanie Rodeffer is a role model of what all parents and professors dream for their offspring and students. She is a leader with dedication, determination, great intelligence, compassion, and a big heart. She has been the heart of the Society for Historical Archaeology for over one and one-half decades.

RONALD L. MICHAEL

Carol V. Ruppé Distinguished Service Award: Ronald L. Michael, 1998. Volume 32, Number 2 (1998): 2-6.
By Stephanie Holschlag Rodeffer.

Carol V. Ruppé Distinguished Service Award

RONALD L. MICHAEL 1998

The Society for Historical Archaeology created the Carol V. Ruppé Distinguished Service Award in 1990 to honor those individuals who have contributed sustained, outstanding service to the society. These award winners have promoted "archaeological and historical studies by advocating scientific research, interdisciplinary cooperation, professional standards, conservation of historical resources, and dissemination of knowledge" (The Society for Historical Archaeology 1996:A5-2). Our 1998 recipient, Dr. Ronald L. Michael, is a model of dedication and commitment to the organization and to those cherished ideals. Every member of this society who has received an early morning, late night, or weekend call from Ronn in pursuit of his editorial responsibilities, recognizes the vast amount of time he has so generously committed to the advancement of historical archaeology and the society. As the beneficiary of thousands of these calls myself, not to mention being the person who pays Ronn's telephone bills, I can attest to the diligence with which he has served the society as its editor for nearly twenty years.

Like many historical archaeologists, Ronn came to the field by a circuitous route through other disciplines. Ronn began reassessing his undergraduate physics major when he realized that he was not interested in spending his professional life in a laboratory. He refocused his studies to incorporate history after experiencing the enticements of a summer ranger-historian position at Grand

Historical Archaeology, 1998, 32(2):2–6.
Permission to reprint required.

Portage National Monument and observing Alan Woolworth's excavations. After receiving a Bachelor of Science degree in physics and history from Jamestown College, North Dakota, in 1963, he completed a Master of Arts degree in American history with an anthropology minor at the University of North Dakota in 1965. Membership in Lambda Alpha and Phi Alpha Theta, national honor societies in anthropology and history, respectively, recognized his commitment to excellence. With aspirations to teach history in a wealthy suburban Chicago high school, Ronn received offers from those schools to teach physics and coach tennis. Finally he accepted a position as instructor of history and tennis coach at Lakeland College, Sheboygan, Wisconsin.

Shortly thereafter Ronn began seeking a doctoral program in historical archaeology that would enable him to combine American history and anthropology, but he found little encouragement from most universities. The graduate history program at Ball State University was receptive to incorporating archaeology, and Ronn received an Doctorate of Education degree in 1969 in social science with an emphasis in anthropology/archaeology. He accepted the position of Associate Professor of Anthropology in the Social Science Department at California University of Pennsylvania in 1969 and was elevated to Professor in 1972. Ronn has chaired and participated on a variety of university committees and since 1970 has directed the university's archaeology programs and administered the Center for Prehistoric and Historic Site Archaeology. These duties have included supervising field and laboratory programs at prehistoric and historic sites, managing field records and artifact collections, and soliciting grants and foundation support for the program. As Project Manager/Principal Investigator, Ronn directed the completion of nearly twenty grants and contracts he secured from 1979 to 1988.

In 1973, Ronn began his extensive suite of volunteer activities by accepting editorship of *Pennsylvania Archaeologist,* a position he held for 21 years. In the late 1970s he edited *Northeast Historical Archaeology* and served as an executive board member of the Council for Northeast Historical Archaeology. During the next decade Ronn also edited the *Eastern States Archaeological Federation Bulletin* and served as a member and chair of the Pennsylvania Review Committee for the National Register of Historic Places, vice-chair of the Commonwealth Historic Preservation Board, President of the Pennsylvania Archaeological Council, and the Pennsylvania Representative to the Committee on Public Archaeology, Society for American Archaeology. Ronn directed more than 150 survey, determination of eligibility, and data recovery projects under the auspices of his corporation, NPW Consultants, Inc., from 1978 to 1994.

Ronn accepted the position as SHA editor in early 1978, just as the society was beginning to experience a membership explosion and the diversification that accompanied the emergence of cultural resource management (Deagan 1992:19). Many new members were not historical archaeologists, but sought information to recognize and address historic archaeological resources in the context of their new responsibilities. Despite this urgent need for visibility, production of the annual journal was two years in arrears and the society's only active outlets for promoting historical archaeology were the quarterly newsletter and the annual conference (Schuyler 1992:36). The need for a committed, productive editor was critical.

The society was extremely fortunate that Ronn's accomplishments in his life before SHA and the society's needs were so closely aligned when he accepted the editorship. His personal struggle to secure a PhD that combined American history and anthropology paralleled the difficulties of the emerging discipline of historical archaeology. His service as editor of *Northeast Historical Archaeology, Pennsylvania Archaeologist,* and the *Eastern States Archaeological Federation Bulletin* honed his editorial skills, established an enviable record of producing timely publications, and provided critical experience with the operation of other voluntary organizations. Ronn's personal diversification also paralleled the changes experienced by the society. His position in the academic community provided a strong foothold in the traditional home of historic archaeological interests. Simultaneously, his service on the Pennsylvania Historical Review Board and the Pennsylvania Archaeological Council and his corporate involvement in conducting cultural resource management projects embraced the profound changes in the profession. Ronn's multidimensional experiences positioned him well to be responsive to the rapidly changing needs of the society.

Ronn has executed his responsibilities as editor with energy, enthusiasm, dedication, and creativity and his tenure is marked by expansion, change, and constancy. In 1978 he inherited an annual journal with an uncertain future and a checkered past, and few "exceptionally brilliant or especially enlightening manuscripts" (Adams 1993:26) awaiting publication. Through his personal commitment and dedication, and the help of Associate Editors Ronald Carlisle and later Donna Seifert, Ronn quickly transformed the annual journal into a timely and respected professional publication. Despite early opposition from some quarters, Ronn promoted the critical need to expand the journal to improve recognition of historical archaeology. The first semi-annual issues appeared in 1981 and *Historical Archaeology* emerged as a quarterly in 1990.

As the number of journals increased, Ronn refined the infrastructure to support their production. The initial associate editor and book reviews editor became a cadre of ten associate editors (now constituting the core of the Editorial Advisory Committee), without whose countless hours of nurturing manuscripts the journal could not be produced at such a reasonable cost to the membership. Ronn coordinates their activities, solicits their counsel, and personally encourages their voluntary contributions. Sarah Turnbaugh began part-time service as the society's copy editor in 1988 and has served with distinction to improve the quality and consistency of the society's publications. Ronn's personal involvement in and commitment to this volunteer editorial "staff" have enabled the society's journal to expand far beyond the level that only membership dues could support.

Despite the challenges of managing this ambitious editorial enterprise primarily through volunteers, Ronn has continually sought new avenues to expand the publications program. During 1984 he revitalized the *Special Publications Series* that had languished for nearly a decade, as an outlet for thematic issues before they became a regular feature of *Historical Archaeology*. He experimented with the production of the *Proceedings of the Conference on Underwater Archaeology* as *Special Publication* No. 4 in 1985 before accepting the opportunity to produce the volume annually in a new series beginning in 1987, now titled *Underwater Archaeology*. This new responsibility required Ronn to develop a different editorial structure and work with an annually rotating editor who also serves as the underwater program chair for the annual conference. Although the complexities involved in editing and producing this volume greatly increased Ronn's personal contribution to the society, he embraced this additional work to emphasize the society's commitment to our underwater colleagues.

In honor of the Columbus Quincentenary the society inaugurated a new publication entitled, *Guides to the Archaeological Literature of the Immigrant Experience in America* in 1990. Ronn again expanded his commitment to the organization to oversee the production of five guides from 1990 to 1997. These bibliographies, with their critical analysis of the literature, were designed to facilitate the identification and use of the diverse, often obscure, published references on historical archaeology. The society's first reader, entitled *Approaches to Material Culture Research for Historical Archaeologists*, developed primarily by George Miller in 1991 for the academic market, has become a widely accepted text in many universities for courses in historical archaeology.

Recently Ronn initiated alternative format publications for the society. Just last year he coordinated the production of the society's first CD-ROM containing the initial 23 volumes of *Historical*

Archaeology. This already promises to be a best seller—it allows the society to offer the knowledge contained in the earliest issues of the journal at an affordable price. The integral search engine replaces the need for separate, but financially taxing indexes.

Ronn also has realigned the editorial infrastructure in response to recognized needs and technological improvements. For example, nearly a decade ago the society discovered during a survey that some groups in the organization believed themselves to be underrepresented in the percentages of published papers and disenfranchised from the book review process. Although a review of journal articles and reviews revealed the opposite trend, Ronn initiated workshops at the annual conference to help new authors and worked diligently with the reviews editor to expand review opportunities.

During the past two years Ronn has grappled with the myriad of changes necessary to incorporate the society's new corporate image into the publications program, the full magnitude of which were not known until implementation began. As the society moves to disseminating information through electronic media, his involvement in the inception of the society's web page and continued contributions to its development and maintenance bring new dimensions to the editorship. Ronn's current challenge is the conversion of the editorial process to electronic publishing, an effort not without difficulty in 1997. His already considerable skill in the publishing process is augmented daily as he and the publishing industry adapt to the "benefits" of new technology.

Throughout the expansion of the publications program and the changes in infrastructure and technology, Ronn's constant commitment to furthering the goals of the society has never wavered. The profession would greatly benefit from archaeologists, young and old, who emulate Ronn's extensive and generous contributions to historical archaeology. Just as Ronn has given freely of his time and talents to historical archaeology, the extraordinary value of his contributions should challenge each of us to make these commitments to our profession and to ourselves:

—to be satisfied with nothing less than the advancement of knowledge about historical archaeology through active publication of scholarly documentation;

—to invest our personal time and resources in advancing the interests of this organization and historical archaeology in the broader public context; and

—to explore creatively new opportunities, as he has done, to expand the society's horizons and promote historical archaeology in ways that reach beyond the organization's limited financial resources.

Ronn, your legacy to the society is more than 10,000 printed pages that document the evolution of the discipline. These pages are the voice of our society for the future, enabling researchers to build on the record of the past. The chosen media, including the emerging electronic formats, have enabled historical archaeologists to reach wider and wider audiences with new ideas. Your work is a selfless example of dedication to the goals and ideals of the society and an inspiration for the future, challenging new scholars to build on the past you have given us with equal enthusiasm, fairness, creativity, and tenacity. Your friends and colleagues salute you for your leadership and devotion to this organization and to all it represents.

REFERENCES

ADAMS, WILLIAM HAMPTON
    1993 Historical Archaeology Strove for Maturity in the Mid-1980s. *Historical Archaeology* 27(1):23-31.

DEAGAN, KATHLEEN
    1993 Retrospective on The Society for Historical Archaeology 1997-1982. *Historical Archaeology* 27(1):19-22.

SCHUYLER, ROBERT L.
1993   The Society for Historical Archaeology, 1967-1992: A Quarter Century of a National Archaeological Society. *Historical Archaeology* 27(1):35-41.

THE SOCIETY FOR HISTORICAL ARCHAEOLOGY
1996   Procedures Manual. Manuscript, Business Office, The Society for Historical Archaeology, Tucson, AZ.

STEPHANIE HOLSCHLAG RODEFFER
6828 EAST TIVANI DRIVE
TUCSON, AZ 85715

Carol V. Ruppé Distinguished Service Award: Norman F. Barka, 2001. Volume 35, Number 4 (2001): 4-7. By Marley R. Brown III.

Carol V. Ruppé Distinguished Service Award

Norman F. Barka 2001

Dr. Norman F. Barka was in attendance at the first annual meeting of The Society for Historical Archaeology when it was convened at the Williamsburg Lodge in January 1968 under the auspices of Colonial Williamsburg and its then Director of Archaeology, Ivor Noël Hume. That year Norm was beginning the sixth semester of his distinguished career as a faculty member in the Department of Anthropology at the College of William and Mary, a position he took up in the academic year immediately following the award of his Ph.D. in Anthropology by Harvard University in 1965. At William and Mary Norm has created one of the most important academic programs in historical archaeology anywhere in the world. Thirty-five years of extremely effective pedagogy later, Norm's students, undergraduate and graduate, are placed at all levels of our profession, including prominent positions in academe, the museum world, and government.

Norm's track record with undergraduates reaches back to the beginning of his appointment at William and Mary and in a very important way he has established a tradition much like that of Beloit College, where he did his own undergraduate training in anthropology, graduating in 1960.

Both Beloit and the College of William and Mary have produced an unusually large number of very successful professional anthropologists relative to the overall size of their student bodies and their faculties in anthropology. In the fall of 1979 Norm welcomed the first class of Master's degree students to the Department of Anthropology, at the College of William and Mary and began his more than twenty years as graduate director, a job that he has done with the greatest of skill and compassion. This month, Norm will be able to add his carefully considered opinions to the selection of the first group of Ph.D. students in Anthropology to be admitted to the graduate program at William and Mary. The new doctoral program, emphasizing historical archaeology, was brought into being through Norm's own distinctive brand of single-minded (and quiet) persistence, and it is one that will depend on his contributions through both new Ph.D. course offerings he is preparing and through his active summer program of fieldwork, now centered on the islands of Bermuda and Guana (British Virgin Islands).

It is not Norman F. Barka's outstanding record of field research and teaching, however, that is being recognized by the society with the 2001 Carol V. Ruppe Distinguished Service Award. It is Norm Barka's tireless advocacy of historical archaeology through dedicated service to The Society for Historical Archaeology. After a decade of participating in the annual meeting, Norm joined the society's Board as president-elect in 1979, beginning what is now over two decades of year-in and year-out work for the society. Norm has done many noteworthy things for the society, including serving as President in 1980, staging an extremely successful 1984 annual meeting at the same hotel where the first one took place, representing the SHA to the Society for Post Medieval Archaeology, and helping put on the joint thirtieth anniversary observance of the two organizations. Most noteworthy of all, however, is Norman Barka's willingness to produce the society's *Newsletter*, four times a year for the past nineteen years (76 issues with a total of nearly 4,000 pages and still counting), and it is this commitment that has earned him the society's award for distinguished service in the year 2001.

The *Newsletter* has always been one of the most important benefits of membership in The Society for Historical Archaeology and it has improved with every passing year, testimony to the talents and dedication of all of its editors. At that first meeting in Dallas, the society's founding fathers, a group that came to be known as the "Special Committee," were very concerned that an annual publication of some sort begin as soon as possible. After a motion was passed to that effect, committee member Charles Fairbanks suggested that the society also publish a newsletter modeled after the Council For British Archaeology Calendar, a newsletter that would be the yearly responsibility of the society's officers. Others saw this as too time-consuming but a consensus emerged among the assembled group that some kind of reporting on current research should be done on a yearly basis. No clear decision about a newsletter format emerged during the organizational meeting, but the first issue of *Historical Archaeology* does contain a summary of research activities for 1967. Shortly thereafter the first volume of the society's official *Newsletter* appeared, under the editorship of David Armour. With the second volume, the *Newsletter* moved to Canada, where it would remain for thirteen years. With the support of Parks Canada in Ottawa, the *Newsletter* was produced by a series of editors including, successively, Jervis Swannack, Karlis Karklins, Charles Lindsey, and Lester Ross.

True to the vision of the society's original Special Committee, whose members agreed during their 1967 deliberations that an annual review of fieldwork was essential, the *Newsletter* served mainly a vehicle for communicating what society members were doing in the field. Organized by region from the beginning, the *Newsletter* became, for all of us, the main way to learn about what sites were being excavated, where, and by whom. From the *Newsletter* sent to society members in August 1971, for example, we learned that Dr. Barka had begun work on the excavation of the Poor Potter's site, arguably the best excavated and studied colonial pottery production site on record anywhere. The *Newsletter* of June 1973 identified Dr. Barka as the discoverer of the first enclosed settlement associated with an early 17th-century Virginia community known as a "Hundred," in this case, Flowerdew Hundred. It would be another several years before the better known (in the popular mind) Wolstenholme Town at Martin's Hundred was found. Frequent entries in the

Newsletter describe results of what has been the most sustained single research project in the historical archaeology of the Caribbean, when in 1981 Dr. Barka began fieldwork in St. Eustatius, a very small island still part of the Netherlands Antilles, that derives much of its historical significance from its status as a true free port during the colonial period. Subsequent issues report on his work on Bermuda, where along with colleague Edward Harris of the Bermuda Maritime Museum, Norm has excavated several of the earliest English colonial fortifications in the New World, as well as what may fairly be described as the oldest standing house built by English colonists to the New World, the Captain's House at King's Castle, a fort built in 1612.

These later references are in issues of the *Newsletter* produced under Norm Barka's editorship, but he has never used the office of *Newsletter* Editor to blow his own horn. These references are included simply to remind readers of the journal that despite the many hours that Norm has spent making sure that the rest of us have had a chance to report on our discoveries in the field or have our say on other professional and scholarly matters, he has managed to conduct his own annual research program, thereby exposing hundreds of students to his exacting standards of archaeological fieldwork.

Dr. Barka has had plenty of need to call upon the *Newsletter* to report his active field research. His effort has resulted in the discovery and recording of many of the most important archaeological sites excavated within the Chesapeake, the Caribbean, and Bermuda over the past three decades. Norm has been doing archaeology in the field since the mid 1950s, having had six full seasons of experience behind him before entering graduate school, including several stints with the River Basin Surveys, college semesters in Mexico, and two seasons with Bill Ritchie unraveling Owasco-Iroquois sites in upstate New York. At Harvard Norm became a Canadian specialist, working first in Saskatchewan, and subsequently in New Brunswick and Quebec. His dissertation at Harvard is concerned with materials he recovered from an early French fort and later loyalist trading post located in what he describes as a "slum neighborhood covered with derelict cars, drunken homeless people who slept in the cars, and bootleggers who were regularly raided by the Royal Canadian Mounted Police as we dug at the site." Perhaps this early experience with one kind of urban archaeology in St. John, New Brunswick explains Dr. Barka's more recent interests in places like Bermuda and the privately owned island of Guana, where he is researching the fascinating story of refugee Quakers who made their living growing sugar with slave labor.

In remaining true to his own calling as an academic historical archaeologist who believes in the importance instructing students within the context of careful and sustained field work, Norm has also had the foresight and energy to ensure that The Society for Historical Archaeology's *Newsletter* kept pace with the many changes that the profession has undergone since 1982. Twice, in 1988 and again in 1997, Norm has overseen substantial changes in the format of the *Newsletter*. Every year of his editorship he has added at least one, and usually two new features, ranging from columns and forums, to greatly expanded illustrations. In his nomination of Dr. Norman F. Barka for the Carol V. Ruppé Distinguished Service Award, Robert Schuyler observed that because of Norm Barka's ability to keep up with the changing times and anticipate features that would be of interest to the readership "the SHA *Newsletter* is without question the most impressive research summation outlet and one of the most recognized newsletters in world."

When asked to reflect on why he became an archaeologist, Norm Barka responded, "Its what I always wanted to be." He observed at last year's SHA meeting in Quebec City "In the end, historical archaeology is fun, an enjoyable way of life. I have been very fortunate in feeling that my job is really not a job. It is just something I do and think about for 24 hours a day." Among the things that Norm has done during his 24-hour days is put thousands of hours of his own time into making sure that all of us have the most up-to-date *Newsletter* we can have, four times a year, every year. It should also be noted that despite his already busy schedule, one made all the more hectic by the production of his first edition of the *Newsletter*, Norm Barka found the time to welcome me to Williamsburg in February, 1982. These nineteen years of SHA *Newsletters* later, he is still willing to find the time, and without his support and friendship I would never have been able to make any kind of success out of my position at Colonial Williamsburg.

Many of us who are members of The Society for Historical Archaeology are every bit as fortunate as Dr. Barka in that we also view our jobs as that which we think about and do 24 hours a day. Norm, however, unlike most of us, has made The Society for Historical Archaeology a substantial and integral part of his professional life. Putting out The Society for Historical Archaeology *Newsletter* on a quarterly basis is a major task. Upon even a moment's reflection, we all realize how much work is must really be and thus we stand in awe of Dr. Barka's accomplishment and congratulate him on the occasion of his recognition by The Society for Historical Archaeology as this year's recipient of the Carol V. Ruppé Distinguished Service Award.

MARLEY R. BROWN III

Carol V. Ruppé Distinguished Service Award

Roderick Sprague 2004

There are those of you who believe I have been the society editor from the beginning of time—part of a package deal when the society was founded. I want you to know that when I became the SHA editor in early 1978, Roderick Sprague was already the "Old Man of the SHA." Volunteerism according to many sources has been steadily declining in the United States for the past 25–50 years. It is now "me first" and "you second," or third, in a list of priorities. Rick either has not heard about this trend or has ignored it. He has actually had a professional career of volunteerism, giving freely of his time to students and his profession, while others found excuses as to why they could not help.

By the time I became the SHA editor, Rick had already served the society by being one of its founders, having attended the organizational meeting as well as being regional coordinator for research in the northwest from 1968 to 1977, general program chairperson for the second annual society meeting in 1969 (held in Tucson), a member of the board of directors for 1970 and 1971, secretary-treasurer from 1971 to 1974, and SHA president in 1976 (actually a three-year term with one year each as president-elect, president, and past president). Shortly before my appointment he had agreed to become a member of the editorial board and book reviews editor for *Historical Archaeology*. Being a gracious person, he offered to step aside so I could select "my own" review editor.

Actually, one of my best editorial decisions was to decline that offer. A better mentor would have been hard to find.

When we started working together I was essentially unknown to him, and I only knew him by professional reputation (had not heard about his personal reputation at that time). I have clear memories of our first contacts, thinking that my telephone company was to blame for bad service to Idaho. I now know that Rick is legendary for his telephone manner, but it was new to me in 1978. I would call Rick and he would answer. I would ask a question or make a comment, and then it seemed like the line had gone dead. I would shake the phone, thinking that maybe something was loose in my receiver, or wait for that dreaded automated voice giving me instructions about how I could make a call. Finally though, we were reconnected and I could hear Rick. As time passed, our telephone contacts normalized, and today I can call my friend and colleague and always share a pleasant but information-filled conversation.

Truly, I have learned that Rick gives of himself to others because he cares. He cares for his students, about historical archaeology, and people and believes part of his reason for existing is to share his talents with others, giving of his time to help others and causes in which he believes.

It would have been extremely easy for a person who had served the society so extensively and effectively during its first decade of existence to feel it was time for others to serve SHA. Fortunately, that is not part of Rick's nature. He has continued to the present to give generously of himself to society service.

Rick remained the SHA reviews editor from 1977 until he decided to retire from the job in 1997. During much of that time, beginning in 1984 and still today, he continues to serve as society parliamentarian; he remains an active member of the society Editorial Advisory Committee, essentially never missing a meeting or never refusing to chair or serve on subcommittees. Rick was society archivist from 1987 until 1998; and in 2002, shortly after resigning from a five-year period of being the society copy-editor contractor during which he standardized many editorial practices, he agreed to accept the position of associate copy editor. During the late 1980s and early 1990s, Rick (in his words) spent "five years of endless drudgery" working to put the historical archaeology bibliography (begun about 20 years earlier by John Cotter) into a publishable format. Shortly after the society established a Web site in the mid 1990s, the bibliography was posted on the SHA site as *A Bibliography of Historical Archaeology in North America*. He gave Cotter full credit for creating the bibliography.

In an unprecedented move, Rick was nominated from the floor to run for a second term as society president. From 1989–1991 he again graciously and actively served the society as its president-elect, president, and past president. Was this enough SHA volunteerism for Rick? Certainly not! Today he still is an active member of the Editorial Advisory Committee, is associate copy editor, serves on the History Committee, is the Inter-Society Relations Committee representative to the Council on America's Military Past, and, in 2003, agreed to chair a subcommittee on curation policy. Rick has served on and chaired many additional SHA committees, but when asked for a list, he responded that there are "far too many" committees to note.

A full career of volunteerism to SHA! However, Rick has and still volunteers his time just as freely to other endeavors, especially the Society of Bead Researchers and editing the *Journal of Northwest Anthropology* for 36 years. All this volunteerism Roderick Sprague has done in addition to having a highly visible, busy, full, and lustrous career as an academician and researcher—contributions already recognized by his receipt in 2000 of The Society for Historical Archaeology J. C. Harrington Medal, an award recognizing individuals for lifetime achievement in historical archaeology. A summary of Rick's professional career and full presentation of all his accomplishments in historical archaeology can be found in *Historical Archaeology* 34 (4):1–6.

Rick is possibly The Society for Historical Archaeology's greatest asset—a volunteer of the highest order for almost four decades.

RONN MICHAEL

Carol V. Ruppé Distinguished Service Award

Vergil E. Noble

January of 1976 saw the United States kick off its bicentennial celebration. It was no coincidence that the Society for Historical Archaeology (SHA) met in Philadelphia that year, a place pivotal in the early history of the nation and where historical archaeology was coming of age under the guidance of scholars such as John Cotter and Robert Schuyler. In 1976, SHA was not yet 10 years old. In attendance at Philadelphia was a young graduate student from Michigan State University by the name of Vergil E. Noble. This was his first SHA conference, and he has not missed one since.

Vergil had joined SHA in 1975 and he soon adopted this organization as his professional home. Through the years he has given freely of his time to support SHA's mission. Dr. Noble is recognized by the SHA by presentation of the Carol V. Ruppé Distinguished Service Award for 2011, "For exceptional and sustained service to the programs, professionalism, and governance of the Society."

The Ruppé Award was established by the SHA in 1988 and is named in honor of Carol V. Ruppé for her many years of service to the organization in creating and managing the bookroom at the annual conference. The award was first presented to Carol Ruppé in 1990 at the conference in Baltimore. The award is given only to SHA members in recognition of their "sustained and truly outstanding service to the Society for Historical Archaeology." This year's award to Dr. Noble is only the fifth Ruppé Award to be presented.

Vergil E. Noble was born in 1952 in Detroit, Michigan, the fourth of four children. His mother, Arliene, was an elementary school teacher, and his father, Vergil, was a crane operator for an automotive parts supplier. He grew up in the suburbs north of Detroit, and according to his recently published account, his "first memorable glimpse of our profession, at age nine or ten, was obtained while watching the Three Stooges short *We Want Our Mummy* (1939)" (Noble 2007:224). He attended Lincoln High School in Warren (this was about 20 years before vocal artist Eminem graced those same halls), where, impressed with his chemistry teacher, he fancied for himself a career teaching high school chemistry. He set his sights on attending college at Michigan State University (MSU) and was admitted for the fall of 1970. During summer orientation, however, he made a life-changing decision by choosing to study archaeology rather than chemistry.

Although he found that he could not pursue Maya archaeology at MSU as he had hoped, he soon found his way to the MSU museum. There he met Professor Charles E. Cleland, who put him to work as a volunteer in the archaeology lab in the fall of 1972. The basement of the museum was an archaeological incubator for many students, as this was where faculty and graduate students focusing on the eastern United States and historical archaeology had their offices.

In 1973, Vergil accompanied graduate student Pat Martin to the Mill Creek site, a late-British–early American milling complex at the Straits of Mackinac. At Mill Creek, Vergil's interest in historical archaeology was unleashed. The next summer he worked for graduate student Judy Tordoff on MSU's project at the 18th-century French colonial site of Fort Ouiatenon, near Lafayette, Indiana. His research interests have ever since included French colonial studies.

Vergil graduated with a B.S. degree with honors in anthropology in spring 1974 and spent the summer and fall working on a variety of archaeological projects in the Great Lakes and upper Midwest. That winter, Vergil decided to apply for graduate study at MSU and was admitted for the fall of 1975.

Vergil's graduate career lasted from 1975 through 1984. In 1976, I began my graduate studies at MSU and soon found myself sharing an office with Vergil in the basement of the museum. We have been close friends ever since, and our paths have crossed repeatedly in SHA, in the former Society of Professional Archaeologists (SOPA), and in the Register of Professional Archaeologists (RPA).

In 1976, Vergil returned to Fort Ouiatenon as Judy Tordoff's field assistant and took over the project in 1977. He worked at this site for three seasons and used this research as the basis for his dissertation. He was awarded an M.A. in 1979 and a Ph.D. in 1983, both in anthropology with a focus in historical archaeology.

His major professor at MSU was Charles Cleland, who instilled in Vergil and many of his other students, myself included, a strong sense of professionalism and service. While completing his doctorate, Vergil held an instructorship with the Department of Anthropology and a research associate position with the MSU museum. Following award of a Ph.D. in 1983, Vergil stayed on at MSU for another year to teach in the anthropology department as a sabbatical replacement for Dr. Cleland and to undertake postdoctoral study in history.

In 1984, Vergil took the position of director of the Midwestern Archaeological Research Center at Illinois State University (ISU) that was open due to the retirement of Ed Jelks. While at ISU, he was also assistant professor in the Department of Sociology and Anthropology. Between 1985 and 1987, he served on the board of directors of the Center for French Colonial Studies (he is a founding member of this organization) and as a councilor of the Illinois Historic Sites Advisory Council (National Register Review Board). In 1985, he received the Research Initiation Award for program development from ISU. In 1987, he received the certificate of merit for "significant contributions to historic preservation" from the Illinois Historic Preservation Agency.

In 1987, Dr. Noble made what he thought would be a brief stop at the Midwest Archeological Center (MWAC) of the National Park Service (NPS) in Lincoln, Nebraska. This year, however, is Vergil's 24th at MWAC. His fieldwork there initially focused on cultural resources at parks within the NPS Midwest Region, including work along the Ohio and Erie Canal, a series of homes of U.S. presidents, and fur-trade sites in Arkansas and Minnesota. He currently works in the external National Register/National Historic Landmarks programs, where he prepares nominations, provides technical assistance to stewards, and monitors conditions of listed properties. Notable was his assistance in coordinating Charlotte King's (University of Maryland) successful nomination of the historic New

Philadelphia town site in Illinois, leading to its designation as a National Historic Landmark in 2009 on the basis of archaeological research significance.

In 1993, Vergil was awarded a special achievement award by the superintendent of Cuyahoga Valley Recreational Area (now National Park), for his research on the Ohio and Erie Canal, and in 1996 the Omaha-Lincoln Federal Executive Association named him employee of the year in the professional/scientific achievement category. In Lincoln, Vergil has also had a long association with the University of Nebraska, where he has served as adjunct professor of anthropology (graduate faculty) since 1987.

The Carol V. Ruppé Distinguished Service Award is presented to Dr. Noble as he attends his 36th consecutive SHA annual meeting. During that time, he has presented 11 papers, co-organized 3 symposia, organized 3 luncheon workshops, served as discussant for 6 symposia, and participated in 5 discussion panels. Since 1979, Vergil has published 9 articles and 11 book reviews in *Historical Archaeology*, and served as coeditor of a thematic issue of the journal. He has published extensively elsewhere as well.

Laudable as his record of attendance and scholarly contribution may be, the SHA is here recognizing Vergil's sustained service that began in 1983 when his name was placed in nomination as a candidate for a seat on the SHA Board of Directors. Although his bid was unsuccessful, he has from that time forward given unselfishly to the organization through service in multiple arenas.

The next year, 1984, he was appointed by *SHA Newsletter* Editor Norman Barka to serve the *SHA Newsletter* as contributing editor for Midwest Current Research. He served in this capacity until 1993, and then between 1994 and 1997 as contributing editor for Great Plains Current Research.

In the early 1990s, Vergil signed on as program coordinator for the SHA Conference on Historical and Underwater Archaeology that was held in January of 1993 in snowbound Kansas City, Missouri. Vergil and I had been talking of organizing an SHA conference for some time, and finally put together an invitation to bring SHA to Kansas City. I talked the Kansas State Historical Society (KSHS) into hosting the conference and volunteered to serve as general conference chair. Vergil agreed to serve as program coordinator and terrestrial program chair, although in reality his contribution was as co-chair of the conference. Another KSHS employee, Carolyn Wallingford, served as local arrangements chair. This is remarkable because Vergil and Carolyn worked so well together that they were married in September following the conference.

In 1994, shortly after Kansas City, Vergil assumed additional responsibility with the SHA Membership Committee. He co-chaired this committee for three years. Also in 1994, Vergil broadened his commitment to the SHA publications program when he agreed to serve as memorials editor for *Historical Archaeology*. This garnered him a position on the editorial advisory committee that he has, fortunately, yet to relinquish. As memorials editor, between 1994 and 1997, he worked with authors during what was inevitably the highly emotional process of preparing memorials for departed colleagues and friends. During his tenure, he coordinated preparation of memorials for Reynold J. Ruppé (by Geoffrey A. Clark and Kent G. Lightfoot), Carlyle Shreeve Smith (by Roger T. Grange, Jr.), John H. Rick (by Max Sutherland), Arnold Remington Pilling (by George L. Miller), and Kenneth Earl Kidd (by Susan M. Jamieson).

The 1994 nominations and elections committee again placed Dr. Noble in nomination as a candidate for the SHA Board of Directors. This time he was duly elected and served on the board from 1995 through 1997. During his term on the board, he was appointed to coordinate a major revision of the SHA Procedures Manual, which he completed in 1997.

That same year he was elected to serve as the SHA representative on the SOPA Board of Directors, a position he held through 1998. He had previously served a term as at-large director on the SOPA board between 1991 and 1993, as grievance coordinator between 1995 and 1997, and as chair of the membership and awards committees. In 1995, he received the SOPA Presidential Recognition Award for service to that organization.

His service as SHA representative to the SOPA board was a critically important assignment, as it was during this period that SOPA went through a very difficult internal analysis. This ultimately led to a decision to disband the organization in favor of a new incarnation, the RPA. Of importance, however, is that this transformation relied on the acceptance of a proposal for the creation of RPA by the board and membership of SOPA, and by the boards of partnering organizations: SHA, the Society for American Archaeology, the American Anthropological Association, and the Archaeological Institute of America; this in itself was no small feat.

I was president of SOPA at that time, and I can personally attest that Vergil's dedication to ethical professional behavior and his precise analytical mind made him a valuable member of the discussion that reinvented SOPA as RPA. His dedication to SHA's interests helped to ensure that the society remained a strong partner in the relationship with RPA. RPA is today succeeding because of the debate and planning that occurred during Vergil's tenure as SHA's representative to the SOPA board during 1997 and 1998.

With the creation of RPA in 1998, the SOPA board went into suspension, and the officers and directors became the transitional board for RPA. Vergil continued to represent the interests of SHA during these important first few years, serving as SHA's appointed representative on the RPA board from 1998 through 2000.

Between 1997 and 2001, Vergil served as reviews editor for *Historical Archaeology*. During a period of explosive growth in publications relevant to the field, Vergil placed books with reviewers and got most of these reviews into the pages of *Historical Archaeology* through the use of his organizational, editorial, and persuasive skills. Vergil edited 202 reviews published in volumes 31 through 35.

The 2000 SHA Nominations and Elections Committee again called Vergil to service as a candidate for the position of president-elect. Vergil's election was confirmed, and he took office at the business meeting at the 2001 SHA conference in Long Beach, California, aboard the *Queen Mary*.

During his term as president-elect, he chaired a search committee for an association management firm for SHA. The society had conducted a previous failed search, and Vergil was tasked with undertaking another. At that time, SHA was being managed largely by volunteers, but with an annual contract with SHA member Michael Rodeffer's firm, Backcountry Archaeological Services, to provide business office services. The move toward a professional management firm was deemed necessary because of the growing administrative demands of the organization that were increasingly taxing its volunteer base. This was, however, uncharted territory for SHA, and the committee worked diligently to put together a scope of services and a review process that resulted in selection of a firm that managed SHA for the next several years.

Testament to Dr. Noble's breadth of influence, in 2001, while serving as SHA President-Elect, he was asked to serve on the steering committee that led the way for the transformation of the long-standing Midwestern Archaeological Conference from an informal but successful regional meeting to a formally incorporated scholarly organization. On the completion of this task, Vergil was asked to chair the nominations committee charged with selecting the first slate of candidates for office in this new organization.

In January 2002, at a time of great national anxiety following the 11 September terrorist attacks on the United States, Vergil took office as SHA president at the annual meeting in Mobile, Alabama. I joined the board as *SHA Newsletter* editor at the same time. Previously, in 2000, Vergil had put together a proposal for the NPS to host the 2004 SHA conference in St. Louis, for which he would serve as general conference chair. During his year as president, Vergil therefore undertook the normal duties of the president, was involved in general planning for an upcoming SHA conference, and presided over what proved to be a very difficult and ultimately unsuccessful transition to a new professional-association management firm.

As president, Vergil focused attention on defining the proper relationship between the SHA and the Advisory Council on Underwater Archaeology (ACUA) as part of a comprehensive analysis and revision of the SHA constitution and bylaws that was also ongoing at that time. The ACUA had long been associated with SHA, which is duly reflected in the annual meeting carrying the name, "Conference on Historical *and* Underwater Archaeology." But in 2002, ACUA was both an independently incorporated not-for-profit organization and constitutionally defined as a standing committee of the SHA. This was at best administratively awkward, and worked as well as it did only because of the good intentions of parties on both sides of this equation.

During his term, Vergil began formal discussions and committee work with the ACUA leadership that ultimately led to the crafting of a memorandum of agreement between SHA and ACUA that recognized the independence of each while codifying a close relationship based on mutual pursuit of a common good. Almost a decade later, this work that was begun in 2002 has resulted in a strong and increasingly symbiotic relationship between SHA and ACUA, which is a tribute to the vision of Dr. Noble and all who have participated along the way.

At the 2003 conference in Providence, Rhode Island, Vergil began his term as immediate past-president and continued his service as the general conference chair for the following conference in St. Louis. Vergil's service as general conference chair during the period leading up to the 2004 meeting was made difficult by the unreliable performance of SHA's management firm. This and a host of other issues led the SHA board to terminate this management contract during the board meeting at the St. Louis conference. Despite questionable support from SHA's contracted management firm, but because of Vergil's leadership and the strength of the society's volunteer base, the St. Louis conference came off without a hitch and is remembered fondly in a long line of excellent SHA conferences. Vergil has since recovered from that year of exhaustion and frustration.

Also in 2003, in his capacity as immediate past-president, Vergil served as chair of the nominations and elections committee and also agreed to chair a committee formed to search for a new editor for *Historical Archaeology*. Retiring editor Ronald L. Michael had overseen production of the journal since 1978, and it had been a very long time since a search for this position had been conducted. Vergil's committee conducted a successful search that resulted in the recommendation of Rebecca Allen for appointment as the next editor of *Historical Archaeology*.

At the close of his term as immediate past-president in January of 2004, Vergil took a bit of a breather, though he continued service on the editorial advisory committee. In 2007, he agreed to chair the committee to search for my replacement as *SHA Newsletter* editor after two terms in this position. This search committee recommended the appointment of Alasdair Brooks, who has brought a welcome global perspective to the *SHA Newsletter* and to the board.

In 2008, Vergil was appointed as SHA parliamentarian upon the retirement of Roderick Sprague from many years of service in this position. Vergil continues to occupy this position which takes advantage of his keen procedural mind, fairness, and thorough knowledge of SHA that has served him and SHA well throughout the past 25 years. I am pleased to report that his appointment as SHA parliamentarian has been renewed for another three years.

Since 1984, Dr. Vergil E. Noble has been involved in constant service to the SHA. During that time, he has helped advance the organization's major programs, especially publications and conferences. He has worked tirelessly to advance the society's standards of ethics and professionalism, as is exemplified by his important service as SHA's representative during the reinvention of SOPA as RPA. He has been steadfast in his dedication to SHA governance, as evident by his two terms on the board of directors (one as president), by his work on committees and task forces, and by his current service as parliamentarian. Best of all, however, is that I can confidently say that Dr. Noble is far from being finished with SHA. For what he has done, and for what he will accomplish for the organization in the future, SHA offers its respectful gratitude.

References

NOBLE, VERGIL E.
    2007   When the Legend Becomes Fact: Reconciling Hollywood Realism and Archaeological Realities. In *Box Office Archaeology; Refining Hollywood's Portrayal of the Past*, Julie Schablitsky, editor, pp. 223–244. Left Coast Press, Walnut Creek, CA.

WILLIAM B. LEES

Carol V. Ruppé Distinguished Service Award

Karlis Karklins

The Carol V. Ruppé Distinguished Service Award was established by the Society for Historical Archaeology (SHA) in 1988 to honor Carol Ruppé for her many years of service to the organization. Karlis Karkins received the 2013 Ruppé Award at the annual conference in Leicester, United Kingdom, in recognition of his tireless efforts for nearly 40 years to further and promote the field of historical archaeology and SHA around the world. It is only the sixth Ruppé Award to be presented.

Karlis Karklins was born in Riga, Latvia, in 1944, during German occupation of the country. As Soviet troops began to advance into Latvia in the fall of 1944, his parents, remembering the horrors of the initial Soviet occupation in 1940–1941, decided to abandon their homeland and head for Germany, the only place the German government would let them relocate. After the war, his parents emigrated to the United States, seeking to continue their careers as professors of German and Russian language and literature. Karlis learned English in New York City, and fortunately his mother soon found a job teaching at Syracuse University, where, in the upstate environment, Karlis was able to divest himself of his distinct Bronx accent.

Karlis became interested in archaeology while in junior high school. Living in White Plains, New York, at the time, he was fascinated by Indians and their diverse cultures. Upon hearing of his interest, a friend gave him a small box of arrowheads that purportedly had been found locally. This piqued his curiosity, and he began to assemble a library of books related to ancient humans and archaeology. Charles Darwin was his hero at the time (and continues to be). The pride of his collection was a worn copy of Henry C. Shetrone, *The Mound-Builders*, and he spent hours poring over its pages, fascinated by the complexity of these ancient peoples' lifeways and their amazing material culture.

By the time he began college in 1962, his family had moved to Tampa, Florida. Although he was interested in the natural sciences at this point, especially mineralogy and paleontology, a friend urged him to attend several anthropology classes that were "cool." This led to a major in anthropology at the University of South Florida, with minors in biology and geology. His first paying job as an anthropologist was cleaning artifacts excavated by University of South Florida archaeologist Roger T. Grange at Castle Hill, Newfoundland, where Karlis too would eventually work. While working on a bachelor degree at the university, a minor event would have a life-long effect on Karlis. The director of the tiny Tampa Museum of Science and Natural History called him one day to inquire if he would be interested in visiting a burial mound in central Florida, where treasure hunters had found glass trade beads. They went to the site, found some beads, and Karlis has been fascinated by trade beads ever since. Today he is a leading expert on trade beads, has learned a lot about them over the last 50 years, but feels there is still a lot more to discover.

After graduation in 1966, Karlis selected the University of Kansas to begin his graduate training. During summer break from those studies in 1967, Karlis accepted a job as an archaeological crew member at Lower Fort Garry National Historic Park, Selkirk, Manitoba, for the National Historic Parks and Sites Service (NHPSS), Ottawa, Canada (later NHPSS would become Parks Canada). He returned in 1968 and was then invited to join the fledgling archaeology section created at the NHPSS by John H. Rick and Jervis D. Swannack, who would become early presidents of the SHA. Karlis began as an archaeologist and was involved in the survey and excavation of a number of sites across Canada. His interest in beads led him to become involved in the Western Canadian Fur Trade Project, the purpose of which was to identify and locate fur-trade sites that were worthy of being commemorated and excavated for interpretation to the public.

When Parks Canada regionalized in 1977, he chose to remain with the headquarters unit in Ottawa and became a material culture researcher. At this point in his career, Karlis decided it was time to complete the graduate studies he had begun at the University of Kansas and applied for educational leave. Instead of returning to Kansas, he chose the University of Idaho, as it was one of the few places at the time that offered courses in historical archaeology. He earned his master's degree in anthropology in 1979 under the tutelage of Roderick Sprague, another bead aficionado, who would become a dear friend. Until retiring as head of the Material Culture Research Section in 2002, Karlis conducted research on various artifact categories, most notably beads, and produced numerous reports on his findings. He also undertook several cultural assessment surveys in the Wager Bay region of Nunavut for Parks Canada in anticipation of this area being designated a national park.

It was during his early days at NHPSS that Karlis became involved with the SHA. His boss, Jervis Swannack, who was then editor of SHA's newsletter, suggested that taking over this job would be a wise career move. After some arm twisting, Karlis agreed and served as newsletter editor from 1971 to 1975. In 1975, he was elected to the SHA Board of Directors, serving until 1978. While on the board he was an active member of the planning committee for the 1977 society meeting, held in Ottawa. In 1980, he took on the role of the SHA Ontario Current Research Editor and also became the Canadian book review editor the following year. He gave up these positions when he was elected president of the society in 1986.

This was an exciting time, as the society was lobbying the U.S. Congress to pass the Abandoned Shipwreck Act. There were visits to Capitol Hill and meetings with several members of Congress. It was also the time that the society was being sued for purportedly libeling an individual who had illegally raised components of the Confederate blockade runner, *Rattlesnake*, situated off the South Carolina coast. Although the lawsuit was eventually dropped, it was a shaky time for the SHA and nerve-racking for its officers. During his presidency, Karlis was also responsible for designing and producing the society's first promotional brochure. Following his term as president, he chaired the Nominations and Elections Committee, and subsequently served on the Newsletter Editorial Advisory Committee during Norman Barka's lengthy term as newsletter editor.

In the years that followed, Karlis continued as unofficial liaison officer between the SHA and Parks Canada, an agency that played a pivotal role in North American historical archaeology and material culture research. Through Karlis's efforts, a number of important research articles prepared by members of the Parks Canada Material Culture Researcher Section (PC MCR) were made available for publication in *Historical Archaeology*. In the late 1990s, Karlis approached the SHA with a plan to compile a reader for publication with papers contributed by PC MCR staff if the society would provide a publication conduit. Unselfishly, Karlis worked the manuscripts into publishable form and had appropriate artwork prepared. He then worked with Parks legal staff to get the papers, considered "Crown" property, released to the SHA for publication. This resulted in the *Studies in Material Culture Research* volume, published in 2000. Karlis also conducted luncheon roundtable workshops, workshop sessions, and symposia on beads at several SHA meetings.

For years, Karlis was active in seeking Canadian nominees for the SHA Board of Directors and recommending them to the nominating committee. He felt strongly that Canadian representation should, if possible, always exist on the board, and he was the most active Canadian in the early development of the SHA. When it comes to the SHA in Canada, Karlis was and is Mr. Canadian SHA. To this day, Karlis is a storehouse of knowledge relative to the history of the SHA, not only in Canada but for the society at large. He seems to have made it an unconscious career goal to do everything in his power to promote the SHA and to see that it thrives. More than possibly any other SHA member Karlis has, for well over 30 years, traveled across Canada, to Western and Eastern Europe, and to Southeast Asia to attend bead conferences and promote historical archaeology and the SHA. Karlis has been a worldwide "SHA Ombudsman!"

Since the early 1980s, Karlis has actively sought to disseminate information relevant to historical archaeology and has been a near-permanent fixture in the SHA conference book room, offering Parks Canada and other publications of interest to the historical archaeological community. Karlis has had a long-standing interest in the SHA and has promoted it whenever and wherever possible. He has attended all but a handful of the SHA's annual meetings since his first one in Bethlehem, Pennsylvania, in 1970. He maintains a serious interest in the society and always attends the business meetings, making comments and suggestions when he sees fit.

Through all the years that Karlis has worked to promote and serve the SHA, he has been a strong supporter of student participation. Recently he has become a financial supporter for student receptions, although he is reticent to acknowledge his contributions.

In addition to his work for SHA, Karlis has been very active in the Society of Bead Researchers. He became a member shortly after it was formed in 1981 and took over as editor in 1983, producing the *Bead Forum*, the society's newsletter. While interest in beads was increasing dramatically worldwide at the time, most archaeological journals were reluctant to devote their limited page space to reports that dealt solely with beads. Furthermore, those that were willing to publish such reports could not afford color illustrations, something bead researchers deemed essential. So it was that Karlis created a scholarly journal devoted solely to beads and beadwork. Its title was short and to the point: *Beads*. The first issue rolled off the presses in 1989 and is still in production, with Karlis as its able editor. Since retiring in 2002, Karlis has continued to research beads and beadwork, and has been invited to present papers at various conferences, some as far away as Istanbul and Borneo. He is always willing to give a helping hand to other researchers and promotes sound scholarship.

What does all of the above mean? Karlis Karklins is a person who, throughout his entire professional career, has been and continues to be selfless, to the extreme, in volunteering his time and talents to serve the society. Rick Sprague commented many times over the years, with great admiration, that Karlis really cared about the society, giving considerably of himself to ensure that the then-young SHA and the field of historical archaeology would survive, thrive, and mature as a discipline. That's what it means!

RONN MICHAEL

Carol V. Ruppé Distinguished Service Award

James Edward Ayres

At the 47th Annual Conference on Historical and Underwater Archaeology in Quebec City, Canada, James Edward Ayres was honored as the recipient of the 2014 Carol V. Ruppé Distinguished Service Award, which was created by the Society for Historical Archaeology (SHA) to recognize individuals who have a "sustained and truly outstanding" record of service to the organization. It should come as no surprise that the award has been conferred on relatively few occasions. Created in 1988 and publicly announced in 1990, Jim Ayres is only the seventh Ruppé recipient to date. Given his years of dedication to the society and extensive contributions, it is only possible to touch upon the highlights of Jim's extraordinary service in the ensuing paragraphs.

Fortunately, the task was eased a bit by the fact that Jim's distinguished career in historical archaeology has already been thoroughly summarized in a testimonial prepared by Charles E. Cleland and Teresita Majewski (2008) when Jim received the J. C. Harrington Medal in Historical Archaeology at the 2008 SHA awards banquet. (It is worth noting in passing that only one other person, the late Roderick Sprague, has ever won the high honor of both a Harrington Medal *and* a Ruppé Award.) That testimonial reviews Jim's interesting personal history, his academic background, and his many and varied scholarly accomplishments. However, it is appropriate to quote from the conclusion of that earlier publication, for it is relevant to the subject at hand.

In praise of Jim Ayres, Cleland and Majewski (2008:5) had this to say:

> For more than 40 years, he has focused on promoting historical archaeology through tireless service as well as broad-ranging and lasting scholarly contributions. For Jim, service and scholarly contributions are inextricably linked in a circle of cause and effect. He has never been a self-promoter, but his work has inspired countless others to pursue service and scholarship in historical archaeology.

So, let us examine more closely this remarkable record of SHA service, mindful that Jim also capably served other organizations—always with the same passionate commitment to duty, but hardly to the same degree as his contributions to the SHA, where he has dedicated so much of his time and energy.

Jim Ayres joined the SHA soon after the organization's 1967 founding, and it was not long before he began volunteering. In 1971, he began serving as a regional news coordinator for the *SHA Newsletter*, a duty that he continued to discharge faithfully for the next 28 years through 1999, which could well be a record tenure among newsletter coordinators. In that capacity, Jim regularly filed items on current research in the American Southwest that he had solicited from colleagues in the region. He also served on the SHA Newsletter Editorial Advisory Committee, once Norman Barka took over the newsletter editorship and organized that committee. Jim was an active member of that committee over the years, participating fully in the deliberations on content and policy development.

Jim quickly was recognized as a thoughtful and dedicated member of the SHA, and consequently he was nominated and elected to the SHA Board of Directors, serving from 1972 through 1975. His work on the board was clearly extraordinary, for in the final year of his term he was nominated for the office of president-elect. Winning the election as he did, Jim continued service on the board for another three years without a break—as president-elect (1976), president (1977), and immediate past president (1978). Jim provided steady leadership as president of the society, serving capably and deliberately during a time of membership growth and diversification of the discipline.

Several years after his presidency ended, Jim had the idea for a gathering of fellow past presidents each year at the conference. Initially conceived as an advisory body to the SHA leadership, Jim and Rick Sprague began organizing those meetings in the 1980s. In time, the gathering evolved into the Past Presidents' Luncheon, which has since become a standard feature of the annual conference. Now more of a social event than political, perhaps, the luncheon still provides an important sense of camaraderie and continuity among those who have held SHA's highest office.

Jim's stellar performance as president earned him a much-deserved reputation for sound judgment and hard work on behalf of the SHA. For that reason, his successor as president, Kathleen Gilmore, appointed Jim to chair a search committee to find a new editor for *Historical Archaeology* at a time when the annual journal was a few years in arrears and in dire need of firm stewardship. Identifying a capable individual to fulfill that role, therefore, was critical to the success of the society's still-fledgling publications program, and Jim's committee went about its charge with great care and efficiency—ultimately recommending Ronald L. Michael to the board for appointment. As the new editor of *Historical Archaeology*, Ronn quickly formed an editorial advisory committee, and naturally Jim was one of the initial members appointed in 1978. Jim served on the committee throughout Ronn's long tenure as editor and beyond that to the present day for a total of 35 years, which is unquestionably a record for service on that now more-encompassing body reborn as the Journal and Co-Publications Editorial Advisory Committee.

Other organizations also have benefited from Jim's leadership. It merits mentioning that he served from 1975 to 1982 as SHA's representative to the Advisory Council for Historic Preservation's International Centre Committee. Then, from 1983 through 1987, Jim also ably served as the SHA's representative to the board of the former Society of Professional Archeologists—now the Register of Professional Archaeologists. The task of representing one organization's interests on a committee or board of another organization is a challenge requiring considerable political skill, as well as a sense of purpose to do right by both organizations, and Jim proved equal to that challenge during those years of service. SHA placed its absolute trust in Jim Ayres as a spokesperson for the organization and was never disappointed in the results.

A further testament to Jim's reputed leadership and dedication to governance of the SHA is the fact that, 20 years after he was first elected to the SHA Board of Directors, he was elected to a second three-year term, serving from 1992 through 1995. I overlapped with Jim for a year on the board during his second term (in 1995), so I had the opportunity to witness firsthand his keen intellect in deliberations and his ability to offer insightful contributions to the discussion of matters at hand. Indeed, Jim's knowledge and experience often proved invaluable to moving discussions quickly along to a satisfactory conclusion. By the fine example he set, Jim was an unassuming role model to those like me who were new to service on the SHA Board.

Last, but certainly not least, is Jim's long service to the SHA on the Dissertation Prize Subcommittee (which has morphed into the selection panel for the prize, renamed in 2011 as the Kathleen Kirk Gilmore Dissertation Award). He joined the subcommittee as a member in 2001 and chaired it from 2003 through 2012. As many will realize, this assembly of dedicated volunteers undertakes a huge annual workload within a very short timeframe, reading and evaluating many worthy submissions each year, and it was largely through Jim's strong leadership that it always concluded its important business in timely fashion. That he was willing to take on and continue this very consuming responsibility late in his career—completing his assignment more than 40 years after he began volunteering for the society—is an incredible reflection of Jim's steady devotion to scholarship in historical archaeology and the organization whose mission is to promote it. Indeed, perhaps nowhere in Jim's illustrious career is the aforementioned linkage between service and scholarship more clearly evident than in his exceptional performance on the Dissertation Prize Subcommittee.

In conclusion, let me point out again that the foregoing outline of Jim's service represents a review of the most remarkable highlights only, for he has served the SHA in many other capacities and on many other occasions over the years. To give but one example, I immediately called upon Jim to serve on the search committee for Ronn Michael's successor as journal editor when I chaired that undertaking in 2003. I felt from the start that Jim's presence on the committee would lend important continuity to the effort, since he had chaired the previous editor search 25 years earlier. If agreeable to the proposition, it seemed to me that his unique perspective on the proceedings would be very useful in our pursuit of a new editor. To my delight, but not to my surprise, Jim did not hesitate for a moment to honor my request, and he proved to be an invaluable member of the search committee during teleconferenced candidate interviews and our deliberations. This is so typical of the man—always willing to serve the society no matter what the task and always to be counted on for a job well done. Jim's professionalism in behalf of the SHA is exemplary, and the organization could not possibly wish for a more steadfast volunteer.

Jim Ayres has repeatedly and competently volunteered his valuable time and considerable energy to the SHA for more than four decades, and so it is with heartfelt thanks and extreme gratitude for his extensive, inspirational dedication to SHA affairs that the Society for Historical Archaeology now honors him with the Carol V. Ruppé Distinguished Service Award.

Reference

CLELAND, CHARLES E., AND TERESITA MAJEWSKI
    2008   J. C. Harrington Medal in Historical Archaeology 2008: James Edward Ayres. *Historical Archaeology* 42(2):1–5.

VERGIL E. NOBLE

Carol V. Ruppé Distinguished Service Award: Patrick H. Garrow, 2015. Volume 49, Number 2 (2015): 10-11. By Della A. Scott-Ireton and Annalies Corbin.

Carol V. Ruppé Distinguished Service Award

Patrick H. Garrow

The Society for Historical Archaeology (SHA) established the prestigious Carol V. Ruppé Distinguished Service Award to honor individuals who have a record of sustained and truly outstanding service to the society. In January 2015, at the 48th Annual Conference on Historical and Underwater Archaeology in Seattle, Washington, SHA presented the Ruppé Award to an archaeologist who exemplifies a life of service to his profession and to his colleagues: Patrick H. Garrow. A true gentleman scholar, his dedication to our science and to our society is reflected in his many years devoted to making SHA, and especially the annual conference, what it is today. Pat's service to SHA spans decades and numerous positions. His selfless contributions include leadership roles on the SHA Board of Directors and organizing and chairing the now-legendary 1998 SHA conference in Atlanta.

Although Pat has served SHA in several capacities, perhaps his most substantial and lasting contribution is as chair of the SHA Conference Committee, a position that is also, by default, SHA Conference Coordinator. Serving in this position for many years, Pat oversaw the growth of the SHA annual meeting from a rather small gathering of a few hundred people to a major annual conference of international proportions attended by over a thousand archaeologists. Pat steered the planning of conferences into an organized, efficient, and repeatable process through his careful and detailed stewardship, including a major revision and updating of the official SHA Conference Manual. Moreover, Pat worked for years to establish a process and pattern for securing conference venues well into the future, giving SHA and local conference committees ample time to plan the meeting. Today, thanks to his efforts, SHA strives to secure conference venues at least five years in advance, sustaining Pat's vision of successful, affordable, and exciting annual meetings. Furthermore, his careful mentoring enabled the smooth transition to a new conference coordinator, who took over planning in 2012 with the goal of keeping Pat's vision focused and progressing.

Pat served as a member of the SHA Board of Directors from 2009 to 2012, as chair of the SHA Conference Committee and conference coordinator from 1999 to 2013 (co-chair with Barbara Garrow 1999–2002), and as conference chair for the 31st Annual Conference on Historical and Underwater Archaeology in Atlanta, Georgia, in 1998. He extensively revised the SHA Conference Manual in 2006 and over the years has made significant personal donations to the annual conference and to the silent auction.

In addition to his direct service to SHA, Pat is a leading researcher and scholar in historical archaeology, dedicating his nearly 50-year career to the cultural resource management (CRM) and academic sectors, and producing numerous publications on a variety of topics, ranging from 19th-century coffin hardware to historical ceramic analysis to Civil War encampments. Furthermore, Pat has been a consummate mentor to hundreds of new professionals. It is a rare historical archaeologist in the state of Georgia who has not been mentored by Pat in one way or another while navigating the ins and outs of CRM archaeology. Pat continues to serve the field of historical archaeology, currently as president of the Register of Professional Archaeologists and through present and past leadership positions in other organizations, including the Society for American Archaeology and the Society for Georgia Archaeology.

Pat's dedication to SHA, commitment to mentoring students and young professionals, promotion of public outreach and education in archaeology, and devotion to the field of historical archaeology make him the ideal recipient of the 2015 Carol V. Ruppé Distinguished Service Award.

DELLA A. SCOTT-IRETON
ANNALIES CORBIN

Carol V. Ruppé Distinguished Service Award: William Moss, 2016. Volume 50, Number 2 (2016): 9-10. By Dena Doroszenko and Réginald Auger.

Carol V. Ruppé Distinguished Service Award

William Moss

The Society for Historical Archaeology (SHA) established the prestigious Carol V. Ruppé Distinguished Service Award to honor individuals who have a record of sustained and truly outstanding service to the society. In January 2016, at the 49th Annual Conference on Historical and Underwater Archaeology in Washington, D.C., SHA presented the Ruppé Award to an archaeologist who exemplifies a life of service to his profession and to his colleagues—William Moss.

After receiving an honors degree in anthropology at the University of Waterloo in Ontario and a master's degree in historical archeology at Laval University, William Moss became principal archaeologist at Quebec City in 1985. This post, created to coordinate municipal action on archaeological heritage management, was the first of its kind in Canada. Together with the city's partners, including the Ministry of Culture and Communications and Laval University, William Moss has led more than 200 archaeological studies of Quebec City over the years. The results have been published as articles in national and international journals, and as scientific works on archaeological collections unique in the world for their quality and context. William Moss has also participated in numerous national and international conferences, communicating the rich heritage of Quebec, a UNESCO World Heritage city. As a result, William Moss is an eponymous figure for the archaeology of the historical period in Quebec.

William Moss has a long and distinguished record of service to SHA. This service has been colored by one constant theme: the promotion of the society and of the discipline of historical archaeology to the scientific community and the general public within the French-speaking world. William served as a valued member of the SHA Board of Directors for two consecutive terms from 2000 to 2005, the latter term as president-elect, president (2004), and immediate past-president. His terms spanned the transition of the organization to management by professional firms, marking a watershed in the evolution of SHA as an international society.

William organized two highly successful annual meetings: the first, in 2000, as co-chair (with Pierre Beaudet) of the 33rd Conference on Historical and Underwater Archaeology, and the second as chair of the 47th Conference on Historical and Underwater Archaeology in 2014. Organizing a conference on the scale of SHA's is a continuous effort spanning many years; the sum of his volunteer contributions to the 2000 and 2014 meetings represents over a decade of constant action. In addition to meeting high scientific standards, both conferences attained the goals of wide international participation and a strong French-language presence. William has notably managed the promotion and the selection process for the SHA Quebec City Award/ Bourse de Québec since 2003. This travel award, created with funds generated by the 2000 meeting in Quebec City, assists French-language students participating in the annual conference. William also served on several SHA committees, particularly the Conference Committee, but also the Collections Management, Public Education and Information, and Awards committees.

William has been an active member in the promotion of historical archaeology in Quebec and Canada for more than three decades. The attribution, in 2000, of SHA Awards of Merit to the Ville de Québec, the Ministère de la Culture et des Communications, Parks Canada, and Laval University recognized and helped to consolidate the success of efforts to promote historical archaeology in the province of Quebec. His career is characterized by a series of well-articulated national and international contributions to the cultural heritage community. William was a proactive agent in several of the programs recognized by these awards, and he was instrumental in having them bestowed. Laval University awarded a doctorate *honoris causa* to William in recognition of his contribution to the consolidation of archaeology as an instrument of economic development in Quebec. This degree was bestowed in 2014 during a colorful ceremony that marked the opening of the 47th Annual Conference on Historical and Underwater Archaeology in Quebec City.

For his dedication to the management of SHA through service on the board, for his promotion of the vitality of the society by organizing two highly successful conferences, and, generally, for his constant efforts to promote the French-language presence of SHA in the world, William Moss is the ideal recipient of the Carol V. Ruppé Distinguished Service Award.

DENA DOROSZENKO
RÉGINALD AUGER

Appendices

Appendix A: Presidents of the Society for Historical Archaelology, 1967–2017

YEAR	PRESIDENT
1967	John L. Cotter
1968	Edward B. Jelks
1969	John H. Rick
1970	Bernard L. Fontana
1971	Charles H. Fairbanks
1972	Vincent P. Foley
1973	Charles E. Cleland
1974	James F. Deetz
1975	Jervis Swannack
1976	Roderick Sprague
1977	James E. Ayres
1978	Kathleen Kirk Gilmore
1979	Lyle M. Stone
1980	Norman Barka
1981	Bert Salwen
1982	Robert L. Schuyler
1983	Edwin Dethlefsen
1984	William H. Adams
1985	Kathleen A. Deagan
1986	Karlis Karklins
1987	Donald L. Hardesty
1988	Garry Wheeler Stone
1989	Mary C. Beaudry
1990	Roderick Sprague
1991	Julia G. Costello
1992	Leland Ferguson
1993	J. Barto Arnold III
1994	Elzabeth J. Reitz
1995	Donna J. Seifert
1996	Glenn J. Farris
1997	Henry M. Miller
1998	Pamela J. Cressey
1999	Teresita Majewski
2000	Susan L. Henry Renaud
2001	Douglas V. Armstrong
2002	Vergil E. Noble
2003	Julia A. King
2004	William Moss
2005	Judith Bense
2006–07	Douglas D. Scott
2008–09	Lu Ann De Cunzo
2010–11	William B. Lees
2012–13	Paul Mullins
2014–15	Charles Ewen
2016–17	Joe W. Joseph

Appendix B: Recipients of the J. C. Harrington Medal in Historical Archaeology, 1982–2017

YEAR	NAME
1982[1]	Jean Carl Harrington
1983	Charles H. Fairbanks
1984	John L. Cotter
1985	Kenneth E. Kidd
1986	George Irving Quimby
1987[2]	Arthur Woodward
1987[2]	Stanley A. South
1988	Edward B. Jelks
1989	Carlyle Shreeve Smith
1990	Bert Salwen
1991	Ivor Noel Hume
1992[3]	
1993	Bernard L. Fontana
1994[3]	
1995	Kathleen Kirk Gilmore
1996[3]	
1997	James Deetz
1998[3]	
1999	George F. Bass
2000	Roderick Sprague
2001	Roberta S. Greenwood
2002	Charles E. Cleland
2003	Merrick Posnansky
2004	Kathleen A. Deagan
2005	Marcel Moussette
2006	Donald L. Hardesty
2007	William M. Kelso
2008	James Edward Ayres
2009	Robert L. Schuyler
2010	Judith Ann Bense
2011	Maria del Pilar Luna Erreguerena
2012	George L. Miller
2013	Mary C. Beaudry
2014	Theresa A. Singleton
2015	Douglas D. Scott
2016	Mark P. Leone
2017[4]	Leland Ferguson

[1] The Society for Historical Archaeology awarded the first J. C. Harrington Medal to its namesake, Jean Carl Harrington, in 1982 (see page 401 of this volume). Although articles highlighting the accomplishments of all other recipients of the medal have been published in the society's journal Historical Archaeology (all of which are reproduced in this volume), the article detailing Harrington's career was published in the March 1982 Newsletter of the Society for Historical Archaeology, which is not reproduced in this volume. A memorial highlighting Harrington's numerous accomplishments does, however, appear in this volume on page 293.

[2] The Society for Historical Archaeology awarded two J. C. Harrington Medals in 1987. One was awarded posthumously to Arthur Woodward, who had passed away the year before. The other was awarded to Stanley A. South.

[3] The J. C. Harrington Medal was not awarded this year.

[4] At the time this list was created, the Society for Historical Archaeology had announced Leland Ferguson as the recipient of the 2017 J. C. Harrington Medal in Historical Archaeology, but the article highlighting his career had not yet been published in the journal Historical Archaeology. Hence, that article is not included in this volume.

Appendix C: Recipients of the Carol V. Ruppé Distinguished Service Award, 1990–2017

YEAR[1]	NAME
1990	Carol V. Ruppe
1994	Stephanie Holschlag Rodeffer
1998	Ronald L. Michael
2001	Norman F. Barka
2004	Roderick Sprague
2011	Virgil E. Noble
2013	Karlis Karklins
2014	James Edward Ayres
2015	Patrick H. Garrow
2016	William Moss
2017[2]	Annalies Corbin

[1] *The Carol V. Ruppé Distinguished Service Award is not awarded every year by the Society for Historical Archaeology. This list comprises all of the award recipients to date.*

[2] *At the time this list was created, the Society for Historical Archaeology had announced Annalies Corbin as the recipient of the 2017 Carol V. Ruppé Distinguished Service Award, but the article highlighting her service to the society had not yet been published in the journal* Historical Archaeology. *Hence, that article is not included in this volume.*

Appendix D: Locations of the Annual Meetings of the Society for Historical Archaeology, 1968–2017

YEAR	LOCATION
1968[1]	Williamsburg, Virginia
1969	Tucson, Arizona
1970	Bethlehem, Pennsylvania
1971	Washington, D.C.
1972	Tallahassee, Florida
1973	St. Paul, Minnesota
1974	Berkeley/Oakland, California
1975	Charleston, South Carolina
1976	Philadelphia, Pennsylvania
1977	Ottawa, Canada
1978	San Antonio, Texas
1979	Nashville, Tennessee
1980	Albuquerque, New Mexico
1981	New Orleans, Louisiana
1982	Philadelphia, Pennsylvania
1983	Denver, Colorado
1984	Williamsburg, Virginia
1985	Boston, Massachusetts
1986	Sacramento, California
1987	Savannah, Georgia
1988	Reno, Nevada
1989	Baltimore, Maryland
1990	Tucson, Arizona
1991	Richmond, Virginia
1992	Kingston, Jamaica
1993	Kansas City, Missouri
1994	Vancouver, British Columbia
1995	Washington, D.C.
1996	Cincinnati, Ohio
1997	Corpus Christi, Texas
1998	Atlanta, Georgia
1999	Salt Lake City, Utah
2000	Quebec City, Quebec
2001	Long Beach, California
2002	Mobile, Alabama
2003	Providence, Rhode Island
2004	St. Louis, Missouri
2005	York, England
2006	Sacramento, California
2007	Williamsburg, Virginia
2008	Albuquerque, New Mexico
2009	Toronto, Ontario
2010	Amelia Island, Florida
2011	Austin, Texas
2012	Baltimore, Maryland
2013	Leicester, England
2014	Quebec City, Quebec
2015	Seattle, Washington
2016	Washington, D.C.
2017	Fort Worth, Texas

[1] *The Society for Historical Archaeology was officially formed at an "International Conference on Historic Archeology" held in Dallas, Texas on 6 January 1967 (see page 9 of this volume). During this conference, the society's newly elected board decided to hold the society's first annual meeting at Colonial Williamsburg, Virginia, at the invitation of Ivor Noël Hume.*

Individuals Featured in this Volume